Born in Scotland in 1924, Margaret Fulton moved to Australia at the age of four where she grew up as one of six children in northern New South Wales. It was here where she began honing her craft while cooking with her mother, along with some of the best country cooks. She began writing her cookery column in *Woman* magazine in 1954 and has contributed to numerous publications over the years, including *The Australian Women's Weekly*, but it was the 1968 publication of *The Margaret Fulton Cookbook* that made her a household name.

Margaret's pre-eminence in the food world was officially heralded when she was honoured with the O.A.M. (Medal of the Order of Australia), and was recognised as one of the National Trust's 100 Living Australian National Treasures. She is also a passionate traveller and her work has taken her around the world. Her friends include some of the world's leading cookery writers, cooks and food experts.

For Margaret Fulton, her greatest enjoyment is to share her cooking knowledge and recipes, and to bring good food into all our homes.

Margaret Fulton's
ENCYCLOPEDIA OF
FOOD & COOKERY

The complete kitchen companion from A to Z

APPLE

*I would like to dedicate this book to my family
and friends, and all those caring and curious cooks.*

This edition first published
in the UK in 2007 by
Apple Press
7 Greenland Street
London NW1 0ND
United Kingdom
www.apple-press.com

First published
in Australia in 1983
This revised and updated edition
published in 2005 by
Hardie Grant Books
85 High Street
Prahran, Victoria 3181, Australia
www.hardiegrant.com.au

ISBN 978 1 84543 229 4.

Cover and text design by Pfisterer+Freeman
Printed and bound in China by SNP Leefung

10 9 8 7 6 5 4 3 2 1

Introduction

I'm delighted to share with you my life's work in this revised and updated edition of *Margaret Fulton's Encyclopedia of Food & Cookery*.

Ever since the 1983 edition was published, readers have been telling me it's the first book they reach for when they need to find an ingredient or recipe. I do the same.

I consider it to be my greatest achievement. It was a book I just had to write, and was borne out of a desire to record my years of notes about the foods we use in everyday cooking: details to consider when buying ingredients, basic and unusual ways to prepare foods, as well as recipes and dishes that have worked their way into our culture and history.

This new edition reveals our changing food trends and includes the diversity of ingredients now commonly available.

I have always believed that good food and good cooking are part of all that's best in life, and hope to encourage a new generation of curious and interested cooks.

Happy cooking.

Margaret Fulton

Weights, Measures and Temperatures

The metric weights and liquids used in this book are those of the Standard Association of Australia.

To make these recipes you need a few inexpensive pieces of equipment obtainable at most supermarkets.

These are:

- A standard graduated 250 ml (8 oz) fluid measuring jug for measuring liquids.

- A nest of 4 graduated metric measuring cups comprising: 250 ml cup, 1/2, 1/3, and 1/4 cup – used for measuring dry ingredients.

- A set of standard measuring spoons comprising:
  1 tablespoon (20 ml)
  1 teaspoon (5 ml)
  1/2 teaspoon (2.5 ml)
  1/4 teaspoon (1.25 ml).

- American and UK measuring cups and spoons are also sold. These vary from the Australian standards. Follow one set of measures; do not mix them.

How to Measure Correctly

DRY INGREDIENTS: In measuring dry ingredients (flour, sugar, etc.) heap the cup or spoon and level off the excess with a knife or spatula.

LIQUID INGREDIENTS: The metric measuring cup shows 1 cup, 3/4, 2/3, 1/2, 1/4 and 1/8 cup measures and their metric equivalents. The litre jug has a similar breakdown from litre to 1/4 litre and also shows graduations in millilitres (1000 ml – 4 cups – 1 litre). All cup and spoon measures are level.

- Many ingredients are given in rounded metric gram/kilogram weights; imperial measurements are given in brackets. A small set of scales is a bonus in the kitchen. A measuring tape or ruler that gives both metric and imperial measurements is also a help.

- The recipes in this book have been made with the 250 ml cup.

- 55 g–60 g eggs have been used unless otherwise specified.

- Can, pack and bottle sizes are given in metric. As a guide, refer to table below. Some cans and packs may vary a little from exact sizes given according to the different brands available. It is best to use the nearest size.

METRIC	IMPERIAL
56 g	2 oz
130 g	4 oz
200 g	6 1/2 oz
230 g	7 1/2 oz
310 g	10 oz
425 g	13 1/2 oz
440 g	14 oz
470 g	15 oz
825 g	1 lb 14 oz

ABBREVIATIONS USED	
gram	g
kilogram	kg
centimetre	cm
millimetre	mm
millilitre	ml
tablespoon	tbs
teaspoon	tsp

Oven Temperature Guide

Oven temperatures are expressed in degrees Celsius (°C) and Fahrenheit (°F). Oven temperatures vary according to make; therefore, refer to the instruction book that accompanies each oven. All ovens should be preheated to the specified temperature particularly for cakes, biscuits and pastry recipes.

a

ABALONE

The beautiful single ear-shaped shell of the abalone is lined with mother of pearl, which is used to make buttons. The tough, fleshy mollusc in the shell is the edible part, and has a delicious clam-like flavour. Abalone is considered a great delicacy and is available fresh or canned.

If fresh, it should be cut into thin slices and pounded to tenderise it before sautéeing briefly (45–55 seconds). It will toughen if overcooked. Dried abalone has to be soaked for 4 days before using and is not recommended.

Sautéed Abalone: Slice abalone into strips against the grain. If fresh, pound with a meat mallet until soft and limp. Coat with egg and breadcrumbs or flour, and cook very quickly in hot oil or butter until golden. Season with salt and pepper and serve with lemon wedges or Tartare Sauce (see page 256).

ABERDEEN SAUSAGE

A Scottish favourite. Serve cold, with salads.

Aberdeen Sausage

250 g (8 oz) bacon, rind removed;
500 g (1 lb) topside mince; 1 cup fresh
breadcrumbs; 2 tsp Worcestershire sauce;
1 tbs finely chopped parsley; 1 tsp salt; freshly
ground black pepper; 1/2 tsp nutmeg; grated rind
1/2 lemon; 1 egg; flour for dusting;
fine, dry breadcrumbs.

Mince bacon and combine with remaining ingredients except flour and dry breadcrumbs. Form into a roll about 8 cm (3 in) wide and dust with flour. Tie securely in a scalded, floured cloth and plunge into a saucepan of boiling water. Boil steadily for 2 hours, replacing water if necessary. Unwrap while hot and roll in dry breadcrumbs. Place on a baking tray and dry in a preheated slow oven (150°C/300°F) for 15 minutes. Serves 6.

AIOLI

A garlic-flavoured sauce from Provence in France. Serve it with hot or cold fish, cold meats, cooked or raw vegetables and hard-boiled eggs.

Aïoli

4 fat cloves of garlic; salt; 1 egg yolk; 1 cup olive oil;
1 tbs lemon juice.

Crush garlic to a pulp with 1/4 tsp salt. Beat in egg yolk, then 3 tbs olive oil drop by drop, then lemon juice. Beat in remaining oil a little at a time. Mixture should be smooth and thick, like mayonnaise. Taste and adjust seasoning. Makes 1 1/4 cups.

ALLSPICE

A spice which seems to combine the flavours of cinnamon, cloves and nutmeg. The source is the berry of the pimento tree and allspice is sometimes bought as 'pimento'. Whole berries are used in pickles and preserves. Crushed, they flavour cakes, puddings, biscuits and some meat and fish dishes.

ALMOND

Whole, slivered, chopped, crushed or ground, plain or toasted, almonds are one of the pleasures of the kitchen.

TO BLANCH ALMONDS (remove brown skin): Cover whole almonds with boiling water and leave until skins are wrinkled (about 5 minutes). Drain, pinch off skins and dry, without colouring, in a preheated very cool oven (120°C/250°F).

TO SLIVER OR FLAKE ALMONDS: Cover freshly blanched nuts with boiling water and simmer 2–3 minutes; drain. Using a very sharp paring knife, cut almonds horizontally into flakes, or split in 2 and cut each half lengthways into fine slivers. Dry, without colouring, in a preheated very cool oven (120°C/250°F).

TO TOAST ALMONDS: Spread in a single layer on a baking tray and bake in a preheated slow oven (150°C/300°F), turning them frequently until golden.

TO GRIND ALMONDS: Use a special rotary nut mill or process in small batches in a blender or food processor. Use high speed but be careful to stop as soon as the almonds become a dry meal. Over-processing makes them pasty and oily. See recipes.

Almond Soup

1 cup ground almonds; 3 cups chicken stock;
1 small onion stuck with 2 cloves; 1 bay leaf;
1/2 cup milk; pinch nutmeg; salt and freshly
ground pepper; 30 g (1 oz) butter; 2 tbs flour;
1 cup cream; slivered toasted almonds to garnish.

Combine ground almonds, stock, onion and bay leaf in a saucepan. Simmer, covered, 30 minutes. Remove onion and bay leaf, pour mixture into a jug and add milk, nutmeg, salt and pepper. Melt butter, add flour and stir on low heat for 1 minute. Remove from heat, and blend in stock mixture. Stir over heat until boiling. Simmer 5 minutes. Add cream and reheat but do not boil. Serve hot or cold, with a sprinkle of slivered almonds. Serves 4.

Almond Macaroons (Amaretti)

2 egg whites; 1 1/3 cups freshly ground almonds;
1 cup caster sugar; 2 tbs icing sugar, sifted;
extra sifted icing sugar for dusting.

Beat egg whites to a firm snow and fold in almonds and sugars. Pipe mixture on to squares of greaseproof paper in small round or oval shapes. Dust with icing sugar and leave about 4 hours. Bake macaroons in a preheated moderately slow oven (160°C/325°F) for 15 minutes or until delicately browned. Cool before removing from paper squares. Store in an airtight container. Makes 14–16.

Almond Tart

PASTRY: 1 cup flour; 2 tbs sugar; ¼ tsp baking powder; 90 g (3 oz) butter; 1 egg, lightly beaten; 1 tbs iced water.

FILLING: 125 g (4 oz) butter; 1 cup caster sugar; ¼ cup flour, sifted; ¼ cup cream; 1½ cups flaked almonds, lightly toasted.

PASTRY: Sift together flour, sugar and baking powder; rub in butter until mixture resembles fine bread-crumbs. Quickly stir in egg and add enough iced water to form a ball. Knead very lightly, wrap in plastic wrap and chill for 1 hour. Place dough on a lightly floured surface and roll out to line a 20 cm (8 in) flan ring. Chill for 30 minutes.

FILLING: Cream butter, add sugar and beat until light and fluffy. Stir in flour and cream, mixing well. Add almonds and spoon mixture evenly into tart shell. Bake in a preheated hot oven (200°C/400°F) for 30–40 minutes (the filling will not be quite firm). Remove from oven and cool on a wire rack until filling is firm. Serve cold with whipped cream. Serves 8.

Almond–Chicken Party Salad

3 cups cooked, diced chicken; ½ cup sultanas; ½ cup slivered almonds, toasted; 3 sticks celery, finely sliced; 6 spring onions chopped; ¾ cup Mayonnaise (page 256); ¼ cup orange juice; salt and freshly ground black pepper.

GARNISH: lettuce leaves; orange slices; extra toasted almonds.

Combine all ingredients for salad. Spoon into a bowl lined with lettuce leaves and garnish with orange slices and almonds. Serves 4–6.

ALMOND PASTE

This sweet pale paste, made from ground almonds, is used to cover fruit cakes before they are iced, as a filling in pastries, as an ingredient in biscuits, etc.

Almond Paste

3 cups pure icing sugar, sifted; 250 g (8 oz) ground almonds; 2 tbs lemon juice; 2 tbs sweet sherry; 1 egg yolk; 2–3 drops almond essence; 1 egg white; ½ cup apricot jam.

Combine icing sugar and ground almonds. Combine lemon juice, sherry, egg yolk and essence. Mix with sugar-almond mixture to form a firm paste which can be rolled out. If necessary, add a little more sherry. Will cover the tops of 2 x 20 cm (8 in) cakes.

To apply almond paste to the top of a cake: trim top of cake, if necessary, to give a flat surface, or turn cake upside-down and use the bottom. Brush lightly with lightly beaten egg white or warm, sieved apricot jam. On a board dusted with sifted icing sugar, roll out paste to fit cake, place on top and press gently with a rolling pin. Leave several hours or overnight before icing cake.

AMARETTI (ITALIAN MACAROONS)

See *Almond*: Almond Macaroons.

ANCHOVY

A member of the herring family. Anchovies are often eaten fresh where caught, but are more familiar to most people as salted fillets packed in oil. They are also made into a paste, which is used as a spread for toast, or an essence to flavour sauces, etc. **See recipes.**

Anchovy Butter

Spread on bread, toast, crisp crackers or croûtons, or slice and place on hot cooked steaks. For a milder flavour, soak anchovies in a little milk for 20 minutes before using.

125 g (4 oz) butter; 1 tbs mashed, drained anchovy fillets; squeeze lemon juice.

Cream butter, then beat in anchovies and lemon juice. Store, covered, in refrigerator. Keeps for 1–2 weeks.

Fettucine with Butter and Anchovies

500 g (1 lb) fettucine (ribbon noodles), freshly cooked and drained; 125 g (4 oz) butter; ¼ cup drained, chopped anchovy fillets; freshly ground white pepper; 1 cup grated Parmesan cheese.

Place fettucine on a heated serving dish. Heat butter with anchovies, stirring well. Grind white pepper over noodles, sprinkle with half the cheese and pour anchovy butter over. Serve remaining cheese separately. Serves 6.

Anchoiade

This spicy, anchovy and garlic spread is delicious served on hot dry toast or crunchy French bread. Small black olives and crisp radish make an interesting addition to the plate. Use the anchovies packed in rough salt for preference; otherwise use those canned in oil.

20 anchovy fillets, rinsed; 2 cloves garlic, crushed; 1 tbs red wine vinegar or lemon juice; freshly ground black pepper; 4 tbs olive oil; 6 slices white bread, or 12 slices French bread.

GARNISH: lemon wedges; red radish; black olives.

Mash anchovies in a mortar (or use a blender or food processor for this). Add garlic, vinegar and pepper, and drizzle oil in very slowly so sauce does not separate. Sprinkle slices of bread with olive oil, place on a baking tray and toast under a preheated grill for 2–3 minutes or until slightly crisp. Turn over, spread with anchovy paste and return to heat for 3–5 minutes. Cut each slice into 4 triangles and serve immediately while piping hot. Arrange on a platter with lemon, radish and black olives. Serves 6.

ANGEL CAKE

A delicate American speciality. Because of its light texture it is not cut, but separated into pieces with 2 forks. You should be able to find an angel cake pan – a high tube pan, often with a removable base – in a good kitchen shop.

Angel Cake

I cup flour, sifted; I $^{1}/_{2}$ cups caster sugar;
I $^{1}/_{4}$ cups egg whites (10–12 medium eggs);
$^{1}/_{4}$ tsp salt; I $^{1}/_{2}$ tsp cream of tartar; I $^{1}/_{2}$ tsp vanilla;
few drops almond essence.

Sift flour and ¾ cup sugar together 3 times. Beat egg whites with salt and cream of tartar until soft peaks form. Sprinkle rest of sugar over egg whites 2 tbs at a time, beating well after each addition. Continue beating until whites stand in stiff peaks, then fold in vanilla and almond essence. Sift about a quarter of the dry ingredients over egg whites and fold in gently. Repeat until all the mixture is used. Pour batter into an ungreased 23 cm (9 in) angel cake pan – if there is a speck of grease on the pan, the cake will not rise. Cut gently through batter with a spatula to remove any large air bubbles. Bake in a preheated moderate oven (180°C/350°F) for 45–50 minutes or until crust is golden-brown. Take cake from oven and place tube on a funnel or bottle, so cake hangs upside-down. When cool, use a thin knife to help remove cake from pan. Serve plain, iced or topped with whipped cream and strawberries. Serves 10–12.

ANGELICA

An aromatic herb, which most home cooks know as bright green, candied stalks used to decorate desserts, cakes and biscuits. Keep candied angelica airtight to avoid drying out, and if necessary wash in warm water to remove excess sugar, and dry before using.

ANGELS ON HORSEBACK

The intriguing name for oysters wrapped in thin rashers of bacon and grilled until bacon is crisp. Serve on small rounds of buttered toast or fried bread. Can be served as an hors d'oeuvre or as a savoury at the end of a meal.

ANISE/ANISEED

A tall plant which has a pronounced licorice flavour. It is also known as sweet cumin. The tiny, greyish-brown seeds are dried for use in cooking and are called aniseed. To release the full flavour of the seeds, they may be crushed – but use them with a light hand, especially in savoury dishes, as the flavour can dominate. Aniseed is used in fish dishes, in particular some fish and vegetable curries and mussels. It is also added to cheeses, cakes, breads and confectionery, as well as some alcoholic drinks.

Anise Drop Biscuits

These tiny biscuits bake to a puffed top on a soft biscuit base.

3 eggs; I cup caster sugar, $^{1}/_{2}$ tsp vanilla;
2 cups flour; I tsp baking powder;
I $^{1}/_{2}$ tbs crushed aniseeds.

Beat eggs until light, then beat in sugar, a little at a time. Mixture should be thick and pale yellow. Add vanilla, then flour and baking powder, sifted together. Add aniseed and beat for 5 minutes. Drop mixture in half-teaspoonfuls, well apart, on a baking tray lined with lightly greased foil. Bake in a preheated moderately slow oven (160°C/325°F) for about 12 minutes or until lightly coloured.

Remove from oven, loosen biscuits on foil and leave them on it, uncovered and at room temperature, for 18 hours to dry. Store in airtight containers. Makes about 90.

ANTIPASTI

The Italian version of appetisers or hors d'oeuvre. They may be hot or cold and, in Italy, are most often served at the table as a first course. Antipasti may be arranged on one large platter for guests to serve themselves, or in individual plates. They may also be served as an accompaniment to aperitifs or cocktails.

Popular ingredients for cold antipasti (Antipasti Freddi) include crisp raw vegetables, lightly cooked vegetables marinated in dressing, slices of ham, prosciutto and salami, marinated mushrooms, stuffed eggs, caviar, smoked salmon and eel, tuna, herring fillets and sardines. Hot antipasti might include chicken livers on crisp fried bread, grilled cheese fingers, dumplings stuffed with spinach or cheese, grilled sardines and batter-fried seafood. **See recipes.**

Antipasto Variato: Use a large, round platter. In the centre, put a mound of drained tuna. Coat with Mayonnaise (see page 256) and sprinkle with capers. Arrange around tuna overlapping slices of prosciutto, then sliced salami. Add thinly sliced fennel, then a circle of hard-boiled eggs, cut into quarters, and topped with strips of anchovy. Arrange celery sticks, radishes and olives around the edge. Serve with salt and freshly ground black pepper, separate jugs of oil and vinegar, crusty bread and butter.

Antipasto Misto: On a long dish arrange an assortment of salads – raw peppers, seeded and cut into rings; raw mushrooms, sliced; potato salad; whole small red tomatoes (the plum-shaped, egg tomatoes are ideal); fennel or celery, finely sliced. Sprinkle with a little Vinaigrette Dressing (see page 442), top with hard-boiled eggs, cut into quarters, and sprinkle with chopped parsley.

See also *Appetisers* and *Hors d'oeuvre.*

Neapolitan Tomato Salad

6 tomatoes, peeled and sliced;
$^{1}/_{4}$ cup Vinaigrette Dressing (page 442);
2 cloves garlic, finely chopped;
6–8 leaves fresh basil.

Arrange tomato slices overlapping on a large platter and pour over dressing mixed with the garlic. Scatter with freshly cut ribbons of basil. Serves 6–8.

Green Beans and Tuna

500 g (1 lb) green beans, topped and tailed and stringed if necessary; salt; $^{1}/_{4}$ cup olive oil;
1 tsp lemon juice; freshly ground black pepper;
1 x 200 g can tuna in oil.

Drop beans into boiling salted water and cook just until crisp tender; drain. While still hot, sprinkle with salt and pepper. Drain tuna, break into large chunks and toss with beans. Cover and chill before serving. Serves 4–6.

Stuffed Eggs with Anchovies

Use as part of an antipasto tray, or serve on a bed of finely shredded lettuce as a first course (allow 2 per serving).

6 hard-boiled eggs; 5 anchovy fillets, mashed;
30 g (1 oz) butter; 1 tbs finely chopped parsley;
2 tbs Mayonnaise (page 256); freshly ground black pepper.

Shell eggs, cut in half lengthways and remove yolks. Mash yolks with anchovies, butter, parsley, mayonnaise and pepper. Refill whites with mixture. Serve slightly chilled. Makes 12.

Crostini con Gorgonzola
(Gorgonzola on Fried Bread Fingers)

BASE: 6 slices white bread, crusts removed and cut into 4 strips each; 30 g (1 oz) unsalted butter; 3 tbs olive oil.

TOPPING: $^{1}/_{2}$ cup crumbled Gorgonzola cheese at room temperature; 60 g (2 oz) unsalted butter, softened; 1 tbs brandy; 1 tsp paprika; freshly ground black pepper.

BASE: Fry bread strips in hot butter and oil until golden-brown on both sides. Drain on paper towels.
TOPPING: Cream Gorgonzola and butter, and mix in brandy, paprika and pepper. Spread on fried bread and serve at once. This mixture may also be spread on biscuits or toast. Serves 4–6.

Marinated Mushrooms

500 g (1 lb) button mushrooms; 2 tbs olive oil, $^{1}/_{2}$ cup Vinaigrette Dressing (page 442); 2 cloves of garlic, split in half; finely chopped parsley to garnish.

Lightly brown mushrooms in hot olive oil. Do not overcook – they should stay firm. Turn into a bowl, add dressing and garlic and marinate, covered, in refrigerator for several hours. Bring mushrooms to room temperature to serve, sprinkled with chopped parsley. Serves 4–6.

ANZAC BISCUITS

Crunchy and economical – an Australian favourite, made popular during World War I when there were egg shortages. Sent in food parcels to the troops who became famous as Anzacs (Australian and New Zealand Army Corps).

Anzac Biscuits

125 g (4 oz) butter; 1 tbs golden syrup; 2 tbs boiling water; $1^{1}/_{2}$ tsp bicarbonate of soda; 1 cup rolled oats; $^{3}/_{4}$ cup desiccated coconut; 1 cup flour; 1 cup sugar.

Melt butter and syrup over low heat. Add boiling water mixed with soda. Pour into mixed dry ingredients and mix well. Drop teaspoonfuls of mixture on to greased baking trays, leaving room for spreading. Bake in a preheated slow oven (150°C/300°F) for 20 minutes. Cool on trays for a few minutes, then remove to wire racks. Store in airtight containers. Makes about 48.

APPETISERS

The name covers a wide variety of food served in small portions with drinks before a meal, or as the first course. They may include vegetables with a light dressing, dips, small fancy sandwiches, pâtés, cold meats and fish, skewered foods and tiny, hot pastries. See recipes.

See also *Antipasti, Canapés, Hors d'oeuvre* and *Sandwiches.*

Anchovy Appetiser Turnovers

$1/2$ x 375 g (12 oz) packet frozen puff pastry, thawed; 2 x 56 g cans rolled, stuffed anchovy fillets, drained; 1 egg yolk, lightly beaten.

Roll out thawed packet pastry thinly. Cut out 5 cm (2 in) rounds, wet edges and place an anchovy on one side of each. Fold other sides over, press with a fork to seal and chill 30 minutes. Brush tops with egg yolk and bake in a preheated very hot oven (230°C/450°F) for 15 minutes or until turnovers are puffed and golden. Makes about 24.

Chicken Satés

3 chicken fillets (skinless, boneless half-breasts); 1 chilli, halved and seeded; $1/2$ medium onion, chopped; 2 tsp grated fresh ginger; juice $1/2$ lemon; 1 tsp salt; 2 tbs water; 2 tbs light soy sauce; 1 tbs peanut oil; extra oil for brushing.

Cut chicken into 2 cm (¾ in) cubes. Put chilli, onion, ginger, lemon juice, salt, water, soy sauce and oil in a blender and blend until smooth. Pour over chicken, cover and marinate for 2 hours in refrigerator. Thread on skewers, brush with extra oil and grill under a preheated grill for 5–8 minutes, turning often, until chicken is crisp and brown. Serves 6.

Ham and Chicken Rolls

A popular Chinese appetiser, may also be served as a first course with a sweet and sour sauce.

4 chicken fillets (skinless, boneless and half-breasts); 1 tsp salt; $1/4$ tsp white pepper; $1/4$ tsp five-spice powder; 1 clove garlic, crushed; 4 slices cooked ham; $1/2$ cup flour; 1 egg, lightly beaten; 2 tbs milk; 4 spring roll wrappers; oil for deep-frying.

Separate strip of fillet which runs lengthways along each half-breast. Pound breast and fillet pieces separately until very thin, being careful not to tear meat. Lay a fillet piece on top of each breast and pound lightly. Spread chicken pieces with combined mixture of salt, pepper, five-spice powder and garlic. Separately roll each slice of ham and place on top of each chicken piece. Roll up firmly, folding ends in securely. Dip chicken rolls in flour, then in egg

beaten with milk. Place chicken roll diagonally across spring roll wrapper, fold in ends and roll up securely. Seal with a little of the egg mixture. Deep-fry rolls in hot oil for 3–5 minutes until golden-brown and cooked through. Do not have the oil too hot or the rolls will brown too much before they are cooked through. Drain on crumpled paper towels. Serve cut into diagonal slices. If serving as a first course, serve accompanied by Sweet and Sour Sauce (see page 520). Serves 4–6.

APPLE

Since the days of the Garden of Eden, apples have been munched with enjoyment at any time of the day in most parts of the world. Although there are many varieties, in general they can be divided into apples for cooking and those for eating, though in many cases they overlap. The Australian Granny Smith, a self-planted tree, discovered by 'Granny' Smith in her garden and nurtured to produce the beautiful green apples that carry her name, is a superb example of the 'all-purpose' apple, with tart-sweet flesh just right for cooking and also for eating.

Apples are used in a great number of ways. They can be baked, stewed, puréed, and used to make tarts and puddings; they can be preserved as jam or jelly, in pickles and chutney, or dried. Raw, they feature in salads, can be eaten with cheese, and are used with savoury meats. Roast pork with apple sauce is enjoyed in many countries.

Store small quantities of apples in the refrigerator crisper, large quantities in a cool, dark place where plenty of air can circulate. If raw apples are cut for salads etc., sprinkle with a little lemon juice to prevent discolouring.

■ **TO COOK:** If you want apple pieces to hold their shape, cook them in syrup ($1/2$ cup sugar to 1 cup water for tart apples, less sugar for sweeter apples). If you want the apples to break up (e.g. for apple sauce), add sugar to taste after cooking in water. For best flavour and colour in apple sauce, slice apples but do not peel or core, and rub through a sieve or put through a food mill after cooking. Flavour with lemon juice or grated rind and a little butter. See recipes.

Apple Sauce (Chunky)

Serve with roast or grilled pork or ham.

4 large cooking apples, peeled, cored and quartered; $1/2$ cup water; $1/4$–$1/2$ cup sugar; 2 tsp lemon juice; $1/4$ tsp cinnamon.

Cook apples until soft in covered saucepan, using just enough water to keep them from scorching. Stir occasionally during cooking. Break up apple a little and add sugar to taste. Stir in lemon juice and cinnamon. Makes about 1½ cups.

NOTE: Vary by adding nutmeg, ground cloves, a few raisins or chopped nuts.

Apple Sauce (Smooth)

Serve hot or cold with roast duck or pork.

**4 cooking apples, quartered;
about ¹/₂ cup water; ¹/₄–¹/₂ cup sugar;
2 tsp lemon juice.**

Do not peel or core apples. Cook until soft in covered saucepan, using just enough water to keep them from scorching. Stir occasionally during cooking. Force through a sieve or food mill and stir in sugar to taste and lemon juice. Vary as in Apple Sauce (Chunky). Makes about 1¹/₂ cups.

Apple Bavarian Slaw

**1 Spanish onion, sliced; 2 red apples, cored and thinly sliced; 4 cups shredded red cabbage;
¹/₂ cup sliced dill pickles; ¹/₂ cup Vinaigrette Dressing (page 442).**

Separate onion into rings. Combine onion, apples, cabbage and pickles. Chill. Just before serving, toss with dressing. Serves 6.

Apple Butter

**2 kg (4 lb) well-flavoured apples, quartered;
2 cups cider or water; sugar;
3 tsp cinnamon; 1¹/₂ tsp ground cloves;
¹/₂ tsp ground allspice.**

Cook apples in cider or water until soft. Strain pulp. To each cup of pulp, add ¹/₂ cup sugar. Stir in remaining ingredients. Cook over low heat, stirring constantly, until mixture is thick. Pour into hot sterilised jars, cool and seal. Store in a cool dry place. Makes about 5 x 1 cup jars.

Deep Dish Apple Pie

Use frozen shortcrust, puff or flaky pastry for this pie.

**3 tbs quick-cooking tapioca; ³/₄ cup white sugar;
¹/₃ cup firmly packed dark brown sugar; ¹/₄ tsp salt;
1 tsp cinnamon; ¹/₂ tsp nutmeg; 6 tart apples,
peeled, cored and sliced; ¹/₂ x 375 g (12 oz) packet
frozen shortcrust, puff or flaky pastry, thawed;
whipped cream flavoured with a little sugar and
nutmeg to serve (optional).**

Mix all ingredients except pastry and whipped cream. Pour into buttered deep 20 cm (8 in) round or square dish. Roll out pastry to fit top of dish. Cut several slits near the centre and lay pastry over apple mixture. Bake in a preheated hot oven (220°C/425°F) for about 35 minutes; reduce heat to moderate (180°C/350°F) and bake for a further 30 minutes. Serve with whipped cream if desired. Serves 6.

Apple Crisp

**5 large cooking apples, peeled, cored and sliced;
¹/₄ cup water; ¹/₂ cup white sugar; ¹/₂ cup firmly
packed light brown sugar; ¹/₂ tsp nutmeg;
¹/₂ tsp cinnamon; ¹/₄ tsp salt; ³/₄ cup flour;
125 g (4 oz) butter or margarine.**

Put apples in shallow 4-cup ovenproof dish and add water. Combine sugars, nutmeg, cinnamon, salt and flour. Cut in butter with pastry blender, knife or fingertips. Spoon evenly over apples. Cover and bake in a preheated moderate oven (180°C/350°F) for 30 minutes. Uncover and bake for 30 minutes longer. Serves 6.

Apple Slices in Brandy and Cream

**6 medium cooking apples, peeled, cored and thinly
sliced; 60 g (2 oz) unsalted butter; 3 tbs brandy;
3 tbs water; ³/₄ cup firmly packed brown sugar;
1 tsp nutmeg; 1 cup currants or dried mixed fruit;
1 cup cream.**

Place apples in a buttered shallow baking dish and dot with remaining butter. Stir rest of ingredients together and spoon over apples. Bake in a preheated moderate oven (180°C/350°F) for 30 minutes or until apples are tender. Serve warm with crisp biscuits or plain cake. Serves 6–8.

Quick Apple Strudel

An Austrian specialty – paper-thin pastry enveloping buttery, spiced apple slices. This version is simplified by using commercial puff pastry, rolled as thin as possible. The same method is used when making with classic Strudel Pastry (see *Strudel*).

**4 large cooking apples, peeled, cored and thinly
sliced; 2 tbs brown sugar; 1 tsp vanilla;
250 g (8 oz) puff pastry; 125 g (4 oz) unsalted butter;
¹/₂ cup fresh breadcrumbs; 2 tbs redcurrant jelly;
¹/₂ cup chopped almonds; sifted icing sugar;
whipped cream to serve.**

Sprinkle apples with brown sugar and vanilla, toss well to coat apples and stand for 1 hour. Roll out pastry on a floured tea-towel to an oblong shape about 35 x 50 cm (14 x 20 in). Melt half the butter and sauté breadcrumbs until golden. Melt remaining butter and brush half over pastry, leaving a 5 cm (2 in) margin along each side. Spread half apples over crumbs, dot with 1 tbs of redcurrant jelly and sprinkle with half the almonds. Top with remaining apples, jelly, almonds and breadcrumbs. Fold in edges of pastry and brush with remaining melted butter. Roll up like a Swiss roll and place strudel, seam side down, on a greased baking tray, curving it if necessary to fit. Brush top with butter and bake in a preheated moderately hot oven (190°C/375°F) for 45 minutes, brushing again with butter every 10 minutes. Remove from oven and dust generously with icing sugar. Serve warm, with whipped cream. Serves 6–8.

Baked Apples

6 large Granny Smith or other cooking apples, cored; $^{1}/_{2}$ cup sugar; I cup water; I tsp cinnamon or nutmeg.

Make a slit around the centre of each apple to prevent splitting. Arrange close together in a shallow baking dish. Boil sugar and water together for 2–3 minutes and stir in spice. Pour over apples and bake in a preheated moderate oven (180°C/350°F) for 50 minutes to 1 hour, basting often with syrup. Serve warm with custard, cream or ice cream. Serves 6.
NOTE: Cavities of apples may be filled with chopped dates or raisins if wished. Brown sugar may be used instead of white for a caramel flavour, and grated lemon rind added to the syrup instead of spice.

Fresh Apple Chutney

2 medium cooking apples, peeled, cored and grated; 3 tbs apricot jam; I tbs vinegar; I tbs finely chopped fresh mint; salt; pinch cayenne.

Mix apples with remaining ingredients, seasoning to taste with salt and cayenne. Serve at once with curries or cold meats. Makes about 2 cups.

Buttered Apples

3–4 cooking apples, peeled, cored and sliced; I tbs brown sugar; 30 g (I oz) butter, cut into small pieces; piece lemon peel.

Put apples into a small, heavy saucepan. Sprinkle with sugar, dot with butter and lay peel on top. Cover and cook on low heat for 15–20 minutes or until tender, turning slices over gently from time to time. Serve hot or cold with cream. Serves 4.

Normandy Pork Chops

6 large pork chops; 60 g (2 oz) butter; 2 large onions, sliced; I clove garlic, crushed; 3 large cooking apples, peeled, cored and sliced;

salt and freshly ground black pepper; I tbs sugar; 2 cups cider.

Trim excess fat from chops and fry them in butter until golden-brown on both sides. Remove to a shallow casserole, arranging them in a single layer. In the same pan fry onions, garlic and apple slices until beginning to soften. Arrange over chops. Add salt, pepper, sugar and cider to pan and bring to the boil, stirring to get up brown bits from bottom. Pour over chops, cover tightly and bake in a preheated moderate oven (180°C/350°F) for 45 minutes or until chops are tender. Serve with noodles and braised red or green cabbage. Serves 6.

Apple Fritters

Serve with grilled bacon for breakfast, or as a dessert with ice cream.

3 large cooking apples, peeled and cored; $^{1}/_{2}$ cup sugar; 2 tbs brandy; 2 tsp grated lemon rind; I$^{1}/_{2}$ cups flour, sifted; $^{1}/_{2}$ tsp baking powder; $^{1}/_{4}$ tsp salt; 2 eggs, lightly beaten; I tsp oil; $^{1}/_{3}$ cup beer; oil for deep frying; sifted icing sugar (for dessert fritters).

Cut each apple crossways into 4 rings. Mix ¼ cup of the sugar with the brandy and lemon rind, pour over apples and stand 2–3 hours. Mix remaining ¼ cup sugar with flour, baking powder, salt, eggs, oil and beer to make a batter. Let batter stand 1 hour. Drain and dry apple rings. Dip in batter one at a time and deep-fry in hot oil until golden-brown and crisp. Drain on crumpled paper towels. Sprinkle dessert fritters with icing sugar. Serve hot. Serves 4.

Apple Pie

Sweet Rich Shortcrust Pastry (page 342); 6 large cooking apples, peeled, cored and thinly sliced; $^{3}/_{4}$ cup sugar; I tbs flour; I tsp cinnamon; $^{1}/_{4}$ tsp nutmeg; pinch salt; 30 g (I oz) butter; I egg white, lightly beaten; extra sugar.

Reserve a third of pastry for lid of pie. Roll out remainder to line a greased 23 cm (9 in) pie plate. Toss apples with sugar, flour, spices and salt. Spread evenly in pastry case and dot with butter. Roll out remaining pastry to cover top of pie, moisten edges and press firmly together. Press edges with tines of a fork to decorate. Make a few slits in top crust for steam to escape, brush with egg white and sprinkle with extra sugar. Bake in a preheated hot oven (200°C/400°F) for 10 minutes. Lower heat to moderately slow (160°C/325°F) and bake for a further 45 minutes or until pastry is golden and apples are tender. Serve warm. Serves 6–8.

Apple Kuchen

A soft yeast bread of German origin.

2 cups flour; ¹/₂ tsp salt; 15 g (¹/₂ oz) compressed yeast; 2 tbs sugar; 1 egg, beaten; ¹/₂ cup warm milk; 30–60 g (1–2 oz) butter, melted; ¹/₄ cup raisins; 1 apple, peeled, cored and sliced; syrup or water; caster sugar; 1 tsp cinnamon.

Sift flour and salt. Cream yeast with sugar. Mix into flour with egg, milk and butter. Beat thoroughly, then leave to rise in a warm place until double its bulk. Turn out on to a floured board and knead lightly. Work raisins into dough. Shape into a large bun with the hand and put into a lightly greased cake or deep sandwich tin. Flatten top with your fist and cover with sliced apple, pressing the sharp edge of the slices into the dough. Brush lightly with a thin syrup (3 tbs water and 1 tbs sugar boiled 1 minute) or water, sprinkle thickly with caster sugar mixed with a little cinnamon, and leave to prove 20 minutes. Bake in a preheated moderately hot oven (190°C/375°F) for 40–45 minutes. Serves 6–8.

German Apple Cake

60 g (2 oz) butter; ¹/₃ cup sugar; 1 egg; 1 cup self-raising flour, sifted; ¹/₄ cup milk; 4 medium apples, peeled, quartered and cored; juice 1 lemon; sugar; cinnamon.

Cream butter with sugar. Add egg and beat well. Add half flour and beat to combine. Add milk and remaining flour alternately (this will make a thick mixture). Spread mixture over bottom of greased 23 cm (9 in) springform tin. Cut quartered apples into thin slices but not all the way through. Put apples as you are preparing them in a bowl and squeeze over lemon juice. Place drained apples, cored side down, on cake. Bake in a preheated moderate oven (180°C/350°F) for 1 hour. While still warm sprinkle with sugar and cinnamon. Serves 6–8.

APRICOT

This small, round, golden fruit grows on a tree that is a member of the peach family. Canned and dried apricots make it possible to enjoy the flavour of this lovely fruit all year round. Keep fresh apricots in the refrigerator in a covered container, or in a plastic bag perforated with a few holes. If apricots are not quite ripe, ripen them at room temperature before storing.

■ **TO COOK FRESH APRICOTS:** Poach gently in a syrup so that they keep their shape. Bring to the boil 1 cup water, ³/₄ cup sugar and 4 cloves or a piece of cinnamon stick. Simmer 5 minutes. Add 12–15 washed apricots, whole, or halved and stoned. Simmer 10 minutes or until just tender. Serve warm or chilled. If desired, liquid may be flavoured with lemon rind instead of spice, or you may use half white wine and half water.

■ **TO COOK DRIED APRICOTS:** Simmer in water to cover for 20 minutes or until tender. Sweeten after cooking with sugar or honey. Dried apricots will also become plump and tender without cooking, if soaked overnight in water, fruit juice or cold tea. Keep covered in the refrigerator. **See recipes.**

Apricot Glaze: This simple glaze is much used in French home and professional cooking to give brilliance and glitter to any fruit tart, since the taste of apricot blends very well with that of other fruits. It can be used as a simple icing for cakes and pies, or used inside a pastry case to moisture-proof it before the filling goes in. Simply boil 1 cup apricot jam with ¹/₄ cup water, stirring frequently until mixture is clear and will just drop from the spoon. Use a pastry brush to apply it. (Redcurrant jelly may be treated and used in the same way.)

Fresh Apricot Crumble Pie

1 kg (2 lb) fresh apricots, halved and stoned; ³/₄ cup sugar; pinch salt; 1 tbs grated lemon rind; 2 tbs lemon juice; 1 tbs cornflour; 1 x 23 cm (9 in) unbaked Rich Shortcrust Pie Shell (page 342).

TOPPING: ¹/₃ cup firmly packed brown sugar; ¹/₂ cup flour; 1 tsp cinnamon; 90 g (3 oz) butter.

Mix together apricots, sugar, salt, lemon rind and juice and cornflour. Pack into pie shell. For topping, combine sugar, flour and cinnamon and rub in butter to form crumbs. Sprinkle over apricots. Bake in a preheated hot oven (200°C/400°F) for 15 minutes. Reduce heat to moderate (180°C/350°F) and bake 30 minutes longer or until apricots are tender. Serve warm with cream or custard. Serves 6–8.

Apricot Chicken

A recipe that swept the world – a way of turning chicken pieces into an exotic dish with only 3 ingredients.

1 large roasting chicken, cut into serving pieces; 1 packet French onion soup mix; 1 x 250 ml can (1 cup) apricot nectar; canned apricot halves to garnish (optional).

Arrange chicken pieces in one layer in a casserole. Sprinkle with soup mix and pour nectar over. Cover and bake in a preheated moderate oven (180°C/350°F) for 40 minutes or until chicken is tender, turning the pieces once or twice. If desired, garnish with canned apricots heated in a little syrup from the can. Serves 4.

Dried Apricot Jam

250 g (8 oz) dried apricots; 2 lemons; 4 cups water; 4 cups sugar; 6 blanched almonds.

Cut each apricot in half. Halve the lemons, squeeze 3 tbs of the juice and reserve. Gather lemon pips and tie in a muslin bag. Soak apricots and lemon pips in the water for several hours. Put apricots, pips and water into saucepan and cook slowly until fruit is soft. Remove pips. Warm sugar in a preheated very slow oven (120°C/250°F) for 10 minutes and add to fruit with strained lemon juice. Stir with a wooden spoon until sugar has dissolved.

Boil the fruit mixture quickly until setting point is reached (place a small teaspoon of jam on a saucer and wait 20 seconds, then run a finger through it; if it wrinkles at the edges and stays in 2 separate parts the jam is right for bottling). Cool slightly and stir once to distribute fruit evenly. Ladle into warm dry jars, including 1–2 almonds in each jar to represent kernels. Moisten clear preserve covers with cloth dipped in vinegar and cover, or cover with sterilised screw-on lids. Tie down, then cool. Makes about 3 cups.

Apricot Crescents

125 g (4 oz) butter or margarine; 90 g (3 oz) cream or Neufchâtel cheese, softened; 3/4 cup flour, sifted; 1/8 tsp salt; 1 tbs cold water; apricot conserve; chopped nuts; sifted icing sugar.

Cut butter and cheese into flour and salt. Add water and mix lightly with fork until blended. Chill until firm, then cut into 24 pieces. Keep dough chilled before rolling. Roll each piece very thin on floured board to form 8 cm (3 in) squares. Spread each with apricot conserve and sprinkle with nuts. Roll up from one corner and bend ends in slightly to form crescents. Put folded side down on ungreased baking trays and bake in a preheated very hot oven (230°C/450°F) for about 10 minutes. Dust icing sugar over cooled crescents. Makes 24.

Spiced Apricots

1 x 825 g can apricots; 8 whole cloves; 1 x 3 cm (1 in) cinnamon stick; 8 whole allspice; 1/4 cup white vinegar; 1/2 cup sugar; 1 small orange, sliced; extra whole cloves (optional).

Drain apricots, reserving 1 cup syrup. Tie whole cloves, cinnamon and allspice in a piece of muslin or cheesecloth and put into saucepan with reserved apricot syrup, vinegar, sugar and orange slices. Bring to the boil. Add apricot halves and simmer 5 minutes. Cover and allow to cool at room temperature. Remove spice bag. Serve warm or chilled. If liked, stud some apricots with extra whole cloves. Spiced apricots improve on keeping; after 1 week they are at their best. Serve with baked ham, roast pork or cold meats. Serves 8.

Apricot Mousse

500 g (1 lb) dried apricots; 1/2 cup sugar; 3/4 cup cream; 1 tsp vanilla.

DECORATION: whipped cream; slivered, toasted almonds.

Simmer apricots in water to cover for 25 minutes. Stir in sugar and cook a further 5 minutes. Rub through a sieve or purée in a blender or food processor. Cool. Whip cream, add vanilla and fold into apricot purée. Spoon into small mousse pots or dessert bowls and chill. Decorate with whipped cream and almonds. Serves 6.

ARROZ CON POLLO (RICE WITH CHICKEN)

One of the best-known dishes from Spain. Recipes may vary slightly from region to region, but flavourings should always include olive oil, garlic and saffron. **See recipes.**

Arroz con Pollo

1 chicken, about 2 kg (4 lb), cut into serving pieces; 1/4 cup olive oil; 1 x 130 g can pimientos, drained and sliced; 1 large onion, chopped; 2 cloves garlic, crushed; 2 large ripe tomatoes, peeled, seeded and chopped; 12 large green olives, stoned and sliced; 1 cup shelled fresh or frozen peas; 3 cups chicken stock; 1/2 tsp saffron threads; 2 cups long-grain rice; salt and freshly ground black pepper.

Brown chicken pieces on all sides in hot oil. Add pimientos, onion, garlic, tomatoes, olives and peas. Fry together for a few minutes, stirring. Meanwhile, heat chicken stock and soak saffron threads in it for 5 minutes. Add stock to pan, bring to the boil, add rice and stir. Taste, and season with salt and pepper. Simmer, covered, for 30 minutes or until chicken is tender and rice has absorbed the liquid. Serves 4.

Arroz con Pollo Mexicano
(Mexican Rice with Chicken)

Arroz con Pollo travelled from Spain to Mexico, then to Peru, Colombia and Cuba and each country has its own adaptation. In Mexico, oregano and cilantro are used. Cilantro is the Mexican name for coriander or Chinese parsley.

6 chicken pieces (breasts, thighs, etc.); 1/2 cup olive oil; 1 onion, chopped; 2 cloves garlic, chopped; 1 1/2 cups long-grain rice; 1 x 425 g can tomatoes, drained; 1 tsp salt; freshly ground black pepper; 1 tbs chopped fresh oregano; 3 cups chicken stock.

GARNISH: 1 x 130 g can pimientos, drained and sliced; fresh cilantro (coriander or Chinese parsley) or chopped parsley.

Wipe over chicken and cut into small serving-sized pieces. Heat oil in a large frying pan and sauté chicken until just browned. Remove chicken and sauté onion and garlic. Add rice and cook until grains are coated with oil, shaking pan and stirring rice around. Add tomatoes, salt, pepper, oregano and chicken stock, mixing gently. Return chicken pieces to pan, pushing them down into rice. Simmer, covered (foil will do), until all liquid has been absorbed and chicken and rice are tender. Garnish dish with strips of pimiento and sprigs of cilantro or chopped parsley. Serves 6.

ARTICHOKE

THE GLOBE OR COMMON ARTICHOKE

The leafy bud of a plant of the thistle family. When buying fresh artichokes, look for solid heads with tightly packed leaves. They should be used as soon as possible after buying. If not cooking the same day, store in a closed container in the refrigerator.

■ **BASIC PREPARATION:** Wash and drain artichokes and trim stems. Pull off any coarse outer leaves then cut one-third off the top of the artichokes or cut off the thorny tips of the remaining leaves with kitchen scissors. As each artichoke is prepared, drop at once into a bowl of cold water containing lemon juice or vinegar; use about 3 tbs to each litre (4 cups) of water. This will prevent discolouration. It is possible to remove the hairy choke before cooking, to form little cups which are boiled and then filled with a savoury sauce or stuffing.

■ **TO COOK:** The basic cooking methods for artichokes are boiling and braising. **See also recipes.**

BOILED ARTICHOKES: Bring a large pan of salted water to the boil, add artichokes and boil, uncovered, until they are tender (from 20–45 minutes depending on size and freshness). A leaf will pull away easily when cooked. Drain upside-down and serve hot with melted butter, warmed cream or Hollandaise Sauce, or allow to cool and serve with Vinaigrette Dressing, Mayonnaise or Tartare Sauce (see pages 442 and 256).

TO EAT: Using fingers, pull off one leaf at a time, and dip the base in butter, cream or sauce. Pull the leaf between the teeth to scrape away the soft fleshy base and discard the rest of the leaf. In the centre of older artichokes you will find the fuzzy portion called the choke. Lift up and discard the choke and eat the soft fond (bottom) underneath. This is the most delicate part, and the one often canned for use in salads and antipasti (as are hearts of artichokes).

PRESERVED ARTICHOKES: Hearts and fonds of artichokes are available canned or bottled in brine or in oil. They are used in the preparation of antipasti and hors d'oeuvre. Artichoke hearts in brine are drained, dressed with Vinaigrette Dressing (see page 442) and chopped parsley and served chilled.

Italian Artichokes in Wine: Use young artichokes with slender elongated heads.

Cut the artichokes lengthways into quarters. Put in cold water to cover with some lemon slices as you prepare them. Heat a little olive oil in a heavy pan with a sprig of fresh, or a pinch of dried oregano, and 1 clove garlic. Add artichokes and cook over a moderate heat, tossing the artichokes until they are burnished and crispy on the outside. Remove garlic clove, add ½ cup white wine, season with salt and black pepper, cover and simmer gently until artichokes are tender, 10–15 minutes. Serve as a first course.

THE JERUSALEM ARTICHOKE

Despite the name, this vegetable is quite different from the globe artichoke. The globe is a bud, the Jerusalem artichoke is a tuber. About the size of a small potato, it is creamy-brown with a knobbly shape.

■ **TO COOK:** Wash well, peel and cut to the size of pigeons' eggs, then drop into boiling salted water with a squeeze of lemon juice or a little wine added to prevent discolouration. Cook with the lid on for about 5 minutes. Drain, return to pan, add a good knob of butter and cook gently for about 10 minutes or until tender. Season with salt and pepper and toss with a few chopped fresh herbs.

Purée of Jerusalem Artichokes: Peel and quarter artichokes and cook as above. Rub through a sieve, return to saucepan and heat gently with a few tablespoons of milk or cream and a touch of nutmeg.

Jerusalem Artichoke Soup: Prepare Purée of Jerusalem Artichokes (above). Add enough chicken stock or milk to make a cream soup consistency. Swirl with cream.

Braised Artichokes

Artichokes cooked gently with oil, wine and aromatics are an epicurean treat.

6 globe artichokes; 3 tbs olive oil; 1 cup dry white wine; 2 cloves garlic; 1 small onion, finely chopped; 1 tbs chopped parsley; 2 sprigs fresh oregano, or pinch dried; salt and freshly ground black pepper.

Prepare artichokes (see above). Combine remaining ingredients in a heavy saucepan, add artichokes and cook, covered, for 30–45 minutes or until tender. Add a little more oil and wine if liquid is drying out. Serve hot or warm with pan juices poured over.

Alternatively, drain and chill and serve with Vinaigrette Dressing (see page 442). Serves 6.

VARIATION

ARTICHOKES A LA GRECQUE: Prepare as for Braised Artichokes, adding 2 peeled, seeded and chopped tomatoes. Serve warm with some of the pan sauce spooned over, or cold, cut into quarters, again with some of the delicious sauce in which they were cooked. Top with chopped parsley. Serves 6.

Artichokes Clamart

Choose very small, young artichokes for this dish. Prepare in a heavy enamelled cast iron pan or flame-proof casserole and serve in the same dish.

8 small, young globe artichokes; 75 g (2 ½ oz) butter; I lettuce, shredded; 2 cups shelled fresh peas; ½ tsp salt; I tsp sugar; ½ cup stock.

Trim artichokes down to tender hearts. Melt 60 g (2 oz) butter in a heavy saucepan, add lettuce and place artichokes and peas on top. Add salt and sugar to taste and moisten with stock. Cover and simmer about 30 minutes or until vegetables are tender. Add remaining butter and serve immediately. Serves 4.

VARIATION

ARTICHOKES CRECY: Prepare as for Artichokes Clamart, replacing peas with an equal quantity of small young carrots, or larger carrots, diced.

Artichoke Heart Salad

I x 400 g can artichoke hearts; I small firm lettuce, shredded; I cup small, uncooked cauliflower florets; I large tomato, peeled, seeded and diced; I tbs snipped chives; 2 tbs sliced stuffed olives; 2 tbs chopped dill pickle; about ½ cup Vinaigrette Dressing (page 442).

Drain artichokes and chill. Combine with remaining ingredients, adding enough dressing to moisten well. Serve at once as a first course, or as a luncheon salad with cold meat. Serves 6.

Artichoke Halves Greek–Style

6 large globe artichokes; 4½ cups water; 3 lemons; I tbs flour; 2 onions, chopped; I cup olive oil; salt and freshly ground black pepper.

Cut stems off artichokes. Remove bottom leaves and with scissors trim off brown thorny tips of all remaining leaves. Cut off tops and halve each artichoke lengthways. Soak in 4 cups water and juice of 2 of the lemons. Meanwhile, sprinkle flour over onions and sauté in olive oil until lightly browned. Arrange artichoke halves, cut sides up, in roasting tin or large heavy frying pan. Add salt and pepper and juice of remaining lemon to onion and oil, and pour over artichokes. Add remaining water. Cover and simmer over low heat for 35–40 minutes or until artichokes are tender. Serve warm or cold. Serves 6.

Artichokes Roman–Style

Carciofi fritti vecchia Roma, the fried artichokes found on menus in Rome, are a treat. Young, tender artichokes, about 60 g (2 oz) in weight, are used for this dish.

6 baby globe artichokes; flour for dredging; I large egg, lightly beaten; 2 cups fresh breadcrumbs; I cup olive oil; 2 cups vegetable oil; salt.

Trim artichoke stems even with their bases and remove any hard exterior leaves. Blanch artichokes in boiling water for 7 minutes or until just tender. Drain in a colander and refresh under cold running water. Spread leaves of artichokes gently outward. Flatten them with the side of a large knife, being careful not to crack them, and pat dry. Dredge artichokes lightly in flour, then coat with egg, letting excess drip off. Finally coat with breadcrumbs, and shake off excess. Heat oils in a deep heavy saucepan over moderate heat and fry artichokes, a few at a time, for 3–5 minutes or until leaves are golden. Drain on paper towels. Sprinkle with salt and arrange on a heated platter. Serves 6 as a first course.

ASPARAGUS

This edible member of the lily family with its crisp stalks and closed, tender tips is considered a luxury vegetable throughout the world. Stalks may range from slender and green to thick, white and fleshy. Violet asparagus is favoured in Italy and wild asparagus is found in some places. Asparagus is delicious served hot, warm or cold. It may be served as an accompaniment, a first course, with salads, or combined with ingredients such as ham, cheese and eggs in main courses. When served as a separate course, it is best eaten with the fingers. When buying fresh asparagus look for firm, straight stalks with tightly closed, well-formed tips. Allow 6–8 spears per person when serving as a separate course.

Canned asparagus is one of the most versatile and popular of canned vegetables. It is used to make salads, sandwiches or a lovely mousse (see page 13), and may be used in any of the ways suggested for hot, boiled asparagus.

■ **BASIC PREPARATION:** Wash gently in cold, running water. Break off the bottom of the stalks at the point where they will snap easily. If stalks seem woody or scaly, peel them thinly with a vegetable peeler or sharp knife.

■ **TO STORE:** To keep fresh for longer stand the bunch in 2.5 cm (1 in) water and store in the fridge. Change the water frequently.

■ **TO COOK:** Asparagus is usually boiled, but may also be prepared Chinese-style (see page 13). **See also recipes.**

BOILED ASPARAGUS: Put prepared stalks into a large, shallow pan of boiling, salted water. Cook, uncovered, for 8–10 minutes or until just tender. Lift out of pan and drain on paper towels or a napkin.

CHINESE-STYLE ASPARAGUS: Slice prepared stalks in slanted pieces, leaving tips whole. Heat enough butter to cover the bottom of a frying pan, add asparagus pieces and season with salt and pepper. When steam rises, cover the pan, lower the heat and cook for about 4 minutes until tender-crisp.

WAYS TO SERVE ASPARAGUS

Devotees enjoy asparagus in many different ways. See opposite for preparation and cooking of asparagus. Good canned asparagus may also be treated in the following ways.

Asparagus Flamande: Prepare, boil and drain 24–30 asparagus spears, or use drained canned asparagus. Hard-boil 4 eggs for 8–10 minutes. Melt 90 g (3 oz) butter. Serve asparagus to each guest with 2 hard-boiled egg halves and melted butter. Each guest mashes the hard-boiled eggs, then adds them to the butter, and dips the asparagus into the mixture. Serves 4.

Asparagus au Gratin: Prepare, boil and drain 24–30 asparagus spears, or use drained canned asparagus. Make Mornay Sauce (see page 457), adding 2–3 tsp French mustard. Arrange asparagus in a buttered flameproof dish, spoon sauce over spears, sprinkle with ½ cup grated Parmasan cheese and 1 tbs melted butter, and brown under a preheated grill. Serves 4.

Asparagus Milanese: Proceed as in the recipe for Asparagus au Gratin, but omit Mornay Sauce. Serves 4.

Asparagus Hollandaise: Prepare, boil and drain 24–30 asparagus spears, or use drained canned asparagus. Keep warm. Make 1 quantity Hollandaise Sauce (see page 459). Serve asparagus with sauce spooned over tips. Serves 4.

Asparagus with Melted Butter: Prepare, boil and drain 24–30 asparagus spears, or use drained canned asparagus. Keep warm. Melt 125 g (4 oz) butter with a grinding of white pepper and a squeeze of lemon juice. Serve asparagus with melted butter. Serves 4.

Asparagus Polonaise: Prepare, boil and drain 24–30 asparagus spears, or use drained canned asparagus. Keep warm. To make Polonaise Butter: combine 3 hard-boiled egg yolks, chopped, with 1 tbs chopped parsley. Heat 2 tbs butter and fry ¾ cup fresh bread-crumbs until golden. Add egg yolks and parsley. Serve asparagus with polonaise butter. Serves 4.

Asparagus Noisette: Prepare, boil and drain 24–30 asparagus spears, or use drained canned asparagus. Keep warm. Heat 90 g (3 oz) butter until a light hazelnut (noisette) colour. Serve asparagus with browned butter. Serves 4.

Asparagus and Ham au Gratin

An excellent dish for a first course or light luncheon.

18 large, cooked asparagus spears (fresh or canned); 18 paper-thin slices cooked ham or prosciutto; 125 g (4 oz) butter, melted; 1 cup grated Parmesan cheese; 6 slices white bread, crusts removed; butter for frying.

Wrap each asparagus spear in a slice of ham. Arrange seam sides down, close together, in a shallow baking dish greased with a little of the butter. Sprinkle with half the remaining butter, then the cheese, then top with rest of butter. Bake in a preheated very hot oven (230°C/450°F) for 10 minutes or until topping is golden-brown. Meanwhile, cut bread into triangles and fry on both sides in a little butter until crisp and golden. Serve asparagus garnished with triangles of fried bread. Serves 6.

Cream of Fresh Asparagus Soup

500 g (1 lb) fresh asparagus; salt; 6 cups chicken stock; 1 medium onion, finely chopped; 2 sticks celery, finely chopped; 45 g (1½ oz) butter; 2 tbs flour; ½ cup cream; freshly ground white pepper; paprika; 2 finely chopped hard-boiled eggs, to garnish.

Wash asparagus and remove tips. Simmer tips in lightly salted water for 4–6 minutes or until tender. Drain and reserve. Cut stalks into small pieces and place in saucepan with stock, onion and celery. Simmer, covered, for 20 minutes or until vegetables are tender. Drain, reserving liquid, and rub vegetables through a sieve. Melt butter in a large saucepan, stir in flour, then slowly stir in cream over low heat. Add warm asparagus stock and stir until soup thickens. Add vegetable purée and reserved asparagus tips and heat through. Season with salt and pepper. Ladle into heated bowls and top each serving with a sprinkle of paprika and a spoonful of chopped egg. Serves 6.

Asparagus Mousse

2 x 440 g cans asparagus spears; 2 tbs gelatine; 6 tbs water; 1½ cups cream; salt and freshly ground white pepper; 3 egg whites; few drops green food colouring (optional).

GARNISH: extra asparagus spears; canned pimiento strips.

Drain asparagus and rub through a sieve, or purée in a blender then rub through a sieve to remove any stringy stalk. Soften gelatine in water, then stand container in hot water until dissolved. Add to asparagus purée, stirring continuously. Cool, then chill until mixture begins to thicken round edges.

Whip cream lightly and gradually stir into asparagus mixture until smooth. Season with salt and pepper. Beat egg whites to a firm snow and fold in with a few drops of green food colouring, if desired. Pour into a 7-cup mould which has been rinsed with cold water. Chill. To serve, unmould and garnish with extra asparagus spears and pimiento strips. Serve very cold. Serves 8.

Asparagus Rolls

Popular on the afternoon tea tray, or with pre-dinner drinks. Also suitable for large receptions.

12 slices sandwich bread, crusts removed; 60 g (2 oz) butter, softened; 1 x 440 g can asparagus spears, drained; salt and freshly ground white pepper.

Butter bread and place 1 asparagus spear diagonally on each slice. Season with salt and pepper, roll up and secure with a toothpick. Store, seam sides down, in shallow containers, covered with a slightly dampened tea-towel, in refrigerator. Take out 15 minutes before serving, and remove toothpicks to serve. Makes 12.

ASPIC

This is a clear, savoury jelly in which cold fish, poultry, meat or vegetables may be served. Aspic is also used to cover food, chopped for a garnish, or mixed with Mayonnaise (see page 256) to coat cold dishes. It is sold in powdered form with instructions for use on the package, or can be made at home.

TO MAKE AN ASPIC MOULD: After preparing aspic, allow it to cool until it is the consistency of unbeaten egg white. Have the mould chilled. Spoon a little aspic into the mould and run it round to cover the inside completely. Keep aspic jelly moving until it sets, to ensure only a thin coating. Allow to set firm. Pour a little aspic into a saucer, dip decorations – hard-boiled egg slices, raw or cooked vegetable or fruit pieces – into it and arrange them over base and sides of mould. (Place small decorations on the end of a skewer for dipping and arranging.) When design is completed, put to chill until set firm before adding filling.

TO COAT FOOD WITH ASPIC: Have food well dried and chilled. Place on a rack over a tray. Cool aspic to consistency of unbeaten egg white and spoon over food. Allow to set firm. Pour a little aspic into a saucer, dip decorations into it and arrange on food. Allow to set firm again, then spoon over 2–3 more layers aspic, allowing each to set firm before adding the next. Aspic that runs on to the tray can be warmed and re-used.

Quick Aspic: Soften 1½ tbs powdered gelatine in ¼ cup cold water, then dissolve by standing container in hot water. Heat the contents of 1 x 440 g can consommé, and stir in gelatine mixture and 2 tbs port, sherry or Madeira. Pour through a scalded cloth into a bowl. Makes about 2 cups.

AUBERGINE

See *Eggplant*.

AVGOLEMONO

The name indicates an egg-lemon mixture, whipped into stock to make a delicate, creamy sauce. It is famous in Greek cookery and popular throughout the Balkans. The mixture is also used to thicken soup. The sauce is always made from the liquid in which meats or vegetables have been cooked, thickened with beaten egg and fresh lemon juice. Fish may be poached and the liquor used to make an avgolemono sauce. Chicken, lamb, meatballs and dolmas may all be served with this sauce. **See recipes.**

See also *Dolma, Dolmades*.

Soupa Avgolemono

½ cup short-grain rice or tiny pasta shapes; 6 cups chicken or fish stock; salt and freshly ground white pepper; 3 eggs, separated; ½ cup lemon juice.

Cook rice or pasta in boiling stock until tender. Season with salt and pepper. Beat egg whites to a firm snow, add yolks and lemon juice and beat until creamy. Whisk a large ladleful of soup into egg mixture, then remove soup from heat and gradually add egg mixture. Stir vigorously while adding it, and for 1 minute longer. Serve at once. Serves 6–8.

Avgolemono

1 cup stock; 2 eggs; juice 1 lemon.

Heat stock in a small saucepan. Beat eggs and add lemon juice. Slowly add some of the hot stock to eggs while continuing to beat. Stir egg mixture into remaining stock. Remove from heat. Cover and let stand for 5 minutes to thicken. Serve at once. Do not reheat. Serves 4–6.

Meatballs with Avgolemono

500 g (1 lb) lean minced steak; 1 small onion, chopped; 2 tsp chopped fresh mint; 1 tbs chopped parsley; 1 tbs cooked rice; salt and freshly ground black pepper; 1½ cups beef stock; 1 cup water; 2 egg yolks; juice 1 lemon.

Mix together steak, onion, mint, parsley, rice, salt, pepper and ¼ cup beef stock. Form into balls the size of a walnut. Bring remaining stock and the water to the boil in a saucepan and drop in meatballs. Simmer for 30 minutes. Beat egg yolks with lemon juice. Slowly add some of the hot stock, beating constantly. Stir egg yolk mixture into remaining stock in pan, cover and stand for 5 minutes off heat before serving. Serves 4.

Chicken Macerata

Chicken is cooked this way in the little town of Macerata, in the Umbria region of Italy.

1 roasting chicken; salt; 2 tbs olive oil; 60 g (2 oz) butter; 2 cups chicken stock (cubes may be used); 2 egg yolks; grated rind and juice 1 lemon.

Rub chicken inside and out with salt, and tie into a good shape. Heat oil and butter in a flameproof casserole, preferably an oval one, into which chicken will fit snugly. Add chicken and cook, turning it, until golden-brown all over. Turn chicken breast side up. Add stock – there should be enough to come halfway up bird. Cover casserole with greaseproof paper, then lid and cook over a low heat for about 1 hour or until chicken is tender. Remove bird and boil liquid over a high heat to reduce it by about a third. Cut the chicken into serving pieces and arrange on a flameproof platter. Keep warm. (For a crispy-skin finish, place it under a preheated grill.)

Beat egg yolks until well mixed but not frothy. Add lemon rind and juice and salt. Add to liquid in casserole and cook, lightly beating, over a gentle heat for 1 minute. Do not boil, and be careful not to overcook; keep beating or eggs will set in strands. Allow to stand off heat for a few minutes. Spoon sauce over chicken. Serve with crusty bread to mop up juices. Serves 4.

AVOCADO

Avocados are the fruit of trees native to Central and South America. They are easy to eat, easy to digest and are rich in oils, proteins and vitamins, particularly vitamin C. They may be pear-shaped or round, and green, purple or blackish-coloured. Some have a thin skin and some a hard, knobbly shell. All have pale, creamy flesh and are ready to eat when they yield slightly if pressed gently between the hands. Choose fruit that is heavy and even-coloured without cracks, bruises or very soft spots. Avocados that are firm and hard will ripen if kept at room temperature for 2–3 days.

■ **BASIC PREPARATION:** Using a stainless steel knife to prevent discolouration, cut in half downward from the stem end. Twist halves slightly to separate, and lift out stone by impaling it on the sharp point of a knife. If you are removing the skin, peel off with a knife if thin, or pry off with a teaspoon handle if thick and hard. Halves can be diced, sliced or mashed. Since the flesh darkens quickly on contact with air, brush or toss immediately with lemon juice or vinegar.

WAYS TO USE AVOCADOS

AS AN APPETISER OR FIRST COURSE: Serve halves in the shell, one half per person. The hollows can be filled with Viniagrette Dressing (see page 442), or seafood mixed with Mayonnaise (see page 256). Some people like just salt, freshly ground black pepper and lemon juice or a sprinkle of Worcestershire sauce.

AS A SANDWICH FILLING OR AS A TOPPING FOR SAVOURIES: Mash flesh with lemon juice, salt and freshly ground black pepper and a touch of crushed garlic or grated onion. A little crumbled crisp bacon sprinkled on top is delicious.

AS A GARNISH: Add cubes of avocado to consommé, or cut in crescents to top potato, chicken or mixed salad.

TO SERVE HOT: Fill cavities of halved avocados in the shell with hot creamed seafood, ham or chicken. Top with grated cheese or buttered breadcrumbs and bake in a preheated moderate oven (180°C/350°F) for 10 minutes or just until heated through. **See recipes.**

See also *Guacamole*.

Guacamole Salad

2 large avocados, peeled, stoned and cut into large dice; 2 medium tomatoes, peeled, seeded and chopped; 2 spring onions, finely sliced; crisp lettuce leaves; chopped parsley; 2 canned pimientos, drained.

DRESSING: 2 tbs oil; 1 tbs vinegar; few drops Tabasco sauce; juice ¹/₂ lemon; salt and freshly ground black pepper.

DRESSING: Beat all ingredients together in a small bowl until mixture thickens.

Put avocado into a bowl and toss gently with dressing. Add tomatoes and spring onions. Cover and chill. To serve, line individual plates with lettuce leaves. Place avocado mixture on lettuce. Sprinkle with parsley. Finely dice or sieve pimientos and spoon over. Serves 4.

Avocado Soup

A creamy soup that can be served hot or cold.

2 medium avocados, peeled, stoned and sliced; 1 cup cream; 4 cups chicken stock; salt and freshly ground white pepper; pinch nutmeg; 1 tbs lemon juice; extra cream to finish.

Purée avocados with cream in a blender or food processor, or mash together and rub through a sieve. For a cold soup, add purée to cold stock, season with salt, pepper, nutmeg and lemon juice and chill. For hot soup, add purée to hot stock and heat to just below boiling point. Season, and serve immediately. Finish hot or cold soup with a swirl of cream on each serving. Serves 6–8.

Avocado Mousse

1 envelope (3 tsp) gelatine; 1 cup chicken stock; 2 large avocados, peeled, stoned and mashed; 2 tsp snipped chives; salt and freshly ground white pepper; 2 tbs lemon juice; 1 tsp Worcestershire sauce; few drops Tabasco sauce; ¹/₂ cup cream; ³/₄ cup Mayonnaise (page 256); 2 egg whites.

Soften gelatine in a little cold stock, then stand container in hot water until dissolved. Add remaining stock, avocados and chives, and beat until smooth. Add salt, pepper, lemon juice, and Worcestershire and Tabasco sauces. Chill until mixture is consistency of unbeaten egg white. Whip cream and fold in with mayonnaise. Beat egg whites until they hold soft peaks and fold in. Adjust seasoning and pour into a wet 6-cup mould. Chill until set. To serve, unmould mousse on to a chilled platter. Serves 8–10.

Avocado and Bacon Salad

This makes a lovely main course salad for 4 or a first course for 8.

2 avocados, peeled, stoned and sliced;
1/2 cup Vinaigrette Dressing (page 442);
4 rashers bacon, rind removed; crisp lettuce leaves;
2 tomatoes, peeled and cut into wedges;
8 black olives; chopped fresh parsley to garnish.

Sprinkle avocado slices with a little of the vinaigrette. Cut each bacon rasher into 3 and pan-fry; drain on crumpled paper towels. Place lettuce leaves on 4 plates and arrange avocado slices on top and tomato wedges at one side. Strew bacon over avocado, add olives and drizzle with remaining vinaigrette. Sprinkle with plenty of chopped parsley. Serves 4 or 8.

Avocado Grand Duc

3/4 cup crabmeat, canned or fresh,
picked over well; 2 tbs Mayonnaise (page 256);
1 tbs tomato paste; juice 1/2 lemon; salt and freshly
ground black pepper; 1 avocado, halved and stoned;
1 hard-boiled egg, chopped; 1 tsp chopped parsley;
1 tsp chopped fresh tarragon; 1 tsp chopped fresh
chervil; 2 tsp caviar (optional).

Combine crabmeat, mayonnaise, tomato paste, lemon juice, salt and pepper. Mix lightly and fill avocado halves with mixture. Mix together egg, parsley, tarragon and chervil, and sprinkle over avocado halves. If wished, top each half with a teaspoonful of caviar. Serves 2.

Avocado Sauce

A sauce for cold fish or chicken.

1 large avocado, halved and stoned;
1 tbs tarragon vinegar; 4 tbs olive oil;
2 tbs lemon juice; pinch cayenne;
salt and freshly ground black pepper; 1 egg yolk.

Scoop flesh from avocado halves and beat with vinegar, oil, lemon juice, cayenne, salt and pepper. Chill. Just before serving add egg yolk and beat again. Makes about 1½ cups.

Avocado Dressing

Similar to guacamole but smoother and not so hot. Use with chicken or fish salads. May also be added to coleslaw.

1 large avocado, peeled and stoned; 3 tbs lime or
lemon juice; 1 tbs finely chopped onion; 1 clove
garlic; 1 tsp salt; freshly ground black pepper.

Mash avocado to a soft purée. Add lime or lemon juice, onion and garlic which has been finely chopped or crushed with the salt and pepper. Blend ingredients well. Cover dressing. The avocado stone can be placed in the mixture – it is said this prevents the avocado from discolouring. Makes about 1¼ cups.

Spanish Avocado Salad

This filling salad makes a delicious lunch dish served with chicken or ham.

1 avocado, peeled, stoned and thickly sliced
crossways; juice 1 lemon; 1 lettuce; 4 ripe tomatoes,
peeled and thickly sliced; 1 green pepper, cored,
seeded, blanched and cut into thick strips;
1/2 cup Vinaigrette Dressing (page 442);
1 small onion, finely sliced.

Brush avocado slices with lemon juice to preserve colour. Line a salad bowl with lettuce leaves. Toss prepared vegetables lightly in dressing and arrange in lettuce-lined bowl. Pour remaining dressing over salad and garnish with onion rings. Serves 4–6.

Avocado Pimiento Salad

crisp lettuce leaves; 2 avocados, peeled, stone and
sliced; 2 canned pimientos, diced or cut into strips;
8 black olives, halved and stoned; 3 tsp lemon juice;
finely chopped parsley.

DRESSING: 2½ tbs oil; 2 tsp lemon juice;
1/4 tsp French mustard; few drops Tabasco sauce;
salt and freshly ground black pepper.

Beat together dressing ingredients or shake them in a jar. Place lettuce leaves on 4 plates and arrange avocados on leaves. Sprinkle with dressing. Add pimiento, olives and lemon juice. Top with parsley. Serves 4.

b

BABA (AU RHUM)

A delectable French dessert cake made of yeast dough containing currants and soaked in rum-flavoured syrup. Large babas are baked in a tall, cylindrical mould and small ones in individual baba, dariole or castle pudding moulds.

Baba au Rhum

$^1/_4$ cup currants; $^1/_2$ cup sultanas; $^1/_4$ cup dark rum; 15 g ($^1/_2$ oz) compressed yeast; $^1/_2$ cup lukewarm milk; 3 tbs plus pinch sugar; 2 cups flour; $^1/_2$ tsp salt; 4 eggs, lightly beaten; 125 g (4 oz) butter, softened.

SYRUP: $1^1/_2$ cups water; $1^1/_2$ cups sugar; 4 tbs dark rum.

GLAZE: 1 cup apricot jam; 2 tbs water; 2 tbs dark rum.

Soak currants and sultanas in rum overnight. To make dough, cream yeast with milk and pinch sugar and stand for 10 minutes. Sift flour, remaining sugar and salt into a large warmed bowl, make a well in centre and add yeast mixture. Sprinkle a little flour from sides over liquid, cover with a cloth and leave in a warm place for 20 minutes. Add eggs and butter to flour-yeast mixture and beat vigorously until dough is smooth and elastic. Drain fruit and mix into dough. Cover with greased plastic wrap and a cloth and leave in a warm place to rise for about 1 hour until doubled in bulk.

Pipe or spoon the baba dough into 16–18 buttered individual baba moulds, filling one-third full. Let dough rise until it reaches tops of moulds. Place baba in a preheated very hot oven (230°C/450°F), then immediately reduce the oven heat to hot (200°C/400°F). Bake for 15 minutes or until well browned. Remove babas from moulds and cool on a wire rack until lukewarm.

SYRUP: Combine water and sugar and cook, stirring, until sugar dissolves. Boil for 10 minutes without stirring, then remove from heat and add rum. Cool until warm. Place rack of babas over a tray and slowly spoon warm syrup over babas so they absorb as much as possible. As syrup collects in tray, re-spoon over babas.

GLAZE: Heat jam and water together, stirring until jam melts. Stir in rum, then rub through a sieve. Brush over babas. Makes 16–18.

NOTE: Dry yeast can be used. See *Yeast Cookery*.

BABA GHANNOUJ

This Middle Eastern eggplant (aubergine) purée with tahini is served as a dip with flat bread, or as a salad with meats and fish.

Baba Ghannouj

3 medium eggplants; 3 cloves garlic, crushed with 1 tsp salt; $^1/_2$ cup tahini (sesame paste); juice 2 medium lemons; 1 tsp ground cumin.

GARNISH: 2 tbs finely chopped parsley; black olives; sliced tomato.

Sear eggplants over a gas flame or under a grill, turning often. Continue searing until skins are blackened and blistered, and flesh soft. Scrape or peel charred skin from eggplants, rinse under cold water and squeeze in a tea-towel to remove as much juice as possible. Mash eggplant flesh with a fork or potato masher. Add garlic and pound to a smooth purée. (This may also be done in a blender or food processor.) Add tahini and lemon juice alternately, beating or blending between each addition. Add cumin and blend. Taste, and add more lemon juice, garlic, tahini or salt if necessary. Mixture should be highly flavoured. Spoon into a bowl or individual serving dishes, sprinkle with parsley, and garnish with olives and tomato slices. Serves 8–12 as a dip.

BACON

This is the fat and lean meat from the side and back of the pig, cured (i.e. preserved) by dry salting or brining. It is frequently smoked as well, for extra flavour and keeping qualities.

TYPES OF BACON

Streaky bacon has alternate streaks of fat and lean, and is sold in narrow strips called rashers. It is delicious grilled or fried with eggs, tomatoes, kidneys; on grilled sandwiches, etc. It crumbles easily when cooked, to make a crisp garnish for vegetables, savoury creamed dishes and salads.

Middle cut bacon, also called 'prime', is lean meat with an edging of fat. It may have a 'tail' of streaky bacon, or the streaky rasher may be removed and sold separately.

Canadian bacon is sugar-cured, smoked pork loin, boned and with the fillet removed. It is very choice and may be eaten hot or cold. In some countries it is not sold as bacon but as 'smoked pork loin'.

Shoulder bacon is lean meat from the shoulder, with little or no fat. Slices are squarish, and are usually thicker than other cuts. They are often used in dishes calling for ham, and can be a main course, fried or grilled with pineapple slices, tomatoes, etc.

Gammon of bacon is particularly popular in Britain. In recipes, gammon and ham may often be interchanged. The flavour is not quite the same as ham, however, because of the different breed of pig and the different curing method.

NOTE: A pig bred for bacon is called a baconer and a pig bred for ham is called a porker.

Speck is highly flavoured, cured and smoked pork which contains a very high proportion of fat. It is sold in slabs and is particularly popular in Germany and other European countries where it is used as the basic fat for browning and adding flavour to vegetables, soups, stews, savoury pastries, etc. It is easy to cut into slices, squares or dice and, when the fat is rendered, there are delicious crispy bits left to add extra flavour and texture to a dish. When a recipe calls for speck and it is not available, fatty streaky bacon or pickled belly of pork with a good proportion of fat, may be used instead.

Green bacon has been lightly cured but not smoked. It has a milder flavour than smoked bacon. If a recipe has green bacon in it, you can blanch ordinary bacon by covering it with cold water and bringing to the boil. Boil 1 minute and drain. This will remove some of the salty and smoky flavour.

See also Pancetta (Italian Bacon).

■ **TO COOK:** Bacon rashers may be grilled, fried or baked. **See also recipes.**

GRILLED BACON: Remove rind, if desired. Snip bacon edges with kitchen scissors to prevent curling. Place rashers on a rack over the grill pan and grill about 10 cm (4 in) from the heat for 2–3 minutes on each side.

FRIED BACON: Remove rind, if desired, and snip edges of bacon. Streaky bacon should be placed in a cold frying pan without extra fat and cooked over very low heat, turning frequently, until done to your liking. If you want the bacon crisp, pour off fat as it collects. Never allow the fat to smoke or the bacon will have a burnt flavour. For lean bacon, grease the frying pan with lard or butter and heat before adding bacon. Cook over medium heat, turning once or twice. Add a little extra fat if necessary to prevent sticking.

BAKED BACON: This is a useful method when you have a large quantity of bacon to cook, as it requires less watching and doesn't need turning. Remove rind from bacon, if desired. Arrange bacon rashers on a wire rack placed over a baking dish, and bake in a preheated hot oven (200°C/400°F) for 10–15 minutes.

Green Salad with Bacon: Tear washed and dried, crisp salad greens into bite-size pieces and place in a bowl. Season with salt and pepper and sprinkle with chopped fresh herbs. Fry streaky bacon rashers, rinds removed, until crisp, chop or crumble coarsely and add to salad. To the fat in the pan add a little vinegar to sharpen taste, pour hot over greens, toss lightly and serve at once.

Grilled Cheese and Bacon Sandwich: A favourite everywhere. Toast bread on one side, butter untoasted side and cover with sliced cheese. Arrange bacon rashers, rinds removed, on top and grill until bacon is crisp and cheese melted.

Variation: Spread butter with chutney or mustard before adding cheese, or add a layer of thinly sliced tomato or thinly sliced pineapple.

Warm Bacon, Avocado and Lettuce Salad

1 large or 2 small lettuce, preferably a soft-leaved variety such as cos or mignonette; 3 thick rashers bacon, rind removed; 2 tomatoes, peeled, seeded and cut into wedges; 2 large avocados, peeled, stoned and cut into chunks.

DRESSING: 3 tsp wine vinegar; pinch salt; freshly ground black pepper; 2 tbs olive oil.

Rinse and dry lettuce, and crisp in refrigerator. Cut bacon into strips the size of a little finger. Line a bowl with lettuce leaves and add tomatoes.

DRESSING: Whisk ingredients together. Add avocado to dressing and toss to coat. Place in bowl. Toss bacon strips in a frying pan over high heat until lightly browned. Pour over salad and serve at once. Serves 6.

Wilted Salad with Bacon

4 tbs vinegar; 1^1/$_2$ tsp sugar; 1 clove garlic, crushed; ^{1}/$_2$ tsp pepper; 6 rashers bacon, rind removed and cut into 2.5 cm (1 in) strips; 1 cos lettuce, rinsed and dried; 2 large ripe tomatoes, each cut into 4 thick slices; 3–4 spring onions, finely sliced.

Mix vinegar, sugar, garlic and pepper in a small bowl. Let stand at least 30 minutes. Fry bacon in a large pan until crisp. Remove pan from heat and add lettuce to hot bacon fat. Gently stir for a minute or until lettuce wilts a little. Add vinegar mixture and mix well. Arrange tomato slices on a large plate or individual salad plates, mound the lettuce on top and sprinkle the spring onions over before serving. Serves 4.

Bacon Appetisers

Before you begin, soak 30 small wooden skewers in water. This will prevent their catching fire during cooking.

500 g (1 lb) chicken livers; 1 x 338 g can water chestnuts, drained; 10–15 rashers bacon, rind removed.

Cut each liver in 2 or 3 pieces. Halve the water chestnuts. Cut each bacon rasher in 4 pieces, and wrap a piece around each water chestnut half. On each skewer, thread a piece of liver and a piece of bacon-wrapped water chestnut. Repeat so that each skewer has at least 2 pieces of liver. Place threaded skewers on a grilling rack and cook under a preheated grill for 3 minutes each side or until the bacon is lightly browned. Makes 30.

Bacon Muffins

2 cups flour; 3 tsp baking powder; ^{1}/$_2$ tsp salt; 1 tbs sugar; 1 egg, lightly beaten; 1 cup milk; ^{1}/$_4$ cup melted butter; 3 rashers bacon, rind removed, crisp fried and crumbled.

Sift flour, baking powder, salt and sugar into a large bowl. Add egg, milk, butter and bacon, stirring only enough to dampen the flour; the batter should not be smooth. Spoon into buttered muffin pans, filling each cup about two-thirds full. Bake in a preheated moderately hot oven (190°C/375°F) for 20–25 minutes. Makes 12.

Bacon and Scallops en Brochette

750 g (1¹/₂ lb) scallops; ¹/₂ cup white wine; 1 tbs soy sauce; 1 tbs olive oil; 2 cloves garlic, finely chopped; grated rind 1 lemon; ¹/₂ cup chopped parsley; 250 g (8 oz) rashers bacon, rind removed.

Trim off any dark parts from scallops but retain coral. Cover scallops with a mixture of white wine, soy sauce and olive oil. Let them marinate for about 20 minutes, then drain. Mix garlic, lemon rind and parsley. Cut each bacon rasher into 4 and curl into rolls. Roll each scallop in parsley mixture and thread scallops on to skewers alternately with bacon rolls. Grill, turning frequently, until scallops are just cooked but not dry, about 8–10 minutes. Serve with rice, plain or saffron-flavoured. Serves 6.

BAGEL

A doughnut-shaped roll which is a distinctive part of Jewish cuisine. It is first cooked in water, then baked, which gives the bagel its characteristic hard, glazed crust. A traditional filling for bagels is cream cheese and lox (smoked salmon).

BAGNA CAUDA

An Italian garlicky sauce served hot as a dip for crisp, raw vegetables.

Bagna Cauda

250 g (8 oz) butter; 4 tbs olive oil; 4 cloves garlic, crushed; 6 anchovy fillets, finely chopped; salt if necessary.

Heat butter and oil together in a shallow pan, add garlic and stir over medium heat until garlic is soft but not brown. Remove pan from heat and add anchovies. Return to low heat and continue cooking, stirring well with a wooden spoon, until anchovies have dissolved to a paste. Taste and season with salt if necessary. Keep hot over a candle warmer or other burner, and serve surrounded by cold, crisp raw vegetables. Serves 6–8.

BAGUETTE (FRENCH BREAD)

This is the name for the flattened, cylindrical loaf which is the everyday bread of France, bought warm and crisp from the bakery, often twice a day. Baguettes may come in different lengths, but are always distinguished by their shape and crisp crust which is slashed on top.

BAKLAVA

A superb sweet pastry, typical of the luscious pastries of Greece and the Middle East.

Baklava

20 sheets filo pastry (about 1 x 375 g/12 oz packet); 185 g (6 oz) butter, melted; 1¹/₂ cups finely chopped walnuts; ³/₄ cup finely chopped almonds; ¹/₄ cup caster sugar; 2 tsp cinnamon; ¹/₈ tsp ground cloves.

SYRUP: 2 cups sugar; 2 cups water; 2 whole cloves; 1 x 8 cm (3 in) cinnamon stick; 1 tbs lemon juice; thin strip lemon rind; 2 tbs honey.

Unwrap filo pastry, spread flat on a tea-towel and cover with a dry tea-towel then a damp one to stop drying out while assembling baklava. Place one sheet of filo in a buttered 33 x 23 x 5 cm (13 x 9 x 2 in) baking dish, brush all over with melted butter and place another sheet on top. Continue adding sheets of filo, buttering in between, until 9 sheets are used. Mix nuts with sugar and spices and sprinkle half over filo. Add 2 more sheets of filo, brushing each with butter. Top with remaining nuts and then 9 more sheets of buttered filo. Trim edges and brush top layer with butter. With a sharp knife, cut through top few sheets of filo to make a diamond pattern. Sprinkle a little water over surface to keep pastry flat while baking, and bake in centre of a preheated moderately slow oven (160°C/325°F) for 30 minutes. Move baklava to a shelf placed above centre and bake for a further 30 minutes. If pastry is browning too much, cover with foil, but do not reduce cooking time.

SYRUP: Place all the ingredients in a saucepan and stir over high heat until sugar dissolves. Bring to the boil and boil over moderate heat for 10 minutes. Strain and cool before using. Spoon syrup over hot baklava as soon as it comes from the oven. Allow to cool, and cut into diamonds to serve. Makes 30.

BALMAIN BUGS

These small crustaceans are also known as shovel-nosed, bay or sand lobsters. They and their close relatives, Moreton Bay Bugs, are widely distributed in Australia's offshore waters. Their flesh, contained mostly in the tail, is rather like that of lobster, and they can be prepared in any way, hot or cold, that is suitable for lobster or other shellfish. They can be bought cooked or uncooked. When buying cooked bugs, be sure that the tails are tightly curled against the undersides and will snap back if straightened. A limp tail means freshness is suspect.

TO REMOVE MEAT FROM A COOKED BUG: Cut round the underside of the body and tail shells with a heavy knife or kitchen scissors and lift out the meat. Discard any soft matter. The upper shell of the body can be washed and used as a container for the meat with its sauce or dressing. If preferred, the bug can be cut in half down the middle, as for lobster, and the meat removed.

TO COOK OR KILL LIVE BUGS: See *Lobster* and follow the same techniques.

BAMBOO SHOOTS

The tender, inner part of young shoots of the bamboo tree are used as an ingredient in Chinese, Japanese and other Oriental dishes. Canned bamboo shoots are widely available today. They should be drained and rinsed in cold water before using.

Bamboo Shoots with Broccoli and Mushrooms

500 g (1 lb) broccoli; 8–10 dried Chinese mushrooms; 6 spring onions; 4 tbs peanut oil; 1 cup drained, canned bamboo shoots; 1 tsp salt; 1 tsp sugar; 1 tbs light soy sauce; 1 tbs dry sherry or rice wine; hot boiled rice to serve.

Cut thick stems from broccoli and save for another use. Cut flower part into pieces 2.5–5 cm (1–2 in) long. Soak dried mushrooms in warm water for 15 minutes. Drain, reserving ¼ cup water. Cut each spring onion into 3 pieces. Drop broccoli into boiling water. When water boils again, drain and refresh under cold running water. Heat oil in a wok or frying pan, add mushrooms, bamboo shoots and spring onions and stir-fry on high heat 1 minute. Add broccoli, salt, sugar, soy sauce, sherry and soaking water from mushrooms. Toss gently for 2 minutes and serve immediately with hot boiled rice. Serves 4.

BANANA

Buy bananas with smooth, unblemished skins and, if possible, in a bunch rather than separately as they keep better. Slightly green bananas may be used for cooking; for eating, allow to ripen at room temperature. Never store in the refrigerator. If slicing or chopping bananas for fruit salads or to decorate cakes, pies, etc., toss with a little lemon or other citrus fruit juice to prevent their turning brown. See recipes.

Baked Bananas: To cook green bananas as a vegetable, place unpeeled bananas in a baking dish and cook in a preheated moderate oven (180°C/350°F) for about 20 minutes until soft when tested with a fork. Peel when cool enough to handle, and season with salt and pepper. Ripe bananas may be cooked in the same way, though cooking time will be less. Serve as a vegetable, or sprinkle with a little brown sugar and lemon juice or rum and serve with ice cream as a dessert.

Banana Custard: Slice 1 ripe banana for each person into a heatproof serving bowl, and sprinkle with lemon juice and a little sugar. Make Stirred Custard (see page 111), using 2 cups milk for 4 bananas. Pour hot custard over the sliced bananas. Sprinkle with nutmeg and serve warm or chilled. For a quick dessert, bought dairy custard may be heated and used instead of home-made custard.

Banana Fritters

4 medium firm bananas; 3 tbs lemon juice; 2 tbs icing sugar, sifted; 1 cup flour; pinch salt; ²/₃ cup warm water; 2 tbs oil; 2 egg whites; oil for deep frying.

TO SERVE: lemon juice; sifted icing sugar.

Peel bananas and cut each into 3 chunks. Sprinkle with lemon juice and icing sugar. Let stand 30 minutes. Meanwhile, sift flour and salt into a bowl, make a well in centre and add water and oil. Stir from centre, gradually drawing in flour, and beat until smooth. Cover and stand 30 minutes. Beat egg whites to a firm snow and fold into batter. Dry banana chunks, dip in batter and deep-fry in hot oil until golden-brown. Drain on paper towels. Serve at once, sprinkled with extra lemon juice and icing sugar. Serves 4.

Bananas au Rhum

A quick dessert that tastes delicious.

60 g (2 oz) butter; 1 tsp grated lemon rind; 1 tbs lemon juice; 4 firm ripe bananas; 4 tbs brown sugar; ¼ cup rum; cream to serve.

Put the butter and lemon rind and juice in a baking dish and place it in a preheated moderate oven (180°C/350°F) for 2–3 minutes, just long enough to melt the butter. Remove and stir. Put bananas in baking dish, turning so they are coated with butter mixture. Sprinkle brown sugar over them and bake for 15 minutes. Heat rum, pour over bananas and set alight. Spoon burning liquor over bananas until flames die down. Serve hot with cream. Serves 4.

Bananas Caribbean

Bananas baked with flavourings make a superb dessert. For a party, they can be flamed at the table.

8 medium, firm bananas; ¼ cup firmly packed brown sugar; ½ cup orange juice; grated rind 1 orange; ¼ tsp cinnamon; ¼ tsp nutmeg; ½ cup sherry; 30 g (1 oz) butter; 4 tbs rum; 30 g (1 oz) desiccated coconut; vanilla ice cream or whipped cream to serve.

Peel bananas and arrange in a buttered, shallow, baking dish. Heat brown sugar, orange juice and rind, spices

b

and sherry together. Pour over bananas and dot butter over top. Bake in a preheated moderately hot oven (190°C/375°F) for 10–15 minutes or until soft, basting now and again. Transfer bananas and sauce to a serving dish. Heat rum, pour over bananas and set alight. Spoon sauce over bananas until flames die down. Sprinkle with coconut and serve with ice cream. Serves 4–6.

Sautéed Bananas

This makes a lovely dessert, and also a fine accompaniment to curry or chicken dishes without the icing sugar.

60 g (2 oz) butter; 4 firm ripe bananas, halve lengthways; 4 tbs icing sugar.

Melt butter in a frying pan. Add bananas and cook over moderate heat for 5 minutes, turning once. Remove to a heated dish and spoon butter from pan over them. Sift icing sugar on top. Serves 3–4.

Banana Nut Bread

This is a simple banana bread, heavy, moist and dark.

3 ripe bananas, well mashed; 2 eggs, well beaten; 2 cups flour; 3/4 cup sugar; I tsp salt; I tsp bicarbonate of soda; 1/2 cup coarsely chopped walnuts.

Mix bananas and eggs together in a large bowl. Sift in flour, sugar, salt and bicarbonate of soda. Add walnuts and blend. Put batter in greased 21 x 11 cm (8½ x 4½ in) loaf tin and bake in a preheated moderate oven (180°C/350°F) for 1 hour. Remove from pan to a wire rack. Serve still warm or cooled, as you like, with butter.

BANBURY TART

A sweet pastry from Banbury in Oxfordshire, England, a town whose name is known to many from the old rhyme, 'Ride a cock horse to Banbury Cross'.

Banbury Tarts

I x 375 g (12 oz) packet frozen puff pastry, thawed; 1/2 cup raisins; 1/2 cup currants; 1/2 cup chopped mixed candied peel; 1/2 cup sugar; grated rind and juice I large lemon; I tsp ground allspice; 1/2 cup water; 2 tbs flour.

GLAZE: beaten egg; sugar.

Roll out pastry thinly and cut into rounds about 8 cm (3 in) in diameter. Combine remaining ingredients (except glaze) in a saucepan and stir over low heat until thick. Allow to cool. Dampen edges of half the pastry rounds and place about 2 tsp filling in centre of each. Top with remaining pastry rounds. Press edges firmly together and decorate with tines of a fork.

Glaze with egg and sprinkle with sugar. Place on baking trays and bake in a preheated hot oven (220°C/425°F) for 15–20 minutes or until golden-brown. Cool on a wire rack. Makes about 12.

BANNOCK

The word 'bannock' comes from the Gaelic for 'cake' and this flat, substantial cake has been part of traditional Scottish fare for centuries. The everyday bannock is not to be confused with the Selkirk Bannock, which is a rich fruit cake made from a yeast dough.

Oatmeal Bannocks

2/3 cup medium oatmeal; pinch bicarbonate of soda; pinch salt; 2 tsp melted lard, dripping or bacon fat; about 1/4 cup hot water; extra oatmeal.

Place oatmeal in a basin with soda and salt and stir to combine. Make a well in the centre and pour in melted fat. Add enough hot water to bind mixture to a stiff paste. Turn out on to a work surface spread thickly with oatmeal. Roll mixture into a ball, using oatmeal to prevent sticking. Knead a few times, then pat out to a round about 5 cm (1/4 in) thick. Sprinkle with a little extra oatmeal, and cut into quarters. Place on a lightly greased hot griddle or frying pan and cook over medium heat until the underside is brown and the edges curl slightly. Turn over with a spatula and brown the other side. Serve warm with butter and honey or jam. Makes 4.

BAP

Baps are the breakfast rolls of Scotland – to the Scot, as indispensable as croissants are to the French. They are light, white and soft (not crusty), and delicious eaten hot with butter. Buttery baps contain extra butter, while floury baps are a less rich mixture, lightly dusted with flour to give them their characteristic appearance.

Floury Baps

4 cups flour; I tsp salt; 3/4 cup milk; 1/2 cup water; 60 g (2 oz) butter; 15 g (1/2 oz) compressed yeast; I tsp sugar; little extra milk and flour.

Sift flour with salt into a bowl. Heat milk and water together to blood heat; add butter and remove from heat when butter has melted. Cream yeast with sugar and stir into warm liquid. Make a well in centre of flour and pour in yeast mixture. Stir in a little flour from the sides until yeast mixture is consistency of thick batter. Cover with a folded cloth and place in a warm spot. When yeast mixture has doubled, and bubbles have formed, mix in remaining flour. Turn dough on to a floured board and knead for about 5 minutes until smooth. Place in a clean, greased bowl and turn over so top surface is also lightly greased. Cover with greased plastic wrap and leave in a warm place for 2 hours or until doubled in bulk. Knock down, and turn on to a floured board. Knead lightly, divide into 12 pieces and shape each into a ball. Place balls of dough on a greased baking tray; cover and allow to rise in a warm place for 20 minutes. Brush with a little milk and sprinkle lightly with flour. Bake in a preheated hot oven (200°C/400°F) for 15–20 minutes or until very pale golden. Makes 12.

NOTE: If using dry yeast see also *Yeast Cookery*.

BARBECUE SAUCE

A sauce can add flavour and promote juiciness in barbecued fish, chicken or meat. Some barbecue sauces are used both to marinate the food before cooking and to baste it while cooking, others are used for basting only. Some commercial Asian sauces are thick amber- or honey-coloured and are often brushed on meat, poultry or fish before cooking, giving the food a delicious flavour and glistening finish. See recipes.

See also *Hoisin Sauce*.

Barbecue Basting Sauce

3/4 cup tomato ketchup; 2 tsp celery seeds; 1 clove garlic, crushed; 1 tbs Worcestershire sauce; 2 tbs vinegar; 2 tbs sugar; dash cayenne or black pepper; 3 tbs oil.

Combine all ingredients in a saucepan, bring to the boil and simmer for 3 minutes. Cool before using. Brush over steak, chops, sausages or hamburgers in the last 5–10 minutes of cooking. Don't use too early or sauce may become bitter or make meat stick. Pass leftover sauce separately. Makes about 1 cup.

Herb and Lemon Marinade

Use for barbecued fish or chicken.

1/3 cup olive oil; 150 ml white wine; juice 1 lemon; 1 onion; sliced; 1 carrot, sliced; 1 celery stalk, sliced; 1 sprig parsley; 1 bay leaf; 1 tbs chopped fresh thyme, dill or rosemary, or 1 tsp dried; 6 peppercorns.

Combine all ingredients and marinate fish for 20–30 minutes, chicken for 1 hour or more before barbecuing. Brush remaining marinade over food while cooking. Makes about 2/3 cup.

BARLEY

Barley is a cereal related to wheat and grows in the same grass-like form. As food prices continue to rise, barley is receiving increased attention from cooks everywhere who appreciate its economy and good nutty flavour. It is excellent in vegetarian dishes, soups and stews and, in addition to its high carbohydrate content, contains useful amounts of protein, calcium and phosphorus and small amounts of B vitamins.

Pot barley (also called Scotch or hulled barley) is the grain with only the outer husk removed. It requires 2–3 hours cooking.

Pearl barley has had the complete husk removed and is then steamed and polished. This is probably the most familiar type of barley, used for barley water and side dishes as well as soups and stews. It needs 1½–2 hours cooking to become tender. See recipes.

Barley Water

This refreshing drink, very popular in Victorian times, is enjoying a revival today. It keeps well in the refrigerator.

1/4 cup pearl barley; 4 cups water; thinly peeled rind and juice 2 medium lemons; sugar to taste.

Place barley, water and lemon rind in a saucepan and bring to the boil. Lower heat and simmer as gently as possible, with lid on, for 2 hours. Strain into a container and add lemon juice and sugar to taste. Cool, then chill. Serves 4–6.

Lamb and Barley Casserole

A nourishing, inexpensive and easily made dish from the Middle East.

2 breasts of lamb, cut into serving-size pieces; 2 tbs oil; salt and freshly ground black pepper; 1/2 cup pearl barley; 4 ripe tomatoes, peeled and chopped; 1 tbs chopped fresh basil or oregano, or 1 tsp dried; 1 tbs sugar; 1/2 medium cabbage, cut into wedges; 1/2 cup finely chopped parsley to serve.

Trim excess fat from lamb. Heat oil in a heavy frying pan and brown lamb on both sides. Season well with salt and pepper, and transfer to a deep saucepan. Add barley and enough water to cover, and simmer with lid on for 1 hour. Skim any fat from top, and add tomatoes, herbs, sugar and cabbage. Simmer, covered, for a further 30 minutes or until barley is tender. Adjust seasoning and sprinkle with chopped parsley to serve. Serves 6.

Scotch Broth (Barley Broth)

1 kg (2 lb) lamb neck chops, or 4 lamb shanks; 8 cups water; 1 tsp salt; 1/2 cup pearl barley; 2 medium onions, chopped; 2 medium carrots, chopped; 1 medium turnip, chopped; 1/2 cup finely chopped parsley.

Remove surplus fat from meat and place in a large saucepan with water and salt. Bring slowly to the boil, cover and simmer for 1 hour, removing any scum that comes to the surface. Add remaining ingredients except parsley. Simmer, covered, for a further

b

1½–2 hours or until tender. Remove meat from pot, and discard bones. Skim any fat from soup. Chop meat into small pieces, return to soup and reheat. Adjust seasoning and stir in parsley just before serving. Serves 6.

BARQUETTES

Made of pastry and meaning 'little boats', these are filled with hot or cold fillings to serve as hors d'oeuvre. They are shaped in special little boat-shaped tin moulds. For pastry recipes see *Pastry*; for suitable fillings, see *Hors d'oeuvre*.

TO SHAPE BARQUETTES: Place moulds close together, about 6 in a group. Roll out shortcrust or flaky pastry thinly, lift on to rolling pin and lay it over all tins together. Form a small piece of pastry into a ball, dip it in flour and use it to press pastry into moulds. Flour rolling pin and roll first one way, then the other, over moulds to remove surplus pastry. Fold trimmings together and roll out again to line more moulds in the same way. Take each mould, press edges lightly up with the thumb and prick bottom before baking.

BASIL

This fragrant, aromatic herb is a member of the mint family and is widely used in Italian cooking. They call it the tomato herb because it goes so well in all dishes containing tomatoes.

It is an annual, so basil is available fresh only during summer, but keeps well packed in oil for winter cooking. Simply snip leaves from the stems, pack in a jar and cover with olive oil. Store tightly covered in the refrigerator and remove leaves as required.

Use fresh basil leaves, cut into thin strips or tear roughly just before using, in all salads, particularly with tomatoes. Add to salad dressings, and blend into butter for sandwiches. Use to add fresh flavour to scrambled eggs and cheese sauces, sprinkle on pizzas before baking and over pasta dishes. Sprinkle lamb chops and liver with chopped basil before cooking, and stir a little into the pan juices after cooking chicken, meat or fish. For a simple but superb Mediterranean-style salad, alternate slices of fresh tomato and baby mozzarella cheese on a serving platter and sprinkle with olive oil, salt and fine ribbons of basil.

Just a word of caution – unlike some herbs, the flavour of fresh basil bears little relation to the dried variety. To enjoy the true aromatic taste, it is necessary to grow your own, or patronise a greengrocer who sells fresh herbs in season. See recipes.

See also *Pasta Sauces*.

Baked Tomatoes with Basil

6 large ripe tomatoes; salt and freshly ground black pepper; 6 spring onions, chopped; 8 leaves fresh basil, shredded or torn; 1 cup fresh breadcrumbs; 1 tbs butter.

Cut each tomato in half and remove cores. Season the cut surfaces generously with salt and lightly with pepper, sprinkle with onions and basil, top with breadcrumbs, and put a generous dot of butter on each half. Arrange in a buttered baking dish, and bake in a preheated moderate oven (180°C/350°F) for 10 minutes. Remove from the oven and brown under a moderate grill for about 3 minutes. Alternatively, if the oven is in use, simply grill under a moderate heat for 10–12 minutes, taking care not to burn. Serves 6.

Stewed Tomatoes with Basil

4 large ripe tomatoes, peeled, seeded and diced; 2 tbs butter; salt and freshly ground black pepper; 10 leaves fresh basil, shredded or torn; ½ cup fresh breadcrumbs.

Place tomatoes in a saucepan. Add butter, salt and pepper. Cover and stew gently for about 5 minutes, stirring occasionally. Add basil and cook 5 minutes longer. Add crumbs and mix well. Cook until tomatoes are soft. The crumbs will take up the excess liquid. Serves 4.

Tomato Salad

A simple yet striking way to serve tomatoes.

4 firm, ripe tomatoes; salt and freshly ground black pepper; 3 tbs olive oil; 1 tsp lemon juice or wine vinegar; 6–8 spring onions, chopped; 8–10 leaves fresh basil, shredded or torn.

Cut tomatoes crossways into thin slices (use serrated-edge knife) and arrange overlapping on a flat dish. Season well with salt and pepper. Mix oil with lemon juice or vinegar and sprinkle over tomatoes. Blanch spring onions in boiling water for 30 seconds, refresh under cold water and drain well. Sprinkle over tomatoes with shredded basil leaves. Serves 4.

BASMATI

See *Rice*.

BATTER

This is flour and liquid, and usually eggs and other ingredients, that are mixed to a consistency that can be stirred or 'battered'. Batters are used for crêpes, pancakes and fritters, waffles and doughnuts, for coating foods for frying, for making Yorkshire Pudding and baked desserts, and sometimes for making small, crisp cases to hold a filling, in the same way as pastry cases. In America, the word is also used for cake mixtures, though they may be thicker than the batter used for other foods.

Depending on the purpose of the batter, ingredients and consistency vary. A batter for crêpes contains a high proportion of eggs and milk to flour, and should be the consistency of pouring cream. Coating batters for fish, etc., are often thicker, and may contain beer or soda water for extra lightness and crispness (the gases have this lightening effect). Whisked egg white is also added to some batters to give lightness. Yeast batters are also used for particular recipes (see *Blini*).

Recipes often advise to rest the batter for anything from 20 minutes to 3–4 hours. During this time the starch cells swell and are more easily broken down in cooking, giving better flavour and texture. Batter may thicken while resting, and more liquid may have to be added to bring it back to the right consistency.

Before dipping foods in batter be sure they are dry or the batter will not cling. **See recipes.**

Basic Batter

The method described below is the basic one for mixing most batters when making by hand. Batter may also be made by putting all the ingredients into a blender, liquid ingredients first then dry ones, and blending until smooth, or by putting dry ingredients into a food processor and, with the motor running, adding liquid ingredients through the feed tube.

I cup flour; pinch salt; I egg; I¹/₄ cups milk.

Sift flour and salt into a large bowl and make a well in centre so that you can see the bottom of the bowl. Put in egg and about ⅓ milk and stir them together with a wooden spatula or spoon. Use a rapid circular motion, gradually extending it to allow flour to wash into liquid little by little. Add more liquid as flour is drawn in. Beat batter until very smooth. Cover and stand at least 30 minutes or up to 3–4 hours. Check consistency before using and stir in a little water, if needed, for the thickness specified in particular recipes.

Use Basic Batter when frying fish, and for Toad-in-the-Hole (see separate entries), and for Yorkshire Pudding and Breakfast Fritters, following.

For other batter recipes, see *Crêpes, Fritters, Pancakes* and *Waffles*.

Yorkshire Pudding

I quantity Basic Batter (above); melted dripping or butter.

Set batter aside for 1 hour. Stir in a little water if necessary to make batter consistency of thick cream. Pour into a jug. Brush deep muffin tins generously with beef dripping from roast or melted butter. Place tins on top shelf of a preheated hot oven (220°C/425°F) for 2–3 minutes or until the fat begins to smoke. Remove from oven, stir batter and pour in quickly to fill each tin about two-thirds full. Replace on top shelf of oven and bake for 15–20 minutes or until well

risen, crisp and golden-brown. Serve immediately as an accompaniment to roast beef. Makes 12.

NOTE: If you prefer, make one large pudding and cut it into squares. In this case, heat 3 tbs dripping or butter in a 25 x 23 x 5 cm (10 x 9 x 2 in) baking tin, pour in the batter and bake as above but in a preheated hot oven (200°C/400°F) for 30–40 minutes or until puffed around the edges, crisp and golden-brown.

Breakfast Fritters

I quantity Basic Batter (opposite); flavouring ingredients chosen from: I cup finely diced corned beef, sausage or other cold cooked meat, mixed with I tsp French mustard and I tbs grated onion; I x 440 g can sweetcorn, drained, mixed with 2 rashers bacon, cooked and crumbled; I cup cooked vegetables (carrots, peas, beans, cabbage, spinach, cauliflower), diced and mixed with I tbs grated onion, I tbs chopped parsley and I rasher bacon, cooked and crumbled; oil for frying; chutney, Tomato Sauce (page 460) or grilled tomato to accompany, if desired.

Mix batter with chosen flavouring ingredients. Heat 1 cm (½ in) oil in a frying pan until it gives off a slight haze. Drop mixture in large spoonfuls into oil and fry about 2 minutes on each side. Turn heat down and cook 2 minutes more. Drain on crumpled paper towels and serve very hot, with chutney, tomato sauce or grilled tomato if desired. Serves 4–6.

BAY

No kitchen should be without bay leaves, which come from the sweet bay or laurel tree. (Do not confuse with varieties of laurel which are poisonous.) If you have a bay tree, use the leaves 3–4 days after picking. To dry them for later use, cut a small twig or branch and hang it for a week or two in a cool, dry place, then pick off the leaves and store in an airtight jar.

In a supermarket the leaves are usually sold in packets, but try to avoid the very old, dried, brownish leaves which have little flavour. Use bay leaves sparingly for best results.

WAYS TO USE BAY LEAVES
- Place a small leaf on top of terrines and meat loaves.
- When making kebabs, secure small pieces of bay between cubes of meat.
- Add a small leaf to the liquid when cooking ham, tongue, corned beef or other boiled meats.
- Always remember to add a small bay leaf to the bouquet garni which is used to flavour marinades, stocks, court bouillon, pickles and many other dishes.
- Add a piece of bay leaf when cooking eggplant, cauliflower, carrots, beetroot, tomatoes or onion.
- Transform sauces, sweet custards and rice puddings by infusing a small bay leaf in the milk.
- Add a bay leaf to vegetable and fish soups.

BEANS, BROAD AND LIMA

These are annual plants cultivated mainly for their seeds, which are used both fresh and dried; see also *Pulses: Dried Beans, Peas and Lentils.*

Fresh broad beans, with their large, lumpy pods, are usually shelled immediately before going into the pot. When the seeds are large, it is necessary also to remove the rather tough outer skin before cooking. If the beans are very young, they can be cut up, cooked and eaten, pods and all.

■ **TO COOK:** Drop beans into boiling, salted water and cook until just tender. Drain and add a little butter, freshly ground black pepper and salt.

They are also delicious with chopped ham: heat cooked beans and ham gently together until warmed through. A few spoonfuls of cream with a dash of nutmeg is another delicious dressing for broad beans: heat until cream just begins to thicken. The herb savory is a natural with broad beans: chop and add to cooked beans just before serving.

Lima beans, named after the capital of Peru, are also known better as butter beans. Cook as for broad beans.

BEANS, DRIED

See *Pulses: Dried Beans, Peas and Lentils.*

BEANS, GREEN

'Green Beans' is the general term for beans with edible pods. There is a great variety on the market – they actually come in colours ranging from deep green and purple to pale yellow. The main types are French beans and runner or pole beans. *French beans* include snap beans, which are fleshy and should snap in half juicily if they are fresh, and yellow wax beans. *Runner beans* grow on a climbing vine. Often the pods are purple but turn green on cooking.

Snake beans are long, thin and dark green. They are delicious served hot; boil, drain well then toss in melted butter. Or serve them in a green salad, blanch in boiling water then rinse in cold water and drain well.

Buy beans as you need them. Store in the vegetable compartment of the refrigerator and use within 2–3 days while they are still crisp fresh.

■ **BASIC PREPARATION:** Many beans are now stringless but some types still need stringing. Young, small beans are nicest cooked whole; larger beans may be snapped in half or sliced in diagonal lengths. Top and tail, if preferred.

■ **TO COOK:** Wash beans in cold water, then drop into a small amount of boiling, salted water – just enough to cover. Simmer without a lid for 6–15 minutes, depending on size and type, until they are tender but still a little crisp. Be careful not to overcook. Drain in a colander and, if not required immediately, plunge into cold water to stop the cooking process. Beans may then stand for an hour or more before finishing.

To reheat, place them in a large frying pan and shake over a moderate heat for a minute or two to heat and rid them of excess moisture, then dress as desired. **See recipes.**

WAYS TO SERVE BEANS

Runner beans and French beans of any kind may be used interchangeably in these recipes.

Buttered Green Beans: Prepare, cook and drain 750 g (1½ lb) green beans. Place in a large pan and shake over high heat while adding 2 tbs butter, bit by bit. Season to taste with salt and freshly ground black pepper. Serves 4–6.

Green Beans Amandine: Prepare, cook and drain 750 g (1½ lb) green beans. Melt 1–2 tbs butter in a large pan, add 2 tbs slivered almonds and toss until golden. Add beans, toss gently together and season to taste with salt and freshly ground black pepper. Serves 4–6.

Green Beans with Onion: Prepare, cook and drain 750 g (1½ lb) green beans. Melt 2 tbs butter in a large pan, add a finely chopped onion and cook until golden. Add the beans and shake pan over high heat to mix beans and onions. Season to taste with salt and freshly ground black pepper and sprinkle with chopped parsley. Serves 4–6.

Green Beans Paysanne: Prepare, cook and drain 750 g (1½ lb) green beans. Cook 2 diced rindless rashers bacon in a large pan. Remove bacon with a slotted spoon, add 2 tbs butter and 2 finely chopped onions to the pan and cook until onion is soft. Add 2 peeled, seeded and chopped tomatoes and, if liked, 1 cup diced potato. Add beans, bacon and ½ cup water and simmer, covered, about 20 minutes. Season with salt and freshly ground black pepper. Serves 4–6.

Green Beans with Mustard Vinaigrette: Prepare, cook and drain 750 g (1½ lb) green beans. Mix 2 tsp French mustard, 2 tbs olive oil, 2 tsp vinegar, 1 small clove garlic, crushed, and salt and freshly ground black pepper to taste. Toss beans gently in dressing, place in a chilled serving dish and sprinkle with chopped parsley. Serve cold. Serves 4–6.

Green Beans Smitane: Prepare, cook and drain 750 g (1½ lb) green beans. Place in a large pan and stir in ½ cup thick sour cream mixed with 1 tsp flour and 1 tsp each finely chopped parsley, chives and dill. Heat gently about 5 minutes. Season with salt and freshly ground black pepper. Serves 4–6.

Spiced Green Beans: Wash and trim 750 g (1½ lb) green beans, and cut into 4 cm (1½ in) lengths. Combine 1 tsp salt, 2 cloves garlic, crushed, 2 slices fresh ginger and 1 tbs lemon juice in a small bowl and add cayenne to taste. Heat ⅓ cup oil in a frying pan, add ½ tsp cumin seeds and fry a few seconds. Add beans and stir 1 minute. Add garlic mixture, cover pan and cook over low heat for 10 minutes or until beans are just tender, stirring occasionally. Remove cover, increase heat and stir constantly until liquid has evaporated. Serves 4–6.

Green Bean Bhaji

2 tbs oil; I tsp black mustard seeds; I tsp turmeric;
I tsp salt; 2 tbs chopped onion; 500 g (I lb) green
beans, trimmed and cut into 2 cm (³/₄ in) lengths;
2–4 tbs water; ¹/₃–¹/₂ cup desiccated coconut
(optional).

Heat oil in a large, heavy pan. Add mustard seed, cover
and allow to brown, but not to burn. Stir in turmeric
and salt. Add onion and sauté until softened. Add
green beans and water. Turn down the heat and cook
until beans are tender, adding a little more water as
needed. If you like, stir in coconut a few minutes
before beans finish cooking. Good with curries, or
grilled or barbecued meats. Serves 4.

BEAN SPROUTS

The young shoots from dried green mung beans. Crunchy,
nutritious sprouts are delicious, not only in Asian recipes
but in salads and sandwich fillings. Popular types for
sprouting include alfalfa, soya beans and tiny, green mung
peas. If fresh sprouts are not available at your health food
shop, greengrocer or Asian food store, it is easy to grow
your own.

TO GROW YOUR OWN: Use enough dried soya beans,
mung peas or alfalfa seeds to come about one sixth of
the way up a glass jar. Fill the jar with cold water, then
drain the water off through a piece of muslin or other
fabric, secured tightly over the top with a rubber band.
Leave in a cool, dark place until next day. Repeat the
watering and draining each day until sprouts are about
2.5 cm (1 in) long. Drain, then keep refrigerated.

NOTE: Sprouts should appear in 2–3 days and will be
large enough to eat in 5–6 days. Use fresh and, if liked,
remove hair-like tails.

Bean Sprout and Mushroom Salad

2 cups fresh bean sprouts; 250 g (8 oz) mushroom
caps, finely sliced; I large carrot, grated; 6 spring
onions, chopped; ¹/₄ cup olive oil or walnut oil;
I tbs wine vinegar; 2 tbs light soy sauce;
I tbs sugar; I clove garlic, crushed; I tsp finely
chopped fresh ginger; 2 tbs dry sherry.

Place sprouts, mushrooms, carrot and onions in a
bowl. Combine remaining ingredients and toss lightly
with vegetables. Serve immediately. Serves 6.

Chinese Noodle Salad

375 g (12 oz) Chinese noodles; salt; I tbs oil;
500 g (I lb) fresh bean sprouts; ¹/₂ cup finely sliced
spring onions; toasted sesame seeds to garnish.

SESAME PEANUT SAUCE: 2 tbs shredded fresh ginger;
1¹/₂ tbs sesame oil; 2¹/₂ tsp sugar; 2 tbs sesame seeds;
I tbs peanut oil; 4 tbs peanut butter; 4 tbs water;

2 tbs soy sauce; 2 tsp vinegar; ¹/₂ tsp Tabasco sauce;
¹/₂ tsp black pepper.

Cook noodles in plenty of boiling salted water for
about 7 minutes or until tender. Drain, rinse under
cold water, drain again and toss lightly with oil to
prevent sticking. Place noodles in a serving bowl and
top with bean sprouts.

SESAME PEANUT SAUCE: Marinate ginger in ¹/₂ tbs
sesame oil mixed with ¹/₂ tsp sugar. Leave for 30 minutes. Toast sesame seeds in a dry, heavy frying pan
over very gentle heat until golden. Place in a bowl and
crush lightly with a pestle or end of a rolling pin until
aroma of seeds is released. Combine peanut oil and
peanut butter with rest of sesame oil and crushed
seeds. Add remaining ingredients, stirring until
mixed. Pour sauce over bean sprouts, and sprinkle
with spring onions and sesame seeds. Toss well.
Serves 4–6.

Vegetarian Egg Fu Yung

4 dried Chinese mushrooms;
4 eggs, lightly beaten; ¹/₄ tsp salt;
¹/₄ tsp white pepper; 2 spring onions,
finely chopped; 6 water chestnuts, chopped;
I cup fresh bean sprouts; I tsp light soy sauce;
I tbs peanut oil; sliced spring onions to garnish.

Soak mushrooms in hot water for 30 minutes;
squeeze out excess water and discard stems. Chop
mushroom caps. Season eggs with salt and pepper
and stir in mushrooms and remaining ingredients
except oil. Heat a wok or frying pan, add 1 tsp oil and
swirl to coat bottom of pan. Pour in about one third
of egg mixture and cook on medium heat until lightly
browned underneath. Turn and cook until other side
is set. Keep warm.

Repeat with remaining mixture to make 2 more
omelettes. Stack omelettes on top of each other, garnish
with sliced spring onions and serve with Sweet and
Sour Sauce (see page 520), if liked. Serves 2–4.

Bean Threads with Bean Sprouts

A simple cold dish that is made easily in minutes. Use the transparent pea-starch noodles and, if liked, vary the bean sprouts – julienne (matchstick) strips of crispy cucumber are ideal. The hot mustard dip makes all the difference.

30 g (1 oz) transparent noodles; 3 cups fresh bean sprouts; 3 spring onions, thinly bias cut.

MARINADE: 4 tbs vinegar; 2 tsp salt; 2 tsp sesame oil.

First prepare marinade by combining ingredients in a bowl. Cover noodles with boiling water and soak until soft and transparent, about 15 minutes. Drain and cut into 8 cm (3 in) pieces. Drop bean sprouts into boiling salted water, bring back to the boil, then quickly drain in a colander. While bean sprouts are still hot, toss quickly in marinade. Add spring onions and drained noodles and mix well. Refrigerate and serve cold with a little dish of made hot English mustard for dipping. Serves 6.

BEARNAISE SAUCE

A classic French egg and butter sauce. The creamy texture and piquant flavour of Bearnaise Sauce make it the perfect partner for grilled steak or roast fillet of beef. It also goes well with roast or grilled chicken.

See *Sauces* for recipe.

BECHAMEL SAUCE

The French call Béchamel Sauce a *sauce mère* or mother sauce because it is the basic white sauce from which so many others are made. It can be made as a flowing sauce, to serve as a separate accompaniment or as a base for cream soups. Made thicker, it becomes a coating sauce to cover food in the dish in which it is to be served (for instance, in Mornay or creamed dishes). Thicker still, it is called a panada and is used for soufflés, croquettes, etc.

See *Sauces* for recipe.

BEEF

In general, the characteristics of good beef, freshly cut, are a rich red to dark red colour, fairly fine grain, marbling (flecks of fat) through the thicker parts, and firm, smooth fat which is white or yellowish according to the breed of animal, its age and the way it was fed.

See *Meat* for amount to buy, factors determining tenderness, testing meat for doneness, etc. **See recipes.**

ROAST BEEF

■ **CHOICE CUTS FOR ROASTING:**

Sirloin: May be boneless or on the bone.
Wing Rib and Standing Rib (bone-in): The best rib meat is from the fore rib, nearest the loin.
Rolled Rib: Boneless.

Rump: Boneless.
Fillet: Small, boneless and fatless – the most tender (and expensive) cut of all, though less full-flavoured than the cuts mentioned above.
Scotch Fillet: Boneless, not quite so tender as true fillet but still a luxury cut.

■ **TO ROAST CHOICE CUTS:** Have the meat at room temperature; tie it into a compact shape if necessary, so that it will cook evenly. Weigh it and place, fatty side up, on a greased rack in a roasting tin. If meat has no fat layer, spread with dripping or butter or brush with oil. Place in the centre of a preheated hot oven (220°C/425°F) for 20 minutes, then reduce heat to moderate (180°C/350°F) and continue to roast, basting with pan juices every 20 minutes in turned-off oven with door ajar, or other warm place, before carving.

ALLOW APPROXIMATELY:

- 15 minutes per 500 g (1 lb) plus 15 minutes for rare meat
- 20 minutes per 500 g (1 lb) plus 20 minutes for medium-done meat
- 25 minutes per 500 g (1 lb) plus 25 minutes for well-done meat.

Roast Fillet of Beef: Use this special method. Remove all fat and covering tissue, tie into a neat shape, folding tail under, and brown well in butter in flameproof baking dish on top of the stove. Flame with brandy if desired, place in a preheated hot oven (200°C/400°F) and roast 15 minutes per 500 g for rare beef, 20 minutes per 500 g for medium-done. Leave in turned-off oven with door ajar, or other warm place, for 15 minutes before carving.

Roast Scotch Fillet: Prepare, brown and flame in the same way as fillet, and then roast in a preheated hot oven (220°C/425°F) for 10 minutes, then reduce the heat to moderately hot (190°C/375°F) and continue to roast for a further 15–20 minutes for rare beef, 25–35 minutes for medium-done beef. Rest as for fillet before carving.

■ **ECONOMICAL CUTS FOR ROASTING:** The following cuts are good for roasting if they come from a high-quality, young carcase.

Topside: Preferably a corner of topside, which often has a pocket cut in it for a stuffing.
Silverside (unsalted): Like a topside, a lean, boneless cut.
Blade: Boneless or bone-in.
Rolled Roast: This may vary in tenderness according to the cuts the butcher has used to make it up. It often consists of rib meat rolled with some meat from other areas.

■ **TO ROAST ECONOMICAL CUTS:** Make sure the meat is at room temperature and, if necessary, tie it into a compact shape for even cooking. Weigh it and place, fatty side up, on a greased rack in a roasting tin. If meat has little or no fat layer, brush with melted butter or dripping. Place in the centre of a preheated moderately slow oven (160°C/325°F) and roast at this temperature for the whole of cooking time. Baste every 15 minutes with pan juices to which a little stock or wine may be added to promote juiciness. Rest for 15–20 minutes in turned-off oven with door ajar, or other warm place, before carving.

ALLOW APPROXIMATELY:

- 20 minutes per 500 g (1 lb) plus 20 minutes for rare meat
- 25 minutes per 500 g (1 lb) plus 25 minutes for medium-done meat
- 30 minutes per 500 g (1 lb) plus 30 minutes for well-done meat.

GRILLED STEAK

For best results, cut steak thick, about 4 cm (1½ in).

■ **CHOICE CUTS FOR GRILLING:**
Fillet, Rump, Sirloin (T-bone and *boneless steaks), Rib Steak.*

■ **TO GRILL CHOICE CUTS:** Have the steak at room temperature. If it has been marinated, dry well. If steak is edged with fat, cut right through fat to lean meat in several places to prevent buckling. Season with salt and pepper but do not salt until after cooking. Brush the steak with melted butter or oil and the grill rack with oil. Grill thick steaks close to high heat under a preheated grill for a minute or two on each side until seared, then lower heat to moderate or move meat further away and continue to cook, turning once, until cooked as desired. If steak is cut thin, grill close to high heat for the whole cooking time.

A steak about 4 cm (1½ in) thick will take 10–15 minutes total cooking time for medium-rare meat; steak 2 cm (¾ in) thick will take 7–10 minutes. Times vary with different cuts and different grills. To test for doneness, see *Meat*.

■ **ECONOMICAL CUTS FOR GRILLING:** *Oyster Blade, Crosscut Blade* and *Top Round*. These are satisfactory if they come from a high-quality young carcase. Tenderness may be promoted by marinating.

■ **TO GRILL ECONOMICAL CUTS:** Follow same procedure as for grilling choice cuts, above.

Pan-grilled Steak: The following method may be used for both the choice cuts and the economical cuts listed above for Grilled Steak.

Steak can be pan-grilled for a crusty outside and juicy inside – especially useful if you are not sure of the efficiency of your grill. Use a thick, heavy pan. Heat on high heat for a few minutes, add just enough oil to coat the base and, when it gives off a slight haze, put in the steak. Cook 30–60 seconds on each side, until seared, then lower heat to moderate and continue to cook, turning once, until cooked as desired. When beads of pink juice appear on surface steak is medium-rare. For other ways to test for doneness, see *Meat*.

BRAISED AND CASSEROLED BEEF

Cuts for casseroling and braising (browning, then simmering with a little liquid) include *Round, Blade, Topside, Skirt, Chuck, Shin* and *Beef Cheeks*.

Meat may be cut into steaks, then into serving-size pieces, or smaller pieces, or may be cooked in one large piece – this is called a pot roast. See *Meat*.

Braised Steak and Onions

750 g (1½ lb) braising steak; seasoned flour; 1 tbs oil; 1 tbs butter; 3 onions, sliced; 1 clove garlic, crushed; 1½ cups beef stock; 1 bouquet garni; salt and freshly ground black pepper.

Trim excess fat from beef, cut into serving-sized pieces and dredge with seasoned flour. Brown, a few pieces at a time, in hot oil and butter in a heavy saucepan or flameproof casserole. Remove meat. Add onions and garlic and cook gently until beginning to brown. Pour off surplus fat, leaving about 1 tbs. Add stock and bouquet garni and bring to the boil, stirring once or twice. Add meat, cover tightly and simmer gently on top of the stove or in a preheated moderately slow oven (160°C/325°F) for 1½–2 hours or until meat is tender. Remove bouquet garni, adjust seasoning and serve with mashed potatoes and a green vegetable. Serves 4.

Braised Steak with Red Wine

1 kg (2 lb) braising steak; seasoned flour; 1 tbs oil; 30 g (1 oz) butter; 1 clove garlic, crushed; 2 onions, coarsely chopped; 1 tbs sugar; 1 tbs Dijon mustard; 1 tbs vinegar; 1 cup red wine; ½ cup beef stock; 1 bouquet garni; salt and freshly ground black pepper.

Trim excess fat from beef, cut into cubes and dredge with seasoned flour. Brown, a few pieces at a time, in hot oil and butter in a heavy saucepan or flameproof casserole. Remove meat. Add garlic and onions and cook gently until beginning to brown. Pour off surplus fat, leaving about 1 tbs. Add sugar, mustard, vinegar, wine, stock and bouquet garni. Add meat, cover tightly and simmer gently on top of the stove or in a preheated moderately slow oven (160°C/325°F) for 1½–2 hours or until meat is tender. Remove bouquet garni and adjust seasoning. Serves 4–6.

Old–fashioned Beef Casserole

750 g (1½ lb) braising steak; 30 g (1 oz) lard or dripping; 1½ tbs flour; 2 cups warm beef stock; 3 onions, sliced; 2 carrots, sliced; 1 turnip, cut into neat chunks; 2 sticks celery, sliced; 1 bouquet garni; salt and freshly ground black pepper.

Trim excess fat from meat and cut into bite-sized pieces. Brown in hot fat in a heavy saucepan or flameproof casserole. Remove meat. Stir flour into fat and cook until browned. Remove from heat, cool a little and add stock, stirring until smoothly blended. Stir over heat until boiling. Add vegetables and bouquet garni, and place meat on top. Cover tightly and simmer gently on top of the stove or in a preheated moderately slow oven (160°C/325°F) for 1½–2 hours or until meat and vegetables are tender. Remove bouquet garni, adjust seasoning and serve. Serves 4.

Beef Pot Roast

1–1.5 kg (2–3 lb) piece braising beef; 1 tbs oil;
1 tbs butter; 2 large carrots, diced; 2 large onions,
chopped; 2 sticks celery, chopped; 1 small turnip,
diced; 1 bouquet garni; 1½ cups beef stock or mixed
stock and red wine; salt and freshly ground black
pepper; vegetables to garnish (see below).

Brown meat all over in hot oil and butter in a flameproof casserole. Remove meat. Add diced and
chopped vegetables, cover and cook gently 5 minutes.
Place meat on vegetables, add bouquet garni and
stock, and season lightly with salt and pepper. Cover
and cook in a preheated moderately slow oven
(160°C/325°F) for 2 hours or until meat is very tender.
Remove meat from casserole. Boil down gravy until it
is syrupy, then strain it. Slice meat and arrange on a
heated platter. Spoon gravy over and surround with
vegetables. Serves 4–6.
VEGETABLE GARNISH: Cook new potatoes, carrots
and green beans or peas separately and toss in melted
butter. Sprinkle potatoes with chopped mint and
carrots with chopped parsley.

Stir-fried Beef with Oyster Sauce

250 g (8 oz) Scotch fillet or skirt steak; ⅔ cup oil;
4 spring onions, cut into finger lengths (include
some green tops); 6 thin slices fresh ginger, finely
chopped; shredded spring onions or coriander
sprigs to garnish.

MARINADE: 1 tbs soy sauce; 1 tsp Chinese rice wine,
sake or dry sherry; 5 tbs water; 2 tsp cornflour;
1 tbs oil.

GRAVY: ½ tbs Chinese rice wine, sake or dry sherry;
1½ tbs oyster sauce; ½ tsp sugar; ¼ tsp black
pepper; ¼ tsp Chinese sesame oil; 1½ tbs water;
1 tsp cornflour.

Remove fat or membrane from beef and cut across
grain into thinnest possible slices. Mix all ingredients
for marinade, pour over beef and allow to stand for
1 hour. Heat ⅔ cup oil in a wok or deep, heavy frying
pan and stir-fry meat slices for about 20 seconds until
they change colour. Drain beef. Pour off all but 2 tbs
oil from wok. Reheat oil, and add spring onions and
ginger to pan. Stir-fry over medium heat for about 30
seconds, then add beef slices and all ingredients for
gravy. Continue cooking, stirring lightly, for about
30 seconds or until gravy thickens and turns translucent. Transfer to a heated platter and serve garnished
with shredded spring onions or sprigs of coriander.
Serves 4–6 as part of a Chinese meal, or 2 as a main
course with rice or noodles.
NOTE: Tender hearts of Chinese spinach (soup greens)
may accompany the beef. These are tossed in a little
hot vegetable oil, moistened with stock and cooked

only until tender-crisp, about 1 minute, and then
decoratively arranged on the plate.

Oriental 'Snakes' of Beef

Thin strips of beef are marinated and then threaded in
zig-zag or 'snake' fashion on skewers – more interesting
and much more economical than serving large steaks
to everyone.

750 g (1½ lb) grilling steak, 4 cm (1½ in) thick;
½ cup soy sauce; 2 tbs honey; 1 tbs dry sherry;
2 cloves garlic, crushed; 1 tbs grated fresh ginger;
few drops Chinese sesame oil.

Slice steak across grain into 5 mm (¼ in) strips and
place in a bowl. Mix remaining ingredients and pour
over. Leave to marinate, covered, at room temperature
for 1 hour, turning meat over several times to
coat evenly.

Soak the bamboo skewers in hot water for 30 minutes. Remove beef strips from marinade and thread on
to skewers, zig-zag or 'snake' fashion. Cook under a
preheated very hot grill for about 3 minutes, turning
once and brushing with marinade. Beef should be rare
on the inside. Serve skewers on a bed of rice, or push
meat off skewers into Lebanese bread pockets, with
addition of chopped celery, peppers or bean sprouts.
Serves 4–6.

Thai Beef Salad

One of the greatest things to have changed in our
greengrocers in the last decade is the availability of a
large selection of salad greens. Each has its unique
quality: some pale, some bright, in reds and greens.
Look for the mixed selection of mesclun or choose
two or three of your favourites, wash them as soon as
you are home, dry, wrap in a paper towels and store
in plastic bags in the refrigerator.

750 g (1½ lb) rump or sirloin steak;
freshly ground pepper; ½ cup mint leaves;
1 large red or 2 large spring onions, thinly sliced;
2 red chillies, sliced; juice of 1 large lime or
½ lemon; 2 tbs fish sauce (nam pla); 1 tsp sugar;
2 tbs roasted peanuts; mixed salad greens;
1 cup cherry tomatoes; Crispy Noodles (optional).

Season the steak with pepper and cook on a hot ribbed grill or under a preheated grill for 5 minutes on each side or until done to taste. Remove, allow to stand 5–10 minutes. Cut into very thin slices and place in a bowl. Meanwhile, combine the mint with the onion, chillies, lime or lemon juice, fish sauce and sugar. Stir well and add to the beef slices, tossing. Toss with roasted peanuts, the salad greens, cherry tomatoes, and pile on top of crispy noodles. Serves 4–6.

CRISPY NOODLES: Heat some vegetable oil in a wok and test the heat with a few strands of vermicelli. It should swell to many times its size immediately if oil is hot enough. Fry the vermicelli in small handfuls, scooping out with a wire strainer as soon as they puff and turn pale golden. Drain well on paper towels and cool.

Potted Meat

Eat this very cold, accompanied by hot English mustard and vinegar, which points up the flavour of the meat. For a summer meal, serve with cucumber slices, tomatoes and potato salad.

1.5 kg (3 lb) shin of beef on the bone, cut into thick slices; 750 g (1¹/₂ lb) pickled (salt) belly pork; 6 black peppercorns; 1 bay leaf; 2 tsp anchovy essence; salt and freshly ground black pepper.

Put beef, pork, peppercorns and bay leaf into a large saucepan and cover with cold water. Bring to the boil and skim. Cover and simmer for 3 hours. Cool. Remove meat from broth and strain broth. Trim away beef fat and gristle and remove bones from beef and pork. Chop meats finely and return to broth. Boil uncovered for 20 minutes, until broth is reduced. Add anchovy essence and season with salt and pepper. Boil a further 5 minutes to blend flavours. Put into a 6-cup bowl which has been rinsed with cold water. Cover with plastic wrap and chill until firm. Turn out and cut in thick slices to serve. Serves 8–10.

Beef Niçoise

Black olives gives this special beef dish a traditional Mediterranean touch and interesting smoky flavour.

1–1.5 kg (2–3 lb) shin of beef; 2 tbs oil; 125 g (4 oz) streaky bacon or pickled (salt) pork, rind removed and cut into strips; 3 cloves garlic, crushed; 6 medium carrots, sliced; 6 medium onions, sliced; 5 sprigs parsley, coarsely chopped; 2 tbs chopped fresh mixed herbs (rosemary, thyme, basil, oregano), or 1 tsp dried; 1 x 425 g can tomatoes with their juice; 2 tbs wine vinegar; salt and freshly ground black pepper; 8–12 stoned black olives (optional).

GARNISH: chopped parsley; croûtons.

Trim fat and sinews from beef and cut into thick slices or cubes. Heat oil in a large flameproof casserole and fry bacon until fat starts to run. Add meat and brown well on both sides. Stir in garlic, carrots, onions, parsley, herbs, tomatoes and vinegar.

Season with salt and pepper and stir gently until liquid reaches simmering point. Place lid on casserole and cook in a preheated moderate oven (180°C/350°F) for 2–2¹/₂ hours or until meat is tender. During this time, check once or twice to see if the liquid has evaporated too much. If so, add a little water, but finished gravy should be thick. Add olives to casserole and cook for a further 20 minutes, covered, so flavours can blend. Turn into a heated serving dish and garnish with chopped parsley and croûtons. Serves 6–8.

NOTE: Cut round or heart-shaped croûtons from white bread and fry in a little hot oil until golden-brown on both sides.

Sailor's Stew

This traditional stew from Scandinavia is a cousin of Irish stew. The name probably indicates that sailors, when they come ashore, appreciate a change from fish! In Scandinavia, this might be offered with rye bread and butter, dill pickles, and a salad.

750 g (1¹/₂ lb) stewing beef (chuck, blade, gravy beef); 750 g (1¹/₂ lb) old potatoes, peeled and thickly sliced; 2 large onions, thickly sliced; 2 cups boiling water; 1 small bay leaf; 2 tsp salt; 6 black peppercorns; 60 g (2 oz) butter; chopped parsley to garnish.

Remove excess fat from beef and cut into bite-sized cubes. Place beef, potatoes and onions in a pan with remaining ingredients. Bring to the boil, and remove any scum that comes to surface. Reduce heat to low, cover pan and simmer for 1¹/₂–2 hours or until meat is very tender and potatoes are reduced to a mash. Stir well to combine potatoes with gravy. Adjust seasoning, discard bay leaf, and serve sprinkled with chopped parsley. Serves 4.

Paprika Beef Stew

Use any lean stewing beef for this rich, heart-warming and economical stew.

1 kg (2 lb) stewing beef; 60 g (2 oz) speck or streaky bacon, rind removed and diced; 3 large onions, chopped; 1 tbs paprika; 1 x 820 g can tomatoes, drained and chopped; 2–3 cups water; 1 clove garlic, crushed; 1 bay leaf; 2 tbs flour; ¹/₂ cup sour cream; salt and freshly ground black pepper.

Cut beef into bite-sized cubes. Sauté speck or bacon in a heavy saucepan or flameproof casserole until golden-brown. Add beef cubes, a few at a time, and brown on all sides. Remove meat from pan with a slotted spoon. Add onions and paprika to pan. Cook gently for 4–5 minutes until onions soften a little, stirring so they do not stick. Return meat to pan and add tomatoes with enough water to come halfway up the meat. Stir well and add garlic and bay leaf. Cover and simmer for 1½ hours or until meat is very tender. Stir flour with sour cream, add to stew and simmer for 2–3 minutes until gravy is smooth and thickened. Adjust seasoning, and discard bay leaf. Serves 6.

Roasted Scotch Fillet

Easy to prepare, cook, carve and serve – this is an ideal buffet dish. Don't overcook this cut and it will be every bit as tender as true fillet. Take care to trim away any sinews and excess fat.

1.5–2.5 kg (3–5 lb) piece Scotch fillet; freshly ground black pepper, or 2 tbs crushed green peppercorns; 30 g (1 oz) butter; 2 tbs oil; 3 tbs brandy; 2 tbs each chopped parsley, chives and capers.

Trim fillet and tie with string to keep a good shape. Season well with freshly ground black pepper or press crushed green peppercorns firmly on to meat. Melt butter and oil in a flameproof baking dish and sear meat quickly to brown the surface, turning with 2 spoons. Heat brandy, set alight and pour over meat, shaking dish so that meat burns with the flame. Roast in a preheated very hot oven (220°C/425°F) for 10 minutes, then reduce heat to moderately hot (190°C/375°F) and roast for a further 25–35 minutes. The smaller yearling beef will not take as long. Top beef with herbs and capers, pressing them in well, and allow to stand 20 minutes before slicing. Transfer to a board and slice two thirds of the beef. Arrange uncut beef with sliced meat on a large heated platter and accompany with a choice of mustards and horseradish sauce. Serves 8.

Piquant Beef Roulades

This makes an interesting dinner party main course, served with buttered noodles and a fresh green or mixed salad.

4 thin slices topside steak; 1 clove garlic, crushed; salt and freshly ground black pepper; 250 g (8 oz) sausage mince; 1 small onion, finely chopped; ¼ tsp dried thyme or oregano; 1 small carrot, quartered; 60 g (2 oz) butter; 1 cup red wine; 1 tbs tomato paste; 1 tbs Worcestershire sauce; 1 tsp sugar; 2 tbs chopped parsley or sliced olives.

If steaks are cut very thin, there is no need to pound them. Otherwise, place between 2 sheets of plastic wrap and flatten with a rolling pin, being careful not to tear the meat. Spread a little garlic over each steak and season with salt and pepper. Combine sausage mince with onion and thyme or oregano and spread a layer of mince over each steak. Place a slice of carrot in the middle, then roll up the steaks neatly, tucking in ends to give a good shape. Melt butter in a flame-proof casserole and gently brown steak rolls on all sides. Pour in wine and tomato paste combined with the Worcestershire sauce and sugar, and cover casserole tightly with a lid or foil.

Bake in a preheated moderate oven (180°C/350°F) for about 1 hour, or until the roulades are very tender. Stir in parsley or sliced olives and adjust seasoning. Serve in the casserole, or transfer to a heated platter. Nice with mashed potatoes, corn bread or buttered rice instead of noodles. Serves 4.

NOTE: The roulades may also be cooked in a saucepan on top of the stove if desired. Choose one large enough to hold them in a single layer.

Budapest Beef Goulash

60 g (2 oz) butter; 750 g (1½ lb) onions, coarsely chopped; 1 kg (2 lb) chuck steak, cubed; 1½ tsp salt; 1 tbs paprika; 3 tbs tomato paste.

Heat butter in a heavy saucepan, add onions and sauté until golden-brown. Add beef and cook over moderate heat, stirring, until beef loses its bright redness. Add remaining ingredients. Simmer very gently, covered, for 1½–2 hours until beef is tender. If necessary, to prevent sticking, ¼ cup water may be added. If liked, stir in ½ cup sour cream before serving. Serves 6.

Ragoût of Beef

45 g (1½ oz) butter; 1 medium onion, chopped; 1 clove garlic; 1 kg (2 lb) shin of beef, cut into large cubes; 1 tsp paprika; salt and freshly ground black pepper; 2 large tomatoes, peeled and chopped; 15 g (½ oz) dried Continental mushrooms; 1 cup water; 1 cup diced celery; 3 tbs Beurre Manié (page 35).

Heat butter in a large frying pan. Add onion and garlic and sauté until onion is transparent. Discard garlic. Add meat, paprika, salt and pepper. Cook over moderate heat, stirring, until meat is browned. Add tomatoes. Cover and simmer very gently 1 hour. Meanwhile, soak mushrooms in water for 15 minutes. Boil for 3 minutes in their soaking liquid. Add celery to frying pan and cook 15 minutes, then add mushrooms and their liquid and continue to simmer gently until meat is tender. The total cooking time is 1½–2 hours. When meat is tender, add beurre manié, bit by bit, stirring constantly until liquid is thickened. Serve with steamed rice, buttered noodles or polenta. Serves 6.

BEEF WELLINGTON

This is the name given to fillet of beef, topped with a good liver pâté (preferably Pâté de Foie Gras) and sometimes sautéed mushrooms, wrapped in pastry and baked. A great luxury dish and quite easy to manage for a dinner party. Prepare up to 1 day in advance, except for glazing with egg and baking. Refrigerate if keeping overnight, but take out and leave at room temperature for 2 hours before baking so that timing will be accurate.

Beef Wellington

1.25 kg (2½ lb) piece beef fillet (the thick end of a fillet should weigh about this much); freshly ground black pepper; 1 tbs oil; 60 g (2 oz) butter; ¼ cup brandy; 60 g (2 oz) mushrooms, sliced; 90 g (3 oz) good liver pâté; 1 x 375 g (12 oz) packet frozen puff pastry, thawed; 1 egg, lightly beaten; watercress or parsley to garnish.

Trim fillet of all fat and gristle, fold tail under and tie into a neat shape. Season with pepper. Brown meat well on all sides in hot oil and butter. Warm brandy, set alight and pour over meat, shaking pan until flames subside. Remove fillet to a rack and allow to get quite cold. Sauté mushrooms in the same pan until tender, cool. Spread fillet with pâté and top with mushrooms. Roll out pastry thinly, trim edges and brush them with beaten egg. Place fillet on one half, fold other half over, press edges to seal and tuck under neatly. Cut strips of pastry from trimmings. Brush pastry around fillet with egg, arrange strips lattice-fashion on top and brush with egg. Chill for 30 minutes, then place on a dampened baking tray. Bake in a preheated very hot oven (230°C/450°F) for 15 minutes more or until golden-brown. Serve on a platter, garnished with a bouquet of watercress or parsley. Serves 6.

BEER

Cooking with beer is popular in many countries. The Germans have their beer soup and cook sausages in beer, the Belgians their beef and beer stew; Australians use beer to add extra lightness and crispness to batter for fish, and the Americans like it as a cooking liquid for prawns.

See also *Carbonnade de Boeuf, Fish*: Fish Fried in Batter and *Welsh Rarebit (Rabbit)*.

Sauerkraut with Apples and Beer

1 x 825 g can sauerkraut; 60 g (2 oz) butter; 2 rashers streaky bacon, or 30 g (1 oz) speck, rind removed and diced; 1 large onion, finely chopped; 1 large tart apple, peeled, cored and diced; 4 juniper berries, crushed; 2½ cups beer; 1 large potato, peeled and grated; 2 tbs sugar; salt and freshly ground black pepper.

Place sauerkraut in a colander, rinse under running hot water and drain well. Heat butter in a large heavy saucepan and fry bacon or speck for 1–2 minutes, then add onion and cook, stirring, until onion is softened. Add sauerkraut, apple and crushed juniper berries and cook over low heat for 15 minutes, stirring frequently. Pour in beer and simmer for 30 minutes, then add potato and simmer another 30 minutes, adding more beer if necessary to keep mixture moist. Season with sugar, salt and black pepper. Excellent with pork and sausage dishes. Serves 6.

BEETROOT

A root vegetable with a bulbous shape and rich sweet, red flesh of a unique texture. To avoid losing any of the rich red colour, beetroot are not peeled or cut before cooking. Cooked beetroot is delicious sliced and heated with a little chopped onion and garlic, or with a spoonful of chopped horseradish folded through. Diced freshly cooked beetroot, heated through in the juice and grated rind of an orange, is delicious. Grated raw beetroot, seasoned with salt and freshly ground black pepper and a squeeze of lemon juice is often added to a salad plate.

When buying fresh beetroot, look for those that are smooth and firm to touch and a good, round shape. Choose small to medium size ones as they are usually more tender. Raw beetroot should stay fresh in the vegetable compartment of the refrigerator for up to a week.

Beetroot have always been one of the most popular canned vegetables. Usually pickled in a mild vinegar solution, they come in various ways: whole baby beetroot; sliced, diced or cut into julienne (matchstick) strips.

■ **TO COOK:** Beetroot is usually boiled whole, but may also be baked in the oven. **See also recipes.**

BOILED BEETROOT: Cut off the tops about 5 cm (2 in) above the beetroot. Wash, but leave whole and do not peel. Place in cold unsalted water to cover and cook, with the lid on, until tender when pierced with a skewer. Very old beetroot may take anything up to 3 hours, although most beetroot will be cooked in 30–40 minutes. When tender, drain (reserving a little of the liquid) and slip off the skins. To serve beetroot hot, leave whole or cut into slices, dice or cut into segments. Reheat gently in reserved liquid, season with salt and freshly ground black pepper and add butter and vinegar or lemon juice as desired.

BAKED BEETROOT: Beetroot may be baked in a preheated moderate oven (180°C/350°F) for 1 hour or until tender. Leave whole and unpeeled, as for Boiled Beetroot, above, and peel when cooked.

Cold Beetroot: Cook and peel beetroot as above, then slice, dice or quarter. Marinate in vinegar or Vinaigrette Dressing (see page 442), with a little cooking liquid added to preserve the colour, and chill until required. Seasonings such as sugar, spring onions or parsley may be added to suit your own taste.

Sautéed Beetroot: Peel and dice 3 medium size beetroot. Melt 60 g (2 oz) butter in a frying pan, add beetroot and season lightly with salt and freshly ground black pepper. Stir over medium heat for 1 minute; reduce heat, cover and cook for about 15 minutes, stirring frequently, until tender. Sprinkle with chopped Italian parsley. Serves 4.

Shredded Beetroot: Peel 3 medium size beetroot and grate coarsely. Melt 60 g (2 oz) butter in a heavy saucepan, add beetroot and season with salt and freshly ground black pepper. Stir over low heat for 2–3 minutes until beetroot is well coated with butter, then add 2 tbs water, cover and cook for 7–10 minutes, stirring frequently until crisp-tender. Remove from heat and toss with 1 tbs lemon juice, 2 tsp chopped parsley and chives and ½ tsp chopped fresh tarragon or a pinch of dried. Serves 4.

Beetroot with Orange Glaze: Boil 3 medium size beetroot as above; peel and dice and set aside. Melt 30 g (1 oz) butter in a heavy saucepan, stir in 2 tbs brown sugar and 2 tsp flour and cook on low heat for 1 minute. Blend in ¾ cup orange juice and stir until boiling. Season with salt and freshly ground black pepper. Add beetroot and heat, stirring gently, until beetroot is heated through. Serves 4.

Glazed Beetroot

1 x 825 g can whole baby beetroot, or 2 cups peeled, diced, cooked beetroot; 60 g (2 oz) butter; 2 tbs sugar; salt and freshly ground black pepper.

Drain beetroot. Heat butter in a heavy frying pan, add beetroot and shake pan to coat with butter. Cook over medium heat for 3 minutes. Sprinkle with sugar and continue shaking pan gently until beetroot are glazed. Season with salt and pepper. Serves 4.

Finnish Beetroot Salad

An unusual salad which is delicious with cold meats or fish.

4 medium beetroot, freshly cooked and peeled; 1 tsp coarse sea salt; 1 tbs grated fresh horseradish or prepared horseradish (not creamed type); ½ cup sour cream; 1 tbs grated orange rind.

Cut beetroot into julienne (matchstick) strips. Combine remaining ingredients and toss with beetroot. Cover and chill for at least 1–2 hours to blend flavours. Serves 4–6.

Beetroot and Herring Salad

2 cups peeled, diced, cooked beetroot; 1 cup peeled, diced, cooked potatoes; 1 cup diced, cooked carrots; ½ cup diced dill pickles or gherkins; 1 large tart apple, peeled, cored, diced and moistened with lemon juice; 1 medium onion, finely chopped; 1 tsp coarse sea salt; freshly ground black pepper; 1 tbs snipped fresh dill, or 1 tsp dried dill weed; 2–3 herring fillets (matjes), cut into strips, to garnish.

DRESSING: ½ cup cream; 1 tbs wine vinegar; 2 tsp sugar.

Combine salad ingredients, cover and chill. Just before serving, whip cream with vinegar and sugar until stiff. Serve salad, dressing and herring strips separately, each diner combining them to suit their own taste. Serves 6–8.

Beetroot Smitane

Beetroot in sour cream, a Russian dish. Delicious with boiled meats or chicken.

6 beetroot, freshly cooked and peeled; 1½ cups sour cream; 15 g (½ oz) butter; salt and freshly ground black pepper; cayenne.

Mash or grate beetroot (this can be done in a food processor). Gently heat sour cream with butter, salt, pepper and a dash of cayenne. Beat sauce until it is light and creamy, and mix with beetroot. Serves 6.

BEIGNETS SOUFFLES (FRENCH FRITTERS)

Light and fluffy fritters of deep-fried choux pastry appear in several cuisines. French *Beignets Soufflés* and German *Crullers* are shaped with a spoon; Spanish *Churros* and German *Strauben* are piped directly into the hot oil (see *Churros*).

Beignets Soufflés

1 quantity Choux Pastry (page 345); oil for deep frying; sifted icing sugar; Quick Apricot Sauce (page 462).

Prepare choux pastry. Heat oil for deep-frying. With a dessertspoon or large teaspoon, take up portions of pastry. Dip another spoon in hot oil, then mould off pieces of choux pastry the size of a walnut into the hot oil. Cook 5–6 at a time, turning them over in oil from time to time. When golden (about 5–6 minutes), drain on crumpled paper towels. Dredge well with icing sugar and serve with apricot sauce. Makes 15–20.

NOTE: If liked, the beignets may be twice-fried. Fry the quantity you want to serve until pale golden, drain, then just before serving return to hot oil for a few minutes. Twice-frying helps when you want to serve a whole quantity for a dinner party.

CRULLERS: Prepare in the same way as Beignets Soufflés, above, but shape with 2 small teaspoons. Crullers are usually served as a snack with coffee.

BEURRE MANIE

A mixture of flour and butter blended to a paste, and used to thicken stews, sauces, casseroles, etc., at the end of cooking. Use 1 tbs butter to 1 tbs flour. Have butter at room temperature and work in the flour with a fork or your fingers until smooth. Whisk beurre manié, a little at a time, into the simmering liquid until thickened as desired.

BIGARADE, SAUCE

An orange sauce served with roast duck. In the original French recipe, bitter Seville oranges are used. If they are not available, look for oranges that are not too sweet. The duck is roasted in the usual way (see *Duck*), then served with the sauce.

Sauce Bigarade

I cup rich chicken stock; I tsp arrowroot or cornflour; 2 tbs wine vinegar; 2 tbs sugar; 2 tbs finely shredded, blanched orange rind; $^{1}/_{2}$ cup hot, fresh orange juice; I tsp lemon juice; 2 tbs Curaçao (optional); salt and freshly ground white pepper; peeled orange sections to garnish.

When duck is cooked, remove to a serving platter and keep warm. Pour off fat from roasting tin and add stock to tin. Bring to the boil, stirring well, and thicken with arrowroot mixed to a cream with a little water. Remove from heat. In a saucepan, cook vinegar and sugar together over low heat until a light brown colour. Add liquid from roasting tin and simmer 4–5 minutes. Stir in orange rind, juices and Curaçao, if using. Bring to the boil and season with salt and pepper. Pour a little sauce over duck to glaze (it may be carved first, if desired). Garnish platter with orange sections and serve remaining sauce separately. Serves 2–4, depending on size of duck.

BIRYANI (BIVIANI)

A great and traditional Mogul dish from India, consisting of layers of delicately perfumed pilau rice and lamb in spiced gravy. A biryani is a festive dish, ideal for a party, and can easily be made ahead and reheated. Accompany it with chutneys, sambals and pappadams.

Lamb Biryani

LAMB: I.5–2 kg (3–4 lb) boned leg of lamb; 125 g (4 oz) ghee, or $^{1}/_{2}$ cup oil; 3 large onions, sliced; 5–6 cloves garlic, finely chopped; 5 cm (2 in) piece fresh ginger, finely chopped; 6 tbs curry powder; I tsp chilli powder (optional); 4 tsp salt; 2 tbs vinegar; 2 tsp Garam Masala (page 171); 2 fresh hot chillies; $^{1}/_{2}$ cup chopped fresh mint; 2 large ripe tomatoes, peeled, seeded and chopped.

PILAU: I kg (2 lb) long-grain rice, preferably Basmati; 125 g (4 oz) ghee; I cinnamon stick; 10 cardamom pods; 5 cloves; 2 onions, sliced; $^{1}/_{2}$ tsp saffron threads, crumbled and soaked in 2 tsp hot water; 8 cups boiling stock; salt.

GARNISH: I cup sultanas; $^{1}/_{2}$ cup blanched almonds; I onion, sliced; little ghee; I cup cooked peas.

LAMB: Trim excess fat from lamb and cut into 2.5 cm (1 in) cubes. Heat ghee or oil in a large pan and fry onions, garlic and ginger until soft and golden. Add curry and chilli powder (if using) and fry 1 minute longer, then add salt and vinegar. Add lamb and stir until well coated with curry mixture. Add garam masala, whole chillies, mint and tomatoes. Cover and cook, stirring from time to time, on very low heat for 1 hour or until lamb is tender and gravy thick. Add a little water if mixture is drying out. Remove whole chillies.

PILAU: While lamb is cooking, wash rice under running water and drain well. Melt ghee in a large pan and add cinnamon stick broken into pieces, cardamom, cloves and onions. Fry until onions are golden. Add rice and fry, stirring, until grains are well coated with ghee. Add saffron and boiling stock, season with salt and stir until boiling. Turn heat very low, cover tightly and cook without uncovering for 10–15 minutes or until rice is tender and liquid absorbed. Remove lid, turn off heat and fluff up rice with a fork.

Put a generous layer of cooked rice in a large, buttered ovenproof casserole and cover with a layer of lamb mixture. Repeat these layers, ending with a layer of rice. Depending on the size of the dish, there should be about 3 layers of rice and 2 of lamb. Cover with foil, then a lid, and reheat over low heat on top of the stove or in a preheated moderately slow oven (160°C/325°F) for 40–50 minutes.

GARNISH: Fry sultanas, almonds and onion in a little ghee. Leave biryani in casserole or turn it out into a heap on a serving dish. Garnish with sultanas, almonds, onion rings and peas. Serves 10–12.

NOTE: The biryani can be prepared ahead, except for final reheating and garnishing, and can be stored, in the refrigerator, for up to 2 days.

BISCUITS

The first biscuits were small, flat cakes which were baked twice to make them crisp. The word now covers an infinite variety of crunchy, crisp, chewy or brittle baked goods, from the plain water biscuit to sweet confections nibbled with coffee. **See recipes.**

Cherry Wink Cookies

1³/4 cups flour; 2 tsp baking powder;
pinch salt; 125 g (4 oz) butter or margarine;
1/2 cup caster sugar; 1¹/2 tsp vanilla; 2 tbs honey;
I egg; 2 tbs milk; 2 cups cornflakes, lightly crushed;
1/2 cup glacé cherries, halved.

Sift flour, baking powder and salt. Cream butter or margarine with sugar and vanilla. Add honey and egg and beat well. Fold in dry ingredients, a little at a time, alternating with milk. Drop teaspoonfuls of mixture into lightly crushed cornflakes and toss gently to coat. Place on greased baking trays and press a halved glacé cherry in centre of each. Bake the cookies in a preheated hot oven (200°C/400°F) for 10 minutes or until golden. Makes about 36.

Cinnamon Crinkles

125 g (4 oz) butter; ³/4 cup sugar; I egg;
1¹/3 cups self-raising flour; extra 2 tbs sugar;
2 tbs cinnamon.

Cream butter with ¾ cup sugar, add egg and beat well. Sift flour and add to creamed mixture. Mix well. Form into small balls and roll in combined extra sugar and cinnamon. Place on ungreased baking trays and bake in a preheated moderate oven (180°C/350°F) for 15 minutes or until golden. Cool on trays until biscuits are crisp. Makes about 36.

French Fingers

125 g (4 oz) butter; 1/2 cup caster sugar;
1/2 tsp vanilla; I egg; 1¹/2 cups self-raising flour;
1/2 cup cornflour.

Cream butter with sugar and vanilla until light and fluffy. Add egg and beat well. Mix in sifted dry ingredients. Spoon or pipe mixture, using a large rose pipe, in 5 cm (2 in) lengths on greased baking trays. Bake in a preheated moderate oven (180°C/350°F) for about 15 minutes. Allow to cool on trays. Makes about 46.

Almond Biscuits

125 g (4 oz) butter; 1/4 cup sugar;
I tsp vanilla; I egg yolk;
2 cups self-raising flour; pinch salt;
I egg white; I cup icing sugar, sifted;
finely chopped blanched almonds.

Cream butter with sugar and vanilla, add egg yolk and beat well. Mix in sifted flour and salt to form a firm dough. Place dough on floured surface and roll out to 5 mm (1/4 in) thickness. Beat egg white until stiff, add icing sugar gradually and beat until smooth.

Spread icing over prepared biscuit mixture. Sprinkle with almonds and cut into diamond or other decorative shapes. Place on greased baking trays and bake in a preheated moderately hot oven (190°C/375°F) for 10–12 minutes. Makes about 60.

Ginger Shortbread Biscuits

250 g (8 oz) butter, softened; 1/2 cup caster sugar;
250 g (8 oz) plain flour; 2 tsp ground ginger;
caster sugar for sprinkling.

Cream together butter and sugar until light and fluffy. Sift together flour and ginger and gradually work into butter mixture. Knead lightly then roll out on a lightly floured surface until 5 mm (1/4 in) thick. Cut into round or star shapes using a biscuit cutter. Transfer to a baking sheet and bake in a preheated slow oven (160°C/325°F) until golden. Sprinkle with caster sugar while warm. Makes about 40.

VARIATIONS

SPICED BISCUITS: Omit ginger but sift 1 tsp ground cinnamon and 1 tsp ground mace with the flour.
BUTTER SHORTBREAD BISCUITS: Omit ginger and add a few drops of vanilla to mixture.

Orange and Lemon Shortbread

185 g (6 oz) butter; 1/2 cup sugar; 2 tsp each finely grated lemon and orange rind; 2 cups flour;
pinch salt; extra 2 tbs sugar.

Cream butter with sugar until fluffy. Mix in fruit rinds and flour sifted with salt. Divide dough in half and mould each portion into a sausage shape. Wrap dough in plastic wrap and chill for 1–2 hours. Cut into 5 mm (1/4 in) thick slices and arrange on greased baking trays. Sprinkle with extra sugar and bake in a preheated moderate oven (180°C/350°F) for 20 minutes or until golden-brown. Cool on a wire rack and store in an airtight container. Makes about 30.

Butter Wafers

A good basic biscuit recipe. Vary the flavour by using brown sugar instead of white, adding poppy or sesame seeds, etc., or a little instant coffee powder. For chocolate butter wafers add a little cocoa but reduce flour in proportion.

125 g (4 oz) butter; 1/3 cup sugar; I egg; I tsp vanilla;
³/4 cup flour, sifted; pinch salt.

Cream butter with sugar, then beat in egg and vanilla. Stir in flour and salt. Drop teaspoonfuls of mixture on to greased baking trays, spacing well apart. Bake in a preheated moderately hot oven (190°C/375°F) for 10 minutes or until biscuits are golden-brown around the edges. Makes about 36.

Coconut Drops

I¹/₂ cups self-raising flour; pinch salt;
I cup sugar; I egg, lightly beaten; I tsp vanilla;
few drops almond essence; 125 g (4 oz) butter,
melted; I¹/₂ cups desiccated coconut.

Sift flour and salt into a bowl and stir in sugar. Add remaining ingredients, except coconut, and combine. Form mixture into small balls about the size of a marble and roll in coconut. Arrange on greased baking trays, spacing well apart. Bake in a preheated moderate oven (180°C/350°F) for 15 minutes or until golden. Cool on a wire rack. Makes about 30.

Highland Oatmeal Cookies

These hearty oatmeal cookies have sustained many a hungry Scottish child in search of a snack.

250 g (8 oz) butter; I cup firmly packed brown sugar;
¹/₂ cup white sugar; I egg; 2 tsp vanilla;
¹/₄ cup water; 2 cups flour; ¹/₂ tsp salt;
I¹/₂ tsp bicarbonate of soda; I tsp cinnamon;
¹/₂ cup chopped nuts; I cup raisins;
2¹/₂ cups rolled oats; walnuts or
glacé cherries to decorate.

Cream butter with sugars, egg and vanilla until light and fluffy. Beat in water. Sift dry ingredients and stir in with nuts, raisins and oats. Drop heaped teaspoonfuls of mixture, about 5 cm (2 in) apart, on to greased baking trays. Press a walnut or cherry into the top of each biscuit. Bake in a preheated moderately hot oven (190°C/375°F) for 12–15 minutes or until lightly browned. Cool on a wire rack. Makes about 60.

Refrigerator Biscuits

This biscuit dough can be stored, wrapped, in the freezer for months. Take a few slices as you need them and have freshly baked biscuits as required. You can decorate the biscuits with cherries or sliced almonds, or brush them with egg white and sprinkle well with caster sugar, before baking.

185 g (6 oz) butter; I cup firmly packed brown sugar;
I egg; I tsp vanilla; 2¹/₄ cups flour; ¹/₂ tsp salt;
¹/₂ tsp baking powder.

Cream butter with brown sugar. Add egg and vanilla and beat well. Sift flour with salt and baking powder. Stir into creamed mixture. Shape into long rolls about 5 cm (2 in) in diameter. Wrap in plastic wrap or foil and freeze until needed. Slice thinly, put on a baking tray and bake in a preheated moderate oven (180°C/350°F) for 7–10 minutes. If wished, store in a refrigerator, wrapped in foil, for up to 2 weeks. Makes 6 dozen.

Drop Biscuits

Drop biscuits vary in texture. Some fall easily from the spoon and flatten into wafers when baking. Stiffer doughs need a push with the finger or the use of a second spoon to release them. To get uniform drops use a standard measuring teaspoon, and if you want the biscuits thinner make a crisscross on top with a fork dipped in caster sugar. During very hot weather, put the dough in the refrigerator for 20 minutes before using.

I³/₄ cups flour; 2 tsp baking powder; pinch salt;
125 g (4 oz) butter; ¹/₂ cup firmly packed brown
sugar; 2 tbs golden syrup; I egg; I¹/₂ tsp vanilla;
3–4 tbs milk.

Sift flour, baking powder and salt together. Cream butter with sugar until fluffy. Add golden syrup, egg and vanilla and beat well. Blend in sifted dry ingredients a little at a time alternately with milk until you have a stiff dough. Drop teaspoonfuls of the mixture on to greased baking trays and bake in a preheated hot oven (200°C/400°F) for 10–12 minutes or until golden. Cool on a wire rack and store in an airtight container. Makes 36.

VARIATIONS

CHOCOLATE DROP BISCUITS: Add 60 g (2 oz) cooled, melted chocolate to the creamed butter and sugar. Bake as directed.

CHERRY DROP BISCUITS: Add ¹/₃ cup chopped glacé cherries with the flour and milk. Bake as directed.

NUT DROP BISCUITS: Add ¹/₂ cup chopped nuts – almonds, walnuts or pecans – with the flour and milk. Bake as directed.

BISCUIT TORTONI

A rich Italian iced dessert made from cream and crushed macaroons, which is spooned into small custard cups, or soufflé dishes, decorated with fruit chocolate and nuts, then frozen.

Biscuit Tortoni

³/₄ cup crushed macaroons, home-made
or purchased; I³/₄ cups cream;
¹/₄ cup icing sugar, sifted; tiny pinch salt;
I tsp vanilla.

DECORATION: halved maraschino cherries;
grated chocolate; chopped, toasted almonds;
shreds candied angelica.

Combine macaroons, ³/₄ cup cream, the icing sugar and salt. Allow to stand for 1 hour. Whip remaining cream until thick enough to stand in soft peaks (but not stiff) and fold into macaroon mixture with vanilla. Spoon into 8–10 small custard cups or small soufflé dishes arranged in a shallow tray that will fit in freezer. Decorate tops with cherries, grated chocolate, toasted almonds and angelica and freeze overnight or until firm. Serves 8–10.

BISHOP'S CAKE

An old English fruit cake that got its name from the stained-glass window appearance of each slice. It is sometimes known as American Christmas Cake, and is more of a fruit-and-nut slab than a cake. This cake should be stored in the refrigerator, wrapped in foil and, being so rich and sweet, only a thin slice is necessary. Bishop's Cake may be cut in finger blocks and served with sherry.

Bishop's Cake

500 g (1 lb) whole, shelled Brazil nuts;
12 dates, stoned; 1 cup glacé cherries, red and green mixed; $^3/_4$ cup flour; $^1/_2$ tsp baking powder;
$^1/_2$ tsp salt; $^3/_4$ cup caster sugar; 3 eggs, beaten;
1 tsp vanilla.

Grease a 21 x 11 cm ($8^1/_2$ x $4^1/_4$ in) loaf tin and line base and sides with greased greaseproof paper. Put whole Brazil nuts, whole dates and whole glacé cherries into a large mixing bowl. Sift dry ingredients over and mix thoroughly. Pour in eggs and vanilla. Stir well and spoon into the prepared tin. Bake in a preheated slow oven (150°C/300°F) for about $1^1/_2$ hours or until a skewer inserted in centre comes out clean. Remove from tin, peel away paper and cool completely on a wire rack. When cold wrap in foil and store in the refrigerator. It will keep for up to 3 weeks.

BISQUE

This French term describes a particular type of cream soup, frequently made of seafood and enriched with cream or egg yolks or both. Bisques are customarily served hot, but may be chilled for a splendid first course on a hot day. See recipes.

Oyster Bisque

90 g (3 oz) butter; 2 tsp grated onion; $1^1/_2$ cups milk;
$^1/_2$ cup cream; salt and freshly ground white pepper;
2 egg yolks, beaten; $1^1/_2$ cups oysters and their liquor (bottled or from the shell); 2 tbs chopped parsley.

Place butter and onion in top half of a double saucepan over hot water. Melt butter, then add milk and cream and season with salt and pepper. Increase heat so water in lower half of saucepan reaches boiling point. When milk is just about to boil, remove from heat and pour a little over beaten egg yolks. Mix well, then return to the pan. Add oysters and liquor, and place over boiling water again. Heat until bisque is very hot but not boiling. Pour into a heated tureen and sprinkle with chopped parsley. Serves 4.

Mushroom Bisque

500 g (1 lb) young mushroom caps, stems removed and reserved; 4 cups chicken stock; 1 medium onion, chopped; 90 g (3 oz) butter; 4 tbs flour;
3 cups milk; 1 cup cream; 1 tsp salt; freshly ground white pepper; Tabasco sauce; 2 tbs sherry.

Slice 6 mushroom caps and reserve. Chop remaining caps and stems. Simmer chopped mushrooms, covered, in stock with onion for 30 minutes. Sauté reserved sliced mushroom caps in 1 tbs of the butter and reserve for garnish. Melt remaining butter in a saucepan, add flour and stir with a wire whisk until blended. Meanwhile bring milk to the boil. Add milk all at once to butter-flour mixture, stirring vigorously with whisk until sauce is thickened and smooth. Stir in cream. Combine mushroom-broth mixture with sauce and season with salt, pepper and Tabasco sauce. Reheat, add sherry and top with reserved mushrooms. Serves 6–8.

BLACKBERRY

A large luscious berry that is cultivated and also grows wild. Blackberries are delicious eaten fresh or stewed, or in jams, pies and tarts.

Blackberry Pie

Rich Shortcrust Pastry for a 2-crust, 23 cm (9 in) pie (page 342); 4 cups fresh or frozen blackberries, or 3 cups drained, canned blackberries;
$^3/_4$ cup sugar; $1^1/_2$ tbs cornflour; 2 tbs lemon juice.

Roll out just over half the pastry and use to line a greased 23 cm (9 in) pie plate. If using fresh blackberries, toss gently with $^3/_4$ cup sugar, the cornflour and lemon juice. For sweetened, frozen blackberries or for canned blackberries, use less sugar. Spoon into pie crust. Dampen edges and roll out remaining pastry to make lid. Press into place, trim and crimp edges and make a few slashes in the top for steam to escape. Bake in a preheated hot oven (200°C/400°F) for 10 minutes, then reduce the oven heat to moderate (180°C/350°F) and bake for a further 25 minutes or until pastry is cooked and golden-brown. Serve warm with cream, ice cream or custard. Serves 6.

BLACK BUN, SCOTTISH

Not a bun in the usual sense but a rich fruit mixture enclosed in pastry. Black bun is traditionally eaten at Hogmanay (New Year) and should be made at least a few weeks ahead to allow it to mature. It will keep for up to a year in an airtight tin.

Scottish Black Bun

I quantity Plain Shortcrust Pastry (page 342);
2 cups flour; $^1/_2$ tsp baking powder; $^1/_4$ tsp black
pepper; I tsp ground ginger; I tsp ground cloves;
$^1/_2$ cup firmly packed brown sugar;
500 g (I lb) raisins; 500 g (I lb) currants;
60 g (2 oz) chopped mixed candied peel;
60 g (2 oz) blanched almonds, chopped;
I apple, peeled, cored and grated; 2 eggs, beaten.

Roll out two thirds of pastry thinly and use to line a greased and lined 20 cm (8 in) cake tin. Sift flour, baking powder, pepper and spices into a bowl and stir in sugar, fruit, peel, nuts and grated apple. Add eggs and mix thoroughly. Turn into tin. Roll out remaining pastry for lid and place on top, pinching edges together. Makes 4 holes right through to bottom with a skewer. Bake in a preheated moderate oven (180°C/350°F) for 3 hours. Turn out carefully and cool. When completely cold, store in an airtight tin. Serve cut into thin fingers.

BLACK FOREST CHERRY TORTE

This famous German torte originated in Swabia in the Black Forest region. The basic combination consists of chocolate cake, chocolate, Kirsch and cherries with a wickedly rich amount of whipped cream.

Black Forest Cherry Torte

CAKE: 90 g (3 oz) dark chocolate; I tbs water or black coffee; 4 eggs; $^3/_4$ cup caster sugar; $^3/_4$ cup self-raising flour; I tsp vanilla; grated rind $^1/_2$ lemon; 45 g (I $^1/_2$ oz) butter, melted and cooled.

TOPPING AND FILLING: 280 g (9 oz) milk chocolate, at room temperature; I x 700 g (I lb 7 oz) jar German sour cherries; 3 tbs Kirsch; 2 cups cream.

CAKE: Place chocolate and water or coffee in a heatproof basin and melt over hot water. Beat eggs with sugar until very light and fluffy. Sift in flour and fold into egg mixture with vanilla, lemon rind, melted butter and chocolate mixture. Turn into a greased, lined and floured 23 cm (9 in) springform tin. Bake in a preheated moderate oven (180°C/350°F) for 1 hour. Cool with the spring released.

TOPPING AND FILLING: Shave thin curls from side of block of chocolate with a swivel-bladed vegetable peeler. Chill. Drain syrup from cherries and mix syrup with Kirsch. Halve cherries, leaving a few whole to

decorate cake. Cut cake into 2 layers and prick bottom layer with a fork. Place bottom layer on a serving plate and soak with half kirsch-flavoured syrup. Whip cream until it just holds its shape and pile about one third over bottom cake layer. Spoon over half the halved cherries. Place top cake layer in position, prick with a fork and spoon remaining syrup over. Arrange remaining cherry halves on top. Cover cake with remaining cream, piling most of it on top. Press chocolate curls around side of cake and sprinkle some on top. Decorate with reserved whole cherries and chill for 1–2 hours before serving. Serves 10–12.

BLACKCURRANT

A small black, juicy berry. Fresh, it is used to make jam, tarts, mousses and other desserts, and to flavour syrup, cordial, and the delicious liqueur called Cassis. Blackcurrants are also available frozen and canned.

BLANCMANGE

A white pudding made of milk, flavourings and cornflour and set in a mould.

Blancmange

2 cups milk; 2 thin strips lemon rind;
4 tbs cornflour; 2 tbs sugar.

Put all but 4 tbs milk into a saucepan with lemon rind and bring slowly to the boil. Remove rind. Mix cornflour and sugar to a smooth paste with remaining milk. Slowly pour boiling milk into cornflour paste, stirring constantly, then return mixture to the saucepan. Simmer for 5 minutes, stirring. Pour into a dampened mould. Cool, then chill until set. To serve, dip mould into hot water 2–3 seconds, wipe mould, shake and unmould on to a serving dish. Serves 4.

BLANQUETTE

A blanquette is a French-inspired stew made of lamb, chicken, veal or sweetbreads. It differs from other stews in that the meat is not browned before cooking, and the addition of cream and egg yolks to the cooking liquid results in a white sauce.

Blanquette de Veau
(White Veal Stew)

1.5 kg (3 lb) boneless veal, cut into large cubes;
salt and freshly ground white pepper; I large onion,
studded with I clove; I large carrot, coarsely
chopped; I stick celery, sliced; I bouquet garni;
5 cups veal or chicken stock; 20 small white onions,
blanched; 125 g (4 oz) button mushrooms;
2 tbs flour; 2 tbs butter; 3 egg yolks, beaten with
$^1/_2$ cup cream; 2 tbs lemon juice.

GARNISH: chopped parsley; croûtons or Puff
Pastry Fleurons (page 155).

Blanch veal for 2 minutes in boiling salted water,
drain and rinse under cold running water. Place
meat in a deep, heavy saucepan with whole onion,
carrot, celery and bouquet garni. Pour stock over,
bring to the boil, then cover and simmer 1½ hours
or until veal is very tender. Remove vegetables and
bouquet garni with a slotted spoon. Add small
onions and mushrooms to the saucepan. Simmer 10
minutes. Blend flour and butter together, and whisk
a little at a time into simmering liquid. Simmer
another 10 minutes, then remove pan from heat. Stir
2 tbs of liquid into egg and cream mixture. Add this
mixture to pan with lemon juice and reheat gently
but do not boil. Adjust seasoning with salt and
pepper. Serve in a heated serving bowl, sprinkled
with chopped parsley and garnished with croûtons
or fleurons. Serves 6.

BLINI

Blini (bliny) are small Russian yeast pancakes made
with buckwheat flour. The classic and superb topping is
a tablespoon of sour cream surmounted by a teaspoon
of caviar. Cottage cheese with herbs, smoked salmon,
vegetable purées, chopped egg or liver may also be
used. For dessert, blini may be topped with sour cream
and jam.

Blini

30 g (1 oz) compressed yeast; 2 cups milk, scalded
and cooled to lukewarm; 1½ cups each plain flour
and buckwheat flour, sifted together; 2 tbs sugar;
3 eggs, separated; 125 g (4 oz) butter, melted;
1 tsp salt; little melted butter for cooking.

Dissolve yeast in warm milk, then stir in 1½ cups
flour and the sugar. Cover with greased plastic
wrap and a cloth and stand in a warm place for 1½
hours or until covered with bubbles. Beat egg yolks
in another bowl, combine with melted butter and
salt and stir in remaining flour. Beat this mixture
into yeast mixture, cover as before and stand in a
warm place for another 1½ hours or until almost
doubled in bulk. Beat egg whites until they form
soft peaks and fold into batter. Stand 10 minutes.
Without stirring batter again, drop a tablespoonful
at a time on to a heated greased griddle or heavy
frying pan. When undersides are brown, sprinkle a
little melted butter over the tops, turn over and
cook other side. Stack on a heated serving platter
and keep covered with a warm cloth until all are
cooked. Makes about 24.
NOTE: If using dry yeast, see *Yeast Cookery*.

BLINTZ

Blintzes are one of the many joys of Jewish cooking –
tender pancakes filled with cottage cheese, then
fried. They are served hot with sugar, cinnamon and
sour cream.

Blintzes

PANCAKES: ¾ cup flour, sifted; ½ tsp salt;
1 tsp baking powder; 2 tbs caster sugar; 2 eggs;
⅔ cup milk/⅓ cup water; ½ tsp vanilla;
oil for cooking.

FILLING: 1½ cups cottage cheese; 1 egg yolk;
1 tsp softened butter; 2 tsp sugar; 1 tsp grated
lemon rind.

TO FINISH: oil and butter for frying; sugar;
cinnamon; sour cream.

PANCAKES: Sift flour, salt, baking powder and sugar
into a bowl. Beat eggs with milk, water and vanilla.
Make a well in centre of dry ingredients, add liquid
mixture and combine very quickly and lightly. Batter
will still be lumpy and must not be overbeaten. Heat
a pancake pan, about 13 cm (5 in) in diameter, and
grease with a few drops of oil. Pour in just enough
batter to cover bottom of pan and cook over moderate
heat until golden-brown underneath. Remove without cooking other side and repeat with remaining
batter. Stack pancakes on a dampened tea-towel,
cooked side up, with squares of greaseproof paper
between them to prevent sticking, and cover with
ends of towel.
FILLING: Mix all ingredients well together.
TO FINISH: Place about 2 tbs filling in middle of each
pancake on cooked side. Turn edges in and roll up
like a cigar. Heat about 2 tsp each oil and butter in a
large, heavy frying pan and put in several blintzes,
seam sides down. Fry over medium heat until golden-
brown on each side. Add more oil and butter to pan
and continue cooking blintzes until all are browned.
Serve hot, sprinkled with sugar and cinnamon, and
pass a bowl of sour cream. Makes about 14.

BOK CHOY

Cultivated in China since ancient times, bok choy
is found in soups and stir-fries, appetisers and main
dishes. Its popularity comes from its light, sweet
flavour, crisp texture and nutritional value. Not only is
bok choy high in vitamins A and C and calcium, it is also
low in calories.
  Bok choy, or *Brassica chinensis* to use its scientific
name, is classified as a cabbage. The Chinese also refer
to bok choy as pak choi or 'white vegetable'. Another
common name is white cabbage. In China over 20
varieties are available. Shanghai or baby bok choy, a
small version of bok choy, is readily available.

Another member of the bok choy family is choy sum, distinguishable by its light green leaves and tiny yellow flowers. Also known as Chinese flowering cabbage, choy sum is the cream of the bok choys. Grocers often sell the trimmed leaves and stalks of choy sum instead of the whole plant. Some sell bok choy sum 'hearts'.

Squid with Baby Bok Choy

You can purchase cleaned squid these days. This dish is relatively quick and worth the effort. The squid is lightly scored in a cross-hatch pattern before being cut into pieces to give an attractive look if you like and to add texture. This is a delicious way of cooking squid and turning it into a light meal.

4–6 squid tubes, about 500 g (1 lb), cleaned; 2 tsp sesame oil; salt and freshly ground pepper; 3 tbs light olive oil; 2.5 cm (1 in) piece fresh ginger, finely shredded; 4 baby bok choy; 4 spring onions, cut into 4 cm (1½ in) lengths; 1 tsp soy sauce; 1 tbs oyster sauce; 1 tbs freshly chopped coriander; coriander sprigs to garnish.

Wash squid and pat dry with paper towels. Score the tubes in crisscross fashion, not cutting through completely. Cut the sacs, flaps, fins and tentacles into 4 cm (1½ in) squares. Place in a bowl with the sesame oil, season lightly with salt and pepper, and keep in the refrigerator until ready to cook.

Trim the base of the bok choy and halve or quarter if large. Wash and dry and set aside. Heat the oil in a wok or a heavy-based frying pan. Add the ginger and cook over a moderate heat for a few seconds. Add the squid and stir-fry over a high heat for 2–3 minutes. Remove the squid with a slotted spoon and set aside.

Add the bok choy and spring onions and cook for 1–2 minutes until the bok choy is tender-crisp. Add the soy and oyster sauces and coriander and cook, turning gently. Return the squid to the pan and toss to combine for a further minute. Garnish with the coriander sprigs and serve immediately. Serves 4–6.

Baby Bok Choy with Oyster Sauce

This dish looks so attractive, with the vivid green of the bok choy, the dark earthy brown shades of the shiitake mushrooms and creamy elegant oyster mushrooms.

500 g (1 lb) baby bok choy; 125 g (4 oz) shiitake mushrooms; 125g (4 oz) oyster mushrooms; 2 tbs vegetable oil; 1 tsp sesame oil; 4 cloves garlic, chopped; 1 tbs finely grated ginger; 1 tsp soy sauce; 2 teaspoons rice wine vinegar; ½ tsp cornflour; 1 tbs oyster sauce.

Baby bok choy may be left whole. If large, trim the bases and halve or quarter, trim the rough tops off leaves but keep plenty of stalk on each leaf. Wash and dry the leaves and cut each across into 2 or 3 pieces. Trim stalks of the mushrooms, slash a cross or star on rounded side of shiitake mushrooms.

Heat the oils in a wok or large pan and stir-fry the mushrooms over a medium heat. Cook the mushrooms until they give up some juice and reabsorb it.

Add the garlic and ginger and stir-fry for 1 minute. Add the bok choy and continue to stir-fry until wilted. Have ready the soy sauce, vinegar, cornflour and oyster sauce combined in a small bowl. Add this mixture to the vegetables and cook for about 1 minute or until the vegetables are glazed. Serves 4.

BOMBE

A frozen dessert set in a mould. The name comes from the spherical moulds traditionally used to shape the dessert. In the absence of a special mould, a bombe can be made in a pudding basin or soufflé dish. It usually consists of an outer layer of ice cream or sherbet and a softer, inner layer of custard, mousse, fruit purée or cream. However, layers of ice cream in different colours and flavours can be used to make a simple, attractive bombe. Using the following recipe as a starting point, it is easy to experiment with variations. **See recipes.**

Strawberry Bombe

500 g (1 lb) strawberries; 1 cup cream; ¼ cup icing sugar, sifted; 2 tbs Kirsch or other fruit liqueur; 1 litre (4 cups) strawberry or vanilla ice cream, slightly softened; extra whipped cream to decorate.

Chill an 8-cup mould in the freezer. Hull and purée enough strawberries to make 1 cup. Whip cream with icing sugar until stiff, then fold in Kirsch and puréed strawberries. Remove mould from freezer and quickly line it with ice cream. Fill centre with strawberry cream, cover with foil and freeze until firm. Unmould to serve, decorate with remaining strawberries and whipped cream. Serves 6.

Bombe Alaska

A spectacular dessert. For a party, set a broken egg shell in the meringue, put a sugar lump soaked in brandy in the shell, and flame; it then becomes Bombe Vesuvius.

1 x 23 cm (9 in) round or square sponge cake layer (see page 176); 1 litre (4 cups) ice cream; 4 egg whites; ½ tsp cream of tartar; 6 tbs caster sugar.

Place sponge on a wooden board and top with ice cream, leaving a small margin of cake uncovered round the edge. Freeze until ice cream is very hard. Beat egg whites with cream of tartar until soft peaks form, then gradually beat in sugar until meringue is stiff and glossy. Swirl meringue over cake and ice cream to cover completely. Bake in a preheated very hot oven (230°C/450°F) for 2–3 minutes until just lightly tinted. Serve at once. Serves 6.

BORAGE

This large herb has greyish-green leaves, covered with a fuzz of grey hairs, and its clusters of blue, star-shaped flowers make it an attractive addition to the garden. Young, fresh borage leaves may be cooked and eaten like spinach or added to salads. With their faint cucumber flavour, they are also one of the traditional ingredients in Pimms, the long, refreshing alcoholic drink once so popular in Britain.

BOREK

A savoury pastry from Turkey, served hot. Feather-light pastry is wrapped around fillings made from spinach and eggs, pumpkin, cheese, meat or fruit. Borek vary in size from small, cigar-shaped mouthfuls to cushion-shapes to serve 3 or 4, or enormous ones baked on a tray for parties.

Meat Borek

This simplified recipe is made with filo pastry.

375 g (12 oz) minced lean beef or lamb;
2 tbs olive oil; 1 clove garlic, crushed;
1 large onion, finely chopped; 2 tbs finely chopped parsley; salt and freshly ground black pepper;
1 egg, beaten; 6 sheets filo pastry;
60 g (2 oz) butter, melted.

Brown meat in olive oil, stirring with a fork to break up any lumps. Add garlic and onion and continue to cook and stir until onion is soft. Stir in parsley and season well with salt and pepper. Allow to cool, then stir in beaten egg. Layer 3 sheets of filo in a greased 28 x 19 cm (11 x 7½ in) lamington tin, brushing generously with melted butter between layers. Spread meat filling over and cover with 3 more buttered sheets of filo. Press edges together. Pour any remaining butter over top. Bake in a preheated moderate oven (180°C/350°F) for about 25 minutes or until pastry is crisp and golden-brown. Serve hot or cold, cut into squares. Serves 18 as an appetiser, 4 as a lunch dish.

VARIATION

COCKTAIL BOREKLER: Small cigar-shaped borekler are made by folding a buttered sheet of filo into 4. Brush with butter, put a spoonful of meat filling in a cigar shape on the centre, fold in ends and roll up. Repeat with remaining ingredients. Place rolls seam sides down, on a baking tray, brush with butter and bake in a preheated moderately hot oven (190°C/375°F) for 20 minutes or until golden. Makes 24.

BORSCH (BORTSCH)

A basic soup of Russia and Poland, mainly characterised by its use of beetroot, which gives the soup a lovely wine-red colour. There are thick and thin versions as well as hot and cold. All borschs are served with a sour cream garnish. **See recipes.**

Borsch

This recipe is for hearty borsch from Russia – a meal in itself.

750 g (1½ lb) stewing beef in one piece (shin of beef is good); 7 cups beef stock; 1 bay leaf; 90 g (3 oz) butter; 1 large onion, chopped; 2 carrots, sliced;
½ medium cabbage, shredded; 2 medium potatoes, peeled and sliced; ¼ cup chopped parsley, including stalks; ½ cup tomato paste;
1 tbs vinegar; 3 medium raw beetroot, peeled and grated; salt and freshly ground black pepper;
¼ cup fresh beetroot juice (while grating beetroot, sieve a little to give juice).

GARNISH: lemon slices; sour cream.

Place beef in a large saucepan with stock and bay leaf and bring to the boil. Skim, then lower heat and simmer, covered, for 1½ hours or until beef is almost tender. Heat butter in another saucepan and gently fry onions, carrots, cabbage and potatoes for 2–3 minutes, stirring to coat with butter. Add vegetables to soup pot and simmer, covered, until beef and vegetables are very tender, another 30–40 minutes. Stir in parsley, tomato paste, vinegar and grated beetroot and simmer uncovered a further 5 minutes. Taste and season well with salt and pepper. Remove beef from pot, cut into slices and divide among 6 large bowls. Stir beetroot juice into soup (this gives a good red colour) and ladle into bowls. Garnish each bowl with a slice of lemon and a spoonful of sour cream. Serves 6.

NOTE: If desired, the meat could be served separately as a second course with rye bread, dill pickles and mustard.

Iced Borsch

A clear, iced borsch, when made with excellent stock will jell slightly. Canned consommé may be used.

4 cups strong beef stock; 4 raw beetroot, peeled and grated; ½ cup red wine; 2 tbs tomato paste;
2 bay leaves; 3 egg whites, stiffly beaten; grated rind 1 lemon; salt; cayenne; 5 tbs sour cream.

Put stock in a large pan. Add beetroot, wine, tomato paste, bay leaves and egg whites. Heat over moderate heat until borsch comes to the boil, then draw off heat and leave for 10 minutes. Pour through a fine damp cloth and place in refrigerator until cold. Add grated lemon rind, salt and cayenne to sour cream and serve separately. Serves 4–6.

BOUCHEES

Tiny mouthful-sized cases for sweet or savoury food, made of choux pastry or puff pastry. Choux pastry bouchées are shaped in the same way as Cream Puffs and puff pastry bouchées in the same way as Vol-au-Vent.

See *Pastry, Cream Puffs* and *Vol-au-Vent*.

BOUILLABAISSE

The superb fish stew of the French Mediterranean coast. It is made with a rich assortment of fish and seafood peculiar to the region, cooked in a highly flavoured stock with olive oil, spices and herbs. Saffron adds the authentic golden colour and flavour to the broth.

BOUILLON

The word comes from the French *bouillir* (to boil) and refers to a broth made by simmering meat, chicken, fish or vegetables in water. When the flavour is extracted the liquid is strained and seasoned, and may be served as it is or with rice, pasta or vegetables added. See *Soups*.

BOUQUET GARNI

A bundle or 'faggot' of herbs and aromatics for flavouring soups, stocks and casseroles. The classic combination is bay leaf, parsley stalks, thyme and celery, but the ingredients may be varied. A bouquet garni is tied in a bundle, or in muslin if dried herbs are used, with a string long enough to tie to the handle of the pan for easy removal.

BOURGUIGNONNE, BOEUF A LA

The famous beef-in-red-wine dish from the French province of Burgundy. The flavour is improved if the dish is made ahead and reheated in a slow oven.

Boeuf à la Bourguignonne

1.5 kg (3 lb) shin of beef or chuck steak; 125 g (4 oz) pickled (salt) pork, diced; 2 tbs olive oil; 60 g (2 oz) butter; 18 small onions, peeled; ¼ cup brandy; 1 tbs flour; 1 cup dry red wine; 1 cup beef stock; 1 bouquet garni containing 1 clove garlic; salt and freshly ground black pepper; 250 g (8 oz) button mushrooms.

TO SERVE: boiled rice; chopped parsley.

Cut beef into 5 cm (2 in) cubes. Brown pork in oil and half the butter in a heavy flameproof casserole. Remove pork and brown onions. Remove onions and brown beef. Warm brandy, set alight and pour over beef. Stir in flour, then wine. Simmer 1 minute, then add stock, bouquet garni, garlic and salt and pepper. Cover and cook in a preheated slow oven (150°C/300°F) for 3–3½ hours or until beef is very tender. Sauté mushrooms in remaining butter. Add to beef with reserved pork and onions, cover and cook 30 minutes more. Remove bouquet garni and serve with boiled rice sprinkled with parsley. Serves 8.

BOURRIDE

A creamy Provençal fish stew with Aïoli (garlic sauce). Some recipes include a chopped tomato, and a little dried orange peel and saffron in addition to the ingredients given below.

Bourride

500 g (1 lb) mixed small white fish; 5 cups fish stock; 1 bay leaf; 1 sprig fresh thyme or pinch dried; 1 onion, chopped; salt; 6 black peppercorns; 1 cup cream; sliced French bread, crisped in oven; 1 cup Aïoli (page 2).

Place fish in saucepan with stock, bay leaf, thyme, onion, salt and peppercorns. Simmer gently 15–25 minutes or until fish is cooked. Remove fish and keep hot. Add cream to pan and simmer a few moments. Arrange bread in a heated soup tureen and add fish. Strain cooking liquid into aïoli, stir to blend and pour over bread and fish. Serve immediately. Serves 6.

BRAINS

Lamb and calf brains are considered a delicacy. They are very perishable and should be used as soon as possible after buying. Allow one set of lamb brains per person, or one set of calf brains for 2 people. If buying frozen brains, make sure they are completely frozen. Unlike most other frozen foods, brains are best thawed quickly by plunging them into hot water.

■ BASIC PREPARATION: Soak brains in lightly salted cold water for 2 hours, changing the water every 30 minutes. Drain them, carefully peel off the membrane with a sharp knife (more difficult when brains have been frozen), and soak in tepid water to remove any blood. Place brains in a saucepan and cover with water, add salt and a little lemon juice or white vinegar. Bring just to simmering point and simmer over very gentle heat for 15 minutes for lamb brains, 20 minutes for calf brains. Allow to cool in liquid, then drain and dry on paper towels. Brains are now ready for use as directed in recipe.

NOTE: If not using brains immediately, do not drain from cooking liquid, cover and then keep in refrigerator for up to 24 hours. See recipes.

Brain Fritters

2 sets lamb brains; 1 tbs lemon juice; 4 spring onions, finely chopped; freshly ground white pepper; oil for frying.

BATTER: 1 cup flour; 1 tsp baking powder; ¼ tsp salt; 2 eggs; 1 cup milk.

Prepare brains as described above and cut into pieces (not too small). Mix gently with lemon juice, spring onions and pepper.

BATTER: Sift flour, baking powder and salt into a bowl and make a well in centre. Beat eggs and milk together, pour into well and gradually stir in flour. Beat until batter is smooth. Cover and stand 20 minutes. Fold brains into batter. Drop by tablespoonfuls into hot oil about 1 cm (½ in) deep. When fritters are crisp and golden on the bottom, turn with a spatula and cook other side. Drain on paper towels and serve very hot. Serves 4.

Brains with Black Butter
(Cervelles au Beurre Noisette)

A dish perhaps better known by its French name, finished off with butter browned to a 'nut' colour, with a touch of vinegar, parsley and a few capers. It has many devotees.

2 sets lamb brains, or 1 set calf brains; 90 g (3 oz) butter; 1 tbs finely chopped parsley; 1 tbs chopped capers; 1 tbs vinegar.

Prepare and cook brains as described above and slice. Heat gently in a little of the butter, place on a heated serving plate and keep warm. Heat remaining butter slowly in a small frying pan until it is nut-brown (not black). Add parsley and capers, stir quickly and pour at once over brains. Add vinegar to pan, swirl it round and pour over brains. Serve immediately. Serves 2.

BRAN

This is the outer layer or husk of cereal grains and is a major source of fibre, the dietary component vital in ensuring that food passes efficiently through the digestive system. Bran is missing from refined white flour but is wholly or partly retained in wholemeal and wholegrain flours.

Bran is also available in unprocessed form and in some dry breakfast cereals. It can be sprinkled on other cereals, fruit or other foods, added to drinks, mixed with crumbs or cheese to top au gratin dishes or added to biscuits, cakes, casseroles and other dishes during preparation.

Bran Muffins

A marvellous recipe for busy households. The batter will keep for up to one month, covered, in the refrigerator. All you have to do to enjoy hot muffins at any time is fill the pans and bake. Delicious served with butter and honey or with ham and bacon.

6 cups flour; 5 tsp bicarbonate of soda; 1 tsp salt; 2 cups firmly packed brown sugar; 2 cups raisins; 3 cups All-Bran; 3 eggs; 1 cup vegetable oil; ¹/₄ cup molasses; 4 cups buttermilk, or 4 cups fresh milk soured with 4 tbs white vinegar; 1¹/₂ cups water.

Sift flour, soda and salt into a large bowl. Stir in brown sugar, raisins and All-Bran. Beat eggs with oil and molasses and mix in buttermilk and water. Pour into dry mixture and stir well. Cover with plastic wrap and refrigerate for at least 1 day (or up to 1 month). Stir mixture lightly, then pour into greased muffin pans, filling three-quarters full. Bake in a pre-heated hot oven (200°C/400°F) for 20 minutes. Serve warm. Makes about 70.

BRANDADE

A thick, creamy fish purée which may be served warm or cold as a first course, as a main dish for a casual meal, or on croûtes as an hors d'oeuvre.

Brandade de Morue
(Cream of Salt Cod)

500 g (1 lb) salt cod; 2 cloves garlic, chopped; ¹/₂ cup cream; ¹/₂ cup olive oil; 1–2 potatoes, peeled and cooked (optional); grated rind and juice 1 lemon; freshly ground black pepper; nutmeg; triangular croûtes of bread to serve.

Soak cod overnight in cold water. Drain, cover with fresh cold water and bring to the boil. Drain, cover again with cold water and bring to the boil. Remove from heat and leave to soak in hot water 10 minutes. Drain cod, remove skin and bones and flake flesh coarsely. Place in a food processor or blender, add garlic and a little cream or oil and process, adding remaining cream and oil gradually as if making mayonnaise. If making by hand, work mixture constantly with a pestle and mortar or a wooden spoon in a bowl while adding cream and oil gradually. Blend in potato, if using (you may need it to reduce saltiness). Beat in lemon rind and juice, pepper and nutmeg. Serve warm or cold, mounded in a dish and surrounded by croûtes. Serves 4–6 as a first course.

VARIATION

OEUFS BENEDICTINE: Top warm Brandade de Morue with hot poached eggs and cover the eggs with warm Hollandaise Sauce (page 459). A good brunch or luncheon dish.

BRANDY

A spirit distilled principally from grape wine but also from the fermented juice of other fruits. Grape brandy is widely used in cooking, especially French cooking, adding depth and flavour to sauces, casseroles, consommés, flambés and other dishes.

WAYS TO USE BRANDY

WITH FRUIT: Sprinkle a little brandy, lemon juice and sugar over summer fruits such as strawberries, peaches or apricots. By the time you have prepared the rest of the meal, they will have formed their own brandy-flavoured syrup.

WITH CHEESE: Grate leftover pieces of cheese, place in a bowl or food processor and work in some freshly ground black pepper, softened butter and brandy to make a soft paste. Stir in some chopped nuts and store, covered, in the refrigerator for a few days to mellow. Serve at room temperature with biscuits or French bread.

WITH PAN JUICES: After sautéeing steak, chops, hamburgers or vegetables, deglaze the pan with cream and a spoonful of brandy for a delectable sauce to serve on the food.

IN SAVOURY DISHES: A spoonful of brandy, added just before serving, makes all the difference to French Onion Soup (see pages 492–3). Add a sprinkle of brandy to the butter in which Carrots Vichy (see *Carrots*) are glazed.

Brandied Fruit: Use one kind of fruit or add different fruits as they come into season. Suitable fruits are strawberries, raspberries, gooseberries, peeled peaches, apricots, grapes and plums, peeled and sliced pineapple. Fruits such as peaches and apricots may be left whole or halved.

Choose a large crock or jar with a well-fitting lid and scald with boiling water. Put in prepared fruit, brandy and sugar in equal quantities – 1 cup sugar and 1 cup brandy for every 1 cup fruit – and cover. Stir gently every day until the last of the fruit has been added, securing the lid after each addition, and store for at least a month or two in a cool place before using. The mixture will keep indefinitely and can be added to as you wish. Serve the drained brandied fruit as a dessert, and enjoy the liqueur with after-dinner coffee.

■ **COOKING WITH BRANDY:** This is not as extravagant as it sounds – the French have been cooking with brandy for centuries. It is perfectly normal to find a bottle of brandy in a French kitchen, kept just for cooking, but it is always used with discretion and for certain dishes only.

Brandy is perhaps the main spirit used in cooking, certainly it is the most traditional, but most good cooks like to vary the spirit, or use a fortified wine. Prawns may be flamed in brandy, but Pernod or whisky may also be used.

Pâtés and terrines are flavoured with brandy, and brandy can lift a consommé or hearty soup like French Onion. Brandy, and other spirits, can be added at different stages of cooking; it is often flamed, whether added halfway through or at the last minute. When you flame food with spirits (all the alcohol in it is burnt away, leaving just the flavour), you also burn off some of the fatty bits on the food; this singeing the surface of the food gives it a distinctive taste.

To get a flame, it is necessary to warm the spirit first; sometimes just adding it to the hot pan is enough. When flaming the Christmas pudding, dip a sugar cube in the spirit (brandy, whisky or rum) and place it on top of the pudding, then warm the spirit, ignite and carefully pour it over the pudding. **See recipes.**

Sweet Potatoes with Brandy: Layer parboiled, thickly sliced, sweet potatoes in a shallow baking dish, dotting each layer with butter and sprinkling with salt, freshly ground black pepper, brown sugar and brandy. Dot top with butter. Cover and bake in a preheated moderate oven (180°C/350°F) for 20 minutes, then remove cover and baste with juices from dish. Return to oven and bake, uncovered, for a further 10 minutes until top is golden.

BRANDY SAUCES

Brandy flavours two simple but delicious dessert sauces that are especially associated with Christmas,

Brandy Custard Sauce: Stir brandy into Créme Anglaise (see page 111) in the proportion of 1 tbs per cup, or to taste. Serve Brandy Custard Sauce warm or cold with Christmas pudding.

Brandy Hard Sauce (Brandy Butter): See *Hard Sauce*.

Flambéed Peaches

A simple way to turn canned peaches into a special occasion dessert.

1 x 825 g can peach halves; 1 cinnamon stick; 2 tsp arrowroot; ¼ cup brandy; ½ cup slivered, toasted almonds.

Pour ¾ cup syrup from can of peaches into a large pan, add cinnamon stick and bring to the boil. Blend arrowroot with a little cold water, stir into peach syrup and stir until slightly thickened. Add peaches and baste with sauce until they are heated through. Warm brandy, set alight and pour over peaches. Top with almonds and serve with ice cream and crisp sweet biscuits. Serves 6.

Ice Cream with Mincemeat Flambé

Serve ice cream with festive hot fruit mince, and for a gala touch flame with brandy.

1 litre (4 cups) vanilla ice cream; 1 x 275 g (9 oz) jar fruit mince; ½ cup brandy.

At serving time, pile scoops of ice cream into a serving bowl. Gently heat mincemeat and spoon over ice cream. Warm brandy in a small pan, ignite, and pour flaming over mincemeat. Serve immediately. Serves 6.

Brandied Chicken Sauté

This is the basic sauté method for poultry or small, tender cuts of meat. You can do veal steaks and lamb noisettes or cutlets in the same way.

4 half-breasts of chicken; 1 tbs olive oil; 30 g (1 oz) butter; 6–8 mushrooms; 8 button onions or golden shallots, peeled; 3 tbs brandy; salt and freshly ground black pepper; 1 clove garlic, crushed; ¼ cup white wine; ½ cup chicken stock; extra nut of butter.

Trim chicken neatly and dry with paper towels. Heat oil and butter and sauté mushrooms and onions on high heat until lightly browned. Remove vegetables

b

with a slotted spoon. Add chicken to pan and brown all over. Warm brandy and pour over chicken. Set alight and shake pan until flames subside. Season with salt and pepper and add garlic, wine, stock and fried vegetables. When liquid boils lower heat, cover pan and simmer gently for 10 minutes or until chicken is tender. Place chicken and vegetables on a heated serving dish. Boil sauce rapidly until slightly reduced, swirl in extra butter off heat and pour over chicken. Serves 4.

Brandy Snaps

These crisp, lacy, rolled wafers are elegant for afternoon tea or to accompany a fruit dessert.

60 g (2 oz) butter; ¹/₃ cup lightly packed brown sugar, ¹/₃ cup golden syrup; ¹/₂ cup flour; 1 tsp ground ginger; grated rind ¹/₂ lemon.

TO SERVE: 1 cup cream; 1 tbs brandy.

Heat butter, brown sugar and golden syrup together until butter melts. Cool, then add flour sifted with ginger. Stir in lemon rind. Drop teaspoonfuls on to buttered baking trays, spacing at least 15 cm (6 in) apart and allowing only 2 biscuits to each tray. Bake one tray at a time in a preheated moderate oven (180°C/350°F) for about 10 minutes or until golden-brown. Remove from oven, allow to set for a few seconds, then ease biscuits off tray with a palette knife and wrap loosely round handle of a wooden spoon, lacy side out. When crisp, remove from spoon. As soon as completely cold, store in an airtight container unless using immediately. To serve, whip cream, fold in brandy and pipe into both ends of each rolled biscuit. Makes about 12.

BRAWN

A preparation of meat stewed with spices and seasonings until soft. The meat is boned, chopped and set in moulds with some of the cooking liquor. Brawn is served cold and thinly sliced, with mustard and vinegar.

Brawn

500 g (1 lb) pickled (salt) pork; 1 kg (2 lb) shin of beef on the bone, sawn in half; 2 veal knuckles, each cut into 4; 1 bay leaf; 1 large onion, halved; 6 black peppercorns; 1 bouquet garni; freshly ground black pepper; salt; nutmeg.

Put all meat into a large saucepan, cover with cold water, bring to the boil and drain. Add fresh water barely to cover meat. Add remaining ingredients except pepper, salt and nutmeg. Cover and simmer about 2 hours, skimming occasionally, until meat comes off bones. Lift out meat and strain stock. Skim stock and return to rinsed-out saucepan. Bring to the boil while cutting meat into 2.5 cm (1 in) pieces.

Strain stock through 2 thicknesses of butter muslin to clear. Layer meat in a 23 x 12 cm (9 x 5 in) loaf tin, grinding pepper liberally over each layer. Season stock to taste with salt and nutmeg and spoon into tin to come just level with meat. Cover with foil or plastic wrap and top with weighted lid or another loaf tin filled with heavy weights. Chill until set. Turn out to serve. Serves 8.

BRAZIL NUT

Hard-shelled, angular seed of the fruit of a large tree native to Brazil. They are particularly rich in oil. Brazil nuts may be chopped or thinly shaved and used in place of almonds with fish or vegetables. They are also very good in fruit cakes, biscuits and sweets.

TO SHAVE BRAZIL NUTS: Cover the shelled nuts with cold water, bring slowly to the boil and simmer 5 minutes. Drain and slice thinly lengthways with a sharp knife or shave off layers with a vegetable peeler. The slices may be toasted in a preheated moderate oven (180°C/350°F) for about 12 minutes until pale brown.

Butterscotch Brazils: Make Butterscotch Toffee (see page 54). Have ready about 2 cups shelled Brazil nuts, a large, greased darning needle, a buttered knife and a buttered baking tray or marble slab. Impale each nut on the needle, dip into hot toffee, let drip a moment and push off with the knife on to the tray. When cool, store in airtight jars.

BREAD

The products we call breads today are an agreed group of preparations rather than a rigidly defined category. The group may differ somewhat from place to place and from time to time. The Germans and Austrians specialise in black bread and rye breads, or bread flavoured with caraway seeds and poppy seeds. The Scandinavians have a large array of dark breads and crispbreads. Ireland has its soda bread. *Pita* bread from the Middle East, and *Chapati* (see page 69), *Puri*, *Paratha* and *Nan* from India, are now enjoyed by the Western world.

However, it can be said that the main ingredient of all bread is flour of some kind and that 'bread' always means a wholesome and sustaining food.

Bread containing yeast as the raising agent is the basic bread of the Western world. Baking bread offers the home cook one of the most satisfying pleasures of the kitchen. It is not difficult to achieve a good result at the first attempt, and one of the joys of breadmaking is that you get better and better as you repeat a recipe, developing the judgment that comes with a little practice. See recipes.

See also *Yeast Cookery*.

BREADMAKING INGREDIENTS

YEAST: A living plant which grows when given moisture and food, and in the process produces the gas which causes bread to rise. It grows best in warm conditions but will also do its work of leavening, though more slowly, in cool conditions.

Fresh compressed yeast is available from many cake shops and health food stores. It should be fresh smelling, even coloured and easily crumbled. It can be kept for several days, well wrapped, in the refrigerator or can be frozen. (Thaw in the refrigerator before using.)

Dried yeast is usually sold by most supermarkets. It takes a little longer to dissolve and needs warm rather than lukewarm water for this; the dough may also take a little longer to rise. Dried yeast will keep for a year or more in an airtight container in a cool place. For use follow directions on packet.

FLOUR: The basic ingredient of all bread. Special bread flour, called strong flour or baker's flour, is best for most breadmaking as it is high in gluten and gives the bread its characteristic chewy texture. For brown bread, use a mixture of wholemeal and white flour or all wholemeal, if you like a more dense and solid loaf. Bread flours are available from health food shops.

RISING TIMES FOR BREAD: Recipes usually say that yeast dough should be allowed to rise in a warm place, but if it suits you better, you can allow it to rise more slowly in a cool place or even in the refrigerator. A dough will take 30–60 minutes to double in bulk in a warm place, about 2 hours at normal room temperature, or up to 12 hours in a cool room or refrigerator. Keep the bowl covered with oiled plastic wrap and a cloth, or place the dough in a plastic bag, large enough to allow for expansion, loosely tie the mouth. A slow rise is considered by many experts to give bread a better texture and flavour than a quickly risen loaf.

BREADCRUMBS

FRESH BREADCRUMBS: Use bread that is 1 or 2 days old. Rub through a wire sieve, or process in a food processor, using the metal chopping blade, or drop a few pieces at a time through the hole in the lid of a blender while motor is running at high speed.

DRIED BREADCRUMBS: Use whole slices of bread, with crusts removed, and spread on baking trays. Bake in a slow oven (160°C/325°F) until golden. Remove from oven and process to very fine crumbs in a food processor or blender, crush with a rolling pin, or rub though a sieve. Store in airtight containers. About 6 slices of bread will make 1 cup fine dry crumbs.

TO COAT FOOD WITH EGG AND BREADCRUMBS: Food to be coated must be quite dry – pat meat, chicken, fish, cut vegetables, etc., with paper towels. Dip in flour, shake off the surplus, dip in beaten egg and allow excess to drip off. Place in fresh or dried breadcrumbs and turn about to coat well, patting crumbs on with your fingers. Shake off excess crumbs, press coating lightly with a spatula and chill the food in the refrigerator for 20 minutes, to allow the egg to harden, before cooking. To ensure even browning, crumbs should be sieved so that they will be of uniform size. To give the food the finish known as *pané à l'Anglaise*, mark it trellis-fashion with the back of a knife before chilling.

Basic Bread

5 cups strong white flour (baker's flour), or for wholemeal bread a mixture of half strong white flour and half plain wholemeal flour; $1^1/_2$ tsp salt; 30 g (1 oz) compressed yeast, or $2^1/_2$ tsp dry yeast; $1^1/_2$–2 cups lukewarm water (or warm for dry yeast); 60 g (2 oz) butter or margarine, melted.

Sift flour and salt into a large warmed bowl, then take out $1/_2$ cup and sift it on to a work surface. Mix yeast with $1/_4$ cup of water in a small bowl, stirring to dissolve. Run your fingers through flour in large bowl and make a well in centre. Pour yeast mixture into well and add butter or margarine (which should be warm, not hot) and $1^1/_2$ cups water. Mix flour and liquid ingredients with the fingers, then beat with your hand, adding a little more water if necessary to make a firm dough. With your hand, fold and slap dough against sides of bowl until it begins to feel elastic and leaves the sides.

Turn the dough out of the bowl on to the floured work surface and knead by folding the far edge towards you, then pushing it firmly away with the heel of the hand. Turn dough a little and repeat. Continue kneading until dough is smooth and elastic and springs back when you make a dent with your finger. Place dough in a clean, warm, oiled bowl, turn it so that it is lightly oiled all over, and cover with oiled plastic wrap and a cloth. Leave to rise in a warm place for 30 minutes to 1 hour (or in a cool place for longer – see Rising Times for Bread). Test by pushing a finger into the dough. If the indentation remains, it is ready. Knock back dough by punching with your fist several times, squeezing out any large bubbles. Turn it out on to a lightly floured surface and knead 3 or 4 times.

For tin loaves, divide dough equally and pat each piece into a round, then fold sides under to form a neat oblong. Press together to seal and place in lightly oiled 12 x 23 cm (5 x 9 in) bread tins. Cover loosely with oiled plastic wrap and a cloth and leave in a warm place until risen to the tops of the tins. The dough may also be formed into any shape such as plaits, twists, cottage rounds or crescents and baked on a greased baking tray. Bake in a preheated very hot oven (230°C/450°F) for 15 minutes, then turn tins round, reduce heat to moderate (180°C/350°F) and bake for a further 20–25 minutes. If you want a crisp crust all over, take bread out of tins and bake directly on oven bars for last 10 minutes. Bread is cooked if it sounds hollow when underside is knocked with the knuckles. If not, return to the oven for more baking. Turn bread out of tins as soon as it comes from oven, and cool on a wire rack. Makes 2 loaves.

VARIATIONS

VIENNA TWIST: Break off about one fifth of the dough and set aside. Pat remaining dough into a rectangle and roll it up towards you from a long side, tapering dough toward ends with your hands to make a long shape with pointed ends. Squeeze edges together to seal and place, seam side down, on a greased baking tray. Divide spare piece of dough in half, roll each piece into a long rope between your hands, twist ropes together and lay on top of loaf, pressing ends to seal. Cover loosely with oiled plastic wrap and allow to rise in a warm place until doubled in bulk. Bake as for tin loaves.

BREAD ROLLS: Pat dough out into a rectangle, cut into 24 equal parts and shape each into a thick round. Turn under all round to make balls, pressing edges together underneath to seal. Place on greased baking trays, cover loosely with oiled plastic wrap and leave in a warm place until almost doubled in bulk. Bake in a preheated hot oven (200°C/400°F) for about 25 minutes, turning trays round halfway through baking time.

TOPPINGS: These may be varied. For a crisp crust, brush dough with cold water and repeat several times during baking. For a golden shiny crust, brush with a little beaten egg; for a cottage loaf, dust the bread lightly with flour and for a rich crust, brush with melted butter. Coarse salt, poppy, sesame or caraway seeds, or coarse wheat can be sprinkled over the bread before baking for an attractive loaf with good flavour.

Farmhouse Bread

6 cups wholewheat flour; 2 tsp salt; I tbs sugar;
30 g (I oz) compressed yeast, or 2$^{1}/_{2}$ tsp dry yeast;
I$^{3}/_{4}$ cups lukewarm water; I tbs oil;
beaten egg to glaze.

Mix the flour, salt and sugar in a warmed bowl. Blend the yeast with a little of the water, then stir into the remaining water and add to the dry ingredients with the oil. Mix to a soft dough. Turn out on to a lightly floured surface and knead for 10 minutes, until dough is smooth and does not stick to the fingers. Place dough in a lightly oiled plastic bag, and leave in a warm place for 1 hour or until doubled in size.

Knock back firmly with the knuckles to remove air bubbles, then turn out on to a floured surface and knead again for 5 minutes. Divide dough into two pieces. Pat each one out to a rectangle, then fold into three and place in 2 greased 500 g (1 lb) loaf tins. Cover

with a damp cloth and leave in a warm place for 30–40 minutes, until dough has risen to the tops of the tins. Brush the tops with beaten egg and bake in a preheated very hot oven (230°C/450°F) for 40 minutes, or until well risen, brown, and hollow when tapped on the bottom. Cool on a wire rack. Makes 2 x 500 g (1 lb) loaves.

Bread Sauce

The traditional English sauce to serve with roast chicken, turkey and pheasant.

I$^{1}/_{4}$ cups milk; I onion stuck with 2 cloves;
I small bay leaf; 30 g (I oz) butter; I slice stale white bread about 2 cm ($^{3}/_{4}$ in) thick, crusts removed;
salt and freshly ground white pepper;
extra milk if needed; I tbs fresh breadcrumbs,
fried in butter (optional).

Put milk, onion, bay leaf, butter and bread, torn into large pieces, in a small saucepan. Season with salt and pepper. Place on very low heat half-covered with a lid. As milk heats, break bread down with fork, then beat until consistency is porridge-like but free of lumps. Simmer, stirring gently, for 5 minutes, then cover and stand off the heat for 30 minutes or longer. Remove onion and bay leaf. Reheat gently, adding a little milk if necessary to give a thick consistency. Adjust seasoning and serve in a heated bowl, sprinkled with crisp fried breadcrumbs, if liked. Serves 4.

Bread and Butter Custard

6 thin slices buttered stale white or fruit bread,
crusts removed; sugar; 2 tbs currants or sultanas
or a mixture of both; 2 tsp chopped mixed
candied peel.

CUSTARD: 2 eggs; I egg yolk; I tbs sugar;
$^{1}/_{2}$ tsp vanilla; I$^{1}/_{2}$ cups milk.

Cut bread into triangles and layer in a buttered pie dish, sprinkling each layer with sugar, fruit and peel. **CUSTARD:** Beat eggs and yolk together. Heat sugar, vanilla and milk, stir into eggs and strain into dish. Stand 30 minutes. Bake in a preheated moderate oven (180°C/350°F) for about 45 minutes or until pudding is set and puffy with a firm crusty top. Serve hot from the dish. Serve 4.

Bread Pudding

9 slices day-old bread; 185 g (6 oz) mixed dried
fruit; 90 g (3 oz) brown sugar; 2 tsp mixed spice;
grated rind I lemon; 60 g (2 oz) butter, softened;
white sugar for sprinkling.

Soak bread in cold water to cover for 30 minutes, then squeeze out excess water and beat with a fork until smooth. Stir in fruit, sugar, spice and lemon rind and beat in butter in small pieces. Put mixture into a soufflé dish or deep ovenproof dish and bake in a preheated moderately hot oven (190°C/375°F) for 1½ hours. Sprinkle surface generously with sugar before serving, accompanied by custard or cream. Serves 6.

BRESAOLA

An Italian specialty of air-dried and cured beef which is usually cut in paper-thin slices and served a little like Carpaccio (see page 65). It has not yet become part of the supermarket range but is available at good delicatessens and butchers. Bresaola is delicious laid over a bed of baby rocket leaves and drizzled with lemon juice and extra virgin olive oil to taste. Top with a few shavings of Parmesan and a good grinding of pepper and serve with bread.

BRIOCHE

A little topknot-shaped yeast bread which, along with croissants, spells breakfast to millions in France. Eat brioche warm with chilled butter, preferably unsalted, and fruit conserve. They are also delicious toasted, or may be hollowed out and used as a case for cooked savoury food such as seafood, pâté or mushrooms. **See recipes.**

See also *Yeast Cookery.*

Brioche

15 g (¹/₂ oz) compressed yeast; ¹/₄ cup lukewarm water; 4 cups flour; pinch salt; 2 tbs sugar; 3 eggs, lightly beaten; ³/₄ cup lukewarm milk; 105 g (3¹/₂ oz) butter, softened; beaten egg to glaze.

Dissolve yeast in water. Sift flour and salt into a large bowl. Take out ½ cup flour and work gradually into dissolved yeast to form a soft dough. Form dough into a ball and cut a cross in the top. Place ball in a bowl of warm water and leave for about 5 minutes or until it doubles in bulk (it will rise to the surface when ready). Meanwhile, make a well in centre of remaining flour, put in sugar, eggs and milk and stir them together. Drain yeast sponge, place it in the well and combine with egg mixture. Stir in flour gradually to form a soft dough. Beat dough vigorously with the hand until thoroughly mixed, then beat in butter.

Place the dough in a greased bowl, sprinkle lightly with flour, cover bowl with plastic wrap and let rise in refrigerator overnight or for at least 6 hours. Remove from refrigerator, punch dough down, and turn on to a floured board, Knead lightly, then divide into pieces the size of an egg. Cut off one third of each piece; roll remainder of each piece into a ball and put into greased brioche moulds (deep fluted moulds). Roll small pieces of dough into little 'tadpole'-shaped tops with tails. Cut a cross in top of each brioche, open a little and push tops in, tail down. Leave to rise 10–15 minutes in a warm place. Brush with beaten egg and bake in a preheated hot oven (220°C/425°F) about 15 minutes or until golden-brown. Makes 12.

BRISLING

Small herring which may be smoked or canned. Also known as sprats or sild, but canned under the name 'brisling' by Norwegian canners.

BROCCOLI

A member of the cabbage and cauliflower family. Choose broccoli with tight heads which are dark green with no hint of yellow. **See also** *Gai Larn.*

■ **BASIC PREPARATION:** Cut off most of the stalks, leaving 5–8 cm (2–3 in) attached to flower heads.

■ **TO COOK:** Drop into boiling salted water and cook, uncovered, about 8 minutes until just tender. Drain and serve immediately or refresh under cold running water to be served cold, or reheated later according to recipe instructions. **See recipes.**

WAYS TO SERVE BROCCOLI

- Serve hot with melted butter and lemon juice or with Hollandaise Sauce (see page 459).
- Cover partially cooked broccoli in cheese sauce, sprinkle with grated cheese and bake in a preheated moderate oven (180°C/350°F) for 20 minutes.
- Serve cooked broccoli cold, coated with Mayonnaise (see page 256).
- Combine hot chopped broccoli, melted butter, finely chopped parsley, snipped chives and crumbled crisp bacon or chopped canned anchovies in a sauce to pour over hot pasta.

Broccoli Parmesan

2 bunches broccoli, lightly cooked; 60 g (2 oz) butter; ¹/₂ cup grated Parmesan or Romano cheese.

Sauté broccoli in butter until heated through. Arrange on heated platter and sprinkle with cheese. Serve very hot. Serves 4.

Broccoli Florentine

2 bunches broccoli, lightly cooked; 2–3 cloves garlic, chopped; ¹/₂ cup olive oil; salt and freshly ground black pepper.

Cut broccoli into large pieces. Lightly sauté garlic in oil; do not allow to brown. Add broccoli and sauté until tender and heated through, turning pieces frequently. Season with salt and pepper. Serve as a separate course or as an accompaniment. Serves 4.

Broccoli Amandine

2 large bunches broccoli; 90 g (3 oz) butter; ¹/₄ cup slivered or flaked blanched almonds; 1 tbs lemon juice.

b

Wash broccoli, pull off large, coarse leaves and cut off tough lower parts of stalks. Cook in rapidly boiling water until just tender, about 15 minutes. Drain and arrange on heated serving platter. Melt butter and fry almonds until golden. Add lemon juice and pour over broccoli. Serves 4.

BROCHE, BROCHETTE

Broche is the French word for a spit or skewer, *brochette* is a little skewer, and foods *en broche* or *en brochette* are the French version of skewer cookery. **See recipes.**

Coquilles St Jacques en Brochette

16 scallops; 2 tbs olive oil; 1 tbs lemon juice; 1 tsp chopped fresh basil, or $^1/_4$ tsp dried; 16 button mushrooms; 2 tbs melted butter; salt and freshly ground black pepper; fresh breadcrumbs; lemon wedges to serve.

Marinate scallops for 1 hour in olive oil, lemon juice and basil. Thread 4 skewers with scallops and mushrooms, alternating them. Brush with melted butter, season with salt and pepper and roll in breadcrumbs. Grill gently until crumbs are browned, about 2 minutes each side. Serve with lemon wedges. Serves 4 as a first course.

Broche Provençale

500 g (1 lb) lean lamb from the leg; $^1/_4$ cup dry white wine; 2 tbs olive oil; 1 tbs chopped mixed fresh herbs, or 2 tsp dried mixed herbs chopped with 2 tbs fresh parsley; 1 clove garlic, crushed; bay leaves; 250 g (8 oz) fatty belly pork; salt and freshly ground black pepper.

Trim skin and any gristle from lamb and cut it into 3 cm (1¼ in) cubes. Marinate for several hours, or overnight, in wine, oil, herbs and garlic. Cut bay leaves in half if large. Cut pork into 2.5 cm (1 in) pieces, about 1 cm (½ in) thick Thread 4 skewers with lamb, bay leaf and pork, in that order, not pushing pieces too tightly together. Season with salt and pepper. Grill close to a preheated very hot grill for 3–4 minutes on each side or until meats are well browned but lamb cubes are still a little pink inside. Serves 4.

BROWNIES

These are American – a delicious cross between a cake and a biscuit. There are 2 basic types. One is very moist and chewy and called a 'fudge-type' brownie. The other is lighter and fluffier, more like a cake. They keep well in an airtight container, and carry well in lunch-boxes. **See recipes.**

Fudge Brownies

250 g (8 oz) butter, softened; 2 cups sugar; 3 eggs; 1 tsp vanilla; 125 g (4 oz) dark chocolate, broken into pieces; 1 cup flour, sifted; $^1/_2$ tsp salt; 1 cup chopped walnuts, almonds or pecans.

Cream half the butter with sugar until light and fluffy. Add eggs, one at a time, and beat until light. Stir in vanilla. Place remaining butter and chocolate in a heatproof basin over hot water and stir until melted. Cool, then combine well with creamed butter and sugar mixture. Stir in flour, salt and nuts. Pour into a greased shallow cake tin about 32 x 23 cm (13 x 9 in). Bake in a preheated moderate oven (180°C/350°F) for 45 minutes or until a skewer inserted in centre comes out clean. Allow brownie mixture to cool in the tin. Cut into small squares to serve. Makes about 48.

Two–Tone Brownies (Cake Type)

250 g (8 oz) butter, softened; 1 tsp vanilla; $^1/_4$ tsp almond essence; 2 cups sugar; 4 eggs; 2 cups flour, sifted with $^1/_2$ tsp salt; 2 cups chopped almonds, pecans, walnuts or Brazil nuts; 60 g (2 oz) dark chocolate, broken into pieces.

CHOCOLATE ICING: 1$^1/_2$ cups icing sugar, sifted; 1 tbs cocoa; $^1/_2$ tsp vanilla; $^1/_2$ tsp cinnamon; 1 tsp butter, softened; about 1 tbs hot water.

Cream butter with essences and sugar until light and fluffy. Add eggs one at a time, beating well after each addition. Stir in flour and nuts, mixing well. Divide mixture in half. Melt chocolate in a heatproof basin placed over hot water. Stir melted chocolate into one half of batter. Drop alternate teaspoonfuls of dark and white batter into a greased 32 x 23 cm (13 x 9 cm) cake tin. Cut through batter several times, down and across, to give a marbled effect. Bake in a preheated moderate oven (180°C/350°F) for 45 minutes or until a skewer inserted in centre comes out clean. Turn out on to a wire rack and cool.
ICING: Combine icing sugar, cocoa, vanilla, cinnamon and butter. Stir in hot water little by little to give a good spreading consistency. Ice brownie cake when cold, and cut into bars to serve. Makes 24.

BROWN SAUCE

See *Sauces*.

BRUSSELS SPROUTS

These look like tiny cabbages. The smaller they are, the better the flavour and texture. They are an excellent vegetable cooked until tender but not too soft and finished off with a little butter and pepper. Choose small, tight, bright green heads with no trace of yellow. Use them soon after buying as they fade quickly. Store, covered, in the refrigerator for a few days only.

■ **BASIC PREPARATION:** Remove any faded leaves and trim stems level with base of leaves. Unless sprouts are very tiny, cut a cross in the end of each stem to speed cooking. Rinse in cold water.

■ **TO COOK:** Drop into boiling salted water, cover and cook until tender but still firm (test a stem with a knife), 6–12 minutes depending on size. Drain and serve immediately with butter, freshly ground black pepper and a few drops of lemon juice. Breadcrumbs, fried in butter and tossed through, give a contrast in texture. See recipes.

Butter-braised Sprouts: This recipe is an exception to the basic cooking method for Brussels Sprouts, but it is too delicious to omit. When chestnuts are added, the dish is a traditional accompaniment to roast turkey or goose.

Partially cook sprouts in boiling, salted water. Drain and dry. Heat 60 g (2 oz) butter in a shallow flameproof dish, add sprouts and turn them to coat evenly with butter. Cover with buttered paper and bake in a preheated moderate oven (180°C/350°F) for about 20 minutes. Cooked or canned chestnuts may be baked in the butter with the sprouts. A little cream is a nice addition, or the sprouts may be covered with buttered breadcrumbs and grated cheese and the top browned under a preheated grill.

Brussels Sprouts à la Crème

500–750 g (1–1½ lb) baby Brussels sprouts; ⅔ cup cream; nut of butter; salt; freshly ground white pepper.

Cook sprouts in boiling salted water for 7 minutes. Drain thoroughly. It is important that the sprouts are absolutely dry when added to the cream. Care must therefore be taken not to overcook them and to allow time for draining. Meanwhile, put cream in the pan and bring to the boil. Add sprouts, butter, salt and pepper. Cover pan and shake well to mix the contents thoroughly. Set on a very low heat and simmer for a few minutes to allow flavour of cream to mix with that of sprouts and for cream to reduce and thicken. Serves 4–6.

Brussels Sprouts with Croûtons

500–750 g (1–1½ lb) Brussels sprouts; 30 g (1 oz) butter; 1 spring onion, chopped; ½ clove garlic, crushed; salt and freshly ground black pepper; lemon juice.

GARNISH: 1 cup croûtons (bread cubes fried in oil until crisp).

Cook sprouts in boiling water, drain well and chop. Heat butter in a frying pan, add spring onion and garlic and cook gently without browning too much. Add sprouts, season well with salt and pepper, and add a good squeeze of lemon juice. Serve garnished with croûtons. Serves 4–6.

Brussels Sprouts with Celery

500–750 g (1–1½ lb) Brussels sprouts; 2 sticks celery, sliced; 45 g (1½ oz) butter; 1 onion, chopped; 1 tbs flour; 1½ cups milk; salt and freshly ground black pepper.

TOPPING: melted butter; breadcrumbs.

Cook sprouts in boiling water until tender and drain well. Blanch celery for 1 minute and drain. Melt butter and soften onion and celery for a few minutes. Sprinkle in flour, add milk and stir until blended. Add sprouts, season with salt and pepper and continue cooking for a few minutes to blend the whole, then turn into a flameproof dish. Sprinkle with melted butter and crumbs and brown in a preheated hot oven or under a preheated hot grill. Serves 4–6.

Sautéed Brussels Sprouts

500–750 g (1–1½ lb) Brussels sprouts; 60 g (2 oz) butter; salt and freshly ground black pepper; finely chopped parsley; squeeze of lemon juice.

Cook sprouts in boiling water until tender and drain well. Heat 45 g (1½ oz) of the butter in a saucepan, put in the sprouts, and toss and shake over high heat for 4–5 minutes. Do this by shaking the saucepan and not by using a fork or spoon. The sprouts will then be crisped very lightly on the outside. Season well with salt and pepper. Add parsley, a squeeze of lemon juice, and remaining butter and shake well. Serves 4–6.

BUBBLE AND SQUEAK

Surely one of the most charming names given to any dish. It is believed to have sprung from the sound effects made by the ingredients as they sizzle in the pan.

■ **TO MAKE BUBBLE AND SQUEAK:** Simply combine equal amounts of cold mashed potato and chopped, cooked cabbage (well drained). Season well and brown both sides in a little hot fat. It is good for breakfast with grilled bacon, sausages or tomatoes.

BUN

Buns are usually made from a yeast dough, like bread, but are soft on top instead of having a crisp crust. They come in great variety – sweet, savoury, steamed or baked. The name 'bun' is also given to some small cakes that don't contain yeast, and to the famous Scottish delicacy, Black Bun, a rich fruit filling enclosed in shortcrust pastry (see page 39).

See also *Yeast Cookery:* Hot Cross Buns and Chelsea Buns.

BUTTER

The delicate flavour and enriching qualities of butter are important to the cooking of many nations. It is used as a spread, as a dressing, as a cooking medium and as an ingredient in a great range of recipes from sauces to cakes. Butter should be stored in the refrigerator, in its original protective wrapping or container, or in a covered container kept especially for it. It may also be stored in the freezer for up to 6 months, with a moisture-proof wrapping over the original wrapping.

Salted or Unsalted Butter: Salting improves the keeping quality of butter. It is a matter of preference which to use as a spread, but be sure to use unsalted butter if it is specified in a recipe – the flavour of some Continental cakes and biscuits depends on it, and some foods are less inclined to stick if fried in unsalted rather than salted butter.

Cultured Butter: Is made from a special culture (as with cheese), each maker having its own distinctive culture and flavour.

Clarified Butter: This has had the water and non-fat solids removed. It is sold as *ghee* (its name in Indian and other Asian cooking where it is extensively used), or you can make it yourself. Cut salted or unsalted butter into pieces, melt and heat slowly, without browning. Remove from heat and allow to stand for a few minutes: a milky residue will sink to the bottom and the clear yellow liquid above it is the clarified butter. Pour off the butter and allow to solidify. The residue may be added to soups or sauces to enrich them.

SAVOURY BUTTERS

Butter creamed with flavourings such as mustard, curry powder, nuts, garlic, capers, herbs or cheese, can be used as a spread for sandwiches or canapés , or chilled and cut into slices to melt on top of steak, fish and other foods.

Maître d'Hôtel Butter: Cream 125 g (4 oz) butter with 2 tbs finely chopped parsley, freshly ground white pepper and 1 tbs lemon juice, beaten in little by little. Add salt to taste, form into a roll about 2.5 cm (1 in) in diameter, wrap in plastic wrap and chill until firm. Serve in slices on grilled steak, chops, liver and fish.

Mustard Butter: Cream 125 g (4 oz) butter with 2 tbs Dijon mustard and 1 tbs finely chopped parsley. Add salt and freshly ground white pepper to taste. Use as a spread for ham or roast beef sandwiches or canapés, or form into a chilled roll as for Maître d'Hôtel Butter, above, and serve on grilled or fried steak, grilled kidneys or liver.

Tarragon Butter: Cream 125 g (4 oz) butter with 2 tbs chopped fresh tarragon, or 2 tsp dried tarragon chopped with 2 tbs parsley. Beat in 1 tbs lemon juice, little by little, and add salt and freshly ground white pepper to taste. Use as a spread for chicken sandwiches or canapés, or form into a chilled roll as for Maître d'Hôtel Butter, above, and serve on grilled or roast chicken or grilled fish.

Marchand de Vin Butter: Boil 1/3 cup red wine and 1/3 cup beef stock with 2 tbs chopped shallots and freshly ground black pepper until reduced to about 2 tbs. Cool. Cream 125 g (4 oz) butter and, little by little, beat in wine mixture. Add 1 tbs chopped parsley and salt and pepper to taste. Form into a chilled roll as for Maître d'Hôtel Butter, above, and serve on steak, hamburgers or calf's liver, or stir into gravies, casseroles and pan sauces to enrich them.

See also *Anchovy:* Anchovy Butter.

SWEET BUTTERS

Sweet butters are excellent for topping waffles, crumpets, pancakes, toast and muffins. Cream unsalted butter and beat in, a little at a time, clear or creamed honey, golden syrup or maple syrup, brown sugar and cinnamon.

BUTTERMILK

Traditionally, the thin liquid left after butter has been churned from milk. Nowadays, the term usually refers to a different product, made commercially by adding a culture to skim milk to give a slightly acid-flavoured beverage. Chilled buttermilk is refreshing alone, mixed with equal parts of orange juice or blended with soft fruit such as strawberries. Buttermilk adds lightness and flavour to pancakes, scones, muffins and cakes, and is a good low-kilojoule (low-calorie) substitute for oil or cream in salad dressings. **See recipes.**

Buttermilk Date Cream

The combination of buttermilk and orange juice always gives a marvellous flavour, and the addition of fresh dates put this superb dessert in the dinner party class.

3/4 cup sugar; 1/2 cup water; 1 1/2 tbs gelatine;
extra 1/3 cup water; 1 cup buttermilk;
2/3 cup orange juice; pinch salt; 1 cup cream;
1 1/2 cups fresh dates, stoned and cut into slivers.

DECORATION: (optional, see method):
1 orange; 1/2 cup water; 1 tbs sugar.

Heat sugar with 1/2 cup water, stirring until sugar has dissolved. Bring to the boil and remove from heat. Soften gelatine in 1/3 cup cold water for 10 minutes. Stir gelatine mixture into sugar syrup until dissolved, then combine with buttermilk, orange juice and salt. Chill mixture until it thickens to the consistency of unbeaten egg white, but do not let it set. Whip cream until it holds soft peaks and fold it into buttermilk mixture together with slivered dates. Pour into a serving bowl. Cover and chill until set.

OPTIONAL DECORATION: For special occasions decorate this dessert with strips of rind from orange, using a vegetable peeler (the rind is the orange part of the skin, not including white pith). Cut rind into fine matchstick lengths and cook gently in water with sugar for about 5 minutes or until the rind becomes clear. Peel white pith from orange and cut between the dividing membranes to take out skinless segments. Arrange them cartwheel fashion on the dessert and strew over the drained strips of rind. Serves 8.

Buttermilk Scones

2 cups self-raising flour; I tsp salt; I tsp sugar; $^1/_2$ tsp bicarbonate of soda; 60 g (2 oz) butter; $^2/_3$–$^3/_4$ cup buttermilk.

Sift all dry ingredients into a mixing bowl. Rub in butter until mixture resembles breadcrumbs. Add enough buttermilk to make a fairly soft dough. Turn out on to a floured board. Knead lightly, then pat or roll the dough to about 1 cm ($^1/_2$ in) thickness. Cut into rounds with a 5 cm (2 in) cutter. Place on ungreased baking trays and bake in a preheated very hot oven (230°C/450°F) for 10–12 minutes or until golden. Makes about 16 scones.

Buttermilk Bread

A Canadian recipe for quick-bread. Serve buttered with salads and soups.

$2^1/_2$ cups flour; $^1/_4$ tsp bicarbonate of soda; I tsp salt; $^3/_4$ cup buttermilk; 90 g (3 oz) butter, melted; I tbs molasses or golden syrup.

Sift flour; bicarbonate of soda and salt into a bowl. Stir in buttermilk, 60 g (2 oz) butter and the molasses or golden syrup to form a soft dough. Transfer dough to a floured surface and knead for 5 minutes or until smooth and elastic. Pat into a round loaf about 15 cm (6 in) in diameter. With a sharp knife, score loaf to make 6 wedges, cutting about 1 cm ($^1/_2$ in) into dough. Place on a baking tray. Bake in a preheated moderately hot oven (190°C/375°F) for 30 minutes or until a skewer inserted in centre comes out clean. Brush hot loaf with remaining melted butter and cool on a wire rack. Serve cut into wedges. Serves 6.

BUTTERNUT PUMPKIN / SQUASH

A member of the gourd family, with a smooth, tender yellow skin which gives it its name. Butternut pumpkins are usually small (one will serve 4–6 as an accompanying vegetable), and are good value for money as there is very little waste. The flavour is similar to that of the hard-skinned pumpkin – perhaps a little sweeter – and the texture is lighter and less mealy. Butternut is excellent baked or steamed and mashed, like other pumpkin. It may also be stuffed for a main course.

Stuffed Butternut Pumpkin

I small butternut pumpkin; $^1/_4$ cup water; 30 g (I oz) butter; I onion, finely chopped; I rasher streaky bacon, rind removed and chopped;

185 g (6 oz) cooked or uncooked beef, pork, veal or lamb, minced, or 125 g (4 oz) grated cheese; I large, ripe tomato, peeled, seeded and chopped; I tbs chopped mixed fresh herbs, or I tsp dried herbs mixed with I tbs chopped, fresh parsley; I cup fresh breadcrumbs; salt and freshly ground black pepper.

Cut pumpkin in half lengthways and scoop out seeds and fibres. Place cut sides down in a baking dish, add water and bake in a preheated moderate oven (180°C/350°F) for about 30 minutes until just tender. Meanwhile, heat butter and cook onion and bacon gently until onion is soft. If using uncooked meat, add it and cook, stirring and breaking down lumps with a fork, until lightly browned. Otherwise, mix onion with meat or cheese off the heat. Add tomato, herbs, half the breadcrumbs and salt and pepper. Scoop out flesh from pumpkin, leaving a thin wall. Dice flesh, add to stuffing mixture and fill pumpkin shells. Sprinkle with remaining breadcrumbs. Return to oven and bake for 15–20 minutes or until topping is brown and crisp. Serves 4.

BUTTERSCOTCH

The name of a hard toffee made from butter, sugar and water, and of a popular flavouring for cakes, biscuits, sauces, icing and puddings. Butterscotch Sauce is delicious over ice cream and waffles, and Butterscotch Filling adds glamour to a simple cake. See recipes.

Easy Butterscotch Sauce

60 g (2 oz) butter; $^1/_2$ cup firmly packed brown sugar; 2 tbs cold water; I egg yolk, beaten; $^1/_4$ cup cream, whipped; $^1/_2$ tsp vanilla.

Melt butter over low heat, add brown sugar and cook 2 minutes, stirring. Add cold water and egg yolk and continue cooking gently, stirring, until mixture thickens. Do not allow to boil. Remove from heat and cool, then chill. Fold in whipped cream and vanilla just before serving. Serves 4.

Butterscotch Filling

45 g ($1^1/_2$ oz) butter; $^1/_2$ cup firmly packed brown sugar; I cup milk; 3 tbs flour; $^1/_2$ tsp salt; 2 eggs, lightly beaten; $^1/_2$ tsp vanilla.

Mix butter and sugar in a heavy saucepan and heat gently, stirring, until melted. Stir in $^1/_2$ cup milk and cook 2 minutes. Blend flour, salt and remaining milk together, stir into hot mixture and cook, stirring, until boiling. Stir a little of this mixture into beaten eggs, pour back into saucepan and stir over low heat until thickened a little more. Do not allow to boil. Stir in vanilla. Cool and use as a cake or pie filling. Makes about 2 cups.

Butterscotch Toffee

**¹/₂ cup water; pinch salt; 3 cups sugar;
¹/₂ tsp cream of tartar; 30 g (1 oz) butter.**

Bring water to the boil in a large, heavy saucepan. Remove from heat, add salt and sugar and stir until dissolved. Return to fairly high heat, cover and return to the boil. Add cream of tartar mixed with a little water and boil, covered, 2 minutes. Remove lid and boil without stirring until mixture reaches hard crack stage (155°C/315°F or when a little dropped in cold water will break). Remove from heat and stir in butter. Pour into buttered shallow tins and mark into squares or bars when almost set, or drop teaspoonfuls on to a buttered marble slab or foil. Makes about 60 small pieces.

NOTE: Butterscotch can be dropped over nuts to make nut toffees.

CABBAGE

Cabbage is king of the cruciferous vegetable family and can be the most delicious of vegetables if not over-cooked. Sadly, cooked cabbage has been wrongfully accused of smelling up kitchens everywhere. It's not the cabbage to blame, but the cook. The notorious odour problem is a result of overcooking. Cabbage should be cooked just until tender, preferably using stainless steel pans.

There are many varieties available: the tightly packed round green cabbage; the elongated sugar-loaf; the striking red cabbage and the crinkly Savoy are the most familiar. Readily available also are the popular Chinese relatives of cabbage such as bok choy, gai, choy and wong bok, among others.

As with broccoli, cabbage is a cruciferous vegetable and may reduce the risk of some forms of cancer, including colorectal cancers. Cabbage is also high in beta-carotene, vitamin C and fibre.

Look for tight, heavy, unblemished heads. Fresh, uncut heads of cabbage can be stored in the refrigerator for up to two weeks. Cover loosely with a plastic bag or use per-forated bags. Do not wash cabbage before storing; the extra moisture will hasten deterioration. If you plan to eat the cabbage raw, use within a few days. Cabbage that you plan to cook can be stored in the refrigerator for about two weeks.

The most popular and successful method of preserv-ing cabbage is pickling. Kimchee and sauerkraut are fermented, pickled products that take days to make. Cabbage flavour is compatible with many herbs and spices. Steamed cabbage can be seasoned with anise, basil, caraway and celery seeds, dill, mustard, fennel, nutmeg, oregano, black pepper, savory and tarragon.

Savoy cabbage: Crinkly, with waves of blue-green leaves, Savoy cabbage has thin, richly flavoured leaves, which are ideal served raw in salads, or cooked. Cooked Savoys do not have the strong sulphur odour of green cabbage. Savoy only keep for about 4 days in the refrigerator, so buy it when you plan to use it.

Red cabbage: The heads are usually smaller and denser than green cabbage. Red cabbage needs to be cooked longer than the green types and is often braised with vinegar (or other acidic ingredient) to help retain its beautiful red colour. Always use stainless steel when preparing red cabbage to prevent discoloration.

■ **BASIC PREPARATION:** It is usually cut into wedges or shredded for cooking. Trim heavy stem and inside ribs from wedges. To shred, cut a head downward, into quarters. Hold each quarter by the stem, with the top pressed firmly on a board, and use a sharp knife to cut thin slices from the side. Discard heavy ribs and stems.

■ **TO COOK:** The old way to cook cabbage is to boil it for hours. The new way is to steam it until just crisp-tender, or for quite a different effect, gently braise in stock with added flavourings. **See recipes.**

Steamed Cabbage: Shred cabbage or cut into wedges. Wash in a colander under cold running water. Melt a knob of butter in a heavy saucepan and add cabbage. Season with salt and pepper, plus a grating of nutmeg if desired. Cover tightly and steam on brisk heat until cabbage is just tender, with slight crunch – about 5 minutes for shredded cabbage, 8–10 minutes for wedges. Shake pan frequently to toss cabbage with butter and to prevent scorching.

Braised Cabbage: Shred half a small red or green cabbage. Heat enough butter to cover the bottom of a heavy flameproof casserole, and toss cabbage until coated in butter. Season with salt and pepper and add enough stock to come to top of cabbage, plus a spoonful of vinegar for red cabbage. Cover tightly and bake in a preheated moderately slow oven (160°C/325°F) or cook over a gentle heat for about 1 hour or until cabbage is very tender and stock absorbed. If desired, aniseed, nutmeg, caraway seeds or other flavourings may be added to the cabbage. Serves 4.

Cabbage Rolls (Dolmas)

10 cabbage leaves; 500 g (1 lb) minced beef or pork and veal mince; 1 small onion, finely chopped; 2 tbs finely chopped parsley; 1 clove garlic, crushed; 1/2 tsp dried thyme; 1 tsp salt; pinch cayenne; 2 tbs vinegar; 3 tbs brown sugar; 2 tsp chopped capers; 1 egg, beaten; 30 g (1 oz) butter; 1 x 425 g can tomatoes, drained, chopped, juice reserved.

Blanch cabbage leaves in boiling salted water for 2 minutes, then drain and plunge into cold water. Drain again and pat dry with paper towels. Combine all remaining ingredients except butter and tomato juice. Divide into 8 portions and place one portion on the stem end of each cabbage leaf. Fold sides over filling and roll up into a cylinder. Place stuffed rolls close together in a buttered casserole dish, seam sides down. Dot with butter and pour tomatoes over. Cover tightly and bake in a preheated moderate oven (180°C/350°F) for 1 hour or until rolls are very tender. Serve with pan juices. Serves 4.

Sweet and Sour Red Cabbage

1 small red cabbage, shredded; 90 g (3 oz) butter; 1 large onion, finely chopped; 2 large cooking apples, cored and thinly sliced; pinch caraway seeds; 2 tbs honey; 2 tbs vinegar; salt and freshly ground black pepper.

Soak cabbage in cold water to cover for 15 minutes. Heat butter in a wide heavy saucepan or deep frying pan and fry onion gently until soft. Lift cabbage from water with hands, leaving it moist, and add to pan with remaining ingredients. Stir to combine, then cover and simmer very gently for 1½ hours. By this time, cabbage should be very tender and all liquid absorbed. (If necessary, add a little boiling water during cooking to prevent cabbage from sticking.) Adjust seasoning, and spoon into a heated serving dish. Excellent with roast pork, duck, venison or any game. Serves 4.

Cabbage with Pancetta, Garlic and Rosemary

100 g (3½ oz) pancetta (Italian bacon), cut into thin strips; 1 large clove garlic; good pinch chopped rosemary leaves; 1 tbs olive oil; 1 kg (2 lb) cabbage, shredded; ½ cup chicken stock or white wine; freshly ground black pepper.

Mix together the pancetta, garlic and rosemary. In a large pan heat the oil and gently fry the pancetta mixture until aromatic and sizzling. Add the shredded cabbage and toss to coat well. Add the stock and pepper and cover very tightly with a close-fitting lid. Cook over a gentle heat for 30–45 minutes until done to taste. This is an Italian dish and the cabbage is usually fairly well cooked. Because it hasn't been boiled in water it doesn't impart a strong unpleasant smell despite the long cooking. Serves 4–6.

Cabbage au Gratin

1 medium cabbage, quartered; 1½ cups Béchamel Sauce (page 456); salt and freshly ground black pepper; pinch nutmeg; 60 g (2 oz) Gruyère cheese, grated.

TOPPING: fresh white breadcrumbs; melted butter.

Cook cabbage in plenty of boiling salted water until just tender. Drain, refresh and press well to remove water. Remove core and chop moderately finely. Mix with the sauce, using sufficient to give a creamy mixture. Season well with salt and pepper, add a little nutmeg, and cook gently for 10 minutes. Stir in grated cheese, reserving a little for the top. Put mixture in flameproof dish and sprinkle with reserved cheese mixed with crumbs and melted butter. Brown in a hot oven or under a preheated grill. Serves 6.

Asian–Style Coleslaw

This appeals to those who appreciate the flavours of Asian seasonings in a light, crisp, fresh-tasting cabbage salad over a heavier coleslaw.

½ small white and red cabbage, halved and cored; a few leaves English spinach; 2 tbs toasted sesame seeds; 1 small onion, halved and finely sliced;

¼ cup snipped coriander leaves; salt and freshly ground pepper.

SESAME DRESSING: ⅓ cup sesame seeds; 4 tbs soy sauce; 1 tbs sugar; 4 tbs rice vinegar; 1 tsp sesame oil; 1 tbs light olive oil.

First make sesame dressing. Place sesame seeds in a dry frying pan and toast until they are golden. Add all dressing ingredients to a bowl and mix with a fork. Place dressing in a small saucepan over a medium heat and bring to the boil. Simmer for 2 minutes or until dressing thickens and set aside. For a fuller sesame flavour, grind sesame seeds in mortar and pestle with 1 tbs soy, then add to other sauce ingredients before cooking.

Hold each cabbage quarter by the stem, with the top pressing firmly on a board, and use a sharp knife to cut into long thin shreds. Discard heavy ribs and stems. Cut off the stems of the spinach at the base of the leaves. Wash in several changes of cold water, dry well and cut into thin shreds. In a bowl place the cabbage and spinach and toss to combine. Add the sesame seeds with the onion and coriander. Drizzle over the dressing and season to taste with salt and pepper. Serves 8.

CABINET PUDDING

A traditional English pudding made of cubed bread or cake, dried fruit and custard. It may be baked or steamed in a mould. It is an economical family pudding – nice in winter.

Steamed Cabinet Pudding

30 g (1 oz) butter; 2 tbs sugar; 4 slices white bread, crust removed and diced; ½ cup sultanas, raisins or mixed dried fruit; 2 eggs; 1 cup milk; pinch salt; ½ tsp vanilla.

Use all the butter to grease a 4-cup pudding basin and sprinkle with 1 tbs sugar. Put bread into a bowl with fruit. Beat eggs, add remaining ingredients, including remaining sugar, and pour over bread. Allow to soak for 30 minutes, then spoon into prepared basin. Cover with greased greaseproof paper and a snap-on lid, or tie down with 2 layers of foil. Place in a saucepan, with boiling water to come halfway up sides of basin, cover with a lid and steam for 1 hour. Replenish boiling water as necessary. Unmould and serve with custard, cream or ice cream. Serves 4.

NOTE: Cabinet pudding maybe baked. Grease a 4-cup ovenproof dish. Follow recipe instructions and spoon mixture into prepared dish. Cover with greased foil and bake in a preheated moderate oven (180°C/350°F) for 35–40 minutes or until set.

CAESAR SALAD

One of the world's great salads, created by chef Alexander Cardini, working at the San Diego race track, in honour of his brother Caesar – also a chef, working in England. There are many variations of the salad today, but this is the original one.

Caesar Salad

1 cos (romaine) lettuce; 4 anchovy fillets;
1 clove garlic, crushed; 2 tbs butter;
8 slices French bread; 1 egg;
salt and freshly ground black pepper;
1 tbs lemon juice; 3 tbs olive oil;
1 tsp Worcestershire sauce;
3 tbs grated Parmesan cheese.

Wash and dry lettuce leaves and crisp in refrigerator. Mash anchovies with garlic and butter, and spread on bread. Bake bread in a preheated slow oven (150°C/300°F) for 25–30 minutes or until crisp. Allow to cool. Place egg in boiling water for 50 seconds and remove. Place lettuce in a large bowl, season with salt and pepper and break egg over. Beat the lemon juice, oil and Worcestershire sauce together and pour over lettuce. Add bread slices and cheese and very gently roll lettuce in the dressing until each leaf glistens (the egg becomes part of the dressing). Serve at once. Serves 2 as a main course, 4 as a side salad or first course.

CAFE AU LAIT

French for coffee with milk. In France and most European countries it means coffee and hot milk in equal proportions. The coffee and milk are served in separate pots, and poured into the cup at the same time.

CAKES

Most cakes fall into one of four main categories – Butter Cakes, Sponge Cakes, Quick-mix Cakes and rich Continental Cakes, which are often served for dessert with coffee. They are classified according to the proportion of fat, sugar and eggs they contain and the method by which they are made. Each has something special to offer.

Butter Cakes

One of the most popular categories of cakes, having the fine flavour that butter can give. They are enjoyed, too, for their own particular flavour, whether it be the basic butter mixture or flavoured with vanilla, lemon, orange, ginger or chocolate, etc. They can stand on their own, unadorned, or can be dressed up with various icings and fillings. Butter cakes keep well because of the high proportion of butter to flour. Cooking margarines may replace the butter, if liked. You will, however, trade the distinctive flavour for a measure of economy, a spongier texture and a somewhat greater volume.

Butter cakes include such favourites as Madeira Cake, Dundee Cake and Fruit Cake (see separate entries). **See recipes.**

Basic Butter Cake

125 g (4 oz) butter; 3/4 cup caster sugar; 1 tsp vanilla; 2 eggs, lightly beaten; 2 cups self-raising flour; pinch salt; 1/2 cup milk.

Cream butter with sugar and vanilla until light and fluffy. Gradually beat in eggs (if using an electric mixer, add eggs one at a time and beat well after each). Sift flour and salt together 3 times and fold into creamed mixture alternately with milk, beginning and ending with flour. Pout into 2 greased and bottom-lined 20 cm (8 in) sandwich tins.

Lightly smooth tops and bake in a preheated moderate oven (180°C/350°F) for 25–30 minutes or until a fine skewer inserted in centre comes out clean. Cool on a wire rack and fill and ice as desired.

NOTE: The cake may also be baked in a deep, 20 cm (8 in) square or round tin. It will then take 45–50 minutes to bake.

VARIATIONS

LEMON CAKE: Add grated rind 1 lemon and 2 tsp lemon juice. Omit vanilla.

CHERRY CAKE: Add 1/2 cup halved, glacé cherries (dusted with flour to prevent them sinking).

SEED CAKE: Add 1 tbs caraway seeds to batter and sprinkle 1 tsp on top before baking.

FRUIT SQUARES: Add 1/2 cup mixed fruit, bake in a 28 x 19 cm (11 x 7½ in) lamington tin.

Cup Cakes

Bake cup cakes in muffin or patty tins. For children's parties and informal occasions, bake and serve in fluted paper cases; they retain their shape better if the cases are placed in muffin tins for baking.

125 g (4 oz) butter; 3/4 cup sugar; 1 tsp vanilla; 2 eggs, lightly beaten; 2 cups self-raising flour; pinch salt; 3/4 cup milk; Glacé Icing (page 205).

DECORATIONS: nuts, glacé cherries, candied angelica, etc.

Cream butter with sugar until light and fluffy. Add vanilla, then beat in eggs a little at a time. Sift flour and salt 3 times and fold into creamed mixture alternately with milk, beginning and ending with flour. Spoon into patty cases set in muffin tins. Bake in a preheated moderately hot oven (190°C/375°F) for 15 minutes or until golden and when a skewer inserted in centre comes out clean. Cool on a wire rack. When cool, ice with glacé icing. Decorate as desired. Makes about 20.

VARIATIONS

BUTTERFLY CAKES: Use the same mixture as for Cup Cakes, but increase oven temperature to hot

(200°C/400°F) and bake cakes in hottest part of the oven. The tops of the cakes will rise in a peak. When cool, cut a slice from the top of each cake and reserve. Top cakes with a peak of sweetened whipped cream. Cut cake slices in half, arrange on top of cream to form 'wings' and dust with sifted icing sugar.

SULTANA CUP CAKES: Omit vanilla and add 1 tsp grated lemon rind. Fold ½ cup sultanas into creamed mixture with flour.

CHERRY CUP CAKES: Fold ½ cup sliced glacé cherries into creamed mixture with flour.

Orange Cake

125 g (4 oz) butter or soft margarine; grated rind and juice 1 medium orange; ³/4 cup caster sugar; 2 eggs, separated; 2 cups self-raising flour; pinch salt; 2–3 tbs milk; sifted icing sugar.

Cream butter with orange rind and sugar until light and fluffy. Add egg yolks one at a time and beat well after each. Sift flour with salt and fold into creamed mixture alternately with strained orange juice and milk, beginning and ending with flour. Beat egg whites until stiff peaks form and gently fold in. Spoon into 20 cm (8 in) round or square tin, or 21 x 11 cm (8½ x 4½ in) loaf tin, that has been greased with melted butter, bottom-lined with greased greaseproof paper and dusted with flour. Bake in a preheated moderate oven (180°C/350°F) for 35–40 minutes or until a skewer inserted in centre comes out clean. Turn out on to a wire rack and when cool dust with sifted icing sugar.

Chocolate Sandwich Cake

A light, fine-textured chocolate cake with the special flavour of raspberry jam.

2 tbs cocoa powder; 2 tbs raspberry jam; 125 g (4 oz) butter; ³/4 cup caster sugar; 1 tsp vanilla; 2 eggs, lightly beaten; 2 cups self-raising flour, sifted; extra raspberry jam for filling; icing sugar, sifted or Chocolate Glaze (page 83).

Mix cocoa to a smooth thin paste with a little boiling water. Add jam and mix in sufficient boiling water to make ³/4 cup. Allow to cool. Cream butter with sugar until light and fluffy. Beat in vanilla, then gradually add eggs, mixing well after each addition. Fold in flour alternately with cocoa and jam mixture. Spread evenly in 2 greased and bottom-lined 18 cm (7 in) sandwich tins. Bake in a preheated moderate oven (180°C/350°F) for 25–30 minutes or until cake springs back when lightly touched with the finger. Turn out on to wire racks to cool. Sandwich together with raspberry jam and top with sifted icing sugar or with chocolate glaze.

Sponge Cakes

There are two ways of making a sponge cake. The first method is to beat whole eggs with sugar until thick and light, then fold in the flour – this is called a Whisked Sponge. The second way is to separate the eggs, make a meringue of the whites and sugar, then add beaten yolks and flour. This is called a Sponge Sandwich.

The French, however, make a slight different version called *Génoise* (see page 176), with melted butter added. It is used as the basis for Petits Fours (see page 357) and other decorated cakes. Swiss Rolls (see pages 522) also belong to the sponge family, but are baked in a shallow tin, rolled while warm, then re-rolled around a filling.

Sponge cakes (except Génoise) contain only a tiny amount of butter, so they don't keep as well as butter cakes, and are at their best when eaten freshly made. See recipes.

Whisked Sponge

3 eggs; ³/4 cup caster sugar; grated rind; ¹/4 lemon; 1 cup self-raising flour; pinch salt; 1 tsp melted butter; 2 tbs hot water.

FILLING AND TOPPING: 1 cup cream; few drops vanilla; 1–2 tsp sugar; pulp 2 passionfruit, 1 cup sliced strawberries, or 2 sliced bananas tossed with a little lemon juice; 1 tbs icing sugar, sifted.

Combine eggs, sugar and lemon rid in a heatproof bowl and place it over a saucepan of simmering water. Whisk for 10 minutes or until a little of the mixture when lifted on the whisk falls in a smooth, steady ribbon on to mixture in the bowl. Remove from heat and continue whisking for about 5 minutes until cool. Sift flour and salt and, using a metal spoon, gently fold flour into egg mixture, alternately with combined butter and hot water. Turn into 2 x 18 cm (7 in) sandwich tins that have been greased, bottom-lined with greased grease-proof paper and dusted with a mixture of 1 tsp each flour and sugar. Bake cakes in a preheated moderate oven (180°C/350°F) for 20–25 minutes or until cakes spring back when touched lightly with the finger. Immediately turn out on to a wire rack to cool.

FILLING AND TOPPING: Whip cream with vanilla and sugar until stiff. Combine half the cream with selected fruit and use to sandwich cakes together. Decorate top with rosettes of remaining whipped cream and dust with icing sugar.

Sponge Sandwich

3 eggs, separated; $^3/_4$ cup caster sugar;
1 cup self-raising flour; pinch salt; 1 tsp melted
butter; 3 tbs hot water.

TO FINISH: jam; whipped cream or sifted icing sugar.

Beat egg whites until stiff. Gradually add sugar and
continue whisking until thick and glossy. Add egg
yolks at once and whisk only until combined. Sift
flour and salt together twice. Sift flour again directly
over egg mixture, and fold in lightly and evenly.
Sprinkle melted butter and hot water over top, and
fold in quickly and lightly. Pour into 2 greased and
floured 18 cm (7 in) sandwich tins. Bake in a preheated
moderate oven (180°C/350°F) for 20 minutes. Turn
out and cool on a wire rack. When cold, sandwich
together with jam and decorate with whipped cream,
or dust top with icing sugar.

Blowaway Sponge

Extremely light, and best eaten the day it is made.

4 eggs, separated; $^1/_2$ cup caster sugar;
$^1/_2$ cup arrowroot; 1 tbs flour;
1 tsp cream of tartar; $^1/_2$ tsp bicarbonate of soda;
1 tsp vanilla.

**FILLING AND DECORATION: sweetened whipped
cream; sifted icing sugar.**

Beat egg whites until stiff. Gradually add sugar and
continue whisking until thick and glossy. Add egg
yolks all at once and whisk only until combined.
Sift together arrowroot, flour, cream of tartar and
bicarbonate of soda and fold lightly into egg mixture
with vanilla. Gently pour at once into 2 greased and
floured 20 cm (8 in) sandwich tins. Bake in a preheated
moderate oven (180°C/350°F) for 25 minutes or until
cakes have shrunk slightly from sides of tins and
centres spring back when touched with a finger. Cool
on wire racks. Sandwich together with whipped
cream and dust top of cake with icing sugar.
    See also *Swiss Roll*.

Australian Chocolate Cake

90 g (3 oz) cooking chocolate; 2 tbs water or coffee;
5 eggs; $^3/_4$ cup caster sugar; $^3/_4$ cup self-raising
flour, sifted; 1 tsp vanilla; grated rind 1 lemon;
60 g (2 oz) butter, melted; walnut halves to decorate
(optional).

**FILLING AND FROSTING: 185 g (6 oz) cooking
chocolate; 1 cup cream; 2 tbs icing sugar, sifted;
1 tbs rum.**

Melt chocolate in a heatproof basin over simmering
water. Stir in water or coffee and cool slightly. Beat
eggs until light and frothy. Add sugar and beat until
very thick and mousse-like. Fold flour into egg mixture
with vanilla, lemon rind, butter and chocolate mixture.
Pour into a greased, lined and floured 23 cm (9 in)
springform tin. Bake in a preheated moderate oven
(180°C/350°F) for 40–45 minutes or until cake springs
back when lightly pressed in the centre. Leave to cool
with the spring released.
FILLING AND FROSTING: Melt chocolate in a heatproof
basin over simmering water and cool. Whip cream,
fold in icing sugar and rum. Reserve a little melted
chocolate and fold remainder through cream to create
a ripple effect. When cold, split cake in half and
sandwich together with half the filling and frosting
mixture. Spread remainder over top of cake. Decorate
with walnut halves, if desired, and drizzle reserved
melted chocolate over.

Quick–mix Cakes

These are also sometimes referred to as 'one bowl' cakes,
because they are made by mixing all the ingredients
simultaneously in one bowl. To make mixing easy, the fat
type specified is often melted butter, but can be oil or
sour cream.
    There are many delicious cakes made by the Quick-mix
method, including Australia's Boiled Fruit Cake. Don't try
to adapt ordinary recipes to this method, but use those
especially created for quick mixing. **See recipes.**

Boiled Fruit Cake

An economical and easy cake that keeps well. For
Christmas, it may be topped with almonds before
baking, or iced and decorated.

750 g ($1^1/_2$ lb) mixed dried fruit;
185 g (6 oz) butter or margarine;
$1^1/_4$ cups firmly packed brown sugar;
1 tbs grated lemon rind; 2 tsp mixed spice;
1 cup water; 2 tsp rum or sherry; 1 cup plain flour;
$1^1/_2$ cups self-raising flour; $^1/_4$ tsp salt;
3 eggs; $^1/_2$ tsp bicarbonate of soda.

Place fruit, butter, sugar, lemon rind, spice, water and
rum or sherry in a saucepan and bring to the boil.
Reduce heat and simmer for 5 minutes, then remove
from heat and leave until lukewarm. Sift flours and
salt together. Beat eggs with bicarbonate of soda. Stir
flour and beaten eggs alternately into fruit mixture.
Pour into a deep 20 cm (8 in) cake tin that has been
greased and lined with 2 layers of greaseproof paper.
Bake in a preheated moderate oven (180°C/350°F) for
45 minutes, then reduce heat to moderately slow
(160°C/325°F) and bake further 45 minutes or until a
skewer inserted in centre comes out clean. Turn out
of tin and cool on a wire rack before removing paper.
Store in an airtight container. This fruit cake will
keep for up to 2 weeks.

Melt and Mix Chocolate Cake

I tbs white vinegar; I cup evaporated milk;
I¹/₂ cups flour; pinch salt; ¹/₂ cup cocoa powder;
I¹/₂ tsp bicarbonate of soda; I¹/₄ cups caster sugar;
155 g (5 oz) butter, melted; I tsp vanilla; 2 eggs.

TO FINISH: raspberry jam or whipped cream;
Rich Chocolate Icing (page 206)
or sifted icing sugar.

Mix vinegar with evaporated milk. Sift flour, salt, cocoa, bicarbonate of soda and sugar into a bowl. Add butter and dry ingredients with soured milk, vanilla and eggs. Beat vigorously until smooth, about 2 minutes. Pour into 2 greased and bottom-lined 20 cm (8 in) sandwich tins. Bake in a preheated moderate oven (180°C/350°F) for 30–35 minutes or until a skewer inserted in centre comes out clean. Cool on a wire rack. Sandwich together with raspberry jam or whipped cream and ice with chocolate icing or dust with icing sugar.

Caramel Nut Cake

I³/₄ cups flour; pinch salt; I³/₄ tsp baking powder;
I cup firmly packed brown sugar;
125 g (4 oz) butter, softened (or soft margarine);
2 eggs; ¹/₂ cup milk; I tsp vanilla;
³/₄ cup chopped walnuts, almonds or pecans;
sifted icing sugar.

Sift flour, salt, baking powder and sugar into a bowl. Add butter, eggs, milk and vanilla and beat vigorously until well blended. Fold in nuts. Spoon into a greased and bottom-lined 23 x 33 cm (9 x 13 in) cake tin. Bake cake in a preheated moderate oven (180°C/350°F) for 30–35 minutes or until a skewer inserted in centre comes out clean. Cool on a wire rack, then dust with icing sugar. Cut into squares to serve.

Continental Cakes

Europe has given us a heritage of superb cakes. Generally speaking, Continental cakes have a richer, closer texture than butter, sponge or quick-mix cakes. When they contain a high proportion of ground nuts instead of flour they are often referred to as tortes, and when they are split into many layers and decorated they may be called *gâteaux*. Rich butter-cream fillings are used, and different types of liqueurs, chocolate or coffee are favourite flavourings. Nuts and fruit are used as decorations, and frequently the cake is chilled before serving.

Springform tins make it easy to turn out the richer mixtures, and the interestingly shaped *gugelhopf, bundt* and ring tins give authentic shapes to Continental cakes. See recipes.

See also *Gâteau*.

Bienenstich

The much-loved 'honey-bee sting' cake of Germany with its creamy filling.

I³/₄ cups flour; 2 tsp baking powder; pinch salt;
75 g (2¹/₂ oz) butter; ¹/₃ cup caster sugar;
2 tbs milk; I egg.

TOPPING: 75 g (2¹/₂ oz) butter; ¹/₂ cup sugar;
125 g (4 oz) blanched, slivered almonds;
I tsp vanilla.

FILLING: 125 g (4 oz) butter; 4 tbs caster sugar;
I cup thick cold egg custard (custard powder custard may be used); 2 tsp vanilla.

Sift together flour, baking powder and salt. Cream butter with sugar until light and fluffy. Combine milk and egg and gradually add to creamed mixture. Work in dry ingredients to make a soft dough. Press dough evenly over bottom of greased 20 cm (8 in) springform cake tin.
TOPPING: Melt butter in a saucepan over low heat, add sugar and stir until combined. Remove from heat, stir until combined. Remove from heat, stir in almonds and vanilla and allow to cool. Spread over dough. Bake in a preheated moderately hot oven (190°C/375°F) for 40 minutes. Release spring and cool on a wire rack.
FILLING: Cream butter and sugar together until light and fluffy, then gradually beat in cold custard and vanilla. When cold split cake into 2 layers and sandwich together with filling.

Finnish Sour Cream Cake

A moist, richly flavoured cake that needs no decoration. An excellent family cake, it is easily made with sour cream and keeps well in an airtight container. It has a spicy cardamom flavour.

2 eggs, beaten; 2 cups sour cream;
2 cups caster sugar; 3 drops almond essence;
3 cups flour; I tsp bicarbonate of soda; ¹/₂ tsp salt;
I tsp cinnamon; I tsp ground cardamom.

Place eggs, sour cream, sugar and almond essence in a large bowl and mix until combined. Sift flour with bicarbonate of soda, salt and spices and add gradually to egg mixture, beating until batter is smooth. Pour into greased 23 cm (9 in) *gugelhopf, bundt* or ring tin that has been dusted with sugar. Bake in a preheated moderate oven (180°C/350°F) for 1¼ hours or until a skewer inserted into centre comes out clean. Leave in tin for 10 minutes before turning out to cool on a wire rack.

Mocha Nut Cake

5 eggs, separated; I cup caster sugar; I tsp instant coffee powder; ¹/₂ cup flour, sifted; ¹/₂ cup finely ground hazelnuts or walnuts; sifted icing sugar.

FILLING: 2 cups cream; 2 tbs icing sugar, sifted; 1 tbs instant coffee powder dissolved in 1 tbs brandy.

Beat eggs whites until soft peaks form. Gradually beat in sugar until mixture stands in stiff peaks. Beat egg yolks separately until thick and light, then fold into whites. Mix coffee, flour and nuts together and fold into egg mixture gently but thoroughly until no white streaks remain. Spoon into greased and floured 23 cm (9 in) springform or ring tin. Bake in a preheated moderately slow oven (160°C/325°F) for 50–55 minutes or until cake springs back when lightly pressed with a finger. Cool on a wire rack.

FILLING: Whip cream until thick, then fold in sugar and coffee dissolved in brandy. Split cake into 4 layers. Just before serving, sandwich together with filling and sprinkle icing sugar on top.

Chocolate Toffee Cake

125 g (4 oz) butter; ²/₃ cup firmly packed brown sugar; 2 eggs; ¹/₂ cup self-raising flour; ¹/₂ cup ground almonds; 75 g (2¹/₂ oz) dark chocolate, grated; extra grated chocolate (optional).

TOFFEE ICING: 60 g (2 oz) butter; ²/₃ cup firmly packed brown sugar; 2 tbs golden syrup; ¹/₂ cup cream; sifted icing sugar (optional).

Cream butter with sugar until light and fluffy. Beat in eggs one at a time, then fold in flour and ground almonds. Add chocolate and mix well. Pour into a greased and lined 20 cm (8 in) cake tin. Bake in a preheated moderate oven (180°C/350°F) for 1¼ hours or until firm to a light touch. Leave in the tin for 5 minutes, then turn carefully on to a wire rack to cool.

TOFFEE ICING: Put butter, sugar and syrup into a saucepan. Stir over a gentle heat until sugar has dissolved. Bring to the boil, reduce heat immediately and simmer, without stirring for 5 minutes. Remove from the heat and slowly pour in cream in a steady stream, beating well with a wooden spoon. Leave to cool and thicken. If you prefer a thicker icing, add sufficient icing sugar to give the desired consistency. Spread over cake and swirl surface with a spoon. Decorate with extra grated chocolate, if wished.

Vienna Cakes

Attractive, buttery-flavoured cakes.

185 g (6 oz) butter, softened; ¹/₂ tsp vanilla; ¹/₂ cup icing sugar, sifted; 1³/₄ cups flour; extra sifted icing sugar; raspberry jam.

Cream butter with vanilla and sugar until light and fluffy. Fold in flour. Pipe or spoon mixture into paper patty cases set in tartlet pans and make a slight dent in the tip of each cake. Bake in a preheated moderately hot oven (190°C/375°F) for 10–12 minutes. Leave to cool. Sift extra icing sugar over each cake and drop a little raspberry jam into the centres. Makes 12.

Children's Cakes

Plain, or lightly flavoured butter cakes are usually the best to use when the party is for tiny children, since not all children like the stronger flavours of some other cakes. See recipes.

Little Bear Maypole Cake

2 x 20 cm (8 in) Basic Butter Cakes (page 58); 1¹/₂ quantities Butter Cream (page 207); ¹/₄ cup raspberry jam; 2 packets chocolate-coated finger biscuits; 2–3 drops green food colouring; 1 cup desiccated coconut; stick and narrow ribbons for maypole; 5–6 small model bears; artificial or sugar flowers.

Sandwich cakes together with a little of the butter cream and some of the raspberry jam. Place cake on a board or tray covered with foil and spread a thin layer of butter cream around sides of cake. Stick chocolate-coated finger biscuits all around sides of cake with the tops just showing above edge to represent a fence. Add food colouring to coconut and mix through with your finger-tips to distribute evenly. You may need to add more colour according to the shade desired. Brush top of cake with remaining jam and cover it with an even layer of coconut. Make maypole with a long thin stick covered with foil, with one of the ribbons wound around it. Position the maypole in the centre of the cake, pushing the stick through until it reaches the board. Stand the little model bears around edge of cake. Attach several ribbons to top of maypole with a drawing pin or sellotape, cover pin with a rosette of butter cream and arrange the ribbons over the cake, taking them out to the bears. The maypole and the edge of the cake may be decorated with artificial flowers, if you wish. Use remaining butter cream to decorate the biscuit fence.

Winifred White Mouse

1 packet butter cake mix, or 1 quantity Basic Butter Cake mixture (page 58); 1 quantity Butter Cream (page 207); 1¹/₂ cups desiccated coconut; 1 licorice stick; 2 pink marshmallows; 4 white pipe cleaners.

Make cake mixture according to the directions on the packet, or follow the recipe. Pour into a well-greased 1 litre (4 cup) ovenproof pudding basin and bake in a preheated moderate oven (180°C/350°F) for 1 hour or until a skewer inserted in centre comes out clean. Turn on to wire rack to cool. Cover a board with foil. Trim flat top of cake so the mouse will sit evenly and invert cake on to the board. Cut the cake into a mouse shape by trimming away one side from top to base so that it is narrower and slopes more, and trimming base of this slope into a slight point for the nose. Cover cake evenly with butter cream and sprinkle thickly with coconut, pressing on firmly. Position a long piece of licorice at the broad end of the mouse to form a tail and cut 2 small pieces of licorice to make the eyes. Halve one of the marshmallows and use for the ears; use the whole marshmallow for the nose. Halve pipe cleaners and place in each side of the nose for the whiskers.

CALAMARI

The Italian name for squid. Squid are saltwater molluscs, related to the octopus and cuttlefish, and found in many parts of the world, where they are prized for their sweet, tender flesh. The baby squid, call *calamaretti* in Italy, are especially sweet. See *Squid*.

CAMOMILE

A plant which resembles a daisy, and is cultivated for the pleasantly aromatic flavour and scent of its flower heads. Dried, they are used in the preparation of camomile tea (said to soothe as well as refresh), in aperitifs and hair rinses.

CANAPES

A French word meaning 'couch', which is used to describe bite-sized pieces of bread, toast, biscuits or pastry topped with savoury food. Canapés may be served whenever a savoury tid-bit is called for – with drinks, at tea and coffee time, for supper or as part of an hors d'oeuvre selection. They can be hot or cold, as simple as a biscuit spread with savoury butter, or as elaborate as pastry shapes baked with a lobster mornay topping. Canapés should look decorative, but remember to keep toppings and garnishes manageable for eating with the fingers, to keep them bite-size, and not to serve too many. Like appetisers, they are designed to whet the appetite, not to satisfy it.

CANAPE BASES
White or wholemeal toast, cut into strips, squares or circles; crispbreads; Melba toast; pumpernickel and rye breads; plain or flavoured savoury biscuits; fried bread (croûtes); pastry rounds; sliced French bread, bread sticks or rolls; home-made quick breads, tiny split hot scones or pancakes.

CANAPE BUTTERS
Use these alone, or garnish as desired; the garnish may be a dab of the flavouring – caviar, sardine, olive, etc.
Sardine Butter: Soften 60 g (2 oz) butter and combine with 1 cup mashed sardines, 1 tsp Worcestershire sauce, 1 tsp Tomato Ketchup, 1 tsp lemon juice and salt and freshly ground black pepper to taste.
Caviar Butter: Soften 60 g (2 oz) butter and combine with 2 tbs caviar or lumpfish roe, 1 tsp grated onion, 1 tsp lemon juice and salt and freshly ground black pepper to taste.
Olive Butter: Soften 60 g (2 oz) butter and combine with 2 tbs finely chopped stuffed olives and 1 tsp grated onion.

CANAPE TOPPINGS
Blend all ingredients well together.
Liverwurst and Bacon: 90 g (3 oz) liverwurst (Latvian, chicken etc.); 2 bacon rashers, rind removed, grilled and crumbled; few drops Tabasco or chilli sauce; 1 tbs lemon juice.
Roquefort: 90 g (3 oz) cream cheese; 30 g (1 oz) Roquefort cheese; 1/4 cup cream; salt and freshly ground black pepper to taste.
Cheese and Ham: 3/4 cup grated mature Cheddar cheese; 1/3 cup devilled ham spread; 1 tsp Worcestershire sauce; 1/4 cup cream.
Egg and Walnut: 4 hard-boiled eggs, finely chopped; 1/4 cup finely chopped walnuts; 1 tbs finely chopped shallot; Mayonnaise (page 256) to bind.
Camembert Canapés: A make-your-own canapé plate – this is a German favourite, great with beer. On individual plates place a wedge of Camembert, a small mound of finely chopped onion and smaller mounds of finely chopped anchovies and canned pimientos. Salt shakers, peppermills and oil and vinegar cruets should be on the table, with platters of thickly buttered rye and pumpernickel bread. Each person mixes their own canapé toppings according to taste.

HOT CANAPES
Snails: Use any of the canapé toppings suggested. Roll out Plain Shortcrust Pastry (page 342) into an oblong shape, spread generously with chosen filling and roll up like a Swiss roll. Chill for 1 hour, then cut into 1 cm (1/2 in) slices and arrange on greased baking trays. Bake in a preheated hot oven (200°C/400°F) until golden. Serve hot.
Rarebit Puffs: Beat 2 egg whites until they form stiff peaks. Fold in 1 cup grated mature Cheddar cheese, 1 tsp Worcestershire sauce, 1 tsp paprika, 1/2 tsp dry mustard, salt and ground black pepper. Spread over round cracker biscuits. Place under a hot grill until topping is puffed and brown. Makes 24.
Hot Crabmeat Canapés: Flake 1 x 185 g can drained crabmeat and mix in 1 tsp chopped onion, 1 tsp chilli sauce, 3 tbs mayonnaise. Spread on crustless toast triangles, going right to the edges. Place under a hot grill until browned. Makes 24.

CANNELLONI

Meaning 'big pipes' these are an Italian specialty – tubes of pasta which are filled with a savoury stuffing. The pasta is usually cooked first and, after filling, the cannelloni are sprinkled with melted butter and grated cheese or with a sauce, and browned in the oven. Fillings may vary from cheese and spinach to a rich chicken or meat mixture.

Cannelloni are usually bought as dried pasta, already

formed into tubes. If you prefer, you can make your own fresh pasta dough, cut it into squares and roll round the filling (in some areas, you can buy fresh pasta from a specialty shop). Thin crêpes, fried on one side only, may be used instead of pasta dough. There are pre-cooked cannelloni tubes sold in packages, ready for filling. For cannelloni recipe see *Pasta*.

CANTELOUPE

See *Melon*.

CAPER

The small, olive-green bud of a bush native to the Mediterranean and North Africa. Capers are hand-picked, salted and pickled in vinegar. Their piquant flavour adds zest to white sauces, mayonnaise, salads, creamed foods and fish dishes; they also make an excellent garnish for open sandwiches, appetisers and so on.

Caper Sauce: The traditional sauce for boiling mutton and lamb. Add creamed capers to Velouté or Béchamel Sauce (see *Sauces*) in the proportion of 1 tbs per cup of sauce, or according to taste.

Egg and Caper Sauce: Add 1 chopped hard-boiled egg per cup to Caper Sauce, above, and serve on poached or steamed fish, smoked fish, vegetables or hot corned beef.

CAPSICUM

See *Pepper*.

CARAMEL

The familiar flavour of caramel results when sugar is cooked long enough to form a rich golden-brown syrup. It is used in cakes, sauces and puddings, to line moulds for creams and custards, and to colour Parisian Essence. It is also used to make a clear brittle topping, for profiteroles and cakes such as Gâteau St Honoré (see page 174).

TO CARAMELISE: This means to dissolve sugar slowly and boil steadily without stirring until a dark brown colour. Put 1 cup sugar and ½ cup water in a small saucepan and stir over gentle heat, until sugar dissolves. Bring to the boil and cook quickly without stirring, until golden-brown. Dip pan in cold water (it will make a loud hissing noise but there's no need for alarm) to prevent caramel from getting darker. **See recipes.**

Caramel Syrup: This syrup, used to flavour cakes and biscuits, keeps indefinitely if stored in a covered container in the refrigerator. Gently melt 1 cup sugar in a heavy-based pan until golden. When bubbles appear over the whole surface, remove from heat and very slowly pour in 1 cup boiling water. Cool. Makes 1½ cups.

Creamy Caramel Sauce

125 g (4 oz) butter; 1 cup firmly packed brown sugar;
1 x 125 g can (³/4 cup) reduced cream.

Melt butter in a heavy saucepan, add sugar and stir over low heat until dissolved. Increase heat and boil for 3 minutes. Remove from heat and when bubbles subside, carefully stir in cream. Makes about 1½ cups.

Butter Caramels

Caramels should be soft and chewy; the longer you cook them, the harder they become so be sure to stop when they are the colour of milky coffee.

125 g (4 oz) butter; 2 tbs golden syrup;
1¹/2 cups sugar; 1 x 400 g can sweetened condensed milk; ¹/2 cup water; large pinch cream of tartar;
1 tsp vanilla.

Place all ingredients except vanilla in a heavy saucepan and stir constantly over fairly low heat until mixture is pale brown – a little dropped into cold water should form a firm but pliable ball. Remove from heat. Stir in vanilla and pour into a buttered 15 cm (6 in) square tin. When nearly set, mark into squares. Wrap squares in wax paper or cellophane when cold. Makes about 36.

VARIATION

WALNUT OR ALMOND CARAMELS: Stir 1 cup chopped walnuts or unblanched almonds into the mixture just before pouring into tin.

CARAWAY

Tiny pungent seeds used in many popular sweet and savoury dishes in Europe, which add flavour to cheeses and cakes, rye breads, casseroles, salads, sauerkraut and potatoes. In Europe the root of the plant is boiled and eaten with parsley sauce. The seeds can be mixed with melted butter, chopped parsley and tossed through ribbon noodles to accompany goulash and other paprika-flavoured dishes.

CARBONNADE DE BOEUF (CARBONADE FLAMANDE)

A traditional dish from Belgium with a rich sauce based on beer.

Carbonnade de Boeuf

750g (1¹/2 lb) chuck steak, cubed; 2 tbs dripping;
2 onions, sliced; 1 tbs flour; 1 cup beer;
1 cup hot beef stock; 1 clove garlic, crushed;
1 bouquet garni; salt and freshly ground black
pepper; ¹/2 tsp nutmeg; ¹/2 tsp sugar; 1 tsp vinegar;
8 slices French bread, 5 mm (¹/4 in) thick;
French mustard.

Brown meat in hot dripping in flameproof casserole, then lower heat and add onions. Cook for 2 minutes. Sprinkle with flour, pour on beer and hot stock and stir until boiling. Add garlic, bouquet garni, salt, pepper, nutmeg, sugar and vinegar. Cover and cook in a preheated moderately slow oven (160°C/325°F) for 2 hours or until meat is tender. Remove casserole from oven, remove bouquet garni, skim off fat and spoon it over bread slices. Spread bread thickly with mustard. Arrange on top of casserole, pushing bread well into gravy (it will float again to the top). Cook uncovered for a further 30 minutes or until bread forms a good brown crust. Serves 4–6.

CARDAMOM

The dried seed pods and the little aromatic dark brown seeds of cardamom are used in curry, pickles, pilau and sweet dishes. There are several varieties – green, white and black – and it is best to buy the seed pods and grind the seeds as needed, since they quickly lose their pungent aroma and distinctive flavour after grinding.
See recipes.

Cardamom Chicken

8 chicken legs or thighs; I clove garlic, crushed; $^1/_2$ tsp salt; I tsp chopped fresh ginger; I tsp ground cardamom; $^1/_2$ tsp nutmeg; $^1/_2$ tsp black pepper; I tsp chilli powder; I tbs butter; 2 tbs oil; $^1/_2$ cup toasted almonds; $^1/_2$ cup water.

GARNISH: I hard-boiled egg, sliced; 2 tomatoes, sliced.

Dry chicken legs on paper towels. Combine garlic, salt, ginger, cardamom, nutmeg, pepper and chilli and rub over chicken legs. Allow to stand for 1 hour. Heat butter and oil in frying pan and fry chicken until golden-brown. Add almonds and cook for 2 minutes. Stir in water, cover and simmer over low heat for about 15–20 minutes or until chicken is cooked. Serve chicken on a bed of boiled rice, garnished with egg and tomato slices. Serves 4–6.

Cardamom Creams

Cardamom-flavoured delicious custard creams. A perfect finale to a curry meal.

$2^1/_2$ cups desiccated coconut; $2^1/_2$ cups milk; 6 whole cardamom pods; 4 eggs; $^1/_4$ cup caster sugar; I tsp freshly ground cardamom; I cup cream.

To make cardamom coconut milk, place coconut, milk and cardamom pods in a heavy saucepan. Bring to the boil slowly, then reduce heat and simmer for 5 minutes to extract flavour from cardamom pods. Cool slightly. Strain through a sieve and squeeze out as much of the milk as possible from coconut. Beat eggs, sugar and freshly ground cardamom until well blended. Add cardamom coconut milk (this should measure 1 cup) and cream and mix well. Strain custard mixture into 6–8 individual moulds or mousse custard pots and set in a roasting tin of hot water. Bake in a preheated moderately slow oven (160°C/325°F) for 35 minutes or until custard is set and a knife inserted near centre comes out clean. Allow to cool, then chill for several hours or overnight. Unmould on to serving dish or plates, or leave in mousse pots. Serves 6–8.

Rice Blancmange

3 cups milk; 3 tbs rice flour; 3 tbs sugar; $^1/_2$ tsp ground cardamom; $^1/_4$ tsp nutmeg; I tsp vanilla; 2 tbs blanched, slivered almonds.

Mix $^1/_2$ cup of the milk with flour to make a smooth paste. Add sugar to remaining $2^1/_2$ cups of milk and bring to the boil. Remove from heat, stir in milk and flour mixture, return to heat and stir constantly until mixture boils and thickens. Boil, stirring, for 3–5 minutes. Remove from heat and stir in cardamom, nutmeg, vanilla and half the almonds. Pour into 6 individual little pots or a 3-cup dish and chill thoroughly. Sprinkle remaining nuts over top before serving. Serves 6.

CARPACCIO

A specialty of good Italian restaurants, the simplest carpaccio is very thin slices of good quality fillet beef, arranged overlapping on plates, rosette-style. It is then simply dressed with a good olive oil, lemon juice and freshly ground pepper and offered as a first course. Good quality tuna may be prepared the same way.

Carpaccio with Rocket and Parmesan

375 g (12 oz) trimmed beef fillet; a handful of baby rocket leaves, washed and dried; a small wedge of Parmesan; freshly ground black pepper; 2 tbs fresh lemon juice; $^1/_4$ cup extra virgin olive oil.

Wrap the beef well in plastic wrap and semi-freeze for 1 hour, or until it is firm but not frozen solid. Using a very sharp knife cut the fillet across the grain into very thin slices. To make the slices even thinner, arrange on sheets of plastic wrap, cover with additional sheets of wrap and gently roll them using a rolling pin, testing a slice as you roll to make sure they are not too thin to transfer to serving plates. Roll up the sheets loosely between sheets of baking paper or plastic wrap and chill the beef for at least an hour.

Divide the beef among 4 chilled plates, lining the plates with a single layer of the slices. Mound the rocket in the centre with shavings of Parmesan made by shaving the wedge of cheese with a vegetable peeler. Each plate should have about 5 shavings, or to taste. Give each serving a good grinding of pepper and drizzle a little of the lemon juice and olive oil over each. Serves 4.

CARPETBAG STEAK

Claimed as an Australian contribution to gastronomy. A thick cut of steak becomes a 'carpetbag' when it has a pocket cut into it and is filled with oysters.

Carpetbag Steak

250 g (8 oz) rump, boned sirloin or fillet steak, cut 2.5 cm (1 in) thick; 4 canned oysters, drained; freshly ground black pepper; parsley to garnish.

Trim excess fat and any gristle from steak and cut a deep pocket in it, about halfway through. Fill pocket with oysters, season with pepper and close opening with wooden toothpicks or poultry pins. Place steak under a preheated very hot grill, and cook on each side for about 5 minutes for medium-rare. Serve garnished with parsley. Steak may also be pan-fried. Use a thick frying pan, oil bottom lightly and cook steak over high heat for 1 minute each side or until a brown crust forms. Lower heat to moderate and continue cooking 3–4 minutes each side for medium-rare. Serves 1.

CARROT

Carrots are one of the three great aromatic vegetables, the others being onion and celery. They are used constantly in casseroles, soups and stews and they are the traditional accompaniment to boiled beef. There is also an excellent carrot soup, Potage Crécy (see page 487).

■ **BASIC PREPARATION:** Young carrots need only be lightly scraped and, if they are tiny, cooked whole. They are delicious cooked in a very little water and a little butter, in a tightly closed pan that permits them to steam until they are just tender. A little sugar or honey added to the water brings out the natural sweetness of the carrots.

Older carrots should be scraped or skins peeled with a swivel-bladed vegetable peeler, and sliced or cut into strips or diced and lightly boiled.

■ **TO BOIL:** Cook, with lid on, in boiling salted water until tender. Young whole carrots will take about 15–20 minutes, older carrots, cut in thick slices, will take 15 minutes. Drain, glaze with butter and toss in chopped parsley or coat with a creamy white sauce. **See also** recipes.

Golden Carrots: Scrub 500 g (1lb) young carrots and slice thinly. Drop into a small saucepan containing 3–4 tbs boiling chicken stock, cover and simmer 3 minutes or until tender but still crisp. Sprinkle with salt and, if liked, add a dab of butter. Serves 4.

Carrots Vichy: Scrub 500 g (1 lb) young carrots and cut into slices. Melt 60 g (2 oz) butter in a heavy saucepan, add carrots, 2 tbs water and 2 tsp sugar. Cover and cook gently until almost tender, then remove lid and continue cooking until water evaporates leaving a light syrup. Toss carrots to glaze and sprinkle with salt and chopped parsley. Serves 4.

Carrots Julienne: Scrap 500 g (1 lb) carrots and cut into julienne (matchstick) strips. Put into a saucepan with 2 tbs each of butter and water and cook, covered, for 6–7 minutes or until tender. Drain off any remaining liquid; add salt, freshly ground black pepper and 5–6 mint leaves, cut into fine strips. Toss over low heat for 1 minute and serve immediately. Serves 4–6.

Dilled Carrots: Scrub 500 g (1 lb) young carrots cut lengthways into quarters. Place in a saucepan with ¾ cup dill-pickle juice and simmer, covered, 10–15 minutes until crisp-tender. Cool, then chill overnight in the liquid. Drain carrots and toss them with 1½ tbs each snipped fresh dill and chives and ¾ cup sour cream. Serve with fish or other salads. Serves 4–6.

Lemon-glazed Carrots: Scrub 500 g (1 lb) young carrots and cut lengthways into quarters, or leave whole if very small. Simmer, covered, in salted water for 10–15 minutes or until crisp-tender; drain. Melt 60 g (2 oz) butter in a frying pan, add 1 tbs sugar, 2 tsp chopped parsley and 1½ tbs lemon juice and heat gently. Add carrots and toss over medium heat until glazed. Serves 4.

Minted Ginger Carrots: Scrub 500 g (1 lb) carrots, cut into batons and put into a baking dish with ½ cup orange juice, ¼ cup olive oil, 1 tsp grated fresh ginger and ½ tsp each salt and sugar. Cover and bake in a preheated moderate oven (180°C/350°F) for 45 minutes or until tender. Serve hot or chilled, sprinkle generously with mint. Serves 4.

Carrot Cake

3 cups flour; 2 cups caster sugar; 1 tsp salt; 1½ tsp bicarbonate of soda; 1 cup undrained canned crushed pineapple; 2 cups grated carrot; 4 eggs; 1½ cups salad oil; 1 tsp vanilla; 1 cup chopped nuts.

Sift flour, sugar, salt and bicarbonate of soda together into a large mixing bowl. Add pineapple, carrot, eggs, oil and vanilla and beat until combined. Stir in chopped nuts. Spoon batter into a well-greased bundt tin or 2 deep 20 cm (8 in) ring tins. Bake in a preheated moderate oven (180°C/350°F) for 1 hour or until a skewer inserted in centre comes out clean.

CASHEW

The nut of a tree indigenous to Brazil but now grown in many tropical countries. Cashews are sold raw or roasted, salted or unsalted. They are delicious as a snack food or made into a butter like peanut butter. They are also used as an ingredient for sweet and savoury dishes in both Western and Eastern cuisines.

Chinese Chicken with Cashews

1 egg white; 2 tbs dry sherry; 1 tsp salt; pinch white pepper; 1 tsp cornflour; 2 half-breasts of chicken, skinned and boned; ½ cup peanut oil; 1 cup shelled

roasted cashews; I shallot, chopped; I small green or red pepper, seeded and cut into I cm ($^{1}/_{2}$ in) squares; I cup canned, sliced bamboo shoots; I tbs soy sauce; I tsp sugar; I extra tsp cornflour, mixed with I tbs water; hot boiled rice to serve.

Beat egg white lightly with a fork and mix in 1 tbs sherry, the salt, pepper and cornflour. Slice chicken into 2.5 cm (1 in) slices, add to egg white mixture and turn pieces to coat them. Heat 3 tbs oil in wok or frying pan over high heat. In another pan, heat 3 tbs oil and fry cashews gently until golden-brown. Remove with a slotted spoon and drain on paper towel. Add remaining oil to pan, heat and stir-fry shallot, green pepper and bamboo shoots for 1 minute. Add remaining sherry with soy sauce, sugar and cornflour mixed with water. Stir until thickened. Add chicken, turn to coat with sauce and heat through. Sprinkle with cashews and serve hot with boiled rice. Serves 3–4.

CASSATA

Meaning 'in a case or chest', *cassata* is the name of two famous Italian desserts. As the name suggests, both were traditionally made in the form of a case with a filling, but they are often made in layers instead.
Cassata Gelata: Line a mould with softened ice cream, fill centre with lightly sweetened, whipped cream, mixed with chopped glacé (candied) fruit and chopped sugared almonds, and freeze until firm. If preferred, ice cream and whipped cream mixture can be arranged in layers.

Cassata Siciliana

500 g (I lb) ricotta cheese; I cup caster sugar; pinch cinnamon; 60 g (2 oz) dark chocolate, grated; 2 tbs sweet liqueur; 2 tbs chopped pistachios or pine nuts; 3 tbs chopped glacé (candied) fruit; I x 20 cm (8 in) round or square sponge cake (page 59).

DECORATION: sifted icing sugar; extra glacé fruit.

Beat ricotta and sugar together until fluffy. Reserve half for topping. Add cinnamon, chocolate and liqueur to remaining mixture and mix well. Fold in nuts and fruit. Line bottom of a 5-cup bowl or mould with greaseproof paper. Cut cake into 1 cm ($^{1}/_{2}$ in) slices and use about three quarters of them to line mould. Fill centre with ricotta mixture, cover with remaining slices of cake and chill, covered, for several hours or overnight. Turn out of mould, coat with reserve topping, dust with icing sugar and decorate with glacé fruit. Alternatively the sponge cake may be split into 3 or 4 layers and filled with the ricotta mixture. Chill, coat with topping, and decorate as described. Serves 8–10.

CAULIFLOWER

A fresh head of cauliflower has very white, closely packed florets, and surrounding leaves still fresh and green. Before cooking, all the dark outside leaves should be broken off. Boiling cauliflower needs a sauce of some kind; cauliflower and cheese have an affinity. Raw cauliflower sprigs are often served as part of a dish of *crudités* with garlic mayonnaise.

■ TO COOK: Separate florets, leaving no more than about 2.5 cm (1 in) of stem. Drop into boiling salted water and cook, uncovered for about 5 minutes. Drain, and serve with a cheese sauce or a sprinkling of cheese.
Boiled Whole Cauliflower: Cut off thick stems and make deep incisions with a sharp knife in remaining smaller stems, so that heat will penetrate them more easily. Sometimes tender young leaves are left on; when lightly cooked they enhance the look of the dish.

Boil head of cauliflower, stem down, in a large pan of lightly salted water, uncovered, for about 15–20 minutes. When stems can be easily pierced with a fork, it is fully cooked. Drain it carefully without breaking off any of florets and place on a heated serving platter. Pour on melted butter, Mornay Sauce (see page 457) or fried, buttered crumbs. See recipes.

Cauliflower Parmigiana

I large cauliflower, trimmed into florets; salt; 3 tbs butter; 2 cups fresh breadcrumbs; $^{1}/_{2}$ cup grated Parmesan cheese; 2 tbs chopped parsley.

Cook florets in boiling salted water for about 8 minutes or until tender. Drain carefully in a colander. Melt butter and fry breadcrumbs until golden. Butter a shallow baking dish, sprinkle with a little grated Parmesan cheese and arrange florets in dish. Sprinkle with breadcrumbs mixed with remaining Parmesan cheese. Bake in a preheated very hot oven (230°C/450°F) for about 5 minutes or until top is golden. Remove from oven and sprinkle parsley over. Serves 6.

Cauliflower au Gratin

I cauliflower, trimmed into florets; salt; I cup Mornay Sauce (page 457); $^{1}/_{2}$ cup grated Parmesan cheese; 2 tbs butter, melted.

Cook florets in boiling salted water for about 8 minutes or until tender. Drain. Arrange stems side down in a baking dish, cover with mornay sauce, sprinkle with cheese, and then with melted butter. Bake in a preheated hot oven (200°C/400°F) for 5–6 minutes or until the surface is golden. Serves 6.

CAVIAR

The salted roe of the sturgeon, which is considered a great delicacy. The caviar from Russia, and from the Beluga sturgeon in particular, is thought by many people to be the finest. Caviar varies in colour from grey to shiny, jet black, and in size from tiny eggs the size of a pin head to eggs the size of seed pearls.

Iced champagne or vodka usually accompany caviar.

WAYS TO SERVE CAVIAR

- Well chilled, with small, neat triangles of hot toast, fresh unsalted butter and thin slices of lemon.
- In a dish surrounded with crushed ice, accompanied by Melba toast, finely chopped onion, sour cream and freshly ground black pepper.
- Accompanied by very finely chopped egg white and egg yolk, with hot toast.
- Spread savoury butters on canapés and top with caviar.
- As an accompaniment to Blini, which are small buckwheat pancakes made with yeast. (See *Blini*.)

CAYENNE PEPPER

This hot, pungent spice is a member of the pepper family and is sold as a powder, ground from dried red chillies. Cayenne is used to flavour curry and chilli and to season sauces, cheese and fish dishes. Just a pinch of cayenne can add sufficient piquancy to a dish – it should be used sparingly.

CELERIAC

The edible turnip-like root of a variety of celery, and with a similar flavour. The root is peeled, the flesh sliced or diced and cooked in boiling salted water for 20–30 minutes or until tender. It is drained and served with a good white sauce, or melted butter and pepper.

Celeriac is often used raw in salad. The flesh is grated or cut in julienne (matchstick) strips and dressed with Vinaigrette Dressing (see page 442). Raw celeriac discolours quickly, so the minute it is exposed to air and cut, it should be put into a bowl of acidulated water until required.

CELERY

This features in many salads and is a favourite flavouring for soups and stews. It is also an excellent vegetable served in its own right as a special dish or accompaniment to meats.

■ **BASIC PREPARATION** (this is always the same): The root ends should be trimmed off and the top leaves removed (these may be reserved for the stock pot). Trim a whole bunch down to about 18 cm (7 in) long and cut in 2. The tough, fibrous strings on the outer stalks should be scraped off, or if using large bunches, the outer stalks may be removed and reserved for the stock pot. Wash the stalks under running cold water.

■ **TO COOK:** Drop into a small quantity of lightly salted boiling water and boil, uncovered, for 10 minutes. Drain, return to pan, heat gently to dry off any moisture. Add 1 tsp butter, pepper, salt, a little grated cheese and chopped parsley to enhance flavour. **See recipes.**

Celery Poulette

1 bunch celery; 1 tbs chopped onion; salt and freshly ground black pepper; 2 tbs butter; 2 tsp flour; 1/4 cup cream; 3/4 cup chicken stock.

Prepare celery as described above, cutting it into roughly 8 cm (3 in) lengths. Place celery, onion, salt and pepper in a saucepan with a tight-fitting lid. Cook slowly, shaking pan often, until celery is almost tender, about 10 minutes. If the lid does not fit tightly, it will be necessary to add a little water, but celery should be almost dry at end of cooking time. Place in a heated serving dish. Melt butter, blend in flour and gradually add cream and chicken stock. Bring to boil, stirring, then reduce heat and simmer for 3 minutes. Spoon over celery. Serves 6.

VARIATIONS

CELERY AMANDINE: Sprinkle 1/4 cup shredded, toasted almonds over Celery Poulette.

SCALLOPED CELERY IN CHEESE SAUCE: Prepare Celery Poulette and add 3/4 cup grated cheese to the sauce. Stir until cheese has melted. Place celery in a casserole, pour over sauce and sprinkle top with additional grated cheese or with buttered breadcrumbs. Brown under a preheated grill or in a preheated oven (180°C/350°F).

Celery and Mushroom Salad

1 bunch celery, trimmed and sliced diagonally; 250 g (8 oz) mushrooms, finely sliced; 1 large canned pimiento, drained and sliced; 2 spring onions, sliced; 2 tbs chopped parsley; 1/4 cup red wine vinegar; 2 tbs Dijon mustard; 1/4 cup olive oil; 1/4 cup vegetable oil; juice 1 lemon; salt and freshly ground black pepper.

Combine celery and mushrooms in a salad bowl, cover and chill. Place pimiento in blender or food processor, add spring onions, parsley, vinegar and mustard, and pureé; or place in a small bowl and pound with a pestle or the end of a rolling pin. Gradually add olive and vegetable oils, then mix in lemon juice, salt and pepper. Pour over celery and mushroom, toss well. Cover and chill for 2 hours. Serves 4–6.

CEREALS

Cereals are cultivated grasses essential for good health. The seeds and grain contain protein, vitamins and minerals to provide a cheap source of energy in the form of carbohydrate. Wholegrain cereals are the most nutritious and add fibre to the diet. Wheat and rice are the major sources of cereal food for man.

See also *Barley; Cornmeal (Polenta); Muesli; Oatmeal; Porridge; Rice; Semolina; Wheat.*

CEVICHE

The name given to marinated raw fish, which is very popular in South America and the South Pacific. The fish fillets are cut into pieces, then 'cooked' or marinated in lemon or lime juice until the flesh becomes opaque. From here on the treatment varies from one place to another; the excess lemon or lime is squeezed from the fish and the fish is dressed in a sauce like Vinaigrette Dressing (see page 442) or coconut milk, and may be mixed with salad vegetables, onion rings, tomato cubes or wedges, chopped chilli, green or red peppers. In Mexico avocado is added, while in the Pacific Islands coconut milk is used. While raw fish fillets are mostly used, raw scallops or fresh green prawns may be treated in the same way. See recipes.

Ceviche *(Tahitian Fish Salad)*

1 kg (2 lb) firm-fleshed fish fillets; juice 5–6 lemons or limes; 1 green or red pepper, seeded and diced; 3 sticks celery, cut into strips; 4 spring onions, chopped; 3 hard-boiled eggs, chopped; salt and freshly ground black pepper; 1/2–3/4 cup Coconut Milk (page 91).

Remove skin and bones from fish, then cut into thick strips. Place in glass or plastic container and pour lemon or lime juice over. Cover and chill at least 3 hours, turning with wooden spoon from time to time. (Do not use a metal spoon.) The juice will turn fish white and opaque and it will look cooked. Squeeze out all juice from the fish by placing fish in a plastic colander and pressing with a wooden spoon. Put into a clean bowl and add vegetables, eggs, salt and pepper. Stir in coconut milk and toss to coat well. Place fish salad in large serving dish or shell and chill. Alternatively, serve in small individual dishes or shells. Serve 8.

Ceviche of Scallops

The combination of ceviche made with scallops and avocado is perfect is serve as a dinner party starter or at a light luncheon followed by a green salad.

375 g (12 oz) scallops; juice 1 lemon; 1 stick celery, diced; 1 small onion, sliced; 4 scallop shells; chopped parsley or snipped chives; lemon wedges to serve.

DRESSING: 1 tbs lemon juice; 1 small clove garlic, crushed with little salt; 1 tbs olive oil; salt and freshly ground black pepper; dash Tabasco sauce.

Wash scallops and trim off any brown bits. Place in a bowl, add lemon juice and marinate for 2–3 hours. Squeeze out excess lemon juice. Mix all ingredients for dressing in a small bowl and pour over scallops. Add celery and onion. Cover and chill for about 1 hour. Spoon marinated seafood into each scallop shell and sprinkle with parsley or chives. Serve with lemon wedges. Serves 4.

VARIATION

CEVICHE OF SCALLOPS WITH AVOCADO: Halve 2 chilled avocados and remove stones. Scoop out some of the flesh and add to above seafood mixture. Mix lightly and spoon into avocado shells.

CHAMPIGNON

The French name for mushroom, but particularly associated with button mushrooms.
See *Mushroom*.

CHAPATI

An Indian unleavened bread made from wholemeal or *atta* flour. Chapatis are eaten with curries and all Indian savoury dishes. Break off a piece and use it to scoop up the food.

Chapatis

2 cups fine wholemeal or *atta* flour; 1 tsp salt; 1 tsp ghee or peanut oil; 1 cup lukewarm water.

Place 1¾ cups flour in a bowl. Add salt and rub in ghee or add oil. Make a well in the centre and add water all at once. Mix with one hand to form a dough and knead for at least 10 minutes. Wrap dough in plastic wrap and chill for at least 1 hour. (It is preferable to chill the dough overnight for lighter chapatis.)

Shape dough into 12–14 small balls about the size of large walnuts. Roll out each one on a board, sprinkled with remaining flour, to a 13 cm (5 in) round. Heat a heavy frying pan until a drop of water spits when dropped on pan. Place chapatis in pan and press edge with a folded tea-towel to encourage bubbles to form and make chapatis light. Cook for 1 minute, then turn to cook other side. Wrap each chapati in a tea-towel as soon as it is cooked. Serve hot to accompany curries or vegetable dishes. Makes 12–14.

CHARLOTTE

A name given to two entirely different desserts. One is cold: a mould is lined with sponge fingers or sponge cake filled with a creamy mousse or Bavarian Cream (*Bavarois*), fruit- or nut-flavoured. The other is hot: the mould is often lined with buttered bread fingers, and usually filled with apples, then baked.

The traditional charlotte mould is made of tin, with sloping sides and has 2 lugs on either side. A charlotte may, however, be made in a loaf tin or a soufflé dish. **See recipes.**

Strawberry Charlotte

1kg (2lb) strawberries; ³/₄ cup caster sugar; 2¹/₂ tbs Kirsch; 16–18 sponge fingers (Savoy biscuits); ¹/₂ cup sherry; 1¹/₂ cups cream.

Hull strawberries and cut them in half. Put in a bowl with half the sugar and the Kirsch. Moisten sponge fingers with sherry (just dip in and out quickly) and use some to line bottom and sides of a charlotte mould. Whip cream with remaining sugar. Put a layer of strawberries in mould, then whipped cream and cover with moistened sponge fingers. Continue layering ingredients, finishing with sponge fingers. Chill at least 4 hours. Unmould and serve in slices with additional whipped cream. Serves 8.

VARIATION

CHOCOLATE CHARLOTTE: Prepare and line charlotte mould with sponge fingers as described in Strawberry Charlotte. Make Chocolate Mousse (see page 85). Fill the sponge finger-lined mould with alternate layers of mousse and sponge fingers. Chill for 4 hours. Unmould and serve in slices. Serves 8.

Apple Charlotte

1 loaf white bread, sliced; 2 eggs, beaten; 2 cups fresh white breadcrumbs.

FILLING: 60 g (2 oz) butter; 5 large apples, peeled, cored and sliced; 2 tbs caster sugar; ¹/₄ tsp cinnamon; ¹/₂ tsp grated lemon rind; 3–4 tbs apricot jam.

Remove crusts from bread and cut each slice into 2 strips. Dip into beaten eggs, then coat with breadcrumbs. Arrange around the sides of a greased 5–6-cup charlotte mould or soufflé dish, overlapping slightly. Line bottom of mould keeping a few slices to cover top.

FILLING: Melt butter in a saucepan, add apples, sugar, cinnamon and lemon rind and cook over a high heat, stirring continuously. When apples are reduced to a thick purée, stir in jam. Spoon into prepared mould and top with reserved bread slices. Bake in a moderate oven (180°C/350°F) for 35–40 minutes. Allow charlotte to stand for a few minutes before turning out on to a heated dish. Serve with whipped cream. Serves 6.

CHATEAUBRIAND

This is large piece of steak, cut from the thick part of the fillet, usually 5–8 cm (2–3 in) thick, and weighing 500–750 g (1–1½ lb). It usually appears on menus as a serving for 2.

■ **TO COOK:** Trim meat, sprinkle both sides with salt, spread with a little butter and grill meat under a preheated grill for about 6 minutes on each side. Transfer meat to a hot frying pan, spread it with additional butter and continue to cook over medium heat, about 10 minutes for rare, 15 minutes for medium-rare. To test: if you look carefully, you will notice that when meat reaches medium-rare stage, tiny drops of pink juice appear on the surface. Touch meat at this stage with the first and second fingers; it will be firm but still retain a noticeable springiness. If it feels soft it is not done; if it is quite firm, it is well done.

Serve with Béarnaise Sauce (see pages 459–60) or Maître d'Hôtel butter (see page 52), watercress and French Fried Potatoes (see page 383).

CHEESE

There are hundreds of varieties of cheese, and it is infinitely versatile. It can appear on the menu at any time of day and in any course; it makes a splendid snack and is one of the most useful 'emergency' foods; it is a good companion to drinks from coffee and beer to fine wine. Cheese is remarkable in its ability to complement other foods and plays a vital part in the cuisines of many countries. Cheese can be made from cow, sheep, buffalo or goat milk, each with its own character.

TYPES OF CHEESE

All natural cheese, no matter how they may vary in individual character, can be divided into four basic types: soft unripened, soft ripened, firm, and hard. Processed cheeses are usually treated to resemble one of these types, and can be used in the same way.

Soft Unripened Cheeses: These include fresh Cottage Cheese and Ricotta and processed Creamed Cottage Cheese, all low in fat. Cream Cheese and Neufchâtel, usually in processed form, are rich and smooth. Fresh Mascarpone is luscious and creamy.

Store these cheeses, closely covered, in the refrigerator. Use fresh varieties within a day or two of purchase, processed varieties within a week or two. They are used in salads, for savouries and desserts, as spreads, and in cooking both savoury and sweet dishes.

Salty Feta, though firm in texture, is classified in the group because of its high moisture content. Store in a covered container in the refrigerator and use with in a week or so. Feta is sliced or diced and served with black olives as an appetiser, or in a salad.

Soft Ripened Cheeses: These vary from richly flowing Camembert and Brie to the great blue cheeses, namely, Stilton, Roquefort, Gorgonzola and Dolcelatte, and buttery Danish Blues. Tangy Port Salut, mild Bel Paese and Chevre (made with goat's milk) are others. Mozzarella, an Italian soft cheese, melts readily in cooking and is used in such well-known Italian dishes as pizza and lasagne.

Many manufacturers produce soft cheeses combined with walnuts, Kirsch, pepper, herbs and other flavourings.

Serve these cheeses as part of the cheese board, on biscuits or bread as a snack or with drinks, or with fruit and nuts for dessert. Small whole Camemberts may be dipped in egg and breadcrumbs and quickly crisped in hot oil for the 'Fried Camembert' featured in some top restaurants as a first course.

Store soft cheeses, loosely wrapped in foil, in the refrigerator and use within a week or so of purchase. If you are lucky enough to have a whole Stilton, give it special care. Store it, covered with a damp cloth wrung out in salt water, in the refrigerator. If it is going to be used fairly quickly, the cheese may be cut in half horizontally, one half wrapped round with a napkin and scooped from the centre to serve. There is a tradition of pouring a little port into the centre, but purists disapprove of this. If the cheese is to be used slowly, cut slices across the face as this lessens the risk of drying out.

Firm Cheeses: These are the all-rounders, and every cheese-making country has its specialties. Cheddar, originally from the west of England, is probably the most famous of all; Cheddar-style cheeses are not made in many countries. Salty Cheshire, Leicester, Sage Derby (so-named because it is flecked with sage) and sharp, white Caerphilly from Wales or Somerset are other well-known British cheeses.

Holland produces smooth-bodied Gouda (shaped like a yellow wheel) and Edam (shaped like a red ball); Denmark makes mild Havarti (formerly called Tilsit) and fuller-flavoured Samsöe. Swiss Emmenthal (smooth and nutty, with large holes) and Gruyère (stronger, with smaller holes) are the originals on which Swiss cheeses around the world are styled.

Firm cheeses are excellent for snacks, savouries, sandwiches, for toasting, for the cheese board and cooking. Store them in the refrigerator in a covered container, cut sides covered with foil, or use within a few weeks of purchase.

Hard Cheeses: These are strong-flavoured and dry, perfect for grating over pasta, rice, vegetables or soups, or for cooking with. For best flavour, buy in the piece and grate off as you need it. This is practical as these cheeses, low in moisture, do not need refrigeration and keep for a long time provided they have good air circulation. Cheese sellers simply hang them from hooks in a cool, airy place. The great names in hard cheeses are Parmesan, Pecorino and Romano, all originally produced in Italy but now much-copied elsewhere.

■ **SERVING CHEESE:** Always bring cheese to room temperature before serving, so that it can release its flavour. Cheese which should be buttery or melting-soft may be hard or rubbery if served too cold.

Put flowing cheeses, such as Brie and Camembert, on to the board uncut if possible. French bread, water biscuits or other crisp, thin crackers, crispbreads or oatcakes (Scottish or Irish) are good accompaniments. Serve with butter or not, as you prefer.

Serve cheese, as the French do, after the main course so that diners can finish their red wine with it, or serve at the end of the meal.

There is no need to serve a great variety of types on a cheese board or platter. One beautiful Brie, or 2 generous wedges of different types are far more tempting than an array of little pieces.

■ **COOKING WITH CHEESE:** Cooking for too long or at too high a heat makes cheese tough and stringy. Always add it at the end of cooking and heat gently for no longer than it takes to melt. Grate hard cheese finely so that it will melt readily; shred firm or soft cheese, or chop it finely. **See recipes.**

Cheese and Bacon Balls

Serve with pre-dinner drinks.

250 g (8 oz) Cheddar cheese;
4 rashers streaky bacon, rinds removed.

Cut cheese in 2.5 cm (1 in) cubes. Cut rashers into strips and wrap around the cheese, securing with wooden toothpicks. Grill, turning once, under a preheated very hot grill so that bacon is crisp before cheese melts. Serve immediately. Makes about 24.

Cheese Feathers

$^1/_2$ cup cold water; I tbs butter; $^1/_2$ cup flour;
6 tbs grated mature cheese; 2 eggs, beaten;
freshly ground black pepper; oil for deep-frying.

Put water and butter into a small, heavy saucepan and bring slowly to the boil. Add flour, stirring all the time. Remove from heat and beat in cheese, then eggs, a little at a time. Season with pepper. Drop teaspoonfuls into hot oil and fry until pale brown. Drain on crumpled paper towels and serve as an hors d'oeuvre with drinks, as an accompaniment to soup, or, with more cheese grated over, as a first course. Makes 60–70.

Devilled Cheese

A good quick breakfast or late-night snack.

60 g (2 oz) grated mature cheese; I tsp chopped
mixed pickle; I tsp curry powder; butter;
2 slices toast.

Mix cheese, pickle and curry powder together. Butter toast lightly and spread with cheese mixture. Place slices side by side on a buttered baking tray. Bake in a preheated hot oven (200°C/400°F) for about *c*

4 minutes or grill under a preheated grill until browned. Serves 1–2.

Cheese and Almond Fingers

A simple cheese savoury.

**3 tbs chopped blanched almonds;
60 g (2 oz) butter; 3 tbs cream;
6 tbs grated mature cheese; salt and
freshly ground black pepper; toast fingers.**

Fry almonds in about one third of the butter until pale gold. Mix together remaining ingredients except toast and spread mixture on toast. Sprinkle with almonds and place under a preheated grill for a few moments to heat through. Serve at once. Makes 15–18.

Edam Tea Ring

A quickly made, cheesy scone ring.

**2 cups flour; 4 tsp baking powder;
1 tsp salt; 1 tsp paprika; 1¹/₂ cups grated Edam
cheese; 4 tbs piccalilli pickle, chopped;
1 egg; ²/₃ cup milk.**

Sift the flour, baking powder, salt and paprika. Stir in cheese and piccalilli. Beat together egg and milk. Pour into flour mixture to make a soft dough, reserving a little milk for glazing. Knead dough very lightly and divide into 6 pieces. Form each into a roll and place on a greased baking tray to form a circle with rolls just touching each other. Brush with reserved milk and egg mixture. Bake in a preheated hot oven (220°C/425°F) for 25 minutes or until golden-brown. Cool on a wire rack. Separate rolls and serve split and buttered, either hot or cold. Serves 6.

CHEESECAKE

Most cheesecakes are made from fresh, unripened cheeses such as cream cheese, cottage cheese or Neufchâtel cream cheese, available in bulk from most delicatessens and cheese counters. Cottage cheese is sold creamed, or as Farm Cheese which has a more dense, smooth consistency and is available in bulk, or as Baker's Cheese, which is a low-fat cottage cheese, also sold in bulk.

All cottage cheeses should be rubbed through a sieve or puréed in a blender before using to give a smooth texture to the finished cheesecake. Ricotta cheese is very white and creamy and may be substituted for any other kind, as well as being used in recipes specifically needing it. It is a low-fat cheese, blends easily and is sold in bulk or in pre-wrapped packages. Italy's beautiful Cassata Siciliana (see page 67) is made with Ricotta cheese. See recipes.

Lindy's Cheesecake
(Bistro Cheesecake)

**CRUST: 250 g (8 oz) plain sweet biscuits, crushed;
1 tbs sugar; ¹/₂ tsp mixed spice;
90 g (3 oz) butter, melted.**

**FILLING: 750 g (1¹/₂ lb) cream cheese; ¹/₂ cup caster
sugar; 1 tsp vanilla; grated rind 1 lemon;
1 tbs lemon juice; 4 eggs, separated; 1 cup cream;
1 tbs flour, sifted.**

TOPPING: 1 cup chilled cream, whipped; nutmeg.

Combine all ingredients for crust and press on to side and bottom of greased 23 cm (9 in) springform tin. Chill.
FILLING: Beat cheese until soft, then add sugar, vanilla and lemon rind and juice and beat until creamy. Beat in egg yolks one at a time, then cream. Fold in flour. Beat egg whites until stiff and fold in. Pour into crust and bake in a preheated moderately slow oven (160°C/325°F) for 1 hour 10 minutes. Turn off heat and leave cake in oven until cold. Release spring and remove sides of tin. Chill until ready to serve, topped with whipped cream and sprinkle with nutmeg. Serves 10–12.
VARIATIONS
Instead of nutmeg, decorate with passionfruit, strawberries, grated chocolate or sliced kiwi fruit.

Sultana Cheese Slice

**PASTRY: 2 cups flour; 125 g (4 oz) butter;
1 egg yolk, beaten; egg beaten with water to glaze.**

**FILLING: 250 g (8 oz) cream cheese;
60 g (2 oz) butter; ¹/₄ cup caster sugar; 1 tbs flour;
2 tbs cream; 3 eggs, separated; ¹/₂ cup sultanas.**

PASTRY: Sift flour into a bowl. Rub in butter until mixture resembles fine breadcrumbs. Add egg yolk and enough iced water to make a firm dough. Chill for 1 hour. Roll out two thirds of dough thinly and use to line a greased 28 x 19 cm (11 x 7 in) tin. Chill.
FILLING: Combine cheese, butter and sugar, beating well. Add flour, cream and egg yolks, then sultanas. Beat egg whites until they form stiff peaks and fold into cheese mixture. Pour into pastry-lined tin. Roll out remaining dough and cut into 1 cm (¹/₂ in) wide strips. Use to decorate the top. Join strips with egg glaze if too short. Brush dough with egg glaze. Bake in a preheated hot oven (200°C/400°F) for 10–15 minutes, then reduce oven heat to moderately hot (190°C/375°F) and bake for a further 15–20 minutes. Cool and cut into squares. Makes about 16.

Manhattan Cheesecake

**500 g (1 lb) cream cheese; 500 g (1 lb) ricotta
cheese; 1¹/₂ cups caster sugar; 4 large eggs;**

60 g (2 oz) butter, melted; 3 tbs each flour and cornflour, sifted together; 2¹/₂ tsp vanilla; 2 cups sour cream.

DECORATION: 1 cup cream, whipped; cherries or other fresh fruit; cinnamon or nutmeg.

Combine cheeses and beat well until creamy. Gradually add sugar, then beat in eggs one at a time. Stir in melted butter, flour, cornflour and vanilla. Fold in sour cream. Spoon mixture into an ungreased 23 cm (9 in) springform tin. Bake in centre of a preheated moderately slow oven (160°C/325°F) for 1 hour (cake will still be soft in centre). Turn off heat and leave cake in oven for 2 hours. Remove and cool complexly in tin, standing on a wire rack. When quite cold, chill for at least 2 hours before removing sides of tin and transferring to a serving plate. Decorate as wished, using whipped cream, fruit, cinnamon or nutmeg. Serves 10–12.

Torta di Ricotta

PASTRY: 2 cups flour; 125 g (4 oz) butter; 1 egg yolk, beaten.

FILLING: 750 g (1¹/₂ lb) ricotta cheese; ¹/₂ cup caster sugar; ¹/₂ cup ground almonds; grated rind 1 lemon; ¹/₂ tsp vanilla; 4 eggs.

PASTRY: Sift flour into bowl and rub in butter until mixture resembles fine breadcrumbs. Add egg yolk and enough iced water to make a firm dough. Chill for 1 hour. Roll out dough and use to line a greased 23 cm (9 in) pie plate. Chill for 1 hour.
FILLING: Combine ricotta, sugar, almonds and lemon rind. Beat in vanilla and eggs, one at a time. Pour into chilled pastry case and bake in a preheated hot oven (220°C/425°F) for 5 minutes, then reduce heat to moderate (180°C/350°F) and bake for a further 30 minutes or until centre of filling is firm. Cool and chill. Serves 8.

Country Cheesecake

CRUST: 2 tbs finely ground unblanched almonds; 1¹/₂ cups plain sweet biscuit crumbs; 2 tbs sugar; ¹/₃ cup melted butter.

FILLING: 375 g (12 oz) cream cheese; 2 eggs, beaten; ¹/₂ cup plus 1 tbs caster sugar; 1 tsp lemon juice; salt; 1¹/₂ cups sour cream; ¹/₂ tsp vanilla.

DECORATION (optional): whipped cream; toasted flaked almonds.

Combine almonds, crumbs and sugar. Pour in melted butter and mix well. Press into bottom and side of a greased 20 cm (8 in) springform tin. Bake in a preheated moderately hot oven (190°C/375°F) for 10 minutes. Allow to cool thoroughly.
FILLING: Beat cream cheese, eggs, ¹/₂ cup sugar, lemon juice and ¹/₂ tsp salt until smooth and creamy. Put into prepared crust and bake in oven for about 20 minutes, or until just set. Turn off heat and allow cake to cool in oven. Combine sour cream, remaining sugar and vanilla and pinch salt. Pour over filling and bake in a preheated very hot oven (230°C/450°F) for 10 minutes. Allow to cool in oven as before. Chill before serving and decorate, if liked, with a thin layer of whipped cream and almonds. Serves 8.

Semolina Cheesecake

CRUST: 1¹/₂ cups flour; pinch salt; 90 g (3 oz) butter; 1 tsp caster sugar; 1 egg yolk, beaten.

FILLING: 60 g (2 oz) butter; ¹/₂ cup caster sugar; 2 eggs, separated; grated rind and juice 1 lemon; ¹/₄ cup ground almonds; 250 g (8 oz) cottage cheese, sieved; 2 tbs semolina; ¹/₂ cup raisins, chopped.

Sift flour and salt into a bowl and rub in butter until mixture resembles fine breadcrumbs. Add sugar and mix to a firm dough with egg yolk. If necessary, add a little water. Roll out on a lightly floured board and line a 20 cm (8 in) springform tin, pressing the pastry 4 cm (1¹/₂ in) up side of tin. Press down well to remove any air bubbles and trim edges neatly.
FILLING: Cream butter and sugar together until light and fluffy. Lightly beat egg yolks with lemon rind and juice, ground almonds, cottage cheese, semolina and raisins. Mix into creamed butter and sugar. Stiffly beat egg whites and fold in. Turn filling into pastry-lined tin and bake in a preheated moderately slow oven (160°C/325°F) for 50–60 minutes or until pastry is golden and filling is set. Remove side of tin and allow cake to cool on base. Chill before serving. Serves 18.

CHELSEA BUN

See *Yeast Cookery*.

CHERRY

Cherries are delicious fruit eaten fresh or stewed 5–10 minutes in sugar syrup, flavoured with a piece of cinnamon stick, lemon peel, and with a little brandy stirred in before they cool. They have a very short season and are worth preserving so you can enjoy them later in the year. One of the best ways to do this is by preserving them in brandy, when they can be used over ice cream, and the brandy syrup folded through whipped cream or stirred into fruit salad or fruit desserts to give a rich flavour.
See recipes.
Rancin: Line an ovenproof dish with thinly sliced white bread and butter. Fill nearly to top with cherries which have been stoned and cooked for a few minutes with plenty of sugar. Do not add any of the syrup. Cover with a second layer of bread and butter and sprinkle

with sugar. Bake in a preheated hot oven (200°C/400°F) for about 20 minutes or until the top is golden and crisp. Dust with caster or sifted icing sugar and serve warm with cream.

NOTE: Brioche or any rich yeast bread (see separate entries) may be used in place of white bread.

Brandied Cherries

185 g (6 oz) sugar; 1 cup water; 1 strip lemon peel; 1.5 kg (3 lb) dark cherries, stoned; brandy.

Place sugar, water and lemon peel in a saucepan and heat, stirring to dissolve sugar. Bring to the boil and boil for 10 minutes. Add cherries and simmer for 5 minutes more. Pack cherries into warm sterilised jars, half fill with brandy and top up with syrup. Seal and store in a cool, dark place for at least 1 month before using.

CHERVIL

One of the classic French *fine herbes* (the others are parsley, tarragon and chives), used to flavour Omelette aux Fines Herbes and to sprinkle on salads. Chervil is good in all egg dishes and with fish and shellfish. Its leaves are lacy, like those parsley, but a softer and a more delicate green. The flavour is light and distinctive with a hint of anise. It is also available dried.

CHESTNUT

The edible nut is available fresh in winter, and also in cans (whole or puréed) and dried (soak overnight in water, then use as fresh). The kernel is sweet and slightly floury. Chestnuts roasted in the shell are a traditional cold-weather snack; chestnut kernels may be simmered in stock and served as a vegetable or chopped for stuffings; sweetened chestnut purée makes the Italian dessert, *Monte Bianco* (or French, *Mont Blanc*). *Marrons glacés* (glazed chestnuts) are luxurious sweetmeats, served in paper cases or used to decorate cakes.

TO SHELL CHESTNUTS: With a small, sharp knife, cut gashes in the shape of a cross on flat side of brown outer shell. Put nuts in a pan of cold water, bring quickly to the boil and boil 1 minute. Turn off heat. Remove one nut at a time, peel off shell and rub off inner skin. Any nut which resists peeling may be returned to the hot water for a few minutes.

TO ROAST CHESTNUTS: Cut a cross in outer shells as described above. Place in a pan with an ovenproof handle. Add 1 tbs oil for each 500 g (1 lb) nuts. Shake over moderate heat until sizzling, then place in a preheated moderate oven (180°C/350°F) for about 30 minutes, when shells and skins will come off easily. See recipes.

Monte Bianco *(Mont Blanc)*

Prepare as close to serving time as possible to achieve the best effect.

1/4 cup sugar; 1/3 cup milk; 1 x 440 g can unsweetened chestnut purée; 1 cup cream; 1 tbs rum; grated chocolate to decorate.

Dissolve sugar in milk over a gentle heat. Add chestnut purée and stir until smooth. Cool, then chill. Whip cream and fold half into chestnut mixture with rum. Fill a greaseproof paper funnel with chestnut cream and pipe so that it falls loosely into cone shape on 6 individual serving plates. Top with remaining cream and sprinkle with grated chocolate. Serves 6.

NOTE: If using sweetened chestnut purée omit sugar and milk; simply fold whipped cream and rum into purée.

Chestnut Soup

45 g (1 1/2 oz) butter; 2 onions, chopped; 1 rasher bacon, rind removed and finely chopped; 1 carrot, diced; 1 stick celery, chopped; 1 x 440 g can unsweetened chestnut purée; salt and freshly ground black pepper; 6 cups chicken stock; Croûtons (page 105) to garnish.

Melt butter in a heavy saucepan, add onion, bacon, carrot and celery and cook until softened. Stir in chestnut purée, salt and pepper and stock. Simmer for about 30 minutes. Put soup through a sieve or purée in a blender or food processor. Reheat and serve garnished with croûtons. Serves 6.

Chestnut Stuffing

250 g (8 oz) butter; 2 large onions, very finely chopped; 1 tsp dried thnyme; 1 tsp dried sage; 1 1/2 tsp salt; 1/2 tsp pepper; 1/3 cup chopped parsley; 3/4 cup chopped celery; 4 cups fresh breadcrumbs; 500 g (1 lb) chestnuts, cooked, shelled, skinned and chopped.

Melt butter in a frying pan and add all ingredients except breadcrumbs and chestnuts. Cook for 5 minutes, then add crumbs and chestnuts. Cook, stirring until crumbs are crisp. Use as a stuffing for turkey. Makes about 8 cups.

NOTE: Canned whole chestnuts may be used in the recipe.

Whole Braised Chestnuts

500 g (1 lb) chestnuts, shelled and skinned; 1 cup chicken stock; 3 tsp cornflour; 2 tbs dry sherry; salt and freshly ground black pepper; 60 g (2 oz) butter.

Place chestnuts in a heavy saucepan. Cover with stock to a depth of 1 cm (1/2 in). Mix cornflour and sherry to a smooth paste, pour over chestnuts, add salt and pepper and dot with butter. Simmer, covered, over lowest possible heat for 50 minutes or until chestnuts are tender. Serve as a separate dish or mix with red cabbage or Brussels sprouts as an accompaniment to turkey.

NOTE: Canned whole chestnuts may be used in this recipe, but simmer for 10 minutes.

Frozen Chestnut Soufflé

1¹/₂ cups icing sugar, sifted; 6 egg yolks; 2 cups milk; 2 cups cream; 1 x 440 g can unsweetened chestnut purée; 1 quantity Crème Anglaise (page 111) to serve.

Whisk sugar and egg yolks together in a heatproof bowl until very light and fluffy. Scald milk and gradually add to egg yolk mixture in a steady stream, beating slowly. Place bowl over simmering water and cook custard until it is thickened. Strain, cool and chill for 1 hour, stirring occasionally. Whip cream until it holds soft peaks and fold it gently but thoroughly into chestnut purée. Combine chestnut mixture with custard. Freeze, covered, for 24 hours. Soften a little before serving with will-chilled crème anglaise and crisp biscuits. Serves 8–10.

CHICKEN

Modern poultry-raising has put chicken on everyone's table at a reasonable price. The wide availability of chicken fillets (skinless, boneless half-breasts) or suprêmes (see *Supreme of Chicken*) makes it one of the most convenient meats. It has always been one of the most adaptable. As good cold as hot, as ready to go on a picnic, to provide cocktail tid-bits or a speedy meal for one, as to appear, superbly sauced, at a dinner party.

You can be reasonably confident that packaged chicken will be tender. In unpackaged chicken, check that the end of the breastbone will bend readily when pressed – the sign of a young bird.

Organic chicken is the best purchase. Free-range, organic poultry that has been carefully fed and has had time to scratch and peck around the ground rewards with a bird that will taste as it should and has had some sort of a life. Such a bird you pay extra for, but it seems preferable to eat chicken less often and make a meal more special.

WHAT SIZE: Chickens are sold by weight. Another indication of size is by numbers. A size 12 weighs 1.2 kg, size 15 weighs 1.5 kg, size 16 weighs 1.6 kg, size 18 weighs 1.8 kg, etc. A very young chicken is called a spatchcock and usually weighs 0.5 kg. A small chicken (size 12) can be grilled or barbecued. A size 12 to 18 or 20 roasted, poached or used in the recipes as indicated. In this book we have used the various terms, a medium chicken is size 14 to 16, a large chicken size 18 to 26.

TO TRUSS A CHICKEN: Shape the bird neatly with your hands, tucking the neck flap underneath. Take a piece of string and place its centre below the breastbone at the neck end. Bring the ends of the string down over the wings to cross underneath, then up to tie the legs and parson's nose together.

TO JOINT A CHICKEN: Cut off legs at the joints. Cut either side of backbone and remove. Turn bird over and cut either side of breastbone, discard. Cut each side of chicken in half, removing wings if liked.

■ **TO COOK:** Chicken may be cooked in any of the following ways. **See recipes.**

Roast Chicken: Put a little butter and a piece of lemon or a few herbs inside chicken; or if using stuffing, spoon it loosely into cavity. Truss bird and lay it on its side on a greased rack in a roasting tin. Spread chicken with a little butter and place in a preheated hot oven (200°C/400°F) for 10 minutes. Turn chicken over and continue cooking, turning and basting every 15 minutes. Turn chicken on its back for last 20 minutes of cooking. Allow about 25 minutes cooking time per 500 g (1 lb). Chicken is done when juices run clear if a skewer is inserted in thickest part of thigh near body. Allow chicken to rest in a warm place for 20 minutes before carving. Make Clear Gravy or Thickened Gravy to accompany the chicken if desired (see *Gravy*).

French Roast Chicken: This method of roasting gives a beautifully moist chicken, and the skin crisps in the last 10–15 minutes of cooking. Put a few strips of orange peel, a few tarragon or parsley stalks and a little salt and freshly cracked black pepper inside the chicken.

Truss and roast as for Roast Chicken, above, but add ³⁄4 cup chicken stock to the pan at the start of cooking and baste bird with pan juices every 15 minutes. Add more stock if it dries up.

Fried Chicken: Dust pieces with flour and coat with egg and breadcrumbs. Chill 20 minutes to firm crumbs. Shallow-fry in oil and butter over moderate heat, turning once, until golden-brown and cooked through. Breasts will take about 15 minutes, thicker pieces will take about 25 minutes. Drain on crumpled paper towels.

Poached Chicken: Place chicken on its back in a heavy saucepan and add water to come to top of thighs (or just to cover chicken pieces). Add salt, pepper, a few slices of carrot, celery, onion, and a few herbs. Cover and simmer gently, just until thigh meat feels tender when tested with a skewer – about 30 minutes for a young bird. Cool in the liquid.

Braised Chicken (Chicken Casserole): Use pieces or a whole, trussed bird. Brown all over in a little butter in a heavy saucepan or flameproof casserole. Remove chicken, add a little sliced carrot, celery and onion to pan and fry until golden. Place chicken on top of vegetables, add a few herbs, salt and freshly ground black pepper and 2 cups water or stock, with a little wine if liked. Cover and simmer on top of stove or in a preheated moderately slow oven (160°C/325°F) until juices run clear when tested with a skewer in the thickest part. Chicken pieces will take about 30 minutes, a whole bird 1 hour or more. Thicken liquid, if liked, with Beurre Manié (see page 35) at the end of cooking.

Sautéed Chicken: Heat a little oil and butter in a heavy frying pan. Add well-dried chicken pieces, a few at a time, sauté on brisk heat until golden on both sides. Replace leg and thigh pieces in pan, cover and cook on low heat 8 minutes. Add breast and wing pieces, cover and cook 15 minutes more. Turn and baste several times during cooking.

Grilled Chicken: Use very small chickens, or chicken pieces. For whole birds, split in half and cut away back and rib bones. Arrange chicken, skin side down, on a greased rack under a preheated grill. Brush with melted butter and grill at moderate heat, turning once and basting with butter several times. Chicken halves will take 25–30 minutes, pieces 10–15 minutes.

Poached Chicken Breasts

Store in the poaching liquor in a covered bowl to keep them moist and fresh-tasting. Good for any recipe calling for cooked chicken, salads, sandwiches, etc.

4 cups water; $^{1}/_{2}$ carrot, sliced; 2 slices onion; small piece celery; 4 black peppercorns; 2 parsley stalks; I sprig fresh thyme, or pinch dried; I tsp salt; 6 half-breasts of chicken.

Put all ingredients except chicken into a large saucepan and bring to the boil. Place chicken in pan, skin side up, turn heat to low, cover and simmer very gently for 10–15 minutes or until meat is tender when tested with a fine skewer. Place chicken breasts in a refrigerator container and strain liquor over. Cool then refrigerate, covered. If you prefer dark to white meat, use chicken thighs and poach according to this recipe.

Chicken Pie

This recipe is not only good for family meals, but also for winter entertaining.

I large roasting chicken (size 18); I carrot, sliced; I onion, sliced; I bay leaf; I tsp salt; 6 black peppercorns; 90 g (3 oz) butter; 6 mushrooms, halved or quartered; 2 tbs flour; $^{1}/_{2}$ cup cream; freshly ground black pepper; I x 375 g packet frozen puff pastry, thawed; beaten egg yolk to glaze.

Put chicken in a large pan. Add carrot, onion, bay leaf, salt and peppercorns. Cover with hot water to top of thighs and bring to the boil, skimming occasionally. Simmer gently for 20 minutes. Allow chicken to cool in stock for about 1 hour, then remove to a dish. Joint chicken and remove all flesh from bones. Skin and cut into large chunky pieces.

Place chicken meat in pie dish and cover with a little stock to keep flesh moist. Return bones to stock and boil for 10–15 minutes to reduce it. Strain and leave to cool. Measure 2 cups of stock and chill so that fat will rise to the surface and settle for easy removal. (The remaining stock can be used as a base for soups or sauces.)

Melt 1 tbs of the butter in a small frying pan and fry mushrooms over high heat for a few minutes. Remove and add to chicken. Melt remaining butter in a saucepan and blend in flour. Add reserved 2 cups stock, stirring to make a smooth sauce. Stir in cream and season with salt and pepper. Spoon sauce over chicken and mushrooms and mix gently. If you have a pie funnel, place it in centre. Roll out pastry to size which fits pie dish. From remaining pastry, make strip long enough to go around top rim of pie dish. Moisten rim of dish and attach strip to it. Moisten strip and firmly press lid of pastry into place. Cut small leaves of pastry from trimmings and arrange on top. Brush top with beaten egg yolk. Bake in a preheated hot oven (200°C/400°F) for 10 minutes, then reduce heat to moderate (180°C/350°F) and bake for a further 20 minutes. Serve with green vegetables or salad. Serves 4–6.

Chicken Kebabs

Boneless chicken breasts are ideal for kebabs.

4 chicken fillets (skinless, boneless half-breasts); I tbs soy sauce; I tbs Dijon mustard; I tbs brown sugar; I tbs sherry or whisky; I tbs oil; I red or green pepper.

Cut chicken breasts into cubes, about 2 cm ($^{3}/_{4}$ in). Combine remaining ingredients, except pepper, in shallow dish (not metal). Add chicken and marinate, covered, for at least 2 hours. Cut pepper into squares, same size as chicken. Drain chicken, reserving marinade. Thread pieces of pepper and chicken alternately on 8 metal skewers. Grill kebabs under preheated grill, about 13 cm (5 in) from heat, turning and basting with reserved marinade, for 5 minutes or until cooked to taste. Serve with hot buttered rice and, if liked, halved tomatoes, seasoned and grilled with kebabs. For a more informal meal serve a split round of flat Lebanese bread on each plate. The chicken may be slipped off skewers into bread pocket and eaten in hand. Serves 4.

Chicken Schnitzels

The schnitzels are not crumbed in this recipe, but dipped in egg only and then quickly fried for a crisp, light coating.

4 chicken fillets (skinless, boneless half-breasts); salt and freshly ground black pepper; about $^{1}/_{2}$ cup flour; 2 eggs, beaten; 60 g (2 oz) butter; 3 tbs oil.

GARNISH: 4 thin slices lemon; 8 anchovy fillets; capers.

Place chicken fillets between 2 sheets of plastic wrap and flatten them out slightly with a rolling pin. Trim off any very ragged edges with a sharp knife. Season fillets well with salt and pepper and dust lightly with flour. Have beaten eggs in a shallow dish beside stove, and floured fillets on a plate. Heat butter and oil together in a large, heavy pan over medium heat. When foam subsides, quickly dip fillets into egg, then place them at once in pan. Cook until underside is crisp and golden, about 2 minutes, then turn fillets with a spatula and cook other side for 2–3 minutes. Serve at once on heated plates, garnishing each fillet with a thin slice of lemon, 2 drained anchovy fillets arranged crisscross fashion on the lemon, and a few capers. Serves 4.

Fried Chicken Florentine

Anyone who has visited lovely Florence will remember the crispy, succulent fried chicken of that city. Serve with crusty bread and a fresh green salad.

1 x 1.5 kg (3 lb) chicken, or 4–6 chicken pieces;
3 tbs olive oil; 2 tbs lemon juice;
$^1/_2$ tsp salt; freshly ground black pepper;
1 tbs chopped parsley; flour for coating;
oil for frying; 1 egg, beaten.

TO SERVE: lemon wedges; Fried Parsley (page 331).

Cut whole chicken into serving pieces. Combine oil, lemon juice, salt, pepper and parsley and marinate chicken in this mixture for 2 hours, turning pieces occasionally. Dry chicken thoroughly, and coat well with flour. Heat enough oil in a heavy frying pan to come about halfway up sides of chicken pieces. When oil is hot, dip chicken pieces in egg then place at once in oil. Cook over medium heat, turning several times, until chicken is golden and crusty outside and juices run clear when flesh is pierced with a skewer. This will take about 15 minutes. Drain on paper towels, and serve with wedges of lemon and fried parsley. Serves 4.

Roast Chicken with Honey and Orange Sauce

60 g (2 oz) butter; 3 tbs honey; salt; 1 tsp paprika;
1 x 1.5 kg (3 lb) chicken; 1$^1/_4$ cups orange juice;
4 spring onions, chopped; 1 green pepper,
seeded and diced; $^1/_2$ tsp ground ginger;
1 tsp prepared horseradish; 2 tsp cornflour;
orange slices to garnish.

Melt half the butter in a saucepan, remove from heat and blend in honey, salt and paprika. Place chicken in a roasting tin and brush with honey mixture. Pour over $^1/_2$ cup orange juice. Roast in a preheated moderately hot oven (190°C/375°F) for 1–1$^1/_2$ hours or until juices run clear when pierced with a skewer.

Baste every 15 minutes. About 10 minutes before chicken is ready, make sauce. Melt remaining 30 g (1 oz) butter and gently cook spring onions and green pepper. Add remaining $^3/_4$ cup orange juice, the ginger, horseradish and salt and bring slowly to the boil. Simmer for 3–5 minutes. Transfer chicken to a heated platter. Pour pan juices into sauce. Blend cornflour with a little cold water, then stir briskly into sauce. Stir over low heat until thickened. Pour into a heated sauceboat and garnish chicken with orange slices. Serves 6.

Chicken Pilaff

4 half-breasts of chicken, or 6 thighs; 2 onions,
sliced; 90 g (3 oz) butter; 1 cup long-grain rice;
$^1/_2$ cup raisins; 2 cardamom pods; 1 bay leaf;
1 tsp turmeric; 3$^3/_4$ cups water or chicken stock;
$^1/_4$ tsp cloves; $^1/_4$ tsp cinnamon; salt and freshly
ground black pepper.

If using chicken breasts, cut into 2–3 pieces. Fry chicken and onions in butter in a heavy frying pan for a few minutes until golden. Add rice, raisins and turmeric, stir to coat with buttery mixture. Place water or stock in a saucepan and bring to the boil. Add spices, season with salt and pepper and return to the boil. Pour over chicken and rice and mix lightly. Cover, reduce heat and simmer gently for about 25 minutes or until rice and chicken are tender. Serves 4.
VARIATION
BARBECUED CHICKEN PILAFF: Thread chicken on to Satay skewers (soaked in water), and cook over hot coals. Cook rice mixture as above and serve separately.

Roast Chicken Chinese–Style

Take a group to a Chinese restaurant for a meal and invariably one person will choose a crispy chicken to share with the table. Here's how it's done at home. Serve with boiled rice and, if liked, a simple Chinese vegetable dish.

1 x 1.5 kg (3 lb) chicken; 3 tbs soy sauce; 1 tbs honey;
$^1/_2$ tsp ground ginger; 1 tbs dry sherry; 2 tbs finely
chopped spring onions; 3 cloves garlic, crushed;
1 tsp five-spice powder; 3 tsp salt.

Remove any loose fat from inside chicken and wipe inside with paper towels. Combine soy sauce, honey, ginger, sherry, spring onions, garlic and $^1/_2$ tsp five-spice powder. Brush all over chicken and in cavity. Loosen skin of breast and thighs and brush mixture on chicken flesh. Cover and leave in refrigerator for 1–2 hours, turning occasionally. Drain chicken, reserving marinade. Place on rack in roasting tin containing 2 cm ($^3/_4$ in) water to prevent drippings from burning. Roast in a preheated moderate oven (180°C/350°F) for about 1$^1/_4$ hours, turning occasionally and brushing frequently with reserved marinade. Chicken is cooked when juices run clear when thickest part of flesh is pierced with a fine skewer. Chop chicken into serving portions and serve with remaining five-spice powder mixed with salt for dipping. Usually accompanied by rice. Serves 4.

NOTE: Five-spice powder is available at Chinese grocery stores.

Smoked Chicken Hunan-Style

In Hunan they have a way of smoking chicken which is superb – moist, tender meat with a rich smoky flavour and glistening skin. If you haven't got a wok with a lid, use a deep, heavy frying pan with a tight-fitting lid or an electric frying pan.

$^{1}/_{4}$ **cup black tea leaves; 2 tbs brown sugar; I cooked White Chicken (Chinese Steamed Chicken, page 79); I tbs Chinese sesame oil.**

Line inside of a wok and its lid with heavy-duty foil. Mix tea leaves with brown sugar and place in bottom of wok. Put a rack in wok which will keep chicken about 5 cm (2 in) above tea leaves – a round wire cake rack is ideal. If using a wire cake rack in a frying pan, you will probably need to rest it on something else to bring it to required height – e.g., 4 metal egg rings, or the outside rim of a loose-bottomed flan tin. Arrange chicken on rack, breast side up. Cover wok tightly and heat over a moderate heat for 5 minutes or until tea mixture begins to smoke. (If using an electric frying pan, set dial at medium.) Smoke chicken for 10 minutes, then turn it breast side down and smoke for a further 10 minutes. Take wok from heat and allow chicken to stand, with lid on for 15 minutes. Remove chicken and brush skin all over with sesame oil. Place on a cutting board and, using a sharp chopper, cut through bones into serving pieces. The wings should be cut in 2, thighs in 3–4 portions each, drumsticks in 3, and breast into 6–8 pieces. Serve as an appetiser, or part of a Chinese meal. Serves 6–8.

Chicken Japonais

Chicken breasts are first coated with a Japanese-style marinade, then grilled with a sweet glaze. The crispy golden skin is delicious and the flesh moist and tender. Serve with noodles and a salad.

4 half-breasts of chicken; $^{1}/_{2}$ cup dry sherry; $^{1}/_{4}$ cup light soy sauce; I tsp finely chopped fresh ginger; I clove garlic, crushed; I tbs sugar; 2 tbs honey.

Place chicken breasts in a shallow baking dish. Combine sherry, soy sauce, ginger, garlic and sugar and pour over breasts, turning them so all sides are coated with marinade. Cover dish and chill overnight. Drain breasts, reserving marinade, and arrange in grill pan, skin side down. Place under preheated grill for 12 minutes. Meanwhile, make glaze by combining honey and 2 tbs of the marinade. Turn breasts skin side up and continue grilling for a further 8 minutes, brushing several times with glaze. Serves 4.

Thai Chicken Curry

There is little that is plain or bland about the cooking of Thailand, which is rich and highly seasoned, happily blending the themes of Indian and Chinese cooking – as in this recipe. Both whole and ground spices are used and the chicken is stir-fried.

6 chicken pieces (breasts or thighs); juice I lemon; 60 g (2 oz) butter; I tbs oil; 2 onions, finely sliced; I clove garlic, crushed; I cinnamon stick; 4 cardamom pods, crushed; 4 whole cloves; $I^{1}/_{2}$ tbs ground coriander; $I^{1}/_{2}$ tsp turmeric; $^{1}/_{2}$ tsp ground ginger; $^{1}/_{2}$ tsp ground cumin; I small red chilli (optional); I cup chicken stock; 6 dried apricots, soaked, drained and cut into strips; salt; coriander (Chinese parsley) or a few shredded spring onions to garnish.

Remove skin and bones from chicken and cut meat into 2.5 cm (1 in) strips. Sprinkle chicken with lemon juice. Heat butter and oil in a heavy frying pan and stir-fry onions and garlic until onions are soft but not brown. Stir in spices. If a hot curry is desired add chilli or part of chilli. Cook mixture, stirring, for 2–3 minutes, then add chicken and stir-fry until it is well coated with spices and just white. Add stock and simmer for about 10 minutes or until chicken is cooked through. Add apricots with a squeeze of lemon juice and salt to taste. Remove cinnamon and serve in 4 individual dishes. Strew over a few sprigs of coriander, or shredded spring onions, and serve with bowls of boiled rice. Serves 4.

Devilled Drumsticks

8 chicken drumsticks; 3 tbs oil; 2 tsp Worcestershire sauce; 2 tsp finely chopped mango or fruit chutney;

2 tsp cider vinegar; I tbs each English and French mustard; $^{1}/_{4}$ tsp Tabasco sauce; I clove garlic, finely chopped; pinch salt; freshly ground black pepper.

Slash chicken flesh in several places. Mix all remaining ingredients together and spread over chicken, pressing it into slashes. Cover and leave 6 hours, or overnight, in refrigerator, turning pieces over several times. Grill, bony side up, under a preheated moderate grill for 10 minutes, Turn, baste with marinade and grill a further 10 minutes or until done. Serves 4–8.

Velvet Chicken

Visitors to Chinese restaurants know how good velvet chicken can be. It is fairly simple and makes a great contribution to a Chinese meal.

I egg white; $^{1}/_{2}$ tsp salt; I tbs rice wine; I tbs cornflour; 500 g (I lb) skinless chicken breast, sliced into strips; 4 cups water; 3 tbs vegetable oil; $^{1}/_{2}$ cup blanched almonds; 2 tsp finely sliced fresh ginger; I bundle asparagus, cut into diagonal lengths and blanched.

Whisk egg white lightly in a large bowl (it should not be frothy). Add salt, rice wine and cornflour and whisk again lightly just to mix. Add chicken strips and mix well. Cover and refrigerate for 30 minutes.

Bring the water to the boil with 1 tbs of the oil in a wok or wide pan. Add the chicken and keep stirring to separate the strips until the chicken looks white, about 1 minute. Tip into a colander and shake off the liquid. Heat 1 tbs of the oil in the pan and fry the almonds until golden. Scoop out on to paper towels. Heat the remaining oil in the wok, sear the ginger, then quickly toss the chicken strips for 1 minute. Add the asparagus, tossing the mixture. Serve on an oval platter and scatter with fried almonds. Serves 4.

Lotus White Chicken

5 egg whites; $^{1}/_{2}$ cup chicken stock; I tsp salt; I tsp dry sherry; 2 tsp cornflour; 125 g (4 oz) chicken breast meat, skinned and finely chopped; oil for deep-frying; 30 g (I oz) cooked ham, shredded, to garnish.

Put egg whites in a bowl. Stir in 3 tbs of the chicken stock, the salt, sherry and half the cornflour. Add chicken and mix well. Heat oil to 180°C/350°F in a wok or deep-fat fryer. Gently pour in about one third of egg and chicken mixture. Deep-fry for 10 seconds or until mixture begins to rise to surface, then carefully turn over. Fry until golden, then remove from pan with a slotted spoon. Drain and place on a heated serving dish. Keep hot while cooking remaining chicken mixture in same way. Heat remaining stock in a small pan. Mix the rest of the cornflour to a paste with a little cold water, add

to stock and simmer, stirring, until thickened. Pour over the chicken. Garnish with ham. Serve hot. Serves 4.

White Chicken
(Chinese Steamed Chicken)

This method is excellent and may be used for any recipes specifying cooked chicken. You will find it makes the flesh firm, white, tender and juicy. Use a fresh, unfrozen chicken for best results.

I x I.5 kg (3 lb) chicken; about 3 litres (12 cups) water; I tsp salt; 2 spring onions, chopped; $^{1}/_{4}$ cup peanut oil; extra salt.

Place chicken in a large, heavy saucepan and add sufficient water to cover the chicken well. When you have established the amount of water you will need, remove chicken. Add salt and spring onions to water and bring to the boil. Lower chicken back into pan, bring back to the boil and simmer for 5 minutes. Cover pan, remove from heat and let chicken cool in the liquid for 2 hours. Remove chicken from pan, rinse under cold water and dry with paper towels. Brush skin all over with peanut oil and sprinkle generously with extra salt. Use as desired for Coriander Chicken, pages 95–6, or for chicken salads, creamed chicken etc. The cooking liquid makes a very good light chicken stock, for light soups, sauces and gravies.

NOTE: When cool and just before serving, chop chicken into 5 x 2 cm (2 x 1 in) pieces and arrange on plate.

Chicken à la King

3 tbs butter; 3 tbs flour; I$^{1}/_{2}$ cups chicken stock or cream; 2 cups cooked chicken, diced (see Poached Chicken, page 76); $^{1}/_{2}$ cup sliced mushrooms, sautéed; $^{1}/_{4}$ cup canned pimiento, cut into strips; I egg yolk, beaten; salt and freshly ground black pepper; $^{1}/_{4}$ cup slivered, blanched almonds; I tbs dry sherry.

Melt butter in a heavy saucepan, stir in flour and cook for 2 minutes over low heat. Gradually add chicken stock or cream, stirring until sauce thickens and boils. Add chicken, mushrooms and pimiento. Pour some sauce over egg yolk and mix well, then return to mixture in pan. Cook gently, stirring until thickened slightly. Season with salt and pepper and fold in almonds and sherry. Serve at once with boiled rice or noodles. Serves 4–6.

NOTE: To reheat, place in a heatproof bowl over boiling water.

CHICKEN KIEV

Chicken Kiev at its finest is simply a boned and flattened chicken breast wrapped around chilled butter lightly flavoured with chives. It is then dipped in egg and breadcrumbs and fried golden-crisp. Pierced with a fork, the chicken releases a jet of golden butter (unwary diners should be warned!) and the combination of liquid butter and juicy chicken is perfection, with no further dressing-up needed. If you order chicken Kiev and find it flavoured with garlic, or with mushrooms added to the filling, it is a chef's unnecessary variation. Follow the recipe below, and you will be making it as it was created in Kiev in Russia, and is still served there today.

Chicken Kiev

1 whole chicken breast, cut from a large chicken, with wing attached; 30 g (1 oz) butter; salt and freshly ground black pepper; 2 tbs finely snipped chives; flour for coating; 1 egg, lightly beaten; 1 cup fresh white breadcrumbs, rubbed through a sieve; oil for deep-frying.

Cut chicken breast in half. With a sharp, pointed knife remove bones from breast, leaving wing joints (including bones) attached. Cut wing off at first joint and scrape meat off bone so it is clean and attached to breast. Peel away skin. Place 2 pieces of breast between 2 sheets of greaseproof paper or plastic wrap and pound until thin with a mallet or the end of an empty wine bottle. Cut butter into 2 pieces and roll each into a cork shape. Chill. Place a roll of butter at base of each chicken breast, diagonally in line with wing bone. Sprinkle with salt, pepper and chives. Fold chicken flesh over butter, then roll up towards bone, folding sides in as you go to enclose butter completely inside chicken. The flesh will adhere without skewers. Coat each rolled breast lightly with flour, dip in egg and roll in breadcrumbs. Refrigerate for at least 2 hours. Heat oil in large saucepan, using enough to cover chicken breasts. To test if oil is hot enough, drop a cube of bread into it. The bread should rise to the surface immediately. Gently lower chicken into oil and fry for $4\frac{1}{2}$–5 minutes or until golden-brown. (This is the only tricky part to chicken Kiev. The oil must be hot enough to brown chicken breast, but not colour it too much before chicken is cooked through.) If chicken starts to brown too quickly during this time, lower the heat. Remove from oil, drain on paper towels and serve immediately, with warm straw potatoes (the packaged variety will do). Serves 2.

NOTE: If you are buying chicken breasts already cut and boned, the wing joint may be removed. If this is so, proceed with the recipe ignoring the missing wing joint.

CHICKEN WINGS

Many people think the wing is the best part of the chicken. Certainly the wings contain meat that is tender, full of flavour and can be prepared in an endless variety of ways. They make an economical dish to serve a crowd, provide delectable mini-drumsticks to serve with drinks, and are perfect in dishes from China, Italy, Spain or in almost any cuisine imaginable. Chicken wing tips, which are usually removed, make well-flavoured chicken stock, and the trimmed wing can then be used according to your recipe. Buy chicken wings from delicatessens, poultry shops, or supermarkets. **See recipes.**

Barbecue Chicken Wings

Guests can nibble these while waiting for the main barbecued food.

1 kg (2 lb) chicken wings, tips removed; 2 tbs tomato purée; 2 tbs cider or wine vinegar; 2 tbs oil; 1 tbs Dijon mustard; 2 cloves garlic, crushed, 1 tbs salt.

Place wings in a large bowl. Mix together remaining ingredients and spoon over wings. Marinate, covered, for several hours or overnight in refrigerator, turning wings occasionally to coat evenly. Drain wings of marinade, and barbecue or grill under a preheated moderate grill until crisp and brown on both sides. Or bake in a preheated moderately hot oven (190°C/375°F), turning once. Cooking time on grill or in oven will be 10–15 minutes. Serves 4.

Southern Fried Chicken Wings

1 kg (2 lb) chicken wings, tips removed; 3 cups milk; 1 cup flour; salt; $^{1}/_{4}$ tsp white pepper; $^{3}/_{4}$ cup vegetable oil; 2 tbs butter; 3 cloves garlic, unpeeled; 1 onion, finely chopped; $^{1}/_{4}$ tsp dried sage; extra 4 tsp flour; 1 cup chicken stock; $^{1}/_{4}$ cup cream; $^{1}/_{2}$ tsp Worcestershire sauce; $^{1}/_{4}$ tsp cayenne.

Place chicken wings in a bowl, cover with 2 cups milk and chill for 1 hour; drain. In a plastic bag combine flour, salt and pepper. Shake wings in bag until they are well coated with flour. Shake off excess flour. Heat oil in a deep frying pan until very hot. Add butter, whole garlic cloves and chicken wings and fry for about 7 minutes or until tender and golden-brown. Turn every now and then with a spoon. Drain on crumpled paper towels and keep warm. Pour off all but 2 tbs fat from pan and discard garlic. Add onion and sage and cook until onion softens. Mix in extra 4 tsp flour and cook, stirring, until gravy thickens and boils. Stir in the cream, Worcestershire sauce and cayenne, bring to the boil, and strain gravy into a sauceboat. Serve gravy with chicken wings. Serves 6.

Chicken Wings Provençale

1 kg (2 lb) chicken wings, tips removed; 2 tbs olive oil; 1 butter; 1 onion, finely chopped; 2 cloves garlic, crushed; 1 large green pepper,

cored, seeded and cut in 2.5 cm (1 in) pieces;
1/2 cup dry white wine; 1 cup chicken stock;
1 x 425 g can tomatoes; 1 tsp tomato paste;
2 tsp chopped fresh marjoram, or 1/2 tsp dried;
2 tsp chopped thyme, or 1/2 tsp dried; 1 bay leaf;
12 black olives; chopped parsley to garnish.

Halve wings at joints. Heat olive oil and butter in a
frying pan and fry chicken wings over moderately
high heat until golden-brown. Remove and keep
warm. Add onion, garlic and green pepper and cook
until onion is softened. Add wine and reduce over
high heat for 1 minute. Add chicken wings, stock,
tomatoes and juice, tomato paste, marjoram, thyme
and bay leaf. Bring to the boil, then lower heat and
simmer, covered, for 15 minutes longer or until
chicken wings are tender. Transfer chicken wings to
heated serving platter. Reduce liquid over moderately
high heat to about 1 cup, discard bay leaf, and pour
over chicken wings. Garnish with chopped parsley.
Serves 4–6.

Chicken Wings Italian–Style

1/2 cup olive oil; juice 1 lemon; 1 tbs chopped
parsley; salt and freshly ground black pepper;
1 kg (2 lb) chicken wings, tips removed; 1 cup flour;
2 eggs, lightly beaten; oil for deep-frying.

Combine olive oil, lemon juice, parsley, salt and pepper.
Add chicken wings, turning to coat thoroughly.
Marinate, covered, for 1 hour at room temperature or
overnight in refrigerator. Drain chicken and dredge
with flour to give a light coating. Dip in beaten egg
and deep-fry in hot oil for about 5 minutes or until
tender and golden-brown. Drain on crumpled paper
towels and serve immediately. Serves 4–6.

Chicken Wings in Black Bean and Oyster Sauce

1 kg (2 lb) chicken wings, tips removed;
2 tbs soy sauce; 2 tbs dry sherry; 1 tbs peanut oil;
2 tsp cornflour; 1 tsp sugar; 3 tsp very finely chopped
fresh ginger; 2 tbs canned black beans; 2 tbs very
finely chopped spring onions; 2 cloves garlic,
crushed with pinch salt; 1/2 cup chicken stock;
2 tbs oyster sauce; 2 tsp sesame oil; 1/4 cup sliced
spring onions to garnish.

Halve wings at joints. Combine soy sauce, sherry,
peanut oil, 1 tsp cornflour, the sugar and 1 tsp ginger.
Add wings, coat well with marinade and marinate,
covered, at room temperature for 1 hour. Rinse, drain
and chop black beans. Combine with chopped spring
onions, remaining ginger and garlic. Preheat a wok or
frying pan, add black bean mixture and stir-fry for 30
seconds. Add wings and marinade and stir-fry for
3 minutes or until wings are browned lightly. Stir in

remaining cornflour dissolved in stock and simmer,
covered, for 15 minutes or until wings are tender.
Cook uncovered, over high heat, tossing wings until
they are glazed and sauce thickened. Stir in oyster
sauce and sesame oil and cook mixture, tossing it, for
1 minute. Serve on a heated platter, sprinkled with
sliced spring onions. Serves 4–6.

NOTE: Buy canned black beans, oyster sauce and
sesame oil from Chinese grocery stores, health food
shops, delicatessens and most supermarkets.

Spiced Chicken Wings with Chick Peas

1 kg (2 lb) chicken wings, tips removed; salt;
1/2 tsp ground ginger; 1/2 cup oil; 2 large onions,
finely chopped; 2 cloves garlic, crushed;
2 tsp ground coriander; 2 tsp ground cumin;
1 tsp cinnamon; pinch cayenne; 2 cups chicken
stock; freshly ground black pepper; 2 cups canned
chick peas (garbanzos), drained.

Sprinkle wings with salt and ginger. Heat oil in a
large frying pan and brown wings over moderately
high heat. Transfer to a casserole dish. Add onions
and garlic to frying pan and cook until onions soften.
Stir in spices and cook for 1 minute, then add chicken
stock, salt and pepper. Arrange drained chick peas
over chicken wings and pour stock mixture over.
Cover and cook in a preheated moderate oven
(180°C/350°F) for 25 minutes. Remove lid and bake
5 minutes longer. Serve with plenty of crusty bread
and a salad. Serves 4–6.

CHICK PEA

See *Pulses: Dried Beans, Peas and Lentils.*

CHICORY

A group of plants cultivated for their leaves. Chicory or
Belgian endive was first grown in Belgium, where it is
called *witlof*. Its elongated yellowish leaves, with pale
green tips, are tightly bunched together. Sliced across,
with leaves separated, it makes a lovely salad, dressed
with a little lemon juice and olive or walnut oil. It can
be mixed with julienne (matchstick) strips of cooked
beetroot or slices of orange.

BRAISED CHICORY: Blanch whole heads in a little boiling
salted water, drain, then cook in a little melted butter and
stock. In this way it is particularly good with veal, chicken
or ham. **See recipes.**

Creamed Chicory

6 heads chicory; 90 g (3 oz) butter; salt and freshly
ground white pepper; pinch nutmeg; 1/2 cup cream.

Cook chicory in boiling salted water for 10–15 minutes.
Drain, pressing well to remove as much water as

possible. Heat butter in a frying pan, add chicory, salt, pepper and nutmeg and sauté over brisk heat for about 3 minutes. Add cream and bring to the boil, shaking pan until cream thickens a little. Serves 4–6.

VARIATION

PUREE OF CHICORY: Prepare 6 heads chicory as for Creamed Chicory. When cooked, purée in a food processor fitted with a steel blade or in a blender. Reheat before serving. Good with roast beef, pork or duckling. Serves 4–6.

Chicory Flamande

A version of braised chicory served as a first course or as a vegetable accompaniment.

6 heads chicory; 60 g (2 oz) butter;
juice 1 lemon; ^{2}/3 cup chicken stock; 1 tsp salt;
1 tsp sugar; freshly ground white pepper;
paprika or chopped parsley to garnish.

Arrange chicory in a buttered ovenproof dish. Melt butter with lemon juice, stock, salt, sugar and pepper and pour over chicory. Cover with lid or a piece of buttered greaseproof paper and cook in preheated moderate oven (180°C/350°F) for 35–40 minutes. Remove lid and brown top under a preheated grill. Sprinkle with paprika or chopped parsley. Serve 6.

Chicory and Walnut Salad

A lovely salad. If liked, a tablespoon of walnut oil may replace the same amount of olive oil used in the recipe.

2 tbs red wine vinegar; 1 tsp Dijon mustard; 2 tsp salt; ^{1}/3 cup olive oil; 1 tsp black pepper; ^{1}/2 cup coarsely chopped walnuts; 4 firm heads chicory, quartered lengthways; 2 cups watercress sprigs.

Mix together vinegar, mustard and salt in a bowl, then add olive oil, pepper, and walnuts. Wrap chicory and watercress in a tea-towel and refrigerate to chill and crisp them. When ready to serve, put greens in a salad bowl, pour dressing over them, and toss gently. Serves 4.

CHILE CON CARNE

A Texan dish of beans and beef in a chilli sauce, now popular all over the USA and in other parts of the world. The meat may be diced or minced, and the amount of chilli depends on the cook – though the original version was fiery.

Chile Con Carne

2 tbs bacon dripping or butter; 1 large onion, finely chopped; 1 large clove garlic, finely chopped; 750 g (1^1/2 lb) stewing beef, minced or diced; 1 x 425 g can tomatoes; 2 x 310 g cans kidney beans,

drained; ^{1}/2 bay leaf; 2 tsp–2 tbs chilli powder (to taste); salt; pinch brown sugar.

Melt fat in a large, heavy saucepan and cook onion and garlic gently until golden. Add beef and brown lightly. Chop tomatoes and add with the juice, the beans, bay leaf, chilli powder, salt and brown sugar. Stir, cover tightly and simmer very gently for about 1 hour for minced meat, 1^1/2 hours or until tender for diced meat. Discard bay leaf. Serve with Tortillas or Corn Bread (see pages 545 and 96). Serves 8.

CHILLIES

These small, fiery members of the pepper family are essential to Latin American, Indian and much of Southeast Asian cuisine. They are used in cooking, as condiments and garnishes and as a flavouring for vinegar and pickles. Unripe (green or yellow) chillies are juicier, with more flavour; ripe (red) chillies, either fresh or dried, are hotter. The dried ones give brighter colour but are less fragrant than the fresh ones. The heat of chillies also differs from one variety to another – the tiny bird's-eye chilli is particularly fiery.

TO HANDLE WHOLE CHILLIES: Working under cold, running water, make a slit down the side of the chilli and scrape out the seeds with the point of a knife. Take care not to touch your nose or eyes as the juice will burn them, and always wash your hands well after handling chillies. Before chopping or grinding dried chillies, tear each one into 3–4 pieces and soak in hot water for 10 minutes. Squeeze out excess moisture before using.

OTHER WAYS TO ADD CHILLI FLAVOUR: Chilli powder is made from ground, dried chilli flesh. Asian-style powder is hotter than Mexican-style powder, which contains cumin and other spices as well as chilli. Sambal ulek (or oelek) is a paste of fresh chillies ground with salt. Chilli sauce combines chillies with other aromatics and comes in various degrees of heat.

See also *Tabasco*.

CHINESE PARSLEY

See *Coriander*.

CHIPOLATA

Chipolatas are especially small sausages, often pan-fried or grilled and served with cocktail sticks and a sauce for dunking. Chipolatas are also used to garnish roast chicken or the Christmas turkey, in which case they are not separated, but cooked in a string and draped around the festive bird like a necklace.

CHIVES

A member of the onion family. Chives grow in clumps of slender green tubular leaves. With their delicate flavour and bright green colour, chives go particularly well with cheese, eggs and potatoes – especially baked potatoes, split open and piled with sour cream, topped with snipped chives.

Chives grow easily in the garden or in pots; they need plenty of sun and the more you cut them the more they grow. Chives are usually cut up small with scissors to prevent their bruising, and added to foods just before serving.

Use them fresh in any of the following ways: sprinkle over puréed soups (e.g. tomato, avocado, vichyssoise, potato); add to beaten eggs for an omelette; sprinkle over scrambled eggs; add to a cheese sandwich; snip over cooked potato or add to creamy mashed potatoes; sprinkle over glazed carrots, green salads, or raw or cooked tomatoes.

GARLIC CHIVES: Garlic chives, Chinese chives, Chinese leek, ku chai or nira is a relatively new vegetable in the English-speaking world. The plant has a distinctive growth habit with strap-shaped leaves. Regular chives, on the other hand, have hollow round spears. The subtle garlic flavour of these chives is perfect for use in dishes where raw regular garlic would be overwhelming or too spicy. The flowers and stems of the budding or flowering chives are edible; simply discard the tough ends. Garlic chives are used regularly in Chinese stir-fries, vegetable dumplings and soups.

Shredded Beef with Garlic Chives

500 g (1 lb) rump or porterhouse beef steaks; 3 tbs soy sauce; 2 tbs Chinese rice wine (Shaoshing) or dry sherry; 2 cloves garlic, finely chopped; 1 tsp grated ginger; 3 tbs vegetable oil; 2 onions, peeled and cut into eighths, lengthways; 1 bunch garlic or Chinese chives, cut into short lengths; 1/2 red chilli, seeded and sliced.

Trim beef of fat and sinews and shred finely. In a bowl mix the beef shreds with soy sauce, wine, garlic and ginger, allowing about 30 minutes for seasonings to be absorbed. Heat the oil a heavy-based frying pan or wok. Add the onions, tossing and stirring until they soften, about 2–3 minutes. Keeping the heat high, add beef with seasonings, chives and chilli, and continue frying for 3 minutes longer, stirring and tossing all the while. Serve hot with steamed rice. Serves 4.

CHOCOLATE

Chocolate and cocoa are made from the bean of the cacao tree. Chocolate was first enjoyed as a hot drink, later it was used for baking, then a great development took place in Switzerland when someone thought of combining milk and chocolate for eating.

Chocolate is more than a delicacy; it is good solid food and nourishment and is considered as such by many nations. Chocolate is part of army rations in time of stress. Mountaineers carry it with them as a matter of course. French children eat it on bread instead of butter and jam, and the comfort derived from a bar of chocolate when one is feeling tired is not to be underestimated.

Chocolate is also used in baking – chocolate cake is an international favourite. It is essential to some of the world's most delicious cakes and sweets – truffles, éclairs, chocolate mousse. Chocolate sauce is superb with ice creams or spooned over profiteroles. **See recipes.**

See also *Cocoa.*

TYPES OF CHOCOLATE AND THEIR USES

Dark chocolate is semi-sweet (the less sugar that is added to chocolate, the stronger its flavour) and ideal for cooking. Use for icings, mousse, sauces etc.; it has a high fat content so is easy to melt and the sugar in it helps to produce a good sheen.

Milk chocolate, available in bars, has dried milk added to the formula. It is lighter and milder than chocolate without milk added, and is used primarily as an eating chocolate.

Chocolate pieces, packaged in bits, is a semi-sweet dark chocolate. They retain their shape to some extent in baking, and are especially adapted to biscuit or cookie making – see Tollhouse Cookies, page 84.

Powdered or drinking chocolate was introduced before eating chocolate; use in hot or cold milk drinks.

Cooking chocolate is a semi-sweet dark chocolate. Cheap cooking chocolate compounds are available and are suitable for use in cakes.

TO MELT CHOCOLATE: It burns so easily it is best to melt it on a plate or in a bowl over a pan of hot water – if chocolate is overheated it scorches. Break up or grate chocolate first so it melts more evenly and quickly.

TO MAKE CHOCOLATE CURLS (or thin chocolate shavings for topping pies, ice cream or desserts): Use a swivel-bladed vegetable parer. Have chocolate at room temperature, pare little curls of chocolate from edge of the block. Store in refrigerator until required.

TO MAKE CHOCOLATE CARAQUE: This is the classic chocolate decoration for cakes and many desserts. It takes practice and skill to make, but is well worth the trouble. Shred or grate 90 g (3 oz) good dark chocolate and melt it on a plate over a pan of hot water. Do not allow the plate to get too hot and work chocolate with a palette knife. Spread it thinly on a marble slab. When just on point of setting, curl it off with a thin knife – the chocolate will form long scrolls or flakes. Place these on greaseproof paper and chill in refrigerator; handle carefully. Keep in an airtight container if necessary.

Chocolate Glaze: Melt together 60 g (2 oz) butter and 60 g (2 oz) dark chocolate in a bowl over a pan of hot water. Beat in 2 tbs boiling water, 1 cup icing sugar, sifted, a pinch of salt and 1/4 tsp vanilla. Use as a glaze over chocolate cake.

Rum Chocolate Frosting: Melt 90 g (3 oz) dark chocolate with 1/2 cup rum over a low heat. Add 4 cups icing sugar, sifted, 1 cup at a time, beating well after each addition. Beat in 60 g (2 oz) soft butter. Add a little more rum, if necessary, to make frosting of spreading consistency. Use to frost and fill chocolate cakes or gâteaux.

Chocolate Mint Sauce: This is one of the easiest recipes for chocolate sauce. Put 12 chocolate peppermint creams in a small bowl that will fit over a pan of boiling water. Melt creams, then stir in ½ cup cream. Serve warm or cool, spooned over ice cream, or poached or canned pears. Serve 4.

Mexican Chocolate: This is especially prepared for making into drinks, and is strongly flavoured with cinnamon. You can get the same effect by melting 30 g (1 oz) grated dark chocolate in a mug of hot milk, with ¼–½ tsp cinnamon added. Beat with a whisk until foamy, adding a little brown sugar if you prefer it sweeter.

Chocolate Cake *(For a Crowd)*

½ cup cocoa powder; ½ cup boiling water; 185 g (6 oz) butter; 1½ cups caster sugar; 1 tsp vanilla; 3 eggs, beaten; 2 cups self-raising flour; pinch salt; ¼ tsp bicarbonate of soda; ¾ cup milk.

TO SERVE: raspberry jam; whipped cream.

Blend cocoa with boiling water and cool. Cream butter with sugar until light and fluffy. Beat in vanilla and eggs. Gradually mix in cooled cocoa mixture. Sift flour, salt and bicarbonate of soda and fold into creamed mixture alternately with milk. Spoon into a greased and floured 28 x 19 x 4 cm (11 x 7½ x 1½ in) lamington tin. Bake in a preheated moderate oven (180°C/350°F) for 30–35 minutes or until a fine skewer inserted in the centre comes out clean. Leave to stand in the tin for a few minutes, then turn out on to a wire rack to cool. Cut into squares and serve with raspberry jam and a bowl of whipped cream.

Honey Chocolate Cake

185 g (6 oz) butter; 1 cup lightly packed brown sugar; ⅓ cup honey; 2 eggs, beaten; 3 tsp rum; ½ tsp vanilla; 2 tbs cocoa powder; 1¾ cups self-raising flour; pinch salt; ½ cup sweet sherry.

TO FINISH: whipped cream; almond essence; icing sugar or Chocolate Glaze (see above).

Cream butter with brown sugar and honey until light and fluffy. Add eggs one at a time, beating well after each addition. Add rum and vanilla. Sift cocoa, flour and salt together 3 times. Fold into creamed mixture alternately with sherry. Spoon into a greased and bottom-lined 23 cm (9 in) round cake tin. Bake in a preheated moderate oven (180°C/350°F) for 45 minutes or until a skewer inserted in the centre comes out clean. Cool in tin for 5 minutes, then turn out on to a wire rack. When cold, split cake into 2 layers and fill with whipped cream flavoured with a few drops of almond essence. Dust top with sifted icing sugar or top with chocolate glaze.

Chocolate Syrup

Serve over ice cream, pancakes, steamed puddings or use to flavour milk drinks.

185 g (6 oz) dark chocolate, melted, or 1 cup cocoa powder; nut of butter (optional); 1½ cups sugar; ¼ tsp salt; 1 cup boiling water; 1 tsp vanilla.

Blend melted chocolate or cocoa with sugar and salt. Add butter, if liked, for a richer syrup. Place in a saucepan with boiling water and cook over medium heat for 5 minutes, stirring constantly. Cool, then stir in vanilla. Makes 2 cups.

Chocolate Sauce

An inexpensive but great recipe. Serve hot or cold over ice cream.

½ cup drinking chocolate powder; 1 cup evaporated milk; 1 tbs golden syrup; ½ tsp vanilla; 2 tsp butter.

Combine drinking chocolate with evaporated milk and golden syrup in a saucepan. Bring to the boil, stirring constantly, then simmer for 5 minutes. Remove from heat and add vanilla and butter. Makes 1¼ cups.

Tollhouse Cookies

An old-time American cookie which has become very popular since the availability of chocolate bits in the packet.

1¼ cups flour; ½ tsp bicarbonate of soda; ½ tsp salt; 125 g (4 oz) butter; ¼ cup firmly packed brown sugar; ½ cup white sugar; 1 egg, beaten; 1 tsp vanilla; 1 x 100 g packet choc-bits.

Sift flour, bicarbonate of soda and salt together. Cream butter with sugars until light and fluffy. Add egg and vanilla and beat well. Stir in sifted dry ingredients and choc-bits. Drop teaspoonfuls on to greased baking trays, leaving room for spreading. Bake in a preheated moderate oven (180°C/350°F) for 10 minutes. Cool on wire racks. Makes about 36.

Chocolate Roll

A lovely, light-as-air chocolate roll with very little flour, can have a rich brandy cream filling or, if you want a dessert, a filling of strawberries and cream.

$^1/_2$ cup flour; $^1/_4$ tsp salt; $^1/_2$ tsp baking powder;
60 g (2 oz) cooking chocolate, broken up; 4 eggs;
$^3/_4$ cup caster sugar; I tsp vanilla; 2 tbs cold water;
$^1/_2$ tsp bicarbonate of soda; sifted icing sugar.

Sift together flour, salt and baking powder. Melt chocolate gently in a heatproof bowl over hot water. Cool slightly. Beat eggs with caster sugar until very light and thick. Fold flour mixture and vanilla all at once into egg mixture. Add water and bicarbonate of soda to chocolate, stirring until smooth. Fold quickly and lightly into egg and flour mixture. Turn mixture into a greased and lined 38 x 25 x 2.5 cm (15 x 10 x 1 in) Swiss roll tin, or a paper case (see below). Bake in a preheated hot oven (200°C/400°F) for about 15 minutes or until cake springs back when centre is gently pressed. Loosen edges and turn cake out on to a tea-towel generously dredged with icing sugar. Peel off lining paper and trim edges of cake with a sharp knife. Roll immediately in towel, first folding hem of towel over edge of cake, and rolling towel in the cake to prevent sticking. After cake is rolled, cool on a wire rack for at least 1 hour.

Before serving, carefully unroll cake and quickly spread with whipped cream sweetened with a little sugar and flavoured with vanilla or brandy, then sprinkle with sliced strawberries if you wish. Re-roll cake, using tea-towel to help, and dust with more icing sugar. The cake can be decorated with rosettes of whipped cream and the rosettes topped with chocolate caraque (see page 83) or whole strawberries.

TO MAKE A PAPER BAKING CASE: Choose a fairly thick greaseproof paper or non-stick paper. Take a piece 30 x 43 cm (12 x 17 in) and fold over ends and sides to form a border about 2.5 cm (1 in). Cut a slit at each corner and fold one cut piece over the other to mitre corner. Fasten each corner with a paper clip so borders stand up. Slide case on to a baking tray before filling with mixture.

Hot Chocolate Soufflés

This is an easy way to make last-minute soufflés in individual dishes.

125 g (4 oz) dark chocolate; 3 tbs brandy or coffee;
5 eggs, separated; 4 tbs sugar; I cup cream,
whipped, to serve.

Melt chocolate with brandy or coffee in a heatproof bowl over hot water. Beat egg yolks with sugar until very pale and thick. Beat in chocolate mixture. Beat egg whites until firm but not dry and fold in egg yolk mixture with a large metal spoon. Spoon into 4 x $^3/_4$-cup, or 6 x $^1/_2$-cup, individual soufflé dishes that have been greased with unsalted butter, filling them about three quarters full. Place on a baking tray, arranging so the dishes do not touch each other. Bake on the bottom shelf of a preheated moderately hot oven (190°C/375°F) for 15–18 minutes. Serve immediately on heated plates. Pass whipped cream: each guest makes a hole in the centre of soufflé and fills it with a dollop of whipped cream. Serves 4–6.

Chocolate Cherry Squares

185 g (6 oz) dark chocolate; 60 g (2 oz) butter;
220 g (7 oz) digestive biscuits, crushed; grated rind
I orange; $^1/_2$ cup sultanas; $^1/_4$ cup chopped glacé
cherries; glacé cherries to decorate.

Melt chocolate and butter in a bowl over a pan of hot water. Remove from heat. Add crushed biscuits with orange rind, sultanas and cherries. Mix well and press into a greased 18 cm (7 in) square tin. Mark into 9 squares and decorate with halved cherries. Chill before cutting into squares. Makes 9.

No Bake Fruit Bars

150 g (5 oz) sweet biscuits, crushed; $^1/_2$ cup chopped
walnuts; $^1/_2$ cup sultanas; 2 tbs golden syrup;
75 g (2$^1/_2$ oz) butter; 60 g (2 oz) dark chocolate.

Grease a shallow 18 cm (7 in) square tin. Mix biscuits with walnuts and sultanas. Heat golden syrup, butter and chocolate in a bowl over a pan of hot water. Pour into biscuit mixture and mix well. Spoon into the prepared tin and smooth surface with a palette knife. Chill until set, then cut into small bars. Makes 14.

Chocolate Mousse

125 g (4 oz) dark chocolate, broken up; 2 tsp instant
coffee powder, dissolved in I tbs hot water; 4 eggs,
separated; 2 tsp rum or brandy; cream to serve.

Place chocolate and coffee in a small heatproof bowl over hot water and stir until chocolate is smooth and melted. Remove from heat and blend in egg yolks one at a time, stirring until thoroughly combined. Beat egg whites until stiff and gently fold into chocolate mixture with rum or brandy. Spoon into 6 mousse pots and chill for 4 hours or overnight. Serve with pouring or whipped cream, or pipe a swirl of whipped cream on top and finish off with chocolate curls or caraque (see page 83) or candied violets. Serves 6.

CHOKO

A delicate pale green, pear-shaped vegetable which makes its first appearance at the end of summer and continues on until early winter. It is one of the most attractive and delicious of vegetables. The choko, which is related to the gourd family, originally came from

Mexico, where it is still considered a great delicacy. In Mexico it is known as chayote.

When you buy chokos, look for young, tender ones, with a pale green, almost translucent, skin. The spikes on the skin should be short and soft. Older chokos have a lighter coloured, opaque skin, and the spikes are quite brittle. Often, towards the end of the season, you may notice the seed protruding from the bottom of the choko, another indication that the choko is likely to be old and possibly tough.

■ **BASIC PREPARATION:** Cut choko into quarters along the natural grooves, peel and remove the centre core. It is best to do this under cold running water, as the choko exudes a sticky liquid which stains the hands. Very young chokos need not be peeled, just halved – the skin is quite tender.

■ **TO COOK:** Drop choko quarters into boiling salted water and simmer for 5–8 minutes until just tender. Drain them, toss in butter and chopped fresh herbs.

Chokos with Ham: Drain cooked chokos, cut in dice or in wedge shapes. Return to heat. Season with salt and pepper, stir in ¼ cup cream, ½ cup diced ham and 1–2 tbs chopped parsley. Heat through over gentle heat.

CHOP SUEY

The name literally means 'bits and pieces' and is a Chinese way of dealing with leftovers or small quantities of food. It originated in the USA, and is served over steamed rice.

Chop Suey

2 tbs peanut oil; 250 g (8 oz) pork loin or fillet, very finely sliced; ½ Chinese cabbage, shredded; 125 g (4 oz) green beans, sliced diagonally; 2 onions, halved and sliced lengthways; 2 sticks celery, sliced diagonally; 2 tsp cornflour; I cup chicken stock; I tbs soy sauce; 250 g (8 oz) cooked chicken (Chinese Steamed Chicken, page 79); 250 g (8 oz) green prawns, shelled and deveined; I cup sliced bamboo shoots.

Heat oil in a wok or large frying pan, add pork and cook until well browned, about 5 minutes. Add cabbage, beans, onions and celery and toss until all ingredients are well combined. Stir-fry a further 3 minutes. Mix cornflour with a little stock and add to remaining stock with soy sauce. Pour into wok and stir until sauce boils and thickens. Add chicken, prawns and bamboo shoots and cook 3 minutes or until prawns are cooked. Served with Chinese-Style Rice (see page 414). Serves 4.

CHORIZO

A spicy, coarse-textured sausage very popular in Spain. It can be sliced and eaten alone or with crusty bread, cheese and black olives, or used in cooking.

Chicken Catalonia

¼ cup olive oil; I kg (2 lb) chicken pieces; 125 g (4 oz) chorizo sausage, finely sliced; 125 g (4 oz) boned pork leg or loin, cubed; 125 g (4 oz) cooked ham, cubed; I large onion, chopped; I tomato, chopped; I green pepper, cored, seeded and sliced; I¼ cups long-grain rice; 2½ cups boiling stock; ½ tsp saffron, crumbled; ½ cup sliced green beans; I tsp salt; ½ tsp black pepper; ½ cup frozen or shelled fresh peas; I canned pimiento, sliced; chopped parsley to garnish.

Heat oil in a large frying pan or paella dish. Brown chicken on both sides, then transfer to a plate. Add sausage, pork and ham, brown lightly and remove to a plate. Put onion in frying pan and brown lightly over gentle heat. Add tomato and green pepper, and cook for 2 minutes. Stir in rice and cook, stirring, for 3 minutes. Add stock, saffron, beans, sausage, pork, ham and chicken and bring back to the boil. Season with salt and pepper. Cook over gentle heat for 25–30 minutes or until rice and chicken are tender and liquid is absorbed. It may be necessary to add more stock or water during cooking to prevent dish becoming too dry. Stir in peas and pimiento for last 10 minutes of cooking. Sprinkle with chopped parsley before serving. Serves 6–8.

CHOWDER

A thick fish or seafood soup to which salt pork or bacon and diced vegetables are added, cream or milk making up part of the stock. It takes its name from the French word for pot or cauldron, *chaudière*, but is now more associated with New England and Newfoundland. Manhattan Clam Chowder and New England Clam Chowder vie with each other for popularity in the United States.

Old–fashioned Fish Chowder

This recipe may also be made with smoked fish. Poach the fish to remove excess salt, then flake and use as for fresh fish.

125 g (4 oz) pickled (salt) pork, diced, or 4 rashers bacon, rind removed and diced; 2 onions, finely sliced; 3 potatoes, peeled and diced; 2 tbs flour; 4 cups Fish Stock (page 509); I kg (2 lb) cod, gemfish or any firm white fish fillet, cut in chunks; 2 cups hot cream or milk; 2 tbs butter; salt and freshly ground white pepper; 2 tbs chopped parsley.

Cook pork or bacon very gently in a heavy saucepan, until fat has melted and meat is brown. Remove and reserve pork or bacon. Add onions to fat in pan and cook over low heat until golden. Stir in potatoes and flour, and toss until coated. Add fish stock and cook about 10 minutes. Add fish chunks and simmer, partially covered, until fish is tender, about 10 minutes. Stir in hot, but not boiling, cream or milk and heat very slowly, without boiling. Add pork or bacon and butter, then season with salt and pepper and stir in parsley. Serves 6.

NOTE: Use head and bones from filleted fish to make stock. A good brand of packaged fish soup may be used in place of the home-made stock.

VARIATIONS

MANHATTAN CLAM CHOWDER: Make as for Old-fashioned Fish Chowder, substituting 2 cups chopped clams (canned do very well) for fish and 3 cups cooked or canned tomatoes for the fish stock. Add also ½ cup diced green pepper with the potato.

NEW ENGLAND CLAM CHOWDER: Make as for Old-fashioned Fish Chowder, substituting 2 cups chopped clams (canned or fresh) for the fish.

CHOW MEIN

'Food with noodles' is the literal translation. Diced chicken, pork or seafood is stir-fried in oil with Chinese vegetables, then finished with a sauce and served with fried noodles.

Chow Mein with Seafood

3½ tbs oil; I onion, sliced; 2 rashers bacon, rind removed and chopped; I x 185 g can crabmeat, drained; 3 tbs soy sauce; 375 g (12 oz) Chinese noodles, cooked in boiling water and drained well; 2½ tbs butter; 3 slices fresh ginger, chopped; 3 cloves garlic, crushed; I small red pepper, seeded and shredded; 6 oysters; 250 g (8 oz) green prawns, shelled and deveined; 3 spring onions, sliced; salt and freshly ground white pepper; I tsp sugar; 2 tbs dry sherry.

Heat oil, add onion and bacon and stir-fry for 1 minute. Add crabmeat and 2 tbs soy sauce, and stir-fry for 1 minute. Mix in noodles and remaining soy sauce and stir-fry for 1 minute. Reduce heat to low and simmer gently 3–4 minutes. Heat butter in a separate small frying pan over medium heat, add ginger, garlic, red pepper, oysters and prawns. Stir-fry for 1 minute. Sprinkle with spring onions, salt, pepper, sugar and sherry. Stir-fry for a further 1 minute. Spoon the noodles mixture into a large serving bowl and spoon prawn mixture over. Serves 2–4.

CHRISTMAS CAKE

The rich and spicy fruit cake of England, made a few months before 25 December so that it will mature into a festive cake, is one of the joys of Christmas. It may be topped with halved almonds before baking, and finished off with a sprig of holly. Some prefer a more elaborate iced version: a coating of almond paste, then an icing. A few Christmas decorations, a fir tree, a toy Santa Claus, Christmas bells or an appropriate greeting may be used to give a dash of colour.

Christmas Cake

I Rich Fruit Cake (pages 164–5); ½ quantity Almond Paste (page 3).

GLAZE: 3 tbs apricot jam; 2 tbs water; I tsp lemon juice.

ICING: 2 egg whites; 500 g (I lb) pure icing sugar, sifted; I–2 tsp lemon juice.

Make cake 2 months before Christmas, and store in an airtight tin until required.

GLAZE: Bring apricot jam and water to the boil and boil for 4 minutes. Push through a sieve, return to saucepan with lemon juice and heat through. Brush hot glaze over top of cake. Roll out almond paste into a round to fit top of cake. Place on cake and gently press with edge of rolling pin. Leave at least 24 hours before icing.

ICING: Whisk egg whites to a light froth and gradually add icing sugar, beating well. Stir in lemon juice and continue beating until icing stands in soft peaks. Spread icing over top and sides of cake. Rough up icing around sides and edge of cake to resemble drifting snow. Decorate with any suitable Christmas decoration. A little of the icing may be set aside, coloured, and used to write Merry Christmas on the cake. Leave icing to set overnight.

CHRISTMAS PUDDING

The Christmas pudding, stuck with a piece of holly, flaming with lighted brandy or rum, served with brandy or rum butter or with a rich custard or cream, is one of the highlights of an English Christmas dinner. Plum or Christmas puddings always improve with keeping, which allows the mixture to mature.

Rich Christmas Pudding

250 g (8 oz) raisins, chopped; 60 g (2 oz) chopped mixed candied peel; 250 g (8 oz) currants; 250 g (8 oz) sultanas; 3 tbs overproof rum or brandy; 250 g (8 oz) butter; 250 g (8 oz) brown sugar; grated rind I orange and I lemon; 4 eggs, lightly beaten; 60 g (2 oz) blanched almonds, chopped; I cup flour, sifted; ½ tsp each salt, mixed spice, nutmeg, ground ginger, cinnamon and bicarbonate of soda; 2 cups fresh breadcrumbs; extra rum or brandy to serve.

The day before, mix raisins, candied peel, currants and sultanas, sprinkle with rum or brandy and leave overnight. The next day, cream butter with sugar and fruit rinds until light and fluffy. Add eggs a little at a time, then stir in fruit and almonds alternately with dry ingredients and breadcrumbs. Put into a large well-buttered 6-cup pudding basin bottom-lined with a round of greased greaseproof paper. Cover with another round of greased greaseproof paper (to fit over top of pudding basin) then with a pudding cloth which has been scalded, wrung out and floured lightly, or use a large sheet of foil. Tie firmly with string. Steam, covered, in a saucepan with boiling water to come halfway up sides of pudding basin, for 6 hours. Add more boiling water as necessary. Remove from water and when cold cover with fresh greaseproof paper. On Christmas Day put pudding into a saucepan of boiling water as described above and steam for 2½ hours. Turn hot pudding on to a heated serving plate. Warm a little rum or brandy in a soup ladle or small saucepan, set alight and pour over pudding at the table. Serve immediately. Serves 8.

CHURRO

This golden choux pastry fritter is a Spanish favourite. Churros make a lovely dessert, though in Spain they are usually served with a mug of hot chocolate as a recklessly fattening snack.

Churros

Oil for deep-frying; I quantity Choux Pastry (page 345), sweetened; sifted icing sugar.

Heat 10–13 cm (4–5 in) oil in a large, deep saucepan until it gives off a slight haze. Using a pastry bag fitted with an 8 mm (⅜ in) star pipe, pipe 13 cm (5 in) lengths of choux pastry into the oil, holding bag high so that pastry falls in thin strips, and cutting off with a knife as each churros is formed. Fry for 3–5 minutes or until golden-brown all over, rolling with a spoon to brown evenly. As churros are cooked, lift out with a slotted spoon and drain on crumpled paper towels. Dredge generously with icing sugar while still warm. Serve immediately. Makes about 12.

VARIATION

STRAUBEN (RUFFLES): The German equivalent of churros. Prepare in the same way, but cut pastry in 5 cm (2 in) lengths as it is piped into the hot oil.

CHUTNEY

This word, of Hindustani origin, describes a well-seasoned relish or pickle that originates in India. Chutney is the standard accompaniment to curried dishes. It may be made from a mixture of chopped fruits, spices, acids and sugar, cooked slowly until thick, while some chutneys are a combination of fresh fruits, chopped, seasoned and served uncooked. Chutney can also be served with cold meat, cheese, or as a sandwich filling. **See recipes.**

Mango Chutney

2 cups cider vinegar; 2¼ cups sugar; 2 large firm mangoes, peeled and sliced; ¾ cup preserved ginger, chopped; 2 cloves garlic; I tsp mustard seeds; ½ tsp salt; ½ cup raisins; ½ cup sultanas.

Combine vinegar and sugar in a heavy saucepan and bring to the boil. Add remaining ingredients and cook for 8–10 minutes or until mango slices are almost tender. Remove fruit with a slotted spoon. Bring syrup back to the boil and continue cooking until reduced to half original volume and quite thick, about 15 minutes. Return fruit to syrup, return to the boil and pour into hot sterilised jars. Seal. Makes about 6 cups.

NOTE: May be made with other fruits, such as 4 peaches or 12 apricots.

Pineapple Chutney

6 small dried hot red chillies; 2 x 425 g cans pineapple chunks; 3 cups white vinegar; 2 cups firmly packed brown sugar; 2 tsp salt; I cup raisins; 2 tbs finely chopped preserved ginger; 3 cloves garlic, crushed; I cup chopped blanched almonds.

Soak chillies in cold water for 30 minutes, then drain and remove seeds. Chop chillies. Drain syrup from pineapple into heavy saucepan. Add chillies, vinegar, sugar, salt, raisins, ginger and garlic. Bring to the boil, reduce heat and simmer for 10 minutes. Add pineapple and simmer for 45 minutes longer or until thick. Add almonds. Pour into hot sterilised jars and seal. Makes 6 cups.

Tomato Chutney

I kg (2 lb) ripe tomatoes, peeled; I½ cups sugar; I cup cider vinegar; I tsp chopped garlic; I tsp salt; ¼ tsp cayenne; I tsp ground ginger.

Cut tomatoes into eighths. Combine with sugar, vinegar, garlic, salt and cayenne in a saucepan. Cook until syrup thickens and tomatoes are soft, about 45 minutes. Add ginger and cook for 5 minutes more. Pour into hot sterilised jars. Cool and seal. Makes about 2½ cups.

Apple Chutney

4 large cooking apples, peeled, cored and chopped; ¾ cup sultanas; 4 medium onions, finely chopped; I clove garlic, chopped; ½ cup sugar; I tsp salt; 2 tsp ground ginger; 2 tsp dry mustard; ¼ tsp cayenne; ⅓ cup chopped dates; ⅓ cup chopped preserved ginger.

SPICED VINEGAR: 2 cups white vinegar; 2 tsp black peppercorns; I tsp mustard seeds; I tsp whole allspice; 2 tsp brown sugar.

SPICED VINEGAR: Place ingredients in an enamel-lined saucepan, bring to the boil, remove from heat and leave until cold. Strain. Combine with ingredients for chutney in enamel-lined saucepan and simmer gently for about 1½ hours or until thick. Spoon into sterilised jars. Cool and seal. Makes 6 cups.

Apple and Plum Chutney

5 large cooking apples, peeled, cored and chopped; 12 small dark plums, stoned and sliced; 2 large onions, chopped; 1 cup sugar; ³/4 cup sultanas; 2 tsp dry mustard; 2 tsp salt; 2 tsp ground ginger; ¹/4 tsp cayenne; 2 cups white vinegar.

Combine ingredients in an enamel-lined saucepan, and simmer very gently for about 2 hours, until thick. Spoon into hot sterilised jars. Cool and seal. Makes about 6 cups.

Apricot Chutney

250 g (8 oz) dried apricots, soaked overnight in water to cover; 4 chillies, seeded and chopped; 1¹/2 cups firmly packed brown sugar; 1¹/2 tsp salt; chopped fresh ginger; 2 cups brown vinegar.

Combine apricots and soaking water with remaining ingredients in an enamel-lined saucepan and simmer gently for about 1 hour or until mixture is thick. Spoon into sterilised jars. Cool and seal. Makes 3 cups.

Bengal Chutney

3 cloves garlic, chopped; 4 medium onions, finely chopped; 7 cooking apples, peeled, cored and chopped; 3¹/2 cups brown vinegar; ³/4 cup firmly packed brown sugar; 3 tsp salt; ¹/2 tsp cayenne; 1 tbs chopped fresh ginger; 1 tbs black mustard seeds; ³/4 cup raisins.

Combine garlic, onions, apples and vinegar in an enamel-lined saucepan. Simmer about 15 minutes or until onions and apples are soft. Cool, then add remaining ingredients and bring back to the boil. Simmer for about 30 minutes or until thick. Spoon into hot sterilised jars. Cool and seal. Makes 6 cups.

Choko Chutney

3 medium chokos, peeled, seeded and chopped; 3 large cooking apples, peeled, cored and chopped; 3 medium onions, chopped; 1 cup sugar; 2 cloves garlic, chopped; 2 tsp ground ginger; ¹/2 tsp ground cloves; ¹/2 tsp cayenne; 3 ¹/3 cups white vinegar; ¹/2 cup treacle; 3 tsp salt.

Combine ingredients in an enamel-lined saucepan and simmer for about 1 hour or until mixture is thick. Spoon into hot sterilised jars. Cool and seal. Makes about 4 cups.

CIDER

The juice of apples that have been ground to a pulp and pressed to extract their juice; the juice is then fermented to make alcoholic cider or processed without fermenting to make non-alcoholic cider. Cider is consumed with much relish in Central Europe, Germany, Austria and Switzerland. Sparkling cider, made sparkling by a number of processes, is a great favourite of the British.

Cider is enjoyed mainly as a drink but is also used, like beer, in batter, casseroles or in baking. Unless otherwise stated, alcoholic and non-alcoholic ciders are interchangeable in cooking. **See recipes.**

Cider Muffins

2 cups flour; 2 tsp baking powder; ¹/3 tsp salt; ¹/2 cup sultanas; 1 cup apple cider; 90 g (3 oz) butter, melted; 1 egg, lightly beaten.

TOPPING: ¹/4 cup sugar; 1¹/2 tsp cinnamon.

Sift flour, baking powder and salt into a bowl. Add sultanas and toss to coat evenly with flour. Combine cider, butter and egg, then pour over flour mixture, stirring until just blended. The batter will be lumpy. Spoon into well-greased muffin pans, filling two thirds full. Combine sugar and cinnamon, and sprinkle over muffins. Bake in a preheated hot oven (200°C/400°F) for 20–25 minutes or until browned and risen. Makes 12.

Apple Cider Cup

2 dessert apples, peeled, cored and thinly sliced; thinly pared rind and juice 1 lemon; 8 cloves; 4 tbs sugar; 4 cups cider; 2 cups soda water (or ¹/2 syphon soda water).

Put apples into a bowl with lemon rind and juice and cloves. Heat sugar and 1 cup cider until boiling, then pour over ingredients in bowl and leave to cool. When cold add rest of cider and soda water. Makes 7 cups.

CIGARETTES RUSSE

The name means 'Russian cigarettes'. These crisp, rolled biscuits are a classic accompaniment to creamy or fruit desserts.

Cigarettes Russe

2 egg whites; ¹/2 cup caster sugar; 90 g (3 oz) butter, melted; 2–3 drops vanilla; ¹/2 cup flour, sifted.

Beat egg whites and sugar with a fork until smooth. Stir in melted butter, vanilla and flour. Place 1 small teaspoonful of mixture on one half of a buttered and floured baking tray and, using a metal spatula, spread to an oblong shape about 13 x 8 cm (5 x 3 in) in size. Spread out another teaspoonful of mixture on other half of tray, spacing well apart. Bake in a preheated moderately hot oven (190°C/375°F) for 5–6 minutes or until golden. Remove immediately from oven and cool 1–2 minutes, then lift from tray with a thin-bladed knife and place upside-down on the table. Working quickly, wind each biscuit round the handle a wooden spoon. Remove at once, and cool. Bake the remaining biscuits in the same way. Store in an airtight container. Makes 15–20.

NOTE: To test whether mixture is the correct consistency, bake 1 biscuit first. If it is too firm and hard to remove from tray, add an extra 1–2 tsp melted butter. If too soft and difficult to handle, add 1–2 tsp flour.

CINNAMON

With its sweet, spicy smell, cinnamon gives an indefinable, delicious haunting quality to many foods, It is the bark of a tropical tree, trimmed from the thin branches and dried in the sun to form curled-up 'quills'. The finest quality is pale yellow-buff in colour and looks like a roll of dried paper. It is also sold ground, in powder form.

Whole cinnamon, in sticks, is used when cooking corned beef or smoked pork, for the court bouillon for fish or in curry dishes and in many rice dishes like Pilau or Pilaff (see *Rice*). It is also used in pickling, in the cooking of many dried pea, bean and lentil dishes, and pears and apples poached with a piece of cinnamon are delicious.

Ground cinnamon is widely used in baking and in flavouring fruits and desserts, also rice custard, custard and eggnog. In Middle Eastern, Oriental and South American cooking, ground cinnamon is used in meat, seafood and sauce cookery. **See recipes.**

Cinnamon Sticks

Apple sauce and whipped cream are good to serve with cinnamon sticks, and they are also good with coffee.

4 very thick slices fresh white bread, crusts removed; 45 g (1¹/₂ oz) butter, softened; 4 tbs caster sugar; 2 tsp cinnamon.

Cut each slice of bread into 3 sticks, spread with butter and roll in a mixture of sugar and cinnamon. Place on greased baking tray and bake in preheated hot oven (200°C/400°F) for about 8 minutes. Makes 12.

Cinnamon Toast

4 thick slices fresh white bread; 30g (1 oz) butter; 2 tbs sugar; 1 tsp cinnamon.

Toast bread under a preheated hot grill. Butter each slice, then sprinkle with mixture of sugar and cinnamon. Return to grill until topping bubbles. Remove crusts and cut into fingers or triangles. Serves 2–4.

Cinnamon Tea Cake

1 egg, separated; ¹/₂ cup sugar; ¹/₂ cup milk; ¹/₂ tsp vanilla; 1 cup self-raising flour, sifted; 30 g (1 oz) butter, melted.

TOPPING: butter for brushing; ¹/₂ tsp cinnamon ; 1 tbs sugar.

Beat egg white until stiff. Add egg yolk, and gradually beat in sugar, beating well between additions. Mix milk and vanilla, and add a little at a time. Gently stir in flour and melted butter. Pour into a greased 18 cm (7 in) sandwich tin. Bake in a preheated moderately hot oven (190°C/375°F) for 20–25 minutes. While still hot, brush with melted butter and sprinkle with a mixture of sugar and cinnamon. Serve warm or cold with butter.

Cinnamon – Ricotta Mousse

A lovely dessert, like a beautiful cheesecake in a glass – can be mixed in 5 minutes.

250 g (8 oz) ricotta cheese; 1 tsp grated lemon rind; 2 egg yolks; ¹/₄ cup caster sugar; 1 tsp cinnamon; 2 tbs dark rum; ¹/₂ cup grated chocolate; strawberries or grated chocolate to decorate.

Beat ricotta and lemon rind until very smooth and creamy. In a separate bowl, beat egg yolks until light, then add sugar, cinnamon and rum and beat for 2 minutes. Combine the 2 mixtures and fold in chocolate. Spoon into 4 glass bowls or tall glasses, and chill for 1 hour. Top with fresh strawberries or grated chocolate to serve. Serves 4.

CLAM

There are many different kinds of saltwater bivalves called clams, the word being an American term for a shell that closes tightly. North America is the place to appreciate clams. But there are similar and equally fine varieties of clam to be found elsewhere in the world. In France, you may be offered *clovisses*, *palourdes* or *praires*; in Italy, *vongole*, *tartufi di mare*; in Spain, *almejas* or *margaritas*; while in Australia cockles and pipis are to be found on the seashores and in fish markets.

Clams are available fresh all the year round; they can also be bought canned or bottled in a liquid brine. The giant Pacific clam, with its tough flesh, is usually minced and canned or frozen for use in soups etc., mainly for consumption on the Asian market.

Fresh clams are best eaten raw with just a squeeze of lemon juice, like oysters. The Italians use tiny clams as a sauce with pasta, the Japanese eat them raw and in soups; and American clam chowder is an international dish (see page 86). They are a good addition to risotto, fritters or they can be stewed in their own juices in a thick tomato sauce for serving with pasta.

Clams are opened much like mussels or oysters – a flat

knife is inserted between the 2 shells in front of the muscle that holds them together; then they are dipped in water to remove sand. They may also be steamed open.

CLOVE

One of the best known and loved of all spices. The little brown clove buds shaped like nails vary in size, depending on their age and where they come from. Cloves should be bought whole, not ground. If a little is needed in powder form, the central 'bobble' can easily be crushed.

Cloves are often stuck in an onion and put in the stock pot, into ham, or used to flavour milk for white or cream sauces and bread sauces. They are also used with stewed apple, in mincemeat, and a single clove will do wonders for a beef stew. In the East cloves go into many types of curry and they are also used in pickles.

Kourambiedes

These little morsels pierced with a clove and coated with icing sugar are sometimes known as Greek shortbreads.

250 g (8 oz) butter, softened; ¹/₃ cup caster sugar; 1 egg yolk; 3 cups flour, sifted; ¹/₂ cup finely chopped almonds; whole cloves; sifted icing sugar.

Cream butter with sugar until light and fluffy. Add egg yolk and beat well. Stir in flour alternately with almonds. Knead mixture lightly and form into a ball. Roll small pieces of dough into balls the size of hazelnuts, and press a whole clove into centre of each. Place on greased baking trays and bake in a preheated slow oven (150°C/350°F) for 25–30 minutes. While still warm, toss biscuits in icing sugar and place on wire racks to cool. Serve in tiny paper patty cases, if you wish. Makes about 70.

COCK-A-LEEKIE

Nourishing soups are a great tradition of Scottish cooking. You can serve cock-a-leekie with the chicken in it, or serve the broth first and the chicken as the main course. Some recipes include a little chopped bacon and a few prunes in the ingredients.

Cock–a–Leekie

1 large chicken (size 18) with its giblets; 10 cups water; 2 tsp salt; 6 leeks, shredded; 1 onion, chopped; 2 tbs rice; good pinch white pepper; 1 tbs chopped parsley.

Truss chicken and put it into a large saucepan with water, salt and giblets. Bring slowly to the boil and skim well. Cover and simmer gently for 1 hour. Add leeks, onion and rice and continue to simmer until chicken is tender. Remove chicken and giblets, and skim off any excess fat from top of soup, remove meat from bones and cut it into chunks. Cut giblets into pieces and return with chicken meat to the pot. Add pepper, parsley and more salt if required, and reheat soup. Serves 6–8.

COCOA

A product of the cacao bean which, when fermented, roasted, hulled and ground, produces a rich, reddish-brown liquid which contains about 50 per cent of the fat called cocoa butter. It is at this stage that cocoa and chocolate undergo their separate processes. To make cocoa a proportion of the cocoa butter is removed; the remaining liquid sets rock hard and is then pulverised. This needs to be sweetened before it becomes palatable. Unlike cocoa, chocolate retains all the natural cocoa butter found in the liquid extracted from the beans, so is a richer product than cocoa.

When using cocoa to make a hot drink, it should be mixed to a paste with a little cold milk or water before being added to the hot milk, otherwise it will be lumpy. To improve the flavour of drinking cocoa, let it simmer a minute or two, then whisk it to a froth before serving.

Instant cocoa, known as drinking chocolate, is pre-cooked cocoa to which sugar and flavourings have been added. It mixes into hot milk easily and does not require cooking. Cocoa powder is used in flavouring cakes, biscuits and desserts, indeed some people prefer cocoa to chocolate for a chocolate cake or sauce.

See also *Chocolate*.

COCONUT

The fruit of the coconut palm, which is one of the most important trees of the tropics. The hard, brown hairy shell, with 3 basal pores commonly known as 'eyes', protects a layer of white, sweet, edible flesh, and the coconut juice, which can be extracted by puncturing 2 of the eyes. Chilled, it makes a refreshing drink or it can be used to make coconut milk (see below). The flesh of the coconut can be grated or shredded and eaten as is or used for cooking. Or it may be dried to make desiccated and shredded coconut, which may be dry or semi-moist.

■ **BASIC PREPARATION:** Pierce eyes with a screwdriver or ice pick. Drain juice and reserve for drinking or cooking. Tap all over shell with a hammer, then break open. To grate white flesh, use grater or work pieces in a blender. See recipes.

Coconut Milk: It may be made with fresh or desiccated coconut. For 1 cup coconut milk, combine in a saucepan 1½ cups flaked, grated or desiccated coconut and 1½ cups milk. Simmer over low heat, stirring once or twice, about 2 minutes. Strain, pressing mixture well to extract milk. Use in a curry sauce or other recipes that call for coconut milk, or chill and serve as a drink.

Coconut Cream: is made by chilling coconut milk; the

'cream' that rises to the top is skimmed off and used in curry sauces or desserts.

TO TOAST COCONUT: Spread desiccated or shredded coconut on a baking tray. Bake in a preheated moderate oven (180°C/350°F) for about 15 minutes until light brown, stirring frequently, or toast under a hot grill.

TO TINT COCONUT: Mix a few drops of food colouring into desiccated or shredded coconut and toss lightly until evenly coloured. Tinted coconut is used for decorating cakes, biscuits, etc.

Raspberry Slices

125 g (4 oz) butter; 1 cup caster sugar; 2 eggs; 1¹/₂ cups self-raising flour, sifted; pinch salt; raspberry jam; 1 cup desiccated coconut.

Cream butter with ½ cup sugar until light and fluffy. Add 1 egg. Mix in flour and salt. Spread in a well-greased or lined 35 x 25 x 2 cm (14 x 10 x ¾ in) tin. Spread with raspberry jam. Beat remaining egg and sugar together, add coconut, and spread mixture over jam. Bake in a preheated moderate oven (180°C/350°F) for about 20 minutes. When cold, cut into thin slices. Makes 24.

Coconut Pyramids

pinch salt; 2 egg whites; 1 cup caster sugar; 1 tsp vanilla; 1¹/₂ cups desiccated coconut.

Add salt to egg whites and whisk until stiff. Fold in sugar, vanilla and coconut using a metal spoon. Pile in small pyramids on a baking tray lined with buttered foil or rice paper and press into neat shapes. Bake in a preheated cool oven (140°C/275°F) for 45 minutes or until pale fawn. Cool on trays. Makes about 14.

Coconut Cones

¹/₂ x 400 g can sweetened condensed milk; 1 tsp vanilla; 2²/₃ cups desiccated coconut.

Put condensed milk, vanilla and coconut in a bowl and mix well. Scoop out in small portions, about the size of a walnut, and shape into cones. Place on greased baking trays (lined with rice paper, if liked). Bake in a preheated moderate oven (180°C/350°F) for about 10 minutes or until lightly tinted. Cool on trays. Makes about 18.

Coconut Tarts

1 quantity Biscuit Pastry (page 343); 12 tsp jam; 1 cup desiccated coconut; ¹/₂ cup sugar; 1 egg, beaten.

Roll out dough and use to line 12 small tart tins, about 8 cm (3 in) in diameter. Place 1 tsp jam in bottom of each pastry case. Combine coconut and sugar and beat in egg. Place spoonfuls in cases on top of jam. Bake the tarts in a preheated moderate oven (180°C/350°F) for about 20 minutes or until golden-brown. Stand in tins for a few minutes, then transfer to a wire rack to cool. Makes 12.

Coconut Ice

One of the easiest sweets to make, coconut ice is a long-time favourite. It has a soft yet firm texture, keeps well without refrigeration and the combination of white and the palest of pale pinks makes it irresistible.

500 g (1 lb) icing sugar; 250 g (8 oz) desiccated coconut; 2 egg whites, lightly beaten; 1 tsp vanilla; 125 g (4 oz) solid white vegetable shortening, melted and cooled; pink food colouring.

Sift icing sugar into a bowl and stir in coconut. Make a well in the centre and add egg whites and vanilla. Add shortening and stir thoroughly into sugar mixture. Divide mixture in half and tint one half pink with food colouring. Press white half evenly over bottom of greased and foil-lined 8 x 25 cm (3 x 10 in) bar tin. Press pink half evenly over white. Allow to set, then cut into pieces. Makes about 30 pieces.

COEUR A LA CREME

One of the simple, pastoral, sweet dishes of France.

Coeur à la Crème

250 g (8 oz) cream cheese; 1¹/₄ cups cream; 1 tbs caster sugar; 2 egg whites; extra 1 cup cream to serve.

Press cheese through a fine wire sieve, then beat in cream and sugar. Beat egg whites until they hold soft white peaks and lightly but thoroughly fold them in to cheese mixture. Turn into a muslin-lined mould (see below), place over a bowl and leave in refrigerator to drain overnight. When ready to serve, unmould on to a serving dish, remove muslin and pour cream over. Surround with strawberries, or serve with other fresh lightly poached fruits or with redcurrant jelly. French Bar-le-Duc jelly, famed for its excellence, is the traditional choice. Serves 4.

NOTE: The classic Coeur à la Crème mould is a little heart-shaped basket or perforated porcelain mould. You can improvise by piercing holes in a cream or cottage cheese carton, or simply use a round sieve.

COFFEE

Coffee is not only a beverage without which many of us would find life impossible, but one of the great flavours in cooking. Its distinctive fragrance enhances cakes, meringues, icings and fillings, and desserts both hot and cold. Whole coffee beans are used to flavour one of the most superb of ice creams and instant coffee granules are the secret of a brilliant 'instant' ice cream dessert. See recipes.

Ice Cream, Coffee and Scotch

A formidable combination.

**2 scoops best quality vanilla ice cream;
1–2 tsp instant coffee granules; 1 tbs Scotch whisky.**

Spoon ice cream into an individual bowl, sprinkle over coffee and pour over whisky. Serve immediately. Serves 1.

Coffee Ice Cream

2 cups cream; 4 egg yolks, beaten; 1 cup freshly roasted coffee beans, cracked; 3/4 cup sugar.

Stir cream into egg yolks, add coffee beans and cook in a heatproof bowl over simmering water, stirring constantly, until thickened. Remove from heat and add sugar, stirring until dissolved. Stand custard for several hours to develop a good coffee flavour, then strain through a nylon sieve into ice cream trays. Cover tightly with foil and freeze until it forms a solid rim about 2.5 cm (1 in) wide. Transfer to a chilled bowl and beat vigorously with an electric or rotary beater. Return to trays and freeze until firm and creamy. Place in refrigerator for 30 minutes before serving to soften a little. Serve with a crisp biscuit. Serves 6.

Coffee Almond Layer Cake

CAKE: 125 g (4 oz) unsalted butter; 1/2 cup caster sugar; 3/4 cup flour; 1 tsp baking powder; 2 tsp instant coffee powder; pinch salt; 2 eggs, lightly beaten; 1/2 cup ground almonds; flaked almonds to decorate.

FROSTING: 185 g (6 oz) butter; 2 cups icing sugar, sifted; 2 tsp instant coffee powder, dissolved in tsp hot water.

CAKE: Cream butter with sugar. Sift together flour, coffee and salt, and stir into creamed mixture alternately with eggs. Stir in ground almonds. Divide mixture evenly between 2 greased and bottom-lined 18 cm (7 in) sandwich tins. Bake in a preheated moderately hot oven (190°C/375°F) for about 25 minutes or until a skewer inserted in the centre comes out clean. Turn cakes out and cool on a wire rack.
FROSTING: Cream butter with sugar until light and fluffy, then beat in coffee. Use frosting to sandwich cake layers and to cover top and sides. Press flaked almonds lightly into top and sides to decorate.

Coffee Kisses

1 cup very strong black coffee; 1 cup water; 2 cups sugar; 5 egg whites; pinch salt; whipped cream to serve.

Heat coffee, water and sugar together, stirring until sugar has dissolved, then boil without stirring to make a thick syrup. Beat egg whites in a heatproof bowl until foamy, add salt and beat whites to a firm snow. Pour on the syrup in a steady stream, beating all the time. Place bowl over simmering water and beat 5 minutes. Drop the meringue from a teaspoon in small peaked mounds on to a baking tray lined with cooking parchment or foil, spacing the mounds a little apart. Bake in a preheated slow oven (150°C/300°F) for 40 minutes or until lightly browned at the top and firm to the touch. Cool. Store meringues in an airtight container. To serve, join together in pairs with whipped cream. Makes about 24.

COLCANNON

The splendid Irish relation of Bubble and Squeak (see page 51).

Colcannon

4 medium, old potatoes, peeled and quartered; salt and freshly ground black pepper; 1 medium onion, finely chopped; 3/4 cup milk; 60 g (2 oz) butter; 2 cups lightly cooked, finely chopped cabbage; finely chopped parsley to garnish.

Cook potatoes in boiling water until tender. Drain them, return to saucepan and shake over low heat until they are dry and mealy. Mash them and season well. Put chopped onion and milk into a saucepan and bring to the boil; beat into potatoes until they are soft and light. Melt butter and toss cabbage in it. Fold into potato mixture and check seasoning. Transfer to a heated serving dish and sprinkle with parsley. Serves 4–6.
NOTE: Colcannon is often served with bacon rashers, or a little cooked bacon can be chopped and added with the cabbage. If desired, colcannon can be fried. Press it in an even layer into a frying pan containing a little hot bacon fat or butter. Cook until brown and crusty underneath, then cut into pieces and turn over to make a fresh layer. Repeat until you have a cake with crisp brown bits through it.

COLESLAW

An American invention, Coleslaw derives from the Dutch words '*kool sla*', meaning cabbage salad. It can be hot or cold, crisp or wilted, and is an excellent accompaniment to sausages and cold or barbecued meats.

Choose green, red, Savoy or Chinese cabbage and shred fine (see directions under *Cabbage*). Put cabbage into iced water and leave 30 minutes. Drain and dry well. For a crisp slaw, refrigerate in a plastic bag and mix with dressing shortly before serving. For wilted slaw, mix immediately with dressing, cover and refrigerate until needed. See recipes.

See also *Salads*.

Walnut Coleslaw with Watercress

4 cups shredded, crisped green cabbage; 3 sticks celery, finely sliced; $^3/_4$ cup Mayonnaise (page 256); 2 tsp honey; I tbs lemon juice; 2 tsp Dijon mustard, $^1/_2$ cup walnut pieces; I cup watercress sprigs.

Put cabbage and celery into a bowl. Mix mayonnaise, honey, lemon juice and mustard, add to vegetables and toss. Fold walnuts through. Transfer to a serving bowl and scatter watercress round edges. Serve immediately. Serves 4–6.

Apple and Caraway Coleslaw

Caraway seeds sharpen the flavour of coleslaw.

$^1/_2$ cup sour cream; 2 tbs caraway seeds; I large red apple, cored and thinly sliced; I tbs lemon juice; $^1/_2$ medium green or red cabbage, shredded and crisped; salt and freshly ground pepper; I small onion, finely chopped.

Mix sour cream and caraway seeds and chill 30 minutes. Sprinkle apple with lemon juice. Sprinkle cabbage with salt and pepper, mix in onion and apple and toss gently with sour cream mixture. Serves 4–6.

COMPOTE

A dish of fresh, canned or dried fruits, cooked gently in a syrup to preserve their shape and served in the syrup as a 'composition' of beautiful colour and form. A compote may be hot or cold and may be made of one kind or a combination of fruits – usually whole, sometimes halved or sliced. A well-made compote is one of the simplest but most elegant of desserts.

Compote of Fresh Fruit

500–750 g (1–1$^1/_2$ lb) fresh fruit (plums, peaches, apricots, cherries, apples, pears, rhubarb); I cup sugar; 2 cups water; flavouring (see note).

TO SERVE: cream or Crème Anglaise (page 111); crisp biscuits or Pain Perdu (page 158).

First prepare fruit: cover plums or peaches with boiling water, stand 3 minutes, drain and slip skins off; wash, halve and stone apricots; remove stems from cherries; peel apples or pears; trim rhubarb and cut into short lengths. Stir sugar, water and chosen flavouring in a wide saucepan over moderate heat until sugar has dissolved, then simmer 3 minutes. Place fruit in syrup, one kind at a time, and poach just below simmering point until tender but still firm. Spoon syrup over fruit frequently and turn fruit over once or twice with 2 wooden spoons while cooking. Remove fruit to a serving bowl, arranging it carefully. Boil syrup down a little and strain over fruit. A little strained lemon juice to sharpen flavour or 1–2 tbs brandy, rum, Kirsch or other liqueur may be added to

syrup if desired. Serve hot or chilled, with cream or crème anglaise and crisp biscuits or pain perdu. Serves 4–6.

NOTE: For flavourings choose from: 2 strips orange rind and $^1/_2$ vanilla bean; 2 strips lemon rind; $^1/_2$ tsp cinnamon, nutmeg or ginger, 3 cloves, or a mixture of spices, with $^1/_2$ cup red or white wine if desired.

CONFECTIONERY

See *Butterscotch, Caramel, Coconut, Fudge*, etc.

CONSERVE

A kind of jam with whole or sliced fruit which is unbroken and retains its original shape. It is pleasant to make a few pots of conserve of a fruit whose season is short, such as cherry. **See recipes.**

Cherry Conserve

I kg (2 lb) halved and stone cherries; 875 g (1$^3/_4$ lb) sugar; 2 tbs lemon juice; finely sliced peel, including white pith, I lemon.

Layer cherries and sugar in a large bowl, cover and leave 24 hours for sugar to extract juice. Place in large, heavy saucepan with lemon juice, and peel in a muslin bag tied to saucepan handle (pith provides extra pectin to aid setting). Bring to a rapid boil and boil until setting point is reached (when a little of the liquid dropped on to a cold plate and cooled appears stiff and wrinkled if pushed with the finger). Remove from heat, remove bag of peel and allow to cool slightly. Stir gently to distribute fruit evenly and pour into hot sterilised jars. Cool and seal. Makes 4 x 500 g (1 lb) jars.

Strawberry Conserve

I kg (2 lb) small strawberries, hulled; I kg (2 lb) sugar; 2 tbs lemon juice; finely sliced peel, including white pith, I lemon.

Layer strawberries and sugar in a large bowl, cover and leave 24 hours for sugar to extract the juice. Place in a large heavy saucepan with lemon juice, and peel in a muslin bag tied to the saucepan handle. Bring to a rapid boil and boil for 5 minutes. Remove bag of peel, reserving it and return conserve mixture to bowl. Cover and leave 8 hours, then replace in saucepan with bag of peel and boil until setting point is reached (see Cherry Conserve). Remove from heat, remove bag of peel and allow to cool slightly. Stir gently to distribute fruit evenly and pour into hot sterilised jars. Cool and seal. Makes 4 x 500 g (1 lb) jars.

CONSOMME

See *Soup* (Consommé and Clear Soups).

COQ AU VIN

A robust Burgundian dish of chicken cooked in red wine with onions, mushrooms and diced bacon.

Coq au Vin

1 x 1.5 kg (3 lb) chicken; 2 cups red wine;
2 bay leaves; 1 sprig fresh thyme; 1 clove garlic,
crushed; 250 g (8 oz) button mushrooms, stalks
trimmed; 125 g (4 oz) shoulder bacon in one piece,
diced; 60 g (2 oz) butter; 2 tbs olive oil; 12 button
onions, peeled; 1/4 cup brandy; 1 bouquet garni;
1 extra clove garlic, peeled; salt and freshly ground
black pepper; 2 tbs flour.

CHICKEN STOCK: giblets from chicken; 1 onion,
halved; 1 carrot, cut into chunks; 1 bouquet garni;
2 cups water; pinch salt.

GARNISH: chopped parsley; triangular Croûtes
of bread (page 105) fried in oil.

Cut chicken into quarters. Make stock by simmering all ingredients together for 1 hour, then strain. Place red wine in a saucepan with bay leaves, thyme, crushed garlic and chicken stock. Boil until reduced to about 1¼ cups, adding mushrooms about 5 minutes before reduction is complete. Remove mushrooms with a slotted spoon, strain wine mixture and set aside. Fry bacon in 30 g (1 oz) butter and the oil until fat runs. Add onions and fry until golden-brown. Dry chicken well, add to pan and fry until golden. Warm brandy, set alight and pour over chicken, shaking pan until flames die. Add bouquet garni, extra garlic clove and wine mixture. Bring to simmering point, season, and cook very gently, covered, for 40 minutes or until chicken is tender. Add mushrooms and cook 5 minutes more. Transfer chicken, mushrooms, onions and bacon to a heated serving dish. Mix remaining butter with flour to a paste and whisk, a small piece at a time, into the simmering sauce until it thickens. Adjust seasoning, discard bouquet garni, and spoon sauce over chicken. Sprinkle with parsley and serve garnished with croûtes. Serves 4.

COQUILLE ST JACQUES

The French name for scallop, so-called because the scallop shell is the emblem of St James of Compostela. The name is often also applied to a recipe in which scallops are the main feature.

See *Scallops*.

CORIANDER (CHINESE PARSLEY)

In talking about coriander, a distinction must first be made between the green leaf and the ripe seed, as their taste and uses are quite different.

Fresh coriander can be recognised by its refreshing smell. The lower leaves are fan-like, the upper leaves are feathery, and it is often sold with the roots still attached. This is also known as Chinese parsley. In Spain and Mexico it is called *cilantro*, and in India *dhania*, and throughout these countries and the Middle East, its odour and taste are much treasured. It adds a great deal to many curries and, ground with coconut, green chilli, salt, a squeeze of lemon and sometimes a little yogurt, is the basis for a delicious and very common Indian chutney. The Chinese sprinkle it over fish and chicken dishes, and it also adds distinction to a Bloody Mary. Use leaves only – no coarse stems – and do not chop.

Coriander seeds taste sweet, aromatic and vaguely like orange peel. In India coriander seeds are roasted before grinding to bring out a more curry-like flavour. Because of their mild flavour, they are used in large quantities in curry-making. In France the seeds are used to flavour a delicious mushroom dish and are almost always used in dishes cooked *à la grecque*.

The seeds are also used in the spicing of some sausages. Roughly powdered, they are the flavouring for roast pork, lamb or kid or spicy meat dishes of many kinds from North Africa and Lebanon, and are a most important spice in Arab cooking. Use ground seeds in cakes, biscuits and chutneys.

You can easily germinate coriander seeds and grow your own green coriander. Sow the seeds in rich soil and full sun. Sow thinly where they are to mature and thin them out as they grow, removing each plant complete with root. In a warm climate, they mature in 4–6 weeks. See recipes.

Mushrooms Coriander

juice 1/2 lemon; 500 g (1 lb) button mushrooms,
quartered or left whole; 1 tbs coriander seeds;
4 tbs olive oil; 2 bay leaves; salt and freshly ground
black pepper.

Squeeze lemon juice over mushrooms. Crush coriander lightly in a mortar or use end of a rolling pin. Heat olive oil in a heavy frying pan, add coriander seeds and cook for 10–15 seconds. Add mushrooms, bay leaves, salt and pepper. Cook 3–4 minutes, tossing mushrooms to cook lightly. Cool. Remove bay leaves and serve in individual bowls with crusty French bread to mop up juices. Serves 4.

Coriander Chicken

1 cooked White Chicken (Chinese Steamed
Chicken, page 79); 6–8 spring onions, shredded;
1 tbs finely shredded fresh ginger; 2–3 tbs toasted
sesame seeds; 1 cup coriander sprigs; 2 tbs peanut
oil; 2 tbs light soy sauce; 1 tsp sesame oil.

Arrange chopped cooked chicken on a plate. Top with spring onions and shredded ginger. (The shreds should be very fine and free from fibres.) Add sesame seeds and coriander. Just before serving heat oil, soy sauce and sesame oil and pour over chicken. Serves 6.

Coriander Chutney

A bright herby green chutney to accompany Indian samoosas or pakoras, little meatballs or dried fish. Makes a good dip for crudités too. You will need a good ½ cup chopped fresh coriander and ¼ cup mint.

2 bunches fresh coriander, stalks removed; 1 small bunch fresh mint, stalks removed; 6 spring onions, chopped; 1 tbs grated fresh ginger; 1 clove garlic, crushed; 1 tsp salt; 1 tsp sugar; 1 tbs lemon juice; ¹⁄₂ cup plain yogurt.

Put all ingredients, except yogurt, into a blender or food processor fitted with a steel blade. Blend until finely chopped. If you don't have a blender, then chop everything finely. Add yogurt and whirl in blender only long enough to mix through. Serve in a small bowl. Makes about 1 cup.

Steamed Fish Coriander

The garnish of shredded spring onions, coriander and ginger makes a perfect finishing touch to this Chinese way with fish.

1 whole fish weighing about 1 kg (2 lb); salt; 2 spring onions, sliced; 2 slices fresh ginger; fresh coriander; 4–6 extra spring onions, green parts only, shredded; 2 extra slices fresh ginger, shredded.

GARNISH: 4 spring onions, white parts only, shredded lengthways; ¹⁄₂ cup fresh coriander; 2 slices fresh ginger, finely shredded; 2 tsp sesame oil; 2 tbs peanut oil; 2 tsp soy sauce.

Clean, scale and remove head from fish. Slash in thickest part and lightly salt inside and out. Place sliced spring onions, 2 slices ginger and fresh coriander in cavity. Lay shredded green ends of extra spring onions, extra shredded ginger and more fresh coriander in top part of a steamer. Place fish on herb bed and steam for 15–20 minutes or until fish flesh is opaque and flakes when tested with a fine skewer.

GARNISH: Remove to a heated serving platter and garnish with white ends of spring onions, coriander and ginger. Warm sesame and peanut oils, pour over fish and sprinkle with soy sauce. Serve immediately. Serves 2–4.

CORN (SWEETCORN)

Choose corn with fresh, dark green husks and plump yellow kernels. Fresh corn looks moist and has a sweet taste. Old corn looks hard and shrunken and tastes floury. Corn deteriorates quickly after picking, so ideally it should be cooked as soon as possible. If storing corn before cooking, refrigerate with husks left on.

■ **TO COOK:** Remove husks and silk tassels from corn. Put in deep saucepan with enough boiling water to cover cobs. 1 tsp sugar can be added to water, but do not add salt – it toughens corn. Return water to the boil and boil for 8 minutes. Overcooking will toughen, not soften, kernels. Serve with butter, salt and freshly ground black pepper, or serve a butter sauce to which has been added fresh or dried tarragon.

Barbecued Corn on the Cob: Remove husks and silk tassels. Rub cobs generously with butter, salt and freshly ground black pepper and wrap each cob in foil, folding in ends to seal it well. Place on grid of barbecue over hot coals. Cook about 15 minutes, depending on the size of the cob, turning frequently. A dash of soy sauce may be added to each cob with the butter before wrapping in oil.

Cobs can also be boiled for 5 minutes, removed from water and drained, brushed generously with melted butter, then barbecued on a grid for 10 minutes. Brush occasionally with melted butter.

CORN KERNELS

These can be used in soufflés, omelettes, and quiches, or added to cream soups, stuffings, macaroni cheese, or mixed with cream or butter and served as an accompaniment to other dishes.

■ **TO COOK KERNELS:** Cut kernels from cob, place in saucepan, cover and simmer in their juice and a little butter for several minutes until tender. Season and moisten with milk or cream.

Devilled Kernels: Add 1 tbs Worcestershire sauce and finely chopped garlic to cooked kernels.

Creamed Sweetcorn: Combine 2 cups cooked or canned sweetcorn kernels with 1 cup Béchamel Sauce (see page 456) or cream, ¹⁄₂ tsp salt and freshly ground black pepper. Simmer 5 minutes. Chopped parsley may be added if liked. Serves 4–6.

Creole Sweetcorn: Cook 1 chopped onion and ¹⁄₂ chopped green pepper in 45–60 g (1¹⁄₂–2 oz) butter until lightly browned. Add 2¹⁄₂ cups peeled, chopped tomatoes, 1 tsp sugar, 1 tsp salt, ¼ tsp black pepper and 2 cups cooked or canned sweetcorn kernels. Simmer 10 minutes. Serves 6.

Corn Bread or Muffins

4 tbs melted butter or bacon dripping; ¹⁄₂ cup flour; 2¹⁄₂ tsp baking powder; 1 tbs sugar; ¹⁄₂ tsp salt; 1¹⁄₂ cups yellow cornmeal; 1 egg; ³⁄₄ cup milk.

Use 1¹⁄₂ tbs melted fat to grease a shallow 29 x 18 cm (11 x 7 in) cake tin or 12 x 8 cm (3 in) muffin tins. Place in top half of a preheated hot oven (220°C/425°F) until sizzling hot. Have all other ingredients at room temperature. Sift flour, baking powder, sugar and salt into a bowl and stir in cornmeal. Beat together egg, milk and remaining butter or bacon drippings, pour into dry ingredients and combine with a few rapid strokes; batter will be lumpy. Turn batter into hot tin or muffin tins and bake in oven for about 25 minutes or until well risen and browned. Serve immediately, cutting bread into squares. Makes 12.

CORNED BEEF

Beef is corned (the old name for salting) by soaking and injecting it with brine, plus a little sodium nitrite to make it pink. The cuts usually used are silverside, solid lean meat with a layer of fat on one side, and brisket, alternating layers of fat and lean meat – this is often rolled and tied. Corned beef is excellent hot, served with vegetables, which may be cooked with it – carrots and cabbage are the classic choice – or cold, with salads.

Corned Beef

1 x 1.5–2 kg (3–4 lb) joint corned beef, either silverside or rolled brisket; 1 large onion, peeled and studded with 6 cloves; 1 tbs vinegar; 12 black peppercorns; 1 blade mace; 1 stick celery, cut into several pieces; 1 bay leaf; 1 bouquet garni; 2 tbs brown sugar; 1 carrot, cut into chunks.

Put all ingredients into a large saucepan and cover with cold water. Simmer, covered, until tender – about 30 minutes per 500 g (1 lb) after liquid reaches simmering point. Beef is done when a fine skewer inserted through thick part comes out easily. If serving hot, allow beef to rest in liquid for 30 minutes after cooking, then remove and carve it in thick slices. If serving cold, allow to cool completely in liquid before removing and slicing thinly. Serves 6–8 hot, 8–10 cold.

CORNISH PASTY

A Cornish pasty is the sturdy pastry-enclosed meal which was the standard food carried to work by 19th-century tin miners in Cornwall, England. Pasties sometimes contained a savoury filling at one end and sweetened apple at the other, separated by a wall of pastry. Nowadays the filling is usually meat and vegetables only. It is cooked in the pastry so that it forms its own gravy; a little kidney should be included to make the gravy richer. The pasty's traditional long shape was designed to fit in a workman's deep pocket. It is still one of the best and most convenient picnic foods.

Cornish Pasties

double quantity Plain Shortcrust Pastry (page 342); 250 g (8 oz) braising beef, cut into thin slivers; 90 g (3 oz) kidney, finely chopped; 1 large onion, finely chopped; 1 large potato, diced; 1 large carrot, diced; 1 small turnip, diced; salt and freshly ground black pepper; 30 g (1 oz) butter, beaten egg to glaze.

Divide pastry into 4 equal pieces and roll out each to a 18 cm (7 in) round. Mix beef and kidney together; mix vegetables together. Season both mixtures with salt and pepper. Put a layer of vegetables on one side of each pastry round, leaving edge uncovered. Put meat in a layer on top of vegetables. Dot with butter and sprinkle lightly with water. Dampen edges of pastry and fold uncovered half over filling. Press edges of pastry together and pinch firmly, turning edge over like a hem, to seal well. This makes a flat pasty – if preferred, filling can be placed down centre of pastry and sides brought up to make a high pasty with a ridge across the centre. Chill pasties 20 minutes, then place on a baking tray and brush with beaten egg. Bake in a preheated hot oven (200°C/400°F) for 20 minutes, then reduce heat to slow (150°C/300°F) and bake a further 35 minutes. If pastry is browning too much, cover tops loosely with dampened greaseproof paper. Makes 4.

CORNMEAL

Cornmeal is important in the cooking of the southern USA and of northern Italy, where it is called *polenta*. The meal may be yellow or white, and is processed in one of two ways: old-style stone-ground, in which some skin and most of the germ are retained, and modern-style steel-milled, in which skin and germ are almost entirely removed.

Stone-ground cornmeal is softer in texture and is superior in nutrition and flavour, but does not keep so well. It should be stored in the refrigerator. Steel-milled cornmeal can be kept on a shelf in an airtight container. See also *Polenta*.

COULIBIAC

A Russian delicacy which is a larger relation of Pirog and Piroshki. Coulibiac is a plump savoury turnover filed with layers of salmon, rice (or rice vermicelli) and eggs. In Russia it would be made with fresh salmon but it is delicious made with a good quality canned salmon. The pastry can be a cream cheese pastry or puff pastry. Coulibiac is excellent served warm – it can be made ahead and reheated – or cold, with sour cream.

Coulibiac

1 x 375 g (14 oz) packet frozen puff pastry, thawed; beaten egg to glaze.

FILLING: 1 x 220 g can red salmon, drained; 30 g (1 oz) butter; 1 small onion, chopped; 6–8 mushrooms, sliced; 1 cup boiled rice; 1 tbs chopped parsley; 2 hard-boiled eggs, sliced; salt and freshly ground black pepper.

TO SERVE: 1/2 cup melted butter mixed with juice 1/2 lemon or 1 cup sour cream (optional).

FILLING: Flake drained salmon coarsely, discarding skin and bones. Melt about half butter in a frying pan, add onion and cook gently until soft. Add mushrooms, toss a few moments and remove pan from heat.

Roll out about three quarters of the thawed puff pastry on a lightly floured surface to a neat rectangle about 18 x 30 cm (7 x 12 in). Place pastry on a baking tray and trim edges neatly, reserving trimmings. Leaving a clear border of 2.5 cm (1 in) all round, place filling ingredients in layers on pastry. Begin with a layer of rice, sprinkled with parsley and dotted with a little butter. Cover with a layer of salmon, then a layer of onion and mushroom mixture, then sliced eggs. Season each layer with salt and pepper.

Roll out remaining pastry to a rectangle that will cover the filling, and place it on top. Brush uncovered border with a little beaten egg and fold up to overlap the covering piece of dough. Press edges together to seal. Make 2 slits in top and decorate coulibiac with pastry fish or other shapes made from trimmings. Secure the decorations with beaten egg. Chill at least 30 minutes, longer if desired.

Brush with beaten egg and bake in centre of a preheated hot oven (200°C/400°F) for 30 minutes. Remove from oven and pour a little melted butter through slits in top – or serve coulibiac with a melted butter and lemon sauce or sour cream. Serves 6.

COURT BOUILLON

Court Bouillon is a flavoured, acidulated liquid used for cooking shellfish and whole or large pieces of fish. It may be based on water with a little vinegar or lemon juice added, or on a mixture of water and wine, with the addition of aromatic vegetables and herbs.

The purpose of Court Bouillon is to add flavour and to keep the flesh of the fish a good colour. Court Bouillon is prepared ahead, strained and sometimes cooled before the fish is placed in it.

Court Bouillon

6 cups water; $^1/_4$ cup lemon juice or white vinegar; 2 tsp salt; $^1/_2$ bay leaf; 1 carrot; $^1/_2$ stick celery; 1 onion, sliced; 6 parsley stalks; 3–4 sprigs fresh tarragon, dill or chervil (optional); 6 black peppercorns.

Put all ingredients except peppercorns into a covered saucepan (not aluminium). Simmer 45 minutes, then add peppercorns and simmer 10 minutes more. Strain before using. It will keep, refrigerated, about 1 week. Makes $5^1/_2$ – 6 cups.

NOTE: Half water and half dry white wine may be used instead of water and lemon juice or vinegar.

COUSCOUS

The cereal dish of North Africa, consisting of fine semolina combined with flour, salt and water into tiny, pasta-like pellets. In Morocco, Algeria and Tunisia, it is usually served as an accompaniment to savoury dishes of meat and vegetables. In Egypt it is more often served with sugar and nuts as a dessert.

■ **TO COOK:** Cover couscous with cold water, stir with the fingers and drain. Stand 15 minutes to allow couscous to swell. Turn couscous into a fine sieve or muslin-lined colander, which will fit snugly over a deep saucepan. For 500 g (1 lb) couscous, put 4 cups water or stock into saucepan, bring to the boil and place container over it (container must not touch liquid). Drape a tea-towel over the top, fit the lid on tightly and bring ends of cloth up over lid. Steam 15 minutes, then turn couscous into a bowl. Fork over, breaking up any lumps, and sprinkle with 2 tbs cold water. Replenish water in saucepan if necessary and return couscous to steaming container. Steam as before for 30 minutes. Turn into a bowl, fork over again and toss with 125 g (4 oz) melted butter. Use as an accompaniment to stews, etc., or (for couscous cooked over plain water only) sprinkle with icing sugar and peanuts or almonds and serve as a dessert.

INSTANT COUSCOUS: This is a fast and convenient product readily available at most supermarkets. Pour the same quantity of warm stock or water over the couscous, let it rest for 5 minutes then warm it up slowly with some olive oil or butter, stirring with a fork quite often.

Couscous with Grilled Vegetables

1 tbs olive oil; 1 tsp ground cumin; $^1/_2$ tsp salt; $1^1/_2$ cups water or chicken stock; 2 cups couscous; 2 ripe tomatoes, seeded and cubed; 2 tsp lemon juice; salt and freshly ground black pepper; 1 bunch coriander, chopped; olive oil; 2 green and 2 red peppers cut into quarters lengthways; 6 small eggplant, halved; 6 small zucchini, halved.

Heat the oil in a small saucepan, add the cumin, and heat until fragrant. Add the salt, water or stock, and bring to the boil. Stir in the couscous and let the mixture stand, covered, off the heat for 5 minutes. Fluff the mixture with a fork and stir in the tomatoes and lemon juice. Add salt and pepper to taste. Toss all the vegetables in olive oil and place under a preheated griller, turning, until tender and golden. Alternatively, cook on the stove using a grill pan. Cool, leave whole or cut into small pieces and set aside.

Toss the coriander through the couscous, adding half the vegetables. To serve, pile the couscous on to a serving platter and top with the remaining vegetables. Top with extra coriander or torn mint leaves before serving. Serves 4–6.

CRAB

The large *Mud Crab*, with its fierce, awesome claws and large, bulky body, is one of the delicacies of the table. It ranges in colour from dark olive-green to brown and turns a bright red when cooked. The weight can be up to 2.5 kg (5 lb) for a large specimen; however, the weight most commonly sold is about 750 g (1½ lb). The meat from the claws is of exceptional flavour, the flesh from the body, picked from between the thin shell walls, is sweet and delicate.

The *Blue Swimmer Crab* is one of the smallest and best eating crabs. Also called sand or blue manna crab, it is bluish-green, the long legs, paddles and claws a vibrant cobalt blue – hence the name; it changes its colour to orange-red when cooked. The average size is around 250 – 375 g (8–12 oz), although they can reach a weight of over 1 kg (2 lb).

The *Giant Tasmanian Crab* is one of the largest of all crabs and is rivalled only by the Alaskan King crab and huge spider crabs caught off Japan. It makes excellent eating, being very meaty with a fine flavour and texture; however, it is not fished commercially in any quantity, and so does not often appear in fish markets.

When buying crab, alive or cooked, choose crabs that feel heavy for their size, and smell fresh and sweet with no hint of ammonia.

Crabmeat is available in cans. Picked crabmeat is also available in packets, both fresh and frozen – useful when crabmeat flesh is used in a recipe.

■ **TO COOK:** First drown the crab (or crabs) in fresh water. Bring a large saucepan of fresh seawater (or salted water) to the boil, drop in a bouquet garni; 1 sliced carrot; 1 onion, halved; 2 sticks celery, sliced, and simmer gently for 10–15 minutes, depending on the size. The crabs will turn red. Remove the crabs.

■ **TO PREPARE A COOKED CRAB FOR EATING:** At all times work with a cloth to protect the hands. Remove the big claws and set aside, twist off the legs. Remove the undershell by using thumbs to prise out round body section from underside. Remove and discard the beige, spongy gills lying flat against inner side of body shell. Cut the undershell body in two. You now have 2 semi-circles, each semi-circle is divided by thin shell partitions, into 4 segments. Split through the semi-circle horizontally, then you can scoop out the meat from between the partitions with a small spoon. Place the flesh in a bowl and discard the rest.

TO CRACK THE CLAWS: Fold double newspaper over them, crack with a hammer, then pull out the meat. Sometimes the claws and legs are cracked and served with a fork, the diner extracting the flesh.

TO CRACK CRABS: Remove claws and legs, crack with a hammer. Remove the undershell, discarding spongy gills. Cut undershell in two, then cut each semi-circle horizontally (see To prepare a cooked crab for eating).

NOTE: There is a mustardy curd present in all crustacea – its presence in abundance indicates not only freshness but quality. This curd is often added to a little cream or mayonnaise and served with the crab. **See recipes.**

Hot Crabs with Butter: Cook crabs as above, crack them open, and arrange on a large plate.

Melt 125 g (4 oz) butter with ½ cup white wine, 3 tbs chopped parsley, 1 tsp chopped fresh thyme and ¼ cup chopped spring onions; pour butter mixture over cracked crabs. The meat is extracted, then dipped in butter. Place plenty of paper napkins nearby, and a finger bowl.

Crab Salad: Prepare crab as above. The flesh may be returned to cleaned and washed crab shell or set on a bed of shredded lettuce. Surround with cracked claws and legs. Send to table with freshly made mustard, the curd from the crab, mixed with cream or mayonnaise, some good mild vinegar and brown bread and butter.

NOTE: Mustard enhances the flavour of crab and should always be used in crab sandwiches.

Chilli Crab

A lovely way of treating crab, from Malaysia.

**1 raw mud crab, or 3 blue swimmers;
½ cup peanut oil; 6 thin slices fresh ginger,
cut in strips; 3 cloves garlic, finely chopped;
1–2 fresh chillies, seeded and chopped;
⅓ cup chilli sauce (Malaysian); 1 tbs soy sauce;
1 tbs sugar; 1 tsp salt.**

Remove large claws from crab and crack. Remove undershell and discard gills. Cut body in 2 or 3 pieces, depending on size. Crack legs. Heat a wok or large frying pan, add oil and when hot, fry crab pieces until they change colour, turning so they cook on all sides. Remove to a plate. Turn heat to low, add ginger, garlic and chillies and fry for 1 minute. Add sauce, sugar and salt and bring to the boil. Return crab and cook gently, turning crab, in sauce to cook and flavour. Rice may accompany crab. Serve with finger bowls and napkins. Serves 2–3.

Crab in Black Bean Sauce

A Chinese specialty – best eaten with fingers and a fork or, if adept, with chopsticks.

I raw mud crab, or 3 blue swimmers; $^{1}/_{2}$ cup peanut oil; 6 thin slices fresh ginger, cut in strips; 2 cloves garlic, crushed; 2 tbs canned black beans; 2 tsp soy sauce; $^{2}/_{3}$ cup hot chicken stock; I tsp cornflour, blended with a little water.

Remove large claws from crab and crack. Remove undershell and discard gills. Cut body in 2 or 3 pieces, depending on size. Crack legs. Heat oil in wok or large frying pan, add ginger, garlic and black beans and fry, crushing beans with back of spoon. Add crab and cook over fairly high heat, tossing and turning until crabs change colour. Add soy sauce, stock and cornflour. Cook for 2–3 minutes. Serve crab and sauce with boiled rice and finger bowls and large napkins. Serves 2–3.

Stir–fried Crab

In the province of Hunan, small crabs are cut up and stir-fried. Provide finger bowls and large napkins when serving.

3–4 raw blue swimmers, or I large mud crab; 3 tbs cornflour; 3 tbs light soy sauce; 2 tbs Chinese rice wine or sherry; I tbs sugar; I$^{1}/_{2}$ tbs vinegar; I tbs chopped shallot; I tsp chopped fresh ginger; $^{1}/_{4}$ cup water; $^{1}/_{4}$ cup peanut oil; 2 tsp sesame oil.

Remove large claws and shells from crabs and crack. Remove undershell and discard gills. Cut bodies into 4 or more pieces. Crack legs. Coat crab pieces with cornflour. Combine remaining ingredients except peanut and sesame oil. Heat a wok or large frying pan, add peanut oil and when hot, fry crab pieces until they change colour, stirring well. Add flavouring mixture and cook over low heat, stirring, for about 5 minutes. Place crab on heated platter and sprinkle with sesame oil. Serves 2–3.

Devilled Crab

45 g (I$^{1}/_{2}$ oz) butter; I tbs flour; $^{3}/_{4}$ cup milk or cream; 2 hard-boiled eggs, chopped; I tbs French mustard; pinch cayenne; I$^{1}/_{2}$ cups canned, frozen or cooked fresh crabmeat, picked over; I cup fresh white breadcrumbs.

Melt 30 g (I oz) butter in a saucepan, blend in flour and stir in milk or cream. Bring to the boil, stirring. Fold in eggs, mustard, cayenne and crabmeat and heat gently. Put mixture into 4 buttered ramekins or crab or scallop shells. Top with breadcrumbs and dot with remaining butter. Brown in a preheated hot oven (200°C/400°F) or under a preheated grill. Serves 4.

Crab Egg Fu Yung

Delicious omelettes, a specialty of Canton.

250 g (8 oz) canned, frozen or cooked fresh crabmeat, picked over; I cup cooked peas; I tsp sherry; 2 spring onions, sliced; 3 slices fresh ginger, finely chopped; $^{1}/_{2}$ cup sliced water chestnuts; I tsp salt; pinch freshly ground black pepper; 6 eggs, beaten; 4 tbs vegetable oil.

Combine crabmeat with peas, sherry, spring onions, ginger, water chestnuts, salt and pepper. Add eggs. Heat oil in a frying pan and fry large spoonfuls of omelette mixture, turning once, until golden-brown on both sides. Serve with soy sauce. Makes 6.

Crab Bisque

90 g (3 oz) butter; 2 tbs grated onion; 2 tsp flour; 2 cups canned, frozen or cooked fresh crabmeat, picked over; 3 cups warm milk; I cup cream; salt and freshly ground white pepper; pinch nutmeg; 3 tbs sherry; 2 tbs chopped parsley or chives.

Melt butter in saucepan, add onion and cook gently for 2 minutes. Stir in flour. Add crabmeat and heat through, then stir in warm milk. Heat through but do not boil. Add cream, salt, pepper, nutmeg, sherry and parsley or chives. Serves 6.

Crab Cakes

Can be made in miniature for little cocktail-sized crab cakes.

2 thick slices crustless bread; milk to cover; 500 g (I lb) picked over crabmeat; I tbs Mayonnaise; $^{1}/_{2}$ tsp salt; I tbs Worcestershire sauce; I tbs baking powder; I tbs chopped parsley; flour for dusting; light olive oil for frying.

Soak the bread in milk to cover for 15 minutes. Squeeze out excess milk gently and place bread in a bowl with the crab, mayonnaise, salt, Worcestershire sauce, baking powder and parsley. Work into a combined mixture. Using slightly wetted hands shape mixture into 8–10 patties, dust with flour and fry in light olive oil on each side until golden. Drain on paper towels and serve as soon as possible. Serves 4.

CRABAPPLE

Crabapple trees are grown mainly for their beauty, but the small, sour fruits make excellent preserves and jelly. Crabapple Jelly is made in the same way as Quince Jelly. See *Quince*.

Spiced Crabapples

500 g (I lb) crabapples; 3 cups boiling water; 2 strips lemon peel; I$^{1}/_{2}$ cups sugar; 6 cloves;

4 whole allspice; 1 x 5 cm (2 in) cinnamon stick; 4 black peppercorns; ¹/₂ tsp salt; 2 tbs wine vinegar.

Simmer crabbapples, water and lemon peel together in a covered saucepan until crabapples are barely tender. Lift out fruit and discard lemon peel. Add sugar, spices tied in a bag, salt and vinegar to pan and stir until sugar has dissolved, then boil without stirring for 5 minutes. Replace crabapples in liquid and simmer 35–45 minutes, or until liquid is syrupy, removing spice bag after 30 minutes. Put the crabapples into sterilised jars and strain syrup over. Cool and seal. Serve with pork, ham, goose or duck. Makes 1¹/₂–2 cups.

CRANBERRY

A tart fruit cultivated in North America and used in jellies, tarts, poultry glazes and pies. Cranberry Sauce is a thick fruity sauce, the traditional accompaniment for roast turkey at Christmas and, in America, at Thanksgiving feasts. You can buy it ready-made from good food stores.

Dried cranberries are nibbled as for other dried fruit, added to salads, or used in baking.

CRAYFISH (AUSTRALIAN ROCK LOBSTER)

See *Lobster*.

CREAM

The fatty part of whole milk which rises to the surface on standing, or it can be separated from the milk. There are few dishes which do not improve with the addition of cream. It adds richness and smoothness to sauces, soups and casseroles. It is often used to decorate and fill cakes, and as an ingredient in flavoured creams and custards. Cream is served with puddings, fruits and many desserts.

The following terms are used throughout this book:

Cream: Fresh cream is just 'cream'; it has a minimum fat content of 35 per cent.

Thickened Cream: This is cream with a small amount of gelatine added to thicken and stabilise it. It holds well when whipped, and has a longer storage life than ordinary cream.

Sour Cream: This is cream with a culture added to give it a sharp tangy flavour. Its thick consistency can be swirled through soups, either hot or chilled. It is used to accompany paprikas and goulash; or use with chopped spring onions and fried crumbled bacon in potato salad. Serve sour cream in a separate bowl with smoked fish such as mackerel and trout. It is the traditional accompaniment with caviar for the buckwheat pancakes called *Blini* (see page 40), and is used as a topping for Idaho potatoes baked in their skins.

Sour Light Cream: This has a lower fat content than sour cream, and is not as thick or sharp. It adds freshness and lightness to salad dressing, soups and sauces. It is particularly good with iced soups such as cucumber, lettuce, spinach and pumpkin.

Reduced Cream and Light Cream: These have lower fat contents than ordinary cream. They provide richness without adding so many kilojoules (calories). However, because of the lower fat content, these creams do not whip successfully.

Canned Creams: These are heat treated to last without refrigeration. Treat as fresh cream and refrigerate after opening.

UHT Creams: These are subject to ultra-high heat treatment, which gives them a long shelf life. Once opened they should be refrigerated. They usually whip successfully.

WAY TO USE CREAM

PAN SAUCES: Add 2–3 tbs cream with ¼ cup stock or wine to pan after sautéeing fillet steaks, chicken fillets, fish fillets or pork chops. Stir rapidly and continuously until thickened, scraping up pan juices. Season as desired and pour over previously cooked meat, fish or poultry. Pan gravy for roast chicken may be made in the same way. Remove chicken and all but 1 tbs fat from the pan, then proceed as above, using more cream and stock.

WHIPPED CREAM: For best and fastest results, chill cream and bowl first. If it is a hot day, place bowl of chilled cream over ice. Whip with a whisk, rotary or electric beater until it reaches the consistency desired. Be careful not to over-beat, as the cream will turn to butter. Whip until soft peaks form and hold their shape. Stop beating immediately if the colour darkens and cream clings heavily to the beaters.

You may whip 1 cup of cream with 1 egg white if you want to use the cream for piping. This helps to stabilise the cream and it holds its shape better. It is best to add flavour to cream after whipping by folding through quickly and lightly. Avoid using sugar if possible, as the cream can separate and does not retain its freshness for as long as plain whipped cram. Flavour whipped cream with liqueurs, wines such as sherry or port, essence or sweet spice. If making Crème Chantilly (see page 102), which is sweetened, use as soon as possible.

Ice Cream: Cream is essential to all true ice creams. This is a rich, quickly made ice cream. Beat 4 egg whites with 4 tbs caster sugar until stiff and glossy. Beat in 4 egg yolks, with 1 tbs brandy, 2 tbs strong black coffee or 1 tsp vanilla. Fold 1 cup whipped cream through egg mixture. Pour into ice cream trays, cover and freeze 4 hours or overnight. Serves 6–8.

See also *Ice cream*.

Frozen Fruit Cream: Whip 2 cups cream and fold through 1 cup sweetened fruit purée. Freeze until beginning to set around edges, remove and beat well. Replace in freezer and allow to freeze 4 hours. This cream is served slightly soft. Place container in refrigerator for 30 minutes before serving, if it has been frozen for longer than 4 hours. Serves 6–8.

CREAM PUFF

This is delectable little puff of feather-light choux pastry, filled with sweetened whipped cream or Crème Pâtissière (see page 207). Poached or fresh fruit can also be added if liked.

See Pastry: Choux Pastry and *Profiterole*.

CREME BRULEE

A beautiful rich French custard, with a glaze of hard, caramelised sugar.

See *Custards*.

CREME CARAMEL

See *Custards*.

CREME CHANTILLY

The French name for sweetened whipped cream. It is particularly delicious with fresh fruits, but can also be used as a cake filling or frosting, and as an accompaniment for many desserts.

Crème Chantilly
(Sweetened Whipped Cream)

1 cup cream; 1 tbs icing sugar, sifted; ½ tsp vanilla.

Whip cream until soft peaks form, then fold in sugar and vanilla. Makes about 1½ cups.

VARIATIONS

JAMAICAN CREAM: Fold into Crème Chantilly ½ cup toasted desiccated coconut and 1 tbs dark rum.

COFFEE-NUT CREAM: Fold into Crème Chantilly 1 tsp instant coffee powder and ¾ cup crushed peanut or almond brittle.

RASPBERRY CREAM: Fold into Crème Chantilly ½ cup raspberry jam.

CREME FRAICHE

In France, the cream called crème fraîche is treated with a special culture which helps it to stay fresh longer, makes it thick and gives it a delicious, slight tang. It is an important ingredient in the light style of cooking called nouvelle cuisine, where it is used in sauces, soups and with fresh fruits. The original crème fraîche is not available in other countries but a good substitute can be made. **See recipes.**

TO WHIP CREME FRAICHE: Measure crème fraîche to calculate one third of its volume. Then add this calculated amount of cold milk, water or chipped ice and a little sugar to taste, and whip until thick.

WAYS TO USE CREME FRAICHE

- Use instead of cream with fresh fruits and fruit desserts.
- Use to enrich sauces such as Velouté and Béchamel (see *Sauces*).
- Swirl on top of individual bowls of cream soups such as Vichyssoise, Asparagus, Pumpkin or Spinach (see *Soups*).
- Use with creamy salad dressings and fold through chicken salads and potato salads.
- Use to top baked jacket potatoes and crumble grilled bacon over.
- Stir 1 tbs through scrambled eggs after cooking.

Crème Fraîche

150 ml (½ cup plus 1 tbs) cream; 1 tbs plain yogurt.

Stir cream and yogurt together in a jar. Cover and keep warm overnight or for 8 hours. One method of doing this is to put jar into an electric frying pan on lowest temperature and with a few centimetres of warm water in it. Another method is to keep container well wrapped and leave it above – not in – an oven on lowest possible setting. Chill cream well before using; it will thicken as it chills. Makes about 1 cup.

CREME PATISSIERE

A classic French cream used for cakes, tarts, flans and pastries.

See *Icings, Frostings and Fillings*.

CREPES

These light and lacy pancakes of France can be enjoyed simply with a squeeze of lemon juice and a sprinkling of sugar, or they can be folded around savoury or sweet fillings and topped with sauces, creams, fruit syrups or liqueurs. The are used to make that most evocative dessert, Crêpes Suzette.

TO STORE CREPES: They can be made freshly each time they are required but they also freeze well. Stack crêpes in groups of 8 or 10 (depending on how many you intend serving at one time), separating each with a square of greaseproof paper. Wrap in foil and place in freezer bags, then store in the freezer.

Crepe pans are made of cast-iron and should not be used for any purpose other than cooking crêpes. They should not be washed after use but wiped out with a paper towel. If a pan becomes sticky, rub it with salt, then finish with an oiled cloth.

TO SEASON A NEW PAN: Fill with oil and bring to smoking point. Remove from heat at once, then stand 24 hours. Pour off the oil, wipe well with paper towels and the pan is ready to use. **See recipes.**

See also *Pancakes*.

Basic Crêpes

1¼ cups flour; pinch salt; 3 eggs, beaten;
1½ cups milk; 1 tbs brandy; 2 tsp melted butter;
extra butter for frying.

Sift flour and salt into a bowl. Make a well in centre and add eggs and milk. Using a wooden spoon, mix well, drawing in flour from sides. Beat well, then stir in brandy and melted butter. Cover and stand 1 hour. Strain as the batter must be free of lumps.

To make crêpes, heat a little butter in a crêpe pan and pour off excess. Use a jug and pour about 1 tbs batter into an 18 cm (7 in) pan. Rotate pan quickly to coat bottom thinly and evenly, then pour off any excess batter. Heat gently and when small bubbles appear (after about 1 minute) use a spatula to flip crêpe over. Cook for 1 minute on other side. Makes 20–24.

Seafood Crêpes

6 spring onions, finely chopped; 60 g (2 oz) butter; 125 g (4 oz) shelled prawns; 125 g (4 oz) shelled mussels; 6–8 scallops, poached for 1 minute; 6–8 oysters (optional); 1 egg yolk; 2 tsp dry sherry; 3 hard-boiled eggs, chopped; 2 tsp snipped chives; 8–12 crêpes (see Basic Crêpe Batter); 2 tbs whipped cream; slivered toasted almonds to garnish.

CREAM SAUCE: 2 cups milk; 1 bay leaf; $^1/_2$ onion, chopped; 5 black peppercorns; 60 g (2 oz) butter; 4 tbs flour; $^1/_2$ cup cream; salt and white pepper.

CREAM SAUCE: Heat milk slowly in a saucepan over low heat with bay leaf, onion and peppercorns. When bubbles form around edge, remove from heat, cover and stand for 10 minutes. Melt butter over low heat, stir in flour and cook, stirring, for 1 minute. Remove from heat, cool a little, then strain in warm milk and cream. Stir until smoothly blended, then return to heat and stir until boiling. Season.

Cook the spring onions gently in butter until softened. Add prawns, mussels, scallops and oysters. Set aside 4 tbs cream sauce and fold egg yolk, sherry, chopped eggs, chives and seafood mixture into the remainder. Spread on crêpes, roll up and arrange in one layer in a buttered, ovenproof serving dish. Cover dish with foil and warm in a preheated moderate oven (180°C/350°F) for 15 minutes. Fold cream into reserved 4 tbs sauce. Uncover crêpes and spoon sauce along centre of dish. Return to oven and bake, uncovered, for 5 minutes. Garnish with toasted almonds and serve immediately. Serves 4–6.

Spinach and Ricotta Crêpes

1 kg (2 lb) spinach; 30 g (1 oz) plus 1 tbs butter; 1$^1/_2$ cups ricotta cheese; pinch nutmeg; 1 tsp salt; $^1/_4$ tsp black pepper; 10–12 crêpes (see Basic Crêpe Batter); $^1/_2$ cup sour light cream.

Cook spinach, covered, in large saucepan in a little water for 10 minutes over a moderate heat. Drain thoroughly, squeezing the leaves in your hands to remove all moisture. Chop and purée in a blender with 1 tbs butter. Press ricotta cheese through a sieve. Add it to cooled spinach with beaten egg yolks, half of the Parmesan cheese, the nutmeg, salt and pepper.

Blend to a smooth paste. Fill crêpes with this stuffing. Roll up and place in a greased ovenproof dish. Dot with remaining butter. Cover with foil and cook in a preheated moderate oven (180°C/350°F) for 20–25 minutes or until well heated through. Remove foil, spoon over sour cream and sprinkle with remaining Parmesan cheese. Return to oven and cook a further 10 minutes. Serves 5–6.

Hungarian Pancakes

60 g (2 oz) butter; 1 small onion, finely chopped; 1 tbs paprika; 1 cup Béchamel Sauce (see page 456); 125 g (4 oz) mushrooms, sliced; 1 cup fresh, cannned or frozen crabmeat, drained and flaked; $^3/_4$ cup cream; salt and freshly ground black pepper; $^1/_4$ cup brandy; 8 crêpes (see Basic Crêpe Batter); 30 g (1 oz) Parmesan cheese, grated.

Melt half the butter in a saucepan, add onion and cook gently for 10 minutes or until soft. Stir in paprika and cook gently for 2 minutes, then add béchamel sauce and continue cooking over a low heat for 5 minutes. Allow mixture to cool slightly. Sauté mushrooms in remaining butter and add half of them to paprika sauce with crab, half the cream, salt, pepper and 2 tsp of the brandy. Fill crêpes with this mixture, roll them up and arrange in a buttered ovenproof dish. Warm remaining brandy, set alight and pour over remaining mushrooms. Shake over heat until flames die out, then add remaining cream. Cook, stirring, until sauce thickens slightly, then spoon over crêpes. Sprinkle with cheese and bake in a preheated moderate oven (180°C/350°F) for 10–15 minutes or until glazed. Serves 8 as a first course, 4 as a main course.

Crêpes Suzette

8 crêpes (see Basic Crêpe Batter); 30 g (1 oz) butter, melted; 4 cubes sugar; 2 oranges; extra 60 g (2 oz) butter, softened; 2 tbs Grand Marnier, Cointreau or Curaçao; sifted icing sugar for dusting; 3 tbs brandy.

Brush cooked crêpes with melted butter and keep warm in oven. Rub each sugar cube over skin of oranges to remove zest or oil. This process saturates sugar with oil from the orange rind and the oranges will look as though their rinds have been grated. Crush sugar and work in softened butter and liqueur. Spread each warm crêpe with orange butter and fold into a triangle. Arrange crêpes overlapping down the centre of a heated serving dish and dust with icing sugar. Heat brandy in a small saucepan, set alight and pour over the crêpes. Serves 4.

Soufflé in a Crêpe

Paper-thin crêpes encasing a light-as-air soufflé taste and look splendid when carried to the table. The crêpes can be made ahead and the soufflé up to the point of adding the beaten egg whites. Then, just as you are finishing the main course, add the whites to the mixture, and spoon into the crêpes – they take only 5–8 minutes to bake.

3 tbs flour; 3 tbs caster sugar; pinch salt; 3/4 cup milk; 3 eggs, separated, few drops vanilla; about 12 crêpes (see Basic Crêpe Batter); icing sugar; 1/4 cup Grand Marnier or other orange-flavoured liqueur.

Mix flour, sugar and salt in a saucepan and stir in milk. Cook over a gentle heat, stirring constantly, until thickened and simmer for 2 minutes. Remove from heat and beat in egg yolks. Whisk egg whites until stiff and fold into yolk mixture with vanilla. Put a good tablespoon of this soufflé mixture in centre of each crepe. Fold crêpes loosely in quarters and arrange in a buttered ovenproof serving dish. Bake in a preheated hot oven (200°C/400°F) for 5–8 minutes. Sift over icing sugar, sprinkle with Grand Marnier and serve immediately. Serves 6.

Apricot Pancakes

10–12 crêpes (see Basic Crêpe Batter); apricot conserve; lemon juice; finely chopped walnuts; sifted icing sugar; whipped cream to serve.

Spread each crêpe with apricot conserve mixed with a few drops of lemon juice. Roll them up loosely and arrange in a greased ovenproof dish. Heat a preheated cool oven (100°C/200°F) for 10 minutes. Serve sprinkled with nuts and icing sugar, with a bowl of whipped cream. Serves 5–6.

VARIATIONS

Combine 125 g (4 oz) ricotta or cream cheese with 1 tbs chopped mixed candied peel, grated rind 1 orange and 1 tbs caster sugar. Use to fill crêpes instead of apricot conserve, then heat as above.

Fill crêpes with sweetened stewed apple flavoured with cinnamon or sweetened stewed peaches, plums or apricots instead of apricot conserve, then heat as above.

Fill crêpes with sweetened chestnut purée flavoured with a little rum instead of apricot conserve, then heat as above.

CRESS

Mustard and Cress: Mustard seeds and cress seeds are planted together. Cress is sown 2 or 3 days before the mustard. Use while they are still seedlings about 2.5–5 cm (1–2 in) high. Strew freshly snipped mustard and cress over hard-boiled egg slices, salmon salads, Cheddar cheese and tomato slices.

Watercress: Small sprigs of dark green watercress leaves make a beautiful garnish for roast lamb or chicken, grilled lamb cutlets or kidneys, and green or orange salads. When buying watercress choose bunches with very dark green, quite large leaves. Try to use it as soon as possible after purchase or store tied in small bunches in refrigerator in sealed plastic bags. The bunches can be put in a vase of water and stored in a cool place or submerged in a bowl of water.

Watercress and Walnut Salad: Discard any yellowing leaves or thick stems from a bunch of watercress. Wash quickly, drain and dry. Put 2 cups watercress and 1/2 cup halved walnuts in salad bowl. When ready to serve, toss with a dressing made with 1 tbs olive or walnut oil and a squeeze of lemon juice. Serve with chicken or pork. Serves 6.

Watercress Sauce: Make 1 cup Béchamel Sauce (see page 456). Fold in 1/2 cup watercress purée (see below). Season with salt, freshly ground black pepper and lemon juice. Use with lamb, chicken or fish dishes.

Watercress Purée: Blanch 2 cups watercress in 1/2 cup boiling water for 2 minutes. Purée in blender or rub through a sieve. Stir in 1 tbs butter.

Watercress Soup: See *Soups.*

CROISSANT

Croissants are crescent-shaped rolls which make breakfast for millions of people in France and the Continent. The classic croissant is made of a yeast milk dough that has been rolled, spread with butter and folded several times. It is light, flaky and buttery, and is served warm either on its own or with jam or preserves.

JAM CROISSANT: A type of croissant using puff pastry. A little jam is placed along the base of a triangle of puff pastry, which is then rolled into a crescent. After baking they are sprinkled with caster sugar, and served warm.

CROQUE MONSIEUR

This French favourite is virtually a toasted cheese sandwich with ham added and is sold in nearly every sidewalk and open-air café. Delicious with a glass of wine or hot coffee. Use crusty French bread or a sandwich loaf.

Croque Monsieur

8 slices white bread; butter; 4 slices lean cooked ham; 1 cup grated Emmenthal or Gruyère cheese; freshly ground black pepper.

Spread bread generously with butter and make into sandwiches with ham, cheese and a grinding of black pepper. Press firmly together and trim crusts if liked. Fry in butter until golden-brown on both sides. Drain on crumpled paper towels. Serve hot. Serves 4.

VARIATION

Prepare Croque Monsieur as above, but before frying dip sandwiches in a mixture of 2 eggs beaten with 1/2 cup milk.

CROQUEMBOUCHE
(CROQUE-EN-BOUCHE)

The French *croque-en-bouche* translated means 'crunch and crumble in the mouth'. Croquembouche is usually made with little choux puffs filled with cream, toffee-glazed and arranged in a pyramid shape on a circular base. When the pyramid is decorated with spun sugar and crystallised fruit or flowers, it becomes a traditional French wedding cake. Other croquembouche can be made with tiny, crisp meringues filled with cream, or even with orange segments, dipped in sugar syrup, resting on a base of pastry.

CROQUETTE

A mixture of chopped savoury food, bound with sauce, formed into a small cork or cylinder shape, then dipped in egg crumbed and fried. Well-made croquettes make a delicious entrée or luncheon dish. Their texture should be such that the creamy inside contrasts deliciously with the crisp crumb covering. They can be made with freshly cooked ingredients but are also an attractive way of using leftover food.

Chicken Croquettes

2 tsp lemon juice; 1 egg yolk; 1 cup panada-thickness Béchamel Sauce (page 456); 2 cups finely chopped cooked chicken; 1 tbs each finely chopped chives and parsley; pinch nutmeg; little melted butter; flour; 1 egg; 1 tsp oil; pinch salt; dry white breadcrumbs; oil for deep-frying; parsley sprigs to garnish.

Beat lemon juice and egg yolk into hot sauce, then mix in chicken, chives, parsley and nutmeg, combining thoroughly. Cover surface with plastic wrap and leave in pan until cool. Turn mixture out on to a buttered baking tray and shape to a rectangle about 2 cm (¾ in) thick. Brush surface with melted butter and chill well. Divide into 8 equal parts. Working on a lightly floured surface with floured hands, form into cork shapes, rolling with the side of the hand and flattening ends. Beat egg with oil and salt. Flour croquettes lightly, then coat with egg mixture and breadcrumbs. Chill 30 minutes. Deep-fry, a few at a time, in hot oil (temperature is right when a bread cube fries golden-brown in 20 seconds). Drain on paper towels and serve hot, garnished with parsley. Serves 4.

CROUSTADE

A bread case made to hold a savoury filling, usually of sauced mixtures based on ham, poultry, seafood or vegetables.

Use one-day-old bread, cut into 5 cm (2 in) slices and remove the crust. Scoop out the centre leaving a rim 1 cm (½ in) thick around the sides and base. Brush inside and out with melted butter and bake in a preheated moderate oven (180°C/350°F) for about 30 minutes or until crisp and golden-brown.

You can make one large croustade by using a whole loaf of white bread. Remove the crusts, do not slice and proceed as for individual croustades, above.

CROUTE AND CROUTON

Croûtes can be small triangles, heart shapes or rounds of bread, varying from 2.5 cm (1 in) to 7.5 cm (3 in) in diameter. They are fried in oil, butter or a mixture of these, and used as a base on which to set Tournedos (see page 545), as a base for Canapés (see page 63) and to accompany mornays or other dishes.

Croûtons are tiny cubes of bread that have been fried to golden crispness in oil, butter, or a mixture of these. They are used as a garnish for soups, fricassés and vegetable purées, or in salads.

Garlic Croûtons: Fry 1–2 cloves sliced garlic in oil or butter and remove before bread cubes are added.

Oven Baked Croûtes: Remove crusts from sliced bread and cut each slice into 4. Brush with oil and bake in a slow oven until golden.

CROWN ROAST

This is made with 2 racks of lamb, bent round and sewn together at each end, with bones on the outside and the meat on the inside. Each rack consists of 7 or 8 cutlets and is chined (the bone cut through between each cutlet) trimmed of all the skin and some of the fat, and the meat is cleaned away from the bones to about 4 cm (1½ in) from the ends.

Your butcher will prepare a crown roast for you if you ask a day or two ahead. Order it by the number of cutlets, according to how many people you wish to serve; allow 2–3 cutlets per person.

■ TO ROAST: Cover ends of bones with foil and stand prepared crown roast in a baking dish. Roast in a preheated hot oven (200°C/400°F) for about 1 hour or until meat juice runs clear when tested with a skewer. If desired, the centre may be filled with stuffing after first 30 minutes cooking (see *Stuffings*). Remove from oven and allow meat to stand for 15 minutes in a warm place while making gravy. When ready to serve, cover ends of each cutlet bone with a paper cutlet frill, and slice meat into double cutlets for serving.

CRUDITES (RAW VEGETABLES)

One of the favourite hors d'oeuvre of provincial France. Prepare a variety of fresh, crisp, young raw vegetables and arrange decoratively on a large platter. You might have carrot, celery or pepper sticks; cauliflower florets, zucchini chunks, tiny tomatoes, baby squash, button mushrooms, etc.

Serve with a dip or sauce for dunking such as Mayonnaise, Aïoli (see pages 256 and 2), or natural yogurt flavoured with herbs and crushed garlic.

CUCUMBER

This member of the gourd family is usually eaten as a salad vegetable, but its delicate and distinctive flavour is very good in soups and hot vegetable dishes too. Hot or cold, it makes an attractive container for other foods; its refreshing coolness makes it important as a curry accompaniment. It makes the most elegant of tea sandwiches, and an outstandingly good and easily prepared pickle.

Varieties include green cucumbers, some as long as 50 cm (20 in), pale round apple cucumbers and small rough-skinned, pickling cucumbers. White or golden-skinned, long varieties are claimed to be 'burpless' and easy to digest. Store cucumbers in the refrigerator crisper and use within a week,

■ **BASIC PREPARATION:** Green cucumbers may be left unpeeled, scored lengthways with a fork and sliced into thin rounds, or may be lightly peeled so that some of the green remains and cut into slices, sticks or cubes. Seeds may be scooped out or not, as preferred. Apple cucumbers are peeled and cut up as desired. Raw cucumber may be dégorged to make it more digestible and make the flavour milder (this also will wilt it). To dégorge, sprinkle slices with salt and leave to drain in colander for 30 minutes. Rinse before using. **See recipes.**

Hot Cucumbers with Basil and Tomatoes

A superb accompaniment to grilled chicken or fish.

2 medium green cucumbers; salt; 30 g (1 oz) butter;
2 spring onions, including green tops;
$^{1}/_{2}$ cup Crème Fraiche (page 102); freshly ground
black pepper; 1 tbs fresh basil leaves;
3 medium tomatoes, peeled, seeded and diced.

Peel cucumbers thinly, halve lengthways and scoop out seeds. Cut crossways into crescents about 5 mm (¼ in) thick. Sprinkle with salt and leave to drain in a colander for 20 minutes. Rinse and dry well. Heat butter, add cucumber and cook on high heat 2–3 minutes, turning pieces over to seal them. Cut spring onions on the long diagonal into slivers and add to pan with crème fraîche. Season with salt and pepper and cook gently 5 minutes more. Serve at once, scattered with reserved basil. Serves 6.

Chilled Cucumber Yogurt Soup

Quick, light and healthy, with a pleasant tang.

1 green cucumber, lightly peeled, seeded and
chopped; 2 spring onions, including some green
part, cut into short lengths; 1 tsp chopped fresh
mint; $1^{1}/_{2}$ cups plain yogurt; salt and freshly ground
white pepper; paper-thin cucumber slices to garnish.

Purée vegetables, mint and yogurt in a food processor or blender. Season with salt and pepper and chill. Serve in chilled bowls with a slice of cucumber floated on each serving. Serves 4.

Cucumber Pickles

These crisp pickles can be eaten after 8 hours. They're lovely with sandwiches or with hot or cold corned beef or other meats.

12 green cucumbers, 13–15 cm (5–6 in) long;
1 tbs salt; 1 large clove garlic, quartered;
4 tiny onions (pickling onions), peeled and halved;
8 bay leaves; 4 small cinnamon sticks; 4 tsp mustard
seeds; 2 tsp prepared horseradish; $^{3}/_{4}$ cup white
vinegar; $^{1}/_{2}$ cup sugar; $^{1}/_{2}$ cup water.

Peel cucumbers, slice lengthways into quarters and remove seeds. Place in a bowl, sprinkle with salt and leave 2 hours. Lift cucumber out but do not rinse, and pack quarters lengthways into warm, sterilised 2½-cup (1-pint) jars, allowing 3 cucumbers per jar. Into each jar tuck ¼ garlic clove, 2 onion halves, 2 bay leaves, 1 cinnamon stick, 1 tsp mustard seeds and ½ tsp horseradish. Heat vinegar, sugar and water together, stirring until sugar has dissolved. Bring to the boil and pour into jars. Seal at once. Makes 4 x 2½-cup (1-pint) jars.

Cucumber Appetiser

1 medium green cucumber, lightly peeled and
finely sliced; salt; 1 tbs wine vinegar;
2 tsp sugar; 3 tbs olive oil; 1 tbs chopped
fresh dill or mint; freshly ground black pepper;
60 g (2 oz) cream cheese, at room temperature;
3 tbs sour cream; 1 tbs lemon juice;
1 small clove garlic, crushed;
sprigs fresh dill or mint to garnish.

Sprinkle cucumber with salt and leave to drain in a colander for 20 minutes. Place vinegar, sugar, oil and chopped herbs in a screwtop jar and shake until emulsified. Season with salt and pepper. Beat cream cheese until soft, then gradually beat in sour cream, lemon juice, garlic, salt and pepper. Rinse cucumber and dry well. Toss with oil and vinegar dressing, and divide evenly among 4 individual serving plates. Spoon cream cheese mixture on top and garnish with a sprig of dill or mint. Serves 4.

CUMBERLAND SAUCE

This is an excellent fruity sauce served cold with hot or cold ham, lamb or game.

Cumberland Sauce

3 tbs redcurrant jelly; 1 tbs lemon juice; 1 tbs orange
marmalade; 2 tbs port; 1 tsp prepared English
mustard, or 2 tsp French mustard.

Combine all ingredients in a bowl and mix together thoroughly. Makes ½ cup.

CUMIN

Spicy, aromatic seeds, used whole or ground, but in common with most spices, cumin is best ground as needed to retain its peak. It is used to spice chicken, rice, lamb and vegetables such as eggplant, in Middle Eastern and North African dishes and it is an essential ingredient in most curry powders used throughout India.

Although cumin looks similar to aniseed and caraway seeds, its aroma is quite different, and you cannot substitute one for the other without changing the dish.

Lamb and Eggplant Stew

An Iranian dish beautifully scented with cumin.

2 small eggplant; salt; 4 tbs oil; 1 large onion, sliced; 750 g–1 kg (1½–2 lb) lamb shoulder, boned and cubed; 2 tbs chopped fresh mint, or 2 tsp dried; ½ tsp white pepper; 3 tomatoes, peeled and chopped; 1 clove garlic, crushed; 2 tsp ground cumin; chopped fresh mint to garnish; boiled rice to serve.

Cut eggplant into small cubes, place in a colander, sprinkle with 1 tbs salt and leave for 1 hour to allow bitter juices to drain away. Dry on paper towels. Heat oil in a heavy pan and sauté onion until golden. Add lamb, mint, salt and pepper and fry until lamb is well browned, stirring frequently to brown on all sides. Remove lamb and onion from pan and keep warm. Add eggplant cubes to pan, cover and fry gently for 10 minutes, stirring occasionally. Return lamb and onion to pan and add tomatoes, garlic and cumin. Cover pan and simmer very gently for 1 hour or until lamb is very tender. Serve sprinkled with extra chopped mint and a dish of boiled rice. Serves 4–6.

CUMQUAT

The cumquat tree has small, decorative citrus fruits resembling tiny oranges. Cumquats are extremely bitter. They are delicious when preserved in a sugar syrup, sometimes with brandy added, or glazed in a syrup reduction.

Glacé Cumquats: Use about 12–18 fresh cumquats for this delicious recipe. Using a fine skewer, pierce skin of each cumquat about 8 times. Place in a bowl with cold water to cover and add 1 tbs salt. Leave overnight, then drain. Put into a pan with fresh water to cover, bring to the boil and simmer until tender, about 30 minutes. Drain and place in a heavy syrup to cover (2 cups sugar to every 2½ cups water). Simmer cumquats in the syrup until they are clear and transparent. Put in a bowl and stand overnight. Next day, drain syrup into a saucepan, add ¼ cup sugar, bring to the boil and pour back over cumquats. Leave for

4 hours. Repeat this process once more, adding another ¼ cup sugar and leaving a further 4 hours. Lastly, drain cumquats from syrup, roll in crystal sugar and place on a wire rack to dry, preferably in a very slow oven. Store in an airtight container in a cool place. Serve in small paper cases or use to flavour ice cream, decorate creamy desserts, or serve with after-dinner coffee.
Cumquats in Brandy: See *Brandy*: Brandied Fruit.

CUP CAKE

See *Cakes*.

CURRANT

See *Fruit, Dried and Candied*.

CURRY

A good curry meal, with its accompaniments and bowls of steaming rice, is something we all look forward to. A curry meal may consist of meat, chicken or fish curry, several vegetables dishes, a lentil and a rice dish. Some curries are very rich, the palate being refreshed with yogurt or salad. Fiery curries are balanced by cooling, bland accompaniments (see below). There should be a dry dish and a moist, a rich dish and a light one. These dishes are all put on the table at the same time; each person then makes a selection to suit personal taste and palate.

A variety of accompaniments may be served with curry. They include cucumber or sliced banana, chutneys, pickles and fresh sambals (see below). You might like to make Chapatis or Puris (see pages 69 and 400), the flat Indian breads that are used to scoop up the curry and its delicious gravy.

Curries are eaten with a spoon and fork. Each spoonful is mixed separately and should consist of rice, curry and different accompaniment. This way, the contrasting tastes and textures are appreciated and it is possible to adjust the hotness of the curries with the rice and the chutney.

Curry Powder: This is probable the world's earliest spice blend. In India housewives daily grind or bruise their curry spices on a 'curry stone', and throughout the world, curry enthusiasts are now blending their own spices.

Thanks to certain spices, all curry powders have a characteristic flavour. Turmeric, fenugreek, cumin, coriander and chilli are the basic spices. Beyond that curry powder may include allspice, cinnamon, cardamom, cloves, fennel and ginger; the various combinations and amounts determine the flavour of the curry.

If you prefer to rely on a favourite brand of curry powder or curry paste, you will know by experience it is better to purchase it in small amounts and use it as quickly as possible. **See recipes.**

SAMBALS AND ACCOMPANIMENTS

Accompaniments are an essential part of every curry

meal. They are easy to make and proved intriguing contrasts in flavour and texture which are most enjoyable. Sambals can be red or white, that is heating or cooling. Red sambals are made by grinding together chillies with ingredients like onion, dried fish, or grated coconut. When the amount of chillies is reduced, the sambal is white or cooling.

Serve one or two of the following sambals, plus a few commercially-made chutneys and nuts with your choice of curried food.

Banana Sambal: Peel and slice bananas at the last moment and sprinkle with a little lemon juice.

Coconut Sambal: Blend ½ cup desiccated coconut with 1 tbs finely chopped onion, ¼ tsp chilli powder or a little finely chopped chilli, add salt and lemon juice to taste.

Cucumber Sambal: Dice or finely slice 1 peeled cucumber. If seeds are large, cut cucumber in 2 and remove sees before slicing. Crush 1 clove garlic with a good pinch salt. Beat ½ cup plain yogurt with a fork, add cucumber and garlic. Blend well.

Fruit Sambal: Sour apples, firm plums, green mangoes or any firm fruit in season may be used. Cut fruit into small dice, mix with a little finely chopped red chilli, salt and lemon juice to taste.

Potato Sambal: Boil 2 medium potatoes, peel and cut into dice. Lightly mix with a little finely chopped green chilli and 2 tbs finely chopped onion, preferably golden shallots. Sprinkle over a little olive oil, add salt and lemon juice to taste.

Tomato Sambal: Combine 2 tomatoes, cut into thin slices, 1 finely sliced small onion, and a little green chilli, finely chopped. Mix lightly with a squeeze of lemon juice and season with salt and freshly ground black pepper. A little desiccated coconut may be sprinkled over top.

Pappadams: These spicy lentil wafers are fried in about 1 cm (¾ in) hot oil for only 3–4 seconds. They increase in size and become crispy and golden.

Bombay Duck: This is actually fish, which is salted and dried. Fry in hot oil or grill until crisp. Crumble over curry.

See also *Chapati, Dhal, Lassi* and *Puri.*

Curry Powder

A simple recipe: use about 1 tbs for every 500 g (1 lb) meat, fish or poultry, substituting it for the spices or curry powder in a recipe.

⅓ cup cardamom seeds; 6 large cinnamon sticks; I tbs whole cloves; I½ tbs cumin seeds; large pinch each ground mace and nutmeg.

Grind all ingredients in a blender or coffee grinder. Pass mixture through a sieve and store in an airtight jar, preferably in the refrigerator. Will keep fresh and aromatic for 4–5 weeks.

Madras–Style Curry Paste

Use about 1 tbs of this paste for each 500 g (1 lb) meat, fish or poultry, substituting it for garlic, ginger and spices in a recipe.

½ cup coriander seeds; 2 tbs cumin seeds; I tsp each black peppercorns, turmeric, black mustard seeds, chilli powder and salt; 3 cloves garlic, peeled; I nob fresh ginger (about walnut-size), grated; I tbs vinegar; ⅓ cup oil.

Combine spices, garlic, ginger and vinegar in food processor or coffee grinder and grind until a paste, adding more vinegar if needed. Heat oil in small saucepan and when very hot add spice mixture. Reduce heat and cook gently, stirring, for a few minutes or until oil separates from spices. Cool and store in airtight jar in refrigerator.

Red Curry Paste

Red and green curry pastes are called for in many Thai recipes. Make a batch of each and store in airtight jars in the refrigerator. It lasts for months and a small amount may be added to soups or stews or other Asian dishes to give them a lift.

5 dried long red chillies, seeded and chopped; 6 cloves garlic, peeled and chopped; 4 golden shallots, chopped; I stalk lemongrass, finely sliced; 2 cm (¾ in) piece of galangal, peeled and chopped; I tbs coriander roots, chopped; ½ tbs kaffir lime peel; I tsp shrimp paste; I tsp ground white pepper; I tsp coriander seeds, roasted; ½ tsp cumin seeds, roasted; I tsp ground nutmeg; pinch of salt; 2 tbs peanuts, roasted and ground.

In a food processor or blender, purée the chillies with the garlic, golden shallots, lemongrass, galangal, coriander roots and lime peel. Add enough water to make a paste. Wrap the shrimp paste in foil and 'roast' in a dry frying pan over a moderate heat for several minutes, turning once, to release the aroma. Add with the pepper, coriander, cumin, nutmeg, salt and blend until combined, and then add the peanuts.
GREEN CURRY PASTE: Make as above but use fresh green chillies in place of red chillies. You may add some green chilli leaves, fresh coriander leaves or even English spinach to increase the green colour.

Lamb with Cashew Nut Curry (Korma)

MASALA SAUCE: 3 dried red chillies, seeded; 2.5 cm (I in) piece fresh ginger, peeled and quartered; ½ cup unsalted cashew nuts; ¾ cup water; 2 large cloves garlic; ½ tsp cinnamon; ½ tsp cardamom seeds; 3 whole cloves; 2½ tsp coriander seeds; I tsp cumin seeds.**

LAMB: $^{1}/_{2}$ tsp saffron threads, crumbled;
3 tbs boiling water; 90 g (3 oz) ghee; 2 medium
onions, finely chopped; $1^{1}/_{2}$ tsp salt; $^{1}/_{2}$ cup plain
yogurt; 750 g ($1^{1}/_{2}$ lb) boned lamb shoulder, cubed;
$1^{1}/_{2}$ tbs chopped fresh coriander; juice $^{1}/_{2}$ lemon.

MASALA SAUCE: Purée chillies, ginger and cashew
nuts in blender with water until smooth. Peel garlic
cloves and add to cashew nut purée with remaining
masala ingredients. Blend again until mixture is
completely ground. Set aside. Soak saffron in boiling
water for about 10 minutes. Heat ghee and cook
onions slowly until soft and golden-brown, about 10
minutes. Stir in salt and masala, then add yogurt.
Cook over a gentle heat, stirring, until ghee covers
the surface. Add lamb and saffron and stir gently.
Cover and cook gently for about 20 minutes.
Sprinkle 1 tbs coriander over lamb and continue
cooking for 10 minutes or until lamb is tender. To
serve, transfer to a heated serving dish and sprinkle
top with lemon juice and remaining coriander. Serve
with boiled rice and accompaniments. Serves 4–6.

Prawn Curry

500 g (1 lb) shelled green prawns, or
1 kg (2 lb) whole green prawns;
30 g (1 oz) ghee or butter; 10 curry leaves;
1 large onion, finely chopped; 3 cloves garlic,
crushed; 5 cm (2 in) piece fresh ginger,
peeled and grated; 2 tbs curry powder or paste;
$^{1}/_{2}$–1 red chilli, seeded and chopped; 1 cup Coconut
Milk (page 91); 2 tsp ground rice; 1 cinnamon stick;
juice 1 lemon; 1 tsp salt.

Devein prawns (shell and devein whole prawns).
Heat ghee in pan, add curry leaves, onion, garlic and
ginger and fry over gentle heat until golden. Add
curry powder and chilli, and fry for 1 minute. Stir in
coconut milk, ground rice (mixed with a little
coconut milk), cinnamon, lemon juice and salt.
Cover and simmer gently for 15 minutes. Add
prawns, stir well, then cover and simmer gently for
10 minutes. Serves 4.
NOTE: If using cooked prawns, it is only necessary to
heat gently, about 5 minutes.
VARIATION
CHICKEN CURRY: Prepare as for Prawn Curry but use
750 g (1½ lb) chicken fillets, each fillet cut into 3, in
place of prawns. Add to curry sauce and simmer
gently for 20 minutes or until tender. Serves 4.

Lamb Almond Curry

Many good curries are cooked by this method of
gently braising the meat and spices, adding more
water as the meat browns and cooks. The result is
tender, excellent meat with a rich brown gravy.

3 tbs ghee or butter; 2 medium onions, finely
sliced; 1 kg (2 lb) boneless lamb, cut into large
cubes; 1 tbs finely sliced fresh ginger;
4–5 cardamom pods; 2 tsp salt; 2–3 red chillies,
seeded and ground to a paste; 2 bay leaves; 4 cloves
garlic, chopped; 1 onion, finely chopped;
1–1½ cups hot water; 1 cup plain yogurt;
12 almonds, blanched and halved.

Heat ghee in a heavy saucepan and sauté sliced onions
until tender. Add meat, ginger, cardamom, salt,
ground chilli paste, bay leaves and half the garlic.
Cook, stirring, for 10 minutes. Add chopped onion
and remaining garlic. Cover and when simmering
add some of the hot water. Stir and cover again.
When simmering again add more water. Repeat
process 3 or 4 times. Add 2 tbs yogurt and more hot
water and cook until meat is tender, adding more hot
water when necessary. Add remaining yogurt and
blanched almonds. Simmer for 5–7 minutes or until
gravy is well blended and rich golden-brown. Serve
with boiled rice and a few accompaniments as liked
(see *Sambals*). Serves 4–6.

Fish Curry with Tomato

500 g (1 lb) fish steaks; 2 tbs ghee; 1 onion, finely
chopped; 2 cloves garlic, crushed; 2 tbs chopped
fresh mint or coriander; 1 tsp ground cumin;
1 tsp ground turmeric; $^{1}/_{2}$ tsp chilli power;
1 tomato, chopped; 1 tsp salt; $^{1}/_{2}$ tsp black pepper;
juice $^{1}/_{2}$ lemon.

Cut fish into serving pieces. Heat ghee in a heavy
saucepan and fry onion and garlic over low heat until
translucent. Mix in mint or coriander, cumin,
turmeric and chilli powder, and stir for 2 minutes.
Add tomato, salt and pepper, and cook until tomato
becomes soft and pulpy. Add lemon juice and fish
pieces, and spoon sauce over fish. Cover pan and simmer gently for 10 minutes or until fish flakes easily
when tested with a fine skewer. Serve with boiled
rice and lemon wedges. Serves 4.

Memsahib's Lamb Curry

An English-style curry quickly made with lamb left
over from the weekend roast. Serve it with simple
accompaniments from the store cupboard such as
sultanas, chutneys, coconut and cashew nuts or try
grated apple moistened with mint sauce.

60 g (2 oz) butter; 2 onions, finely chopped;
1 cup diced celery; 1 clove garlic, crushed;
1–2 tbs curry power; 2 tsp flour; 2 cups chicken
stock; 1 green apple, peeled and diced;
2 cups diced cooked lamb.

Melt butter in frying pan and sauté onions, celery
and garlic until soft. Stir in curry powder and flour

and cook, stirring, for 2 minutes Remove from heat and stir in stock. Bring to the boil, add apple and lamb and simmer, covered, for 30 minutes. Serves 4.

Vegetable Curry

¹/₂ cup oil or melted ghee; I tsp mustard seeds; 6–8 curry leaves (optional); I tsp turmeric; 2 cloves garlic, crushed; 2 cm (³/₄ in) piece fresh ginger, peeled and grated; ¹/₂ red chilli, seeded and chopped; ¹/₂ cauliflower, broken into florets; I carrot, sliced; 250 g (8 oz) green beans, strung and chopped; I cup shelled green peas; salt.

Heat oil in large saucepan, add mustard seeds, curry leaves, turmeric, garlic, ginger and chilli and fry for 1–2 minutes. Add vegetables and fry over a medium heat, stirring, for 10–12 minutes or until vegetables are almost tender but still a little crisp. Add salt, cover and simmer for 2–3 minutes. Serve at once. Serves 4.

NOTE: You may vary the vegetables for this dish, using diced potato, Brussels sprouts, cabbage, silverbeet leaves, green peppers, spinach, etc.

Chicken Curry

2 medium onions, finely chopped; I clove garlic, crushed; 2 cm (I in) piece fresh ginger, peeled and grated; 60 g (2 oz) ghee; I tbs curry powder; 2 large tomatoes, peeled, seeded and diced; 2 tsp paprika; 2 whole cloves; 8 cm (3 in) cinnamon stick; 2 cups Coconut Milk (page 91); 2 tsp salt; 2 green peppers, seeded and shredded; I x 1.5 kg (3 lb) chicken; 2 tbs cream; I tbs chopped fresh mint.

Cook onions, garlic and ginger gently in hot ghee until beginning to turn golden. Add curry powder and cook 3–4 minutes. Add tomatoes, paprika, cloves, cinnamon, coconut milk, salt and green peppers. Simmer, covered, for about 15 minutes, then add chicken, cut into serving pieces, and simmer 30–40 minutes, until chicken is tender. Add cream and fresh, chopped mint. Heat curry through and serve with boiled rice and accompaniments (see pages 107–8). Serves 4.

Burma Beef Curry

I medium onion, finely chopped; I clove garlic, crushed; 30 g (I oz) butter or ghee; I tbs curry powder; 2 ripe tomatoes, peeled and diced; 500 g (I lb) stewing steak, cubed; ¹/₂ cup milk; 2 tsp lemon juice; salt and freshly ground black pepper; 2 tsp sugar.

Fry onion with garlic in butter or ghee for 3–4 minutes. Add curry powder and fry for a further 2 minutes. Add tomatoes and meat with just enough water to barely cover meat. Simmer very gently for about 1¹/₂ hours or until meat is tender. Stir in milk and lemon juice, season to taste and add sugar. Serve with boiled rice and accompaniments (see pages 107–8). Serves 4.

Pork Vindaloo

I kg (2 lb) pork; 1¹/₂ cups boiling water; ¹/₄ cup tamarind pulp; ¹/₄ cup mustard oil; 12 whole peppercorns; 2–3 bay leaves.

MARINADE: 3 large cloves garlic, crushed; I tbs ground ginger; I tsp ground chilli; I tbs curry powder; ¹/₂ tsp ground cloves; ¹/₂ tsp ground cardamom; I tsp cinnamon; ¹/₂ tsp salt; ¹/₂ cup malt vinegar.

Combine all the ingredients for the marinade in a bowl. Cut the pork into large cubes and add to the marinade. Leave for 18–24 hours. Pour the boiling water over tamarind pulp and cool. When cold, push through a sieve and reserve the liquid. Heat the oil in a frying pan, add the meat, marinade, peppercorns, bay leaves and tamarind juice. Simmer gently 2 hours or until meat is tender. Serves 4.

Singaras

500 g (I lb) potatoes; 2 tsp curry power; 2 tsp salt; I tsp cumin seeds; I tsp fennel seeds; ¹/₂ tsp black mustard seeds; 30 g (I oz) ghee or butter; 4 cups flour; 1¹/₄ cups water; oil for frying.

Boil potatoes in their skins and when cooked, but still firm, peel and cut into 6 mm (¹/₄ in) dice. Sprinkle curry power, salt and seeds evenly over and mix lightly. Rub soft ghee or butter into flour. Make a well in the centre, then add all the water at once to make a soft dough. Knead well until smooth and elastic. Divide into 32 pieces and roll each into a ball. Roll out each one thinly on a floured board, with a lightly floured rolling pin, to a circle about 10 cm (4 in) across. Cut each circle in 2 with a sharp knife. Moisten edges of each half circle and put a spoonful of potato mixture on each. Fold over and press edges well together. From each circle, you will get 2 triangular-shaped pastries. When all are made, fry in deep hot oil until puffed and golden. Drain on paper towels. Serve hot or cold. Makes 64.

CUSTARD

Whether or not a custard is a simple, baked one flavoured with nutmeg or an elegant Crème Brulée (opposite) with soft cream covered with a brittle crust of burnt sugar, the custard base is milk and/or cream and eggs or egg yolks. Gentle cooking is essential to ensure the perfect smoothness of texture necessary for any custard.

There are two basic kinds of custard: stirred custard, cooked on top of the stove, and baked custard, cooked in the oven. Once these have been mastered a great many variations can be made, such as Crème Pâtissière (see page 207) which is used to fill French tarts, tartlets, éclairs and profiteroles, or such classic custards as Crème Caramel or Petits Pots de Crème. **See recipes.**

Baked Custard

2 cups milk; 2 eggs; I egg yolk; 2 tbs sugar; pinch salt; $^1/_2$ tsp vanilla or nutmeg.

Heat milk in heavy saucepan over low heat. Mix together eggs, egg yolk, sugar, salt and vanilla or nutmeg. Mix well, but do not beat. When small bubbles appear around edge of milk pan, pour about one third into egg mixture and mix until well blended. Add this mixture to remaining milk and mix again. Put 6 buttered custard cups or 1 large ovenproof dish in a baking tin and fill with strained custard. Carefully pour hot water into baking tin to come halfway up sides of cups or dish. Bake in a preheated moderately slow oven (160°C/325°F) for 30 minutes or until a knife inserted in centre of custard comes out clean. Remove custard cups or large dish from water. Cool. Serves 6.

Stirred Custard

This is the simple custard sauce that accompanies many English steamed puddings and poached fruit.

I cup milk; I tsp cornflour; I egg; I tbs sugar; vanilla to taste.

Heat most of the milk in the top of a double saucepan. Blend cornflour with remaining cold milk. Blend in a little of the hot milk, then return to saucepan and cook for 1 minute. Allow to cool. Add egg and sugar beaten together. Stand pan over boiling water and cook, stirring until custard coats spoon. Stir in vanilla. Makes 1 cup.

Crème Anglaise

This is the rich custard sauce, velvety and smooth, created in England and adopted by France.

$^1/_2$ cup sugar; 4 large or 5 small egg yolks; I tsp cornflour; 2 cups milk; I vanilla bean.

Beat sugar into egg yolks gradually and continue to beat for 2–3 minutes until pale yellow. Beat in cornflour, then gradually stir in milk, scalded with vanilla bean. Pour mixture into top part of double saucepan, place over hot water and stir slowly and continuously until custard thickens sufficiently to coat back of spoon. Keep custard well under simmering point. Remove from heat and stir for 1–2 minutes to cool slightly. Strain. Serve warm or cold. If serving cold, cover surface with damp greaseproof paper to prevent skin forming on top, and chill. Serves 6–8.

Crème Brûlée

Make as for Crème Anglaise, using only $^1/_4$ cup sugar and substituting cream for milk. Pour into 4 individual or 1 larger serving dish and chill well. Just before serving, stand custard in shallow baking dish surrounded with ice to keep custard chilled. Sprinkle white or brown sugar in a 3 mm ($^1/_8$ in) layer over top and put under preheated grill until sugar melts and forms a toffee glaze. Serve immediately. Serves 4.

Petits Pots de Crème

These rich custard creams can be flavoured with vanilla, coffee or chocolate. Offer a choice of flavours or make all the Pots de Crème in one flavour.

$2^1/_2$ cups milk; I vanilla bean, or $^1/_2$ tsp vanilla; $^1/_4$ cup caster sugar; 4 egg yolks; I whole egg; I tsp instant coffee powder; I tbs warm water; 30–45 g (I–I$^1/_2$ oz) cooking chocolate, chopped.

Scald milk with vanilla bean and sugar. Remove bean. Lightly beat egg yolks with whole egg. Add milk and vanilla if vanilla bean is not being used. Strain custard and divide into 3 equal parts. Flavour one part with coffee dissolved in the warm water; one with chocolate melted on a plate over hot water; and leave the third plain. Pour carefully into 9–10 little pots. Stand these in a shallow baking dish and half fill tin with hot water to surround pots. Cover pots and bake in a preheated moderate oven (180°C/350°F) for 12–20 minutes or until set depending on your oven and thickness of pots. Cool and serve with crisp dessert biscuits. Serves 6.

Oeufs à la Neige

This classic of the custard world is sometimes mistaken for the French dessert *Ile Flottante* (Floating Island).

$2^1/_2$ cups milk; I vanilla bean; I tbs sugar or vanilla sugar; I quantity Crème Anglaise (page III); 2 tbs slivered, toasted almonds, to decorate.

MERINGUE: 4 egg whites; I cup caster sugar.

MERINGUE: Whisk egg whites until peaks form. Gradually beat in sugar 1 tbs at a time until stiff peaks form and hold their shape.

Put milk, vanilla bean and sugar into shallow pan and bring to simmering point. Poach tablespoons of meringue in the milk, turning to cook evenly, for 3–5 minutes or until set. Lift out carefully with slotted spoon, drain and put on top of custard (Crème Anglaise) in a glass or china bowl. Serve decorated with almonds. Serves 6–8.

NOTE: The milk in which meringues were poached can be used for custard or sweet sauce.

Crème Caramel

CARAMEL: $^1/_2$ cup water; I cup sugar.

CUSTARD: I cup cream, I cup milk; $^1/_2$ tsp vanilla; 3 whole eggs; 2 egg yolks; $^1/_2$ cup sugar.

CARAMEL: Put water and sugar in a small saucepan over low heat and stir until sugar dissolves. Boil, without stirring, until golden-brown. Pour into 6 individual $^1/_2$-cup moulds, turning moulds to coat bottom and sides.

CUSTARD: Warm cream and milk together, remove from heat and add vanilla. Beat whole eggs, egg yolks and sugar, and stir into warmed cream and milk. Strain, then pour into prepared moulds. Set in a baking tin of hot water and bake in a preheated moderately slow oven (160°C/325°F) for 25 minutes or until custard is set and a knife inserted in centre comes out clean. Cool and chill overnight. Unmould on to serving plates. Serves 6.

Ile Flottante aux Praline
(Floating Island)

This classic dish with its 'island' of baked, toffee-coated meringue in a lake of rich custard is one of the greats of the dessert world.

$^1/_2$ cup sugar; 2 tbs water; pinch cream of tartar; $^1/_3$ cup crushed Praline (page 387); I quantity of Crème Anglaise (page III), very well chilled.

MERINGUE: 4 egg whites; pinch cream of tartar; pinch salt; $^2/_3$ cup caster sugar; $^1/_2$ tsp vanilla.

In a heavy saucepan combine sugar, water and cream of tartar. Heat gently, stirring, until sugar has dissolved. Wash sugar crystals frequently from sides of pan with a brush dipped in water. Cook over moderate heat, without stirring, until mixture caramelises and turns a deep golden-brown. Pour caramel carefully into a 4-cup ovenproof mould, tilting it to coat bottom and sides. Set aside.

MERINGUE: Whisk egg whites with cream of tartar and salt until they form soft peaks. Beat in sugar, a little at a time, and vanilla, and continue beating until mixture holds stiff glossy peaks.

Spoon half meringue into caramel-lined mould, sprinkle with crushed praline and spoon in remaining meringue. Smooth top with a spatula. Place mould in a baking tin and add enough hot water to reach halfway up sides of mould. Bake in centre of a preheated cool oven (140°C/275°F) for 40 minutes or until a skewer inserted in the centre comes out clean. Invert meringue on to a serving dish, surround with Crème Anglaise and hand remaining Crème Anglaise separately. Serves 4.

Maple Syrup Custard

Creamy custard with a subtle maple flavour, baked in individual pots or one large dish.

4 eggs; 2 cups milk; $^1/_2$ cup maple syrup; pinch salt.

TO SERVE: whipped cream; maple syrup.

Beat eggs, then add milk, maple syrup and salt and combine well. Pour into 6 buttered custard cups or a buttered 4-cup casserole. Set container in a baking tin with enough warm water to come halfway up sides of container Bake in a preheated moderate oven (180°C/350°F) for about 30 minutes for individual cups, or 45–50 minutes for larger dish, or until set. Serve warm, with cream and a drizzle of maple syrup. Serves 6.

CUSTARD APPLE

The fleshy, round or heart-shaped fruit of the Anona tree, found in the tropics. The fruit is cut open and the creamy white flesh is spooned out of the knobbly green shell. The flesh is soft, sweet, aromatic and custard-flavoured; the shiny black seeds should be discarded.

CUTTLEFISH

A saltwater mollusc, closely related to squid. Like squid, the eyes, long central bone, sac of ink and yellowish deposit under the head must be removed. More tender than octopus and squid, cuttlefish can be cooked in the same way as squid.

See *Squid*.

DAMPER

The traditional Australian bush bread, damper was once made from flour, salt, water and perhaps some dripping. It was baked directly in the ashes of the fire or in a camp oven. Today, milk and butter may be used and the damper is baked in a hot oven or, if cooked in the fire, is usually wrapped in foil so that there is no need to knock the ashes off before eating it.

Damper

4 cups self-raising flour; 1 tsp salt; 30 g (1 oz) butter or dripping; 1 cup milk; ½ cup water.

Sift flour and salt into a large mixing bowl. Rub in fat. Make a well in flour and pour in milk and water. Mix with a knife until dough leaves sides of bowl; you may need a little more flour if dough is too slack. Place on a greased and well-floured baking tray and pat out to a round about 20 cm (8 in) across. Cut a cross in the top. Bake in a preheated hot oven (200°C/400°F) for 25 minutes, then reduce oven heat to moderate (180°C/350°F) and bake a further 15–20 minutes or until damper sounds hollow when tapped. Serve sliced with butter, and golden syrup or jam if liked. Makes 1 x 20 cm (8 in) loaf.

DANISH OPEN SANDWICHES (SMØRREBRØD)

Smørrebrød means 'buttered bread', but Danish open sandwiches are very much more than that. They are special to the Danes and have been copied throughout the world as one of the great Danish inspirations. They are made with thin slices of any type of rye bread, crusty French bread, toasted or plain, or crispbreads. These are spread with butter, or fat such as spiced pork dripping, right to the edge of the bread to prevent any moisture from the topping making the bread soggy. The fat helps to hold everything in place.

The generous toppings turn the sandwiches into a meal; they are eaten at lunch, and always with a knife and fork.

Toppings are generally made up from foods found in the household pantry or refrigerator. Cold roast meats or poultry; canned or spiced fish; potato salad; cheese; mayonnaise; cold scrambled or hard-boiled eggs. The delicatessen supplies salami, smoked pork and beef, ham, liver sausage, smoked salmon or mackerel, along with capers, horseradish, gherkins and pickles.

Fresh vegetables play an important role – tomatoes, cucumber, lettuce, onions – and herbs, such as chives, dill, parsley and cress, are all used.

TOPPINGS FOR DANISH OPEN SANDWICHES

Egg with Anchovy and Capers: Place flat anchovy fillets in parallel rows on a piece of buttered rye bread.

Hard-boil and finely chop an egg before arranging it between the rows. Garnish with capers.

Sardine with Sliced Tomato: Place tomato on buttered rye or French bread in overlapping slices; on these put a whole sardine or several small ones. Garnish with a twist of lemon.

Danish Blue with Raw Egg Yolk: Cover buttered rye bread with a very thin slice of Danish Blue cheese. Place an onion ring in the centre and put the egg yolk in the centre of ring, to stop egg from running off.

Roast Beef with Potato Salad and Chives: Place thin, furled slices of roast beef on buttered bread and heap a generous mound of potato salad in the centre. Sprinkle salad with snipped chives.

Bacon and Kidney with Tomato: Fry rindless streaky bacon rashers until crisp, drain and cool. Place bacon on buttered rye bread and top with a slice of tomato. Place chopped grilled kidney over tomato and garnish with a parsley sprig.

Smoked Mussels: Place mussels on buttered French bread or crispbread; garnish with dill sprays and a sliver of lemon zest.

Smoked Salmon with Scrambled Egg: Place a slice of smoked salmon on buttered French or rye bread and across it spread a strip of scrambled egg. Garnish with sour cream.

Spiced Herring with Onion Rings: Place herrings on buttered dark rye bread, top with overlapping raw onion rings and garnish with capers or cress.

Roast Pork and Orange: Top buttered light rye bread with thinly sliced pork; garnish with an orange twist and a stoned prune or a spoonful of apple sauce.

Roast Pork and Beetroot: Place slices of roast pork on buttered light rye bread or crispbread; garnish with a slice of cooked beetroot and a strip of crisp crackling.

Ham with Vegetable Salad: Make vegetable salad with equal quantities of chopped cooked beetroot and apple, and a little chopped gherkin. Add some stiff Mayonnaise (see page 256) to bind. Place ham slice on buttered dark or light rye bread, French bread or crispbread. Mound salad neatly on top and garnish with watercress sprigs.

Salami with Potato and Chives: Spread rye or French bread or crispbread with spiced lard (see below) and place slices of salami on it; arrange slightly overlapping slices of boiled new potato and sprinkle with snipped chives.

Spiced Lard: Melt some pure lard, or gently fry some fat pork or fat bacon dice until the fat runs. Add a little finely chopped onion and a few leaves of thyme and fry until onion is softened. Allow fat to solidify before using on bread for *smørrebrød*.

DANISH PASTRY

Light-as-air Danish pastries are made from a rich, buttery, yeast dough with a variety of toppings and fillings. The pastries may be filled with preserves, dried fruit, nuts or Crème Pâtissière (see page 207); glazed with icing, sprinkled with spices, coarse sugar or ground nuts and then shaped into knots, twists or little parcels.

They are served with steaming hot cups of coffee but are sometimes eaten after the main course at lunch. Most people buy their favourite Danish pastries from good pastry shops; even in Denmark, home cooks consider they require the special skills of a pastry cook.

DATE

Dates grow in huge, hanging bunches, often weighing up to 15 kg (33 lb), on the date palm, and are eaten either fresh or dried. The best dried dates are soft and juicy, packed whole in small boxes. These can be eaten as they are or used in recipes for stuffed dates. The hard, dry variety comes in blocks and is good for cooking.

Fresh dates can be bought from many greengrocers and should be purchased when their skins are a smooth, shiny brown and the fruit is plump and not sticky.

WAYS TO USE DATES

WHOLE DRIED DATES: Removes the stones and stuff with any of the following – marzipan; whole or ground nuts; flavoured fondant; cream cheese, sweetened with vanilla sugar; glacé fruits such as cherries or pineapple; or very thick Crème Pâtissière, see page 207, flavoured with Kirsch and sprinkled with sugar. Serve in frilly paper sweet cases as petits fours.

DRIED DATES SOLD IN BLOCKS: Use, finely chopped, in puddings, cakes, breads, scones or sandwiches.

FRESH DATES: Serve with a bowl of thick, creamy plain yogurt; ricotta cheese, flavoured with grated lemon or orange rind; in a fruit salad or simply enjoy them on their own. They also make a good addition to a cheese board. See recipes.

Date Bars

I cup flour; I3/4 cups rolled oats (plain or quick-cooking); 250 g (8 oz) butter or firm margarine.

FILLING: I cup chopped, stoned dates; I tbs lemon juice; 2 tbs rum or water; 2 tsp grated lemon rind; 1/4 cup firmly packed brown sugar; I tsp cinnamon or allspice.

FILLING: Place dates in a saucepan with remaining filling ingredients and simmer 20 minutes, stirring often, or until dates are soft. Cool. Sift flour into a bowl. Add oats and rub in butter or margarine until well blended. Divide mixture in half and press one portion into a greased 18 cm (7 in) square cake tin. Spoon date mixture evenly on top, then sprinkle with remaining rolled oats mixture and press it into place to cover filling. Bake in a preheated moderate oven (180°C/350°F) for 25 minutes. Cut into bars and allow to cool in tin. Makes 12–14.

Frosted Date Bars

These nutty, economical fruit bars stay moist for weeks. Make them 2–3 weeks ahead if liked, but don't roll in the icing sugar until you serve them.

3/4 cup evaporated milk; I cup chopped dates; I cup self-raising flour; 1/2 tsp salt; 125 g (4 oz) butter; 1/2 cup caster sugar; I egg, beaten; I tsp vanilla; 1/2 cup chopped walnuts; sifted icing sugar.

Place evaporated milk in a small saucepan and heat until small bubbles appear at edge of saucepan. Pour over dates and allow to cool. Sift flour and salt together. Cream butter with sugar until light and fluffy. Add egg and vanilla and beat well. Fold in sifted flour alternately with milk and date mixture. Stir in nuts. Spoon mixture into a greased 23 cm (9 in) square cake tin. Bake in a preheated moderate oven (180°C/350°F) for 30–35 minutes or until a skewer inserted into the centre comes out clean. Turn out and cool on a wire rack. Cut into bars and toss in icing sugar. Makes 24.

Date and Nut Rolls

These are easily made and are popular sliced and buttered for morning tea or in packed lunches. They can be baked in loaf tins, but the traditional roll tins seem just perfect.

I cup chopped dates; 3/4 cup firmly packed brown sugar; I tsp bicarbonate of soda; 60 g (2 oz) butter; I tsp grated lemon rind; I cup boiling water; 2 cups self-raising flour; I tsp mixed spice; I egg, beaten; 1/2 cup chopped walnuts.

Put dates in a large mixing bowl with brown sugar, soda, butter and lemon rind. Pour boiling water over and stir until butter has melted. Leave to cool. Sift flour and spice together and add to cooled date mixture alternately with egg and walnuts. Stir well, spoon into 2 well-greased nut roll tins or 21 x 11 cm (8½ x 4½ in) tins and bake in a preheated moderate oven (180°C/350°F) for 45 minutes. Leave to cool in tins for 5 minutes before turning out. Makes 2.

Date and Nut Cake

250 g (8 oz) stoned dates; I cup boiling water; 90 g (3 oz) butter, softened; I cup sugar; I tsp vanilla; I egg, beaten; I1/2 cups self-raising flour; I tsp bicarbonate of soda; I tsp cinnamon; 1/4 tsp salt; 1/2 cup chopped walnuts.

Place dates in a large bowl and pour boiling water over. Leave for 2–3 minutes or until they soften. Add butter and sugar and beat well until combined. Blend in vanilla and egg. Sift flour with bicarbonate of soda, and fold in with cinnamon and salt. Stir in the nuts.

Turn into a greased and lined 21 x 11 cm (8½ x 4½ in) loaf tin or a 20 cm (8 in) round or square cake tin. Bake in a preheated moderate oven (180°C/350°F) for 25–30 minutes or until cooked when tested with a skewer. Leave in the tin for 2 minutes, then turn on to a wire rack to cool. Serve warm as a dessert accompanied by whipped cream, or store in an airtight container ready to eat on its own or sliced and buttered.

DESSERTS AND PUDDINGS

The name for the sweet course of a meal varies from country to country and even from family to family – 'dessert' and 'pudding' are both widely used to mean sweet dishes ranging from substantial hot pies and steamed puddings to such cold sweets as jellies, soufflés, moulds, sweet rice dishes and fruits. Here we have elected to call our 'just desserts' pudding (part of the author's Scottish heritage).

Desserts and puddings fall into one of the following categories:

BAKED PUDDINGS: This large class includes baked fruit pies, flans and tarts, such as Lemon Meringue Pie, and Rhubarb Pie; cake and yeast mixtures like Cottage Pudding, Babas and savarins; scone mixtures like Fruit Cobbler and Fruit Crumble (see individual recipes).

MILK PUDDINGS: These are made with milk and cereals such as rice, sago or semolina, and either cooked on top of the stove or in the oven. They can be served hot or cold. Junkets are an example of cold milk puddings (see individual recipes).

STEAMED PUDDINGS: These may be made with a cake-like batter, sponge mixtures, custard or breadcrumb mixtures, and may be light or rich with fruit and nuts like Sultana Pudding, Steamed Pineapple Pudding, Chocolate Pudding and Rich Christmas Pudding (see individual recipes).

BATTER PUDDINGS: Those made with a thin mixture of eggs, flour and milk, which may be fried like fritters, cooked on a griddle like pancakes, or cooked in special irons like waffles (see individual recipes).

JELLIES, CREAMS, MOUSSES AND MOULDS: Innumerable cold sweets come into this category. They are usually set with jelly, sago or cornflour, can be made in a mould and turned out or served in a glass bowl or sundae glasses etc.; e.g. jellies, Bavarian creams, mousses and cold soufflés (see individual recipes).

ICED SWEET PUDDINGS: These include ice creams, water ices, sorbets, sherbets and sundaes (see individual recipes).

FRUIT SWEET PUDDINGS: Fruits make lovely puddings; e.g. Baked Apples, Poached Pears, fruit fools, Fruit Trifle, Strawberries Romanoff, Apricots in Brandy and Bananas Flambé (see individual recipes).

EGG PUDDINGS: These include puddings where eggs are the main ingredients; e.g. Crème Caramel, Queen of Puddings, sweet or soufflé omelettes, soufflés, meringues and meringue-based sweets. See individual entries for other puddings, also *Custards*, *Baba au Rhum*, *Flummery*, *Fritters*, *Jelly*, *Soufflé*, etc. **See recipes.**

Baked Puddings

Butter the dish, tin or mould well, so that the pudding is easily turned out or served. Wipe round edges of container before baking. The pudding is easier to handle if it is placed on a baking tray while cooking. Oven settings may vary with different cookers, so that average settings in recipes are given for general guidance.

Spiced Apple Charlotte

**4 apples, peeled, cored and finely diced;
3/4 cup sugar; 1/4 tsp salt; 1/2 tsp ground cloves;
1/2 tsp grated lemon rind; 1/2 cup orange juice;
3 tbs sherry; 60 g (2 oz) butter, melted;
3 cups fresh breadcrumbs.**

Mix apples with sugar, salt, cloves, lemon rind, orange juice and sherry. Set aside. Combine melted butter and breadcrumbs, mixing well. Fill a buttered 5-cup charlotte mould or casserole with alternate layers of breadcrumbs and the apple mixture, beginning and ending with breadcrumbs. Cover pudding and bake in a preheated moderate oven (180°C/350°F) for 30 minutes. Remove cover and bake for about 15 minutes longer or until crumbs are brown and apples are tender. Serve warm, with cream. Serves 6.

Apple and Date Crisp

**1 cup dates, stoned; 1/2 cup water; 1 tsp grated lemon rind; 1/2 cup plus 2 tbs sugar; juice 1/2 lemon;
1 1/2 cups self-raising flour; 1/2 tsp cinnamon;
125 g (4 oz) butter; 1 cup rolled oats; 2 large cooking apples; peeled, cored and thinly sliced.**

Combine dates, water, lemon rind and 2 tbs sugar in a saucepan and cook 2–3 minutes or until dates are soft. Remove from heat, add lemon juice and beat with a wooden spoon until smooth. Allow to cool. Sift flour and cinnamon into a bowl. Rub in butter and mix in remaining sugar and oats. Press about ⅔ oat mixture into a greased and lined 19 cm (7½ in) square cake tin. Spread this with date mixture. Arrange apple slices on top. Place remaining oat mixture on top of apples and press down. Bake in a preheated moderate oven (180°C/350°F) for 45 minutes. Serve with cream or ice cream. Serves 6.

Wholemeal Apple Crisp

**3 cooking apples, peeled, cored and sliced;
1 cup honey; 1 tbs lemon juice; 1/2 cup wholemeal flour; 60 g (2 oz) butter; 1/4 cup firmly packed brown sugar; 1 tsp grated lemon rind;
2 tsp cinnamon.**

d

Place apples in a well-greased pie dish. Heat honey, add lemon juice and pour over apples. Put flour in a bowl and rub in butter until mixture resembles dry breadcrumbs. Add sugar and lemon rind and spread over apples. Sprinkle with cinnamon. Bake in a pre-heated moderately hot oven (190°C/375°F) for 30–40 minutes, or until apples are tender and the topping crispy brown. Serves 4–6.

Almond Castles

90 g (3 oz) butter; $^1/_3$ cup caster sugar;
3 eggs, separated; 3 tbs cream or milk;
1 tbs brandy (optional); $1^1/_2$ cups ground almonds.

Cream together butter and sugar. Stir in egg yolks, cream or milk, brandy, if used, and almonds. Whisk egg whites to a stiff froth and fold lightly into almond mixture. Spoon into 8 greased dariole moulds, filling them three quarters full. Bake in a preheated moderately slow oven (160°C/325°F) for 20–25 minutes or until the puddings are firm in the centre and golden-brown. Turn out and serve with custard. If liked, the puddings may be steamed – cover with greased greaseproof paper and steam 40–50 minutes or until firm. Serves 8.

Pineapple Delicious Pudding

$^1/_4$ cup self-raising flour; $^1/_4$ tsp salt; $^1/_2$ cup sugar;
2 eggs, separated; $^1/_2$ cup milk; 1 tbs lemon juice;
$^1/_4$ cup crushed, drained pineapple;
$^1/_4$ cup pineapple juice.

Sift flour, salt and sugar into a bowl. Beat egg yolks and add to flour mixture with milk, lemon juice and crushed pineapple and juice, and mix well. Fold in stiffly beaten egg whites. Pour into ovenproof dish and stand dish in a roasting tin of water. Bake in a preheated moderate oven (180°C/350°F) for 40–45 minutes or until set. Serve with cream or ice cream. Serves 4.

Sultana Bread Pudding

$3^1/_2$ cups milk; 1 piece vanilla bean, or 1 tsp vanilla;
$^1/_4$ cup butter, softened; 8 slices French bread
(centre portion, not the crusty end); $^1/_2$ cup sultanas;
3 eggs, or 5 egg yolks; $^1/_3$ cup sugar;
$^1/_8$ tsp salt; nutmeg.

Scald milk, then add vanilla bean, if used. Simmer 15 minutes. Cool. Discard vanilla bean, if used, or add vanilla. Butter one side of each slice of bread. Arrange slices in a 6-cup casserole, buttered sides down, sprinkling the sultanas between the layers. Beat eggs or yolks with sugar and salt and add the scalded milk, stirring. Pour over the bread. Let stand 30 minutes. Sprinkle with nutmeg. Set casserole in a roasting tin of hot water and bake in a preheated

moderate oven (180°C/350°F) for about 1 hour or until a knife inserted in the centre comes out clean. Serve warm. Serves 6–8.

Orange Bread Pudding

3 slices bread, cubed; 1 cup milk, scalded;
$^3/_4$ cup orange juice; grated rind 1 orange;
4 egg yolks, beaten; $^1/_2$ cup sugar;
$^1/_8$ tsp salt; butter; whipped cream to serve.

Soak bread cubes in milk for 10 minutes. Add orange juice and rind, egg yolks, sugar and salt. Stir until sugar has dissolved. Pour into 4 well-buttered individual moulds, dot with butter and place in a roasting tin of hot water. Bake in a preheated moderately hot oven (190°C/375°F) for 30 minutes or until the tip of a knife inserted 2.5 cm (1 in) from the outside edge comes away clean. Chill. Unmould and serve with whipped cream. Serves 4.

New England Bread Pudding

$3^1/_2$ cups milk; $^1/_4$ cup butter; 3 cups stale bread
cubes; $^1/_2$ cup sugar; 2 eggs, lightly beaten;
$^1/_2$ cup sherry; 1 tsp cinnamon; 1 tsp nutmeg;
1 cup seedless raisins; $^1/_2$ cup chopped mixed
candied peel.

Heat milk, add butter and pour hot liquid over bread cubes. Soak about 5 minutes, then stir in sugar, eggs, sherry and spices. Add raisins and peel. Pour mixture into a buttered baking dish. Set dish in a roasting tin of hot water and bake in a preheated moderately hot oven (190°C/375°F) for about 1 hour or until a knife inserted in the centre comes out clean. Serves 6.

Fruit Sponge

500 g (1 lb) fresh fruit (e.g. apricots, peaches,
apples); sugar; 90 g (3 oz) butter; 2 eggs, beaten;
1 cup self-raising flour.

Prepare fruit according to kind and arrange in a greased 4-cup pie dish. Sprinkle with sugar to taste and add a little water if required. Cream together butter and $^1/_2$ cup sugar. Add eggs gradually, beating well between each addition – if there is a sign of curdling, add some flour. Sift flour and stir lightly into creamed mixture. Spread mixture over fruit. Bake in the middle of a preheated moderate oven (180°C/350°F) for 35–40 minutes. Serve hot or cold with cream or custard. Serves 6.
NOTE: This can be made with canned fruit if liked. Drain juice from the fruit before arranging in the pie dish.
VARIATION
Use 6 individual ovenproof dishes and bake as above for about 20 minutes.

Winter Fruit Brown Betty

1 cup dried apricots; 2 cups dried apples;
2 cups fresh breadcrumbs; 60 g (2 oz) butter,
melted; $^{1}/_{3}$ cup chopped blanched almonds; grated
rind 1 orange; $^{1}/_{2}$ cup firmly packed brown sugar;
15 g ($^{1}/_{2}$ oz) butter.

Soak apricots and apples overnight in plenty of water
to cover. Drain and chop roughly. Toss breadcrumbs
in melted butter. Spread a thin layer of crumbs in
bottom of baking or soufflé dish. Cover with a little of
the chopped fruit. Sprinkle over a little of the
almonds, orange rind and sugar. Repeat layers until
dish is full, finishing with a layer of crumbs. Dot with
butter and sprinkle with any remaining sugar. Bake
in a preheated hot oven (200°C/400°F) for 30 minutes
or until golden and crisp. Serve very hot with cream.
Serves 6.
NOTE: To make fresh breadcrumbs, cut 6–8 thick
slices of white bread into cubes and rub through a
sieve, or whirl in electric blender or food processor.

Baked Apple Roly-Poly

PASTRY: $1^{1}/_{2}$ cups flour; $^{1}/_{2}$ tsp bicarbonate of soda;
1 tsp cream of tartar; 1 tbs butter;
about 4 tbs iced water.

FILLING: 3 cooking apples, peeled, cored and sliced.

SYRUP: $^{3}/_{4}$ cup sugar; 60 g (2 oz) butter;
1 cup boiling water.

To make pastry, sift dry ingredients together, rub in
butter with fingertips and mix in enough water to
make a soft dough. Roll out pastry to a rectangle.
Spread apples over pastry and roll up like a Swiss roll.
Lift roly-poly into a greased shallow ovenproof dish,
seam side down. Mix sugar, butter and boiling water
and pour over. Bake in a preheated moderate oven
(180°C/350°F) for 1 hour, basting roly-poly every 10
minutes with syrup. Serve hot, cut into slices, with
custard or cream. Serves 6.
VARIATIONS
JAM OR GOLDEN SYRUP ROLY-POLY: Follow recipe for
Apple Roly-Poly, but substitute jam or golden syrup
for apples. Roll out pastry fairly thin.
FRUIT ROLY-POLY: Follow recipe for Apple Roly-Poly
but substitute $^{3}/_{4}$ cup dried fruit for apples.

Batter Puddings

Batters are made from a basic mixture of flour, milk and
egg. The flour is worked to a very soft consistency with
the eggs and some of the liquid, so that it can be beaten
more easily until smooth. The rest of the liquid is then
stirred in. The mixture is left to stand for 30 minutes
before use.

The lightness of a batter depends on the quick formation of steam within the mixture and quick cooking. A

baked batter therefore needs to be cooked in a preheated
hot oven (220°C/425°F) and the temperature can be
reduced when the flour is almost cooked. It is best to put
the batter at the top of the oven to begin with; then to
move it to a lower shelf at reduced heat to finish cooking.
See also *Fritters* and *Pancakes*.

Batter Pudding

2 cups flour; $^{1}/_{4}$ tsp salt; 2 eggs; $2^{1}/_{2}$ cups milk;
1 tbs cooking fat or lard.

Sift flour and salt into a bowl. Make a well in the
centre of the flour and break eggs into this. Add about
$^{1}/_{2}$ cup of the milk. Stir, gradually working flour down
from sides and adding more milk as required to make
a stiff batter consistency. Beat well for about 5 minutes.
Add rest of the milk. Cover and leave to stand for 30
minutes. Put fat into a Yorkshire pudding tin about
20 x 25 cm (8 x 10 in) and heat in a preheated hot oven
(220°C/425°F). The fat should just be beginning to
smoke. Quickly pour in the batter and return to the
oven, placing the tin at the top of the oven. Bake for
about 25 minutes or until nicely browned. Reduce
heat to moderately hot (190°C/375°F) and continue
baking for 10–15 minutes. Serve with wine, syrup or
jam sauce. Serves 6.
VARIATION
BATTER PUDDING WITH APPLES: Prepare batter as
for Batter Pudding. Cover and leave to stand for 30
minutes. Spread 500 g (1 lb) peeled, cored and sliced
apples over bottom of well-greased tin and sprinkle
with 6 tsp sugar and $^{1}/_{4}$ tsp cinnamon or grated lemon
rind. Pour batter over and flake 15 g ($^{1}/_{2}$ oz) butter on
top. Bake pudding in a preheated hot oven
(220°C/425°F) for about 25 minutes or until nicely
browned, then reduce heat to moderately hot
(190°C/375°F) and continue baking for 10–15
minutes. Dredge with sugar before serving.

Milk Puddings

These are basically made with a farinaceous ingredient,
sugar and milk. Eggs may be added, if liked, or any other
suitable flavouring such as grated lemon or orange rind,
nutmeg, cinnamon, vanilla or other flavouring essences.

The addition of egg to a milk pudding increases the
nutritive value, and the pudding is made much lighter if
the whites are whisked before being added. The egg must
not be added until the rice, macaroni or other grain is fully
cooked, otherwise the long cooking necessary to cook
the grain would overcook the eggs and cause them to
curdle. Baking for about 30 minutes in a preheated warm
oven (160°C/325°F) is usually long enough to cook the
eggs and brown the top of a 2–3 cup pudding. The correct
consistency of a boiled or baked milk pudding is such that
it will just flow over the plate when served. This result is
achieved by using the correct quantities of ingredients

d

and slow cooking to prevent excessive evaporation. Extra milk can sometimes be added if the pudding becomes too thick.

GENERAL POINTS: Silverstone-lined, heavy saucepans are ideal. Avoid using thin saucepans; rinse out the saucepan with cold water before using, or lightly grease with butter to lessen the risk of burning. Puddings cooked in a saucepan must be stirred well from the bottom of the pan and only just allowed to simmer.

Grease the baking dish to facilitate cleaning afterwards.

In puddings where eggs are included, the mixture must be cooled slightly before the egg yolks are added.

Sago Fluff

3 tbs sago; 3 cups milk; 2 eggs, separated; 3 tbs sugar; pinch salt; 1 tsp vanilla; stewed dried apricots or prunes.

Cook sago in 2 cups of the milk until all grains disappear, being careful it does not burn. Beat egg yolks with sugar, salt and remaining milk. Add to sago, stirring until thick. Remove from heat. When cool, fold in stiffly beaten egg whites and vanilla. Pile into a serving dish when cold. Arrange apricots or prunes around edge of dish. Syrup from fruit may be served with pudding. Serves 6.

Coconut Meringue Custard

3 cups milk; 3 eggs, separated; 3 tbs sugar; 4 tbs desiccated coconut; 2 tbs glacé cherries; 2 tbs plum jam; 2 tbs caster sugar.

Scald milk in a heavy saucepan. Beat egg yolks and sugar together and add to milk, stirring all the time. Scatter 2 tbs coconut over bottom of a greased pie dish and strain custard over this. Leave for 30 minutes. Add glacé cherries (leaving a few for decoration) and stir through. Stand dish in a roasting tin of cold water and bake in the coolest part of a preheated moderately slow oven (160°C/325°F) for 1 hour, or until mixture is set. Remove from oven and spread jam over top of custard. Beat egg whites until stiff and fold in caster sugar. Pile this on to custard. Top with rest of coconut and cherries and return to the oven. Bake for 20 minutes longer. Serve hot with cream. Serves 6.

Cloud Custard

1¹/₂ cups milk; 2 tsp cornflour; 1 large egg, separated; pinch salt; ¹/₂ tsp vanilla; 4 tsp sugar.

Place milk (reserving about 1 tbs) in a small saucepan and bring to the boil. Meanwhile, mix cornflour to a smooth paste with reserved milk, and blend in egg yolk, salt, vanilla and 2 tsp of the sugar. When milk boils, pour a little on to cornflour mixture, stir well and return to saucepan. Stir over low heat for

3–4 minutes until custard is smooth and thick. Remove from heat and cool. Beat egg white until stiff, then beat in remaining sugar. Spoon custard into bowl with meringue, and lightly fold together for a pretty yellow and white effect. Chill until serving time. Serves 4.

Creamy Rice Pudding

4 tbs short-grain rice; 1 tbs sugar; 3¹/₂ cups milk; 15 g (¹/₂ oz) butter; nutmeg; 1 tbs cream.

Place rice in buttered pie dish. Add sugar and milk and stir well. Add butter in small pieces and top with nutmeg. Bake in a preheated moderately slow oven (160°C/325°F) for 1¹/₂ hours, stirring every 30 minutes. Stir well, then add the cream and leave to cook a further 30 minutes or until brown. Serve with cream or jam. Serves 6.

Geneva Pudding

¹/₂ cup rice; 4 cups milk; pinch salt; 1 kg (2 lb) cooking apples, roughly chopped; 30 g (1 oz) butter; ¹/₄ tsp cinnamon; 3 tbs water; ¹/₃ cup sugar.

Simmer rice in milk, with salt, until tender. Meanwhile, put apples in a saucepan with butter, cinnamon and water. Simmer very gently until tender, then rub the mixture through a fine sieve. Stir 1 tbs sugar into rice and add rest to apple purée. Arrange rice and apple purée in alternate layers in a well-buttered pie dish, with rice forming bottom and top layers. Bake in a preheated moderate oven (180°C/350°F) for about 1¹/₄ hours or until brown. Serves 6.

Swedish Rice

2 cups rice; salt; 750 g (1¹/₂ lb) cooking apples, peeled, cored and thinly sliced; 2 cups milk; pared rind 1 lemon; ¹/₃ cup sugar; pinch cinnamon; ¹/₂ cup sherry; ³/₄ cup seedless raisins, roughly chopped.

Add rice to a pan of salted boiling water. Boil for 3 minutes, then drain off the water. Add apples, milk and lemon rind to rice and cook until tender. Remove lemon rind. Add sugar, cinnamon, sherry and raisins and mix well. Cook for 3–4 minutes longer. Serve with cream. Serves 6.

Tapioca Cream Pudding

¹/₄ cup tapioca; 4 cups milk; pinch salt; 15 g (¹/₂ oz) butter; 2 tbs sugar; ¹/₄ tsp almond essence; 3 eggs, separated; 6 coconut macaroons, crushed.

Soak tapioca in milk, with salt, for 1–2 hours, then tip mixture into a saucepan. Bring to the boil and simmer until tapioca is cooked. Add butter, sugar and almond essence and mix well. Cool slightly, then add egg yolks.

Pour into a well-buttered pie dish and bake pudding in a preheated moderate oven (180°C/350°F) until just set. Whisk egg whites stiffly and fold in crushed macaroons lightly. Pile on top of tapioca pudding. Reduce heat of oven to slow (150°C/300°F) and bake for a further 30 minutes or until a pale golden-brown on top. Serves 6.

Steamed Puddings

The mould or basin in which a pudding is steamed should be well greased with fresh butter. Always prepare the steamer, the mould or basin, and the covering before the pudding is mixed.

There should be plenty of boiling water in the steamer. If a steamer is not available, the pudding can be partly steamed by standing it on an old plate, saucer or pastry cutter (to prevent direct contact with the source of heat) in a saucepan, with just enough water to reach halfway up the mould or basin. Put a tightly-fitting lid on the saucepan and simmer gently. If the water boils down, add more boiling water to replace it. Do not let the pan boil dry.

Where gentle steaming is indicated in the recipe, the water below the steamer should only simmer. The basin or mould should not be more than three quarters full.

Always cover the pudding with greased paper before steaming; this acts as a waterproof cover against condensing steam. Use a piece of strong paper, such as greaseproof, grease it well, make a pleat down the centre and place it, greased side down, over the top of the basin. Turn the edges of the paper under and twist them securely below the rim of the basin. If liked, tie with string, looping it to make a handle for easy removal of the basin.

After taking the pudding out of the steamer, leave it for a minute or two to allow it time to shrink slightly from the sides of the mould or basin, before turning it out on to a warm serving plate.

Madeira Pudding

4 slices bread, diced; ¹/₃ cup caster sugar; I tsp grated lemon rind; 2 cups milk; 3 eggs, beaten; ¹/₂ cup sherry or Madeira.

Mix together bread, sugar and lemon rind. Heat milk to about blood heat and pour it on to eggs, stirring well. Add sherry or Madeira and pour over bread mixture. Leave to soak for 15–20 minutes. Pour into a well-buttered mould or pudding basin, cover with greased greaseproof paper and steam very gently for 2 hours. Serve with custard, wine or jam sauce. Serves 6.

Windsor Pudding

2¹/₂ tbs rice; 2 cups milk; I kg (2 lb) cooking apples, cored and roughly chopped; ¹/₄ cup caster sugar; grated rind and juice ¹/₂ lemon; 3–4 egg whites.

Simmer rice in milk until tender and all the milk has

been absorbed. Meanwhile, cook apples in as little water as possible, until soft. Sieve or purée in a blender, then stir in sugar, rice, and lemon rind and juice. Whisk egg whites stiffly and fold lightly into the mixture. Put into a greased pudding basin, cover with greased greaseproof paper and steam very gently for about 40 minutes. Serve with custard sauce made from the egg yolks. Serves 6.

Chocolate Puddings

Cook these little puddings in your electric frying pan, or use any large flameproof dish with foil fitted over to make a good cover.

3 tbs cocoa powder; 90 g (3 oz) butter; ¹/₂ cup caster sugar; I egg; ¹/₂ tsp vanilla; I¹/₂ cups self-raising flour; pinch salt; 6 tsp raspberry jam.

Put cocoa into a measuring cup, fill to half cup line with boiling water and mix together until blended. Cool. Cream butter with sugar, then add egg and vanilla and beat in thoroughly. Sift in flour and salt. Add cocoa mixture and combine thoroughly. Put 1 tsp jam in bottom of each of 6 greased individual moulds. Divide chocolate mixture between moulds. Have frying pan heated, with water to a depth of about 2 cm (³/₄ in). Place moulds in pan, cover with pan lid and simmer for 20 minutes. Turn out and serve hot with cream or custard sauce. Serves 6.

Chocolate Sauce Pudding

A light chocolate sponge, floating on top of a rich chocolate sauce.

30 g (I oz) butter; ¹/₂ cup caster sugar; ¹/₂ tsp vanilla; I egg; I cup self-raising flour; 2 tsp cocoa powder; ¹/₂ tsp salt; ¹/₂ cup milk.

SAUCE: ¹/₂ cup sugar; 2 tsp cocoa powder; I¹/₂ cups hot water.

Cream butter with sugar and vanilla. Add egg and beat well until creamy. Fold in sifted flour, cocoa and salt alternately with milk. Pour into greased 4–5-cup pudding basin. To make sauce, mix sugar and cocoa and sprinkle over sponge mixture. Lastly pour over hot water. Cover basin with greased greaseproof paper and steam for 1–1¹/₂ hours. Serves 4.

Light Cottage Pudding

This is the basic steamed pudding that has been part of the winter scene for many generations. It may be varied by the sauce or custard served with it.

60 g (2 oz) butter; ¹/₄ cup sugar; I egg; ¹/₂ tsp vanilla; I cup self-raising flour; 3 tbs milk.

Cream butter with sugar. Beat in egg and vanilla. Stir in sifted flour and milk. Turn into a greased pudding basin, cover with greased greaseproof paper and steam 1¼ hours. Serve with jam, golden syrup or sweet sauce. Serves 4.

Sultana Pudding

A light steamed pudding is something we all enjoy, especially on a wintry evening.

1½ cups self-raising flour; pinch salt; 125 g (4 oz) butter; ⅔ cup firmly packed soft brown sugar; 2 eggs, lightly beaten; ½ tsp vanilla; ⅓ cup sultanas; 4 tbs milk.

Sift flour with salt. Cream butter with sugar until light, then gradually beat in eggs and vanilla. (Add a little flour with the last few additions.) Fold in remaining flour, sultanas and milk. Spoon into a well-buttered pudding basin, cover with double thickness of greased greaseproof paper and steam for 2 hours. Serve with stirred custard or cream. Serves 6.

Steamed Pineapple Pudding

3–4 slices canned pineapple; 6–8 glacé cherries.

BUTTERSCOTCH: 75 g (2½ oz) butter; 1½ cups firmly packed brown sugar.

PUDDING: 1 cup self-raising flour; pinch salt; 90 g (3 oz) butter; ½ cup caster sugar; 1 tsp vanilla; 2 eggs; 4 tbs milk.

Cut pineapple slices in half to make 6–8 circles. Make butterscotch by creaming butter and sugar together. Spread over bottom and sides of a greased 4-cup pudding basin or charlotte mould. Arrange pineapple circles on top and decorate with cherries. Sift flour and salt. Cream butter with sugar and vanilla until light. Beat in eggs one at a time, then fold in milk alternately with flour. Spoon into basin. Cover with 2 thicknesses of pleated greased paper and steam for 1½ hours. Serve with cream or custard sauce. Serves 6.

Steamed Ginger Pudding

2½ cups flour; 1 tsp ground ginger; pinch mixed spice; 1 tsp bicarbonate of soda; 155 g (5 oz) finely grated suet; 1 egg; ¾ cup golden syrup; ¾ cup warmed milk; 3 tbs finely chopped preserved ginger.

Sift flour, spices and bicarbonate of soda into a bowl. Add suet. Make a well in the centre and pour in beaten egg mixed with syrup and milk. Stir well to a batter that will fall easily from spoon. Spoon preserved ginger over bottom of greased 5-cup pudding basin. Pour in mixture, cover basin with a pleated piece of greased greaseproof paper and steam for 2½–3 hours. Serve with warmed golden syrup or custard. Serves 4–6.

Steamed Jam Puddings

60 g (2 oz) butter; ¼ cup sugar; 1 egg; ½ tsp vanilla; 1 cup self-raising flour; 3 tbs milk; 2 tbs jam.

Cream butter with sugar. Beat in egg and vanilla, then fold in sifted flour and milk. Place jam in 4 greased individual pudding or dariole moulds and pour in mixture. Cover with greased greaseproof paper and steam for 25 minutes. Serve with custard or cream. Serves 4.

Sago Plum Pudding

2 tbs sago; 1 cup milk; 60 g (2 oz) butter; 1 cup sugar; 1 tsp bicarbonate of soda; pinch salt; 1 cup fresh breadcrumbs; 1 cup sultanas or mixed dried fruit; 1 tbs chopped mixed candied peel; ½ tsp mixed spice.

Soak sago overnight in the milk. Beat butter and sugar together, then beat in soaked sago and milk, bicarbonate of soda and salt. Add breadcrumbs, fruit, peel and spice. Mix well and turn into a well-greased pudding basin or mould. Cover top with greased greaseproof paper and steam for 2 hours. Serve with custard or cream. Serves 6.

NOTE: The pudding mixture may be divided into 6 individual moulds and steamed for 1 hour, if preferred.

Quick Steamed Pudding

Easy, inexpensive and good.

1 egg; 2 tbs sugar; ½ tsp vanilla; 1 cup self-raising flour; ½ cup milk; 1 tbs melted butter; 2 tbs jam or golden syrup.

Place all ingredients except jam or golden syrup in a bowl and beat until smooth. Put jam or golden syrup into bottom of a greased 4-cup pudding basin, add pudding mixture and cover with greased greaseproof paper. Steam for 40 minutes. Serve with custard, sweet white sauce or cream. Serves 4–6.

VARIATION

FRUIT PUDDING: Make basic pudding mixture and stir in ¼ cup sultanas, chopped dates or mixed dried fruit. Omit jam or golden syrup. Turn into basin and steam as directed.

Iced Sweet Puddings

Ices may be broadly divided into 2 categories: water ices, sorbets, sherbets, etc., and ice creams. But there is also a large selection of iced sweet puddings. These include frozen soufflés; creamy cake-like concoctions and layered ice cream and fruit combinations.

See also *Ice Cream*; *Ices, Sorbets, Granite and Sherbets* and *Cassata*.

Vanilla Soufflé Glacé
(Frozen Vanilla Soufflé)

I cup milk; I cup cream; I vanilla bean, or
I tsp vanilla; 4 egg yolks; $^1/_2$ cup sugar;
2 cups cream, whipped; I tsp cocoa powder.

Heat milk, cream and vanilla bean in a heavy saucepan to boiling. Meanwhile, beat egg yolks with sugar until thick and light-coloured. Discard vanilla bean from liquid, if used, or stir in the vanilla. Beat some of the hot liquid into the egg mixture, then mix into remainder in pan and heat, stirring, until mixture coats the back of the spoon. Strain through a fine sieve and cool to room temperature. Fold in whipped cream. Pour into a 5-cup soufflé dish fitted with a lightly greased greaseproof paper collar. Freeze until firm. Before serving, remove paper collar and sprinkle top with sifted cocoa. Serves 6.

VARIATIONS
There are many ways to vary the composition of a frozen soufflé. The basic mixture may be seasoned with very strong coffee, with numerous spirits and liqueurs, such as rum, Cognac or Grand Marnier, and with melted chocolate. Toasted almonds or pistachio nuts are delicious folded into the basic mixture.

Frozen Soufflé with Glacé Fruit

To make this dessert it is best to have both a portable electric beater and a standard electric beater with a good motor.

5 egg yolks; 5 whole eggs; $1^1/_2$ cups sugar;
$^3/_4$ cup chopped candied fruit (cherries, apricots, angelica); $^1/_4$ cup Kirsch or Cognac; 2 cups cream.

Put egg yolks and whole eggs in the heatproof mixing bowl of an electric beater. Set bowl in a saucepan containing hot water and set over low heat. Start beating using a portable beater and gradually add sugar. The egg yolk mixture should become thick and like a soft meringue, several times the original volume (10–15 minutes). Remove mixing bowl from saucepan and set in place in the standard beater. Beat until the egg yolk mixture reaches room temperature. Meanwhile, soak fruit in Kirsch or Cognac. Fold fruit and liqueur into egg yolk mixture. Whip cream until stiff and fold into mixture. Pour into a 7-cup soufflé dish fitted with a greaseproof paper or foil collar. Place in the freezer and freeze until fairly solid. Remove collar before serving. Serves 8–10.

Frozen Lemon Creams

I cup milk; I cup cream; I cup sugar; grated rind and juice 2 lemons; 6 large lemons.

Combine milk, cream and sugar, stirring until sugar has thoroughly dissolved. Pour into an ice cream tray and freeze until mushy. Add lemon rind and juice and beat mixture well with a rotary beater. Freeze again for 2 hours. Beat mixture again thoroughly, return to the freezer, and freeze until solid. (Alternatively, use a sorbetière; see To Freeze Ice Cream, page 202.) Slice off tops of lemons and remove all the pulp. (Discard the pulp or save it for another use.) Cut a thin slice from the bottom of each lemon shell so that it will stand upright. Fill shells with frozen mixture, piling it high. Serve decorated with a green lemon leaf or other green leaf. Serves 6.

Pavé au Chocolat

185 g (6 oz) unsweetened chocolate;
125 g (4 oz) butter, softened;
$^3/_4$ cup sugar; 4 egg yolks; $^1/_4$ cup brandy;
$^3/_4$ cup water; 2 packages sponge fingers.

Melt chocolate over hot, not boiling, water. Cream butter with sugar until smooth. Add egg yolks, one at a time, and stir them in thoroughly. Add melted chocolate and mix well. Combine brandy with water in a shallow pan. Dip sponge fingers quickly into liquid to moisten, then arrange one third side by side down an oblong platter. Cover with a coating of the chocolate mixture (allow one third of the mixture for between the layers and use the remainder for the top and sides). Build up 2 more layers of sponge fingers with chocolate mixture between them. Ice the top and sides of loaf with chocolate mixture and refrigerate 3 hours. Serves 8.

Velvet Ice Cream

An economical ice cream that take only minutes to prepare.

I x 410 g can evaporated milk, chilled; 2 tsp vinegar;
$1^1/_4$ cups cream; I x 400 g can condensed milk;
I cup fresh milk; I tsp vanilla.

Beat together evaporated milk and vinegar until frothy. Add cream slowly. Add condensed milk, fresh milk and vanilla. Pour into an ice cream tray and freeze 1 hour or until mushy. Beat 5 minutes, then return to freezer and freeze until firm. Makes about 2 litres (8 cups).

Jellies, Creams, Mousses and Moulds

Jellies are usually fruit juices or wines jelled with dissolved gelatine but they can also be made from milk or custard. They may be set in bowls or in jelly moulds and turned out when set (see *Gelatine* and *Jelly, Sweet and Savoury*).

Creams are also set in gelatine; those known as Bavarian creams are compounds of custard, cream and flavouring. These may also be set in bowls or in moulds and turned out.

A mousse is a light creamy dish; it may be hot or cold, sweet or savoury. A cold mousse can be frozen, but when a gelatine mixture is used, it is merely chilled. Sweet mousses can be flavoured with puréed fruit, liqueur, coffee or chocolate, one of the world's favourite mousses (see *Chocolate*).

Amor Frio

1 tbs gelatine; 2 tbs water; $3/4$ cup orange juice; $1/4$ cup sherry; 1 x 410 g can evaporated milk, well chilled; $1/2$ cup sugar.

Soften gelatine in water, then place over simmering water until dissolved. Remove from heat, add orange juice and sherry and mix together. Beat milk with sugar for a few minutes, then add orange mixture and beat until thick and fluffy. Place in serving bowl and chill until set. Serves 6.

Apricot Marshmallow

$1/4$ cup sugar; 1 cup water; 500 g (1 lb) apricots, halved and stoned; 1 tbs lemon juice; 3 tsp (1 envelope) gelatine; whipped cream to decorate.

Dissolve sugar in water and bring to the boil. Add apricots and poach gently until fruit is soft. Measure 2 cups of fruit and syrup, add lemon juice and set aside to cool. Dissolve gelatine in $1/4$ cup of remaining hot syrup. Add to cooled apricots and stir well. Leave until mixture is almost on setting point, then beat until very thick. Spoon into parfait glasses. Chill. Decorate with whipped cream. Serves 6.

Vanilla Bavarian Cream

This is a basic recipe for Bavarian cream. Vary it by adding different flavourings and decoration.

$1^{1}/2$ cups milk; 4 egg yolks; $3/4$ cup caster sugar; pinch salt; 1 tbs gelatine, softened in $1/4$ cup cold water; 2 tsp vanilla; $1^{1}/2$ cups cream.

DECORATION: strawberries or other fruit, grated chocolate, toasted almonds etc.

TO SERVE: fruit, Creamy Caramel or Chocolate Sauce (see pages 64 and 84).

Scald milk and cool. Beat egg yolks with sugar and salt until thick and lemon-coloured. Place in a heavy saucepan with milk and stir over low heat until mixture coats spoon. Add softened gelatine, stir until dissolved, then add vanilla. Cool, then chill until mixture is beginning to set. Whip cream until stiff and fold in. Pour into a 6-cup mould rinsed with cold water and chill for at least 5 hours. Unmould carefully on to a chilled serving plate. Decorate as desired and serve with a fruit, caramel or chocolate sauce. Serves 6.

VARIATIONS

CHOCOLATE BAVARIAN CREAM: Add 60 g (2 oz) chocolate, roughly chopped, to the hot milk and stir until melted, then proceed with recipe.

ORANGE BAVARIAN CREAM: Add grated rind 1 orange to the hot milk, then proceed with recipe.

GINGER BAVARIAN CREAM: Add 2 tbs finely chopped ginger in syrup to the hot milk, then proceed with recipe.

Berry Bavarian Cream

$1^{1}/2$ cups berries, fresh or frozen and thawed; $1/2$ cup sugar; 3 tsp (1 envelope) gelatine; 6 tbs water; 1 tbs lemon juice; $2/3$ cup cream, whipped.

Crush berries and add sugar. Leave to stand for 30 minutes. Meanwhile, soften gelatine in water, then place over simmering water until dissolved. Stir into berries. Add lemon juice and refrigerate until thickened slightly. Lightly fold in whipped cream and pour into a bowl. Chill. Serves 4–6.

Coffee Bavarian Cream

3 tsp (1 envelope) gelatine; $1/4$ cup cold water; 2 eggs, separated; $1/2$ cup sugar; $1/4$ tsp salt; $1/2$ cup milk; $1/2$ tsp vanilla; $1/2$ cup strong black coffee; 1 cup cream.

Sprinkle gelatine over the water and allow to soften. Beat egg yolks in top part of a double saucepan and add $1/4$ cup sugar and the salt. Gradually add milk. Cook over hot water, stirring constantly, until slightly thickened. Beat egg whites until stiff. Gradually add remaining sugar, beating constantly. Whip cream until slightly stiff. Fold into gelatine mixture with the egg whites. Pour mixture into a wetted 5-cup mould and chill until firm. Unmould and serve. Serves 4–6.

Chestnut Mousse

$1^{1}/2$ tbs (2 envelopes) gelatine; $1/4$ cup water; 1 x 500 g can unsweetened chestnut purée; 2 cups milk; $3/4$ cup sugar; $1/2$ tsp vanilla; 6 egg yolks; 2 tbs dark rum or Grand Marnier; 1 cup cream.

Soften gelatine in water. Blend chestnut purée with milk in a saucepan and stir in sugar. Beat with an electric beater until smooth. Add gelatine mixture, bring almost to the boil, stirring to dissolve gelatine. Stir in vanilla. Beat egg yolks in a mixing bowl. Beat in a little of the hot chestnut mixture, then stir into the remaining mixture in the pan. Cook, stirring, until mixture thickens slightly. Do not boil. Stir in rum or Grand Marnier. Sieve mixture into a mixing bowl. Allow to cool, but do not let it start to set. Whip cream and fold into the chestnut mixture. Pour into a lightly oiled 7-cup mould and refrigerate until firm. Unmould and serve, with custard sauce. Serves 6–8.

Caramel Cream

I tbs gelatine; ¼ cup water; 2½ cups milk; I tbs sugar; 2 eggs, beaten; ½ cup cream, whipped.

CARAMEL: 3 tbs sugar; I tbs lemon juice; 2 tbs water.

Soften gelatine in water. Meanwhile, heat milk with sugar in a heavy saucepan, stirring until sugar has dissolved. Add eggs and cook gently, stirring, until custard thickens enough to coat back of spoon. Add gelatine mixture and stir until dissolved. Cool. For caramel, put sugar and lemon juice into a saucepan and cook until brown, taking care it does not burn. Add water, then stir into custard mixture. When cold and beginning to set, fold in whipped cream. Pour into a mould and chill until set. Serves 6.

Hazelnut Cream

You can buy ground hazelnuts at good health food shops and delicatessens. Better still, for the best flavour, grind your own (nut mills are available at kitchen shops): toast hazelnuts, rub off the skins, then grind. Serve the cream with crisp biscuits.

250 g (8 oz) hazelnuts, ground; 2½ cups milk; 6 egg yolks; I cup caster sugar; I tbs gelatine; 2 tbs water; 2 tsp vanilla; 2 cups cream.

DECORATION: whipped cream; whole hazelnuts.

Combine ground hazelnuts and milk in a heavy saucepan and bring to the boil. Cool. Beat egg yolks and sugar together until pale and thick. Pour on milk mixture, stirring constantly. Place in the top of a double saucepan and cook, stirring, until custard has thickened. Cool. Soften gelatine in water for 5 minutes, then dissolve over hot water. Stir into custard with vanilla. Cool until mixture has the consistency of unbeaten egg white. Whip cream and fold into mixture. Pour into 8 individual serving dishes and chill until firm. Decorate with whipped cream and hazelnuts. Serves 8.

Raspberry Mousse

This is a simple, yet light mousse recipe that can be made using any canned fruit.

I x 425 g can raspberries; 3 tsp (I envelope) gelatine; ⅔ cup cream; I egg white.

Drain raspberries, reserving ½ cup can syrup. Place syrup in a pan, sprinkle over gelatine and let soften; then heat, stirring, until gelatine has dissolved. Pour over berries and stir thoroughly. Chill until beginning to thicken. Whip cream and fold into berry mixture. Whisk egg white stiffly and fold in. Pour into a dish or 6 individual dishes and chill. Serves 6.

Egg Nog Rum Cream

5 eggs, separated; ⅔ cup caster sugar; ½ cup rum; I tbs gelatine; 4 tbs water; 2 cups cream; Clear Raspberry Sauce (page 410) to serve.

DECORATION: ¾ cup cream, whipped; 6–8 glacé cherries; few strips angelica; nutmeg.

Beat egg yolks with sugar until thick and foaming. Stir in rum. Soften gelatine in water, then dissolve over simmering water. Whip cream until it holds its shape. Beat egg whites until stiff. Fold cream and gelatine into egg yolk mixture, then fold in egg whites. Pour into a large glass bowl or other pretty dessert bowl and leave to set. Decorate with piped rosettes of whipped cream, or pile cream around the edge. Sprinkle with chopped cherries, angelica and nutmeg. Serve with sauce. Serves 6–8.

Puréed Fruit Mould

½ cup sugar; I cup water; 750 g (1½ lb) apricots or red plums, halved and stoned; blanched almonds; 3 tsp (I envelope) gelatine.

Dissolve sugar in water, then bring to the boil. Add fruit to syrup and poach gently for 10 minutes. Lift fruit out of syrup and pick out a few of the best halves. Place half a blanched almond in each of these reserved halves and arrange them rounded side up in a 20–23 cm (8–9 in) sandwich tin. Allow to cool, then place in refrigerator. Sieve remaining poached fruit and make resulting purée up to 1¾ cups with the cooking syrup. Heat an extra ½ cup syrup and stir in gelatine briskly until dissolved. Add to fruit purée, stir well and allow to cool. When purée is almost on the point of setting, pour carefully over fruit halves arranged in the tin. Chill until set. Turn out, and serve with whipped cream. Serves 4–6.

Pineapple Mist

3½ tsp gelatine; ½ cup water; ¼ cup sugar; ¾ cup canned pineapple juice; 2 tsp lemon juice; 2 egg whites.

d

Soften gelatine in water, then place over simmering water until dissolved. Add sugar, stirring until dissolved. Stir in pineapple and lemon juices. Refrigerate until slightly thickened. Beat mixture until thick, adding the stiffly beaten egg whites. When quite thick, spoon into a serving bowl or 6 individual dishes. Serves 6.

Maple Mousse

I tbs gelatine; I tbs cold water; $^1/_2$ cup maple syrup;
3 egg yolks; 30 g (I oz) toasted slivered almonds;
$2^1/_2$ cups cream; 2 tsp rum.

Soften gelatine in water, then dissolve over simmering water. Heat maple syrup in a heavy saucepan and stir in gelatine mixture. Beat egg yolks until very light. Add a little of the hot syrup mixture to them, then add remaining syrup mixture, stirring constantly. Cool maple mixture in the refrigerator for 30 minutes or until the consistency of unbeaten egg white. Fold in almonds. Whip 2 cups cream and fold into maple mixture. Place in a large serving dish or individual serving dishes and chill until set. Whip remaining cream and flavour with rum. Serve with the maple mousse. Serves 4–6.

Fruit Sweet Puddings

Fruits make lovely desserts. There are single fruits to be enjoyed at their peak, fragrant and warm from the sun, which make the perfect ending to a meal. In summer months set them in a bowl of ice cubes, and enjoy them lightly chilled. Or use them to make brilliant fruit sauces to be enjoyed with meringues, creams, ice cream and little pastries.

Discover light, airy fools and snows, fruit mousses and soufflés (see individual recipes), enjoy fruits baked, poached in wine, flambéed with spirits or marinated into fruit juice or liqueurs.

For other fruit desserts, see entries under names of individual fruits.

Apple Snow

4–6 cooking apples, cored and thickly sliced;
I cup caster sugar; juice $^1/_2$ lemon; 2 egg whites.

DECORATION: whipped cream;
toasted slivered almonds.

Put apples in a saucepan with very little water. Cover and cook until soft. Drain. Sieve or purée in a blender and measure 1 cup purée. Add sugar and lemon juice and cool. Whisk egg whites until stiff, fold in apple mixture and continue whisking until fluffy. Pile into tall glasses and decorate with a swirl of whipped cream and toasted almond slivers. Serves 6.

Apples and Sago

$2^1/_2$ cups water; $^1/_4$ cup fine sago; 6 cooking apples,
peeled and cored; $^1/_2$ cup sugar; pared rind and
juice $^1/_2$ lemon; few drops red food colouring.

Bring water to the boil in a large saucepan. Sprinkle in sago and cook until mixture is clear, about 15 minutes. Add apples, sugar, and lemon rind and juice to the sago. Cover and simmer very gently 10–20 minutes or until apples are tender. Lift apples out on to a heated serving dish. Remove lemon rind from sago mixture and add a few drops of food colouring. Pour it over and around the apples. Serves 6.

Bananas Brazilian

6 bananas, cut in half lengthways;
$^1/_2$ cup fresh orange juice; I tbs fresh lemon juice;
$^1/_4$ cup firmly packed brown sugar; $^1/_8$ tsp salt;
60 g (2 oz) butter; I cup grated fresh or
desiccated coconut.

Place bananas in a buttered casserole. Combine orange and lemon juices, sugar and salt and pour over bananas. Dot with butter. Bake in a preheated hot oven (200°C/400°F) for 10–15 minutes. Sprinkle bananas with coconut and serve immediately. Serves 6.

Cherries Jubilee

I cup sugar; 2 cups water; $^1/_8$ tsp salt;
750 g ($1^1/_2$ lb) fresh cherries, stoned;
I tbs cornflour; $^1/_2$ cup Cognac, warmed;
French Vanilla Ice Cream (page 202) to serve.

Place sugar, water and salt in a saucepan and bring to the boil, stirring to dissolve sugar. Add cherries, reduce heat and simmer until tender. Drain cherries, reserving 1 cup of the syrup. Combine cornflour with reserved syrup in a saucepan, bring to the boil and simmer 3 minutes, stirring constantly. Add cherries. Pour Cognac into cherries and ignite. Spoon juices over cherries and serve, flaming, over French vanilla ice cream. Serves 6.

Baked Figs

Orange liqueur and cloves enhance the flavour of fresh figs in this recipe.

12–18 ripe figs; 1/2 cup firmly packed brown sugar; 3/4 cup water; 1/2 tsp ground cloves; 2 tbs Cointreau or Grand Marnier.

Prick figs with fork. Place in an ovenproof dish and sprinkle with brown sugar. Add water. Bake in a pre-heated slow oven (150°C/300°F) for about 30 minutes, basting occasionally with syrup in dish. Drain figs. Dust with cloves and sprinkle over liqueur. Serve warm with whipped cream or ice cream. Serves 6.

Melon with White Grapes and Grand Marnier

Use seedless white sultana grapes or big white grapes, halved and seeded, or canned grapes for this recipe.

1 large rockmelon, peeled, seeded and cubed; 1 large bunch grapes; 1/2 cup Grand Marnier.

Place melon cubes in a crystal bowl. Cover with a layer of grapes. Pour Grand Marnier over. Cover bowl with foil to keep in all the fragrance of the Grand Marnier. Chill thoroughly. Serve with crisp, dainty biscuits or small sponge fingers. Serves 6–8.

Melon Compote

1 honeydew melon; 1 rockmelon; 2–3 pieces preserved ginger, chopped; 2 tsp ginger syrup; 1 cup water; 1/2 cup white wine or dry sherry; 3/4 cup sugar.

Halve melons, remove seeds and scoop out flesh in dessertspoon-sized pieces. Put melon into earthenware basin with preserved ginger and ginger syrup. Make a syrup by simmering together water, wine or sherry and sugar. Pour boiling syrup over melon. Cool and chill well before serving. Serves 6.

Pears in Port Wine

6 firm, ripe pears; juice 1/2 lemon; 2 cups water; 1 cup port wine; 1 1/4 cups sugar; 1 cinnamon stick; pared rind 1/2 orange; strip lemon rind.

Peel pears and drop them into a bowl of cold water, with lemon juice added. This will keep them from darkening. Combine the 2 cups water with remaining ingredients in a saucepan and bring to the boil, stirring until sugar has dissolved. Add drained pears and simmer until fruit is tender. Do not overcook. Let pears cool in the syrup, then chill before serving. Serves 6.

Pineapple Flambé

1/4 cup sugar; 1/2 cup sherry; 1/2 cup water; 1 ripe pineapple, peeled, cored and sliced; 1 1/2 cups redcurrant jelly; 1/2 cup Cognac or Kirsch.

TO SERVE: French Vanilla Ice Cream (page 202); 8–10 macaroons, crumbled.

Combine sugar, sherry and water in a saucepan and bring to the boil. Add pineapple slices and poach for about 5 minutes. Drain. Melt currant jelly in a frying pan over low heat. Add pineapple slices and simmer, spooning syrup over fruit, for about 5 minutes. Add Cognac or Kirsch directly into centre of fruit mixture and let it heat for several minutes without stirring. When well warmed, light Cognac or Kirsch and spoon over fruit while flaming. Serve fruit over ice cream and top with macaroon crumbs. Serves 6.

Italian Fruits in Marsala

1 cup sugar; 1/2 cup water; juice 1 lemon; 1/2 cup Marsala; 4–6 small peaches, skinned; 1 small pineapple, peeled, cored and thickly sliced; 1 punnet (250 g/8 oz) strawberries, hulled.

Dissolve sugar in water with lemon juice, and boil to form a heavy syrup. Allow to cool. Stir in Marsala and leave to become quite cold. Immerse peaches, pineapple and strawberries in the syrup. Chill thoroughly before serving. Serves 6.

Oranges with Grand Marnier Syrup

6 large navel oranges; 1/2 cup water; 1 1/2 cups sugar; 1/4 cup orange juice; 1/4 cup Grand Marnier.

Thinly pare rind from 3 of the oranges and cut into very thin julienne (matchstick) strips. Place rind strips in a small saucepan, barely cover with water, bring to the boil and simmer 10 minutes. Drain and run cold water over rind. Place the 1/2 cup water and the sugar in another saucepan. Heat, stirring, until sugar dissolves. Bring to the boil and boil until syrup thickens and turns a pale straw colour. Immediately remove from the heat, add blanched orange rind strips and stir gently. Let the rind soak in the syrup for 30 minutes, then stir in orange juice and Grand Marnier. Remove peel and pith from all of the oranges. Slice each orange into 3 or more slices and place in a shallow serving dish. Top with the glazed rind and spoon syrup over oranges. Chill well before serving, spooning syrup over oranges occasionally. Serves 6.

Mangoes Flambé

**1 punnet (250 g/8 oz) strawberries, hulled;
1/4 cup plus 2 tbs sugar; 30 g (1 oz) butter;
2 tbs Cointreau; 2 large mangoes, peeled, halved
and stoned; 2 tbs Kirsch, warmed.**

Sprinkle strawberries with 2 tbs sugar and let stand
for 2 hours. Place remaining sugar and butter in a
saucepan and heat gently, stirring to melt sugar.
Increase heat and cook, stirring constantly, until just
starting to brown, then add strawberries. Pour
Cointreau over them. Lower heat to moderate and
stir mixture to a thick syrup. When lightly bubbling,
add mangoes and baste with the sauce. Flame with
Kirsch and serve immediately with vanilla ice cream.
Serves 4.

Strawberries in Liqueur

**2 punnets (500 g/1 lb) strawberries, hulled and
sliced; 1/2 cup icing sugar; 1 tbs Cointreau;
1 tbs Kirsch; 2 tbs brandy or Cognac,
6 sponge fingers.**

Sprinkle strawberries with icing sugar and mix gently.
Pour liqueurs over berries and mix carefully. Cover
and let stand at room temperature for 1 hour, then
refrigerate for 3–4 hours. Serve with sponge fingers.
Serves 6.

Pineapple Romanoff

**1 large pineapple, peeled, cored and diced;
6 tbs icing sugar; 4 tbs Cointreau; 2 tbs rum;
1 cup cream; 2 tbs Kirsch; grated rind 1 orange.**

Toss pineapple in a bowl with 2 tbs icing sugar. Pour
over Cointreau and rum. Cover and chill for several
hours. Whip cream, add remaining icing sugar and
flavour with Kirsch. Add whipped cream to marinated
pineapple and toss until every piece is coated with
creamy liqueur mixture. Spoon into a glass bowl or 6
individual dishes and sprinkle with grated orange
rind. Keep cold until time to serve. Serves 6.

Rhubarb and Ginger Compote

An unusual combination, but rhubarb, spices and gin
complement one another beautifully.

**1 cup sugar; 1/2 cup water; 1 kg (2 lb) rhubarb,
chopped; 1 tbs finely grated orange rind;
1/4 tsp nutmeg; 1/2 tsp ground ginger; 1/2 cup gin;
1 tbs finely chopped preserved ginger.**

Dissolve sugar in water in a large saucepan over low
heat. Increase the heat and bring to the boil, without
stirring. Add rhubarb, orange rind, nutmeg and
ground ginger and reduce heat to low. Simmer for 5
minutes or until rhubarb is tender. Using a slotted
spoon, transfer rhubarb to a serving dish. Increase

heat to high and bring cooking liquid to the boil. Boil
for 10–12 minutes or until liquid has reduced by
about one third. Remove pan from heat, add gin and
pour over rhubarb. Sprinkle chopped preserved ginger
over the top, cover and chill for at leat 30 minutes.
Serves 6.

Pineapple Ambrosia

**2 bananas, sliced; juice 1/2 large lemon;
1 ripe pineapple, peeled, cored and diced;
2 oranges, peeled and sliced; 1 punnet (250 g/8 oz)
strawberries, hulled; 1/2 cup icing sugar;
90 g (3 oz) grated fresh or desiccated coconut.**

Toss banana slices in lemon juice to prevent discolouring. Layer fruit in a glass bowl, sifting a little
icing sugar to taste between each layer. Sprinkle with
coconut and chill. Serves 6.

Cardamom Pears

**6 pears, peeled, cored and sliced; 2 tbs soft brown
sugar; 3/4 cup water, 2 tsp ground cardamom;
1/2 cup Grand Marnier or Cointreau;
1 cup cream, whipped, to serve.**

Arrange pears in a shallow ovenproof dish and sprinkle
over sugar. Pour water over top, then sprinkle over
cardamom. Bake in a preheated moderate oven
(180°C/350°F) for 40 minutes or until pear slices are
tender. Transfer pear mixture to a serving bowl, add
liqueur, cover and set aside to cool completely. Serve
well chilled, with whipped cream. Serve 6.

DEVILS ON HORSEBACK

The name given to one of the classic savouries, now
most often served as appetisers. Poach some prunes in
red wine until they are plump. Drain, stone and stuff with
an almond and anchovy fillet and wrap in bacon. Cook
quickly under a preheated grill or in a hot oven
(220°C/425°F) for 4–5 minutes. Serve on hot buttered
toast. Allow 3 per person.

DHAL

Dhal is a lentil purée served with curry meals, boiled rice
or Indian breads. Any type of lentils can be used, but red
lentils or moong dhal are the quickest cooking types, and
don't need soaking.
   See *Pulses: Beans, Peas and Lentils*.

DILL

Dark green, feathery dill has a delicate flavour some-
where between parsley and fennel; it is one of the most
beautiful herbs for garnishing. It is much used in
Scandinavian, Russian and Balkan cooking, especially
with cucumbers and fish, and in combination with yogurt
and sour cream. Dill seeds are a favourite flavouring in

sauerkraut and in pickled cucumbers (in the USA these are known as dill pickles). Fresh dill tends to lose its aroma during cooking so it is usually added toward the end of cooking time.

Sprinkle chopped fresh dill on potato salads or hot new potatoes; add a little to mayonnaise to be served with cold fish or shellfish, or stir it into a cream sauce to serve with hot fish; add stalks and seeds to cooking water for lobster or prawns; add chopped dill and a little vinegar to melted butter for a sauce to pour over freshly cooked beetroot. **See recipes.**

Dill Pickles

These fresh-tasting pickles are quick and easy to make and are ready to use after a week. As they do not keep well, make just a jar or two at a time.

500 g (1 lb) small green cucumbers;
1 cup white vinegar; 1 cup water; 1 tbs salt;
2 tbs dill seeds; 6 peppercorns.

Wash cucumbers thoroughly and cut in half lengthways unless very small. Pack into warm sterilised jars. Bring vinegar, water and salt to the boil and pour into jars. Add dill seeds and peppercorns, and cover immediately. Use after a week. Makes about 1½ litres (6 cups).

VARIATION
KOSHER PICKLES: Follow recipe for Dill Pickles but add 4 peeled, sliced cloves garlic to the jars with dill seeds and peppercorns.

Dilled Herring Pâté

This is one of those magically easy recipes that produce surprising results. Guests find it difficult to identify the taste but are always appreciative.

1 x 200 g can herring in tomato sauce;
125 g (4 oz) butter, softened; lemon juice;
chopped fresh dill leaves or dill seeds;
chopped fresh lemon balm, lemon thyme,
or grated lemon rind.

Purée herring with their sauce in a blender or food processor. With motor running, add butter, a little at a time, and lemon juice to taste, then just a little chopped dill or dill seeds – keep tasting. Transfer to a bowl and stir in a little chopped lemon balm or lemon thyme, or grated lemon rind. Chill before using. Serve with fingers of hot wholemeal toast. Makes about ¾ cup.

DIPS

People of many lands enjoy scooping up a savoury mixture with pieces of food for relaxed nibbling. Some dips are famous – Mexico's Guacamole, Middle Eastern Baba Ghannouj and Hummus, Italy's Bagna Cauda, Provence's Aïoli, Greek Tzatziki (see separate entries).

The dipping idea gains new interest with crisp, chilled pieces of vegetables or fruit, cold seafood, flat Lebanese (pita) bread, spears of ham or sausage, pumpernickel or fingers of home-made pastry as a change from biscuits or potato chips for the dipping food. **See recipes.**

Brandied Cheese Dip for Fruit

125 g (4 oz) blue cheese; 125 g (4 oz) cream cheese;
1 tbs cream; 2 tbs brandy.

Mash blue cheese, add cream cheese and cream and beat until smooth. Stir in brandy. Serve at room temperature with chilled wedges of apple, pear or melon. Makes about 1 cup.

Tuna and Green Peppercorn Dip

1 x 200 g can tuna in oil, drained;
¹/₂ cup Mayonnaise (page 256);
¹/₂ tsp green peppercorns, crushed; salt.

Mash tuna and blend with remaining ingredients, adding salt to taste. Spoon into a bowl and chill. Serve with small rounds of pumpernickel. Makes about 1¼ cups.

Hot Clam Dip

2 x 100 g cans minced clams; 60 g (2 oz) butter;
³/₄ cup cracker biscuit crumbs; 1 small onion,
finely chopped; 1 tsp lemon juice,
dash Tabasco sauce.

Drain juice from 1 can of clams. Melt butter, add drained clams and other can of clams with juice. Stir in remaining ingredients. Pour into an ovenproof serving dish and bake in a preheated moderate oven (180°C/350°F) for 30 minutes. Place in centre of a platter and surround with chilled celery or cucumber sticks, tiny crisp lettuce leaves, cauliflower florets or cooked shelled prawns for dipping. Makes about 2 cups.

Refried Bean Dip

A dipping version of Mexican Refried Beans *(Frijoles Refritos)*.

2 x 310 g cans of red kidney beans; I onion, finely chopped; I clove garlic, crushed; I small red chilli, seeded and chopped, or I tsp Mexican chilli powder (or to taste); 4 tbs bacon dripping or oil; I cup grated cheese; salt.

Drain beans, reserving liquid. Gently fry onion, garlic and chilli or chilli powder in fat until onion is soft. Add beans a little at a time, mashing them into mixture. Add ½ cup bean liquid, mix well and stir in cheese. Remove from heat as soon as cheese melts. Taste and add a little salt if necessary. Serve hot with corn chips or crackers. If mixture gets too stiff for dipping, add a little more hot bean liquid or water. Makes about 3 cups.

DOLMA, DOLMADES

A dolma is any dish prepared by stuffing a vine, fig, cabbage or other edible leaf with a savoury mixture and braising the packages.

Dolmades – stuffed vine leaves – are a specialty throughout Greece and Turkey. They may be served hot with a sauce or cold as an appetiser. The stuffing is based on rice and herbs, often with minced lamb, or pine nuts and currants. Dolmades freeze well so it is worth making a good batch at a time.

If making dolmades to serve as an appetiser, use the following recipe but do not make the sauce. Arrange cooked dolmades in an oiled dish, sprinkle with a little olive oil and store, covered, in refrigerator until required. Serve with lemon wedges, and if liked, squares of feta cheese. **See recipes.**

See also *Cabbage*: Cabbage Rolls.

Dolmades with Avgolemono

about 80 young fresh vine leaves, or 500 g (I lb) preserved vine leaves (available in bulk from Continental delicatessens); 2 onions, finely chopped; 3/4 cup olive oil; 1/4 cup short-grain rice; 500 g (I lb) minced lamb; I tbs finely chopped fresh mint; 1/4 cup finely chopped parsley; 2 tbs currants; salt and freshly ground black pepper; I cup lamb, beef or chicken stock; 1/4 cup dry white wine.

SAUCE: 4 egg yolks; juice I lemon.

Rinse fresh or preserved vine leaves and drop into boiling water, a few at a time. Blanch for 3 minutes. Remove to a bowl of cold water, then drain. Cook onions gently in 2 tbs oil until soft. Add rice and stir 2 minutes. Put meat into a bowl, add mint, parsley, currants, onion mixture, salt and pepper and blend well.

Place a vine leaf, shiny side down, on a flat surface and put a heaped teaspoon of stuffing in centre. Fold stem end and sides over, then roll up tightly towards the point. Repeat with remaining stuffing and leaves, reserving about 10 leaves. Line a heavy saucepan with a few reserved leaves and pack rolls in, seam sides down, close together in layers, sprinkling each layer with remaining oil. Pour stock and wine over and cover top of rolls with remaining leaves. Weight with a heavy plate, cover saucepan tightly and simmer gently 1 hour.

Remove dolmades to a heated platter and keep warm while making sauce. Add a little water if necessary to liquid in saucepan to make 1 cup and bring to the boil. Beat egg yolks and add lemon juice, then hot liquid, beating constantly. Pour over dolmades and serve immediately. Makes about 70, to serve 15–20 as an appetiser.

Stuffed Grape Vine leaves
(Dolmathakia Latheres)

about 80 young fresh vine leaves, or 500 g (I lb) preserved vine leaves (available in bulk from Continental delicatessens); 2 large onions, finely chopped; 3/4 cup olive oil; I cup short-grain rice; 3 tbs pine nuts; 3 tbs chopped parsley; 2 tsp chopped fresh mint; 2 tsp chopped fresh dill; 3 tbs currants; salt and freshly ground black pepper; 2 cups water; juice I lemon.

Rinse fresh or preserved vine leaves and blanch in boiling water for 3 minutes, a few at a time. Put in a bowl of cold water, drain and cut off stems. Gently fry onions in ½ cup olive oil until translucent. Add rice and pine nuts and stir over heat for 2 minutes. Stir in herbs, currants, salt, pepper and 1 cup water. Cover tightly and cook over low heat for 15 minutes until water is absorbed.

Place a vine leaf, shiny side down, on flat surface and put a heaped teaspoon of stuffing in centre. Fold stem end and sides over stuffing and roll up tightly toward point. Repeat with remaining stuffing and leaves, reserving about 12 leaves. Line a heavy-based saucepan with half reserved vine leaves. Pack rolls close together, seam sides down, in layers in pan. Sprinkle each layer with oil and the lemon juice. Add remaining cup of water and cover top of rolls with rest of leaves. Invert a plate on top to keep rolls in shape during cooking. Cover saucepan tightly, bring to the boil and simmer gently for 1 hour. Remove from heat and leave for 1–2 hours until liquid is absorbed. Lift rolls out carefully into a dish and chill for several hours before serving. Garnish with lemon slices and serve with a bowl of chilled plain yogurt. Makes about 70.

DRIED FRUIT

See *Fruit, Dried and Candied.*

DUCHESS POTATOES (POMMES DUCHESSE)

A rich potato and egg mixture that is piped into decorative borders or rosettes, then browned under a grill or in a hot oven. It is one of the few potato recipes that can be prepared ahead.

Duchess Potatoes

1 kg (2 lb) medium, old potatoes, peeled and quartered; 30 g (1 oz) butter; 1 tsp salt; pinch white pepper; pinch nutmeg; 2 whole eggs; 2 egg yolks.

Cook potatoes in lightly salted boiling water to cover until they are soft. Drain well, then return to pan and shake over low heat for a few minutes to dry them. Force through a sieve into a hot saucepan, or push through potato ricer. Beat with a wooden spoon until very smooth. Add butter, salt, pepper, nutmeg and lightly beaten eggs and egg yolks. Mix thoroughly. If made ahead of time, brush surface with a little butter to prevent a crust from forming. When ready to use, reheat over low heat, stirring constantly. Pipe mixture through a piping tube to make a border around heatproof platters, and brown under grill. Or pipe into rosettes on a greased baking tray and brown in a preheated very hot oven (220°C/425°F) to serve as a vegetable. Serves 6–8.

DUCK

A bird prized by gourmets for its rich flavour and succulence it can be prepared in a great variety of ways. A duck has more fat, a larger frame and less meat than a chicken of the same weight, so allow about 375–500 g (12 oz–1 lb) raw weight per person. For a dinner party, it is pleasant (and certainly very convenient for the carver) to serve half a small duckling for each person. A good young duck has creamy skin and a plump breast, with a pliable breastbone.

TO TRUSS A DUCK: Truss in the same way as chicken. Shape the bird neatly with your hands, tucking the neck flap underneath. Take a piece of string and place its centre below the breastbone at the neck end. Bring the ends of the string down over the wings to cross underneath, then up to tie the legs and tail together.

ROAST DUCK: Pull out loose fat around neck and inside body. Press the 2 little oil glands near base of tail to empty them. Wipe bird inside and out with damp paper towels. If using stuffing, spoon it loosely into the body cavity. Or, instead of stuffing, a few lemon slices or a quartered green apple, with some sliced onion and a little sage or other herbs, may be placed inside duck to flavour it.

Truss bird and place it, breast side up, on a rack set in a roasting tin.

Roast in the centre of a preheated moderately hot oven (190°C/375°F) for 15 minutes, then reduce heat to moderate (180°C/350°F) and continue roasting, allowing about 25 minutes per 500 g (1 lb). Very small birds will take a little less and very large ones a little more than this time. Baste with pan juices every 15 minutes and, 20 minutes before end of cooking time, prick breast all over to allow excess fat to escape and make skin crisp.

Test for doneness by inserting a fine skewer into thickest part of the thigh near the body; juices should run clear with no tinge of pink. Allow duck to rest in a warm place for 20 minutes before carving.

Make Clear Gravy or Thickened Gravy to accompany duck, if desired (see *Gravy*). A little orange or lemon juice may be added to gravy.

Roast duck may also be served with apple sauce or another tart sauce such as Sauce Bigarade (see page 35). Young green peas, braised celery, glazed turnips and onions are classic accompaniments. A crisp green salad is a good alternative.

NOTE: If you have any doubt about the tenderness of a duck, it is advisable to braise it instead of roasting it. The slower, longer cooking ensures moist tender flesh, and you can still achieve a crisp skin if you uncover the bird for the last 15 minutes of cooking.

Duck breasts are available at many good butchers, the marylands being used for duck confit. They are excellent for easy cooking and entertaining. **See recipes.**

Braised Duck with Glazed Turnips

1 x 1.5 kg (3 lb) duckling, 30 g (1 oz) butter; 1 carrot, chopped; 1 stick celery, chopped; 1 onion, chopped; 1 cup dry white wine; 1 bouquet garni; salt and freshly ground black pepper; 2 tsp cornflour.

VEGETABLES: 1 kg (2 lb) small white turnips, peeled and quartered; 1 kg (2 lb) small white onions, peeled; 2 tbs sugar; 60 g (2 oz) butter; 1 cup water.

Remove excess fat from duck, empty oil glands near tail and truss bird. Heat butter in a flameproof casserole to fit the duck, put bird in and brown all over. Lift duck out and discard all but 1 tbs fat from casserole. Add carrot, celery and onion and cook gently until golden. Replace duck on top of vegetables and add wine, bouquet garni, salt and pepper. Cover and cook in a preheated moderately hot oven (190°C/375°F) for 1½ hours. Meanwhile, trim turnips to pigeon's egg shapes, if desired. Place turnips and onions in a heavy saucepan with sugar, butter and water. Cover and cook until just tender, then remove lid and cook until liquid is reduced to a glaze, rolling vegetables to glaze them. Remove duck to a heated serving dish, remove trussing string and keep warm. Strain liquid from casserole into a saucepan, spoon fat from top and bring to the boil. Stir in cornflour mixed with a little water and, when sauce is thickened, adjust seasoning and pour into a heated gravyboat. Surround duck with glazed turnips and onions, and serve sauce separately. Serves 4.

Duck Breasts with Balsamic Vinegar

1–2 tbs light olive oil or sunflower oil;
4 duck breasts; 1 tbs red wine vinegar; good pinch sugar; salt and freshly ground pepper;
$^{1}/_{4}$ tsp ground cinnamon; 4 tbs blueberries or raspberries; 1 tbs balsamic vinegar.

Heat the oil in a frying pan. Fry the duck breasts, skin side down, gently until skin is golden. Turn and add the red wine vinegar, sugar, salt, pepper, cinnamon and berries. Cover and cook gently for 10–15 minutes until the duck breasts are tender and still juicy inside and the berries have melted into a delicious sauce. Lastly swirl in the balsamic vinegar, let it bubble a few seconds and check the sauce for seasoning. Serve the duck breasts cut into thick slices with the sauce poured over. Serves 4.

Grilled Duckling with Mandarin and Green Peppercorn Sauce

Duckling is marinated then grilled to produce crisp skin and succulent flesh. It is served with a lovely citrus sauce.

1 x 1.5 kg (3 lb) duckling, quartered; $^{1}/_{2}$ cup lemon juice; 1 small onion, thinly sliced; salt; 1 tsp cracked black peppercorns; $^{1}/_{2}$ cup oil; 30 g (1 oz) butter, melted; 2 small mandarins, thinly sliced.

SAUCE: $1^{1}/_{2}$ tbs sugar; 1 tbs red wine vinegar;
$^{2}/_{3}$ cup duck stock or canned chicken stock;
$^{1}/_{3}$ cup orange juice; 2 tbs lemon juice, or to taste;
$1^{1}/_{2}$ tsp arrowroot; 1 tbs water; $1^{1}/_{2}$ tbs drained green peppercorns, crushed; salt.

Remove backbone from duck, trim pieces neatly and cut off wing tips. Use trimmings, with giblets, if these were included with duck, to make duck stock for the sauce (see *Stock*). Remove visible fat from inside duck and wipe all over with damp paper towels. Mix lemon juice, onion, 1 tsp salt, cracked peppercorns and oil in a bowl. Add duck and turn pieces about so that they are coated with marinade. Cover, refrigerate overnight, turning pieces occasionally.

Drain duck, pat pieces dry with paper towels and prick skin all over with a skewer. Brush duck all over with melted butter and place, skin side down, on a grill rack. Cook under a preheated grill, about 13 cm

(5 in) from heat, for 20 minutes, basting pieces with pan juices after 10 minutes. Turn duck skin side up, brush with melted butter again and sprinkle with salt. Grill, basting frequently with pan juices, for 15–20 minutes more or until the skin is crisp and juices run clear when fatty part of thigh is pricked with a skewer. If necessary, prop up legs with crumpled foil to achieve even browning; also reduce heat to prevent duck browning too quickly.

SAUCE: In a small heavy saucepan mix sugar and vinegar and bring to the boil over moderate heat, stirring until sugar dissolves. Cook, watching carefully, until vinegar evaporates and sugar is slightly caramelised. Remove saucepan from heat, cool slightly, then pour stock into caramel and stir until caramel has dissolved. Place back on heat and boil until reduced to about $^{1}/_{2}$ cup. Add orange and lemon juice and simmer, stirring, for 1 minute. Mix arrowroot with water and stir into the sauce. Simmer, stirring, until thickened. Add green peppercorns and salt, and simmer for 1 minute.

Arrange duck on heated platter with mandarin slices in an overlapping circle round it. Serve sauce separately in a heated sauceboat. Serves 4.

Duckling Casserole

1 x 1.5 kg (3 lb) duckling, quartered;
salt and freshly ground black pepper;
1 stick celery, chopped; 2 carrots, chopped;
1 onion, sliced; 6 tbs Cognac or brandy; 1 strip lemon peel; 1 cup red wine; 1 rasher bacon, cut thick, rind removed and diced; 2 tbs olive oil;
$^{1}/_{2}$ cup rich duck stock, made with trimmings and giblets; 1 bouquet garni; 2 cloves garlic.

GARNISH: 12 small new potatoes, boiled;
250 g (8 oz) mushrooms; butter; lemon juice.

Remove backbone from duck pieces and place in a porcelain or earthenware bowl. Add salt, pepper, celery, carrots, onion, Cognac, lemon peel and red wine, and marinate duck in this mixture overnight. Remove duck pieces from marinade and dry with paper towels. Reserve marinade. Sauté bacon in olive oil in flameproof casserole until golden. Remove bacon and brown duck pieces in bacon fat. Return bacon to casserole and cook, covered, over a moderate heat for 20 minutes. Add reserved marinade, stock, bouquet garni and garlic. Cook over a low heat for $1^{1}/_{2}$ hours or until duck is tender. Remove bouquet garni, skim fat and adjust seasoning. Remove duck pieces and bacon to a heated serving platter. Strain over sauce and garnish with boiled potatoes and sliced mushrooms which have been cooked quickly in butter and lemon juice. Serve immediately. Serves 4.

d

Sauté of Duck with Burgundy

This recipe is also good to use for wild duck.

1 x 1.5 kg (3 lb) duckling; 1 tbs oil; 1 onion, finely sliced; 15 g (¹/₂ oz) butter; 175–250 g (6–8 oz) button mushrooms; ³/₄ cup red Burgundy; ¹/₂ cup duck stock; salt and freshly ground black pepper; 4 tsp Beurre Manié (see page 35); fried bread croûtes to garnish (see page 105).

Quickly brown duck all over in oil in a large pan. Remove from pan and leave to cool a little, then quarter: first cut down through breastbone with kitchen scissors and then on either side of backbone through rib cage. Cut each half into 2 just above the leg, and set aside. (The backbones can be used for stock for a stew.) Add onion to pan in which there should be about 1–2 tbs of duck fat. Brown onion slightly, then add butter and mushrooms, whole or sliced according to size, and sauté briskly for 2–3 minutes. Heat wine in a small saucepan, then add to pan with stock. Stir until it boils. Season with salt and pepper. Put in pieces of duck, cover and simmer for 20 minutes. The duck should still be slightly pink. When ready to serve, trim duck pieces with scissors or poultry shears if necessary to remove any ugly bones, and arrange in a heated serving dish. Thicken sauce slightly with beurre manié, reboil and spoon over duck. This dish may be garnished with fried bread croûtes. Serves 4.

Peking–Style Duck Pancakes

A great first course or cocktail party dish if you live near Chinatown where it is convenient to buy a whole barbecued duck. Usually, you can also buy the pancakes to go with the duck, which saves time.

1 barbecued duck; Mandarin Pancakes (see below); bean paste (hoisin sauce), to serve; shredded spring onions and Lebanese cucumber.

MANDARIN PANCAKES: 2 cups plain flour; ¹/₂–³/₄ cup boiling water; 1¹/₂ tbs Chinese sesame oil.

Cut the duck into pieces from the bone, and using fingers, shred into small pieces. Spread each pancake with a little hoisin sauce and top with a few pieces of duck and strips of spring onions and cucumber. Serves 8 as a first course or part of a Chinese meal.
PANCAKES: Sift flour into a bowl and make a well in the centre. Pour in boiling water a little at a time, gradually stirring in the flour (use just enough water to make a soft dough). Knead dough for 5–10 minutes or until it feels pliable and elastic, then wrap in plastic wrap and allow to rest for 15 minutes. Roll out dough to 5 mm (¹/₈ in) thickness on a lightly floured surface and cut into 7 cm (3 in) circles. Brush tops of circles with sesame oil and press oiled surfaces together in pairs. Roll out each 'sandwich' again into a bigger circle, about 10 cm (4 in) across. Lightly grease a heavy-based frying pan. Cook the pancakes over moderate heat for 1 minute on each side. As they are cooked, peel apart and stack on a warm plate until ready to serve. A dab of bean paste is spread on each pancake, then some spring onion and a spoonful of chicken. The pancake is rolled up and eaten in the hand. The pancakes can be made ahead and placed in a steamer over boiling water for a few minutes. Diners help themselves to the filling and pancakes. It is best to cover the stack of pancakes loosely to prevent them drying out through the meal.

Caneton à l'Orange
(Duckling with Orange)

2 x 1.5 kg (3 lb) ducklings, salt; 90 g (3 oz) butter; 2 large oranges; 1 tbs brandy; watercress to garnish.

ORANGE SAUCE: 1 tsp sugar; 1 tbs flour; 1 cup duck stock or water; ¹/₂ cup dry white wine; juice 2 oranges; salt and freshly ground black pepper; 3 tbs port wine (optional).

Season ducklings with salt, rub all over with butter and place a few strips of orange rind inside each bird. Put in baking dish. Roast in a preheated hot oven (200°C/400°F) for 15 minutes, then reduce heat to moderate (180°C/350°F) and continue roasting until tender, 1¹/₂–2 hours. Baste frequently with butter while cooking. Peel remaining rind from oranges very thinly, using a potato peeler, and cut rind into very fine shreds. Cover with hot water, simmer 3 minutes, then drain. Cool and reserve for garnish. Remove pith from oranges and cut into sections. Sprinkle with brandy and leave until required. Remove duck from pan and keep warm on heated serving dish. Pour off all but 2 tbs butter and drippings from baking dish. Add sugar and cook until caramelised a pale golden colour. Stir in flour and cook a few minutes until light brown. Stir in stock (this should be made with ducks' feet, neck, etc.) or water and cook gently until thickened. Strain into saucepan. Add wine, orange juice, salt and pepper. Cook gently for 5–10 minutes. Add a few of the blanched shreds of orange rind and the port wine, if liked. Garnish duck with orange sections, remaining shreds of orange rind and watercress, and serve with sauce. Serves 6.

DUMPLING

Light, fluffy and flavoursome – that's what good dumplings should be. They are a treasured part of home cooking in many countries from China to Central Europe and the British Isles.

Dumplings come in a great variety of shapes, textures and flavours: they may be made with flour, semolina, cornmeal, potato, soft cheese or even stiffly beaten egg whites, and contain ingredients such as salt, butter, yeast, spices, herbs or fruit. Some dumplings are steamed on top of a stew or casserole, some are simmered in stock or, for sweet dumplings, in a syrup, and others are baked.

When making dumplings, if they are too soft and fall apart, add a little more flour; if too heavy, add a little liquid. Dumplings made with a raising agent are always cooked with the lid on the pot.

Test dough by cooking one small dumpling ahead of the rest. The kind of stew and amount of liquid can make a difference.

Cook dumplings just before serving. The dough can be made ahead and refrigerated until needed. **See recipes.**

Fluffy Dumplings

Superbly light and tender dumplings to cook on top of a stew.

**I cup flour; I tsp baking powder;
$^1/_2$ tsp salt; pinch nutmeg;
30 g (I oz) butter; $^1/_4$–$^1/_3$ cup milk.**

Sift dry ingredients into a bowl and rub in butter. Add milk, blending with a fork until a fairly wet dough is formed. Shape with wet hands or between 2 wet tablespoons (or whatever size you like) and drop on top of a simmering stew 15 minutes before the end of cooking time, making sure dumplings sit on meat and do not sink into gravy. Cover and simmer 15 minutes without lifting lid. Serve dumplings with stew. Makes about 12.

VARIATIONS

BACON DUMPLINGS: Follow the recipe for Fluffy Dumplings, adding 2 tbs crisp-fried and crumbled bacon (about 1 large rasher) to flour-butter mixture.

CARAWAY DUMPLINGS: Follow the recipe for Fluffy Dumplings, adding 1 tsp caraway seeds to the dry ingredients.

CHEESE DUMPLINGS: Follow the recipe for Fluffy Dumplings, adding 2 tbs grated cheese, $^1/_2$ tsp dry mustard and a pinch cayenne to the dry ingredients.

HERB DUMPLINGS: Follow the recipe for Fluffy Dumplings, omitting nutmeg and adding $1^1/_2$ tbs chopped parsley or other fresh herbs to the flour-butter mixture.

GOLDEN SYRUP DUMPLINGS: See *Golden Syrup*.

DUNDEE CAKE

Many a Scottish housewife makes this traditional light fruit cake every week so that there is always some on hand for family and visitors.

Dundee Cake

**250 g (8 oz) butter; I cup caster sugar; grated rind
2 oranges; 5 eggs, beaten; $2^1/_2$ half cups flour;
I tsp baking powder; pinch salt; $^1/_4$ cup chopped
blanched almonds; I cup sultanas; I cup currants;
$^1/_2$ cup chopped mixed candied peel; I tbs orange
juice; extra blanched almonds to decorate.**

Cream butter with sugar and orange rind until light and fluffy. Gradually beat in eggs. Sift flour, baking powder and salt. Mix in chopped almonds, fruit and peel. Stir into creamed mixture with strained orange juice. Turn into a greased 20 cm (8 in) round deep cake tin lined with greased brown and greaseproof papers. Smooth surface and arrange extra almonds in pattern on top. Bake cake in a preheated slow oven (150°C/300°F) for 2–$2^1/_2$ hours or until a skewer inserted in centre comes out clean. Allow to cool in tin.

DUXELLES

French name for mushrooms finely chopped and sautéed in butter, used for many kinds of stuffings and quick mushroom sauces.

See *Mushroom*.

e

e

ECCLES CAKES

These little English pastries, filled with fruit and spices, were once part of the Eccles Wakes. These festival holidays were held 300 years ago in the Lancashire town of Eccles to celebrate the dedication of the local parish church. They can be made using frozen or home-made puff pastry.

Eccles Cakes

2 tbs butter, softened; 2 tbs brown sugar; 2 tbs finely chopped mixed candied peel; $^1/_3$ cup currants; $^1/_4$ tsp mixed spice; I x 375 g (12 oz) packet frozen puff pastry, thawed; I egg white, lightly beaten; $^1/_4$ cup caster sugar.

Mix together butter, brown sugar, peel, currants and mixed spice. Roll out pastry dough thinly and cut into 8 cm (3 in) rounds. Place a spoonful of fruit mixture in centre of each round. Moisten edges of rounds with water and draw up edges of each round to meet in the centre and completely enclose filling. Press well together and turn over so join is underneath. Roll out lightly until currants just show through dough and cake is about 8 mm ($^1/_3$ in) thick. Place on greased baking trays and leave in a cool place for 10 minutes. Make 3 slits in top of each cake, then brush with lightly beaten egg white and dredge with caster sugar. Bake in a preheated very hot oven (230°C/450°F) for about 15 minutes or until golden-brown and crisp. Remove from baking tray and cool on a wire rack. Makes about 12.

ECLAIR

A finger-shaped puff of choux pastry. Eclairs make one of the most delicate confections for afternoon tea or dessert or, filled with a savoury mixture, are served as a first course or as party savouries.

The shells for savoury éclairs are made from unsweetened choux pastry, shaped and baked in the same way as for sweet éclairs. They may be filled with a hot or cold savoury mixture.

For fillings, see *Profiteroles*; for sweet éclairs, **see recipes.**

Party Eclairs: For miniature éclairs to serve as party savouries, place 1 quantity savoury Choux Pastry (see page 345) in a piping bag fitted with a 1 cm ($^1/_2$ in) plain tube, and pipe into 4 cm (1$^1/_2$ in lengths) about 5 cm (2 in) apart on lightly greased baking trays. Bake in a preheated very hot oven (230°C/450°F) for 10 minutes, then reduce the heat to moderate (180°C/350°F) and bake for a further 10 minutes or until golden-brown, firm and light in the hand. Slit each éclair along the side and dry out in the turned-off oven for 20 minutes. Fill with hot or cold savoury mixture of your choice. Makes about 24.

Chocolate Eclairs

I quantity sweetened Choux pastry (page 345); I cup cream; I tsp caster sugar.

GLOSSY CHOCOLATE ICING: 2 tbs cocoa powder, sifted; I$^1/_2$ tbs sugar; 3 tbs water; I cup icing sugar, sifted; few drops vanilla.

Spoon choux pastry into a large piping bag fitted with a 1 cm ($^1/_2$ in) plain tube. Pipe mixture in 8 cm (3 in) lengths about 5 cm (2 in) apart on 2 lightly greased baking trays. Bake in a preheated very hot oven (230°C/450°F) for 12 minutes, then reduce heat to moderate (180°C/350°F) and bake for 15–20 minutes more or until golden-brown, firm and light in the hand. Slit each éclair along the side, turn off the oven and leave eclairs in the oven to cool for 20 minutes with the door half open. Remove and cool completely on a wire rack. When cold, whip cream with sugar and fill the eclairs.

GLOSSY CHOCOLATE ICING: Stir cocoa, sugar and water over low heat until sugar has dissolved, then bring to the boil without stirring. Remove from the heat and stir in icing sugar and vanilla. Add a little boiling water if necessary to make a coating consistency. Spread over tops of eclairs and leave to set. Makes about 12.

VARIATIONS

RASPBERRY OR STRAWBERRY ECLAIRS: Make as for Chocolate Eclairs but fill with whole raspberries or sliced strawberries and whipped cream. Ice with Lemon Glacé Icing (see page 205) tinted pink.

COFFEE ECLAIRS: Make as for Chocolate Eclairs but fill with whipped cream flavoured with 1 tbs coffee liqueur and ice with Coffee Glacé Icing (see page 205).

EEL

Fresh eel is firm and delicately flavoured; its high oil content makes it rich eating. Smoked eel makes a luxury first course or canapé topping.

■ **BASIC PREPARATION:** Fresh eel is cleaned in the same way as other fish, and is always skinned before cooking. Cut it, on the diagonal, into 5–8 cm (2–3 in) pieces and peel off skin, then proceed according to the recipe.

Smoked eel is ready to eat. Simply remove the skin and lift fillets off the bone. Serve as a first course with lemon wedges and brown bread and butter, or place on small pieces of buttered brown bread, add a squeeze of lemon juice, a grinding of black pepper and a dab of mayonnaise, and serve with drinks.

Sautéed Eel Provençale

750 g (1¹/₂ lb) eel; seasoned flour; 2 tbs olive oil; 60 g (2 oz) butter; 6 golden shallots, finely chopped; 2 cloves garlic, crushed; ¹/₂ cup fresh breadcrumbs; 2 tbs chopped parsley; salt and freshly ground black pepper; lemon wedges to serve.

Cut eel into pieces and skin as described above. Cut fillets from bones, roll in seasoned flour and sauté in the oil and half the butter until golden-brown. Remove from pan and keep warm. Add remaining butter to pan and keep warm. Add remaining butter to pan and sauté spring onions, garlic and breadcrumbs until crumbs are crisp. Stir in parsley, season with salt and pepper and spoon over eel. Serve immediately, with lemon wedges. Serves 4.

EGG

An egg is a remarkably efficient package of nutrition, being rich in protein, vitamins and minerals. Eggs are indispensable in the kitchen. They are used to thicken, as in custards or puddings; to leaven, as in soufflés, cakes and puffy omelettes; to emulsify, as in mayonnaise. A beaten egg stirred into hot, not boiling, liquid will thicken and enrich soups and sauces. Use a beaten egg to bind mixtures for croquettes, meatballs and stuffings, and if you want to fry foods, a coating of egg will protect the food and keep the outer coating of breadcrumbs in place. Beaten egg gives a beautiful shiny glaze when brushed over pastry before baking.

TO BUY AND STORE: Eggs are bought graded according to weight; the medium (55 g/2 oz) ones are used in most recipes unless otherwise stated. Choose the freshest eggs possible by purchasing them from a busy shop with a fast turnover. A fresh egg when broken into a saucer, should be quite highly domed, with the white thick and compact.

Never wash eggs before storing as this will destroy the natural protective film over the shells; store them in the refrigerator away from highly flavoured foods as the shells are porous and absorb odours. Place the pointed ends down to allow the air space at the rounded end to 'breathe'.

Egg whites can be stored for 2–3 weeks in an airtight container in the refrigerator. To use: measure 1¹/₂ tbs for each egg white. Egg yolks may be covered with water, and refrigerated. Use within 5 days.

For best results in cooking, remove eggs from the refrigerator a few hours before using. Eggs used at room temperature mix with other ingredients more readily and the whites whisk to a greater volume.

TO WHISK EGG WHITES: These can be beaten by hand, with a whisk or rotary beater, or with an electric mixer. Whether you beat egg whites by hand or use a machine the basic principle is the same. The bowl and beater should be very clean, and the whites have no trace of yolk.

Start beating slowly until a soft foam forms, then add a pinch of salt and ¹/₂ tsp cream of tartar for 4 egg whites. Gradually increase the beating speed and circulate the beaters right round the bowl, to incorporate all the egg white and beat in as much air as possible. Beat until the whites are glossy and creamy. Their volume by now should be 7 times greater than when you started beating and should hold a soft peak when the beater is raised. Stop beating before the whites form very stiff peaks as they become dry and brittle and will not mix well with other ingredients.

■ **TO COOK:** Eggs, cooked on their own, can be baked, boiled, coddled, fried, poached, scrambled and made into an omelette. **See also recipes.**

Baked Eggs: Butter small ramekins and break an egg into each. Season with salt and freshly ground white pepper, cover with 1 tsp warm cream or melted butter, and bake in a preheated moderate oven (180°C/350°F) for 8–10 minutes until the white is set and the yolk still runny.

Diced bacon, ham, salami or chopped spinach may be placed in the bottom of each ramekin before adding the egg if you wish. Cheese can be sprinkled over the egg before adding the cream or butter.

Boiled Eggs: Place eggs in a pan with cold water to cover. Bring to the boil and cook for: 3 minutes for soft-boiled, 4 minutes for medium-boiled and 10 minutes for hard-boiled. Cool hard-boiled eggs rapidly under cold running water and tap gently all over to crack the shell and prevent an unsightly dark ring forming around the yolk. Store shelled hard-boiled eggs in cold water in the refrigerator.

Coddled Eggs: Butter inside of egg coddler lightly and drop in 1–2 eggs. Add a tiny piece of butter and season with salt and pepper. Screw on lid and cook for 10 minutes in a saucepan of boiling water. The yolks should be soft, the whites just set. For variety, add grated cheese, chopped fresh herbs, sliced mushrooms or diced cooked ham.

Fried Eggs: Melt enough bacon fat or butter to cover the bottom of a frying pan. When it begins to sizzle break the eggs, one at a time, into a cup and slide them into the pan. Fry gently, basting from time to time with the fat, until the eggs are cooked with firm whites and soft yolks or as you like them. Remove with an egg slice and serve at once.

Omelettes: For 1–2 people, beat 3 eggs lightly with 1 tbs water, season with salt and freshly ground white pepper. Melt 15 g (¹/₂ oz) butter in a small frying pan and, when the foam subsides, pour in the eggs. Lift the cooked egg from the edges towards the centre – the uncooked egg will run underneath. Repeat until the eggs have set underneath but are still moist on top. Fold one third of the omelette towards the centre and roll out on to a heated plate, tilting the pan so that the omelette folds over again. Serve at once.

TO FILL OMELETTES: Heat the filling and spoon it across the centre just before the omelette is folded over. Use about 3 tbs of any of the following fillings: chopped cooked mushrooms; chopped fresh herbs; chopped cooked bacon and onion; warm asparagus tips; grated cheese; salmon or crab mixed with a little cream.

Poached Eggs: Use very fresh eggs, straight from the refrigerator, as they hold their shape better. Half fill a shallow pan with water, add ¼ tsp vinegar and bring to the boil. Break each egg into a cup, slide it into the water, cover the pan, remove from the heat and leave for 3½ minutes for soft eggs or 4 minutes for firmer ones. Remove, using an egg slice, drain and serve at once.

Scrambled Eggs: For one person, beat together 2 eggs, 1 tbs milk or cream, salt and freshly ground pepper. Melt 2 tsp butter in a pan, pour in the eggs and cook over low heat, stirring gently until the eggs are creamy and soft. Serve immediately.

Eggs Florentine

1½ cups cooked, chopped spinach, well drained; 2 tbs cream; salt and freshly ground black pepper; 4 eggs, poached and kept hot; 4 slices Gruyère or Emmenthal cheese; 4 black olives to garnish (optional).

Combine spinach, cream, salt and pepper and put into a gratin dish or 4 individual ramekins. Arrange eggs on spinach purée. Place a slice of cheese on each egg and put into a preheated hot oven (200°C/400°F), or under a preheated hot grill, until cheese melts and turns golden. Garnish with olives if liked and serve immediately. Serves 4.

Eggs New Orleans

3 tomatoes, peeled, seeded and chopped; I green pepper, cored, seeded and chopped; I onion, chopped; 2 sticks celery, chopped; 3 tbs tomato paste; I tsp sugar; ½ tsp salt; ¼ tsp black pepper; I bay leaf; I cup fresh breadcrumbs; 4 eggs; ½ cup grated cheese.

In a saucepan combine all ingredients except breadcrumbs, eggs and cheese. Simmer, stirring occasionally, for 10 minutes. Remove bay leaf, then stir in breadcrumbs. Place mixture in a shallow ovenproof dish. Make 4 depressions on surface and break an egg into each. Sprinkle with grated cheese and bake in a preheated moderate oven (180°C/350°F) for 15–20 minutes or until cheese has melted and the eggs are firm. Serves 4.

Eggs with Watercress Mayonnaise

3 cups watercress sprigs; ½ cup thick Mayonnaise (page 256); squeeze lemon juice; cayenne or Tabasco sauce; ¼ cup Vinaigrette Dressing (page 442); 4–5 hard-boiled eggs, halved.

Boil 1 cup watercress sprigs in water for 2 minutes. Drain well and purée in a blender or push through a sieve. Add to mayonnaise with lemon juice and cayenne or Tabasco. Toss remaining cress through vinaigrette dressing and arrange down centre of a platter. Place egg halves on cress and coat with mayonnaise. Serves 4.

Salmon–Stuffed Eggs

16 (2 x 50 g cans) flat anchovy fillets; milk; 8 hard-boiled eggs, halved; 90 g (3 oz) smoked salmon, chopped; ½ cup Mayonnaise (page 256); freshly ground black pepper; capers; I tbs snipped fresh dill or chives; watercress or shredded lettuce.

Drain oil from anchovies and put fillets in a shallow dish with a little milk to cover. Remove yolks from the egg halves and mash with smoked salmon, mayonnaise and pepper. Spoon mixture back into egg whites, mounding it. Drain anchovies, pat dry and cut each fillet lengthways into 2 strips. Garnish each egg with 2 strips anchovy, crossed in the centre. Place a caper on each quarter of yolk and sprinkle with dill or chives. Arrange on cress or lettuce. Serves 8.

Tea Eggs (*Marbled Eggs*)

In China eggs are often pickled, (known in the West as Thousand Year Old Eggs), or preserved by salting. The Chinese also braise eggs in this mixture of tea and soy sauce.

6 eggs; 2 tbs Indian tea leaves; 2½ cups water; 2 tbs soy sauce.

Place eggs in a saucepan, cover with cold water and bring gently to the boil. Simmer for 10 minutes. Drain eggs and crack shells all over with a spoon without removing any shell. Boil tea leaves in the 2½ cups water for 5–6 minutes until liquid is strong and dark. Add soy sauce and stir. Remove from heat. Put eggs into liquid and leave for at least 1 hour or until liquid is cool. To serve, remove shells. You will find that some of the tea mixture has seeped through the cracks in shells to form a marble-like pattern on the whites. Makes 6.

Eggs Mornay

250 g (8 oz) macaroni; 90 g (3 oz) butter; 3 tbs flour; 2½ cups milk; 90 g (3 oz) Cheddar cheese, grated; salt and freshly ground black pepper; pinch nutmeg; 6 hard-boiled eggs, halved; parsley to garnish.

Bring a large saucepan of salted water to the boil. Add macaroni and cook rapidly for 15–20 minutes, or until tender. Meanwhile, melt 60 g (2 oz) butter in a saucepan, stir in flour and cook, stirring for 2 minutes. Add milk and stir until sauce boils and thickens. Beat in 60 g (2 oz) cheese, and season with salt, pepper and nutmeg. Do not allow sauce to boil once cheese has been added. Drain macaroni and toss with remaining butter. Spoon hot macaroni into flameproof serving dish, top with eggs and spoon sauce over. Sprinkle with remaining cheese and put under preheated hot grill until cheese melts and browns. Garnish with parsley and serve immediately. Serves 6.

Egg Croquettes

60 g (2 oz) butter; 3 tbs flour; 1 cup milk;
1 tbs chopped parsley; 4 hard-boiled eggs, chopped;
2 eggs; salt and freshly ground black pepper; pinch nutmeg; flour; dry breadcrumbs; oil or dripping for deep-frying; parsley to garnish.

Melt butter in small saucepan, add flour and cook for 2 minutes. Add milk and cook until thick, stirring constantly. Remove from heat and, while sauce is still hot, stir in parsley, hard-boiled eggs, and 1 beaten egg. Season well with salt, pepper and nutmeg. Turn into a shallow dish or tin and smooth over with palette knife. Chill until ready to use (several hours if possible). Turn croquette mixture on to a floured board and cut into small sausage shapes. Dip into flour, then second egg beaten with ½ tsp salt. Roll in breadcrumbs. Deep-fry in hot fat until golden-brown. Drain on paper towels and serve immediately, garnished with parsley. Serves 4.

Curried Eggs

45 g (1½ oz) butter; 1 small onion, finely chopped;
½ cooking apple, peeled, cored and finely chopped; 2 tbs curry powder; 2 tbs flour;
2½ cups stock or water; 1 tsp curry paste (optional);
1 tbs chopped mango chutney; 1 tbs brown sugar;
juice ½ lemon; ½ tsp salt; 30 g (1 oz) sultanas;
8 hard-boiled eggs, halved.

Melt butter in a heavy saucepan, add onion and apple and cook gently for 5–6 minutes. Stir in curry powder and flour, then gradually stir in stock or water and bring to the boil. Add remaining ingredients (except eggs), cover and simmer for 20–30 minutes. Arrange eggs in a heated serving dish. Pour over sauce, and serve with boiled rice and chutney. Serves 4–6.

Straciatella alla Romana
(Egg and Cheese Soup)

3 eggs; 1½ tbs grated Parmesan cheese;
1 tbs chopped parsley; 6 cups chicken stock.

Beat eggs until frothy. Add cheese and parsley. Bring stock to a rolling boil. Pour egg mixture into it, stirring all the time until eggs are set. Serve immediately. Serves 6.

Stuffed Eggs

8 hard-boiled eggs, halved; 60 g (2 oz) butter;
2 tbs cream; ½ tsp dry mustard; salt and freshly ground black pepper; paprika.

Remove yolks from eggs, mash and mix with butter, cream, mustard, salt and pepper. Stuff egg whites with the mixture, sprinkle with paprika, and chill before serving. Serves 4–8.

VARIATIONS

STUFFED EGGS WITH LIVER PATE: Use Stuffed Egg recipe, adding 2 tbs chopped pickle relish and ½ cup liver pâté to egg yolks.

STUFFED EGGS WITH ANCHOVIES: Use Stuffed Egg recipe, adding 1 small can anchovy fillets, drained and crushed, or 1 tbs anchovy paste to egg yolks. Garnish with capers.

STUFFED EGGS WITH DEVILLED HAM: Use Stuffed Egg recipe, adding 2 or more tbs devilled ham to egg yolks. Garnish with chopped parsley.

STUFFED EGGS WITH OLIVES: Use Stuffed Egg recipe, adding 2 tbs chopped stuffed green or black olives to egg yolks.

STUFFED EGGS WITH MUSHROOMS: Use Stuffed Egg recipe, adding 2–3 tbs chopped, sautéed or raw mushrooms to egg yolks. Garnish with a bit of canned pimiento.

STUFFED EGGS WITH CAVIAR: Use Stuffed Egg recipe, adding 2 or more tbs caviar to egg yolks. Garnish with chutney.

CURRIED STUFFED EGGS: Use Stuffed Egg recipe, adding 1 tsp curry powder to egg yolks. Garnish with chutney.

STUFFED EGGS WITH HERBS: Use Stuffed Egg recipe, adding chopped fresh chives, chervil, parsley, savory or other herbs to egg yolks.

EGG FLIP

A nutritious meal-in-a-glass which should be in every-one's repertoire. An egg flip is the perfect breakfast-on-the-run and an instant, light, digestible meal at any time of day.

Egg Flip

1 egg; 1 tsp sugar; $^1/_4$ tsp vanilla, or 1 tsp brandy or sherry; 1 cup hot or cold milk.

Beat egg, sugar and vanilla, brandy or sherry thoroughly together. Add milk and beat until frothy. Pour into a glass and serve immediately. Serves 1.

VARIATIONS

FLUFFY EGG FLIP: Follow recipe for Egg Flip but separate the egg. Beat yolk, sugar and flavouring together, and stir in milk. Beat egg white until stiff, fold into mixture and serve immediately.

FRUIT EGG FLIP: Follow recipe for Egg Flip but substitute orange or pineapple juice for milk.

EGG NOG

A smooth but potent blend of eggs, cream and brandy, rum or whisky. Egg nog is a festive drink, associated especially with Christmas.

Egg Nog

6 eggs, separated; $^1/_2$ cup caster sugar; 2 cups brandy, rum or whisky; 4 cups cream; pinch salt; freshly grated nutmeg.

Beat egg yolks with sugar until thick. Beat in spirit and cream. Beat egg whites with salt until they form soft peaks, then fold into cream mixture. Serve in small punch cups or coffee cups, sprinkled with grated nutmeg. Serves 10–12.

EGGPLANT (AUBERGINE)

Although there are many varieties of eggplant, ranging from white to almost black, the rich, purple one is the most familiar. Eggplant combines well with other veget-ables such as tomatoes, zucchini and peppers. It makes a wonderful pickle. Cooked and mashed with spices, it is served as a dip (see *Baba Ghannouj*). It makes a case for savoury stuffings, and adds distinction to meat dishes and stews. Eggplant, diced or sliced and fried in butter or oil, can be served with eggs, fried or grilled fish, lamb chops, steaks or chicken. Small finger eggplant are known as Lebanese and Long Tom Eggplant.

When buying eggplants, look for smooth, firm, shiny vegetables with no blemishes and a fresh, green calyx. Avoid the very large ones as they can be spongy with little taste. Eggplants should be used as soon as possible after buying as they deteriorate quickly. If not using immediately, store, covered, in the refrigerator.

■ **BASIC PREPARATION:** Eggplants are often 'dégorged' (treated with salt to remove excess liquid) before cook-ing. This process is aimed at removing any bitterness and also prevents them from becoming soggy when cooked, and from soaking up too much oil if fried.

TO DEGORGE: Remove stem and calyx and cut the egg-plant in half lengthways, or cut into slices. Score the surface of the flesh, sprinkle with salt and leave on a tilted plate or in a colander for 30 minutes or so, for liquid to run off. Rinse off excess salt and dry thoroughly with paper towels before proceeding with the recipe.

■ **TO COOK:** Eggplant may be grilled, pan-fried, sautéed or baked. **See also recipes.**

GRILLED EGGPLANT: Slice eggplant thickly (do not peel) and dégorge (see above). Brush both sides with oil and season with freshly ground black pepper. Grill under a preheated grill, turning once, until surface is flecked with brown and flesh is soft. Season with salt after cooking.

Serve with grilled meats.

FRIED EGGPLANT: Slice eggplant thickly (do not peel) and dégorge (see above). Dip in flour and fry in olive oil over medium heat until golden-brown. Drain on paper towels and season with salt and freshly ground black pepper. Serve as a hot vegetable, or as a first course with a sauce of chilled plain yogurt, flavoured with garlic and mint.

Eggplant may also be cut into large dice and fried as above.

BAKED EGGPLANT: Brush whole, unpeeled eggplants with oil and bake in a preheated moderate oven (180°C/350°F) for 30 minutes or until soft. Halve the egg-plants lengthways and scoop the flesh into a bowl. Mash with a little butter, freshly ground black pepper, salt, crushed garlic and chopped fresh herbs such as parsley, basil or mint. Replace in shells, sprinkle with grated cheese or buttered breadcrumbs and reheat in the oven or under a preheated grill until golden and bubbling.

Eggplant Pickle

Serve with shish kebabs, meatballs, chicken or curry dishes.

2 medium eggplants; 1 cup vinegar; $^1/_4$ cup lemon juice; 2 tsp mustard seeds; 2 tsp coriander seeds, toasted; 1 tsp fennel seeds; 3 cloves garlic; 2 tsp fresh ginger, chopped; pinch chilli powder; salt and freshly ground black pepper.

Pierce eggplants all over with a fork and place on rack in a preheated hot oven (200°C/400°F), with a dish on the shelf below to catch juices. Bake for about 30 minutes or until soft. Halve lengthways, scoop out flesh and chop finely. Mix with $^1/_2$ cup vinegar to prevent discolouring. Put lemon juice and remaining vinegar into a blender with mustard, coriander and fennel seeds, garlic and ginger and blend until smooth. Add to eggplant flesh and season to taste with chilli powder, salt and pepper. Spoon into sterilised jars and store, covered, in the refrigerator. Makes 3–4 cups.

Eggplant Parmigiana

2 medium eggplants; thickly sliced; salt; 1 small onion, finely chopped; 2 cloves garlic, crushed; ¹/₂ cup olive oil; 1 cup chopped canned tomatoes; freshly ground black pepper; 90 g (3 oz) prosciutto, finely sliced; ¹/₂ cup grated Parmesan cheese; 15 g (¹/₂ oz) butter.

Sprinkle eggplant slices with salt. Toss and let stand for 1 hour. Meanwhile, make sauce: fry onion and garlic in 1 tbs oil until soft. Add tomatoes and simmer, covered, for 10 minutes. Season with salt and pepper. Rinse and dry eggplant slices. Fry over fairly high heat in remaining oil until golden-brown on both sides. Drain on paper towels. Arrange slices overlapping in a shallow baking dish, covering each slice with a slice of prosciutto, a spoonful of tomato sauce, a grinding of pepper and a sprinkling of Parmesan. Dot with butter and bake in a preheated moderate oven (180°C/350°F) for 30–40 minutes. Serves 4.

Stuffed Eggplant

2 large eggplants; salt; 4 tbs oil; 1 onion, chopped; 4 tomatoes, peeled and chopped; 1 clove garlic, crushed; 2 tbs chopped parsley; freshly ground black pepper; ¹/₂ cup beef stock; 2 tbs butter; 1¹/₂ cups fresh white breadcrumbs; ¹/₂ cup grated Cheddar cheese.

Cut eggplants in half lengthways, slash cut edges, sprinkle with salt and leave to stand upside-down for 1 hour. Drain and dry on paper towels. Heat oil in a frying pan and fry eggplant gently for a few minutes, cut sides down. Remove from heat, carefully scoop out flesh, not damaging skins, and chop it finely. Mix together eggplant flesh, onion, tomatoes, garlic, parsley and pepper. Fill eggplant shells and place them in a flameproof gratin dish with stock. Cover with foil and bake in a preheated moderate oven (180°C/350°F) for 30–40 minutes or until eggplant is tender. Melt butter in a small frying pan and fry breadcrumbs until crisp and golden. Sprinkle crumbs over cooked eggplant, top with cheese and grill until cheese melts. Serves 4.

Eggplant Mousse

This delicious mousse is wonderfully versatile. Use it to fill halves of tomatoes, or serve it as an appetiser in a brightly coloured bowl with corn chips or crusty bread, or sticks of cucumber, zucchini and fennel for dipping. The mousse improves when made a day ahead and left in the refrigerator.

3 large eggplants, sliced; salt; 2 tbs olive oil; 2 onions, very finely chopped; 3 cloves garlic, crushed; 2 anchovies, finely chopped; freshly ground black pepper; 2 tbs chopped fresh parsley or basil; juice ¹/₂ lemon.

Sprinkle eggplant slices with salt. Toss and let stand for 1 hour. Rinse and dry eggplant slices. Sprinkle with olive oil and place in an oiled baking dish. Bake in a preheated moderately hot oven (190°C/375°F) for 1 hour or until soft. Pass eggplant through a food mill or lightly purée in a food processor. Add onions, garlic, anchovies, salt and pepper (it should be highly seasoned). Chill. Before serving, sprinkle on parsley and lemon juice and, if you like, a few drops of olive oil. Makes 2 cups.

Eggplant Provençale

Halved eggplants, filled with a minced meat mixture and served hot with tomato sauce.

3 medium eggplants; 2 tbs olive oil; 1 medium onion, chopped; 2 cloves garlic, crushed; 1 green pepper, cored, seeded and chopped; 500 g (1 lb) minced steak; 1¹/₄ tsp salt; ¹/₄ tsp black pepper; ¹/₂ tsp dried oregano; ¹/₂ cup grated Romano cheese; ¹/₄ cup dry breadcrumbs; 2 tbs tomato paste; 1 quantity Basic Tomato Sauce (page 538).

Cook eggplants in boiling water, covered, for 15 minutes. Drain and cut in half lengthways. Carefully remove flesh, leaving a shell 1 cm (¹/₂ in) thick. Chop flesh. Heat oil in a heavy frying pan, add onion, garlic and green pepper and sauté until just tender. Combine eggplant flesh with sautéed mixture. Add remaining ingredients, except tomato sauce, and mix well. Fill eggplant shells with mixture and place in a greased baking pan. Brush tops with additional oil and bake in a preheated moderate oven (180°C/350°F) for about 45 minutes. Serve with tomato sauce. Serves 6.

EMPANADAS

These spicy meat turnovers are popular in several Latin American countries. Fillings vary from region to region, and the empanadas may be baked or deep-fried.

Empanadas

PASTRY: 4 cups flour; 2 tsp paprika; $^1/_2$ tsp salt; 185 g (6 oz) butter or lard; cold water.

FILLING: $^1/_2$ cup oil; I onion, finely chopped; I tomato, peeled, seeded and chopped; I tsp paprika; I kg (2 lb) lean stewing beef, trimmed and cut into 6 mm ($^1/_4$ in) dice; 2 tsp flour; $^1/_2$ cup beef stock; $^1/_2$ tsp ground cumin; salt; $^1/_2$ tsp chilli powder; I hard-boiled egg, chopped; $^1/_4$ cup stoned, chopped green olives; $^1/_3$ cup sultanas.

To make pastry, sift flour, paprika and salt together, and rub in fat. Using a knife, stir in enough water to make a fairly stiff dough. Knead lightly, wrap in plastic wrap and chill.

To prepare filling: heat oil in a large frying pan, add onion and fry gently until golden-brown. Add tomato and paprika and cook slowly until soft. Add meat, flour, stock, cumin, salt to taste and chilli. Stir until mixture comes to the boil. Cover and simmer for 15 minutes, then remove lid and cook rapidly for 5–10 minutes to reduce liquid by half. Cool mixture.

Divide pastry into pieces about the size of an egg. Roll each piece thin to form an 18 cm (7 in) circle. Put 2 tbs meat filling, 1 tsp chopped egg, $^1/_2$ tsp chopped olives and a few sultanas in the centre of each pastry circle.

Spread filling over half the circle, leaving a 2 cm ($^3/_4$ in) margin. Moisten edges of pastry and fold over to make turnovers, pressing edges firmly together. Pinch edge between thumb and finger and fold pinched part over on to unpinched part, or fold pastry circle to within 1 cm ($^1/_2$ in) of opposite edge, fold lower half over the upper and crimp. Chill empanadas for 20 minutes, then bake in a preheated hot oven (200°C/400°F) for 15 minutes. Alternatively, deep-fry in oil until golden-brown and drain on crumpled paper towels. Makes 18.

ENCHILADAS

Spicy enchiladas are a Mexican dish made of flat, soft tortillas (see *Tortilla*) dipped in a chilli and cumin-flavoured sauce, rolled around a filling and topped with more sauce. Traditionally they are sprinkled with grated cheese and garnished with hard-boiled egg, radish and lettuce. There are many different enchiladas; cooked or leftover meat, fish or poultry can be used. Follow recipe for Enchiladas de Pollo using meat of your choice.

Enchiladas de Pollo
(Chicken–Stuffed Tortillas in Sauce)

2 eggs, beaten; 2 tbs water; $^1/_4$ tsp cinnamon; 12 Tortillas, about 13 cm (5 in) in diameter (page 545); oil for frying.

SAUCE: 2 tbs olive oil; 6 tomatoes, peeled, seeded and chopped; I onion, chopped; I green or red pepper, seeded and chopped; $^1/_2$ tsp ground cumin; $^1/_2$ tsp chilli powder; salt and freshly ground black pepper.

FILLING: 250 g (8 oz) cooked chicken meat, chopped; $^1/_4$ cup raisins; $^1/_2$ cup chopped blanched almonds; 2 tbs chopped green olives.

GARNISH: $^1/_2$ small lettuce, shredded; 3 radishes, finely sliced; I Spanish onion, finely sliced into rings; I hard-boiled egg, sliced.

SAUCE: Heat the oil in a frying pan and sauté tomatoes, onion and green or red pepper until tender. Add cumin, chilli powder, salt and pepper. Remove from heat and keep warm.

Combine all the filling ingredients and mix well. Beat eggs with water and cinnamon until frothy, then dip each tortilla into this mixture to coat. Place some of the filling in centre of each tortilla, roll up and secure with wooden toothpicks. Heat oil in a frying pan and sauté enchiladas for about 2 minutes on each side or until golden-brown. Drain on paper towels. Place on a heated serving dish, pour sauce over and arrange garnish around edge. Serves 4–6.

ENDIVE, CURLY

A member of the chicory family whose decorative, curly-fringed leaves and pleasantly bitter taste make it a good partner to other greens, fruit or other robust-flavoured ingredients in a salad.

■ **BASIC PREPARATION:** Discard tough outer green leaves and break tender leaves off tough stalks. Wash leaves in cold water, dry in a salad dryer or on a tea-towel and store in a closed plastic bag in the refrigerator to crisp. See recipes.

Endive, Apple and Walnut Salad

Serve with grilled chicken or with cold meats.

$^1/_2$ bunch curly endive, trimmed and crisped; I red and I green apple, cored and cut into thin wedges; 2 tsp lemon juice; $^1/_4$ cup walnut pieces.

DRESSING: 2 tsp lemon juice; salt and freshly ground black pepper; 2 tbs walnut or olive oil; 2 tbs sour cream.

Place endive in a salad bowl. Toss apples with lemon juice and add to bowl. Make dressing: mix lemon juice with a little salt and pepper, beat in oil a little at a time, then sour cream. Pour over salad and toss lightly. Add walnuts, toss again and serve immediately. Serves 6.

Ensalada Sevillana
(Seville Winter Salad)

1 bunch curly endive, trimmed and crisped;
1 red pepper, cored, seeded and sliced;
2 small onions, finely sliced into rings;
16 black olives, stoned; 2 oranges, peeled and finely sliced into rounds.

DRESSING: $^1/_4$ cup olive oil; 1 tbs white wine vinegar; 1 clove garlic, crushed; $^1/_2$ tsp salt; $^1/_4$ tsp sugar; little fresh or dried tarragon.

Mix all salad ingredients together in a salad bowl. Combine ingredients for dressing in a screw-top jar, shake well and pour over salad just before serving. Serves 4–6.

ENTRECOTE

Meaning 'between the ribs', entrecôte was originally the French name for a beef steak from the rib section, but the term is now widely used on menus to denote any fine steak dish. The dish is named after its sauce or garnish, e.g. Entrecôte Chasseur is a grilled or pan-fried steak with Sauce Chasseur (see page 458).

Entrecôtes Vert–Pré

4 rib, sirloin or rump steaks, cut 2.5–4 cm (1–1$^1/_2$ in) thick, each weighing about 200 g (7 oz); Straw Potatoes (page 384); watercress; Maître d'Hôtel Butter (page 52).

Grill or pan-fry steaks until rare or medium, as desired. Put each steak on to a heated plate and garnish with a portion of straw potatoes and a small bouquet of watercress. Place a slice of maître d'hôtel butter on each steak and serve immediately. Serves 4.

ENTREE

Today, an entrée describes a made-up dish, served as a first course or as a light supper or luncheon dish – it may even be the main dish of a meal.

The French word *entrée* means 'way in' or 'entrance'. At a formal dinner, these dishes follow the soup and fish course and come before the main meat course. It is amusing to go through the menus of old-fashioned books – one cannot help but wonder how they did it. Today, much simpler menus are in favour and the separate hors d'oeuvre, soup, fish and entrée courses have practically combined into a first or starter course, and any one of these courses may be served.

Since entrées are usually 'dressed' or 'made' dishes, they are considered the first course to show the cook's

skill to the full. Attractive presentation is vital and, luckily, by their nature these small portions of meat, fish and so on, and their accompaniments, can be arranged in myriad different ways; in a pretty pastry case, *en brochette*, in individual ramekins or shells. They may also be individual feather-light soufflés, golden croquettes, fritters, filled crêpes or bouchées, dainty portions of Beef Stroganoff (see page 511), or sautéed calf's liver (see *Liver*).

ESCABECHE (ESCOVITCH)

This dish is a form of pickled fish; the sauce preserves the fish with or without refrigeration for 2 days. It is served throughout the West Indies, but in Jamaica it is called Escovitch.

Escabeche

1 kg (2 lb) fish fillets; flour for coating; 1 quantity Basic Fritter Batter (page 159); olive oil for deep-frying.

SAUCE: 1 cup dry white wine; 1 cup white wine vinegar; 1 cup olive oil; 1 tsp salt; 6 black peppercorns.

PICKLES: 2 cups finely sliced mixed vegetables (carrots, turnips, onions and green beans); 1 red pepper, seeded and sliced; 1 green pepper, seeded and sliced; 2 cloves garlic, sliced; 1 chilli, seeded and finely chopped (optional); 1 cup white vinegar; 1 tbs sugar.

Cut fish into bite-sized strips or cubes. Roll in flour, dip into batter and fry in oil until golden-brown. Drain on paper towels and cool. Mix together ingredients for sauce and set aside. Cover pickle vegetables with vinegar, add sugar and boil for 3 minutes. Cool. Place fish in an earthenware bowl, cover with sauce and pickles and marinate for 24 hours. Drain before serving, with a salad. Serves 8.

ESCALOPE

Escalope is a French word which may mean any thin, boneless and skinless slice of meat or fish, but it is mainly used for fine slices of veal, beaten thin. The same delicate slices feature in the cuisines of various countries and take different names accordingly. The French *escalope* becomes *scaloppine* (plural, *scaloppini*) or sometimes *costolette* (cutlet) in Italian; the German name is *schnitzel*; in English, it is a scallop or simply a veal steak. You may find it under any of these names in butchers' shops. Classically, escalopes are cut from the top of the leg, across the grain. Thin veal steaks from other sections are often sold as escalopes, schnitzel etc., and they may also be satisfactory.

■ BASIC PREPARATION: If you buy large veal steaks which separate into natural divisions, divide them. Snip around the edges so that escalopes will cook without curling. If not already beaten out, place each one between 2 sheets of greaseproof paper and beat gently with a cutlet bat, rolling pin or the flat side of a meat mallet (not the knobbly side which would tear the meat) to a thickness of 5 mm (¼ in).

Tiny escalopines (Italian *piccati*) can be prepared at home from a loin or set of rib cutlets. Cut the eye of meat from the bone and slice across about 2 cm (¾ in) thick. Beat each slice out as described.

See also *Schnitzel* and *Scaloppine*.

Escalopes de Veau au Beurre
(Veal with Butter Sauce)

6 large or 12 small veal escalopes, beaten thin; seasoned flour; 60 g (2 oz) clarified butter; ¼ cup white wine; finely chopped parsley.

Coat escalopes lightly with flour, patting off excess. Heat butter in a large, heavy frying pan, add escalopes just as it begins to brown and sauté on fairly high heat until golden-brown on both sides (do this in 2 batches if necessary). Remove them to a heated serving dish and pour the butter over them. Add wine to the pan and boil 1–2 minutes, stirring in all the brown bits. Pour over meat, sprinkle with chopped parsley and serve at once. Serves 6.

VARIATIONS

ESCALOPES DE VEAU A LA CREME: Sauté the escalopes as described in Escalopes de Veau au Beurre. Remove them to a heated serving dish. Pour out fat from sauté pan, add 1 tbs dry sherry and ¼ cup cream and boil 1–2 minutes, stirring in all the brown bits. Pour sauce over meat and serve at once.

ESCALOPES DE VEAU A LA CREME ET CHAMPIGNONS: Follow the recipe for Escalopes de Veau a la Crème, but do not pour off fat from pan after removing the escalopes. Sauté 90 g (3 oz) sliced button mushrooms in the fat before adding sherry and cream.

ESCAROLE (BATAVIAN ENDIVE)

Escarole has broad, crinkled leaves and comes from the same group of green-leaved vegetables as curly endive. It is used in salads and should be prepared in the same way as curly endive.

See *Endive*.

FENNEL

Both the herb and vegetable varieties of fennel are of ancient origin. The herb plant is tall, with green stalks and feathery leaves, and the vegetable, known as Florence fennel, is a bulbous root that looks somewhat like celery. The flavour depends on the variety and ranges from bitter to sweet, tasting quite strongly of anise. Wild fennel often grows by the roadside in temperate climates.

FENNEL AS A VEGETABLE: Use the fennel bulb raw, sliced into a tomato or green salad or on its own dressed with Vinaigrette Dressing (see page 442). The distinctive flavour lends itself well as a salad accompaniment to fish, pork or lamb. The bulbs can also be used and prepared in the same way as celery.

FENNEL AS A HERB: The feathery leaves, so often used in the south of France, lend a delicate flavour to fish, fish soups or cream sauces to accompany seafood. In Italy the stalks and leaves are used, chopped with garlic, to make a stuffing for roast pork. Fennel leaves are also delicious cooked with barbecued lamb, and dried fennel branches give an intriguingly smoky taste to barbecued fish. Use fresh leaves to stuff a whole fish before baking.

FENNEL SEEDS: These are aromatic and are used to flavour foods such as pickles, biscuits, pastries and fish. See recipes.

Fennel Smoked Fish

1 x 1.25 kg (1¼ lb) whole fish, scaled and cleaned; 6 short pieces dried fennel; olive oil; 1 large bunch dried fennel branches; ½ cup brandy).

Cut 3 incisions on each side of fish. Put a piece of fennel in each incision and brush fish with oil. Place in a barbecue grid and grill fish for 7–10 minutes on each side. Lay dried fennel branches on a large flame-proof dish and place fish in grid on top. Warm brandy, set alight and pour flaming over dried fennel branches which catch alight and give out a strong scent to flavour the fish. When flames die down, remove fish from grid to a heated serving plate. Serves 2.

NOTE: Any white-fleshed fish is suitable for this dish. Salt or fresh water fish may be used and small fish can be prepared this way.

Fennel with Butter and Cheese

4 bulbs fennel, trimmed and cut into segments; 1 tbs olive oil; 1 clove garlic; 1 slice lemon; 1 tsp salt; 2 tbs butter; 2 tbs grated Parmesan cheese; freshly ground black pepper.

Put fennel into a saucepan containing enough boiling water to cover. Add oil, garlic, lemon and salt. Bring back to the boil, reduce heat, cover and simmer for 30–35 minutes or until just tender. Melt butter in a shallow gratin dish. Drain fennel well, put into dish and turn gently to coat with butter. Sprinkle with cheese and pepper. Brown lightly under a preheated grill before serving. Serves 4.

Fennel and Tomatoes with Dill

oil for frying; 4 bulbs fennel, trimmed and finely sliced lengthways; salt and freshly ground black pepper; 4 ripe tomatoes, peeled and sliced; 3 tbs chopped fresh dill.

Heat enough oil to cover bottom of a heavy pan and stew fennel gently, stirring often, until almost soft. Add salt, pepper and tomatoes and continue to cook gently for 5 minutes, stirring occasionally with a spatula to avoid breaking up tomatoes. Remove from heat, stir in dill and turn into a serving dish. Serve cold but not chilled. Serves 4–6.

Braised Fennel

A French way with this anise-scented vegetable, gently braised, to complement fish or lamb dishes.

4 bulbs fennel, trimmed; 2 tbs olive oil; 1 tsp salt; ½ cup water, stock or dry white wine.

Halve or quarter fennel lengthways, depending on size. Heat olive oil in a frying pan or heavy flame-proof casserole, add fennel and salt and cook gently, turning vegetable, for about 10 minutes. Add water, stock or wine, cover and cook over low heat for about 25 minutes or until tender. Serves 4.

FENUGREEK

Both the leaves and seeds of fenugreek are used in Indian cooking. The small flat, beige-coloured seeds are ground and used in curry powders and are especially good in fish curries. The hard seeds should be lightly roasted before they are ground, but don't roast them for too long or a bitter flavour will develop. The fresh leaves can be used to give a distinctive tang to salads. Fenugreek seeds are also used to give a maple flavour to sweets and candies.

Sour Fish Curry

1 tbs tamarind pulp; ½ cup hot water; 1 medium onion, chopped; 3 cloves garlic, crushed; 1 tsp chopped fresh ginger; 1 tbs ground coriander; 2 tsp ground cumin; 1 tsp turmeric; 1 tsp chilli powder; ½ tsp ground fenugreek; 3 tbs oil; 1 tbs vinegar or lemon juice; 1½ tsp salt; 500 g (1 lb) fish fillets or steaks, cut into serving pieces.

Soak tamarind pulp in hot water for 10 minutes, then rub pulp off seeds and soften it in the water. Strain and discard seeds and fibres. Purée onion, garlic, ginger and 1 tbs tamarind liquid in a blender or food processor, or pound in a mortar with a pestle. Mix in spices. Heat oil in a saucepan and fry spice mixture, stirring, until it thickens and darkens. Add rest of tamarind liquid, the vinegar or lemon juice, salt and enough hot water just to cover fish. When this comes to the boil put in fish and simmer very gently for 10–15 minutes or until it flakes easily when tested with a fine skewer. Serves 4.

FETTUCINE

See *Pasta*.

FIG

Fresh figs are sweet and luscious eaten raw when they are very soft and ripe. Pick them from the tree if you have the chance and eat while still warm from the sun. There are more than 150 varieties of fig, ranging in colour from greenish-yellow to very dark purple, and the entire fruit is edible. Figs should be eaten at room temperature; if they are too cold their delicate flavour is lost. Dried figs are extremely sweet and can be used in cakes and puddings or stewed.

WAYS TO USE FIGS

Fig Salad: Slice fresh figs, sprinkle with brandy and serve with cream, or sprinkle with sweet white wine and serve with yogurt.

Prosciutto and Figs: Halve figs and arrange paper-thin slices of prosciutto around them.

Figs with Orange Juice: Cut stalks from 4 fresh figs, quarter them and place in a serving bowl. Pour over them the freshly squeezed juice of 1 large orange and set aside for an hour before eating. Serves 2.

Baked Figs: In an ovenproof dish arrange 5–6 slightly underripe whole figs. Pour in ¼ cup water, sprinkle with ¼ cup sugar and bake in a preheated moderate oven (180°C/350°F) for 20 minutes. Serve chilled with cream. Serves 2–3.

See also *Fruit, Dried* and *Candied*.

Caramelised Figs

A gas blowtorch purchased from the local hardware store is a boon for dishes like this.

6 fresh figs, halved lengthwise; 2 tbs port or marsala; 2 tbs sugar; natural yogurt or mascarpone; fresh mint sprigs to decorate.

Preheat the griller or oven to very hot (250°C/450°F). Arrange the figs cut side up, in a flameproof dish. Spoon some port or marsala and sugar over each. Place under the grill and cook for a few minutes or until softened and glazed. Alternatively, use a gas blowtorch to caramelise the figs. Carefully arrange 3 caramelised fig halves on each of 4 dessert plates. Set a large scoop of the natural yogurt alongside the figs and drizzle over the juices in the dish. Garnish if liked with mint sprigs. You may like to offer a dessert biscuit with this. Serves 4–6.

Rich Fig Pudding

1¼ cups chopped dried figs; ¾ cup raisins; 1½ cups chopped stoned dates; ¼ cup chopped preserved ginger, drained; 2–3 tbs brandy or rum; 3 cups fresh breadcrumbs; 2 cups self-raising flour; 1 cup shredded suet; pinch salt; 3 eggs; grated rind and juice 1 lemon; ¼ cup milk.

Combine figs, raisins, dates and ginger. Sprinkle with brandy or rum, cover and leave for 1 hour. Mix together breadcrumbs, flour, suet and salt. Beat eggs to a froth and mix into dry ingredients with lemon rind and juice and prepared fruit. Mix thoroughly, adding milk to bring mixture to dropping consistency. Spoon mixture into greased 5-cup pudding basin, cover with 2 thicknesses buttered greaseproof paper and tie securely with string. Place in a large saucepan with enough water to come halfway up sides of basin. Cover and steam for 4 hours. Serve in wedges with cream or custard. Serves 6.

FILET MIGNON

A small, choice steak cut from the narrow (tail) end of a fillet of beef, which should be trimmed of all fat and surrounding filament. A *filet mignon* should be about 4 cm (1½ in) thick when it is ready for cooking, but as the tail of fillet may be very narrow, the fillet is often cut thicker and beaten gently with the flat of a cleaver or large knife to the required thickness. Shape it with your hands into a neat circular shape, and tie string round it to keep the shape before cooking it.

It can be prepared in any of the ways described for *Tournedos* (see page 545), or in the classic way, Filets Mignons Henri IV.

Filets Mignons Henri IV

4 filets mignons; 1 tbs oil; 30 g (1 oz) butter; 4 round croûtes white bread sautéed in clarified butter (see page 52); Straw Potatoes (page 384); artichoke hearts or asparagus tips sautéed in butter, or watercress sprigs; 1 quantity Béarnaise Sauce (pages 459–60).

Sauté filets mignons in oil and butter, heated until just turning brown, for 3–4 minutes on each side for rare, or a few minutes longer for medium-rare. Remove strings from filets and place each on a hot croûte set on a heated plate. Garnish plates with straw potatoes and artichoke hearts, asparagus tips or watercress. Serve immediately with béarnaise sauce. Serves 4.

FILO PASTRY (FILLO/PHYLLO)

A very light, thin and delicate pastry widely used in cookery of the Middle East, for both sweet and savoury dishes. Filo is available either fresh or frozen in 375 g (12 oz) packs from supermarkets, groceries, delicatessens and health food stores. You will find the pastry ready to use, separated into thin sheets. Despite its delicate texture, filo is one of the easiest of all pastries to use.

■ **TO USE:** The main point to remember is that filo dries very quickly and becomes brittle when exposed to the air. Spread a dry tea-towel on your work surface, remove the filo sheets from their plastic pack and unfold on to the tea-towel. Do not separate the sheets. Cover with another dry tea-towel and cover that with a lightly dampened tea-towel. Remove each sheet as you need it, making sure you keep the remainder covered. Brush each sheet lightly with melted butter (for sweet or savoury dishes) or oil (for savoury dishes) before using.

Filo pastries freeze well and are ideal for entertaining. They may be baked from the frozen state at the temperature given in the recipe, although they may need extra cooking time. A sprinkling of cold water on the top layer of the pastry will help make it crisp. **See recipes.**

Tiropitakia (Greek Cheese Pastries)

2 onions, finely chopped; 30 g (1 oz) butter; 500 g (1 lb) feta cheese, crumbled; 375 g (12 oz) ricotta cheese; 3 eggs; 1/2 cup finely chopped parsley; salt and freshly ground black pepper; 1 tsp nutmeg; 24 sheets filo pastry; 350 g (8 oz) butter, melted.

Cook onions gently in 30 g (1 oz) butter until soft. Turn them on to a plate to cool a little. Mix feta and ricotta cheeses. Add eggs, beat thoroughly and fold in onions and parsley. Season with salt, pepper and nutmeg. Unfold filo pastry and, leaving it stacked, cut lengthways in three strips. Stack strips between 2 dry tea-towels with a dampened towel on top. Lay 1 strip on work surface. Brush lightly with melted butter, fold lengthways in half and brush again with butter. Place a teaspoon of cheese filling on one end of pastry strip. Fold corner of pastry over filling until it meets the folded edge of pastry to form a triangle. Continue to fold pastry over in triangles until you come to end of strip. Brush top with melted butter and place, seam side down, on a lightly greased baking tray. Repeat with remaining filling and pastry. Bake Tiropitakia in a preheated moderately hot oven (190°C/375°F) 15–20 minutes or until puffed and golden-brown. Serve hot. Makes about 72.

NOTE: Tiropitakia can be prepared and frozen unbaked until required. Bake straight from the freezer, allowing 10 more minutes' cooking time.

VARIATION

SPINACH TIROPITAKIA: Follow recipe for Tiropitakia, but use filling for Spanakopita (Greek Spinach Pie, below) instead of cheese filling.

Spanakopita (Greek Spinach Pie)

1 bunch (1 kg/2 lb) spinach, finely chopped; 12 spring onions, chopped; 1/2 cup vegetable oil; 1 onion, chopped; 4 eggs, beaten; 250 g (8 oz) feta cheese, crumbled; 250 g (8 oz) Cheddar cheese, grated; 1/4 tsp cinnamon; 1/4 tsp nutmeg; 1/4 tsp salt; freshly ground black pepper; 20 sheets filo pastry.

Combine spinach, spring onions and parsley in a large bowl. Heat 2 tbs of the oil and gently fry onion until soft. Add to spinach mixture with eggs, feta and Cheddar cheeses, cinnamon, nutmeg, salt and pepper and mix well. Stack filo sheets between 2 dry tea-towels with a dampened towel on top. Lightly brush 1 sheet of filo pastry with oil and place in a greased baking dish, about 33 x 23 cm (13 x 9 in). Repeat until 10 sheets of filo have been used, brushing each with oil. Spread spinach mixture over filo. Cover with remaining sheets of filo pastry, brushing each with oil. Sprinkle water over top sheet of filo. Bake in a preheated moderate oven (180°C/350°F) for 45 minutes or until golden-brown. Using a sharp knife, cut into diamond shapes for serving. Serves 6–8.

Lamb Filo Pie

2 tbs olive oil; 2 onions, chopped; 1.25 kg (2 1/2 lb) minced lamb; 1/4 cup chopped fresh mint; 1 tsp cinnamon; 1/4 tsp nutmeg; salt; 3/4 cup pine nuts; 24 sheets filo pastry; 250 g (8 oz) butter, melted.

Heat oil in a large frying pan, add onions and cook until softened. Add lamb and sauté until browned. Drain off excess fat. Stir in mint, cinnamon, nutmeg, salt and pine nuts. Set aside. Stack filo sheets between 2 dry tea-towels with a dampened towel on top. Line a buttered 33 x 23 cm (13 x 9 in) baking dish with 4 sheets of filo, brushing each lightly with butter, and allowing ends to hang over sides of dish. Spread one quarter of lamb mixture over filo and top with 4 more filo sheets, each lightly brushed with butter. Continue layering filo and lamb mixture, reserving 4 sheets of filo and ending with lamb mixture. Fold overhanging ends of filo over lamb mixture in dish. Top with remaining 4 sheets of filo, each brushed with butter, and tuck ends down inside edge of dish to enclose filling completely. Bake in a preheated moderately hot oven (190°C/375°F) for 45 minutes or until top is golden. Serve hot, cut into diamond shapes. Serves 10–12.

Ricotta and Artichoke Pie

olive oil; 3 shallots, chopped; 500 g (1 lb) ricotta cheese; 1 cup grated Gruyère cheese; 3/4 cup grated Parmesan cheese; 1/2 cup sour cream; 4 eggs, beaten; 1/2 tsp dried tarragon; 1 x 400 g can artichoke hearts, drained and quartered; salt and freshly ground black pepper; 24 sheets filo pastry.

Heat 1 tbs olive oil in a small frying pan, add shallots and cook until softened. Set aside. Place ricotta, Gruyère and Parmesan cheeses in a large bowl and add sour cream, eggs and tarragon. Mix until thoroughly combined. Stir in shallots, artichoke hearts, salt and pepper. Stack sheets of filo between 2 dry tea-towels with a dampened towel on top. Brush a 25 cm (10 in) spring-form tin with olive oil. Line tin with 5 sheets of filo pastry, each brushed lightly with olive oil, overlapping them and allowing ends to hang over sides of tin. Spread half cheese mixture over filo. Top with 5 more sheets of filo, each brushed with oil. Add remaining cheese mixture, spreading evenly, fold in overhanging pastry and then top with remaining filo sheets, each lightly brushed with oil. Tuck overhanging ends down inside tin, enclosing filling completely. Bake in a preheated hot oven (200°C/400°F) for 40–45 minutes or until top is golden. Let pie cool completely in tin. Serves 8–10.

Indian Beef Triangles

155 g (5 oz) butter; 1 large onion, chopped; 2 cloves garlic, crushed; 2 tbs curry powder; 1 1/2 tsp grated fresh ginger; 1 1/2 tsp salt, 1 tsp sugar; 1/4 tsp cayenne; 750 g (1 1/2 lb) minced beef; 24 sheets filo pastry.

Melt 30 g (1 oz) butter in a large, heavy frying pan. Add onion and garlic and cook until onion has softened. Stir in curry powder, ginger, salt, sugar and cayenne and cook for 1 minute. Add beef and cook until browned and crumbly. Set aside. Melt remaining butter and cool slightly. Stack sheets of filo between 2 dry tea-towels with a dampened towel on top. Brush 1 sheet of filo with melted butter, cut in half lengthways, and fold each half in half lengthways. Brush halves with butter. Place 1 1/2 tsp of meat mixture in corner of one end of each half. Fold filo over filling, enclosing it to form a triangle. Continue to fold pastry over in triangles until you come to the end of strip. Make triangles with remaining filo and meat filling. Place on a buttered baking tray and brush with melted butter. Bake in a pre-heated moderately hot oven (190°C/375°F) for 20–25 minutes or until golden. Makes 48.

Greek Custard Pie

4 cups milk; 3/4 cup sugar; 3/4 cup fine semolina; 1 cinnamon stick; 1 tsp grated lemon rind; pinch salt; 5 eggs, lightly beaten; 1 tsp vanilla; 250 g (8 oz) filo pastry; 185 g (6 oz) unsalted butter, melted.

SYRUP: 1 cup water; 1 cup sugar; 1 cinnamon stick; 1 tbs lemon juice; 1 strip lemon rind.

Mix milk, sugar, semolina, cinnamon, lemon and salt in a heavy saucepan and stir over low heat until thickened. Simmer 5 minutes, then remove from heat. Discard cinnamon stick. Cover surface of mixture with plastic wrap to prevent a skin from forming, and cool. When cool, add eggs and vanilla and mix thoroughly. Stack sheets of filo between 2 dry tea-towels with a dampened towel on top. Place 1 sheet of filo in a greased 33 x 23 cm (13 x 9 in) oven-proof dish and brush it with melted butter. Repeat until you have used half the filo. Pour in custard mixture and top with remaining filo, brushing each sheet with butter before it is placed in position.

Trim edges of filo to fit dish and brush top with remaining butter. With a sharp knife, cut through top 3 sheets of filo in a diamond pattern. Bake in a preheated moderate oven (180°C/350°F) for 45 minutes or until pastry is golden-brown and a thin knife inserted into custard comes out clean. Remove from oven and cool in dish.

SYRUP: Place all ingredients in a saucepan and bring to the boil, stirring until sugar has dissolved. Boil over moderate heat 10 minutes, then strain and cool to lukewarm. When pie is cold, pour over lukewarm syrup and leave to cool completely before serving. Serves 10–12.

Cream Cheese Slices

250 g (8 oz) cream cheese or ricotta cheese; 2 eggs; 1/2 cup sugar; 1 tbs lemon juice; 1/2 cup sultanas; 6 sheets filo pastry, cut in half; 125 g (4 oz) butter, melted.

Place cheese, eggs, sugar and lemon juice in a mixing bowl and beat well until smooth. Stir in sultanas. Stack filo between 2 dry tea-towels with a dampened towel on top. Place 1 sheet of filo in a greased 28 x 18 cm (11 x 7 in) baking dish, first brushing sheet with melted butter. Repeat until you have used half the filo. Spoon over cheese filling, and continue adding remaining filo sheets, brushing each with butter. Using a sharp knife, mark top filo layers into diamond shapes 6 x 4 cm (2 1/2 x 1 3/4 in) Bake in a preheated moderate oven (180°C/350°F) for 20–30 minutes or until golden and filling is set. Serve cold. Makes about 18.

Nut Rolls

3/4 cup finely chopped walnuts; 1/2 cup finely chopped almonds; I tsp sugar; 1/4 tsp cinnamon; 1/8 tsp nutmeg; IO sheets filo pastry; 250 g (8 oz) butter, melted.

CINNAMON HONEY SYRUP: I cup sugar; 2/3 cup water; 1/4 cup honey; I small cinnamon stick; I tsp fresh lemon juice.

Mix together nuts, sugar and spices. Stack filo between 2 dry tea-towels with a dampened towel on top. Brush half of a sheet of filo with melted butter, fold other half over and brush with butter so that you have a piece of filo 18 x 30 cm (7 x 12 in). Sprinkle with 1 tbs of nut mixture. Beginning at one end, roll filo as you would a jam roll. Cut into 3. Place on greased baking tray with smooth side of pastry rolls up and brush with melted butter. Repeat with remaining filo and nut filling. Bake in a preheated moderate oven (180°C/350°F) for 20 minutes or until golden-brown.

CINNAMON HONEY SYRUP: Mix all ingredients together and simmer for 30 minutes. Cook only until light brown. Dip hot nut rolls into warm syrup. Makes 30.

FINNAN HADDIE

The smoked haddock of Scotland, which is split, flattened and smoked to a beautiful pale gold. The flavour is light and delicate and mixes well with cream, eggs, rice or potatoes.

■ TO COOK: Finnan Haddie can be grilled, poached or baked. See also recipes.

GRILLED FINNAN HADDIE: Rub with butter, place skin side down on a greased grill tray and cook under a preheated moderate grill on one side only for about 7 minutes. Serve with extra melted butter.

POACHED FINNAN HADDIE: Place skin side down in a shallow flameproof dish, cover with water, milk or a combination of both, and simmer very gently for 5–7 minutes or until flesh flakes. Drain well and remove skin and bones. Serve with melted butter or a Béchamel Sauce (see page 456), garnished with sliced hard-boiled eggs.

BAKED FINNAN HADDIE: Place skin side down in a baking dish, dot with butter and add 1 cup water. Bake, uncovered, in a preheated moderate oven (180°C/350°F) for 15 minutes or until flesh flakes. Remove fish, take off skin and bones and serve garnished with fresh dill, or accompany with Mushroom Sauce or fresh Tomato Sauce (see *Sauces*).

Creamed Finnan Haddie

500 g (I lb) smoked haddock, cooked in half water, half milk; I 1/2 tbs butter; I 1/2 tbs flour; I cup cream; I cup fish stock; freshly ground black pepper; 1/4 tsp nutmeg.

GARNISH: triangles of bread; butter for frying; I tbs chopped parsley.

Skin, bone and flake haddock and set aside. Melt butter in a saucepan, add flour and stir until smooth. Add cream and fish stock, stirring constantly until boiling. Simmer for 3 minutes. Season with pepper and nutmeg. Fry bread triangles in butter until golden-brown and drain on paper towels. Fold fish through cream sauce, reheat gently and pile into a heated serving dish. Serve surrounded with bread triangles and sprinkled with parsley. Serves 2–4.

Far Eastern Kedgeree

250 g (8 oz) smoked haddock, cooked, skinned, boned and flaked; 2 cups warm freshly boiled long-grain rice; 60 g (2 oz) butter, melted; freshly ground black pepper; 2 tbs oil; 60 g (2 oz) raw peanuts, shelled and skinned; 2 tbs sultanas; 2 hard-boiled eggs, I chopped and I sliced; 2–3 tbs cream (optional); chopped parsley.

Fork fish into warm rice, add butter and pepper and keep warm. Heat oil and fry peanuts until they are pale gold. Add sultanas and continue frying for a few seconds until they are plump. Add these to fish and rice together with chopped egg and cream, if using. Pile on a heated dish, garnish with slices of hard-boiled egg and sprinkle with chopped parsley. Serves 4.

Omelette Arnold Bennett

This is an elegant dish which was created for the writer Arnold Bennett by the Savoy Grill in London.

60 g (2 oz) butter; 1/2 cup cream; 4 tbs cooked, skinned, boned and flaked smoked haddock; 4 eggs, separated; 3 tbs grated Parmesan cheese; salt and freshly ground white pepper.

Melt 30 g (1 oz) butter and 2 tbs cream in a frying pan over medium heat, add haddock and stir for 2–3 minutes. Leave to cool. Beat egg yolks with 1 tbs cream. Whisk egg whites to form very soft peaks and fold into yolks with haddock and half the cheese. Season with salt and pepper. Melt rest of butter in a pan, pour in omelette mixture and cook until golden and set underneath. Do not fold omelette but slide on to a heated flameproof serving dish. Sprinkle on rest of cheese and pour remaining cream over it. Brown quickly under a preheated hot grill and serve at once. Serves 2.

FISH

Fish is the gourmet's joy, the hurried cook's friend, a boon to weight-watchers and the cholesterol-conscious, being highly nutritious, digestible and always tender.

Select fish carefully, use it promptly and cook it briefly and it will reward you with fine eating.

Freshness is all-important. A fish which has been kept a day too long in the shop or in your refrigerator may still be perfectly edible, but the best of its pure and delicate flavour will have disappeared. When buying a whole fish, check for full, bright eyes, flat gills, which are red underneath, and a clenched mouth. It should feel slippery not tacky, and should smell 'of the sea' – fishy but fresh.

When buying fish steaks or fillets, be especially careful. Sometimes stale fish are filleted and labelled 'fresh fillets'. Again, they should smell fishy but fresh, and have a sheen, not a dull surface. If pressed, the flesh should feel springy and the indentation should quickly disappear. If the flesh oozes and the indentation fills with moisture, then the steak or fillet has been frozen and thawed and should not be offered as fresh fish.

Buy fish on the day you will eat it, if possible. If you must keep it overnight, store it, loosely covered in foil, in the coldest part of the refrigerator.

Fish can be divided into 2 types, fat and lean.

Fat Fish includes mullet and all those which are commercially canned or smoked – salmon, trout, herring, sardines, tuna, mackerel, tailor, gemfish and so on. These are technically classified as 'oily' fish, though they come in many variations of texture and fat content from the undoubtedly oily mullet to the succulent but delicate trout and salmon. In general, dark-fleshed fish are the oiliest.

Fat fish are a good choice for grilling, baking, barbecuing or hot-plate griddling: the more delicate ones are also good pan-fried or poached.

Lean (white) Fish includes whiting, bream, John Dory, snapper, mulloway (jewfish), sole, flounder, perch and flathead. They are a good choice for pan-frying, deep-frying or poaching. If baked or grilled, they should be protected from drying out by basting; a stuffing also helps to keep the flesh moist.

Like your butcher, the fishmonger can be a useful guide to the best fish to buy for a particular recipe.

■ **BASIC PREPARATION:** If you are buying fish, ask the fishmonger to clean and scale it for you. They will also skin, fillet or cut it into steaks if you ask. If you have caught it or been given it, you can prepare it at home.

TO SCALE A FISH: Working on plenty of newspaper, grasp the tail and scrape firmly from the tail toward the head with a small rigid knife or a serrated, fish-scaling knife. Repeat on the other side.

TO CLEAN A FISH: Cut open along the belly from the vent (near the tail) to the head, and pull out the entrails. Wash the fish inside and out under cold running water. With a small knife, remove any dark stomach lining or dark vein inside under the backbone. Wash again and dry the fish well.

TO FILLET ROUND FISH: Place fish on a board and grasp firmly. With a sharp, flexible knife, remove head and cut

along the backbone to the tail. Starting at the head end, slide the knife closely along the backbone, cutting away the fillet all the way to the tail. Turn the fish over and repeat on the other side, cutting off the tail.

TO FILLET FLAT FISH: These fish yield 4 fillets – 2 on each side. Place fish on a board and grasp the head firmly. Cut round behind the head and down the backbone from head to tail. Using a sharp, flexible knife slide the blade closely down the backbone to the tail on one side, cutting away the fillet. Remove the second fillet in the same way. Turn fish over and repeat on the other side.

TO SKIN A FISH FILLET: Place the fillet, skin side down, on a board with the tail towards you. Make a small cut through the flesh at the tail end. Dip the fingers of one hand in salt and hold the tail firmly, while with the other hand you ease a sharp, flexible knife between flesh and skin, pushing the flesh off the skin.

■ **TO COOK:** Fish should be moist and juicy when served, and must not be cooked beyond the moment when the flesh turns from translucent to opaque. This usually takes minutes only. If cooking a whole fish, start testing halfway through the recommended cooking time by pushing a fine skewer into the thickest part near the bone. When it slides in easily and you can push the flesh away from the bone just a little, the fish is cooked. **See recipes.**

PAN-FRIED FISH: Use clarified butter (see page 52) or a mixture of oil and butter, enough to cover the base of the pan. When sizzling well, place fish in and cook quickly. Before frying, the fish may be coated with seasoned flour or with egg and breadcrumbs.

FISH MEUNIERE: Skin fillets of white fish, dust with seasoned flour and pan-fry as above. Remove to a heated plate when done. Add a little more butter to the pan and while it is foaming, add the strained juice of a lemon, chopped parsley, salt and freshly ground black pepper. Pour over the fish, garnish with lemon and serve at once.

DEEP-FRIED FISH: Coat fish with egg and breadcrumbs or with batter; very small fish such as whitebait may simply be dipped in milk and seasoned flour. Deep-fry in very hot oil (190°C/375°F) or test oil with a bread cube, if it browns in 30 seconds the oil is hot enough. Drain on crumpled paper towels.

POACHED FISH: Use Court Bouillon (see page 98), water acidulated with vinegar or lemon juice or a mixture of wine and water – there should be just enough to cover fish. Cover dish with buttered greaseproof paper and cook very gently so that the liquid barely shivers, never bubbles, on top of the stove, or in a preheated moderately slow oven (160°C/325°F). The poaching liquor is often used for a sauce to accompany the fish.

GRILLED FISH: Preheat the grill so that fish will grill as fast as possible. For fillets and small steaks, line the grill pan with foil, melt a little butter in it and grill the fish on one side only – the heat of the pan will cook the underside. Baste once or twice with pan juices.

Large steaks and small whole fish can be grilled in the same way, but turn them halfway through cooking. Slash whole fish in the thickest part so that heat can penetrate.

BARBECUED FISH: Place fish in an oiled, hinged grill for ease of turning. Cook close to very hot coals, brushing several times with oil or melted butter.

BAKED FISH: Brush fish with oil or melted butter, place in a well-greased ovenproof dish and season with salt, freshly ground black pepper and a sprinkling of lemon juice or white wine. Cover loosely with buttered foil or greaseproof paper and bake in a preheated hot oven (200°C/400°F), allowing 6–10 minutes (depending on thickness of the fish) per 500 g (1 lb), plus 6–10 minutes over. Uncover and brush once or twice with pan juices during cooking.

WAYS TO USE PRESERVED FISH

SMOKED FISH: See *Finnan Haddie* and use the same methods for grilling, poaching or baking any smoked fish.

PICKLED FISH: Pickling is an excellent way of preserving oily-fleshed fish such as herrings. Pickled herrings are available packed in jars from many supermarkets and delicatessens, and they are delicious with rye breads, sour cream and fresh onion rings.

Pickled rollmops are boned, halved herrings, rolled around peppercorns and onion slices. Try them on black bread spread with unsalted butter and accompanied with a salad of baby beetroot.

Soused herrings may be prepared at home, using a vinegary marinade to which herbs and spices are added; enjoy them with rye breads and potato salad.

DRIED FISH: Fish such as cod and haddock can be dried to a flatness and hardness resembling hide. It is reconstituted by soaking in water for at least 12 hours. Change the water several times during this period.

SALTED FISH: Use salt cod to make *Brandade de Morue* (see page 44), a deliciously light dish from Provence, which is almost a fish purée.

Grilled Sardines: Grilled or barbecued fresh sardines make a memorable first course. Rub off scales with a cloth or soft paper. Leave sardines whole or butterfly them. If leaving whole, there is no need to gut them – eat flesh off bone in same way as you would eat corn on the cob.

To butterfly them, cut the head almost through from backbone; pull, and as head comes off the gut will come with it. Slit fish along belly and lift out backbone, cutting it off with scissors close to the tail (leave tail on).

Rinse and dry sardines; turn them in seasoned flour, brush with oil and arrange side by side in an oiled, hinged grill. Grill or barbecue close to high heat, brushing several times with oil, for 2–3 minutes each side. Serve with lemon wedges and crusty bread. Allow 500 g (1 lb) sardines to serve 4 as a first course.

See also *Anchovy* and *Tuna*.

Whiting or John Dory Fillets with Vermouth Sauce

90 g (3 oz) butter, melted; 8 whiting or John Dory fillets, skinned; 4 tbs dry vermouth; 1 tbs lemon juice; 1 tsp tomato paste; salt and freshly ground black pepper; $^{1}/_{2}$ cup cream; chopped parsley; Puff Pastry Fleurons (page 155) to garnish.

Brush a large, flameproof baking dish generously with some of the butter and lay fillets in it side by side. Blend remaining butter with vermouth, lemon juice and tomato paste. Pour over fish, season with salt and pepper and place over high heat. Cook, basting fish with pan juices, until flesh turns white. Lift fish on to a heated serving dish. Add cream to baking dish and stir until sauce thickens a little. Pour over fish, sprinkle with parsley and serve immediately, garnished with fleurons. Serves 4.

Mullet Baked with Rosemary

8 slices lemon (unpeeled); 4 medium mullet, scaled and cleaned; 2 tbs lemon juice; 2 cloves garlic, finely chopped; 1 tsp chopped fresh rosemary, or $^{1}/_{2}$ tsp dried; salt and freshly ground black pepper.

Place 2 slices lemon inside each mullet. Mix lemon juice, garlic and rosemary. Place mullet side by side in a greased baking dish and drizzle rosemary mixture over them. Season with salt and pepper. Cover dish with foil or a lid and bake in a preheated hot oven (200°C/400°F) for 10 minutes. Uncover, brush with pan juices and bake for a further 5 minutes or until fish flakes easily when tested with a fine skewer. Serves 4.

Oven-fried Fillets Niçoise

2 tsp salt; 1 cup milk; 1$^{1}/_{2}$ cups fresh breadcrumbs; 3 tbs chopped parsley; 2 cloves garlic, finely chopped; 1 tsp grated lemon rind; 1 tsp chopped fresh thyme, or $^{1}/_{4}$ tsp dried; 6 white fish fillets (bream, flathead, flounder, redfish), skinned; 90 g (3 oz) butter, melted; paprika; lemon wedges to garnish.

Mix salt and milk. Mix breadcrumbs, parsley, garlic, lemon rind and thyme. Dip fillets in milk, then in breadcrumb mixture. Arrange side by side in a well-buttered baking dish and drizzle melted butter over. Bake on top shelf of a preheated very hot oven (230°C/450°F) for about 12 minutes or until the fish flakes easily when tested with a fine skewer. Sprinkle with a little paprika and serve immediately, garnished with lemon wedges. Serves 4–6.

Fish Steaks Baked in Cream

4 thick fish steaks (snapper, jewfish); salt and freshly ground black pepper; I cup cream; I tbs lemon juice; I tbs Dijon mustard; I tsp Worcestershire sauce; fresh coriander leaves or chopped parsley.

Arrange fish steaks side by side in a buttered, shallow flameproof dish. Season with salt and pepper. Blend cream with lemon juice, mustard and Worcestershire sauce and pour over fish. Cover dish with buttered greaseproof paper and bake in a preheated moderately slow oven (160°C/325°F) for 20 minutes or until fish flakes easily when tested with a fine skewer. Lift steaks on to a heated serving platter and keep warm. Place flameproof dish over high heat and boil liquid, stirring, until it is slightly reduced and thickened. Adjust seasoning and spoon over fish. Scatter with coriander leaves or chopped parsley and serve immediately. Serves 4.

Mediterranean Mullet

3 tbs butter; 2 tomatoes, peeled and sliced; I small green pepper, cored, seeded and sliced; 125 g (4 oz) mushrooms, sliced; salt and freshly ground black pepper; 4 red mullet, whiting or other small whole fish, scaled and cleaned; 1/4 cup red wine; 2 tbs chopped chives.

Melt 2 tbs butter in a shallow flameproof casserole or gratin dish. Add vegetables and cook gently for 5 minutes, stirring occasionally. Season with salt and pepper. Place fish side by side on top of vegetables and pour over wine. Sprinkle with chives and dot with remaining butter. Cover and bake in a preheated moderate oven (180°C/350°F) for 20–30 minutes or until the fish flakes easily when tested with a fine skewer. Serves 4.

Sardinian–Style Tuna

4 tuna fish steaks, 2.5 cm (I in) thick; salt and freshly ground black pepper; flour for dusting; 3 tbs olive oil; I small onion, chopped; I clove garlic, crushed; 750 g (1 1/2 lb) tomatoes, peeled; 2 tbs chopped parsley; I bay leaf; 4 anchovy fillets, mashed; few black olives.

Season fish with salt and pepper and dust with flour. Heat 2 tbs oil in a large shallow pan and fry fish quickly until golden on each side. Transfer to a plate. Add remaining oil to pan and fry onion and garlic gently for 5 minutes. Press tomatoes through a coarse sieve or purée in a blender. Add parsley, bay leaf and anchovy to pan and stir for a few seconds. Add tomatoes, bring to the boil and continue boiling until mixture has reduced to a thin sauce consistency. Season with pepper. Replace fish and simmer gently for 15 minutes, turning tuna steaks once during cooking. Turn off heat, add olives and leave for 5 minutes before serving with a crisp green salad. Serves 4.

Deep–fried Szechuan Fish

I x 750 g (1 1/2 lb) whole fish (flounder, sole or bream), scaled and cleaned; I tsp grated fresh ginger; 3 spring onions, chopped; 2 tsp salt; 2 tbs dry sherry; oil for deep-frying; I tsp ground Szechuan pepper or black pepper; 2 tbs sesame oil; lemon slices to garnish.

Dry fish on paper towels and score each side diagonally to make a diamond pattern. Place ginger, spring onions, 1 tsp salt and the sherry in a dish. Add fish, spoon marinade over and leave for 30 minutes. Drain fish and dry on paper towels. Heat oil to medium, and deep-fry fish until golden-brown, about 7–10 minutes depending on thickness of fish. Remove and drain on crumpled paper towels. Sprinkle with pepper and remaining salt. Heat sesame oil to moderately hot, pour over fish and serve immediately, garnished with lemon slices. Serves 2–4.

Fried Marinated Fish

Marinating fish after frying is a good way of adding flavour to fresh water fish or eel.

500 g (I lb) filleted fresh water fish (perch, fresh water cod or eel), cut into 2.5 cm (I in) wide strips; 2 tbs milk; seasoned flour for coating; oil for shallow-frying.

MARINADE: 2 tbs oil; I small onion, finely sliced; I large clove garlic, crushed; I yellow or green pepper, grilled, skinned, cored and seeded; 4 tbs dry white wine; 2 tbs wine vinegar; 3 leaves fresh sage; I tsp sugar; salt and freshly ground black pepper.

Dip fish strips in milk, drain and then coat in seasoned flour. Heat enough oil in a shallow frying pan to give a depth of about 5 mm (1/4 in). Fry fish until crisp and golden on both sides and cooked through. Drain on paper towels and arrange, closely packed, in a shallow serving dish.

MARINADE: Heat oil in a saucepan and fry onion and garlic very gently for about 8 minutes or until soft and golden. Cut pepper into fine strips, add to pan and fry for 3–4 minutes. Stir in wine, vinegar, sage leaves, sugar, salt and pepper. Bring to the boil and simmer for 1–2 minutes, then pour over fish. Cover and leave in a cold place overnight. Serve cold as antipasto. Serves 4.

Soused Fish

I onion, sliced; 6 small mullet, herring or mackerel, filleted; 2 bay leaves; I clove; 4 whole allspice or black peppercorns; I tsp salt; ¹/₂ cup vinegar.

Place slices of onion on the centre of each fillet and roll up, skin side out, from head to tail, securing with a wooden toothpick if necessary. Place fish in a flameproof casserole with bay leaves, clove, allspice or peppercorns and salt. Pour over vinegar and just cover with water. Cover casserole and heat very gently until simmering point is reached. Transfer dish to a preheated moderately slow oven (160°C/325°F) and cook for about 1 hour or until fish flakes easily when tested with a fine skewer. Transfer fish to a serving dish, deep enough so that the rolls can be covered with liquid. Strain over sufficient cooking liquid to cover. Cool, then chill. Serves 6.

NOTE: This dish will keep for up to 2 weeks in the refrigerator.

Fish Fried in Batter

For the classic fish-and-chip shop style, use Basic Batter to coat the fish. For a light, crisp coating, use Crisp Fritter Batter (page 159).

4 large or 6 small white fish fillets; flour for coating; I quantity Basic Batter (page 25); oil for shallow-frying.

Check that fillets are well scaled and remove as many bones as possible (long-nose pliers or strong tweezers are a help). Coat fillets with flour and pat off excess. Dip each into batter, holding by the tail and allowing surplus batter to drip back into bowl. Have 1 cm (½ in) hot oil ready in a frying pan (oil is hot enough when a slight haze rises from it). Place fillets in oil, skinless side down first, and fry 3–4 minutes on each side. Do not crowd pan: fry fish in batches if necessary, adding a little more oil as required. Drain on crumpled paper towels. Keep cooked fish hot on paper towels in a warm oven until all are done, then serve immediately. Serves 4–6.

Baked Fish with Oysters and Herbs

I x I.5–2 kg (3–4 lb) whole fish; 60 g (2 oz) butter, melted; 2 cups fresh white breadcrumbs; I tsp dried marjoram; 2 tbs chopped parsley;

salt and freshly ground black pepper; cayenne; 2 thin rashers bacon; I cup oysters.

Have fish cleaned and scaled but leave head and tail intact. Heat butter in a frying pan and lightly brown crumbs. Add marjoram, parsley, salt, pepper and cayenne and mix well. Stuff fish loosely with herb mixture and close with skewers and string. Place fish in baking pan lined with greased foil and arrange bacon on top. Bake, uncovered, in a preheated moderate oven (180°C/350°F) for 30–40 minutes or until fish flakes easily when tested with a fine skewer. Using foil as handles, transfer fish to a heated platter. Discard bacon. Garnish with oysters that have been simmered in their juices 1 minute. Serves 6–8.

Fish Cakes

60 g (2 oz) butter; 4 tsp finely chopped onion or chives; 2 cups mashed potatoes; I x 250g can tuna in oil or salmon, drained and flaked; squeeze lemon juice; salt and freshly ground black pepper; I egg, beaten; I cup dry breadcrumbs; oil or butter for frying.

Beat butter and onion into mashed potatoes. Add tuna or salmon and season with lemon juice, salt and pepper. Form into 6 small cakes. Dip in beaten egg, then in breadcrumbs. Fry in a little oil or butter until nicely browned. Serve with Sauce Tartare (page 256) or dill mayonnaise made by combining ½ cup Mayonnaise (page 256) with 1 tbs chopped fresh dill or 1 tsp dried dill.

Skate with Black Butter Sauce

I x 750 g–I kg (I ¹/₂–2 lb) wing skate, scaled and cleaned; 3 tbs vinegar; 3 tsp salt; I bay leaf; I onion, sliced; 4 black peppercorns; few stalks parsley; 3 tsp finely chopped parsley; 3 tsp chopped capers; 60 g (2 oz) butter.

Place skate in a pan sufficiently wide for fish to lie flat while cooking. Cover with cold water, add 1 tbs vinegar, the salt, bay leaf, onion, peppercorns and parsley stalks and bring gently to the boil. Simmer very gently for 20–25 minutes, depending on the thickness of fish. Lift with a fish slice on to a board or clean folded tea-towel. Scrape away the skin from both sides and remove flesh from the large bone. Transfer to a heated serving dish, sprinkle with chopped parsley and capers and keep hot. Heat butter in a small frying pan until it turns brown but not in the least burnt. Pour quickly over fish. Add remaining 2 tbs vinegar to pan and reduce to half. Pour over fish and serve. Serves 4.

Fish à la Grecque

I x I.5 kg (3 lb) whole fish (snapper, jewfish
or bream), scaled and cleaned;
salt and freshly ground black pepper;
lemon juice; I onion, chopped;
I clove garlic, crushed; I tbs finely chopped
parsley; I tbs olive oil; 3 tomatoes, peeled, seeded
and chopped; ¹/₂ cup dry white wine;
lemon wedges to garnish.

Sprinkle fish inside and out with salt, pepper and
lemon juice and place in a baking dish lined with
greased foil. Sauté onion and garlic with parsley in
olive oil until soft. Add tomatoes to onion mixture.
Fry gently for a few minutes, then add a little water
and simmer a few minutes longer. Spoon this mixture
over fish. Pour wine over and around fish. Cook in a
preheated moderate oven (180°C/350°F) for about 40
minutes or until fish flakes easily when tested with a
fine skewer. Garnish with lemon. Serves 4.

FLAN

An open round pastry case, filled with fruit, cream or a
savoury mixture.
A *flan case* is a pastry shell which is either baked blind
(see *Pastry*), or with the required filling. Use 1 quantity of
Pâte Brisée for a savoury flan or 1 quantity of Pâte Sucrée
for a sweet flan to line a 20 cm (8 in) flan ring (see *Pastry*).
Ease the uncooked dough in from the edge of the flan
ring before baking to help prevent pastry from sticking.
Flan tins have a moveable base so you can easily remove
the tin from the sides of the pastry. When flan is baked, sit
it on a jar, carefully ease the sides away from the pastry
and let outer ring fall on to the table, leaving the pastry
sides exposed. Carefully slide the flan off the metal base,
using a spatula, and place on a serving platter. See
recipes.
See also *Quiches* and *Tarts and Tartlets*.

Glazed Strawberry Flan

I quantity Pâte Sucrée (page 344–5).

FILLING: 250 g (8 oz) cream cheese;
¹/₂ cup sugar; I tsp grated lemon rind;
I tbs orange juice; I tbs cream; I punnet (250 g/8 oz)
strawberries, hulled.

GLAZE: ¹/₂ cup redcurrant jelly; I tbs water;
2 tsp Cointreau or Grand Marnier,
or 2 tbs orange juice.

Roll out pastry thinly and use to line a 20 cm (8 in)
flan ring. Chill for at least 30 minutes. Prick bottom
all over with a fork, then bake blind in a preheated
moderately hot oven (190°C/375°F) for about 20
minutes or until pastry is a pale biscuit colour. Allow
to cool.

FILLING: Cream together all ingredients except strawberries and chill.
GLAZE: Heat jelly and water in a small saucepan,
stirring until smooth. Cool slightly. Stir in liqueur or
orange juice.
TO ASSEMBLE: Put cream cheese filling in flan case
and smooth surface with a spatula. Carefully decorate
with strawberries. Spoon glaze over them and chill.
Serves 6.

French Apple Flan

I quantity Pâte Sucrée (pages 344–5); I kg (2 lb)
Granny Smith apples, peeled, cored and sliced;
60 g (2 oz) butter; 2 tbs sugar;
caster sugar for sprinkling.

APRICOT GLAZE: ¹/₂ cup apricot jam; I tbs water;
2 tbs orange juice.

Roll out pastry thinly and use to line a 20 cm (8 in) flan
ring. Chill for at least 30 minutes. Prick bottom all over
with a fork. Put apple slices in a frying pan with butter
and sugar, and cook over a low heat for about 3
minutes. Fill pastry case with apples, reserving best
slices for the top. Arrange them in overlapping circles,
by starting at the edge of the pastry and forming
smaller and smaller circles until apples underneath are
completely covered. Brush top with a little of the
butter in which apples were cooked and sprinkle with
caster sugar. Bake in a preheated moderately hot oven
(190°C/375°F) for 20–25 minutes or until the edges of
apple slices are tinged a golden-brown.
APRICOT GLAZE: Heat jam and water in a small
saucepan, stirring until blended. Rub through a sieve
and cool a little. Stir in orange juice and keep warm.
Remove flan from oven and, while still warm, brush
with apricot glaze. Serve flan warm with cream.
Serves 8.

Flan aux Pruneaux (Prune Tart)

I tsp tea leaves; 500 g (I lb) large dessert prunes;
I quantity Rich Shortcrust Pastry (page 342);
I egg; ¹/₂ cup cream; I tsp cornflour; ¹/₄ cup caster
sugar; 2 tbs Cointreau or Grand Marnier;
30 g (I oz) butter.

Make a weak tea, strain and pour over prunes. Soak
for 4 hours. Roll out pastry and use to line a greased
20 cm (8 in) flan ring. Drain and stone prunes, then
spread out in pastry case. Bake in a preheated hot
oven (200°C/400°F) for about 20 minutes. Meanwhile,
beat egg with cream, cornflour, sugar and liqueur.
Remove tart from oven, pour custard mixture over
and dot with butter. Return to oven and bake for
further 10–15 minutes to set custard. Cool on wire
rack and serve with cream. Serves 6–8.

FLAPJACKS

A favourite breakfast all over North America consists of a stack of thick pancakes with butter and maple syrup accompanied by bacon, ham or sausage. The pancakes are large, but tender and light. They are known by many names – griddle cakes, hot cakes, flannel cakes, wheat cakes and, in the West and Northwest of the USA and in Canada, flapjacks.

Flapjacks

2 cups self-raising flour; ¹/₂ tsp salt; 2 tsp sugar; 3 eggs; 1³/₄ cups milk; 60 g (2 oz) butter, melted.

Sift flour and salt together into a bowl and sprinkle sugar over. Beat eggs with milk and pour over flour. Stir just until all the flour is moistened – batter will be lumpy. Lightly stir in melted butter. Heat a heavy, greased frying pan or griddle until a drop of cold water, flicked on to the surface, bounces and sputters. Pour batter on to make pancakes spaced a little apart, using a 1-tablespoon ladle for small pancakes or a ¹/₄-cup measure for larger ones. Cook until pancakes are full of bubbles on top and undersides are browned, then turn and cook other sides. Serve flapjacks in a stack with butter in between. Makes 12–15 x 15 cm (6 in) flapjacks.

FLEURONS

Small ovals, diamonds or crescents of puff pastry, which are used to garnish certain dishes finished with a rich sauce, or are served with elegant soups.

TO MAKE FLEURONS: Roll out trimmings of puff pastry thinly, brush the surface with beaten egg and cut shapes 6–8 cm (2¹/₂–3 in) in length. Bake in a preheated very hot oven (230°C/450°F) for 6–8 minutes or until golden. Serve 1 or 2 with each portion.

FLOATING ISLAND (ILE FLOTTANTE)

See *Custards.*

FLORENTINES

These great European favourites are flavoured with fruit and nuts, and spread with chocolate after baking.

Florentines

90 g (3 oz) butter; ¹/₂ cup sugar; 1 cup roughly chopped, blanched almonds; 3 tbs chopped raisins; ¹/₄ cup chopped mixed candied peel; ¹/₄ cup chopped glacé cherries; 2 tbs cream, whipped; finely grated rind ¹/₄ lemon; 185 g (6 oz) plain chocolate, broken in pieces.

Melt butter and sugar in a saucepan and boil for 1 minute. Remove from heat and stir in all remaining ingredients except the chocolate. Leave to cool. Put teaspoons of the mixture on greased, foil-lined baking trays in heaps well apart – 4 or 5 per sheet. Bake in the centre of a preheated moderate oven (180°C/350°F) for 10–12 minutes or until golden-brown. Remove and cool until just firm, pressing edges back to a neat shape. Remove carefully to a wire rack and leave until cold. Melt chocolate in a heatproof bowl over a saucepan of hot water. Spread over smooth side of each Florentine; as chocolate sets, mark into wavy lines with a fork. Leave to harden. The florentines can be stored (without chocolate) for about a week in an airtight container with greaseproof paper separating them. Makes 24.

FLOUR

The indispensable item in store cupboards, milled from grains or cereals such as rye, wheat, rice and corn. Wheat flour is most used in cooking and is classified according to the type of wheat milled, which varies through hard to soft. Wheat flours can be highly refined white or coarse ground wholewheat.

TYPES OF FLOUR

All-purpose flour is used for all types of cooking in the USA; it has no raising agent. It is milled from a blend of medium to strong wheats.

Arrowroot is an excellent thickening agent, especially for fruit sauces or pie fillings as it becomes clear when cooked. Do not overcook arrowroot as it has a tendency to become thin again.

Atta flour is a fine ground wholewheat flour used to make Indian flatbreads.

Buckwheat flour is also known as saracen corn or beechwheat. It is used to make Blini (see page 40), the traditional little yeast pancakes of Russia which are eaten with caviar and sour cream. It is also used for some crêpes, and added to other flours in breadmaking.

Chick pea (Besan) flour is used for batters, especially for *pakoras*, little Indian fritters, or to thicken soups, stews and gravies.

Cornflour is used as a thickening agent; also in short-breads and biscuits when a particularly short texture is needed and in cakes and puddings for extra lightness. Pure cornflour is made from the heart of the maize kernel which is ground to a very fine, silky powder. Some cornflour is made from wheat, and this is stated on the packet.

Plain flour is produced from soft wheat grain that is refined and bleached to give the familiar fine white flour. The low gluten content gives a light, short texture which makes it excellent for baking cakes, biscuits, pastries and scones. Plain flour can be substituted for self-raising flour by adding 2 tbs (30 g/1 oz) baking powder to 4 cups flour. Sift together 3 times before using.

Potato flour has much the same qualities as arrowroot and can be used in the same way.

Rice flour is made from very finely ground, polished rice

grains. It is used as a thickening agent, and if you wish to freeze a dish, rice flour will help prevent the sauce separating during reheating. Ground rice is a thicker form of rice flour, used in some shortbreads and some baking.

Roti flour has a granular texture and is cream colour. It is made from part of the wheat grain and is used for unleavened breads.

Rye flour is used for breads and crispbreads. Coarsely ground whole rye flour is used in pumpernickel, more finely ground in black bread, and a blend of rye and wheat flours is used in lightly coloured rye breads.

Self-raising flour is plain flour with the addition of baking powder as the raising agent. It is used to make standard butter cakes, sponge cakes, scones, etc. Use 2 tsp baking powder to 1 cup plain flour if you do not have self-raising flour on hand.

Strong plain white flour is a mixture of soft and hard wheat with a higher gluten content than plain flour. Strong flour is the one to use when baking breads, buns and pizzas as the gluten strands stretch and become flexible and elastic during kneading.

Wholewheat or wholemeal flour is milled from whole wheat grains, retaining most of their original vitamins, minerals, salts and fibre. Breads made from wholewheat taste delicious and produce loaves with a more dense texture than those made with plain white flour.

If you prefer a lighter loaf, use a mixture of half wholewheat flour and half strong flour. For wholewheat pastry, sift the flour and use the fine part to make the dough. Retain the particles of grain and roll the dough in them before shaping. Do not buy more wholewheat flour than you need at one time and store in a very cool dry place.

FLUMMERY

The charming name of a very good old-fashioned, fluffy fruit dessert. In Australia it is usually made when the abundant fresh passionfruit is in season – probably the nicest flummery of all.

Passionfruit Flummery

1 tbs gelatine; ¹/₂ cup cold water;
2 tbs flour; 1 cup sugar; ¹/₂ cup orange juice;
1 cup hot water; 1 tbs lemon juice;
¹/₂ cup passionfruit pulp;
cream or ice cream to serve.

Soak gelatine in cold water. Mix flour and sugar in a saucepan, blend to a smooth paste with a little orange juice, then stir in remaining orange juice and hot water. Stir over medium heat until mixture boils. Remove from heat, add soaked gelatine and stir until dissolved. Turn into a mixing bowl and chill until mixture is starting to thicken. Beat until very thick and at least doubled in volume. Add lemon juice and passionfruit, and chill until set. Serve with cream or ice cream. Serves 6.

FOIE GRAS

A great delicacy, made from the liver of especially fattened geese or from the livers of ducks or chickens. The finest *foie gras* comes from Alsace-Lorraine and Toulouse in France. *Pâté de foie gras* is a subtle mixture of goose liver, finely chopped veal and truffles enveloped in a rich pastry.

A slice of *foie gras* basted with Madeira and stock is an essential part of the classic French dish Tournedos Rossini. The steaks are placed on warm artichoke bottoms, covered with a slice of *foie gras*, topped with slivers of truffles and served with a spoonful of Madeira Sauce (see page 458).

See also *Tournedos*.

FONDANT

See *Icings, Frostings and Fillings*.

FONDUE

This means 'melted' in French, and the name now applies to a number of dishes. It is the name of a cheese dish, melted in wine, which originally came from Switzerland; under the same name comes a beef fondue from France, and a dessert fondue. Certain vegetable preparations are also called fondue. The vegetables in question are cooked for a very long time, often in butter, until they are reduced to pulp. Tomato Fondue is used in the preparation of many other dishes. **See recipes.**

FONDUE UTENSILS: Fondues are cooked and served in one communal pot. This is a legacy from the Switzerland of long ago when cooking and eating utensils were scarce. Today we still use just one pot, placed over a table burner in the centre of the table. Each person is given a fork and spears a cube of bread, meat or fruit for dunking before eating.

The traditional fondue pot for cheese is made of earthenware and is wide and shallow, though cast-iron pots can also be used. Those for beef fondue are of metal – copper or stainless steel. Spirit burners, used for cheese and meat fondues, should be sturdy and easily regulated. For dessert fondues, use decorative ceramic pots kept warm over the gentle heat of a candle.

Fondue Bourguignonne: Pieces of tender steak are speared and cooked in melted butter or a mixture of oil and butter for a minute or so until done to the guest's taste. The meat is then dipped into one of several sauces before it is eaten. The sauces may be tomato, curry, Béarnaise or soy, and it is traditional to try all the sauces on the table.

Dessert Fondue: Made with hot chocolate melted in cream and flavoured with a liqueur. Squares of cake, marshmallows or fruit are dipped first into the sauce, then into dishes of desiccated coconut or nuts.

Tomato Fondue

This recipe can be used as a garnish for eggs, vegetables or grilled meats, fish or poultry or as an ingredient in dishes called provençale, portugaise, or madrilène.

60 g (2 oz) butter, or 30 g (1 oz) butter and 2 tbs oil; 1 onion, chopped; 6–8 tomatoes, peeled, seeded and chopped; salt and freshly ground black pepper; 1 clove garlic, crushed; 1 tbs chopped parsley.

Melt butter, or butter and oil, in a heavy saucepan and gently cook onion until golden. Add tomatoes, salt, pepper and garlic. Cover and simmer very gently for about 1 hour or until tomatoes have reduced to a thick pulp and liquid has almost disappeared. Stir in parsley. Makes about 1½ cups.

Swiss Fondue

1 clove garlic, halved; 375 g (12 oz) Emmenthal cheese, grated; 375 g (12 oz) Gruyère cheese, grated; 2 tsp flour; 1½ cups dry white wine; 1 tsp lemon juice; 1 tbs Kirsch; ¼ tsp nutmeg; ¼ tsp black pepper; French bread cubes.

Rub inside of a deep flameproof casserole with garlic. Mix cheeses with flour and place in casserole with wine, lemon juice, Kirsch, nutmeg and pepper. Cook over a very low heat, stirring occasionally (the fondue should be a creamy consistency). Keep mixture hot over a table spirit burner and serve with cubes of bread. Guests spear the bread and dip it into cheese mixture. Serves 8.

FOOL

Fruit fool is a superbly simple, delicate dessert made with sweetened puréed fruit, thick cream and sometimes home-made or commercial custard.

Fool

⅔ cup cream, or ½ cup cream and ⅓ cup thick custard; 1¾ cups fruit purée, sweetened to taste (choose fresh, frozen or canned strawberries, raspberries, rhubarb, apricots, blackcurrants or gooseberries (see below); sponge fingers to serve.

Whip cream and fold into fruit. If using cream and custard, beat custard into fruit purée before folding in whipped cream. Pile into individual serving dishes. Chill and serve with sponge fingers. Decorate with additional cream if liked. Serves 4.

NOTE: Purée fresh strawberries and raspberries; lightly poach fresh rhubarb, apricots, blackcurrants or gooseberries and drain before puréeing; thaw and drain frozen fruits before puréeing; drain canned fruits before puréeing. The purée should be the consistency of thick cream and may be sweetened to taste.

FORCEMEAT

See *Stuffings.*

FOUR SPICES (QUATRE EPICES)

A blend of round white pepper, cloves, nutmeg and ginger, sold everywhere in France and used in making pâtés, pies, sausages and brawns.

To make your own Four Spices, grind 30 g (1 oz) white peppercorns and 1 tbs whole cloves, coarsely chopped, to a fine powder in a blender. Mix with 1 tbs freshly grated nutmeg and 1 scant tbs ground ginger. Store in an airtight jar in a cool, preferably dark place.

Pâté de Campagne
(Country-Style Pâté)

375 g (12 oz) chicken livers; 250 g (8 oz) streaky bacon; 250 g (8 oz) stewing veal; 2 cloves garlic, crushed; 8 juniper berries, crushed; ¼ tsp cracked black peppercorns; ½ cup dry white wine; 2 tsp brandy; 1 large egg; 1 cup fresh white breadcrumbs; 1 tsp dried sage; 1 tsp dried thyme; 1½ tsp Quatre Epices (Four Spices); 1 small onion, chopped; 60 g (2 oz) butter; 1½ tsp salt; 1 thin slice pork back fat, beaten flat with side of a cleaver (ask butcher to do this), or 2 extra rashers streaky bacon.

Trim chicken livers, removing membranes and any discoloured parts. Chop fine and place in a bowl. Cover bacon with boiling water, stand 5 minutes, drain and remove rind. Mince bacon and veal coarsely, or chop in a food processor. Add to livers with garlic, juniper berries, cracked peppercorns, wine, brandy, egg, breadcrumbs, herbs and quatre épices. Mix well. Cover and leave 2–3 hours. Cook onion gently in butter until soft and add to meat mixture with salt. Press mixture into a greased terrine. Cut pork fat or extra bacon into strips and arrange in a lattice over top of pâté. Cover terrine with a lid of foil. Place terrine in a baking tin of warm water and bake in a preheated moderate oven (180°C/350°F) for 2 hours. Remove from oven, remove terrine lid and place a light weight on top of pâté (e.g. a plate with a couple of cans of food on it). Leave pâté in refrigerator for 2 days before serving, cut into slices. Serves 6 as a lunch dish with salad.

FRANKFURT

Frankfurt sausages are fully cooked when bought and need only heating through. They are usually made from spiced beef and pork (kosher frankfurts are all beef) and are lightly smoked. Manufacturers usually call their more lightly spiced varieties 'Continental' or 'Vienna' frankfurts.

Frankfurts are good poached, grilled, barbecued, baked in a sauce or added to baked beans or to pea or *f*

potato soup. Serve them with hot or cold potato salad, creamy mashed potatoes, braised red cabbage, sauerkraut or coleslaw, and such condiments as mustard, dill pickles, tomato sauce or chutney. Cocktail frankfurts have the charm of the miniature and are a favourite with children, also with grown-ups if served with an interesting mustard or sauce. **See recipes.**

POACHED FRANKFURTS: Place in hot water to cover and heat through at just below boiling point. Do not boil or the frankfurts may split.

GRILLED OR BARBECUED FRANKFURTS: Cut 2 or 3 diagonal slashes in the frankfurts and grill or barbecue at high heat until lightly browned. Baste with barbecue sauce if you wish.

BAKED FRANKFURTS IN A SAUCE: Pour 1 cup of a well-flavoured sauce such as Barbecue Basting or Tomato Sauce (see pages 23 and 460) over 6 frankfurts arranged in a shallow ovenproof dish. Bake, uncovered, in a preheated moderate oven (180°C/350°F) for about 20 minutes until heated through. Sprinkle top with grated cheese after 10 minutes, if desired. Tomato based pasta sauce may be used.

Potato Frankfurt Goulash

This European-style main course is easy. Serve with buttered cabbage, or sauerkraut drained, rinsed, and heated with a little salt, pepper, sugar and vinegar. Vary the sausage using any smoked sausage.

5 large potatoes; 2 onions; 2 tbs olive oil; 125 g (4 oz) streaky bacon or speck, diced; I tsp ground paprika; $^{1}/_{4}$ tsp caraway seeds (optional); I$^{1}/_{2}$ cups stock or water; salt and freshly ground pepper; 4 plump Continental frankfurts.

Peel the potatoes and cut into large chunks. Peel and thinly slice the onions. Heat the oil in a large saucepan and gently fry the bacon for a few minutes. Add the onions and stir until they start to turn golden. Add potatoes and remaining ingredients except the sausage, bring to the boil, then simmer with the lid on for 30 minutes. Cut frankfurts into diagonal chunks; add to the pot and simmer for another 3–5 minutes or until heated through. Serves 4.

Piglets in Blankets

4–5 Vienna frankfurts; $^{1}/_{2}$ quantity Sour Cream Pastry (page 343); French or German mustard; I egg, beaten.

Poach frankfurts for 5 minutes, cool and skin. Roll out half the pastry into a rectangular sheet and place a frankfurt on one end. Spread frankfurt with a little mustard, then turn pastry over to enclose frankfurt as if making a sausage roll and cut off excess pastry. Brush edges with beaten egg and press to seal. Repeat with remaining frankfurts and pastry. Brush pastry

tops with beaten egg and cut each 'pig in a blanket' into 4 or 5 'piglets'. Cut pastry scraps into little leaves or fancy shapes and use to decorate piglets, securing and brushing decorations with egg. Place on a buttered baking tray, keeping each frankfurt in shape (so that ends do not dry out). Bake in a preheated hot oven (200°C/400°F) for 15–20 minutes or until pastry is golden. Makes 16–25.

FRAPPE

The French word for 'iced', or 'chilled'. A frappé is made from sweetened fruit juice, frozen until mushy and served as a refreshing finish to a rich meal. It looks very pretty topped with whipped cream and served in parfait or sherbet glasses. A frappé can also be an iced drink. Various liqueurs are served over shaved ice in a cocktail glass and sipped through a short straw as the ice melts. Crème de Menthe, Tia Maria and Cointreau make delicious liqueur frappés.

FRENCH FRIES

See *Potato*.

FRENCH TOAST

Home cooks of many countries have had the same excellent idea – to transform bread into a delectable, comforting breakfast or dessert by dipping it into an egg-and-milk mixture and frying it in butter. It is variously called French Toast, German Toast or Nun's Toast. In Austria it is *Arme Ritter* (Poor Knights), in England, Poor Knights of Windsor. Spanish Toast, *Pain Perdu* and Orange French Toast are variations.

French Toast

2 eggs; pinch salt; I tbs sugar (optional); $^{2}/_{3}$ cup milk; 6 slices day-old bread, crusts removed; about 60 g (2 oz) butter; sugar and cinnamon, jam, maple syrup or bacon etc. to serve.

Beat eggs with salt and sugar, if using, and mix with milk. Cut bread into triangles or strips. Heat a little butter in a frying pan. Dip bread, a few pieces at a time, into egg mixture and fry in butter until golden-brown on both sides. Add more butter to pan as needed. Serve French toast very hot, as a dessert, with sugar and cinnamon or warmed jam, or (omitting sugar from dipping mixture) with maple syrup and grilled bacon for breakfast. Serves 3–6.

VARIATIONS

PAIN PERDU: Follow recipe for French Toast but use half milk and half cream in the dipping mixture, and flavour it with a dash of vanilla. Serve Pain Perdu sprinkled with sugar and cinnamon, alone or as an accompaniment to poached fruit.

SPANISH TOAST: Follow recipe for French Toast but substitute ½ cup sweet sherry for the milk. Fry toast until crisp and serve dusted with sifted icing sugar and cinnamon.

ORANGE FRENCH TOAST: Follow recipe for French Toast but substitute orange juice for the milk. Serve sprinkled with a mixture of sugar and grated orange rind.

FRIKADELLER

Danish meat patties, very light and moist. They can be made according to various recipes; the pork and veal version is a favourite.

Frikadeller

500 g (1 lb) pork and veal mince;
½ cup fresh white breadcrumbs; ½ cup milk;
1 medium onion, grated; 1 egg; 1 tsp nutmeg;
½ tsp salt; ½ tsp white pepper; seasoned flour;
30 g (1 oz) butter; 2 tbs oil.

GARNISH: sour cream; beetroot or dill pickles.

Place meat in a large bowl. Soak breadcrumbs in milk and beat, a little at a time, into meat. Beat in onion, egg, nutmeg, salt and pepper. Mixture should be light and fluffy. Cover and chill 1 hour to firm. Shape into small, thick round or oblong patties and coat in seasoned flour. Heat butter and oil; when foam subsides, add frikadeller and fry 8–10 minutes on each side. Serve very hot, garnished with sour cream and beetroot or dill pickles. Boiled or mashed potatoes, cucumber salad and red cabbage are traditional accompaniments. Serves 4.

FRITTERS

Deep or shallow-fried delicacies, either sweet or savoury, made by encasing slices of food in a special batter, or mixing chopped food through a batter before frying. Well-made and perfectly fried fritters should be light, crisp and golden outside, soft and creamy inside and served as soon as they are cooked.

Tiny bite-size fritters can be served as appetisers. Larger ones make perfect lunches, served with a crisp green salad and fresh fruit. Sweet fritters are delicious finales to have as dessert at dinner.

The French also make a type of fritter called *beignets* using choux pastry, sometimes mixed with cheese, which are deep-fried and served as hors d'oeuvre. Sweet ones are filled with cream, custard or jam after deep-frying (see *Beignets Soufflés*). In Vienna fritters can be made with a light pastry or rich yeast dough (see *Yeast Cookery*), shaped into little buns with a filling of cream, custard, jam or fruit and deep-fried. There are also the Spanish churros (see page 88), which are made with choux pastry. **See recipes.**

■ **TO DEEP-FRY FRITTERS:** Use an electric fryer, deep frying pan or deep wide saucepan. Pour in vegetable oil to reach halfway up the sides of the frying utensil, making certain it is at least 8 cm (3 in) deep. Heat oil to moderate (185°C/360°F), test with a thermometer or by immersing a cube of bread in the hot oil. It is ready to use when the bread turns pale brown in 45 seconds. Place 5-6 pieces of food into hot oil, fry for 2–3 minutes until golden. Lift out the fritters and drain on crumpled paper towels, keep warm and fry the remaining batches in the same way. Serve immediately. Use a slotted spoon or tongs to lower the food into the oil and remove when cooked.

■ **TO SHALLOW-FRY FRITTERS:** Put equal quantities of oil and butter into a heavy frying pan to a depth of not more than 5 mm (¼ in). Heat the fat and cook fritters 2–3 minutes each side or until golden-brown. Drain well on paper towels and serve immediately.

Basic Fritter Batter

Use for fish, vegetables and meat.

1 cup flour; 1½ tsp baking powder; ½ tsp salt;
2 eggs; ⅔ cup milk.

Sift flour, baking powder and salt into a bowl. Beat eggs with milk. Make a well in centre of flour. Add egg mixture in a steady pouring stream, stirring in flour gradually, and beat to a smooth batter. Stand for several hours before using. Makes enough to coat about 2 cups food.

Fluffy Fritter Batter

Use for small seafood fritters – oysters, prawns, fish fillet strips etc. – or fruit, such as sliced apples, bananas, whole strawberries, pineapple circles. Can also be used for chopped cooked meats like leftover beef, lamb, chicken or brains.

1⅓ cups flour; ½ tsp salt; 1 tbs melted butter;
2 eggs, separated; ¾ cup flat beer or soda water.

Sift flour and salt into a bowl. Make a well in centre and add melted butter, egg yolks and beer. Gradually work in flour and beat to a smooth batter. Allow to stand several hours. Just before using whisk egg whites until stiff and fold into batter. Makes enough to coat 2 cups prepared food.

Crisp Fritter Batter

1 cup flour; pinch salt; 1 whole egg; 1 egg, separated;
60 g (2 oz) butter or margarine, melted;
1 cup beer or soda water.

Sift flour with salt into a bowl and make a well in centre. Beat 1 whole egg and 1 egg yolk (keep second white for later) and pour into well with melted butter or margarine. Stir, incorporating flour gradually and adding beer or soda water little by little, until mixture is smooth. Cover and stand 1 hour. Just before using, whisk remaining egg white to a firm snow and fold into batter. Makes enough batter for 4 thick fish fillets.

Sweet Fritter Batter

Use for fruit fritters.

2 eggs, separated; ²/₃ cup milk; I tbs melted butter; I cup flour; I tbs caster sugar.

Beat together egg yolks, milk and melted butter. Sift flour and sugar into a bowl, make a well in centre and stir in egg mixture. Gradually work in flour, beating to a smooth batter. Allow to stand several hours. Just before using, whisk egg whites until stiff and fold into batter. Makes enough to coat 2 cups prepared food.

Cooked Meat Fritters

Cooked lamb, beef, veal or chicken meat, chopped and fried in fritter batter makes a delicious meal, accompanied by a crisp salad.

2 cups chopped cooked meat; I tbs finely chopped onion; salt and freshly ground black pepper; I quantity Basic Fritter Batter (page 159); oil and butter for shallow-frying.

Combine chopped meat and onion, season with salt and pepper and fold into batter. Heat oil and butter in a frying pan (see To Shallow-Fry Fritters, page 159). Drop meat mixture in large tablespoonfuls into hot fat and fry on both sides until golden and crisp. Drain on crumpled paper towels. Serve hot. Serves 4.

Fresh Vegetable Fritters

Use the freshest possible vegetables, sliced mushrooms or whole button mushrooms, blanched and dried slices of zucchini or patty pan squash, salted and dried, thin slices of eggplant, red or green peppers or onion rings.

2 cups sliced or prepared vegetables (see above); oil for deep-frying; I quantity Basic Fritter Batter (page 159).

Prepare vegetables. Heat oil in a deep-fryer or saucepan to 185°C/360°F (see To Deep-Fry Fritters, page 159). Dip sliced vegetables into batter, allow excess batter to drain off, and drop into oil, 4 or 5 pieces at a time. Fry for 2–3 minutes or until golden-brown. Drain on crumpled paper towels and serve hot. Serves 4.

Cooked Vegetable Fritters

Drained canned or leftover vegetables are first chopped then added to fritter batter and fried.

2 cups cooked, chopped vegetables; I quantity Basic Fritter Batter (page 159); oil and butter for shallow-frying.

Add chopped vegetables to prepared batter. Heat oil and butter in a frying pan (see To Shallow-Fry Fritters, page 159). Drop vegetable mixture in tablespoonfuls into hot fat and fry on both sides until golden and crisp. Do not crowd the pan. Drain the fritters on crumpled paper towels and serve hot. Serves 4.

Fresh Fruit Fritters

Sliced fruit such as apples, pears and bananas as well as whole berry fruit, strawberries and boysenberries, may be frittered. Keep apple, pear and pineapple slices about 1.2 cm (½ in) thick; bananas may be cut in 3 diagonal slices. Apricots and plums may be halved and stoned.

oil for deep-frying; 2 cups (or equivalent) prepared fruit; I quantity Sweet Fritter Batter (opposite); sifted icing sugar (optional).

Heat oil in deep-fryer or saucepan to 185°C/360°F (see To Deep-Fry Fritters, page 159). Coat fruit with batter. Drop into hot oil, 3 or 4 pieces at a time, and fry until crisp and golden. Drain on crumpled paper towels. Sprinkle with icing sugar, if liked, and serve hot with whipped cream or a sauce like Sabayon (see page 428). Serves 4.

Fruity Rice Fritters

An unusual Danish specialty to enjoy as a dessert or for brunch with bacon or ham.

2 cups cold boiled rice; 2 eggs, lightly beaten; pinch salt; I tbs grated lemon or orange rind; ¹/₂ cup chopped raisins or sultanas; ¹/₄ cup chopped blanched almonds; 2 tbs flour; 60 g (2 oz) butter.

TO SERVE: sifted icing sugar; jam; thick cream (optional).

Mix together rice, eggs, salt, lemon or orange rind, raisins or sultanas, nuts and flour. Heat butter in a large frying pan and drop mixture into the pan in large spoonfuls. Cook fritters until golden on both sides and cooked through, turning once, about 3 minutes each side. Drain on paper towels. If serving as a dessert, sprinkle with icing sugar and serve hot with apricot or raspberry jam and thick cream. Serves 4.

FRITTO MISTO

A Fritto Misto, or 'mixed fry', is an Italian dish of small pieces of tender meats, young fresh vegetables or succulent seafood encased in a light, fluffy batter which are quickly deep-fried. Fritto misto, like all fried food in batter, must be eaten as soon as it is cooked to be at the peak of perfection. Choose the freshest possible ingredients, small slices of zucchini, eggplant, artichoke hearts, mushrooms or tiny cauliflower florets, or very thin slices of veal escalope or lamb's brains. Dip them in batter (see *Fritters*) and deep-fry for 2–3 minutes until golden.

Fritto Misto di Mare, the famous Italian fisherman's fish fry, can include small whole fish or strips of fillet, calamari, prawns, or scallops – whatever combination of seafood is best and freshest on the day.

Fritto Misto di Mare
(Mixed Fried Seafood)

1 kg (2 lb) fish (a mixture of very small whole fish, fish fillets, prawns, scallops, calamari);
juice 1 lemon; oil for deep-frying;
flour for coating.

BATTER: 1 cup self-raising flour; 1/4 tsp salt;
1 tbs brandy; 1 tbs oil; 3/4 cup warm water;
1 egg white.

TO SERVE: lemon wedges; 1 1/2 cups Mayonnaise (page 256); 1 tbs chopped capers; 1 tbs chopped parsley; 1 tbs chopped canned pimiento (optional).

Remove heads of small whole fish, open out and remove backbone (see *Fish*: Grilled Sardines for method). Cut fillets into 5 cm (2 in) strips. Shell prawns, leaving tails on, and devein. Discard any dark beards from scallops. Wash and clean calamari (see *Squid*) and cut into rings. Dry all seafood on paper towels and sprinkle with lemon juice.
BATTER: Sift flour and salt into a bowl, make a well in centre and add brandy and oil. Gradually add water, stirring from centre until mixed, then beat batter until smooth. Leave 30 minutes. Just before cooking seafood, whisk egg white until it stands in soft peaks and fold gently into batter.

Heat oil in a deep fryer or saucepan (a cube of bread should brown in 30 seconds). Toss seafood in flour and dip in batter. Deep-fry a few pieces at a time, for 1–2 minutes or until golden. To prevent toughness, do not overcook. Drain on crumpled paper towels and keep hot in a cool oven until all pieces are fried. Arrange on a heated serving platter and serve immediately with lemon wedges, and mayonnaise mixed with capers, parsley and pimiento, if using. Serves 4.

FROMAGE BLANC (WHITE CHEESE)

This refreshingly tangy, versatile cheese is one of the main ingredients in sauces of the *Cuisine Minceur* for meat, poultry, fish and vegetables. Try it, too, mixed with puréed vegetables, with crisp green salads, as a topping on fresh tomato slices or as a dipping sauce to accompany a platter of crudités (see page 105). It is also delicious served with fresh fruits, especially berry fruits.

In France fromage blanc is made from skimmed milk soured with a culture, but you can make an excellent substitute at home by blending together cottage cheese, plain yogurt and lemon juice.

Fromage Blanc

100 g (3 1/2 oz) cottage cheese;
125 g (4 oz) plain yogurt; 3 tsp lemon juice.

Place all ingredients in a food processor or blender, and blend thoroughly until mixture is smooth, shiny and as thick as whipped cream. Cover and store in refrigerator for 12 hours before using. You may use a food mill if you wish, beating mixture thoroughly after pushing through mill. Makes about 1 cup.

FROSTING

See *Icings, Frostings and Fillings*.

FRUIT

Fruit is such a pleasure to look at and to eat, it seems a pure bonus that it's so good for us as well. Every bite contains vitamins, minerals and fibre, that most important food component for a healthy digestive system. Eat the peel when possible for the best investment in good health.

Keep fruit at room temperature until fully ripened; the process can be hastened by leaving it in a paper bag with the top closed. Once ripe, most fruits should be refrigerated to slow further changes. The exceptions are bananas, which blacken under refrigeration, and citrus fruit that will be used within a week or two – citrus does not ripen further after picking, and will stay in good condition at room temperature for some time before beginning to deteriorate.

WAYS TO USE FRUIT

Of course, a piece of choice fruit is a splendid way to finish a meal. Fresh fruit is also a favourite food to nibble or munch between meals. Fruit can be poached, baked, sautéed, deep-fried, grilled or barbecued. It combines with other ingredients for hundreds of lovely desserts, cakes, pies and tarts. Don't forget how well fruit goes with savoury foods, too – fried apples with sausage or pork chops, apricots with lamb, pears with cheese, green grapes with fish, melon or figs with prosciutto, orange with duck, apple with roast pork, and pineapple with ham or cheese are some of the best known combinations.

Fruit and vegetable salads, fruit stuffings for meat, fruit relishes, sauces and soups add verve to the first or main course. Ideas such as quinces stuffed with a savoury meat mixture; cherries simmered in red wine and orange juice and served with ham or poultry; an apple and mint water ice to accompany roast lamb or game birds; hot curried fruit or chilled pears with tarragon cream dressing served as a first course, are more unusual ways to add a happy surprise to a meal.

Fresh Fruit Salad: The nicest fruit salads have the fruit left in fairly big pieces – about 2–2.5 cm (¾–1 in) so that their beautiful appearance and contrasting textures are not lost. Leave skin on where practicable. Two or three good fruits are often better than a big variety. Sprinkle salad with sugar and lemon juice, cover and leave to chill and develop flavours for 30 minutes or more before serving. Fruits which darken quickly after cutting (peaches, bananas, apples, pears) should be turned in a little lemon juice and added only a short time before serving.

Add interest to fresh fruit salads with the addition of a little white wine or liqueur or just a sprinkling of rum or brandy. Crème Fraîche (see page 102), sour cream lightly sweetened with brown sugar, or cream half-whipped with a few drops of liqueur, rum or brandy, are good fruit salad toppings. Serve with Tuiles, Cigarettes Russe (see pages 550 and 89) or other crisp delicate biscuits.

FRUIT BOTTLING

Successful fruit bottling depends on efficient sterilisation – this means anything that will cause the fruit to ferment or turn mouldy must be killed by heat. This can be done in an oven, in one of the excellent preserving kits (e.g. Fowler's), in a deep saucepan or, if you still have one, in a copper. Make sure you have good preserving jars of heat-treated glass, with a strong lid and clamp to effectively seal the contents. If you buy a preserving kit with its deep steriliser and jars, etc., it comes complete with instructions. If you want to experiment with the French-type jars, with clamp-on lids, you can do them in the oven – it is simple and effective, and it is the method often used for only a few bottles. It is most important to have good preserving jars.

BASIC RULES

- Preserve only choice and sound fruit.
- Prepare small quantities at a time.
- Ensure that jars and rubbers are sterile: wash in hot soapy water, rinse in boiling water.
- Check all jars to be used, to make sure these are free from flaws (no chopped rims).
- Use only new rubber rings, not old ones.

PREPARATION OF FRUIT: Most fruits are suitable for bottling, but because of their short season, stone and berry fruits are particular favourites.

Fruits should be washed first then prepared as for stewing. Apricots, plums and peaches are halved and stones removed and peeled if liked. Pears are peeled and halved, pineapples are trimmed and sliced. Berry fruits are washed lightly and drained. Tomatoes are left whole in salted water, or tomato juice made from softened tomatoes.

BLANCHING FRUIT: Tomatoes, peaches and plums usually have the skins removed as these varieties have skins which split on heating. Hold the fruit in a square of muslin or cheesecloth and immerse in boiling water for a brief period, depending on ripeness – usually 30 seconds is sufficient. A metal strainer may be used to hold more fruit. Then plunge into cold water. Gentle rubbing will now remove the skin or, if this is not successful, the skin may be peeled off with a sharp knife.

After peeling, drop the fruit into cold water to prevent discolouration. Pears, apples and peaches should be dropped into a light brine (1 tsp salt to 5 cups water), then rinsed.

Blanching as described above sets the colour of the fruit and, by reducing the size of some fruits, makes possible a more economical pack.

PREPARING OF SYRUP: Make the syrup while the fruit is heating in the oven – ½–¾ cup will be needed for each 500 ml (2 cup) jar. Its strength is largely a matter of personal taste. Light syrup – 1 cup sugar to 3 cups water. Medium syrup – 2 cups sugar to 3 cups water. Heavy syrup – 3 cups sugar to 3 cups water.

Figs require a heavy syrup, while apples are better done in a light syrup. For most fruits a medium strength is fine.

BOTTLING IN WATER FOR DIABETICS AND DIETERS: Home-bottled fruit is excellent for diabetic people. Simply use boiling water instead of syrup. The best size of jar to use is 500 ml (2 cup). If desired, the fruit may be sweetened to taste with a proprietary sweetener before serving.

TESTING OF SEAL: 24 hours after bottling, the lids should be tested to make sure the vacuum has formed and the lid is firmly sealed. To test clip-type jars: remove the clip and lift the jar gently by the lid. If the jar is a screw-band type, remove the band and tilt until the weight of the liquid is against the lid. Make the same test for jars sealed with rubber solution. If the seals have not formed, the jars should be reprocessed, or the contents eaten the same day.

If lids are secure, label the jars, mark the date of preserving on each and store in a cool, dark place. If preserves are subjected to bright light, the colour of the fruit in the jars will fade.

OVEN METHOD

The procedure of sterilising bottled fruit in the oven is one of the simplest of all methods. The oven method is convenient when only a small quantity of fruit is to be preserved. For this and other reasons, the berry fruits or just a few jars of cherries, or special stone fruits may be processed for use later in the year.

Fruit	Style of Pack	Syrup Recommended	Processing times at boiling point for 2 and 4 cup jars at 0–1000 feet	
			500ml (2 cups)	1 litre (4 cups)
Apples	Cold pack	Water or light syrup	20 minutes	25 minutes
	Steam or boil to wilt		15 minutes	20 minutes
	Bake or boil whole hot pack*		15 minutes	15 minutes
	Apple sauce, hot pack*		10 minutes	10 minutes
Apricots	Pack raw with boiling syrup	Medium	25 minutes	30 minutes
	Boil with syrup 3–4 minutes		15 minutes	20 minutes
Berries				
Blackberries	Pack raw; cover with boiling syrup	Medium	20 minutes	25 minutes
Loganberries, Mulberries	Boil 3–4 minutes with equal weight Sugar, stand overnight; hot pack*	In own syrup	10 minutes	15 minutes
Raspberries, Gooseberries	Pack raw; cover with boiling syrup; hot pack*	Medium	15 minutes	20 minutes
Cherries	Pack raw; cover with boiling syrup	Medium	15 minutes	20 minutes
	Precook; hot pack*	Medium	10 minutes	15 minutes
Figs	Wash, stew, bring to boil in syrup. Pack; add lemon juice 1 tbs each 4 cup jar	Heavy	45 minutes	50 minutes
Grapefruit	Immerse in boiling water 3–6 minutes. Peel, remove all pith, quarter, drop or pack in jars. Cover with boiling syrup	Heavy	Lids on loosely 15 minutes at 82°C/180°F. Seal, cover with water 35 minutes at 82°C/180°F	Lids on loosely 15 minutes at 82°C/180°F. Seal, cover with water 40 minutes at 80°C/180°F
Grapes	Wash, stem, pack; cover with boiling syrup	Light	15 minutes	20 minutes
Nectarines	Halve, stone, cover with boiling syrup	Medium	25 minutes	30 minutes
Oranges	Immerse 4 minutes in boiling water then in cold. Peel, remove pith, quarter, drop or pack in jars. Cover with boiling syrup	Heavy	30 minutes	35 minutes
Peaches	Pack raw; cover with boiling syrup			
	Clingstones	Medium	35 minutes	40 minutes
	Slipstones	Medium	25 minutes	30 minutes
	Precook; hot pack*	Medium	15 minutes	20 minutes
Pears	Pack raw; cover with boiling syrup	Medium	25 minutes	30 minutes
	Precook 6 minutes; hot pack*	Medium	20 minutes	25 minutes
Pineapples	Pack raw; cover with boiling syrup	Medium	25 minutes	30 minutes
Plums	Pack raw, cover with boiling syrup	Medium	25 minutes	30 minutes
	Precook; hot pack*	In own juice	10 minutes	15 minutes
Quinces	Precook 3 minutes; pack	Medium	25 minutes	30 minutes
Rhubarb	Precook; hot pack* (not necessary to use sugar)	In own juice	10 minutes	15 minutes
Tomatoes	Peel, pack raw; cover with hot brine	Brine (1 tsp salt to 1 litre/4 cups water) or own juice	45 minutes	45 minutes
	Peel, simmer 8 minutes; hot pack*		10 minutes	10 minutes

*Fruits referred to on timetable as 'hot pack' should be put into a pan and brought to a gentle boil in syrup, or a little water (which may be poured into the jar with the fruit). Small soft fruits should be simmered approximately 2 minutes, large or firm fruits approximately 2–4 minutes, depending on ripeness and maturity. This cuts down the processing time as fruits have been heated prior to being packed into the sterilised preserving jars.

The method for oven bottling is as follows:

1 Slow cooking of the fruit is required. If the fruit cooks too quickly it will burst, go pulpy, and lose its shape.

2 Pack fruit into the jars prepared as described in Preparation of Fruit, page 162. The fruit will shrink during cooking, so jars must be well filled.

3 Stand the jars on a heatproof mat or baking tin on a shelf in the bottom half of a preheated cool oven (120°C/250°F). Jars must not touch each other. Put on lids of jars, but not rubber rings and do not clip on.

4 Leave the fruit in the oven until it looks cooked, has shrunk and changed colour slightly. This normally takes 45–60 minutes. Pears and tomatoes need 1½ hours.

5 Prepare the syrup; when required, bring back to boiling point. Remove one jar from the oven and stand on a double thickness of paper towel or tea-towel.

6 Have rubber rings soaking in water, place rubber ring on the lid of the jar. Add boiling syrup to fill the jar, until it just overflows. Clip lid on jar tightly.

7 Repeat step 6 with remaining jars. The procedure is the same for tomatoes, except that salted water or tomato juice replaces the sugar syrup.

NOTE: It is very important to perform steps 5 and 6 as quickly as possible, and with only one jar at a time.

BOILING WATER BATH METHOD

Use suitable preserving jars and a lidded cooker or boiler, deep enough for the jars to be covered by at least 5 cm (2 in) boiling water. The jars of fruit or tomatoes being preserved must be covered completely by 5 cm (2 in) water, they must also stand in the cooker on a rack so that the water flows freely under them; an ordinary cake rack will do.

Except when preserving grapefruit, it is not necessary to use a thermometer, because the temperature required for preserving by this boiling water bath method is reached when the water boils.

The boiling water bath has many advantages – it is safe, economical (no special equipment is necessary), and it is time-saving compared with the 'slow sterilising' method recommended for commercial outfits. For example, slipstone peaches, pineapples or pears sterilised slowly will take approximately 3½ hours and require careful watching; bottled in the boiling water bath they will take 25 minutes.

Thoroughly clean jars, rubbers and lids in hot water, and make the syrup, the fruit to be preserved should be sorted and simultaneously blanched and peeled by scalding, see Blanching Fruit, page 162.

PACKING AND PROCESSING: Pack fruit into jars. Before adding the syrup, run water gently in and out of the jars to remove any particles of fruit and keep the syrup clear. The syrup, which should be boiling, will be clearer if strained through a cloth. Fill only to within 1 cm (½ in) of the top of 500 ml (2 cup) jars and wipe the rim of the jar with a moist cloth before sealing. A skewer worked gently between the

fruit and the jar will release the air bubbles. If the screwband type of jar is used, do not seal tightly.

Lower jars into the boiling water in the cooker or boiler with tongs, or by holding the top of the jar with a cloth. Count the processing time from the time the water returns to the boil. As soon as the water is seen to be boiling, put the lid on the cooker and process according to the times given in the table on page 163.

Remove jars from cooker after processing and place on a wooden surface or a folded cloth, away from draughts. Hot jars may break if placed on marble or other cold materials. Tightly seal screw-bound jars immediately on removal from cooker. Test seal after 24 hours, see page 162.

FRUIT CAKE

The rich aroma of fruit cake-baking conjures up memories of Christmas, birthdays or exciting special occasions in every household. Rich fruit cake keeps for months wrapped and stored in a cool dry place and is best made well ahead to allow the flavour to ripen before cutting. Light fruit cakes are ideal for any occasion and many people prefer them to the very rich ones. They keep well for up to 3 weeks when stored wrapped in an airtight container.

Boiled Fruit Cake (see *Cakes*) is mixed using a particularly easy method and is excellent for families who love to have fruit cake at any time. It may be kept for 2 weeks in an airtight container. **See recipes.**

For more fruit cakes, see *Cakes:* Sultana Cake, *Dundee Cake* and *Bishop's Cake.*

Rich Fruit Cake

Suitable for a wedding or Christmas cake or any celebration cake that calls for a good-keeping, rich cake.

FRUIT: 250 g (8 oz) raisins, chopped; 250 g (8 oz) sultanas; 250 g (8 oz) currants; 185 g (6 oz) mixed candied peel, finely chopped; 60 g (2 oz) glacé cherries, diced; 60 g (2 oz) glacé apricots, diced; 6 tbs brandy or rum; 3 tbs sherry.

CAKE MIXTURE: 250 g (8 oz) butter; 1¹/3 cups firmly
packed brown sugar; grated rind 1 lemon;
2 tbs marmalade; 5 eggs; 2¹/2 cups flour;
1 tsp mixed spice; 1 tsp cinnamon; ¹/4 tsp salt;
125 g (4 oz) blanched almonds, chopped;
extra blanched almonds (optional); extra brandy.

FRUIT: Put all fruit into a bowl and sprinkle with
brandy or rum and sherry. Leave overnight.
CAKE MIXTURE: Beat butter and brown sugar with
lemon rind until light and creamy. Add marmalade
and beat well. Add eggs one at a time, beating well
after each addition. Add 1 tbs flour with the last egg.
Sift together remaining flour, mixed spice, cinnamon
and salt, and stir into creamed mixture alternately
with fruit and chopped almonds. Turn mixture into a
20 cm (8 in) round or square deep cake tin lined with
1 layer of brown paper and 2 layers of greased greaseproof paper. If not icing cake with almond paste and
royal icing, decorate with whole almonds arranged in
a pattern on top. Bake in a preheated slow oven
(150°C/300°F) for 3–3½ hours or until a skewer
inserted in centre comes out clean. Remove from oven
and immediately sprinkle with about 1 tbs extra
brandy. Remove cake from tin, leaving paper on cake.
Wrap in a tea-towel and leave on a wire rack until
cool. Store in an airtight tin.

Light Fruit Cake

1¹/3 cups sultanas; ¹/3 cup currants; ¹/3 cup raisins;
¹/3 cup chopped mixed candied peel;
¹/3 cup roughly chopped glacé cherries;
grated rind ¹/2 lemon or orange;
250 g (8 oz) butter; ²/3 cup caster sugar;
²/3 cup firmly packed brown sugar;
2¹/2 cups plain flour; ¹/2 cup self-raising flour;
5 eggs; 1–2 tbs lemon juice.

Combine dried fruit with peel, cherries and lemon or
orange rind. Cream butter with sugars until very
light and fluffy. Sift flours together. Beat eggs into
creamed mixture one at a time, following each with
1 tbs flour. Fold in remaining flour, then fruit. Add
lemon juice. Turn into a greased and lined 20 cm
(8 in) round or square deep cake tin. Bake cake in a
preheated slow oven(150°C/300°F) for 2½ hours or
until a skewer inserted in centre comes out clean.
Turn on to a wire rack and leave to cool. When cold,
remove paper lining and store in an airtight tin.
NOTE: Spices can be sifted with the flour if liked. Use
½ tsp cinnamon, 1 tsp mixed spice and ¼ tsp nutmeg.

FRUIT COCKTAIL

A first-course fruit cocktail should delight the eye and
refresh the palate. Avoid formless canned fruit, pieces
cut too small and over-sweetening. Use just one fruit, or
2 or 3 which contrast in colour and texture; melon and

grapes, grapefruit and cherries, orange and strawberries,
pineapple with pawpaw and Kiwi fruit.
   Leave fruit in good-size chunks. Macerate in a little
lemon juice and just a touch of honey or sugar, plus, if you
wish, ground or grated fresh ginger or mint leaves, cut
into thin ribbons. Serve in stemmed, clear glass bowls
and garnish each with a sprig of mint, a Maraschino cherry
or fine slivers of orange or lemon rind.

FRUIT CUP

This is a deliciously refreshing drink based on fresh fruit
and fruit juices. You can mix the fruit with iced water,
soda water or mineral water and sweeten to taste. Some
fruit cups use orangeade, lemonade or ginger ale to add
some fizz. All fruit cups look inviting served in long glasses,
decorated with slices of fruit or sprigs of mint. See
recipes.

Festive Fruit Cup

1¹/2 cups sugar; 4 cups water; 1 pineapple;
juice 6 lemons; juice 6 oranges;
pulp 6 passionfruit; 1 x 1250ml bottle (5 cups)
lemonade; 1 x 1250ml bottle (5 cups) orangeade.

Heat sugar and water together, stirring until sugar
has dissolved. Boil without stirring for 5 minutes.
Cool, then chill. Peel, core and grate pineapple (or use
a food processor if you have one). Mix sugar syrup,
pineapple, fruit juices and passionfruit pulp and chill
well. Two hours before serving, stir in lemonade and
orangeade. Serve chilled. Makes 20–25 cups.

Citrus Grape Cooler

3 tbs caster sugar; 1 cup orange juice;
¹/2 cup lemon juice; ¹/2 cup grape juice;
2 cups water; ice cubes;
orange slices to decorate.

Combine sugar and fruit juices and stir until sugar
dissolves. Add water and ice and mix well. Serve in
tall glasses, each decorated with a twist of orange.
Serves 4–5.

FRUIT, DRIED AND CANDIED

DRIED FRUIT
The preservation of fruits by drying gives us a sweet,
nourishing food available all year round. Dried fruits have
a high concentration of sugar for a quick boost of energy,
and contain valuable minerals and vitamin A. Many kinds
of fruit are dried, from larger ones such as peaches,
pears, apples, bananas and apricots, to dates and all the
grape family: dessert muscatels, raisins, sultanas and
currants, or a mixture of these with peel and cherries
ready to use in baking.
   When buying dried fruits, choose clean, well-washed
fruit, which has no musty smell, and store, tightly covered,

f

in a cool, dry, airy place. Buy only as much as you use within 6–8 weeks.

Dried fruits make marvellous snacks on their own, so are ideal to carry outdoors or for busy mothers when children arrive home from school feeling hungry. Add dried fruits to cakes, puddings, breads, buns, biscuits and pastries. They are especially good with rice in pilaffs and in rice-based stuffings flavoured with spices, herbs and nuts for meats, poultry or vegetables.

TO RECONSTITUTE DRIED FRUIT: The very best quality dried fruits are graded as 'dessert'. Such fruit as prunes, dates, apricots, figs, peaches and pears can be purchased in this grade and reconstituted without cooking, by soaking in water (or cold tea for prunes) for 3 hours. They can also be stewed without prior soaking.

Dessert peaches and pears are delicious eaten raw, they have a delicate taste and are best cooked only lightly.

To plump raisins, sultanas or currants, cover with boiling water or tea; leave 10 minutes then drain. They can also be plumped by washing briefly and then heating, closely covered, in a preheated moderate oven (180°C/350°F) until they puff up.

TO STEW DRIED FRUIT: Place the fruit in a saucepan and cover with cold water. Simmer, covered, until the fruit is soft and plump. The length of time this takes depends on the type and size of fruit.

To retain whole fruit, add sugar to water before cooking. Most fruit will take ¼ cup sugar to 1 cup fruit, but this depends on your taste and which fruit you are cooking, some are more tart than others. Flavour apricots with a piece of cinnamon stick, pears with a little ground or fresh ginger, and prunes with a whole clove. Serve with thick whipped cream or custard.

If fruit is very hard and dry, soak overnight in cold water to cover before cooking it in the same water.

When stewing to a purée, sweeten fruit with sugar after cooking.

CANDIED FRUIT

Glacé Fruit: The word refers to the glossy coating found on candied fruits such as cherries, apricots, peaches, pineapple rings and whole baby figs, oranges or mandarins.

Glacé fruits are eaten as a sweetmeat – lovely with after-dinner coffee – and are also used as an ingredient in sweet dishes or as a decoration. One of the prettiest ways to use the fruits is in the traditional Bishop's Cake (see page 38). When the cake is cut the slices look like stained glass windows.

Crystallised Fruit: Candied fruit with a coating of granulated sugar. Candied peel and angelica may not have the addition of a sugar coating; both are used to decorate cakes, puddings, custards, breads and biscuits while mixed candied peel is used in fruit cakes, loaves, and breads, puddings and sweet cheese desserts. **See recipes.**

Grilled Stuffed Figs: Soak dried figs in sherry or port for 36 hours. Split and fill with nuts or cream cheese, or a combination of the two, or with Cheddar cheese. Wrap with partially cooked bacon strips and secure with a wooden toothpick. Grill until bacon is crisp and figs are heated through.

Savoury Stuffed Dates: Fill dates with whole or chopped nuts, cream cheese and peanut butter, or a stuffing made by combining cream cheese with a little mayonnaise, finely chopped celery and onion, pepper and salt to taste.

Prune Snow: To 1½ cups sieved cooked prunes add 1 tbs lemon juice, 1 tsp grated lemon rind, pinch cinnamon. Fold in 2 egg whites, beaten until stiff, with 1–2 tbs sugar. Spoon into serving dishes, top with cream. Serves 3–4.

Macerated Prunes, Apricots and Figs: Macerate dried fruit in large sealed jars. Prunes can be macerated in sherry or red wine, apricots in sherry or brandy, figs in brandy. Allow to macerate for at least 1 week before using and use the liquid left in the jars for making another batch. Serve prunes on their own or with a sprinkling of chopped nuts as a dessert, or as an accompaniment to curry. Figs are delicious served with coffee after dinner.

See also *Fruit Cake, Dundee Cake, Eccles Cakes, Christmas Cake*, etc.

Riesling Rice

Rice flavoured with white wine, spices and currants is an elegant accompaniment to grilled chicken, fish or lamb.

1½ cups long-grain rice; 3 cups boiling water; ½ cup currants; 60 g (2 oz) butter; 1 cup riesling or other dry white wine; 2 tsp salt; ¼ tsp white pepper; ¼ tsp nutmeg; ¼ tsp ground allspice; 1 tsp sugar.

Wash rice under cold running water and drain well. Pour 1 cup boiling water over currants and soak for 10 minutes, then drain and set aside. Melt butter in a large saucepan, add rice and stir over medium heat for 5 minutes. Add rest of boiling water and remaining ingredients. Boil until liquid is absorbed and steam holes appear in rice. Turn heat very low, cover tightly and steam 10 minutes or until rice is just tender. Remove from heat, add currants and fork through. Serves 6.

Date and Raisin Crunch

125 g (4 oz) dates, chopped; ⅓ cup raisins; grated rind and juice 2 oranges; 2½ cups rolled oats; ⅓ cup flour; 185 g (6 oz) butter; ⅓ cup sugar.

Combine dates and raisins in a saucepan. Make up orange juice to 1 cup liquid with water. Add liquid to dates and raisins and cook gently until fruit is a thick pulp. Remove from heat and cool. Mix rolled oats and flour, rub in butter and add sugar and orange rind. Press half the mixture into a greased 28 x 19 cm (11 x 7½ in) lamington tin. Spread with fruit filling and sprinkle rest of oat mixture on top. Press down lightly. Bake in a preheated moderately hot oven (190°C/375°F) for 45 minutes. Serve warm as a dessert or cut in wedges when cold and serve as a biscuit bar for tea. Serves 6–8 as a dessert or makes 30 pieces.

Plumped Prunes with Oranges

375 g (12 oz) dessert prunes; 2 large oranges, peeled and cut into segments; 2 cups boiling water.

Toss prunes and oranges in a bowl. Pour in boiling water to cover fruit, seal with plastic wrap and refrigerate overnight. If liked, add 1 tbs Grand Marnier before serving, with whipped cream or sour light cream. Serves 4.

Apricot Sauce

250 g (8 oz) dried apricots; 1 cinnamon stick; ¹/₂ cup sugar; 1 tsp grated orange rind; 1 tbs Grand Marnier (optional).

Soak apricots in water to cover for several hours. Bring to the boil with cinnamon stick and simmer until soft. Remove cinnamon stick. Rub apricots through a sieve or purée in a food processor or blender, then add sugar. Return to saucepan and cook until sugar has dissolved. A little more water may be added if sauce is too thick. Stir in orange rind and Grand Marnier, if using. Allow to cool before serving. Serve with vanilla ice cream; fold through whipped cream for a pavlova filling; or serve with tiny meringues sandwiched together with Crème Chantilly (see page 102) as a dessert. Makes 1¹/₂ cups.

Gingered Figs

500 g (1 lb) dried figs; 1 tsp ground ginger; 3 tbs sugar; 1 large orange; 4 slices lemon.

Wash figs and clip off stems. Put into a saucepan with cold water to cover, add ginger and bring to the boil. Simmer until figs are plump and soft, 30–35 minutes. Drain, reserving liquid. Place figs in a serving dish. Measure liquid and return 1 cup to saucepan. Add sugar and cook gently about 5 minutes. Peel rind thinly from orange and cut into julienne (matchstick) strips. Remove white pith and cut orange flesh into segments or thin slices. Add to syrup with orange strips and lemon slices. Pour syrup over figs, chill and serve, with plain yogurt or sour cream flavoured with some finely chopped ginger in syrup. Serves 6.

Apricot Soufflé

¹/₂ cup dried apricots; ¹/₂ cup water; 5 tbs sugar; 2 tbs orange juice or Grand Marnier; grated rind ¹/₂ orange; 3 egg whites.

Soak apricots in water to cover for 3 hours. Drain and place in a saucepan with the ¹/₂ cup water. Cook over very gentle heat until tender. Drain again and add 2 tbs sugar. Push apricots through a sieve or purée in a blender. Stir in orange juice or liqueur and orange rind. Whisk egg whites until stiff, then gradually beat in remaining sugar. Fold gently into cooled apricot purée. Turn into a buttered 18 cm (7 in) soufflé dish which has been lightly sprinkled with sugar. Bake in a preheated hot oven (200°C/400°F) for about 20 minutes. Serve immediately. Serves 4.

Fruit, Nut and Rice Casserole

1 cup dried apricots; ¹/₂ cup sultanas; 1 cup long-grain rice; 60 g (2 oz) butter; 2 onions, chopped; 1 small green pepper, cored, seeded and chopped; ¹/₂ tsp curry powder; ¹/₂ cup toasted almonds, chopped.

Cover apricots and sultanas with water and soak for 2 hours. Drain and chop apricots. Melt butter until tender, drain and set aside. Melt butter in a frying pan and sauté onions, green pepper and curry powder over gentle heat until onion is beginning to soften. Add almonds, apricots, sultanas and rice. Pile into a greased baking dish and bake in a preheated moderate oven (180°C/350°F) for about 20 minutes. Serve with roast or grilled chicken or lamb. Serves 6.

Mediterranean Stuffing

1 chicken liver, finely chopped; 1 cup cooked rice; ¹/₄ cup raisins; ¹/₂ cup ground almonds, 1 onion, finely chopped; ¹/₂ cup chopped parsley; 2–3 leaves fresh basil, chopped; 60 g (2 oz) butter, softened; 1 egg, beaten; salt and freshly ground black pepper.

Mix all ingredients together. Use to stuff a chicken before roasting.

FUDGE

A soft, creamy sweet or candy made with sugar and milk or cream to which are added various flavourings and other ingredients. Fudge makes a lovely gift at Christmas time. Wrap the pieces in coloured cellophane and pack in a pretty box or basket, or serve with black coffee after dinner.

Chocolate Fudge

$1^1/_2$ cups sugar; $^1/_3$ cup evaporated milk;
125 g (4 oz) cream cheese, softened and chopped;
$1^1/_4$ cups chopped marshmallows;
90 g (3 oz) milk chocolate, chopped;
90 g (3 oz) dark chocolate, chopped;
$^1/_2$ cup chopped walnuts; $^1/_2$ tsp vanilla,
or 1 tbs brandy.

Combine sugar and milk in a heavy saucepan. Stir over medium heat until boiling. Add cheese and marshmallows and cook, stirring, for 5 minutes. Remove from heat and stir in chocolate, walnuts and vanilla or brandy. Pour into an oiled 18 cm (7 in) square cake tin. Cool, cut into squares and store in refrigerator. Makes about 24 large pieces.

g

GAI LARN (CHINESE BROCCOLI)

Also called Chinese kale, this is one of the most popular Asian vegetables, often appearing as a dish at banquets and on its own trolley at yum cha. Gai larn has dark green leaves, fat yet tender stems, and small white flowers. For the Chinese it is the stem that is the choice part of this vegetable, the leaves being largely neglected.

If the stems have a tough skin they are best lightly peeled. Gai larn may be steamed, boiled, stir-fried or braised. The simplest way to prepare gai larn is to discard the large outer leaves, cut the stems into finger lengths, drop them into lightly salted boiling water with a few drops of peanut oil added, and cook until tender-crisp. Drain well, splash a little oyster sauce over and serve hot.

GALETTE

A galette is a flat cake traditionally made with flaky pastry or yeast dough. It is the symbolic cake eaten on Twelfth Night in France. A more elaborate version can consist of meringue, fruit and nuts. Savoury galettes made with vegetables, shaped into rounds, and served hot or cold cut into wedges are also delicious. **See recipes.**

Almond and Hazelnut Galette

4 egg whites; $1^{1}/_{2}$ tbs flour; 45 g ($^{1}/_{2}$ oz) ground hazelnuts; 75 g ($2^{1}/_{2}$ oz) ground almonds; $^{1}/_{2}$ cup caster sugar; 45 g ($1^{1}/_{2}$ oz) butter, melted; $1^{1}/_{2}$ cups cream; $^{1}/_{2}$ tsp vanilla; $1^{1}/_{2}$ cups sliced peaches, fresh or drained canned; sifted icing sugar.

Cut out 3 rounds of greaseproof paper 20 cm (8 in) in diameter. Spray with non-stick cooking spray, and place on baking trays. Whisk egg whites until very stiff peaks form. Sift flour, nuts and sugar into egg whites, add melted butter and fold together gently using a metal spoon. Divide the mixture into 3 and spread out on each greaseproof round. Bake in a preheated moderate oven (180°C/350°F) for 25–30 minutes or until pale gold. Place on wire racks to cool and remove paper bases when cold. Whip cream and flavour with vanilla. Place one meringue round on a serving platter, spoon one third of the cream over and arrange sliced peaches on cream. Cover with second meringue round. Repeat layering with cream and peaches and place last meringue round on top. Dust with icing sugar and decorate with remaining one third whipped cream. Serves 8.

Potato Galette

This is a beautifully crisp, golden-brown potato cake. Serve hot or cold.

500 g (1 lb) potatoes, cooked; 30 g (1 oz) butter; 1 medium onion, chopped; 2 eggs, beaten; $^{1}/_{4}$ cup hot milk; salt and freshly ground black pepper; $^{1}/_{4}$ tsp nutmeg.

Mash potatoes well, then push through a sieve. Melt butter in a saucepan and soften onions over low heat. Remove from heat and beat in potatoes, eggs, hot milk, salt, pepper and nutmeg. Turn into a greased 20 cm (8 in) sandwich tin. Smooth top with a spatula and bake in a preheated moderate oven (180°C/350°F) for 1 hour. Turn out cake and serve cut into wedges. Serves 8.

Galette Normandy

PASTRY: 2 cups flour; 150 g (5 oz) butter; 5 tbs icing sugar, sifted; 2 egg yolks; $^{1}/_{4}$ tsp vanilla.

FILLING: 30 g (1 oz) butter; 1 kg (2 lb) cooking apples, peeled, cored and quartered; grated rind and juice $^{1}/_{2}$ lemon; $^{1}/_{2}$ cup sugar.

TO FINISH: Glacé Icing (page 205); 1 tbs redcurrant jelly (optional).

PASTRY: Sift flour on to a board, make a well in the centre and put in butter, sugar, egg yolks and vanilla. Work together into a smooth paste. Divide into 3 portions and chill for 30 minutes.

FILLING: Melt butter in a heavy saucepan, add apples and lemon rind and juice, cover and cook gently until soft and pulpy. Mix in sugar and purée in a food processor or blender or push through a sieve. Roll out pastry into 3 equal-sized rounds about 20 cm (8 in) diameter. Bake on baking trays in a preheated moderate oven (180°C/350°F) for about 15 minutes or until a pale golden colour. When pastry is cold sandwich layers together with apple mixture. Cover the top with a thin layer of glacé icing and marble with redcurrant jelly, if using. Serves 8.

GAME

For culinary purposes, 'game' means the meat of wild animals and birds or of traditional game species which are now farmed for the table. Farmed game is usually milder in flavour, fatter and more tender than the wild variety.

Game is prized for its rich flavours and textures. The powerful aroma and taste referred to as 'gamey' develop with lengthy hanging – a necessity with much wild game in order to tenderise it, but less necessary for the farmed kind.

Most game tends to be dry, so game is often marinated or barded or larded with fat before cooking to promote juiciness.

TO BARD GAME: Cover the breast of the bird with fat bacon or pork fat before roasting; toward the end of cooking the covering is removed and the breast dredged with flour and basted. This is called 'frothing' and is done to brown the breast.

TO LARD GAME: Cut strips of pork fat and thread or insert through the flesh, using a larding needle.

Roasting is the best way to cook good, young game, but if you have any doubts about tenderness, it is advisable to casserole it to ensure moist, tender meat. Game also makes a luxurious soup or pie. Small game birds are often placed on a piece of toast for roasting and are served on the toast. **See recipes.**

ACCOMPANIMENTS FOR GAME: Game Chips (see page 383), wild rice and browned breadcrumbs (see page 47) are classic accompaniments to game. Other accompaniments should be robustly flavoured, e.g. braised celery, Brussels sprouts and chestnuts, glazed onions or turnips; spiced fruits; Watercress and Walnut Salad (see page 104), or orange salad.

See also *Pheasant, Quail, Rabbit,* and *Venison.*

Game Pie

**1 pheasant or 2–3 smaller game birds;
2 slices each onion, carrot and celery;
1 bouquet garni; 2 cups water; 250 g (8 oz) skinless belly pork, diced; 125 g (4 oz) cooked ham, diced;
1 onion, finely chopped; 1 tbs chopped parsley;
1 tsp chopped fresh thyme, or 1/2 tsp dried;
1 leaf fresh sage, finely chopped, or pinch dried;
4 juniper berries, crushed; 1/4 tsp ground mace;
1/2 cup port; 2 tbs brandy; 1 tsp salt;
freshly ground black pepper;
90 g (3 oz) mushrooms, sliced; 30 g (1 oz) butter;
1 tbs flour; 250 g (8 oz) frozen puff pastry, thawed;
1 egg yolk, beaten.**

Cut meat off pheasant or other birds. Put carcase into a saucepan with slices of onion, carrot and celery, bouquet garni and water and simmer, covered, for 1½ hours. Strain, chill and remove fat from surface. Cut pheasant meat into bite-size pieces and place in a bowl with pork, ham, chopped onion, herbs, berries, mace, port, brandy, salt and pepper. Cover and leave 6–8 hours, turning over occasionally. Put meat mixture into a pie dish just big enough to hold it. Sauté mushrooms in butter and place them on top of meat mixture. Add flour to fat in sauté pan and stir until golden, then add 1 cup stock from carcase and stir until boiling. Season with salt and pepper and pour over pie filling. Cool completely. Cover dish with puff pastry, make a hole in the centre and decorate with pastry leaves. Brush with egg yolk and bake in a preheated very hot oven (230°C/450°F) for 15 minutes or until pastry is well-risen, then reduce heat to moderately hot (190°C/375°F) and bake for a further 1½ hours or until meat is tender (test with a skewer through hole in crust). If crust is browning too much, cover loosely with foil. Serves 4–6.

Game Soup

**2–3 game bird carcases, cooked or raw; 6 cups good beef stock; 2 tsp chopped mixed fresh herbs, or 1/2 tsp dried; 3 juniper berries, crushed;
60 g (2 oz) butter; 60 g (2 oz) cooked ham, diced;
1 onion, diced; 1 small carrot, diced; 1 tender stick celery, diced; 60 g (2 oz) mushrooms, sliced;
3 tbs flour; salt and freshly ground black pepper;
1/4 cup port or sherry; 60–90 g (2–3 oz) cooked game bird meat, cut into small strips;
croûtons to garnish.**

Simmer carcases, stock, herbs and juniper berries together for 1½ hours. Strain into a bowl and wash out the saucepan. In same saucepan, melt butter and brown ham and vegetables. Stir in flour and cook 2 minutes. Remove from heat, cool a little, then add 5 cups warm stock and stir until smoothly blended. Return to heat and stir until boiling. Season with salt and pepper and add port or sherry and the meat. Cover and simmer 20–30 minutes or until vegetables are tender. Serve garnished with croûtons. Serves 6.

GARAM MASALA

A fragrant blend of spices used in curries. There are dry masalas in powder form and wet masalas ground into a paste with water, oil or vinegar. The spices are roasted to bring out the flavour and make it easier when grinding to a fine powder. Commercial blends are available.

There are many versions of garam masala, and most cooks use their own favourite combinations of spices according to their preference. Some use hot spices such as pepper, while others use only the fragrant aromatic ones. Always use good quality spices, and buy them from a store that has a rapid turnover to ensure freshness. After grinding the spices (use a blender or a mortar and pestle), store in an airtight jar in a cool, dry place.

Garam masala is sometimes added to recipes with other spices at the frying stage, but it is more often used during the last few minutes of cooking when it is sprinkled over the food. **See recipes.**

Garam Masala

**4 tbs coriander seeds; 2 tbs cumin seeds;
1 tbs black peppercorns; 2 tsp cardamom seeds;
4 x 8 cm (3 in) cinnamon sticks; 1 tsp whole cloves;
1 whole nutmeg, finely grated.**

Over medium heat in a small pan roast separately first coriander, then cumin, peppercorns, cardamom, cinnamon and lastly cloves. Remove each spice from the pan as it begins to smell fragrant and cool it on a plate. Put all into a blender and blend to a fine powder or pound using a mortar and pestle. Mix in nutmeg and store in an airtight jar. Will keep several months. Makes ¾ cup.

g

Fragrant Garam Masala

3 x 8 cm (3 in) cinnamon sticks;
2 tsp cardamom seeds; 1 tsp whole cloves;
¹/₂ nutmeg, grated.

Over medium heat in a small pan roast separately first cinnamon, then cardamom, then cloves. Remove each spice from the pan when it begins to smell fragrant and cool on a plate. When all are roasted and cooled, blend to a fine powder in a blender or pound using a mortar and pestle. Finally add nutmeg. Makes ¼ cup.

GARLIC

The distinctive taste of garlic makes it one of the best-known herbs. A perennial plant of the onion family, it is the small bulbous root that is used for flavouring. When fully grown, the bulb is made up of a number of small sections, known as cloves. One clove is usually sufficient to bring out the flavours in a savoury dish, although there is a famous chicken dish that calls for 40 cloves of garlic – yet the flavour is surprisingly gentle (see page 173).

Garlic is an essential ingredient in the cuisines of France, Spain and Italy, the Middle East and Far Eastern countries. In the south of France and in Spain, garlic is used lavishly – in sauces, salads, meat and fish dishes, as a vegetable, or crushed and spread on crusty bread which has been liberally sprinkled with fruity olive oil. In Italy, on the other hand, its use is generally more discreet. The garlic clove is added whole and then removed from the dish before serving. In the south of Italy, however, a more lusty flavour is enjoyed.

For some, garlic's odour is a deterrent to its enjoyment, but for those who love garlic there are ways to render it inoffensive. The aroma of a garlic-flavoured meal is less offensive when accompanied by salad greens, providing garlic is not used in the dressing. Fresh parsley neutralises garlic on the breath most effectively. If a whole clove of garlic is cooked peeled but not cut, a much milder flavour results. The smell of garlic can be removed from the hands by sprinkling them with salt, then rinsing with cold water.

Organic garlic is available and well worth looking for in the organic section in most supermarkets.

WAYS TO USE GARLIC

- Garlic is an essential ingredient in curries.
- It perks up otherwise bland dishes such as yogurt, soups and some side salads. Try sliced cucumber in sour cream and see what a difference a little garlic makes (good as an accompaniment to curries).
- Crushed and lightly fried with some butter, garlic gives boiled vegetables a delicious flavour – try it with spinach, beans or zucchini.
- One clove, blended with 30 g (1 oz) butter, makes the butter for garlic bread that everyone loves (see below).
- A whole peeled clove, steeped in Vinaigrette Dressing (see page 442) for a few hours makes a difference to green salads.
- It is a basic ingredient of many rich casseroles and seafood soups.
- Its robust flavour turns mayonnaise into Aïoli (see page 2), the renowned garlic mayonnaise of Provence. See recipes.

TO CRUSH GARLIC: Garlic may be crushed in a garlic press but by far the easier method is to crush it with salt.

Take an unpeeled garlic clove. Place it on a board. Place the flat part of the knife blade on top and give the blade a sharp crack with the side of the palm. This flattens the garlic clove and makes the skin easy to remove. Remove the thin papery skin of the garlic. Sprinkle the garlic with 1 tsp salt. Using the flat edge of the knife blade, work the garlic and salt to a pulp.

Garlic Bread: Cut a loaf of Italian or French bread into thin diagonal slices, almost through to bottom crust but so loaf still holds together. Spread cut surfaces with Garlic Butter (see below). Wrap bread in foil. Bake in a preheated moderately hot oven (190°C/375°F) for 15 minutes, loosen foil and bake for a further 5 minutes to make crust crispy. Serve hot.

Garlic Butter: Cream 125 g (4 oz) butter. Crush 1 or more garlic cloves (to taste), and blend into butter. Use to make Garlic Bread, or use on snails, mussels, over boiled fish, or vegetables.

Garlic Chapons: This is the name given, in the south-west of France, to crusts of bread or slices of crusty French bread which have been rubbed with raw garlic, seasoned with oil, vinegar, salt and pepper and added to green salad, especially to curly endive. Sometimes seasoned chapons are put into a preheated slow oven (150°C/300°F) for 15–20 minutes to allow them to dry out and become crispy.

Garlic Oil: Use for seasoning salads. Peel 10 garlic cloves, drop into boiling salted water for 3–4 minutes. Drain them, then pound in a mortar to a fine paste. Add 1 cup good olive oil, then push through a muslin cloth or sieve.

It can also be made by adding chopped garlic to oil and allowing it to stand 24 hours, then passing through a fine sieve.

Garlic and Oil Sauce: Cook 2–3 finely chopped garlic cloves gently in ¼ cup olive oil. Season with salt and pepper to taste and serve at once over well-drained hot pasta or boiled potatoes.

Tomatoes Provençale

2 medium tomatoes, halved; salt and freshly ground black pepper; ¼ cup fresh breadcrumbs; 2 tsp melted butter; I clove garlic, crushed.

Season tomatoes with salt and pepper. Mix breadcrumbs with butter and garlic and season with salt and pepper. Spoon on to tomato halves. Grill under a preheated moderate grill until crumbs have browned and tomatoes heated through, or bake in a preheated moderately hot oven (190°C/375°F) for 15 minutes. Serves 4.

Garlic Prawns

A Spanish specialty traditionally prepared in individual flameproof ramekins and served sizzling hot. They can be prepared in a frying pan and transferred to 4 hot ramekins for serving.

500 g (I lb) large green prawns; ¾ cup olive oil; 4 cloves garlic, finely chopped; ½ tsp chopped red chilli, or pinch chilli powder; 2 tsp salt; I tbs chopped parsley and I tbs snipped chives (optional).

Shell and devein prawns or leave whole, unshelled. Place in covered container with ½ cup olive oil, the garlic, chilli and salt. Cover and refrigerate for at least 2 hours. When ready to serve, heat remaining oil in 4 flameproof dishes. Drain prawns, reserving marinade. Divide prawns between dishes and cook for 3–4 minutes or until prawns turn pink. Pour reserved marinade over, add parsley and chives and cook for further 1 minute. Serve with crusty French bread. Serves 4.

Lamb Aillade

Leg of lamb cooked with garlic, anchovies, rosemary and thyme is a specialty of Provence. It is traditionally served at Easter with a green salad garnished with hard-boiled eggs.

I leg of lamb, about 2 kg (4 lb); 12 cloves garlic, 6 whole and 6 slivered; 12 anchovy fillets, chopped; 3 tbs olive oil; I tsp chopped fresh rosemary; I tsp chopped fresh thyme; salt and freshly ground black pepper; ½ cup dry white wine; 2 tbs chopped parsley or mint.

Make slits in lamb and insert a sliver of garlic and a piece of anchovy in each incision. Rub lamb with 2 tbs of the olive oil, the rosemary, thyme, salt and pepper. Let it stand for 1–2 hours. Place meat on a rack in a roasting tin and roast in a preheated hot oven (200°C/400°F) for 20 minutes. Reduce heat to moderate (180°C/350°F) and cook for a further 1–1¼ hours. Heat remaining 1 tbs olive oil in a frying pan and cook whole garlic cloves slowly for about 10 minutes or until they are soft (do not let edges become crisp). Set aside in a small bowl. Remove lamb from roasting tin and pour off excess fat. Pour wine into tin, scrape up brown bits and boil wine over high heat to reduce it by half. Add reduced liquid to garlic cloves. Mash well with a fork and add salt and pepper. Slice lamb and sprinkle with pepper. Spoon sauce over it and sprinkle with parsley or mint. Serves 6–8.

Chicken with 40 Cloves of Garlic

A dish from the French provincial area of Dauphine. Don't be startled by the quantity of garlic in this recipe. The chicken will emerge golden, meltingly tender and with the most wonderful aroma of herbs and garlic. Serve with plenty of thick slices of crusty bread. The French spread the bread with tender garlic; a treat for garlic lovers.

I x I.75 kg (3½ lb) chicken; salt and freshly ground black pepper; small bouquet fresh parsley, thyme, rosemary and tarragon; ¾ cup olive oil; 40 unpeeled garlic cloves; bunch fresh rosemary, thyme, sage, bay leaf, parsley and celery leaves; I cup flour mixed to a thick paste with ¼ cup water.

Season chicken inside and out with salt and pepper. Place bouquet of fresh herbs inside. Pour oil into a flameproof casserole just large enough to hold chicken and add unpeeled garlic cloves. Place the larger bunch of fresh herbs on top of garlic. Gently warm oil, then add chicken and turn to coat all over. Cover dish and seal lid to base with flour and water paste. Bake in a preheated moderate oven (180°C/350°F) for 1½ hours. Break pastry seal, clean seal from the edge and serve in the dish with crusty bread. Serves 4–6.

GATEAU

The French word for a cake of all types – plain or decorated, large or small, used for dessert, with coffee or celebrations and parties. In other parts of the world the word gâteau is synonymous with a rich, highly decorated cake, often layered with cream or butter cream, flavoured with liqueur, and decorated with cream, chocolate, nuts or fruits. **See recipes.**

See also *Cakes.*

Gâteau Caraque

A rich chocolate sponge filled and covered with chocolate butter cream and decorated with chocolate caraque. It keeps well.

75 g (2 ¹/₂ oz) unsweetened chocolate, broken into small pieces; 2 tbs coffee; 3 eggs; ¹/₂ cup plus 3 tsp caster sugar; ¹/₂ cup plus 3 tsp flour;
I quantity Chocolate Crème au Beurre (page 207); Chocolate Caraque or Curls (page 83).

Melt chocolate with coffee over warm water. Set aside to cool. Whisk eggs with sugar until very thick and pale. This will take 8–10 minutes. Sift in flour and fold it in quickly and carefully with the melted chocolate. Turn mixture into a 20 cm (8 in) cake tin that has been greased, bottom-lined with greased greaseproof paper, and floured. Bake in a preheated moderate oven (180°C/350°F) for 30–40 minutes or until a skewer inserted in centre comes out clean. Cool on a wire rack. When cold, split cake into 2 layers and sandwich with one third of the chocolate crème au beurre. Spread sides and top with rest of cream and cover with chocolate caraque or curls. Serves 8.

Gâteau Progres

This cake is a speciality of France, made as a reward for success, something to help celebrate a special achievement in one's life. There are three basic steps in its preparation: first, the making of the nut meringue layers; second, the butter cream; and third, the laying together and finishing off. The first two steps can be done well ahead of time, and the finishing off can be done a few hours before the cake is needed.

It is traditional to dredge the top with icing sugar and pipe 'Progres' across the centre of the cake, or sometimes, the word 'Succes'.

²/₃ cup caster sugar; 1¹/₄ cups ground almonds; 5 egg whites; 3 drops vanilla essence; I quantity Coffee Butter Cream (see below); almonds, blanched, toasted and chopped, to decorate; icing sugar, for dusting.

COFFEE BUTTER CREAM: ¹/₂ cup sugar; ¹/₂ cup very strong coffee; 5 egg yolks; ¹/₂ tsp vanilla essence; 250 g unsalted butter.

Have ready 3 baking trays, each lined with baking paper on which has been marked a 20 cm (8 in) circle. Preheat the oven to moderate (180°C/350°F). Sift the sugar, reserving 3 tbs, and ground almonds together. Whisk the egg whites in an electric mixer until stiff peaks form, but the mixture is not dry. Beat in the reserved sugar until the mixture is thick and glossy. Fold in the sifted sugar and almond mixture quickly and lightly.

Divide the mixture into 3 portions and spread on the baking paper circles neatly. Bake in the preheated oven for about 20 minutes or until firm to the touch. Cool on wire racks.

To assemble, lay a meringue round on a serving plate and spread with half the coffee butter cream, lay the second round on top and spread with the remaining butter cream. Top with the last round and spread the sides only of the cake with the reserved coffee butter cream, keeping a little aside if you are going to pipe the top. Press the toasted almonds into the butter cream at the sides and dust the top of the cake with icing sugar. Finish by piping 'Progres' or 'Succes' on top. When the cake is assembled store in the refrigerator to firm the butter cream, it also makes the cake easier to slice.

COFFEE BUTTER CREAM: Dissolve the sugar in the coffee over a very gentle heat, then bring to the boil, boiling until the syrup falls in a thread from the spoon – if you have a sugar thermometer it should register (112°C/234°F). Beat the yolks for 1 minute, preferably using an electric beater; while still beating, add the hot syrup in a very slow stream. Continue beating until the mixture has cooled. Add the vanilla essence and then the butter in small pieces, beating well until thoroughly incorporated and the butter cream is light and fluffy. If it seems too soft, allow to chill for a few minutes.

Gâteau St Honoré

This is the traditional French birthday cake.

¹/₂ quantity Pâte Sucrée (pages 344–5); I egg beaten, to glaze; I quantity Choux Pastry (page 345); ¹/₂ cup cream; vanilla; I cup sugar; ¹/₂ cup water.

CREME ST HONORE: I egg, separated; I egg yolk; ¹/₄ cup caster sugar; 2 tbs flour; I tbs cornflour; 1¹/₂ cups milk; I vanilla bean; ¹/₂ cup cream.

Roll out pâte sucrée to a 20 cm (8 in) round and place on a greased baking tray. Prick well with a fork, and brush edge with beaten egg. Fill a piping bag fitted with a 1 cm (¹/₂ in) plain tube with choux pastry. Make a border around edge of pastry round, 1 cm (¹/₂ in) in from outside to allow for spreading. Brush with beaten egg. Pipe remaining choux on to a greased baking tray in 15 small rounds the size of a walnut. Brush with beaten egg. Bake all the pastry in a preheated hot oven (200°C/400°F) for 25 minutes for the choux puffs and 35 minutes for the pastry base or until crisp and golden. Remove from oven. Prick base of each choux puff 2 or 3 times to allow steam to escape and cool on a wire rack. While choux puffs and choux ring are cooling, prepare crème St Honoré.

CREME ST HONORE: Beat 2 egg yolks with sugar until creamy and very light in colour. Mix flour and cornflour with a little cold milk to make a smooth paste and add to egg yolk mixture. Scald remaining milk with vanilla bean, strain on to egg yolk mixture, blend and return to saucepan. Stir over a gentle heat until mixture boils. Whisk egg white until peaks form, add a little of the hot custard, mix thoroughly and pour back into pan. Stir gently over low heat for 2–3 minutes. Chill. Whip cream and fold through just before serving.

Whip cream, flavour with vanilla and put in a piping bag. Cut a tiny hole in the side of each puff with the point of a knife and force in cream through the hole. In a small heavy saucepan heat sugar with water until dissolved. Bring to the boil and boil, without stirring, until golden. Spoon a little caramel syrup on to choux pastry rim and secure choux puffs on top. Fill centre of gâteau with crème St Honoré. Return caramel to the heat and cook until a rich amber colour. Immediately put saucepan into cold water to prevent further cooking. Spoon over the puffs. For a spectacular effect, dip 2 spoons into caramel, then pull and spin caramel strands around the gâteau. Serve immediately. Serves 8.

NOTE: The gâteau may be prepared ahead if desired. Make pâte sucrée 2 days ahead, wrap and store in refrigerator.

THE DAY BEFORE: Make choux pastry. Roll out pâte sucrée and pipe on choux pastry border. Bake. Prepare and bake puffs. When cool, store base and individual puffs in an airtight tin. Make basic custard but do not fold in whipped cream. Store, covered, in refrigerator.

A FEW HOURS BEFORE ASSEMBLING: Place case and puffs in a preheated moderate oven (180°C/350°F) for 10 minutes until crisp. Cool completely.

JUST BEFORE ASSEMBLING AND SERVING: Whip cream and fold into basic custard. Fill puffs with vanilla-flavoured cream and continue as directed in recipe.

GAZPACHO

The refreshing, spicy, chilled soup-salad which is served in almost every Spanish home and restaurant. It is a favourite alfresco dish and, accompanied by separate bowls of garnishes, is almost a meal in itself. Gazpacho varies a little from region to region but is always a flavoursome mixture of vegetables and aromatics, served over ice.

Gazpacho

6 ripe, red tomatoes, peeled, or
1 x 425 g can tomatoes, drained,
plus 2 fresh tomatoes, peeled; 1 cup white
wine or stock; 2 cloves garlic, crushed;
$^{1}/_{2}$ tsp ground cumin; salt and freshly ground black
pepper; $^{1}/_{2}$ cups fresh breadcrumbs;
$^{1}/_{3}$ cup olive oil; $^{1}/_{4}$ cup wine vinegar;
3 cups tomato juice; 1 large onion, diced;
1 green pepper, cored, seeded and diced;
1 cucumber, peeled, seeded and diced;
12–16 ice cubes; 3 hard-boiled eggs, chopped;
1 cup small garlic croûtons (page 105).

Seed 6 fresh or the canned tomatoes. Coarsely chop half the fresh or all the canned tomatoes and simmer 5 minutes with wine or stock. Purée in a blender or rub through a sieve. Set aside. Cut remaining tomatoes into small dice. Mix garlic, cumin, salt and pepper. Mix in breadcrumbs, then very gradually beat in oil to form a thick paste. Stir in vinegar little by little, then puréed tomatoes and tomato juice. Combine with half the diced vegetables. Adjust seasoning and chill 2–3 hours before serving. Place 2–3 ice cubes in each bowl, then ladle gazapacho over. Serve remaining vegetables, chopped hard-boiled egg and garlic croûtons in separate bowls for each diner to add their own choice of garnish. Serves 6–8.

GELATINE

An extract of the animal protein, collagen, gelatine makes possible a great range of culinary triumphs both sweet and savoury – a delicate Bavaroise (Bavarian Cream, page 123), an airy cold soufflé, a beautifully shaped salmon or vegetable mousse, a sparkling aspic – as well as dozens of family dishes from simple jellies and whips to cake and pie fillings, smooth and economical ice cream, home-made confectionery and appetising moulds of meat, fish and vegetables. It is sold in powdered form, often in individual envelopes, also in leaf form.

Leaf gelatine once came in thick sheets – now it is available in very thin sheets. As it is available in varying degrees of strengths and qualities it is advisable to use powdered gelatine unless you are sure of the leaf gelatine. Many professional cooks use leaf gelatine but they have shopped around for the best quality. Generally speaking, 6 sheets of gelatine is the equivalent of 3 teaspoons of powdered gelatine (a 10 g/$^{1}/_{3}$ oz sachet), which is enough to soft-set 480 ml (2 cups) of liquid.

Gelatine can be used with almost any food except uncooked pineapple and pawpaw, which contain an enzyme that prevents jelling. As the enzyme is inactivated by heat, cooked or canned pineapple or pawpaw present no problem.

Do not boil gelatine mixtures, as this will weaken the jelling power, nor freeze them unless their fat content is very high, as in ice creams.

AMOUNT TO USE: Proportions of gelatine to liquid may vary from recipe to recipe, depending on other ingredients. As a general guide, 1 envelope or 3 tsp gelatine will set 2 cups liquid into jelly. If the jelly is to be unmoulded, use 1 tbs gelatine to 2 cups liquid to give a slightly firmer texture.

TO ADD GELATINE TO A MIXTURE: Sprinkle gelatine over cold water or some of the liquid used in the recipe, using about 3 times the volume of liquid to gelatine. Do not stir but leave the liquid to absorb the gelatine, undisturbed. If gelatine is to be added to a cold mixture, soften it first. Place the gelatine container in hot water on gentle heat, and leave until mixture is clear. Never let it boil. Stir or fold into the cold mixture and continue to stir or fold carefully until mixture is on the point of setting (when it has the consistency of unbeaten egg whites), before turning into a mould or serving dish to set.

TO UNMOULD A GELATINE MIXTURE: This is not difficult if you don't try to rush it. Have ready a chilled, dampened serving plate and a sink or pan of comfortably hand-warm water, deep enough to come up to the rim of the mould. Remove mould from refrigerator and, with your fingers, gently pull the edge of the gelatine away from the mould all round. Dip the mould into warm water for about 4 seconds if it is metal, 8 seconds if it is china or glass.

Lift out and invert the serving plate on top. Hold mould and plate firmly together, turn over and shake gently up and down until the gelatine slips from the mould on to the plate. If it doesn't, repeat the process. Centre the gelatine on the dampened plate, then wipe the edges dry. **See recipes.**

Jambon Persillé *(Cold Parsleyed Ham)*

A traditional dish from Burgundy, splendid for a buffet or picnic.

1 kg (2 lb) cooked or canned ham, cut into 2.5 cm (1 in) cubes; 1 1/2 cups well-flavoured chicken stock; 1/2 cup dry white wine; freshly ground black pepper; nutmeg; 1 cup finely chopped parsley; 2 tbs gelatine; 1/2 cup cold water; 1–2 tbs tarragon vinegar.

Simmer ham in stock and white wine, seasoned with pepper and nutmeg, for 5 minutes. Drain, reserving liquid. Put ham into a bowl or loaf tin which has been rinsed out with cold water and lightly dusted with parsley. Soften gelatine in water, then stir into hot liquid. When gelatine has dissolved, add remaining parsley and tarragon vinegar to taste. Allow to cool and when syrupy pour over the ham. Chill in refrigerator until well set, then unmould. Serves 8–10.

Fresh Orange Jelly

A reminder of why jellies were once served at the most elegant dinners.

thinly peeled rind 1 orange; thinly peeled rind and juice 1/2 lemon; 1/3 cup sugar; 1 1/2 cups hot water; 2 tbs plus 3 tsp gelatine; 2 1/2 cups freshly squeezed orange juice, strained; extra sugar or lemon juice; cream to serve.

Put orange and lemon rind, lemon juice, sugar and half the water into a saucepan and warm on low heat for 10 minutes to infuse. Dissolve gelatine in remaining hot water. Stir into ingredients in saucepan, strain and cool. Stir in orange juice, taste and add a little more sugar or lemon juice, if needed. Pour into a mould or glass bowl. Chill until set. Serve with cream. Serves 6–8.

GENOISE CAKE (GENOESE)

A basic sponge-type cake used for filled cakes, sponge fingers, petits fours or Bombe Alaska. The eggs and

sugar are beaten with a balloon whisk over gentle heat until they are warm, thick and pale lemon-coloured, and the beating continues at room temperature until the mixture is cool and even thicker. These 2 steps can be done using a hand-held electric mixer, with or without the use of heat, although the volume of the cake will not be quite as great as it would when hand-mixed with a balloon whisk. Flour and melted butter are then mixed in very quickly and lightly to preserve the masses of air bubbles formed through whisking.

To make filled, layered cakes, use whipped cream or butter cream (see page 205), flavoured with liqueur, and decorate with fruit or nuts.

Ice single cakes with Butter Icing, flavoured to your taste (see *Icings, Frostings and Fillings*).

Genoise Cake

4 eggs; 1/2 cup caster sugar; 1/2 tsp vanilla; 1 cup flour; sifted; 60 g (2 oz) butter, melted and cooled.

Put eggs, sugar and vanilla in a heatproof bowl, place over warm water over a gentle heat and whisk until mixture is pale lemon-coloured, thick and doubled in bulk. This will take about 7 minutes. Remove bowl from heat and beat a further 3–4 minutes or until cool and very thick. Fold in flour, then add butter. Mix as lightly and rapidly as possible. Turn at once into 2 greased 20 cm (8 in) round or 18 cm (7 in) square tins that have been bottom-lined with greased grease-proof paper. Bake in a preheated moderate oven (180°C/350°F) for 20–30 minutes or until cooked. To test, gently press centre with finger – if cake springs back it is cooked. If impression remains, leave cake for further 5 minutes and test again. Cool on a wire rack. This recipe will make 2 x 20 cm (8 in) round cakes or 2 x 18 cm (7 in) squares.

GHEE

See *Butter*.

GHERKIN (CORNICHON)

Gherkins or cornichons ('little horns') are very small cucumbers which are grown for pickling. The best are about 3 cm (1 1/2 in) long. Serve pickled gherkins with hot boiled beef, corned beef or frankfurts, or with cold meats and cheese. They are also part of the flavouring for Tartare, Gribiche and Rémoulade Sauces (see page 256).

Gherkins

1 kg (2 lb) firm gherkins; 1 cup salt; 4 cups water; 1 tbs whole cloves; 1 tbs white peppercorns; 1 tbs blade mace; 1 tbs whole allspice; 1 x 8 cm (3 in) cinnamon stick; 2 slices fresh ginger; 4 cups white vinegar; grape leaves (optional).

Place gherkins in a large bowl. Dissolve salt in water and pour over gherkins. Cove and leave 3 days. Meantime, tie spices and flavourings in a muslin bag, place in vinegar and bring to the boil. Cool, with spice bag in vinegar, for 2 hours, then remove bag. After 3 days, drain, rinse and dry gherkins. Pack them into scalded wide-mouthed jars. Bring vinegar to the boil, pour over gherkins, cover tightly and leave 24 hours. Pour off vinegar into a saucepan, bring to the boil again, pour over gherkins and leave as before. Repeat this process once more. Add a few grape leaves to each jar, if desired, to help keep gherkins crisp. Cover tightly and leave 6 weeks. Makes 2 x 500 g (1 lb) jars.

GIBLETS

The name for the neck, heart, gizzard and liver of poultry (though livers may or may not be included in giblets that you buy). If giblets are sold with a bird, they are packaged and placed in the body cavity, so always be sure to check before cooking. If they are there, use them to enrich the gravy to be served with the bird. Giblets are also sold separately. They make excellent soup or can be served, in a sauce made from their cooking liquid, on toast.

■ **BASIC PREPARATION:** Remove all fat and membrane from giblets and cut off any discoloured or dark parts from liver. Clean all grit from gizzard and scrape the lining well. Wash giblets under cold running water.

Giblet Gravy: Put all giblets, except liver, into a saucepan and add a slice each of onion and carrot, a small piece of celery and a few fresh herbs if you have them. Cover with cold water and simmer 45 minutes or until giblets are tender. It is best to cook liver separately because of its strong flavour. If you are roasting a bird, cook liver under it for 5–10 minutes; otherwise sauté it in a little butter.

Strain liquid from the pan of giblets and reserve, and discard neck. Finely dice the heart, gizzard and cooked liver. Use reserved liquid when making gravy and add diced giblets at the end.

GINGER

A bold perennial, with the most heavenly scented flower. The 'root', which is known as the 'hand' (it looks rather like a hand with plump, deformed fingers) is the edible part of the plant. Whole, fresh ginger should be smooth-skinned and kept dry or it will sprout and lose its flavour. It has been used in Asia, from India to China since long ago, and dried ginger was one of the first spices to reach Europe from Asia.

FRESH GINGER: It can be peeled and grated or ground to a pulp and used in many types of curries. (See Prawn Curry and Lamb with Cashew Nut Curry, pages 108–9). In Chinese dishes, a slice of fresh ginger is added to oil and sautéed for a minute to give its distinctive but delicate flavour to the oil. Peeled and cut into fine strips,

it is often used in Chinese and Japanese dishes (see Coriander Chicken and Steamed Fish Coriander, pages 95–6). Peeled and sliced, it can be rubbed over chicken, fish or duck, as you would garlic. It may also be added to marinades, soups or stews.

DRIED GINGER: The root is often dried. To use, cut into pieces and soak in cold water for several hours. Dried ginger is also ground to a powder, and it is a popular spice for flavouring cakes, biscuits and puddings.

PRESERVED GINGER: The peeled root is often preserved in syrup and eaten as a sweetmeat. Preserved ginger is used in fruit and cream desserts and steamed puddings. The syrup may be poured over ice cream, fruit salad, etc.

RED PICKLED GINGER AND BRINED GINGER: Called *gari* or *sushoga* in Japanese, finely sliced red pickled ginger is a traditional accompaniment to sushi and sashimi. Although its pretty pink colour can be natural if young ginger is used and enough time is allowed, it is often dyed using natural foods, such as beetroot. Sugar, salt and vinegar are used to preserve the thinly sliced ginger.

Ginger preserved in brine is used in stir-fry dishes; it is available sliced, diced, in julienne strips and used as a substitute for fresh ginger.

CANDIED GINGER: This is another popular treatment; chopped or sliced it is used in baking or as a sweetmeat.

Finally, ginger is widely used for flavouring ginger ale and ginger beer, one of the most popular beverages.

TO KEEP FRESH GINGER: Juicy young roots that have not become too fibrous may be peeled and cut into small knobs. Place in a clean glass jar and cover with dry sherry. Keep, covered, in refrigerator and use as for fresh ginger. See recipes.

Gingered Honeydew Melon: Peel and slice a ripe chilled honeydew melon. Discard seeds and arrange slices in an overlapping design on a chilled platter. Sprinkle them with a mixture of 1 tbs icing sugar, sifted, and ½ tsp ground ginger. Serve as a first course or dessert with ice cream.

Ginger Ice Cream: Take 500 ml (2 cups) vanilla ice cream from freezer and allow to soften slightly. Swirl in 2 tbs finely chopped, preserved ginger and return to freezer. Serve with a crisp sweet biscuit. Good with poached pears, peaches or sliced fresh melon.

Oriental Chicken Wings

A popular starter for barbecues or casual entertaining. Best eaten in your fingers.

1 kg (2 lb) chicken wings; 4 tbs soy sauce; 2 tbs lemon juice; 1 tbs grated fresh ginger, or ½ tsp ground ginger; 2 tsp honey; 2 tbs tomato ketchup.

Cut tips off wings. Mix remaining ingredients together, add wings and turn to coat. Leave to marinate, covered, for several hours in refrigerator. Drain and arrange wings on a greased grill rack. Grill under a preheated grill for about 10 minutes, then turn, brush with marinade, and grill for a further 10 minutes. Serve hot and offer a pile of paper napkins. Serves 6.

Ginger Marinade

1 tbs grated fresh ginger; 2 tbs soy sauce; 1 tbs lemon juice; 2 tbs oil.

Combine ingredients. Use to marinate 500 g (1 lb) shelled green prawns or scallops, diced chicken or pork, fish fillets or chicken pieces. Marinate, covered, about 30 minutes to 2 hours. Thread marinated food on skewers or place fish fillets or chicken joints on grill rack. Cook under preheated grill, turning several times and brushing with extra marinade during cooking.

Chinese Gingered Roast Chicken

3 tbs soy sauce; 1 tbs honey; 2.5 cm (1 in) piece fresh ginger, grated, or ¹/₂ tsp ground ginger; 3 cloves garlic, crushed; 1¹/₂ tsp five-spice powder; 1 x 1.5 kg (3 lb) roasting chicken; 3 tbs salt.

Combine soy sauce, honey, ginger, garlic and ½ tsp five-spice powder, and rub over chicken and in cavity. Cover and refrigerate 1–2 hours, turning occasionally. Drain chicken, reserving marinade. Put on a rack in roasting tin containing a little water (to prevent drippings from burning). Roast in a preheated moderate oven (180°C/350°F) for 1¼ hours, brushing 3 or 4 times with reserved marinade and turning chicken occasionally. Chop chicken through skin and bones into bite-sized pieces. Arrange on a heated serving dish. Serve remaining five-spice powder mixed with salt for dipping. Serves 6.
NOTE: Five-spice powder is available from Asian grocery shops or Asian sections at supermarkets.

Rich Ginger Cake

A marvellously rich, moist cake with excellent keeping qualities; an old family favourite that is splendid for picnics, lunch-boxes and morning and afternoon snacks.

125 g (4 oz) butter; ³/₄ cup firmly packed brown sugar; 2 cups flour; 1 tsp ground ginger; pinch salt; 2 eggs; 1 cup treacle; ¹/₃ cup sultanas; ¹/₃ cup sliced preserved ginger; ¹/₄ cup milk; ¹/₂ tsp bicarbonate of soda.

Cream butter with sugar until light and fluffy. Sift flour with ground ginger and salt. Beat eggs into creamed butter mixture one at a time, sprinkling mixture each time with 2 tsp flour. Stir in treacle, sultanas, preserved ginger and remaining flour. Warm milk gently, add soda and stir at once into cake mixture. Turn into a greased and floured 18 cm (7 in) round deep cake tin or 21 x 11 x 6 cm (8½ x 4½ x 2½ in) loaf tin. Bake cake in a preheated moderate oven (180°C/350°F) for 1 hour, then reduce heat to moderately slow (160°C/325°F) and bake for a further 30 minutes. If cake begins to brown too much on top, cover loosely with a piece of greaseproof paper. Cool for 5 minutes in tin before turning out.

Crystal Prawns

Soaking prawns in water with bicarbonate of soda gives the prawn meat a clear colour – thus the name. It also slightly changes the texture of the meat.

1¹/₂ tbs bicarbonate of soda; 2¹/₄ cups water; 500 g (1 lb) green king prawns, shelled and deveined; 1¹/₂ tbs cornflour; ¹/₂ tsp salt; ¹/₂ tsp sugar; 2 tbs shredded fresh ginger; 2 tbs shredded red pepper; ¹/₄ cup sliced spring onions.

Dissolve bicarbonate of soda in 2 cups water, add prawns and soak for 2 hours. Drain and rinse well under cold running water, then soak again in fresh cold water to cover for a further 1 hour. Drain. Blanch in boiling water for 2 minutes, drain well and dry. Combine remaining ¼ cup water, the cornflour, salt and sugar and heat in a wok or frying pan, stirring, until boiling. Add prawns and toss until well coated and heated through. Place ginger and vegetables on a heated serving platter, spoons prawns on top and toss through. Serves 4.

GINGER BEER

Home-made ginger beer is one of the joys of childhood. It is made by fermenting a simple syrup with a yeast, ginger and sugar mixture (called 'plant'). As fermentation causes strong pressure inside bottles, be sure to use sturdy bottles, seal them with patent clip-on bottle seals or screw-tops and store them in a cool place where a burst bottle will do no harm. Make ginger beer in small batches so that it will not be kept too long.

Ginger Beer

GINGER BEER PLANT: 1 tsp compressed yeast, or ¹/₂ tsp dry yeast; 9 tsp sugar; 1 cup warm water; 9 tsp ground ginger.

SYRUP: 4 cups sugar; 6 litres (24 cups) warm water; ¹/₂ cup strained lemon juice.

PLANT: Mix yeast and ½ tsp sugar in a large jar and add water (lukewarm for compressed yeast, comfortably hand-warm for dry yeast) and ½ tsp ginger. Cover jar with muslin and leave 8 days, adding ½ tsp each of ginger and sugar every day.
SYRUP: Heat sugar and 6 cups water, stirring, until sugar dissolves. Remove from heat and add remaining

water and lemon juice. Strain yeast mixture through 2 thicknesses of muslin. Reserve sediment on muslin. Add strained liquid to syrup. Stir well. Pour into bottles, filling only to base of necks, and seal. Leave about 5 days before drinking, depending on weather – in hot weather, the ginger beer will be ready in 3–4 days.

To make further batches of ginger beer, halve plant left on muslin and place in 2 jars with 1 tsp ground ginger, 1 tsp sugar and 1 cup water in each (no more yeast is added after first start). Repeat process as before, adding sugar and ginger daily. Makes 8 x 750ml (3 cups) bottles.

GINGERBREAD AND GINGERBREAD MEN

These lovely old favourites are easy to make, keep well and are immensely popular with all members of the family. See recipes.

Gingerbread

This is a moist, sticky gingerbread.

1¹/₂ cups flour; 2 tsp baking powder; 1 tsp ground ginger; ¹/₂ tsp mixed spice; pinch salt; 60 g (2 oz) butter; 2 tbs treacle; ¹/₂ cup loosely packed brown sugar; 2 eggs, beaten; ³/₄ cup milk; 1 tsp bicarbonate of soda; Lemon Glacé Icing (page 205).

Sift flour, baking powder, ginger, spice and salt. Cream butter with treacle and sugar until light and fluffy. Stir in flour mixture, eggs and milk in which bicarbonate of soda has been dissolved. Beat vigorously until surface of batter is covered with bubbles. Pour into a greased 20 cm (8 in) round or square cake tin that has been bottom-lined with greased greaseproof paper. Bake in a preheated moderate oven (180°C/350°F) for 30–35 minutes. Keep cake airtight for 1–2 days before cutting, to develop flavours. Ice with lemon glacé icing.

Nutty Gingerbread

This gingerbread should be somewhat dry and chewy. It is delicious topped with lemon or orange icing, or simply served sliced and buttered.

2¹/₂ cups flour; ¹/₂ tsp bicarbonate of soda; ¹/₂ tsp salt; 1¹/₂ tsp ground ginger; ²/₃ cup sultanas; ¹/₃ cup chopped almonds; ²/₃ cup firmly packed brown sugar; ¹/₂ cup treacle; ¹/₄ cup golden syrup; 185 g (6 oz) butter; 2 large eggs, beaten.

TO FINISH: lemon or orange Vienna Icing (page 205); glacé ginger (optional).

Sift flour, bicarbonate of soda, salt, cinnamon and ginger; and stir in sultanas and almonds. Put sugar, treacle, golden syrup and butter in a saucepan and heat gently until butter melts. Add to flour mixture.

Mix in eggs and beat well. Pour into a greased 28 x 19 cm (11 x 7¹/₂ in) lamington tin that has been bottom-lined with greased greaseproof paper. Bake in a preheated moderate oven (180°C/350°F) for 30–35 minutes or until a skewer inserted in centre comes out clean. Allow to cool, then ice with lemon or orange Vienna icing and decorate with slices of glacé ginger, if using.

Gingerbread Men

Children love gingerbread men and this easy recipe makes them fun to make.

125 g (4 oz) butter; ¹/₃ cup sugar; ¹/₃ cup golden syrup; 3 cups flour; ¹/₂ tsp ground ginger; 1 tsp cinnamon; 3 tsp bicarbonate of soda; 1 egg; 2 tsp vanilla.

DECORATION: currants; glacé cherries.

Put butter, sugar and golden syrup in a saucepan and heat gently, stirring occasionally, until butter melts. Allow to cool. Sift flour, ginger and cinnamon. Add bicarbonate of soda to cooled butter mixture and pour on to flour mixture. Add egg and vanilla, and mix to a soft dough. Roll out to a thickness of 5 mm (¹/₄ in) and cut out shapes with a gingerbread man cutter or a sharp knife. Place on greased baking trays. Put currants in place for eyes and buttons, and cherries cut into strips for mouths. Bake in a preheated moderate oven (180°C/350°F) for 10 minutes. Cool on a wire rack. Makes about 20 small gingerbread men.

GINGERNUT BISCUITS

Who doesn't remember the hard, crunchy texture of gingernut biscuits with their wonderfully spicy flavour? Try the recipe and recall the past.

Gingernuts

1 cup flour; 2 tbs sugar; 1 tsp bicarbonate of soda; 1 tsp mixed spice; 1 tsp cinnamon; 1 tsp ground ginger; 60 g (2 oz) butter; 2 tbs golden syrup; extra ¹/₄ cup sugar (optional).

Sift dry ingredients. Melt butter with golden syrup and pour into flour mixture. Mix well and roll into balls the size of a walnut. If liked, roll the balls in extra sugar before baking for super crunchiness. Place on greased baking trays and press lightly. Bake in a preheated very hot oven (230°C/450°F) for 5 minutes, then reduce the oven heat to moderate (180°C/350°F) and bake for a further 7–10 minutes. Cool on trays. Makes about 20.

GNOCCHI

The delectable little savoury dumplings or cakes of Italy, mostly made from mixtures containing semolina or polenta (see page 373), mashed potatoes or ricotta cheese and spinach. They are served with a variety of sauces or simply with melted butter and grated cheese, and hold the same place as pasta in a meal. They can also make a satisfying meal when served alone with salad, or can accompany grilled meats or roast chicken. Gnocchi can be shaped like little dumplings and poached in lightly salted water, or cut into cakes and baked in the oven. **See recipes.**

Gnocchi alla Romana
(Semolina Gnocchi)

I medium onion, halved; I bay leaf; 3³/4 cups milk; ³/4 cup semolina or polenta; I¹/2 tsp salt; freshly ground white pepper; ³/4 cup grated Parmesan cheese; 60 g (2 oz) butter; ¹/2 tsp dry mustard.

Put onion halves in a saucepan with bay leaf and milk. Bring slowly to the boil. Remove onion and bay leaf, and add semolina or polenta, salt and pepper. Cook, stirring, over a low heat for 15–20 minutes or until very thick. Remove from heat and stir in half the cheese, 15 g (¹/2 oz) butter and the mustard. Spread on an oiled baking tray to about 1 cm (¹/2 in) thick. Cool. When cold, cut into rounds with a 5 cm (2 in) cutter or into squares with a knife. Arrange in rings, slightly overlapping, in a well-oiled shallow ovenproof dish. Sprinkle with remaining cheese. Melt remaining butter and sprinkle over top. Bake in a preheated moderate oven (180°C/350°F) for 15 minutes, then place under a preheated hot grill until top is brown and crisp. Serve immediately, while still bubbling. Serves 4.

VARIATION

GNOCCHI IN TOMATO SAUCE: Prepare gnocchi as above and arrange in a well-oiled shallow ovenproof dish. Spoon over Tomato Sauce (see page 460), sprinkle generously with grated Parmesan cheese and bake in a preheated moderately hot oven (190°C/375°F) for 30 minutes or until golden-brown.

Potato Gnocchi

2 kg (4 lb) potatoes, cooked, mashed and kept warm; 2 tsp salt; 2 eggs, beaten; 3 cups flour, sifted; I quantity of Bolognese Sauce (page 340); grated Parmesan cheese.

Make dough for potato gnocchi just before cooking as it becomes damp if allowed to stand. Mix together warm mashed potatoes, salt and eggs. Work in enough flour to make a firm but soft dough. Divide dough into pieces and roll in well-floured hands to thick pencil shapes about 1 cm (¹/2 in) diameter. Cut into 3.5 cm (1 in) lengths and pinch centre of each one lightly between finger and thumb.

Place gnocchi on a lightly floured tea-towel, making sure they do not touch each other and stick together. Bring a large saucepan of salted water to a simmer and drop in gnocchi, a few at a time. Do not crowd pan. As soon as gnocchi float to surface, remove with a slotted spoon. When all are cooked and drained, stir into hot sauce and serve topped with grated Parmesan cheese. Serves 6.

NOTE: Potato gnocchi can be served simply tossed with melted butter and grated Parmesan cheese, or with Tomato Sauce (see page 460).

Herb Gnocchi

250 g (8 oz) fresh or frozen spinach; 125 g (4 oz) fresh sorrel leaves (if not available substitute same amount of extra spinach); I cup watercress sprigs; I cup parsley sprigs; I tbs chopped fresh chervil; I tbs chopped fresh tarragon; I tbs chopped fresh dill; 185 g (6 oz) ricotta cheese; 30 g (I oz) butter, cut into small pieces; salt and freshly ground black pepper; ³/4 cup grated Parmesan cheese; 2 eggs, beaten; 2¹/2 tbs flour; melted butter to serve (optional).

Wash and drain spinach, sorrel, watercress and parsley (if using frozen spinach, allow to thaw and do not wash). Boil ¹/2 cup water in a large saucepan, add spinach, sorrel, watercress and parsley and boil for 4 minutes. Drain well, squeezing out as much water as possible, and chop finely. Add chervil, tarragon and dill. Stir mixture in a saucepan over a low heat for several minutes to dry out as much as possible. This gives a good dry mixture for shaping gnocchi. Beat ricotta cheese until smooth and add to green mixture with butter, salt and pepper. Stir in one third of the Parmesan cheese. Remove pan from heat. Beat in eggs and flour until smooth. Pour into a shallow dish and leave, uncovered, in refrigerator overnight.

After chilling, mixture should be firm enough to handle; if it is not, add a little more sifted flour but not too much or gnocchi will be heavy. Heat a large pan of salted water to just below simmering point. Form mixture into egg-shaped gnocchi by using 2 teaspoons and rolling very lightly on a floured board. Drop gnocchi in batches into water, making certain they do not stick together. When they float to the surface, after 4–5 minutes, lift them out with a slotted spoon and drain on a clean cloth. Test one to make sure they are cooked enough. Keep drained gnocchi warm in a heated serving dish while you cook remainder.

Sprinkle gnocchi with a little Parmesan cheese and serve with remaining Parmesan and a jug of melted butter. Serves 4.

GOAT'S MILK

This is more easily digestible than cow's milk, and is excellent for people who are allergic to cow's milk. Goat's milk cheeses are delicious, velvet-textured and fresh. They are found all over France and in countries around the Mediterranean. Goat's cheeses vary in flavour according to the region and the length of time taken for ripening, but most taste nutty and sweet. Garlic, chives and herbs can be used as flavourings.

GOLDEN SYRUP

This light, pale golden syrup is a by-product of sugar refining. It is used in cakes, puddings, sweet sauces, confectionery, tart fillings and gingerbreads. See recipes.

See also *Treacle*.

Golden Syrup Dumplings

**2 cups self-raising flour; pinch salt;
45 g (1¹/₂ oz) butter; 2 eggs, beaten; little milk.**

**SYRUP: 2 cups water; ¹/₃ cup sugar;
2 tbs golden syrup; 30 g (1 oz) butter.**

Sift flour and salt and rub in butter. Add eggs and stir in with a knife, adding enough milk to make a soft dough. Divide dough into 12 pieces and roll into balls. In a large saucepan, heat water with sugar and golden syrup, stirring until sugar dissolves. Add butter and bring to the boil. Place dumplings in syrup, cover and simmer for 20 minutes without lifting lid. Serve dumplings at once, with syrup spooned over them. Serve with custard or cream. Serves 6.

Golden Sponge Pudding

**125 g (4 oz) butter; ¹/₂ cup caster sugar; 2 eggs;
1 cup self-raising flour; 2–3 tbs milk;
6–8 tbs golden syrup.**

Cream butter with sugar. Beat in eggs and stir in flour. Add sufficient milk to lighten mixture, which should be soft enough to drop lightly from a spoon. Put golden syrup in bottom of greased 4-cup pudding basin. Spoon mixture into basin, cover and steam for 2 hours. Turn out on to a heated serving dish and serve with thick cream and more hot syrup if you wish. Serves 6.

GOOSE

A festive bird, which is traditionally eaten at Christmas, Michaelmas (29 September) or Martinmas (11 November).

A young roast goose makes succulent eating, though if there is any doubt about tenderness it is better to braise the bird in the same manner as duck. The meat is rich and goose releases quite a lot of fat during cooking, so roast goose is usually stuffed with a sharp sage-and-onion or fruit stuffing. Many cooks prefer to bake the stuffing separately with some of the fat that runs from the goose, and to place an apple and some aromatic vegetables or herbs inside the bird – these flavourings are not served with it.

A pliable breastbone is the sign of a young goose, and a good bird should have a plump breast and a creamy-colour. As the bird has a large, bony frame, allow 500–700 g (1–1¹/₂ lb) uncooked weight per serving. A 3.5 kg (8 lb) goose will serve 6; a 4.5 kg (10 lb) one will serve 8.

Roast Goose

**1 young goose; salt and freshly ground black pepper;
2 apples, halved; 1 onion, halved;
3–4 fresh leaves sage, or ¹/₄ tsp dried;
1 tbs oil; 2 tbs flour; ¹/₄ cup brandy.**

Remove excess fat from inside goose and press or cut oil sacs at base of tail to empty them. Wipe bird inside and out with a damp towel and rub inside and out with salt and pepper. Place apples, onion and sage in cavity; sew up opening or close with poultry pins laced with string. Truss goose: tuck wing tips under back, pull loose skin of neck to back and fasten these with small skewers. Tie ends of legs together with string, drawing them close to tail. Prick breast all over with a skewer and dry bird well. Brush a roasting tin with the oil and place over high heat. Dust goose with flour and place in tin, turning to sear all over. Warm brandy, set alight and pour over bird. (This adds flavour and also sears off any remaining pin feathers.)

Place goose, breast up, on a rack in the tin, cover loosely with foil and roast in a preheated moderate oven (180°C/350°F) for 25 minutes per 500 g (1 lb) or until juice runs clear when a fine skewer is inserted between top of leg and body. Remove fat with a spoon or bulb baster as it accumulates, and remove foil for last 30 minutes to give goose a good golden colour. For a crisp skin, increase heat to very hot (220°C/425°F) 10 minutes before end of cooking time, and flick a little ice water over breast once or twice during this time. Leave goose on a heated platter in a warm place for 20 minutes before carving. Serves 6.

NOTE: The goose may be loosely stuffed with a mixture such as Apple, Prune and Nut Stuffing (see page 514), or stuffing may be baked separately with some of the fat that runs from goose. Any leftover fat, lifted from the chilled pan juice, is delicious spread on bread or used for frying potatoes.

GOOSEBERRY

A summer fruit that can have red, yellow or green berries that are either sweet or tart. Gooseberries are grown in cool climates and are widely used in the *g*

northern countries of Europe. In English home-cooking, gooseberries are used in tarts, desserts, jams, jellies and sauces, or poached in syrup flavoured with elder-flower. Gooseberry Sauce is traditionally served with mackerel, but is good with any oily-fleshed fish, and with roast duck or roast pork. Gooseberry Fool (see page 157) is also a delicious favourite for dessert.

If you cannot buy or grow fresh gooseberries, canned or frozen ones can be used for tart fillings, sauces and fools.

Gooseberry Sauce

250 g (8 oz) fresh gooseberries, or 2 cups drained canned gooseberries; 2 tsp caster sugar; 60 g (2 oz) butter; 1 tbs flour; 1 cup hot water; 1/2 tsp ground ginger; salt and freshly ground white pepper; 1/4 tsp nutmeg.

If using fresh gooseberries, top and tail them, cover with cold water and simmer gently until tender. Purée drained fresh or canned gooseberries and sweeten with sugar. Melt half the butter in a small saucepan, stir in flour and pour on hot water. Stir until boiling and simmer for 2 minutes. Remove from heat, stir in remaining butter and then gooseberry purée. Finish with ground ginger, salt, pepper and nutmeg. Serve hot with baked or poached mackerel, mullet, tailor or other oily-fleshed fish, or with roast duck or pork. Makes about ¾ cup.

GOUGÈRE

From Burgundy in France, a gougère is a savoury cheese-flavoured choux pastry ring that may be cut into slices and served with drinks, served plain and offered as a light meal with a salad, or made more elaborate with a meat, seafood or chicken filling as a main dish. The smaller bite-sized 'gougères' are the perfect food to serve with drinks, especially a glass of red wine.

1 cup plain flour, sifted; pinch each of salt, pepper and nutmeg; 1 cup water; 125 g (4 oz) unsalted butter, cut into small pieces; 1 tsp sugar; 1/2 tsp salt; 4 eggs; 125 g (4 oz) Gruyère cheese, half grated, the rest cut into small dice; a little beaten egg.

Place the water, salt, pepper and nutmeg with the but-ter in a saucepan. Bring to the boil, ensuring that the butter has melted by the time the water boils. Remove from the heat and add the sifted flour and sugar, all at once. Incorporate quickly and thoroughly with a wooden spoon and continue beating until the mixture balls around the spoon and leaves the sides of the pan.

Remove from the heat and allow to cool a minute or so before beating in the eggs, one at a time. Beat each egg fully into the mixture before proceeding with the next. Fold in the grated cheese and put the mixture into a piping bag fitted with a 1 cm (½ in) plain tube.

Grease and flour a baking tray and mark a 20 cm (8 in) circle on it. Pipe a circle of pastry on the tray, following the outline, then pipe another circle on top of the first. Brush with beaten egg and stud with the diced cheese. Bake in a preheated very hot oven (220°C/430°F) for 25-30 minutes or until well risen, crisp and golden-brown. Serve warm, cut into thin slices. For a lunch dish, fill centre with Chicken à la King (page 79), creamed seafood or any savoury mixture desired and cut Gougère in wedges to serve. Serves 4–6.

GOUGERES: Spoon small balls of the mixture on a buttered baking tray. Prick a piece of diced cheese into each puff, brush with a little beaten egg and bake in a very hot oven (220°C/430°F) for 20 minutes until risen and golden. Serve piping hot. Make ahead by shaping on to baking paper-lined tray and freezing the uncooked gougères. When they are firm and frozen they can be transferred into freezer bags ready for baking any time. Gougères become cheese 'beignets' when deep-fried until puffed and golden. Makes 30.

GOULASH (GULYAS)

The Hungarian word *gulyas* means 'herdsman's stew'. Goulash is popular all over the world, and in Hungary is regarded as the national meat dish. It is an enticingly rich stew that always contains meat, usually beef or veal, onions and sweet or spicy paprika. Goulash should never be thickened except with the use of diced potato. The meat is best cut into large pieces, about 5 cm (2 in), to prevent breaking up during the long slow cooking process, and the paprika should not be cooked over high heat without liquid as the heat turns it bitter. Sour cream should be served in a bowl on the table for the diners to help themselves.

Hungarian Goulash

2 tbs lard; 4 onions, finely chopped; 2 cloves garlic, finely chopped; 1.5 kg (3 lb) veal neck chops or steaks, cut into 5 cm (2 in) cubes; 1 tbs paprika; 2 green peppers, cored, seeded and chopped; 2 tomatoes, peeled and chopped; salt and freshly ground black pepper.

TO SERVE: noodles; sour cream.

Heat lard in a flameproof casserole and add onions and garlic. Cover and cook gently for about 10 minutes or until soft and translucent, stirring occasionally. Add veal cubes and sauté until golden. Reduce heat, sprinkle with paprika and cook very gently for about 10 minutes. Add green peppers and tomatoes. Bring to the boil, cover and cook goulash in a preheated slow oven (150°C/300°F) for about 2 hours or until the meat is tender. Season with salt and pepper. Serve with buttered noodles and a bowl of sour cream handed separately. Serves 6–8.

GRANITA (GRANITE)

Granita and *spumone* are the Italian names for the soft, water ices which are also called sorbets or sherbets elsewhere, though they are unlike some sorbets. Granita should have a slightly granular texture; it can be made from sweetened fruit juices, soft fruit or coffee.

See also *Ices, Sorbets, Granite* and *Sherbets*.

Granita die Caffé (Coffee Water Ice)

150 g (5 oz) freshly ground Continental roast coffee; 6 tbs sugar; 4¼ cups boiling water.

TO SERVE: whipped cream;
extra ground coffee (optional).

Put coffee and sugar into a warmed earthenware jug and pour boiling water over. Cover jug, stand in a saucepan of boiling water and leave to infuse off the heat for 20–30 minutes. Cool. When cold, strain through a filter paper. Pour into a shallow ice cream tray and freeze, without stirring, until frozen to a granular but solid mush. Serve in tall glasses, topped with whipped cream and a sprinkling of ground coffee. Serves 4–6.

GRAPES

Grapes from the vine have been celebrated down the centuries as much for their decorative qualities as for the pleasure of eating them. A fine bunch, served at the end of a meal with creamy cheese or, in the Italian way, on ice, has an air of luxury and refreshes the eye as well as the palate.

When buying grapes, look for those which are fully ripe but still fresh. Dark grapes should have lost any tinge of green, and white grapes should be just beginning to show an amber tone. All varieties should be plump, with a bloom on the skin, and be firmly attached to the stem. Stems should not be withered, though they should be showing some brown. Store grapes unwashed on a plate, loosely covered with plastic wrap, in the refrigerator.

Canned grapes are also available and make an attractive addition to many sweet or savoury dishes.

WAYS TO USE GRAPES

- Chilled grapes are a perfect picnic dessert – carry them in a covered container with a few ice cubes.
- Use grapes in fruit salads, bowls and platters; serve them on ice or with creamy cheese at the end of a meal.
- Grapes combine well with poultry, ham or crab in main course salads, and with ingredients such as apples, pears, watercress, hearts of palm, melon, celery, cottage cheese, walnuts or endive in first-course or side salads.
- They also make a good garnish or sauce for hot ham, tongue or game birds and for fish, particularly sole. A grape garnish gives the name *véronique* to a dish.

TO PEEL GRAPES: Most grapes can be peeled easily with the fingers or a small knife. If they prove difficult, dip them in boiling water while you count to 4, before peeling.

TO SEED GRAPES: The seeds are easily flipped out with the point of a knife if grapes are halved. If you want to keep grapes whole, push the prongs of a bobby-pin into a cork and use the other end to hook out seeds through the stem end of the grapes.

FROSTED GRAPES: One of the prettiest decorations for a holiday cake, dessert or fruit bowl. Beat 1 egg white just until frothy and brush over a bunch of grapes, coating each fruit. Dredge with caster sugar, turning to cover all over, shake off excess and dry on a wire rack. See recipes.

Grape Jelly

underripe grapes; sugar.

Put grapes into a heavy saucepan with just enough water to prevent scorching. Stir and crush. Stew over gentle heat until juice runs freely, then strain through a colander lined with several layers of cheesecloth and set over a bowl. Do not press grapes, just allow juice to drip through slowly. Chill juice, then measure it by transferring with a cup measure from the bowl into a saucepan. Do not use sediment. Add ¾ cup sugar for every cup of juice. Stir over heat until sugar has dissolved, then boil rapidly until a few drops of the mixture, dropped on to a chilled plate, will jell as they cool. Pour into clean, warm jars and seal.

Grape Ice Cream

A simple and delicate ice cream, the colour of lilacs.

2½ cups cream; 1¼ cups unsweetened grape juice; ⅓ cup caster sugar; little fresh lemon or lime juice.

Mix cream, grape juice and stir until sugar has dissolved. Add lemon or lime juice to taste. Freeze in an electric ice cream maker or sorbetière (see *Ice Cream*). Serves 6.

Grapes Brûlée

3 cups seedless white grapes (sultana grapes); 1½ cups sour cream; ¼ tsp vanilla; ¾ cup firmly packed brown sugar.

Arrange grapes in an even layer in a 23 cm (9 in) heatproof glass pie plate or other shallow dish. Mix sour cream and vanilla, and spread over grapes, covering them. Chill for at least 2 hours. Cover with a layer of brown sugar so that none of the cream shows through, then place dish under a preheated very hot grill until sugar melts – watch carefully and remove before it blackens. Cool, then refrigerate for several hours before serving. Serves 6–8.

GRAVLAX (MARINATED SALMON)

A dish synonymous with Scandinavia, fresh fish, traditionally salmon, is cured for 3 days before serving. It is often accompanied by Mustard and Dill Sauce (see page 290), or mustard-flavoured sour cream. It is a tradition to pack the prepared fish in the snow; however, modern refrigeration has largely replaced this practice.

Gravlax (Marinated Salmon)

750 g (1¹/₂ lb) fillets fresh salmon, salmon trout or large trout; ¹/₄ cup sugar; ¹/₄ cup coarse salt; 1 tsp white peppercorns, cracked; 1 large bunch fresh dill; ¹/₄ cup Cognac or brandy; ¹/₄ cup dry white wine.

Place 1 fillet skin side down on a plate, sprinkle thickly with sugar, salt and white pepper, cover with plenty of dill sprigs and press seasonings on to fish. Cover with second fillet of fish, skin side uppermost. Sandwich remaining fillets in the same way. Select a ceramic or glass dish just large enough to hold the fish, pour in Cognac or brandy and white wine and place fillets in it, with seasonings sandwiched between them. Cover with plastic wrap, weight with a 1 kg (2 lb) weight, and let marinate in refrigerator for 3 days. Turn fish every 12 hours, basting with marinade and separating fillets a little to baste fish inside. After 3 days remove weight and plastic wrap. Transfer with a slotted spoon to a cutting board. Separate fillets, scrape off dill, and cut fish horizontally into 5 mm (¹/₄ in) slices, cutting it off without the skin. Place slices on black bread, top with a swirl of sour cream mixed with mustard and a sprig of dill, or serve with Mustard and Dill Sauce (see page 290). Serves 6–8 as an appetiser.

GRAVY

A sauce made in the pan from the browned, coagulated juices left after meat is roasted or pan-fried. It is made by deglazing, that is by adding liquid to the pan and scraping and stirring the flavoursome bits into it as it boils. The liquid used may be vegetable cooking water, stock, wine, cream or a mixture of these.

A good gravy should be well flavoured and light-bodied so that it 'shows the meat'. It is usually rather scant since the rich meat flavours are lost if too much liquid is added. A thin or clear gravy (in French, *jus*), achieves its body by reduction and perhaps a little butter swirled in at the end.

Purists frown on the use of flour to thicken a gravy, but since a great many people like gravy made this way, and since it is, after all, simply a roux-based sauce like many respected classics, it seems unreasonable to decry it. The points to watch are that the flour is browned slowly to give good flavour and colour and that you use just enough to give body, without making the gravy heavy and blanketing.

For a gravy which is lightly thickened but still clear, make *jus lié* by thickening clear gravy with a little arrowroot, or add body with two or three spoonfuls of vegetable purée, (see below).

Clear Gravy: Put a few slices of onion or carrot under meat in roasting tin, if desired, to strengthen flavour of the juices. After meat is cooked, transfer it to a heated platter and keep warm. Heat tin gently on top of stove, allowing juices and sediment to colour without burning. Pour fat off slowly without disturbing sediment.

Off the heat, add 1–2 cups hot vegetable water or stock and stir thoroughly, scraping up sediment. Return to heat and boil until reduced by about a quarter, stirring and scraping several more times. Add any juices that have escaped from meat. Season, strain and serve very hot. If desired, a walnut of butter may be swirled into the gravy, off the heat, at the last moment.

Wine Gravy: Follow recipe for Clear Gravy, above, using half vegetable water or stock and half red or white wine as the liquid. Or make clear gravy, using all stock and add a glass of dry sherry before reducing gravy.

Cream Gravy: Follow recipe for Clear Gravy, above, using cream or a mixture of cream and stock or vegetable water as the liquid.

Jus Lié: Follow recipe for Clear Gravy, above. Mix a little arrowroot to a cream with cold water, using 2 tsp arrowroot per cup of gravy. Pour into boiling gravy, stirring until it is clear and lightly thickened. A spoonful of Madeira, port or brandy may be added per each cup gravy, simmer for a few minutes longer before serving.

Vegetable-thickened Gravy: To make a thickened gravy without starch, follow recipe for Clear Gravy, above, and stir in some vegetable purée at the end. Use 2–3 tbs purée per cup gravy. For the purée, choose a mixture from mushrooms, cauliflower, spinach, onions, carrots, celery and canned or fresh tomatoes. Simmer in a little stock, or water and a stock cube, with a few fresh herbs or a pinch of dried herbs, and drain well. Purée in a blender or food processor, then sieve. Any leftover purée may be frozen in small portions for future use.

Thickened Gravy: Put a few slices of onion or carrot under meat in roasting tin, if desired, to strengthen flavour of the juices. After meat is cooked, transfer it to a heated platter and keep warm. Slowly pour off all but 2 tbs fat from tin, leaving sediment undisturbed. Off the heat, sprinkle 1 tbs flour into tin and blend well with fat. Place over low heat, stirring constantly, until mixture is nut-brown. Slowly pour in 1–1¹/₂ cups vegetable water or stock, stirring constantly until smooth. Stir until boiling, then add any juices that have escaped from meat and simmer 5 minutes. Season, strain to remove lumps and serve very hot.

Thickened Wine Gravy or Cream Gravy: Prepare by varying liquid used, in the same way as for the Wine and Cream variations of Clear Gravy.

Onion Gravy: After meat is cooked, pour off all but 2 tbs fat, add 1 onion, finely chopped, and sauté until softened. Add 1 tbs flour and 1 tsp dry mustard, stir on low heat until browned. Stir in ¾ cup beef stock; ½ cup flat beer, ½ tsp sugar and 1 tsp chopped fresh thyme, or ¼ tsp dried. Stir until boiling, simmer 5 minutes and season to taste with salt and freshly ground black pepper. Use for sausages or pork chops.

Mushroom Gravy: Follow recipe for Thickened Gravy, above, but pour off all fat from pan, add 2 tbs butter and sauté 1 cup sliced mushrooms before blending in flour. Use cream or a mixture of cream and stock or vegetable water as the liquid. Use for beef steaks, pork or veal chops, meat loaves or hamburgers.

GREEN GODDESS DRESSING

A salad dressing with a subtle piquancy which complements seafood. Try serving Green Goddess Dressing with prawns, lobster or crabmeat arranged on a bed of watercress for a luxurious entrée, as part of a cold buffet table.

Green Goddess Dressing

I cup Mayonnaise (page 256); ¹/₂ cup sour cream;
¹/₃ cup chopped parsley; 2 tbs snipped chives;
I tbs lemon juice; 2 tbs anchovy paste;
2 tbs tarragon vinegar;
salt and freshly ground black pepper.

Combine mayonnaise and sour cream, then add remaining ingredients and mix well. Makes about 2 cups.

GREEN PEPPER

See *Peppers, Sweet*.

GRIBICHE SAUCE

Use this lovely hard-boiled egg mayonnaise with fish or cold meats.

Gribiche Sauce

3 hard-boiled eggs, halved; ¹/₂ tsp salt;
¹/₄ tsp white pepper; I tsp Dijon mustard;
I¹/₂ cups olive oil; ¹/₂ cup vinegar;
¹/₂ cup finely chopped sour gherkins and capers,
mixed together and drained of moisture;
2 tbs finely chopped mixed fresh parsley,
chives, tarragon and chervil.

Separate egg yolks from whites; cut whites in julienne (matchstick) strips and set aside. Mash egg yolks and add salt, pepper and mustard. Add, very gradually and while beating constantly, the olive oil and vinegar. Stir in egg white strips, gherkins, capers and mixed herbs. Makes about 3 cups.

GRIDDLE CAKES (GIRDLE CAKES)

These little flat cakes were originally cooked on the griddle or girdle irons which gave them their names. Today, they are cooked on a griddle iron, a hotplate or in a frying pan. Griddle cakes can be sweet or savoury and eaten at any meal or as a snack during the day. They are usually based on a batter mixture of varying thickness, according to the type of griddle cake being made.

There are as many varieties of griddle cakes as there are different types of flour or meal – Russian Blini (see page 40), are made with buckwheat flour, Scottish Oatmeal Bannocks (see page 22), and Australian Pikelets (see page 366), with refined wheat flour. Each is a type of griddle cake.

When you cook griddle cakes, make sure the iron, hotplate or frying pan is hot enough. Test by sprinkling the heated surface with a few drops of water; if the drops dance, the heat is right, and if they splatter and break up, it is too hot. The iron can be greased or not, depending on recipe and batter mixture. **See recipes.**

See also *Pancakes* and *Flapjacks*.

Irish Potato Cakes

500 g (I lb) old potatoes, cooked,
mashed and kept warm; 60 g (2 oz) butter;
salt and freshly ground black pepper;
about I cup flour; butter to serve.

Beat potatoes with butter. Season with salt and pepper, and work in enough flour to bind into a dough. Divide dough in half. Place on a floured surface and pat out into 2 rounds, about 1 cm (½ in) thick. Cut each round into 8 triangles. Grease and heat a griddle, hotplate or frying pan and cook potato cakes for about 5 minutes on each side until brown. Split in 2 and spread with butter. For breakfast, serve very hot with sausages, bacon, grilled tomatoes or fried eggs. Makes 16.

Wholemeal Griddle Cakes

An American breakfast favourite.

3/4 cup self-raising flour; 3/4 cup wholemeal
self-raising flour; I tsp salt; 2 tbs sugar; 2 eggs,
separated; I cup milk; 30 g (I oz) butter, melted.

Sift flours with salt and sugar. Beat egg yolks with milk and melted butter. Whisk egg whites until they stand in peaks. Stir milk mixture into flour, then fold in egg whites. Grease and heat a griddle, hotplate or frying pan. Place tablespoonfuls of mixture on pan and cook for about 3 minutes on each side or until brown. Serve hot at breakfast with butter, maple syrup and grilled sausages or bacon. Makes about 14. **NOTE:** In America, these griddle cakes are served in stacks, with butter melting in-between. Allow about 4 to a stack.

g

Crisp Corn Griddle Cakes

These are good served at breakfast with bacon and grilled tomatoes.

$^1/_2$ cup plain flour; $^2/_3$ cup yellow cornmeal (polenta); 1 tsp salt; $^1/_2$ tsp bicarbonate of soda; 1 tsp baking powder; $^1/_4$ cup self-raising flour; 60 g (2 oz) butter, melted; 2 cups buttermilk; 1 egg, beaten.

Sift together plain flour, cornmeal, salt, bicarbonate of soda, baking powder and self-raising flour. Blend together the butter, buttermilk and egg. Make a well in the centre of the cornmeal mixture and pour in the liquid. Stir from the centre with a wooden spoon until dry ingredients have been moistened and you have a smooth batter. Do not overmix. Drop spoonfuls of batter on to a hot preheated griddle or frying pan, making cakes about 10 cm (4 in) in diameter. When undersides are brown, turn over and cook the other sides. If batter thickens while cakes are cooking, stir in a little extra buttermilk. Serve straight from the pan. Makes about 10.

GUACAMOLE

A savoury dip or spread of Mexican origin now famous throughout the world. The superb combination of creamy avocado laced with lemon and chilli is at its best with hot corn chips or crackers. It also adds zing served with cold chicken or seafood.

Guacamole

2 ripe avocados, peeled and stoned; 1 clove garlic, crushed; $^1/_4$ tsp salt; 1 small onion, finely chopped; 2 tsp lemon or lime juice; 1 small fresh chilli, seeded and chopped, or few drops Tabasco sauce.

Cut avocado flesh into chunks and blend at high speed until smooth or push through a nylon sieve. Add garlic, salt, onion, lemon or lime juice and chilli or Tabasco, and blend a further 30 seconds. Transfer to a serving dish. Makes about 1 cup.

NOTE: If you prepare guacamole a few hours before it is needed, leave an avocado stone in mixture to prevent browning, cover and refrigerate. Remove stone before serving.

GUAVA

A tropical fruit with a thick rind and soft flesh, embedded with a mass of seeds. It is green when underripe, yellow or pink-flushed when ripe. There is also a red variety. The flavour is light, sweet, a little musky. Guavas can be eaten fresh with sugar and cream, stewed or made into jam or a jelly which is served in the same way as redcurrant jelly with meat or game. They are also made into one of the best of the fruit 'cheeses' (see Quince Cheese, page 405).

Guava Jelly

slightly underripe guavas, cut up; rind and pith 1 lime or lemon; sugar; lime or lemon juice.

Put guavas, lime or lemon rind and pith into a saucepan with enough water to cover. Boil until fruit is very soft. Strain through a colander lined with 2 thicknesses of cheesecloth and set over a bowl. Do not squeeze or press fruit, just allow juice to drip through slowly. Measure juice and add 1 cup of sugar for each cup of juice, and juice of 1 lime or lemon for each litre (4 cups) of juice. Bring to the boil, stirring until sugar has dissolved, then boil until a few drops of the mixture, dropped on to a chilled plate, will jell as they cool. Pour into clean, hot jars and seal.

GUGELHOPF (KUGELHUPF)

The yeast cake of Alsace from which babas and savarins were developed. Gugelhopf is studded with rum-soaked currants and is cooked in a distinctive fluted ring mould.

Gugelhopf

$^1/_3$ cup slivered almonds; $^1/_2$ cup currants; $^1/_2$ cup raisins; 3 tbs rum; $^3/_4$ cup milk; 30 g (1 oz) compressed yeast; 3 cups flour; pinch salt; $1^1/_2$ tbs caster sugar; 3 eggs, lightly beaten; 125 g (4 oz) butter, melted and slightly cooled; sifted icing sugar.

Generously butter a 20 cm (8 in) gugelhopf tin or fluted ring tin and press slivered almonds into butter. Refrigerate until needed. Soak currants and raisins in rum. Warm milk to blood heat, pour on to yeast and stir until dissolved. Sift flour and salt into a warm bowl. Make a well in centre and add milk mixture, sugar, eggs and melted butter. Beat well and add soaked fruits. Pour well-mixed batter into prepared tin (tin should be three quarters full).

Cover with a damp cloth and stand in a warm place for 20–30 minutes or until mixture has risen to 2.5 cm (1 in) below the top. Bake in a preheated moderately hot oven (190°C/375°F) for 50–60 minutes or until a fine skewer inserted in centre comes out clean. Stand a few minutes, then turn out on to a wire rack to cool.

Dust with icing sugar and serve in slices with coffee or white wine.

NOTE: Dry yeast can be used. See *Yeast Cookery*.

GUMBO

Creole cookery, centred on New Orleans in the USA, is a blend of Spanish, French, Negro and Indian influences. A gumbo is a Creole soup-stew which uses okra for flavouring and thickening – the word 'gumbo' comes from an African word for okra. A gumbo may be based on chicken, pork or ham, seafood or a mixture of these, but it will always have the typical satin-smooth texture which okra's jelly-like juice provides.

Chicken and Oyster Gumbo

1 x 1.5 kg (3 lb) chicken, cut into 8 pieces;
3 tbs bacon fat or butter; 1 onion, chopped;
250 g (8 oz) smoked ham, diced; 4 cups sliced okra;
4 large ripe tomatoes, peeled and chopped,
or 1 x 425 g can tomatoes, chopped, with their juice;
1 bay leaf; 3 cups boiling water; salt and freshly
ground black pepper; dash cayenne;
12 large oysters; hot boiled rice to serve.

Brown chicken pieces all over in bacon fat or butter. Remove chicken from pan and set aside. Add onion, ham and okra, and stir over medium heat 5 minutes. Add tomatoes, bay leaf, water, salt, pepper and cayenne. Return chicken to pan, cover and simmer 45 minutes or until chicken is tender. Adjust seasoning, add oysters and simmer 1 minute. Serve immediately over rice in soup bowls. Serves 6.

h

HAM

The cured meat of the hind leg of the pig, ham is extremely versatile. It runs the gamut from being sliced for a filling in a sandwich to a whole ham leg, beautifully glazed, holding pride of place on any celebration table. There are many different types of ham throughout the world depending on the method of curing, the breed of pig and the feed they eat.

Ham can be purchased as a whole leg on the bone, in smaller cuts with or without the bone, or sliced. It is also canned, or pressed into long boneless rounds of rectangles for slicing.

TYPES OF HAM

Coppa is the cured, raw shoulder and neck part of the pig. It is fattier and less expensive than prosciutto, and is excellent in recipes calling for raw ham.

Double-smoked ham has a particularly rich smoky flavour as the name implies, from extra smoking.

Ham steaks are popular pan-fried or grilled on the family barbecue and served with pineapple slices and fruit chutneys.

Prosciutto Crudo is a delicate raw ham which can be purchased at specialist delicatessens. It is served as an entrée, sliced paper-thin, with fresh melon slices, fresh figs or simply with a pat of country butter.

Shoulder (picnic shoulder), loin or forehock meat can be cured in a similar way to ham, which gives it a similar flavour. It can be used in recipes specifying chopped, diced, minced or sliced ham.

Wiltshire ham or gammon is cured as part of the whole pig before being divided into cuts.

WAYS TO USE LEFTOVER HAM

- *Croquettes*, *Rissoles*, *Fritters* (see separate entries for recipes).
- Serve slices of ham with fried, poached or scrambled eggs.
- Mash hard-boiled egg yolks with sour cream and minced ham, and pile into egg white halves for stuffed eggs.
- As fillings for *Vol-au-vent*, *Croustades* or *Tartlets*. Add ½ cup finely diced ham to 1 cup Mornay or Béchamel Sauce (see page 456): stir in 1 tbs finely chopped parsley and season with pepper. Pile into selected bread or pastry cases and warm in a preheated moderate oven (180°C/350°F) for about 15 minutes. Makes sufficient filling for 15 small individual cases.
- Add ham strips to chicken, pasta, potato or rice salads with mayonnaise dressing (see page 256).
- Mince ham with a little onion and season with fruit, chutney or mustard. Spread on buttered bread or in bread rolls.
- Add small chunks of ham to pea, potato, pumpkin or lentil soups, and chicken or corn chowder. See recipes.

See also *Prosciutto*.

Baked Glazed Ham

A traditional recipe for baked ham.

1 x 7 kg (14 lb) cured leg of ham.

GLAZE: 1 ½ cups firmly packed brown sugar; 2 tsp dry mustard; 3/4 cup clear honey; whole cloves; ½ cup orange juice.

Cut a scallop pattern around thick end of ham shank and ease skin away from fat. Turn ham over and ease away rest of skin, which should come off in one piece. Place ham, fat side uppermost, on a rack in a roasting tin containing 3.5 cm (½ in) of water. Cover tin with foil, making it as airtight as possible, and bake in a preheated moderately slow oven (160°C/325°F) for 2½ hours. Remove from oven and pour off liquid in tin. Using a sharp knife, score fat with 5 mm (¼ in) deep diagonal cuts, first one way, then opposite way to form a diamond pattern.

GLAZE: Mix sugar, mustard and honey together and using a brush spread half the mixture over ham. Stud each diamond with a clove. Mix remaining glaze with orange juice. Increase oven temperature to hot (200°C/400°F) and bake ham for a further 30–40 minutes, basting it every 10 minutes with remaining glaze. Serve hot or cold. Serves 20–25.

VARIATIONS

Apply any one of the following glazes in the same way as in the preceding recipe and continue baking:

CIDER GLAZE: Combine 1 cup firmly packed brown sugar with 1 cup apple cider and spread over ham. Use extra ½ cup apple cider for basting.

APPLE SAUCE GLAZE: Combine 1 cup apple sauce or apple purée with 2 tbs prepared mustard and ½ cup honey, and spread over ham. Use ½ cup apple juice for basting.

MARMALADE GLAZE: Combine 1 cup orange marmalade with ¼ cup cider vinegar and ¼ tsp nutmeg, and spread over ham. Use ½ cup orange juice for basting.

PEACH NECTAR GLAZE: Combine 1 cup peach nectar with ½ cup honey and ¼ tsp cinnamon, and spread over ham. Use extra ½ cup peach nectar for basting if necessary.

Ham au Gratin

8 slices cooked ham; 2 tbs white wine; 1 cup Béchamel Sauce (page 456); 1 tsp French mustard; 2 tbs grated Parmesan cheese; 1 tbs dry breadcrumbs.

Place ham in a buttered ovenproof dish, overlapping slices. Moisten with white wine. Season béchamel sauce with mustard and 1 tbs of the cheese and spoon over ham. Mix remaining cheese and crumbs and scatter over the top. Bake in a preheated moderate oven (180°C/350°F) for 30 minutes. Serves 4.

Croissants with Ham and Cheese

Serve these next time you have a picnic and want a glamorous touch.

4 croissants, fresh or frozen;
4 thin slices cooked ham, or 8 slices prosciutto;
4 slices Emmenthal, Gruyère or Jarlsberg cheese.

Warm and crisp croissants in a preheated moderate oven (180°C/350°F). Using a serrated knife, slice through each croissant from the outer curve, but don't cut right through. Layer ham and cheese slices in the warm croissants, wrap in a clean tea-towel and then wrap tightly in several sheets of newspaper to retain warmth. They should keep warm for about 3 hours. Serves 2–4.

Baked Ginger Ham with Sweet Potato

I small sweet potato, peeled and thickly sliced;
2 ham steaks; I tsp butter; I tsp brown sugar;
¹/₄ tsp ground ginger; ¹/₄ cup fruit juice
(orange, pineapple, apricot).

Cook sweet potato in lightly salted boiling water until tender, about 10 minutes. Drain well. Place ham steaks in a flat casserole or pie dish and arrange sweet potato slices around them. Mix together butter, brown sugar and ginger, and spread over ham. Pour fruit juice around ham. Bake in a preheated hot oven (200°C/400°F) for 15 minutes, basting several times with juice. Serve with a green salad. Serves 2.

Ham with Orange and Chicory Salad

8–10 slices cooked ham; 3 heads chicory, sliced;
3 large oranges, peeled and sliced;
I medium onion, finely sliced;
¹/₂ cup Vinaigrette Dressing (page 442);
chopped parsley; 6–8 black olives to garnish.

Arrange sliced ham around edge of serving platter. Lightly toss chicory, orange and onion slices in vinaigrette and pile in centre. Sprinkle with chopped parsley and garnish with black olives. Serves 4–6.

HAMBURGER

A first-rate hamburger can stand comparison with its grand relation, a fine steak. Like steak, a good hamburger is juicy within, crusty outside and full of flavour. The first secret of success is to build flavour and moistness into the mixture, the second is to handle it lightly when shaping so that it holds together without compacting. If you want the inside rare, make the patties about 4 cm (1½ in) thick; for a well-cooked interior, make patties 2–2.5 cm (¾–1 in) thick. Cook a hamburger as you would a steak: whether pan-frying or grilling, sear the outside at high heat, then turn heat down to medium to finish cooking.

Basic Hamburgers

4 slices bread, crusts removed;
³/₄ cup fresh or evaporated milk;
I kg (2 lb) best quality minced steak;
2 tsp salt; freshly ground black pepper;
¹/₂ tsp dry mustard; ¹/₄ tsp Worcestershire sauce;
I small onion, grated or very finely chopped; 2 eggs.

Tear bread into pieces and soak in milk 10 minutes, then beat with a fork. Lightly mix together all ingredients except eggs, then stir in eggs with a fork. With wet hands, shape into 8 equal-size patties. Heat grill or pan, brush hamburgers with oil or butter and cook at high heat to sear the outsides, then turn down heat to medium and finish cooking. Pan-fry for a total of 4–6 minutes on each side, or grill for 7–10 minutes on each side for medium done. Serve, on buns or toast if desired, with a selection of garnishes or sauce of your choice. Serves 8.

VARIATIONS

HERBED HAMBURGERS: Add 1 tbs chopped fresh dill, thyme or other herbs, or 1 tsp dried, to Basic Hamburger mixture.

GARLIC HAMBURGERS: Add 1 fat clove garlic, crushed, and 2 tbs chopped parsley to Basic Hamburger mixture.

DEVILLED HAMBURGERS: Add 2 tbs tomato sauce; 1½ tsp prepared English mustard, 2 tsp lemon juice and a dash of Tabasco sauce to Basic Hamburger mixture.

STUFFED HAMBURGERS: Shape Basic Hamburger mixture into 16 thin patties. On 8 of the patties place one of the following: 1 tbs chopped, sautéed mushrooms, bacon or onion; small piece Cheddar, Swiss, Camembert or blue cheese; 1 tbs chopped, mixed apple, celery and walnuts; 1 canned anchovy fillet chopped with a few capers. Top with remaining patties and press edges to join.

HAMBURGER TOPPINGS

Top each freshly cooked hamburger with one of the following:

- A thick slice of sautéed tomato and 2–3 sautéed mushrooms threaded on a toothpick.

- 1 tsp sour cream or plain yogurt, seasoned with salt and pepper and sprinkled with snipped chives.
- A slice of Maître d'Hôtel, Anchovy or other flavoured butter (see *Butter*).
- A thin slice of raw onion, topped with a spoonful of Mayonnaise (see page 256) and a sprig of parsley.

SAUCES FOR HAMBURGERS

RED WINE SAUCE: Pan-fry hamburgers, remove and keep warm. Add 2 tbs chopped spring onions to pan and sauté 1 minute, then add ½ cup red wine. Boil rapidly 2 minutes, season with salt and pepper, remove from heat and swirl in 30 g (1 oz) butter. Pour over hamburgers and serve immediately.

STROGANOFF SAUCE: Pan-fry hamburgers, remove and keep warm. Add 1 small onion, finely chopped, to pan and sauté, stirring, 2 minutes. Add 125 g (4 oz) sliced mushrooms and cook, stirring, until limp. Stir in ½ cup sour cream. Season with salt and pepper, heat through and spoon over hamburgers. Sprinkle with paprika and serve immediately.

HARD SAUCE

A traditional accompaniment to Christmas Pudding and Mince Pies. It is also good with other steamed puddings and with baked apples. As the name suggests, it becomes firm when chilled. Hard sauce is also called Brandy or Rum Butter.

Hard Sauce

90 g (3 oz) unsalted butter; I cup icing sugar; sifted; I tbs brandy, rum, Grand Marnier or Cointreau, or more to taste; I egg white (optional).

Beat butter until creamy, then add sugar a little at a time, beating until white and fluffy. Add liquor gradually, beating constantly. If using egg white, beat until soft peaks form and fold in. Pile sauce into a bowl and chill. Makes about 2 cups.

NOTE: If liked, ½ cup ground almonds can be substituted for ¼ cup of the icing sugar, and 1 tsp vanilla can be used instead of the brandy, rum or liqueur.

HARE

Hare is akin to rabbit in flavour, though it is darker and more gamey. Young hare (up to 1 year old) is called 'leveret'; it may be roasted whole, or with fore and hind legs removed (saddle of hare), or forelegs only removed (baron of hare). It is often first marinated for a day or so before cooking as it tends to be dry, and is then roasted in the same way as rabbit. However, if there is any doubt about tenderness, hare is best casseroled or used for a pie.

The most famous hare dish, Jugged Hare (immortalised by Mrs Beeton with the purported advice 'first you must catch your hare'), used to be made by putting hare pieces, vegetables, herbs and port into a pot or jug and standing it in boiling water to cook. It was then thickened with the hare's blood. Nowadays it is more usual to braise the hare and to thicken the sauce with Beurre Manié (see page 35).

Casserole of Hare

I hare, jointed; seasoned flour; I tbs oil; 15 g (½ oz) butter; 125 g (4 oz) streaky bacon, rind removed and diced; 12 small onions; I stick celery, sliced; 2 carrots, sliced; I bouquet garni; ¼ cup port; I cup beef or game stock; juice I lemon; salt and freshly ground pepper; 1–2 tbs Beurre Manié (page 35); 1–2 tbs redcurrant jelly; fried croûtons to serve (see page 105).

MARINADE: I cup red wine, 2 tbs oil; I onion, finely chopped; I bay leaf; 3 cloves; 4–5 juniper berries, crushed; freshly ground black pepper.

Combine marinade ingredients, bring to the boil, cool and pour over hare. Marinate 12 hours, turning pieces occasionally. Remove hare; strain marinade and reserve liquid. Dry hare, dust with seasoned flour and brown in hot oil and butter in a flameproof casserole. Remove hare. Add bacon and vegetables to casserole and sauté until onions are coloured. Place hare on top of vegetables and add bouquet garni, port, stock, lemon juice and strained marinade. Season lightly with salt and pepper, bring to simmering point, cover tightly and bake in a preheated slow oven (150°C/300°F) for 2–3 hours or until hare is tender. Transfer hare, bacon and vegetables to a heated serving dish. Skim fat from liquid in casserole, discard bouquet garni and thicken a little with beurre manié. Stir in redcurrant jelly to taste, adjust seasoning and pour over hare. Garnish the casserole with croûtons and serve immediately. Serves 6.

HARICOT (OF MUTTON OR LAMB)

Despite the name, haricots (beans) are not a traditional ingredient in this ancient dish. The word 'haricot' here is thought to have come from the Old French word *halicoter*, to cut into morsels. The dish is a casserole of mutton or lamb with potatoes, turnips and onions.

Haricot of Mutton or Lamb

125 g (4 oz) fatty pork, diced; 750 g (1½ lb) lean stewing mutton or lamb, cut into bite-sized cubes; I medium onion, sliced; pinch sugar; 2 tbs flour; I clove garlic, crushed; 4 cups mutton or beef stock; 2 tbs tomato purée; I bouquet garni; salt and freshly ground black pepper; 4 medium potatoes, quartered; 2 small turnips, quartered; 24 tiny onions.

Put diced pork into a flameproof casserole and fry until fat runs and dice are browned. Remove pork with a slotted spoon. Add mutton or lamb and sliced onion to casserole and brown. Add sugar and allow it to caramelise, then sprinkle in the flour and stir until well mixed. Add garlic, then stock a little at a time, stirring until smoothly blended. Add tomato purée and bouquet garni, season lightly, cover and place casserole in a preheated moderate oven (180°C/350°F). Cook for 1 hour. Add vegetables and pork dice, and cook another hour or until meat is tender. Adjust seasoning, discard bouquet garni and serve. Serves 6.

HARICOT BEAN

See *Pulses: Dried Beans, Peas and Lentils.*

HARISSA

A hot chilli paste often eaten with couscous in northern African countries. It can be bought in jars and tubes but home-made harissa is fantastic. Try a little with grilled meats, in a soup or stew to which you want give a good spicing. Remember just a little goes a very long way.

Harissa

1 tbs coriander seeds; 2 tbs cumin seeds;
1 tbs peppercorns; 1 tsp ground cinnamon;
1 cup whole birds-eye chillies, stalks removed;
10 cloves garlic, peeled; 10 mint leaves;
1 bunch fresh coriander leaves, roots included;
1 tsp salt; 6 tbs olive oil.

Grind the coriander and cumin seeds and peppercorns in a food processor or blender. Add the cinnamon, chillies, garlic, mint, coriander and salt, and blend to a thick paste. Keep in a sterilised screw-top jar in the refrigerator. Makes $1\frac{1}{2}$ cups.

HASH

A dish made from a mixture of diced and usually cooked food; it is a marvellous way of using leftovers. Vegetables, meats, poultry or fish are mixed with sufficient sauce, gravy or cream to moisten, seasoned well and heated through. Serve hash on buttered toast, in a pastry shell, over rice or noodles, with creamy mashed potatoes or on its own.

Heavenly Hash is a sweet variation made using canned fruits. It is a superbly simple dessert to prepare and is always popular with children. See recipes.

Corned Beef and Potato Hash

2 tbs butter; 1 large onion, chopped;
2 sticks celery, chopped; 1 small green pepper,
cored, seeded and diced; 3 cups minced
corned beef; 2 cups diced cooked potatoes;
1 tbs Worcestershire sauce; 2 tbs chopped
parsley or chives; salt and freshly ground
black pepper; $\frac{1}{3}$–$\frac{2}{3}$ cup stock or cream;
6 hot poached eggs (optional).

Melt butter in a large saucepan, add onion, celery and green pepper and simmer very gently until tender. Stir in corned beef, potatoes, Worcestershire sauce, parsley or chives, salt and pepper. Stir over medium heat while gradually adding stock or cream. Cook until well blended and thoroughly heated. Place on a heated platter and serve topped with poached eggs, if using. Alternatively, sauté hash on a greased griddle or in a shallow-sided frying pan until well browned underneath. Remove carefully, folding like an omelette and roll on to a heated serving platter. Serves 6.

Heavenly Hash

1 x 310 g can mandarin segments;
1 x 280 g jar maraschino cherries;
1 x 425 g can pineapple pieces;
2 x 100 g packets marshmallows, one pink
and one white; $1\frac{1}{4}$ cups sour light cream;
$\frac{1}{4}$ tsp ground cardamom; $\frac{1}{4}$ tsp ground ginger;
1 tsp grated orange rind; 1 tbs Cointreau or
Grand Marnier (optional).

Drain fruit. Halve marshmallows and toss carefully with fruit. Whip sour cream with remaining ingredients. Fold cream mixture through fruit and marshmallows. Chill for about 2 hours. Serves 6.
NOTE: If sour light cream is not available, use fresh cream and add 1 tbs lemon juice to the fruit mixture.

HAZELNUT (COBNUT OR FILBERT)

The shiny brown shell of the hazelnut encloses a juicy, milky kernel much used in puddings, cakes and ice creams, especially in European cookery. The mealy texture of the nuts makes them perfect for use in Continental tortes (see *Tortes*), in which the ground nuts take the place of flour.

Hazelnuts can be eaten on their own, roasted or freshly shelled, and their texture should be crisp and brittle. They are delicious in mushroom sauce, or tossed through a watercress salad, and as an extra bonus are highly nutritious, being rich in protein, fat, iron and thiamine. Hazelnuts can be purchased packaged or in the shell from most supermarkets, health food stores and good delicatessens.

TO SKIN HAZELNUTS: Place kernels on a baking tray in a preheated moderate oven (180°C/350°F) for 5–6 minutes, turning once. Put the warm nuts in a paper bag or a clean cloth and rub against one another to break the skin fibres, and remove the skins from the kernels.
TO ROAST HAZELNUTS: Spread skinned kernels on a baking tray and roast in a preheated hot oven

(200°C/400°F) for 7–10 minutes, stirring frequently to prevent scorching.

TO GRIND HAZELNUTS: Remove skins first and use a special nut grinder or a blender.

TO SALT HAZELNUTS: Skin kernels if desired. Roast as above and add 1 tsp salt to 1 cup kernels while still warm. See recipes.

See also *Galette*.

Hazelnut and Mushroom Sauce

60 g (2 oz) butter; ¹/₂ cup halved hazelnuts; 1 small onion, finely chopped; 6 mushroom caps, finely sliced; 2 tbs flour; 2 cups chicken stock; salt and freshly ground black pepper.

Melt butter and add hazelnuts, onion and mushrooms. Stir over gentle heat until just browned. Remove from pan with a slotted spoon. Mix flour into butter remaining in pan, then add stock and stir over gentle heat until thickened. Return hazelnut mixture, season with salt and pepper and serve with grilled chicken breasts, roast chicken or sautéed veal steaks. Makes 2¹/₂ cups.

Hazelnut Meringue

4 egg whites; 1 cup caster sugar; ¹/₄ tsp vanilla; ¹/₂ tsp vinegar; 1 cup ground hazelnuts, toasted in oven for 5 minutes; 1 cup cream, whipped; 1 punnet (250g/8 oz) strawberries, hulled; sifted icing sugar.

Whisk egg whites until they stand in soft peaks, then gradually whisk in caster sugar a tablespoonful at a time. Continue beating until mixture is very stiff and standing in peaks. Whisk in vanilla and vinegar, then fold in nuts with a metal spoon. Divide mixture between 2 greased and floured 20 cm (8 in) sandwich tins that have been bottom-lined with greased greaseproof paper. Bake in a preheated moderately hot oven (190°C/375°F) for 35–40 minutes. Turn out on to wire racks to cool. When cool, sandwich together with whipped cream and strawberries and dust top with icing sugar. Serves 8.

NOTE: Always fill the meringues at least 3 hours before serving to prevent their splintering when cut into portions.

Hazelnut Ice Cream

1 litre (4 cups) vanilla ice cream, preferably home-made (page 202); 1 cup chopped toasted hazelnuts; 1 tbs coffee liqueur.

Soften frozen ice cream to a partially frozen state and fold chopped hazelnuts through. Stir in coffee liqueur and refreeze. Serves 8.

VARIATIONS

CHOCOLATE HAZELNUT ICE CREAM: Substitute chocolate ice cream for vanilla ice cream and proceed as for Hazelnut Ice Cream.

HAZELNUT ORANGE ICE CREAM: Use recipe for Hazelnut Ice Cream, substituting 1 tbs Curaçao and 1 tbs chopped candied orange peel for coffee liqueur.

Hazelnut and Chocolate Roulade

3 eggs, separated; 2 tsp water; ³/₄ cup caster sugar; 1 cup flour; 1 tsp baking powder; pinch salt; 1 cup ground hazelnuts; 2 tbs icing sugar, sifted.

FILLING: 1 punnet (250g/8 oz) strawberries, hulled; 3 tbs icing sugar, sifted; 185 g (6 oz) dark chocolate; 1 tbs water; 2 egg yolks; 90 g (3 oz) unsalted butter, well softened and at room temperature.

Whisk egg whites with water to a firm snow, then add sugar a spoonful at a time and continue beating until stiff. Beat in egg yolks. Sift flour with baking powder and salt, mix with hazelnuts and fold gently into egg mixture. Turn into a greased and lined 30 x 25 cm (12 x 10 in) Swiss roll tin and level the top with a palette knife. Bake in a preheated hot oven (200°C/400°F) for 12–15 minutes or until firm to the touch. Turn roulade out quickly on to a sugared sheet of greaseproof paper and roll up with greaseproof paper on the inside. Leave to cool.

FILLING: Purée strawberries and stir in icing sugar. Melt chocolate with water in a heatproof bowl placed over hot water. Remove from heat and add egg yolks one at a time. Beat well, then gradually mix in butter. Tip into a bowl and blend in strawberry purée. Uncurl sponge roll very carefully and remove paper. Spread with filling and re-roll. Dust with icing sugar before serving. Serves 6–8.

Hazelnut Cookies

1¹/₂ cups toasted, ground hazelnuts; 2 cups flour; pinch salt; ¹/₃ cup caster sugar; 250 g (8 oz) butter; 1 cup icing sugar, sifted; 1 tbs hot water; chopped hazelnuts or pistachios to decorate.

Put ground nuts into a bowl. Sift flour with salt and add to bowl with caster sugar. Rub in butter and combine well until smooth. Form into a ball, wrap in plastic wrap and chill for 1 hour. Roll out dough thin and cut into rounds with a plain or fluted 4 cm (1¹/₂ in) cutter. Place rounds on greased baking trays and bake in a preheated moderate oven (180°C/350°F) for about 15 minutes. Allow to cool for 1 minute on trays, then transfer to a wire rack to cool completely. Combine icing sugar with hot water to make a stiff icing and spread a little on top of each biscuit. Sprinkle over chopped nuts. Makes about 80.

NOTE: If liked, half the biscuits may be left un-iced and pairs joined together with a little raspberry jam.

HEART

Heart has a mild flavour somewhat like liver, although not so pronounced in taste. The flesh is lean and dry with a close texture. The most tender hearts are those from lambs, pigs and calves, while ox heart needs longer, slower cooking. Hearts can be stuffed and baked, casseroled or sautéed.

■ **BASIC PREPARATION:** Cut away the veins and arteries with a sharp pair of scissors and trim off the fat. Wash well in cold running water. Cover with warm water with the addition of 1 tbs vinegar to 2 cups water. Soak for at least 3 hours, or overnight if using ox heart. Change the water several times. Drain, rinse and dry before proceeding with recipe.

Baked Stuff Heart: Use 4 lambs' hearts or 1 ox heart prepared as above. Make Apple, Prune and Nut Stuffing (see page 514), fill heart cavities and sew up with a needle and thread. Put hearts in a baking dish with 1 cup stock. Cover with buttered foil and bake in a preheated moderate oven (180°C/350°F) for 1½–2 hours for lambs' hearts and 2–2½ hours for ox heart, basting often with juices and extra 1 cup stock. When cooked, make a gravy with pan juices, thickened with flour (see page 184), and serve with redcurrant jelly and mashed potatoes. Serves 4.

Sautéed Heart: Prepare 4 lambs' hearts as above. Cut into 1 cm (½ in) slices and sauté in 3 tbs butter and 1 tbs oil. Add 2 tsp chopped fresh rosemary or 1 tsp dried, salt and freshly ground black pepper. Cook over gentle heat, stirring, for 10–12 minutes. Remove from heat, place on a warm platter, sprinkle with 1 cup buttered toasted breadcrumbs and serve with a fruit chutney. Serves 4–6.

Lambs' Hearts with Orange Sauce

**4 prepared lambs' hearts; 60 g (2 oz) butter;
1 tbs oil; 1–2 onions, chopped; 2 rashers bacon,
rind removed and chopped; 2 tbs flour;
2 cups stock; ½ cup red or white wine; 1 clove garlic,
crushed; salt and freshly ground black pepper;
2 tbs bitter marmalade; grated rind and juice
1 large orange; ¼ cup Grand Marnier or
Cointreau; finely chopped parsley.**

Brown hearts in butter and oil in a heavy frying pan together with onion and bacon. Remove hearts, onion and bacon and place in a flameproof casserole Stir flour into oil and butter in frying pan, then add stock and wine. Cook over low heat, stirring, until thickened. Add garlic, salt, pepper and marmalade. Pour sauce into casserole and simmer gently until hearts are done, about 1½ hours. Remove hearts, slice them thin and arrange in a shallow ovenproof dish. Skim fat off sauce, and boil for 4–5 minutes if necessary to reduce and thicken. Stir in orange rind, juice and liqueur. Cover hearts with half the sauce, keeping the rest warm in a sauceboat to hand separately. Warm

hearts through in a preheated moderate oven (180°C/350°F), then sprinkle with chopped parsley. Serve with boiled new potatoes and an orange and tomato salad. Serves 4–6.

HERBS

The generous but discriminating use of herbs is one of the easiest ways of adding flavour to food. Herbs owe their flavouring qualities to essential oils which quickly permeate the foods with which they are mixed. Sometimes the seeds of the plant are the seasoning agent, sometimes it is the foliage. You will find that most herbs are at their best when home-grown and plucked fresh for use – so do start a small herb garden.

Herbs are easy to cultivate – in a backyard garden, in pots or in a box on the kitchen window-sill – preferring a light, moderately rich soil and a sunny exposure. Few gardening efforts are less troublesome or more rewarding than growing herbs of one's own, for nothing adds such interest and flavour to cooking as a snip or two of a favourite herb.

Discover the joy of cooking with herbs by starting with the major ones. Parsley, thyme, sage, mint, marjoram, basil, chives, oregano and bay leaf (see separate entries) are the ones most often used.

With fresh parsley and mint we are on familiar ground. To cook without parsley is almost unthinkable. The curly, attractive, bright green leaves can be chopped and sprinkled over dishes before serving to give flavour, colour and nutrition to soups, casseroles, grills, sautés and salads.

A sprig or stalk goes into flavouring many savoury dishes. Flat-leaf Italian parsley is also good in flavour, and Chinese parsley is becoming popular (see *Coriander*).

Mint sauce is a favourite with lamb and vegetables such as green peas and carrots.

Thyme, marjoram and sage are used in stuffings; sprigs or a few little chopped leaves are added to roasts, casseroles, meat loaves and sausages.

Chives and garlic, those well-known members of the onion family long used in Mediterranean countries, are becoming more acceptable throughout the world. Garlic bread is an international favourite. Chives snipped over omelettes and salads, or jacket potatoes with butter or sour cream and snipped chives are all a great treat.

No kitchen should be without bay leaves – the foundation of bouquet garni, bay flavours stocks, soups and stews. And an infusion of bay leaf and milk transforms rice puddings and many cream sauces.

FRESH OR DRIED? Fresh is almost always best. Parsley, chives, mint and basil should always be fresh. Thyme, marjoram and oregano can be used both fresh and dried. Bay leaves should not be absolutely fresh; they are picked and kept for 3 or 4 days to allow them to lose their bitterness. Or they may be purchased dried. Good quality tarragon is often dried.

Use 1 tsp dried herbs for every tbs fresh herbs. Crumble dried herbs before using, to release their odour. If using dried herbs, it helps to chop the herbs along with some fresh parsley, it gives a nice look and fresh flavour to the otherwise colourless herbs.

When buying dried and rubbed herbs, the rougher looking ones are usually the best. With very fine or powdered herbs the flavour seems to get lost. Do not expect dried herbs to last forever; buy in small quantities, keep them airtight and in a cool dark place.

See separate entries for individual herbs.

FINES HERBES

A mixture of fresh parsley, tarragon, chives and chervil, all finely chopped, is called *Fines Herbes* in classical French cooking. This is virtually the bouquet garni of uncooked or briefly cooked dishes. Nowadays, the term is commonly applied to other combinations of fresh herbs which may include only one or more of the original fine herbes. They are used in the following traditional ways.

Omelettes: The best-known use for this delicate herb mixture. Stir 1 tbs fines herbes into a 2-egg omelette mixture before cooking, and garnish the omelette with a fresh herb sprig. Other fresh herbs, or parsley alone, may be substituted if classic fines herbes are not available.

Other Egg Dishes: Flavour scrambled eggs or soufflés with fine herbes; shell soft-boiled eggs and serve in little dishes, with a mixture of melted butter and fines herbes poured over them.

With Chicken or Veal: Mix fines herbes with melted butter and a squeeze of lemon for a simple sauce to spoon over grilled or roast chicken, veal scallops or veal cutlets.

Sauces: Mix fines herbes into Mayonnaise or Tartare Sauce (see page 256), or Hollandaise or Béarnaise Sauce (see pages 459–60), to serve with fish, shellfish, vegetables or eggs.

Salads: Sprinkle fines herbes over a green, potato or pasta salad.

HERMITS

Little cookies from America with raisins, nuts and spices in the mixture. Enjoy them with morning coffee.

Hermits

$^1/_4$ cup raisins; $^1/_4$ cup chopped nuts; 2 cups flour;
60 g (2 oz) butter; $^1/_2$ cup caster sugar; $^1/_2$ tsp salt;
2 eggs; $^1/_2$ cup molasses; $^1/_2$ tsp bicarbonate of soda;
$^1/_4$ tsp cream of tartar; 1 tsp cinnamon;
$^1/_2$ tsp ground cloves; $^1/_4$ tsp mace; $^1/_4$ tsp nutmeg.

Toss raisins and nuts in $^1/_4$ cup of the flour and set aside. Cream butter with sugar until light and fluffy. Add salt, eggs and molasses and beat well. Mix together remaining $1^3/_4$ cups flour, the bicarbonate of soda, cream of tartar, cinnamon, cloves, mace and nutmeg and add to creamed mixture. Beat thoroughly, then stir in raisin and nut mixture. Spread in a greased 25 x 30 cm (10 x 12 in) Swiss roll tin or drop in teaspoonfuls on greased baking trays. Bake in a preheated moderate oven (180°C/350°F) for 15–20 minutes if using Swiss roll tin or for 8–10 minutes for drop cookies. In each case when baked the tops should be firm and golden and centres chewy. Cut mixture in Swiss roll tin into 5 cm (2 in) squares while still warm. Makes about 30 squares or 60 drops.

VARIATION

CONCORD HERMITS: Substitute 1 cup firmly packed brown sugar for white sugar and molasses and add $^1/_2$ cup sour cream. You may also add 3 tbs chopped mixed candied peel if you wish.

HERRING

One of the richest and most succulent of the fat fish (see *Fish*). It is not available fresh in the Southern Hemisphere, but can be bought frozen in some fine food stores and delicatessens. Herring is picked, dried and cured by salting and smoking in a great variety of ways, some of the most famous being kippers, bloaters, salts, rollmops, Bismarck herring and red herring. Fresh or frozen herring can be cooked in any of the ways suitable for fat fish, or in the traditional Scots way with oatmeal, a marvellous breakfast dish.

In Scandinavia and Germany, where herring is a favourite food, Schnapps, Aquavit, or Russian vodka are often served ice-cold with herring, sometimes followed by a cold Pilsener chaser.

See also *Kippers*.

HERRING, CANNED AND SALTED

In addition to the many prepared herring and herring salads available in delicatessens, there are dozens of versions in jars and cans, in grocery stores, gourmet food departments and supermarkets. Depending on the type of herring, its sauce and its flavour, you can do a lot to these preparations by adding, as needed, sour cream, vinegar or sugar if the herring is too sweet or too sour, fresh snipped dill or slivers of onions, a pinch of curry powder or a dab of prepared mustard, a slice of lemon or a few spoonfuls of white wine.

All of the herring sold in barrels for preparation at home is cured in brine and must be kept soaking in the refrigerator in several changes of cold water before you can proceed with a recipe. Salt herring is a firm fish which, as you might expect from its name, is extremely salty.

Matjes denotes a reddish, salt-cured herring that has not yet spawned. It is quite salty and richly flavoured, very tender and delicate in texture. It is almost always sold in fillets and is at its best chilled on ice and served with sprays of dill and hot boiled new potatoes; it may be soaked first in milk or buttermilk.

Bismarck is a sharply flavoured herring, pickled whole in a spicy mixture of vinegar, onions, spices and lots of dried red chillies. **See recipes.**

Matjes Rolls

6 herring fillets (matjes); milk or buttermilk; 6 thick slices apple, cored; ¹/₂ cup white wine; 6 tbs Horseradish Cream (page 199); 3 tbs snipped chives.

GARNISH: pickled baby beetroot; pickled gherkins.

Rinse herring, cover with milk or buttermilk and soak for 2 hours, changing milk several times for a milder flavour. Let apple slices marinate in white wine 30 minutes–1 hour. Remove herring fillets from milk and drain on paper towels. Put 1 tbs horseradish cream into the centre of each fillet. Roll up and fasten rolled fillets with a toothpick. Sprinkle top with snipped chives. Set each roll on an apple slice that has been drained on paper towels. Serve on individual plates garnished with a few pickled baby beetroot and gherkins. Serves 6.

Crispy Herring in Oatmeal

4 herring; milk; medium oatmeal (from health food shops); 185 g (6 oz) butter.

GARNISH: lemon wedges; parsley sprigs.

Check that fish is well scaled and cleaned. Slit each down belly to tail. Cut off head, tail and fins. Open out flat and place skin side up on a board. With Press down with knuckles of other hand along backbone to loosen it. Turn the herring over and carefully ease out backbone with point of a knife. Pull out as many small bones as possible (a pair of long-nose pliers or tweezers helps). Wipe fish with damp paper towels, dip in milk and then in oatmeal. Fry in hot butter, skinless side first, until outside is crisp. Drain on crumpled paper towels and serve very hot, garnished with lemon wedges and parsley sprigs. Serves 4.

NOTE: If the herring has roe, coat it with milk and oatmeal, fry separately and place down centre of each fish.

If fresh or frozen herring is unobtainable, mullet or mackerel fillets may be substituted.

Pickled Herring Salad

Most Scandinavian buffets will include a salad such as this. It may be served as a first-course salad, or as part of a buffet.

8 herring fillets (matjes would be ideal); milk or buttermilk; 2 beetroot, cooked, peeled and diced; 3 potatoes, cooked and diced; 4 hard-boiled eggs, chopped; 2 sour pickled cucumbers, chopped; ¹/₂ red salad onion or 4 spring onions, chopped.

DRESSING: ³/₄ cup sour cream; I tbs wine vinegar; 2 tsp dry mustard; I tsp salt; 2 tsp lemon juice.

GARNISH: sour cream; snipped chives.

Rinse herring, cover with milk or buttermilk and allow to soak for 2 hours, changing milk several times. Drain, pat dry with paper towels and cut into bite-size pieces. Combine beetroot, potatoes, eggs, cucumbers, onion and herring in a salad bowl. In a small bowl combine dressing ingredients and fold through salad, tossing lightly to combine. Chill salad, covered with plastic wrap, for 1 hour. Garnish salad with a dollop of sour cream and snipped chives. Serves 6.

HOISIN SAUCE

This reddish brown Chinese sauce is both sweet and spicy. Brewed from fermented soybeans, sugar, garlic, vinegar and spices, hoisin is used as a dipping sauce for Chinese food or a basting sauce for barbecued meats. A darker version is often called Peking or barbecue sauce and is the one used for preparing the popular Chinese barbecued pork and Peking duck. When adding to a dish, it's a good idea to cook the hoisin in oil for a few minutes to rid it of the raw bean flavour.

HOLLANDAISE SAUCE

See *Sauces*.

HONEY

The natural, unrefined substance bees make from flower nectar. It varies greatly in colour, flavour and consistency, depending on the kind of blossom from which the nectar is gathered. In general, the honey lightest in colour will have the mildest flavour.

Honeycomb gives us honey as it is made and stored by the bees. The honey is sealed in the cells capped with wax. It is sold by some specialist health food shops and should be served cut into small squares.

h

Cut honeycomb is honeycomb cut into bars, wrapped separately and sold in health food stores.

Chunk is chunks of honeycomb suspended in liquid honey. It is sold in jars at specialist delicatessens and health food shops.

Liquid honey is obtained by uncapping the comb and extracting the honey. It is usually sold in jars and heat-treated to prevent crystallisation during storage.

Candied, creamed or solid honey is granulated honey from which some of the moisture has been removed. Buy from supermarkets, delicatessens or health food shops.

WAYS TO USE HONEY

- Substitute honey for sugar on hot porridge.
- Sweeten whipped cream with honey for cakes and desserts.
- Serve fresh fruit for dessert with ¼ cup honey stirred into ¾ cup sour cream.
- Top chocolate, vanilla or coffee ice cream with honey and sprinkle with chopped nuts.
- Mix half honey and half butter to spread on hot toast, crumpets, muffins, pancakes or scones.
- Top sautéed apple rings, pineapple or banana slices with honey, cinnamon and a little grated orange rind; cook a few moments longer to glaze.
- Mix honey with ricotta or cream cheese, nuts and chopped dried fruit to fill baked tartlet shells, or serve with plain sweet biscuits.
- Add 1 tsp honey with a little mustard and ground ginger to pep up baked beans.
- Make a hot syrup of ¾ cup honey and ¼ cup lemon juice and pour over a freshly baked nut and fruit loaf. Prick the loaf first before using the syrup.
- Glaze carrots, turnips, onions or new potatoes with honey. Cook vegetables, covered, in a very little salted water with a spoonful of butter and one of honey. Remove lid when vegetables are almost cooked and continue cooking until water has evaporated leaving a golden glaze. Tilt saucepan to roll vegetables in the glaze before serving. **See recipes.**

Honey – Ginger Glazed Shoulder of Lamb

I shoulder lamb, boned and rolled; ¹/₂ cup warmed honey; 2 tbs lemon juice; I tbs soy sauce; pinch ground cloves; I tsp ground ginger; ¹/₂ cup hot chicken or veal stock.

Place lamb on a rack in a roasting tin and roast in a preheated hot oven (200°C/400°F) for 15 minutes. Reduce heat to moderate (180°C/350°F) and roast for a further 30 minutes. Mix together honey, lemon juice, soy sauce and spices, and brush lamb with this mixture. Continue to roast, brushing with glaze every 10 minutes, allowing in total 20 minutes per 500 g (1 lb), plus 20 minutes, for lamb that is pink inside, or 25 minutes per 500 g (1 lb), plus 25 minutes, for well-done lamb. When cooked, leave for 15 minutes before carving. Meantime, skim fat from pan juices, add stock and stir until boiling. Pour gravy into a sauceboat and serve with the lamb. Serves 6.

Honey Prawns

750 g (I ¹/₂ lb) green king prawns, shelled and deveined; ¹/₄ cup cornflour; I cup self-raising flour; ¹/₂ tsp salt; ¹/₄ tsp white pepper; I¹/₄ cups water; I egg, beaten; oil for frying; 2 tbs honey; 2 tbs sesame seeds.

Dust prawns lightly with cornflour. Sift flour, salt and pepper into a bowl, make a well in centre and gradually add water and egg, mixing to a smooth batter free of lumps. Put 3 or 4 prawns in a bowl, pour over a small amount of batter to coat and remove. Repeat with remaining prawns. Heat oil in a large frying pan or wok, add prawns a few at a time and fry for 2 minutes or until prawns are golden and cooked through. Drain and keep warm. Remove oil from pan and wipe clean. heat 1 tbs fresh oil in pan, add honey and stir over gentle heat until warm. Add prawns, toss quickly, remove and sprinkle with sesame seeds. Serve immediately. Serves 4–6.

Honey Buns

125 g (4 oz) butter; ¹/₂ cup firmly packed brown sugar; I egg, beaten; 2 tbs honey; I³/₄ cups self-raising flour; pinch salt; creamed honey for spreading.

Cream butter with brown sugar. Beat in egg and honey. Sift flour with salt and work into mixture until it forms a soft dough. Chill until firm. Shape dough into small balls the size of a walnut and place well apart on greased baking trays. Bake in a preheated moderate oven (180°C/350°F) for 12 minutes or until risen and golden. Cool and sandwich in pairs with creamed honey. Makes 10–12.

Honey Cheesecake

I quantity Rich Shortcrust Pastry (page 342); lightly beaten egg white to glaze; 500 g (I lb) ricotta cheese; ¹/₂ cup sugar; ²/₃ cup honey; 4 eggs; 2 tsp cinnamon.

Roll out pastry to line a greased 20 cm (8 in) square cake tin. Brush pastry with a little egg white, prick bottom and sides well and bake blind in a preheated moderately hot oven (190°C/375°F) for 10 minutes. Remove and cool while preparing filling. Beat together cheese, sugar and honey, add eggs and beat until combined. Pour into cooled pastry shell. Reduce oven temperature to moderate (180°C/350°F) and bake cheesecake for 45–50 minutes or until top is golden-brown. Turn off heat and allow to cool in oven. Sprinkle with cinnamon and cut into squares or diamond shapes to serve. Makes about 16 squares.

Honey Rum Chocolate Cake

185 g (6 oz) butter; 1 cup lightly packed brown sugar; $^{1}/_{3}$ cup honey; 2 eggs; 1 tbs rum; $^{1}/_{2}$ tsp vanilla; 2 tbs cocoa powder; $1^{3}/_{4}$ cups self-raising flour; pinch salt; $^{1}/_{2}$ cup sweet sherry; 1 cup cream, whipped; sifted icing sugar.

Cream butter with brown sugar, add honey and beat until light and fluffy. Beat in eggs one at a time, then stir in rum and vanilla. Sift cocoa, flour and salt and fold into the creamed mixture alternately with sherry, beginning and ending with flour. Turn into a greased and lined 23 cm (9 in) round cake tin. Bake in a pre-heated moderate oven (180°C/350°F) for 45 minutes or until a fine skewer inserted in centre comes out clean. Allow to cool in the tin for a few minutes, then turn out on to a wire rack to finish cooling. Split cake into two layers, fill with whipped cream and dust the top with icing sugar. Serves 8–10.

NOTE: If desired the top may be iced with Chocolate Butter Cream Icing (see page 205).

HONEYDEW MELON

The flesh of honeydew melon, pale green, crisp and delicately fragrant, is superb alone or in combination with other foods both sweet and savoury. It is perhaps the best melon to serve with prosciutto, and can be used in any of the ways suitable for other melons.

See also *Ginger, Melon* and *Prosciutto*.

HORS D'OEUVRE

Hors d'oeuvre means 'outside the main body of work', that is, outside the main part of the meal. The term is the French equivalent of appetisers: small portions of savoury food served at the table to introduce a luncheon or dinner, or in another room with drinks before the meal. In English-speaking countries hors d'oeuvre are usually associated with a party or special occasion. But in France, the midday meal almost invariably begins with a slice of pâté, egg or fish mayonnaise, cold meat dressed with a piquant vinaigrette or *les hors d'oeuvre variés* – the plate of mixed hors d'oeuvre which displays the skill of the French cook at transforming small quantities of food, including leftovers, into a delicious and thrifty first course.

SERVING HORS D'OEUVRE

The function of hors d'oeuvre is to delight and invite the diner, and their appearance is very important.

- Slice meats thin and overlap them neatly; very thin slices of meat such as prosciutto can be rolled or folded loosely into triangles.
- Cut salad ingredients into uniform pieces or shreds.
- Arrange hot pastries geometrically on a tray or pile them into a napkin-lined basket.
- Sprinkle chopped herbs in a narrow strip down the centre of the dish or in a border round the edge, or scatter them lightly over the surface – never in damp clumps.
- Add colour and pattern with canned pimiento or an-chovy strips, neatly crossed or arranged trellis-fashion.
- Consider the balance of colour, texture and flavour; juicy red tomato, crisp green pepper, salty black olives; rich golden mayonnaise topped with piquant capers; a slice of pâté with a bright radish, still retaining some of its green leaves, and a few tiny gherkins (cornichons).
- Avoid an over-contrived or zealously worked-on appearance – aim to make each arrangement light and fresh, as if it had just been imagined for the first time.

HORS D'OEUVRE VARIES

These cold hors d'oeuvre can be mixture of little salads which you have prepared yourself, such as those given below, and other foods from the kitchen cupboard or delicatessen – smoked fish such as eel, tailor, mackerel; good canned or pickled fish; meats such as salami, ham, sausage, liverwurst; fresh, pickled or canned vegetables; eggs; feta and other cheeses. Leftovers of meat, fish or vegetables can be combined with Vinaigrette Dressing (see page 442) or Mayonnaise (see page 256) to add to the platter. Garnish with olives, capers, chopped herbs or fresh herb sprays, watercress or tiny lettuce leaves, canned pimiento, cherry tomatoes or tomato wedges, sieved hard-boiled egg, lemon slices or wedges. Serve with fresh crusty bread and butter.

Egg Mayonnaise: Halve hard-boiled eggs lengthways and arrange, rounded sides up, on a serving platter. Coat with Mayonnaise (see page 256) and garnish with drained canned pimiento, cut into strips and arranged trellis-fashion, and with a stoned half of black olive in each square. Scatter with parsley and serve at room temperature.

Fish Mayonnaise: Follow recipe for Egg Mayonnaise but substitute about $^{1}/_{3}$ cup poached or canned fish, skin and bones removed and broken into large flakes for each egg, and capers for black olives.

Salade de Boeuf (Beef Salad): Very lightly mix together equal quantities of diced, cooked beef and diced, cooked new potatoes. Add a little finely chopped onion and peeled, seeded and diced tomato. Moisten with Mustard Vinaigrette (see page 442), season with salt and freshly ground black pepper, cover and chill lightly. Dress neatly in a shallow dish and sprinkle generously with chopped parsley just before serving.

Vegetable à la Grecque: Follow recipe for Zucchini à la Grecque using a selection of young vegetables, (see page 600).

HOT FILLED HORS D'OEUVRE

Ahead of time, prepare miniature tartlet or barquette cases in short or flaky pasty, puff pastry Bouchées or choux pastry Profiteroles or Eclairs (see separate entries). Also prepare a savoury filling such as those which follow. Just before serving, put cases into a preheated slow oven (150°C/300°F) to warm, and reheat filling over low heat or by standing the container in boiling water. Fill cases with hot filling and serve immediately, or finish as directed.

Chicken Filling: To 1 cup finely chopped, cooked chicken, add 1 tbs each finely chopped celery and spring onions. Mix with 1¼ cups hot, thick Cream Sauce (see page 457) and season with salt, pepper and a dash of Worcestershire sauce. Reheat gently, fill cases and sprinkle with paprika.

Florentine Filling: Chop enough spinach to make 1 cup, firmly packed. Cook, uncovered, with 1 tbs butter until soft, then uncover, season with salt, freshly ground black pepper and nutmeg and cook, stirring and watching carefully, until moisture evaporates. Add 3–4 tbs hot thick Béchamel Sauce (see page 456) and 2 tbs grated Parmesan cheese. Fill cases, sprinkle with more cheese and return to oven until cheese melts.

See also *Antipasti, Appetisers, Canapés, Sandwiches, Savouries* and *Smörgasbord*.

HORSERADISH

The thick taproot of the horseradish plant is ground or grated to give the hot stinging flavour of the traditional sauce which accompanies roast beef of old England. In Germany the root is grated and mixed with vinegar as a sauce for fish or mixed with mayonnaise as a dressing for hard-boiled eggs. Some specialist greengrocers stock fresh horseradish roots in season. Grated horseradish may be purchased preserved or as a relish from good delicatessens. Manufacturers use it in horseradish cream, easily obtainable from most grocery stores and supermarkets.

NOTE: Preserved horseradish or relish may be used instead of fresh in the recipe below, in which case use half the quantity of fresh specified in each recipe. See recipes.

Horseradish Butter

125 g (4 oz) butter; 1 tbs chopped parsley; juice ½ lemon; 2 tbs grated horseradish; ½ tsp Dijon mustard; 1 tbs wine vinegar.

Mix ingredients together well and refrigerate. Use sliced, on grilled steak, chops, kidneys or fried fish. Serves 8.

Horseradish Cream

⅔ cup cream; squeeze lemon juice; 2 tbs grated horseradish; ½ tsp salt; freshly ground black pepper; pinch sugar.

Whip cream. Add lemon juice, horseradish, salt, pepper and sugar, and fold in lightly. If using bottled horseradish, press out moisture before using. Serve 6–8.

Horseradish Sauce

3 tbs grated horseradish; ½ cup cream; 1 tsp Dijon mustard; 1 tbs white wine vinegar; pinch sugar.

Whisk ingredients together until thick. Taste and add more vinegar or an extra pinch of sugar if necessary. Serve with hot or cold roast beef. For a milder flavour omit vinegar and add a little more sugar. Serves 4.

HOT WATER CRUST

See *Pastry*.

HUEVOS RANCHEROS (RANCH-STYLE EGGS)

A Latin-American dish which makes a splendid week-end breakfast or lunch. There are several versions; the eggs can be poached or fried separately or cooked in the sauce.

Huevos Rancheros

3 tbs olive oil; 1 small onion, chopped; 1 clove garlic, crushed; 1 small green pepper, cored, seeded and chopped; 2 ripe tomatoes, peeled, seeded and chopped; salt and freshly ground black pepper; dash Tabasco sauce; 1 tbs chopped fresh coriander, or ¼ tsp ground cumin; 4 eggs; 4 Tortillas (pages 544–5); coriander sprigs to garnish.

Heat half the oil in a frying pan and cook onion, garlic and green pepper gently until soft. Add tomatoes and simmer until thick. Season with salt, pepper, Tabasco and coriander or cumin. Make 4 depressions in the sauce and break an egg into each. Cover pan and cook 3–4 minutes or until eggs are set. Meantime, heat remaining oil and fry tortillas 30 seconds on each side or until crispy. Place tortillas on 2 heated plates. Use an egg slice to lift 2 eggs and surrounding sauce on to each tortilla and strew coriander sprigs over eggs. Serve at once. Serves 2.

HUMMUS BI TAHINI (CHICK PEA AND SESAME PUREE)

Chick pea purée or dip is one of the most widely known and appreciated of all the Middle Eastern dishes. Tahini is a paste made from sesame seeds and can be bought from most delicatessens, health food stores and some super-markets. Hummus should have the consistency of thick mayonnaise and be well seasoned, but neither the flavour of garlic nor that of lemon juice should predominate.

Hummus bi Tahini

500 g (1 lb) dried chick peas; juice 2–3 lemons; 2–3 cloves garlic; salt; 3/4 cup tahini; 1 tbs olive oil; 1 tsp paprika; 1 tbs finely chopped parsley to garnish.

Soak chick peas overnight in cold water to cover. Next day drain and place in a saucepan with fresh water to cover. Bring to the boil, then reduce heat to low and cook, covered, for 2–3 hours or until tender. Drain peas, reserving ½ cup liquid. Set aside ½ cup whole chick peas and purée remainder, adding a little of reserved cooking liquid or lemon juice if necessary. Crush garlic with salt and add to purée.

Gradually mix in tahini paste with lemon juice and beat vigorously. Add more cooking liquid to give the consistency of thick mayonnaise. Check seasoning and add more lemon juice, garlic or salt if desired. Hummus is traditionally served spread on a flat plate. Make a shallow depression in the centre and pour in olive oil, then sprinkle with paprika, or mix paprika with oil and drizzle over surface. Garnish with chopped parsley and reserved whole chick peas. Serve as a dip with flat Lebanese bread. Makes about 4 cups.

NOTE: 4 cups drained canned chick peas can be substituted for cooked dried ones.

ICE CREAM

Ice cream just has to be one of the world's favourite desserts. While fine commercial ice creams are available, good, home-made ice cream, made from pure cream and eggs and carefully churned, is the richest, best-textured and finest ice cream of all.

There are many types of ice cream, from the French Vanilla, rich Italian to the economical ones. You can use milk and eggs or half milk or full-cream, powdered milk. Each has its merit. The custard-based ice creams are rich, creamy and smooth. Those based on whipped evaporated milk are inexpensive to make, and the powdered milk base, also inexpensive, brings ice cream to remote areas where fresh milk or cream is unavailable (see *Milk*).

The way to achieve a smooth texture in home-made ice cream is to churn it, which prevents ice crystals from forming as the mixture is freezing. You can do this by freezing the mixture in metal ice cream trays and beating the partially frozen cream with a rotary or electric mixer, or by using one of the excellent small electric sorbetières or ice cream makers, complete with paddles, that constantly churn the mixture until it is the right consistency. These small machines make approximately 1 litre (4 cups) of ice cream at a time. Larger ice cream makers are also available; these require salt and crushed ice and may be hand or electrically driven.

TO FREEZE ICE CREAM AND ICES

In Freezing Compartment: Turn freezing compartment to maximum or coldest setting about 1 hour before the mixture is prepared. Place prepared mixture in metal ice cream trays and put the trays back into the freezing compartment. Allow the mixture to semi-freeze. Transfer the mixture to a mixing bowl, whisk it thoroughly with a rotary or electric mixer, replace it in the ice cream trays, cover with foil and freeze again for 1–4 hours until frozen hard. Store in freezing compartment at normal setting. If liked, the beating process may be repeated when the ice cream is just firming. The time required to freeze ice cream varies greatly according to the freezing compartment and the mixture used.

In an Electric Ice Cream Maker or Sorbetière: Turn freezing compartment to maximum or coldest setting about an hour before the mixture is prepared. Read instruction booklet that usually accompanies these machines – as a general guide: make the ice cream mixture, pour it into the sorbetière and put it in the freezer, preferably in the coldest part, making sure the sorbetière stands level.

The sorbetière has a flat cord which passes under the freezer door and is plugged in to the nearest power point. The ice cream (or water ice if making) is constantly churned by paddles, and when it reaches the right consistency (after about 1–1½ hours), the paddles lift up automatically. Remove paddles, smooth over surface of ice cream, cover and allow to freeze until hard. Store in freezer compartment at normal setting.

When ice cream is frozen, return freezer control to normal. Home-made ice creams and ices tend to freeze harder than the commercial ones. They reach the peak of flavour and texture after ripening (mellowing) for 2–6 hours and are best eaten within 48 hours of being made. Allow hard ice cream or ices to soften in the refrigerator for about 30–60 minutes before serving. See recipes.

Rich Vanilla Ice Cream
(Custard base)

1 cup milk; 1½ cups cream; ½ vanilla bean, or 1 tsp vanilla; 2 eggs; 2 egg yolks; ½ cup sugar; ¼ tsp salt.

Scald milk, cream and vanilla bean, if using, in a heavy saucepan over a low heat. Remove vanilla bean, or add vanilla, if using. Beat the eggs and egg yolks, sugar and salt together in a heatproof bowl until thick and mousse-like. Stir in some of the scalded liquid. Place bowl over a saucepan of boiling water, add remaining liquid and cook, stirring, until thick (the mixture should coat a metal spoon). Remove from heat and cool quickly over cold water, stirring occasionally. Pour mixture into container of a sorbetière or metal ice cream trays. Cover, place in freezer and process as directed (see *To Freeze Ice Cream and Ices*). Makes about 3½ cups. Serves 6.

French Vanilla Ice Cream
(Mousse base)

1¾ cups cream; ½ vanilla bean, or 1 tsp vanilla; ¼ cup sugar; ½ cup water; 3 egg yolks.

Place cream and vanilla bean, if using, in a heavy saucepan and heat gently, without boiling, for 5 minutes. Set aside and add vanilla, if using. Place the sugar and water in a small saucepan, dissolve sugar, then bring to the boil. Boil for 5 minutes without stirring. Allow to cool for 30 seconds. Beat egg yolks until pale and frothy. Pour hot sugar syrup over yolks, whisking constantly until thick. Strain cream, add to egg mixture and whisk until frothy. Pour into container of a sorbetière or metal ice cream trays. Cover, place in freezer and process as directed (see *To Freeze Ice Cream and Ices*). Makes about 3 cups. Serves 5–6.

VARIATIONS

CHOCOLATE ICE CREAM: Use French or Rich Vanilla Ice Cream, but melt 125 g (4 oz) cooking chocolate in the warm cream or milk and cream.

COFFEE ICE CREAM: Use French or Rich Vanilla Ice Cream, but add 1 tbs instant coffee powder to the cream or milk and cream.

COCONUT ICE CREAM: Use French or Rich Vanilla Ice Cream, but add 1 cup desiccated coconut to cream or milk and cream and heat gently to infuse. Push mixture through a sieve, squeezing out as much of the coconut-flavoured creamy milk as possible. Discard the coconut.

ALMOND ICE CREAM: Use French or Rich Vanilla Ice Cream, but add ½ cup ground almonds to the cream or milk and cream and heat gently to infuse. Push mixture through a sieve, squeezing out as much almond-flavoured milk as possible. Discard meal.

BURNT ALMOND ICE CREAM: Use French or Rich Vanilla Ice Cream, but add ¾ tsp almond essence instead of vanilla. When frozen, stir in ½ cup flaked almonds which have been toasted to a golden colour. Cover and return to freezer with temperature control set at normal and allow to ripen 2–6 hours (see *To Freeze Ice Cream and Ices*).

PEACH VANILLA ICE CREAM: Make up and freezer-churn French or Rich Vanilla Ice Cream. When frozen, stir in 1½ cups mashed ripe peaches. Transfer mixture to suitable mould or container. Cover and return to freezer with temperature control set at normal and allow to ripen 2–4 hours (see *To Freeze Ice Cream and Ices*).

STRAWBERRY VANILLA ICE CREAM Prepare as for Peach Vanilla Ice Cream but add 1½ cups mashed strawberries.

NOTE: Any frozen fruits may be used as indicated in Peach and Strawberry Ice Cream. Allow fruits to thaw partially and crush in a blender.

Strawberry Ice Cream

1 punnet (250 g/8 oz) strawberries, hulled;
3 egg yolks; ¾ cup sugar; 1¼ cups cream,
lightly whipped; almond essence.

Place strawberries in bowl of a blender or food processor and purée, then fold in whipped cream. Beat egg yolks and sugar until pale and light. Mix in strawberry purée. Add a few drops of almond essence to taste. Pour into container of a sorbetière or metal ice cream trays. Cover, place in freezer and process as directed (see *To Freeze Ice Cream and Ices*). Makes about 1 litre (4 cups). Serves 8.

Italian Apricot Ice Cream

185 g (6 oz) dried apricots; 2 cups cream; 6 egg yolks;
⅓ cup sugar.

Cook apricots in a little water until they are tender. Drain and push fruit through a sieve to make a thick purée. In the top of a double saucepan, gradually stir cream into beaten egg yolks and cook gently over simmering water, stirring occasionally, until thickened. Remove custard from heat and add sugar immediately, adding more to taste if necessary. Stir until dissolved. Cool custard, then stir in apricot purée. Pour into container of a sorbetière or metal ice cream trays. Cover, place in freezer and process as directed (see *To Freeze Ice Cream and Ices*). Makes about 1 litre (4 cups). Serves 8.

ICES, SORBETS, GRANITE AND SHERBETS

Freshly made water ices are among the most delectable of frozen ices – whether called sorbets as in France, sherbets in the USA or granite in Italy. Sorbets are generally accepted to be fruit juices, sweetened and frozen. However, they may also be made with tea, coffee, champagne or a spirit. Granite are softened fruit purées frozen until granular in texture; sherbet is the American version of granita. For a finer-grained ice, a lightly beaten egg white or softened gelatine may be folded into the mixture to be frozen. Buttermilk or milk is often added to the fruit mixture.

Ices combine magnificently with a scoop of ice cream, or with fresh fruit. They may be served in fruit shells – scooped-out oranges or lemons, half a poached pear, half a small melon – and garnished with fresh garden leaves. Meringues are often shaped into containers for ices, and pretty crystal or glass plates and goblets can be enhanced with the delicate colours of fruit ices.

Sorbets may be served before the main course to refresh the palate or with other creams or fruit as a dessert. Three-star restaurants all over the world are featuring sorbets and ices on their menus, and offer different flavoured sorbets on a plate, together with the fresh fruits from which they were made.

Ices, sorbets, granite, sherbets – neither solid nor liquid – are most refreshing concoctions to be enjoyed at any time of the day, and can do much to refresh the palate during a rich meal.

TO FREEZE ICES: Follow the directions, *To Freeze Ice Cream and Ices*. See recipes.

Lemon Sorbet (1)

125 g (4 oz) cube sugar; 4 lemons;
1½ cups water; 1 small egg white.

Rub sugar cubes over rind of 2 lemons until cubes are impregnated with lemon oil (zest). Place in saucepan with water and stir over low heat until sugar dissolves. Bring to the boil and boil 6 minutes. Cool. Squeeze juice from all 4 lemons and strain. Add to sugar syrup and mix well. Beat egg white with a few tbs of the lemon syrup. Fold into remaining syrup. Pour mixture into metal ice cream trays or container of sorbetière. Cover, place in freezer and process as directed (see *To Freeze Ice Cream and Ices*). The sorbet may be transferred to a separate dish or mould, depending on how you want to serve or store it. Makes 1 litre (4 cups). Serves 6–8.

Lemon Sorbet (2)

³/₄ cup lemon juice; juice 1 orange, strained; grated rind 2 lemons; 1 cup sugar; 1¹/₂ cups water.

Mix lemon and orange juice with grated rind. Put sugar and 1 cup water in a small saucepan and bring to the boil. Boil for 5 minutes. Remove from heat and cool, then add remaining water and fruit juices. Chill. Pour mixture into metal ice cream trays or container of a sorbetière. Cover, place in freezer and process as directed (see *To Freeze Ice Cream and Ices*). Makes about 1 litre (4 cups). Serves 6–8.

NOTE: If a fine-grained sorbet is desired beat an egg white until soft but fluffy and stir into the mixture before freezing.

VARIATION

LIME SORBET: Make as for Lemon Sorbet (2) but replace half the lemon juice with lime juice.

Orange Sorbet (1)

juice 6 oranges; juice 1 lemon; 1 cup icing sugar, sifted.

Mix the orange and lemon juices and measure. If necessary squeeze more oranges to make 2 cups juice. Stir in sugar, whisking thoroughly until it dissolves. Transfer to an ice cream maker or metal ice cream tray, cover with foil and freeze to a slush. Purée in a food processor or blender or beat with a rotary beater until the slush becomes very light and fine grained. Transfer to a 2-cup freezerproof soufflé dish or mould and freeze. Take sorbet out of freezer 30–45 minutes before serving and leave to soften in refrigerator. Makes 3 cups. Serves 4–6.

Orange Sorbet (2)

1¹/₂ cups orange juice; grated rind 1 orange; 1 cup sugar; ³/₄ cup water; juice 2 lemons, strained; 1 egg white.

Mix orange juice with grated rind. Place sugar and water in a saucepan, dissolve sugar over a gentle heat and bring to the boil. Boil for 5 minutes, then cool. Add orange and lemon juices and mix well. Beat egg white with 2–3 tbs of the orange mixture, then fold through remaining orange mixture. Pour into metal ice cream trays or container of a sorbetière. Cover, place in freezer and process as directed (see *To Freeze Ice Cream and Ices*). Makes about 1 litre (4 cups). Serves 6–8.

VARIATIONS

ORANGE RUM SORBET: Make Orange Sorbet, using ¹/₂ cup white rum for ¹/₂ cup of the water.

GRAPEFRUIT SORBET: Make as for Orange Sorbet replacing orange juice and rind with grapefruit.

Earl Grey Sorbet

3 cups water; ²/₃ cup sugar; 1 tbs Earl Grey tea; juice 1 orange; lemon slices to serve.

Combine 2 cups water with the sugar, bring to the boil and boil for 5 minutes. Bring remaining water to the boil, add tea leaves and leave to infuse. Add strained tea infusion to sugar syrup with orange juice to taste; see that the mixture has a good tea taste. Cool. Pour into metal ice cream trays or container of a sorbetière. Cover, place in freezer and process as directed (see *To Freeze Ice Cream and Ices*). Serve with lemon slices. Makes about 3¹/₂ cups. Serves 4–6.

Apricot Buttermilk Sherbet

12 ripe apricots to yield 1 cup puréed fruit; about ¹/₄ cup sugar; 2 tbs lemon juice; pinch salt; 1¹/₂ cups buttermilk.

Combine fruit purée, sugar, lemon juice, salt and buttermilk, stirring well until sugar has dissolved. (This can be done in a blender or food processor fitted with a steel blade in which case the fruit need not be puréed first.) Taste and add more sugar if necessary. The flavour should be sharp, not sweet. Pour into metal ice cream trays or container of a sorbetière. Cover, place in freezer and process as directed (see *To Freeze Ice Cream and Ices*). Makes about 3 cups. Serves 4–6.

VARIATIONS

MANGO BUTTERMILK SHERBET: Prepare as for Apricot Buttermilk Sherbet, replacing 1 cup apricot purée with 1 cup puréed fresh or canned mangoes.

PEACH BUTTERMILK SHERBET: Prepare as for Apricot Buttermilk Sherbet, replacing 1 cup apricot purée with 1 cup puréed fresh or canned peaches.

STRAWBERRY BUTTERMILK SHERBET: Prepare as for Apricot Buttermilk Sherbet, replacing 1 cup apricot purée with 1 cup puréed strawberries (1 punnet).

Watermelon Ice

4 cups watermelon, without seeds; ¹/₂ cup sugar; juice 1 lemon, strained; sprigs fresh mint to decorate.

Place watermelon in a blender and blend at medium speed for 30 seconds, or crush with a potato masher and push through a coarse sieve. Combine sugar and lemon juice and stir well. Add to watermelon purée. Pour into metal ice cream trays or container of a sorbetière. Cover, place in freezer and process as directed (see *To Freeze Ice Cream and Ices*). Serve with lemon slices. Makes about 3¹/₂ cups. Serves with mint sprigs.

Strawberry Sherbet

**4 punnets (1 kg/2 lb) strawberries, hulled;
juice 1 orange; juice 1 lemon; 1³/4 cups sugar;
¹/2 cup water.**

Blend or purée fruit and push through a sieve. Add fruit juices. Combine sugar and water in a small saucepan, bring slowly to the boil to dissolve sugar and boil for 2–3 minutes. Combine fruit pulp and sugar syrup. Pour into container of a sorbetière or metal ice cream trays. Cover, place in freezer and process as directed (see *To Freeze Ice Cream and Ices*). Makes about 1 litre (4 cups). Serves 6–8.

VARIATIONS

MELON SHERBET: Prepare as for Strawberry Sherbet using 1 ripe, well-flavoured melon weighing about 1 kg (2 lb), or 2 smaller melons. Halve melon, scoop out seeds and remove flesh. Purée as for strawberries. You should have about 2 cups purée.

APRICOT OR PEACH SHERBET: Prepare as for Strawberry Sherbet using 1 kg (2 lb) ripe apricots or peaches. Drop fruit into boiling water for 5 minutes, then chill and peel fruit. Halve and remove stones, then purée flesh as for strawberries. You should have about 2 cups purée.

ICINGS, FROSTINGS AND FILLINGS

ICING

The sweet coating that goes on the outside of a cake. Icings add flavour to cakes, give texture contrast, help them stay fresh and moist and, of course, add to their appearance. Popular icings include the following:

Almond Paste: For coating and moulding into fruits, flowers, etc. (see page 3).

Butter Cream Icing: For coating and piping.

Glacé Icing: For coating and simple decoration.

Royal Icing: For coating and elaborate decoration.

Plastic Fondant Icing: For covering and modelling.

FROSTING

Similar to icing; use for coating.

FILLINGS

The range of cake fillings seems almost endless, but there are some universal favourites. Sponges are popular with a simple jam filling or whipped cream and fruit. Lemon Cheese transforms a plain butter cake or sponge sandwich. The smooth butter cream called *Crème au Beurre* in France is often sandwiched between many layers of cake to make a Continental gateau. Cream cheese and ricotta cheese are the basis of other European cake fillings. Dried fruits, nuts, rum, chocolate, ginger and other flavourings are often added to a rich custard cream (Crème Pâtissière) for luscious dessert cakes. See recipes.

See also *Mock Cream*.

Butter Cream Icing (*Vienna Icing*)

A soft and creamy icing that can be swirled into decorative shapes and also used for piping.

**125 g (4 oz) butter; 1¹/2 cups pure icing sugar, sifted;
1 tbs sherry; few drops vanilla.**

Beat butter until light and creamy, then gradually beat in half the icing sugar. Beat in sherry alternately with remaining sugar. Stir in vanilla. Sufficient to fill a Swiss roll or top a 20 cm (8 in) cake.

VARIATIONS

CHOCOLATE BUTTER CREAM ICING: Sift 1 tbs cocoa powder with icing sugar.

ORANGE BUTTER CREAM ICING: Add 1 tsp grated orange rind to icing sugar, and use 1 tbs orange juice in place of sherry.

LEMON BUTTER CREAM ICING: Add 1 tsp grated lemon rind to icing sugar, and use 1 tbs lemon juice in place of sherry.

WALNUT BUTTER CREAM ICING: Fold in 2 tbs finely chopped walnuts after mixing.

LIQUEUR BUTTER CREAM ICING: Use 1 tbs Grand Marnier, Crème de Menthe, Crème de Cacao, etc., in place of sherry.

Glacé or Warm Icing

A quickly mixed, easily flavoured icing that sets firmly to a decorative glaze. Decorations should be added quickly before the icing sets.

**1¹/4 cups pure icing sugar; 1 tbs boiling water;
few drops flavouring essence;
food colouring as desired.**

Sift icing sugar into a small, heatproof bowl. Add boiling water gradually, mixing to a smooth, thick paste that will coat the back of the spoon. Place bowl over a small amount of boiling water and stir icing for 1 minute. Add flavouring and colouring as desired. Pour icing quickly over cake and smooth surface with a spatula or knife dipped in hot water. Sufficient to cover top of a 20 cm (8 in) cake.

VARIATIONS

CHOCOLATE GLACE ICING: Sift 1 tbs cocoa powder with icing sugar. Melt 1 tsp butter in boiling water before adding to icing sugar.

COFFEE GLACE ICING: Add 1 tsp instant coffee powder dissolved in 1 tbs boiling water to icing sugar.

LEMON GLACE ICING: Use 1 tbs lemon juice instead of boiling water.

SPICE GLACE ICING: Add ¹/2 tsp each cinnamon and nutmeg and ¹/4 tsp ground cloves to icing sugar.

Royal Icing

**2 egg whites; 4 cups pure icing sugar, sifted;
1 tsp lemon juice; food colouring as desired.**

Place egg white in a bowl and beat lightly. Add icing sugar 1 tbs at a time, beating continuously until mixture is very stiff and stands in peaks. Blend in lemon juice and food colouring. Keep icing covered with a damp cloth to prevent it hardening too quickly. This will cover a 20 cm (8 in) cake and can be used for piped decorations, lettering, etc.

Plastic Fondant Icing

A roll-out type of icing used to cover rich fruit cakes. It gives a very smooth surface for decoration.

500 g (1 lb) pure icing sugar, sifted; 1¹/₄ tsp gelatine; 1 tbs cold water; 2 tsp glycerine; ¹/₄ cup liquid glucose; flavouring and food colouring as desired; maize cornflour for dusting.

Sift icing sugar into a bowl. Soften gelatine in cold water, then place over hot water and stir until dissolved. Remove from heat and add glycerine and glucose, stirring well. Add to icing sugar with flavouring, kneading with the hands until mixture forms a firm dough-like paste. Remove to a board sprinkled with cornflour and knead until smooth and pliable. Food colouring may be added, if desired, and kneaded through. Roll out to fit top and sides of cake. Fit carefully on cake, smoothing with hands dusted with cornflour. Plastic icing may be kept in an airtight container until needed, but do not store in refrigerator as this will harden fondant. Sufficient to cover top and sides of a 20 cm (8 in) cake. Use Modelling Fondant for moulded decorations.

Modelling Fondant

Excellent for moulded decorations, such as fruit and flowers.

¹/₂ tsp gelatine; 1 tbs cold water; 3 tsp liquid glucose; 500 g (1 lb) pure icing sugar, sifted; maize cornflour for dusting; food colouring as desired.

Soften gelatine in water, then place over hot water and stir until dissolved. Remove from heat and stir in glucose. Add to icing sugar, kneading well until all sugar has been absorbed. Put on a board dusted with cornflour and knead until pliable, adding colouring if desired. Keep mixture well wrapped in an airtight container until ready to use. Makes about 2 cups.
NOTE: If the mixture is too dry add a little boiled water, and if too moist add extra sifted icing sugar.

Rich Chocolate Icing

185 g (6 oz) dark chocolate, roughly chopped; ¹/₄ cup dark rum; ¹/₂ tsp vanilla; 2 cups icing sugar, sifted; 30 g (1 oz) butter, softened; 1 tbs hot milk.

Melt chocolate in a heatproof bowl set over simmering water. Stir in rum and vanilla. Add icing sugar, butter and milk. Stir vigorously over the hot water until icing is smooth and glossy. If too thick, add a little more milk. Spread at once over cake. Sufficient to cover top of a 23 cm (9 in) square cake.

Economical Chocolate Icing

1¹/₂ cups icing sugar, sifted; ¹/₂ tsp cinnamon; 1 tbs cocoa powder; 30 g (1 oz) butter; 1 tbs hot water.

Mix icing sugar, cinnamon and cocoa in a bowl, then stir in softened butter and water. Mix to a smooth paste, adding a little more hot water if necessary. Sufficient to cover top of a 20 cm (8 in) cake.

Seven-Minute Frosting

1 cup sugar; ¹/₂ tsp cream of tartar; 1 egg white; 2 tbs water; ¹/₄ tsp vanilla.

Place sugar, cream of tartar, egg white and water in the top of a double saucepan or in a heatproof bowl placed over simmering water (do not allow bottom of bowl to touch water). Beat with an electric beater on slow, or with a rotary beater, until mixture is thick enough to hold its shape. This takes about 7 minutes, which gives the frosting its name. Cool a little, then stir in vanilla or other desired flavourings and spread roughly over cake. Sufficient to cover a bar cake or an 18 cm (7 in) round cake.
NOTE: Quantities may be doubled for larger cakes, in which case the frosting takes about 10 minutes to make.

VARIATIONS
PEPPERMINT SEVEN-MINUTE FROSTING: Add 2–3 drops peppermint essence instead of vanilla and a little pink or green food colouring.
MARSHMALLOW SEVEN-MINUTE FROSTING: When mixture is thick, after cooking for 7 minutes, stir in 1 cup chopped marshmallows. Stir until melted.
CHOCOLATE SEVEN-MINUTE FROSTING: Stir in 90 g (3 oz) melted dark chocolate after cooking for 7 minutes.

Chocolate Cream Cheese Frosting

90 g (3 oz) dark chocolate, roughly chopped; 90 g (3 oz) cream cheese, softened; ¹/₄ cup milk; 4 cups icing sugar, sifted; ¹/₂ tsp salt.

Melt chocolate in a heatproof bowl over hot water. Remove from heat, and gradually beat in cream cheese and milk. Add icing sugar and salt, beating until mixture is smooth and spreadable. Add a little more milk if necessary. Sufficient to cover tops of two 23 cm (9 in) cakes.

Crème au Beurre *(Butter Cream)*

2 egg yolks; ¹/₄ cup sugar; ¹/₂ cup milk;
250 g (8 oz) unsalted butter; ¹/₂ tsp vanilla.

Beat egg yolks with half the sugar until light and creamy. Place remaining sugar and the milk in a heavy saucepan and bring to the boil, stirring to dissolve sugar. Pour milk on to yolk mixture and blend well. Return to pan and stir over gentle heat until custard coats the back of the spoon. Do not allow to boil. Strain and cool. Cream butter and when soft add cooled custard little by little. Flavour with vanilla. Makes about 2 cups.

VARIATIONS

COFFEE CREME AU BEURRE: Stir 2 tsp instant coffee powder into hot custard. Omit vanilla.
CHOCOLATE CREME AU BEURRE: Melt 60 g (2 oz) chopped dark chocolate over hot water. Beat into creamed butter with custard.
RUM CREME AU BEURRE: Beat 1–2 tbs dark rum into creamed butter with custard. Omit vanilla.

Ricotta Rum Filling

Use for small tarts, cakes or with Savoy fingers and a glass of Madeira.

250 g (8 oz) ricotta cheese; ¹/₂ cup sugar;
¹/₂ tsp vanilla; 2 tbs dark rum; 2 tbs grated dark chocolate; 1 tbs chopped glacé fruit
(ginger, apricots, pineapple, etc.).

Combine ricotta, sugar, vanilla and rum and beat until light and fluffy. Fold in chocolate and fruit. Fill sponge or layer cake, wrap in foil, and leave in refrigerator for 2–3 hours before serving. Makes about 2 cups.

Crème Pâtissière
(Custard Cream Filling)

This filling is good for éclairs and cream puffs as well as sponges, cakes and pastries.

1¹/₂ cups milk; 1 vanilla bean; ¹/₂ cup sugar;
¹/₄ cup flour; 2 eggs; 2 egg yolks.

Bring milk to the boil with vanilla bean. Put aside. Mix sugar and flour together, add eggs and egg yolks and beat until light. Remove vanilla bean from milk and gradually pour milk into egg mixture, stirring until well blended. Return to pan and cook over gentle heat, stirring constantly, just until boiling point. Remove from heat and continue stirring for a few minutes to release steam. Turn into a bowl to cook, then chill, covered, until ready to use. Makes about 2 cups.

VARIATIONS

RICH CREME PATISSIERE: After cooling, fold in ³/₄ cup whipped cream.

TUTTI-FRUTTI CREME PATISSIERE: Omit vanilla bean. After cooling, fold in 2 tbs rum, brandy or fruit liqueur, and ¹/₄ cup chopped glacé fruits.
FRANGIPANE CREAM: After removing Crème Pâtissière from heat, beat in 6 g (2 oz) butter and ¹/₄ cup crushed macaroons or chopped blanched almonds.

Lemon Cheese Filling

Delicious as a filling for sponges and cakes, or spread on hot, buttered toast.

60 g (2 oz) butter; grated rind and juice 2 medium lemons; 2 egg yolks (60 g/2 oz eggs); ¹/₂ cup sugar.

Melt butter in top of double saucepan or heatproof bowl set over hot water. Add lemon rind and juice, egg yolks and sugar and stir with a wooden spoon over simmering water until mixture thickens. Allow to cool before using. Mixture may be made in double quantities and will keep well in a covered jar in the refrigerator. Makes 1 cup.

VARIATION

PASSIONFRUIT CHEESE FILLING: Use pulp from 4 large passionfruit in place of lemon rind and juice.

IRISH COFFEE

The success of this famous coffee depends entirely on the use of the finest ingredients – true Irish whiskey, fresh roasted, freshly brewed coffee, and cream, lightly whipped so that it floats on top of the hot coffee. An excellent end to a meal.

Irish coffee is served in tall coffee cups or heatproof glasses. An enterprising manufacturer has made a small burner to take a special Irish Coffee glass. This is used to heat the whiskey in the glass, and it ensures that the coffee is piping hot – part of the charm is to sip the hot whiskey-laced coffee through the layer of cold cream. If serving to guests, arrange ingredients on a tray, take to the table and prepare.

Irish Coffee

8 tbs Irish whiskey; sugar; 3 cups very hot freshly brewed strong coffee; 1 cup cream,
lightly whipped until it holds soft peaks.

Set out 4 heated Irish Coffee glasses or cups. In each glass stir together 2 tbs whiskey (heated over a burner for preference) and 1¹/₂ tsp sugar. Add hot, strong black coffee, and stir until sugar is dissolved. Spoon cream gently on top. Serves 4.

IRISH SODA BREAD

Irish soda bread is one of the specialties of that country, and is baked in countless farmhouses and homes all over Ireland. It is made in white and brown loaves and the Irish enjoy the taste of soda which is used as the raising agent.

White Soda Bread

6 cups flour; I tsp bicarbonate of soda; I tsp salt; I cup buttermilk or sour milk.

Sift dry ingredients into a bowl and make a well in the centre. Add buttermilk in a steady pouring stream, working in flour with a large fork. The dough should be slack but not wet and the mixing done lightly and quickly. Add a little more milk if dough seems too stiff. With floured hands, put dough on to a lightly floured surface and flatten into a round about 4 cm (1½ in) thick. Put on to a baking tray and make a large cross on top with a floured knife. (This is to ensure even distribution of heat.) Bake in a preheated moderately hot oven (190°C/375°C) for about 40 minutes. Test centre with a skewer before removing from oven. To keep bread soft, wrap in a clean tea-towel. Makes 1 large loaf or 2 small ones.

NOTE: If buttermilk or sour milk is not available, 1 cup fresh milk may be used, in which case add 1 tsp cream of tartar to the dry ingredients.

VARIATIONS

BROWN SODA BREAD: Make as for White Soda Bread, using 4 cups wholewheat flour and 2 cups white flour. A little more milk will be needed to mix the dough. If a brittle texture is required, add 1 tbs melted butter. The bread should not be cut until it is quite cold. This takes 4–6 hours.

TREACLE SODA BREAD: Make as for White Soda Bread, but heat 2 tbs black treacle (molasses) with the milk, and add 1½ tsp sugar and ½ cup sultanas, if liked, to the dough.

IRISH STEW

Authentic Irish stew uses 1 kg (2 lb) potatoes and 250 g (8 oz) onions to each 500 g (1 lb) quantities of meat and potatoes, but the gravy may need to be slightly thickened before serving. It was originally made with either mutton or kid.

Irish Stew

I kg (2 lb) lamb neck chops; 2 kg (4 lb) potatoes, peeled; 500 g (I lb) onions, thickly sliced; salt and freshly ground black pepper; 2 cups water; I bouquet garni; 2 bay leaves.

Trim excess fat from chops. Slice a few of the potatoes and halve the rest. Put sliced potatoes into a deep saucepan, then add meat, then halved potatoes and then all the other ingredients. Cover tightly and simmer gently for 2–2½ hours. Shake pan from time to time to prevent stew sticking. This stew should not be thin. It should be thick, well seasoned and creamy. Remove bouquet garni and bay leaves before serving. Serves 6–8.

j

JAMS

Though few of us now want to devote a day to jam-making, or indeed feel the need for a large store of jam, a new generation of cooks is discovering the pleasure of making just a few pots when a favourite fruit is in season. Jam is made by boiling fruit with sugar (firm fruits are first cooked without sugar until tender) until the mixture is pulpy and will set, when cool, to a soft jelly-like consistency. It is perfectly practical to make a small quantity and does not take long providing you understand a few basic points.

PECTIN: The substance in fruit which, with the right balance of acid and sugar, causes jam to set. The fruit used should be firm-ripe as it contains more pectin than when fully ripe. When making jam with fruits that are low in pectin, such as cherries, apricots and strawberries, the setting can be helped by adding some high-pectin fruit (apple, plum, quince, black or red currants) or a bag of lemon peel, including the high-pectin white pith. Commercial pectin is also available.

SETTING POINT: The fruit is usually simmered until soft, then sugar is added and the jam is boiled vigorously until setting point is reached. Test for this by the spoon method or the saucer method.

The Spoon Method: Dip a clean wooden spoon into the jam and remove a spoonful. Allow to cool for a few moments, then turn spoon over gently. If jam breaks distinctly from the spoon in heavy, jelly-like drops or flakes, it is ready.

The Saucer Method: Place a small teaspoon of jam on a cold saucer, cool for 20 seconds, then run a finger through it. If it wrinkles at the edges and stays in two separate sections, it is ready.

POTTING AND SEALING: Wash jars in hot water, drain thoroughly and heat in a low oven before filling. Remove jam from heat, cool slightly and stir gently to distribute the fruit evenly. Use a clean, hot jug or cup and fill to within 3 mm (1/8 in) of the top of jar. Cover surface of hot jam with a greaseproof disc, and seal with screw-top lids or cellophane covers with rubber bands (moisten outside of cellophane first to ensure a tight fit). Label and store in a cool, dark, dry place. See recipes.

Plum Jam

Blood plums, satsumas or angelinas make particularly good plum jam, rich and tart, so try to get one of these varieties.

**1 kg (2 lb) firm plums, halved; butter;
1/2 cup water; 1 kg (2 lb) sugar, warmed.**

Remove stones from plums, crack a few and remove kernels. Butter a large heavy saucepan, add plums and water and cook gently until tender, 15–20 minutes. Add warm sugar and heat until sugar dissolves, stirring occasionally. Add kernels, bring to the boil rapidly and boil vigorously about 20 minutes or until setting point is reached. Remove pan from heat immediately, cool a little, stir gently and pour into hot sterilised jars. Cover and seal. Makes 3–4 x 500 g (1 lb) jars.

Blackberry Jam

**1.5 kg (3 lb) firm blackberries, including a few red ones; 1/4 cup water; 2 tbs lemon juice;
sliced peel (including white pith) 1 lemon;
1.5 kg (3 lb) sugar, warmed.**

Place blackberries in a large, heavy buttered pan. Add water, lemon juice and peel tied in a muslin bag. Press berries with a wooden spoon to release juice. Bring slowly to boiling point and simmer 30 minutes. Remove bag of peel. Add sugar gradually to berries, stirring until dissolved, then boil quickly until setting point is reached. Remove pan from heat immediately and cool jam a little. Stir gently and pour into hot sterilised jars. Cover and seal. Makes 4–5 x 500 g (1 lb) jars.

Tomato Jam

**butter; 1.5 kg (3 lb) very firm, red tomatoes,
peeled and thickly sliced; 1.5 kg (3 lb) sugar;
3 tbs lemon juice; sliced peel (including white pith)
1 lemon; pinch salt.**

Butter a large heavy saucepan and add tomatoes and sugar. Bring to the boil slowly, stirring until sugar has dissolved, then add lemon juice and peel tied in a muslin bag. Boil quickly until setting point is reached. Stir in salt and remove pan from heat immediately. Remove bag of peel, cool jam a little and pour into hot sterilised jars. Cover and seal. Makes 4–5 x 500 g (1 lb) jars.

Peach and Passionfruit Jam

**10–12 passionfruit; 6–8 large, firm peaches,
peeled, stoned and chopped; sugar; lemon juice.**

Cut passionfruit in half and scoop out flesh. Mix with peaches. Measure fruit and for every 5 cups, allow 1 kg (2 lb) sugar and 2 tbs lemon juice. Put all ingredients into a heavy saucepan and bring to the boil slowly, stirring until sugar has dissolved. Boil rapidly until setting point is reached. Remove from heat immediately, cool a little, stir gently and pour into hot sterilised jars. Cover and seal. Makes 3–4 x 500 g (1 lb) jars.

JELLY, PRESERVE

Jelly preserves are made from the pure juice of fruit cleared of all other matter, to which sugar is added and the mixture boiled until it reaches setting point. As in jam, pectin, sugar and acid must be present in the right proportions.

The fruit used should be slightly underripe because it has more pectin than when fully ripe. Choose fruit such as grapes, crab apples, guavas, quinces or any fruit high in pectin and acid to establish a good firm jel. Good jelly must be clear in colour, well flavoured and set so that it holds its shape.

Jelly preserves are made by boiling fruit, cut into small pieces with the skin on, with just enough cold water to cover, until fruit is tender. This dissolves out the pectin and acid. Soft fruits such as berries need very little water. The pulp is then strained through a jelly bag and allowed to drain quite undisturbed, usually for about 12 hours. The liquid is measured into a pan and sugar added in the correct proportion. The mixture is then boiled rapidly until setting point is reached.

The Jelly Bag can be purchased ready for use, fixed in a stand, or can be made at home: buy a square of coarse flannel and sew strong white tape across each corner to make a loop just big enough to fit the legs of a chair. Fix an inverted chair firmly into the corner of a table (never stand it on the side of a table), slip the tape firmly on to the legs and pour boiling water through the flannel to cleanse and open the cloth. Have a large earthenware bowl under the strainer; empty and replace the bowl. When fruit has been boiled until soft and broken down, pour the contents of the saucepan into the jelly bag and leave to drain undisturbed. Do not press fruit or squeeze bag as this will give a cloudy jelly. Measure juice back into the saucepan by dipping with a cup measure, leaving any sediment behind in the bowl.

Small quantities of fruit can be drained through several thicknesses of cheesecloth in a colander over a bowl, instead of a jelly bag. Setting Point is tested in the same way as jam. For Potting and Sealing see *Jams*.

See also *Grape Jelly* (page 183); *Guava Jelly* (page 186); *Redcurrant Jelly* (page 411).

Quince Jelly

1 kg (2 lb) firm, ripe quinces; about 1 kg (2 lb) sugar.

Cut quinces into chunks and put them in a saucepan with 6 cups water. Bring to the boil and simmer until fruit is soft.

Strain liquid from quinces through a jelly bag, or a colander lined with several thicknesses of cheesecloth, into a bowl; allow to drip undisturbed without pressing or squeezing. Measure juice by dipping with a cup measure from bowl into saucepan. Do not use sediment. Add 500 g (1 lb) sugar for every 2½ cups juice. Bring slowly to the boil, stirring to dissolve sugar before liquid starts to boil, then boil rapidly until a few drops of the mixture, dropped on to a chilled plate, will set as they cool. Skim if necessary and pour into clean, warm jars. Seal while hot. Makes 3–4 x 500 g (1 lb) jars.

NOTE: A good jelly can be made using a mixture of quince and apples. Quinces or apples may be used in combination with fruits that have a low pectin

content, such as raspberries or blackberries, either fresh or frozen.

VARIATION

APPLE JELLY: Make in exactly the same way as Quince Jelly, using good tart apples.

JELLY, SWEET AND SAVOURY

Many of us first associate the word 'jelly' with those high moulded puddings, in bright shimmering colours, served at children's birthday parties, but popular sweets such as Turkish Delight are jellies, too, and other types of table jellies can be clear or opaque.

JELLY (SWEET): Popular sweets such as Marshmallows (see page 255), fruit jellies, jujubes and Turkish Delight (see page 555) come into this category. These are based on a sugar syrup which is stiffened by adding gelatine, gum Arabic, cornflour, or arrowroot, and reduced by boiling.

JELLY (TABLE): A sweet mixture to which a setting agent such as gelatine is added to give a set firm enough to hold its shape when unmoulded. For savoury dishes, an aspic jelly is often used (see *Aspic*). Vegetable juices, tomatoes, cooked vegetables or seafoods are often set in jelly form.

There are three main types of table jelly – Clear, Whipped, and made with Milk, Cream and Egg.

Clear Jellies: Transparent jellies of good colour, made from fruit juices or commercial jelly crystals. These are usually set in moulds and turned out to serve, or set in glass dishes. A very attractive effect can be achieved by setting fruit in layers in the jelly.

Whipped Jellies or Jelly Whips: The jellies are whipped when they are just on the point of setting, and resemble the consistency of unbeaten egg white.

Milk, Cream and Egg Jellies: Milk, custards and creams set with gelatine. Some classic desserts such as Bavarian Cream (see page 123) come into this category. See recipes.

TO UNMOULD JELLIES: See *Gelatine*.

Orange Jelly Baskets

**6–8 large oranges (enough to give 2 cups juice);
3–4 lemons; 2 cups water; 1 cup sugar;
thinly peeled rind 2 oranges; 3 tbs gelatine;
12–14 thin strips angelica, 13 cm (5 in) long.**

Halve oranges and lemons, scoop out flesh and press it through a sieve, or put in a blender, to remove juice. Gently press orange skins to flatten their bases so that the halves will sit flat. Put water, sugar, orange rind and gelatine in a saucepan and stir over gentle heat until sugar and gelatine are dissolved. Cover, remove from heat, and set aside for 10 minutes. Strain through a fine nylon sieve and add strained orange and lemon juice. When cool, pour into prepared orange skins and leave to set. Dip strips of angelica into boiling water to make them pliable and bend each into a half circle. Before serving, fix angelica handles over jellies. Makes 12–16.

Port Wine Jelly

An old-fashioned dessert, definitely not for children.

**2 tbs gelatine; 1¹/₄ cups water; 2 tbs sugar;
2 tsp redcurrant jelly; 2 cups port wine;
few drops red food colouring (optional);
whipped cream.**

Soften gelatine in water in a saucepan for 2 minutes. Add sugar and redcurrant jelly and stir over a gentle heat until dissolved. Stir in port and food colouring, if using. Strain through muslin or disposable cloth, pour into a wetted mould or into individual wine glasses and chill until set. Top with whipped cream, or unmould and serve with whipped cream. Serves 6–8.

Strawberry Jelly Whip

**1 packet strawberry jelly crystals; 2 egg whites;
whipped cream and fresh strawberries to decorate.**

Make jelly according to packet instructions and leave until just beginning to set, then whip it until light and frothy. Whisk egg whites until standing in soft peaks and fold into whipped jelly mixture. Pour into 6 individual glass dishes and refrigerate until set. Serve decorated with a swirl of whipped cream and a whole strawberry. Serves 6.
NOTE: This recipe can be varied by using other jelly flavours and proceeding as above.

Milk Jelly

**2 cups milk; ¹/₄ cup caster sugar;
3 thin strips lemon rind or ¹/₂ tsp vanilla;
1 tsp gelatine; 3 tbs water.**

Place milk in a saucepan with sugar and lemon rind, if using. Place over gentle heat and stir until sugar dissolves. Turn off heat and allow to infuse for 10 minutes if using lemon rind, or stir in vanilla. Soften gelatine in water and dissolve over gentle heat. Add to cooled milk, strain into wetted 2¹/₂-cup mould and refrigerate until set. Turn out and serve. Serves 4.

Seafood Mousse

**1 tbs gelatine; ¹/₄ cup cold water;
3/4 cup very finely chopped celery;
1¹/₂ cups flaked canned or cooked lobster, crab or salmon; ¹/₄ tsp salt; ¹/₄ tsp paprika;
3/4 cup Mayonnaise (page 256); 3 tbs lemon juice;
¹/₄ tsp Tabasco sauce; 1 small clove garlic, crushed;
¹/₂ cup cream, whipped; shredded lettuce or watercress to garnish.**

Soften gelatine in cold water, then dissolve over hot water. Combine celery and seafood. Season with salt and paprika. Stir gelatine into mayonnaise, and add lemon juice, Tabasco and garlic. Stir in seafood mixture. Fold whipped cream gently into mixture. Spoon into a wetted 4-cup mould and chill until set. To serve, unmould on to a platter garnished with shredded lettuce or watercress. Serves 6–8.

Jellied Beetroot

**1¹/₂ tbs gelatine; ¹/₂ cup cold water;
3¹/₂ cups chicken stock; juice ¹/₂ lemon;
1 tbs dry sherry; 3 whole cloves; 1 bay leaf;
1 sprig parsley; 1 sprig fresh thyme; salt and freshly ground white pepper; 500 g (1 lb) cooked beetroot, peeled and sliced; watercress to serve.**

Soften gelatine in cold water, then dissolve over simmering water. Heat stock, lemon juice, sherry, cloves, bay leaf, parsley, thyme, salt and pepper and when just at the boil remove from heat and stir in dissolved gelatine. Cover and keep warm for 10 minutes. Strain into an 8-cup mould and add beetroot. To serve, unmould on to a bed of watercress. Serves 6–8.

JUNIPER BERRY

The flavour of ripe juniper berries is sweet, aromatic and rather like pine because they contain elements of turpentine. Juniper berries are used to flavour gin and other spirits. In fact, it is considered that 6–8 of these berries soaked in a marinade for a long time – or cooked slowly in a stew – give a seasoning equivalent of ¹/₄ cup gin.

Juniper berries are used in marinades for wild boar, pork and venison, in stuffings for chicken and other small birds, and in pâté. In Germany, juniper berries are a common flavouring for Sauerkraut, and in Britain they are used in the curing of country hams.

The berries are usually crushed before use. They go well with herbs – parsley, thyme, fennel, marjoram, bay and garlic – as well as with brandy or port, and with other spices when used in meat dishes. The berries may be bought dried – look for ones that are still plump.

JUNKET

This favourite English dish is made of warmed milk, sweetened and flavoured, and coagulated with rennet or junket tablets made with the enzyme rennin extracted from calves' stomachs. Vanilla-flavoured junket tablets are available, or some packs offer an assortment of flavours.

Junket

2 cups milk; 2 tsp sugar; $^1\!/_2$ tsp vanilla; 1 junket tablet; $^1\!/_2$ cup thickened cream; nutmeg (optional).

Warm milk just to blood heat. Add sugar and vanilla. Crush junket tablet in a little water. Pour milk into a china dish, stir in dissolved junket tablet and leave to set in a cool place (not the refrigerator). Pour cream over surface of the junket. If liked, a little nutmeg may be sprinkled over the top. Serves 4.

k

KASHA

Outside Russia kasha is the name of a coarse buckwheat meal, but in Russia both buckwheat and other cooked grains are called kasha. Buckwheat kasha has an assertive almond-like flavour; it can be served with all meat dishes, especially with rich meats like pork, duck or goose.

Buckwheat Kasha

2 cups buckwheat meal (kasha), or 1 cup buckwheat and 1 cup burghul (cracked wheat);
3 cups stock or water; 1 tsp salt (optional);
45 g (1¹/₂ oz) butter.

If grain is not toasted (brown) already, place it in a dry frying pan and toast over medium heat, stirring often, until golden-brown. Bring stock or water to the boil in a heavy saucepan, adding salt unless stock is already seasoned. Pour toasted grain in slowly, stirring constantly. Return to the boil over gentle heat and simmer for a few minutes until thick. Stir in butter, cover and cook gently 10 minutes. Remove lid and fluff up kasha with a fork. Leave uncovered over very low heat for 1 hour, tossing and turning it with a fork every 5 minutes to separate grains. Serves 4–5 as an accompaniment.

VARIATIONS

KASHA WITH MUSHROOMS AND ONIONS: Cook Buckwheat Kasha as described in recipe, and fold through 90 g (3 oz) sliced mushrooms and 1 large chopped onion which have been sautéed together in butter.

KASHA WITH PORK AND ONIONS: Cook Buckwheat Kasha as described in recipe, and fold through 125 g (4 oz) diced pickled (salt) pork and 1 large chopped onion which have been sautéed together in a little butter until pork is crisp and brown.

HERBED SESAME KASHA: Cook Buckwheat Kasha as described in recipe, and fold through 2 tbs each toasted sesame seeds and chopped fresh herbs (parsley, thyme, chives, oregano, basil).

KEBAB

Strictly speaking, a kebab is a piece of meat, but what is generally referred to today as a kebab is, in fact, a shish kebab which is derived from the Turkish words *shish*, meaning skewer, and *kebab*, meaning grilled (known as *shashlik* in Russia). It consists of small pieces of meat threaded on to the skewers or swords and grilled.

The secret of all skewer cookery is in the seasoning or marinades used to flavour the meats. The meats are well seasoned and sometimes marinated beforehand, and may be combined with onions, mushrooms, peppers and so on, threaded on the same skewers. For best results, shish kebab should be cooked over a charcoal fire; next best is under a preheated grill.

Shish kebab is often served with boiled or saffron rice or with the flat pita or Lebanese bread, which should be toasted lightly over the charcoal or under the grill before filling. If served with the flat bread, make a pocket by cutting open one side of the bread; then when the kebab is ready, lay the skewer in the bread pocket, squeeze it together gently to hold the meat etc., at the same time pulling out the skewer. Tabouleh (see page 524) may be added to the pocket.

■ **TO PREPARE:** After soaking in the marinade (if used), the food is threaded on skewers. Flat metal ones are good as the food won't slip around on them as they're turned. Bamboo or wooden skewers are used in Asia, and if the wood is still green, they won't char during cooking. Otherwise, soak them in cold water for an hour before using so they won't burn.

■ **TO COOK:** Place skewered food about 8–10 cm (3–4 in) from the heat on grill or barbecue, brushing with marinade and turning several times as it cooks. Don't overcook. Lamb or beef should be well browned on the outside, but still moist and pink on the inside. Vegetables are often cooked on skewers, by themselves or alternated with pieces of meat or seafood. Squares of red or green pepper, small onions, mushrooms, slices of eggplant or tomatoes, slices of corn on the cob or chunks of zucchini are all good additions. **See recipes.**

Marinated Kebabs

This is one of the simplest but best marinades. Use it for lamb, beef, pork or chicken. It is also good with scallops, green prawns or other seafood.

1.5 kg (3 lb) boneless lamb, tender steak, or other meat, trimmed of excess fat and gristle and cut into bite-sized cubes.

MARINADE: 4 tbs oil; 4 tbs lemon juice; 2 tbs chopped parsley; 2 bay leaves, crumbled; 1 clove garlic, finely chopped; salt and freshly ground black pepper.

Combine marinade ingredients in a glass or pottery dish and add meat. Marinate for 2 hours, turning now and again. Thread meat cubes on to 6 metal skewers, spacing them a little apart. Reserve marinade. Brush grill rack with oil and barbecue kebabs over hot coals or cook under a preheated grill for 4–5 minutes on each side. The meat cubes should be brown outside but still pink inside for beef or lamb – pork is usually preferred cooked through. Brush with reserved marinade several times as they cook. Serve with rice noodles, or inside soft buns or flat Lebanese bread, with a selection of fresh salads. Serves 6.

Middle East Kebabs

Minced beef is mixed with yogurt and a special spice mix, Baharat, and moulded on to skewers to make interesting kebabs. The finished kebabs are served in flat bread with salad vegetables.

500 g (1 lb) best quality minced beef;
1 small onion, grated; 2 tbs plain yogurt;
2 tsp Baharat (see page 499); 1 tsp salt;
1 clove garlic, crushed; 1 tbs lemon juice.

TO SERVE: flat Lebanese bread; Tabouleh (page 524); shredded lettuce or sliced tomato.

Place all ingredients in a bowl and combine very thoroughly by hand, kneading until mixture becomes smooth and compact. Divide into 8 portions, and mould each one around the top of the flat metal skewer (not a round one, or meat will slip) in a cigar shape. Barbecue close to hot coals or cook under a preheated grill for 6–8 minutes, turning to brown all sides. Slip inside pockets of flat Lebanese bread with tabouleh and shredded lettuce or sliced tomato. A little plain yogurt spooned over makes a nice sauce. Serves 4–6.

Kufteh Kebabs
(Rolled Kebabs)

Called Kufteh Kebab, or Luleh Kebab, a favourite Iranian dish. 'Luleh' means rolled: the meat is shaped into long rolls or shaped around a skewer. If you enter a Teheran bazaar you may see merchants sitting in their shops and eating this dish with nane lavash, a flat crisp bread, and spring onions.

500 g (1 lb) minced beef or lamb; 1 large onion, grated; 1 egg, beaten; 1/2 tsp black pepper;
1/4 tsp cinnamon.

Combine meat with remaining ingredients, beating well with a wooden spoon until meat seems lighter in colour. Take a handful of mixture and roll in into a flat cigar shape. Or, if you have flat skewers, shape meat around skewers into sausages 13 cm (5 in) in length and 2.5 cm (1 in) in diameter. Barbecue over hot coals or cook under a preheated hot grill for 5–8 minutes or to your own taste, turning to brown all sides. Serve with boiled rice and, if liked, grilled tomatoes. May also be eaten with flat Lebanese bread. Serves 4.

Moroccan Kebabs

The fresh, lemon flavour of cumin gives an intriguing taste to these kebabs. The other spice is ground ginger. If you want to be a little more exotic, use 1 tbs grated fresh ginger instead of ground ginger, and add 3 tbs plain yogurt to the marinade.

1.5 kg (3 lb) boneless lamb, cut from leg, chump or shoulder, trimmed of excess fat and gristle and cut into bite-size cubes; 2 small green peppers, cored, seeded and cut into squares; 1 small onion,

quartered; Saffron Rice or Tabouleh (pages 415 and 524) to serve.

MARINADE: 1 small onion, finely chopped;
1/2 tsp salt; 1 tsp ground cumin; 1 tsp ground ginger;
1/2 tsp black pepper; 4 tbs olive oil;
1 tsp paprika; dash cayenne.

Combine marinade ingredients in a glass or pottery dish, add meat and leave for 2 hours, turning meat now and again. Separate onion quarters into petals. Thread meat, peppers and onion alternately on to 6 metal skewers, not too close together. Reserve marinade. Brush grill rack with oil and barbecue kebabs over hot coals or cook under a preheated grill for 8–10 minutes or until brown outside and still pink inside. Turn skewers as they cook, and brush with reserved marinade from time to time. Serve with saffron rice, or push skewers into pockets of flat Lebanese bread with tabouleh. Serves 6.

Oriental Lamb Kebabs

Lamb is popular in northern China and a beautifully seasoned dish of skewered lamb is featured at the famous Peking Duck restaurant in Beijing (formerly called Peking). Szechuan peppercorns and sweet bean paste can be found at Asian food stores.

1 tsp Szechuan peppercorns or black peppercorns;
1/4 cup light soy sauce; 2 tbs Chinese rice wine;
1 tbs finely chopped garlic; 1 tbs finely chopped fresh ginger; 2 tsp Oriental sesame oil;
1 tsp five-spice powder; 1/4 tsp white pepper;
1 kg (2 lb) boneless lamb shoulder, trimmed of excess fat and gristle and cut into bite-sized cubes; sweet bean paste to serve.

Place peppercorns in a small, heavy frying pan and stir over moderate heat for 3 minutes or until fragrant. Pulverize in a blender, or by hand with a mortal and pestle, and place in a large bowl. Add remaining ingredients, except lamb, and stir to combine. Add lamb cubes to marinade, tossing to coat each piece. Cover and leave to marinate for 3 hours at room temperature or overnight in refrigerator. Soak 6 long bamboo skewers in water for 1 hour (to prevent charring).

Thread lamb cubes on to skewers, leaving a little space between each cube. Reserve marinade. Arrange skewers on a rack placed over grill pan and grill about 10 cm (4 in) from heat for 8–10 minutes. While lamb is cooking, turn skewers to brown evenly and baste several times with reserved marinade. Serve with boiled rice and sweet bean paste for dipping. Serves 6.

KEDGEREE

See Finnan Haddie.

KID

The meat of a young goat, kid is beginning to appear in some of our more enterprising butchers' shops. A whole roast kid is the festive dish of the Greeks and other Mediterranean peoples who cook it with oil and wine, garlic and aromatic herbs, while Saudi Arabians stuff it with rice, fruit and nuts and rub it with spices. These approaches bring out the best in this sweet and tender but somewhat dry and bland-flavoured meat.

You can use kid in any recipe for lamb, but it is advisable to marinate it for up to 24 hours before cooking, and to protect roast kid against dryness by barding (covering with fat bacon or pork fat) or larding (threading strips of pork fat through the meat) (see page 171).

KIDNEY

Known as offal or variety meat, the kidneys of beef, lamb, veal and, less frequently, pork are used in cookery. Kidneys may be used alone or combined with other meats.

Lambs' kidneys are one of the most delicious morsels; calves' kidneys are even more delectable, especially for those who find other kidneys, especially ox kidneys, too strong. Ox kidneys are mostly used in steak and kidney pudding or pie, though they can be quite tasty cooked in a casserole.

Unless directed to cook them whole with some of their skin and fat still around them, kidneys should be cleared of their fat, membrane and white core before cooking. Eat them as fresh as possible and store in the refrigerator for no longer then 24 hours.

If cooked for too long, kidneys tend to be tough and coarse in flavour. **See recipes.**

Grilled Lambs' Kidneys: Cut out core from kidneys with scissors and remove skin. Split kidneys in half, taking care not to sever them completely. Open kidneys out and run 2 skewers horizontally through them to keep them flat while grilling. Place 2 or 3 kidneys on each skewer. Season with salt and freshly ground black pepper, brush with melted butter or oil and place back on the grill rack, cut sides uppermost. Cook under a preheated very hot grill for 3 minutes on each side. Remove skewers and serve the kidneys immediately.

See also *Steak and Kidney Pudding/Pie.*

Lamb's Kidney in Potato

4 potatoes; 15 g (¹/₂ oz) butter; 4 lambs' kidneys; salt and freshly ground black pepper.

Scrub potatoes, dry and pierce skins in several places with a fork. Rub butter over surface of each potato. Cut a good slice off top and scoop out a hole inside big enough to hold a whole lamb's kidney on which you have left a little of the fat. Skin kidneys and remove core. Put a kidney into each potato, season with salt and pepper, then put top slice of potato on as a lid, tying it on firmly. Bake in preheated moderate oven (180°C/350°F) for about 1¹/₂ hours. When potato is tender, the kidney will be cooked. Serves 4.

Ox Kidney Casserole

1 whole ox kidney; 30 g (1 oz) butter; 10 mushrooms, sliced; 1 small onion, chopped; 1 tbs flour; 5 tbs warm red or white wine; 5 tbs warm good stock; salt and freshly ground black pepper; 2 tbs cream; 2 tbs chopped parsley; toast points to serve.

Cut kidney in half and remove all trace of fat. Cut each half in half and then into slices. Plunge (for a second only) into boiling water, then drain on a cloth and dry well. Chop the kidney coarsely and fry quickly in butter. Remove with a slotted spoon and put aside. Brown mushrooms and onion in the butter. Stir in flour, then wine and stock. Season with salt and pepper and simmer for 5 minutes. Add chopped kidney, having first carefully drained off any fat or exudation from it. Stir in cream and heat through gently. Serve sprinkled with chopped parsley, with toast points. Serves 4.

Veal Kidney à la Crème

2 veal kidneys, skinned and split in half; 45 g (1¹/₂ oz) butter; 2 tbs brandy, warmed; 3 tbs sherry; 6 mushrooms, sliced; 1 cup cream; freshly grated horseradish.

Soak kidneys in cold water for 30 minutes. Drain, remove cores and slice. Brown quickly in butter. As soon as raw look has disappeared, pour brandy over kidney slices and set it alight. Shake pan until flames die down, then add sherry and mushrooms. Cook for 10 minutes. Stir in cream and horseradish to taste. Bring to just on boiling point and serve at once, with boiled rice. Serves 3–4.

Kidneys in Mustard Sauce

2 veal kidneys, or 6 lambs' kidneys, skinned and split in half; seasoned flour; 90 g (3 oz) butter; 2 tsp French mustard; 2 tbs chopped spring onions; ¹/₂ cup dry white wine; 2 tsp lemon juice; ¹/₄ cup chopped parsley.

Soak kidneys in cold water for 30 minutes. Drain, remove cores and slice thinly. Coat kidney slices in seasoned flour and brown in half the butter. Remove and keep hot. Stir mustard into fat in pan with remaining butter, add spring onions, cook for 1 minute stirring, then add wine and lemon juice. Return kidneys and cook gently until liquid is reduced by half. Add parsley and cook for 1 minute. Serve with fluffy boiled rice or noodles, or with toast. Serves 4.

Veal Kidney Liègeoise

**2 veal kidneys, skinned and cored;
30 g (1 oz) plus 2 tsp butter; salt and freshly ground black pepper; 1/4 cup gin, warmed;
4 juniper berries, crushed; 1/4 cup stock.**

Leave a very thin layer of fat all round kidneys. Heat 30 g (1 oz) butter in or stewpan or cocotte just large enough to hold kidneys. Season kidneys with salt and pepper, place in pan and cook gently for about 30 minutes, turning often. Five minutes before serving, pour in gin, flame and shake pan until flames die down. Add juniper berries and stock and boil to reduce a little, then swirl in remaining butter. Serve with boiled rice or toast points. Serves 3–4.

KIPPER

The word 'kipper' generally refers to a split, cleaned herring which is then brined, dried and smoked. The best-tasting kippers are those that have been cured in the traditional way without added dyes or artificial smoking.

Buy kippers fresh and loose if you can; although the frozen ones keep their texture well, they lose a little flavour. Kippers are also available canned or vacuum-packed. Fresh, loose kippers can sometimes be very salty; if so, place them in a shallow dish, cover with boiling water and stand for 5 minutes before grilling. See recipes.

Grilled Kippers

4 kippers, fresh or frozen; 30 g (1 oz) butter, softened.

TO SERVE: butter; lemon wedges.

Place kippers in a shallow dish, cover with boiling water and stand for 5 minutes. Drain and dry well. Spread softened butter over each kipper, place skin side down on a grill rack and cook under a preheated moderate grill on one side only for about 8 minutes or until brown and crisp. Remove from heat and serve topped with a pat of butter and lemon wedges. Serves 4.

VARIATION

GRILLED KIPPERS WITH MUSTARD BUTTER: Combine 60 g (2 oz) butter with 2 tsp prepared English mustard, pinch sugar and salt to taste. Chill before serving with kippers, grilled as above.

Baked Kippers

This dish is perfect for Sunday brunch. Serve with creamy scrambled eggs (see page 137) accompanied by hot bread rolls or hot buttered rice.

**6 kippers, canned or packaged; 60 g (2 oz) butter; juice 1/2 lemon; few drops Tabasco sauce;
1/2 tsp Worcestershire sauce (optional);
chopped parsley.**

Lightly butter a baking dish and arrange kippers in it. Dot with butter and bake in a preheated hot oven (200°C/400°F) about 15 minutes or until butter melts and fish is heated through. In a small saucepan combine remaining butter, lemon juice, Tabasco and Worcestershire sauce, if using. Pour over hot kippers and sprinkle with chopped parsley. Serves 6.

KOHLRABI

A member of the cabbage family which is a native of northern Europe. The name comes from the German and means 'cabbage turnip'.

This vegetable is the globular swelling of the stem of the plant which grows above the ground; it is not, as is commonly thought, a root vegetable. Prepare in the same manner as turnip; its flavour is rather like that of a turnip, but more delicate. It may be boiled and puréed; cooked in slices and finished off *au gratin*, or boiled and finished off by sautéeing in butter. It is also excellent raw, finely shredded or cut in julienne (matchstick) strips in a salad.

■ **TO COOK:** Cut off tops of 4 kohlrabi and pare roots. Slice and drop into boiling salted water, then cook, uncovered, until tender. Drain well and peel. Purée with 15 g (1/2 oz) butter, or toss slices in butter and finish off with a dusting of freshly grated nutmeg. Serves 4.

Turkish Grated Salad

A very pretty salad, with mounds of different coloured raw vegetables and bright garnishes.

**1 lettuce; 3 medium carrots, grated;
2 kohlrabi, grated; 1 large yellow swede turnip,
or 2 beetroot, grated; 1/2 small, firm cabbage,
finely shredded; olive oil; salt and freshly ground black pepper; ground cumin.**

**GARNISH: black olives; red radishes; parsley;
lemon wedges.**

Rinse and dry lettuce leaves and use to line a large platter. Arrange separate mounds of each vegetable on lettuce leaves. Sprinkle generously with olive oil, and season with salt, pepper and a sprinkle of cumin. Garnish platter decoratively with olives, radishes, parsley and lemon wedges. Serves 6–8.

KUGELHUPF

See *Gugelhopf*.

LADIES' FINGERS

This name belongs to two completely different foods: the first is okra with its tapering green pods (see *Okra*). The second kind of fingers are cigarette-shaped pastries which may have a savoury meat filling and form part of the Middle Eastern array of hors d'oeuvre called *mezze*, or, with a sweet filling, are a Cypriot accompaniment to coffee.

In some sweet recipes, Ladies' Fingers may refer to sponge fingers or boudoir biscuits.

Ladies' Fingers (Bahem Bahgen)

3 large onions, finely chopped; 3 tbs olive oil; 750 g (1^1/2 lb) minced lamb; 2 x 425 g cans tomatoes, drained; 3 tbs tomato paste; 1 tsp sugar; ^{3}/4 tsp ground allspice; 2 tbs lemon juice; 1^1/2 tsp salt; freshly ground black pepper; 3 tbs pine nuts; 375 g (12 oz) filo pastry; 125 g (4 oz) butter, melted.

Fry onions in oil until soft. Combine meat, tomatoes and tomato paste in a bowl. Add onions, sugar, allspice, lemon juice, salt and a good grinding of pepper. Mix with your hands, squeezing and kneading mixture for 2 minutes to blend smoothly. Add pine nuts and mix through. Unfold pastry on dry tea-towel. Cover with another dry tea-towel, then with a damp one. Keep pastry covered while you are working to prevent it drying out.

Remove one sheet, brush lightly with melted butter and place another sheet on top. Brush again with butter. Continue until you have 4 layers of pastry. Cut into 13 cm (5 in) squares. Spoon a line of meat filling on one side of each square. Fold edges in and roll up like a cigarette. Repeat with remaining pastry and filling. Brush tops of pastry rolls with butter, place on greased baking trays and bake in a preheated hot oven (200°C/400°F) for 20 minutes until crisp and lightly browned. Serve hot. Makes about 24.

LAKSA

A Singapore–Malaysian soupy noodle dish, said to be first created by the ancient Chinese who migrated to Malaysia, laksa is sold as a meal from hundreds of soup vendors, all of whom have their own special recipe. This Southeast Asian fast food provides the diner with a rich, filling, many-layered experience.

Laksa starts off with a spice paste, which is made into a rich coconut broth. Then crab or fishcakes or prawns or chicken are added with noodles and a few or great many garnishes. The word 'laksa' means 'ten thousand', because there are so many garnishes added.

Laksa can be elaborate or simple and these days is easy to make at home by using one of the many laksa pastes commercially available. Chinese chopsticks and china spoons are a must for laksa.

Chicken Laksa

For a feast, finish this hot and spicy noodle soup, with garnishes such as quartered hard-boiled eggs, matchsticks of cucumber, coriander or mint sprigs. Offer wedges of lime or lemon for diners to squeeze over the laksa.

1 x size 15 chicken, preferably free-range; 1 onion, halved; 1 x 2.5 cm (1 in) piece ginger, sliced; 1 tbs oil; 2 tbs commercial laksa paste; about 3 cups chicken stock or water; 3 cups coconut milk; ^{1}/2 cup coconut cream; 500 g (1 lb) rice vermicelli, soaked in cold water; 2 cups bean sprouts, tailed; ^{1}/2 cup crisp fried shallots.

Wash the chicken inside and out. Place in a large saucepan with enough water to cover. Add the onion and ginger. Bring to the boil, skim the surface, lower the heat, and simmer, covered, for 40 minutes. Remove the chicken, straining and reserving the cooking liquid. Cool, cut the chicken into large pieces and remove the skin and bones. Shred as much chicken as you wish to use into strips.

Heat the oil in a large saucepan. Add the laksa paste mixture, stir until aromatic and oil separates from the paste. Add chicken stock or water and coconut milk, stirring constantly until boiling. Do not stop stirring, or coconut milk may curdle. Slowly add coconut cream, stirring to combine.

Drain the soaked vermicelli and drop into the coconut milk mixture, adding extra stock if necessary to make enough of the soup liquor. Bring back to the boil then remove from heat. Drain the noodles, using a slotted spoon or tongs, and divide between 4 deep soup bowls. Add the bean sprouts and chicken. Carefully ladle the hot soup on to the noodles. Top with fried shallots and, if liked, some chilli paste. Serves 4.

CRISP-FRIED SHALLOTS: Either fry thinly sliced shallots until crisp and golden in oil or toss in a little oil and cook in a microwave oven on High until golden, turning frequently.

LAMB

You can always be sure that you are buying true lamb because the carcase must, by law, be stamped for its full length with the word 'lamb' after passing inspection. As it comes from young animals, lamb is basically a tender, succulent meant. Top-quality lamb, freshly cut, has fine-grained, light reddish-pink meat, with an even edge of firm, white fat. Avoid meat which is coarse-grained, dull in colour or lacking in fat, or whose fat is discoloured. These can indicate an animal which was in poor condition.

Please see *Meat* for amount to buy, factors determining tenderness, testing meat for doneness, carving, etc.

ROAST LAMB

■ CHOICE CUTS FOR ROASTING:

Leg: May be cut short or long (to include some of the chump). Many butchers crack the shank bone but it looks better and is easier to carve if the bone is left in one piece. A leg of lamb may also be boned and stuffed.

Loin: The juiciest cut. It may be roasted on the bone or boned, rolled and tied. Loin is easy to carve – just cut across between the bones, or, if boneless, into thick slices. Make sure the butcher has chined a bone-in loin (chopped through the backbone at intervals, or removed it) so that it is ready to carve.

Saddle: Consists of 2 loins still joined together – an impressive party piece but harder to carve than a single loin, as the backbone is retained (for carving, see *Meat*).

Chump: A superb small, compact roast with only a small proportion of bone.

Rack of Lamb: Consists of 6–8 rib cutlets. It is a luxurious little roast and you can get just the size you want by specifying the number of cutlets. Rack is easy to carve – just cut down between the bones. The butcher will remove the chine bone (backbone), trim off excess fat and clean the ends of the rib bones. A full rack may be cut into single portion racks of 2–4 cutlets each before roasting, or may be roasted whole, then cut into single or 2–4 cutlet portions.

Crown Roast: Made from 2 racks of lamb, bent round and tied together, with the meat inside and bones outside. The skin and excess fat are removed before tying.

■ ECONOMICAL CUTS FOR ROASTING:

Shoulder: Excellent eating but fattier than the leg, making it especially suitable for eating cold. Shoulder can be roasted on the bone but for easier carving it is often boned, rolled and tied. It may be stuffed before being tied. It may be stuffed before being tied.

Forequarter: Similar to shoulder, usually sold boned and rolled.

■ TO ROAST LAMB: Both choice and economical cuts

may be roasted in the same way. Have the meat at room temperature; remove skin if desired. Tie meat into a compact shape if necessary so that it will cook evenly. Weigh it and place, fatty side up, on a greased rack in a roasting tin. If lamb is lean, add 2 tbs butter or dripping to pan. Place in the centre of a preheated hot oven (220°C/425°F) for 20 minutes, then reduce heat to moderate (180°C/350°F) and continue to roast, basting with pan juices every 20 minutes. Rest for 15–20 minutes in turned-off oven with door ajar, or other warm place, before carving.

Allow a total roasting time of approximately 20 minutes per 500 g (1 lb) plus 20 minutes, for lamb pink in the centre, or 30 minutes for 500 g (1 lb) plus 30 minutes, for well-done lamb.

Roast Rack of Lamb: Prepare racks as described above. Slice away skin and excess fat, leaving a good, even layer of fat. Score fat with shallow, diagonal cuts in a lattice pattern. Season with freshly ground pepper. Place rack, fatty side up, in a roasting tin and roast in a preheated moderately hot oven (190°C/375°F) for 15–20 minutes for lamb which is juicy and pink near the bone. Cook a further 5–10 minutes for medium-to-well-done meat.

Herbed Racks of Lamb: For 2 racks of lamb (6–7 cutlets each), combine ¹⁄₂ cup olive oil with juice and grated rind 1 lemon, pinch salt, freshly ground black pepper and 2 cloves garlic, chopped. Place lamb in this mixture, turning to coat it all over. Sprinkle with chopped fresh rosemary, or a combination of chopped fresh parsley and thyme, and leave to marinate for at least 2 hours, turning occasionally. Roast as for Roast Rack of Lamb.

Parslied Racks of Lamb: Score and season 2 racks of lamb as for Roast Rack of Lamb. Melt 60 g (2 oz) butter and combine with ¹⁄₄ cup chopped parsley, 1¹⁄₂ cups fresh breadcrumbs, salt, freshly ground black pepper and a few drops of lemon juice. Toss lightly. Cover scored side of lamb with a thick compact layer of breadcrumb mixture, pressing crumbs firmly on to meat. Roast as for Roast Rack of Lamb.

GRILLED LAMB

It is best to have lamb steaks, chops or cutlets cut 2–2.5 cm (1³⁄₄ in) thick for grilling or cooking over coals.

■ CHOICE CUTS FOR GRILLING: Chump and Loin chops,

Cutlets (ask the butcher not to fatten them), or Noisettes (from a loin or rack of lamb which has been skinned, boned, rolled and tied, then cut across into slices).

■ TO GRILL CHOICE CUTS: Have meat at room temperat-

ure. Trim off skin and, if edged with fat, cut through fat to lean meat in several places to prevent buckling. Roll up tails of loin chops and secure with poultry pins or small skewers.

Preheat grill, brush meat with melted butter or oil and the grill rack with oil. Grill close to high heat for a minute or two on each side until seared, then continue to cook 6–8 minutes longer, turning once. To test for doneness, see *Meat*.

■ ECONOMICAL CUTS FOR GRILLING: Leg steaks or

Chops, Shoulder and Forequarter chops. Not as tender as the choice cuts and usually need marinating for best results.

■ TO GRILL ECONOMICAL CUTS: Prepare the meat and

the grill as for choice cuts, above. Grill close to high heat for a minute or two on each side until seared, then lower heat to moderate and continue to cook, turning once and brushing once or twice more with butter or oil. Allow 10–12 minutes total cooking. To test for doneness, see *Meat*.

SAUTEED LAMB

This method is suitable for cutlets, noisettes and marinated economical cuts. Prepare meat as for grilling, above. Use a thick, heavy pan: heat on high heat for a few minutes, add just enough oil to coat the base and when it gives off a slight haze, put in the meat. Cook

30–60 seconds on each side until seared, then lower heat to moderate and continue to cook, turning once, until cooked as desired. When beads of pink juice appear on surface, meat is cooked but still pink in centre. For other ways to test for doneness, see *Meat*.

PAN-FRIED CRUMBED LAMB

Cutlets are the usual cut for this cooking method, but lamb steaks can also be used. Coat with egg and breadcrumbs and chill 20 minutes. In a heavy frying pan, heat enough butter and oil to come halfway up the pieces of lamb. When foam subsides, arrange the pieces in one layer without crowding pan. Cook over moderate heat until golden-brown, then turn and cook other side. Drain on crumpled paper towels and serve immediately.

BRAISED AND STEWED LAMB

Some of the great lamb dishes – Irish Stew (page 208), curries (page 109) and Navarin of Lamb (page 295) – come into this category. Braising and stewing, involving long slow cooking with liquid, are ideal ways to cook some of the less tender cuts, such as neck or shoulder chops, breast of lamb or lamb shanks. **See recipes.**

WAYS TO SERVE LAMB CHOPS, STEAKS AND CUTLETS

Herbed Lamb Chops: Melt 30 g (1 oz) butter and stir in 2 tbs finely chopped fresh mint, thyme or rosemary, or 1 tsp dried. Score 4 thick lamb chops or noisettes on both sides with a sharp knife, place in one layer in a dish and drizzle herb butter over. Turn chops or noisettes to coat all over and leave to marinate 1 hour, then grill or cook over hot coals as usual.

Lamb Cutlets Dijonnaise: Melt 30 g (1 oz) butter and stir in 1 tbs Dijon mustard. Place 6 lamb cutlets in one layer in a dish and drizzle mustard butter over. Turn cutlets to coat all over and leave to marinate 1 hour, then dust them on both sides with flour and sauté in a little butter and oil.

Lamb Steaks with Orange: Dust 4 lamb steaks with seasoned flour and brown in butter and oil. Pour off fat, and add grated rind 1 orange and 4 tbs orange juice to pan. Cover and simmer gently 30 minutes or until lamb is tender. Adjust seasoning and serve.

Chutney Chops: Score thick chump shops with a sharp knife on both sides and rub in a highly spiced chutney. Leave to marinate at room temperature about 1 hour, then grill or cook over hot coals as usual.

Oriental Lamb Chops: Mix ½ cup pineapple juice, 2 cloves garlic, crushed, and 2 tbs soy sauce. Marinate 4 forequarter chops in mixture for 3–4 hours, then remove chops, dry them and sauté in butter and oil.

BONING A LEG OF LAMB: Using a sharp pointed knife, clear meat from protruding hip bone at wider end of leg, remove bone. Cut away meat from shank bone and pull out bone. Working from wider end, clean meat from middle bone then remove from hip cavity. Fill hip cavity with stuffing and tie leg into a neat shape, tucking shank end into cavity.

PREPARING A CROWN ROAST: Using 2 racks lamb, remove chine or bony part from meat end and scrape meat and fat from narrow end of each rib. Cut bone between each cutlet and tie racks into a circle with meat inside.

Braised Lamb Shanks

6 lamb shanks; flour for dredging; salt and freshly ground black pepper; 1 tbs chopped fresh oregano, or 1 tsp dried; ⅓ cup oil; grated rind 1 lemon; 1 onion, chopped; 1 cup chopped celery; 1 cup chopped carrots; 1 clove garlic, crushed; ¾ cup red wine; ¾ cup stock.

Wipe shanks with a damp cloth. Dredge with flour, season with salt and pepper and press oregano on to surface. Heat oil in a frying pan and brown shanks a few at a time. Transfer to a large casserole and sprinkle with lemon rind. Add onion, celery, carrots and garlic to frying pan and cook, stirring, 5 minutes. Add wine and stock, bring to the boil and simmer, stirring well, for a few minutes. Pour contents of pan over meat in casserole. Cover and bake in a preheated moderate oven (180°C/350°F) for 1–1½ hours or until meat is tender. Thicken gravy with 1 tbs flour mixed with a little cold water. Serve with creamy mashed potatoes or boiled rice. Serves 6.

Lamb Boulangère

French housewives used to send Sunday's leg of lamb on its bed of sliced vegetables to be cooked in the baker's oven (after the bread came out) while the family were at church. The name (Lamb Baker's Wife) remains but today's lamb is baked at home.

30 g (1 oz) butter; 1 tbs olive oil; 500 g (1 lb) onions, sliced; 1 kg (2 lb) potatoes, peeled and finely sliced; 1 clove garlic, chopped; salt and freshly ground black pepper; 1 leg of lamb; 1 cup beef stock; chopped parsley.

Heat butter and oil in a roasting tin and fry onions gently on top of stove until soft. Push onions to one side. Arrange a bed of potato slices in bottom of tin and spoon onions over them. Scatter garlic over and season with salt and pepper. Place lamb on top, pour stock over and place in a preheated very hot oven (220°C/425°F). Roast for 20 minutes, then reduce heat to moderate (180°C/350°F) and continue to roast, spooning pan juices over vegetables once or twice, until lamb is done as you like it. For lamb pink in the centre, allow, altogether, 20 minutes per 500 g (1 lb) plus 20 minutes. For well-done lamb, allow 30 minutes per 500 g (1 lb) plus 30 minutes. Rest 15 minutes in turned-off oven with door ajar, then remove lamb, carve it and arrange meat on bed of vegetables. Sprinkle with chopped parsley and serve immediately. Serves 4–6, depending on size of leg.

NOTE: For easier carving the lamb may be boned and tied. Carve across into thick slices.

Leg of Lamb Breton

When a Breton housewife roasts the lamb which is a specialty of the region, it comes to the table on a bed of delicious white beans to soak up the garlic-flavoured juices.

BEANS: 1¹/₂ cups dried haricot beans, soaked overnight and drained; 1 onion, quartered; 1 clove garlic; 8 black peppercorns; 1 bouquet garni (celery, bay leaf, thyme, parsley); salt; 1 tbs butter; 1 onion, chopped; 1 tomato, peeled, seeded and chopped; chopped parsley.

LAMB: 1 x 1.5 kg (3 lb) leg of lamb; 1 large clove garlic, sliced; freshly ground black pepper; 30 g (1 oz) butter, softened; 1 cup water; large pinch salt.

Cook beans as usual (see *Pulses*). When beans soften, add quartered onion, garlic, peppercorns, bouquet garni and a little salt to the cooking water. Meanwhile cut several incisions between skin and flesh of lamb and push garlic slices into them. Season lightly with pepper and spread with softened butter. Put lamb on a rack in a roasting tin. Pour water into tin, add salt and place in preheated moderately hot oven (190°C/375°F). Roast the lamb for 1¹/₄ hours, basting every 15 minutes with pan juices and adding a little extra water if juices dry up. This will produce lamb that is still quite pink. Roast for a further 20–30 minutes for well-done lamb. Remove lamb from oven and rest in a warm place for 20 minutes. Skim excess fat from pan juices. Drain beans when tender and remove onion, garlic, bouquet garni and peppercorns. Melt butter and cook chopped onion and tomato gently until soft. Add ¹/₂ cup juice from roasting tin and the beans, stirring gently so as not to crush them. Season with salt and pepper. Spoon beans on to a heated serving platter, sprinkle with parsley and place lamb on top. Serve any remaining pan juices separately. Serves 6–8.

French Roast Lamb

Lamb cooked the French way is always moist and juicy. The lamb is basted throughout cooking with buttery stock.

1 x 2 kg (4 lb) leg of lamb; 2 cloves garlic, finely sliced; 60 g (2 oz) butter, melted; 1 tsp salt; 1³/₄ cups chicken stock; little white wine.

Cut 5–6 slits in lamb with a sharp-pointed knife. Insert slices of garlic into each. Brush lamb with approximately 30 g (1 oz) melted butter and sprinkle with salt. Place lamb on a rack in a roasting tin and add 1¹/₄ cups stock and remaining butter. Roast in a preheated moderate oven (180°C/350°F), allowing 18–20 minutes per 500 g (1 lb). Baste lamb ever 15 minutes. Place lamb on a heated serving dish and keep warm. Skim fat from top of liquid in roasting tin then place tin over heat on top of stove. Bring to the boil, add a little white wine and remaining stock and allow to bubble, stirring, for a few minutes. Serve with lamb. Serves 6.

Swedish Lamb

In Sweden lamb is roasted on a bed of vegetables, with coffee and stock basting the meat for great flavour.

1 x 2–2.5 kg (4–5 lb) leg of lamb; 2 tsp salt; 2 tsp black pepper; 3 onions, sliced; 3 carrots, sliced; 1 cup hot beef stock; 1¹/₂ cups hot strong black coffee; 1 tbs sugar; ¹/₂ cup cream.

Trim any excess fat from lamb. Rub salt and pepper into lamb and place on rack in a roasting tin over onions and carrots. Roast in a preheated hot oven (200°C/400°F) for 30 minutes. Reduce oven temperature to moderate (180°C/350°F) and add stock, coffee and sugar to tin. Continue cooking, basting frequently, until done to your taste. One hour longer gives meat tender and pink on the inside; in 1¹/₂ hours the meat becomes medium to well-done. Transfer lamb to a heated platter and rest 15–20 minutes. (This helps to settle juice back in the meat and makes carving easy. If carved as soon as it is cooked juices run too freely on the plate, making it all look rather unappetising.) Rub vegetables and cooking liquid through a sieve or purée in a blender. Reheat with cream and serve with lamb. Serves 6–8.

Roast Leg of Lamb Bengal

Indian cooks working in British households in the days of the Raj gave new dimensions to familiar foods – such as this exotic roast lamb.

1 leg of lamb.

MARINADE: 1 cup plain yogurt; 1 onion, chopped; 3 cloves garlic; 2 tsp tomato paste; 1 tbs olive oil; 2 tsp salt; freshly ground black pepper; 1 cm (¹/₂ in) piece fresh ginger.

Remove thin outer skin from lamb and trim off most of the fat. Place in a dish just large enough to hold it and prick all over with a fork. Put ingredients for marinade into a blender or food processor and process until smooth. If making by hand, chop onion, garlic and ginger finely and mix with other ingredients. Pour marinade over lamb, cover and leave in refrigerator overnight or for at least 6 hours, turning lamb once or twice. Place lamb on rack in a roasting tin. Roast in centre of a preheated very hot oven (230°C/450°F) for 15 minutes, then reduce heat to moderate (180°C/350°F) and continue to roast, basting frequently with marinade. Allow a total cooking time of 20 minutes per 500 g (1 lb) for lamb that is pink at the centre, or 25 minutes per 500 g (1 lb) for well-done. Test with a fine skewer in the thickest part; juice will run pink for medium-done lamb and clear for well-done. Rest lamb for 20 minutes in a warm place (such as turned-off oven with door ajar) before carving. Serve with a purée of potatoes or lentils flavoured with coriander and cumin and a salad of tomatoes, mint and cucumber. Serves 6.

Spiced Shoulder of Lamb

In India, tough mutton is tenderised by marinating it in yogurt and spices. It is a delicious way to treat a shoulder of lamb.

**1 shoulder of lamb, boned; juice 1 lemon;
1 tsp ground cardamom; 2 tsp ground coriander;
good pinch saffron, crumbled (optional);
salt and freshly ground black pepper;
1 cup plain yogurt; 2 onions, finely sliced;
30 g (1 oz) butter.**

Score surface of lamb in a diamond pattern using a sharp knife. Rub in lemon juice, spices, salt and pepper. Spread yogurt over lamb. Leave to marinate in a glass or ceramic dish for 1–2 hours. Spread lamb on a rack in a roasting tin, cover with any marinade and roast in a preheated moderate oven (180°C/350°F) for 30 minutes. Meanwhile, fry sliced onions in butter until lightly coloured. Spoon onions over meat and continue to roast for further 30 minutes. Serve, cut in strips, with boiled rice or a rice pilaf flavoured with sultanas and cinnamon. Serves 6.

Herbed Loin of Lamb

Give your butcher warning and he will bone the loin for this dish. The pungent flavour of garlic, parsley, rosemary and thyme gives a deliciously aromatic and gamey flavour to the lamb. Serve with creamy mashed potatoes and, if liked, Tomatoes á la Provençale (see page 539).

**1 x 1.5 kg (3 lb) loin of lamb; 3 cloves garlic;
salt; 2 tbs mixed chopped fresh parsley, rosemary
and thyme; freshly ground black pepper;
30 g (1 oz) butter; 3/4 cup white wine;
1 tbs flour; watercress or parsley to garnish.**

Ask the butcher to bone the loin of lamb. Otherwise, trim meat of any excess fat, remove fillet and bone. Crush garlic to a fine paste with 1 tsp salt. Mix garlic and herbs together and spread over inside of lamb. Replace fillet, roll up and tie at 2.5 cm (1 in) intervals. This may be done hours ahead for a more 'gamey' taste. Place meat in a roasting tin, sprinkle with salt and pepper, add butter to tin and pour in wine. Roast

in a preheated moderately hot oven (190°C/375°F), basting often, for 45 minutes or until meat juices are clear. Remove meat to a heated serving platter and rest in a warm place for 10–15 minutes before serving. The juices will be re-absorbed by meat, making carving easier. Skim fat from the cooking juices. Mix 1 tbs of fat with the flour in a cup. Stir into pan juices, bring to the boil and simmer for a few minutes. Season with salt and pepper. If gravy is too thick, add a little stock or water. Remove string from meat and carve into thick slices, serving gravy separately. Garnish with a small bunch of watercress or parsley. Serves 6.

Herbed Shoulder of Lamb

Boned should of lamb rolled around a generous layer of fresh herbs results in a roast with a great flavour.

**1 shoulder of lamb, boned; 2 tbs chopped chives;
4 tbs chopped parsley; 1 tsp chopped fresh lemon
thyme or oregano; 1 tsp chopped fresh rosemary;
1 tbs chopped fresh ginger; 2 tbs oil;
salt and freshly ground black pepper.**

GRAVY: 1/2 cup red wine; 1/2 cup stock; salt.

Spread boned meat out so it lies flat, cover it with waxed paper or plastic wrap and pound it with a mallet or rolling pin so it is of more or less even thickness. In a small bowl combine herbs, ginger and oil. Sprinkle surface of lamb with salt and pepper and spread herb mixture evenly over it. Roll up lamb tightly and tie at 5 cm (2 in) intervals with kitchen string. Brush lamb with a little oil, sprinkle with salt and pepper and place in a roasting tin. Roast in a preheated moderate oven (180°C/350°F) for 1–1½ hours. Transfer to a heated platter and keep warm.
GRAVY: Skim any excess fat from cooking juices and deglaze tin with wine and stock, stirring in brown bits clinging to bottom and sides. Reduce gravy by boiling over a high heat until thickened slightly, season with salt and pour into a heated sauceboat. Carve lamb in thick slices and serve it with gravy. Creamy mashed potatoes make a good accompaniment and help mop up the delicious juices. Serves 4–6.

NOTE: If you don't have a supply of fresh herbs use 6 tbs chopped parsley and ¼–½ tsp each of the dried herbs indicated as fresh in the recipe.

Italian Lamb Stew

2 tbs oil; 250 g (8 oz) bacon, rind removed and diced; I onion, sliced; 2 cloves garlic, crushed; I kg (2 lb) leg or shoulder of lamb, boned, trimmed of excess fat and cut into 4 cm (1½ in) cubes; salt and freshly ground black pepper; I tsp chopped fresh rosemary, or ¼ tsp dried; I tsp chopped fresh marjoram or ½ tsp dried; ½ cup plus 2 tbs red wine; 2 tbs tomato paste.

Heat oil in a large, heavy frying pan. Add bacon, onion and garlic and sauté until golden. Remove to a plate. Add half the meat and brown on all sides. Remove, and brown remaining meat. Place meat in a heavy flameproof saucepan, add sautéed bacon, onion and garlic and season with salt, pepper, rosemary and marjoram. Stir in ½ cup red wine, bring to the boil and simmer until wine is reduced by half. Add tomato paste and enough water to cover meat. Cover and simmer gently about 1½ hours or until meat is tender. Add remaining red wine just before serving to deepen flavour, and serve directly from pan. Serve with flat ribbon noodles or fluffy boiled rice. Serves 4–6.

Haricot Beans and Lamb

¾ cup dried haricot beans, soaked overnight and drained; I kg (2 lb) lamb neck or shoulder shops, trimmed of excess fat and cubed; I–2 tbs oil; 2 medium onions, sliced; 2 large tomatoes, peeled and sliced; 2 tbs tomato paste; 2 cups chicken stock or water; I tbs lemon juice; I sprig fresh rosemary, or I tsp dried; salt and freshly ground black pepper.

Cook beans in boiling water for 1 hour. Fry lamb cubes in oil in a frying pan until brown. Add onions and cook until soft. Remove from pan and place in large flameproof casserole. Drain beans and add to casserole with tomatoes. Blend tomato paste with stock or water, lemon juice, rosemary, salt and pepper. Pour into casserole and bring to the boil on top of the stove. Reduce heat, cover and simmer about 1 hour or until meat and beans are tender. Or cook in a preheated slow oven (150°C/300°F) for 1½ hours after bringing to the boil. Serves 6.

Pot Roasted Lamb Shoulder

I small shoulder of lamb, trimmed of excess fat, boned, rolled and tied; I clove garlic, cut into slivers; 2 tbs seasoned flour; 2 tbs oil; 2 medium potatoes, peeled; 2 medium carrots, scraped; 2 tbs chopped fresh mint, parsley or other herbs; ½ cup water; salt and freshly ground black pepper.

Make small slits in lamb and insert slivers of garlic. Roll lamb in seasoned flour. Heat oil in large, heavy saucepan and slowly brown lamb on all sides. Add vegetables, herbs and water and season with salt and pepper. Cover and simmer on very low heat for 1–1½ hours or until lamb is tender. Serve with pan juices as gravy. Serves 4.

Lamb with Parsley Sauce

Simple, old-fashioned and very good. Neck chops are beautifully sweet.

1.5 kg (3 lb) lamb neck chops; I tsp salt; 2 cups water; freshly ground black pepper; 1½ tbs flour; ¾ cup chopped parsley; I–2 tsp lemon juice.

Place chops in a saucepan with salt and water. Bring to the boil, cover and simmer gently for 1 hour or until tender. Lift chops on to a heated serving dish, season with salt and pepper and keep hot. Blend flour with a little cold water and stir into cooking liquid. Bring to the boil, stirring constantly, and simmer a few minutes. Add parsley and lemon juice to taste and spoon over chops. Serve with boiled potatoes and carrots. Serves 6.

Spiced Lamb in Sour Cream

5 tbs ghee or butter; I kg (2 lb) boned lamb shoulder, trimmed of excess fat and cut into 2.5 cm (I in) cubes; 15 cardamom pods, bruised; 6 curry leaves, or I bay leaf; 6–8 cloves; 6–8 black peppercorns; I cup sour cream; ⅓ cup plain yogurt; I tsp salt; ½ tsp saffron threads, crumbled.

TOMATO AND MINT SAMBAL: 2 tomatoes, chopped; ½ onion, sliced; I tbs chopped fresh mint.

BANANA SAMBAL: 2 bananas, sliced; squeeze lemon juice.

CUCUMBER AND YOGURT SAMBAL: I green cucumber, peeled, seeded and diced; I clove garlic, crushed; ½ cup plain yogurt.

Heat ghee in a heavy flameproof casserole or saucepan and fry lamb cubes in several batches, transferring them to a dish as they are browned. In remaining fat, sauté cardamom pods, curry leaves or bay leaf, cloves and peppercorns until cloves begin to pop. Return lamb to casserole with remaining ingredients and bring to the boil, stirring. Cover tightly with foil and lid and simmer, stirring once or twice, for 1½ hours, or until lamb is tender. Meanwhile, mix ingredients for fresh sambals.

Remove lamb with a slotted spoon to a dish and strain sauce into a bowl, discarding the solids. Return sauce to pan, add lamb and cook over a moderate heat, stirring occasionally, until sauce is reduced by about half. Transfer mixture to a heated serving dish and serve with boiled rice, fresh sambals and a choice of chutneys. Serves 6.

Gormeh Sabzee

This is a Persian stew made with lamb, a very large bunch of parsley (3 cups chopped) and kidney beans. It is economical, nutritious and delicious.

90 g (3 oz) butter; 3 cups chopped parsley; I bunch spring onions, chopped; 1.5 kg (3 lb) lean boneless lamb (leg, chuck, shoulder), trimmed of excess fat and gristle and cut into 2.5 cm (I in) cubes; salt and freshly ground black pepper; 2 lemons; 2 cups dried kidney beans, soaked overnight and drained; I onion.

Melt half the butter in a heavy flameproof casserole or saucepan and fry parsley and spring onions until bright green. Heat remaining butter in a frying pan, add meat and brown lightly. Do not crowd pan, but fry meat in several batches if necessary. Season with salt and pepper and add to parsley mixture. Add juice of 1 lemon and remaining lemon cut into 6 (use skin and flesh). Add water just to cover – about 1½ cups. Cover and simmer until meat is almost tender, about 1 hour. Meanwhile, place beans in a saucepan with whole onion and water to cover, bring to the boil, reduce heat, cover and simmer until tender, 30–45 minutes. Drain and discard onion. Add beans to casserole and continue cooking until lamb is tender, about 25 minutes. Serve with pilaf or boiled rice. Serves 6–8.

NOTE: 4 cups drained, canned kidney beans may be used instead of dried.

Dilled Lamb Shanks with Sour Cream Sauce

6 lamb shanks; salt and freshly ground black pepper; I tbs oil; 60 g (2 oz) butter; I large onion, chopped; 1½ cups dry white wine; ½ cup beef stock; I bay leaf; 2 tbs flour; 3 tbs chopped fresh dill, or 2 tsp dried; I cup sour cream.

Trim excess fat from lamb shanks and season shanks with salt and pepper. Heat oil and half the butter in a frying pan and brown lamb shanks on all sides. Transfer to a flameproof casserole or heavy saucepan. Gently cook onion in fat remaining in frying pan until onion is transparent. Pour in wine and stock and bring to the boil. Add to lamb shanks in casserole with bay leaf. Simmer, covered, for about 1½ hours or until shanks are tender. Remove shanks to a heated plate and keep warm. Strain stock. Melt remaining butter in the casserole, add flour and stir

over moderate heat for 2 minutes. Gradually add stock. Stir until mixture boils and thickens. Add dill and sour cream. Season with salt and pepper. Return lamb, heat through but do not boil. Serve with boiled new potatoes, tossed in butter, or boiled rice. Serves 6.

Lamb Pilau

An old and traditional Middle Eastern recipe. If liked, the spices can be tied in a muslin bag and removed before serving. The spices enhance the look of the finished dish; put them to one side when serving or eating.

90 g (3 oz) ghee or butter; I shoulder of lamb, boned, trimmed of excess fat and cubed; ½ cinnamon stick; 12 cloves; 5 black peppercorns; 6 cardamom pods, bruised; I tsp salt; freshly ground black pepper; 6 cups water; 2 cups rice; 2 onions, sliced; ¼ cup oil or ghee; ¼ cup toasted slivered almonds.

Heat half the ghee in a frying pan and brown meat cubes. This is best done in 2 batches (do not over-crowd pan or you will get a stewed result). Place in a large flameproof casserole or saucepan. Add spices, salt, pepper and 1 cup water. Cover and cool gently until meat is tender, about 30 minutes. Rinse rice well and drain. Heat remaining ghee in a saucepan, add rice and cook, stirring, about 5 minutes. Add remaining water, bring to the boil and cook 8–10 minutes. Make 3 or 4 holes in rice with handle of a wooden spoon. Place cooked meat on top of rice with about ¾ cup of the meat juices. Cover and cook gently about 15 minutes. Meanwhile, fry onions in oil until pale golden and slightly crispy (but do not burn). Fork meat through rice to mix and fluff up rice. Turn on to heated platter and top with fried onion rings and toasted slivered almonds. Serves 6.

Lamb and Potato Curry

The added bonus of this Indian curry dish is that it makes a little lamb go a long way!

2 medium onions; 4 slices fresh ginger; 3 cloves garlic; I red chilli, seeded; 3 tbs ghee; 500 g (I lb) potatoes, peeled and cut into chunks; I onion, finely sliced; 500 g (I lb) boneless lamb (leg or shoulder), trimmed of excess fat and cubed; 1½ tsp salt; I bay leaf; ½ cup plain yogurt blended with ½ cup water; I cup hot water; 2 tbs tomato paste; I tsp Garam Masala (page 171); fresh coriander leaves to garnish.

Chop the 2 onions, ginger, garlic and chilli finely together (this may be done in a food processor). Heat ghee in a large, heavy frying pan and sauté potatoes until golden on all sides. Remove with a slotted spoon. Add sliced onion to hot ghee and fry until golden. Stir in meat, salt, bay leaf and chilli mixture and stir until golden, adding a little yogurt mixture from time to time. When meat is browned add any remaining yogurt mixture and hot water and cook gently for 30 minutes or until meat is almost tender. Add potatoes to pan and cook for another 10 minutes, stirring frequently, until potatoes are almost tender. Stir in tomato paste and continue cooking until potatoes are tender. Turn into a heated serving bowl, sprinkle with garam masala and garnish with coriander leaves. Serve with plain boiled rice, chutney, and fresh salad or a selection of sambals. Serves 4.

NOTE: It is best to make your own garam masala although it is available from most health food shops and Asian food stores, and many supermarkets.

Lamb Shanks in White Wine

4 small lamb shanks, cracked; 1 clove garlic, slivered; salt and freshly ground black pepper; 1 tbs oil; 1 onion, finely chopped; 1 cup dry white wine; 500 g (1 lb) small new potatoes; 8 small or medium carrots, halved.

Make small incisions in meat of lamb shanks using a sharp knife, and insert garlic slivers. Season shanks with salt and pepper and brown in hot oil. Transfer to an ovenproof casserole and add onion and wine. Cover and bake in a preheated moderate oven (180°C/350°F) for 1 hour. Add potatoes and carrots, cover again and bake for a further 1–1½ hours or until meat and vegetables are tender. Serves 4.

Lamb Chops Provençal

The Provençal shepherds' way of cooking lamb chops: the chops are barbecued or grilled, then served with a simple rustic sauce containing garlic, parsley and white wine, on croûtes of fried bread to catch the delicious juices.

4 thick lamb loin or chump chops; 4 thick slices bread; olive oil; 1 medium onion, finely chopped; 1 clove garlic, crushed; 2 tbs chopped parsley; 3 tbs hot water; 1 cup dry white wine; salt and freshly ground black pepper; extra chopped parley to garnish.

Grill chops over a charcoal fire or under a preheated hot grill for about 4 minutes on each side. This will give meat that is well browned but pink in the centre. Grill for a few minutes longer if you want chops well done. Meantime, lightly fry bread in a little olive oil in a frying pan, drain on crumpled paper towel and keep warm. Heat 2 tbs olive oil in pan, add onion, garlic and parsley and fry until onion is golden-brown. Add water, wine, salt and pepper and simmer for 5 minutes. Arrange fried bread croûtes on a heated serving platter or individual plates, place a lamb chop on each croute and spoon sauce over all. Sprinkle with a little chopped parsley and serve immediately. Serves 4.

Sautéed Strips of Lamb

Serve with rice pilaf and green salad.

750 g (1½ lb) lamb leg steaks, cut 2 cm (¾ in) thick; 4 tbs olive oil; 3 tbs wine vinegar; ½ tsp salt; freshly ground black pepper; 1 small onion, grated; 1 tbs finely chopped parsley; ½ tsp chopped fresh rosemary or pinch dried; 30 g (1 oz) butter.

Trim skin, fat and gristle from steaks and cut meat off bones into strips about 6 cm (2½ in) long. Pound strips with the edge of a saucer to break down fibres. Mix 2 tbs olive oil with vinegar, salt, pepper, onion, parsley and rosemary in a bowl. Add lamb and turn to coat strips with marinade and dry well on paper towels. Sauté in butter and remaining oil over high heat, about 2 minutes each side. Serves 4–5.

Lamb Brochettes

The lamb is cut into cubes and marinated overnight, so it is ready for threading on skewers and grilling. A boned shoulder is the most economical cut for this dish, trimmed of fat and any gristle.

1 kg (2 lb) boneless lamb, cut into bite-sized cubes; 6 tbs oil; 1 clove garlic, crushed; 2 tbs lemon juice; salt and freshly ground black pepper; 1 tbs chopped fresh oregano, or ½ tsp dried; 1 bay leaf, crumbled.

Place lamb cubes in a bowl. Combine remaining ingredients and pour over lamb. Stir, cover, and refrigerate overnight until needed. At serving time, thread lamb on to 6 metal skewers and cook under a preheated high grill for 10–12 minutes or until cooked through, turning skewers occasionally so meat cooks evenly. Serve on a bed of rice pilaf. Serves 6.

Spiced Lamb Chops with Prunes

There's a Moroccan influence in this dish, with the combination of meat and fruit. To offset its richness, serve with plain boiled rice and green salad.

60 g (2 oz) butter; 6 thick lamb chops, cut from leg or shoulder; salt and freshly ground black pepper; 1 large onion, finely sliced; 12 large, soft prunes; ¾ cup red wine; ¾ cup water; 4 whole cloves; 1 x 2.5 cm (1 in) cinnamon stick; 4 strips lemon rind; 1½ tbs sugar.

Heat butter in a large, heavy frying pan (an electric frypan is ideal) and brown chops on both sides over medium heat. Season generously with salt and pepper and cover with onion slices. Add remaining ingredients to pan, bring to boil, than reduce heat and cover tightly. Simmer for 45 minutes or until chops are very tender. Taste for seasoning, and add more salt, pepper or sugar if required (sauce should be well flavoured). Remove cloves, cinnamon stick and lemon rind before serving. Serves 6.

Lamb in Chilindron Sauce

750 g (1½ lb) boned shoulder or leg of lamb, trimmed of excess fat and cubed; I tsp salt; freshly ground black pepper; 6 tbs olive oil; 3 cloves garlic; I onion, chopped; 4 red peppers, cored, seeded and sliced; 4 large tomatoes, peeled and chopped ; 2 tsp paprika ; I tsp saffron, crumbled; I chilli, seeded and sliced; 10 black or green olives, halved and stoned.

Sprinkle meat with salt and pepper. Heat oil in a flameproof casserole with garlic cloves. Add meat and fry until evenly browned. Remove meat. Discard garlic cloves if a milder flavour is preferred. Add onion and red peppers and sauté until they start to soften. Stir in tomatoes, paprika, saffron and chilli. Return meat to pan, cover and cook very gently for about 1 hour or until meat is tender, adding olives about 10 minutes before serving. If meat becomes dry during cooking add a little water to moisten, but dish should contain very little liquid. Transfer to a heated serving dish and serve immediately. Serves 4–6.

Red–Cooked Lamb

'Red-cooked' is a traditional Chinese method of slow cooking. Soy sauce is the predominant flavouring ingredient, followed by sherry, ginger, garlic and onion. Pork, beef and poultry can all be used in this recipe.

1 kg (2 lb) shoulder of lamb, boned and cubed; salt and freshly ground black pepper; 2 tbs oil; I onion, chopped; I clove garlic, crushed; 3 tbs soy sauce; 4 tbs sherry; 2 tsp sugar; ½ cup brown stock; 2 slices fresh ginger; 2 bay leaves; 2 tsp cornflour mixed to a thin paste with I tbs cold water; I small red pepper, cored, seeded and cut into strips.

Season meat well with salt and pepper. Heat oil in a wok or frying pan and brown meat on all sides. Remove to a flameproof casserole, then fry onion and garlic for 3 minutes. Drain and transfer to casserole. Mix together soy sauce, sherry, sugar and stock. Pour over meat, mix well and add ginger and bay leaves. Simmer very gently until meat is tender, about 1½ hours. Just before serving stir in blended cornflour and continue simmering until thickened. Remove bay leaves. Serve garnished with red pepper and with a dish of boiled rice. Serves 4–6.

Lamb Satay

I tbs tamarind pulp soaked in ¼ cup water for 10 minutes; 500 g (I lb) boneless lamb (from leg), cut into 2 cm (¾ in) cubes; I onion, grated; 2 cloves garlic, crushed; ½ tsp dried shrimp paste (trasi); I tbs dark soy sauce; 2 tbs desiccated or grated fresh coconut.

Strain tamarind over a bowl, squeezing out and reserving as much water as possible. Discard tamarind. Place lamb cubes in a bowl and pour over remaining ingredients, including tamarind water. If using desiccated coconut, moisten with 1 tbs hot water. Mix marinade well into meat, then cover and leave at room temperature for 2 hours, or overnight in the refrigerator. Drain lamb cubes. Thread on to bamboo skewers (previously soaked in water for 2 hours to prevent burning). Grill under a preheated grill for about 10 minutes, turning frequently and take care that coconut does not burn. Serve with steamed rice and Malaysian Satay Sauce (see pages 454–5). Serves 4–6.

LAMINGTON

A popular Australian cake made from genoise or butter cake, cut into squares, dipped in chocolate icing and coated with desiccated coconut.

Lamingtons

Make the basic genoise that day before required to make it easier to cut into neat squares. If you have frozen the cake, allow it to thaw for a full 24 hours before using for Lamingtons.

I quantity Basic Genoise (page 176); desiccated coconut; 3 cups icing sugar; ⅓ cup cocoa powder; ½ cup boiling water; few drops vanilla.

Bake genoise in a greased and base-lined shallow lamington tin, 28 x 19 cm (11 x 7½ in). Cut cake into 3 strips lengthways, then cut each strip into 8 even pieces. Scatter a thick bed of coconut on a large sheet of greaseproof paper. Sift icing sugar and cocoa into a heatproof bowl, add water and vanilla and stir over hot water until smooth and shiny. The icing should be thin – add a little more boiling water if necessary, and keep the bowl over hot water while working. Spear each piece of cake on a fork and dip into icing. Hold over the bowl a moment to allow icing to set slightly, then roll in coconut, using the paper to help. Place on a wire rack to dry. Makes 24.

VARIATION

JAM LAMINGTONS: Each piece of cake may be cut in half and sandwiched together with a little jam before dipping into icing and rolling in coconut. Be careful to use only a small amount of jam so that it does not run out while the cake is being coated.

LANCASHIRE HOTPOT

A world-famous English hotpot with a wonderful flavour. Very warm and comforting on cold winter nights, this hotpot is topped with a delicious crust of crisp, brown potatoes. It originally contained oysters, from the days when oysters were plentiful and very cheap.

Lancashire Hotpot

750 g (1½ lb) best end of neck lamb stewing chops; 1 tbs flour; salt and freshly ground black pepper; 4 medium onions, sliced; 2 lamb's kidneys, skinned, cored and sliced; 6 mushrooms, sliced; 6 medium potatoes, peeled and sliced; 18 oysters (optional); 1½ cups stock.

Trim off any excess fat from chops and coat with flour, seasoned with salt and pepper. Place layers of meat, onions, kidneys, mushrooms and potatoes in a large casserole, seasoning each layer lightly with salt and pepper and finishing with a layer of potatoes. If using oysters, arrange them in a layer on top of mushrooms. Pour over stock. Cover and cook in a preheated moderate oven (180°C/350°F) for 2 hours. Remove lid of casserole and cook for a further 30 minutes to brown potatoes. Serves 6.

LANGUES DES CHATS (CATS' TONGUES)

A flat, crisp biscuit, finger- or cat's tongue-shaped, served with liqueurs, sparkling wines, ice and ice creams, also used as an ingredient in some puddings. The biscuits keep well in an airtight container.

Langues des Chats

60 g (2 oz) butter; ¼ cup caster sugar; 2 eggs whites; ½ cup flour; ¼ tsp vanilla.

Cream butter with sugar until very light and fluffy. Beat whites to a snow and add to butter mixture alternately with sifted flour, beating vigorously. Add vanilla. Spoon into a piping bag fitted with a 1 cm (½ in) plain tube. Pipe on to a greased and floured baking tray in the shape of éclairs. Bang tray sharply on the work surface once or twice to flatten biscuits slightly. Bake in a preheated moderately hot oven (190°C/375°F) for 10–12 minutes or until biscuits are pale golden with edges tinged brown. Leave to cool on baking tray. Makes about 24.

LASAGNE

One of the most popular pasta dishes, the usual combination of meat and cream sauce topped with cheese is delicious. Lasagne noodles can be shaped like postcards or long and flat with wavy edges. The precooked noodles, now readily available, are excellent and simplify preparation. Lasagne is a good dish to choose when entertaining a crowd. Make the meat sauce ahead and freeze, assemble the dish early on the day and heat when required, or as lasagne freezes well, the whole dish may be made ahead and stored, frozen, until required. Serve with a bowl of crisp green salad and plenty of crusty bread, and finish with fresh fruit.

See *Pasta* for Lasagne recipe.

LASSI

A most refreshing drink, made with plain yogurt; it may be sweet, salty or sour. Found all over the Middle East and parts of India, it is perfect to drink on a hot summer's day or with spicy foods.

Lassi

½ cup plain yogurt; 2½ cups iced water; salt and pepper to taste; ice cubes.

Pour yogurt into a jug and beat with a whisk until very smooth and free of lumps. Gradually add iced water, whisking well. Season with salt and pepper and serve, poured over ice cubes. Makes 3 cups.

VARIATION

SWEET LASSI: Beat 2 tbs plain yogurt with 2 tsp sugar, gradually add about 1 cup iced soda water and serve poured over ice cubes in a tall glass. Serves 1.

LEEK

A member of the onion family, grown for its fleshy stem which is banked with soil while growing so that it remains white. Its flavour is sweeter and more delicate than that of onions. Leeks are much used in soups and are an essential ingredient in Vichyssoise, perhaps the greatest cold soup of all (see pages 493–4). They are also one of the nicest vegetables to serve cold as a first course or part of an hors d'oeuvre platter (see *Zucchini à la Grecque*, page 600); they make an interesting and delicious hot vegetable too.

When buying leeks, look for medium to small ones, with firm, unblemished stems and unwilted green tops. Trim tops a little but leave roots on; stand in a little cold water in a jug, cover with a plastic bag and store in the refrigerator. Use within a week.

■ **BASIC PREPARATION:** Because of the way they are grown, leeks are usually gritty and need careful cleaning. Cut off all but 4–5 cm (1–1½ in) of the green tops, cutting to a point so that you retain more of the tender inside layers than the outside (use tops to flavour soup or stock). Trim off roots.

If using as a whole vegetable, slit down the middle to within about 2.5 cm (1 in) of the root end and wash very thoroughly under running water, spreading layers gently to be sure all grit is washed out.

If leeks are to be chopped or sliced, it is easiest to cut them up first, then place in a colander and wash grit off under cold running water. **See recipes.**

Braised Leeks

6 leeks, trimmed and washed; 45 g (1¹/₂ oz) butter; ¹/₂ tsp salt; freshly ground black pepper.

Put leeks into a saucepan with butter, salt, pepper and water barely to cover. Bring to the boil, half-cover and simmer 10 minutes. Remove lid and continue cooking about 10 more minutes or until leeks are tender and liquid reduced to about ¹/₂ cup. Transfer leeks to a shallow baking dish, pour cooking juices over them and cover loosely with foil. Place in a preheated very hot oven (230°C/450°F) and cook for about 8 minutes or until leeks are golden. Serves 6.

VARIATION

LEEKS PARMIGIANA: Prepare Braised Leeks, transfer to a shallow flameproof dish and pour cooking juices over them. Sprinkle with ¹/₂ cup grated Parmesan cheese and place under a preheated grill 1–2 minutes to brown the surface. Serve immediately.

Purée of Leeks

4 leeks, finely sliced; 30 g (1 oz) butter; salt and freshly ground black pepper; sugar; nutmeg; 1–2 tbs cream.

Put leeks into a heavy saucepan with only the water that clings to them after washing. Add butter and a pinch each of salt and sugar. Cover tightly and place on low heat until butter has melted and leeks have exuded some juice. Increase heat to moderate and continue to cook until leeks are tender, then remove lid and cook quickly until liquid evaporates, stirring and watching carefully that leeks do not scorch on bottom. Purée in a food processor or food mill or rub through a sieve. Season with pepper and nutmeg and stir in sufficient cream to give a smooth consistency. Reheat gently in the saucepan or in a covered dish in the oven. Serves 4.

Leek Filo Pie

Good served hot, warm or cold – nice for a picnic.

6 medium leeks, cut into 1 cm (¹/₂ in) thick slices; 1 egg; 125 g (4 oz) feta cheese; salt and freshly ground black pepper; 8 sheets filo pastry; 3 tbs olive oil or melted butter.

Simmer leeks in a little lightly salted water 8 minutes; drain and refresh under cold running water. Drain again and leave until cold. Purée egg and feta cheese in a blender or food processor, or mash together with a fork. Combine with leeks and season with salt and pepper (remembering that feta tends to be rather salty).

Place filo between 2 dry tea-towels with a damp tea-towel on top. Brush one sheet of filo lightly with oil or butter, fold in half and brush again. Use to line an oiled or buttered shallow 20 cm (8 in) square cake tin. Place 2 more sheets of filo, each lightly brushed with oil or butter, on top, overlapping them and allowing ends to hang over sides of tin. Add leek filling and spread evenly in tin. Top with remaining filo folded in half and lightly brushed with oil or butter as before. Fold overhanging ends over top and tuck down inside tin to enclose filling completely. Brush top with oil or butter. Bake in a preheated moderately hot oven (190°C/375°F) for 45 minutes or until top is golden. Cut into squares to serve. Serves 4–6.

Leek and Potato Scallop

30 g (1 oz) butter; 4 old potatoes, peeled and finely sliced; 2 leeks, finely sliced; 60 g (2 oz) Gruyère or Cheddar cheese, grated; salt and freshly ground black pepper; nutmeg; ³/₄ cup milk; ³/₄ cup cream.

Butter a shallow ovenproof dish and layer potatoes and leeks in it, dotting each layer with butter, sprinkling with half the cheese and seasoning lightly with salt, pepper and nutmeg. Scald milk and cream and pour over. Sprinkle remaining cheese on top. Bake in a preheated moderate oven (180°C/350°F) for 1¹/₄ hours or until potato is tender. Serves 4–6.

LEGUMES

See *Pulses: Dried Beans, Peas and Lentils.*

LEMON

It is hard to imagine cooking without lemons, indeed lemons have been called 'the fruit with a thousand uses'. The juice and rind, or zest, containing essential citrus oils, are used to season and flavour a great number of dishes, and both are as indispensable as salt and pepper.

LEMON JUICE

A medium-size lemon yields approximately 2 tbs juice. To extract the maximum amount, warm a whole lemon in a preheated moderate oven (180°C/350°F) for 2 minutes, or roll it over a hard surface to soften slightly before halving and squeezing.

- Use lemon juice instead of vinegar in salad dressing.
- When a recipe calls for sour milk, buttermilk or sour cream and you have none on hand, the addition of

1 tsp lemon juice to 1 cup milk or ½ cup cream will provide a good substitute.

- To keep peeled fresh apples, pears or peaches from browning when not using immediately, immerse in 1 cup water plus 2 tsp lemon juice.
- Brush cut avocados or bananas with lemon juice to prevent browning.
- Melt 2 tbs butter, mix in the juice of 1 lemon, some chopped parsley or snipped chives and use as a sauce over boiled new potatoes, green beans, asparagus, patty pan squash, zucchini, grilled fish or chicken.
- Rub juice over a joint of lamb before roasting.

LEMON RIND OR ZEST

The zest can be grated off the surface of the lemon with a fine grater, rubbed off with sugar lumps or removed by paring very thinly with a vegetable peeler. Do not include any white pith because it leaves a bitter taste.

- Add 2 tbs grated lemon zest to 125 g (4 oz) cream cheese and beat until creamy.
- Sweeten with 1 tbs caster sugar and use to fill stoned dates or prunes, or serve with fresh berry fruits.
- Mix grated rind into mixture for meatballs, meat loaves or hamburgers.
- Mix grated rind into rice or bread stuffings for fish or poultry.
- Rub sugar lumps over a lemon and use to flavour custards.
- Stir a little grated rind into cake fillings or frostings.
- Add a small strip of lemon rind to the poaching syrup for fruit.

See also *Zest.*

LEMON SUGAR: Combine grated rind of 2 lemons with ¾ cup caster sugar. Store in an airtight jar and use sprinkled over fresh fruit, hot cereals, fruit pies or pastries.

Add ½ tsp cinnamon to ¼ cup Lemon Sugar and sprinkle over hot buttered toast.

GREMOLATA: The traditional accompaniment to Osso Buco Milanese (see page 321).

LEMON SHELLS: Halve lemons, scrape out the membrane and pulp and use as containers for individual servings of ice cream or sorbet.

LEMON AS GARNISH

Lemon Twists: Slice very thinly and make a cut from the centre to the edge. Twist the 2 sides of the slit in opposite directions to act as a base so the slice will stand up.

Lemon Wedges: Quarter the lemon lengthways, cut the rib off in a small wedge, then cut lemon wedges to size required. The centre rib is removed to prevent squirting when the wedge is squeezed.

Julienne Strips: Pare rind thinly, using a vegetable peeler. Trim into thin strips the size of a matchstick and blanch in boiling water for 2 minutes. Drain and dry before using. **See recipes.**

Skewered Lemon Prawns

½ **cup light soy sauce;** ½ **cup vegetable oil;** ½ **cup lemon juice; 1 small onion, grated; 1 kg (2 lb) green prawns, shelled and deveined.**

Mix together soy sauce, oil, lemon juice and onion. Add prawns, turning to coat in mixture, and marinate for at least 2 hours. Thread on to skewers (if using wooden skewers soak for 1 hour in water to prevent them burning), reserving marinade. Grill for 5–10 minutes depending on size of prawns, brushing often with marinade. Serves 4–6.

Grilled Lemon Chicken

An excellent way with chicken and one that weight watchers will appreciate.

juice 1 large lemon; 1 small onion, grated; 1–2 cloves garlic, crushed with pinch salt (optional); freshly ground black pepper; 4 chicken pieces, half-breasts or legs; 1–2 tbs oil; 1 lemon, sliced wafer-thin.

Combine lemon juice, onion, garlic if using and pepper. Marinate chicken pieces in this mixture for least 1 hour, turning several times. Brush grill rack with oil and add chicken pieces, skin side down. Cook under a preheated grill for about 10 minutes, then turn over and arrange slices of lemon on top. Continue to grill for a further 7 minutes or until chicken is cooked. Serves 4.

NOTE: If cooking boneless, skinless chicken breasts (chicken fillets) for weight watchers, place the chicken on sheet of foil smeared with oil. Protect with lemon slices and grill without turning for about 10 minutes.

Roast Lemon Chicken

A tangy lemon butter is slipped between the chicken flesh and skin and more is smoothed over the skin. The result is a most flavoursome bird with crispy golden skin.

60 g (2 oz) butter; 2 tsp grated lemon rind; 3 tbs lemon juice; salt and freshly ground white pepper; 1 x 2 kg (4 lb) or size 12 chicken; oil; lemon slices to garnish.

Cream butter with lemon rind. Gradually add 1 tbs of the lemon juice, then season with salt and pepper. Carefully loosen skin of chicken from flesh without piercing skin. This can be done by starting at the neck and slipping fingers between skin and flesh. Work towards tail, including tops of drumsticks. Spread two thirds of butter mixture under skin and pat chicken to smooth butter into a uniform layer. Truss chicken and rub with remaining butter mixture. Place breast side down on an oiled rack in a roasting tin. Roast in a preheated hot oven (200°C/400°F) for 20 minutes. Turn chicken, without breaking skin, breast side up and sprinkle with remaining lemon juice. Continue to cook, basting with pan juices every 20 minutes, for 1¼ hours or until juices run clear when thigh is pieced with a skewer. Let chicken rest for 15 minutes, then transfer to a heated platter and garnish with lemon slices. Serves 6.

Lemon Pork

1 kg (2 lb) boneless lean pork, cut into 2.5 cm (1 in) cubes; 2 tbs flour; ¼ cup oil; 1 tbs grated fresh ginger; 2 onions, sliced; ½ cup peeled and chopped tomatoes; 2 tbs chopped parsley; ½ cup lemon juice; 2 cups chicken stock; few drops Tabasco sauce; 2 tbs Mayonnaise (page 256).

GARNISH: lemon wedges; chopped parsley.

Sprinkle pork cubes with flour. Heat oil in a heavy pan and add pork and ginger. Cook over medium heat until pork is brown. Add onions, tomatoes and parsley, cook for a few minutes longer and add lemon juice, stock and Tabasco. Reduce heat and simmer very gently, uncovered, for about 1 hour or until pork is tender and stock reduced. Just before serving stir in mayonnaise. Garnish with lemon wedges and chopped parsley and serve with boiled new potatoes. Serves 6.

Lamb Loaf with Lemon Cream Sauce

Use a small boned shoulder of lamb. Chop the meat finely in a food processor or put through a mincer.

750 g (1½ lb) minced lean lamb;
125 g (4 oz) cooked ham, finely chopped;
2 tsp chopped fresh rosemary, or ½ tsp dried;
¼ tsp nutmeg; salt and freshly ground black pepper; 1 cup fresh white breadcrumbs;
2 eggs, beaten.

SAUCE: ¾ cup cream; 2 tbs lemon juice.

Place lamb in a bowl with remaining ingredients (except those for sauce). Mix lightly together. Shape into a round or oblong and place in a greased baking dish. Bake in a preheated moderate oven (180°/350°F) for 1 hour. Remove loaf from dish to a heated serving platter and pour off any fat left in baking dish. Add cream and lemon juice to dish and heat gently, scraping up brown bits. Season with salt and pepper and pour over loaf to serve. Serves 4–5.

Lemon Delicious Pudding

When the pudding is cooked you will have a delicate cake on top and tangy lemon sauce underneath. Serve hot, with cream or custard.

45 g (1½ oz) butter; ¾ cup caster sugar; 2 tsp finely grated lemon rind; 3 eggs, separated; 3 tbs flour; 1 cup milk; ¼ cup lemon juice; pinch salt.

Cream butter with sugar until light and fluffy. Add lemon rind and egg yolks and beat well. Sprinkle sifted flour over top and stir in with milk and lemon juice. Beat egg whites with salt until stiff and fold lightly into pudding mixture. Spoon into a greased 6-cup ovenproof dish and place in a roasting tin containing enough hot water to come halfway up sides of dish. Bake in preheated moderately slow oven (160°C/325°F) for 1 hour or until cake topping is cooked when tested with a fine skewer. Serves 6.

Lemon Meringue Pie

For an alternative recipe see page 237.

PASTRY: 90 g (3 oz) butter; ⅓ cup sugar; 1 tsp vanilla; 1 egg; ¾ cup self-raising flour; ¾ cup plain flour.

FILLING: 3 egg yolks; ½ cup sugar; 2 tbs flour; grated rind and juice 2 lemons; 4 tbs water.

MERINGUE: 3 egg whites; pinch cream of tartar; ¼ cup sugar.

PASTRY: Cream butter with sugar and vanilla. Add egg and beat well. Stir in sifted flours, turn out on to a floured board and knead lightly. Chill for 1 hour. Roll out on floured surface to fit greased 20–23 cm (8–9 in) pie plate. Pinch edges decoratively and prick base well with a fork. Bake in a preheated hot oven (200°C/400°F) for 15 minutes, then reduce oven temperature to moderate (180°C/350°F) and bake for further 5–10 minutes or until crust is golden. Cool.
FILLING: Mix egg yolks, sugar, flour and lemon rind in the top of a double saucepan and gradually stir in lemon juice and water. Cook, stirring constantly, over boiling water until mixture is smooth and thick. Cool, and pour into pie shell.
MERINGUE: Beat egg whites with cream of tartar until thick. Gradually add sugar, 2 tbs at a time, beating until mixture is thick and glossy and sugar dissolved. Spread over filling in pie shell, sealing completely with meringue. Bake in a preheated moderate oven (180°C/350°F) for 8–10 minutes or until meringue is golden. Serves 8.

Cold Lemon Soufflé

3 eggs, separated; ¾ cup caster sugar; grated rind and strained juice 2 small lemons; 2 tsp gelatine; 3 tbs water; ¾ cup cream, lightly whipped.

DECORATION: whipped cream; toasted flaked almonds.

Prepare a 5–6 cup soufflé dish with a strip of foil or greaseproof paper (see *Soufflé*). If a smooth effect is desired for the sides of the soufflé, brush one side of strip with melted butter. Tie strip around dish, buttered side in, so that it stands like a collar above edge.

Beat egg yolks in a large heatproof bowl, adding sugar gradually until mixture is thick and pale lemon coloured. Add lemon rind and juice. Whisk over simmering water until thick and light. Remove from heat and whisk for a few minutes longer. Soften gelatine in water, then dissolve over simmering water. Add to egg yolk mixture. Fold cream into mixture and then stiffly beaten egg whites. Spoon into prepared soufflé dish and chill until set. Run a heated knife round between 2 layers of paper collar and peel off collar carefully. Decorate with cream and press toasted flaked almonds around sides. Serves 6.

Lemon Butter Biscuits

250 g (8 oz) butter; grated rind 1 lemon; 1 cup icing sugar, sifted; 2 cups flour, sifted.

Beat butter with lemon rind until creamy. Add icing sugar and beat well. Stir in flour. Cover and chill for 30 minutes. Take teaspoons of the mixture and roll lightly into balls. Place on ungreased baking trays and press down with a fork which has been dipped in cold water to prevent sticking. Bake in a preheated moderate oven (180°C/350°F) for 10–12 minutes or until slightly coloured. Transfer to a wire rack. Cool and store in an airtight tin. Makes about 50.

Sour Pickled Lemons

12 lemons; 3 tbs rock salt; 1 tbs paprika; 3 bay leaves; 12 black peppercorns; 1/2 cup olive oil; 2 red chillies (optional).

Cook the whole unpeeled lemons in boiling water for 20 minutes. Drain and cut each lemon into quarters. Layer in a large jar with salt, paprika, bay leaves and peppercorns. When jar is full, pour on oil. Add whole chillies to make a hot pickle if you wish. Cover and store in a cool, dark place. The pickles will be ready in 6 months. Serve with curries and cold meats. Makes 6–8 cups.

Lemon and Sherry Dressing

Try this dressing over fresh fruit salads, apples, grapefruit, peaches, pears, oranges or bananas.

1/4 cup lemon juice; pinch salt; 1/4 cup sugar; 2 tbs dry sherry.

Combine lemon juice and salt, stir in sugar, then add sherry. Mix well. Makes 2/3 cup.

Lemon Tea Loaf

1 1/2 cups flour; 1 cup sugar; 1 tsp baking powder; 1/4 tsp salt; 125 g (4 oz) butter; 2 eggs, beaten; 1/2 cup milk; grated rind 1 lemon; 1/2 cup chopped walnuts.

LEMON SYRUP: juice 1 lemon; 1/4 cup sugar

Sift flour, sugar, baking powder and salt into a bowl. Rub in butter using fingertips. Mix beaten eggs and milk, stir into flour mixture, then fold in lemon rind and walnuts. Pour into a greased and base-lined 21 x 15 cm (8 1/2 x 6 in) loaf tin. Bake in a preheated moderate oven (180°C/350°F) for 1 1/4 hours or until a skewer inserted in centre comes out clean.
LEMON SYRUP: Mix lemon juice and sugar together. When cake is cooked and still hot, pour over the top. Allow to cool in tin.

LEMON CHEESE (LEMON BUTTER)

A preserve made from lemons, sugar, butter and eggs. Its tart-sweet flavour makes it a perfect filling for tartlets, sponge cakes, sponge rolls and short biscuits, or use it as a spread. Lemon cheese is always a welcome gift from your kitchen, especially if accompanied by a dozen little baked, unfilled pastry shells.

Lemon Cheese (Lemon Butter)

3 lemons; 6 sugar lumps; 1/2 cup sugar; 30 g (1 oz) butter; 2 tsp cornflour; 1 tbs water; 2 eggs.

Wash and dry lemons. Rub sugar lumps over lemons until they are saturated with oil (zest) from skins. Put sugar lumps into a saucepan with sugar, butter and strained juice of the lemons. Place over low heat and stir continuously until sugar dissolves. Add cornflour blended with water and bring to the boil; remove from heat. Beat eggs in a heatproof bowl and slowly add hot lemon mixture, beating continuously. Place over simmering water and cook 10 minutes, stirring, or until thick enough to coat the spoon. Pour into hot jars and seal. Lemon cheese keeps for several weeks stored in refrigerator. Makes about 1 1/2 cups.
NOTE: This recipe makes a fairly firm lemon cheese. For a softer lemon cheese see page 207.

LEMONADE

The combination of lemon juice, sugar and water makes one of the most refreshing drinks imaginable. Serve lemonade icy cold in tall glasses garnished with a twist of lemon or a sprig of mint.

Lemonade

2 cups sugar; 1 cup water; 1 cup lemon juice.

Combine sugar and water in a saucepan. Bring to the boil, stirring, over gentle heat. Boil gently for 5 minutes without stirring. Cool, then add lemon juice. Strain and store in a covered container in refrigerator. When ready to serve, add 2 tbs syrup to 1 glass of iced water. Makes 2 1/2 cups syrup.

VARIATION

CLARET LEMONADE: Combine ½ cup made-up lemonade with ½ cup claret. Moisten rims of 2 wine glasses with water and dip into sugar to frost. Pour Claret Lemonade over ice in each glass.

LEMONGRASS

Known as serai in Malaysia, takrai in Thailand. Also known as citronella. Lemongrass is easily grown and is available fresh at many supermarkets and Asian food stores. Fresh lemongrass stem is sold in bunches and looks similar to very long spring onions. It is a very fibrous plant and before cooking it is necessary to remove the tough outer leaves. The lower third of the stalk, the bulb-like portion, is the part to use when a recipe specifies 'chopped or sliced lemongrass'. Alternatively, the whole stalk may be cut into pieces and bruised before adding to dishes that are to be simmered such as curries; remove before serving. Store, loosely wrapped, in the bottom of the refrigerator.

Roasted Chicken with Lemongrass

I large free-range chicken; 2 lemongrass stems, outer leaves removed and thinly sliced; ¹/₃ cup finely chopped coriander leaves; 2 cloves garlic, finely chopped; I lemon, rind finely grated; 2 tbs olive oil; I¹/₂ cups fresh coriander sprigs; freshly ground pepper; I cup dry white wine; I cup chicken stock.

Rinse the chicken well inside and out and dry with paper towels. In a small bowl, mix half the sliced lemongrass, coriander, garlic, lemon rind and 1 tbs of the olive oil. Gently lift the skin (being careful not to break it) from the neck end of the chicken and spread the lemongrass mixture over the flesh. Place the whole lemon inside the cavity with the remaining sliced lemongrass, and coriander sprigs, and tie the chicken into a neat shape with string.

Place the chicken on a rack in a roasting pan and rub the remaining olive oil on to the skin. Season with pepper. Pour in the wine and chicken stock. Place the chicken in a preheated moderate oven (180°C/350°F) and roast for 1½-2 hours, basting every 15 minutes. Remove the chicken from the oven and rest for 10 minutes before serving. Serves 4–5.

Steamed Snapper with Lemongrass

I large or 4 small snapper; salt; 2 spring onions, sliced; 2 slices fresh ginger; I¹/₂ cups water.

GARNISH: ¹/₂ leek, washed and finely shredded into 5 cm (2 in) strips; I stem lemongrass, tender part only, finely chopped; 4 spring onions, finely shredded into 5 cm (2 in) strips;

I red bird's-eye chilli, seeded and cut into strips; I–2 tbs soy sauce; ¹/₃ cup peanut or vegetable oil; 2 tsp sesame oil.

Scale, clean, and lightly rinse the fish and pat dry with paper towels. Slash in thickest part and lightly salt inside and out. Place spring onions and ginger in cavity. Arrange the fish in a single layer on the bottom of a baking dish. Add the water to the dish. Cover with foil or lid and cook gently over a medium heat until the fish is cooked, 10–15 minutes. Scatter over the shredded leek, lemongrass, spring onions and chilli. Cover well with foil or lid and cook gently over a moderate heat until cooked, about 5 minutes.

Remove the fish and place on to 4 large serving plates. Sprinkle with soy sauce. Heat peanut and sesame oils in a small saucepan until very hot, then pour carefully and evenly over fish. Serve immediately (if the oil is hot enough there should be lots of sizzling as the garnish half-cooks). Serves 4.

Thai Sour Spicy Prawn Soup

Also known as Tom Yam Goong, this favourite soup is very hot and spicy with a delicious balance of sour.

9 large or 18 small prawns; 2 stems lemongrass; 4 kaffir lime leaves or a strip of lime rind; 4–5 button mushrooms; 2–3 tiny bird's-eye chillies, split and seeded; 4 cups seafood stock; 4 tablespoons lime juice; 2 tablespoons Thai fish sauce (nam pla); I cup coriander leaves.

Wash the prawns, peel but leave the tails on, then devein. Crush the tender white ends of the lemongrass, and slice finely on the bias. Halve the lime leaves. Slice the mushrooms and chillies (use only 1 chilli if your taste doesn't run to very hot). Heat the stock in a large saucepan. Add the lemongrass, lime leaves, mushrooms, chilli and lime juice and fish sauce. Bring to the boil, reduce the heat, and simmer for 2 minutes. Add the prawns and cook only until the prawns turn pink. Toss in the coriander leaves and serve. Serves 6.

LENTIL

See *Pulses: Dried Beans, Peas and Lentils.*

LETTUCE

It is as true today as when John Evelyn wrote it in the seventeenth century that 'the lettuce ever was and still continues the principal foundation of the universal Tribe of Salads, which is to cool and refresh'. This first family of leafy salad greens has numerous members of which the best-known are long and slender cos (romaine), round, crisp, pale-green iceberg and soft bronze-edged mignonette.

When buying lettuce, look for fresh, unwilted heads with no discolouration. Check that the centre is sound.

If you want to keep it for several days before using, remove any damaged outside leaves, place unwashed in a plastic bag and gently squeeze out air. Fasten tightly and refrigerate. If using the same day, wash, dry and store as follows.

See also *Mesclun* and *Radicchio*.

■ **BASIC PREPARATION:** Remove any damaged or coarse outside leaves (they can be used for soup). Cut out the core and hold upside-down under running cold water. The water will help you to spread the leaves gently so that you can separate them whole. Break off thick base of each centre rib, wash leaves and drain. If you want smaller pieces, tear lettuce rather than cutting it, as cut edges darken. Dry thoroughly. This is best done in one of those wonderful salad dryers that works like hand-operated spin-dryers. Otherwise, you can put lettuce into a salad basket or fold it in a tea-towel and swing vigorously outdoors, or shake over a sink. Pack loosely into plastic bags, close and store in refrigerator for at least an hour to crisp. When making a salad, do not add dressing to lettuce until the last moment or it will lose its crispness.

WAYS TO USE LETTUCE

Lettuce star alone in great salads such as Caesar Salad (see page 58) or classic Green Salad (see *Salads*), or provides a base for other ingredients of every kind. Tiny lettuce leaves or the fine shreds called *chiffonnade* are among the prettiest garnishes. In addition to its many roles as a raw vegetable, lettuce makes a delicately flavoured soup, a meltingly tender braised vegetable or a delicious last-minute addition to a lamb casserole. Blanched lettuce leaves can be used to wrap other food, and lettuce is an essential ingredient in the epicurean green pea dish Petits Pois à La Française (see page 351). **See recipes.**

Cream of Lettuce Soup

60 g (2 oz) butter; 1 small onion, chopped; 1 large lettuce, chopped; salt and freshly ground white pepper; 3 cups chicken stock; 2 eggs yolks, or 2 tsp arrowroot; 1/2 cup cream.

GARNISH: shredded fresh mint; fried croûtons (see page 105).

Melt butter in a large saucepan, add onion and cook gently until soft but not brown. Add lettuce, season with salt and pepper and cook over low heat 5 minutes or until lettuce is soft. Rub through a sieve or purée in a blender with a little of the stock. Heat remaining stock and add lettuce purée. Beat egg yolks or arrowroot with cream; stir in a little hot soup then stir this back into saucepan. Stir over low heat until soup begins to thicken. If using egg yolks remove from heat at this point; do not allow to boil. If using arrowroot, continue to stir until boiling, then remove from heat. Adjust seasoning, and serve sprinkled with mint. Pass croûtons separately. Serves 6–8.

Braised Lettuce

6 small lettuces; salt and freshly ground black pepper; 4 thin rashers streaky bacon, rind removed and chopped; 1 onion, finely chopped; 1 carrot, finely chopped; 1 bouquet garni; about 1 1/2 cups hot chicken or beef stock, or 1 cup stock and 1/2 cup white wine or vermouth; knob butter; squeeze lemon juice.

Plunge lettuces, whole, 2 or 3 at a time, into boiling salted water and parboil 5 minutes. Cool under running water and squeeze to extract as much water as possible. Cut each lengthways in half. Season with pepper and fold crossways in half; tie with string. In a shallow pan that will take lettuces in a single layer, make a bed of bacon, onion and carrot. Add bouquet garni and lay lettuce close together on top. Cover and cook over moderate heat, or in a preheated hot oven (200°C/400°F), 10 minutes. Pour in enough stock barely to cover lettuce. Cover and simmer on low heat, or in a moderate oven (180°C/350°F), 1 hour. Remove lettuce to a heated serving dish, remove string and keep warm. Strain cooking liquid into a clean saucepan, skim off fat and boil rapidly until reduced to about 1/2 cup. Adjust seasoning, remove from heat and swirl in butter and lemon juice. Pour over lettuce and serve immediately. Serves 6.

Five-Minute Lettuce Soup

4 cups chicken stock; 1/2 small lettuce, or outside leaves of 1 large lettuce, finely shredded; 2 eggs; few drops soy sauce.

Heat stock to simmering point, add lettuce and cook 2–3 minutes. Beat eggs with soy sauce, stir in a little of the hot soup then stir this back into soup. Serve immediately. Serves 4.

Chef's Salad

Chef's salads vary according to the ingredients available and the chef's inspiration, but all start with a bed of crisp lettuce.

2 small mignonette or cos lettuces, or 1 firm iceberg lettuce; 1 half-breast of chicken, lightly poached and cooled; 1 thick slice cooked ham; 60 g (2 oz) Swiss cheese; 2 spring onions; 1 small stick celery; 2 hard-boiled eggs, quartered; 1/3 cup Garlic or Herb Vinaigrette Dressing (page 442).

Remove coarse outer leaves of lettuce, cut out cores and rinse under running water without separating leaves. Wrap in a tea-towel and place in refrigerator 1 hour or longer to drain thoroughly and crisp. Cut mignonette or cos lengthways into halves, iceberg into 4 wedges or 4 thick slices from top to bottom. Arrange on serving platter. Remove skin and bone from chicken, cut chicken, ham and cheese into julienne (matchstick) strips. Shred spring onions and celery to about the same size. Pile these ingredients lightly on lettuce, criss-cross fashion. Use eggs to garnish platter. Serve dressing separately at the table so each diner can add their own. Serves 4.

LIMA BEAN

See *Beans, Broad and Lima*.

LIME

This citrus fruit can be pale or dark green and has a tart, greenish flesh; it can be treated as a lemon. Limes make a delicious marmalade and are used commercially to make marvellous cordial. In India they are used to make pickles, and slices or wedges are used as an accompaniment to many curried dishes. Limes are also used in Mexican and Creole cooking. The limed fish of Tahiti and Acapulco is delicious. The rind and juice of limes may be used in the same way as the rind and juice of lemons.

Limes, with their delicious sharpness, make the most refreshing drinks. Gimlets, Margheritas, Daiquiris and Tequilas are not the same without limes. Long cool gin or rum drinks are better for a dash of lime juice. See recipes.

See also *Lemons* and *Ceviche*.

COCKTAILS AND LONG DRINKS

A jigger is the traditional bar measure of 45 ml (1½ fl oz). A jigger measure is available at most bottle shops. A simple sugar syrup is a useful ingredient when mixing drinks. Boil 1 cup sugar with ½ cup water for about 5 minutes. Cool, keep in a bottle in the refrigerator, and use as needed. If you do not possess a cocktail shaker, stir ingredients in a jug or whirl for a few seconds in a blender. Strain the drinks into chilled glasses. When making long drinks the base is mixed and ice added followed by the 'mixer', usually a carbonated water – soda, Vichy, ginger ale – which shoud be well chilled.

Daiquiri: Shake well with ¾ cup cracked ice: ½ jigger sugar syrup; 1½ jiggers lime juice; 6 jiggers rum. Strain into chilled glasses. Makes 4.

Cubana: Shake well with ¾ cup cracked ice: 1 tbs sugar syrup; 1½ jiggers Benedictine; 5½ jiggers rum. Strain into chilled glasses. Makes 4.

Gimlet: Shake well with ¾ cup cracked ice: 1 tbs sugar syrup; 1½ jiggers lime juice; 5 jiggers gin. Strain into tall chilled glasses. Makes 4.

Substituting orange juice for half the lime juice changes a Gimlet into an Orange Blossom. Vodka is becoming increasingly popular and may replace gin in both cocktails.

Margherita: Shake well with ¾ cup cracked ice: 5 jiggers tequila; 1½ jiggers lime juice; ¼ jigger triple sec (white Curaçao). Strain into glasses, the rims of which have been rubbed with citrus rind then spun in salt. Serves 4.

Cuba Libra: Combine in a tall glass: juice 1 lime; ½ squeezed lime; 1 jigger rum. Add 2 large ice cubes, fill glass with cola, stir and serve. Makes 1.

Gin and Tonic: Place 2 ice cubes in a tall glass, add 1 large jigger gin (or Vodka) and fill glass with quinine water (tonic). Add lime or lemon juice to taste. Makes 1.

Tahitian Limed Fish

There are many ways of making this famous raw fish salad. Lemon may replace the lime when limes are unavailable. Serve as a first course.

500 g (1 lb) firm-fleshed fish fillets; 2 limes; 1 tbs olive oil; salt and freshly ground black pepper; 6 spring onions, sliced; 2 tsp green peppercorns, lightly crushed; 1 cos or mignonette lettuce; 2 canned pimientos, diced; 2 tomatoes, peeled and quartered, to garnish.

With a sharp knife cut fish into very thin slices which are almost transparent. Pare rind thinly from limes and reserve. Squeeze juice from limes. Spread out fish on a chilled plate and drizzle over lime juice. Combine oil, salt, pepper, spring onions and peppercorns. Sprinkle over fish and marinate for 1 hour. Cut reserved lime rind into fine julienne (matchstick) strips, about the thickness of pine needles. Drop into boiling water and blanch for 1 minute. Drain. Make a bed of lettuce leaves on 4 plates and arrange slices of marinated fish on top with any of the marinade left over. Scatter blanched lime rind and pimientos over fish and garnish with tomato quarters. Serves 4.

VARIATION

ACAPULCO LIMED FISH: Prepare Tahitian Limed Fish. Peel, stone and mash 1 avocado. Season with salt, freshly ground black pepper, a dash of Tabasco sauce and a squeeze of lime juice. Spoon avocado mixture over fish salad.

Nutbread with Lime Butter

An unusual tea-time combination.

2½ cups flour; 1 tbs baking powder; ½ tsp salt; 1 cup chopped walnuts; 60 g (2 oz) butter; ¾ cup firmly packed brown sugar; 1 egg; ¾ cup plus 2 tbs milk.

LIME BUTTER: 60 g (2 oz) butter; grated rind 1 lime; 1 tbs lime juice; salt.

Sift flour with baking powder and salt, then add walnuts. Cream butter with sugar until light and fluffy, then beat in egg and milk. Fold in flour mixture 1 cup at a time. Allow to stand, covered with plastic wrap, for 40 minutes. Spoon into a battered 21 x 11 cm (8½ x 4½ in) loaf tin that has been lined on the bottom and long sides with greased greaseproof paper. Bake in a preheated moderate oven (180°/350°F) for 1 hour 10 minutes or until a skewer inserted in centre comes out clean. Cool in tin for 15 minutes before turning out on to a wire rack.

LIME BUTTER: Cream butter with lime rind and juice. Add salt to taste. Serve with sliced Nutbread.

Lime Meringue Pie

This recipe is equally delicious when made with lemons, see variation below.

3 tbs cornflour; 1¼ cups plus 6 tbs sugar; ½ cup lime juice; 1 tbs grated lime rind; 3 eggs, separated; 1½ cups boiling water; 1 x 23 cm (9 in) Shortcrust Pastry Tart Shell, baked (page 342).

Combine cornflour, 1¼ cups sugar, and lime juice and rind in a saucepan. Beat egg yolks until thick and fluffy and add to lime juice mixture. Gradually add boiling water. Heat to simmering over very gentle heat, stirring constantly until thickened. Simmer 2–3 minutes. Pour into pastry shell and leave to cool.

Beat egg whites until stiff but not dry and gradually beat in remaining sugar. Spread meringue over top of pie, carefully sealing in all the filling and being sure to touch edge of pastry shell all around. Bake in a preheated hot oven (200°C/400°F) for about 5 minutes or until very pale brown. Cool and serve with whipped cream. Serves 8.

VARIATION

LEMON MERINGUE PIE: Use lemon peel and juice in place of lime peel and juice.

LIME, KAFFIR

The aromatic leaves of the kaffir lime tree are a dark shiny green and shaped with two sections. They are used in many Southeast Asian dishes, particularly Thai, including curries, salads and soups. The leaves may be used whole or finely shredded or pounded to release the aromatic citrus flavour. Use with a light hand; a little makes a big difference, too much can give a bitter flavour.

The fruit of this tree, with its coarse, pitted skin, contains very little juice but the rind is grated and added to dishes. Fresh kaffir lime leaves are available at most supermarkets and greengrocers.

Gaeng Pla Choo Chee
(Fish in Red Curry Sauce with Lime Leaves)

This is a fabulous dish, particularly for those who like it hot. The Thai combination of lime leaves, coconut milk and red curry paste is great with fish.

1 large whole white fish, such as bream, snapper or perch; ¾ cup vegetable oil; 2 tsp Red Curry Paste (page 108); 1 fresh red chilli, seeded and finely sliced; 6 fresh kaffir lime leaves; 1 cup coconut milk; 1 tbs fish sauce (nam pla); 1 tbs sugar.

GARNISH: lime wedges; fresh coriander leaves; 1 small red peppers, cut into very fine strips.

Have the fish scaled and gutted. Wash and pat dry with paper towels. Trim the fish by cutting off the sharp spikes and make 2–3 diagonal cuts along each side of the fish to help it cook evenly. Heat the oil in a wok or large frying pan over a high heat, reserving 1 tbs for later; lower the fish carefully and cook until golden on one side. Lower the heat and gently turn the fish over. Turn up the heat and cook for a further 5 minutes or until golden. Lift the fish gently on to a serving plate.

Meanwhile, gently stir-fry in another pan the red curry paste, chilli and lime leaves in the remaining tbs of oil. Add the coconut milk, fish sauce and sugar, and simmer for about 5 minutes. Pour the sauce over the fish and garnish with the lime wedges, coriander, shredded lime leaves and pepper strips. Serve with steamed rice. Serves 4.

Thai Chicken and Coconut Soup

4 fresh kaffir lime leaves; 5 cm (2 in) piece tender lemongrass; 2 cm (¾ in) fresh ginger; 3 cups chicken stock; 4–6 slices fresh or dried galangal; 3 tbs fish sauce; ½ cup fresh lime or lemon juice; 2 fresh red chillies, seeded and finely sliced; 1 whole chicken breast fillet, cut into strips; 1½ cups coconut milk; ½ cup chopped fresh coriander; salt and pepper to taste.

Finely shred 2 of the kaffir leaves, leaving the others whole. Finely chop the lemongrass; peel and finely slice the ginger. In a large saucepan combine the stock, galangal, fish sauce, lime juice and whole lime leaves, chillies, lemongrass and ginger. Bring the mixture slowly to a simmer. Stir in the chicken and coconut milk and simmer the soup for 3–5 minutes, or until the chicken is tender. Stir in the coriander and add shredded lime leaves and salt and pepper to taste. Serves 4–6.

LINZER TORTE (LINZ JAM TART)

Linzer Torte, named after the town of Linz on the River Danube, is made in many parts of Austria. It is distinguished by its unique pastry made with ground nuts, either almonds or hazelnuts, and spices. This pastry is arranged in lattice strips over a jam filling, either plum or raspberry. Serve Linzer Torte plain or dusted with icing sugar.

Linzer Torte

1 cup flour; ¼ cup caster sugar; 2 tsp cocoa powder; ½ tsp cinnamon; pinch ground cloves; ½ tsp baking powder; pinch salt; 125 g (4 oz) ground almonds; 125 g (4 oz) butter; milk or Kirsch; 1½ cups raspberry or plum jam; beaten egg to glaze; sifted icing sugar (optional).

Sift flour, sugar, cocoa, cinnamon, cloves, baking powder and salt into a mixing bowl. Add ground almonds. Rub in butter, which has been cut into small pieces, and mix lightly with fingertips to a dry dough, adding milk or Kirsch if necessary. Wrap dough in foil and chill for at least 30 minutes. Divide dough; roll out ⅔ and press on to bottom of a greased 18 cm (7 in) springform tin. Spread jam on top. Roll out remaining dough, cut into 1 cm (½ in) wide strips and arrange in lattice fashion on top, using the last one as an edging around the tart. Press down lightly and chill for 30 minutes. Remove tart from refrigerator, brush with beaten egg and bake in a preheated moderately hot oven (190°C/375°F) for 35–40 minutes. Allow to cool in tin. Dust with icing sugar if desired. Serve with whipped cream. Serves 8–10.

LIVER

Liver has outstanding nutritional properties, and, when properly prepared, is delicious. Beef, calf, lamb, pork and poultry livers are used in the cookery of many nations. Liver and bacon is a natural combination enjoyed in Britain, USA and Australia. Lamb, beef or calf livers are all used for the dish. Goose liver is made into the famous pâtés and terrines of France and Hungary. Chicken livers are used in some of the risottos of Italy, in pâté, which is easy to make and a treat, or can be sautéed to make a quick meal.

Beef, calf, lamb and pork livers are all generally available from butchers. Calf's or lamb's liver is best enjoyed cut in thin slices and quickly pan-fried, and served with a flavoursome accompaniment, such as onions, bacon, etc. Beef liver is less tender than calf's or lamb's liver and has a more pronounced flavour; it is often braised with onions. Pork liver has a strong flavour and is less tender than the other kinds; it is not good for frying but makes excellent pâté, or it may be braised whole with vegetables. Poultry livers are tender and mild in flavour, and are usually available from specialty poultry shops.

■ **BASIC PREPARATION:** Pull thin veil of membrane away from liver. Cut away any fat and gristle, and cut out veins, using a small, sharp-pointed knife. Cut into thin slices or leave whole depending on recipe.

■ **TO COOK:** Liver can be pan-fried, grilled or braised. See also recipes.

PAN-FRIED OR SAUTEED LIVER: Calf, lamb and good pork liver are cut into thin slices, seasoned with salt and pepper and lightly dusted on each side with flour. Chicken livers are left whole. Heat a small amount of fat in a frying pan (butter, oil or half butter and half oil). Using tongs, put slices in pan. Cook quickly, turning once, until crisp on both sides but pink inside, about 4 minutes in all. Cook pork liver a little longer.

GRILLED LIVER: Calf, lamb and poultry livers can be grilled. Have calf's or lamb's livers cut 1 cm (½ in) thick. Heat grill. Put liver on greased grill rack and brush with melted butter. Grill 8–10 cm (3–4 in) from heat, turning once, until required doneness, 4–8 minutes in all.

BRAISED LIVER: All livers can be braised. Have beef, calf, lamb or pork livers cut 1 cm (½ in) thick. Sprinkle with flour seasoned with salt and freshly ground black pepper. Brown liver quickly on both sides in hot fat (half butter and half oil is ideal), then add ½ cup stock and seasoning as desired (fresh herbs, diced bacon, sliced mushrooms, sliced onions) and simmer, covered, until tender.

Liver and Bacon

375–500 g (12 oz–1 lb) calf's or lamb's liver, cut into 1 cm (½ in) thick slices; salt and freshly ground black pepper; flour; butter or bacon fat for frying; 4–8 rashers bacon, rinds removed; 2–3 thin slices onion; hot water or stock; lemon juice; chopped parsley.

Season liver slices with salt and pepper and dip in flour. Heat butter or bacon fat in a frying pan and fry liver 2–3 minutes on each side. Put on a heated dish. Fry bacon until crisp and arrange over liver. Put onion into the hot fat and cook until golden-brown. Remove, drain and arrange on the dish. Season with salt and pepper. Add a few tbs of hot water or stock to the pan to make a little brown gravy. Sprinkle liver with lemon juice, gravy and parsley and serve. Serves 4.

Liver Bonne Femme

bacon fat or butter; 500–750 g (1–1½ lb) lamb's or calf's liver; 3 rashers lean bacon, rind removed, or cooked ham, cut into strips; 2–3 potatoes, peeled and cut into olive shapes, or 6–8 tiny new potatoes; 2 mushrooms, quartered; 12 small onions; 1 tbs flour; ⅔ cup white wine or cider; 1 cup stock; salt and freshly ground black pepper; 1 bouquet garni.

Heat fat or butter in a heavy pan or flameproof casserole, put in the piece of liver whole and sauté it quickly on all sides for about 5 minutes. Remove liver from casserole and put in bacon or ham, potatoes, mushrooms and onions. Fry them lightly, then scatter over the flour and mix well. Pour on wine or cider and stock. Bring to the boil, season with salt and pepper and add bouquet garni. Return liver to pan and simmer on top of stove or braise in a preheated moderate oven (180°C/350°F) for 40–50 minutes. Carve liver in thin slices and arrange on a heated serving dish with bacon and vegetables. Boil up sauce, discard bouquet garni and spoon sauce carefully over the liver. Serves 6.

Swiss Liver

750 g (1¹/₂ lb) calf's liver, cut into thin strips; seasoned flour; 60 g (2 oz) butter; ¹/₄ cup oil; 3 tbs chopped onion; 3 tbs chopped parsley; salt and freshly ground black pepper; 1 cup sour light cream.

Dust liver strips with seasoned flour. Heat butter and oil in a frying pan. When hot and bubbly, add onion, parsley and liver strips. Sauté quickly, turning liver strips to brown on all sides. Do not overcook. Strips should be pink in centre. Season and add sour cream. Heat through, but do not boil. Serve on fried bread. Serves 4.

Calf's Liver Tuscan–Style

6–8 slices calf's liver; seasoned flour; 2 tbs oil; 30 g (1 oz) butter; salt and freshly ground black pepper; 4 leaves fresh sage, chopped; 1 lemon, quartered, to garnish.

Dust liver slices with seasoned flour. Heat oil and butter in frying pan. Cook slices 1¹/₂ minutes on each side. Season with salt, pepper and sage and cook another minute on each side. Serve garnished with quarters of lemon. Serves 4.

Venetian Liver with Onions

The way liver is prepared in Venice with lots of onions and the surprising touch of lemon rind is one of the nicest. Traditionally served with thick slices of Polenta (see page 373).

2 tbs oil; 2 large onions, finely sliced; 2 tbs water; 1 tsp grated lemon rind; 500 g (1 lb) calf's or lamb's liver, very finely sliced; salt and freshly ground black pepper.

Heat oil in a large frying pan, add onions, toss to coat with oil and add water. Cover and cook over gentle heat for about 20 minutes. Add lemon rind and mix well. Push onions to one side of pan. Add a little more oil, then the liver and season with salt and pepper. Stir well, cover and cook for 2–3 minutes. If you like a thicker gravy, toss slices of liver in seasoned flour before adding to pan. Serve with mashed potatoes, polenta or fluffy boiled rice. Serves 4.

Devilled Liver on Croustades

A delicious light luncheon or supper dish.

¹/₂ cup oil; 4 slices bread, cut 2 cm (³/₄ in) thick; 60 g (2 oz) butter; 2 onions, sliced; 500 g (1 lb) beef, pork, calf's or lamb's liver, diced; 2 tbs flour; 2 tsp dry mustard; 1 cup hot water; ¹/₂ tsp salt; freshly ground black pepper; ¹/₂ cup sour light cream.

First make the croustades. Heat oil in a frying pan and fry bread until golden and crisp. Drain on crumpled paper towels and keep hot until required. Pour oil from pan and add half the butter. When melted, add onions and fry until browned. Push onions to side of pan and add remaining butter. Coat liver in flour and brown in the butter, adding more butter if needed. Add mustard, water, salt and pepper. Heat gently until sauce thickens, stirring constantly. Add sour cream and serve on croustades. Serves 4.

Sautéed Liver with Basil

500 g (1 lb) calf's or lamb's liver, sliced; seasoned flour; 1 tbs oil; 60 g (2 oz) butter; 2 tbs fresh basil cut into thin strips.

Turn liver slices in seasoned flour and pat off excess. Sauté in the oil and half the butter, then remove to a heated dish. Add remaining butter and basil to pan and heat for a few moments. Pour over liver and serve at once, with grilled or sautéed tomatoes. Serves 4.

VARIATION

SAUTEED LIVER WITH HERBS: Follow recipe for Sautéed Liver with Basil, but substitute 2 tsp lemon juice and 2 tbs chopped fresh herbs (parsley, sage, oregano, thyme, chives) for basil.

Flambéed Liver with Cream

500 g (1 lb) calf's liver, sliced; seasoned flour; 1 tbs oil; 30 g (1 oz) butter; 1 tbs lemon juice; ¹/₄ cup brandy or whisky; ¹/₂ cup cream; salt and freshly ground black pepper.

Turn liver slices in seasoned flour and pat of excess. Sauté liver slices in oil and butter for 1 minute, turn and sauté other side for 2 minutes. Pour over lemon juice and brandy or whisky, and set alight. Shake pan until flames die down, stir in cream, season to taste and serve immediately. Serves 4.

Smothered Liver and Onions

5 medium onions, sliced; 60 g (2 oz) butter;
4 tbs oil; 500 g (1 lb) calf's or lamb's liver, finely
sliced; 2 tbs flour; 1 tsp salt; freshly ground
black pepper; $^3/_4$ cup water.

Cook onions in half the butter and oil in a frying pan
until golden-brown; remove. Dredge liver slices
with flour seasoned with salt and pepper. Fry in
remaining butter and oil until browned on both
sides. Return onions to pan with water, cover and
simmer for 3–4 minutes. Do not overcook or liver
will toughen. Serves 4.

Chicken Liver Pâté

One of the simplest but best ways to make a pâté. The
chopped hard-boiled egg improves the texture.

250 g (8 oz) chicken livers; 1$^1/_4$ cups stock;
$^1/_2$ cup chopped onion; 45 g (1$^1/_2$ oz) butter;
2 hard-boiled eggs, finely chopped;
salt and freshly ground black pepper;
30 g (1 oz) butter, melted, to seal.

Simmer livers in stock until done, 8–10 minutes.
Drain, reserving stock. Remove veins from livers.
Purée livers with a little of the stock in a food
processor or blender. Brown onion lightly in butter
and blend with liver purée and eggs to make a paste.
Season with salt and pepper. If desired, season
further with a pinch of curry powder or a dash of
brandy. Put in a small dish or 4 individual ramekins.
Spoon melted butter over surface to seal pâté and
refrigerate several hours. Serve with buttered toast
fingers. Serves 4.

Chicken Livers Marsala

60 g (2 oz) plus 1 tbs butter; 500 g (1 lb) chicken
livers, halved; $^1/_2$ tsp salt; $^1/_4$ tsp black pepper;
6 leaves fresh sage, chopped; 2 slices prosciutto
or cooked ham, diced; 8 bread triangles, sautéed;
$^1/_4$ cup Marsala.

Melt 60 g (2 oz) butter in a frying pan and add livers,
salt, pepper, sage and prosciutto or ham. Cook 5 minutes. Remove livers from pan and place on sautéed
bread triangles. Add Marsala to pan, stir well and
cook 3 minutes. Add remaining butter, mix well and
pour over livers. Serves 4.

Chicken Liver Risotto

60 g (2 oz) butter; 6 chicken livers, quartered;
$^1/_2$ cup chopped onion; $^1/_2$ cup finely chopped
mushrooms; 1 cup long-grain rice; 2$^1/_2$ cups
boiling chicken stock; 2 tbs chopped parsley;
salt and freshly ground black pepper;
grated Parmesan cheese to serve.

Melt butter in a large heavy saucepan and brown
chicken livers. Remove livers and keep hot. Add
onion to pan and cook until transparent. Add mushrooms and cook 3 minutes longer. Add rice and cook,
stirring constantly, 2 minutes. Stir in stock. Cover and
simmer over low heat until stock is absorbed and rice
is tender but still firm, about 20 minutes. If stock is
absorbed and rice is not tender, add a little more stock
and cook longer. Stir livers and parsley into rice,
season with salt and pepper and serve immediately,
with grated Parmesan cheese. Serves 4.

Rice with Chicken Livers and Mushrooms

60 g (2 oz) butter; 1 onion, chopped;
2 cups long-grain rice; $^1/_4$ cup Marsala;
8 cups hot chicken stock.

SAUCE: 60 g (2 oz) butter; 1 onion, finely sliced;
1 thin slice prosciutto, cut into julienne
(matchstick) strips; 3 leaves fresh sage,
or $^1/_2$ tsp dried; 1 bay leaf; 6 chicken livers, chopped;
6–8 mushrooms, sliced; salt and freshly ground
black pepper; 1 tbs Marsala; 1 cup chicken stock.

Melt butter in a heavy saucepan, add onion and
sauté until brown. Stir in rice and cook, stirring,
until each grain is golden in colour. Add Marsala
and cook gently until it is absorbed into rice. Add
stock, 2 cups at a time, each time covering pan until
liquid is simmering. Allow to cook very slowly,
without stirring, until rice has absorbed all the liquid.
When done, rice should be fairly dry but not too soft.
SAUCE: Melt butter in a saucepan and sauté onion,
ham, sage and bay leaf until mixture takes on a little
colour. Add chicken livers and mushrooms and stir
well. Add salt, pepper, Marsala and stock. Simmer
10 minutes. Stir half the sauce into the risotto. To
serve, place risotto in a heated bowl. Serve remaining
sauce separately. Serves 6.

Liver Dumplings in Soup

There is something very middle-European and old-
fashioned about liver dumplings in soup. It is also
delicious.

125 g (4 oz) beef, calf, lamb, pork or chicken liver;
$^1/_2$ small onion; 1 egg yolk; $^1/_4$ tsp salt; pinch freshly
ground black pepper; pinch dried thyme; pinch
nutmeg; 1$^1/_2$ tbs chopped parsley; 1$^1/_2$ slices bread,
crusts removed; milk or water; about $^1/_2$ cup flour;
8 cups soup stock.

Mince or finely chop liver with the onion. Add egg
yolk, salt, pepper, thyme, nutmeg and parsley. Soak
the bread in milk or water to moisten and squeeze out
excess liquid. Add to liver mixture with enough flour
to make a soft dough. Bring soup stock to the boil.

Dip a teaspoon in the soup, then fill it with liver dough and drop into soup. Re-dip spoon in soup before shaping each dumpling. Cover pan and simmer 10–15 minutes, depending on size of dumplings. Serves 6–8.

Chicken Liver Toasts

These small savouries are equally good served as an antipasto or as light snacks.

3 tbs butter; 1 shallot, finely chopped; 3–4 leaves fresh sage; 250 g (8 oz) chicken livers, finely chopped; freshly ground black pepper; 8 slices French bread, halved, or 8 slices sandwich loaf, cut into triangles; extra butter for shallow-frying; 2 tsp lemon juice; 1 tbs chopped parsley.

Melt 3 tbs butter in a small saucepan and sauté shallot and sage leaves for about 5 minutes. Discard sage leaves. Add livers and pepper and cook gently, stirring, for about 6 minutes or until livers are lightly coloured but still slightly pink. Fry bread pieces in butter until crisp and golden on both sides; drain on paper towels. Stir lemon juice into liver mixture, check seasoning, spread over fried bread and sprinkle with parsley. Serve immediately. Serves 8.

LOBSTER

The Australian rock lobster (spiny lobster or crayfish), with its long antennae and rough, spiny carapace (shell), is one of the delights of the crustacean world. The meat, most of which is found in the tail, is sweet, firm-textured and very white when cooked. It can be used in any recipe needing lobster meat.

Allow ½ large or 1 small lobster per serving. They may be bought live or ready cooked. When buying cooked lobster, make certain the tail is tightly curled into the body and snaps back when straightened, and that the lobster is heavy for its size. The smell should be sweet and fresh. A 1–1.5 kg (2–3 lb) lobster is ideal; larger ones tend to be rather tough so are best avoided.

The European lobster or French *homard* from northern seas differs from the Australian rock lobster in that it has large pincer claws, containing much of the sweet juicy meat, and a smooth, shiny carapace.

■ **TO BOIL LOBSTER:** If a recipe calls for green (uncooked) lobster, it should be killed immediately before cooking. This can be done by leaving it head first in a bucket of cold fresh water for a least 1 hour, or in the following manner.

Take a heavy, sharp, short-bladed knife. Place lobster on a board, underside up. Hold the lobster with a towel and make a firm incision with the point of the knife where the tail joins the body. This will sever the spinal cord and kill the lobster immediately. Any movement of legs or tail after the lobster is killed is due to reflex muscle spasms.

Alternatively put the live lobster into the freezer and leave 30 minutes for each 500 g (1 lb) weight, to stun it.

To boil, place lobster in a large saucepan of fresh cold water and bring slowly to simmering point. Simmer for 10 minutes for the first 500 g (1 lb) weight and 7 minutes for each 500 g (1 lb) over. Remove from water and allow to cool.

You may use frozen green lobster tails instead, if you prefer.

TO CLEAN LOBSTER: Use a heavy sharp knife. Cut the lobster in half lengthways. Insert the point of the knife at the tail, cut towards the head and slit the underside. Remove the intestinal vein that runs the length of the lobster, and all the soft matter in the body and at the top of the head. Retain any orange or pink roe and the thick, dark brown liquid which is the mustard or tomalley. The roe can be gently poached; the mustard can be used in a sauce or butter for the lobster, or can be placed in a small bowl and cooked in a water bath, to be served separately as an accompaniment or used as a spread for canapés.

TO REMOVE MEAT FROM SHELL: Prise the meat from the tail and body with a sharp knife and cut into pieces. The meat may be extracted from the legs by breaking them at the joints and carefully pulling the meat out. Rinse carapace and dry well. It can then be used as a container in which to serve the meat. **See recipes.**

Grilled Lobster with Lemon Butter

1 green (uncooked) lobster or lobster tail; ¹/₂ cup butter, melted; juice ¹/₂ lemon.

Halve lobster or lobster tail and clean if necessary. Mix butter and lemon juice and brush over lobster meat. Place, cut sides down, on oiled grill rack and cook under preheated hot grill for 2 minutes. Turn cut sides up. Reduce heat to moderate and cook a further 8–12 minutes (depending on size), brushing frequently with lemon butter, until flesh is white and firm. Loosen flesh from carapace, and serve in the shell with extra melted butter and lemon wedges. Serves 2.

Lobster Mornay

1 cooked lobster, halved and flesh cut into bite-sized pieces; 1 cup Mornay Sauce (page 457); ¹/₂ cup grated cheese; fried breadcrumbs (optional).

Fold lobster meat through hot sauce and reheat gently. Pile into shells. Top with grated cheese and cook under a preheated medium grill for 1–2 minutes to melt cheese. If liked, sprinkle with fried breadcrumbs. Serves 2.

Lobster Mayonnaise

$^1/_2$ cup Mayonnaise (page 256); 2 tsp chopped mixed
fresh herbs (parsley, thyme, chives); $^1/_2$ tsp Dijon
mustard; 1 cooked lobster, halved and flesh cubed;
lettuce leaves.

GARNISH: hard-boiled egg slices; tomato wedges;
cucumber slices; sprig fresh dill or lemon balm.

Flavour mayonnaise with chopped herbs and
mustard. Spoon over lobster meat in shells. Serve
chilled on crisp lettuce leaves, garnished with egg
slices, tomato wedges, paper-thin cucumber slices
and a sprig of fresh dill or lemon balm. Serves 2.

Lobster Cocktail Salad

1 cup diced celery; 2 tbs Mayonnaise (page 256);
2 tbs tomato paste; 1 tbs chopped fresh tarragon,
or 1 tsp dried; 2 tbs finely chopped parsley;
2 tbs gin; 1 tbs brandy; salt and freshly ground
black pepper; 375 g (12oz) cooked lobster meat,
cut into large dice; lettuce leaves;
celery strips to garnish.

Blanch celery in boiling water for 1 minute, drain
and refresh. Combine celery, mayonnaise, tomato
paste, herbs, gin, brandy, salt and pepper. Fold in
lobster meat and chill, covered, for at least 2 hours or
overnight. Line 4–6 salad plates with lettuce, spoon
lobster mixture into a mound on top and garnish
with celery strips. Serves 4–6.

Lobster Tails Lucullus

2 small live lobsters; $^1/_2$ cup dry white wine.

SAUCE: mirepoix of $^1/_2$ small carrot,
$^1/_2$ small onion, $^1/_2$ small stick celery, all finely
chopped; 250 g (8 oz) butter; $^2/_3$ cup white wine;
bouquet of 1 sprig thyme, 1 sprig marjoram and
1 small piece bay leaf; $^2/_3$ cup cream;
salt; white pepper.

Prepare lobster by plunging head first into fresh water
or by severing spinal cords as described (see page 241),
then separate tails from bodies and cut tails lengthways in half. Set tails aside while making the sauce.

Clean lobster bodies (retaining mustard and any roe
for another use). Smash bodies and sauté with the
mirepoix in 60 g (2 oz) butter. Add wine, boil over
high heat until reduced by half, add herb bouquet
and cream and boil until liquid is syrupy. Strain and
return liquid to rinsed-out saucepan. Cut remaining
butter into about 8 pieces. Bring liquid to simmering
point, remove from heat and beat in 2 pieces of butter
with a wire whisk. Return to low heat and beat in
remaining butter, piece by piece; sauce will thicken
to consistency of pouring cream. Season and turn
off heat.

Arrange halved tails, meat side upward, in one layer
in a baking dish, pour $^1/_2$ cup wine around them
and cover the dish. Place in a hot oven (200°C/400°F)
and steam for 8–10 minutes or until meat turns
white. Holding each half tail in a cloth, prise meat
from shells.

Reheat sauce on low heat whisking constantly; do
not allow to boil. Spoon some sauce on to 4 heated
plates, place tail meat on top and spoon a little more
sauce over. Serve with steamed rice and snow peas.
Serves 4.

Lobster with Basil Sauce and Mangoes

Court Bouillon (page 98); 2 green lobster tails;
2 large, ripe mangos.

SAUCE: 2 tbs good wine vinegar; 6 tbs olive oil;
1 small clove garlic, peeled; 30 fresh basil leaves;
salt and freshly ground black pepper.

Bring the court bouillon to the boil in a large
saucepan. Add lobster tails and simmer for 6–8 minutes or until shells turn red. Remove lobster tails
from pan and when cool enough to handle, remove
shells and cut flesh into slices, 1 cm ($^1/_2$ in) thick.
Meanwhile, make the sauce. Place vinegar, oil, garlic
and basil leaves in a blender or food processor and
process until smooth. Season to taste.

With a sharp knife, make a slit lengthways around
the mangoes and peel off the skin. Cut the flesh into
very thin slices.

Assemble the ingredients on 4 large, individual
plates. First make a circle of mango slices on each
plate, leaving a space in the centre. Heap lobster in
the space and spoon the sauce in a ribbon around the
outside of the mango slices. Serves 4.

LOGANBERRY

A cross between the blackberry and the raspberry,
and its flavour is a blend of these fruits. Ripe loganberries
are dark, purplish-red. Fresh loganberries are only
occasionally seen in the shops, but they are available
commercially frozen and canned. They are excellent for
dessert, and loganberries can be substituted for other
berries in many recipes – for example, for mulberries in
Mulberry Jell and Mulberry Pie (See *Mulberry*), or for
raspberries in Raspberry Jam and Summer Pudding
(see *Raspberry*).

LOQUAT (JAPANESE MEDLAR)

The fruit of an Oriental tree related to the rose. Loquats
are glossy, orange-coloured fruit about the size of a small
plum, with juicy tart-sweet flesh. They are eaten raw or
made into jams and jellies.

LYCHEE (LITCHI, LICHEE)

A small fruit native to South China, with translucent white flesh; the flavour and texture are distinctive but somewhat reminiscent of a luscious grape. Canned lychees are more familiar than fresh ones, but the latter in their knobbly, plum-brown shells appear sometimes in good greengrocers' shops, and are ambrosial eating.

Lychees make a refreshing dessert at the end of a Chinese meal. They are excellent in a fruit salad, and are also used in Chinese pork or duck dishes, rather as apples and oranges are used in European cooking.

Almond Jelly with Lychees

2^1/$_2$ cups water; 3 tsp agar agar powder (see Note); ^{1}/$_2$ cup sugar; I cup evaporated milk; ^{1}/$_2$ tsp almond essence; I x 565 g can lychees in syrup, chilled; 6 maraschino cherries, to decorate.

Place water in a saucepan and sprinkle agar agar powder over the top. Bring to the boil, then simmer for 5 minutes. Add sugar and milk and heat gently, stirring all the time, until sugar dissolves. Add almond essence drop by drop, to suit your taste. Pour into a cake tin or mould, and chill for 1 hour or until set. To serve, cut jelly into squares or diamond shapes. Drain lychees and reserve 1 cup syrup. Arrange jelly pieces and lychees in 6 individual bowls, pour a little syrup over and decorate each serving with a cherry. Serves 6.

NOTE: Agar agar powder is a setting agent, like gelatine and is obtainable from Asian food stores. If not available use 3 tsp (1 envelope) gelatine.

m

m

MACADAMIA NUT

This nut is native to Australia – its old-time name was the 'Queensland bush nut' – but it is also grown in Hawaii and southern USA. Macadamias are expensive but healthy and delicious – crisp, sweet and butter-flavoured. They are about the size of a hazelnut with a round, shiny shell which is so hard that it resists most efforts to crack it at home. Macadamias are sold shelled and usually roasted and salted, in cans or packages. They are excellent served with drinks or as a dessert nut; they can be sliced or chopped for nut breads, cakes, biscuits, ice cream and other desserts, or used in the same way as almonds in butter sauce to serve with fish.

Macadamia oil is good in cooking and salads. **See recipes.**

Barramundi with Macadamias

Snapper steaks, whiting fillets or other fine white fish can be substituted for barramundi.

2 tbs lemon juice; 4 barramundi or other white fish steaks or fillets; 4 tbs ghee or butter; 2 tbs finely chopped spring onions; 3 tbs chopped macadamia nuts; freshly ground black pepper.

GARNISH: lemon wedges; parsley.

Brush lemon juice over fish and leave 10 minutes. Brush fish with 2 tbs ghee and grill. Meantime, heat remaining ghee in a small pan and gently fry spring onions and nuts until golden. Pour over fish, season with pepper and serve garnished with lemon wedges and parsley. Serves 4.

Macadamia Ice Cream

1²/₃ cups milk; 2 eggs, separated; 1¹/₂ cups sugar; 1 tsp vanilla; 1 cup cream; 185 g (6 oz) salted macadamia nuts, finely chopped; 3 tbs rum or brandy.

Heat milk in top of double saucepan over simmering water. Beat egg yolks with sugar, stir in a little of the hot milk. Cook, stirring constantly, until slightly thickened. Cool and add vanilla, unbeaten egg whites and cream, stirring until well combined. Pour into container of sorbetière or metal ice cream trays and freeze until just setting, then stir in about half the nuts and the rum or brandy. Freeze until firm and allow to ripen (mellow) for 24 hours. Transfer from freezer to refrigerator about 30 minutes before serving so that ice cream softens slightly. Serve sprinkled with remaining nuts. Serves 6.

MACARONI

See *Pasta*.

MACAROONS

See *Almond*: Almond Macaroons.

MACE

The lacy outer covering of the nutmeg. It is made up of frond-like tendrils; one tendril, left whole, is called a blade of mace. Mace is also sold ground. Its flavour is similar to that of nutmeg. Mace is the indispensable seasoning for English potted meats and shrimps (prawns). It is part of the classic combination or aromatics which flavours the milk for Béchamel Sauce (see page 456), and enhances the flavour of fish sauces, pies or creamed dishes, and of mashed or scalloped potatoes. A blade of mace is particularly useful for flavouring dishes such as a clear soups, jellies and pale sauces where grated nutmeg would spoil the appearance.

Potted Tongue

250 g (8 oz) cooked salted ox tongue; 155 g (5 oz) ghee or butter; ¹/₄ tsp ground mace; freshly ground black or white pepper; extra ghee for sealing.

Remove any skin and bones from tongue and cut meat into pieces. Place in a food processor fitted with the steel blade, add the 155 g (5 oz) ghee and process until smooth. Beat in mace and a little pepper, then pack into a pot or pots and smooth top. Chill until firm. Melt extra ghee and pour over surface to cover and seal. Cover pots with foil and store in refrigerator. Serve chilled with hot toast as a first course, or with crusty brad and crisp raw vegetables for a summer lunch. Makes about 2 cups.

MACKEREL

Superb smoked mackerel from Scandinavia are known round the world as a delicacy to rival smoked trout. They can be skinned and eaten with lemon, pepper and brown bread and butter, or made into one of the best of pâtés. Mackerel are also canned, and Spanish mackerel are available fresh, usually as cutlets (steaks); they can be cooked in the same ways as other fat fish (see *Fish*), and are often served with a sharp sauce such as mustard, horseradish or gooseberry (which is made from fresh or frozen gooseberries, in the same way as Apple Sauce (Chunky), see page 61.

Smoked Mackerel Pâté

1 smoked mackerel, weighing about 500 g (1 lb); 185 g (6 oz) butter; 1¹/₂ tbs lemon juice; freshly ground black pepper; pinch paprika; 2 tbs cream.

Remove skin and bones from mackerel and flake flesh. Cream butter, add mackerel flesh (which is soft) and beat well. Add lemon juice and season with pepper and paprika. Beat in cream until just combined. Pack into a pot or pots and chill. Serve with hot toast or Melba toast as a first course or with drinks. Makes about 2 cups.

MADEIRA CAKE

This traditional British cake has the refreshing tang of lemon and orange and is usually baked with a slice of candied citron peel on top. If citron peel is difficult to buy, used chopped mixed candied peel or sliced glacé orange. Serve with a glass of Madeira as did the people of Victorian England.

Madeira Cake

250 g (8 oz) butter; I cup caster sugar;
finely grated rind I lemon and I orange;
$^{1}/_{2}$ tsp cinnamon; 5 eggs; $I^{1}/_{2}$ cups plain flour;
$^{1}/_{2}$ cup self-raising flour; $^{1}/_{2}$ tsp salt; I tbs milk;
I tbs diced mixed candied peel,
or I slice glacé orange.

Cream butter with sugar, rinds and cinnamon. When pale and creamy, add eggs one at a time, beating well after each addition. Sift flours with salt. Fold half the flour into creamed mixture and when thoroughly incorporated, mix in milk. Fold in remaining flour. Turn into a greased and lined deep 20 cm (8 in) round cake tin. Bake in a preheated moderately slow oven (160°C/325°F) for 45 minutes. Sprinkle top of cake with peel, or press on the glacé orange slice. Bake for a further 40–45 minutes or until cake has shrunk away from sides of tin and a fine skewer inserted in centre comes out clean. Remove cake from tin and cool on a wire rack.

MADELEINES

These very light little French tea cakes are usually baked in shallow, scallop-shaped moulds which give them their distinctive shell-like appearance. They are served dusted with icing sugar. English Madeleines are a slightly more elaborate version baked in dariole moulds, glazed, coated with coconut and topped with a cherry.

Madeleines

2 eggs, lightly beaten; I cup sugar; I cup flour, sifted; 185 g (6 oz) butter, melted and cooled;
I tbs rum; I tsp vanilla; sifted icing sugar.

Place eggs and sugar in the top of a double saucepan and heat, stirring constantly, until just lukewarm. Remove from heat and beat for about 10 minutes or until thick but light and creamy, incorporating as much air as possible. Gradually fold in sifted flour, then add butter, rum and vanilla. Spoon carefully into greased Madeleine moulds. Bake in a preheated moderately hot oven (190°C/375°F) for 10–15 minutes or until

very pale golden. Remove from moulds, cool on a wire rack and dust with icing sugar. Makes about 15.
NOTE: Dariole moulds or muffin tins can be used if madeleine tins are not available.
VARIATION
ENGLISH MADELEINES: Make Madeleines according to recipe above but bake in dariole moulds. After baking and when cold, level tops with a sharp knife to give a flat base when inverted. Turn out upside-down and brush with warm Apricot or Redcurrant Glaze (see page 9). Roll immediately in desiccated coconut and top each with $^{1}/_{2}$ glacé cherry.

MADRILENE

See *Spiced Tomato Consommé* (pages 484–5).

MAITRE D'HOTEL BUTTER

See *Butter*.

MALT

This is produced from grain – usually barley – which has been soaked, sprouted, dried and ground, a process resulting in the conversion of the grain starch into a sugar called maltose. Malt extract comes in dried and syrup form, and is a nutritious addition to drinks, bread, cakes and puddings. It also imparts a distinctive flavour and, in baked goods, a rather moist texture. Malted milk powder, prepared with dried milk and malt extracts, can be stirred into hot or cold milk for a nourishing drink or whipped with milk, ice cream and flavouring for a soda-fountain style 'malted'.

Malt Bread

4 cups plain wholemeal flour; 2 cups plain flour;
pinch salt; 30 g (I oz) compressed yeast; $I^{3}/_{4}$ cups
lukewarm water; 2 tbs black treacle; 2 tbs syrup-type
malt extract; 60 g (2 oz) sultanas (optional);
60 g (2 oz) butter, melted.

SYRUP: 2 tbs milk; 2 tbs sugar.

Put flours and salt into large warmed mixing bowl. Cream yeast with a little of the water. Make a well in flour mixture and pour in yeast mixture, treacle and malt extract. Add sultanas, if using, and beat vigorously with your hand, mixing in butter and remaining water little by little, to form a soft dough. Turn on to a floured board and knead 5–10 minutes until dough is even-textured and well blended. Place in a greased bowl and turn greased side of dough up. Cover with greased plastic wrap and a damp cloth and leave in a warm place to rise until dough has doubled in bulk, about 2 hours. Knock down dough, divide in half and put each half into a greased 500 g (1 lb) loaf tin, pressing down well. Cover and allow to rise again for about 45 minutes, or until dough has doubled in bulk. Bake in a preheated moderate oven (180°C/350°F) for about 40 minutes, turning tins round after first 25 minutes of cooking time.

For syrup, heat milk and sugar, stirring until sugar has dissolved. Brush tops of loaves with syrup and bake a further 5 minutes. When cooking, loaves will sound hollow when undersides are knocked with knuckles. Remove from tins and cool on wire rack. Makes 2 loaves.

NOTE: If preferred, bread can be shaped into 24 buns and baked on a greased baking tray for 15–20 minutes. Dry yeast may be used. See *Yeast Cookery.*

MANDARIN AND TANGERINE

A small, very sweet type of orange, with a skin that is easily removed and flesh that separates easily into segments. A variety of North African mandarin, grown in Tangiers, is responsible for the name Tangerine. Canned segments are known as mandarins.

Mandarins may be enjoyed as a fruit but may also be used in the making of fruit salad. The small, brightly coloured segments are useful for decorating sweets and gâteaux. Of the same family is the tangelo.

TO REMOVE THE WHITE PITH: Dip segments quickly into boiling water and scrape with a knife.

Glazed Mandarins

A delectable confection to enjoy with chocolate or petits fours with after-dinner coffee.

3 mandarins, peeled and broken into segments; I cup sugar; $^{1}/_{4}$ cup water; $^{1}/_{2}$ tsp cream of tartar.

Remove white pith and large pips from mandarin segments, taking care not to cut or tear the skin too much. Lightly grease a marble slab or baking sheet. Put sugar, water and cream of tartar in a small heavy saucepan and stir over low heat until sugar dissolves. Bring to the boil without stirring. Brush sides of pan with a brush dipped in boiling water to remove any sugar crystals. Boil to hard crack stage (155°C/310°F), or test by dropping a little syrup into cold water: it should immediately become crisp and brittle. Tilt pan and allow bubbles to subside. Secure mandarin segments, one at a time, on end of fine skewer and swirl quickly around in syrup until coated. Put on oiled slab and leave to set, about 5 minutes. Serve in small confectionery paper or waxed paper cases. Serve within 1 hour of making. Makes about 24.

MANGE-TOUT

See *Snowpeas.*

MANGO

This exotic fruit, with its heady perfume, is now cultivated in many tropical countries. As mangoes do not travel well

they are often picked green. Allow the fruit to ripen to a rosy orange-yellow to enjoy its unrivalled flavour, likened to a blend of ripe melon, mixed with peach and a tang of apricots. The choicest fruit should have a firm flesh and smooth texture free of any fibres.

Mango slices are put into curries, made into pickles with salt, oil and chillies, made into chutneys and desserts, or they can be dried to make amchur powder, an important ingredient in some curries.

Like many good fruits, the presentation of a mango contributes greatly to one's pleasure in eating it. It should be neatly skinned, sliced off the stone, laid in small smooth portions, the right size to be picked up and popped in the mouth with a fruit fork. It is best served a little chilled. Alternatively, each side is cut off the stone, turned flesh side up and scored into diamonds or cubes without cutting through the skin. A little pressure on the underside of the skin and the flesh opens like an exotic flower ready for eating.

Mangoes are also available canned in slices or as a pulp, also as a nectar or as chutney. **See recipes.**

Mango Ice Cream: To a litre of softened vanilla ice cream add 2 cups ripe mango pulp. Mix well and freeze again.

Mango Mousse

I tbs gelatine; $^{1}/_{2}$ cup water; 2 cups mango pulp, fresh or canned; $^{1}/_{2}$ cup orange juice; 2 tbs rum; 2 egg whites; 2 tbs sugar; $^{1}/_{2}$ cup cream.

DECORATION: $^{1}/_{2}$ **cup cream, whipped; I orange or mandarin, peeled and cut into segments.**

Sprinkle gelatine over water and leave for 5 minutes to soften, then stir over simmering water to dissolve. Combine mango pulp, orange juice and rum in a bowl. Stir in dissolved gelatine and chill until mixture is on the point of setting. Beat egg whites until stiff peaks form, then add sugar gradually, beating until thick and glossy. Whip chilled cream until soft peaks form. Fold cream into mango mixture, then fold in egg whites. Turn into a serving bowl and chill. Decorate with whipped cream and orange or mandarin segments. Serves 6–8.

Mango Rum Sundae

1 large ripe mango, peeled, stoned and thinly sliced; ¹/₄ cup caster sugar; ¹/₃ cup rum; vanilla ice cream.

Put mango slices in a shallow dish and sprinkle with sugar and rum. Chill, covered, for 1 hour. Put ice cream into 4 serving dishes and top with mango slices and juice. Serves 4.

Mango and Mint Sauce

Tropical fruits go so well with choice seafood. This beautiful sauce is excellent with Atlantic salmon or trout, any fish, even prawn or lobster salad.

1 mango or 1 cup drained canned mango slices; ¹/₃ cup olive oil; 2 tbs balsamic or wine vinegar; 8 mint leaves, shredded.

Cut cheeks off the fresh mango, scrape off all the flesh from the skin and around the stone, and place in a blender or food processor and pureé until smooth. While the motor is still running, add the oil gradually, then the vinegar and mint leaves. The mixture should thicken like a mayonnaise. Transfer to a bowl and keep at room temperature until ready to serve. Makes 1 cup.

Mango Sorbet

A cool fruit sorbet may be served as a dessert or to refresh the palate in between rich courses.

2 tsp gelatine; 2 tbs water; 2 cups mango pulp, fresh or canned; juice ¹/₂ medium lemon; 1 tbs rum; 1 egg white.

Soften gelatine in water, then stir over simmering water until dissolved. Stir into mango pulp with lemon juice and rum. Turn the freezer to maximum temperature. Place mango mixture in an ice cream tray, cover with foil and freeze until mushy. Remove sorbet to a bowl and beat with a rotary beater until smooth but not melted. Fold in stiffly beaten egg white. Return to ice cream tray, turn freezer temperature to normal and freeze sorbet until firm. Leave to ripen (mellow) for 2–6 hours. Allow sorbet to stand at room temperature for a few minutes before serving. Serves 6.

Spiced Mango Chicken

Chicken breasts are baked until golden and tender in yogurt flavoured with spices and topped with mango slices. It takes little cooking and the preparation can be done in advance, making this a marvellous party dish.

8 half-breasts of chicken; 125 g (4 oz) ghee or butter; 2 small onions, finely chopped; 8 cardamom pods; 2 cinnamon sticks; 1 cup water; 16 slices fresh or canned mango.

MARINADE: 1¹/₂ cups plain yogurt; 2 tbs ground coriander; 2 tsp finely chopped fresh ginger; 2 tsp salt; 2 tsp turmeric; ¹/₂ tsp black pepper.

Remove all the tiny rib bones from the chicken breasts, leaving the main breastbone. Combine all ingredients for marinade in a large bowl, add chicken pieces and stir to coat well. Marinate in refrigerator for at least 2 hours or overnight. Melt 60 g (2 oz) ghee or butter in a large frying pan. Sauté onions, cardamom pods and cinnamon sticks for 5 minutes or until onions are soft and golden. Add water and stir well. Remove as much marinade as possible from chicken breasts and reserve. Place chicken in a baking dish and spoon a little of the onion mixture on top of each breast. Top each breast with 2 slices of mango. Dot with remaining ghee or butter and bake in a preheated hot oven (220°C/400°F) for 10 minutes. Spoon reserved marinade over chicken. Continue cooking until chicken is tender, about 10 minutes longer. Place chicken on a heated serving dish and keep warm. Remove cardamom pods and cinnamon sticks from sauce, bring to the boil and spoon over chicken to serve.

Serve Spiced Mango Chicken with plain boiled or saffron rice or a pilaf and interesting sambals (see *Curry*). Tiny cherry tomatoes, pappadams and cucumber slices in natural yogurt would be nice – and fruit chutney. Serves 8.

MANGOSTEEN

A tropical fruit with a shiny purple skin and a delicate creamy white flesh with a sweet-sour taste. It is served skinned and segmented and is delicious either at room temperature or well iced.

MAPLE SYRUP

As its name implies, maple syrup is a product of the sap extracted from various species of the maple tree. Maple syrup has a distinctive but delicate flavour and is used over pancakes, popovers, ice cream and other desserts. It may flavour custard, creams, moulds, ice creams or fillings and frostings for cakes or biscuits.

There are different grades of maple syrup, the best being light in colour. Once opened, maple syrup should be stored in the refrigerator. See recipes.

Maple Jelly

1¹/₂ tsp gelatine; ¹/₃ cup water; 1 cup maple syrup, heated; 1 cup cream, whipped.

Soften gelatine in cold water for 5 minutes, then add to hot maple syrup and stir until completely dissolved. Chill until slightly set, to the consistency of unbeaten egg whites. Fold in cream and turn into a serving dish. Chill for 2 hours. Serves 4–6.

Frozen Maple Cream

3 egg yolks; ³/₄ cup maple syrup; 1 cup cream;
2 egg whites.

Beat egg yolks in top of a double saucepan until light
and lemon-coloured. Add syrup and ¼ cup cream
and cook, stirring constantly, over hot water until
thick. Cool. Beat egg whites until stiff but not dry.
Fold into custard mixture. Pour into ice cream tray
and freeze until mushy. Remove to a bowl and beat
with a rotary beater until smooth but not completely
thawed. Whip remaining cream until stiff and fold
into partially frozen mixture. Return ice cream to tray
and freeze until firm. Serves 4–6.

Baked Apples with Maple Syrup

4 cooking apples; maple syrup.

Prepare apples by peeling top halves and coring. Place
apples in shallow baking dish and fill centres with
maple syrup. Add water to cover bottom of dish.
Bake in preheated moderate oven (180°C/350°F) for
30–40 minutes or until apples are tender. Spoon pan
juices over apples several times during cooking.
Serves 4.

Maple Parfait

6 egg yolks; ²/₃ cup maple syrup; ¹/₈ tsp salt;
2 cups cream, whipped.

Beat egg yolks and syrup together in top of a double
saucepan. Add salt and cook over simmering water
until slightly thickened, stirring constantly. Cool.
Fold in whipped cream. Pour into ice cream tray and
freeze until firm. Serves 6.

Maple Freeze

¹/₂ cup maple syrup; 2 egg whites; 1 cup undiluted
evaporated milk, well chilled.

Boil syrup to soft-ball stage (112°C/238°F). Beat
egg whites until stiff but not dry. Add syrup slowly,
beating constantly, and continue beating until
mixture is cool. Whip milk until thick and fold egg
white and syrup mixture into it. Pour into ice cream
tray and freeze until firm. Serves 8.

NOTE: If you do not have a sugar thermometer, test
syrup by dropping a small quantity into iced water. It
should form a ball which will hold its shape.

MARASCHINO

A liqueur made from a small, sour, black cherry known as
marasca, grown in Dalmatia. The cherry kernels are
distilled together with the leaves, giving a bitter tang to
an otherwise sweet drink.

Maraschino is used to flavour sweets, punches and
cocktails etc. Maraschino cherries are a sweet cherry

bleached, then preserved in maraschino syrup. They are
used as decoration on some pastries and drinks, confectionery, biscuits, cookies, cakes and in sauces.

Maraschino cherries are available red in syrup, with or
without stems. Or they may be candied or glacéed in red,
green or yellow variations, generally used for holiday
cooking at Christmas or Easter.

MARBLE CAKE

This is one of the prettiest of all cakes. The mixture is
divided into three different colours, pink, white and
chocolate, and marbled using a knife to make intriguing
colour patterns which are seen when the cake is sliced.
Children are especially fond of Marble Cake and it is
most popular for birthday parties.

Marble Cake

125 g (4 oz) butter; 1 cup caster sugar;
1 tsp vanilla; 2 eggs, beaten; 2 cups self-raising
flour; ¹/₂ tsp salt; ³/₄ cup milk;
2 tbs cocoa powder; 2 tbs boiling water;
red food colouring.

Cream butter with sugar and vanilla until light and
fluffy. Gradually beat in eggs. Sift flour with salt
and fold into creamed mixture alternating with
milk. Divide mixture into 3 portions. Sift cocoa and
dissolve in boiling water. Stir into one portion of
cake mixture. To another portion add red food
colouring to tint it pink. Leave third portion white.
Drop mixtures by tablespoons into a well-greased
deep 20 cm (8 in) round cake tin, alternating pink,
white and chocolate. Run a knife through to marble
mixture. Bake in a preheated moderate oven
(180°C/350°F) for 50–60 minutes. Turn out on a wire
rack and, when cool, ice and decorate marble cake
as desired.

MARENGO

The battle of Marengo in 1800 was a victory for
Napoleon's army. It marked another victory – for the
little General's chef created a dish, fit for the conquering
hero, from food found in the surrounding fields and
looted gardens. He took a chicken, a head of garlic, a
few tomatoes, some bay, parsley and thyme and a few
field mushrooms. These were sautéed in the oil and
finished with the wine that travelled with the French
army. A few fresh water crayfish were added, a fried egg
and some crisp fried bread. Today, these last three
ingredients may be omitted.

Napoleon enjoyed the dish, claiming, it is said: 'It has
been a glorious day, my children. I am well pleased with
you.' With the battle, the dish created on that day has
entered history.

Chicken Marengo

2 kg (4 lb) chicken pieces; salt and freshly ground black pepper; flour; 1 tbs oil; 1 tbs butter; 2 cloves garlic, crushed; 1 bouquet garni (parsley, thyme, bay leaf); 1 cup white wine; ¹/4 cup brandy; 2 large tomatoes, peeled and quartered; 12 mushrooms; chopped parsley.

Sprinkle chicken pieces with salt and pepper and coat lightly with flour. Heat oil and butter in a frying pan and brown chicken over high heat until golden on all sides, turning frequently. Transfer to a flameproof casserole and add garlic, bouquet garni, white wine, brandy and tomatoes. Cover casserole tightly and cook gently for 30 minutes, turning chicken pieces several times with wooden spoon. Add mushrooms and cook for 10 minutes longer or until chicken is tender. Adjust seasoning and discard bouquet garni. Serve in casserole, sprinkled with chopped parsley. The dish may be garnished with heart-shaped croûtes of bread fried in butter, a fried egg for each serving, and cooked crayfish. Serves 6.

MARGARINE

This is available as Polyunsaturated Table Margarine, Table Margarine, or Cooking Margarine. It is a smooth-textured product, made from vegetable oils only or a combination of both animal fats and vegetable oils, used in varying amounts. The ratio of saturated to unsaturated fats in table margarine is strictly controlled by law and the type of margarine must be specified clearly on the label with other components such as milk products, vitamins, flavouring agents, salt and emulsifiers.

Margarine and butter are both fats and each has the same number of kilojoules or kilocalories (1 tbs has 578 kilojoules/138 kilocalories), providing the same units of energy as each other. The exception is 'whipped' margarine, which may contain slightly fewer kilojoules (kilocalories) since the volume is increased by the air incorporated during the whipping process.

Polyunsaturated Table Margarine: High in polyunsaturated fats in proportion to saturated fats, and made from vegetable oils. It is often recommended for people on low cholesterol diets because the high level of polyun-saturated fats makes it suitable for people who need to restrict their intake of saturated fats. In this case, the margarine to choose is the one with the highest percentage of polyunsaturated fats.

Table Margarine: This has a higher saturated fat content than polyunsaturated table margarine. It is made from vegetable oils and has a smooth easy-spreading con-sistency, although not quite as soft as polyunsaturated table margarine.

Cooking Margarine: Best for cooking only. It contains saturated animal fats and vegetable oils and is usually sold in solid blocks.

MARGARINE IN COOKING

Margarine can be used instead of butter quite success-fully in most baking. When using, substitute the same quantity of margarine for butter as specified in a recipe. It is particularly good for recipes using the quick-mix method (see *Cakes*) because margarine mixes very easily and quickly with other ingredients. Use also in sauces, steamed puddings, shortcrust pastry (see *Pastry*) or cake-type desserts. Table margarine is usually quite successful for shallow-frying as well.

Cooked vegetables may be tossed in margarine for flavour. Polyunsaturated table margarine may be used for some cooking – in making sauces or coating foods to be grilled, etc.

MARINADE

A seasoned liquid used to 'marinate' food before or after cooking in order that it will absorb flavour and/or become more tender. The term 'to marinate' is used for meats, game, poultry, fish and vegetables; for fruits, the term 'macerate' is used when steeping in sugar, liqueurs or spirits.

The first marinades were simple brines, used for preserving fish – the word stems from the same root as the word 'maritime'. In modern usage a marinade consists of oil, an acid (lemon juice, wine or vinegar) and spices or aromatics. As the food stands in the marinade, the oil and aromatics impart flavour and the acid tenderises.

A marinade may be cooked or uncooked, and is used with a large cut of meat for dishes like sauerbraten, or cubes of meat or poultry or tender steaks for grilling or pan-frying.

As a marinade usually contains an acid, it and the foods it serves should be kept in a dish made of glass or glazed china. Never use aluminium or porous containers such as some pottery. Use a wooden spoon for stirring or turning the food. Marinate food in containers just large enough to hold the food and cover them with the marinade. Keep marinating foods well covered and under refrigeration if they are to steep for more than 1 hour.

Higher temperatures hasten marinating but care has to be taken in very hot climates as high temperatures also hasten bacterial action. A marinade is powerful – do not marinate foods too long or use too many herbs and spices or you may destroy the food's own flavour. Frequent basting or turning the food in the marinade assures equal distribution and penetration of flavours and the tenderising process. As a general rule, a whole piece of meat may be marinated for 2–3 days for a 'gamey' taste, but otherwise marinate overnight. Cubes of food or small steaks or cutlets need only be steeped 2–3 hours.

COOKING WITH MARINADES

After food has been marinated, drain it and dry with paper towels. Keep marinade as it may be used in the cooking. Stews and pot roasts are often cooked with some of the marinade – it is a good idea to dilute it with stock or water before adding it to the meat.

Part of a marinade may also be used to baste marinated meat during roasting or grilling, or a spoonful may be added to a gravy or sauce. **See recipes.**

Cooked Marinade

For meats and game to be roasted, pot roasted, grilled, etc.

$^1/_4$ cup oil; $^1/_2$ cup chopped onions; $^1/_2$ cup chopped celery; $^1/_2$ cup chopped carrot; $^1/_2$ cup chopped parsley; 4 cloves garlic, crushed; 2 cups cider vinegar; 2 cups dry red or white wine; 2 cups water; 2 bay leaves; 1 sprig thyme; tiny sprig rosemary; 1 tsp peppercorns; 5 whole cloves; 5 whole juniper berries, crushed.

Heat oil in deep saucepan. Cook onions, celery, carrot, parsley and garlic in oil over medium heat for 5 minutes or until onions are soft but still white. Do not brown. Add remaining ingredients. Simmer, covered, over low heat for 45–60 minutes, stirring occasionally. Strain and cool before using. Makes 4–4$^1/_2$ cups marinade, or enough for about 3 kg (6 lb) meat.
NOTE: The marinade may be strained after use, brought to the boil, cooled and used again, if wished.

Uncooked Marinade

For shellfish, prawns, lobster, to be pan-fried, grilled, etc.

$^3/_4$ cup brandy, dry sherry or dry white wine; $^1/_2$ tsp salt; $^1/_2$ tsp black pepper; $^1/_2$ tsp crushed dried rosemary, basil or thyme, or 1$^1/_2$ tsp fresh.

Combine all ingredients and put in deep bowl. Marinate seafood in mixture for 1–3 hours. Makes about $^1/_2$ cup, or enough for 30 prawns or 1 x 500 g (1 lb) lobster.

Uncooked Marinade

For all meats.

1 cup water; 1 cup wine; 6 peppercorns; 1 bay leaf; 8 whole cloves; 1 medium onion, finely sliced; 1 tsp crushed dried rosemary, thyme or marjoram, or 1 tbs fresh.

Combine all ingredients. Makes 2 cups, or enough for 2.5 kg (5 lb) meat.
NOTE: Dry white wine will give a more delicate flavour, but for red meats and game or venison, dry red wine is preferable.

Beer Marinade

For beef, game or prawns.

1$^1/_2$ cups beer; $^1/_2$ cup salad oil; 1 small onion, finely sliced; 1 clove garlic, crushed; 2 tbs lemon juice; 1 tsp salt; $^1/_2$ tsp black pepper; 1 tsp dry mustard.

Combine all ingredients and blend thoroughly. Makes about 2 cups, or enough for 1–1.5 kg (2–3 lb) meat or prawns.

Larded Braised Beef

1 x 2 kg (4 lb) top round of beef; Uncooked Marinade for meats (see recipe); 250 g (8 oz) picked (salt) pork, cut into long thin strips; 2 tbs oil; 1 tbs tomato paste; 3 tbs brandy; 1 cup stock; salt and freshly ground black pepper; 2 tbs Beurre Manié (page 35, optional).

Place meat in a large bowl, add marinade and let stand in refrigerator 24 hours, turning occasionally. Remove meat and dry thoroughly with paper towels. Strain marinade and reserve 1 cup.

To lard beef, thread a larding needle by placing a strip of pork in the open end. Insert pointed end of needle into beef at right angles to grain. Push, then pull needle through beef. Trim off the pork flush with the beef. If you do not have a larding needle, holes may be made in meat and strips of pork pushed in, using a finger or handle of wooden spoon.

Heat oil with tomato paste in a Dutch oven or heavy flameproof casserole. Stir in brandy, stock, reserved marinade, salt and pepper and bring to the boil. Add meat. Cover, reduce heat and simmer for 2–2$^1/_2$ hours. Carve enough beef for one meal in thin slices (saving the remainder for another meal) and place on a heated serving platter. Thicken gravy, if liked, with beurre manié and spoon a little over meat. Serve remainder separately. Serves 6–8.

Lamb Kebabs

1.5 kg (3 lb) lamb leg chops, cut thick; 1 clove garlic, crushed; $^1/_3$ cup oil; 1 tbs lemon juice; 2 tsp chopped fresh marjoram, or 1 tsp dried; 1 tbs finely chopped onion; salt and freshly ground black pepper; 250 g (8 oz) small, even-sized mushrooms; 3 firm tomatoes, quartered; 1 medium green pepper, cored, seeded and cut into squares; cooked rice to serve.

Trim excess fat from meat and cut into 4 cm (1$^1/_2$ in) cubes. Put into a bowl. Combine garlic, oil, lemon juice, marjoram, onion, salt and pepper and pour over lamb cubes. Let marinate in refrigerator for 4 hours, stirring occasionally. Cut mushroom stalks level with caps. Thread mushrooms on to skewers, alternating with tomato quarters and pepper squares. Drain lamb cubes, reserving marinade, and thread on to separate skewers. Put lamb skewers under a preheated grill and grill for 7 minutes.

Brush vegetable skewers with some of the marinade and put under grill. Cook, brushing lamb and vegetable skewers with marinade and turning frequently, for 10–12 minutes or until meat is done to your liking. Spoon hot rice on to a heated serving platter and arrange skewers on top. Serves 4.

Lemon–Ginger Chops

4 tbs oil; I tsp grated lemon rind; I tbs lemon juice; I tbs brown sugar; I tsp grated fresh ginger; salt and freshly ground black pepper; 4 large lamb chump chops.

Mix together oil, lemon rind and juice, brown sugar, ginger, salt and pepper. Put chops in a shallow dish, in a single layer and pour marinade over. Cover and marinate in refrigerator for at least 8 hours. Drain chops, reserving marinade. Grill under preheated grill for 10–15 minutes or until tender, turning occasionally and basting with marinade. Serves 4.

Marinated Steak

I x 750 g (I¹/₂ lb) slice middle cut rump steak, cut 4 cm (I¹/₂ in) thick; ³/₄ cup dry red wine; ¹/₄ cup oil; I onion, sliced; I bay leaf, crumbled; 4 stalks parsley; ¹/₂ tsp dried tarragon or thyme; salt and freshly ground black pepper.

Trim any fat from steak. Place in a rectangular glass or ceramic dish. Mix remaining ingredients, except salt, and pour over steak. Cover and leave to marinate in refrigerator for several hours, turning steak occasionally. Lift out steak and place on grill rack. Cook under a preheated high grill for 3 minutes each side until sealed, then reduce heat to medium and cook until done to taste. Total cooking time: rare – 15 minutes; medium – 20–25 minutes; well-done – 30–35 minutes. Baste with marinade during cooking and turn steak with tongs so that juices will not escape. To serve, sprinkle with salt and carve in thin slices. Serves 4–6.

Beef Stew with Wine and Herbs

I kg (2 lb) stewing beef, cubed; I cup red wine; I bay leaf; I clove garlic, sliced; I tsp salt; ¹/₂ tsp black pepper; few sprigs parsley; 4 sprigs fresh thyme; 2 tbs bacon dripping or other fat; I¹/₂ cups stock; I stick celery with leaves, diced; I onion, sliced; 4 cloves; I piece fresh ginger; cornflour.

Place meat in a large bowl and add wine, bay leaf, garlic, salt, pepper, all but 2 sprigs parsley, and 2 sprigs of thyme. Marinate, covered, in refrigerator several hours, turning frequently. Remove meat and dry thoroughly with paper towels. Reserve marinade. Heat dripping in a Dutch oven or heavy flameproof casserole, add meat and brown on all sides. Do this in several batches. Meanwhile, place reserved marinade and stock in a saucepan and add celery, onion, remaining herbs and spices tied together in cheesecloth or muslin. Bring to the boil and simmer 10 minutes. Add liquid to meat, cover and simmer until tender, 2–3 hours. Add water if necessary. If desired, when meat is just tender, vegetables such as peas, carrots and onions may be added. Cook until vegetables are tender. Discard herb bag and remove meat to a heated platter. Thicken gravy with cornflour dissolved in a little cold water, using ¹/₂ tbs cornflour for each cup of broth. Boil, stirring, for 2 minutes. Pour gravy over meat, with vegetables, if used, arranged around it. Serves 4–6.

Brochette of Scallops

This simple marinade gives a marvellous flavour to sea scallops, and is also good with green prawns.

750 g (I¹/₂ lb) fresh scallops; ¹/₂ cup dry vermouth; ¹/₂ cup olive oil; I clove garlic, crushed; 2 tbs chopped parsley.

Remove any brown bits from scallops, then place in a bowl. Add remaining ingredients and turn gently to mix. Marinate, covered, for several hours in refrigerator. Drain scallops, reserving marinade. Thread scallops on to 4 large or 8 small skewers and grill under preheated grill for 5–6 minutes, turning occasionally and brushing with marinade. Serve with fluffy boiled rice or crusty bread. Serves 6.

MARJORAM

A strongly perfumed herb, which is one of the most important of all kitchen herbs. There are three types of marjoram – sweet, pot and wild (known also as oregano) – but sweet marjoram is the one found growing in most gardens and it is the most delicate of the three.

Marjoram and thyme team exceptionally well together, and marjoram can be used in almost any dish that is flavoured with thyme. Marjoram, thyme and sage are the favourite combination for old-fashioned poultry seasoning. There are many more dishes in which marjoram is a good flavouring. It goes particularly well with veal, poultry, pork or beef; for flavouring meat loaves and sausages; in liver dishes, and in most stews. Some fish dishes such as baked fish, salmon croquettes or creamed shellfish are enhanced by the addition of marjoram.

Many vegetables are complemented by the flavour of marjoram. Try adding it to mushroom dishes, green beans and peas, potato dishes, broccoli, Brussels sprouts, eggplants, asparagus, carrots, spinach, zucchini, or onions.

In salads, try adding chopped marjoram to greens tossed in Vinaigrette Dressing (see page 442); with sliced green peppers; Coleslaw; stirred through cottage cheese and cream cheese. A little chopped fresh marjoram gives piquancy to tomato juice, chicken noodle soup or onion soups.

Veal Chops with Marjoram

4 veal chops; salt and freshly ground black pepper; 2 tsp chopped fresh marjoram; seasoned flour; 30 g (1 oz) butter; 2 tbs oil; ½ cup stock.

Season veal chops with salt and pepper. Press marjoram into both sides of chops, place on a plate, cover and leave for 1 hour for flavours to penetrate. Coat chops very lightly with seasoned flour and cook in butter and oil over gentle heat until meat is done, about 10–15 minutes, turning once. Remove chops to heated dish and keep warm. Add stock to pan and simmer, stirring in brown bits, to make a gravy. Season and spoon over chops. Serves 4.

MARMALADE

Few British breakfasts are complete without some hot buttered toast and marmalade. Beautifully coloured and flavoured, most marmalades are soft transparent jellies with small pieces of fruit or fruit peel suspended in the jelly.

Marmalades may be made from one, two, three or more fruits, one of which is nearly always a citrus fruit. Orange marmalade is, perhaps, the favourite and can be made from sweet oranges or bitter Seville or Bigarade oranges. These bitter oranges have a short season and are not always easy to come by. Your greengrocer may be able to order some for you if you wish to make the traditional Seville Orange Marmalade.

Try also Apple and Ginger Marmalade, an unusual combination, or Three-Fruit Marmalade made from grapefruit, oranges and lemons.

Marmalades need slightly longer cooking and use less sugar than jams. The peel should be soaked first or cooked in water to help soften it before sugar, warmed for 7 minutes in a very slow oven (120°C/250°F), is added, otherwise it will remain hard. Prolonged boiling after the sugar is added will not soften the peel but darken the colour of the marmalade and break down the pectin, causing it to lose its jelling properties. Pectin is contained in the pith and pips, which are cooked with the marmalade, usually in a muslin bag.

TO TEST FOR SETTING POINT: Place 1 tsp marmalade on a chilled saucer, wait 20 seconds, then run a finger through it. If the marmalade crinkles at the edges and stays in two separate portions, it is ready for bottling. Pack the warm marmalade into warm, dry, sterile jars, cover, seal and label. See recipes.

See also *Jams*.

Seville Orange Marmalade

If you cannot get bitter oranges use sweet ones instead. These will of course give a sweeter flavour to the marmalade.

1.5 kg (3 lb) Seville oranges; 2 lemons; 12 cups water; about 3 kg (6 lb) sugar, warmed.

Scrub fruit, peel and cut peel into fairly coarse strips. Chop fruit pulp, removing pips and any pith. Tie pips and pith in a muslin bag (they contain the pectin that sets the marmalade). Put peel and flesh in a pan with bag of pips, add water and bring to the boil. Simmer gently until volume has reduced by about a third. Squeeze bag of pips to press out all the juice and discard bag. Measure cooked pulp and return it to pan with 500 g (1 lb) sugar to each 2½ cups pulp. Stir over a gentle heat until sugar has dissolved, then boil until setting point is reached, 15–20 minutes. Cool a little and ladle into warm, dry, sterilised jars. Cover and seal. Makes about 8–10 cups.

Three–Fruit Marmalade

Allow 750 g (1½ lb) mixed fruit – 2 lemons, 1 large orange, 1 grapefruit; 7½ cups water; about 6 cups sugar, warmed.

Scrub and dry fruit. Slice lemons and orange finely and put pips in a muslin bag. Peel rind thinly from grapefruit with a vegetable peeler. Shred and add to sliced fruit in a large bowl. Peel pith from grapefruit. Chop pith finely and add to pips in muslin bag. Slice grapefruit flesh and put in bowl with other fruit and water. Tie muslin bag closed at top, put in bowl, weight with a plate on top to keep fruit immersed in water and leave overnight. Next day, empty contents of bowl into a pan and cook gently for about 1½ hours or until fruit is soft and half the liquid has evaporated. Remove muslin bag, squeezing out as much liquid as possible. Measure pulp and return it to pan with 1 cup sugar to each cup of pulp. Stir until sugar has dissolved, then bring to the boil and cook rapidly until setting point is reached, about 15–20 minutes. Remove pan from heat and cool marmalade for about 15 minutes. Ladle into warm, dry, sterilised jars. Cover and seal. Makes about 6 cups.

Apple and Ginger Marmalade

This ginger marmalade is delicious on cream cheese sandwiches or toast. It can also be used as a glaze for cheesecake. Its spiciness is a welcome change from other jams and marmalades.

375 g (12 oz) fresh ginger, peeled; 1.5 kg (3 lb) tart green cooking apples, quartered and cored; 6 cups water; ¼ cup strained lemon juice; 3 cups sugar, warmed.

m

Slice ginger into very thin julienne strips. Place ginger strips in a saucepan and cover with boiling water. Boil for 30 minutes. Drain ginger in a colander and refresh under cold running water. Place ginger in a bowl, cover with fresh water and chill, covered, for at least 12 hours. Drain and pat dry with paper towels. Place apples and the 6 cups water in a large saucepan and bring to the boil. Boil for 40 minutes, stirring occasionally to mash apples with back of spoon. Pour into a colander lined with 4 layers of boiled, rinsed and squeezed-out cheesecloth. Set colander over a heavy saucepan and allow apple pulp to drip through without squeezing. Do not disturb or press fruit in any way. The following day, measure juice. If there is more than 4½ cups of apple juice, reduce by boiling until it measures 4½ cups. Place apple juice in pan with lemon juice and ginger, gradually add sugar and stir until sugar has dissolved. Bring to the boil and boil rapidly for 15 minutes or until setting point is reached. Remove from heat, skim off broth and stir gently for 5 minutes to prevent ginger from floating to surface. Pour into warm, dry, sterilised jars. Cover and seal. Store for at least a week before using to allow flavours to mellow. Makes 4–6 cups.

Old–fashioned Marmalade

A chunky type of marmalade with just a hint of bitterness.

**1 kg (2 lb) oranges; 10 cups water;
8 cups sugar, warmed; juice 1 lemon.**

Scrub oranges and put them whole into a saucepan with the water. Simmer gently until fruit is tender, 1½–2 hours. Test by inserting a skewer. If it penetrates the fruit it is ready. Lift fruit from pan and reserve liquid. Halve cooled fruit and remove pips. Return pips to pan of reserved liquid and simmer gently 15 minutes. Strain liquid to remove pips and set aside. Chop oranges into strips. Make up to 8 cups with strained liquid. If there is not enough liquid, make up with extra water. Pour into pan, add sugar and lemon juice and stir until sugar has dissolved. Bring to boil and cook rapidly until setting point is reached, 15–20 minutes. Remove from heat and cool for about 15 minutes. Ladle into warm, dry, sterilised jars. Cover and seal. Makes about 6–8 cups.

MARROW, VEGETABLE

This large, sausage-shaped member of the gourd family is best eaten when it is young, with tender flesh. Marrow is used as a vegetable – at its best if its bland taste is enhanced by a well-flavoured sauce or stuffing – and for jams or chutneys. It can also be used as a pie filling in much the same way as apple, though again the bland flavour of marrow needs lifting with brown sugar, lemon juice, raisins and spices.

When buying marrow, look for a small, smooth, unblemished one which feels heavy for its size. Store in a cool place and use within a week or two.

■ **BASIC PREPARATION:** Peel and halve marrow, scoop out seeds with a metal spoon and cut flesh into cubes or fingers. For rounds, cut peeled or unpeeled marrow across into thick slices and stamp our seeds with a cutter. Whole or halved marrow may be baked with a stuffing. For whole marrow, cut off stalk end and scrape out seeds from centre with a metal spoon. Peel marrow completely or remove strips of peel to give a striped effect. For halves, cut unpeeled marrow lengthways in half and scoop out seeds. Scoop out some of the flesh, leaving a shell about 2.5 cm (1 in) thick. The scooped-out flesh is usually chopped and used in the stuffing.

■ **TO COOK:** As it has a high water content, marrow is best steamed, baked, fried or stewed gently in its own juices with a little butter. Boiling in water is not advisable. (See also *Minced Meat.*) **See recipes.**

BAKED MARROW: Prepare a whole marrow, halves or slices as described above. Fill centre with a well-flavoured stuffing, preferably based on rice rather then breadcrumbs, which may become too wet. If using a whole marrow, tie the end piece back in place with string. Place in a greased baking dish, brush with oil or melted butter, cover loosely with foil and bake in preheated moderate oven (180°C/350°F) until tender – 45–60 minutes for whole marrow or halves, 15–20 minutes for slices.

BUTTERED MARROW: Put prepared marrow into saucepan with 15 – 30 g (½–1 oz) melted butter, salt and pepper and, if liked, a few chopped or dried herbs or a little finely chopped onion. Cover pan and cook gently 7–10 minutes or until tender, shaking pan from time to time.

FRIED MARROW: Prepare marrow, dry and coat with seasoned flour or with flour, egg and breadcrumbs. Fry over medium heat in oil, butter or a mixture of these.

STEAMED MARROW: Place prepared pieces of marrow in a steamer or colander over boiling water. Season with salt and pepper, cover tightly and steam 20 minutes or until tender.

Marrow with Beurre Noisette

**750 g (1½ lb) marrow, peeled and seeded;
60 g (2 oz) butter; 2 tbs wine vinegar;
2 tbs chopped parsley; freshly ground black pepper.**

Cut marrow into cubes or fingers and steam or cook with butter as described above. Heat the butter in a small frying pan on moderate heat, shaking occasionally to ensure even colour, until it is a light nut-brown. Stir in vinegar, parsley and pepper and pour while still frothing over hot marrow. Serve immediately. Serves 4–6.

Stuffed Marrow

**1 small marrow; 2 tbs oil; 1 onion, chopped;
2 thick rashers streaky bacon, rind removed**

and coarsely chopped; 250 g (8 oz) minced beef; 1¹/₂ cups cooked long-grain rice; 1 tbs grated Parmesan cheese; salt and freshly ground black pepper; chopped parsley; 2 cups Fresh Tomato Sauce (page 339) or Tomato Sauce Neapolitan Style (page 339).

Cut marrow in half, remove seed and scoop out flesh as described on page 254. Chop scooped-out flesh coarsely and reserve. Heat 1 tbs oil in frying pan and cook onion and bacon gently 5 minutes. Add beef and cook, stirring and breaking up lumps with 2 forks, until lightly browned. Stir in rice, cheese and chopped marrow and season with salt and pepper. Divide mixture between marrow halves. Place in a greased baking dish. Brush marrow with remaining oil, cover loosely with foil and bake in preheated moderate oven (180°C/350°F) 45 minutes to 1 hour or until marrow is tender. Sprinkle with chopped parsley and serve with hot tomato sauce. Serves 4–6.

MARSHMALLOW FROSTING

Marshmallow is a whipped confection resulting in a creamy, stiff mixture with a spongy texture. The name comes from the marshmallow plant; a gum formerly used in its cooking was obtained from its roots. Marshmallow makes a delicious frosting for butter cakes and looks most decorative for special occasions when swirled into rough peaks. Marshmallow can also be used to top mugs of hot chocolate. For best results use an electric mixer to beat the mixture.

Marshmallow Frosting

2 tsp gelatine; 1¹/₂ cups boiling water; 2 cups sugar; ¹/₂ tsp vanilla.

Dissolve gelatine in half the boiling water in a saucepan, add remainder of water and mix with sugar. Heat gently, stirring, until boiling, then boil without stirring over medium heat for 15 minutes. Remove from heat, cool slightly and beat until mixture doubles in bulk and becomes thick. Fold in vanilla. Spread quickly over cake with a warm dry spatula or knife, swirling the top into little peaks for a decorative effect. Sufficient to frost a 20 cm (8 in) butter cake.

MARSHMALLOWS

These little puffy pillows of marshmallow are among the most popular sweets found at the confectioner's. They can be coloured pink or white, coated with icing sugar, tinted or toasted coconut, chocolate sprinkles or hundreds and thousands. They make delicious fillings when dipped in melted chocolate. Home-made or commercial marshmallows are also used as an ingredient in other sweets such as Heavenly Hash (see page 192), to make sauces for ice creams or in desserts. See recipes.

Marshmallows

1¹/₂ cups caster sugar; ¹/₂ cup cold water; 4 tsp gelatine; ¹/₂ cup hot water; 1 tsp vanilla; ¹/₂ cup toasted or tinted desiccated coconut, or ¹/₄ cup cornflour and ¹/₄ cup icing sugar, sifted together.

Place sugar and cold water in a large bowl and, using an electric mixer, beat for 3–4 minutes. Dissolve gelatine in hot water and, while still hot, add to sugar mixture. Beat until thick and white. Add vanilla. Pour into a lightly greased lamington tin, 28 x 19 x 4 cm (11 x 7¹/₂ x 1¹/₂ in). Leave at room temperature until firm, Cut marshmallow into squares or other shapes with a warm, dry knife. Place coconut (or cornflour and icing sugar mixture) in a plastic bag and toss the marshmallow pieces to coat thoroughly. Makes about 24.

VARIATION

MARSHMALLOW CONES: Prepare marshmallow mixture. After adding vanilla, spoon immediately into 15 ice cream cones and sprinkle tops with hundreds and thousands. Makes 15.

Coffee Marshmallow Cream

500 g (1 lb) marshmallows, chopped; 1 cup very strong black coffee; 2 cups cream, whipped; slivered toasted almonds, Brazil nuts or crushed Nut Brittle (page 300).

Place marshmallows in a heatproof bowl over hot water. Add coffee and heat, stirring frequently, until marshmallows are melted. Chill mixture until it is about to set, then fold in whipped cream. Pour into an oiled 6-cup ring mould. Chill until set. Invert on to a serving platter and cover the top with nuts or nut brittle. Serves 6.

Marshmallow Sauce

³/₄ cup sugar; 1 tbs golden syrup; ¹/₄ cup milk; 250 g (8 oz) marshmallows, chopped; 2 tbs water; 1 tsp vanilla.

Combine sugar, golden syrup and milk in a heavy saucepan. Stir over low heat until sugar has dissolved. Bring to the boil, then simmer gently for 5 minutes. Place marshmallows and water in top of a double saucepan and heat, stirring frequently, until melted. Pour sugar mixture over marshmallows, beating well. Add vanilla. Serve sauce hot or cold over ice cream, baked apples, poached pears or peaches or with fresh fruit salad. Make about 2 cups.

NOTE: Marshmallow Sauce may be reheated in a double saucepan. Beat well before serving.

MARZIPAN

Another name for Almond Paste (see page 3). Marzipan is often modelled into edible cake and dessert decorations such as miniature fruits. Mould into desired shape and tint, using a small brush and diluted vegetable food colouring. Allow to dry thoroughly before handling.

MAYONNAISE

The delicately flavoured, uniquely light and smooth mixture of oil, egg yolks and lemon juice is perhaps the most popular of the cold sauces.

Deservedly or not, Cardinal Richelieu is credited with the invention of this sauce in the seventeenth century, and it is interesting that it is still made exactly the same way today, except that one may, using great care, combine the emulsion with an electric beater or food processor instead of a wire whisk. Certainly, one should first master the skill of making this sauce in the old way (with a wire whisk) before making it with modern electric beaters.

Making mayonnaise presents only one problem: it may curdle or separate. For consistent success, have the egg yolks and oil at room temperature, and beat the oil into the egg yolks very gradually, drop by drop at first then finally in a thin stream, until the emulsion of the egg and oil forms a smooth sauce. If anything goes wrong and the mayonnaise separates, you can restore the emulsion as follows: wash the beater; in another bowl beat another egg yolk with ½ tsp salt and ½ tsp vinegar; then gradually beat in the curdled mayonnaise a teaspoon at a time at first, then more quickly until emulsified.

Mayonnaise should be stored in a cool place, not in the refrigerator. It will keep for several weeks – the oil is a preservative. Mayonnaise has dozens of uses, can be varied endlessly and will transform such simple ingredients as hard-boiled eggs, fresh cooked or canned fish, poached chicken or diced cooked vegetables into an elegant dish. There are many lovely mayonnaise variations, some of the classics are Sauce Rémoulade, Sauce Tartare, Sauce Niçoise, Aïoli Sauce, Sauce Russe and Sauce à la Ritz. See recipes.

See also *Aïoli*.

Mayonnaise

**2 egg yolks; ¹/₂ tsp salt; pinch white pepper;
¹/₂ tsp dry mustard; 2 tsp vinegar or lemon juice;
1 cup olive oil or salad oil or a mixture of both.**

Have all the ingredients at room temperature. Warm eggs and oil in hot water if they are cold. Rinse out a mixing bowl with hot water and wrap a damp cloth around the base to keep it steady. Place egg yolks, seasonings and 1 tsp vinegar or lemon juice in bowl and beat with a wire whisk to combine. When thick, begin to add oil, drop by drop, from a teaspoon, whisking constantly and incorporating each addition thoroughly before adding the next. As mixture thickens, oil flow can be increased to a steady thin stream but keep beating constantly. Stop pouring every now and then to check that oil is well blended. If mayonnaise should show signs of breaking or curdling beat in 1–2 tsp boiling water before adding more oil. When all oil is incorporated, beat in remaining vinegar or lemon juice. Makes about 1 cup.

NOTE: For lighter mayonnaise, add 1 tbs of very hot water just before using.

VARIATIONS

FOOD PROCESSOR OR BLENDER MAYONNAISE: Place egg yolks, seasonings and 1 tsp vinegar or lemon juice in bowl and blend for a few seconds. With motor running, pour oil in very gradually, ensuring that each addition has been absorbed before adding more. When all the oil has been incorporated, add remaining vinegar or lemon juice.

MAYONNAISE DIJONNAISE: Make Mayonnaise, using 1 tbs Dijon mustard instead of dry mustard.

SAUCE VERTE: Rinse 1 cup watercress sprigs and 8 sprigs parsley stripped from the stems. Cover with boiling water and let stand 5–6 minutes. Drain greens, plunge into cold water, and drain again, pressing out all surplus water. Rub greens through a sieve, or chop finely, then combine with finished Mayonnaise. Serve with cold lobster, salmon, poached fish or other fish and shellfish. Good also for vegetable salads.

SAUCE RUSSE: Add 3 tbs chilli sauce, 1 tbs finely chopped canned pimiento and 1 tsp chives to finished Mayonnaise and mix well. Use for cold eggs and vegetables and for shellfish.

SAUCE A LA RITZ: Add 1 tbs chilli sauce, ¹/₂ tsp Worce-stershire sauce, 1 tomato, peeled, seeded and chopped, and 1 tsp each chopped chives and parsley to the finished Mayonnaise and mix well. Use for seafood cocktails.

SAUCE REMOULADE: Press all moisture from 3 tbs finely chopped sour pickles and 1 tbs chopped capers. Add pickles and capers to the finished Mayonnaise with 1 tsp Dijon mustard and 1 tbs chopped mixed fresh parsley, tarragon and chervil. Use with fried or cold poached fish and shellfish.

SAUCE TARTARE: Add 6 green olives, chopped, and 1 tsp chopped chives to Sauce Rémoulade. Use for fried fish and shellfish.

SAUCE NICOISE: Add 1 tbs tomato paste, 3 tbs finely chopped red pepper and 1 tsp chopped mixed fresh tarragon and chives to Mayonnaise. Use with cold poached fish or shellfish.

MUSTARD MAYONNAISE: Combine ¹/₂ cup Mayonnaise (see recipe), 3 tbs cream, 2 tbs Dijon mustard, 1 clove garlic, crushed, 1 tbs lemon juice, salt and freshly ground black pepper, pinch cayenne.

Thousand Island Dressing

¹/₃ cup Mayonnaise (page 256), 2 tsp tomato sauce,
dash Tabasco sauce; 1 hard-boiled egg, chopped;
2 spring onions, chopped; 6 green or black olives,
stoned and chopped; salt and freshly
ground pepper.

Mix all ingredients together. Makes about ½ cup.

MEAT

Meat is usually the star around which the rest of the meal
revolves. It is the basis of literally thousands of wonderful
dishes. As all meat becomes more expensive, it
becomes more and more important to choose meat
carefully and to get the best from it. For information on
characteristics of good beef, lamb, mutton, pork and
veal, specific cuts and methods of cooking them, please
see entries under individual names of these meats.

BUYING MEAT

You can judge meat to some degree by its appearance,
but you must rely largely on the skill and integrity of your
butcher for first-class meat. Eating is the final test, but for
points to help you appraise quality, please see entries for
individual meats.

TO CHOOSE THE RIGHT CUT FOR THE DISH: As
discussed under 'Cooking Meat', cuts from different
parts of the animal vary greatly in tenderness and, of
course, in cost. This does not mean that you should buy
the most expensive cut you can afford for every dish. The
connective tissue which makes cheaper cuts too tough
for grilling or frying is exactly what gives a rich, melting
texture to a dish when it is cooked slowly with moisture
and broken down into gelatine. For best results, follow
the suggestions for the suitable cuts given in entries for
individual meats and in the recipe you are following.

HOW MUCH TO BUY: The amount of meat for each serving
varies, of course, with appetites and the type of dish.
As a general guide, allow:

- 125–250 g (4–8 oz) per serving on boneless cuts, such
  as stewing meat, roasts, steaks and minced meat.
- 155–250 g (5–8 oz) of meat with some bone, such as
  chops, T–bone steaks and roasts on the bone.
- 375–500 g (12 oz –1 lb) of bony cuts such as spare ribs,
  lamb shanks and bone-in shoulder.

STORING MEAT

As a general rule, the larger the piece of meat and the less
surface area is has for its size, the longer it will store.
Minced meat, sausage and variety meats should be
cooked within 24 hours of purchase. Diced meat should
be used within 48 hours, steaks and chops with 2–4 days,
and roasts within 3–5 days. The bacteria which cause the
surface of meat to become slimy thrive in the absence of
air, so meat should never be stored tightly wrapped in
plastic. Unwrap it, put it on a plate, cover loosely with foil
or greaseproof paper and store in the coldest part of the
refrigerator.

TO FREEZE MEAT: Freeze it as quickly as possible so, if
you want to pack several pieces together, wrap them
individually in foil or freezer wrap and freeze in a single
layer first. It is practical to prepare meat ready for cooking by trimming or cutting it up before freezing. Small
cuts or diced meat can be stewed or casseroled from
frozen, and thin pieces can be fried or grilled from frozen;
but larger pieces will be overdone on the outside before
the inside is fully cooked, so first thaw these completely.
It is better to thaw meat in the refrigerator than at room
temperature as less juices are lost. Allow 5–6 hours for
steak and chops, 6 hours per 500 g (1 lb) for large pieces.

COOKING MEAT

Tenderness in meat depends partly on the age and
condition of the animal, on how the meat was handled
after slaughter and also on the cut. Tender cuts come
from those parts of the animal which had the least
exercise, such as the loin (lower back) and rump. These
cuts respond to dry-heat cooking, so roast, grill, fry or
sauté them.

Tougher cuts, from parts of the animal which had more
exercise, have developed more connective tissue,
which is the main cause of toughness. Slow cooking
with moisture changes connective tissue into gelatine,
so braise, stew, pot-roast or simmer these cuts. In these
slow-cooking processes, the liquid should never go
above simmering point – when the surface shivers
and single bubbles rise slowly. Some meat dishes are
traditionally called 'boiled' but this is a misnomer – meat
that is cooked at full boiling point loses its juices and
becomes tasteless and dry.

Always remove meat from the refrigerator in time for it
to reach room temperature right through before cooking
it. This ensures that the inside will be cooked as desired
before the outside is overdone. Cooking times given in
recipes are based on meat at room temperature.

TO JUDGE WHEN MEAT IS DONE: Cooking times given
in recipes can be used as a guide, but the shape of the
piece, the quality of the meat or the efficiency of your
stove can cause variations. Start testing when about
⅘ of the cooking time is up.

To test large pieces of meat, a meat thermometer is
ideal as it is marked at the correct internal temperatures
for different meats. Insert the thermometer into the

thickest part of the meat, away from fat or bone, leave for a minute, then read it.

Failing a thermometer, or for smaller cuts such as steak, press the meat with your finger. If it is soft and spongy it is not cooked through. If it is soft but quite springy, it is medium-rare. If it is firm with little resilience, it is well-done.

You can also test by inserting a fine skewer or kitchen needle into the thickest part of the meat and checking the colour of the juice that comes out. If it is red, the meat is rare; if pink, medium; if clear, well-done.

CARVING MEAT

The first requisite for good carving is a razor-sharp knife. For meat, it should have a rather long, narrow and slightly flexible blade. The essence of the art is to allow the knife to do the cutting – the carver guides the blade with a long, light, slightly sawing action, rather than driving it. Electric carving knives make the job easier for many people, though purists prefer their traditional tools.

It is easier to carve on a board than on a platter; the board should have a channel to catch the juices. You will also need a fork and a hot plate for the carved meat.

Always allow the cooked joint to rest in a warm place for 15–30 minutes before carving (the larger the piece, the longer the time) so that the juices can settle back into the tissues.

Meat is usually carved across the grain, though some joints may be carved with the grain, parallel to the bone.

Boneless Rolled Joints (e.g. rib or other cuts of beef; loin or shoulder of lamb, mutton, veal or pork; breast of veal, rolled corned beef). Lay the piece on its side and carve downwards in slices – thinly for beef and veal, more thickly for lamb, mutton and pork.

Other Boneless Joints (e.g. topside, fresh or corned silverside or rump of beef): Carve in slices across the grain, changing the direction of the knife and turning the joint as needed.

Leg of Lamb, Mutton or Pork: This may be carved in two ways. The most economical and easiest way is to carve slices parallel to the surface (with the grain), turning the joint over as needed. The method which gives the juiciest meat, with an edging of the brown outside on each slice, is to start carving in the middle, downwards to the bone. Take out a wedge-shaped piece first, then slices, also slightly wedge-shaped, from each side. Finally, turn joint over and slice off remaining meat parallel to the surface.

NOTE: Before starting to carve roast leg of pork, remove the crackling, break into pieces. Serve a piece of crackling with each portion.

Ham on the Bone: Carve by either of the methods described for leg of lamb, above.

Rack of Lamb, Crown Roast of Lamb or Pork, Rib of Pork on the Bone: Carve downwards into single or double cutlets, making sure beforehand that the butcher has chined the joint properly (chopped through the bone where you will be cutting).

Rib of Beef on the Bone: Cut between meat and bone to separate them, then slice meat at right angles to bone.

Sirloin of Beef on the Bone: First turn the joint over and carve out the undercut (the fillet) in thick slices. Turn upright again, cut between meat and bone to separate them and push bone down slightly. Slice meat thinly at right angles to the bone.

Shoulder of Lamb or Mutton the Bone: First hold up the leg end of the joint with the fork, meaty side uppermost, and carve slices parallel to the surface. Next, put joint flat on dish, turn over and carve slices from either side of the shoulder blade.

Saddle of Lamb: There are two ways of carving a saddle. For either method, start by cutting off the skirt pieces that are tucked underneath. These are fatty and are not always served, but may be cut diagonally into small pieces if you want to serve them.

You may now carve lengthways down either side of the central bone to give long flat strips of meat, or cut between bone and meat to separate them, then cut meat across into small thick slices. Lastly, turn the joint over and cut between bone and meat to remove the 2 fillets, then cut these across into small thick slices. Serve a piece from each part of the saddle for each portion.

Sucking Pig: Cut round the outline of shoulder and leg, pull outwards gently and cut off through joints. Carve meat in slices. Remove head and divide meat down centre of back. Cut pig across the middle to separate rib section. Cut through ribs, dividing into chops.

NOTE: The pig will be easier to carve if the skin is first removed. Break the crisp parts (crackling) into pieces and serve some crackling with each portion.

MEATBALLS

These are made from minced, ground or very finely chopped or shredded meat and are included in nearly every cuisine of the world. They range from tiny meatballs dropped in soup to much larger ones used as a main course. They can be fried, grilled, baked, braised or poached, the mixtures are nearly always economical, often incorporating breadcrumbs, rice, vegetables or sometimes a little fruit, to stretch the quantity and improve the flavour.

Meatballs are often served with or in a sauce, the variety being infinite. Swedish meatballs are served with cream sauce, Greek in egg and lemon sauce (see *Avgolemono*), Italian *Polpette* are served alone or with a tomato sauce, and Germany has a lemon and caper sauce for the famous *Königsberger Klöpse*. In India delicious curried *Koftas* have a curry sauce, while the Chinese make superb smoked meatballs.

Meatballs are marvellous for parties. They can be made, cooked ahead and heated when required. Serve them with a dipping sauce when having drinks. Use beef, lamb, pork, or any suitable combinations, such as pork and veal, according to your recipe. Cuts such as beef topside or round steaks, lamb, veal or pork shoulder are good for mincing at home. The meat should be lean and free of gristle and sinew. Buy it ready-minced from your butcher or mince the higher-quality cuts at home, using a mincer or food processor. It is best to use minced meat within 24 hours after buying. Store in refrigerator, spread evenly in a dish and loosely covered with foil. **See** recipes.

See also *Frikadeller*.

Onion Soup with Meatballs

$^1/_4$ cup barley, soaked overnight and drained;
2 cups water; 4 cups beef stock; 250 g (8oz) minced beef; 1 egg yolk; 1 tbs finely chopped onion;
1 tbs chopped parsley; pinch white pepper;
45 g ($1^1/_2$ oz) butter; 3 large onions, chopped;
$^1/_2$ tsp Worcestershire sauce;
salt and freshly ground black pepper.

GARNISH: sour cream; chopped parsley.

Place barley, water and stock in a saucepan and bring to the boil. Half cover and simmer until barley is tender, about $1^1/_2$ hours. Mix together minced beef, egg yolk, chopped onion, parsley and white pepper and shape into walnut-sized balls. Heat butter in frying pan and brown meatballs on all sides. Drain on crumpled paper towels and set aside. Cook chopped onions in fat in frying pan until tender and lightly browned. Add meatballs, fried onions and Worcestershire sauce to barley soup and simmer for a further 30 minutes. Season with salt and pepper. Serve with a swirl of sour cream and sprinkled with chopped parsley. Serves 4–6.

Königsberger Klöpse
(Meatballs in Lemon and Caper Sauce)

250 g (8 oz) each minced beef, pork and veal,
or 750 g ($1^1/_2$ lb) mixed minced pork and veal;
3 slices stale white break; 1 cup lukewarm water;
1 onion finely chopped; 5 anchovy fillets, chopped;
2 eggs, 1 tbs chopped parsley, grated rind
1 lemon; $^1/_2$ tsp salt; $^1/_4$ tsp pepper;
3–4 cups veal or beef stock; 1 small onion;
1 bay leaf.

LEMON AND CAPER SAUCE: 30 g (1 oz) butter;
$^1/_2$ tsp minced onion; $1^1/_2$ tbs flour; 2 tbs lemon juice; 2 tbs capers; 2–3 tbs sour cream.

Mix meats together. Cut bread into small pieces and soak in lukewarm water for 15 minutes. Drain, squeeze dry and add to meat with chopped onion and anchovies. Mix well or mince again in a food processor or mincer. Add eggs, parsley, lemon rind, salt and pepper and mix thoroughly. With wet hands shape mixture into balls about 5 cm (2 in) in diameter. Place stock, whole onion and bay leaf in large saucepan and bring to the boil. Simmer for 10 minutes, then drop in meatballs. Simmer for 20 minutes longer or until meatballs rise to surface. Using a slotted spoon transfer them to a heated dish and cover. Strain and reserve stock.

LEMON AND CAPER SAUCE: Melt butter in a heavy saucepan, add onion and cook gently until translucent. Stir in flour and allow to brown very slowly. Pour in reserved stock and stir continuously until thickened. Add lemon juice and capers. Add meatballs to sauce and simmer very gently for 15 minutes, stirring occasionally. Stir in sour cream. Serve on a mound of sauerkraut. Serves 4–6.

Swedish Meatballs in Cream Sauce

500 g (1 lb) lean minced steak; 250 g (8 oz) mixed lean minced pork and veal; $1^1/_2$ cups fresh white breadcrumbs; $2^1/_2$ cups cream; $^1/_2$ cup milk;
1 onion finely chopped; 90 g (3 oz) butter;
1 egg beaten; $^1/_4$ tsp ground ginger; salt and freshly ground black pepper; nutmeg; 1 tbs flour;
$^1/_2$ cup stock; chopped fresh dill.

Mix meats together. Soak breadcrumbs in a mixture of $^1/_2$ cup cream and the milk. Cook onion in 30 g (1 oz) butter until tender but not brown. Combine meats, breadcrumbs, egg and onion, and season with ginger, $1^1/_2$ tsp salt, pepper and $^1/_2$ tsp nutmeg. Beat vigorously until very light in texture, then chill. Form into small balls. Melt remaining butter in large frying pan and lightly brown meatballs on all sides, a few at a time. Remove from pan and keep warm in an oven-proof dish in a preheated slow oven (150°C/300°F) while making the sauce. Stir flour into fat in frying pan and cook for 2 minutes, stirring. Remove from heat and add stock and remaining cream. Bring to the boil, stirring constantly. Season with salt, pepper and nutmeg and cook over a low heat for about 10 minutes or until sauce reduces and thickens, stirring frequently. Pour sauce over meatballs and scatter with dill. Serve with boiled rice. Serves 6.

NOTE: The meatballs may be made and cooked the day before and then reheated in the oven, with the sauce poured over just before serving.

Party Meatballs

These economical meatballs are marvellous for a party. They freeze well, so can be made and stored for 3–4 weeks and reheated as required.

2 large potatoes, peeled and diced; 1 medium Granny Smith apple, peeled, cored and diced;
2 large onions finely chopped; 2 rashers bacon, rind removed and finely chopped; 2 eggs, beaten;
1 kg (2 lb) minced steak; 500 g (1 lb) sausage mince;
2 tsp curry powder; 1 tsp ground ginger; 2 tbs sugar;

$^{1}/_{4}$ tsp dry mustard; $^{1}/_{2}$ tsp salt; $^{1}/_{4}$ tsp pepper;
1 tbs tomato sauce; flour, oil for frying.

**SPICY TOMATO SAUCE: 1 cup tomato sauce;
1 tbs brown sugar; 1 tbs Worcestershire sauce;
1 tbs soy sauce.**

Place potatoes, apple and onions in a saucepan and
just cover with water. Bring to the boil, then reduce
heat and simmer until very tender. Drain, and mash
or pureé. Allow to cool. Place all ingredients except
flour and oil in a bowl and mix well together. Using
floured hands, roll into bite-sized balls. Heat a little
oil in a frying pan and fry meatballs until golden on
all sides. Drain on paper towels and serve hot or cold.
The meatballs can also be baked in a preheated
moderately hot oven (190°C/375°F) for 15–20 minutes
or until golden-brown. For sauce, heat all ingredients
together in a saucepan, stirring occasionally. To serve
pour sauce into a bowl on a platter arrange meatballs
around it. Provide a container of toothpicks so guests
can spear the meatballs for dunking. Makes about
130–150 small meatballs.

Smoked Chinese Meatballs

The simple meatball transformed with Chinese
flavourings then smoked over black tea and fennel
seeds makes a stunning first course, especially when
taken to the table in the attractive Chinese bamboo
steamer.

**6 dried Chinese mushrooms; $^{1}/_{2}$ x 230 g can water
chestnuts, drained and finely chopped;
250 g (8oz) lean minced beef; 250 g (8 oz) minced
pork; 2 tbs soy sauce; 2 tbs cornflour; 1 tbs finely
chopped spring onions; 1 tbs finely chopped fresh
ginger; 1 tbs rice wine or dry sherry;
1 tsp Chinese sesame oil.**

**FOR SMOKING: 2 tbs brown sugar;
2 tbs black tea leaves; 2 tbs fennel seeds.**

**TO SERVE: 2 tsp sesame oil mixed with 2 tbs soy sauce;
2 spring onions, finely sliced.**

Soak mushrooms in hot water to cover for 15 minutes
or until soft. Drain, then remove stalks and chop caps
finely. Place mushrooms in a large bowl with remaining
ingredients and mix well by hand until mixture is
firm and compact. Shape into walnut-sized balls and
arrange each on a little square of greaseproof paper.
Set in one layer on a greased cake rack or in a Chinese
bamboo steamer. Cover and steam over boiling water
in a wok or deep frying pan for 15 minutes.
Meanwhile, prepare a container for smoking; use an
old frying pan, wok or other metal container. Line
with foil, pressing it well into shape of container.
Combine brown sugar, tea leaves and fennel seeds
and place in bottom of pan. Set over high heat. When
tea mixture starts to smoke, put rack containing

meatballs into pan. Cover lightly with a lid or foil and
smoke for 5 minutes, then turn heat off and leave for
a further 10 minutes, still covered. To serve, brush
meatballs with oil and soy sauce mixture and sprinkle
with spring onions. Serves 6–8 as a first course, or 4 as
a main course with rice.
NOTE: If using a Chinese bamboo steamer with its
own lid simply place meatballs in bamboo base, cover
and place over burning tea mixture.

Curried Koftas *(Indian Meatballs)*

**500 g (1 lb) finely minced steak; 1 onion finely
chopped; 1–2 chillies, seeded and chopped;
2 tbs chopped fresh coriander or mint;
1–2 cloves garlic, crushed; $^{1}/_{2}$ tsp salt; 1 tbs Garam
Masala (page 171); 1 tsp chilli powder; flour;
oil for frying.**

**SAUCE: 30 g (1 oz) butter or ghee; a large onion,
finely chopped; 1 tbs chopped fresh ginger;
1 tsp turmeric; $^{1}/_{4}$ tsp salt; 2 tsp Garam Masala;
$^{1}/_{4}$ tsp chilli powder; 2 large tomatoes, peeled and
chopped; 1 tbs lemon juice; $^{1}/_{2}$ cup water.**

Mix steak with onion, chillies, coriander or mint,
garlic, salt, garam masala and chilli powder. Knead
mixture until stiff and smooth. Roll into walnut-
sized balls and dust lightly with flour. Shallow-fry in
hot oil until golden on all sides. Drain on crumpled
paper towels.
SAUCE: Heat butter or ghee in a heavy saucepan and fry
onion and ginger until softened. Add turmeric, salt,
garam masala and chilli powder and stir for a minute,
then add tomatoes. Cook, stirring, for a few minutes.
Stir in lemon juice and water. Add meatballs and stir
to coat with sauce. Cover and simmer 15–20 minutes
or until sauce is thick. Serve with rice, a choice of
chutneys and sambals such as minted chopped tomatoes,
sliced bananas, coconut and pappadams. Serves 4.

Polpette *(Italian Meatballs)*

**500 g (1 lb) minced steak, 2 cloves garlic, sliced;
2 tbs chopped parsley; 1 strip lemon rind;
1 thick slice white bread; $^{1}/_{4}$ cup milk; 2 eggs;
$^{1}/_{4}$ tsp salt; $^{1}/_{4}$ tsp pepper; pinch nutmeg;
flour; oil for frying.**

Put steak, garlic, parsley and lemon rind through a
mincer or food processor to mince finely. Soak bread
in milk for 15 minutes, then drain and squeeze dry.
Stir bread into meat mixture. Beat in eggs and add
salt, pepper and nutmeg. Form into little flat cakes
and coat lightly in flour. Fry in hot oil and drain on
crumpled paper towels before serving. Serves 4.
VARIATION
ITALIAN MEATBALLS WITH TOMATO SAUCE: Make
Polpette as above and place in an ovenproof dish after
frying. Pour in 1$^{1}/_{2}$ cups Tomato Sauce Neapolitan

Style (see page 339) and bake, covered, in a preheated moderate oven (180°C/350°F) for about 30 minutes or until heated through. Serve with grated Parmesan cheese handed separately. Serves 4.

Moroccan Meatballs

250 g (8 oz) boned shoulder of lamb, trimmed of excess fat and minced; 250 g (8 oz) potatoes, peeled, boiled and mashed; 2 eggs, beaten; 2 tbs chopped parsley; 2 onions, finely chopped; 1/4 tsp black pepper; 1/2 tsp cayenne; salt; 1/4 cup flour; 1/4 cup oil.

Mix together thoroughly all ingredients except flour and oil. Form into balls the size of small eggs. Flatten slightly and roll lightly in flour. Heat oil in frying pan and fry meatballs for 10–15 minutes or until cooked and golden brown on all sides. Serve very hot. Serves 4.

Porcupines

These are named for the grains of rice, which swell during cooking to stand out resembling porcupine quills.

500 g (1 lb) minced steak. 1/2 cup fresh white breadcrumbs; 3/4 tsp salt; 1/2 tsp paprika; 1/2 green pepper, cored, seeded and diced (optional); 1 egg, beaten; 1/2 cup rice; 1 x 310 g can tomato soup; 1/2 cup water; 1 cup frozen peas.

Combine minced steak, breadcrumbs, salt, paprika, green pepper, if used, and egg. Roll lightly into balls, press into flat cakes and role in rice. Heat soup and water in a heavy saucepan and add meat cakes. Cover and simmer gently for 40 minutes. Add peas and simmer for a further 5 minutes before serving. Serves 4–6.

Keftethes (Greek Meat Patties)

500 g (1 lb) minced veal; 250 g (8 oz) minced pork; 3 thick slices stale bread, crusts removed; 1 onion, finely chopped; 1 clove garlic, crushed; 3 tbs chopped parsley; 1 tsp chopped fresh mint; 1 tsp chopped fresh basil; 1 medium tomato, peeled and chopped; 1 egg; 1 tbs vinegar; 1 tsp bicarbonate of soda; 1 1/2 tsp salt; freshly ground black pepper; flour; oil for shallow-frying.

Combine meats. Soak bread in cold water, drain and squeeze dry. Mix bread with onion, garlic, herbs, tomato, egg and vinegar. Blend in soda, salt and pepper. Add meat and mix in lightly and thoroughly, using hands if necessary. Chill for 1 hour. Roll into balls, dust with flour and flatten into rounds about 5 cm (2 in) in diameter. Shallow-fry in hot oil for 4–5 minutes each side. Patties should puff up. Drain on crumpled paper towels and serve immediately. Serves 5–6.

Zucchini and Lamb Patties

500 g (1 lb) zucchini, grated (unpeeled); salt; 500 g (1 lb) boneless lamb, trimmed of excess fat and minced; 1/4 tsp white pepper; 2 tbs chopped fresh dill; 1 onion grated; 60 g (2 oz) cream cheese, softened; 2 eggs; 2 tbs flour; 2 tbs olive oil.

GARNISH: 1 lemon, cut into 6 wedges; sprigs fresh dill.

Place grated zucchini in a colander, sprinkle with salt and let drain for 30 minutes to extract bitter juices. Squeeze out excess moisture between the palms of your hands and dry zucchini on paper towels. Mix with lamb, pepper, dill, onion, cream cheese and eggs. Add flour and form into 12 round patties. Heat oil in a frying pan and fry patties over medium heat for about 5 minutes on each side or until golden brown. Serve hot, garnished with lemon wedges and dill sprigs. Serves 6–8.

MEAT LOAF

A well-made meat loaf should be light, juicy and hold its shape when cut. Handle the meat lightly when mixing so that the final result is not too dense. A small proportion of fat helps to retain juiciness, and the loaves slice best when bound with egg, and not overcooked. Meat loaf is good eaten hot or cold; it provides an excellent filling for sandwiches or bread rolls, or simply slice and pack in a lunchbox with crisp lettuce wedges and tiny tomatoes. Serve meat loaf at lunch with appropriate salads, or hot for dinner with vegetables and a suitable sauce, such as tomato or barbecue. **See recipes.**

Basic Meat Loaf

1 kg (2 lb) minced steak; 1 tsp salt; 1/4 tsp black pepper; 1 cup fresh breadcrumbs; 1 cup evaporated milk; 1 small onion, finely chopped; 2 tsp chopped fresh herbs or 1/2 tsp dried; 2–3 rashers bacon, rind removed (optional).

GRAVY: 1 tbs flour; 1 1/2 cups beef stock.

Thoroughly combine all ingredients except bacon. Pack lightly into a greased 21 x 15 cm (8 1/2 x 6 in) loaf tin, or shape mixture into a loaf on a shallow baking tray. Top with bacon rashers, if using, and bake in a preheated moderate oven (180°C/350°F) for 1 hour or until loaf shrinks slightly from sides of tin. Pour 2 tbs fat from tin into a saucepan. Add flour and stir over medium heat until brown. Pour in stock, stir until boiling and simmer 3 minutes. Strain into a heated sauceboat. Serve meat loaf hot with gravy and vegetables, or cold with a salad. Alternatively, meat loaf may be served hot with Tomato Sauce or Mushroom Sauce (see *Sauces*). Serves 6.

VARIATIONS

CRUSTY MEAT LOAF: Make Basic Meat Loaf mixture and shape into a loaf on a baking tray. Omit bacon, score top into diamond shapes with the back of a knife. Bake as above, basting every 15 minutes with ½ cup melted butter mixed with ½ cup white wine or stock.

OTHER MEATS: Make Basic Meat Loaf using 1 kg (2 lb) mixed minced veal and pork, or 500 g (1 lb) minced steak and 250 g (8 oz) each minced veal and pork.

EGG LOAF: Place ¼ Basic Meat Loaf mixture in loaf tin, put 3 shelled hard-boiled eggs down the middle and pack remaining meat mixture over and around them. Top with bacon and bake as above.

OTHER SEASONINGS: Add any of the following to Basic Meat Loaf mixture: 1 clove garlic, crushed; 1 cup grated cheese; ½ cup sautéed sliced mushrooms; ½ cup chopped green pepper or celery; 1 cup cooked, finely chopped, well-drained spinach; ¼ cup finely chopped parsley and ¼ cup pine nuts.

POTATO FROSTING: Bake Basic Meat Loaf, omitting bacon, in loaf tin and drain off fat. Turn out on to baking tray or ovenproof dish. Spread with 2 cups well-seasoned mashed potatoes and brush with melted butter or sprinkle with grated cheese. Bake in preheated hot oven (200°C/400°F) for 20 minutes or until browned.

PASTRY CRUST: Make Basic Meat Loaf omitting bacon, drain off fat and allow to cool. Roll out 1 x 375 g (12 oz) packet frozen puff pastry, thawed, to rectangle about 25 x 35 cm (10 x 14 in). Put cooled meat loaf, top side down, in the centre of pastry. Fold pastry completely around loaf, sealing edges with water. Turn right side up on a baking tray and brush pastry with 1 egg lightly mixed with 1 tsp milk or water. Decorate with pastry leaves or as desired, attaching decorations with some egg wash. Brush decorations with egg and bake in a preheated hot oven (200°C/400°F) about 15–20 minutes or until nicely browned.

Spicy Meat Loaf with Mustard Sauce

Serve this deliciously tangy meat loaf with lots of creamy mashed potatoes and buttered Brussels sprouts.

1 egg, beaten; ⅓ cup evaporated milk; 1 tbs vinegar; 1 tbs treacle; 1 tbs French mustard; 1½ cups fresh breadcrumbs; 1 small onion, finely chopped; ½ tsp salt; 750 g (1½ lb) minced beef.

SAUCE: 1 cup beef stock; 2 tsp vinegar, 2 tsp dry mustard; 1 tsp treacle; 2 tbs cornflour; ½ cup cold water.

Combine egg, evaporated milk, vinegar, treacle, mustard, breadcrumbs, onion and salt. Add beef and

mix well. Pack mixture lightly into a 21 x 11 cm (8½ x 4½ in) loaf tin. Bake in a preheated moderate oven (180°C/350°F) for 1¼ hours. Meanwhile, make the sauce. Combine stock, vinegar, mustard and treacle in a saucepan and beat until smooth. Blend together cornflour and cold water, add to pan and cook, stirring, until thickened and bubbly. Serve meat loaf hot, with mustard sauce. Serves 6.

Orange Meat Loaf

750 g (1½ lb) minced steak; ¼ cup orange juice; 1 egg; 1½ cups fresh white breadcrumbs; 1 onion, finely chopped; salt; ¼ tsp pepper; 2 tsp chopped parsley; ¼ tsp dried thyme.

TOPPING: ¼ cup tomato paste; ⅓ cup firmly packed brown sugar; ¼ tsp dry mustard; ¼ tsp cinnamon; ¼ tsp ground cardamom or cloves; 3 slices orange, halved.

Combine all meat loaf ingredients and mix well. Lightly pack into greased 21 x 11 cm (8½ x 4½ in) loaf tin. Bake in a preheated moderate oven (180°C/350°F), on the lower shelf, for 30 minutes.

TOPPING: Combine tomato paste, sugar, mustard and spices and mix well. Place orange slices on top of meat loaf, spoon spice mixture over and bake for a further 30 minutes or until cooked and the top nicely glazed. Serve hot or cold. Serves 6.

Meat Loaf with Tahini

750 g (1½ lb) minced lamb or beef; 2 onions, finely chopped; ½ cup chopped parsley; 1 tsp salt; ½ tsp ground allspice.

SAUCE: 3 tbs tomato paste; 2 tbs tahini (sesame paste); 3 tbs white vinegar; salt; ground allspice.

Place meat in bowl. Add onions, parsley, salt and all-spice and knead well, first dipping your fingers in cold water. Press meat mixture into a greased 21 x 11 cm (8½ x 4½ in) loaf tin. Bake in a preheated hot oven (200°C/400°F) about 15 minutes or until loaf is lightly browned. Meanwhile, prepare sauce by mixing together tomato paste, tahini and vinegar. Season with salt and allspice. Add enough water to blend ingredients to a thin but creamy sauce. Pour enough sauce over meat loaf to cover, and return to oven. Bake for a further 1 hour, basting occasionally with the remaining sauce. Serve with rice. Serves 6

Garlic Sausage Meat Loaf

1 onion, finely chopped; 2 cloves garlic, crushed; 2 tbs oil; ½ cup fresh breadcrumbs; 1 egg; 1 tsp chopped parsley; ½ tsp salt; ¼ tsp pepper; 750 g (1½ lb) sausage mince; 1 tsp dried thyme or rosemary.

Cook onion and garlic in 1 tbs oil until soft but not brown. Mix together onion, garlic, breadcrumbs, egg, parsley, salt and pepper. Add sausage mince and mix well. Shape into a sausage-shaped loaf, brush with remaining oil and sprinkle with herbs. Wrap in foil and place in an ovenproof dish. Bake in a moderately hot oven (190°C/375°F) for 50 minutes. Serve hot or cold, or use as a filling for sandwiches or bread rolls. Serves 6.

MELBA TOAST

Originally created for the great diva Dame Nellie Melba, Melba toast is made with very thin slices of bread. They are baked to golden-brown crispness and make a pleasantly crunchy toast accompaniment – perfect with pâté, and as an accompaniment for creamy soups.

■ **TO PREPARE:** Toast bread slices lightly on each side and cut off crusts. Using a very sharp knife, cut each slice through the middle, producing 2 very thin slices. Cut each into 4 triangles and place on an ungreased baking tray, soft side up. Bake in a preheated, very slow oven (120°C/250°F) for about 15–20 minutes until crisp and golden.

MELON

It is hard to say whether the fragrance, the flavour or the cool refreshment of a melon is the most enjoyable thing about it. These luxurious members of the gourd family have been celebrated down the centuries as food fit for kings. There are many varieties which fall into two quite different types, musk or watermelons for eating fresh; and jam melons which have little flavour uncooked but make good jam.

A musk melon (e.g. cantaloupe or rockmelon, honeydew, Charentais) should be firm and heavy for its size. A rockmelon should have a clean scar at the stem end; any roughness or stem left on is a sign that the melon was picked before it was mature and will lack flavour. A honeydew should show a slight yellowing of the skin. There should be no moist or soft spots, but if it is fully ripe, the melon will yield slightly if pressed gently between the hands, and will be fragrant.

A watermelon should have a bloom on the skin, and the underside, where it rested on the ground, should be yellowish, not white or green. The melon should sound hollow when tapped. If buying cut melon, the flesh should be deep pink without white streaks, and the seeds very dark.

Store fully-ripe melons in a cool, airy place, or in a tightly-closed plastic bag to avoid scenting other food, in the refrigerator. Keep slightly underripe melons in a warm room for a few days before refrigerating. Always remove melon from the refrigerator 30 minutes or so before serving, as it should be only slightly chilled for best flavour.

WAYS TO USE MELON
An unadorned wedge of ripe melon, eaten in the sun, can hardly be bettered, but melon is wonderfully versatile – an excellent accompaniment to many savoury foods and superb for dessert.

- Use it, alone or with vegetables, for salads; serve it as a sambal with curries; wrap cubes of rockmelon or honeydew in thin strips of ham and serve on toothpicks as a party savoury.
- Serve with a sprinkle of lemon juice and ground ginger or mace for breakfast.
- Dice it or cut it into balls and dress with lemon juice and chopped mint for a first course.
- Cut it into thin crescents and serve with prosciutto as a classic and beautiful way to start a meal.
- Garnish chicken, lamb or seafood salad with melon.
- Use small melon halves, scooped out, as containers for ice cream or fruit salad, or a large watermelon shell to hold prepared fruits on a buffet table. Use it in fruit cups and fruit salads.
- Cut a small, deep plug out of a ripe watermelon and pour in a little gin or rum every hour or so for a day; chill overnight and serve next day as a refresher that's definitely not for children.

TO CUT MELON WEDGES: To serve a melon wedge ready to eat with a fork, scoop out the seeds with a spoon, then use a sharp knife to cut between flesh and rind, from end to end. Cut the flesh across into small blocks and pull these pieces out, alternating to left and right, to extend 2 cm (¾ in) or so beyond the edge of the rind.

TO MAKE MELON BALLS: Halve musk melons and remove seeds; cut watermelon into large wedges or slices. Leave melon on shell and, holding it in one hand, press the open side of a melon baller firmly into the flesh until the rounded side touches it. Twist the baller to cut out a neat ball of flesh.

TO VANDYKE A MELON: Vandyking or cutting a sawtooth edge is a good finish for melon halves. Mark the equator of the melon with a few toothpicks as a guide, if you wish. Place the point of a small, sharp knife at the equator and holding the knife on the slant, push it in all the way to the centre. Starting at the bottom of the first cut, make another in the same way but slanting in the opposite direction. Make the third cut from the top of the second one and continue, alternating angles, all the way round. Gently pull and twist the melon apart and remove the seeds. If the halves are to be used as shells to hold food, remove most of the flesh with a sharp spoon, leaving a wall about 1 cm (½ in) thick. Cut a very thin slice from the base to make the melon half stand level on the plate. **See recipes.**

Melon Salad

Very good with duck or ham.

1 rockmelon; 1 honeydew melon; freshly ground black pepper; ½ tsp ground ginger; juice 1 lemon or lime.

Halve melons, scoop out seeds and peel. Cut flesh into small cubes and place in a bowl. Add a small grinding of pepper and sprinkle over ginger and lemon or lime juice. Toss melon to coat, then cover and chill. Serves 6–8.

Melon, Chicory and Grape Salad

A fresh combination of textures and flavours with a good minty dressing. Serve as a light first course.

**3 heads Belgian endive or witlof,
or 2 small cos lettuce; I small rockmelon;
I cup grapes.**

**DRESSING: $3/4$ cup oil; $1/4$ cup lemon juice;
$1^1/2$ tbs finely chopped fresh mint; I tbs capers;
salt and freshly ground black pepper.**

Cut endives in quarters lengthways, then cut across in half if large. Treat lettuce the same way. Peel melon, quarter and remove seeds. Cut each quarter into 6 slices. Chill ingredients in refrigerator, then arrange melon alternately with endive on 6 salad plates. Divide grapes among salads. To make the dressing, add oil slowly to lemon juice in a small bowl, beating with a fork or whisk. Stir in mint and capers and season with salt and pepper. Spoon dressing over salads and serve at once. Serves 6.

Melon Rings with Strawberries

**I small honey dew or rockmelon, chilled;
I punnet (250g/8 oz) strawberries, chilled;
caster sugar; lime or lemon wedges.**

Cut melon into 4 thick slices, discarding ends and seeds. Peel slices and place each on an individual serving plate. Choose 4 best strawberries and set aside. Hull remainder and sprinkle with sugar. Pile strawberries into centres of melon slices, place reserved strawberries on top to decorate and serve with lime or lemon wedges. Serves 4.
NOTE: Fresh raspberries may be substituted for strawberries.

Melon and Lemon Jam

**3.5 kg (7 lb) jam melon; I tbs grated fresh ginger;
3 large or 6 small lemons, thinly sliced;
$10^1/2$ cups sugar; $1/4$ tsp cayenne,
or I tsp ginger essence.**

Peel and dice melon, removing seeds, place in a large bowl and sprinkle with fresh ginger. Add lemons, sprinkle with $1^1/2$ cups sugar, cover and stand overnight.

Next morning put mixture into a heavy pan and boil until melon is clear, about $1^1/2$ hours. Add remaining sugar and cayenne pepper or ginger essence. Boil about 20 minutes until mixture is clear and setting point is reached (when a teaspoonful, dropped on to a chilled plate and left 30 seconds, will wrinkle and stay in 2 parts if you run your finger through it). Remove from heat, cool slightly then pour into hot, sterilised jars. Cover and seal. Makes 8–10 x 500 g (1 lb) jars.

MERINGUE

There are many variations of meringue – all based on egg white and sugar beaten to a stiff froth, then baked. They include small meringues, baked in a very slow oven until light and crisp. Glamorous vacherins, dainty petits fours and mountainous fluffy pie toppings are all favourites. Meringues are usually plain but a flavouring may be added such as chopped nuts, chocolate pieces or coconut.

Meringue mixture can be shaped and used in many different ways. Small buttons or rosettes baked until dry and crisp may be joined together with whipped cream to make a delicious sweet for afternoon tea or dessert. These tiny meringues may also be used as a topping for desserts or cakes. Another popular way is to shape meringue with an oval dessertspoon or tablespoon, and these ovals may be joined with whipped cream to form an egg shape. Meringue is often made into a pie shell or basket – individual baskets are very popular, and these may be filled with fruit, whipped cream or any number of creamy desserts.

A light meringue is often piled on to a baked, sweet pie or pudding and placed in a moderately hot oven just long enough to tint the meringue; it should be soft and marshmallow-like inside; the crust may be crisp or soft, depending on the treatment. See Lemon Meringue Pie (page 232) and Lime Meringue Pie (page 237).

Another favourite meringue is the Pavlova (see page 347), which, with whipped cream and tart-sweet passionfruit or strawberries, is a dessert sweet-tooths can never resist.

■ **TO PREPARE MERINGUE:** Egg whites for meringue should be at room temperature and beaten with a pinch of salt, cream of tartar, or a few drops of lemon juice. This may be done in a copper bowl with a wire whisk or a glass bowl and electric beaters. The slightest trace of yolk in the whites will inhibit their rising (yolks contain fat). The same holds true for bowl and beater, both must be totally free of fat or grease. It is best to wash the bowl and beater with hot water and dry them with a clean, fresh towel before beating the whites.

Part of the sugar should be added gradually at first, after the whites become foamy, then the remaining sugar is folded in. The meringue has been sufficiently whipped when the whites form soft peaks and cling to the beater in a mass. You have over-beaten if they look dry and stand in sharp, jagged peaks, and the mixture will probably fall when placed in the oven.

The oven temperature should be as low as possible.

The point is to dry the meringue by getting all the moisture out of the mixture rather than baking it. A temperature of 120°C/250°F is as high as it should go. Higher than this, the meringues brown too quickly, turn leathery, and collapse. Properly baked, a meringue is crisp, feather-light, the palest bisque in colour, almost white. If liked, meringues may be dusted lightly with caster sugar before baking.

Bake meringues for about 1 hour, although they may be left in the turned-off oven to crisp. Once they are completely cool, meringues keep a long time in airtight containers. Excess moisture in the air makes them soggy, so it is best not to bake meringues on a very damp or rainy day or have anything steaming on the stove when they are out of the oven and cooling on wire racks.

The baking trays for meringues should either be lightly buttered, dusted with flour, and the excess flour tapped off, or they may be covered with non-stick cooking parchment. Baking trays coated with non-stick surfaces are also excellent.

Meringues

This basic meringue mixture may be used for tiny miniature meringues, joined together with whipped cream and set in paper cases, or used for different kinds of desserts, meringue baskets, swans, etc.

3 egg whites; scant $^1/_8$ tsp cream of tartar; I cup caster sugar.

Beat egg whites on very low speed of electric mixer until frothy. Add cream of tartar and beat on highest speed until peaks hold their shape. Gradually beat in 2 tbs sugar and continue beating for 2–3 minutes. Add all remaining sugar at once and fold in quickly and lightly with a metal spoon. Pipe on to baking trays that have been lightly oiled and floured or lined with non-stick cooking parchment. Or shape meringue mixture with 2 spoons. Bake in a preheated cool oven (120°C/250°F) for 1 hour. Ease meringues with spatula and leave in oven further 30 minutes or until dry. When cool store in an airtight container. Makes about 36.

VARIATIONS

MERINGUE SHELL: Prepare Meringue mixture as above or Meringue Cuite. Spread or pipe over bottom and sides of a greased 20–23 cm (8–9 in) pie plate, building it up on the outside edge. Bake in a preheated cool oven (120°C/250°F) for 1–1½ hours or until surface is set and crusty but only just coloured. Loosen meringue shell from pie plate while still warm, and cool before filling.

The meringue will crisp as it cools. Use for cream pies. If liked the meringue may be shaped on a baking tray lined with non-stick cooking parchment. Mark an 18–20 cm (7–8 in) circle on the paper and use this as a guide, spreading or piping meringue inside

circle, building up the outer edge. Bake as above.

INDIVIDUAL MERINGUE SHELLS: Prepare basic Meringue mixture as per recipe or Meringue Cuite. Line 3 baking trays with non-stick cooking parchment. Mark 8 cm (3 in) circles on paper, leaving at least 5 cm (2 in) space between circles. Spread or pipe meringue mixture inside circles, building up outer edges. Bake in a preheated cool oven (120°C/250°F) for 1–2 hours. Turn oven off, turn cases over and allow to cool in oven. Use as shells for fresh fruit salad with whipped cream, fruit fool, or other creamy desserts. Makes 12.

Meringue Cuite *(Cooked Meringue)*

Egg whites and sifted icing sugar are beaten over hot water for this meringue. Its advantage is that it will stay thick and firm for some time after it is made. This is a slightly old-fashioned recipe, for with modern efficient electric beaters it is possible to get the same result without heat. Icing sugar gives a smooth finish but when made in an electric mixer, caster sugar is perfectly satisfactory.

4 egg whites; I$^1/_4$ cups pure icing or caster sugar; pinch salt.

Put ingredients in a copper or heatproof glass bowl. Beat over gentle heat until very thick. Use for tiny meringues, meringue baskets, shells, etc.

Meringues Chantilly

These are so called because they are filled with Crème Chantilly (whipped, sweetened, vanilla-flavoured cream, see page 102). Meringues should be made small – just one or two bites, for afternoon teas; when served as a dessert they may be larger.

2 large egg whites; $^1/_2$ cup caster sugar.

FILLING: $^1/_2$ cup cream, I tsp caster sugar; few drops vanilla; chopped walnuts to finish (optional).

Using a rotary beater or an electric mixer, beat egg whites until they form soft peaks. Sift 2 tbs caster sugar over whites and beat again until mixture is stiff and shiny. Sift half the remaining sugar over whites and, using a large metal spoon, fold it in. To do this, cut gently down through mixture and lift some mixture up and over on to the top, repeating until whites and sugar are lightly mixed. Don't worry about mixing thoroughly; it is important not to overwork meringue or air bubbles will break down. Shaping meringues will mix whites and sugar a little more. Use 2 damp dessertspoons or tablespoons (depending on size you want meringues) to shape meringues. With one, scoop up a heaped spoonful of mixture. With other spoon, scoop meringue out on to a baking tray, that has been lightly greased and floured, or lined with non-stick cooking parchment, to form a half-egg shape. Neaten with a knife dipped in cold water. If preferred, meringue can be formed by piping, using a bag fitted with a large plain or rose tube.

Dredge with remaining sugar and bake in a preheated cool oven (120°C/250°F) for about 1 hour or until a delicate beige colour. Peel parchment off meringues, if used, or lift carefully off tray with a thin knife. Gently press base of each meringue, while still warm, to make a hollow. Replace upside-down on tray and return to oven for a further 30 minutes to complete cooking. Cool on a wire rack. An hour or two before required, whip cream with sugar and vanilla until stiff, and use to sandwich meringues together in pairs. The cream may be piped or spread on. Place in refrigerator until serving time. If you wish, sprinkle chopped walnuts on cream just before serving. Makes 12.

Fruit Meringue Pie

Make this with fresh raspberries, strawberries or other fresh or canned fruit such as plums or apricots. Be sure that canned fruits are very well drained. It may be kept in the refrigerator for 1–2 hours before serving.

4 egg whites; I cup caster sugar; $^1/_2$ cup cream; I cup sliced fresh or canned peaches; chopped pistachio nuts to decorate.

Line a baking tray with non-stick cooking parchment. Draw on it 2 circles 18 cm (7 in) in diameter. Make meringue mixture, with egg whites and all the sugar as for Meringues Chantilly. Fit a large plain or rose tube into a piping bag and fill it with meringue mixture. Pipe a ring of meringue round one circle just inside the line. Pipe on to outer edges of paper 8–12 baby rosettes with bases totalling the same width as meringue ring. Pipe remaining meringue mixture inside other circle and spread it evenly into a flat disc. Bake in a preheated cool oven (120°C/250°F) for 45 minutes to 1 hour or until crisp when tapped. Remove from oven. Lift off rosettes with a thin knife and place on a wire rack. Turn paper upside-down and carefully peel it off meringue ring and disc. (If you try to prise these pieces off the paper, they are likely to splinter.) Lift very carefully and place on a wire rack to cool.

Before serving, whip cream until stiff and fill a piping bag fitted with a 1 cm ($^1/_2$ in) rose tube. Place meringue disc on a serving plate and pipe a ring of cream round edge. Set meringue ring on top and press down very gently. Arrange peach slices inside ring in concentric circles. Pipe a little cream on base of each rosette and arrange rosettes evenly spaced on the ring, pressing each one down gently to secure. Pipe remaining cream round ring to decorate and top with chopped pistachios. Chill until serving time, Serves 8.

Meringue Pie Topping

3 egg whites; $^1/_4$ tsp cream of tartar; 5 tbs sugar.

Beat egg whites until light and frothy. Add cream of tartar and continue beating until whites are stiff enough to hold a peak. Gradually beat in sugar and beat until meringue is stiff and glossy. Pile meringue lightly on cooled pie filling, spreading it until it touches edges of pastry to prevent meringue shrinking. Bake in a preheated hot oven (220°C/425°F) until top is brown, 5–6 minutes. For a more decorative effect, use a piping bag fitted with a rose tube to pipe rosettes of meringue over pie filling. Sufficient to top a 20–23 cm (8–9 in) pie.

MESCLUN

Originating from Provence in France, mesclun is the term for mixes of tender young lettuces and other greens. The Provençale tradition calls for chervil, arugula (rocket), lettuce and endive in precise proportions. Elsewhere it is a mixture of baby greens, such as oak-leaf lettuce, tiny cos, butterhead and coral lettuce leaves along with wild or baby rocket, mizuna and snowpea shoots, depending on what is available. Even edible flowers or their petals such as calendulas, chive blossoms, marigolds, nasturtiums and violets may be part of a mesclun mix. It is a very convenient way of buying salad greens. Although the ingredients in mesclun are varied, all mescluns are noted for their tasty combination of flavour, colour and texture. Buy only as much mesclun as you need for that day. It does not keep well because of the extra handling it has received. You can mix your own. If using large leaves, tear into bite-sized pieces.

MILK

Whole milk could be regarded as closest to a complete food since it contains all essential nutrients required by the human body, including proteins, vitamins and minerals, especially calcium. Milk or milk foods should be included in the daily diet. Children and adults enjoy drinking milk. There are many lovely milk drinks, but it can be used in forms other than as a drink. Delicious soups, sauces, custards, milk jellies, junkets, scones, cakes and many other dishes use milk as a major ingredient.

Milk should always be heated slowly and cooked at low temperatures.

TYPES OF MILK

Milk is available in many different forms, depending on the methods of processing.

Fresh whole milk is packaged in cartons or bottles. It has been pasteurised to remove bacteria, and homogenised to disperse the milk fat (about 4.1%) evenly through the liquid and prevent it rising to the surface. This gives the milk a smooth, creamy texture. Keep milk refrigerated and use within 3–4 days after buying. Use according to any recipe calling for milk.

Fresh low fat milk is packaged in cartons. It contains less milk fat – usually about 2% – than whole milk. Use as for whole milk, however, it is unsuitable for babies except when given under medical advice.

Fresh skim milk is packaged in cartons. It contains little milk fat, having about 0.1% of the total content, and is excellent for use by people on low fat diets. It should not, however, be used for babies except when given under medical advice. Use according to special recipes calling for skim milk. Refrigerate after opening and use within 3–4 days.

Fresh flavoured milk is whole milk that contains added flavouring agents and sugar; the sugar increases the energy content. Refrigerate after opening and use within 3–4 days.

UHT milk (ultra high temperature milk) undergoes a special treatment where very high temperatures are used during pasteurisation for a very short time; this preserves proteins and vitamins while destroying bacteria. The milk is packaged in special containers and, unopened, has a long shelf life of about 5–6 months without refrigeration. It is best chilled before serving. Refrigerate after opening and use within 3–4 days. It can also be purchased flavoured and sweetened. Use unsweetened, unflavoured UHT milk in place of whole milk; however, the high temperature treatment alters the protein structure and destroys the enzymes, making UHT milk unsuitable for junket as it will not set.

Evaporated milk is whole milk evaporated to about 40% of the original volume. It is canned and has a very long shelf life. For the equivalent of full cream milk, add 3 parts water to 2 parts evaporated milk. To make 1 cup use a measuring jug and pour in 100 ml evaporated milk, then fill with water to 250 ml. Refrigerate after opening and when reconstituted, and use within 2 days. Use, undiluted, to enrich soups and sauces, or as a binding agent in meat loaves or meatballs. Or use as a topping on desserts and where specified in special recipes calling for evaporated milk.

Evaporated reduced fat milk has a lower milk fat content than ordinary evaporated milk. It is canned, and should be stored and treated as for fresh milk when opened. Reconstitute in the same proportion as for evaporated milk. Use in special recipes calling for evaporated reduced fat milk, or in some recipes in place of fresh whole milk such as scones, quick breads, soups and sauces.

Sweetened condensed milk is canned milk from which the water content is reduced during processing and about 40% sugar is added. The sugar acts as a preservative, and the milk will keep up to 1 week without refrigeration after opening and up to 3 weeks refrigerated. It is much sweeter than normal milk when reconstituted. Use 80 ml (⅓ cup) with water added to make up 250 ml (1 cup). Use in sweet sauces, pie fillings, and desserts which call for sweetened condensed milk.

Sweetened condensed skim milk is canned milk similar to sweetened condensed milk but with a percentage of milk fat removed. Use as specified in special recipes or reconstitute by using 80 ml (⅓ cup) and adding water to make up 250 ml (1 cup). Store and treat as for sweetened condensed milk.

Powdered full cream milk has a long shelf life. Reconstitute powder by adding water in the proportion specified on the packet or use 3 tbs (¼ cup) milk powder and add water to make up 250 ml (1 cup). The milk should then be refrigerated and used within 2 days, and the powder stored in a dry airtight container after opening. It can be substituted for fresh whole milk in most recipes, following the proportion given for reconstituting. Refrigerate milk after reconstituting and use within 3–4 days.

Non-fat skim milk powder has a long shelf life. Reconstitute powder by adding water in the proportion as specified on the packet or use 2 tbs milk powder and add water to make up 250 ml (1 cup). It is unsuitable for babies except under medical advice, but is excellent for people on low fat diets. It may also be used in recipes calling for skim milk. Store powder in a dry, airtight container. Refrigerate milk after reconstituting, and use within 3–4 days.

Milk substitutes are whitener used in tea or coffee. They are usually made from vegetable oil, coconut oil or soya beans. Other additives such as sugar, artificial colour and emulsifiers are often added as well.

See also *Buttermilk*.

Vanilla Milk Shake

Milk shakes can be made using a blender, rotary beater or wire whisk. These help give the drinks a lovely frothy topping.

1 glass chilled milk; 1 scoop vanilla ice cream; ¼ tsp vanilla; nutmeg or cinnamon to decorate (optional).

Combine ingredients and whisk, beat or blend together. Pour into a long glass and sprinkle with nutmeg or cinnamon, if liked. Serves 1.

VARIATIONS

CHOCOLATE MILK SHAKE: Substitute 2 tsp chocolate topping or syrup for vanilla; top with grated chocolate.

STRAWBERRY MILK SHAKE: Use ¼ cup fresh puréed strawberries or 2 tsp strawberry topping instead of vanilla.

BANANA MILK SHAKE: Substitute 1 mashed banana for vanilla.

PEANUT BUTTER MILK SHAKE: Substitute 1 tbs peanut butter for vanilla; sprinkle with nutmeg.

MOCHA MILK SHAKE: Use 2 tsp instant coffee powder and 2 tsp chocolate syrup or topping instead of vanilla. Use coffee or chocolate ice cream instead of vanilla. Top with instant coffee powder.

Lemon Jelly Whip

I cup evaporated milk; I packet lemon jelly crystals;
I cup hot water; $^1/_4$ cup lemon juice;
2 tbs toasted flaked almonds.

Chill evaporated milk in the freezer for 2–3 hours. Dissolve jelly crystals in hot water and allow to cool but not set. Whip evaporated milk until soft peaks form, then beat in lemon juice followed by jelly. Spoon milk mixture into 6 serving glasses and chill until set. Top with toasted flaked almonds. Serves 6.

Basic One Whip Ice Cream

I tsp gelatine; 2 tsp hot water; I tbs butter, softened;
4 tbs caster sugar; I tsp vanilla; I x 375 ml can
($1^1/_4$ cups) evaporated milk, chilled; $^1/_4$ tsp salt;
I tbs lemon juice.

Soften gelatine in hot water, then stir briskly over simmering water until thoroughly dissolved. Add butter and allow to melt. Stir in sugar and vanilla. Cool. Beat chilled evaporated milk with salt and lemon juice until thick. Gradually add cooled gelatine mixture, beating constantly. Pour into ice cream trays, cover and freeze. Makes 5–6 cups.

VARIATIONS

CHOCOLATE ONE WHIP ICE CREAM: Add $^1/_4$ cup chocolate topping to gelatine mixture.

COFFEE WALNUT ONE WHIP ICE CREAM: Dissolve 3 tsp instant coffee powder in gelatine mixture. Fold in $^1/_4$ cup chopped walnuts before freezing.

FRUIT SALAD ONE WHIP ICE CREAM: Fold in juice of 1 orange and 1 lemon, 2 sliced bananas, 1 cup sliced strawberries and the pulp of 1 passionfruit before freezing. Use as soon as frozen or fruit will develop ice crystals.

Vanilla Ice Cream

I tsp gelatine; 2 tbs cold water; $^1/_2$ cup boiling water;
I cup full cream milk powder; $^1/_4$ cup caster sugar;
I x IIO g can ($^1/_2$ cup) reduced cream;
I tsp lemon juice; I tsp vanilla.

Soften gelatine in cold water, add boiling water and stir until dissolved. Whisk in powdered milk and sugar and add reduced cream, lemon juice and vanilla. Pour into ice cream trays. Freeze until beginning to set around the sides, then remove to a chilled bowl and beat until doubled in volume. Cover and freeze until firm. Serves 6–8.

Whipped Dessert Topping

$^1/_2$ cup non-fat skim milk powder;
$^1/_2$ cup well-chilled water; 2 tbs lemon juice;
$^1/_4$ cup caster sugar; $^1/_2$ tsp vanilla.

Mix together skim milk powder and water. Beat for 3–4 minutes or until soft peaks form. Add lemon juice and beat 3–4 minutes longer or until stiff peaks form. Fold in sugar and add vanilla. Serve immediately. Makes about 2 cups.

Fluffy Topping

I x 375 ml can ($1^1/_4$ cups) evaporated milk, chilled overnight; I tsp lemon juice; vanilla; 2 tbs icing sugar, sifted (optional).

Pour milk into a large chilled bowl, add lemon juice and whip using an electric mixer or rotary beater until thick and doubled in volume. Flavour to taste with vanilla and fold in icing sugar, if using, just before serving. Use as a topping on cakes or desserts. Makes about 3 cups.

MILLE-FEUILLES

The name literally means 'a thousand leaves', and refers to the many flaky layers of crisp puff pastry used to make this beautiful French pastry. Puff pastry is layered alternately, usually with whipped cream and raspberry and strawberry jam. The top is glazed with icing or dusted with icing sugar and crushed pastry trimmings decorate the sides. Mille-feuilles are assembled as one whole cake, then cut into rectangles for serving. Crème Pâtissière (see page 207) is sometimes used instead of cream, with a thick fruit purée and a Chocolate Glaze (see page 83).

Savoury mille-feuilles make an elegant and impressive entrée, and provide an unusual variation on the traditionally sweet pastry. Make your own puff pastry (see *Pastry*), or if you prefer, use commercial frozen puff pastry. See recipes.

Mille-Feuilles

$^1/_2$ x 375 g (12 oz) packet frozen puff pastry, thawed,
or I quantity Puff Pastry (page 343);
I cup cream; 3 tbs strawberry or raspberry jam.

ICING: I cup icing sugar, sifted; $1^1/_2$ tbs water;
2–3 drops vanilla.

Roll out pastry as thin as possible to a rectangle about the size of a large baking tray. Lay this over a dampened baking tray, allowing pastry to come right up to the edges. Prick well all over and chill for 15 minutes. Bake in a preheated hot oven (200°C/400°F) for 5–10 minutes or until pale golden-brown. Using a palette knife carefully turn pastry over and bake a further 5 minutes. Remove from oven and cool on a wire rack.

When cold, trim edges and cut into 3 strips about 8 cm (3 in) wide. Crush trimmings lightly. Whip cream until it stands in soft peaks. Spread one strip of pastry with half the jam and half the cream. Lay a second pastry strip on top and press down lightly. Spread with remaining jam and cream. Top with last pastry strip. Press down lightly.

ICING: Mix icing sugar with enough water to make a creamy consistency. Add vanilla. Stir over hot water until icing is warm and glossy. Spread top pastry layer with warm icing and press crushed pastry trimmings around sides to decorate. Cut across into slices 4 cm (1½ in) wide. Makes about 8.

Savoury Mille–Feuilles

This dish is superb for a buffet party or at a luncheon. The pastry may be baked ahead of time, then reheated in the oven at the last moment and the scrambled eggs prepared but not cooked until required.

1 x 375 g (12 oz) packet frozen puff pastry, thawed or 1 quantity Puff Pastry (page 343), rolled into 2 sheets; 1 egg, beaten with 2 tsp water and pinch salt.

FILLING: 8 eggs; salt; ½ tsp white pepper; 45 g (1½ oz) butter; 250 g (8 oz) smoked fish (any kind), cooked and flaked or 125 g (4 oz) smoked salmon; 3 tbs cream; 2 tbs mayonnaise; 2 tbs snipped chives; 1 tsp grated lemon rind.

GARNISH: paper-thin slices lemon, sprays of fresh dill.

Cut each sheet of ready-rolled puff pastry in half, mark halves in a criss-cross pattern and place them on 4 dampened baking trays. Chill 10 minutes, then brush with egg wash and bake in a preheated very hot oven (200°C/400°F) for about 12 minutes or until risen and brown. Remove pastry from baking trays and cool on a wire rack. If using frozen puff pastry, divide packet into 4 and roll out each piece into a rectangle about 25 x 15 cm (10 x 6 in). Chill for 30 minutes, then brush with egg wash and bake and cool as above.

FILLING: Beat eggs, season with salt and pepper and cook gently in butter, stirring occasionally, until set. Add flaked fish and allow to cool. Fold in remaining ingredients. Choose 2 best pieces of pastry for tops of mille-feuilles. Spoon egg mixture on pastry bases and top with pastry to make 2 mille-feuilles. Garnish tops with lemon slices and arrange sprays of dill beside pastry. Use a very sharp knife to cut mille-feuilles into slices. Serves 6–8.

MINCED MEAT

The versatility of minced meat is well known to most cooks. Good quality minced meat is a bargain, being nutritionally sound, full of flavour and less expensive than many other cuts. Ready-minced meat is available from your butcher or supermarket, or, if you prefer, order a specific cut, such as chuck steak or topside, and mince it at home. Your butcher will also mince special cuts for you if you order ahead.

Beef Mince: Pure beef mince is usually sold graded according to the degree of fat included, and either finely or coarsely ground. Use fine ground, lean beef for meatballs, meat loaves, hamburgers and patties. Coarser ground mince is good for stews, pies and meat sauces. Some fat in mince is essential for flavour and to improve the texture of meat loaves, meatballs and similar dishes.

Hamburger Mince: Usually a combination of finely ground beef, lamb, pork or veal. It can be used for most recipes calling for finely minced meat.

Lamb Mince: Contains lamb meat only and is used in many Middle Eastern dishes.

Sausage Mince: Usually beef and lamb, very finely ground, with cereals and seasonings. The percentage of fat and cereal to meat is controlled by state laws. Use to extend dishes using beef mince, or to make stuffings, patties or sausage rolls.

Veal and Pork Mince: Finely ground veal and pork meat, with some pork fat for flavour. Use where recipes specify.

Always use minced meat within 24 hours of purchase, and store, loosely covered with foil, in the refrigerator. See recipes.

See also *Hamburgers, Meatballs, Meat Loaf, Pies.*

Savoury Mince

Serve this savour mince with creamy mashed potatoes or with hot buttered toast. It can be varied by adding chopped fresh herbs or a spoonful of tomato paste.

2 onions, finely chopped; 1 tbs dripping or oil; 500 g (1 lb) minced steak; 1 tbs flour; 1 tsp salt; freshly ground black pepper; 1 cup beef stock; 2 tsp Worcestershire sauce.

Fry onions in dripping or oil in frying pan until soft. Add minced steak, press down with a fork and fry until browned and crumbly. Add flour, salt and pepper and mix well. Stir in beef stock and Worcestershire sauce and bring to the boil, stirring. Reduce heat, cover and simmer gently for 30 minutes. Serves 4.

Meat and Spinach Pinwheels

1 egg; ½ tsp salt; 30 g (1 oz) butter, melted; ½ cup milk; 2 cups self-raising flour, sifted; extra melted butter for brushing; 1 cup cooked, well-drained, chopped spinach; 1 quantity Savoury Mince (see above).

Place egg in mixing bowl with salt and beat lightly. Add melted butter and milk and stir in flour with a fork. Turn out on a floured board and knead lightly. The dough should be dry enough for easy handling.

Roll out dough thinly to an oblong and brush lightly with a little melted butter. Spread spinach over, then cooled savoury mince, leaving a border of 2.5cm (1 in) clear around edges. Roll dough up loosely, enclosing filling. Moisten ends with water and pinch together. Using a sharp knife cut roll in slices 2 cm (3/4 in) thick. Place in a greased ovenproof serving dish. Brush with melted butter and bake in a preheated hot oven (200°C/400°F) for 15–20 minutes or until golden-brown. Serves 4–6.

NOTE: A scone dough may be used for this recipe if preferred. The rolls can be prepared in advance and kept, covered, in the refrigerator for a few hours before baking.

Beef and Bean Casserole

2 tbs butter; 750 g (1¹/₂ lb) minced steak;
1 onion, finely chopped; 1 x 425 g can tomatoes, drained and chopped; 1 cup hot beef stock;
125 g (4 oz) pasta shells; ¹/₂ tsp dried mixed herbs;
1 tsp chilli powder; 2 tsp Worcestershire sauce;
salt and freshly ground black pepper;
1 x 225 g can baked beans; finely chopped parsley to garnish.

Melt butter in a saucepan and brown meat and onion. Stir in all the remaining ingredients except baked beans and parsley. Mix together well and simmer gently for 30 minutes, stirring occasionally. Add more water if necessary. When meat is cooked and pasta is tender, stir in baked beans and heat through. Garnish with chopped parsley. Serves 6.

Swedish Meat Cakes

Beetroot and capers add piquancy to these little meat cakes.

750 g (1¹/₂ lb) minced beef; 1 tbs capers; 1 egg, lightly beaten; ¹/₂ cup finely chopped, cooked beetroot;
1 small onion, finely chopped; 2 slices white bread, soaked in 1 tbs milk; ¹/₄ tsp Worcestershire sauce;
¹/₂ tsp salt; freshly ground black pepper; oil.

Combine all ingredients, except oil, in a bowl, mixing well with a fork. Form into 8 flat patties, handling lightly. Grease an ovenproof dish with a little oil and place patties in it. Bake in a preheated moderate oven (180°C/350°F) for 30 minutes, turning once to brown both sides. Serve with mashed potatoes and a salad or green vegetables. Serves 4.

NOTE: These little cakes may also be pan-fried. Allow 7–8 minutes on each side.

Beef Patties with Horseradish

1 kg (2 lb) topside mince; salt and freshly ground black pepper; 1 cup fresh breadcrumbs;
60 g (2 oz) butter, softened; 3 tbs grated horseradish; 3 tbs snipped chives; oil;
chopped parsley.

SAUCE: 2 tbs lemon juice; 1 cup stock;
¹/₂ cup sour cream; salt.

Season meat with salt and pepper and fork in breadcrumbs. Cream together butter, horseradish and chives and combine with meat. The mixture should be handled lightly; do not compact it too much. Shape into 6 generous patties. Heat a little oil in a heavy frying pan, just enough oil to grease the bottom, and cook patties over a high heat for about 5 minutes on each side. The centres should still be pink, but the outsides well browned. Transfer to a heated platter and keep warm while sauce is being made. Put lemon juice and stock into frying pan and cook over a high heat until reduced to about half. Remove pan from and stir in sour cream. Heat gently, stirring in any brown bits. Season with salt. Pour sauce over patties and sprinkle with chopped parsley. Serve with creamy mashed potatoes or buttered noodles. Serves 6.

MINCEMEAT

This preserve consists of minced or finely chopped fruit and spices with the addition of brandy, rum or other spirits. It is used as a filling for sweet mince pies which are part of the traditional Christmas fare in Britain. As the name suggests, the original recipes included cooked minced meat. Today suet is the only part of meat used, but in many recipes this is replaced with butter. There are numerous treasured family recipes, all differing slightly. For example, some contain oranges, others apples, some shredded suet, others butter.

A rich mincemeat is best allowed to mature for a month or two after it is made. The brandy helps preserve the mincemeat. If butter is the fat used, the mincemeat should be stored in a cool place, or in very hot weather in the refrigerator.

Mincemeat is usually made into mince pies or mince tarts. It also makes a delicious topping for ice cream, or it can be used in fruit slices and tea loaves. Make your own mincemeat or use the commercial variety available in jars from supermarkets and delicatessens. **See recipes.**

Mincemeat

375 g (12 oz) seedless raisins; 250 g (8 oz) mixed candied peel; 185 g (6 oz) sultanas;
3 medium apples, peeled and cored;
60 g (2 oz) glacé cherries; 125 g (4 oz) blanched almonds; 100 g (3¹/₂ oz) dried apricots;
185 g (6 oz) currants; 2 cups firmly packed brown sugar, grated rind and juice 1 lemon; grated rind
1 orange; 2 tsp mixed spice; ¹/₂ tsp nutmeg;
125–185 g (4–6 oz) butter, melted;
¹/₃ cup brandy or rum.

Finely chop or mince raisins, mixed peel, half the sultanas, the apples, cherries, almonds and apricots. Add remaining sultanas and currants. Stir in brown sugar, lemon rind and juice, orange rind, spices, butter and brandy or rum. Mix well and put into a large jar. Cover and chill. Stir every day for a week. Mincemeat can be kept for a few weeks in the refrigerator. Makes about 6 cups.

NOTE: Brandy can be replaced with the juice of 1 orange in which case mixture should not be made in advance.

English Mincemeat (with suet)

250 g (8 oz) each currants, sultanas, seedless raisins and mixed candied peel; 250 g (8 oz) cooking apples, peeled and cored; 125 g (4 oz) blanched almonds, chopped; 1^1/$_2$ cups firmly packed brown sugar; 125 g (4 oz) shredded suet; ^{1}/$_2$ tsp nutmeg; ^{1}/$_2$ tsp cinnamon; grated rind and juice 1 lemon; ^{1}/$_2$ cup brandy or rum.

Finely chop currants, sultanas, raisins, mixed peel and apples. Add nuts, sugar, suet, spices and lemon rind and juice and mix all ingredients thoroughly. Cover mincemeat and leave to stand for 2 days. Add brandy or rum, stir well and put into jars. Cover and allow to mature for at least 2 weeks before using. Makes about 5 cups.

Mince Pies

Mince Pies can be made ahead, frozen and reheated when required.

90 g (3 oz) butter; ^{1}/$_4$ cup caster sugar; 1 egg; 1^1/$_2$ cups flour; ^{1}/$_2$ tsp baking powder; beaten egg to glaze; 1 cup Mincemeat (above); sifted icing sugar.

Cream butter with sugar. Add egg and beat well. Sift flour and baking powder and stir into creamed mixture. Knead lightly on floured board. Wrap dough in plastic wrap and chill for 1 hour. Roll out thin and cut into rounds to fit lightly greased patty tins. Cut same number of smaller circles to fit tops of pies. Moisten edges with beaten egg and put 1 heaped teaspoon mincemeat into each. Make a small slit in each pastry lid or cut with a small star cutter. Top each filled pie with lid and press edges of pastry well to seal. Glaze with beaten egg. Bake in a preheated moderate oven (180°C/350°F) for 20–30 minutes or until pale golden-brown. Remove from oven and dust with icing sugar. Makes about 12.

Mincemeat Tea Loaf

This loaf slices beautifully and when wrapped and stored in an airtight container will keep for several weeks. It also freezes well.

2 cups flour; ^{1}/$_2$ tsp salt; ^{1}/$_2$ tsp bicarbonate of soda; 1 tsp baking powder; 125 g (4 oz) butter; ^{2}/$_3$ cup firmly packed brown sugar; 2 eggs; 3 tbs sour light cream; 1 cup Mincemeat (see recipe); ^{1}/$_2$ cup coarsely chopped walnuts or pecans.

Sift flour, salt, bicarbonate of soda and baking powder. Cream butter with sugar until light and fluffy. Add eggs one at a time, beating well. Mix in sour cream. Gently fold in dry ingredients; do not overmix. The batter should be stiff. Stir in mincemeat and nuts. Spoon into a greased 21 x 15 cm (8^1/$_2$ x 6 in) loaf tin, pressing with the back of a spoon to pack mixture solidly in tin. Bake in a preheated moderate oven (180°C/350°F) for 50–60 minutes or until a skewer inserted in centre comes out clean. Cool on a wire rack before slicing.

Fruit Squares

This is a rich, crumbly slice, delicious with coffee.

1 cup firmly packed brown sugar; 1^1/$_2$ cups rolled oats; 1^1/$_2$ cups flour, sifted; ^{1}/$_2$ tsp salt; 185 g (6 oz) butter; 3 cups Mincemeat (opposite); 1 egg, beaten.

Combine brown sugar, rolled oats, flour and salt and mix well. Rub in butter until mixture resembles coarse breadcrumbs. Spread half mixture into a 28 x 19 cm (11 x 7^1/$_2$ in) lamington tin. Cover with mincemeat, spread remaining crumb mixture over the top. Gently brush with beaten egg. Bake in a preheated hot oven (200°C/400°F) for 20–25 minutes. Allow to cool in tin, then cut into squares, bars or diamond shapes. Makes about 20.

Mincemeat Tart

1^1/$_2$ cups seedless raisins; 3 medium apples, peeled and cored; ^{1}/$_2$ orange, including rind; ^{1}/$_2$ lemon, including rind; ^{1}/$_2$ cup cider vinegar; 1^1/$_2$ cups firmly packed brown sugar; ^{1}/$_2$ tsp salt; ^{1}/$_2$ tsp cinnamon; ^{1}/$_2$ tsp nutmeg; ^{1}/$_2$ tsp ground cloves; 1 x 20 cm (8 in) Rich Shortcrust Pastry Shell, baked (page 342).

TOPPING: 1^1/$_2$ cups cream; 1 tbs icing sugar.

Coarsely chop raisins, apples, orange and lemon. Place in an enamel-lined saucepan, add vinegar and heat to boiling point. Reduce heat and simmer for 10 minutes. Add sugar, salt, cinnamon, nutmeg and cloves and simmer 15 minutes more. Let cool. Fill pastry shell with cooled mincemeat. Whip cream, sweeten with icing sugar and pile over mincemeat filling. Serves 6–8.

NOTE: To serve hot, place filled tart in a preheated moderate oven (180°C/350°F) for 15 minutes and hand around whipped cream separately.

MINCE PIES

See *Mincemeat*.

MINESTRONE

This hearty Italian soup has a fairly broad interpretation since it varies from region to region and cook to cook. In general, the name, *minestrone*, applies to a very thick vegetable soup containing a variety of fresh and dried vegetables, further thickened with some form of pasta or rice. Minestrone are never thin, watery soups and are sometimes so thick they are eaten rather than drunk. Grated Parmesan cheese is nearly always served with minestrone, and in Genoa, the unique basil sauce Pesto alla Genovese (see page 339) is stirred into the soup just before serving.

Minestrone is almost a meal in itself; serve with plenty of crusty bread, followed with a crisp green salad and fresh fruit. Serve the soup in deep bowls so guests may stir in plenty of freshly grated Parmesan cheese. See recipes.

Minestrone Genovese

125 g (4 oz) dried haricot beans, soaked overnight and drained; 8 cups water; 2 large eggplants, peeled and diced; 500 g (1 lb) tomatoes, peeled and chopped; 1 small cabbage, very finely shredded; 2–3 small zucchini, diced or 1 cup diced pumpkin; 185 g (6 oz) mushrooms, sliced; 2–3 tbs olive oil; 90 g (3 oz) vermicelli; 2 tbs Pesto alla Genovese (page 339); grated Parmesan cheese to serve.

Put beans in a saucepan, cover with fresh water and bring to the boil. Simmer for about 1 hour or until nearly tender. Drain beans and return to pan with the 8 cups water. Add all the vegetables and the olive oil and bring to the boil. Simmer until vegetables are almost cooked, then add vermicelli and cook a further 5 minutes or until tender. Stir in pesto. Serve with plenty of freshly grated Parmesan cheese handed separately. Serves 6–8.

NOTE: You may vary the vegetables according to the season. Use peas, beans, spinach, leeks and cauliflower florets, and rice instead of vermicelli if you wish.

Minestrone Borghese

90 g (3 oz) butter; 125 g (4 oz) cooked ham, finely diced; 1 onion, finely chopped; 1 clove garlic, crushed; 2 tomatoes, peeled, seeded and chopped; 3 sticks celery, diced; 1 tsp salt; 1/4 tsp white pepper; 8 cups chicken stock; 4 potatoes, peeled and diced; 1 1/2 cups elbow macaroni or other pasta; 4 zucchini, peeled and sliced; 2 red peppers, cored, seeded and sliced; 2 sprigs fresh basil or 1 tsp dried; grated Parmesan cheese to serve.

Melt butter in a saucepan and cook ham gently until golden. Add onion and garlic and cook until translucent. Add tomatoes, cover and simmer for about 10 minutes. Stir in celery and season with salt and pepper. Add stock and bring to the boil, then reduce heat and simmer for 30 minutes. Mix in potatoes and cook for 15 minutes longer. Add pasta. Cook until nearly tender, then add zucchini, red peppers and basil and cook for a further 10 minutes. Serve with grated Parmesan cheese. Serves 8.

NOTE: If using dried basil add it with the tomatoes.

Minestrone alla Casalinga
(Home-Style Minestrone)

1/2 cup dried haricot beans, soaked overnight and drained; 3 tbs oil, 2 onions, chopped; 2 cloves garlic, crushed; 2–3 rashers bacon, rind removed and chopped; 4 tomatoes, peeled, seeded and chopped; 8 cups beef stock; 1 tsp chopped fresh marjoram; 1/2 tsp chopped fresh thyme; 2 carrots, diced; 2 potatoes, peeled and diced; 1 small turnip, diced; 1–2 sticks celery, finely sliced; 3 cups shredded cabbage; 1/2 cup macaroni pieces or small pasta shells, stars, etc.; 2 tbs chopped fresh parsley; salt and freshly ground black pepper; grated Parmesan cheese.

Put beans in a saucepan, cover with fresh water and bring to the boil. Simmer for 1 hour or until nearly tender. Drain. Heat oil in a large saucepan, add onions, garlic and bacon and sauté for a few minutes. Add tomatoes, drained beans, stock, marjoram and thyme and bring to the boil. Cover and simmer for about 2 hours. Stir in carrots and cook for about 10 minutes, then add potatoes and turnip. Cook for a few more minutes, then add celery, cabbage and pasta. Cook until pasta and all the vegetables are tender. Stir in parsley, salt, pepper and 2–3 tbs Parmesan cheese. Pass around a bowl of Parmesan cheese when serving soup. Serves 8–10.

MINT

There are over 40 varieties of mint. Peppermint and spearmint are perhaps the best known. The round-leafed common or garden mint, the one found in most gardens, originally grew as a wild mint, and is among the best of culinary mints. Spearmint (the name refers to the arrow-head shape of the leaf) is the most widely grown and is sold commercially; it is often given away when buying fresh peas or baby new potatoes, and butchers used to give it away with a leg of lamb.

Mint is one of the easiest herbs to grow; it thrives in most temperate climates, in sun or shade, but likes plenty of water. The leaves can be dried, hung in bunches or laid on a rack, so that the air circulates. Once dried, the leaves should be stripped from the stems and stored in an airtight wrapping or container or in the freezer.

A clean-tasting herb, mint gives a tangy freshness to all dishes in which it is used. It doesn't go well with other herbs or with garlic (although a notable exception is Tabouleh, the lovely parsley and mint salad made with Burghul wheat). However, it does go well with orange – try it in Duckling with Orange (see page 132) or in orange salad – and with lamb or mutton, particularly the fatty cuts. Mint doesn't really do anything for other meats, but it's good with vegetables like fresh beans, peas and potatoes, lentils, tomatoes, eggplants, carrots and mushrooms.

The French rarely, if ever, use mint flavouring except oil of peppermint in sweets, but in most other countries of the old world it is one of the most commonly used herbs. It goes into soups and sauces, omelettes and salads, lentil pureés and even tea. In India it is used in some curries (particularly potato or lamb curry), both at the beginning and end of cooking. It's also used in the cooling chutneys that accompany hot spicy dishes.

In Middle Eastern cuisine, mint is one of the most frequently used herbs. It flavours salads, such as cucumber and yogurt salad; soups; the Lebanese kibbeh, and vegetable dishes. The British like to add a sprig of mint to freshly cooked peas or new potatoes, and to serve a mint sauce or jelly with lamb or mutton. Pea soup is superb when touched with fresh mint.

Mint is one herb that can be used in sweet dishes as well – many fruit salads are better for the addition of finely chopped mint. Pineapple, mint and Kirsch make a delightful combination. And you can garnish drinks with leaves of mint, or drop them into iced tea. See recipes.

VIETNAMESE MINT: Bright green, pungent-flavoured leaves growing on stems from a small bush, Vietnamese mint is widely used in Asian cooking. It grows very easily and is available at most Asian grocers, but if unavailable peppermint or spearmint can be used (though it has quite a different flavour). It is a vital addition to Vietnamese noodle soup (pho), and as a garnish in curries and fresh spring rolls.

Mint Tea: Place fresh or dried mint leaves in a teapot (glass preferably) and pour boiling water over. Leave to infuse 4–5 minutes before serving with a lemon slice and sugar to taste.

Mint Sauce: The sharp flavour of mint sauce with roast lamb once helped counteract the fattiness of mutton in the days when mutton was more easily available than lamb. Many people still prefer roast lamb served with mint sauce to any other way. Use fresh mint leaves whenever possible as they provide a flavour that cannot be matched with dried leaves. See recipes.

Minted Green Peas

2 cups water; pinch salt; 2 sprigs fresh mint;
1 tsp sugar; 1 kg (2 lb) peas, shelled;
30 g (1 oz) butter; 1 tbs chopped fresh mint.

Bring water to the boil, add salt, mint sprigs and sugar, and stir in peas. Cook uncovered for 15 minutes or until tender. Drain peas well, refresh under cold water and return to pan with butter and chopped mint. Shake peas over a low heat until butter has completely melted. Serves 6.

Minted Potatoes en Papillote

New potatoes seasoned with butter and mint are cooked sealed in paper to capture the wonderful natural flavours.

1 kg (2 lb) small new potatoes; 60 g (2 oz) butter;
6–8 leaves fresh mint, finely chopped,
or 1 tsp dried chervil; salt.

Scrub potatoes. Fold large piece of greaseproof paper in half, then cut into a heart shape. Place potatoes on one side of paper with the butter and mint or chervil. Season with salt. Fold other side of paper over and seal edges completely by folding edge over and over in a twist. Place on a baking tray and cook in a preheated moderately hot oven (190°C/375°F) for about 40 minutes. Take to the table in the bag. Serves 6.

NOTE: An oven bag may be used to cook potatoes this way, but be sure to pierce 2 or 3 holes in bag before baking. Take to the table in a dish.

Mint Julep

A refreshing drink to serve on a hot day.

10–12 sprigs fresh young mint; 1 tsp sugar;
1 tbs hot water; crushed ice; 1/4 cup brandy, whisky,
gin or bourbon; fresh fruit in season.

Crush half the mint with the sugar using a spoon. Add water and mix until all mint flavour is extracted. Take a tumbler or a large balloon wine glass, almost fill with crushed ice and push remaining mint in, stalks downwards. Strain crushed mint mixture into glass and pour in spirit. Decorate top of the ice with small pieces of fruit in season, choosing the most colourful available. Put in a couple of drinking straws and serve. If using brandy add just a dash of rum on top. Serves 1.

Cucumber and Mint Refresher

1/3 cup seeded and chopped cucumber;
1 tbs roughly chopped fresh mint leaves;
2/3 cup chilled milk; 2/3 cup plain yogurt;
salt and freshly ground black pepper.

Put cucumber and mint into goblet of a blender with enough milk to cover blades. Blend about 30 seconds at high speed. Add remaining ingredients, blend for a few seconds and serve. Serves 2.

Mint Sauce

1/2 cup fresh mint leaves; I tbs caster sugar;
2 tbs boiling water; 3 tbs wine vinegar; pinch salt.

Finely chop the mint leaves with 1 tsp of sugar. Place in sauceboat or bowl and add boiling water. This will set the colour. Stir in remaining sugar, vinegar and salt and let mint sauce stand for 1 hour before serving to let flavours develop. Makes about 1/2 cup.

MIXED SPICE

Also known as pudding spice, a little jar of this spice-mix is very convenient for those who are addicted to spicy food or make rich fruit cakes or puddings. It is a mixture of the sweet spices used in English cookery – cinnamon, cloves and nutmeg – but it may also contain Jamaica pepper or allspice and sometimes coriander, depending on the manufacturer's recipe.

See *Fruit Cake* and *Christmas Pudding*.

MOCHA

A strongly flavoured coffee, originally grown in the Yemen. Most people find it too rich so it is usually blended with milder coffee beans to make a suitable mix.

The word 'mocha' is also used to describe cakes, desserts, biscuits, etc., flavoured with coffee. It is often applied as well to a mixture of coffee and chocolate, whether it is used as a beverage or flavouring. See recipes.

Mocha Chiffon Pie

I cup milk; I tbs gelatine; 60 g (2 oz) semi-sweet chocolate; 3/4 cup sugar; 1/4 tsp salt;
4 eggs, separated; I tsp vanilla;
2 tbs instant coffee powder;
I x 23 cm (9 in) Sweet Rich Shortcrust
Pastry Shell, baked (page 342).

Put milk in top part of double saucepan. Sprinkle gelatine on milk and soften for 5 minutes. Add chocolate and stir over medium heat until melted and gelatine has dissolved. Beat 1/4 cup sugar and the salt with the egg yolks. Beat in chocolate milk and pour back into double saucepan. Put over simmering water and cook, stirring constantly, until mixture is thickened and coats a metal spoon. Remove from heat and add vanilla and coffee. Chill until thickened but not firm. Beat egg whites until foamy. Gradually add remaining sugar, beating until stiff but not dry. Fold into gelatine mixture. Pile lightly into pastry shell and chill until firm. Serve plain, or spread with sweetened whipped cream. If desired, sprinkle with shaved chocolate, freshly grated nutmeg, chopped candied ginger, flaked coconut or chopped nuts. Serves 6–8.

Mocha Sundae Sauce

125 g (4 oz) semi-sweet chocolate; 2 cups sugar;
2 x 375 ml can (I 1/2 cups) evaporated milk; pinch salt; 2 tbs instant coffee powder; I tsp vanilla.

Melt chocolate in double saucepan over boiling water; stir in sugar. Add evaporated milk and salt. Cover and cook very gently over boiling water for 15–20 minutes. Beat until smooth. Stir in instant coffee and vanilla. Makes 3 cups.

Mocha Chocolate

60 g (2 oz) semi-sweet chocolate; 3/4 cup water;
1/3 cup sugar; 2 1/2 cups milk;
3/4 cup double-strength black coffee; I tsp vanilla.

Put chocolate, water and sugar in saucepan and bring to the boil, stirring until chocolate has melted. Boil for 2 minutes, stirring constantly. Reduce heat and gradually stir in milk. Add coffee and heat to scalding (do not boil). Stir in vanilla. Makes 4 cups.

Frozen Mocha Mousse

125 g (4 oz) semi-sweet chocolate; 1/3 cup water; 3/4 cup sugar; 1/8 tsp salt; 3 egg yolks; I tbs instant coffee powder; I tsp vanilla; 2 cups cream, whipped.

Put chocolate and water in saucepan. Bring to the boil over low heat, stirring until chocolate has melted. Add sugar and salt and simmer for 3 minutes, stirring. Gradually stir into well-beaten egg yolks. Add coffee and cool. Fold in vanilla and cream. Pour into ice cream trays and freeze until firm. Serves 6.

Mocha Rum Punch

2 cups hot milk; I cup hot strong black coffee;
4 tbs drinking chocolate powder; 1/2 cup rum;
1/2 cup cream, whipped with I tbs sugar.

Beat together milk, coffee, chocolate and rum. Fold in sweetened whipped cream. Serve at once. Serves 6.

MOCK CREAM

A mixture that is similar to fresh cream and can be used as a substitute in certain dishes. Nothing can beat real cream, although some mock cream fillings are especially good for buns and cakes. **See recipes.**

Mock Cream

I cup milk; I tbs cornflour; pinch salt;
45 g (I 1/2 oz) butter; I tbs caster sugar; 1/2 tsp vanilla.

Bring all but 2 tbs milk to the boil in a heavy saucepan. Mix cornflour and salt well with reserved cold milk and add to boiling milk. Cook for 3 minutes, stirring, then allow to cool. Beat butter, sugar and vanilla to a cream. Take skin off top of cold milk mixture and add milk a spoonful at a time to butter mixture. Beat well until all is incorporated and mixture is consistency of whipped cream. Makes about 1½ cups.

Mock Whipped Cream

1 tsp gelatine; 3 tsp water; 125 g (4 oz) butter; ½ cup sugar; pinch salt; vanilla or lemon essence; ¼ tsp cream of tartar.

Soften gelatine in water then stir over simmering water until dissolved. Place butter, sugar, salt and flavouring in a bowl. Beat slightly, then add cream of tartar followed by dissolved gelatine. Whip well for about 10 minutes or until mixture is like whipped cream. Use as a filling for puffs, sponges and buns. Makes about 2 cups.

Washed Mock Cream

125 g (4 oz) butter; ½ cup sugar; vanilla.

Cream butter with sugar until light and fluffy (this may be done by hand or with an electric beater). Pour in about 1 cup cold water, give a light beat, then pour off water. Beat again, pour on more water, beat lightly then pour off water. This is repeated until mixture is light and fluffy and there are no sugar grains left in the cream. Flavour with vanilla. Use to fill cakes, buns, etc. Makes about 1½ cups.

MOLASSES

A dark heavy syrup which is a by-product of the various boiling-down processes used to produce sugar finally from sugar cane. There are three main types: light un-sulphured molasses, which is the syrup separated from young sugar canes; dark, sulphured molasses, a direct by-product of sugar manufacture (sulphur fumes are used in the making of sugar, hence the presence of sulphur in molasses); and blackstrap molasses, a dark, bitter syrup which is the residue of a third boiling process to extract most sugar crystals.

Light molasses, although used in cooking, is more often served over waffles, pancakes, muffins or ice cream as a table syrup. Dark molasses is used as an ingredient in recipes, while blackstrap molasses is a popular health food as well as being and additive used in cattle food, and in industry.

Sorghum molasses, as the name implies, is made from the seeds of sorghum grass native to tropical Africa and Asia. The syrup is thinner and more sour than cane molasses.

Molasses is used in making some of the great traditional dishes of the USA such as Boston Baked Beans (see page 394) and Indian Pudding (opposite) from New England. It also makes a delicious sauce for pancakes, and an unusual spicy barbecue sauce that's excellent with barbecued pork spare ribs. Molasses will keep after opening for up to 2 months if tightly covered in the refrigerator. You can buy molasses in jars at some supermarkets or health food shops. **See recipes.**

Molasses Johnnycake

This is a type of cornbread. Delicious cut in squares and served warm with butter.

1 cup flour, sifted; 3 tsp baking powder; 1 tsp salt; 1 cup yellow cornmeal (polenta); 1 egg, beaten; ¼ cup dark molasses; 1 cup milk; ¼ cup butter, melted.

Sift flour, baking powder and salt into a bowl. Mix in cornmeal. Combine egg, molasses and milk, and stir into dry mixture. Blend in melted butter. Pour into greased 20 cm (8 in) square tin. Bake in a preheated hot oven (200°C/400°F) for 25–30 minutes.

Barbecue Sauce

Serve as a sauce with barbecued or baked pork spare ribs, barbecued steak or chicken, or use as a basting sauce during cooking.

½ cup dark molasses; ½ cup mild prepared mustard; ½ cup cider vinegar.

Mix ingredients together well and heat gently until just warm. Makes 1½ cups.

Indian Pudding

This traditional dessert from New England in America was made to celebrate the native Americans' gifts of corn.

4–5 cups milk; ⅓ cup cornmeal (polenta); ¾ cup dark molasses; 125 g (4 oz) butter; 1 tsp salt; 1 tsp ground ginger; 3 tbs sugar; 1 egg, beaten; ½ cup raisins; ½ tsp cinnamon.

Place 4 cups of the milk in the top of a double saucepan over direct heat and bring to the boil. Stir in cornmeal. Place over boiling water and cook, stirring, for about 15 minutes. Stir in molasses and cook for a further 5 minutes. Remove from heat and mix in butter, salt, ginger, sugar, egg, raisins and cinnamon. Pour batter into a well-greased baking dish. If you would like the pudding to have a soft centre pour over the remaining milk. Bake in a preheated moderately slow oven (160°C/325°F) for 1½–2 hours. Serve hot with whipped cream. Serves 8.

Molasses Pancake Sauce

½ cup dark molasses; 1 cup honey; 1 cup golden syrup; 125 g (4 oz) butter; ¼ tsp salt; 1 tsp vanilla, or 2 tsp lemon juice.

Place all ingredients except vanilla or lemon juice in a heavy saucepan. Heat gently, stirring occasionally, until mixture is well combined and hot but below boiling point. Remove from heat and stir in vanilla or lemon juice. Serve poured over pancakes. Makes about 2 cups.

MOUSSAKA

Moussaka is made in many Mediterranean countries, each with a slight variation. But the main ingredients remain the same – a vegetable, usually eggplant, minced lamb (or beef) and a custard-like topping which can be a Béchamel sauce, sour cream or plain yogurt flavoured with cheese, and egg beaten into the mixture to give the characteristic texture. See recipes.

Moussaka

1 large eggplant, thickly sliced; salt; 2 tbs olive oil; 1 large onion, chopped; 1 clove garlic, finely chopped; 500 g (1 lb) minced lamb or steak; 1 tsp flour; ³/₄ cup beef stock; freshly ground black pepper; 500 g (1 lb) tomatoes, peeled and sliced, or 1 x 470 g can tomatoes, drained and sliced; 2–3 tbs grated Parmesan cheese.

SAUCE: 30 g (1 oz) butter; 2 tbs flour; 1¹/₄ cups milk; salt and freshly ground black pepper; 1¹/₂ cups grated Cheddar cheese (Red Malling is excellent); 2 egg yolks, beaten.

Score eggplant slices slightly, place in a dish and sprinkle liberally with salt. Cover with a plate and leave for several hours. Heat 1 tbs oil in a frying pan and gently fry onion and garlic until golden. Add meat, sprinkle with flour and stir for a few minutes, then pour in stock. Season with salt and pepper. Cook gently for a few minutes, stirring constantly. Turn into a greased ovenproof dish. Place tomatoes on top of meat mixture. Drain eggplant slices, rinse well and dry on paper towels. Heat remaining oil in pan in which meat was cooked and fry eggplant slices until golden on both sides. Drain and place on top of tomato slices.
SAUCE: Melt butter in a saucepan, stir in flour and cook over a gentle heat, stirring for 2 minutes. Add milk and stir until sauce boils and thickens. Season with salt and pepper, then stir in cheese until melted. Remove from heat and whisk in egg yolks.

Pour sauce over eggplant slices in casserole and sprinkle with the Parmesan. Bake in a preheated moderately hot oven (190°C/375°F) for about 40 minutes or until top is golden. Serves 8–10.
VARIATIONS
MOUSSAKA WITH YOGURT TOPPING: Prepare Moussaka as above but replace sauce with the following mixture: beat together 2 eggs, blend in 2 tbs flour, and whisk in 1 cup plain yogurt.
MOUSSAKA WITH SOUR CREAM TOPPING: Prepare Moussaka with Yogurt Topping, substituting Sour Cream for yogurt.

Potato Moussaka

A popular Greek variation of moussaka. Good eaten hot or cold.

4 tbs olive oil; 750 g (1¹/₂ lb) potatoes, peeled and finely sliced; 1 large onion, finely chopped; 1 kg (2lb) minced beef or lamb; 1 tbs chopped fresh oregano, or 1 tsp dried; 2 tbs tomato paste; 1 tsp Worcestershire sauce; 2 cloves garlic, crushed; salt and freshly ground black pepper; 4 tbs grated Parmesan cheese.

SAUCE: 30 g (1 oz) butter; 2 tbs flour; 1¹/₄ cups milk; 1 egg, lightly beaten; salt and freshly ground black pepper.

Heat 3 tbs of oil in a frying pan and cook potatoes for 2 minutes on each side; it will be necessary to cook these in 2 or 3 batches. Heat remaining oil in another frying pan or a saucepan and fry onion very gently for about 5 minutes. Add meat, oregano, tomato, pasta, Worcestershire sauce, garlic, salt and pepper to the onion and cook gently for 15 minutes, stirring occasionally. Line a 2-litre (8-cup) casserole with most of potato slices. Put half the meat mixture in the casserole, cover with a layer of remaining potatoes and add rest of meat. Sprinkle over cheese.
SAUCE: Melt butter in a saucepan, blend in flour and cook for 1 minute, then add milk gradually, stirring over a moderate heat until sauce thickens. Remove from heat. Add egg and season with salt and pepper.

Pour sauce over contents of casserole and cover with a lid. Cook in a preheated moderate oven (180°C/350°F) for 45 minutes. Serves 8–10.

MOUSSE

The French name for foam or froth. A mousse is a rich, airy mixture which depends on whisked egg white, whipped cream, or both for its lightness and velvety texture. A mousse can be sweet or savoury; hot, cold or frozen. It can be unmoulded for serving or served in the individual pots or larger dish in which the mousse is set. See recipes.

See also *Apricot Mousse* and *Chocolate Mousse* (pages 10 and 83).

Salmon Mousse

1 tbs gelatine; ¹/₄ cup cold water; 2 tsp sugar; 1 tsp salt; 1 tsp dry mustard; ¹/₄ cup white vinegar; 2 cups drained, flaked, canned red salmon; 1 cup finely diced celery; 2 tsp capers; ¹/₂ cup cream, whipped; fresh dill or tiny lettuce leaves to garnish.

SOUR CREAM SAUCE: ¹/₂ cup sour cream; 1 tbs grated onion; ¹/₂ tsp salt; freshly ground white pepper; 1 tsp horseradish relish (optional); 2 tsp vinegar; paprika.

Sprinkle gelatine over water in a small saucepan. Soften 2 minutes Add sugar, salt, mustard and vinegar, and stir over low heat until gelatine has dissolved. Remove from heat and chill to consistency of unbeaten egg white. Fold in salmon, celery and capers, then fold in whipped cream. Turn into a wetted 4-cup mould or individual moulds and chill until firm. Meanwhile, make sauce. Combine all ingredients except paprika and chill well. Sprinkle with paprika just before serving. Unmould mousse on to serving plate and garnish with dill or lettuce. Serve with sauce. Serves 4.

Tomato Mousse

I kg (2 lb) ripe tomatoes, peeled, seeded and coarsely chopped; 2 tsp tomato paste; salt and freshly ground black pepper; 6 tsp gelatine; 1/2 cup water; 3/4 cup cream; I tbs finely chopped fresh basil, or 2 tsp finely chopped fresh mint; sprigs fresh basil or mint or cherry tomatoes, to garnish.

Place tomatoes in a blender or food processor with tomato paste, salt and pepper and purée until smooth. Sprinkle gelatine over water in a small heatproof bowl and soften, then place bowl over simmering water and stir until dissolved. Stir gelatine mixture into tomato purée. Lightly whip cream and fold into mixture with chopped basil or mint. Spoon into 6 wetted moulds and refrigerate until set. Unmould on to chilled plates and serve garnished with basil, mint or cherry tomatoes. Serves 6.

Hot Ham and Chicken Mousse

375 g (12 oz) cooked chicken meat; 250 g (8 oz) lean cooked ham; salt and freshly ground black pepper; I tbs grated onion; I tbs Dijon mustard; 3 egg whites; I cup cream.

Place chicken and ham in a food processor fitted with the steel blade, and process until smooth. Add salt, if needed, pepper, onion and mustard. Process until well mixed, then add egg whites and process again until smooth. Turn mixture into a bowl and chill 30 minutes. Whip chilled cream until it forms soft peaks and fold into chicken mixture. Turn into a well-buttered 6-cup mould, place in a roasting tin of warm water and cover with a sheet of buttered greaseproof paper. Bake in a preheated moderately hot oven (190°C/375°F) for 40 minutes or until a skewer inserted in centre comes out clean. Unmould on to a heated serving plate and serve with Poulette Sauce or Sauce Suprême (see *Sauces*). Serves 6–8.

Tarama and Cream Cheese Mousse

Tarama is salted roe of grey mullet available from delicatessens. This tangy mousse can be served with sauce as a first course, or with toast points to accompany drinks.

1 1/2 tsp gelatine; 1 1/2 tsp dry sherry; 4 tbs tarama; 235 g (4 oz) cream cheese, softened; 1/3 cup plain yogurt; 1/2 cup sour cream; I tbs lemon juice; 1 1/2 tbs finely chopped fresh dill, or 2 tsp dried; 1/2 cup cream; salt and freshly ground black pepper; sprigs fresh dill, lemon twists or red caviar to garnish.

SAUCE: 1/4 cup plain yogurt; 1/3 cup cream; 2 tbs finely chopped fresh dill or finely chopped cucumber; salt and freshly ground black pepper.

Sprinkle gelatine over sherry in a small bowl and soften. Place bowl over simmering water and stir until gelatine has dissolved. Beat tarama and cream cheese with an electric mixer or rotary mixer until light and fluffy. Add yogurt, sour cream, gelatine mixture and lemon juice and beat until well combined. Stir in dill. Whip cream until it forms soft peaks and fold into tarama mixture. Season with salt and pepper and turn into a wetted 2-cup mould or serving dish, or divide among 6 individual moulds or ramekins. Cover and chill until set. Unmould on to chilled plates, or serve in dishes, garnished with dill, lemon twists or caviar. For sauce, combine all ingredients, seasoning with salt and pepper. Serves 6.

Caramel Mousse

CARAMEL: 1/2 cup sugar; 1/4 cup plus I tbs cold water.

MOUSSE: 1 1/2 tsp gelatine; 2 tbs water; 5 eggs, separated; 2 tbs caster sugar; I tsp vanilla; 1 1/3 cups cream.

DECORATION: whipped cream, strawberries.

To make caramel, combine sugar and 1 tbs water in a small saucepan and stir until sugar dissolves. Increase heat and cook, rotating pan gently, until a rich brown caramel forms. Remove from heat and, protecting your hand with a cloth, gradually stir in remaining water to dilute caramel. Cool 5 minutes.

MOUSSE: Sprinkle gelatine over water and allow to soften, then stir into caramel mixture until dissolved. Beat egg yolks, sugar and vanilla with an electric mixer until thick and lemon coloured. With motor still running, add caramel mixture in a stream, and beat until mixture is thick and fluffy. Whip cream just until it holds firm peaks and fold into caramel mixture. Beat egg whites until they hold soft peaks. Gently but thoroughly fold caramel mixture into whites. Turn mixture into a 6–8-cup serving dish or 6–8 individual dishes. Cover and chill until set. Serve decorated with whipped cream and strawberries. Serves 6–8.

MOUSSELINE

A French word meaning muslin, which is the name given to various preparations that are feather-light as the delicate fabric. Mousselines of fish, poultry or meat are small moulds of the main ingredient, beaten with egg whites and cream, and cooked in a bain marie (water bath). Mousseline Potatoes are puréed potatoes beaten with boiling milk to a consistency of lightly whipped cream (see page 382). Basic sauces which have been lightened by the addition of whipped cream are also described as mousseline, e.g. Mayonnaise Mousseline or Hollandaise Mousseline (the latter often called simply Sauce Mousseline).

See also *Sauces*.

Scallop Mousselines

Other shellfish or fresh fish may be used to make these delicate mousselines.

375 g (12 oz) fresh scallops; salt and freshly ground white pepper; nutmeg; 3 egg whites; 2 cups sour cream.

Remove any dark beards from scallops and place them in a food processor fitted with the steel blade. Add 1 tsp salt and a pinch each of pepper and nutmeg and process until smooth. Add egg whites and process again until smooth. Put container in refrigerator and chill 30 minutes. Return container to processor, switch on motor and pour chilled cream through feed tube. When cream and scallop mixture are combined, switch off. Adjust seasoning, return container to refrigerator and chill 1 hour.

To make mixture by hand, finely mince scallops, place in a bowl and add seasonings. Break up egg whites with a fork and add them gradually to scallops, beating vigorously with a wooden spoon to make a smooth, pliable paste. Cover bowl, place in refrigerator and chill thoroughly, then set bowl over ice and add chilled cream a little at a time, beating thoroughly with a wooden spoon. Adjust seasoning.

Fill 6 buttered ½-cup moulds to brim with mousseline mixture and smooth tops. Place moulds in a large roasting tin and add enough warm water to come halfway up sides of moulds. Cover with a sheet of buttered greaseproof paper and bake in a preheated moderate oven (180°C/350°F) for 10–12 minutes or until a skewer inserted in the centre of a mousseline comes out clean. Turn mousselines out on to heated plates and serve with a sauce such as Beurre Blanc or Velouté (see *Sauces*). Serves 6 as a first course.

NOTE 1: The mousselines may be cooked 24 hours ahead and chilled, covered. To serve, place moulds in a roasting tin of hot water and cover as before, reheat in a preheated hot oven (200°C/400°F) for 10 minutes.

NOTE 2: The coral from the scallops may be removed, poached separately for 30 seconds in white wine, and used to garnish the mousselines. Or the corals can be puréed and added to the sauce.

VARIATION

CHICKEN MOUSSELINES: Make as per recipe, substituting 500 g (1 lb) boneless breast of chicken for the scallops. After egg whites have been added, work mixture through a sieve to remove small sinews. Place mixture in a bowl over ice, then beat in cream a little at a time, as described.

MUESLI

Muesli is a breakfast enjoyed by millions of people throughout the world. The Bircher-Muesli breakfast, formulated by Dr Bircher-Benner in his wonderful sanatorium in the Swiss Alps, was an attempt to make a food as perfect as possible. Muesli is based on a mixture containing raw cereal, such as oats, to which is added dried fruit, bran or wheat germ and sometimes nuts and raw sugar. It is eaten with milk or cream and fresh fruit, usually at breakfast.

Thousands of Swiss thrive upon it, and people from all over the world go to Zurich to eat it at 7 o'clock in the morning and again at 6 o'clock at night. Dr Bircher-Benner believes that the main meal of the day should be taken at noon.

Today, muesli is prepared commercially in many varying forms. It is simple to make, many families developing their own special recipe. **See recipes.**

Muesli

By using the whole apple, skin and all, you increase the minerals in muesli and make it a really 100% natural breakfast. The addition of 1 tbs toasted chopped nuts – almonds, hazelnuts, brazils – can provide a crunch and additional protein.

6 tbs whole oats; 6 tbs water; juice ½ lemon; 2 tbs cream; 3 apples, cored; honey.

Soak oats in the water overnight. In the morning add lemon juice and cream and mix well. Shred apples into oats, sweeten with honey to taste and stir. Serve at once. Serves 4.

Swiss Muesli

Also known as Swiss Health Breakfast. Store wheatgerm in the freezer as this is one food that quickly goes rancid. It is easy to take out enough for each day as you need it. There are as many variations of the Swiss Health Breakfast as there are fruits on the market. Fresh grapes, peaches, bananas, or any other favourite fruit can be mashed or shredded into the cereal.

1 tbs fresh wheatgerm; 1 tbs whole oats; 5 tbs water; 1 tsp lemon juice; honey; cream or milk; 1 apple, cored; chopped nuts (optional).

Soak wheatgerm and oats in the water overnight in the refrigerator. Next morning, add lemon juice, honey and cream or milk and mix well. Shred apple into this, stir and serve at once. Scatter a handful of chopped nuts on top if you like – it makes the cereal more nutritious. Serves 1.

Toasted Muesli

3 cups quick cooking oats; ¹/₂ cup dried apricots, finely chopped; ¹/₂ cup sultanas; ³/₄ cup fresh wheatgerm; ¹/₂ cup raw sugar.

TO SERVE: apples; milk or cream.

Toast oats in a preheated moderate oven (180°C/350°F) for 8–10 minutes. Place oats in a bowl and add apricots, sultanas, wheatgerm and sugar. Mix well. Store in a tightly covered container at room temperature. Serve 3–4 tbs muesli in individual cereal bowls, grate 1 apple over each serving and add milk or cream. Serves 4.

MUFFINS (AMERICAN)

These are one of America's nicest gifts to the culinary world. They are light little quick breads, baked in deep, round tins and served hot for breakfast, with coffee, or with soups or salads.

It is important to remember when mixing American muffins that the liquid ingredients should be mixed into the dry ones with a few swift strokes, just enough to moisten the flour – the mixture should still be lumpy. Overmixing will produce tough, coarse-textured muffins. Spoon the mixture into each tin in one large spoonful, pushing it off with the spoon held low, to avoid stretching the elastic gluten strands in the flour. See recipes.

Basic American Muffins

2 cups flour; 1 tbs baking powder; ¹/₄ tsp salt; 2 tbs sugar; 1 egg, lightly beaten; 1 cup milk; 60 g (2 oz) butter, melted.

Sift dry ingredients into a large bowl. Mix egg, milk and butter together, pour over dry ingredients and mix just until flour is moistened; batter should still be lumpy. Spoon into 12 well-greased ¹/₃-cup muffin tins, filling each one two-thirds full. Bake in a preheated hot oven (200°C/400°F) for 20–25 minutes or until well risen and golden-brown. Makes 12.

VARIATIONS

NUT OR FRUIT MUFFINS: Follow recipe for Basic Muffins, but use ¹/₄ cup sugar and add ¹/₂ cup chopped nuts or dried fruit to the dry ingredients before mixing in liquid. Chopped pecans, walnuts, dried apricots, raisins or mixed dried fruit may be used. After filling muffin tins, sprinkle with sugar.

WHOLEMEAL MUFFINS: Follow recipe for Basic Muffins, using 1 cup of wholemeal and 1 cup white flour.

WHOLEMEAL ORANGE MUFFINS: Follow method for Basic Muffins, using 1 cup wholemeal flour; 1 cup white flour; 1 tbs baking powder; ¹/₄ tsp salt; ¹/₂ cup firmly packed brown sugar; juice 2 oranges; grated rind 1 orange; 2 eggs; and 60 g (2 oz) butter, melted.

BACON OR HAM MUFFINS: Follow recipe for Basic Muffins, reducing sugar to 1 tbs and adding 3 rashers bacon, fried crisp and crumbled, or ¹/₂ cup finely chopped cooked ham, to dry ingredients before mixing in liquid.

Buttermilk Corn Muffins

1 cup flour; 1 cup yellow cornmeal (polenta); 2 tsp baking powder; 1 tsp bicarbonate of soda; 1 tsp salt; 1¹/₂ cups buttermilk; 2 eggs, lightly beaten; 60 g (2 oz) butter, melted.

Sift dry ingredients into a large bowl. Combine buttermilk, eggs and melted butter, pour over dry ingredients and mix just until flour is moistened; batter should still be lumpy. Spoon into 12 well-greased ¹/₃-cup muffin tins, filling each two-thirds full. Bake in a preheated hot oven (200°C/400°F) for 20–25 minutes or until well risen and golden-brown. Makes 12.

MUFFINS (ENGLISH)

These flat, round, unsweetened yeast cakes were sold for many years in the streets of London and other English towns by the muffin man, with his tray and bell. Now they are available, packaged, at most supermarkets and deli-catessens. Muffins are one of the great traditional foods of the English tea. They should be pulled apart (not cut), toasted, buttered and served hot.

They are useful, too, as a base for almost any topping, sweet or savoury. Perhaps their finest hour is as the base for Eggs Benedict, invented at Brennan's Restaurant in New Orleans, USA, as part of the famous 'Breakfast at Brennan's', a leisurely feast which may last most of the day. See recipes.

Eggs Benedict

4 slices cooked ham; 2 English muffins; butter; 4 eggs; 1 quantity warm Hollandaise Sauce (page 459).

Trim ham slices to fit muffins. Fry ham in a little butter until lightly browned. Keep warm. Split and toast muffins. Poach eggs. Butter muffins lightly and place 2 halves each on 2 heated plates. Top each muffin half with a slice of ham, then with a hot poached egg and lastly with hollandaise sauce. Serve immediately. Serves 2.

Hamburger Muffins

When hamburger patties are cooked directly on muffins, all the good juices are absorbed.

$^1/_4$ **cup rolled oats; $^1/_4$ cup evaporated milk; 500 g (1 lb) minced steak; 1 tsp salt; freshly ground black pepper; $^1/_4$ tsp dry mustard; 1 small onion, grated; 1 egg, lightly beaten; 3 English muffins; butter; chutney.**

To make hamburgers, place rolled oats and milk in a blender or food processor and process until oats are finely chopped (or chop oats by hand and mix thoroughly with milk). Lightly mix oats, meat, salt, pepper, mustard and onion in a large bowl, then stir in egg with a fork. Using wet hands, shape into 6 patties the same diameter as a muffin. Split muffins in half and toast both sides under grill. Spread with butter then with chutney. Put a hamburger patty on each muffin and smooth it out to cover top. Pinch it down round edge of muffin so it will not shrink away during cooking. Cook under a preheated medium grill for 10–12 minutes. Serve at once. Serves 6.

Cheese and Bacon Muffins

A good spur-of-the-moment snack if you have muffins in the freezer. These are splendid for picnics, too – wrap in foil then in a tea-towel to keep them warm.

6 English muffins, white or wholemeal; 3 rashers bacon, rind removed and chopped; $^1/_2$ cup milk; 185 g (6 oz) Swiss or other mild cheese, grated; freshly ground black pepper; dash Worcestershire sauce; melted butter.

Split muffins in half and pull out some of the crumb. Fry bacon crisp in frying pan. Remove pan from heat and stir in crumbs, milk, cheese, pepper and Worcestershire sauce. Fill muffins with mixture, press halves together and secure with wooden toothpicks. Brush tops with melted butter and bake in a preheated moderate oven (180°C/350°F) for 15 minutes. Remove toothpicks and serve warm. Serves 6.

Sunday Breakfast Muffin

Serve with orange juice and coffee.

4 English muffins; 45 g (1$^1/_2$ oz) butter, softened; 3 rashers bacon, rind removed and finely chopped; 3 tbs peanut butter; 1 tbs crushed nuts; 2 tbs honey, golden syrup or maple syrup.

Split and toast muffins. Meanwhile, mix all other ingredients together. Spread over muffin halves and cook under a preheated medium grill until bacon is crisp and topping brown and bubbly. Serve immediately. Serves 4.

Muffin Pizzas

Muffins make a good base for individual pizzas

6 English muffins; 3 tbs olive oil; 250 g (8 oz) minced steak, sausage mince or finely chopped salami; 1 clove garlic, crushed; 3 tbs tomato paste; 1 tbs chopped fresh oregano, or 1 tsp dried; salt and freshly ground black pepper; 12 thick slices mozzarella or other mild cheese.

GARNISH: Sliced black or green olives; halved anchovy fillets; strips of green or red pepper.

Split muffins, toast lightly and brush with olive oil. Brown meat and garlic in remaining oil, breaking down lumps of minced steak or sausage mince with a fork. Stir in tomato paste and oregano and season with salt and pepper. Cover each muffin half with meat mixture and top with a slice of cheese. Arrange olives, anchovies or pepper strips on top and bake in a preheated moderately hot oven (190°C/375°F) for 10 minutes or until muffins are heated through and cheese melted. Makes 12.

MULBERRY

A juicy, mild-flavoured berry which grows in many gardens on large, beautiful trees. Unripe mulberries are red, ripe ones purple-black and should be handled with care as the juice is deeply staining. They are good to eat fresh, with a little sugar and lemon juice to bring out the flavour. They also make a splendid pie and can replace other berries in recipes such as Summer Pudding (see pages 518–19). Mulberry jelly is a particularly good preserve. See recipes.

Mulberry Jelly

Slightly underripe mulberries, washed and stalks removed; sugar, warmed.

Put mulberries into a heavy saucepan and cover with cold water. Bring slowly to the oil, mashing down well to extract juice. Simmer gently for about 1 hour or until pulp is very soft. Strain through a colander lined with several layers of cheesecloth, set over a bowl. Do not press pulp, but allow juice to drip through slowly. Measure juice by transferring it from the bowl to a saucepan with a cup measure. Do not use sediment. Bring juice to the boil and add 1 cup sugar for every cup of juice. Stir until sugar is dissolved, then bring back to boil and boil until setting point is reached. Pour into clean, warm jars and seal.

m

Mulberry Pie

5 cups fresh mulberries, stalks removed,
or 4 cups mulberries and I large Granny Smith
apple, peeled, cored and finely sliced;
I¹/₂ tbs cornflour; ¹/₂ cup plus 2 tsp caster sugar;
2 tbs lemon juice; I quantity Sweet Rich Shortcrust
Pastry (page 342).

Toss fruit gently with cornflour and ½ cup sugar,
then with lemon juice. Place in a 4-cup pie dish,
mounding it up in the middle. Roll out pastry to a
shape 4 cm (1½ in) larger than top of dish. Cut off a
1 cm (½ in) strip all round, dampen rim of dish and
press pastry strip on rim. Cut off excess and press join
together. Brush strip with a little water, then lift
remaining pastry with rolling pin and lay over the
top. Press edge down lightly and trim off excess
pastry. Seal pastry by pressing round edge with the
back of a knife, then press around with your thumb
to make a decorative edge. Sprinkle with remaining
sugar. Bake in a preheated moderately hot oven
(190°C/375°F) for about 30 minutes or until filling is
bubbling and crust is golden-brown. Serve hot with
cream. Serves 4–6.

MULLIGATAWNY

A highly spiced dish, not quite a soup, which is a heritage
of the days of the British Raj in India. The name is derived
from the Tamil *molegoo tunee*, meaning 'pepper water'.
Mulligatawny is usually served in large soup plates with a
spoonful of boiled rice in the centre of each plate.
Sometimes a bowl of rice is served on the side instead
and diners spoon the rice at will into the spicy mixture.

Mulligatawny

60 g (2 oz) butter; 3 medium onions, sliced;
12 curry leaves (optional); I tbs curry powder or
curry paste; 8 cups well-flavoured stock (beef, lamb
or chicken); I cup finely sliced celery;
I¹/₂ cups diced cooked meat or chicken;
2 cups Coconut Milk (page 91); salt and freshly
ground black pepper; boiled rice;
lemon wedges to serve.

Heat butter in a large saucepan and gently fry onions
until golden. Add curry leaves and curry powder or
paste, and fry, stirring, 1 minute longer. Add stock
and celery, bring to the boil and simmer 20 minutes.
Add meat or chicken and coconut milk and bring
almost to boiling again. Taste and season with salt
and pepper. Put a spoonful of rice into each heated
soup plate and ladle soup over; alternatively, serve
rice in a separate bowl. Serve with lemon wedges
which are squeezed over soup just before eating.
Serves 6–8.

MUSCATEL

Large, fragrant raisin made from the muscat grape.
Muscatels are available loose or in bunches and are
attractive served as a dessert or on a cheese board.
Seeded, muscatels can be added to pilau and some
sauces.

MUSHROOM

Many a good cook considers the mushroom almost a
kitchen staple which should be always at hand to slice for
a garnish, add to a salad, give wonderful flavour to meat,
chicken, fish, eggs and vegetables or to serve as a
savoury dish in its own right. Mushrooms are remarkable
in their ability to complement both robust and delicate
flavours, and their pretty shape can add much to the
appearance of a dish.

Not really vegetables but edible fungi, mushrooms
were once a luxury but the highly efficient mushroom-
growing industry has put them on everyone's table all
year around at a reasonable price. All cooks prize them
for their versatility and flavour, from the pearly whites to
the larger brown flats. There are many new mushrooms
with a wild taste and different textures finding their way
into our supermarket and greengrocers' shelves.
Oyster mushrooms, which grow upwards on a log like
oysters; fresh strongly flavoured shiitake (once only
available dried from China); wood-ear fungus: each has
its own texture, shape and flavour. Slippery jacks, swiss
browns and pretty bunches of enoki are also worth
looking for. Use them freely in soups and stir-fries,
and mix them up when making a delicious risotto or
pasta sauce.

Fresh cultivated mushrooms are supplied in three
grades.

Button Mushrooms: Also known by their French name,
champignons, button mushrooms are completely
closed. They are attractive in salads or as a garnish and
do not darken when cooked, so are perfect for pale,
creamy dishes.

Cup Mushrooms: These have the membrane just
breaking to expose the pink gills. They darken a little
when cooked but can be kept pale if brushed with
lemon juice. They are good for stuffing and for cooking
in general.

Flat Mushrooms: These are excellent grilled, served
on toast or in brown soups and casseroles; because
they darken with cooking, they can give a grey cast to
pale dishes.

Buy mushrooms in quantities you will use within a few
days. Store, lightly covered with damp paper towels or in
a paper bag or box, in the refrigerator. Avoid plastic wrap
or plastic bags which can cause mushrooms to sweat.

■ **BASIC PREPARATION:** Do not peel cultivated mushrooms.
The skin contains much of the flavour and nutritive value;
it also helps them to stay in shape during cooking and

reduces darkening. Only large, mature wild mushrooms may need peeling; keep the peelings for stock or soup.

Washing or soaking introduces excess water which the mushrooms absorb like a sponge. Cultivated mushrooms need only a wipe with a soft cloth before using. If you must wash wild mushrooms, rinse them quickly and dry well. Do not wipe or cut mushrooms until shortly before using. If they are to be used raw, brush cut surfaces with lemon juice to keep them white.

Trim stems on the diagonal, just beyond the cap, if mushrooms are to be used whole, halved or quartered. Cut stems level with caps if mushrooms are to be sliced downward into little umbrella shapes, or if they are to be stuffed and cooked (the stem helps to keep the shape). Remove stems by twisting, if directed by recipe, but keep all stems and trimmings for stock, soup or sauces.

TO PREPARE DRIED MUSHROOMS: Soak in hot water to cover 20–30 minutes, depending on size. Remove with a slotted spoon and drain on paper towels, then use as recipe directs. The soaking water is often used in the dish, or may be added to stock or soup.

TO MAKE TURNED OR FLUTED MUSHROOMS: Choose very white mushrooms. Hold rounded side up and with a small, sharp, pointed knife make deep swirling cuts from the centre of the mushroom cap down to the edge. The slivered peeling falls off to reveal the petal-like shape. Use as a garnish for main course dishes.

■ **TO COOK:** Mushrooms may be sautéed, grilled or added to stews, casseroles and sauces. See also recipes.

SAUTEED MUSHROOMS: Mushrooms absorb fat in cooking and this can make them soggy. They also release juice and become soft if heat is too low or they are cooked too long. For firm, golden-brown mushrooms, use just enough melted butter, good quality oil or a mixture of both, to cover the bottom of the pan. Heat until it begins to give off a slight haze, add prepared mushrooms and cook briskly without turning, shaking pan gently once or twice, for about 1 minute. Turn and brown other side, then add a little more butter or oil if necessary and toss mushrooms 1 minute more. Do not crowd the pan, and cook in batches if necessary. Do not cover those mushrooms which are already cooked; when they are all done, return them to the pan, toss on high heat for moments only and serve immediately.

GRILLED MUSHROOMS: Wipe with a cloth, wring out in water with a little lemon juice added. Brush with oil or melted butter and place under a preheated grill, skin side uppermost. Cook about 2 minutes, turn and brush again with butter or oil, and cook another 2 minutes. Sprinkle with chopped parsley and serve with grilled steak, chops, bacon or tomatoes, or on toast.

COOKED IN LIQUID: Mushrooms become heavy if cooked too long in liquid, so add to stews or casseroles toward the end of cooking time. Sliced or small whole mushrooms may be simmered for a few minutes in a little

acidulated water to make them firm and white before adding to delicate sauces or using as a garnish.

DUXELLES

A concentrated mushroom paste that will keep well in the refrigerator – a good way of using up mushrooms that might not keep, or leftover stems and peelings.

WAYS TO USE DUXELLES

- Add a spoonful to soups, stews and other dishes when a mushroom flavour is wanted.
- Mix with sour cream for an omelette filling or with a Béchamel Sauce (see page 456) to stuff crêpes.
- Mix with a little cream and put some into each ramekin in which you are baking eggs.
- Mix with cooked rice or buttered breadcrumbs and chopped herbs to stuff meat.
- Mix ½ cup Duxelles with 90 g (3 oz) softened cream cheese and enough cream to make it spreadable. Spoon into baked tartlet shells, sprinkle with grated Parmesan cheese and bake in a preheated moderate oven (180°C/350°F) for 5 minutes.
- Put a teaspoonful of Duxelles into the middle of hamburgers.

Duxelles

**2 tbs finely chopped spring onions;
30 g (1 oz) butter; 250 g (8 oz) mushrooms or mushroom stems and trimmings, finely chopped;
salt and freshly ground black pepper;
1 tbs chopped parsley.**

Cook spring onions gently in butter until soft. Add mushrooms and cook gently for 5 minutes, then raise heat and cook briskly, stirring until almost dry. Season with salt and pepper and stir in parsley. Spoon into a jar, press down and cover with foil. Store in refrigerator. If duxelles is to be kept more than a week, run melted butter over the top to seal before refrigerating, or freeze it. Makes 1 cup.

Stuffed Fresh Mushrooms

Fresh mushroom caps with a savoury stuffing makes a healthy light hors d'oeuvre.

**20–25 cup mushrooms; chopped parsley,
leaves of flat parsley or paprika to garnish.**

**HERB FILLING: 125 g (4 oz) cream cheese;
1 tbs lemon juice; ¼ cup chopped parsley;
¼ cup chopped mixed fresh herbs, or 2 tsp dried herbs mixed with ¼ cup chopped parsley;
salt and freshly ground black pepper.**

Remove mushroom stems and chop fine. Mix ingredients for filling, adding chopped mushroom stems. Fill mushroom caps, mounding mixture up, and garnish each with chopped parsley, a parsley leaf or a sprinkle of paprika. Makes 20–25.

m

VARIATIONS

CHICKEN FILLING: Mix together 1 boneless skinless chicken breast, cooked and finely chopped; 4 tsp Mayonnaise (page 256); 2 tsp chopped parsley or chives; salt and freshly ground black pepper. Use to fill mushroom caps as above.

NUT FILLING: Mix together 125 g (4 oz) cream cheese, or 1 cup ricotta cheese, ¼ cup chopped toasted almonds, walnuts or pecans; 1 tbs finely snipped chives; salt and freshly ground black pepper. Use to fill mushroom caps as above.

Chilled Mushroom Soup

A superb soup with the flavour of fresh mushrooms. Use a good, home-made chicken stock.

185 g (6 oz) flat mushrooms, trimmed; 2 tsp arrowroot; 4 cups strong chicken stock; 3 egg yolks; ¾ cup cream; salt and freshly ground white pepper; snipped chives to garnish.

Put mushrooms through a food mill or purée them in a food processor, then rub through a sieve. Mix arrowroot to a cream with a little of the stock, then bring rest of stock to boil. Add mushroom purée and simmer 3 minutes. Stir a little of the hot soup into arrowroot mixture, then stir this back into boiling soup. Beat egg yolks with cream, stir in a little of the hot soup, then turn heat down under soup and stir in egg yolk mixture. Stir until soup becomes glossy and thickens slightly but do not allow to boil. Season with salt and pepper. Remove from heat, pour soup into a bowl, cool then chill well. Serve garnished with snipped chives. Serves 6.

Cream of Mushroom Soup

The mushrooms are just heated through to preserve their full flavour.

30 g (1 oz) butter; 6 spring onions or 1 small onion, finely chopped; 1 small clove garlic, crushed (optional); 2 tbs flour; pinch nutmeg; 3 cups warm chicken stock; 185 g (6 oz) flat mushrooms, sliced (including stems); 2 egg yolks; ½ cup cream; salt and freshly ground black pepper; lemon juice; 3–4 button mushrooms, finely sliced, or snipped chives or fresh tarragon, to garnish.

Melt butter in heavy saucepan, add spring onions or onion and garlic, if using, and cook gently until soft but not coloured. Stir in flour and nutmeg and cook 1 minute, then remove saucepan from heat and cool a little. Add warm stock, stirring until smoothly blended. Return to medium heat and stir until boiling. In several batches, purée soup with sliced flat mushrooms in a blender or food processor. Return to saucepan and heat to just below boiling point. Beat

eggs with cream, stir in a little of the hot soup and stir this mixture back into pan. Heat gently, stirring constantly, until soup becomes glossy and thickens a little. Season with salt, pepper and lemon juice and serve garnished with mushroom slices or herbs. Serves 4–5.

Mushroom Frittata

A frittata is a flat omelette. It can be served hot or at room temperature – good for lunch or, cut into small squares, with drinks.

125 g (4 oz) mushrooms; 3 tbs olive oil; 2 cloves garlic; 1 small onion, finely chopped; ½ small red or green pepper, cored, seeded and diced; 6 eggs; 3 tbs finely chopped parsley; ¼ cup grated Swiss cheese; ¼ cup grated Parmesan cheese; 1 tsp salt; freshly ground black pepper.

Slice mushrooms, cutting first into halves or quarters if they are large. Heat oil in a heavy frying pan, add garlic, onion, mushrooms and pepper and cook briskly until vegetables are lightly browned. Remove garlic and turn heat low. Beat remaining ingredients together, reserving about 1 tbs Parmesan cheese. Pour mixture into pan, stir to mix in vegetables and cook slowly until edges shrink a little. Sprinkle with reserved cheese and place under a preheated grill until set and lightly browned. Serve hot or cool, cut into wedges or squares. Serves 4 as a main dish.

Baked Mushrooms in Cream

Serve this dish to add interest to a plain grill, with grilled steak, or as part of a leisurely holiday brunch with hot rolls and slices of pan-fried ham.

500 g (1 lb) mushrooms; 60 (2 oz) butter, melted; salt and freshly ground black pepper; 2 tbs snipped chives or finely chopped spring onions; ¼ cup cream; 3 tbs grated Parmesan cheese.

Trim mushroom stems level with caps. Arrange caps, stem side down, in a buttered shallow ovenproof dish and brush tops with the melted butter. Season well with salt and pepper, sprinkle with chives or spring onions, and pour cream over. Bake in a preheated hot oven (220°C/425°F) for 10 minutes. Scatter Parmesan cheese over top and bake 5 minutes more. Serves 4.

Stuffed Grilled Mushrooms

8 large cup mushrooms; 60 g (2 oz) butter; 4 spring onions or ½ small onion, finely chopped; 1 clove garlic, crushed (optional); ¾ cup finely chopped cooked ham; 2 tsp Dijon mustard; pinch nutmeg; ¼ cup fresh breadcrumbs; salt and freshly ground black pepper, rounds of hot fried bread or buttered toast to serve; chopped parsley to garnish.

Trim mushroom stems level with caps and chop stems fine. Melt half the butter and fry stems, spring onions or onion and garlic, if using, until soft. Stir in ham, mustard, nutmeg, breadcrumbs, salt and pepper. Melt remaining butter, brush skin side of mushrooms and grill them, skin side up, under a preheated grill for 2 minutes. Turn caps over, fill with stuffing and return to grill. Cook until stuffing is heated through, Place on rounds of fried bread or toast and garnish with parsley. Serve very hot. Serves 4.
NOTE: Finely chopped corned beef, cooked bacon, sausage or chicken livers, salami or canned luncheon meat may be used instead of ham, and other flavourings such as tomato paste, chutney or Worcestershire sauce may be substituted for mustard and nutmeg.

Funghi Ripieni (Stuffed Mushrooms)

12 large mushrooms; 6 tbs olive oil; I onion, finely chopped; I clove garlic, crushed; I cup fresh breadcrumbs; 2 tbs chopped parsley;
60 g (2 oz) finely chopped cooked ham;
2 tbs grated Parmesan cheese; salt and freshly ground black pepper; extra chopped parsley to garnish.

Remove and chop mushroom stems. Heat 3 tbs oil in a small saucepan and fry onion and garlic gently for 5 minutes. Stir in breadcrumbs and fry for 2–3 minutes until crisp. Add parsley, mushroom stems, ham, cheese, salt and pepper. Mix well. Lightly oil the bottom of a shallow ovenproof dish and arrange mushrooms, cup sides up, in a single layer in dish. Spoon a little filling into each mushroom and sprinkle liberally with oil. Cover loosely with greaseproof paper and bake in a preheated moderately hot oven (190°C/375°F) for 20–30 minutes. Sprinkle with parsley before serving. Serves 4–6.

Poached Eggs Printemps

125 g (4 oz) button or cup mushrooms, sliced;
60 g (2 oz) butter; I small lettuce, shredded;
4 eggs; 1/2 cup cooked peas; salt and freshly ground black pepper; 60 g (2 oz) Gruyère cheese, grated.

Fry mushrooms lightly in butter. Add lettuce, cover and cook gently until soft. Meanwhile, poach eggs. Add peas to mushroom mixture, season with salt and pepper and turn into a shallow flameproof dish. Trim eggs neatly. Use a spoon to make 4 hollows in the bed of vegetables and place a poached egg in each. Season lightly, cover with grated cheese and place under a preheated grill until cheese is golden and bubbly. Serve at once. Serves 4.

Mushrooms in Pastry Cases

I quantity Shortcrust Pastry (page 342);
60 g (2 oz) butter; 500 g (1 lb) open flat mushrooms, sliced; 2 tsp flour; 3/4 cup hot chicken stock; 3/4 cup sour cream; salt and freshly ground black pepper; lemon juice; 1/2 tbs chopped parsley; 1/2 tbs snipped chives; 1/2 tbs chopped fresh tarragon, or 1/2 tsp dried; I egg yolk beaten.

Line 4 x 8–10 cm (3–4 in) individual pie moulds with pastry. Prick well. Bake pastry blind in a preheated moderately hot oven (190°C/375°F) for about 15 minutes and leave to cool. Melt 30 g (1 oz) of the butter in a saucepan. Add mushrooms and cook gently until soft. Drain off juice (use to flavour soup or another sauce) and remove pan from heat. Melt remaining butter in another saucepan and stir in flour. Cook for 1 minute, stirring all the time, then add stock and sour cream and cook, stirring, until thickened and just boiling. Season with salt, pepper and lemon juice and mix in drained mushrooms. Reheat mixture and stir in herbs. Keep hot. Brush pastry cases all over with beaten egg yolk and bake in moderately hot oven for a further 5 minutes. Remove from oven, fill with hot mushroom mixture and serve immediately. Serves 4.

Mushroom Tart

250 g (8 oz) button or cup mushrooms, trimmed;
45 g (1 1/2 oz) butter; 1/2 cup cream; I egg yolk;
2 whole eggs; 60 g (2 oz) Gruyère cheese, grated;
I tsp salt; freshly ground black pepper; tiny pinch cayenne; small pinch nutmeg; I x 20 cm (8 in)
Rich Shortcrust Pastry Shell, baked (page 342).

Sauté mushrooms in butter until golden, and remove from heat. Beat cream with egg yolk and eggs, and stir in mushrooms and butter, cheese, salt, pepper, cayenne and nutmeg. Pour into pastry shell and bake in a preheated moderate oven (180°C/350°F) until filling is set and delicately browned. Serve hot or warm. Serves 4.

Mushrooms on Croûtes

A good first course or light luncheon or supper dish.

185 g (6 oz) button mushrooms; 4 thick slices bread, crusts removed; 90 g (30 oz) ghee or butter;
3 tbs finely chopped parsley; 2 cloves garlic, crushed; I tsp lemon juice;
salt and freshly ground black pepper.

Remove mushroom stems and keep for another dish. Arrange bread slices side by side in a shallow ovenproof dish. Place mushroom caps upside-down on bread. Melt butter, add parsley, garlic and lemon juice and season with salt and pepper. Spoon butter sauce over mushrooms and bread. Bake in a preheated moderately hot oven (190°C/375°F) for 20 minutes. Serve at once. Serves 4.

Mushrooms with Garlic

An Italian way with mushrooms.

**²/₃ cup olive oil; 2 cloves garlic;
1 kg (2 lb) mushrooms, thickly sliced;
1 tbs chopped fresh oregano, or 1 tsp dried;
salt and freshly ground black pepper.**

Heat a little olive oil in a frying pan and add garlic, 1 clove chopped and the other clove whole. When whole clove is brown, remove it from oil and discard it. Add mushrooms in several batches and sauté in remaining oil, as described on page 282. Return all mushrooms to pan, lower heat, sprinkle oregano over and season with salt and pepper. Continue to cook over a gentle heat 3 minutes, stirring occasionally, then turn out on to a heated serving dish. Serves 6–8.

Mushrooms in Cream Sauce

A lovely first course. Serve in individual small bowls or dishes on an entrée plate.

**500 g (1 lb) button mushrooms; 125 g (4 oz) butter;
1¹/₂ cups cream; 1 tbs Dijon mustard; salt and
freshly ground black pepper; 1 cup chopped parsley.**

Trim mushroom stems level with caps. Cut caps into halves or quarters depending on size. Sauté mushrooms in butter, in several batches, as described on page 282. Set mushrooms aside. Add cream, mustard, salt and pepper to pan and cook, stirring over moderately high heat, until sauce thickens slightly. Return mushrooms to pan and fold through sauce. Serve hot, topped with a generous sprinkling of parsley. Offer hot crusty bread rolls or French bread to mop up sauce. Serves 6.

Baked Mushrooms with Ham

A good weekend luncheon dish, served with a crisp salad.

**250 g (8 oz) medium mushrooms;
60 g (2 oz) butter; salt and freshly ground black
pepper; 125 g (4 oz) cooked ham, finely chopped;
¹/₄ cup sour cream; 2 tsp lemon juice;
4 spring onions, finely chopped;
stuffed or stoned black olives to garnish.**

Trim mushroom stems level with caps and chop stems finely. Lightly sauté mushroom caps in butter, as described on page 282. Remove to a buttered baking dish just large enough to hold them in one layer and season with salt and pepper. In the same pan, fry chopped mushroom stems until soft. Remove from heat and stir in ham, sour cream, lemon juice and spring onions. Season with salt and pepper. Fill caps with mixture and bake in a preheated moderately hot oven (190°C/375°F) for 10 minutes. Garnish with olives to serve. Serves 6.

Farmhouse Mushroom Pie

**125 g (4 oz) butter; 125 g (4 oz) cooked ham or
bacon, chopped; 1 large onion, chopped;
2 leaves fresh sage, chopped, or ¹/₄ tsp dried;
1 tsp chopped fresh thyme, or ¹/₄ tsp dried;
500 g (1 lb) mushrooms; salt and freshly ground
black pepper; 2 cups cooked rice;
4 hard boiled eggs, sliced; 1 quantity Flaky
Pastry (page 343), or 1 x 375 g (12 oz) packet frozen
puff pastry, thawed; beaten egg to glaze.**

Melt half the butter and fry ham or bacon until golden. Add onion and cook gently until soft. Stir in sage and thyme. Remove from heat and cool a little. Leave mushrooms whole if small; cut into halves or quarters if large. Generously butter an 8-cup pie dish and put in half the mushrooms in one layer. Dot with butter and season lightly with salt and pepper. Cover with ¹/₃ of the rice then ¹/₃ of the onion mixture and half the eggs. Season again. Repeat these layers and top with remaining ¹/₃ of rice and remaining ¹/₃ of onion mixture. Roll out pastry and cover dish. Chill for 30 minutes. Brush with beaten egg and bake in a preheated very hot oven (230°C/450°F) for 10–15 minutes or until pastry is well risen and lightly coloured, then turn heat down to moderate (180°C/350°F) and bake 20 minutes longer, covering top loosely with foil if browning too much. Serves 6.

Creamed Mushrooms

An excellent quick meal for one.

**185 g (6 oz) button mushrooms, sliced;
30 g (1 oz) butter; 1 tbs flour; salt and freshly ground
black pepper; ³/₄ cup milk; ¹/₄ cup cream;
pinch nutmeg; 2 slices buttered toast;
chopped parsley.**

Sauté mushrooms in butter. Sprinkle over flour and stir until well blended. Season with salt and pepper. Add milk, cream and nutmeg and bring to the boil, stirring. Serve on freshly buttered toast, topped with parsley. Serves 1 as a main dish or 2 as a snack.

Mushroom Salad

250 g (8 oz) small mushrooms, thickly sliced;
1/3 cup Garlic Vinaigrette Dressing (page 342);
1/4 cup finely chopped parsley; bouquet of
parsley to garnish.

Mix mushrooms with vinaigrette and chopped
parsley. Cover and chill. At serving time, put into a
pretty bowl. Garnish with a generous bouquet of
parsley. Serves 4–6.

Chinese Mushroom Omelette

6 dried Chinese mushrooms; 125 g (4 oz) cooked
pork or chicken meat, cut into shreds;
2 tsp light soy sauce; 1/2 tsp grated fresh ginger;
6 eggs; I tsp salt; 1/4 cup vegetable oil;
250 g (8 oz) frozen peas, thawed.

Cover mushrooms with hot water and soak 20 minutes. Drain, reserving soaking water and slice each
mushroom into 3 pieces. Place pork or chicken in a
bowl, add soy sauce and ginger and turn meat about
with chopsticks or 2 forks to coat with sauce. Leave
10 minutes. In a separate bowl, beat eggs lightly with
salt. Heat 2 tbs oil in a heavy frying pan. When it
begins to give off a haze, add meat mixture and stir-
fry on high heat 1 minute. Add 2 tbs soaking water
from mushrooms, then add mushrooms and peas.
Toss on high heat 2 minutes, turn contents of pan into
a bowl and keep warm. Wipe out pan and add
remaining oil. Heat until it gives off a haze, then add
eggs and cook on high heat, without stirring, until
they set underneath into a skin. Lower heat and cook
until top is almost set, then spoon meat mixture over
half the egg and fold the other half over it. Slide on to
a heated platter and serve hot. Serves 4.

Stir-fried Beef with Mushrooms

60 g (2 oz) dried Chinese mushrooms; I egg white;
2 1/2 tbs soy sauce; I tsp cornflour; 500 g (I lb) lean
fillet or rump steak, trimmed of all fat and cut
against grain into thin shreds; 1/2 cup vegetable oil;
125 g (4 oz) canned bamboo shoots, drained and
shredded; I tbs red wine; I tsp sugar; 1/2 tsp salt;
sprigs fresh coriander to garnish.

Cover mushrooms with hot water and soak 20 minutes. Drain. Remove and chop stems and cut caps
into fine strips. Mix egg white, soy sauce and cornflour, add shredded beef and marinate 5 minutes.
Drain beef, reserving soy sauce mixture. Heat 4 tbs
oil in a wok or frying pan. When it begins to give off
a haze add beef and stir-fry over high heat until it
changes colour. Remove beef and set aside. Add
remaining oil to wok and heat. Add bamboo shoots
and mushrooms and stir-fry over high heat I minute.
Return beef to pan and add wine, sugar, salt and

reserved soy sauce mixture. Stir-fry 1 minute and
serve hot, garnished with sprigs of coriander.
Serves 4–6.

Mushroom and Tarragon Sauce

2 tbs finely chopped fresh tarragon, or 3 tsp dried;
2 spring onions, finely chopped; I tbs red wine
vinegar; 125 g (4 oz) mushrooms, finely chopped;
1/2 cup Madeira or dry sherry; 1/2 cup cream;
60 g (2 oz) butter; salt and freshly ground
black pepper.

In a small pan cook tarragon, spring onions and
vinegar until reduced by half. Add mushrooms and
Madeira or sherry and simmer for 5 minutes. Blend
in cream and butter and stir over medium heat a
further minute. Season with salt and pepper, and
serve. Makes 2 cups.

MUSSEL

A bluish-black edible mollusc, found clumped together
on many coastlines and in estuaries, clinging tenaciously
to any available support – rocks, poles, piers.

Whether you gather mussels yourself or buy them at
the market, the rule is the same as for other shellfish; they
must be alive when they are cooked. Live mussels hold
their shells together so tightly it is difficult to pry them
apart. Discard any with open shells, or any with a
bad smell.

You will notice that most recipes call for a little wine to
be used in the cooking of mussels, and that cooked mussels are often served on the half shell with a sauce made
from the cooking liquid. The true devotee will eat the
mussels with a fork, then drink the sauce from the shell,
the remaining sauce being mopped up with crusty bread.

Mussels are also sold bottled, in a briney solution or
canned – and sometimes smoked.

■ **BASIC PREPARATION:** Buy at least 500 g (1 lb) mussels
for each person. When you get home, rinse the mussels
several times in cold running water, then thoroughly
scrub each mussel with a clean, stiff brush or pot scourer
to remove mud, seaweed or any dirt that may cling to
them. Soak for several hours in water with a handful of
oatmeal or cornmeal.

Pull away the beard that clings around the edge of the
shell and discard any mussel which is not tightly closed;
then rinse again in cold running water, and they are ready
to cook. All this preparation may sound a little finicky, but
the time spent is well repaid by the final, delicious results.

There are two methods for opening mussels. Either may
be used when mussels are to be used for salads, etc.
TO OPEN MUSSELS IN THE OVEN: Arrange the cleaned
mussels in a single layer in a baking tin and place the
tin in a preheated very hot oven (230°C/450°F) for 7–8
minutes or until the shells have opened. Throw away any
unopened mussels.

TO STEAM OPEN MUSSELS: Put the cleaned mussels in a large saucepan with 250 ml (1 cup) water over high heat and steam the mussels, covered, shaking the pan once or twice, for 5–6 minutes or until the shells have opened. Discard any unopened shells. **See recipes.**

Barbecued Mussels: If you can buy dried fennel stalks (often available from Continental fruit shops and some delicatessens) or gather them from the roadside, you will be able to enjoy this spectacular way of cooking mussels in the open.

Make a fire on the barbecue in you favourite way. Arrange prepared and cleaned mussels on a metal tray and strew a thick layer of dried fennel stalks over the top. Place the tray over the glowing coals, and then set fire to the fennel stalks. As they burn, the aromatic fennel flavour permeates the opening mussels, a marvellous combination. Remove the tray as soon as the mussels have opened, pick off any remaining stalks and serve on the shell with crusty bread and butter to mop up the juices.

Mussels Marinière (*Moules Marinière*)

The beloved moules of France are, of course, our mussels. Moules Marinière is the classic and best loved way of enjoying mussels. They are steamed in wine and aromatics – parsley, bay leaf, spring onions, etc. – and served with some of the liquor. There are variations which are equally popular throughout the world. Please read instructions on preparation of mussels.

2 kg (4 lb) mussels, prepared; 4 spring onions, finely chopped; 4 parsley stalks; 1 bay leaf; sprig fresh thyme; freshly ground black pepper; 60 g (2 oz) butter; 2 cups dry white wine; 1 tsp flour; little chopped parsley.

Place mussels in a wide pan with spring onions, herbs, pepper, half the butter and the wine. Cover pan and cook over a high heat for 5 minutes, shaking pan occasionally. Remove mussels as soon as they open, discarding the top of each shell. Discard any mussels that do not open. Arrange mussels in heated soup plates. Strain cooking liquid and return to pan. Mix remaining butter with flour and add to liquid. Boil rapidly, stirring, until slightly thickened. Pour over mussels in each soup bowl and sprinkle with chopped parsley. Serve at once with crusty bread, butter and chilled dry white wine. Serves 4.

VARIATIONS

MUSSELS WITH CREAM (MOULES A LA CREME): Replace butter and flour used for thickening with 3/4 cup cream. Reduce mussel cooking liquid by about 1/3 by rapid boiling, then stir in cream and cook gently to thicken a little. Pour over mussels and serve.

MUSSELS WITH PERNOD (MOULES A LA PERNOD): Prepare as for Mussels with Cream, adding 2 tbs Pernod with the wine.

MUSSELS IN EGG AND CREAM SAUCE (MOULES A LA POULETTE): Steam mussels as described and keep warm, covered. Strain cooking liquid and reserve 2 cups. Bring liquid to the boil in a stainless steel, enamelled or non-stick saucepan. Reduce to 1 1/2 cups, then remove from heat. In a bowl whisk together 1/2 cup cream and 3 egg yolks, gradually whisk in 1/2 cup of the liquid in a steady stream and whisk mixture into remaining liquid. Cook, whisking, over a low heat until thickened slightly. Add 2 tsp lemon juice and 2 tbs chopped parsley. Divide mussels among 4 heated soup bowls and spoon sauce over mussels.

Baked Buttered Mussels

Serve with crusty bread, to mop up the lovely garlic butter.

1 tsp oil; 1.5 kg (3 lb) mussels, scrubbed and cleaned (see Basic Preparation); 60 g (2 oz) butter; 2 tbs chopped parsley; 2 cloves garlic, finely chopped.

Rub a large baking dish with oil and place mussels in it in a single layer. Bake in a preheated very hot oven (230°C/450°F) for 5–10 minutes or until the shells open. Do not overcook. Remove upper shell. Melt butter and stir in parsley and garlic. Serve mussels on the lower shell with a little of the butter spooned over and any liquid from the pan. Serves 4.

Mussels in Dilled Cucumber Sauce

1 cucumber, peeled, seeded and chopped; 1/4 cup sour cream; 3 tbs snipped fresh dill, or 1 tbs dried; 1 tsp lemon juice; 1 tsp Dijon mustard; 2 drops Tabasco sauce; salt and freshly ground white pepper; 2 kg (4 lb) mussels, scrubbed, steamed open, shelled, and black rims removed if desired.

GARNISH: soft-leaved lettuce; cucumber slices; sprigs fresh dill.

Squeeze cucumber lightly in a tea-towel to remove excess moisture. Combine cucumber, sour cream, dill, lemon juice, mustard, Tabasco, salt and pepper. Add mussels, and toss the mixture. Serve on chilled salad plates lined with lettuce leaves, garnished with cucumber slices and fresh dill sprigs. Serves 4.

Mussels and Salad Niçoise

250 g (8 oz) potatoes, peeled and sliced; 2 tbs tomato paste; 2 cups Mayonnaise (page 256); 1 red pepper, cored, seeded and chopped; 1/2 tsp chopped fresh tarragon, or pinch dried; 1/2 tsp snipped fresh chives or bottled freeze-dried; 2 kg (4 lb) mussels, scrubbed, steamed open, shelled, and blacked rims removed if desired.

GARNISH: soft-leaved lettuce leaves;
250 g (8 oz) green beans, trimmed, blanched for
1 minute and patted dry; 3 hard-boiled eggs,
quartered lengthways; stoned black olives;
cherry tomatoes.

Place potatoes in a saucepan, cover with cold salted water and bring to the boil. Simmer until just tender. Drain potatoes and let them cool. Mix tomato paste with mayonnaise, red pepper, tarragon and chives. Place mussels in a large bowl, add potatoes and 1½ cups of the tomato mayonnaise, or to taste, and toss gently. Serve salad on chilled plates lined with lettuce leaves, garnished with green beans, egg quarters, olives and tomatoes. Serve remaining tomato mayonnaise separately. Serves 6 as a first course or 4 as a main course.

Mussel Salad

Perfect to serve as a summer lunch dish.

1.5 kg (3 lb) mussels, scrubbed and steamed open;
500 g (1 lb) waxy potatoes, peeled cooked and diced;
185 g (6 oz) green beans or snow peas, cooked; 1 stick
tender celery, cut into fine strips.

GARNISH: 2 tomatoes, each cut into 6 wedges;
6 spring onions, finely shredded.

DRESSING: 3 tbs olive oil; 1 tbs wine vinegar;
1 tsp Dijon Mustard; salt and freshly ground black
pepper; 2 tbs chopped mixed fresh herbs.

Reserve 6 mussels in shells for garnishing; remove remaining mussels from shells and discard shells. Mix together dressing ingredients in a salad bowl, add potatoes, beans or peas, mussels and celery and toss lightly together. Just before serving, garnish with reserved mussels in shells, tomatoes and spring onions. Serves 4.

Mussels Antipasto

½ cup dry white wine or water; 1 kg (2 lb) mussels,
scrubbed; ¾ cup fresh white breadcrumbs;
2 large cloves garlic, chopped; 2 tbs finely chopped
parsley; freshly ground black pepper;
¼ cup olive oil.

Boil wine or water in a large heavy saucepan, add mussels, cover and cook over very high heat for 5–6 minutes, shaking pan frequently, until mussel shells open. Remove from heat. Detach and discard top shells, leaving each mussel in its lower shell. Discard any mussels that have not opened. Arrange side by side in a large shallow gratin dish or in 4 individual gratin dishes. Mix together breadcrumbs, garlic, parsley and pepper and spoon over mussels. Sprinkle oil evenly over the top. Cook in a preheated very hot oven (230°C/450°F) for 3–4 minutes or until

crumbs are just tinged brown. Take care not to overcook and toughen mussels. Alternatively, you may brown the mussels for 1 minute under a preheated hot grill. Serves 4.

Vermicelli with Tomato and Mussel Sauce

1 kg (2 lb) mussels, scrubbed and steamed open;
⅓ cup olive oil; 1 onion finely chopped; 2 cloves
garlic, sliced; 750 g (1½ lb) tomatoes, peeled and
chopped; 375 g (12 oz) vermicelli or spaghetti;
salt and freshly ground black pepper;
2 tbs chopped parsley to garnish.

Reserve a few of the mussels in their shells for garnish. Remove remaining mussels from shells and discard shells. Heat 3 tbs of the oil in a large saucepan and fry onion until soft and golden. Stir in garlic, then tomatoes. Simmer gently for about 30 minutes or until tomatoes have reduced to a pulp.

Cook pasta in boiling salted water for about 10 minutes or until tender. Drain, place in a heated serving dish containing remaining oil and toss until lightly coated. Season sauce with salt and pepper, add shelled mussels and heat through for a few minutes, stirring well. Pile sauce over pasta, garnish with chopped parsley and reserved mussels in shell and serve immediately with a green salad. Serves 4.

MUSTARD

The condiment based on the ground powder of the seeds of the mustard plant. There are three types of mustard seed which may be ground to make mustard – white (*Sinapis alba*), brown (*Brassica juncea*) and black (*Brassica nigra*). Manufactured mustard powder is usually a mixture of one or more varieties of mustard seed.

The pungency of mustard is due to an essential oil, which is not present in the living seed or in dry, ground powder but forms when the crushed dried seed is mixed with water. An enzyme then causes a glucoside (a bitter substance chemically related to sugar) to react with the water and the hot taste of mustard emerges. Mixing with boiling water, as some advocate, kills the enzyme and produces a milder but bitter mustard. Vinegar should not be used to mix mustard either, for salt and vinegar both inhibit the develop of the enzyme – unless of course, one prefers a milder but bitter mustard.

m

Mustard powder should be mixed with cold water and allowed to stand 10–15 minutes, in which time the essential oils will develop. Once the essential oils have developed, they will not be readily degraded by vinegar or salt or even by heat. To preserve mustard's pungency in cooked dishes, however, add towards end of cooking and cook gently.

MAIN TYPES OF MUSTARD

English Mustard: In England mustard is sold in powdered form: it is made from blended seeds of the black mustard seed and yellow-white alba, finely ground, and it is a hot yellow in colour. The powder is mixed with water, at home, and is the pungent but perfect partner for the roast beef of England. It is the proper mustard to use with cheese – the toasted Cheddar cheese that Ben Gunn dreamed of in *Treasure Island* would certainly have had a dash of good English mustard. Welsh rarebits, cheese sauce and cheese soufflés reach their peaks with just the right amount of English mustard. Mixed English mustard is the perfect condiment with ham, roast pork, or pork pie, and beef or pork sausages.

When used in dishes that call for mustard, even English mustard loses much of its pungency if overcooked. In mayonnaise and salad dressing, mustard helps to stabilise the emulsions as well as adding a bite. Mustard is also used in pickles.

Fresh mustard powder should be mixed every time it is needed. Put a few tablespoons of mustard powder in a small dish, add water a teaspoon at a time and mix to a smooth paste. Allow to stand 10–15 minutes to develop the flavours. To make a milder mustard, with a biting after-taste, mix the mustard with wine vinegar or cider.

Stale, mixed mustard loses much of its essential oils and therefore its pungency. However, as a powder, in its small container (Colemans, the oldest traditional English mustard makers have designed an excellent container), mustard will retain its powers, provided it does not get damp. An English prepared mustard is also available.

French Mustard: While most of the mustard consumed in England is dry, the French, and indeed most of Europe, prefer a mixed prepared mustard. Transportation and travel are changing this as more of the world is introduced to the excellent mixed prepared mustards of France and in particular the mustards of Dijon, in Burgundy.

The two types of mustard used in France are the pale Dijon and the darker Bordeaux mustard. Dijon mustards have a particularly clean taste – sharp and salty, not sweet, and with a strong hot taste of mustard.

Dijon mustard is exceptionally good with steak and anything else in which the taste of the dish should not be masked. Dijon mustard is the one used in French sauces – French cooks prefer it in mayonnaise and vinaigrette and for the delicate creamy sauces that go with kidneys, egg dishes, chicken or fish. Pan gravies are often enhanced with Dijon mustard and cream.

The best-known brands of Dijon mustard include Grey-Poupon, who make dozens of different blends and ship them all over the world, as do Maille, Olida and Amora. There is, of course, the grained French mustard called *Moutarde de Meaux*, an interesting mixture of ground and half-ground seeds, with a grainy texture.

Among the additives to French mustards are tarragon; a mixture of French herbs; green peppercorns, called *Moutarde au Poivres Verts*; and tomato purée is added to make a mustard that goes well with hamburgers. None though, really beats the original Dijon mustard of France.

Bordeaux mustard is darker than Dijon (it contains the seed coat). It is sour-sweet with vinegar and sugar, and is heavily flavoured with tarragon and other herbs and spices.

All mixed mustards should be stored, covered, in a cool place and, once opened, they slowly lose their flavour. It is better to buy in small quantities and replace as necessary.

German Mustard: It is of the general type of Bordeaux mustard – dark in colour, sweet-sour and flavoured with herbs and spices. It goes particularly well with German sausage, particularly of the frankfurt kind, like *knack-wurst*, the Dutch *rookwurst*, and Polish *kielbasa*, etc.

Other Mustards: Manufacturers throughout the world prepare mixed mustards for their local markets. In USA, a mustard is made from the alba seeds, and flavoured with sugar, vinegar or white wine. It is the one you get when you order a hot dog or hamburger in America. Manufacturers emulate the famous mustards of France and Germany, but few match up to the genuine article.

OTHER FORMS OF MUSTARD

Mustard Seeds: Spice shops. Oriental or Chinese groceries and health food shops sell mustard seeds. These find their way into pickles and curries, while some are used for home-made mustards. Again, these home-made mustards never match those from France and Germany.

Mustard Greens: The young green plant of the white mustard (*Sinapis alba*) is the mustard in mustard and cress. In these days rape is sometimes substituted. Trays of mustard and cress are sold, already sprouted, although these may contain only small cress. Snip the tops off and use when making sandwiches, add to egg or chicken dishes and use as a garnish over salads. You can also buy the seeds and sprout your own mustard and cress (see *Cress*).

Mustard Oil: This is obtained by pressing the seeds of field mustard, rape as well as other mustards, and is used to great advantage in Indian cooking, particularly that of Bengal, North India and Pakistan. It has a very distinctive flavour and smell, but is not all that pungent when used in cooking as the essential mustard oil is readily driven off with heat. Mustard oil can be bought in most shops specialising in Indian products. See recipes.

White Wine and Mustard Sauce

For sausages, ham steaks or pork chops.

**15 g (¹/₂ oz) butter; 2 tbs chopped spring onions;
¹/₃ cup white wine; ¹/₃ cup cream; 1 tbs French
mustard; salt and freshly ground black pepper.**

Cook sausages or chops with just enough oil to film
pan. Remove meat to a hot dish and slowly pour off
fat from pan. Melt butter in pan, add spring onions
and cook gently 2 minutes. Add wine and bring to the
boil, stirring and scraping up brown bits from bottom
of pan. Stir in cream and mustard and cook gently
1–2 minutes or until sauce becomes glossy and a little
thicker. Season with salt and pepper and spoon over
chops or sausages. Serves 4.

Mustard Sauce

To vary flavour, use some of the many different
mustard mixes available now, adapting the amount
added to taste.

**1 quantity Béchamel Sauce (page 456);
1 tbs dry mustard; 2 tbs water; 2 tsp sugar;
1 tbs vinegar.**

Make sauce using all milk or half milk and half stock
(veal or chicken). Blend mustard with water and
stand for 10 minutes. Blend sugar and vinegar until
smooth and add to hot sauce. Serve with fish. Makes
1¹/₂ cups.

Mustard and Dill Sauce

**4 tbs highly seasoned prepared mustard;
1 tsp dry mustard; 3 tbs sugar; 2 tbs white vinegar;
¹/₃ cup vegetable oil; 3 tbs chopped fresh dill.**

Mix mustards, sugar and vinegar to paste. Using a
whisk, gradually beat in oil until it forms a thick
emulsion. Stir in dill. Keep refrigerated in a tightly
covered container and whisk before using. Sauce will
keep for 3–4 days in refrigerator. Makes about ¹/₂ cup.

Chicken Schnitzels Dijonnaise

**4 chicken fillets (skinless, boneless half-breasts);
salt and freshly ground black pepper;
4 tsp Dijon mustard; about ¹/₂ cup flour;
60 g (2 oz) butter; 3 tbs oil; 2 eggs, beaten;
¹/₂ cup cream.**

Place chicken fillets between 2 sheets of plastic wrap
and flatten them out slightly with a rolling pin. Trim
off any very ragged edges with a sharp knife. Season
fillets well with salt and pepper, smear each with
¹/₂ tsp mustard and dust lightly with flour. Heat butter
and oil together in a large, heavy frying pan over
medium heat. Have beaten eggs in a shallow dish
beside the stove, and floured fillets on a plate. When
foam subsides in pan, quickly dip fillets into egg, then

place them at once in pan. Cook until undersides are
crisp and golden; about 2 minutes, then turn fillets
with a spatula and cook other sides for 2–3 minutes.
Remove and keep warm. To pan add cream and
remaining mustard, swirling gently over a moderate
heat to make a smooth, creamy sauce. Serve chicken
topped with sauce. Serves 4.

Dijon Grilled Chicken

**6 chicken pieces, breasts or legs; or 2 x 500 g (1 lb)
chickens, split; 60 g (2 oz) butter; 1 tbs oil;
2–3 tbs Dijon mustard; 2 tbs chopped spring
onions; ¹/₄ tsp dried thyme; salt and freshly
ground black pepper; pinch cayenne.**

Arrange chicken pieces on grill rack, skin side up.
Melt butter in a small pan, add oil and brush chicken
pieces with some of this mixture. Grill chicken
under a preheated grill for 10 minutes on each side,
brushing or basting frequently with butter and oil.
Blend mustard with spring onions, thyme, salt,
pepper and cayenne and slowly add remaining oil
and butter mixture, drop by drop, to thicken it. Turn
chicken skin side up again, and spread with some of
the mustard mixture. Grill for a further 10 minutes,
reducing heat if necessary, until chicken is golden-
brown and tender, basting with mustard mixture
from time to time. Small chicken pieces will take less
time to cook, 15–20 minutes altogether, so time
accordingly. Serves 4.

Mustard Chicken in Yogurt

**6–8 chicken joints, breasts, thighs, drumsticks;
salt and freshly ground black pepper;
2 tbs French mustard; 1 cup plain yogurt, stirred.**

Season chicken joints with salt and pepper. Place in a
lightly greased shallow ovenproof dish and cover
with foil. Bake in a preheated hot oven (200°C/400°F)
for 25 minutes. Remove foil and spread each chicken
piece with mustard, then cover with yogurt. Return
to hot oven for about 5 minutes. Serve immediately.
Serves 4–6.

Grilled Chicken with Mustard Sauce

**2 x 500 g (1 lb) chickens, split and flattened;
lemon juice; salt and freshly ground black pepper;
2 tbs melted butter; watercress to garnish.**

**SAUCE: 2 spring onions finely chopped;
1 tbs dry sherry; ¹/₂ cup chicken stock;
1 tsp tomato paste; 1 tbs French mustard;
few drops Worcestershire sauce; pinch cayenne.**

Season both sides of chickens with lemon juice, salt
and pepper. Brush chickens with melted butter and
grill very gently, starting with skin side down, for

about 12 minutes, then turn over and continue cooking for 20 minutes, basting occasionally with melted butter. Place chicken on a heated serving dish and keep warm.

SAUCE: Strain pan juices from chicken into a small saucepan, add spring onions and fry gently until golden. Add sherry and stock and bring to the boil. Stir in tomato paste, mustard, a few drops of Worcestershire sauce and cayenne. Garnish chicken with watercress and serve sauce separately. Chicken may also be served on a bed of salad vegetables, to which the chicken gives a delicious taste – the juices from the chicken melt into the salad. Serves 4.

Creamed Onions Dijonnaise

750 g (1¹/₂ lb) medium onions, sliced; ¹/₂ cup water; ²/₃ cup sour light cream; I tbs Dijon mustard; ¹/₂ tsp or more salt; freshly ground black pepper.

Cook onions in water over a gentle heat, about 10 minutes. Drain and place in a greased ovenproof dish. Mix cream, mustard, salt and pepper and pour over onions. Cover and bake in a preheated moderate oven (180°C/350°F) for 30 minutes. Serve with grilled or pan-fried steak or roast beef or lamb. Serves 4–6.

Tomato Salad with Dijon Dressing

4 firm, ripe tomatoes; salt and freshly ground black pepper; 3 tbs olive oil; 2 tsp Dijon mustard; I tsp lemon juice or wine vinegar; 6–8 spring onions, chopped; chopped parsley or chives.

Cut tomatoes crossways into thin slices (use serrated-edge knife) and arrange overlapping on a flat dish or 4 individual plates. Season well with salt and pepper. Mix oil, mustard and lemon juice or vinegar, beating with a fork or shaking in a jar until thick and creamy. Sprinkle over tomatoes. Drop spring onions into boiling water, blanch for 10 seconds and refresh under cold water. Pat dry with paper towels. Strew over tomatoes with some parsley or chives. Serves 4.

Chicken Breasts Dijonnaise

4–6 half-breasts of chicken; salt and freshly ground black pepper; 90 g (3 oz) butter; 2–3 tbs brandy, warmed; ¹/₂ cup cream; I tbs Dijon mustard.

If breasts are large, cut each into 2 serving pieces. Season well with salt and pepper. Melt butter in a large frying pan and saute chicken, 3–4 pieces at a time (do not crowd pan), over medium heat. Cook for 15–20 minutes or until golden and juices run clear when chicken is pierced with a fine skewer. Return all chicken to pan. Ignite brandy and pour flaming over chicken. Shake pan until flames subside, then remove breasts to a heated serving dish and keep hot. Add cream to pan along with mustard.

Bring to the boil, scraping up any brown bits. Stir until the sauce thickens slightly, and season with salt and pepper. Spoon sauce over chicken. Serve with creamy mashed potatoes or boiled rice and follow with a salad. Serves 4.

Chicken Breast en Croûte

4 large chicken fillets (skinless, boneless half-breasts); 60 g (2 oz) butter; salt and freshly ground black pepper; squeeze lemon juice; 185 g (6 oz) cooked ham, very finely chopped; 2 tbs sour cream; I tsp English mustard; I x 375 g (12 oz) packet frozen puff pastry, thawed; beaten egg to glaze; Mushroom and Tarragon Sauce (page 286) to serve.

Fry chicken pieces in butter for 1–2 minutes on each side until colour changes, without browning. Lift from pan and season with salt and pepper. Squeeze a little lemon juice over and put in refrigerator to cool completely. Mix ham with sour cream and mustard. Roll out pastry very thin and divide into 4, making each piece oblong in shape and large enough to enclose a chicken piece. Place a chicken piece on one edge of each piece of pastry and spread chicken with ham mixture. Brush edges of pastry with a little water and fold pastry over to enclose chicken like an envelope, trimming off any excess pastry and forming them into neat, attractive shapes. Place seam side down on a baking tray and decorate with some of the pastry trimmings if liked; use a little beaten egg to secure the decorations. Brush pastry all over with beaten egg. Bake in a preheated hot oven (200°C/400°F) for about 30 minutes or until pastry is golden. Accompany with mushroom and tarragon sauce and buttered green beans, followed by a salad. Serves 4.

Dijon Pork en Croûte

500 g (I lb) pork fillet in one piece, or 2 smaller fillets; 2 tbs brandy; I tbs Dijon mustard; salt and freshly ground black pepper; 30 g (I oz) butter; I tbs oil; 2 tsp chopped mixed fresh herbs (chives, parsley, thyme); I x 375 g (12 oz) packet frozen puff pastry, thawed; I egg, lightly beaten.

Cut pork fillet into 4 portions or cut smaller fillets in half. Trim edges. Mix together brandy, mustard, salt and pepper in a shallow dish. Marinate pork in this mixture for several hours in refrigerator, turning often. Remove and pat dry. Heat butter and oil in a heavy frying pan, and quickly fry fillets until golden on all sides. Sprinkle with herbs. Cool. Roll out pastry thin and cut into 4 portions. Wrap each piece of fillet neatly in pastry, sealing joins with a little beaten egg. Use pastry trimmings to make decorative shapes and attach to pastry with egg. Chill packages for 1 hour.

m

Glaze tops with remaining egg and bake in a preheated moderate oven (180°C/350°F) for 30 minutes. Reduce heat to moderately slow (160°C/325°F) and bake for a further 15 minutes. A crisp green salad is all that is required to accompany this main course. Serves 4.

Pork Patties

500 g (1 lb) minced pork; salt and freshly ground black pepper; 30 g (1 oz) butter;
1 tbs Dijon mustard; ¹/₂ cup cream.

Shape pork into 4 medium patties. Season well with salt and pepper. Heat butter in a heavy frying pan, add patties, press out flat and cook 3 minutes on each side. Remove to a heated serving plate and keep warm. Add mustard and cream to pan, stir in brown bits from bottom of pan and cook until sauce thickens. Spoon sauce over patties. Serves 4

Yorkshire Rarebit

15 g (¹/₂ oz) butter; 1 tbs flour; 2 tbs milk;
2 tbs beer; 2 tsp dry mustard mixed with water;
large pinch salt; freshly ground black pepper;
1 cup grated Cheddar cheese; 2 slices hot buttered toast; 2 thick slices lean cooked ham;
2 hot poached eggs.

Melt butter in a saucepan. Remove from heat and stir in flour to make a smooth paste, then stir in milk, beer, mustard, salt and pepper. Return to low heat and stir until thickened. Add cheese and stir just until cheese has melted – about 2 minutes. Place toast on 2 flameproof serving plates. Spoon cheese mixture over toast, top with ham and place under a preheated grill until cheese is bubbly and ham lightly browned. Remove from heat and top each serving with a poached egg. Serve immediately. Serves 2.

Sour Cream Coleslaw

¹/₂ medium cabbage, finely shredded; 2 tbs oil;
1 tbs vinegar; 1 tbs French mustard; 2 tbs chopped celery; ¹/₂ red pepper, cored, seeded and shredded;
¹/₂ green pepper, cored, seeded and shredded;
4 spring onions, chopped; ¹/₂ cup sour light cream;
3 tbs chopped parsley.

Put cabbage in a large salad bowl. Combine oil, vinegar and mustard and beat with a fork until thick. Add to cabbage and mix well. Top with celery, shredded peppers and spring onions. Chill well. Just before serving, toss in sour cream, mixing lightly. Top with chopped parsley. Serves 6.

MUTTON

The meat of mature sheep over 2 years of age. Good mutton is brick-red when freshly cut and the bones are dry and white. Although not nearly as tender as lamb, many people prefer mutton's richer flavour. Mutton is usually less expensive than lamb though it can be hard to find in butchers' shops – low demand means low supply.

■ **TO COOK:** Mutton can be used in any recipe for pot roasted, casseroled, 'boiled' or stewed lamb. It simply takes longer to cook. The choicest chump or loin chops or cutlets from a top-quality mutton carcase can be pan-fried or grilled in the same way as lamb, though they will be less tender. (See *Lamb*.)

To roast mutton, use the slow method, in a preheated moderate oven (180°C/350°F) throughout. No fat is needed in the pan. Mutton is best well cooked – allow 40–45 minutes per 500 g (1 lb). A sliced onion placed on meat before cooking gives it a delicious flavour.

n

NAM PRIK

This sauce is on the table with most Thai meals. Make a jar and store it in the refrigerator; only a small amount is served at a time, usually in a small dish for dipping. Serve with tiny fresh or crisp fried spring rolls, rice or noodle dishes, or salads.

Nam Prik

3 cloves garlic, chopped; 3 golden shallots, chopped; I stem lemongrass, chopped; 6 fresh red chillies, seeded and chopped; I tbs coriander root, chopped; I tbs dried shrimp paste (belacan, blachan or kapi); I tbs brown sugar; 4 tbs fresh lime juice; 2 tbs soy sauce; 4 tbs fish sauce (nam pla).

Heat the garlic, shallots, lemongrass, chillies and coriander root in a small heavy pan until they start to smoke. Place in a blender with the shrimp paste, sugar, lime juice, soy and fish sauce. Blend to a smooth paste. Stir in 1–3 tbs water to taste and serve in a small bowl.

NAPOLEONS

French pastries each consisting of three layers of thin, crisp puff pastry rectangles, sandwiched with Crème Pâtissière or whipped cream and topped with white icing, rippled with lines of chocolate.

Napoleons are similar to French pastry, Mille-Feuilles (see pages 268–9), although in France the name 'Napoleons' is rarely associated with them in any French recipe. Why these pastries were named 'Napoleons' and why the distinctive decorative icing was used is obscure. The explanation differs from country to country. Probably it was named after *Napolitains*, the imposing, and embellished, layered pastries that used to decorate formal dinner tables. This practice has now been abandoned, and although *Napolitains* are still made, they are now usually small and known as Napoleons. Whatever the reason, Napoleons are light, delicious and found in pastry shops in many parts of the world.

Napoleons

¹/₂ x 375 g (12 oz) packet frozen puff pastry, thawed, or I quantity Puff Pastry (page 343; 2 cups Crème Pâtissière (page 207); I quantity Glacé Icing (page 205).

CHOCOLATE DECORATION: 60 g (2 oz) cooking chocolate; 45 g (1 ¹/₂ oz) butter.

Roll out pastry as thin as possible to a rectangle about the size of a large baking tray. Place on dampened baking tray, pricking well all over and chill for 15 minutes. Bake in a preheated hot oven (200°C/400°F) for 5–10 minutes or until pale golden, then turn pastry over carefully and continue baking for a further 5 minutes. Cool on wire rack. Cut into 3 strips about

8 cm (3 in) wide. Spread one strip of pastry with half the crème pâtissière. Lay a second pastry strip on top and spread with remaining crème. Top with last pastry strip. Press down lightly and spread icing over top.

CHOCOLATE DECORATION: Melt chocolate and butter in a double saucepan over warm water and cool slightly. Pipe in thin rows across the icing at 2.5 cm (1 in) intervals. Before chocolate has set use tines of a fork or back of a sharp knife to draw a line down centre of length of pastry. Draw another line in the opposite direction on each side, thus pulling chocolate into a decorative pattern. When chocolate has set, cut strips crossways into pieces about 5 cm (2 in) wide, using a very sharp knife. Best served on the day they are made. Makes about 8.

NASI GORENG

One of the basic dishes of Indonesia, rather similar to fried rice. A variation is popular in Malaysia also. Meats, vegetables or seafood are cut into smallish chunks and fried in oil and, towards the end of cooking, all the ingredients are stirred together. The dish can vary from region to region but rice is always the major component. *Bami Goreng* is a similar fried dish, but made with cooked noodles instead of cooked rice. **See recipes.**

Nasi Goreng

3 eggs; salt and freshly ground black pepper; oil for frying; 2 onions, chopped; 2 cloves garlic, crushed; ¹/₂ tsp dried shrimp paste (trasi); 500 g (1 lb) pork or lean beef steak, diced; 250 g (8 oz) green prawns, shelled and deveined; 4 cups cold cooked rice; 6 spring onions, finely sliced; 2 tbs light soy sauce; 3 tbs onion flakes; I cucumber, finely sliced.

Beat eggs with salt and pepper. Heat a little oil in a frying pan and make an omelette with half the eggs. Turn on to a plate without folding. Make another omelette with the remaining eggs. When cool, place omelettes on top of each other, roll up and cut into strips. Set aside for garnish. Put chopped onions, garlic and shrimp paste in blender and blend to a paste (or chop onions very finely, crush garlic and dissolve paste in a little hot water; combine these 3 ingredients). Heat 3 tbs oil in frying pan or wok and fry blended ingredients for a few minutes. Add meat and fry, stirring, until cooked. Remove meat and keep warm. Fry prawns, remove and keep warm. Add 2 tbs more oil and when hot stir in rice and spring onions, tossing and mixing thoroughly. Sprinkle with soy sauce and mix evenly. Return meat and prawns to pan and combine with rice. Keep hot. Place onion flakes in a wire strainer and lower them into hot oil for a few seconds or until they turn golden-brown. Drain on paper towels. Pile rice mixture on a heated serving platter and garnish with strips of omelette, fried onion flakes and cucumber slices. Serves 6–8.

NOTE: Dried shrimp paste, also sold as *blachan* or *trasi* and dried onion flakes, known as *bawang goreng,* are available from Asian grocery stores.

Nasi Goreng (Malaysia)

6 cups cold cooked rice; 2 small brown onions, sliced; 4 tbs oil; 2 tbs raisins; I egg, lightly beaten; 2 fresh red chillies, seeded and chopped; 2 cloves garlic, chopped; 250 g (8 oz) green prawns, shelled and deveined; 2 spring onions, finely sliced.

Stir rice to separate grains. Fry one onion gently in oil in wok or frying pan until crisp and golden-brown. Remove with a slotted spoon, drain and set aside for garnish. Fry raisins in same oil for 2 minutes, stirring, then remove and set aside. Pour egg into pan and make thin omelette. Roll up and slice finely. Reserve for garnish. Blend or pound together chillies, garlic and remaining onion, then fry together gently for 3–4 minutes, adding more oil if necessary. Add prawns and stir-fry until cooked. Stir in rice, increase heat and fry for about 3 minutes. Serve on a large heated platter, garnished with fried onions, raisins, omelette strips and spring onions. Serves 6–8.

NAVARIN

A French lamb or mutton stew made with a proportion of onions, carrots, turnips and sometimes potatoes, or in spring with peas and young new vegetables, when it becomes *Navarin à la Printanière.*

This substantial dish is best eaten when reheated; first refrigerate overnight to solidify the fat, then remove the fat next day and finish cooking. The dish should have a rich, full-flavoured gravy, the meat being tender and the vegetables soft without being overcooked. **See recipes.**

Navarin of Lamb

I kg (2 lb) lamb neck chops; salt and freshly ground black pepper; 30 g (I oz) dripping; I tbs flour; 3 cups warm water or stock; I clove garlic, crushed; I tsp tomato paste; I bouquet garni; 30 g (I oz) butter; I tsp sugar; 8 small onions, peeled; 2 large carrots, thickly sliced; I turnip, sliced.

Trim chops and season with salt and pepper. Brown in melted dripping in a flameproof casserole. Remove half the fat, then sprinkle chops with flour, turning to coat well. Cook gently until golden-brown. Add water or stock, garlic and tomato paste and bring to the boil, stirring constantly. Add bouquet garni, cover and simmer gently for 1 hour. Remove meat, strain gravy into a bowl and return meat to gravy. Cover and refrigerate overnight. Next day, remove solidified fat from the surface and place meat and

liquid back in casserole. Heat gently. Melt butter and sugar in a frying pan and fry vegetables quickly until golden. Add vegetables to meat, cover and simmer very gently for 1 hour or until meat and vegetables are tender. Adjust seasoning. Serve with crusty bread or with creamy mashed potatoes seasoned with nutmeg. Serves 4–6.

Navarin à la Printanière

500 g (I lb) boned shoulder of lamb, trimmed and cubed; 500 g (I lb) boned breast of lamb, trimmed and cubed; 60 g (2 oz) dripping; 2 cups stock; 2 tbs tomato paste; 750 g (I¹/₂ lb) new potatoes, scraped; 6 baby carrots, scraped; 18 whole baby onions, peeled; I cup shelled fresh peas, cooked; I cup sliced green beans, cooked; salt and freshly ground black pepper; ¹/₂ cup finely chopped parsley.

Brown meat in melted dripping in a frying pan. Remove and place in a flameproof casserole. Pour off fat from frying pan, then deglaze pan with 1 cup of the stock. Pour stock into casserole over meat and add remaining stock and tomato paste. Bring to the boil, then cover and simmer for 1 hour. Cool and refrigerate overnight. Next day, remove solidified fat from surface. Heat meat and liquid gently. Add potatoes, carrots and onions and simmer about 1 hour or until meat and vegetables are tender. Skim any fat from surface, then fold in peas and beans. Season with salt and pepper and simmer 5 minutes longer. Serve sprinkled with parsley. Serves 6–8.

NECTARINE

A superb summer stone fruit of the peach family, with a smooth skin, flushed a pinky-red. The flesh is firm and fragrant, and varies from creamy white to quite deep orange. Varieties range from small to large, some with clingstones and some with slipstones, and can be used in most recipes calling for peaches. A nectarine is delicious eaten freshly picked on its own or, perhaps, with a glass of chilled Sauterne. **See recipes.**

Baked Nectarines

6–8 ripe nectarines, peeled; juice ¹/₂ lemon; I¹/₂ cups sugar; I cup water; 6–8 cloves.

Cover nectarines with cold water and lemon juice to prevent discoloration. Place sugar and water in a saucepan and stir over medium heat until sugar has dissolved. Bring to the boil and boil for 5 minutes without stirring. Remove each nectarine from water, dry and stick with a clove. Arrange in a baking dish and pour syrup over. Bake in a preheated moderate oven (180°C/350°F) for 20 minutes or until tender, basting 2–3 times with syrup. Remove from oven, cool then chill. Serve with whipped cream. Serves 3–4.

Sugared Nectarines

8 ripe slipstone nectarines; ¹/₄ cup caster sugar; juice 1 lemon.

Slice nectarines into a glass bowl by making an incision down the natural division of the fruit deep enough to reach stone. Make another incision beside it and slice out section. Continue in this way around fruit to give even slices. Sprinkle sugar over fruit, then lemon juice. Serve immediately. Serves 4–6.

Smetna with Nectarines

A marvellous combination of smetna (the Russian name for sour cream) and brown sugar makes the difference in this dessert. Equally good when used with peaches.

³/₄ cup firmly packed brown sugar; 1¹/₂ cups sour light cream; 8 large ripe yellow nectarines, stoned and sliced; toasted flaked almonds to decorate.

Nectarines in White Wine

A simple, yet quite stunning summer dessert.

6 large ripe nectarines, stoned and sliced; ¹/₄ cup caster sugar; white wine, chilled.

Place nectarines in large wine glasses. Sprinkle with sugar, pour over white wine and refrigerate for 30 minutes. Serves 4.
NOTE: Peaches can be used instead of nectarines with equally delicious results.

NESSELRODE PUDDING

Originally this pudding was a very rich frozen confection full of candied fruits, chestnuts and liqueurs. It was invented by the chef to a Russian statesman, Count Nesselrode, who had a taste for lavish living. Today, the pudding is less rich and may be served unfrozen, but is still delicious. Set in an attractive bowl, this smooth, light and creamy dessert looks very festive with its decoration of rum-soaked cherries and a scattering of grated chocolate.

Nesselrode Pudding

3 egg yolks; ³/₄ cup sugar; 2¹/₂ cups cream; 1 tbs gelatine softened in 2 tbs cold water; ¹/₂ cup canned crushed pineapple, drained; ¹/₂ cup raisins; 2 tbs glacé cherries, soaked in 2 tbs rum; ¹/₄ finely chopped dark chocolate.

DECORATION: glacé cherries soaked in rum; dark chocolate, grated.

Combine egg yolks with sugar in the top of a double saucepan. Gradually stir in 1¹/₂ cups of the cream, the softened gelatine and crushed pineapple. Stir over simmering water until custard has thickened slightly. Pour into a chilled ice cream tray and freeze until just firm. Spoon mixture into a chilled bowl and beat with an electric or rotary beater until smooth and creamy. Fold in raisins, cherries and chocolate. Whip remaining cream and fold in. Pour into a decorative freezerproof bowl and return to freezer. Remove to refrigerator 30 minutes before serving to soften slightly. Serve decorated with glacé cherries and grated chocolate. Serves 8–10.

NICOISE

The word 'Niçoise' conjures up foods ripened by the warm sun of southern France. Dishes *à la Niçoise* are made from foods of the region around Nice and can be based on fish or vegetables. They are flavoured with garlic and have as their main ingredients tomatoes, black olives and fruity olive oil.

Salade Niçoise

Salade Niçoise is a rustic country salad, made with ingredients on hand and in season. Tuna fish can be added, or the lettuce omitted as desired.

1 lettuce, washed and dried; 1 x 50 g can anchovy fillets, drained; 3 tomatoes, peeled and quartered; 3 hard-boiled eggs, quartered; 1 cucumber, peeled and sliced; 2 sticks celery, sliced; 1 white onion, sliced; 1 small green or red pepper, cored, seeded and sliced; 1/2 cup black olives; 1 tbs capers (optional).

DRESSING: 1 tsp Dijon mustard; ¹/₂ tsp sugar; ¹/₂ tsp salt; ¹/₄ tsp black pepper; 1 clove garlic, crushed; 1 tbs chopped fresh herbs (parsley, chives, oregano); ¹/₂ cup olive oil; 2 tbs wine vinegar; 2 tsp tarragon vinegar; 1 tbs lemon juice or to taste.

Place lettuce leaves in salad bowl or on a platter. Arrange anchovy fillets, tomatoes, eggs, cucumber, celery and onion slices over lettuce. Garnish with pepper slices, black olives and capers if using.
DRESSING: Mix mustard, sugar, salt, pepper, garlic and herbs. Gradually beat in oil and lastly beat in wine and tarragon vinegars. Add lemon juice to taste. Beat again before using. Spoon dressing over salad and serve. Serves 4.

NOCKERL

These Austrian dumplings are usually served in soups, stews and goulashes or as an accompaniment for other dishes. However, Salzburger Nockerl is a wonderfully light fluffy dessert made from puffs of soufflé that bear little resemblance to the general concept of a dumpling. As the name implies the dish is a specialty of Salzburg but has spread throughout neighbouring Germany. Serve elegantly, with champagne or a chilled moselle wine.

Salzburger Nockerl

2 egg yolks; 1 tsp vanilla; ¹/₂ tsp grated lemon rind; 1 tbs flour; 4 egg whites; pinch salt; 2 tbs caster sugar; icing sugar, sifted.

Beat egg yolks lightly and stir in vanilla, lemon rind and flour. In another bowl, beat egg whites with salt until they hold firm peaks. Beat in sugar and continue beating until stiff and glossy. Stir a large spoonful of egg white into egg yolk mixture, then fold quickly and lightly into remaining egg white. Spoon in 4 mounds in a well-buttered 20 x 25 x 5 cm (8 x 10 x 2 in) ovenproof dish; it does not matter if mounds touch each other. Bake in centre of a preheated moderate oven (180°C/350°F) for about 10 minutes or until very pale brown on the outside but still soft and moist on the inside. Sprinkle generously with icing sugar and serve immediately with whipped Crème Anglaise (see page 111). Serves 4.

NOODLES, CHINESE

In China noodles are the *mein* in *Chow Mein*, and differ from other noodles in that the strands are 'thrown' by hand to form the customary long, thin strands or 'strings'; these vary in diameter from that of Italian spaghetti to that of the finest vermicelli. Many large Chinese restaurants throughout the world are beginning to put on displays of noodle-throwing for their delighted clientele. It is fascinating to see how readily a ball of dough becomes an armful of fine threads in the hands of a true craftsman.

The Chinese have always regarded noodles as a symbol of longevity because of their great length, and therefore they never cut them. However, like all noodles, the Chinese types come in a variety of shapes and sizes, some being small, and often as fine as thread.

Chinese noodles can be served in a sauce of meat or vegetables, in soup or fried. Chinese fried noodles get different treatment in different places. Some restaurants (and recipes) call for the noodles to be parboiled, rinsed in cold water, formed into a nest and then fried until crisp; they are then often topped with a savoury dish of meat or vegetables in a sauce. In China, the noodles are boiled, rinsed, then shallow-fried with meat, vegetables and seasonings or served as a complete dish.

RICE STICK NOODLES OR CELLOPHANE NOODLES: These are also found in Chinese cooking. They are thread-like and clear in colour, and are about the same length as chopsticks. They are found in Chinese food stores and are used more in southern China.

COMMERCIALLY MADE NOODLES: These are sold packaged in fine, medium or wide widths. Some are cut into squares and some fine noodles are shaped into nests. There are also dried soup noodles from Japan, China, Taiwan, Singapore, etc., and packaged noodle dinners.

The method for cooking all of these is usually printed on the packet.

■ TO COOK: The methods of cooking the flat European egg noodles and Chinese noodles differ slightly. Allow 1 bundle Chinese egg noodles for each person. Soak noodles in hot water for about 10 minutes. The strands will separate and enable the noodles to cook evenly. Bring a large saucepan of water to the boil and add a spoonful of peanut oil. Drain the soaked noodles and drop them into the boiling water. When water returns to the boil, cook fine noodles for 2–3 minutes, wide noodles for 3–4 minutes. Do not overcook. Like properly cooked pasta, noodles should be tender but still firm to the bite.

At end of cooking time, drain noodles in a large colander, then run cold water through the noodles to rinse off excess starch and to cool them so they don't continue to cook in their own heat. Drain thoroughly. Use in soups or braised noodle dishes – spread noodles out on a damp (not wet) tea-towel, spreading them apart with chopsticks so they dry out a little before using as directed in recipe.

Soft-fried Chinese Noodles: Cook noodles as described above and spread out to dry. A little peanut oil may be sprinkled over them to prevent them from sticking.

Heat 2 tbs each of peanut oil and sesame oil in a wok or frying pan, and when very hot add a handful of noodles. When golden on one side, turn and fry other side. Repeat with remaining noodles, draining on paper towels before serving at once. It may be necessary to add more oil to the pan if a large quantity of noodles is being fried, but make sure the fresh oil is very hot before adding noodles.

Serve them with beef, pork, poultry or vegetable dishes, or combine with stir-fried ingredients for Chow Mein (see page 87).

Crisp-fried Chinese Noodles: These crisp noodles are used mainly as a garnish. Rice vermicelli and cellophane noodles may be fried in deep hot oil straight from the packet. Egg noodles need to be cooked first as for soft-fried noodles. Use a larger amount of peanut oil and deep-fry in handfuls until crisp and golden-brown. Drain on paper towels before serving.

Noodles and Chicken Broth

This is one of the simplest Chinese noodle dishes to prepare and one which is as excellent as it is substantial. As a quick luncheon dish it cannot be surpassed.

4 tbs vegetable oil; 1 cup shredded chicken meat; ¹/₄ cup light soy sauce; ¹/₄ onion, finely chopped; ¹/₂ tsp grated fresh ginger; ¹/₄ cup Chinese wine or dry sherry; 1–2 cups boiling chicken broth or stock; 250 g (8 oz) Chinese egg noodles; pinch salt.

Heat oil in a wok or deep frying pan. When very hot, add chicken and stir-fry 3–4 minutes. Add soy sauce, onion, ginger and 1 cup broth or enough to cover noodles completely. When boiling hard, add noodles and salt and cook until done. Serve hot. Serves 4.

n

Noodles with Chicken Broth

A soup.

125 g (4 oz) Chinese egg noodles, cooked;
$^1/_2$ cup shredded cooked chicken meat;
2 slices cooked ham, shredded; 3 cups chicken
broth or stock; $^1/_2$ tsp salt; pinch pepper;
2 tsp soy sauce; 4 spring onions, shredded.

Place cooked noodles in heated serving bowl.
Arrange chicken and ham on top of noodles. Heat
broth, adding salt, pepper and soy sauce. Pour hot
broth over noodles, top with spring onions and serve
hot. Serves 4.

Braised Noodles with Chicken

4 bundles wide Chinese egg noodles; 1 tbs soy sauce;
1 tbs Chinese wine or dry sherry; 4 chicken fillets
(skinless, boneless, half-breasts), cubed;
$^1/_2$ Chinese cabbage; 1 tbs cornflour;
2 tbs cold water; 1 tbs oyster sauce; $^1/_2$ tsp salt;
2 tbs peanut oil; 2 cloves garlic, crushed;
1 tsp grated fresh ginger; 1 cup chicken stock;
5 spring onions, chopped.

Soak noodles in hot water for 10 minutes, then cook
as directed on the packet for 3–4 minutes or until
tender but still firm. Do not overcook. Drain in a
colander and rinse under cold running water to stop
cooking. Drain. Pour soy sauce and wine or sherry
over chicken. Mix and leave to marinate. Cut stalks
of Chinese cabbage into bite-sized pieces. Mix cornflour
with cold water, oyster sauce and salt, and set aside.

Heat oil in a wok or frying pan and gently fry
garlic and ginger for a few seconds. Add chicken and
stir-fry over high heat for 2 minutes or until colour
changes. Add cabbage and fry, stirring, for 1 minute
longer. Add stock, bring to the boil, add cornflour
mixture and stir until thick. Add well-drained
noodles and heat through, tossing to mix evenly.
Garnish with spring onions. Serves 4–5.

Chinese Chicken and Noodle Salad

4 half-breasts of chicken; salt; 1 bay leaf;
1 slice onion; few black peppercorns;
375 g (12 oz) Chinese egg noodles; 1 tbs oil;
Sesame Peanut Sauce (page 27).

GARNISH: 3 spring onions, finely sliced;
1 tbs toasted sesame seeds.

Place chicken breasts in a saucepan, and add salted
water to cover, bay leaf, onion and peppercorns.
Simmer gently for 10 minutes. Cool in water. Cook
noodles according to packet directions or as on page
297. Drain, and rinse under cold running water. Drain
thoroughly and toss lightly with oil to prevent sticking.

Drain chicken, remove skin and bones, and slice flesh
finely. Place noodles in a large heated serving dish, top
with chicken and pour sesame peanut sauce over.
Garnish with sliced spring onions and toasted sesame
seeds. Toss salad gently and serve. Serves 6–8.

Fragrant Noodles

20 dried shrimp (from Chinese groceries);
$^1/_2$ cup peanut oil; 3 medium onions, diced;
1 tbs light soy sauce; 2 tsp Chinese wine or
dry sherry; 2 cups water; 500 g (1 lb) Chinese
egg noodles.

Soak dry shrimp in cold water 10 minutes, then drain
and clean. Heat half of the oil in a frying pan or wok,
add onions and stir-fry 2–3 minutes. Lower heat
slightly, add shrimp and cook, stirring, until only
residual moisture is left and oil splatters when in
contact with moisture. Remove from heat. Heat rest
of oil in a small saucepan, add shrimp mixture, soy
sauce and wine or sherry and stir-fry 1–2 minutes.
Add water and simmer 30 minutes or until water has
nearly evaporated. Meanwhile, cook noodles according
to packet directions or as on page 297. Drain, rinse
quickly under cold running water and drain again.
Reheat all ingredients together and serve. Serves 4.

Prawn Chow Mein

250 g (8 oz) Chinese egg noodles; 6 tbs vegetable oil;
1 $^1/_2$ cups small, shelled green prawns, deveined;
3 tbs soy sauce; $^1/_2$ cup Chinese wine or dry sherry;
2 tsp sugar; 1 tsp salt; $^1/_2$ tsp grated fresh ginger;
vinegar to serve.

Cook noodles according to packet directions or as on
page 297. Drain and rinse under cold running water.
Distribute noodles as thinly as possible on a damp
(not wet) cloth and place them in a cool, airy place to
dry. Place one third of the oil in a wok or frying pan
and heat. Add prawns and fry until over half done
(about 3 minutes). Then add half of the soy sauce,
Chinese wine or sherry and sugar. Cook another
3 minutes, then remove from the pan and keep warm.
Put remaining oil into pan and heat. Add noodles,
and fry, turning from time to time with a fork or
chopsticks, until golden-brown. Add remaining soy
sauce, wine and sugar, the salt and ginger. Cook
briskly for a further 2 minutes. Return prawns to pan,
cook another 2 minutes, and serve immediately Some
people prefer a dash of vinegar on 'Ch'ao Mien' and
this should be provided at the table as its use is a
matter of individual taste. Serves 4.

Fried Noodles

250 g (8 oz) Chinese egg noodles; 8 tbs oil;
3 eggs, beaten with $^1/_2$ tsp salt; 250 g (8 oz) boneless
pork, shredded; 2 canned bamboo shoots, shredded;

2 cups chopped vegetables or bean sprouts; 6 dried mushrooms, soaked in water, drained and shredded; 4 spring onions, shredded;
1 tbs Chinese wine or dry sherry; 2 tbs soy sauce;
$^{1}/_{2}$ cup stock; 1 tsp cornflour; 2 tsp salt.

Cook noodles according to packet directions or as on page 297. Drain, rinse under cold running water and drain again. Heat 3 tbs oil in a frying pan, add eggs and fry to a thin omelette. Break omelette into small pieces and remove to a plate. Heat a further 3 tbs oil in a pan and fry pork 3–4 minutes. Add bamboo shoots, vegetables or bean sprouts, mushrooms, spring onions, wine or sherry and soy sauce. Blend stock with cornflour, add to pan and heat, stirring until thickened. Keep hot. Heat remaining oil in a separate frying pan or wok, add noodles and salt and fry for 6 minutes, stirring constantly. Pat into a pancake shape and allow to brown lightly on both sides. Remove noodles to a large heated plate or bowl, pour over pork mixture, top with omelette pieces and serve hot. Serves 4.

Chilled Noodles with Sauce

375 g (12 oz) Chinese egg noodles; 1 tbs sesame oil;
1 tbs vegetable oil; 2 eggs, beaten; 1 cup shredded cooked chicken or pork; 3 slices cooked ham, shredded; 1 cup shredded cucumber;
$^{1}/_{2}$ cup cooked shelled prawns, deveined.

SAUCE: 1 tbs sesame seeds; 1 tbs red pepper oil, or 1 tsp Tabasco sauce; 2 tbs soy sauce;
2 cups chicken broth or stock.

Cook noodles according to packet directions or as on page 297. Drain, mix with sesame oil and chill. Heat vegetable oil in a frying pan, add eggs and fry into a thin omelette. Arrange shredded omelette, chicken or pork, ham, cucumber and prawns on top of chilled noodles.
SAUCE: Grind sesame seeds in a mortar. Add remaining sauce ingredients and mix thoroughly. Serve sauce separately in a bowl. Pour sauce over noodles and shredded ingredients just before eating. Serves 4–6.
NOTE: If you cannot buy red pepper oil, make it by heating 2 tbs sesame oil in a small frying pan and frying 2 red chillies until they turn dark. Drain off the oil and discard chillies.

Lamb Shreds with Cellophane Noodles

375 g (12 oz) lamb chump chops, boned; 1 egg white;
1 tsp salt; 1 tsp cornflour; 1 cup plus 2 tbs peanut oil;
1 tbs soy sauce; $^{1}/_{4}$ tsp red pepper oil or
Tabasco sauce; 30 g (1 oz) cellophane noodles.

Slice lamb into thin, match-like shreds. Mix with egg white, $^{1}/_{2}$ tsp salt and the cornflour. Let stand 5 minutes. Heat 2 tbs peanut oil in a frying pan or wok

and stir-fry lamb for about 2 minutes. Add soy sauce and pepper oil or Tabasco. Mix well and place on a heated platter. Heat remaining peanut oil and deep-fry noodles for 1–2 seconds. Do not burn. Drain on paper towels. Sprinkle with the remaining salt and place at both ends of the lamb shreds. Serves 4.

NOODLES, EGG

A paste made from flour and egg yolks, rolled flat and cut into strips. Egg noodles are a favourite in Germany where they are called *nudeln* or *nockerln*, also in France where they are known as *nouilles*.

Noodles may be cooked and treated in much the same way as spaghetti or other pastas (see *Pasta*). Each country has its own favourite way.

In Germany noodles are generally boiled, drained and mixed with melted butter or bacon fat. They are seasoned with salt, pepper and nutmeg, paprika, poppyseeds, finely chopped dill or parsley, crumbled cooked bacon or chopped ham – the seasoning added depends on the food being served with the noodles. Thin noodles are preferred for chicken, veal and soup, wider noodles are the popular choice for stews, generally those flavoured with paprika, like goulash.

■ TO COOK: Cook egg noodles in plenty of boiling salted water; keep water boiling rapidly to prevent noodles sticking together. Drain, use as directed.

See also *Pasta*.

Chicken Noodle Casserole

500 g (1 lb) egg noodles; 1.5 kg (3 lb) chicken joints;
salt and freshly ground pepper; 60 g (2 oz) butter;
1–2 tbs oil; 1 onion, finely chopped; pinch dried rosemary; $^{1}/_{3}$ cup flour; 2$^{1}/_{2}$ cups chicken stock;
$^{1}/_{2}$ cup dry white wine; $^{1}/_{2}$ cup cream;
$^{1}/_{2}$ cup chopped walnuts.

Cook noodles in plenty of boiling salted water until tender. Drain and put in bottom of large shallow ovenproof serving dish. Sprinkle chicken pieces with salt and pepper. Brown in butter in a frying pan, a few pieces at a time. Place on noodles. Add oil then onion to butter in frying pan and cook gently until soft. Stir in rosemary and flour and cook, stirring, 1–2 minutes. Stir in stock gradually, then wine. Bring to the boil, stirring constantly. Add cream and cook gently for 5–10 minutes. Add nuts, then spoon sauce over chicken. Cover dish with lid or foil and bake in a preheated moderate oven (180°C/350°F) for 1 hour. Serves 6.

NUT BRITTLE

Nut brittle is a clear, hard toffee well flavoured with nuts, either peanuts, pecans, Brazil nuts or some other combination. It is best made with corn syrup, which is available from specialist grocery stores and some delicatessens.

Nut Brittle

**1 cup water; 2 cups sugar; 1 cup light corn syrup;
2 cups shelled raw peanuts, pecans or Brazil nuts;
1 tsp salt; 30 g (1 oz) butter; ¹/₄ tsp bicarbonate
of soda.**

Place water in a large heavy saucepan and bring to
the boil. Remove from heat and stir in sugar until
dissolved. Stir in corn syrup, nuts and salt. Return
to medium heat and cook to hard crack stage
(146°C/295°F), stirring occasionally to keep nuts
submerged so they cook thoroughly and toffee syrup
does not burn. Remove from heat and stir in butter
and bicarbonate of soda. Pour into a well-buttered
lamington tin. When cool, crack into pieces and store
in an airtight container. Makes about 1 kg (2 lb).
NOTE: To test for hard crack stage without a sugar
thermometer, drop ¹/₂ tsp of toffee into cold water. It
should make brittle threads that stay brittle when
removed from water.

NUT BUTTER

This can be smooth or chunky and is made by pounding
or grinding a variety of blanched and roasted nuts to a
butter-like spread. Probably the best known nut butter is
Peanut Butter (see page 349), but others are made from
almonds, cashews, pecans, walnuts, hazelnuts and pine
nuts. Nut butters will keep for months if stored in a cool
dry place.

Nut Butter

**2 cups toasted, unsalted almonds, pecans,
walnuts, cashews or other nuts; 3–6 tbs safflower or
vegetable oil; 1 tsp salt.**

Put nuts, half the oil and the salt in a blender or food
processor. Purée to desired consistency, adding more
oil if necessary. Store in sealed, airtight jars. Makes
about 1 cup.

NUTMEG

The large nutmeg tree is native to the Indonesian
islands and the Philippines, and also grows in the West
Indies. The ripe plum-like fruit dries and then splits
open. The nutmeg seed is encased in a bright red outer
covering, which, when dried in the sun, is known as
mace (see *Mace*). The seed is slowly dried in the tropical
sun or over slow-burning charcoal fires. They will keep
well in an airtight container, sometimes for years.

Nutmeg is at its best when grated fresh into the dish in
which it is required as, once grated, it rapidly loses its
best flavour.

Beautifully aromatic nutmeg is equally at home in
sweet and savoury dishes. The English devotees of the
eighteenth and nineteenth centuries often travelled with
their own, personal nutmeg grater, such was their love of
this lovely spice. In English cooking today, nutmeg is
mainly used in cakes and sweet dishes, but it is equally
important in savoury and meat dishes.

Use it in sausages, terrines, pâtés and potted meats. It
is also good in egg dishes, or with mashed potatoes, and
it is particularly tasty with spinach. A spinach ravioli filling
nearly always contains nutmeg, as does the famous
Bolognese Sauce (see page 340). Nutmeg is excellent in
white or cheese sauce, and a blade of mace is often
infused in the milk for these sauces; in fact, both go well in
any cheese dish.

Nutmeg is a frequent ingredient in many Indian spiced
foods, and in Garam Masala (see page 171) – that fragrant
spice-blend often added at the end of cooking. Nutmeg is
also a common flavouring in Middle Eastern cookery, and
is good with lamb.

For desserts, nutmeg is a natural partner of rice and
other milk puddings, apples pies and spiced fruits. It is
often sprinkled over warm milk, punches or drinks to be
taken at night, and it is claimed that nutmeg has a slightly
soporific effect.

In Indonesia a fresh ripe nutmeg seed is often prepared
as a sweetmeat preserve, as is fresh mace. These are
delicious and well worth looking for in Indian shops
– certainly buy some if you are lucky enough to visit Bali
or elsewhere in Indonesia.

Buy good quality, large nutmegs whole, store in a small
jar, then grate freshly each time nutmeg is needed. Small
tin nutmeg graters are inexpensive and available from
most kitchen shops; more elaborate mills, rather like
pepper mills, are also available. **See recipes.**

Spinach Florentine

**1 large bunch spinach, coarsely shredded;
30 g (1 oz) butter; 1 clove garlic, finely chopped;
salt; ¹/₄ tsp nutmeg; ¹/₄ cup cream; coarsely grated
Parmesan cheese; melted butter.**

Place spinach in large saucepan, cover and cook for 5
minutes, tossing occasionally. Drain well, press out all
excess moisture. Heat butter in frying pan, add garlic,
salt, nutmeg and cream and stir. Add spinach and toss
lightly to heat through. Place in a flameproof serving
dish and sprinkle with cheese and melted butter.
Brown quickly under a preheated grill. Serves 4.

Chicken Liver Mousse

**185 g (6 oz) chicken livers; 2 eggs; 1¹/₂ cups milk;
¹/₄ tsp salt; freshly ground black pepper; nutmeg;
2 clove garlic; 1 tsp chopped parsley.**

Remove any veins and sinew from chicken livers.
Place in a blender with eggs, milk, salt, pepper,
nutmeg, garlic and parsley, and blend to a purée. It
may be necessary to do this in 3 batches. Fill 6 small
buttered soufflé dishes. Place in a roasting tin
containing enough water to come halfway up sides

of dishes. Cover with foil. Bake in a preheated hot oven (220°/445°F) for 30 minutes or until mixture is set. Loosen sides of mousses from dishes with a knife, invert on to a heated plate and drain off any excess juices. Serve hot with Fresh Tomato Sauce (see page 339). Serves 6.

Cauliflower Cream Soup

$^1/_2$ medium cauliflower, broken into florets;
4 cups chicken stock; $^1/_3$ cup milk; 30 g (1 oz) butter;
salt and freshly ground black pepper;
$^1/_4$ tsp nutmeg; 2 egg yolks; $^1/_4$ cup cream.

Reserve a few cauliflower florets for garnish. Drop remaining cauliflower into boiling salted water and cook until tender, about 10 minutes. Drain and press through a sieve, or purée in a blender or food processor. Place in a saucepan, add stock and bring slowly to the boil. Add milk, butter, salt, pepper and nutmeg. Combine egg yolks with cream, add a little of the hot soup, blend well and stir into remaining soup. Cook gently without boiling until soup thickens. Garnish with sprigs of raw cauliflower and serve immediately, sprinkled with a light fresh grating of nutmeg. Serves 6.

Armenian Nutmeg Cake

2 cups firmly packed brown sugar;
2 cups self-raising flower, sifted;
125 g (4 oz) butter; 1 tsp bicarbonate of soda;
1 cup milk; 1 egg, beaten; 1 tsp nutmeg;
$^1/_2$ cup chopped walnuts.

Combine sugar and flour. Rub in butter until mixture resembles fine breadcrumbs. Press half the mixture into a well-greased 20 cm (8 in) square tin. Dissolve soda in milk, add egg and nutmeg and pour over remaining sugar and flour mixture. Mix well, then spoon into tin on top of pressed-in mixture. Sprinkle walnuts over. Bake in a preheated moderate oven (180°C/350°F) for 1 hour. Allow to stand 15 minutes before turning out on to a wire rack to cool.

NUTS

These are one of man's oldest foods and one of the most useful. As well as making sustaining and convenient snacks, they are excellent companions to fruit or cheese for dessert and have dozens of culinary uses from nut butters, salads, savoury dishes, breads, cakes and biscuits to desserts, ice creams and confectionery.

For long storage, nuts should be kept unshelled in a cool place or in the freezer. If shelled, buy in quantities you can use up within a few weeks and keep them in an airtight container in a cool, dark, dry place. Larger quantities of shelled nuts are best stored in the freezer. Since exposure to air and light causes loss of flavour, you will find that nuts that you blanch, chop or grind just before using are much better than the ready-prepared products.

Salted Nuts: Peanuts, cashews, walnuts, almonds, etc., can be salted individually or mixed. Heat about 2 tbs butter or oil for each cup of blanched nuts. Spread nuts in a thin, even layer in the pan and cook slowly, stirring continuously, until nuts are delicate, even brown. Remove from pan, drain on paper towels and sprinkle with salt, allowing about 1/2 tsp per cup of nuts. Toss lightly to coat all nuts and serve, or cool and store in an airtight container.

Curried Nuts: Follow recipe for Salted Nuts, but add 1/2 tsp curry powder per cup of nuts to salt before sprinkling over. Onion or garlic salt may be substituted for plain salt, for added flavour.

Devilled Nuts: Follow recipe for Salted Nuts until nuts are browned, then for each cup of nuts add 1 tsp Worcestershire sauce, 1/2 tsp salt and small pinch cayenne to pan. Stir over gentle heat until nuts are evenly coated, remove from pan and drain on paper towels. Pass around when serving drinks.

See also *Nut Brittle*, *Nut Butter* and individual entries for nuts.

OATCAKE

See *Bannock*.

OATMEAL

Made by grinding hulled oats into flour or meal. Oatmeal is generally prepared in grades according to its texture – coarse, medium or fine; medium is the one we use most.

Oatmeal is among the most nutritious of all the grains, and rolled oats, the steamed grain flattened between rollers for faster cooking, have been used to make breakfast porridge for generations of families throughout the world. Oatmeal is also used to give bulk to sausages, to thicken soups and stews or to bake oatcakes, breads, scones, biscuits (see *Anzac Biscuits*), and puddings. The Scots have many splendid dishes containing oatmeal, including Oatcakes (see *Bannock*), Crispy Herring in Oatmeal (see page 196), and, of course, porridge, while the Swiss breakfast muesli contains uncooked rolled or toasted oats. Quick-cooking oatmeal is readily available from supermarkets and grocery stores, and can be used in many recipes as well as for a quick breakfast cereal.

Rolled oats are said to be invented by the Quaker Oat Company in 1877. Quick-cooking oats are thinner and finer than rolled oats and have been pre-cooked. See recipes.

Ginger Oatmeal Scones

I cup flour; 4 tsp baking powder;
2 tsp ground ginger; $^1/_2$ tsp ground allspice;
$^1/_2$ tsp salt; I cup one-minute oats; 2 tbs butter;
2 tsp honey; $^1/_4$ cup warm water; $^1/_3$ cup milk.

Sift flour, baking powder, spices and salt into a bowl. Add oats and rub in butter. Mix honey, water and milk, blending thoroughly. Pour into dry ingredients and mix to a soft dough. On a floured surface lightly pat dough into a round about 2.5 cm (1 in) thick. Cut into rounds using a scone cutter or sharp knife. Place on an ungreased baking tray and bake in a preheated very hot oven (230°C/450°F) for 10–12 minutes. Serve warm with butter and ginger marmalade or apricot jam. Makes about 12.

Oat and Raisin Bread

A delicious tea bread, served sliced with butter.

I egg, beaten; $^1/_3$ cup firmly packed brown sugar;
2 tbs golden syrup, warmed; $I^1/_4$ cups buttermilk;
60 g (2 oz) butter, melted; $^2/_3$ cup rolled oats;
I cup wholemeal flour; 2 tsp baking powder;
$^3/_4$ tsp salt; $^3/_4$ tsp bicarbonate of soda;
$^2/_3$ cup raisins.

Beat egg with sugar, syrup, buttermilk, butter and rolled oats. Let stand for 5 minutes. Sift flour, baking powder, salt and bicarbonate of soda and fold into oat mixture. Stir in raisins lightly. Turn into a greased

and lined 20 x 10 cm (8 x 4 in) loaf tin and spread batter evenly. Bake in a preheated moderate oven (180°C/350°F) for 1 hour or until a skewer inserted in centre comes out clean. Cool on a wire rack. Serve sliced and spread with butter.

Oatmeal Soda Bread

A quick bread made without yeast.

I cup wholemeal flour; I cup white flour;
I tsp baking powder; I tsp bicarbonate of soda;
I tsp sugar; I tsp salt; $I^1/_2$ cups fine oatmeal;
$I^1/_4$ cups buttermilk or sour milk.

Sift flours, baking powder, soda, sugar and salt into a large bowl and mix in oatmeal. Stir in buttermilk or sour milk and mix lightly and quickly to a soft dough. Put on a floured surface, knead once or twice and shape dough lightly into a round. Place on a greased baking tray. Using a sharp knife cut a cross in top of loaf. Bake in a preheated moderately hot oven (190°C/375°F) for about 1 hour or until bread sounds hollow when tapped underneath. Remove from oven and immediately wrap in a clean tea-towel. Serve while still warm, with plenty of butter.

Cranachan

A marvellous Scottish dessert also known as Cream Crowdie.

4 tbs medium oatmeal; $I^1/_4$ cups cream;
I tbs icing sugar, sifted; 2 tbs whisky,
or I tsp vanilla.

Spread oatmeal on an ungreased baking tray and lightly toast in a preheated moderate oven (180°C/350°F) for about 15 minutes or until crisp. Cool. Whip cream until it holds soft peaks and fold in icing sugar and whisky or vanilla. Gently stir cooled, toasted oatmeal into cream. Serve on its own or with fresh strawberries or raspberries. Serves 4.

Peanut Butter Biscuits

90 g (3 oz) butter; 2 tbs crunchy
peanut butter; $I^1/_2$ cups caster sugar;
$^1/_2$ cup lightly packed brown sugar;
I tsp vanilla; I egg; $I^1/_2$ cups self-raising flour,
sifted; I tsp salt; $^1/_2$ cup rolled oats.

Cream butters, sugars and vanilla. Add egg, beat well, then stir in flour and salt. Mix in oats. Form mixture into 2 rolls about 2.5 cm (1 in) in diameter, wrap in plastic wrap and chill for about 30 minutes. Cut into 2.5 mm ($^1/_4$ in) thick slices and arrange on greased baking trays. Bake in a preheated moderate oven (180°C/350°F) about 20 minutes. Cool on baking trays for 3 minutes, then transfer to wire racks. Store in an airtight container. Makes about 36.

O

Oatmeal Crunch

I cup rolled oats; I cup desiccated coconut;
$^1/_2$ cup raw sugar; $^1/_2$ tsp vanilla; 125 g (4 oz) butter,
melted; $^1/_2$ cup mixed chopped raisins
and dried apricots.

Combine oats, coconut, sugar, vanilla and melted butter and mix thoroughly. Stir in chopped fruits. Spread mixture in greased lamington tin and bake in a preheated moderate oven (180°C/350°F) for 20–30 minutes. Cut into squares while still hot. When cool, remove from tin and store in an airtight container. Makes about 30 squares.

Rolled Oat Biscuits

$2^1/_4$ cups rolled oats; $^1/_2$ cup raw sugar;
125 g (4 oz) butter; 2 tbs honey; 2 tbs golden syrup;
I tsp molasses (optional); I tbs sultanas;
2 tbs chopped dried apricots.

Combine rolled oats and sugar. Melt butter, add honey, syrup and molasses and combine thoroughly. Pour over oats and sugar. Add sultanas and apricots and stir well. Place in a greased lamington tin and smooth top. Bake in a preheated moderate oven (180°C/350°F) for 20–25 minutes. Cut into squares while still warm and remove from tin when cold. Store in an airtight container. Makes about 20.

Cherry Raisin Drops

I cup rolled oats; I cup ricotta or cottage cheese;
I cup self-raising flour, sifted; $^1/_2$ cup caster sugar;
$^1/_4$ cup chopped raisins; $^1/_4$ cup chopped glacé
cherries; 125 g (4 oz) butter, melted; $^1/_3$ cup milk.

Combine all ingredients and mix well to a stiff batter. Place teaspoons of mixture on greased baking trays, allowing space for spreading. Bake in a preheated moderately hot oven (190°C/375°F) for 15–20 minutes. Remove from trays and cool on wire racks. Makes about 36.

OCTOPUS

A cephalopod, as is squid. The two resemble each other in that they have tentacles but no visible external shell. The best edible octopus is the small variety, with a maximum weight of about 500 g (1 lb). Larger octopuses are usually not as tender as their smaller cousins.

Octopus can be stewed, fried or stuffed and baked like squid (see *Squid*). The larger ones need the longest cooking. Little octopuses can be gently fried in olive oil to make up a delicious salad, served warm with plenty of lemon juice, chopped garlic and chopped parsley.

■ **BASIC PREPARATION:** If your recipe calls for only the tentacles, ask the fishmonger to remove the head for you. Otherwise, cut off the tentacles, set aside and clean octopus by pulling out intestines and ink sac, reserving the latter if the octopus is to be cooked in its ink. Using kitchen shears or a very sharp knife, cut out the eyes and beak-like mouth and discard. Rinse well.

If octopus is large, it must be tenderised. After cleaning, pound with a heavy mallet or cleaver then strip off skin by rubbing with salt and rinsing well. Alternatively, simmer in water to cover for 1 hour, then peel off skin and proceed according to your recipe.

If octopus is under 500 g (1 lb), omit pounding or simmering; simply rub off skin, rinse octopus well and proceed with recipe. **See recipes.**

Pickled Octopus

A delicious appetiser served in Greece.

500 g (I lb) octopus, cleaned, skinned and
pounded; I clove garlic, crushed; $^1/_2$ cup olive oil;
$^1/_2$ cup vinegar; salt and freshly ground
black pepper.

GARNISH: lemon wedges; chopped parsley.

Place octopus head and tentacles in a heavy saucepan without any liquid. Cover and cook very gently until octopus turns a deep pink and is tender, which takes about 45 minutes. Drain and, when cool, strip suckers from tentacles into bite-sized strips and place in a bowl. Add garlic, olive oil, vinegar, salt and pepper. Mix well, cover and leave to marinate in refrigerator for at least 12 hours. Stir occasionally. Drain off marinade, and pile octopus into a serving dish. Garnish with lemon wedges and chopped parsley. Serve with crusty bread and provide toothpicks for convenient eating. Serves 6.

Octopus Stewed with Onions

500 g (I lb) octopus, cleaned, skinned and
pounded; $^1/_3$ cup olive oil; 3 onion, sliced;
2 cloves garlic, crushed; I tsp chopped fresh
marjoram, or $^1/_2$ tsp dried; $^1/_2$ tsp sugar; I bay leaf;
2 tbs white wine vinegar; I cup red wine; I cup
canned tomatoes; 2 tsp tomato paste; salt and
freshly ground black pepper; chopped parsley.

Cut octopus into pieces about 5 cm (2 in) long. Heat oil in a deep frying pan and sauté onions and garlic until translucent. Add octopus pieces, marjoram, sugar and bay leaf, and cook gently for 5 minutes. Stir in vinegar, wine, tomatoes and tomato paste, cover pan and simmer gently for 40–45 minutes or until octopus is tender. Remove bay leaf, season with salt and pepper, sprinkle with plenty of chopped parsley and serve with crusty bread. Serves 4.

OEUFS A LA NEIGE (EGGS IN THE SNOW)

See *Custard*.

OFFAL

General term for those parts of an animal left over from cutting up a carcase; they may also be called variety meats. Some types of offal come from inside the animal (e.g. liver, kidneys, sweetbreads, brains, tripe) while others are external (e.g. tongue, tail, feet, head).

See also entries for individual names.

OIL

Oils are distinguished from fats in that they are liquid at room temperature. Edible oils are processed from many seeds, nuts and fruits including olives, peanuts, sunflower seeds, coconuts, walnuts, pumpkin seeds, grape seeds, avocados, sesame seeds, corn, cotton seeds and soy beans.

There are some edible oils of animal origins, but these are mostly used in manufacturing rather than in the kitchen.

Cold-pressed or unrefined oils have been extracted simply by pressing, and retain their full natural flavour. Refined oils, the majority of those available, have been processed to make them relatively flavourless and odourless, and to keep well. Ideally, buy oil in quantities that you will use within a month or two. Delicate salad oils such as walnut, grape seed or pumpkin seed, and other cold-pressed oils, should be stored in the refrigerator. Cooking oils should be stored, tightly sealed, in a cool place away from light. Do not mix together used and unused oil or else the flavour will spoil.

TYPES OF OIL

There are three basic types of oil: polyunsaturated, mono-unsaturated and saturated. They differ from each other in their chemical structure. There is some controversy about their different effects on health, and it is widely believed that the use of polyunsaturated oils, as well as fats, is preferable to that of saturated ones to help control blood fats (cholesterol and triglycerides), which are a risk factor in heart disease and strokes.

Polyunsaturated oils include sunflower, safflower, maize, soy bean and many blended vegetable oils.

Mono-unsaturated oils are usually fairly neutral in context. They include olive and peanut oils.

Saturated oils are mostly of animal origin; coconut oil, however, is saturated.

WAYS TO USE OILS

SALAD DRESSINGS AND SAUCES: Olive oil is the queen of salad oils and is indispensable for pasta sauces. Its flavour varies in character and strength from one country and from one type of olive to another. A trick for developing a fruity flavour is to keep a few black olives in a bottle of oil. The finest olive oil is virgin oil, from the first cold pressing of the olives. It is sometimes blended with the less expensive, blander oil from later pressings to improve its flavour.

Peanut oil or polyunsaturated all-purpose oils, such as sunflower, safflower, corn or blended oils, can be used in salad dressings and sauces though they will contribute little to the flavour. You may like to mix them half-and-half with olive oil.

Aromatic oils, such as walnut, grape seed, pumpkin seed and avocado, give subtle flavour variations to salad dressings.

CAKES AND BREADS: Oil is used instead of butter or margarine in some cakes and breads, but it cannot be substituted for these in other recipes. All-purpose oils such as the polyunsaturated ones are suitable; the flavour of olive oil is usually too strong though it is occasionally called for.

FRYING: The best oils for frying are those which can be heated to fairly high temperatures before beginning to smoke (a sign that the oil is starting to break down and will spoil the flavour of the food; it is also very close to its 'flash' point – when it will burst into flames). Peanut oil (much used in Chinese cooking), corn oil, safflower oil, sunflower and most blended oils are suitable.

So-called 'solid oils' (oils which have been processed to make them solid at room temperature), are much less expensive than polyunsaturated oils; they are recommended by manufacturers for deep-frying and perform particularly well, though the processing makes them more saturated than before.

Olive oil breaks down at high temperatures so can be used for frying only at moderate heat; it is not, therefore, suitable for deep-frying. But its lovely flavour makes it ideal for lightly frying vegetables or for the gentle cooking of onion, which is the first step in so many dishes. It is also used for *Ratatouille* (see page 411) and other Mediterranean dishes, which are simmered in oil rather than fried. Mustard seed oil, which has a distinctive flavour, is often used to fry the onions, garlic and spices for a curry.

Heat oil for frying slowly to the correct temperature. If it is not hot enough, too much will be absorbed by the food, and if it is overheated, it will not only spoil the flavour but can be dangerous. If overheated oil should catch alight, smother the flames by sprinkling with flour (don't thrown on too much at once as this may cause oil to splash); or cover the pan with a lid and leave so that flames will go out from lack of air. Do not use water as this will only spread the flames. After use, strain oil through a sieve lined with a disposable cloth and store, tightly sealed, in the refrigerator or a very cool place. The 'smoke' point is gradually lowered with use.

Oil that smells burnt or looks dark should be discarded. Solid oil or peanut oil, properly used, should last for about 3–5 fryings. Polyunsaturated oils are less robust and will probably last for only 1–2 fryings.

SAUTEEING AND BROWNING CASSEROLE MEAT: Use only a little oil, and heat slowly until it just begins to give off a haze, then add food (which should be well dried or floured) immediately. If you are cooking several batches, wipe pan out quickly with paper towels and use fresh oil for each batch.

SHALLOW-FRYING: Usually used for food which is floured or coated with batter or crumbs. Put in enough oil to come halfway up the pieces of food. Be sure the container is deep enough to allow oil to boil up when food is added. Heat slowly until it just begins to give off a haze and add food immediately.

FRYING WITH BUTTER AND OIL: A mixture of butter and oil is often used for sautéeing and shallow-frying – the butter contributes its distinctive and fine flavour, while the oil with its higher smoking point protects the butter from burning. Heat oil slowly until it just begins to give off a haze, add butter and, as soon as foaming subsides, add food. For sautéeing, use equal quantities of oil and butter unless otherwise instructed. For shallow-frying, use rather more oil and less butter.

DEEP-FRYING: Use a depth of oil sufficient to float the food, but never fill pan more than halfway up as oil will boil up when you add food. Have pieces of food of uniform size so that they cook evenly. A frying basket helps to add and remove food all together so that none is overdone. Heat oil slowly to required temperature – for most deep-frying, this is 180°C/350°F on a kitchen thermometer, or when a cube of day-old bread turns golden and crisp in 1 minute.

OKRA

The rigid green seed pods, elegantly curved and pointed, have a flavour resembling that of eggplants but with a somewhat mucilaginous texture. Okra, also called ladies' fingers or gumbo, is used extensively in Creole cooking, particularly in the soup-stew, *Gumbo* (see page 187). It is also used in Indian curries, and in many Middle Eastern dishes.

Choose crisp, fresh green-coloured pods that are no more than 10 cm (4 in) long. The pods should snap easily and the seeds be firm but not hard. Avoid any pods that are shrivelled, limp, bruised or a dull green.

Okra can also be purchased canned from most supermarkets or delicatessens. Rinse the pods well in cold running water to get rid of the viscous juices before using unless the recipe is for gumbo, curry or meat stew which may need the juices to give the texture required.

■ **BASIC PREPARATION:** Wash the pods, carefully remove the tip and the cap – a fringe-like top where the pod meets the stem. Do not cut the pod and expose the seeds and sticky juices inside. This helps prevent the pods splitting and losing shape during cooking when serving whole. See recipes.

Buttered Okra: Place prepared whole okra pods in lightly salted simmering water. Simmer, uncovered, for 8–10 minutes or until tender and still crisp. Drain and serve tossed in butter.

With Fresh Tomato Sauce: Prepare as for Buttered Okra, but omit the butter and serve in Fresh Tomato Sauce (see page 339), sprinkled with chopped parsley.

Fried Okra Rings

$1/4$ cup milk; I egg, beaten; 375 g (12 oz) okra, trimmed and sliced; $1/2$ cup cornmeal (polenta) or flour; salt and freshly ground black pepper; 60 g (2 oz) butter.

Beat milk and egg together. Drop in okra, drain then coat lightly with cornmeal or flour seasoned with salt and pepper. Sauté okra in butter until golden, turning once. Drain on paper towels and serve immediately. Serves 3–4.

Okra and Tomatoes

3–4 tbs olive oil; 3 onions, chopped; I clove garlic, chopped; 500 g (1 lb) okra, trimmed; 500 g (1 lb) tomatoes, peeled and chopped; juice I lemon; salt and freshly ground black pepper; $1/2$ tsp sugar; I tbs water; finely chopped parsley.

Heat oil in a frying pan, add onions and garlic and cook gently for about 5 minutes or until they soften. Add okra and cook to a light golden colour, turning gently from time to time. Spread out okra in one layer in the pan and put tomatoes on top with lemon juice, salt, pepper and sugar. Sprinkle over water and cook for about 20 minutes or until okra is tender and sauce reduced. Shake pan during cooking but do not stir. Serve warm or cold, sprinkled with parsley. Serves 3–4.

Okra Curry

I tbs ghee or oil; I large onion, sliced; 2 green chillies, seeded and chopped; I clove garlic, chopped; $1/2$ tsp grated fresh ginger; $1/2$ tsp turmeric; 500 g (1 lb) tender okra, trimmed and cut into 5 cm (2 in) lengths; $1/2$ tsp ground coriander; $1/2$ tsp ground cumin; $1^1/2$ cups Coconut Milk (page 91) or buttermilk; I tsp salt.

Heat ghee or oil in a saucepan and fry onion and chillies over medium heat until onions are golden. Add garlic, ginger and turmeric and fry, stirring, for 1 minute. Add okra, coriander, cumin, coconut milk or buttermilk and salt. Simmer uncovered until okra is tender, 10–12 minutes. Serve hot with rice. Serves 4–6.

Chicken with Okra

500 g (1 lb) young okra, trimmed; $1/2$ cup vinegar; 185 g (6 oz) butter; 6–8 chicken joints, legs, wings or thighs; I onion, finely chopped; I clove garlic, crushed; $1^1/2$ cups peeled and chopped tomatoes; I tbs tomato paste; $1/2$ cup dry white wine; I bay leaf; 2 pieces cinnamon stick; $1/2$ tsp sugar; salt and freshly ground black pepper.

Place okra in a bowl, pour over vinegar and toss to coat. Leave 30 minutes, then drain, rinse very well and pat dry. Melt 125 g (4 oz) of the butter in a deep frying pan, add chicken joints and brown on all sides. Remove and keep warm on a plate. Reduce heat and cook onion and garlic in butter in pan until soft. Add tomatoes, tomato paste, wine, bay leaf, cinnamon stick, sugar, salt and pepper and stir well. Cover and simmer for 20 minutes. Return chicken to pan, cover and simmer for a further 15 minutes. Melt remaining butter in another frying pan and cook okra, turning gently, until golden. Add okra to chicken mixture and cook for 20 minutes longer. Remove bay leaf and cinnamon stick. Serve with whole boiled or mashed potatoes. Serves 6.

OLIVE

The fruit of the olive tree, which is a native of the Mediterranean where so many people depend on its oil for a living. So it is only natural that olives and olive oil are the foundation of Mediterranean cooking. The fruit of the olive tree is either black (the ripe fruit) or green (the immature fruit). Black olives are picked ripe and are full-flavoured and mellow, while green ones are picked immature and are firm and tangy. They are often pickled and stuffed with pimiento or anchovy.

Olives are used in sauces, stuffings and salads as well as for garnishes. They add colour to a Neapolitan pizza and flavour to those wondrous Mediterranean stews which simmer away for hours on top of the stove. Stop at any little café or bar around the Mediterranean and you are likely to be offered a plate of hors d'oeuvre – black and green olives, local salami, cheese and some crisp vegetables. Olives have an interesting salty flavour which seems to complement aperitifs better than anything else. Serve them alone or with cubes of cheese, preferably crumbly Greek feta cheese obtainable from Continental delicatessens.

Olives from various countries differ in shape and flavour. In good Continental delicatessens, you can find olives from Greece – mottled, fat and round and stored in olive oil – inky-black Calamata olives, with sharp pointed ends, and green olives, small and very salty. Black olives from Spain are large and ripe and their green olives are very firm with large stones. Sometimes you find enormous olives called Spanish or Queen olives, which are excellent for stuffing with a little pimiento mixed with capers, anchovies or almonds. Very good olives grow in California, South Australia and also along the banks of the Murray River.

Olive oil is produced from small olives which are not considered good eating, and its flavour varies with each grove. Some oils are delicate with a pure flavour, others extremely fruity and some so refined they are almost tasteless. The olive oils of Italy, France, Spain, Greece, and, more recently, Australia, vary enormously in quality and taste. It is simply a matter of preference and how it is to be used. It's worth experimenting to find one you're happy with – it can make so much difference to your cooking, marinades, salads, mayonnaise and dressings.

It is difficult to describe the different tastes of olive oil. However, here are a few generalisations:

- Olive oil ranges in colour from a pale straw yellow to the virgin dark green oil.
- Olive oils range in taste from the French style of fruity and light to the Italian oils, which are usually heavier and more complex.
- Olive oil is usually described as having a light or heavy feel in the mouth.

When it comes to cooking you will learn to use different oils for different dishes. Choose a light olive oil for a dish of subtle flavour and an extra virgin olive oil for more robust flavour. The true extra virgin olive oil is cold-pressed from quality fruit, picked at the 'just ripe' stage. Whenever possible add at just the last moment, even to hot dishes, to ensure its flavour is maintained.

Always store olive oil in a cool, dark place, not in the refrigerator.

See also *Tapenade*.

TO STORE BLACK OLIVES: The best way is in a jar with olive oil to cover. A strip of lemon peel, a sprig of oregano or some garlic cloves and a chilli may be placed in the jar as well to give a subtle flavour. **See recipes.**

Herbed Olives: Put 1 small red chilli, 1 clove garlic, 1 sprig fresh dill and 2 tbs olive oil over 500 g (1 lb) black olives in a jar. Cover and marinate for at least 2 days.

Garlic Olives: Put 500 g (1 lb) olives into a jar with 2–3 cloves garlic, lightly crushed. Cover with olive oil and allow to stand at least 2 days.

Marinated Olives: Put 500 g (1 lb) black olives into a jar and pour over a mixture of 3 parts olive oil and 1 part vinegar. Add 1 clove garlic and 1 tsp finely chopped fresh oregano and allow to marinate for at least 2 days.

Grecian-Style Olives: Place 500 g (1 lb) Calamata olives (black, shiny and pointed) in a jar, cover with vinegar and allow to stand for 2 days. Drain, and pack into sterilised jars, arranging the olives alternately with layers of lemon slices and celery. Cover with olive oil and keep in a cool place for at least a week.

Mixed Italian Olives: With a sharp knife cut slashes in the flesh of 500 g (1 lb) green and black olives. Place in a sterilised jar with 1 small green and 1 small red pepper, 3 sticks celery and 2 cloves garlic, all finely chopped. Add 1/4 cup each olive oil and vinegar and 1 sprig fresh oregano (or good pinch dried). Let stand at room temperature for at least 2 days. Store in the refrigerator until required. Use as an antipasto.

Preserved Olives: Choose fresh black olives and prick them all over with a skewer or pin. Place them on a large cane tray, sprinkle with lots of salt and toss them so that they become well impregnated with salt. Leave for 3–4 days. Continue to toss them 2–3 times a day. On the last day, add a little more salt to replace the salt that has been drained away. When the olives have lost all their bitterness, put them in a jar and pour over some olive oil. Add a few bay leaves and seal the jar. Store in a cool place for 2 months before using, turning the jar occasionally.

Capalatina

A Sicilian pickled eggplant and olive spread or dip. Serve with crudités, cracker biscuits or corn chips or scoop up with Lebanese bread.

2 large eggplants, cut into 2.5 cm (1 in) cubes; salt;
3/4 cup olive oil; 2 large onions, chopped;
3 sticks celery, sliced; 2 x 425 g cans Italian-style tomatoes, seeds removed; 1 cup stoned black olives;
2 tbs drained capers; 2 tbs pine nuts or slivered blanched almonds; 2 tbs sugar;
1/4 cup wine vinegar; 1/2 tsp black pepper.

Place eggplant cubes in a colander, sprinkle with salt and leave for 1 hour, turning cubes several times. Press out liquid, rinse and dry with paper towels. Heat oil, add eggplant in batches (do not crowd pan) and brown on all sides. Remove cubes with a slotted spoon as they are browned. Add onions and celery and sauté until lightly browned. Add tomatoes and olives, bring to the boil and cook over a low heat for 10 minutes. Put eggplant back into pan and add remaining ingredients. Cover and simmer gently for 25 minutes, stirring often. Cool, then chill. Makes 4–5 cups.

Beef with Olives

1 x 125 g (4 oz) piece speck or bacon, cut into 1 cm (1/2 in) cubes; 1 x 1.2 kg (2 1/2 lb) piece chuck or topside beef; 10 small onions, peeled;
2 small carrots, peeled; 1 bouquet garni;
salt and freshly ground black pepper;
pinch nutmeg; 6 golden shallots, halved;
1 clove garlic; 3/4 cup red wine; pinch sugar;
1 cup green olives, stoned;
125 g (4 oz) mushrooms, quartered.

Heat speck or bacon slowly in a heavy pan until fat melts. Remove and set aside. Add piece of meat to speck or bacon fat in pan and brown on all sides. Add

onions, carrots, bouquet garni, salt, pepper and nutmeg. Reduce heat, cover and cook gently for about 20 minutes, turning meat once. Add shallots, garlic, wine, sugar and cubes of speck or bacon and simmer for 1 1/2 hours. Meanwhile, blanch olives in boiling water in order to extract some of their saltiness. Drain and dry. Add mushrooms and olives to beef and simmer for a further 1 hour. Adjust seasoning, and remove bouquet garni. Place beef on heated serving platter, carve into slices and spoon over a little sauce. Serve with noodles or boiled potatoes. Serves 6.

Beef Stew with Wine and Olives

1.5–2 kg (3–4 lb) chuck or blade steak,
cut into 2.5 cm (1 in) cubes; 3–4 tbs flour;
2 tsp salt; freshly ground black pepper;
4 tbs oil; 2 onions, chopped; 1 bay leaf;
1 1/2 cups red wine; 1/2 onion; 5–6 parsley stalks;
6 black peppercorns; 1 cup stuffed green olives.

Coat steak cubes in flour mixed with salt and pepper. Heat oil in a heavy frying pan. Add beef, a few cubes at a time, and cook over high heat, turning until brown on all sides. Transfer meat to a heavy saucepan. Add onions to frying pan and cook gently until golden. Add bay leaf and some of the wine. Bring to the boil, scraping sediment from bottom of pan, then add to saucepan with remaining wine, and onion tied in a muslin bag with parsley stalks and peppercorns. Bring to the boil again, then reduce heat, cover pan and simmer very gently for about 1 1/2 hours or until meat is almost tender when pierced with a skewer or fork. Stir occasionally to prevent sticking. Remove onion and parsley stalks, peppercorns and bay leaf. Stir in olives, and heat through. Serve with crusty bread or creamy mashed potatoes. Serves 6–8.

Onion and Olive Pizza

Some of the simplest pizzas are the most delicious. This one has no tomatoes or cheese, but just two topping ingredients add up to superb flavour.

1 quantity Pizza Dough (pages 371–2); 6 tbs olive oil;
6 medium onions, finely sliced; salt and freshly ground black pepper; 20 black olives, stoned and coarsely chopped.

After dough doubles in bulk, knock down and knead lightly 4 or 5 times. Place in centre of a greased 35 x 30 cm (14 x 12 in) baking tray and pull and push out with the fingers until dough touches all sides of tray. Allow to rise in a warm place for 15 minutes. Heat oil in a large frying pan, add onions and cook over medium heat until golden-brown and softened. Season with salt and pepper. Spread dough with onions and scatter olives over top, then press topping down into dough with the back of a spoon. Bake in a preheated moderately hot oven (190°C/375°F) for 25–30 minutes or until pizza crust is crisp and golden around the edges. Serves 8–10.

Olive Bread

Serve thinly sliced and buttered with salad, or as a sandwich with slices of Cheddar cheese.

2 eggs; 1 cup coarsely chopped stuffed green olives; 2 tbs olive oil; 2 cups flour; 1 tbs sugar; 2 tsp baking powder; $^1/_4$ tsp salt; $^1/_2$ cup milk.

Beat eggs until frothy. Stir in olives and oil. Sift flour, sugar, baking powder and salt and add to olive mixture with milk. Fold in gently. Pour into a greased and lined 20 x 10 cm (8 x 4 in) loaf tin. Bake in a preheated moderate oven (180°C/350°F) for 1 hour or until bread sounds hollow when tapped on the bottom. Cool on a wire rack.

OMELETTE

A good French omelette is a smooth, golden oval that is tender, soft and creamy inside. The perfect omelette must be beaten quickly, cooked in less than half a minute and served immediately.

An omelette is one of the greatest instant gourmet meals. Once you master the simple art of making a good omelette, you are well on your way to being a gourmet cook. Learning to make a good omelette is entirely a matter of practice. A few tips: be sure you have everything ready, the pan at hand, egg bowl and beater, spatula for turning the omelette, butter for cooking, the filling or seasoning, heated plates – and don't forget the diner, who should be sitting at the table before you start cooking the omelette.

Almost every country has its own omelette in its cuisine, there's a Spanish Potato Omelette and one made with peppers; then there's the famous American omelette, Hangtown Fry, an omelette with oysters, and the Egg Foo Yung of China. The French omelette is a world favourite, and the wonderful thing about learning to make an omelette is that you not only have one dish at your fingertips but nine or ten, for with each different filling you have a new taste sensation.

DESSERT OMELETTES

Sweet omelettes for dessert can be made the same way as savoury omelettes of the basic type, but more often they are the fluffy kind and are known as soufflé omelettes. Omelettes in soufflé form are closely related to the dessert soufflé proper, but they offer far fewer problems for the cook other than a few minutes absence from the table. As for all light omelettes, basic, savoury or sweet, the soufflé kind must be served immediately after it is cooked. For spectacle, the dessert omelette should come to the table enveloped in the blue flames of rum, brandy or a liqueur of some kind, or dusted with sifted icing sugar and burnt in a diamond design. Serve with a bowl of whipped sweetened cream.

FLAMING AN OMELETTE: A flamed omelette should be flavoured with the liqueur that will later envelop it in flames. A tablespoon of rum or brandy is sufficient, beaten in with the eggs. If the platter is hot, the omelette straight from the stove, the liqueur heated with a pinch of sugar and ignited as it is poured on, the 'flaming' will be a success. See recipes.

OMELETTE PANS

To produce a really golden omelette you must have a heavy pan. Cast-iron or heavy aluminium are the best because the heat is spread easily; once hot, the pan acts like a hotplate and it is the pan rather than the source of heat that does the cooking. Thinner pans allow the heat to come through, so that the centre of the pan over the flame or element is hotter than the outer part. Don't have your pan bigger than 20–23 cm (8–9 in). This will cook a 3–4 egg omelette nicely and will serve 2; if you are cooking for 4, repeat the recipe.

A new development in pans has been non-stick surfaces; this, combined with strong metals, make the perfect modern omelette pan. The eggs must be able to slip around freely, and eggs will never stick to a pan that is properly cared for. That is why many people keep a pan especially for omelettes. Certainly you should not pan-fry other foods at high heat in your omelette pan, or you may burn food into the pan and omelettes will stick to it forever after.

Basic French Omelette

3 eggs; 1 tbs water; $^1/_2$ tsp salt; freshly ground black pepper; 15 g ($^1/_2$ oz) butter.

Have a plate warmed and waiting and also the diner, and even if making omelettes for several people make and serve each one individually – it only takes a minute. Have eggs at room temperature. Break eggs into a bowl, add water and beat lightly with a fork just to combine whites with yolks. It is important not to overbeat as it makes the omelette tough. Add salt and a grinding of pepper. Melt half of the butter in an omelette pan. When foam has subsided pour in eggs. Leave for 10–15 seconds until eggs start to set on bottom. Using a fork or a metal spatula pull egg mixture into centre of pan and allow runny mixture to run to outside. Do this until eggs have set underneath but the top is still quite moist and soft. If using a filling, spoon across omelette, tilt pan, and using an egg slice flip over one third of the omelette towards the centre, then turn over again so that it is folded into 3 as it rolls out on to a heated plate. Melt remaining butter in same pan and when it is sizzling pour it over omelette, or smear butter over surface of omelette to give a nice glazed finish. Serve at once. Serves 1.

VARIATIONS

ASPARAGUS OMELETTE: Use only the tips of 4–5 cooked fresh or canned asparagus spears. Season with salt and pepper and heat in a little butter. Spoon into centre of a 3-egg omelette and fold over.

MUSHROOM OMELETTE: Slice 3–4 small mushrooms, cook lightly in a little butter, and season with salt and pepper. Spoon into centre of a 3-egg omelette and fold over. For an elegant finish, trim stem of 1 mushroom level with cap, slice downward and just colour slices in butter. Lay them, neatly overlapping, along top of finished omelette.

FINES HERBES OMELETTE: The official fines herbes are parsley, chervil, tarragon and chives. Add any 2 or 3 of these fresh herbs, finely chopped, to the uncooked egg mixture before making the omelette.

ONION OMELETTE: Cook 1 sliced onion in butter for 5 minutes or until soft. Scatter over omelette, then fold over.

CHEESE OMELETTE: Shred ½ cup Gruyère, Emmenthal or a tasty Cheddar cheese and strew over 3-egg omelette before folding it.

BACON AND MUSHROOM OMELETTE: Fry 1 rasher bacon, diced, and remove from pan. Add a small nut of butter to bacon fat in pan and cook 2–3 sliced mushrooms until tender. Mix with bacon and use to fill a 3-egg omelette before folding it.

TOMATO OMELETTE: Peel, seed and coarsely chop 2 tomatoes. Heat a nut of butter in a pan, add 2 slices onion, finely chopped, and the tomatoes, season with salt and pepper and heat through. Add a sprinkling of chopped parsley or chives if liked. Use to fill a 3-egg omelette before folding it.

Supper Omelette

Crispy bacon and crunchy bread croûtons fill this creamy omelette.

**4 rashers streaky bacon, rind removed
and cut into fine strips; 1 thick slice bread,
crusts removed and diced; 4 eggs; salt and freshly
ground black pepper; good pinch dry mustard;
2 tsp butter.**

Put bacon into a cold omelette pan and fry without additional fat over a low heat until crisp. Remove bacon with a slotted spoon. Add bread to pan and fry in bacon fat until crisp and golden-brown on all sides. Remove bread and keep bacon and bread cubes warm while making omelette. Beat eggs with a little salt and pepper and the mustard. Heat butter in omelette pan, pour in egg mixture and cook fairly briskly, lifting edges of omelette with a spatula to let uncooked egg run underneath. When omelette is just set but top is still creamy, sprinkle bacon and bread cubes along centre. Fold omelette in half and serve at once. Serves 2.

Neapolitan Omelette

**2 cups cooked spaghetti; ½ cup tomato purée;
4 eggs, lightly beaten; 1 tbs chopped parsley;
pinch salt; freshly ground black pepper;
1 tbs grated Parmesan cheese; 1 tbs olive oil.**

Cut spaghetti into short lengths. Add tomato purée, eggs, parsley, salt, pepper and Parmesan cheese and mix very well. Heat oil in pan, pour in spaghetti mixture and cook slowly on both sides. Serves 4.
NOTE: Leftover spaghetti in sauce is often used in this dish.

Spanish Potato Omelette
(Tortilla de Patatas)

Cooked, diced potatoes may be used in this omelette or raw potato fried in the pan before eggs are added.

**olive oil for frying; 1 onion, chopped; 2–3 potatoes,
peeled and diced; 6 eggs; salt and freshly ground
black pepper.**

Heat a little oil in an omelette pan, add onion and fry until golden. Remove and set aside. Add more oil to pan and fry potatoes gently until tender but not crisp. Beat eggs well with a few drops of water and season with salt and pepper. Return onion to pan with potatoes and pour eggs over. When set and lightly browned underneath invert carefully or lift on to a large heated plate. Put a little more oil in pan and slide omelette back to cook other side. Cut into wedges and serve immediately. Serves 3–4.
VARIATION
SPANISH PEPPER OMELETTE (TORTILLA DE PIMIENTOS): Fry 1 green or red diced pepper and 1 chopped rasher of bacon (rind removed) with the onion. Omit potatoes.

Spanish Omelette (Tortilla Española)

This is often offered in Spanish bars, cut into small squares, as a little something to enjoy with a glass of wine. Also good cold, it is a favourite Spanish picnic dish.

**1 tbs butter or oil; 2 cooked potatoes, peeled and
diced; 1 onion, chopped; 2 rashers bacon, rind
removed and diced; 4 eggs; salt and freshly ground
black pepper; 1 tomato, sliced; chopped parsley or
chives (optional).**

Heat butter or oil in a frying pan, add potatoes, onion and bacon and fry until edges of potato are golden. Beat eggs with salt and pepper and pour into frying pan. Cook until just set, but no longer. Do not try to fold omelette over – it will be too thick. Serve with sliced tomato and, if liked, a sprinkling of chopped parsley or chives. Serves 4.

Fluffy Omelette

3 eggs, separated; 2 tbs hot water; salt and freshly ground black pepper; 15 g (¹/₂ oz) butter.

Beat egg yolks and water together until pale yellow. Beat egg whites until they form soft peaks, and fold in yolk mixture. Season with salt and pepper. Heat butter in a small omelette pan. Pour in egg mixture and cook until golden-brown underneath. Place pan under a preheated hot grill and cook for a few minutes until golden-brown on top. If using a filling, spoon on to half of omelette, fold other half over and slide out of pan on to a heated plate. Serve immediately. Serves 1.

VARIATIONS

FLUFFY BACON OMELETTE: Make Fluffy Omelette as above and fill with 2 rashers bacon, crisply fried and crumbled, before folding.

FLUFFY HERB OMELETTE: Make Fluffy Omelette as above and sprinkle with 2 tbs finely chopped parsley or other fresh herbs before folding.

FLUFFY SALMON OMELETTE: Make Fluffy Omelette as above and fill with 2 tbs flaked smoked salmon or smoked fish before folding.

FLUFFY HAM AND CHEESE OMELETTE: Make Fluffy Omelette as above and fill with 2 tbs chopped cooked ham, plus ¹/₄ cup grated cheese, if liked, before folding.

FLUFFY MUSHROOM OMELETTE: Make Fluffy Omelette as above and fill with 3–4 sliced mushrooms, cooked in a little butter, before folding.

FLUFFY TOMATO OMELETTE: Make Fluffy Omelette as above and fill with 1 tomato, peeled, sliced and cooked in a little butter with a few onion slices and chopped fresh herbs, before folding.

Hangtown Fry

15 g (¹/₂ oz) butter; 2 bacon rashers, rind removed; 3–4 fresh oysters; 2 eggs, lightly beaten; salt and freshly ground black pepper.

Heat butter in a frying pan, add bacon and fry until cooked but not crisp. Place the oysters on top of the bacon and carefully pour the eggs over them. Season with salt and pepper. Cook without stirring until the eggs set. Turn the omelette out upside-down on to a warm plate and serve immediately. Serves 1.

Omelette Soufflé (Sweet)

A last-minute touch makes this delicious soufflé omelette spectacular. A lovely dessert when there are just two for dinner.

3 eggs, separated; 1 tbs sugar; 2 tsp flour; 1 tbs cream; grated lemon rind (optional); pinch salt; 15 g (¹/₂ oz) butter; 2 tbs good jam; sifted icing sugar.

Place egg whites in a china or copper bowl. Lightly beat egg yolks with sugar, flour, cream and lemon rind, if using. Whisk egg whites with salt until stiff peaks form. Pour in yolk mixture and fold in gently with a large metal spoon. Heat butter in a large omelette pan (if you have it, a heavy cast iron one) and pour in egg mixture. Place in a preheated moderately hot oven (190°C/375°F) and cook for 12–15 minutes or until golden and risen. Slide on to a heated serving dish and spread with jam. Fold over and serve flamed (see page 309) or sprinkle with sifted icing sugar. For a spectacular look, heat 2 metal skewers over a flame and when red-hot, use them to mark a lattice over the icing sugar on the omelette; it will caramelise as you lightly press it. Serve immediately. Serves 2.

ONION

The pungent and aromatic onion acts as both a flavouring agent and a vegetable in its own right. It is indispensable in the kitchen and lends its unique qualities to many savoury dishes.

Onions can be used to flavour stocks, soups, stews, sauces, poultry, meat and vegetable dishes. They appear as vegetable accompaniments, as garnishes, either raw or cooked, shaped or whole. Tiny onions can be glazed as a garnish for roast meats or they can be pickled in spicy vinegar – delicious eaten with good Cheddar cheese and fresh white or brown bread.

When buying onions, choose those that are firm, with no bruising or soft spots. The outer skin should be fine and papery. Always store onions in a cool, dry, airy place.

TYPES OF ONION

Brown Onions: Readily available in supermarkets and greengrocers, these onions have a stronger flavour than the white variety, and can be too strong to eat raw. They keep well for some weeks in a cool, dry place. If your eyes water when preparing stronger onions, try peeling them under cold water, but do not let them soak. Dry well before using. Some people say it helps to hold a slice of bread in your mouth while peeling and chopping onions. Use brown onions in most cooked dishes.

Pickling Onions: Tiny brown pickling onions are sometimes available from greengrocers during the winter months. They are used whole in casseroles (see Boeuf à la Bourguignonne on page 43), glazed as a garnish, or fried whole as well as for pickling.

Spanish Onions: These large red-skinned onions have a purple-tinted flesh. They are sweet, mild and crisp and delicious sliced in rings in salads, especially those containing fresh oranges and black olives.

White Onions: These are readily available in supermarkets and greengrocers through most of the year. White onions are milder than their brown counterparts and do not keep as long. Use in any recipe calling for onions. They can also be sliced into rings and added raw to salads.

Green Onions: An immature onion with an unformed bulb. See *Shallot and Spring Onion*.

■ **BASIC PREPARATION:**

TO DICE OR CHOP ONIONS: Cut the onion in half through the root end. Remove the skin and place flat side down on a chopping board. Using a sharp knife, make 3 or 4 slits lengthways through to the board but not through the root end, so the slices are still attached. Then make 3 or 4 horizontal cuts from one side to the other, still leaving the slices attached to the root. Finally, chop into dice by slicing downwards from the stem to the root end.

TO MAKE ONION RINGS: Peel the onion, cut off the stem end and slice thinly. Carefully push out the consecutive rings of onion from each slice.

TO SLICE ONIONS: Cut the onion in half from stem to root end. Remove the skin, using a sharp knife; lay flat side down on a chopping board and cut slices to required thickness from the stem to the root end.

TO COOK WHOLE ONIONS RETAINING SHAPE: Cut a small slice from the stem end and discard. Remove the skin and scrape the root end, to remove the outer skin and any tiny dried roots remaining. Using a sharp pointed knife, cut a shallow cross through the root base but do not remove or slice off the base.

TO EXTRACT ONION JUICE: Cut onion in half and squeeze on a lemon squeezer the same way you would squeeze a lemon.

TO GRATE ONION: Peel and halve onion. Using short sharp downward strokes, rub it against the medium side of a grater.

■ **TO COOK:** Onions should be cooked over gentle or medium heat; too high a heat may scorch the onions and turn them bitter. **See recipes.**

Fried Onions

Use these fried onions for the old favourite, Steak and Onions.

¹/₂ cup oil; 4 medium onions, sliced; salt and freshly ground black pepper; pinch each paprika and sugar.

Heat oil in a large heavy frying pan and add onions. Cook over a gentle heat, stirring often, for 15–20 minutes or until golden-brown and soft. Season with salt, pepper, paprika and sugar. Serve very hot with grilled rump steak. Serves 4.

VARIATION

QUICK FRIED ONIONS: Dice onions. Melt enough butter to cover bottom of a frying pan and add onions. Stir until well coated with butter, then barely cover with warm water. Cook over high heat until all the water has evaporated. Reduce heat and continue cooking, stirring and adding more butter if necessary, until golden and tender. Season with salt and pepper.

Onions Baked in their Skins

These are delicious cooked with roasts.

4–6 medium onions; butter; parsley sprigs.

Slice stem ends from onions, scrape root end and make a shallow cross in the root core using a sharp knife. Place onions in baking dish around the meat and bake for about 1 hour or until tender but still firm when pierced with a skewer. Remove from oven, slip off outer skins and place in a heated serving dish. Top with knobs of butter and sprigs of parsley. Serves 4–6.

NOTE: If you cook onions in boiling water for 10–15 minutes first, the cooking time in the oven will be reduced. For baked onions when you are not having a roast, arrange prepared onions in a shallow greased baking dish in a preheated moderate oven (180°C/350°F) for 1 hour or until tender.

Boiled Onions with Parsley Sauce

Serve with corned beef, hot pickled (salt) pork or boiled beef.

6 large onions, peeled; 30 g (1 oz) butter; 1 tbs flour; ¹/₂ cup evaporated milk or cream; salt and freshly ground black pepper; 1 tbs finely chopped parsley.

Scrape root end of onions and cut a shallow cross in the base of each. Drop onions into boiling water and cook for about 30 minutes or until tender. Drain, reserving ½ cup cooking liquid. Arrange onions in a heated serving dish and keep warm. Melt butter in a saucepan and blend in flour. Stir in reserved cooking liquid. Cook for 1 minute, stirring, then stir in milk or cream. Heat until boiling, stirring constantly. Season with salt and pepper and stir in parsley. Pour over onions and serve immediately. Serves 4–6.

Crisp Fried Onion Rings

2 cups milk; ¹/₂ tsp salt; 3 large onions, sliced and pushed out into rings; freshly ground black pepper; 1 tsp paprika; 1 cup flour; oil for deep-frying.

Combine milk with ¼ tsp salt in a shallow dish. Add onion rings and soak for 20 minutes. Combine remaining salt, pepper, paprika and flour in a plastic bag. Shake to mix. Drain a few onion rings at a time and dip in seasoned flour. Shake off excess flour, then deep-fry rings in oil until crisp and brown. Place cooked rings on a baking tray lined with paper towels to drain and keep warm in a preheated very slow oven (120°C/250°F) while frying the remainder. Serves 4–6.

NOTE: To test when oil is hot enough, drop a prepared onion ring into oil. Onion should rise to the surface and turn crisp and golden in about 30 seconds. Take care that the oil does not overheat; the rings should be golden and not dark brown. Use only enough oil to come not more than halfway up sides of frying container to avoid splashing or overflowing.

Glazed Onions

**250 g (8 oz) pickling onions, peeled;
30 g (1 oz) butter; 1 tsp sugar;
salt and freshly ground black pepper.**

Cut a shallow cross in centre of root end of each onion. Place onions in a saucepan of cold water. Bring to the boil, simmer for 5 minutes and drain well. Put in a heavy saucepan with butter, sugar, salt and pepper. Cover and cook gently for about 10 minutes or until tender, well glazed and shiny. Shake pan frequently to prevent onions from sticking. Serves 4 (as a garnish).

Braised Onions

**1/2 cup stock; 500 g (1 lb) small onions, peeled;
30 g (1 oz) butter; salt and freshly ground
black pepper.**

Bring stock to the boil and add onions and butter. Cover and cook gently for 10 minutes. Remove lid and cook for a further 5 minutes to reduce liquid. Season with salt and pepper. Serves 4.

Creamed Onions

**500 g (1 lb) pickling onions or small white onions,
peeled; 1/4 tsp salt; 1 cup hot Béchamel or Mornay
Sauce (page 456); 1 tbs chopped parsley (optional).**

Drop onions into boiling water and cook for 10 minutes. Drain and return to pan. Add fresh boiling water and continue cooking until tender but still crisp. Just before cooking is completed add salt. Drain onions thoroughly, place in a heated serving dish and pour sauce over them. Sprinkle with chopped parsley, if using. Serves 4–6.

Italian Salad

**4 medium oranges; 1 Spanish onion, finely sliced
and pushed out into rings; 1/4 cup dry sherry;
juice 1/2 lemon; 1 tbs olive oil; pinch white pepper;
lettuce leaves; 8–10 black olives, stoned.**

Peel oranges, removing all white pith. Cut oranges into 5 mm (1/4 in) slices. Place in a bowl with onion rings and sherry and marinate 1 hour. Drain, reserving sherry marinade. Blend lemon juice, oil, pepper and sherry marinade. Whisk well. Arrange lettuce leaves in a serving dish. Place orange slices on top, and then olives and onion. Add dressing and toss carefully. Serves 6.
NOTE: Use 2 small white onions if you cannot buy Spanish onions.

Creamed Onions with Sherry

**750 g (1 1/2 lb) medium onions, sliced;
1/2 cup water; 1/3 cup sour light cream; 3 tbs sherry;
1/2 tsp salt; freshly ground black pepper.**

Cook onions in water over a gentle heat for about 10 minutes. Drain and place in a greased ovenproof dish. Mix cream, sherry, salt and pepper and pour over onions. Cover and bake in a preheated moderate oven (180°C/350°F) for 30 minutes. Serves 4–6.

Onion Sauce

**3 medium white onions, finely chopped;
1 cup hot Béchamel Sauce (page 456);
30 g (1 oz) butter; pinch cayenne.**

Cook onions in boiling water for 5 minutes or until tender. Drain and add to sauce. Reheat gently until simmering. Stir in butter and season with cayenne. Makes 1 1/2 cups.

Onion Quiche

**30 g (1 oz) butter; 1 tbs oil; 4–5 medium onions,
finely sliced; 1/2 tsp ground cumin or nutmeg;
1/2 tsp salt; 3 egg yolks, beaten; 1/2 cup cream;
1 x 20 cm (8 in) Rich Shortcrust Pastry shell,
baked (page 342).**

Heat butter and oil in a heavy frying pan, add onions and cook over a gentle heat for 15–20 minutes or until soft and golden, shaking pan occasionally. Remove from heat, add cumin and salt and stir in egg yolks and cream. Spoon onion mixture into pastry shell. Bake quiche in preheated hot oven (200°C/400°F) for 10 minutes, then reduce temperature to moderate (180°C/350°F) and bake for a further 20 minutes. Serves 4–6.
NOTE: A less rich version can be made using 2 whole eggs instead of 3 yolks, and 1/4 cup each cream and milk or 1/2 cup evaporated milk instead of cream.

Spiced Pickled Onions

Long soaking in salted water helps keep the onions crisp.

**1 kg (2 lb) small pickling onions; 1/3 cup plus
1 tsp salt; 2 cups white vinegar; 2/3 cup water;
1/3 cup sugar; 1 tbs pickling spice;
1 red chilli (optional).**

Soak onions in boiling water to cover in a large bowl for 15 minutes. Drain and peel. Return onions to bowl and soak in fresh water to cover, with 1/3 cup of the salt, for 48 hours (cover bowl with plastic wrap). Drain and rinse onions. Place vinegar, the 2/3 cup water, sugar, pickling spice, chilli, if used, and remaining salt in a large heavy saucepan and bring to the boil. Add onions and cook for 5 minutes.

Divide onions between sterilised preserving jars and add hot spiced vinegar to cover. Seal jars with lids and let stand in a cool place for at least 2 weeks before serving.

German–Style Herring with Onion

Herring are the basis of many Continental first courses. Here they are marinated in sour cream and garnished with onions for a piquant appetiser. Make several days ahead and use as required.

8 herring fillets (Matjes); milk or buttermilk; 1¹/₂ cups light sour cream; ¹/₄ cup white wine vinegar; 1 tbs olive oil; 2 large tart apples, peeled, cored and diced; 6 black peppercorns, slightly crushed; 1 bay leaf.

GARNISH: 2 medium Spanish or white onions, finely sliced; parsley or dill sprigs.

Rinse herring, cover with milk or buttermilk and allow to soak for 2 hours, changing milk several times. Drain, pat dry with paper towels and cut into bite-sized pieces. Place in glass or pottery bowl. Mix together sour cream, vinegar and olive oil and fold remaining ingredients through. Pour over herring. Cover and marinate in refrigerator for at least 24 hours, turning mixture once or twice before serving. Top with onion rings and parsley or dill. Serve with a plate of buttered rye bread. Serves 8.

Onion Buns

Yeast dough buns filled with bacon and onion.

4 cups flour; 1 tsp salt; 1¹/₄ cups mixed milk and water; 60 g (2 oz) butter; 15 g (¹/₂ oz) compressed yeast (if using dry yeast, see *Yeast Cookery*); 1 tsp sugar; beaten egg to glaze.

FILLING: 4 rashers streaky bacon, rind removed and finely chopped; 1¹/₂ cups grated onion; freshly ground black pepper.

Sift flour and salt into bowl. Warm milk and water, add butter and remove from heat when it has melted. Mash yeast with sugar and stir in warm liquid. Stir a little flour from edges to make a stiff batter, cover with a cloth and leave in a warm place to sponge. When yeast mixture has doubled and bubbles have formed, mix in all the flour. Turn on to a floured surface and knead until smooth. Place in a clean greased bowl, turn dough over so top surface is lightly greased, cover with a damp cloth and leave to rise in a warm place for about 2 hours or until doubled in bulk. Knock dough down and knead lightly. Divide into 20 pieces.

Mix filling ingredients, seasoning well with pepper. Place 1 tbs filling in middle of each piece of dough.

Fold edges over to enclose filling, pinching together to seal, and mould into balls. Arrange buns, seam sides down, on a buttered baking tray and let rise, loosely covered, in a warm place for about 20 minutes. Brush with beaten egg and bake in a preheated hot oven (200°C/400°F) for 15 minutes or until buns are golden and sound hollow when tapped. Serve warm with butter. Makes 20.

Onion Hush Puppies

American fishermen cooked these curiously named buns at their fish fries. Legend says they threw the fatty bits to the dogs at the same time shouting 'Hush puppy'. Serve hot and buttered on their own or to accompany fish chowder, shellfish or baked whole fish.

1¹/₂ cups white cornmeal; ¹/₄ cup flour; 3 tsp baking powder; ¹/₂ tsp salt; pinch cayenne; ³/₄ cup buttermilk, or ³/₄ cup fresh milk soured with 1 tbs vinegar; 2 large eggs, lightly beaten; ¹/₂ cup grated onion; 1 clove garlic, crushed; oil for deep-frying; butter to serve.

Combine cornmeal, flour, baking powder, salt and cayenne. In separate bowl beat together buttermilk, eggs, onion and garlic. Stir into cornmeal mixture and allow to stand for 15 minutes. Heat 8 cm (3 in) oil in a deep-fryer and fry tablespoons of batter, 4–6 at a time, for 3 minutes or until golden-brown. Drain on crumpled paper towels and eat while still piping hot, spread with softened butter. Makes about 20.

Stuffed Onions

6 large onions, peeled; 250 g (8 oz) minced cooked ham, or 250 g (8 oz) minced veal and 2 rashers bacon, rind removed and diced; 1 tbs oil; salt and freshly ground black pepper; cayenne; ¹/₂ cup sour cream; 1 tbs finely chopped celery; 2 tbs chopped chives; 2 tbs chopped parsley; 1 cup fresh white breadcrumbs; butter; 1 cup chicken stock.

Cook onions in boiling water for 10 minutes. Drain. Scoop out centres and chop fine. Sauté chopped onion centres with ham, or veal and bacon in oil in a frying pan. Add remaining ingredients, except butter and stock, and mix well. Push stuffing into onion cases. Place on a greased shallow baking dish. Dot with butter, pour stock around onions and bake in a preheated hot oven (200°C/400°F) for 35–45 minutes or until tender and golden-brown. Serves 6.

Dutch Onion Tart

3 cups finely sliced onions; 60 g (2 oz) butter; 500 g (1 lb) ricotta cheese; ¹/₄ cup cream; 2 eggs; 1 x 23 cm (9 in) Rich Shortcrust Pastry shell, baked (page 342); salt and freshly ground black pepper; ¹/₄ tsp cayenne.

Fry onions in butter over gentle heat until soft. Moisten cheese with cream, then beat in eggs. Pour into tart shell. Season lightly with salt and pepper. Cover with onions, and sprinkle with cayenne. Bake in a preheated hot oven (200°C/400°F) for 20–25 minutes. Serves 8.

Onion Tartlets

1 quantity Rich Shortcrust Pastry (page 342); 8 medium onions, sliced; 125 g (4 oz) butter; salt and freshly ground white pepper; 2 tbs flour; 2 cups beef stock; 2 tbs grated Cheddar cheese; 2–3 tbs grated Parmesan cheese.

Line 6 x 10 cm (4 in) tartlet tins with pasty, prick well and bake blind (see *Pastry*). Cook onions gently in half the butter until soft. Increase heat a little and cook until a rich, even brown, stirring occasionally. Season with salt and pepper and remove from heat. Melt remaining butter in a saucepan, stir in flour and cook over medium heat for 5–6 minutes or until flour turns nut brown. Gradually add stock and simmer, stirring, for 5 minutes. Mix in onions and spoon mixture into pastry cases. Mix cheeses together and sprinkle over the top. Bake in a preheated very hot oven (230°C/450°F) for 5–10 minutes, or cook under a preheated hot grill, until cheese melts and colours slightly. Serves 6.

ORANGE

A golden citrus fruit available all year round. We depend on its refreshing, unique flavour and texture not only as a fresh fruit but also for use in cooking many savoury and sweet dishes.

Orange juice starts the day for many people and fresh squeezed orange juice retains its precious vitamin C. What better snack is there than a naval orange, peeled, divided into segments and eaten just as it is? Or try a bite of fresh fruit and then a mouthful of steaming hot, black coffee as is the way enjoyed by many people in Mediterranean countries.

Valencia oranges have thinner and smoother skins than navels. They are sweet, full of juice and available from October through to April. Navels then come in season, lasting from May through to September.

Bitter oranges, also known as Seville or Bigarade, are not as easily available. They are too bitter to eat fresh but make excellent marmalade and are used in the classic Sauce Bigarade (see page 35). Choose oranges with bright shiny skins and no bruising or very soft spots. They should be firm and quite heavy to hold.

TO SERVE WHOLE: Slit the outer skin into 8 segments, cutting from the stem end to base. Carefully peel the skin away from the orange, leaving the skin attached to the base of the fruit. Tuck the skin points underneath the orange.

TO SEGMENT: Using a sharp knife, remove all the peel and pith then cut each side of each membrane to release segments.

TO CUT SHELLS: Halve fruit and remove pulp, leaving the shell. Pulp may be chopped and mixed with other fruit before piling back into the shell. If you wish to have a scalloped edge, halve the fruit by cutting diagonal slits into the centre of the fruit. Carefully separate the halves and remove the pulp.

TO GRATE RIND: Rub the rind in short light strokes across a grater. Do not grate any of the bitter white pith.

TO MAKE ORANGE RIND STRIPS: Peel strips of rind from one orange using a vegetable peeler. Do not include any bitter white pith. Cut the rind into fine matchstick lengths and cook gently in ¹/₂ cup water and 1 tbs sugar for about 5 minutes or until the rind becomes clear. Use to decorate hot or cold puddings, iced desserts, cakes or as specified in a recipe.

WAYS TO USE ORANGES

- Squeeze orange juice over strawberries.
- Add grated orange rind to stewed rhubarb.
- Make Orange Butter (mash 125 g/4 oz) unsalted butter with 1 tbs orange juice and 1 tbs orange rind) and spread on sweet breads, or buns, scones or pikelets.
- Top pineapple rings with a thick orange slice, drizzle warm honey over and serve with yogurt.
- Cook rice in half orange juice and half water, add chopped mint to the cooked rice and serve with lamb, or add chopped thyme to orange rice and serve with veal or poultry.
- Add grated orange rind to hot, buttery mashed potatoes and serve with fish or veal. **See recipes.**

Citrus Carrot Soup

1 large onion, finely chopped; 90 g (3 oz) butter; 8 medium carrots, sliced; 2 potatoes, peeled and sliced; 3 cups water; salt and freshly ground black pepper; ¹/₂ tsp ground cloves; 3 tbs lemon juice; 2 cups orange juice.

GARNISH: chopped fresh mint; sour cream (optional).

Gently fry onion in butter in a heavy saucepan until golden. Add carrots, potatoes, water, salt, pepper and cloves. Cover and simmer until vegetables are tender, about 20 minutes. Purée soup in a blender until smooth (do this in 2 or 3 batches), or push through a sieve. Add lemon and orange juices. Reheat if soup is to be served hot, or chill for 3–4 hours. Serve sprinkled with chopped mint and add a spoonful of sour cream to each bowl, if desired. Serves 6.

Orange Marinated Steak

500 g (1 lb) round, topside or skirt steak.

MARINADE: ¹/₂ cup orange juice;
1 onion, chopped; 1 tbs ground coriander;
1 tbs olive oil; 1 clove garlic, crushed.

GARNISH: 1 orange, peeled and sliced;
sprigs fresh coriander or parsley.

Lightly score steak in a diamond pattern on each side. Combine ingredients for marinade in a glass dish. Add steak, turn to coat, cover and refrigerate for 6–8 hours, turning occasionally. Drain steak, reserving 2 tbs marinade. Pat steak dry with paper towels. Lightly oil grill rack. Grill steak under a preheated grill, for 5 minutes on each side for medium-rare meat. Transfer meat to a heated platter. Cut it across grain into thin slices and sprinkle with reserved marinade. Garnish platter with orange slices and sprigs of coriander or parsley. Serves 4.

Chicken in Orange Sauce

8 chicken joints, legs, thighs, wings or breasts;
¹/₄ cup olive oil; 1 cup fresh orange juice, strained;
1 cup dry white wine; ¹/₂ cup raisins;
¹/₂ cup chopped blanched almonds;
1 tbs sugar; ¹/₂ tsp ground ginger;
¹/₂ tsp salt; ¹/₂ tsp white pepper; 30 g (1 oz) butter.

Brown chicken joints in hot oil, then place in a shallow baking dish. Combine remaining ingredients, except butter, and pour over chicken. Bake in a preheated moderate oven (180°C/350°F) for about 30 minutes or until tender, basting frequently. Remove chicken to a heated serving platter. Heat sauce, boiling to reduce it if necessary, and swirl in butter. Pour sauce over chicken. Serve with boiled rice and a green salad. Serves 4.

Orange Chicken Salad

4 cups diced cooked chicken;
1 cup finely sliced celery; ¹/₂ cup chopped walnuts;
¹/₂ cup seedless white grapes;
2 oranges, peeled and segmented;
lettuce leaves; extra orange segments to garnish
(optional).

ORANGE CREAM DRESSING: 3 tbs thawed frozen concentrated orange juice; 3 tbs Mayonnaise (page 256); grated rind 1 orange;
few drops Tabasco sauce; ¹/₂ cup cream.

Combine chicken, celery, walnuts, grapes and oranges and chill, covered, several hours.
ORANGE CREAM DRESSING: Mix together orange juice mayonnaise, orange rind and Tabasco. Whip cream until thick and fold in. Add dressing to chicken mixture and fold through gently. Serve on a bed of lettuce leaves, garnished with extra orange segments if desired. Serves 4.

Orange and Watercress Salad

This orange salad with peppery watercress is excellent served with barbecued meats and poultry or cold roast duck, ham or turkey at Christmas.

6 oranges; 1 bunch watercress.

DRESSING: 1 tbs vinegar; salt and freshly
ground black pepper; 4 tbs olive oil;
1 tbs chopped mixed fresh mint and parsley.

Peel oranges, removing all white pith, and cut into thick slices. Break stalks off watercress. Reserve a small bunch of watercress and add remainder to orange slices.
DRESSING: Place vinegar in a small bowl with salt and pepper and gradually whisk in oil until thick. Mix in herbs. Pour dressing over oranges and watercress and toss lightly. Garnish with remaining watercress. Serve immediately. Serves 8.

Orange Vinaigrette

6 oranges; sprigs fresh mint.

SAUCE: 6 tbs olive oil; 2 tbs wine vinegar;
12 black olives, halved and stoned;
1 onion, chopped; 1 tbs chopped fresh mint;
1 tbs chopped parsley; 1 tbs chopped fresh basil;
salt and freshly ground black pepper;
pinch cayenne.

Peel oranges, removing all white pith, and slice.
SAUCE: Combine oil, vinegar, olives, onion and herbs. Season with salt, pepper and cayenne and mix well. Toss orange slices in sauce and arrange on a platter with sprigs of mint. Serve as an accompaniment to veal, ham steaks, lamb or poultry. Serves 6–8.

Beetroot in Orange Sauce

1 tbs grated orange rind; 1 tbs lemon juice;
1 tbs orange juice; ¹/₄ tsp salt; ¹/₄ tsp pepper;
¹/₄ tsp nutmeg; 60 g (2 oz) butter;
2 cups canned baby beetroot, drained;
2 tbs sour cream; 2 tbs snipped chives.

Place all ingredients, except sour cream and chives, in a heavy saucepan and heat gently, stirring occasionally. Serve topped with sour cream and chives. Serves 6.

Buttermilk Orange Cream

I tbs gelatine; 3 tbs cold water; $^1/_2$ cup orange juice; I tbs lemon juice; I$^1/_4$ cups buttermilk; $^1/_3$ cup caster sugar.

DECORATION: orange segments; whipped cream.

Soften gelatine in water, then dissolve over simmering water. Cool. Combine remaining ingredients and stir in cooled gelatine. Spoon into individual serving dishes and chill until set. Decorate with orange segments and whipped cream. Serves 4.

NOTE: Use fresh buttermilk for this recipe, as the longer the buttermilk is stored the more acid-tasting it becomes.

Orange Tea Sticks

A marvellous recipe for those times when the family wants a sweets course and you haven't prepared one. These lovely grilled bread sticks are great with ice cream or whipped cream.

8 slices day-old white bread, crusts removed; $^3/_4$ cup sugar; 6 tbs orange juice; 60 g (2 oz) butter; I tsp grated orange rind.

Cut bread into 2 cm ($^3/_4$ in) wide strips. Combine sugar, orange juice and butter in a small saucepan and cook over low heat for 5 minutes. Add grated orange rind. Dip each bread stick in syrup, then place side by side on a lightly greased baking tray. Cook under a preheated grill until brown on both sides. Serve immediately. Serves 6.

Orange Sherbet

8 oranges; I tbs gelatine; 2 cups milk; $^1/_4$ tsp salt; $^1/_2$ cup sugar; $^1/_4$ cup lemon juice; 2 tsp grated orange rind.

Cut tops off oranges and gently squeeze as much juice as possible from them without damaging skins. Scoop out remaining pulp. Reserve shells. Measure 2 cups orange juice and strain. Soften gelatine in $^1/_2$ cup milk in a small heatproof bowl for 5 minutes. Set bowl over simmering water and stir until gelatine has dissolved. Combine remaining ingredients in a separate bowl and stir in gelatine mixture. Pour into an ice cream tray and freeze until mushy. Turn into a chilled bowl and beat well. Return to tray and freeze until firm. Pile into empty orange shells and serve with an Italian-type biscuit such as amaretti or savoiardi. Serves 8.

Cold Orange Soufflé

2$^1/_2$ cups orange juice; 2 tbs gelatine; 2 tbs sugar; 2 eggs, separated; fresh fruit to decorate.

Place orange juice in a saucepan. Sprinkle gelatine over and allow to soften for 10 minutes. Add sugar and heat gently, stirring to dissolve sugar and gelatine. As soon as mixture starts to boil, remove from heat and strain over well-beaten egg yolks. Stir well to combine and leave until cool and starting to set. Beat egg whites until stiff and fold through orange mixture. Pile into a serving dish and chill until set. Decorate with orange or mandarin segments, strawberries or kiwi fruit. Serves 6.

Oranges in Caramel

8 large seedless oranges.

CARAMEL: 250 g (8 oz) sugar; $^2/_3$ cup cold water; $^2/_3$ cup warm water.

CARAMEL: Put sugar and cold water in a heavy saucepan and heat gently, stirring occasionally, until sugar dissolves. Boil, without stirring, over medium heat until caramel is a rich golden-brown. Remove from heat. Cover hand holding the saucepan with a cloth to prevent possible splashing and scalding and quickly pour in warm water. Heat gently to dissolve caramel in water, then pour into a jug or bowl and leave to cool.

Using a swivel-headed vegetable peeler, thinly pare a little rind from 1 orange and cut into fine shreds. Blanch for 1 minute in boiling water, then drain and dry. Remove all rind and white pith from oranges and cut each orange in thick slices. Re-form each orange and arrange in a deep glass serving dish. Pour caramel over, sprinkle with shredded rind and chill well. Delicious with Brandy Snaps (see page 46) filled with whipped cream. Serves 8.

Moroccan Oranges

This interesting way with fresh oranges couldn't be easier to prepare, but the taste is exotic. Use your prettiest plates for serving and eat with a knife and fork.

I large orange for each person; brown sugar; cinnamon; rosewater (obtainable from the chemist); fresh leaves lemon or mint.

Peel each orange carefully, taking care to remove all white pith. Slice across with a sharp knife into very thin slices. Arrange slices on individual plates, overlapping them slightly to form a pretty circular pattern. Sprinkle liberally with brown sugar and cinnamon and then with rosewater. Garnish with fresh lemon or mint leaves, or even a pretty garden leaf, and serve at once.

Oranges in Spiced Red Wine

3/4 cup sugar; I cup water; I cup dry red wine; 2 cloves; 8 cm (3 in) cinnamon stick; 2 slices lemon; 8 oranges.

Dissolve sugar in water and stir in wine. Add cloves, cinnamon and lemon slices. Bring to the boil and simmer until the mixture is thick and syrupy. Allow to cool a little. Peel oranges, removing all white pith, and cut into 1 cm (½ in) thick slices. Place in a bowl and pour over warm spiced wine. Chill. Serve alone, or with sour cream sweetened with brown sugar. Serves 8.

Orange and Date Loaf

2 cups self-raising flour; 125 g (4 oz) butter; ¹/₂ cup caster sugar; grated rind I orange; I egg, beaten; ¹/₂ cup milk; ¹/₂ cup water; I cup chopped dates; ¹/₂ cup chopped candied orange peel.

Sift flour into a bowl and rub in butter. Stir in sugar and orange rind. Add egg, milk and water and beat well. Stir in dates and candied peel and turn into a greased and base-lined 18 x 10 cm (7 x 4 in) loaf tin. Bake in a preheated moderate oven (180°C/350°F) for 1¼ hours. Serve sliced and buttered.

Orange Quick Bread

An easily made tea bread, delicious eaten still warm with butter. Have one loaf and freeze the other.

3 cups self-raising flour; ¹/₄ tsp salt; I tbs grated orange rind; ³/₄ cup sugar; I egg; ¹/₄ cup orange juice; I¹/₄ cups milk; ³/₄ tbs melted butter; ³/₄ cup chopped walnuts (optional).

Sift flour and salt into a bowl and stir in orange rind and sugar. Beat together egg, orange juice, milk and melted butter and stir in nuts, if using. Pour on to flour mixture and combine ingredients with a few swift strokes, stirring lightly until just blended. Pour into two 20 x 10 cm (8 x 4 in) loaf tins. Bake in a preheated moderate oven (180°C/350°F) for 40–50 minutes or until a skewer inserted in centre comes out clean. Cool on wire racks. Makes 2 loaves.

Orange and Almond Cake

An excellent light cake, good on its own or for dessert at luncheon or dinner.

I¹/₄ cups fine fresh breadcrumbs; grated rind I orange; juice 3 large oranges; 125 g (4 oz) ground almonds; I tbs orange-flower water; 4 eggs, separated; ¹/₂ cup caster sugar; ¹/₂ tsp salt; I cup cream, whipped.

Butter a 20 cm (8 in) square or round cake tin and sprinkle lightly with ¹/₄ cup of the breadcrumbs, orange rind and juice, ground almonds and orange-flower water. Beat egg yolks with sugar and salt until very pale and thick and stir into orange mixture. Beat egg whites until they hold stiff peaks and fold into orange mixture. Turn into prepared cake tin. Bake in a preheated moderate oven (180°C/350°F) for about 40 minutes. Allow cake to cool in tin. When cold, turn out and spread whipped cream over top before serving.

NOTE: Orange-flower water can be purchased from many health food shops and delicatessens, or in concentrated form from chemists. Use only 2–3 drops if using the concentrate.

Orange Tea Bread

I tsp Earl Grey tea; ¹/₂ cup boiling water; 60 g (2 oz) butter; ³/₄ cup sugar; I egg, lightly beaten; I tbs grated orange rind; I tsp grated lemon rind; 3 cups flour; I tsp baking powder; I tsp bicarbonate of soda; ¹/₂ tsp salt; ¹/₂ tsp cinnamon; ³/₄ cup orange juice; ¹/₂ cup chopped pecans or walnuts.

Mix tea with boiling water. Leave to steep for 3 minutes, then strain. Cream butter with sugar until light and fluffy. Add egg and rinds and beat well. Sift flour, baking powder, soda, salt and cinnamon. Add to butter mixture with juice and tea. Stir gently then mix in nuts. Turn into a greased and lined 21 x 15 cm (8¹/₂ x 6 in) loaf tin. Bake in a preheated moderate oven (180°C/350°F) for 45 minutes or until a skewer inserted in centre comes out clean. Cool completely before serving, buttered.

Orange Semolina Cake

This cake will stay moist and light for a week if wrapped in foil and kept in the refrigerator. Allow to stand at room temperature for 30 minutes before serving.

125 g (4 oz) butter; ¹/2 cup caster sugar; I tbs grated
orange rind; 2 eggs; 2 tbs brandy; I cup semolina;
I tsp baking powder; I¹/4 cups ground almonds.

SYRUP: ¹/2 cup sugar; I¹/4 cups orange juice.

Cream butter with sugar and orange rind until
light and fluffy. Beat in eggs one at a time, beating
thoroughly after each addition. Stir in brandy.
Combine semolina, baking powder and almonds
and fold lightly into creamed mixture. Turn into a
greased and lined 20 cm (8 in) round or square cake
tin. Place in a preheated hot oven (200°C/400°F),
then immediately lower the oven temperature to
moderate (180°C/350°F). Bake for 30 minutes or
until a skewer inserted in centre comes out clean.

SYRUP: Place sugar and juice in a saucepan, bring to
the boil and boil briskly for 5 minutes. Cool slightly.
Remove cake from oven, pour syrup over hot cake
and allow to cool in tin. Turn on to a serving plate
and serve with tea or coffee or as a dessert with
whipped cream.

Orange Marmalade Cake

185 g (6 oz) butter; I cup caster sugar; 3 eggs;
3 tbs orange marmalade; 2¹/2 cups self-raising
flour, sifted; ¹/4 tsp salt; grated rind 2 oranges;
¹/2 cup fresh orange juice, strained.

Cream butter with sugar until light and fluffy. Add
eggs, one at a time, beating thoroughly. Stir in
marmalade. Add flour and salt alternately with
orange rind and juice. Spoon into a greased and
lined 20 cm (8 in) round deep cake tin. Bake in a
preheated moderate oven (180°C/350°F) for 30–40
minutes or until a fine skewer inserted in centre
comes out clean. Turn out, cool on a wire rack.

Preserved Orange Rolls

These little confections are a delicacy from Greece.
Serve them in liqueur glasses with a teaspoon.
Delicious served after dinner with black coffee.

6 large, thick-skinned oranges; 3 cups sugar;
3 cups water; I tbs lemon juice.

Lightly grate entire surface of each orange. Score
peel deeply into 6 segments from stem end to base
and remove peel from orange. (Use orange flesh in
another dish.) Tightly roll up peel segments and,
using a needle and thread, pass thread through each
roll to keep it tightly rolled. When 12 rolls are
threaded, tie the ends together to form a circle of
rolls. Continue, to make 3 circles of rolls. Put circles
of rolls into a pan of cold water, bring to the boil and
drain immediately. Repeat boiling and draining
process twice more to remove bitterness from peel.
Cover with fresh cold water and let rolls simmer
gently until tender. Drain and leave until dry.

In a clean saucepan, bring the sugar and the 3 cups
water to the boil. Add the lemon juice and boil for
5 minutes. Add circles of orange rolls and boil for 10
minutes, skimming off any scum when necessary.
Remove from heat, cover and leave overnight. Next
day, bring pan contents to the boil and cook gently
for 20 minutes or until syrup is thick. To test if syrup
is ready, drop a little on to a cold plate. If drops
do not spread, syrup is ready. If you have a sugar
thermometer, cook to 105°C/220°F. Cool a little, then
remove threads and place rolls and syrup in sterilised
jars. Seal and store in a cool place. Makes 36.

ORANGE-FLOWER WATER

This beautiful fragrant liquid, collected from the distillation
of oil from the sweet blossoms of the bitter orange tree,
is used as a delicate and subtle flavouring in cooking,
particularly in Middle East sweet dishes. Orange-flower
water is available from Greek and Middle Eastern
grocery stores, or in a concentrated form from
chemists. The concentrate should be used sparingly in
drops, and not spoon measures. **See recipes.**

Moroccan Beetroot Salad

4 beetroot; 2 tsp sugar; I tbs orange-flower water;
I tsp ground cumin; I tbs chopped fresh coriander
or parsley; sprigs fresh coriander or flat parsley
to garnish.

Cook beetroot in water to cover for 30–40 minutes or
until tender. Drain, slip off skins under cold running
water and cut into small cubes. In a bowl combine
beetroot with remaining ingredients. Cover and chill
for 1 hour. Serve garnished with sprigs of coriander
or flat parsley. Serve with barbecued lamb. Serves 4.

Date Pastries

3 cups flour; ¹/2 cup caster sugar;
250 g (8 oz) unsalted butter;
I tbs orange-flower water; ¹/4 cup water.

FILLING: 45 g (I¹/2 oz) butter; 250 g (8 oz) dates,
stoned and chopped.

Sift flour and sugar into a bowl and rub in butter
until mixture resembles fine breadcrumbs. Mix
orange-flower water and water, sprinkle on to flour
mixture and mix to a firm dough. Knead lightly, then
cover with plastic wrap and set aside for 30 minutes.

FILLING: Melt butter, add dates and stir over gentle
heat to soften. Cool. Take about 1 tbs of dough and
roll it into a ball. Push 1 tsp of filling into the centre
and mould dough around it. Reshape into a ball.
Place on a lightly greased baking tray, flatten slightly
and press with tines of a fork around sides and across
top to give a slight cone shape. Repeat with remaining
dough and filling. Bake in a preheated moderately

slow oven (160°C/325°F) for 30–35 minutes or until pale gold. Cool on baking tray; the pastries will become firm and crisp when cold. Store in an airtight container. Makes about 30.

Khoshaf

Dried fruit salad is prepared throughout the Middle East. Some people use only apricots and raisins with nuts, others prefer to balance the sharpness of apricots with the sweetness of prunes. Prepare a day or two in advance and make enough to eat over a few days; it gets better every day.

500 g (1 lb) dried apricots; 250 g (8 oz) prunes; 250 g (8 oz) raisins or sultanas; 1/2 cup blanched almonds; 1/3 cup pine nuts; 3/4 cup sugar; 2 tbs orange-flower water or rosewater.

Put all ingredients in a large bowl. Add water to cover, stir, cover and put in refrigerator for 1–2 days. Serve chilled with sour cream sweetened with a little brown sugar. Serves 6.

OREGANO

Also known as wild marjoram, oregano is a more potent herb than its close cousins in the marjoram family. It grows well in the warm climates of sunny countries, particularly those of the Mediterranean. Its scent and flavour are robust, strongly aromatic and flavour many dishes from southern Italy including pizza, tomato and garlic sauces for pasta, seafoods and vegetables, such as eggplants, zucchini and mushrooms.

In Italy oregano is used fresh or dried; in either case it is grown for home use or gathered into big bundles and sold in markets.

Oregano also grows in Greece, where it is known as *rigani*, the flavour being even more pungent than in Italy. *Rigani* is often used dried in many beautiful Greek lamb dishes such as *Arni Souvlakia* (Skewered Lamb) and *Arni Lemonato* (Roast Lemon Lamb). See recipes.

Mushrooms with Oregano

3 tbs olive oil; 500 g (1 lb) open mushrooms, thickly sliced; 1 clove garlic, crushed; 1 tsp dried oregano; salt and freshly ground black pepper.

Heat oil in a frying pan, add mushrooms and cook for 5 minutes, stirring. Add garlic and oregano and season with salt and black pepper. Toss well. Serve as a vegetable accompaniment to meats or poultry, or on hot buttered toast at luncheon or supper. Serves 4–6.

Roast Lemon Lamb (Arni Lemonato)

1 x 1.5 kg (3 lb) leg of lamb; 2–3 cloves garlic, slivered; juice 1 lemon; salt and freshly ground black pepper; 1 tsp dried oregano; 1 cup hot water; 2 tbs butter; 1 cup stock or water.

Cut small slits in lamb and insert slivers of garlic. Rub skin with lemon juice and season with salt and pepper. Sprinkle with oregano and place in baking dish. Roast in a preheated moderate oven (180°C/350°F) for 30 minutes. Drain off fat and add hot water to dish. Roast a further 45 minutes or until lamb is done to your liking. Turn once to brown evenly. Allow lamb to rest in a warm place for 15 minutes before carving. Meanwhile, skim fat from pan juices and add 1 cup stock or water, stirring. Boil on top of stove to reduce, if necessary, and serve this sauce separately. Serves 4–6.

NOTE: A nice accompaniment is potatoes, peeled and quartered and cooked with the lamb during the last hour. Sprinkle with extra lemon juice and fresh oregano leaves.

Skewered Lamb (Arni Souvlakia)

1.5–2 kg (3–4 lb) boned leg of lamb, cut into 4 cm (1 1/2 in) cubes; 1/2 cup olive oil; 1/2 cup dry white wine; juice 1 lemon; 2 tsp dried oregano; 2 cloves garlic, crushed; 8 bay leaves, broken into pieces; salt and freshly ground black pepper.

GARNISH: parsley; lemon wedges.

Place lamb cubes in a glass dish. Mix remaining ingredients, reserving about half bay leaves, and add to lamb, turning to coat meat. Cover and refrigerate for 12–24 hours, stirring occasionally. Thread lamb on to metal skewers, with pieces of reserved bay leaf between some cubes of meat. Reserve marinade. Cook under a preheated hot grill or over glowing charcoal, turning and basting frequently with marinade, for 15 minutes or until cooked to taste. Place on a platter and garnish with parsley and lemon wedges. Serves 6–8.

Mexican Meatballs

500 g (1 lb) minced steak; 1/4 cup cornmeal (polenta); 1 egg; 1 clove garlic, crushed; 1 small onion, finely chopped; 1 tsp dried oregano; 1/2 tsp salt; 1/2 tsp pepper.

CHILLI TOMATO SAUCE: 30 g (1 oz) butter; 1 small onion, chopped; 1 clove garlic, crushed; 2–3 tbs chilli powder or to taste; 3 cups tomato juice; 1 tsp dried oregano; salt.

Combine all ingredients for meatballs and shape into balls about 2.5 cm (1 in) in diameter.

CHILLI TOMATO SAUCE: Melt butter in a large saucepan, add onion and garlic and cook gently until lightly browned. Add chilli powder and stir for a few seconds. Stir in tomato juice, oregano and salt. Simmer for 10 minutes. Drop meatballs into simmering sauce, cover and simmer for 10 minutes longer, or until meatballs are cooked. Serve with rice or Cornbread (see *Cornmeal*). Serves 4.

NOTE: Chilli Tomato Sauce can be used with barbecued meats, or as a dipping sauce for cocktail meatballs or sausages. This recipe makes about 3 cups sauce.

OSSO BUCO MILANESE

This dish has spread far beyond Lombardy where it originated and became part of the international cuisine. It is a wonderful dish of veal on the bone, the marrow still intact, gently cooked in wine and tomatoes; it is at its best when made with very young, tender veal. Osso Buco is served sprinkled with *Gremolata*, a mixture of parsley, garlic and lemon rind, and is traditionally accompanied by Risotto Milanese (see page 418).

Osso Buco Milanese
(Stewed Shin of Veal)

1.5 kg (3 lb) shin of veal, cut into 5 cm (2 in) pieces; ¼ cup flour; 60 g (2 oz) butter; ⅔ cup white wine; 3 medium tomatoes, peeled and chopped; 1 cup stock; ½ tsp salt; ½ tsp pepper.

GREMOLATA: ½ cup finely chopped parsley; 1 clove garlic, finely chopped; 2 tsp grated lemon rind.

Dust veal lightly with flour. Melt butter in a large deep pan, add veal, a few pieces at a time, and brown on all sides. Remove browned pieces and keep warm while browning the rest. Return all veal pieces to pan when all are browned, arranging them so they remain upright to prevent the marrow falling out as meat cooks. Pour wine over and simmer for 10 minutes. Add tomatoes and stock and season with salt and pepper. Cover and simmer very gently, basting meat every 15 minutes, for 1½ hours or until meat is tender but not falling off the bones.

GREMOLATA: Mix ingredients together and sprinkle over top of Osso Buco just before serving. Serves 4.

OXTAIL

The tail of a cow or ox. Oxtail soup and stew are among the most comforting dishes of all in winter. The flavour is rich, and the long slow cooking necessary develops the soft gelatinous texture. Oxtail is best cooked the day before serving and refrigerated overnight. The fat will solidify on the surface which makes it easy to remove before the dish is reheated. Preparation the day ahead also allows the richness to develop fully.

Most butchers stock oxtails during the winter months and they are usually sold ready-jointed. Trim as much fat as possible from joints before using (usually only the upper joints need trimming). One whole oxtail serves two to three people. **See recipes.**

Oxtail Soup

A hearty soup that is a meal in itself.

1 oxtail, jointed; 30 g (1 oz) dripping; 2 carrots, sliced; 1 large onion, sliced; 2 stick celery, sliced; 1 bouquet garni; 2 rashers bacon, or 6 bacon rinds; 8 cups beef stock; 2 tsp cornflour; 2 tbs cold water; juice ½ lemon; salt and freshly ground black pepper; 1 tbs brandy (optional); finely chopped parsley.

Place oxtail joints in a large saucepan, cover with cold water and bring to the boil. Drain and pat dry. Melt dripping in saucepan, add oxtail pieces and fry until well browned on all sides. Remove and drain on paper towels. Add vegetables to hot dripping and fry until lightly browned. Return oxtail to pan with bouquet garni, bacon rashers or rinds and beef stock. Bring to the boil, cover and simmer gently for 3–4 hours. Strain off stock and discard bacon, bouquet garni and vegetables.

Refrigerate stock overnight. Remove meat from bones, shred finely and set aside. To finish soup, remove any solidified fat from surface of stock, pour into pan and bring to the boil. Blend cornflour with cold water to make a thin paste. Gradually stir this mixture into stock and simmer, stirring, to thicken slightly. Add reserved meat and lemon juice and season with salt and pepper. Stir in brandy, if using, and sprinkle with finely chopped parsley. Serves 6.

Braised Oxtail

3 tbs oil or dripping; 1 large oxtail, jointed; 2 large onions, quartered; 2 large carrots, quartered; 2 sticks celery, cut into 5 cm (2 in) lengths; 1 tbs flour; 2½ cups beef stock; 1 bouquet garni; salt and freshly ground black pepper; finely chopped parsley.

Heat oil or dripping in a flameproof casserole and brown oxtail joints all over. Remove oxtail. Add onions, carrots and celery to casserole and brown lightly over medium heat. Sprinkle flour over and stir well, then remove from heat and pour on stock. Return to low heat and stir until boiling and thickened. Return oxtail with bouquet garni and season with salt and pepper. Cover casserole and cook in a preheated moderate oven (180°C/350°F) for 1½–2 hours or until meat is very tender and comes away from the bone easily. Skim off fat from the surface, discard bouquet garni and serve very hot, sprinkled with chopped parsley. Accompany with creamy mashed potatoes. Serves 4.

NOTE: Cook oxtail a day ahead if you have time and refrigerate overnight to improve the flavour and make the fat easier to remove.

Oxtail with Grapes

2 medium to large oxtails, cut into 5 cm (2 in) pieces; 4 rashers streaky bacon, rind removed and chopped; 2 large onions, chopped; 2 cloves garlic, crushed; 4 large carrots, sliced; 2 bay leaves; 1 sprig parsley; 1 sprig fresh thyme; salt and freshly ground black pepper; 750 g (1¹/₂ lb) seedless white grapes.

Remove excess fat from oxtail pieces. Place in a pan, cover with cold water and bring to the boil. Simmer for 10 minutes. Drain and dry well on paper towels. Fry bacon in a large flameproof casserole over a gentle heat until the fat runs. Add onions, garlic and carrots and fry gently, stirring a few times, for about 10 minutes. Add oxtail pieces, bay leaves, parsley, thyme, salt and pepper and cook for a further 20 minutes over gentle heat. Remove stalks from grapes and crush them lightly in a bowl. Add to casserole, cover with a sheet of foil then the lid and transfer to a preheated slow oven (150°C/300°F). Cook for 3–3¹/₂ hours or until meat is very tender and comes away easily from the bones. Remove from oven, cool then refrigerate.

The next day remove fat that has risen to top. Take all meat off the bones. Remove carrots and place meat and carrots in a clean saucepan. Remove herbs, place remaining contents of casserole in a blender and blend at high speed for about 30 seconds, or push through a sieve. Pour over meat and carrots and reheat gently on top of stove. Adjust seasoning. Spoon into a heated deep serving dish, garnish with extra grapes if liked and serve with plenty of crusty bread to mop up juices. Serves 8.

OYSTER

A much-prized mollusc, oysters appear on menus throughout the world, their unique flavour and texture being unlike any other mollusc or seafood. Many varieties are extensively cultivated, one of the most highly regarded being the Sydney rock oyster. The best European oysters include the English Whitstable, and the *Belon* and green *Marenne* from France. Most of these are sold raw or sometimes frozen in the half shell; some are bottled in fresh water without preservatives while others can be purchased unopened.

Live rock oysters can survive unopened in the shell for up to 2 weeks if they are stored in a clean damp hessian bag and kept in a cool place. If stored in a plastic bag or in the refrigerator, they will soon die. Always discard oysters with shells that have started to open, or those with an offensive odour.

Select oysters on the half shell from reliable suppliers. They should be plump, creamy and smell of the sea. Opened oysters should always have a fresh sea smell and be eaten on the day of purchase.

Buy fresh bottled oysters only when refrigerated and in clear liquid with no trace of cloudiness. These are excellent for soups and sauces.

Oysters can also be bought canned, smoked, barbecued or natural, either whole or chopped.

■ **BASIC PREPARATION:** To open oysters, a special flat-bladed knife, with a tough triangular point, is used. Insert the knife point under the smooth lip of the joined shells where there is a gap in the corrugated shell edge. Push the knife between the upper and lower shells and lever them apart. Gently detach the oyster from the hinge on the upper shell and serve in the deep bottom shell. It is best to protect your hand with a cloth before grasping the oyster.

WAYS TO USE OYSTERS

They are best eaten raw – *au naturel*, on the half shell, served with lemon wedges and brown bread and butter. There are, however, many other delicious ways to use them.

- Use oysters in beautiful soups and soup stews (see *Gumbo*): serve them hot or cold; baked, grilled or fried.
- In many dishes oysters are traditionally served on rock salt, which can be purchased from health food shops and re-used if stored in a covered container.
- Add 5 or 6 oysters to Steak and Kidney Pie (see page 507) after mixture is cooked.
- Serve oysters *au naturel* accompanied with hot chipolata or bratwurst sausages.
- Serve canned smoked oysters on crackers or croûtes, with a sliver of lemon peel and ground black pepper.
- Place a smoked oyster in a hot mini puff pastry case, top with sour cream and snipped chives or hot crumbled bacon, lemon juice and chopped parsley.
- Fill hot vol-au-vent cases or tartlet shells with whole oysters and top with Béchamel or Mornay Sauce (see page 456). **See recipes.**

Oyster Soup

30 g (1 oz) butter; 2 tbs flour; 3¹/₂ cups Fish Stock (page 509); ¹/₂ cup cream; 24 bottled or fresh oysters, whole or halved, drained; salt and freshly ground white pepper; snipped chives.

Melt butter in a heavy saucepan. Stir in flour and cook over a gentle heat for about 1 minute. Pour on stock and bring to the boil, stirring constantly. Stir in cream. Place oysters in a soup tureen or soup bowls and pour boiling soup over them. Add seasoning and sprinkle with chives. Serves 4.

Oyster Soup Rockefeller

1 bunch spinach or silverbeet; 2 cups Fish Stock (page 509) or chicken stock; 1 small onion, finely chopped; 2 cups milk; 36 bottled oysters, drained; salt and freshly ground black pepper; 2 drops Tabasco sauce; ¹/₂ cup cream, whipped, to garnish.

Place spinach or silverbeet in a saucepan with stock and onion and simmer for 5 minutes. Purée in a blender or push through a sieve. Heat milk, add spinach purée and oysters and heat very gently. Season with salt and pepper. Add Tabasco and serve immediately, garnishing each bowl with a little cream. Serves 6.

Oysters au Naturel

Many people think the delicate flavour is best complemented when oysters are served slightly chilled, with lemon, black pepper and thin brown bread and butter. Others enjoy them with a piquant cocktail sauce, and it is usually best to include a small bowl of sauce on each plate.

24–32 fresh oysters on the half shell; rock salt; 2 thin slices buttered brown bread; I lemon, quartered.

COCKTAIL SAUCE: $^1/_2$ cup tomato purée; 2 drops Tabasco sauce; squeeze lemon juice; 3 tbs cream; salt and freshly ground black pepper.

Chill oysters for 1–2 hours. Place some rock salt on 4 plates and a small bowl for the sauce in the centre of each. Mix sauce ingredients together well and fill bowls. Remove crusts and cut each slice of bread into 4, arrange bread on a small plate. Arrange 6–8 oysters on each plate on rock salt bed and place a lemon wedge on each plate. Serves 4.
NOTE: Horseradish may also be used to flavour the sauce.

Oysters Kilpatrick

24 fresh oysters on the half shell; rock salt; 2 tbs Worcestershire sauce; 30 g (I oz) butter; 4 rashers lean bacon, rind removed and finely chopped; freshly ground black pepper.

Arrange oysters on a bed of rock salt in an ovenproof dish, or directly in the grill pan. Heat Worcestershire sauce and butter to simmering point. Spoon a little butter mixture over each oyster and sprinkle with bacon. Season with pepper. Place under a preheated grill for 3–4 minutes or until oysters are plump and bacon crisp. Serves 2–4.

Oysters Czarina

A marvellously dramatic dish topped with caviar or its close relative, red and black lumpfish roe.

36 fresh oysters on the half shell; $^1/_2$ cup light sour cream; cayenne; I small jar each red and black lumpfish roe; rock salt (optional); snipped chives.

TO SERVE: brown bread and butter sandwiches; lemon wedges.

Remove oysters from shells and smear a little sour cream on bottom of each shell. Return oysters, put a small dab of sour cream on top and sprinkle with a little cayenne. Mask oysters with red and black lumpfish roe, red on one side, black on the other. Arrange on 6 plates, on a bed of rock salt, if desired. Sprinkle oysters with chives and serve with brown bread and butter sandwiches and lemon wedges. Serves 6.

Oysters Mornay

24 fresh oysters on the half shell; I cup Mornay Sauce (page 456); rock salt; $^1/_2$ cup grated cheese.

Remove oysters from shells, smear a little sauce on bottom of each shell and return oysters. Arrange on heatproof plates, on a bed of rock salt. Cover oysters well with sauce. Sprinkle with grated cheese and grill for 2–3 minutes until lightly browned. Serve immediately. Serves 4.

Soufflé Oysters

24 fresh oysters on the half shell; 3 rashers bacon, rind removed and finely chopped; 60 g (2 oz) butter; I$^1/_2$ tbs flour; $^1/_2$ cup milk; I tsp Dijon mustard; salt and freshly ground white pepper; $^1/_2$ cup grated Cheddar cheese; 2 eggs, separated.

Put oysters on a baking tray. Fry bacon in an ungreased frying pan until crisp and crumbly. Drain and sprinkle over oysters. Melt butter in a saucepan, add flour and stir over medium heat for 1–2 minutes. Remove from heat and gradually stir in milk. Add mustard, salt and pepper. Return pan to low heat and cook, stirring continuously, until sauce boils and thickens. Remove from heat and stir in cheese. Add beaten egg yolks and allow mixture to cool until warm. Beat egg whites until soft peaks form and gently fold into cheese mixture. Spread heaped spoonfuls of the mixture over each oyster. Bake in a preheated hot oven (200°C/400°F) for 5 minutes or until puffed and golden. Serve immediately. Serves 4.

Steak with Oyster Sauce

315 g (10 oz) rump steak, cut thick; freshly ground black pepper; 30 g (I oz) butter, softened.

OYSTER SAUCE: 12 bottled or canned oysters; 30 g (I oz) butter; I tbs lemon juice; salt; cayenne; 2 egg yolks; $^1/_2$ cup cream; $^1/_2$ tsp Worcestershire sauce.

Snip fat in several places around sides of steak to prevent curling. Sprinkle both sides with pepper and spread with butter. Grill under a preheated grill 6–8 minutes on each side or until cooked as desired.
OYSTER SAUCE: Combine oysters and $^1/_2$ cup of their liquid in a saucepan with butter, lemon juice, salt and cayenne. Simmer 30 seconds, then add egg yolks

beaten with cream and Worcestershire sauce. Heat through but do not allow to boil or sauce will curdle. Place steak on a heated serving platter and surround with sauce. Garnish with watercress if liked. Serves 2.

Oysters with Garlic Butter

Serve with brown bread, cut into strips, to mop up any juices.

2–3 cloves garlic; ¹/₄ tsp salt; 3 tbs finely chopped parsley; 90 g (3 oz) unsalted butter; 24 fresh oysters on the half shell; I cup fine fresh breadcrumbs.

Crush garlic with salt to a smooth paste. Combine garlic, parsley and butter and cream well. Place about ½ tsp of butter on each oyster, top with breadcrumbs and grill under a preheated hot grill for 3 minutes or until golden. Serves 4.

Oyster Brochettes

24 oysters, bottled or fresh; lemon juice; 6 rashers bacon, rind removed and halved; freshly ground black pepper; 4 slices rye bread; 2 tbs sour cream; 4 lemon wedges to garnish.

Drain and pat dry bottled oysters, or remove fresh oysters from shell. Squeeze lemon juice over. Wrap 2 oysters in each half rasher of bacon and carefully thread on to metal skewers. Season with pepper. Place under a preheated grill, or in a hot, dry frying pan, and cook 2–3 minutes or until bacon is just cooked. Place brochettes on rye bread spread with sour cream and serve garnished with lemon wedges. Serves 4.

Fried Oysters

24 bottled oysters; I egg; fine dry breadcrumbs; oil for deep-frying; freshly ground black pepper.

GARNISH: I lemon, quartered; Fried Parsley (page 331).

Drain oysters over a saucepan, reserving liquid. Bring liquid to the boil, then add oysters and cook for 30 seconds only, just until plump. Cool oysters in the liquid and drain. Beat egg lightly. Dip each oyster in egg then in breadcrumbs, coating well. Heat oil in a deep fryer until hot enough for a bread cube dropped in the oil to turn golden in 30 seconds. Place oysters in a frying basket and fry for 2–3 minutes or until crisp and golden. It is best to fry the oysters in 3–4 batches. Drain on crumpled paper towels, and arrange in bowls on napkins. Grind a little black pepper over before serving. Garnish with lemon quarters and fried parsley. Serves 4.

p

PAELLA

A traditional Spanish rice dish that has become famous all over the world. The ingredients, apart from rice flavoured with olive oil, onion, garlic and saffron, vary from region to region, and even from family to family. Paella from coastal regions usually contains seafood, poultry and a spicy Spanish sausage such as chorizo. Paella from inland Spain often contains meat, chicken, sausage and vegetables. Paella takes its name from the utensil in which it is cooked – a large two-handled, heavy frying pan – but it can be cooked successfully in any frying pan large enough to take all the ingredients. Use Calasparra or Arborio rice for preference. Paella makes an excellent buffet dish, and only a salad and dessert or cheese are needed to complete the meal.

Paella Valenciana

good pinch saffron, crumbled;
5 cups chicken stock; $^{1}/_{2}$ cup olive oil;
6 half-breasts of chicken, or 4 small pork chops,
cut in two; 2 onions, chopped; 2 cloves garlic,
chopped; 2 tomatoes, peeled and chopped;
$4^{1}/_{2}$ cups short-grain rice; salt and freshly
ground black pepper; 250 g (8 oz) shelled green
peas; 500 g (1 lb) cooked prawns;
500 g (1 lb) squid, cleaned and sliced;
1 chorizo or peperoni, sliced;
3 canned pimientos, drained and sliced;
1 cooked crab or crayfish tail (optional);
1 lemon, quartered.

Put saffron and stock into a large saucepan. Bring to the boil and allow stock to take on colour of saffron. Heat oil in either a paella pan or large frying pan. When very hot sauté chicken breasts or pork until golden-brown. Remove and add onions, garlic and tomatoes. When onions are softened, add rice, combine with other ingredients and fry for 3–5 minutes. Add stock mixture and season with salt and pepper. Spread rice evenly to the edge of the pan and return chicken or pork with peas. Cook on a medium heat until rice has absorbed nearly all the liquid in the pan.

At this stage start decorating paella. Arrange chicken breasts or pork pieces to form a star in the centre. Add prawns, squid, slices of peperoni, strips of pimiento and lastly crab meat with legs and cracked claws, or crayfish tail cut in sections. Do not stir at this stage as the decorations are a feature of the paella and must not be disturbed. Continue cooking until rice is tender and other ingredients are cooked. If rice appears too dry or if foods don't appear to be cooking sufficiently add a little more stock. Just before serving garnish with lemon quarters. Serves 8–10.
NOTE: The tiny squid tentacles make a pretty flower-like decoration in the paella.

PALM HEARTS

The pale, tender hearts of the cabbage palm. In many tropical climates these are available fresh. For visitors from more temperate climates who have a cabbage palm in the garden at home, it is intriguing to see these little palms cut down for the delicate, creamy white hearts that find their way to the table – each palm tree has but one heart!

Canned palm hearts are available in most delicatessens, and may be used as a garnish or in a mixed salad with a variety of salad greens, or as an appetiser salad. They may be served whole, halved lengthways or cut into circles. **See recipes.**
Salad of Palm Hearts: Drain canned palm hearts, halved or sliced, toss with Vinaigrette Dressing (see page 442) and chill. Line bowl with washed and dried salad greens, arrange palm hearts on top and pour over dressing. Garnish with fresh herbs, slivers of pimiento, peeled prawns or fine strips of ham.

Palm Hearts and Beetroot Salad with Horseradish Cream

1 mignonette lettuce; 8 canned palm hearts, halved
lengthways; 3 small cooked beetroot, peeled,
quartered and sliced.

DRESSING: $^{3}/_{4}$ cup cream; 1 tbs lemon juice;
1 tbs bottled horseradish, or to taste;
salt and freshly ground white pepper; 2 tbs olive oil.

Line 4 salad plates with lettuce leaves. Divide palm hearts between plates, arranging them decoratively. Scatter beetroot decoratively over palm hearts.
DRESSING: Whisk together cream, lemon juice, horseradish, salt and pepper for 10 seconds or until mixture is frothy. Add olive oil, drop by drop, whisking, and whisk dressing until it is well combined. Spoon it over the salad. Serves 4.

Hearts of Palm Salad Deluxe

1 x 425 g can palm hearts, chilled, drained and
cut into matchsticks; 2 tbs lemon juice;
$^{1}/_{2}$ cup cream, whipped; $^{1}/_{4}$ tsp celery seeds;
$^{1}/_{4}$ tsp sugar; $^{1}/_{2}$ tsp salt, $^{1}/_{4}$ tsp white pepper;
$^{1}/_{2}$ tsp fresh or canned seedless grapes;
$^{1}/_{4}$ cup toasted, shredded almonds.

Sprinkle palm hearts with lemon juice. Fold together remaining ingredients, reserving 1 tbs of almonds. Transfer to a serving bowl and sprinkle with reserved almonds. Serves 4–6.

PANCAKES

Nearly every country in the world has its own version of pancakes. They are endlessly versatile and range from Chinese Egg Rolls to the sophisticated Crêpes Suzette of France (see *Crêpes*), which many people consider to be the ultimate pancake variation. Pancakes usually have a thick, fluffy texture and can be sweet or savoury. They can be served stacked or rolled, with a sauce, or served flat, with a topping; their thin, lacy relative, crêpes, are usually rolled or folded around a filling.

Russian Blini made from buckwheat and served with sour cream and caviar (see *Blini*); Jewish Blintzes, with creamy cheese filling, and topped with conserve and sour cream (see *Blintzes*); Griddle Cakes, Flapjacks and Pikelets (see separate entries) are all part of the pancake family. Whatever variation you choose, pancakes have delicious possibilities for parties, snacks and for every course of a meal, every meal of the day.

THE PANCAKE PAN: Use a heavy, flat pan, preferably made from cast-iron, with sides about 1 cm (½ in) high and about 18 cm (7 in) in diameter. A cast-iron pan should be kept only for making pancakes and their variations. Do not wash after use: simply rub it with paper towels and a few drops of oil. If the pan becomes sticky, rub with salt first and finish with oil.

TO SEASON A NEW PAN: Fill with oil and heat to smoking point. Turn off heat and stand 24 hours. Pour off the oil, and wipe well with paper towels.

TO TOSS PANCAKES: Some people consider the best way to turn over a pancake during cooking is to toss it. Pour the batter from a jug into the pan, tilting the pan to coat the bottom evenly. When bubbles appear on top of the batter and it begins to set, shake the pan to make sure the pancake is not sticking and has browned underneath. Jerk the pan forward quickly until the pancake moves on to the downward sloping part of the pan. Flip the pancake over with a quick movement of the wrist so that the uncooked side is now underneath. This takes practice.

TO STORE PANCAKES: Store as for Crêpes (see page 102)

TO REHEAT PANCAKES: Place on a baking tray, cover with foil and warm in a preheated moderate oven (180°C/350°F) for 5 minutes. Or place a stack of 3–4 pancakes on a heatproof plate, cover with another plate and warm over boiling water for 8–10 minutes.

See also *Crêpes.*

Sweet Pancake Toppings: Squeeze lemon juice over and sprinkle with sugar; spread with butter and pour on hot maple syrup; top with warm mincemeat (see *Mincemeat*) and a spoonful of whipped cream; spread with lemon cheese and top with whipped cream; spread with apple purée, sprinkle with cinnamon and top with sour cream; spread with sour cream and brown sugar, top with sliced strawberries or pineapple pieces; spread with thick cream and top with warmed apricot, plum or blackberry jam. **See recipes.**

Basic Pancake Batter

**I cup flour; I tsp baking powder; ¹/₂ tsp salt; I egg;
I¹/₂ cups milk; 15 g (¹/₂ oz) butter, melted;
oil for frying.**

Sift flour, baking powder and salt into a bowl. Make a well in the centre and add egg, milk and melted butter. Using a wooden spoon, gradually draw in flour. Beat well, cover and leave to stand for 1 hour.

Grease and heat pancake pan. Pour batter into a jug and pour in enough batter while tilting the pan, to coat the bottom. Cook until small bubbles appear on the surface, about 1 minute, then flip over using a metal spatula or toss, see above. Place cooked pancake on a clean tea-towel, fold ends over to cover and continue making pancakes the same way. Drop each directly on top of the last and fold towel over to cover again. Makes 10–12 x 18 cm (7 in) or 14–16 x 15 cm (6 in) pancakes.

Chinese Egg Rolls

**I cup flour; 2 tbs cornflour; ¹/₂ tsp salt;
2 eggs, lightly beaten; 2 cups water;
oil for deep-frying; 2 spring onions, sliced,
to garnish.**

**FILLING: ³/₄ cup cooked prawns, shelled, deveined
and finely chopped; ¹/₂ cup finely diced celery;
¹/₃ cup minced pork; ¹/₃ cup minced canned water
chestnuts; ¹/₃ cup minced canned bamboo shoots;
2 tsp dry sherry; I tbs soy sauce;
I tbs grated onion; I egg.**

Sift flour, cornflour and salt into a bowl and mix in eggs and water. The batter should be as thin as cream; if it is not add a little more water. Cook pancakes as for Basic Pancakes, cooking on one side only. Cool on a wire rack.

FILLING: Combine all ingredients, using the hands and mixing well. Form into little finger-shaped rolls. Put a roll on the cooked side of each pancake and roll up, tucking in edges to seal in filling. Seal with beaten egg or any leftover batter mixture, Chill for 2–3 hours. Pour enough oil into a deep saucepan to come 5 cm (2 in) up the sides. Heat oil until a bread cube dropped in turns brown in 60 seconds. Deep-fry the rolls in batches until golden-brown, about 5 minutes. Drain on paper towels and serve immediately, garnished with sliced spring onions and bowls of soy and chilli sauces for dipping. Makes about 20.

Hungarian Pancake Pie

When you're in the mood to show off to dinner guests, make this superb dessert from Middle Europe. Pancakes are layered with sweet fillings and baked with a coating of meringue. To serve, cut into wedges like a cake.

**12–14 x 18 cm (7 in) Basic Pancakes (see recipe);
³/₄ cup apricot or plum jam; 125 g (4 oz) dark
chocolate, grated; 125 g (4 oz) walnuts or pecans,
crushed; I cup chopped raisins; I cup cream,
whipped; 4 egg whites; ¹/₂ cup sugar.**

Place the first pancake on a greased baking tray. Spread with a little jam and sprinkle with chocolate. Place another pancake on top, and sprinkle with crushed nuts, a few raisins, and a spoonful of cream. Continue with these layers until pancakes are used up, leaving the top one plain. Beat egg whites to a froth, then beat in sugar a little at a time until they form firm peaks. Swirl egg white mixture over pancakes, making sure they are completely covered. Bake in a preheated hot oven (220°C/425°F) for 3–4 minutes or until meringue is lightly tipped with brown. Serves 6.

Green Pancakes with Cream Cheese

I cup flour; ¼ tsp salt; I egg; ¾ cup milk;
½ cup cooked, drained and puréed spinach leaves;
butter for frying.

FILLING: 500 g (I lb) cream cheese;
salt and freshly ground black pepper;
4 tbs snipped chives.

Make batter with flour, salt, beaten egg and milk, beating well until smooth. Stir in spinach purée and allow batter to stand for 30 minutes. In a separate bowl, beat cream cheese with salt and pepper, and stir in chives. Melt a little butter in a pancake or crêpe pan and cook pancakes, as for Basic Pancakes, page 327. Put 2 tbs of the cheese filling on each pancake and roll up. Serve warm. Makes about 10 small pancakes.

Fluffy Chicken Pancake Peking

Serve this light Chinese pancake as a first course, or with rice and stir-fried vegetables as a main course.

3 egg whites; 2 tsp dry sherry; ¼ tsp salt;
freshly ground black pepper;
I chicken fillet (skinless, boneless half-breast),
minced; 3 tbs peanut oil; ¼ tsp Chinese sesame oil;
shredded spring onions to garnish.

Beat egg whites until foamy and mix thoroughly with sherry, salt, pepper and chicken. Heat 1½ tbs peanut oil in a small frying pan on medium heat. When moderately hot, add chicken mixture and tilt pan so that 'pancake' is of even thickness. Cook until top is firm to touch (the underside should be barely coloured). Loosen edges with a metal spatula and slide pancake on to a plate. Add remaining peanut oil to pan and heat. Slide pancake back into pan, cooked side up. Cook 1–2 minutes more, then slide pancake on to a heated platter. Sprinkle with sesame oil and serve immediately, garnished with shredded spring onions. Serves 2.

Dutch Apple Pancake Cake

60 g (2 oz) butter; 10 medium apples, peeled, cored and sliced; pared rind I lemon; 3 tbs sugar;
10 x 18 cm (7 in) Basic Pancakes (page 327);
Apricot Glaze (page 9); whipped cream;
toasted slivered almonds.

Melt 45 g (1½ oz) of the butter in a saucepan, add apples and lemon rind and cook gently for about 10 minutes or until a thick purée has formed. Stir in sugar, remove lemon rind and rub through a sieve. Place a pancake on a heated serving dish and spread with apple purée. Continue layering pancakes and apple purée, ending with a pancake. Spread final pancake with a fine layer of apricot glaze. Pipe rosettes of whipped cream around top and decorate these with toasted slivered almonds. Serve pancake cake as soon as possible, cut into wedges. Pass around a bowl of lightly whipped cream separately. Serves 6.

Shrove Tuesday Fritters

This is a beautiful dish of deep-fried pancake strips dusted with icing sugar, served with a bowl of Kirsch-flavoured plum sauce.

8 x 18 cm (7 in) Basic Pancakes (page 327);
oil for deep-frying; sifted icing sugar.

PLUM SAUCE: ½ cup plum jam; ½ cup water;
piece pared lemon rind; juice ½ lemon;
I tsp arrowroot dissolved in 2 tsp water;
I tbs Kirsch.

Roll up each pancake and cut into strips 1 cm (½ in) wide. Heat oil and when very hot put in 1 pancake strip. If oil sizzles immediately, it is hot enough. Add half the pancake strips and toss with a slotted spoon until golden all over. Remove from oil and drain on crumpled paper towels. Keep hot while frying remaining pancake strips. Serve warm, piled on to a dish and dusted with icing sugar. Accompany with plum sauce.

PLUM SAUCE: Place jam, water, and lemon rind and juice in a saucepan and bring slowly to the boil. Thicken with arrowroot mixture and boil, stirring, until clear. Strain, flavour with Kirsch and serve sauce hot or cold. Serves 4–6.

Swedish Pancakes

This is a famous Swedish dish customarily served with loganberries or fruit conserves. The pancake is extremely light and tender. The basic pancake can be varied by using a choice of flavourings.

3 eggs; I cup milk; I cup flour, sifted;
¾ cup cream; 90 g (3 oz) unsalted butter, melted;
¼ tsp salt; oil for frying.

Beat eggs with ½ cup of the milk for 2–3 minutes. Add flour all at once and beat until mixture is thick and smooth. Beat in remaining milk and cream, then stir in melted butter and salt. Cover and allow to stand for at least 2 hours. Very lightly grease a pancake pan, place over a high heat and when very hot, lower heat and drop in batter in small mounds. Immediately sprinkle surface of each pancake with flavouring, if using (see below). When pancakes begin to set and bubbles appear on surface, carefully lift each one and turn it over. Cook for a further 1–2 minutes to brown other side, Serve as soon as possible. Makes about 24.

VARIATIONS

Sprinkle these on to the batter as soon as it is placed in the pan: chopped mixed candied peel; crushed almond macaroons or amaretti; chopped toasted almonds; chopped dried apricots, soaked; grated eating apple, unpeeled.

PANCETTA (ITALIAN BACON)

Pancetta is the same cut as bacon, the fat and lean meat from the back and side of the pig, cured the Italian way (as they do Prosciutto Crudo, page 391) by rubbing with salt and sometimes spices, and left to air-cure for the winter months during which time the 'cooking' takes place. Coppa is a similar Italian-style product made with pork neck.

Both are usually cut into small lardons or strips and used in countless Italian soups, sauces, stews, and other meat and vegetable dishes (see Cabbage with Pancetta, Garlic and Rosemary, page 57).

Radicchio with Pancetta and Egg Salad

2 heads of radicchio; 100 g (3½ oz) thickly cut
pancetta, cut into thin strips; 2 tbs olive oil;
2–3 eggs, hard-boiled and quartered ;
3 tsp balsamic vinegar;
salt and freshly ground pepper.

Wash and thoroughly dry the radicchio, and shred roughly into a shallow salad bowl. Fry the pancetta in a frying pan for 5 minutes, until the fat is running and the strips are crisp. Take it off the heat and stir in the olive oil, and then reheat slightly for 20 seconds. Pour this hot oil and pancetta all over the radicchio, stirring to mix it in. Scatter the eggs on top and toss. Sprinkle with the vinegar, season with salt and pepper, and toss again. Serve at once. Serves 3–4.

PANETONE (PANETTONE)

An Italian yeast cake, of Milanese origin, enriched with eggs and butter and studded with sultanas and candied peel. It is very similar to the German Gugelhopf (see page 186), and is traditionally associated with Christmas. Imported Italian Panetone may be found in most Italian delicatessens around Christmas time, and some Italian bakers make their own.

PANFORTE

See *Siena Cake*.

PANNA COTTA

This cream dessert set with gelatine is a delicious specialty of Piedmont. It may be flavoured with lemon or orange zest, chocolate, vanilla or a dash of liqueur. The skill in making this dessert relies on using just the right amount of gelatine so that it sets to a silky smoothness without being rubbery. See *Gelatine*.

Panna Cotta

¼ cup water; 3 tsp powdered gelatine;
2 cups cream; 1 cup milk; 6 tbs caster sugar;
a very little light salad oil; grated rind 1 lemon
(or 1 tsp vanilla extract or 2 tbs brandy or liqueur);
sugared fresh berries (sliced strawberries,
raspberries, blueberries) to serve.

In a small bowl combine water and gelatine. Leave for 5 minutes. Slowly heat the cream and milk with the sugar in a saucepan over a moderate heat until it comes to scalding point, stirring every now and then. Remove from the heat and stir in the softened gelatine until well dissolved. Add choice of flavourings. Tip the contents of the pan into a bowl set over another bowl of ice cubes and stir occasionally until the mixture has cooled without starting to set.

Meanwhile have ready 6 individual dariole moulds or ramekins that have been lightly oiled. Pour the cooled mixture into the moulds and place in the refrigerator for several hours or overnight, until set. Unmould each panna cotta by dipping the base of the mould into hot water for 3–4 seconds, turn upside-down to release on to a dessert plate. Surround with prepared berries to serve. Serves 6.

PAPPADAMS (PAPPADOMS, POPPADOMS, PODDADUMS)

These thin, lentil-flour rounds are available packaged in Asian grocery stores, health food stores and many supermarkets and delicatessens. When fried, they swell dramatically into crunchy golden wafers to eat with or crumble over curries and other Indian dishes. Packaged pappadams will keep for months in a cool dry place. Once fried, they will keep crisp for a day or so in an airtight tin; if they soften, crisp them again in a low oven.

■ **TO FRY:** Heat about 2 cm (¾ in) of oil in a wide pan. Have ready a bed of crumpled paper towels on several thicknesses of newspaper. Fry pappadams one at a time, pressing down with a fish slice or 2 spoons so that they will stay fairly flat. Fry only a few seconds on each side until pappadams are a very pale gold (they will darken more after removing from oil). Drain on paper towels.

PAPRIKA

A spice made from a sweet variety of red pepper, grown widely in Europe. It should be a deep, rich red in colour, with a mild, sweet aroma. The best paprika is said to come from Hungary, where it goes into the characteristic meat dish of that country, Goulash (see page 182).

Paprika is also valued for its colour, which enlivens any pale, creamy-coloured dish. Potato salad, cauliflower au gratin or a dish of creamed chicken or fish, is all the more appetising for a light sprinkle of paprika.

Always buy paprika in small quantities, since even the best or 'noble' paprika loses its spicy qualities when stored very long. For that reason, the quantity of paprika for a recipe is not always specified precisely because it depends on individual tastes and the quality of the paprika. See recipes.

Chicken Paprika

1 roast chicken, cut into small joints;
1 onion, chopped; 30 g (1 oz) butter;
1–2 tsp paprika; 1 tbs flour; 1/2 cup chicken stock;
4 ripe tomatoes, peeled, seeded and roughly
chopped; salt and freshly ground black pepper;
1 clove garlic; 1 bay leaf; 1/2 cup sour cream.

Keep chicken warm in turned-off oven. Cook onion in butter in a large saucepan until soft, add paprika and cook 1 minute. Stir in flour, then remove from heat and add stock and tomatoes. Stir well. Return to heat and bring to the boil, stirring. Add salt, pepper, garlic and bay leaf. Simmer until reduced and thickened. Strain sauce and return to pan. Add chicken pieces and simmer 15 minutes. Stir in sour cream just before serving with boiled rice or noodles. Serves 4.

Veal Chops Paprika

6 veal chops; 2 tbs oil; 2 onions, sliced;
1 clove garlic, crushed; 1 tbs flour; 1 tbs paprika
or to taste; 4 ripe tomatoes, peeled and seeded;
salt and freshly ground black pepper;
1/2 cup sour cream.

Brown chops in oil in a large frying pan on both sides, then remove. Add onions and cook until pale brown. Add garlic and return chops. Sprinkle with flour. Stir, then add paprika and cook 2–3 minutes. Add tomatoes, salt and pepper, plus water if necessary just to cover chops. Cover pan and simmer gently until chops are tender, about 1 hour. Just before serving, add sour cream and stir well but do not allow to boil. Serve with steamed potatoes or buttered noodles. Serves 6.

PARFAIT

A French term, meaning 'perfect', which was originally used only for a coffee ice cream, but later came to apply to all kinds of ice creams, served in a tall glass or individual decorative dish.

Today, a parfait glass is usually a tall, narrow, short-stemmed glass, and an ice cream parfait is a combination of scoops of ice cream, a sauce such as chocolate, strawberry or caramel, whipped cream and sometimes chopped nuts or fresh fruit for decoration.

A very fine preparation of chicken or goose liver may also be termed a 'parfait'.

PARSLEY

Surely the most popular and most widely grown herb; indeed, it is one of the essential herbs in the kitchen. Sprigs of parsley are part of Bouquet Garni; fresh parsley is one of the 'fines herbes' (together with tarragon, chives and chervil); and parsley stalks are used for flavour in a Court Bouillon.

Parsley is a biennial herb, which means that it will yield for two years. It is easily grown from seed, and a parsley patch will be self-perpetuating if some plants are allowed to go to seed each year.

The principal varieties of parsley are the curly-leaved, and flat-leaved or Italian, parsley. The latter is usually more flavoursome, and is recommended for Mediterranean dishes such as Tabouleh, while the curly-leaved parsley is often more attractive as a garnish.

Parsley is rich in vitamin C and minerals, and is said to be one of the best natural tonics. It is also said that chewing parsley can get rid of, or at least hide, a garlicky breath.

Small amounts of chopped parsley add flavour interest to mashed potatoes, steamed vegetables, scrambled eggs and omelettes, sauces, stuffings and salads. In large quantities, it goes into Tabouleh and the jellied ham of Burgundy, France, Jambon Persillé (see *Gelatine*). See recipes.

See also *Coriander* (Chinese Parsley).

■ BASIC PREPARATION

TO CHOP PARSLEY BY HAND: Wash parsley and dry in a cloth. Use a chopping-board large enough to allow parsley to scatter a bit. Using a good cook's knife, hold blade at both ends and, keeping pointed end on the board, chop with rapid up-and-down movements. Sweep parsley together and repeat until it is chopped to desired fineness. Put parsley into a cloth and wring well to remove excess moisture – this ensures that it will not clump when sprinkled.

TO CHOP PARSLEY IN A FOOD PROCESSOR: The food processor makes it easy to have chopped parsley always on hand – it is a good idea to chop about half a cup at a time and store it ready to give instant colour and added nutrition to many dishes.

Do not wash parsley before chopping. Put into processor, fitted with steel blade, and process by switching rapidly on-off, on-off, until chopped to desired fineness. Wash in a sieve, put into a cloth and wring well to dry. Store as below.

TO STORE PARSLEY: Wash and dry well and store in a screw-top jar or tightly closed plastic bag, with some air left in it, in the refrigerator. Or freeze chopped in plastic bags or tubs, for up to 6 months.

Fried Parsley Garnish: Allow 2–3 sprigs per person. Wash and dry parsley sprigs between paper towels. Drop into very hot oil and fry very quickly, about 3 seconds – they should be crisp but not burnt. This is easy to manage if you place parsley in a sieve. Use as a garnish for fried fish and seafood.

Persillade Garnish: A mixture of finely chopped parsley, garlic or shallot, added to pan-fried meat, fish or vegetables just before serving. This garnish is typical of southern French cuisine. Mushrooms, zucchini rounds, sliced squid, lamb chops, all take well to a persillade treatment.

Parsley Sauce: Add very finely chopped parsley to a Béchamel or Velouté sauce (see *Sauces*). Use with salted pork, corned beef or lamb, steamed fish, hard-boiled eggs, or chicken.

Parsley and Lemon Stuffing

Use for chicken or turkey – double quantities for a small turkey.

$1/2$ cup dry breadcrumbs; 2 tbs finely chopped parsley; $1/4$ tsp dried marjoram; $1/4$ tsp chopped fresh lemon thyme; grated rind $1/2$ lemon; 2 tsp lemon juice; 1 small egg; 90 g (3 oz) butter, softened; salt and freshly ground black pepper.

Combine breadcrumbs with parsley, marjoram, lemon thyme, and lemon rind and juice. Beat in egg, then blend in softened butter. Season lightly with salt and pepper. Makes about ¾ cup.

Parsley and Garlic Stuffing

Use to stuff a boned leg or shoulder of lamb.

$1/2$ cup chopped parsley; 1 sprig fresh thyme or rosemary; 2 tbs finely chopped shallots; 1 clove garlic, crushed; $1/4$ tsp ground ginger; salt and freshly ground black pepper.

Combine all ingredients (use leaves only of thyme or rosemary). Spread on lamb, roll up, tie and roast as usual. Makes about ¾ cup.

PARSNIP

A carrot-shaped, white root vegetable, most common in the winter months. It has a distinctive, slightly sweet and sometimes strong flavour, and makes a good accompaniment to most roast or grilled meats.

Parsnip may be added to a mixed vegetable soup or stew, but use only half as much parsnip as carrot. Julienne (matchsticks) of carrot and parsnip, cooked in a little water until tender but still firm, then tossed with butter and finely chopped herbs, is a lovely winter vegetable dish – add the parsnip julienne about a minute after the carrot.

Young parsnips can be mashed like potatoes, with butter and cream, pepper and salt and chopped parsley added. This also makes tasty croquettes, in the same way as potato (see *Potato*). Old parsnips are not always suitable for mashing, as they may have a hard, woody core, which should be cut away before cooking. **See recipes.**

Creamed Parsnips

500 g (1 lb) parsnips, peeled and quartered; 60 g (2 oz) butter; salt and freshly ground black pepper; $1/2$ cup cream; 1–2 tbs chopped parsley.

Remove core from parsnips if woody, and cut into smaller pieces if desired. Cook until almost tender in boiling salted water. Drain. Return to pan with butter and complete cooking over low heat, shaking pan from time to time. Season with salt and pepper and add cream. Heat through and serve, sprinkled with parsley. Serves 4.

Roast Parsnips

4 parsnips, peeled and quartered; dripping or oil if necessary.

Remove core from parsnips if woody. Blanch in boiling water for 5 minutes, then drain. Place parsnips around or under meat in roasting tin, or cook in a separate tin of dripping or oil, or cook with potatoes. Allow about 30–45 minutes in a moderately hot oven (190°C/375°F). Serves 4.

PASSIONFRUIT (GRENADILLA)

Although a native of Brazil, passionfruit is grown in many other countries where the climate is warm and there is little risk of frost. It is a small, round pulpy fruit with small black edible seeds and a tough purple skin.

Passionfruit are usually considered a summer fruit, although they are available year-round. Passionfruit pulp can be purchased canned or frozen, and any surplus from home production may be frozen in small quantities for up to 1 year – small ice cube trays are perfect; when frozen transfer to freezer bags.

Passionfruit is a traditional garnish for Pavlova (see page 346–7), and there are few fruits whose flavour is not enhanced by passionfruit. In summer, it goes beautifully with fresh or cooked peaches, as well as nectarines and rockmelon; and in autumn, with fresh sliced or poached pears. **See recipes.**

Passionfruit Mousse

3/4 cup passionfruit pulp; 3–4 tbs caster sugar;
I tbs gelatine; 2 tbs lemon juice; 2 tbs hot water;
3/4 cup orange juice; 2 egg whites; I cup cream.

Mix passionfruit pulp with caster sugar to taste. Sprinkle gelatine over lemon juice, leave to soften, then add hot water and stir until dissolved. Add to orange juice and chill until just starting to set. Whip juice mixture until frothy. Beat egg whites until stiff. Whip cream until thick. Fold passionfruit pulp into juice mixture, then fold in cream and egg whites. Spoon into a serving bowl and place in refrigerator to set. Serves 6.

Passionfruit Ice Cream

1/4 cup caster sugar; 1/2 cup passionfruit pulp;
squeeze lemon juice; 3/4 cup cream.

Stir caster sugar into passionfruit pulp until dissolved, then add lemon juice. Place in freezer to chill. Whip cream until thick. Fold cream into passionfruit mixture, pour into container of sorbetière and freeze. Alternatively, pour into ice cream tray, freeze until mushy, then turn out and beat until smooth before returning to freezer. Serves 6.

Passionfruit Cheese

60 g (2 oz) butter; 4 passionfruit; 2 egg yolks;
1/2 cup sugar.

Melt butter in top of a double boiler or in a bowl over a pan of simmering water. Add passionfruit pulp, egg yolks and sugar. Stir over gentle heat until mixture has thickened. Cool, pour into sterilised jar and seal. Makes about 1 cup.

PASTA

Spaghetti Caruso, Rigatoni Carbonara, Vermicelli Napolitana, Straw and Grass, Lasagne, Cannelloni – the names conjure up pictures of steaming pasta of different shapes and sizes, each with its own delicious complementary sauce.

Pasta is as Italian as opera and as varied. There are said to be about 400 different varieties of pasta, from the fine strands of *vermicelli* to the broad, flat *lasagne* and the giant *cannelloni* (large pipes). Pasta comes in different shapes, too: small and large shells; *cornetti* or elbow macaroni; *trivelle* – shaped like a corkscrew. The long thin strands of *spaghetti* are an all-time favourite, but so too is *bucatini* (spaghetti with a hole in the middle); and there's *linguine* (flat spaghetti) as well. Some pastas are eaten with a sauce, sometimes just with butter; others like *tortellini* are stuffed with meat or cheese, spices and herbs.

Sauces are important (see *Pasta Sauces*) – contrary to popular belief not all the sauces include tomato, but those

that do are legion – the *Ragù alla Bolognese* is, perhaps, the most famous. So too are the fresh tomato sauces that can be made in just a few minutes with fresh or canned tomatoes. And tomato paste (a concentrated reduction of fresh tomatoes) is added to many sauces to enrich them and give them their lovely natural tomato flavour.

When buying pasta, go for quality. Look also for the pre-cooked varieties, especially *cannelloni* and *lasagne*, which eliminate one whole step – cooking the pasta in boiling water – which can be tricky with these shapes as they have a tendency to stick together. Pre-cooked *spaghetti* is a great boon: it takes only 6 minutes to boil, the strands stay separate and in that time you can make a simple tomato sauce, or simply serve the spaghetti with butter flavoured with a crushed clove of garlic and a grating of Parmesan cheese – it's delicious!

There are three main distinctions to be made with types of Italian pasta. One is called *pasta fatta in casa*, meaning fresh, home-made pasta; another is the mass-produced type, sold dried, in packets, and the third is the pasta made in the fresh pasta shops that are now emerging. There is much to be said for all three, but if you have a light hand with pastry, it is well worth trying to make your own pasta. You may even invest in a pasta-making machine. The electric machines actually make the pasta, then roll it out and cut it into a variety of shapes, all done automatically. A great toy and if you really love pasta, a joy.

SERVINGS: 500 g (1 lb) pasta will serve 4 people as a main course, 6 people as a first course.

■ **TO COOK:** Use a large, deep pan with plenty of room for the pasta to cook, without sticking. Allow 3.75 litres (15 cups) water for 250 g (8 oz) pasta. Add about 1 tsp salt for each litre (4 cups) of water, and have the water boiling vigorously before adding pasta. A teaspoon of olive oil may be added to water to help prevent pasta sticking together, a good tip, especially for large pasta like *lasagne*.

Drop pasta into water slowly so water does not go off the boil. Stir a few times at start of cooking to prevent pasta sticking, then allow to boil vigorously, uncovered. When cooked, pasta should be tender but still firm to the bite – *al dente*, as the Italians say, which means just firm enough to bite comfortably, but not so soft that it is mushy. Pasta is meant to be chewed. When cooked, remove pan immediately from heat and drain pasta. Pour boiling water through pasta in a colander or sieve, then allow to drain. Toss in hot sauce or melted butter and serve immediately.

Home-made pasta will not take as long to cook as the bought variety, but it is difficult to give exact times as this depends on the thickness of the dough and also the size and shape of the pasta.

COOKING TIMES: There is a guide to cooking times on most packets, but it is best to start tasting and testing pasta, especially fresh pasta, as soon as it rises to the surface of the water. The following are approximate cooking times for dried packaged pasta.

Spaghetti: 12 minutes

Tagliatelle (long ribbon strips): 8 minutes

Vermicelli (long thin threads): 8–10 minutes

Cannelloni and Lasagne (large pipes or squares): 12 minutes. Pre-cooked cannelloni and lasagne are available. Follow packet instructions.

TO COMBINE PASTA AND SAUCE: Place drained cooked pasta in a heated serving bowl, add part of the sauce (if desired, sprinkle with grated Parmesan cheese). With 2 forks, or spaghetti tongs, toss gently until pasta is coated with sauce. Top with remaining sauce.

TO KEEP PASTA HOT: It is best to serve pasta as soon as it is cooked. However, it can be kept hot for a short while. Return drained cooked pasta to the empty cooking pan, add about 60 g (2 oz) butter, then cover with a lid and keep warm.

Or drain pasta in a colander and set over a pan containing a small amount of simmering water. Coat pasta with 90 g (3 oz) butter (for 6 servings) to keep it from sticking together. Cover colander. **See recipes.**

Egg Pasta *(Pasta all'Uovo)*

2 cups flour; 2 eggs.

Sift flour into a bowl, make a well in centre and add eggs. Stir with a knife, adding a little cold water (about 3 tbs) and form into a firm dough with hands. Turn out on to a floured board and knead, turning and pushing with the heel of your hand for about 15 minutes or until dough is smooth and pliable. The dough will be stiff at first but will become more pliable as you knead. Shape into a ball and wrap in plastic wrap. Leave to rest for 20 minutes. Roll out dough to a paper-thin, even sheet on a lightly floured surface. Sprinkle lightly with flour to prevent sticking. Cut into required shapes as described below, and cook in a large saucepan of boiling salted water. Dough can be left for 30 minutes before cooking, but sprinkle liberally with flour to prevent it sticking.

NOTE: This quantity of dough can be doubled, but divide it in half before rolling out. If using a noodle machine for rolling and cutting, follow manufacturer's directions.

VARIATIONS

GREEN PASTA (PASTA VERDE): Put 1 x 315 g (10 oz) packet frozen chopped spinach in a saucepan and stir over a low heat until melted. Or, if using fresh spinach, cook 2 bunches until tender, about 4–5 minutes. Turn into a fine sieve and press with a spoon to extract all liquid. When cool enough to handle, squeeze spinach with hand to extract as much remaining liquid as possible. Chop or process fresh spinach in a blender or food processor. Make pasta as for Egg Pasta, using 2½ cups flour and 1 egg, and adding spinach purée with egg. It may be necessary to

add a little cold water – or more flour – to make a firm dough.

RIBBON NOODLES (TAGLIATELLE): Roll out Egg or Green Pasta dough to an oblong shape. Starting from the shorter side, roll up dough, then cut across roll into 1 cm (½ in) strips. Unravel each strip and drop into boiling salted water. Cook for about 5 minutes or until pasta is tender. Drain and serve with a sauce or with butter and grated Parmesan cheese.

FINE RIBBON NOODLES (TAGLIOLINI): Roll up dough as for Tagliatelle, but cut in thin, 5 mm (¼ in) strips. Serve similarly or in soup.

LASAGNE AND CANNELLONI: Cut rolled out Egg or Green Pasta dough into oblongs about 8 x 10 cm (3 x 4 in). Place on a floured baking tray so they are not touching. Bring a large pan of salted water to the boil and drop in pasta. Cook about 10 minutes or until tender, then drain and rinse. Spread on a clean cloth, again not touching, and allow to dry. Lasagne and cannelloni can be left 2 hours before cooking. As they are larger than other pasta, they are best cooked in 2–3 lots, or more if your pan is small.

Pasta with Butter
(Pasta al Burro)

500 g (1 lb) pasta, such as ribbon noodles, spaghetti or macaroni; butter; grated Parmesan cheese.

Cook pasta in boiling salted water until 'al dente'. Drain, turn into a heated serving bowl and top generously with butter and grated Parmesan cheese. Stir through pasta until coated. Serve extra butter and cheese at the table. Serves 4.

Ribbon Noodles Alfredo
(Tagliatelle Alfredo)

500 g (1 lb) ribbon noodles; 60 g (2 oz) butter; 1 cup cream; 1 cup grated Parmesan cheese; freshly ground black pepper.

Cook pasta in boiling salted water until 'al dente'. Drain well in a colander. Melt butter in same saucepan over a low heat. Mix in cream, then toss in noodles. Add cheese and a good grind of pepper. Toss well and serve immediately. Serves 4.

Noodles with Pesto
(Pasta col Pesto)

500 g (1 lb) fine ribbon noodles; 1 quantity Pesto alla Genovese (page 339); 60 g (2 oz) butter; grated Pecorino or Parmesan cheese to serve.

Cook pasta in boiling salted water until 'al dente'. Drain and pile into a heated serving bowl. Heap pesto on top with butter and serve. Mix pesto into pasta at the table. Serve with Pecorino or Parmesan cheese. Serves 4.

Spaghetti Bolognese

500 g (1 lb) spaghetti; 1 quantity hot Bolognese Sauce (page 340); grated Parmesan cheese.

Cook spaghetti in boiling salted water until 'al dente'. Drain and turn into a heated serving bowl. Add half the bolognese sauce and toss with 2 forks until each strand is evenly coated. Top with remaining sauce and sprinkle with grated Parmesan cheese. Serve immediately. Serves 4.

Pasta Ammuddicata

Noodles with anchovy sauce accompanied by a bowl of crisp fried crumbs is a specialty from the south of Italy. It is a quick and easy dish but delicious. No cheese is served with this dish.

4–5 canned anchovies, milk; 2/3 cup olive oil; 1 1/2 cups coarse fresh breadcrumbs; pinch chilli powder; 250 g (8 oz) bucatini or tagliatelle.

Soak anchovies in a little milk for 15–20 minutes, then drain and chop. Heat half the olive oil in a small pan, add anchovies and cook them over lowest possible heat until dissolved to a paste. Heat remaining oil in a frying pan and fry breadcrumbs until golden and crispy. Sprinkle with chilli powder and keep warm. Cook pasta in boiling salted water until 'al dente'. Drain and toss with the anchovy sauce. Serve immediately, accompanied by the bread-crumbs in a separate bowl. Serves 3–4.
NOTE: If liked, 2–3 tbs chopped parsley and 1 tsp chopped fresh oregano may be added to the anchovy sauce.

Pasta with Chunky Tomato Sauce
(Pasta Pizzaiola)

A Neapolitan dish. The tomatoes should just be heated through to retain their fresh flavour. If fresh basil or oregano is not available, add extra chopped parsley.

500 g (1 lb) spaghetti or vermicelli; 3/4 cup grated well-flavoured cheese.

SAUCE: 4 firm ripe tomatoes, peeled, seeded and coarsely chopped; 2 cloves garlic, crushed; 3 tbs olive oil; 1 tsp chopped fresh basil or oregano; 2 tbs chopped parsley; salt and freshly ground black pepper.

Cook pasta in boiling salted water until 'al dente'.
SAUCE: Meanwhile, cook tomatoes and garlic gently in oil for 5 minutes. Add basil or oregano. Cook 2 minutes longer, then stir in parsley, season with salt and pepper and remove from heat. Drain pasta and place in a heated serving dish. Pour over sauce and pass grated cheese separately. Serves 4.

Pasta with Basil Sauce

500 g (1 lb) fettucini or spaghetti; 1/2 cup chopped parsley; 1/2 cup chopped fresh basil; 1/2 clove garlic, chopped; 1/2 cup olive oil; 1 cup ricotta cheese; pinch cayenne; grated Parmesan cheese.

Cook pasta in boiling salted water until 'al dente'. Meanwhile, combine parsley, basil and garlic in a mortar. With a pestle pound them into a paste. Gradually work in oil and cheese, then season with cayenne. (This can also be done in a blender or a food processor fitted with a steel blade.) Drain pasta and place in a heated serving dish. Add sauce and gently mix. Serve immediately. Offer some grated Parmesan cheese for topping. Serves 4–6.

Penne with Mushrooms

Tiny, white button mushrooms make a delicious, simple sauce for pasta. Try them with penne or large shells.

4 tbs olive oil; 1 clove garlic, chopped; 500 g (1 lb) button mushrooms, sliced; salt and freshly ground black pepper; 1–2 tbs chopped parsley; 1 tbs butter; 250 g (8 oz) penne or large pasta shells; 4 tbs grated Parmesan cheese.

Heat oil in a large pan, add garlic and mushrooms and cook until soft, about 6–8 minutes. Add salt, pepper, parsley and butter. Keep warm. Cook pasta in boiling salted water until 'al dente'. Drain well. Pour mushroom mixture over and toss lightly. Turn into heated serving dish and sprinkle with grated cheese and, if liked, more parsley. Serves 3–4.

Pasta with Garlic and Fresh Herbs

You really need fresh herbs for this dish. In summer use a mixture of basil, dill, parsley, oregano and coriander which gives a wonderful flavour. In winter, when fewer herbs are growing, use parsley and a little raw grated onion with whatever fresh herbs are available.

500 g (1 lb) noodles/spaghetti, shells, trivelle, or other pasta; 2 tbs olive oil; 3 cloves garlic, sliced; 60 g (2 oz) butter; 3/4 cup chopped mixed fresh herbs; 1/2 tsp salt; freshly ground black pepper; about 2/3 cup milk.

Cook pasta in boiling salted water until 'al dente'. Drain well. Heat oil in saucepan, add garlic and fry until very lightly brown (it must not burn or it will be bitter). Add pasta to heat through. Add butter, then using 2 forks toss pasta to mix in butter. Add herbs, salt and pepper and toss again. Add milk slowly, cooking and tossing pasta as you do. The milk will slowly be absorbed; it should form a little sauce around the pasta. Serve at once. A green salad is a good accompaniment. Serves 4.

Spaghetti Caruso

The speciality of the Restaurant Caruso Belvedere, in Italy. This sauce is also good with bucatini, the fine spaghetti with the hole in the middle.

2 cloves garlic, halved; 3 tbs olive oil;
2 medium onions, chopped; 125 g (4 oz) chicken livers, trimmed and chopped; 250 g (8 oz) mushrooms, sliced; 2 tbs tomato paste;
$^1/_2$ cup water; 2 cups canned tomatoes with juice;
1 tsp chopped fresh thyme, or $^1/_4$ tsp dried;
1 tsp chopped fresh basil, or $^1/_4$ tsp dried; 1 bay leaf;
1 tsp salt; freshly ground black pepper; 1 tsp sugar;
500 g (1 lb) spaghetti or bucatini;
1 cup grated Parmesan cheese.

Sauté garlic in 3 tbs oil in a frying pan for 2 minutes; discard garlic. Add onions and cook gently for 4 minutes, then add chickens livers and mushrooms. Cook, stirring frequently, for 5 minutes, Stir in tomato paste mixed with water, tomatoes and juice, thyme, basil, bay leaf, salt, pepper and sugar. Simmer, covered, 30 minutes. Meanwhile, cook pasta in boiling salted water until 'al dente'. Drain and put on a heated platter with half the cheese. Spoon over half the sauce and toss. Pass remaining sauce and cheese separately. Serves 4–6.

Spaghetti with Broccoli

This dish is a Calabrian speciality.

1 large head broccoli; 1 tbs oil; 3 cloves garlic, crushed; 3–4 tomatoes, peeled, seeded and chopped;
1 tsp salt; $^1/_4$ tsp pepper; 4 tbs raisins; 4 tbs pine nuts;
500 g (1 lb) spaghetti; 1 tbs chopped parsley;
1 cup grated Parmesan cheese.

Separate florets from broccoli stalks. Cut stalks into bite-sized pieces. Cook florets and stalks in boiling salted water for 5 minutes. Drain and keep warm in a covered bowl. Put oil and garlic into pan and cook over medium heat until garlic is soft. Add tomatoes, salt and pepper and cook over moderate heat for 10 minutes. Stir in raisins and pine nuts. Keep hot. Cook spaghetti in boiling salted water until 'al dente'. Drain and place in a heated shallow serving bowl. Pour sauce over and top with broccoli and chopped parsley. Mix gently, then serve, with cheese. Serves 6–8.

Spaghetti with Cheese and Green Peppercorns

One of the simplest spaghetti dishes, flavoured with canned green peppercorns.

250 g (8 oz) spaghetti; $^1/_2$ cup grated Pecorino cheese; 1 tsp canned green peppercorns, crushed;
3 tbs butter.

Cook spaghetti in boiling salted water until 'al dente'. Drain. Reserving a few tablespoons cooking water. Return spaghetti to saucepan and add remaining ingredients with reserved water. Mix gently and serve. Serves 3–4.

Spaghetti con Vongole

If you can get fresh clams, by all means use them for this dish; about 500 g (1 lb) will be required. Scrub and steam open in a little water. Remove clams from shells and rinse out any sand. Canned clams are very good too, and save a visit to the fish market.

3 tbs oil; 2 cloves garlic, crushed; 3 tomatoes, peeled, seeded and chopped; 1 tbs tomato paste;
1 x 290 g can clams, drained; salt and freshly ground black pepper; 250 g (8 oz) spaghetti;
2 tbs chopped parsley.

Heat oil in a saucepan and fry garlic a moment, then add tomatoes and tomato paste. Cook over a gentle heat for about 20 minutes. Add clams and season with salt until 'al dente'. Drain and place in a heated serving dish. Pour sauce over spaghetti and toss to mix well. Sprinkle with chopped parsley. Serves 3–4.

Tortellini

Stuffed pasta rings that can be served with the stock in which they are cooked or with a bolognese sauce.

45 g (1$^1/_2$ oz) butter; 180 g (6 oz) raw turkey breast meat, sliced; 90 g (3 oz) cooked ham;
90 g (3 oz) Italian sausage; 4 tbs grated Parmesan Cheese; 2 eggs, beaten; salt and freshly grounded black pepper; 1 quantity egg pasta (see page 333).

TO SERVE: 1 litre (4 cups) good quality chicken stock; grated Parmesan cheese.

Heat butter and fry turkey gently until golden then finely mince together turkey, ham and sausage. Add cheese, eggs, salt and pepper and mix to form a smooth paste. Cover and refrigerate. Roll pasta dough thinly to form a large rectangle. Dust lightly with a little flour and leave to rest and dry for 15–20 minutes. Cut into about 40 x 3.5 cm (1$^1/_2$ in) squares and place about $^1/_2$ tsp filling on each square. Fold each square over to form a triangle, press edges firmly to seal and enclose filling. Curve each triangle around your fingertip and press the two ends together. Bring stock to the boil. Drop in tortellini and simmer, stirring occasionally, for 5 minutes. Turn off heat, cover pan and leave to stand for 20–30 minutes. To serve, ladle tortellini into soup plates with a little stock and pass around grated Parmesan. Serves 4.

Rigatoni Carbonara

Try to find rigatoni for this dish; these are the large ribbed noodles or penne, shaped like a pen nib. This is a Roman specialty and translated literally means 'charcoal burner's style'. Spaghetti is often served in this way, but the fat tubes of rigatoni seem better able to collect lovely bits of the egg and bacon sauce.

500 g (1 lb) rigatoni, penne or spaghetti; 1 tbs oil; 125 g (4 oz) lean bacon or speck, cut into 2.5 cm (1 in) pieces; 4 eggs; 3/4 cup grated Parmesan cheese; 1 tbs salt; freshly ground black pepper; 1/4 cup cream; 60 g (2 oz) butter.

Cook pasta in boiling salted water until 'al dente'. Meanwhile, heat oil in a heavy frying pan and fry bacon or speck until crisp and brown. Remove from pan. Beat eggs in a bowl with cheese, salt, pepper and cream. Drain pasta and keep warm. Melt butter in frying pan, add egg mixture and cook, stirring constantly until it begins to thicken. Add pasta and bacon, mix together quickly and serve at once. Serves 4–6.

NOTE: It is important to drain pasta before cooking the egg mixture and to add it to the eggs just as they are thickening. They must not overcook and should be moist.

Straw and Grass

A Roman dish, which gets its name from the 2 pastas used. This simple sauce calls for strips of ham; use leg ham or the raw prosciutto.

125 g (4 oz) butter; 1 clove garlic; 500 g (1 lb) button mushrooms, sliced; salt; 1 cup cream; 125 g (4 oz) cooked ham or prosciutto cut into strips; 250 g (8 oz) spaghetti; 250 g (8 oz) tagliatelle; 3/4 cup grated Parmesan cheese.

Heat butter in a large frying pan. Add garlic and mushrooms, sprinkle lightly with salt and sauté for 5–8 minutes. Heat cream in the top of a double saucepan. Add mushrooms and ham and keep warm. Cook the 2 pastas separately in boiling salted water until 'al dente'. Drain, then toss in mushroom sauce. Serve immediately, topped with grated cheese. Serves 6.

Tagliatelle all'Amatriciana

This recipe is one of the most famous of all pasta dishes. It is said to come from Amatrice, a little village in the Sabine country near Rome. The sauce is based on 'pancetta', a type of bacon (available at many Italian delicatessens) which is diced and mixed with tomatoes, peppers and onions. Purists omit the tomatoes. Try to find the very thin tagliatelle, sometimes called tagliarini, or linguine ribbon noodles for this, bought or home-made.

2 tbs oil; 250 g (8 oz) pancetta, bacon or speck, diced; 1 small dried chilli, or pinch cayenne; 1 small onion, chopped; 500 g (1 lb) tomatoes, peeled, seeded and chopped; salt and freshly ground black pepper; 500 g (1 lb) tagliatelle or linguine; 1/2 cup each grated Pecorino and Parmesan cheese.

Heat oil in a heavy frying pan. Add bacon and cook until brown and crisp. Remove from pan, drain on paper towels and set aside. Soak dried chillies in hot water for 5 minutes, then drain, remove seeds and chop finely. Add chilli and onion to the pan and sauté until onion is softened. Stir in tomatoes, season with salt and pepper and add cayenne, if using. Simmer sauce for 10 minutes. While sauce is cooking, cook pasta in boiling salted water until 'al dente'. Drain. Place pasta in a large heated shallow serving dish. Add reserved bacon to sauce and pour over pasta. Sprinkle with grated cheese and serve at once. Serves 4–6.

Macaroni with Four Cheeses

This very simply made sauce relies on a combination of different cheeses for its lovely flavour. A favourite Roman dish.

500 g (1 lb) macaroni (tubular, shell, bow, etc.); 60 g (2 oz) butter; 1 tsp flour; 1 cup milk; 60 g (2 oz) Gruyère cheese; 60 g (2 oz) Edam or Gouda cheese; 60 g (2 oz) Cheddar cheese; salt and freshly ground white pepper; 60 g (2 oz) Parmesan cheese, grated.

Cook macaroni in boiling salted water until 'al dente', about 15–20 minutes. Meanwhile, melt half of the butter in a heavy saucepan and stir in flour. Cook, stirring, for 30 seconds or so. Gradually stir in milk and simmer sauce for 3 minutes, stirring well. Remove from heat. Cut Gruyère, Edam and Cheddar cheeses into match-sized strips and stir into sauce. Season with salt and pepper. Put pan back on stove over medium heat and stir until cheeses are almost melted (this should take only a minute). Drain macaroni well, place in a heated deep serving dish and toss with remaining butter. Pour sauce at once over macaroni, mix lightly, and serve. The Parmesan cheese may be sprinkled on top or served separately. Serves 4–6.

NOTE: This is a substantial dish, full of protein, and needs only a light salad to complete the meal.

Italian Pasta Salad

2 cups macaroni or fancy pasta, shells, bows, etc.;
2 tbs oil; 250 g (8 oz) thickly sliced cooked ham,
cubed; 2/3 cup black olives, halved and stoned;
I cup green peas, cooked; 1/2–I cup Mayonnaise
(page 256); 2 tbs French mustard;
salt and freshly ground black pepper;
2 tomatoes, peeled and quartered.

Cook macaroni in boiling salted water, with 1 tbs oil
added, for 15 minutes or until 'al dente'. Drain and
rinse well. Sprinkle remaining oil over and toss well
to coat – this will prevent macaroni sticking together.
Add ham to macaroni with olives and peas.
Combine 1/2 cup mayonnaise with mustard and stir
through cold macaroni mixture, adding a little
more mayonnaise if necessary to give a creamy
salad. Season with salt and pepper. Spoon into salad
bowl. Place tomatoes around salad. Serve chilled.
Serves 4–6.

Cannelloni with Meat Stuffing

The pre-cooked cannelloni tubes eliminate a big step
in preparing this dish and you are assured of the pasta
being just 'al dente', as it should be.

I x 130 g (4 oz) packet pre-cooked cannelloni tubes;
125 g (4 oz) mozzarella cheese.

SAUCE: I onion, chopped; I clove garlic, crushed;
1/4 cup oil; I tbs chopped parsley; I tsp salt;
freshly ground black pepper; I x 425 g can tomatoes,
chopped with juice; 2 tbs tomato paste;
2 cups boiling water.

FILLING: 500 g (I lb) minced steak; 2 eggs, beaten;
2 tbs oil; 2 tbs grated Parmesan cheese;
I tbs chopped parsley; I tsp chopped oregano or
basil, or 1/4 tsp dried; I tsp salt;
freshly ground black pepper.

If not using pre-cooked cannelloni, cook the tubes in
boiling salted water for 5 minutes. Rinse in cold water
and drain. Cannelloni should be just flexible enough
to handle.
SAUCE: Sauté onion and garlic in oil until brown. Add
parsley, salt and pepper. Stir in tomatoes and tomato
paste. Gradually stir in boiling water and simmer for
20 minutes.
FILLING: Combine steak, eggs, oil, cheese, parsley
and herbs and season with salt and pepper. Pour half
the sauce into a shallow baking dish. Fill cannelloni
with prepared filling. Arrange side by side in the
sauce. Cover with remaining sauce and thin slices of
mozzarella. Bake in a preheated moderate oven
(180°C/350°F) for 45–50 minutes. Serves 4–6.

Cannelloni with Cheese and Ham Stuffing

I x 130 g (4 oz) packet pre-cooked cannelloni tubes;
oil; 1 1/2 cups grated Parmesan cheese; extra grated
Parmesan cheese to serve.

FILLING: 3/4 cup ricotta cheese, sieved;
250 g (8 oz) mozzarella cheese, grated;
60 g (2 oz) cooked ham, chopped; 2 eggs;
salt and freshly ground black pepper.

SAUCE: 90 g (3 oz) butter; 4 large, ripe tomatoes,
peeled, seeded and chopped; I tbs chopped
fresh basil; 1/2 tsp salt; 1/4 tsp black pepper.

If not using pre-cooked cannelloni, cook in boiling
salted water, with a little oil added, for 5 minutes or
until tender but firm. Rinse in cold water and drain.
FILLING: Mix all ingredients together and spoon into
cannelloni. Arrange cannelloni side by side in a
buttered shallow ovenproof dish.
SAUCE: Heat half the butter in a heavy saucepan and
add tomatoes, basil, salt and pepper. Simmer, covered,
for 15 minutes. Spoon sauce over cannelloni, sprinkle
with cheese and dot with remaining butter. Bake in a
preheated moderately hot oven (190°C/375°F) for 15
minutes. Serve very hot, and pass a bowl of grated
Parmesan cheese separately. Serves 6.

Baked Lasagne *(Lasagne al Forno)*

This lasagne may be made with fresh egg pasta
or bought pre-cooked lasagne. Serve with a fresh
green salad.

I quantity Egg Pasta (page 333), or 2 x 250g (8 oz)
packets pre-cooked lasagne; I quantity Bolognese
Sauce (page 340); double quantity Béchamel Sauce
(page 456), flavoured with pinch grated nutmeg;
1/2 cup grated Parmesan cheese.

If using fresh pasta, divide dough in half and roll out
each half thinly to a rectangle 40 x 45 cm (16 x 18 in).
Trim edges and cut dough into 8 x 10 cm (3 x 4 in)
oblongs.
  Drop one at a time into a large pan of boiling salted
water and cook for about 10 minutes or until 'al
dente'. Cook in at least 2 lots. If using bought pasta
that is not pre-cooked, cook it for 15 minutes in
boiling salted water. Turn into a colander and rinse
with cold water, then place pasta sheets on a clean
cloth so they are not touching and leave to dry. Put a
layer of bolognese sauce on the bottom of a large deep
ovenproof dish. Top with some Béchamel sauce, then
add a layer of pasta. Repeat layers until dish is
full, ending with bolognese, then Béchamel sauce.
Sprinkle with Parmesan cheese. Bake lasagne in a
preheated moderate oven (180°C/350°F) for 1 hour or
until heated through. Serves 6–8.

NOTE: A richer dish can be made by including slices of mozzarella cheese after each layer of Béchamel sauce. Sometimes a beaten egg is added to the last layer of Béchamel sauce for a custard-like topping.

Lasagne with Ricotta

This may be made a day or two ahead and stored in the refrigerator. Reheat in a moderate oven for about 30 minutes, and serve cut in squares accompanied by a mixed tossed salad. Good for a crowd.

750 g (1¹/₂ lb) minced steak; salt and freshly ground black pepper; 4 tbs olive oil; I quantity Egg Pasta (page 333), or 2 x 250g (8 oz) packets pre-cooked lasagne; 500 g (1 lb) ricotta or cottage cheese; 500 g (1 lb) mozzarella cheese, sliced; I cup grated Parmesan cheese.

TOMATO SAUCE: 3 tbs olive oil; ¹/₂ stick celery, diced; I onion, finely chopped; I clove garlic, crushed; 750 g (1¹/₂ lb) ripe tomatoes, chopped, or 2 x 425 g cans tomatoes, drained; 3 tbs tomato paste; I cup wine, juice from canned tomatoes or water; salt and freshly ground black pepper; I bay leaf; I bouquet garni.

TOMATO SAUCE: Heat oil in saucepan, add celery, onion and garlic and wine, tomato juice or water. Season with salt and pepper and add bay leaf and bouquet garni. Cook gently for 30 minutes, then remove bay leaf and bouquet garni and rub through a sieve. Set aside.

Season meat with salt and pepper. Shape into balls a little larger than a marble. Heat oil in a frying pan and brown meatballs on all sides. Do this in 3 portions so that oil keeps hot and free from moisture. Place all meatballs back in pan and cook gently for 5 minutes. Drain. If using fresh pasta, divide dough in half and roll out each half thinly to a rectangle, 40 x 45 cm (16 x 18 in). Trim edges and cut dough into 8 x 10 cm (3 x 4 in) oblongs. Drop oblongs, one at a time, into a large pan of boiling salted water and cook for about 10 minutes or until 'al dente'. Cook in at least 2 lots. If using bought pasta that is not pre-cooked, cook it for 15 minutes in boiling salted water. Turn into a colander and rinse with cold water, then place pasta sheets on a clean cloth so they are not touching, and leave to dry.

Butter a large baking dish or ovenproof casserole and spoon about one third of the tomato sauce into it. Arrange half of the pasta sheets on top, then cover with a thin layer of sauce and spoon over one third of the ricotta. Arrange a layer of one third of the mozzarella cheese on top and sprinkle with one third of the Parmesan cheese. Spoon over more tomato sauce, then add meatballs, one third of the cheeses and remaining pasta. Coat with remaining tomato sauce, then add remaining cheeses, ending with a layer of Parmesan cheese. Bake in a preheated moderate oven (180°C/350°F) for 45 minutes or until golden. Serves 12–15.

Ravioli

I quantity Egg Pasta, made with only 1¹/₂ cups flour, 2 eggs and I tbs water (page 333); melted butter; grated Parmesan cheese.

MEAT FILLING: 30 g (1 oz) butter; 250 g (8 oz) minced steak; I small clove garlic, chopped; I tbs finely chopped parsley; 3 tbs fresh breadcrumbs; 2 tbs grated Parmesan cheese; good pinch grated nutmeg; salt and freshly ground black pepper; I egg.

MEAT FILLING: Heat butter in pan and fry meat, stirring, until beginning to brown. Add garlic and parsley and continue cooking, stirring with a fork, until meat is well browned. Place in a bowl and add breadcrumbs, cheese, grated nutmeg, salt and pepper. Mix all together, then stir in beaten egg. Combine thoroughly and set aside. The pasta dough should be softer than for other pasta. Halve kneaded dough. Roll out each portion thinly on a floured board to a long oblong shape. Cover first piece with damp paper towel to prevent drying out. Place teaspoons of filling in mound at 5 cm (2 in) intervals in regular lines on second sheet of pasta. Brush between mounds of filling with water, then place second sheet of dough over top. Press firmly between mounds, sealing the 2 sheets of dough together, then, using a pastry wheel, cut into squares. Drop ravioli into a large pan of boiling salted water and cook 15 minutes or until tender (cooking time depends on thinness of dough). Drain and toss in melted butter and grated Parmesan cheese, or in Bolognese Sauce (see page 340). Serve immediately. Serves 4–6.
NOTE: Meat-filled Ravioli is often served in chicken broth as a soup. Dough for Ravioli can also be cut into 4 cm (1¹/₂ in) rounds, then filled and the dough folded over to make half moons. Press edges well together and mark with a fork.

Tortellini della Nonna

Pasta is often served with cream, Parmesan cheese and a good grinding of black pepper. Here is a famous version made with tortellini (small filled pasta twists), which can be bought frozen from Italian greengrocers and many supermarket freezer chests.

1 x 500 g (1 lb) packet frozen tortellini; 125 g (4 oz) butter; ³/₄ cup cream; 5 thin slices prosciutto, cut into ribbons; ¹/₂ cup cooked peas; I cup grated Parmesan cheese; salt and freshly ground black pepper; extra grated Parmesan cheese to serve.

Plunge tortellini into a large saucepan of boiling salted water and cook for about 25 minutes or until just tender. Drain in a colander. Melt butter in a deep, heavy frying pan over a moderately slow heat. Add tortellini and stir until coated with butter. Add cream, prosciutto and peas, and cook mixture until cream thickens slightly. Add Parmesan, and season with salt and pepper. Serve immediately, with a dish of freshly grated Parmesan cheese and a pepper mill for those who would like extra pepper. Serves 6–8.

PASTA SAUCES

Tomato, Pesto, and Bolognese are, perhaps, the most famous of pasta sauces. They are simple to prepare and cook, and have a certain 'freshness' about them.

The *pomodoro*, or apple of gold as the tomato is often called, sets the stage for many Italian pasta sauces, and tomato sauce is the basis of many regional specialties. Ingredients are added to it as suits local tastes – prosciutto from Bologna, onion and bacon of the Roman countryside, the clams of Naples, and local fresh cheeses and fish.

Flavourings may change, so too may the length of time a sauce is cooked, but this only determines the characteristics of the sauce as it changes from province to province. **See recipes.**

Fresh Tomato Sauce

This light, fresh-tasting sauce is very versatile. Serve it with pasta, roast veal or roast beef and with Chicken Liver Mousse (see pages 300–1).

2 tsp olive oil; 1 clove garlic, crushed; 2 shallots or spring onions, chopped; 4 large tomatoes, peeled, seeded and chopped; 1 tsp tomato paste; pinch sugar; ^{2}/$_3$ cup chicken stock.

Heat oil in a saucepan, add garlic and shallots or spring onions and cook for 2–3 minutes. Add tomatoes, tomato paste, sugar and stock and cook over gentle heat for 10 minutes, stirring occasionally. Purée sauce in a blender or food processor, or push through a sieve. Check seasoning. If sauce is too thin return to pan and reduce by boiling. Makes 1^1/$_2$ cups, or sufficient for 500 g (1 lb) pasta.

Pesto alla Genovese
(Green Sauce Genovese)

This is the famous sauce which is eaten by the Genoese with all kinds of pasta and gnocchi. It is also added to soups – try a tablespoon stirred into minestrone or a chicken broth at the last minute, or spoon over piping hot baked jacket potatoes as an alternative to sour cream.

2–3 cloves garlic, chopped; 4–6 tbs finely chopped fresh basil; 4 tbs chopped parsley; 1 tbs pine nuts or walnuts; ^{1}/$_2$ cup grated Parmesan or Romano cheese; 1 cup olive oil; freshly ground black pepper.

With a mortar and pestle, pound garlic, basil, parsley, pine nuts or walnuts and cheese together until smooth. Gradually add oil, whisking between additions. Add enough oil, whisking all the time, until sauce is thick and smooth. Season with pepper. Makes sufficient for 750 g (1^1/$_2$ lb) pasta.

NOTE: If made in large quantities, sauce can be made in a blender or food processor. Store in a jar in refrigerator, covered with a layer of olive oil.

Tomato Sauce Neapolitan

Known sometimes as Pizzaiola Sauce, this is often served with roasted or grilled chicken or meats. The fresh taste and look of the sauce is preserved by cooking the tomatoes for a relatively short time and by the addition of fresh basil or oregano.

3 tbs butter; 2 tbs olive oil; 1 kg (2 lb) very ripe Italian egg tomatoes, peeled, seeded and diced; 4 leaves fresh basil, or 8 sprigs fresh oregano; salt and freshly ground black pepper.

Place butter, oil, tomatoes and basil or oregano in a saucepan. Cook over low heat for 10 minutes, stirring occasionally. Season with salt and pepper. Discard herbs before serving. Makes 1^1/$_2$ cups, or sufficient for 500 g (1 lb) pasta.

VARIATION

PIZZAIOLA SAUCE: Prepare Tomato Sauce Neapolitan, but add 2 chopped cloves garlic and a little chopped onion to butter and oil, along with tomatoes. Good also with tiny escalopes of veal, grilled beef steaks and chicken breasts.

Tomato Sauce, Sicilian–Style

A good sauce with pasta, or grilled meats.

1 small eggplant, peeled and diced; salt; 1.25 kg (2^1/$_2$ lb) ripe tomatoes, peeled and chopped; ^{1}/$_3$ cup olive oil; 1 clove garlic; 1 red pepper, peeled, cored and chopped; 4 leaves fresh basil, or pinch dried; 4 anchovy fillets, chopped (optional); freshly ground black pepper.

Place eggplant in a bowl, sprinkle with salt and leave at least 30 minutes. Drain well and set aside. Purée tomatoes in a blender, or sieve them. Heat oil in a saucepan and sauté garlic until golden, then discard garlic. Add eggplant and cook for 5 minutes, stirring occasionally. Add tomatoes, red pepper, and basil and simmer gently for 40 minutes or until sauce is thick. Add anchovies, if using, and simmer a further 5 minutes. Season with salt and pepper. Makes about 2^1/$_2$ cups, or sufficient for 750 g (1^1/$_2$ lb) pasta.

Bolognese Sauce *(Ragù alla Bolognese)*

Ragù is the sauce from Bologna that people all over the world love to serve with spaghetti. The true Ragù is not just a sauce of tomato-flavoured minced meat; its ingredients include several kinds of meat, chicken livers and good uncured bacon, pancetta, or better still, prosciutto. Sometimes cream or butter is added to the sauce just before it is tossed with the hot pasta. Bolognese cooks claim that this cream or butter makes for a smoother sauce.

250 g (8 oz) lean steak, finely chopped;
250 g (8 oz) lean boneless pork, finely chopped;
60 g (2 oz) bacon or prosciutto, chopped; 1 tbs olive oil; 1 clove garlic, peeled; 1 small onion, finely chopped; 1 tbs chopped parsley; 1 bay leaf;
1 x 425 g canned tomatoes; 1/2 cup white wine;
1/2 cup water; 2 tbs tomato paste; salt and freshly ground black pepper; grated nutmeg;
1 tbs chopped fresh basil;
butter or cream (optional).

Put steak, pork and bacon or prosciutto, mixed well together, into a saucepan with oil, garlic, onion, parsley and bay leaf. Brown slowly, stirring frequently to prevent meat cooking in lumps. As soon as garlic turns golden, remove it and discard. Add tomatoes (with juice from can), wine, water, tomato paste, salt, pepper and nutmeg. Cover and simmer for 1 hour. Add basil and cook for 1 minute longer. Remove from heat and discard bay leaf. If liked, add a little butter or a few spoonfuls of cream. Makes sufficient for 500 g (1 lb) pasta.

VARIATION

If liked, substitute 250 g (8 oz) chicken livers for the pork and add an extra 60 g (2 oz) chopped bacon.

Tomato Sauce

Made using canned or fresh tomatoes.

2 tbs olive oil; 1 small onion, finely chopped;
1 kg (2 lb) tomatoes, peeled, seeded and chopped, or 2 x 875 g cans tomatoes, drained and chopped;
1/2 tsp salt; 1/2 tsp sugar or to taste;
1/4 tsp black pepper; 2 leaves fresh basil, or 1 sprig fresh oregano; 1 bay leaf; 1 tbs tomato paste.

Heat oil in a saucepan, add onion and cook over a high heat for 5–6 minutes, stirring, until brown. Add tomatoes, salt, sugar, pepper, basil or oregano, bay leaf and tomato paste. Bring to the boil, then cover and simmer for 45 minutes, stirring occasionally. Discard herbs before serving. Sauce may be pushed through a sieve to make a smooth purée if desired. Makes 1½ cups, or sufficient for 500 g (1 lb) pasta.

NOTE: Tomato sauce may be cooked for 15 minutes only; this gives a fresher tomato taste, which is preferred by some.

PASTITSO (PASTICCIO)

The Greek meat pie made of layers of pasta and savoury meat topped with a creamy custard sauce. It is cut into squares and served warm or cold.

Pastitso

125 g (4 oz) butter; 2 medium onions, finely chopped; 500 g (1 lb) minced steak;
2 tomatoes, peeled and chopped; 1 tbs tomato paste;
salt and freshly ground black pepper;
3/4 cup grated cheese; 1 x 250 g (8 oz) packet pre-cooked lasagne; 1 egg, beaten.

CREAM SAUCE: 60 g (2 oz) butter; 3 tbs flour;
2 1/2 cups milk; 3 tbs cream (optional); salt and freshly ground white pepper; grated nutmeg.

Melt butter in frying pan and cook onions and minced steak for 2–3 minutes, stirring constantly. Add tomatoes, tomato paste, salt and pepper and continue cooking over low heat until meat is tender, stirring occasionally. Cover pan if mixture becomes too dry. Remove from heat and stir in 1/2 cup of the cheese.

CREAM SAUCE: Melt butter in a saucepan, blend in flour and cook gently for 2 minutes. Add milk gradually, stirring over a low heat until boiling. Add cream, if using, and season with salt, pepper and nutmeg. Remove sauce from heat.

Place half the lasagne covered in a greased casserole and cover with meat mixture, then remaining lasagne. Blend cream sauce with beaten egg and remaining cheese. Pour over lasagne. Bake in a preheated moderate oven (180°C/350°F) for 40–50 minutes or until top is nicely browned. Serve hot with a green salad. Serves 6.

PASTRY

From crumbly shortcrust and the airy layers of puff and flaky pastry to feathery choux, delicate pâté sucrée, tender sour cream or cream cheese pastry, yeast pastry, hot water pastry, strudel and *filo*, pastry means a world of enjoyment: delicious sweets, puffs, pies and tarts filled with jam, custard, fruit and cream, as well as savoury fillings that make tempting hors d'oeuvre, appetisers, snacks and meals.

Most pastries are a mixture of flour and fat, bound with liquid, but variations in ingredients and in ways of mixing and cooking produce different end results. A good pastry should be light, tender, crisp and somewhat flaky.

As with most cooking, success in pastry-making is really a matter of practice. Certainly there are those whose delicate touch contributes to the lightness and tenderness of the pastry. But experience has shown that by following a few simple rules, anyone can make good pastry. Start with the simple ones such as shortcrust, rich shortcrust, sweet flan or sour cream pastry. Master those and you will then be able to make superb quiches and fruit tarts, and will be inspired to go on to other delights.

COMMERCIAL PASTRIES: Nowadays, manufacturers make it easy and foolproof to produce home-baked pastries. Supermarkets carry pastry mixes, packaged *filo*, frozen shortcrust or puff pastry, ready to roll out, even ready-rolled sheets of pastry and stamped-out vol-au-vent cases, ready to bake.

SHORT PASTRIES

Most short pastries are made by mixing fat with flour and lightly stirring in just enough liquid to make the mixture hold together. Important points for success are:

- Have ingredients and equipment cool before starting, so that the fat will remain in tiny pieces without melting into the flour.
- Handle the pastry quickly and lightly once the liquid is added to avoid overdevelopment of gluten (elastic strands formed by the flour protein and moisture), which makes pastry tough and causes it to shrink when baked.
- Chill pastry for at least 30 minutes after mixing and before rolling out, and again when it has been shaped, before baking. This relaxes the gluten so that the pastry will be tender and won't shrink when baked. The longer it is chilled after mixing, the better – overnight is ideal – but be sure to remove it from refrigerator at least 1 hour before shaping or you will be obliged to overhandle it.

FLAKY PASTRIES

These pastries are made by folding together layers of pastry dough with butter or other fats in between. When baked, the pastry puffs up into separate thin, crisp 'leaves'.

Important points for success are:

- Have ingredients, equipment and your hands cool before starting, so that the fat will remain in firm layers, separating the pastry layers. Chilling the pastry at inter-vals during preparation, as described in recipes, is also designed to keep fat layers firm.
- The basic dough for flaky pastries is damper and more elastic than for short pastries. This allows the pastry to stretch when it is folded, and also allows for taking up extra dredging flour during preparation.
- There is a special way of rolling flaky pastries. First beat lightly and evenly with rolling pin from front to back of pastry, then roll out as follows: bring rolling pin down firmly on pastry, give a short, sharp back-and-forth roll, lift pin and repeat.

   The idea is to roll pastry thinner without pushing the fat about so that it breaks through the surface. Work your way from front to back of pastry with these short, quick rolls but stop just before you get to the back edge so that pastry is not pushed out of shape. If fat does break through, sprinkle it with flour and refrigerate pastry for 10 minutes before continuing.

- Keep corners square and edges straight. Correct the shape by pulling corners out gently rather than pushing sides in.
- Fold pastry exactly in three with edges level. Use a ruler as a guide and mark thirds with a fingertip on a long side before folding.
- Whatever shape you want to make from flaky pastries, always roll them straight along or straight across, keeping the rectangular shape. Rounds, ovals, etc. must be cut from the pastry, not shaped by rolling. Cut cleanly with a sharp knife, and avoid edges when glazing, so that layers can separate as the pastry rises.

■ **TO LINE A FLAN RING:** Place a flan ring on a baking tray, or use a loose-bottomed flan tin. If the pastry you are using contains sugar or egg, lightly grease sides and base – this is not necessary for plain pastry. Roll pastry out to a circle about 3 mm (⅛ in) thick and about 4 cm (1½ in) bigger than the ring. Lift pastry over rolling pin, then lift and lay pastry over the ring using the rolling pin. Ease pastry carefully into the ring, then, with a floured forefinger or small ball of pastry, press pastry into the angle round the base. Use floured fingertips to press pastry firmly against the sides of the ring, holding a loose ring steady with the other hand while you do so.

Roll across the top of the ring with the rolling pin to trim off surplus pastry. Press pastry gently around the top edge to work it very slightly above the rim of the ring, then work round the top, gently thumbing the pastry a fraction away from the ring. Rest 30 minutes before baking as recipe directs.

To release the baked shell or tart from a flan ring, slide it off the tray on to a serving plate and lift ring off. To release it from a loose-bottomed tin, place tin on a jar and allow sides to fall down. Slide tart off the base on to a serving plate, or leave on the base to serve.

■ **TO BAKE BLIND:** Flan cases and tart shells are often baked 'blind', meaning without filling. A case or shell may be baked completely if filling is not to be cooked with it, or partially baked to colour and crisp the pastry before adding the filling and finishing the cooking. Care must be taken to see that an empty case or shell doesn't puff up unevenly or buckle as it cooks. Oven temperatures used for baking blind vary with the type of pastry being used (see recipes).

TO BAKE TARTLET SHELLS BLIND: Prick lightly all over base with a fork, bake 6 minutes then check. If any have puffed up, press down gently with a spoon then finish baking.

TO BAKE A LARGER CASE/SHELL BLIND: Line it with crumpled, light greaseproof paper or tissue paper and fill with rice, crusts of bread or dried beans. For partial pre-baking, bake the shell for about 8 minutes or until sides are just coloured. Lift out paper with rice, crusts or beans, return case or shell to oven and bake about 5 minutes more to dry and colour the base. Remove from oven, add filling and finish cooking. If sides of case or shell are over-browning, protect them with foil.

TO PRE-BAKE COMPLETELY: Bake 10–15 minutes after removing paper and rice, crusts or beans, until case or shell is golden. Remove from oven and cool before filling. **NOTE:** To moisture-proof a pastry case or shell which will have a juice filling, brush inside with lightly beaten egg or egg white or warm jam and place in oven 2–3 minutes to set. **See recipes.**

Plain Shortcrust Pastry
(Pâte Brisée)

Use for savoury pies, pastries, etc.

$1^{1}/_{2}$ **cups flour; pinch salt; 90 g (3 oz) chilled butter or firm cooking margarine, diced; about 3 tbs iced water; squeeze lemon juice.**

Sift flour and salt into a large bowl. Add diced fat and stir round with a knife until pieces are coated with flour. Rub fat into flour between thumbs and fingertips, lifting hands above bowl to aerate mixture, until it resembles coarse breadcrumbs. Shake bowl so that any large lumps come to the surface and rub them in. Mix water and lemon juice. Add 2 tbs liquid to flour mixture and stir in quickly with a round-ended knife. When dough starts to cling together, use fingers of one hand to gather it into a ball. Sprinkle in more liquid only if necessary to dampen any remaining dry mixture in bowl and use ball of dough to gather it up. Dough should leave bowl clean.

Place pastry on a lightly floured surface and knead lightly by turning and pressing with floured heel of hand until smooth. Wrap in plastic wrap and chill 30 minutes. Place dough on lightly floured surface and shape with fingers into a round or other shape as required. Lightly flour rolling pin and roll out, lifting and turning dough frequently and lightly flouring work surface as needed to prevent sticking. Chill again after shaping, before baking. Unless otherwise indicated, bake shortcrust pastry in a preheated very hot oven (230°C/450°F). Makes sufficient dough to line a 20–23 cm (8–9 in) pie plate or flan ring.

VARIATION
• For a 25 cm (10 in) pastry shell or two-crust 20–23 cm (8–9 in) pie: Follow recipe for Plain Shortcrust Pastry, using 2 cups flour, 125 g (4 oz) butter or firm margarine and about 4 tbs iced water with a squeeze of lemon juice added. Use a little more than half the dough for bottom crust, and the remainder for lid.

Shortcrust Pastry with Soft Margarine

Solid cooking margarine makes successful pastry but if using soft table margarine, a slightly different method of mixing is needed since the margarine is too soft to rub in with the fingertips.

125 g (4 oz) soft table margarine; 1 tbs water; $1^{1}/_{2}$ cups flour, sifted.

Using a fork, soften margarine with water and 2 tbs flour. Mash to a paste, then work in remaining flour until you have a smooth ball of dough. Wrap in plastic wrap and refrigerate at least 1 hour. Roll out and use as required. Makes sufficient dough to line a 20 cm (8 in) flan ring or pie plate.

Rich Shortcrust Pastry
(Pâte Brisée à l'oeuf)

This pastry is crisper and more moisture-proof than plain shortcrust. Use it for fruit tarts, quiches and other pies and tarts with rich fillings. It is also ideal to use when making individual savoury or fruit tartlets or barquettes.

$1^{1}/_{2}$ **cups flour; pinch salt; $^{1}/_{4}$ tsp baking powder; 125 g (4 oz) chilled butter, diced; 1 egg yolk; 2 tsp iced water; squeeze lemon juice.**

Make pastry in same way as for Plain Shortcrust Pastry, using egg yolk mixed with water and lemon juice as the liquid. Unless otherwise indicated, bake unsweetened rich shortcrust pastry in a preheated hot oven (220°C/425°F), and sweetened pastry in a preheated moderately hot oven (200°C/400°F). Makes sufficient dough to line a 20–23 cm (8–9 in) pie plate or flan ring.

VARIATION
SWEET RICH SHORTCRUST PASTRY: Follow recipe for Rich Shortcrust Pastry, beating 2 tsp caster sugar with egg and water before mixing with dry ingredients.
• For a 25 cm (10 in) pastry shell or a two-crust 20–23 cm (8–9 in) pie: Follow recipe for Rich Shortcrust Pastry, using 2 cups flour, large pinch salt, $^{1}/_{2}$ tsp baking powder, 185 g (6 oz) butter, 1 egg yolk, about 1 tbs iced water and squeeze of lemon juice. Use a little more than half the dough for bottom crust, and the remainder for lid. Scraps can be used to decorate the pie if liked.

Shortcrust Pastry in the Food Processor

The food processor makes tender, light pastry in moments. It makes sense to keep some diced, frozen butter on hand for this recipe.

2 cups flour; 125 g (4 oz) frozen butter, cooking margarine or a mixture of both, diced; $^{1}/_{4}$ tsp salt; 2 eggs; about 1 tbs cold water; squeeze lemon juice.

Place flour, butter and salt in food processor with steel blade in place. Process, turning on and off rapidly, until butter is cut into flour and mixture looks like coarse breadcrumbs. Mix eggs with water and lemon juice. With motor running, pour liquid quickly through feed tube. Do not use it all unless necessary – stop pouring as soon as a ball of dough forms round blade. Wrap in plastic wrap and chill for 1 hour before using. Bake as for Rich Shortcrust Pastry. Makes sufficient dough to line 2 x 18–20 cm (7–8 in) pie plates or flan rings.

VARIATION
For sweet pastry, add ⅓ cup caster sugar to processor with flour, butter and salt.

Cream Cheese Pastry

A rich, tender pastry for small turnovers and tartlets. Chill well before using and handle carefully.

**125 g (4 oz) packaged cream cheese;
125 g (4 oz) butter; 1½ cups flour.**

Beat cream cheese and butter in a large mixing bowl until soft. Sift in flour and mix to a dough. Wrap in plastic wrap and chill several hours or overnight. (If left overnight allow to stand at room temperature for about 1 hour before rolling out.) Makes sufficient dough for about 24 small pastries.

Sour Cream Pastry

A rich, melting pastry. As it is very soft, chill well before rolling out to make it easier to handle. Use this pastry for turnovers, individual tarts, etc.

2¼ cups flour; 1 tsp salt; 185 g (6 oz) chilled butter, diced; 1 egg; ½ cup sour cream.

Sift flour and salt into a large bowl. Add butter and rub into flour until mixture resembles coarse bread-crumbs. Make a well in centre. Beat egg and sour cream together and pour into well. Stir from centre, gradually incorporating flour to make a soft, pliable dough. Wrap in plastic wrap and chill for 1 hour before using. Unless otherwise indicated, bake sour cream pastry in a preheated hot oven (200°C/400°F). Makes sufficient dough for 12 x 8 cm (3 in) tarts or turnovers.

Biscuit Pastry

This sweet, tender pastry is used for pies, tarts and tartlets and as the base for slices.

125 g (4 oz) butter; ½ cup caster sugar; 1 egg, beaten; 1 cup plain flour; 1 cup self-raising flour.

Cream butter and beat in sugar little by little until mixture is white and fluffy. Beat in egg, then stir in sifted flours. Knead lightly, wrap in plastic wrap and chill about 20 minutes or until firm enough to roll. Makes sufficient for a two-crust 20–23 cm (8–9 in) pie.

Puff Pastry

Use for fine pastries where maximum delicacy and high, even rising are required.

**2 cups flour; 250 g (8 oz) butter;
about ⅔ cup iced water; squeeze lemon juice.**

Sift flour into a mixing bowl, add 30 g (1 oz) of the butter, and rub into flour until mixture resembles coarse breadcrumbs. Add water mixed with lemon juice and stir with a knife, then gather dough together with fingers. Place on a lightly floured surface, knead lightly and shape into a square pat. Wrap in plastic wrap and chill for 1 hour. At the same time chill remaining butter.

Remove chilled dough and butter from refrigerator; put butter into a loose plastic bag and beat with a rolling pin to make it pliable, then with a floured rolling pin roll it into a 15 cm (6 in) square. Butter and dough should both be firm and of same consistency. Lightly flour work surface and roll out dough to a 25 cm (10 in) square, pulling out corners to make a neat shape. Place butter diagonally on centre of dough and fold the 4 corners in, slightly overlapping, to make an envelope of dough completely enclosing the butter.

Flour work surface and rolling pin and, working as described under Flaky Pastries (page 341), roll dough to a rectangle 1 cm (½ in) thick. Fold bottom one third up and top one third down and seal edges by pressing lightly with rolling pin. This is the first fold. Turn dough round at right angles so that top flap is to your right, as if it were a book. Roll as before to a rectangle 3 times as long as it is wide and about 5mm (¼ in) thick. Fold into 3, place in a plastic bag and chill about 30 minutes until firm but not hard. Dough has now had 2 folds. Remove dough from refrigerator and roll and fold twice more in the same manner. Chill again for about 30 minutes, then roll and fold twice more (dough has now had 6 folds). Chill again for 30 minutes, and dough is ready to use. Roll out and cut as desired, then chill again for 30 minutes before baking. Unless otherwise indicated, bake puff pastry in a preheated very hot oven (230°C/450°F). Makes sufficient dough for 2 x 18 cm (7 in) rounds or 12 small pastries or turnovers.

Flaky Pastry

Easier to make and only a little less delicate and high-rise than Puff Pastry. Use for pie toppings, tarts, vol-au-vent cases, etc.

2 cups flour; pinch salt; 90 g (3 oz) butter; about ⅔ cup iced water; 90 g (3 oz) lard.

Sift flour and salt into a mixing bowl, add half the butter and rub in until mixture resembles coarse breadcrumbs. Add water, stir in with a knife and gather dough into a ball with your fingers. Knead lightly on a floured work surface until smooth, then with floured hands shape into a rectangular block. Roll out to a rectangle 3 times as long as it is wide and about 5 mm (¼ in) thick. Divide lard in half and work each portion and remaining butter separately with a wooden spoon until they are of same consistency as dough.

Cut one half of lard into small pieces and place in rows of about 4, keeping well within the edges, on top two thirds of dough. Fold bottom one third of dough up and top one third down and seal edges by pressing lightly with rolling pin. Turn dough round at right angles so that edge of top flap is to your right as if it were a book. Flour work surface and rolling pin and, working as described under Flaky Pastries (page 341), roll dough to a rectangle 5 mm (¼ in) thick. Place remaining butter on top two thirds as you did the lard, then fold, turn and roll out again. Repeat, using remaining lard. Place dough in a plastic bag and chill for at least 30 minutes before using. Rest again after rolling out and cutting, before baking. Unless otherwise indicated, bake flaky pastry in a preheated very hot oven (230°C/450°F). Makes sufficient dough for 2 x 18 cm (7 in) rounds or about 12 small pastries.

Rough Puff Pastry

The simplest of the flaky pastries. Use for sausage rolls, turnovers, etc., where you want crisp tender layers but a very high, even rise is not required.

2 cups flour; pinch salt; 90 g (3 oz) butter, diced; 90 g (3 oz) lard or firm cooking margarine, diced; about ²/₃ cup iced water; squeeze lemon juice.

Sift flour and salt into a large bowl. Have the fats cool and firm but not hard. Add fats to flour and stir around with a knife until pieces are well coated. Mix water and lemon juice and stir into flour with a round-ended knife, without breaking up fat. With floured fingers, gently gather mixture into a ball, then place it on a floured work surface. Do not knead; use floured hands to shape it into a rectangular block.

Working as described under Flaky Pastries (page 341), roll out to a rectangle 1 cm (½ in) thick. Fold bottom one third up and top one third down and seal edges by pressing lightly with rolling pin. Turn dough round at right angles so that top flap is to your right, as if it were a book. Roll again to a rectangle about 5 mm (¼ in) thick and fold as before. Repeat

twice more, then place dough in a plastic bag and chill at least 30 minutes. Dough is now ready for use. Rest again after rolling out and cutting, before baking. Unless otherwise indicated, bake rough puff pastry in a preheated very hot oven (230°C/450°F). Makes sufficient dough for 2 x 20 cm (8 in) rounds or 16–20 small sausage rolls.

Hot Water Pastry

This pastry sets firm enough to stand by itself even before baking. It is used for raised pies and is the traditional pastry for English cold pies such as pork or veal and ham pie, even when these are made in a mould. It must be used while it is still warm since it becomes brittle when cold.

4 cups flour; ³/₄ tsp salt; 250 g (8 oz) lard; ¹/₂ cup plus 2 tbs water.

Warm flour, then sift with salt into a warm mixing bowl and make a well in centre. Heat lard with water and, when boiling, tip into well and mix with a wooden spoon until smooth. Use at once, keeping dough not being worked in a covered bowl over hot water. Makes sufficient dough for a 20 cm (8 in) covered raised pie.

Suet Pastry

Suet pastry can be baked, but is usually boiled or steamed to make a soft crust for puddings or dumplings – the exception to crisp pastries.

2 cups self-raising flour; pinch salt; 125 g (4 oz) fresh suet or packaged shredded suet; about ¹/₃ cup cold water.

Sift flour and salt into a mixing bowl. If using fresh suet, remove any skin and chop fine with a little of the measured flour to prevent it from sticking. Add to flour and stir around with a knife, then add most of the water, and stir with knife until dough begins to cling together. Gather into a ball with your fingers. Sprinkle in more water only if necessary to dampen any remaining dry mixture in bowl, and use ball of dough to gather it up. Place on a lightly floured work surface and knead lightly by turning and pressing with floured heel of hand until smooth. Roll out and use at once. Make sufficient dough to line a 4-cup pudding basin.

VARIATIONS

For an extra light and spongy crust, ½ cup flour may be replaced by 1 cup loosely packed fresh white breadcrumbs. For a sweet pudding, 1 tbs white or brown sugar may be added to the flour.

Pâté Sucrée (Sweet Flan Pastry)

Pâté Sucrée is fine and crisp, and used for the most delicate sweet tarts.

I cup flour; pinch salt; 60 g (2 oz) butter; ¹/₃ cup caster sugar; 2 egg yolks; 2 drops vanilla.

Sift flour and salt on to a work surface and make a well in centre. Place remaining ingredients in well and work them together with the fingertips of one hand. With other hand, use a metal spatula to draw flour quickly into centre. Mix to a ball of dough. Flour work surface and knead dough lightly by turning and pressing with lightly floured heel of hand until smooth. Wrap in plastic wrap and chill for 1 hour before using. Chill again after shaping, before baking, and prick bottom just before placing in oven. Bake in a preheated moderately hot oven (190°C/375°F) until pastry is a pale biscuit colour. This pastry must not brown or the flavour will be spoilt. Makes sufficient dough to line an 18–20 cm (7–8 in) flan ring or 18 tiny tartlet moulds, or 6 individual 8 cm (3 in) tartlet tins.

VARIATION

For a 25 cm (10 in) pastry shell: Follow recipe for Pâté Sucrée using 1½ cups flour, pinch salt, 90 g (3 oz) butter, ½ cup caster sugar, 3 egg yolks and 3 drops vanilla.

Choux Pastry

Choux pastry is softer than other pastries and is shaped with a spoon or by squeezing from a piping bag. When it is cooked, it swells into crisp golden shells that are hollow inside. The secret of making shells that will hold their shape is to be sure that the pastry is cooked and dry right through. First place in a preheated very hot oven (230°C/450°F) so that the pastry puffs quickly, then reduce heat to moderate (180°C/350°F) so that pastry will cook without over-browning. To be fail-safe, leave cooked shells in the turned-off oven with door slightly open for 20 minutes to ensure that they are thoroughly dried out. A well-cooked shell should be golden-brown and firm to the touch and feels very light in the hand.

I cup flour; I cup water; 125 g (4 oz) butter, cut into pieces; ¹/₂ tsp salt; I tsp sugar (for sweet puffs); 4 eggs.

Sift flour on to a sheet of greaseproof paper. Put water, butter, salt and sugar, if using, into a medium-sized saucepan. Bring slowly to the boil (butter must be melted before water boils). Immediately remove from heat, tip in flour all at once and stir vigorously with a wooden spatula. Return to heat and continue stirring until mixture forms a mass, leaves sides of saucepan and begins to film the bottom – this will take only a short time. Remove from heat and cool a little. Turn mixture into bowl of an electric mixer or leave in saucepan. Beat eggs together and add to dough, a little at a time, beating after each addition until thoroughly incorporated. Do not add all the egg

unless necessary; dough is right when it is as shiny as satin and holds its shape on a spoon. Use warm. Makes sufficient dough for 12 medium-sized éclairs or puffs.

PASTRY CREAM (CREME PATISSIERE)

See *Icings, Frostings and Fillings*.

PATE BRISEE AND PATE SUCREE

See *Pastry*.

PATE AND TERRINE

Pâté and terrine are standard features in any French charcuterie, and the basis of many a lunch for those who have travelled in that country.

It is difficult to make a firm distinction between a pâté and terrine. A fine-textured liver pâté is almost always called a pâté, yet a coarse, meaty product might be called either a *pâté de campagne* or a *terrine maison*.

Originally, a pâté was always enclosed in pastry, and was made with almost any sort of meat or fish. Later, it came to be baked in an earthenware dish (a terrine), which was lined with thinly sliced pork fat to keep the mixture moist.

Most pâtés and terrines contain a good proportion of pork, especially fat belly pork. When making a pâté or terrine, if possible choose particular cuts of meat and either mince it yourself or have it minced by the butcher, rather than buying ready-minced meat. Fat is essential to the texture of the pâté or terrine, and enables it to be sliced without crumbling. It also means that a pâté or terrine is served without butter, and with just crusty French bread or a good wholemeal bread, plus some pickled gherkins or olives or a crisp salad.

A pâté or terrine is sometimes served as a first course; in this case it is usually accompanied by thin, crisp melba toast or warm, freshly made white or brown toast or a selection of savoury crackers. **See recipes.**

Pork and Veal Terrine

500 g (I lb) minced pork; 500 g (I lb) minced veal; I clove garlic, crushed with tsp salt; ¹/₂ tsp dried thyme; ¹/₂ tsp ground cloves; freshly ground black pepper; grated rind ½ lemon; I egg; ¹/₂ cup dry sherry or dry vermouth; thin slices pork back fat or bacon rashers, rind removed; 125 g (4 oz) sliced cooked ham, cut into fine strips; I bay leaf.

Combine minced meats, garlic salt, thyme, cloves, pepper, lemon rind, egg and sherry or vermouth. Mix well. Taste and correct seasoning if necessary. Line a 21 x 11 cm (8½ x 4½ in) terrine or loaf tin with pork fat or bacon. Spoon half meat mixture into tin, top with ham strips, then spread remaining meat mixture over. Place bay leaf on top. Cover with foil and lid, if using terrine. Stand in roasting tin filled with water and cook in a preheated moderate oven (180°C/350°F) for about 1½ hours. Cool under heavy weight, then chill. Flavour develops after 1–2 days. Serves 8–10.

VARIATION

Substitute 6 cleaned, sliced chicken livers for ham strips.

Different herbs and spices can be used to vary flavour. Majoram, tarragon, parsley and lemon thyme can be added sparingly; nutmeg, allspice, mace and crushed juniper berries can impart different and distinctive flavours. It is important to taste the mixture to judge how much to add; cook a small ball of mixture for a few minutes in a little butter or oil for a better idea of the final taste of the cooked terrine.

Rabbit Terrine *(Terrine de Lapin)*

I rabbit; 125 g (4 oz) lean belly pork; 125 g (4 oz) boneless shoulder veal; I tsp salt; freshly ground black pepper; I tbs grated onion; ¼ tsp ground allspice; ¼ tsp nutmeg; 2 tbs brandy; ½ cup dry white wine; 2 sprigs fresh thyme or marjoram; I clove garlic, bruised; thin slices pork back fat or bacon rashers, rind removed; I bay leaf.

Remove flesh from rabbit, and mince finely with pork and veal. Season with salt and pepper. Blend in onion, spices, brandy and wine. Bury herbs and bruised garlic in centre of mixture, cover and leave overnight. Line a 21 x 11 cm (8½ x 4½ in) terrine or loaf tin with thin slices pork fat or bacon. Taste meat mixture and correct seasoning. Remove garlic and herbs. Pack meat mixture into prepared tin and place bay leaf on top. Cover well with foil and lid, if using terrine. Stand in roasting tin of water and cook in a preheated moderate oven (180°C/350°F) for about 1½ hours. Cool with weight on top, then chill. Allow to mature 1–2 days before eating. Serves 4–6.

Brandied Chicken Liver Pâté

90 g (3 oz) butter; I onion, chopped; I clove garlic, crushed; 250 g (8 oz) chicken livers; I bay leaf; few sprigs fresh thyme or oregano, or pinch dried herb; 2 tsp brandy; salt and freshly ground black pepper.

Melt 30 g (1 oz) butter in a frying pan and cook onion and garlic over low heat until onion is transparent. Add chicken livers and cook 2–3 minutes, tossing from time to time. Add crumbled bay leaf and thyme or oregano, and cook 1 minute longer. Cool. Chop livers roughly, then pound mixture with wooden spoon or blend in blender. Melt remaining butter and stir into liver mixture with brandy. Season with salt and pepper. Pack into small dish or mould and chill. If desired, unmould before serving. If pâté is to be kept several days, cover with thin film of melted butter. Serves 4.

Chicken Terrine
(Terrine de Poulet)

I chicken, about 1.2–1.5 kg (2½–3 lb); 2 eggs; ½ cup cream; 2 tbs brandy; salt and freshly ground black pepper; 250 g (8 oz) cooked ham, finely chopped; 250 g (8oz) boneless shoulder veal, minced; thin slices pork back fat; ½ cup finely chopped fresh herbs (parsley, tarragon, chives).

Remove meat from chicken and cut into strips. Beat eggs with cream, add brandy and season with salt and pepper. Combine with ham and minced meats. Line a 21 x 11 cm (8½ x 4½ in) terrine or loaf tin with pork fat. Spread layer of minced meat mixture on bottom, cover with strips of chicken and sprinkle with herbs. Continue in layers until all ingredients are used, ending with minced meat mixture. Cover with foil and lid, if using terrine. Stand in roasting tin of water and cook in a preheated hot oven (200°C/400°F) for about 1 hour. Cool under a weight, then chill. If desired, unmould before serving. Serves 6–8.

PAUPIETTES

Thin slices of meat, fish or poultry, wrapped around a stuffing and braised. A French term, *paupiette* is probably most commonly used with veal; thin slices of beef, rolled around a stuffing and braised, are usually referred to as beef olives.

Veal Paupiettes *(Paupiettes de Veau)*

6 thin veal steaks; I clove garlic, crushed with ½ tsp salt; 2–3 leaves fresh sage, finely chopped, or pinch dried; 6 slices cooked ham; 6 tbs fresh white breadcrumbs; I tbs flour; oil; ½ cup dry white wine; 2 ripe tomatoes, peeled, seeded and chopped; 2 tsp tomato paste; salt and freshly ground black pepper.

Flatten veal steaks, then cut each in half. Mix garlic with sage and rub into one side of each piece of veal. Place half a slice of ham in each piece of veal and top with breadcrumbs. Roll up and secure with wooden toothpicks or tie with fine string. Roll in flour. Heat oil in a frying pan and brown veal rolls on all sides. Add wine, tomatoes and tomato paste, and season with salt and pepper. Simmer about 30 minutes, stirring occasionally. Remove toothpicks or string before serving. Serves 6.

PAVLOVA

With a crisp meringue outside, delicate marshmallow-like softness inside, filled with cream and topped with fruit, Australia's most famous contribution to the culinary world was named for the great ballerina Anna Pavlova, and is a queen of desserts.

Pavlova can be baked and served in a fluted china flan dish, moulded in a springform tin or shaped into a free-form dome. Strawberries and passionfruit are two classic toppings, but any fresh, frozen or canned fruits can be used, or the pavlova can be topped with lemon cheese or apricot sauce. **See recipes.**

Basic Pavlova

6 egg whites, at room temperature; pinch salt; 2 cups caster sugar; $1\frac{1}{2}$ tsp vinegar; $1\frac{1}{2}$ tsp vanilla; whipped cream for filling; fruit or other topping of your choice.

If you have a gas oven, preheat it to very hot (230°C/450°F) before starting to mix pavlova. If you have an electric oven, preheat it to slow (150°C/300°F). Beat egg whites with salt at high speed until soft peaks form. Add sugar, 1 tbs at a time, beating well after each addition. Stop beating when all sugar has been incorporated and fold in vinegar and vanilla. Pile mixture into a greased 20 cm (8 in) china flan dish and lightly smooth top. *Or* pile mixture into a greased 20 cm (8 in) spring-form tin and lightly smooth top. *Or* cover a baking tray with greased foil, mark a 20 cm (8 in) circle on it and pile mixture onto the circle; mound up sides with a spatula and make a slight depression on top. If using a gas oven, turn heat to lowest temperature, put pavlova in and bake $1\frac{1}{2}$ hours or until crisp on top and a pale straw colour. If using an electric oven, put pavlova in and bake 45 minutes, then turn oven off and leave with door shut for 1 hour. When pavlova is cooked, remove from oven and cool completely. Remove sides of springform tin. Fill pavlova generously with whipped cream, then with your choice of topping. Serves 6–8.
NOTE: The meringue may be sprinkled with blanched, slivered almonds before baking. They will toast to a golden-brown.

Rolled Pavlova

4 egg whites; pinch salt; $\frac{2}{3}$ cup caster sugar; 1 tsp cornflour; $1\frac{1}{2}$ tsp vinegar; $\frac{1}{2}$ tsp vanilla essence; extra caster sugar; 300 ml (10 fl oz) cream; 1 punnet strawberries, hulled and sliced; pulp from 1–2 passionfruit; sifted icing sugar to dust.

Line a 26 x 30 cm (10 x 12 in) Swiss roll pan with baking paper. Beat egg whites with salt until stiff peaks form. Beat in $\frac{1}{2}$ cup of the sugar, 2 tbs at a time. Gently fold in remaining sugar, cornflour, vinegar and vanilla and spoon into prepared pan. Smooth over surface. Bake in a preheated moderate oven (180°C/350°F) for 12–15 minutes or until set on the top and springy to the touch. Turn out on to a clean tea-towel sprinkled generously with caster

sugar and leave 5 minutes on a wire rack to cool. Roll up gently from the short end, using the tea-towel to assist the rolling. Leave for 30 minutes or until cool.

Whip the cream to soft peaks, add half the sliced strawberries and fold through the cream. Unroll the pavlova, spread with the cream and scatter with the passionfruit and remaining strawberries. Roll up again using the tea-towel to assist and place seam side down on a serving plate. Refrigerate at least 30 minutes and dust with sifted icing sugar to serve. Serve cut into thick slices. Serves 8.

PAWPAW

Also known as papaya, this tropical fruit is found in many Pacific countries. When properly ripe, its skin and flesh should be a deep golden-yellow, one variety is pinkish-red.

The simplest way to enjoy pawpaw is to peel and halve it, remove the tiny black seeds and cut the flesh into cubes or wedges. Sprinkle with a little lemon juice, chill, and serve as a dessert or breakfast dish.

Pawpaw may be combined with other fruits in a fruit salad – it is particularly good with passionfruit. An attractive and refreshing combination is pawpaw with slices of kiwi fruit, mandarin segments and passionfruit pulp, lightly sweetened and sprinkled with Kirsch, and well chilled before serving.

The juice of pawpaw contains an enzyme, papain, which can be used to break down the fibres of meat and tenderise it. **See recipes.**

Pawpaw Sorbet

Pawpaw sorbet makes an excellent dessert after curries or highly spiced foods.

1 ripe pawpaw, peeled, halved and seeded; 1–3 tbs lemon juice; 1 egg white; 2 tbs caster sugar.

Chop pawpaw flesh roughly and blend, a few pieces at a time, or push through a sieve, to make a thick, smooth purée. Combine with lemon juice to taste and pour into chilled ice cream tray. Freeze until just starting to set around edges. Whisk egg white until stiff and gradually beat in sugar. Turn pawpaw mixture into chilled bowl and beat until smooth. Fold in egg white. Return to ice cream tray, cover with foil and freeze until firm. Transfer to refrigerator 15–30 minutes before serving. Serves 6–8.

Pawpaw and Mango Whip

1 large ripe mango, peeled, seeded and chopped, or 1 x 425 g can mango slices, drained and chopped; 1 small ripe pawpaw, peeled, seeded and chopped; 2 tbs rum; 1 tbs lime or lemon juice; 2 tbs sugar; 1 cup cream, whipped.

Purée mango and pawpaw in a food processor or blender, or push through a nylon sieve. Transfer to a bowl and stir in rum, juice and sugar. Fold in cream. Cover and chill several hours. Spoon into a serving dish and serve with extra whipped cream and crisp biscuits. Serves 6.

PEACH

A delicious fruit, which may be white or yellow-fleshed, a slipstone (the fruit readily separates from the stone) or clingstone (as its name suggests, the fruit clings to the stone). Peaches are with us from early summer until autumn, and one of the great joys of these months, and very welcome if they are perfectly ripe and slightly chilled.

Like many other fruits, the peach is thought to have originated in China and to have been introduced to Europe by way of Persia. The best-known are probably Elberta and Hale, both of which produce large, yellow-fleshed slipstone peaches, ideal for eating fresh or for cooking.

Any surplus of peaches may be made into jam or frozen, but canning or home-bottling is the most popular way of preserving them for year-round enjoyment. Canned peaches may be halved or sliced, in heavy or light syrup or in a fruit nectar; they may be substituted for fresh cooked peaches in most recipes.

Peaches combine nicely with other summer fruits in fruit salad or compote. Sliced fresh peaches, covered with passionfruit pulp, make an elegantly simple and most delicious dessert. And in a different context, peaches highlight the flavour of meat and poultry; serve with grilled ham steaks and roast duck.

TO PEEL PEACHES: Pour boiling water over peaches, leave to stand 1–3 minutes. Skins will loosen and slip off easily. If peaches are really ripe, skin may be rubbed off without boiling water treatment.

Sprinkle peaches with lemon juice to prevent discoloration, if they are not to be cooked or eaten immediately.

■ **TO POACH PEACHES:** Peel peaches as above, halve or slice as desired. Prepare syrup, using ½ cup sugar per cup water. Add peaches to hot syrup, simmer very gently for 3–5 minutes, cool in syrup. If desired, remove peaches with slotted spoon, reduce syrup over high heat, pour over cooked peaches. Chill. **See recipes.**

Brandied Peaches

Brandied Peaches may be served as a dinner party dessert with whipped cream or as an accompaniment to roast duck or ham or grilled pork chops.

peaches, peeled, halved and stoned; sugar; brandy.

Prick peaches all over with fine, sharp needle. Prepare sugar syrup with equal quantities sugar and water, and simmer peaches for 5 minutes. Lift out carefully, pack into wide-mouthed jars and half fill with sugar syrup. Cool, then add brandy to cover peaches completely. Seal jars and store in a cool, dark place for 2–3 months before using.

Peaches in Wine

A striking dessert that is very simple to prepare.

1 ripe peach per person, peeled, stoned and sliced; caster sugar if desired; dry red or white or sweet white dessert wine.

Place peach slices in long-stemmed wine glasses. Sprinkle with a little sugar, then fill glasses with wine. Chill 1 hour. Serve with thin, crisp sweet biscuits.

Peaches Aflame

An impressive dinner party dessert.

6 peaches, peeled, halved, stoned and poached, or 1 large can peach halves; ½ tsp arrowroot; ¼ cup brandy; ½ cup toasted, slivered almonds; ice cream to serve.

Pour ½ cup peach syrup (from poaching or can) into top of chafing dish or pan and bring to the boil. Blend arrowroot with a little cold water, stir into syrup and stir until slightly thickened. Add peaches and baste with syrup until heated through. Warm brandy, ignite and pour over peaches. Top with almonds and serve with ice cream. Serves 6.

Spiced Peaches

Grilled peach halves, flavoured with sugar and spice that go well with ham or tongue.

4 large peaches, peeled, halved and stoned; 3 tbs brown sugar; 16 whole cloves; sprinkling cinnamon and nutmeg; 45 g (1½ oz) butter.

Arrange peaches in a heatproof dish. Sprinkle with brown sugar, stud each peach half with 2 cloves and sprinkle with cinnamon and nutmeg. Dot with butter. Grill under a preheated grill about 5 minutes. Serve with hot ham or tongue. Serves 8.

PEANUT

Also known as the groundnut, because, although the flowers of this vine-like plant are borne above ground, the nuts are really edible seeds in pods which form and grow underground.

Peanuts are highly nutritious, being rich in fat and protein, which is why peanut butter is often recommended for children. Peanut oil is a light, almost tasteless oil which can be used for salads or for cooking, and especially for deep-frying.

In cooking the peanut may be used raw, still in its reddish skin, or roasted. Some recipes might call for roasted salted peanuts, which is the usual way peanuts are enjoyed as a snack. Sugar and caramel-coated peanuts are also available commercially.

Peanuts are particularly important in the cooking of many Asian countries. In almost any city from Bangkok to

Singapore, you will find satays – five or six small cubes of meat on bamboo skewers, grilled quickly over a tiny heap of hot coals and served with a spicy-hot peanut sauce. Cans or bottles of ready-made satay sauce may be found in most Asian food shops, but it is easy to make, starting with either fresh roasted peanuts or Peanut Butter. **See recipes.**

Chocolate Peanut Biscuits

125 g (4 oz) butter; 3/4 cup firmly packed brown sugar; 1 egg; 1 tbs cocoa powder; 1 1/2 cups self-raising flour; 250 g (8 oz) raw peanuts.

Cream butter with brown sugar, add egg and beat well. Sift cocoa with flour, stir in, then add peanuts. Drop teaspoons of mixture on to greased baking trays and bake in a preheated moderate oven (180°C/350°F) for 15 minutes. Makes about 30.

Peanut Crispies

2 egg whites; pinch salt; 3/4 cup sugar; 30 g (1 oz) butter, melted; 1/2 tsp vanilla; 4 cups cornflakes; 3/4 cup desiccated coconut; 3/4 cup chopped raw peanuts.

Beat egg whites with salt until stiff. Gradually beat in sugar, then add remaining ingredients and fold in gently but thoroughly. Drop small teaspoons of mixture into patty cases and bake in a preheated moderately hot oven (190°C/375°F) for 20–30 minutes. Makes about 48.

Gado Gado (*Indonesian Vegetable Salad with Peanut Sauce*)

1/2 small cabbage, shredded; 1 small cucumber, finely sliced; 1 cup beans, parboiled; 2 carrots, cut into thin strips; 1 cup green bean sprouts.

PEANUT SAUCE: 1 cup raw peanuts; 1/2 cup oil; 1 large onion, sliced; 2 cloves garlic, crushed; 1 tsp chilli powder; 1/2 tsp shrimp paste or shrimp sauce; 2 cups Coconut Milk (page 91) or water; 1/2 tsp brown sugar; 1/2 tsp grated lemon rind; 1 tbs vinegar; salt.

Arrange vegetables on salad platter.

PEANUT SAUCE: Fry peanuts for 5 minutes in dry pan. Cool. Remove skins, then grind peanuts to a paste. Heat oil in pan and stir-fry onion and garlic with chilli powder and shrimp paste or sauce. Add ground peanuts and coconut milk or water and bring to the boil, stirring constantly. Add remaining ingredients and simmer gently until sauce thickens. Serve at room temperature. Dilute with hot water if too thick. Pour sauce over vegetables or serve separately. Serves 6.
NOTE: Shrimp paste or shrimp sauce can be purchased at Chinese grocery stores.

Beef Satay

1 tbs finely chopped garlic; 2 chillies, finely chopped; 1 tbs finely chopped onion; 1/2 cup Coconut Milk (page 91); 1 tbs ground coriander; 1 tbs soy sauce; salt and freshly ground black pepper; 1 kg (2 lb) sirloin or rump steak, cubed.

PEANUT SAUCE: 3/4 cup peanut oil; 2 tbs dried onion flakes; 1 dried chilli; 1 tbs lemon juice; 1 tbs soy sauce; 375 g (12 oz) crunchy peanut butter; 1 tbs sugar; 1/2–3/4 cup Coconut Milk (page 91) or water.

Combine all ingredients except steak. Add steak to this marinade and leave 1 hour.
PEANUT SAUCE: Heat oil in wok or deep frying pan. Put onion flakes in a small metal strainer and lower into hot oil. Fry until golden, being careful not to burn. Drain on crumpled paper towels. Fry chilli in oil until puffed and crisp. Remove and drain. Discard stalk and seeds and crumble or chop chilli. Set aside. Combine lemon juice, soy sauce, peanut butter, sugar and coconut milk or water in a saucepan and heat gently, stirring. Remove from heat. When cold, add fried onion and crumbled chilli. Mix thoroughly. Add more liquid if necessary to make a dipping sauce consistency. Thread meat on skewers and grill over hot coals or under a preheated grill, brushing occasionally with marinade when turning. Serve hot with sauce. Serves 6.
NOTE: Dried onion flakes are available from most Asian stores and Asian grocery sections of supermarkets.

PEANUT BUTTER

This nutritious paste of ground peanuts is a childhood favourite, and many a peanut-loving adult retains a fondness for it.

Spread on bread, toast or biscuits, peanut butter makes a good snack, and it combines with crisp bacon, celery, dates or raisins for wholesome sandwiches which carry well. Peanut butter cookies and cakes are other ways to enjoy its warm flavour. It is easy to make peanut butter at home in a blender or food processor. **See recipes.**

Peanut Butter

1 1/2–3 tbs peanut oil; 1 cup roasted peanuts; salt.

If using a blender, put 1 1/2 tbs oil into the container and, with motor running, add peanuts through hole in lid. Add more oil as necessary and, if nuts are not already salted, about 1/2 tsp salt. Process until you have consistency you want, from chunky to smooth. If using a processor, put peanuts into the container and process, switching on and off, until coarsely chopped. With motor running, add oil through feed tube until you obtain consistency you want. Salt to taste. Makes about 3/4 cup.

Peanut Butter Cookies

$^1/_2$ cup peanut butter; 125 g (4 oz) butter;
$^1/_2$ cup sugar; $^1/_2$ cup firmly packed brown sugar;
$^1/_2$ tsp vanilla; I egg; $1^1/_4$ cups flour; $^1/_2$ tsp baking
powder; $^3/_4$ tsp bicarbonate of soda; $^1/_4$ tsp salt.

Cream peanut butter, butter and sugars together,
then beat in vanilla and egg. Sift in flour, baking
powder, bicarbonate of soda and salt and mix to a
soft dough. Wrap in plastic wrap and chill for 30
minutes. Roll dough into walnut-sized balls and
place, well apart, on greased baking trays. Flatten,
crisscross fashion, with a fork dipped in flour. Bake
in a preheated moderately hot oven (190°C/375°F)
10–12 minutes until risen and golden-brown. Makes
about 35.

VARIATIONS

PEANUT BUTTER AND RAISIN COOKIES: Follow recipe
for Peanut Butter Cookies, stirring in $^1/_4$ cup chopped
raisins with the flour.

ORANGE PEANUT BUTTER COOKIES: Follow recipe for
Peanut Butter Cookies, substituting 1 tsp grated
orange rind for vanilla.

Peanut Butter Spice Cake

30 g (I oz) butter, softened; $^3/_4$ cup caster sugar;
5 tbs smooth peanut butter (at room temperature);
I large egg; $1^1/_3$ cups self-raising flour; pinch salt;
$^1/_2$ tsp each ground cinnamon, nutmeg and ginger;
$^1/_4$ tsp ground cloves; I cup buttermilk.

Cream butter with sugar until light and fluffy, then
beat in peanut butter. Add egg and mix well. Sift
together flour, salt and spices and fold alternately
into creamed mixture with buttermilk, beginning
and ending with flour. Turn batter into greased and
floured 20 cm (8 in) square cake tin and place in a
preheated moderate oven (180°C/350°F). Bake for 40
minutes or until a skewer inserted in centre comes
out clean. Let cake cool in tin on a wire rack for 10
minutes before turning it out to cool completely.
Serve plain, or ice with chocolate icing.

NOTE: If you have no buttermilk, use 1 cup ordinary
milk soured with 1 tbs lemon juice.

Peanut Butter Chews

$^1/_2$ cup crunchy peanut butter; 3 tbs honey;
I tsp vanilla; $^1/_2$ cup instant skim milk powder;
pinch salt; 3 tbs icing sugar, sifted;
$^1/_2$ cup finely chopped unsalted peanuts.

Mix all ingredients, except chopped peanuts,
kneading them together with your hands until well
blended. Roll mixture into 2.5 cm (1 in) balls and
coat them in peanuts. Store in refrigerator. Makes
about 20.

PEAR

The sweet, juicy pear is one of the most versatile of fruits.
It may be enjoyed as is or cooked, and it blends as well
with wines and liqueurs as it does with other fruits such
as raspberries and blackcurrants.

The first pears usually arrive on the market towards the
end of summer. A succession of varieties and controlled
atmosphere storage allows us to have fresh pears almost
all year. Canned pears can also substitute for fresh
poached pears in most recipes.

The main varieties of pear available are the Williams
(also known as Duchess, Bartlett, Bon Chrétien), the
Winter Cole, Beurré Bosc and the Packham. The
Williams is an early season variety, yellow tinged with
pale green, and is usually very juicy; it is delicious eaten
with Gorgonzola cheese, or freshly sliced and covered
with passionfruit pulp. The Winter Cole is a small pear,
rather round in shape and greenish, turning to russet; it
is characteristically pale yellow when ripe. The Beurré
Bosc is elongated, with a russet skin changing to dark
cinnamon when mature; the flesh is white and juicy. The
Packham, similar in appearance to the Williams, is
greenish-yellow turning to light yellow when ripe, its
flesh being white and juicy when ripe. The Packham is
good for poaching or in a tart.

In France, an *eau de vie* (fruit alcohol) is made from
pears; a judicious dose may be added to a simple pear
dessert for variety.

■ **TO POACH PEARS:** Choose pears which are still
under-ripe, but not too hard. Peel gently with vegetable
peeler, rub with lemon juice to prevent browning. Halve
lengthways, remove cores with a melon baller or
small knife.

Poach in syrup of 1 part sugar to 2 parts water until just
tender. A piece of vanilla bean may be added to syrup.
Remove fruit with slotted spoon and reduce syrup, then
pour over fruit.

Poached pears may be served simply with cream
or custard, or with a blackcurrant or raspberry purée.
See recipes.

Pears in Red Wine

6 small pears; $^1/_2$ cup sugar;
$^1/_2$ cup red wine; $^1/_2$ cup water;
strip lemon rind; I cinnamon stick.

Peel pears, leaving stalks. Dissolve sugar in wine and
water in a saucepan, then add lemon rind and cinnamon and bring to the boil. Boil 1 minute. Arrange
pears upright in ovenproof dish and pour syrup over.
Cover and cook in a preheated moderate oven
(180°C/350°F) until tender, about 1 hour. If pears are
very hard, they may take as long as 2 hours. Arrange
pears in serving dish and pour over wine syrup. Serve
cold, accompanied by whipped cream if desired.
Serves 6.

VARIATION

If pears are almost ripe, they may be cooked over low heat on top of stove in prepared wine syrup. Remove pears with a slotted spoon when tender, reduce syrup over high heat and pour over pears.

Pears with Sabayon Sauce

6 small pears; $^1/_2$ cup sugar; I cup water; I vanilla bean; 4 egg yolks; $^1/_2$ cup sweet white wine; $^1/_3$ cup caster sugar; I tbs Grand Marnier or Cointreau; I tbs flaked almonds, lightly toasted.

Peel pears, leaving stalks. Dissolve sugar in water in a saucepan, add vanilla bean and bring to boil. Boil 5 minutes. Poach pears gently in syrup until tender, then cool in syrup. Place egg yolks, wine, caster sugar and liqueur in top of double saucepan over simmering water. Beat vigorously with rotary beater until mixture becomes thick and creamy. Do not overcook, nor allow water to boil or mixture will curdle. Drain pears, place in serving dish or dishes, coat with sauce and sprinkle with almonds. Serves 6.

VARIATIONS

PEARS WITH RUM SABAYON SAUCE: Poach pears as above and cool. Make sauce using 4 tbs poaching syrup and 2 tbs white rum in place of white wine. Sprinkle with blanched julienne (matchsticks) of orange and lemon rind instead of almonds.

POIRES BELLE HELENE: Peel pears, halve and remove cores. Poach as above and cool. Place in bowls, add a scoop of vanilla ice cream to each and pour hot Chocolate Sauce (see page 84) over.

Pears with Spinach

I bunch spinach; I large ripe pear, peeled and cored; salt and freshly ground black pepper; I tbs cream (optional).

Trim spinach leaves from stems and rinse well. Cook in a large pan, with no additional water, for about 5 minutes. Drain, and squeeze out excess water. Cook pear in water until very soft. Drain. Purée spinach and pear together in a blender. Season with salt and pepper and reheat gently. Blend in cream, if desired. Serves 4–6.

PEAS (GREEN)

Although fresh green peas may be found throughout most of the year, they are really at their best in spring. Freshly picked, while still young and small, they have a sweetness and delicacy which are perhaps best appreciated when the peas are served on their own, as a separate course, although spring peas also make a good accompaniment to spring lamb or veal. The very tiniest peas are what the French call *petis pois*.

Since about half the weight of the peas is in the pods, allow 1 kg (2 lb) fresh peas for 4 servings. Peas may be shelled in advance, but wrap them in a damp cloth or cover them with their pods so they do not lose their moisture. A few pea pods may be cooked with the peas for added flavour, and if they are young and fresh, pea pods can be made into a soup.

Generally, the younger and fresher the peas, the less cooking time they will need. Older peas are still tasty if cooked slowly with additional flavourings, such as ham or herbs. Frozen and canned peas may not equal fresh peas in flavour, but they make up for this in convenience. Their flavour can be improved by treating them in ways similar to those for fresh peas. **See recipes.**

Green Peas

I kg (2 lb) fresh peas, shelled; salt; I sprig fresh mint (optional); 30 g (I oz) butter.

Drop peas into enough boiling salted water to cover. Add mint and cook for 10–15 minutes until just tender. Drain, refresh under cold water, then return to pan with butter. Shake over low heat until hot and coated with butter. Serve immediately. Serves 4.

VARIATION

Chopped fresh mint or summer savory may be added to peas with butter. 125 g (4 oz) sliced sautéed mushrooms may be combined with peas just before serving.

Petits Pois à la Française
(Green Peas, French–Style)

I kg (2 lb) fresh peas, shelled; 6 lettuce leaves, or small lettuce heart, shredded; 12 spring onions, peeled; 60 g (2 oz) butter; 2 sprigs each fresh parsley and chervil; I tsp sugar; salt; 3 tbs water.

Place peas in a large saucepan with half lettuce, the onions, butter, herbs, sugar and salt. Cover with remaining lettuce and add water. Cover and cook over gentle heat for 15–20 minutes, shaking pan from time to time, until peas are tender. Remove herbs and adjust seasoning to taste before serving. Serves 4.

VARIATION

500 g (1 lb) frozen peas may be substituted for fresh peas.

Risi e Bisi *(Rice with Peas)*

In Italy, this dish is considered a soup but it is eaten with a fork. Serve it as a separate course, or as a lunch or supper dish.

30 g (I oz) butter; I tbs olive oil; I rasher lean bacon, rind removed and diced; 2 golden shallots, chopped; 5 cups chicken stock; $^3/_4$ cup Italian short-grain rice; $1^1/_2$ cups shelled fresh peas or frozen peas; salt; I tbs finely chopped parsley; grated Parmesan cheese to serve.

Heat butter and oil in a large saucepan and cook bacon and shallots about 5 minutes. Add stock and rice, bring to the boil and stir well. If using fresh peas, add with rice; add frozen peas after about 15 minutes. Cook over low heat for 20–50 minutes or until rice is moist and tender. Season with salt, and sprinkle with parsley. Serve with Parmesan offered separately. Serves 4–6.

Pea Purée

1¹/₂ cups shelled fresh peas; pinch sugar;
30 g (1 oz) butter; ¹/₄ cup cream;
salt and freshly ground black pepper.

Cook peas in boiling salted water for 15 minutes or until very tender. Drain, then rub through sieve or purée in a blender. Return to saucepan, add sugar and butter and stir until butter is incorporated into purée. Stir in cream, and season with salt and pepper. Serves 4.

VARIATION
Substitute frozen peas for fresh. Cook as for fresh peas but reduce cooking time.

Green Pea Soup

30 g (1 oz) butter; 1 spring onion, finely chopped;
1 slice cooked ham, cut into fine strips;
1 cup shelled fresh peas; pinch sugar;
3¹/₂ cups chicken or veal stock; 1 sprig fresh mint;
salt and freshly ground black pepper;
¹/₄ cup cream.

Melt butter in a saucepan and cook spring onion until soft. Add ham and peas and toss in butter. Add sugar, stock and mint and season with salt and pepper. Simmer until peas are very soft. Remove mint. Rub through a sieve or purée in a blender. Add cream, adjust seasoning and reheat gently. Serves 4.

PECAN

An American nut of the hickory family, rather like a walnut in flavour and appearance; indeed, in many recipes walnuts and pecans are interchangeable.

The name comes from the Indian word for these nuts, which were quickly adopted by the new settlers in North America. Of all the pecan dishes, perhaps the best known is Pecan Pie. **See recipes.**

Pecan Sandwich Spread

¹/₂ cup finely chopped pecans; ¹/₄ cup finely chopped celery; ¹/₄ cup chopped stuffed olives;
1¹/₂ tbs Mayonnaise (page 256).

Combine all ingredients. Spread on lightly buttered wholemeal or white bread. Makes about 1 cup, or sufficient for 4 sandwiches.

Southern Pecan Pie

1 cup sugar; ¹/₄ cup golden syrup; ¹/₄ cup water;
¹/₄ cup melted butter; 3 eggs, well beaten;
1 cup pecan halves; 1 x 23 cm (9 in) unbaked Rich Shortcrust Pastry Shell (page 342).

Mix together sugar, golden syrup, water and melted butter. Add eggs and pecans and stir well. Pour into pastry shell. Bake in a preheated hot oven (200°C/400°F) for 10 minutes, then reduce heat to moderate (180°C/350°F) and continue baking for about 30 minutes. Serve warm or cold. Serves 8.

Pecan Balls

125 g (4 oz) butter, softened; 2 tbs sugar;
1 tsp vanilla; 1 cup ground or finely chopped pecans;
1 cup flour, sifted; ¹/₂ cup icing sugar.

Cream butter with sugar until fluffy. Mix in vanilla and pecans. Add flour in 2 parts, stirring after each addition until thoroughly blended. Roll into small balls, and place about 5 cm (2 in) apart on ungreased baking trays. Bake in a preheated moderate oven (180°C/350°F) for 12–15 minutes or until pale brown. Sift icing sugar on to a flat plate. Roll biscuits in icing sugar as soon as removed from oven. Cool on wire racks. Makes about 20.

Butter Pecan Ice Cream

A toasted-pecan flavoured ice cream.

¹/₂ cup chopped pecans; 60 g (2oz) butter;
1¹/₂ tbs cornflour; ¹/₂ cup sugar; 2 tbs brown sugar;
1 cup milk; 1 tsp vanilla; 1 cup cream.

Toss pecans with butter in a frying pan over gentle heat until lightly toasted. Cool. Mix cornflour and sugars. Blend in milk. Pour into saucepan and cook until thick, stirring constantly. Remove from heat and stir in vanilla. Chill. Whip cream until stiff. Fold in chilled mixture and pecans. Pour into ice cream tray and freeze. Serves 4–6.

PECHE MELBA (PEACH MELBA)

This famous dessert was created by one of the world's greatest chefs, Auguste Escoffier, to honour Dame Nellie Melba, after he had heard her sing in 'Lohengrin'. Melba's performance inspired a dessert of peaches on vanilla ice cream, served between the wings of an ice-carved swan and covered with spun sugar. Later the dish was given its distinctive flavour by dispensing with the swan and spun sugar and covering the peaches and ice cream with fresh raspberry purée. The purée became know as 'Sauce Melba'.

Today, Pêche Melba is served in great restaurants all over the world, and remains as distinctive a dish as it was in Dame Melba's time.

p

Pêche Melba

$^1/_2$ cup sugar; 2 cups water; 1 vanilla bean;
4 fresh peaches, peeled; 500 g (1lb) fresh or frozen
raspberries; $^1/_2$ cup icing sugar, sifted;
2 cups French Vanilla Ice Cream (page 202).

Place sugar, water and vanilla bean in a saucepan over medium heat. Stir until sugar dissolves, then bring to the boil and simmer 5 minutes. Place peaches in syrup, cover and poach gently 5–10 minutes or until just tender. Remove from syrup, drain and chill, covered. Rub raspberries through a nylon sieve or purée in a food processor or blender. Gradually add icing sugar until sauce thickens. Pile ice cream in a glass dish, cover top with peaches, whole or halved according to size, and spoon raspberry sauce over peaches. Serves 4.

PEPPER

The world's most important spice, grown in tropical counties such as Indonesia and India. Highly aromatic and with a pungent biting flavour, pepper is used to season all types of savoury dishes based on meat, poultry, game, fish, eggs, cheese and vegetables. It can even enter into sweet recipes, as a spice rather than as a seasoning, for example in the German biscuits, *Pfeffernüsse*.

The most commonly available types of pepper are black or white, both of which may be found as peppercorns (whole dried berries) or as ground pepper. Like most spices, the flavour deteriorates after grinding, and pepper is best if freshly ground. Ideally, there should always be two pepper grinders, one for black pepper and one for white; ground white pepper should be used in pale-coloured dishes and sauces, where specks of black would spoil appearance.

Black peppercorns are the dried berries of the pepper vine (*Piper nigrum*), picked while still green and not completely ripe; on drying, they become dark brown or black. They are more aromatic than white peppercorns.
White peppercorns are fully ripe berries, from which the outer hull is removed before drying. They are hotter than black peppercorns.
Green peppercorns are the berries picked while still green, then preserved in brine. They are usually available in small cans or jars, and are soft enough to be ground or mashed to a paste. Their flavour is much milder than black or white peppercorns. Green peppercorns are often used with duck, and in pâtés or as an alternative to black peppercorns in Pepper Steak (see below).
Pink or red peppercorns come from an entirely different plant, a tree native to South America and sometimes referred to as Brazilian pepper tree. Recent research has shown that many people have allergic reactions to pink peppercorns, so their use should be approached with caution. See recipes.

Curried Chicken with Green Peppercorns

$^1/_4$ cup vegetable oil; 4 onions finely chopped;
1 tbs green peppercorns, drained and crushed;
1 slice fresh ginger, finely chopped;
$^1/_2$ tsp each turmeric and ground mace;
$^1/_4$ tsp each ground cloves, coriander and
cinnamon; 10 small chicken thighs, cut in half;
2 tsp cornflour; 2 cups chicken stock;
2 apples, peeled, cored and cut in 1 cm ($^1/_2$ in)
cubes; 2 tbs toasted desiccated coconut to garnish.

Heat oil in a large frying pan and cook onions until softened. Add green peppercorns and cook for 1 minute, then add ginger and spices and combine. Add chicken and brown on all sides. Blend cornflour with a little chicken stock, then combine with remaining stock. Add to frying pan and cook, stirring, until thickened. Reduce and simmer for 5 minutes. Add apples and continue to simmer for 10 minutes more or until chicken is tender. Garnish with toasted coconut and serve with fluffy boiled rice. Serves 6–8.

Veal and Pepper Loaf

1–2 tbs black peppercorns; 2 slices white bread, torn
into pieces; 2 cups parsley, stems removed;
3 sticks celery, chopped; $^1/_2$ cup water;
1 kg (2 lb) minced veal; 1 egg, lightly beaten;
1 tsp salt; 6–8 rashers bacon, rind removed.

Crush peppercorns in a mortar with a pestle or in a bowl with end of a rolling pin. Blend bread in a blender or food processor to make fine crumbs. Place parsley, celery and water in the container of the food processor or blender and blend until ingredients are chopped but not mushy. Place meat in a mixing bowl and add peppercorns, parsley mixture, egg, breadcrumbs and salt. Mix well with the fingers. Line a 6-cup loaf tin with bacon rashers, leaving ends hanging over edge of tin. Pack meat mixture into tin and fold overhanging bacon over meat. Cover with a lid or foil and bake in a preheated moderately slow oven (160°C/325°F) 2 hours. Remove from oven, place a weight on top, and allow to cool, then chill. Serves 6–8.

PEPPER STEAK (STEAK AU POIVRE)

There are many versions of steak au poivre. Here are two, one with crushed black peppercorns, the other with green peppercorns and a cream sauce.

Pepper Steak

4 pieces rump or fillet steak;
1¹/2 tbs coarsely cracked black peppercorns;
olive oil; 1 tbs butter; salt;
dash Worcestershire sauce; lemon juice;
2 tbs brandy; chopped fresh parsley and chives.

Trim steaks of excess fat and any gristle. Press pepper into both sides of steaks and leave 30 minutes. Cook in a little oil in heavy frying pan until done to your taste. Dot with butter, and season with salt, Worcestershire sauce and lemon juice. Warm brandy, ignite and pour over meat. Sprinkle with herbs and serve immediately, coating steaks with the sauce. Serves 4.

NOTE: Use a mortar and pestle to crack peppercorns or crack with mallet between 2 sheets of plastic.

VARIATION

Prepare pepper steaks as above. After flaming the steaks with brandy, add ½ cup cream, blending in well with the back of a spoon. Substitute 2 tsp green peppercorns for herbs.

PEPPER (SWEET)

Sweet peppers (also called capsicums) are members of the same large Capsicum family as the hot chilli pepper. Their flesh has a sweet, vigorous flavour, which enlivens salads and many cooked dishes, and their square-ish hollow shape (the name 'capsicum' means box) makes them perfect for stuffing.

Peppers come in a mosaic of colours – brilliant red, yellow or green. Red peppers are fully ripe ones, and are much sweeter and milder than the unripe green ones; they are also twice as rich in vitamin C. When the lovely elongated yellow and orange ones appear on the market, make use of them for their season is all too short.

When buying peppers, avoid any that are wrinkled or have soft spots. They should be smooth, firm and gleaming. Store in the refrigerator crisper and use them within a week or so of purchase.

■ **BASIC PREPARATION:** The fleshy inner ribs or core and the seeds are discarded before using. Cut the pepper in half lengthways, or cut a lid from the top if you want to keep it whole, and pull out ribs or core and seeds with your fingers. Cut away the stem (unless you are retaining it for its decorative effect in a whole or halved stuffed pepper). Wash under cold running water.

TO SKIN PEPPERS: It is very often worth skinning peppers. It makes their flavour more delicate and changes their texture from crisp to richly soft. Spear whole pepper on a long-handled fork and turn it over a gas flame, or put it close to a very hot grill, turning until skin is charred all over. Put pepper into a paper bag for 10 minutes to steam, then rub skin off under cold water. Red or yellow peppers are easier to skin than green ones.

TO BLANCH PEPPERS: Some recipes suggest blanching peppers before stuffing, again to give more delicate flavour. After removing ribs or core and seeds, drop pepper into boiling water for a minute or two, pushing pepper down well under the water. Remove and refresh under cold running water. Drain well and proceed with recipe.

WAYS TO USE PEPPERS

- A simple way to cook peppers is to cut them into strips, discarding ribs or core and seeds, and fry in a little oil, perhaps flavoured with garlic. Season with salt and pepper and serve with grills or roasted meat.
- Halved and drizzled with oil, peppers may be grilled with meat.
- Sliced into rings, cut into strips or diced they are used raw in many salads. Use in stews, soups or casseroles.
- Strips or raw pepper may be part of a dish of Crudités (see *Crudités*) to use with a dipping sauce. **See recipes.**

Chilled Pepper Salad

Arrange this salad in a shallow dish and serve well chilled.

4 large ripe tomatoes, peeled and thickly sliced;
4 peppers (any colour), skinned, cored, seeded and cut into strips; 1 x 50 g can flat anchovy fillets;
¹/2 cup Vinaigrette Dressing (page 442);
freshly ground black pepper; 6–8 black olives, halved and stoned; 3 hard-boiled eggs, quartered;
chopped parsley or fine strips fresh basil to garnish.

Arrange tomato slices in a shallow dish. Place peppers on top of tomatoes. Drain anchovies; mix their oil with vinaigrette and drizzle this mixture over salad. Season with black pepper. Slit anchovy fillets in half lengthways and arrange lattice-fashion on salad. Put an olive half into each square. Chill well. At serving time, arrange eggs round edge and scatter salad with parsley or basil. Serves 6.

Fettucine and Pepper Salad

250 g (8 oz) fettucine (flat noodles); 2 red or green peppers, skinned, cored, seeded and cut into strips;
125 g (4 oz) Gruyère cheese, diced; 6–8 black olives;
¹/4 cup Mustard Vinaigrette Dressing (page 442);
salt and freshly ground black pepper.

Cook fettucine and drain. Mix peppers, cheese and olives in a salad bowl. Mix fettucine with vinaigrette, add to other ingredients and toss lightly. Season and chill 1 hour before serving. Serves 4.

Beef and Peppers in Black Bean Sauce

Hoisin sauce and black beans are available at Asian food stores.

**500 g (1 lb) lean fillet or rump steak;
1 tbs soy sauce; 1 tbs hoisin sauce (optional);
1 tbs tomato paste; 1¹/₂ tbs cornflour;
5 tbs vegetable oil; 1¹/₄ tsp sugar; 2 tbs Chinese salted
black beans; 1 medium red pepper, cored
and seeded; 1 medium green pepper, cored
and seeded; 1 tsp grated fresh ginger;
3 tbs dry sherry.**

Slice beef thinly across the grain and cut into finger-length strips. Mix soy sauce, hoisin sauce, tomato paste, cornflour, 1 tbs oil and sugar. Add beef, turn to coat the strips all over, and leave 15 minutes. Meantime, soak beans in cold water for 15 minutes. Cut peppers into 4 cm (1¹/₂ in) squares. Heat remaining oil in a frying pan or wok over high heat. When it begins to give off a haze, add ginger and drained black beans and stir-fry 30 seconds. Add beef and stir-fry 2 minutes. Add peppers, sprinkle with sherry and stir-fry 1 minute more. Serve at once. Serves 4–6.

Peppers, Onions and Corn

An excellent vegetable mixture to serve with grills, sausages, sautéed liver or bacon.

**90 g (3 oz) butter; 3 medium onions, thickly sliced;
2 red or green peppers, cored, seeded and cut into
strips; 1 cup cooked fresh, or drained canned,
corn kernels; salt and freshly ground black pepper.**

Heat butter and cook onions gently until soft. Add peppers to pan and cook, stirring, on medium heat for 5 minutes. Stir in corn, heat through and season with salt and pepper. Serves 4–6.

Stewed Peppers (Papriche Stufate)

One of the many Italian dishes starring peppers. Serve hot with grilled chops or sausages, or at room temperature as part of an antipasto tray.

**¹/₂ cup olive oil; 1 clove garlic, flattened with a heavy
knife; 6 green or yellow peppers, cored, seeded and
cut into strips; 4 large, ripe tomatoes, peeled and
chopped; salt and freshly ground black pepper;
2 tbs finely chopped parsley to garnish.**

Heat oil in a frying pan and fry garlic gently until golden-brown, then discard garlic. Add pepper strips and cook gently 5 minutes. Cover with tomatoes and season with salt and pepper. Continue cooking until tomatoes are reduced to a thick sauce. Serve hot or cold, garnished with parsley. Serves 4.

Peppers with Bacon

A savoury dish which needs no other accompaniment than crusty bread.

**2 tbs olive oil; 250 g (8 oz) lean rashers bacon,
rind removed and cut into 4 cm (1¹/₂ in) pieces;
1 onion, finely sliced, 2 tbs water; 4 large, ripe
tomatoes, peeled, seeded and chopped;
4 green or yellow peppers, skinned, cored,
seeded and cut into strips; salt and freshly
ground black pepper.**

Heat oil in a frying pan over low heat and fry bacon gently until lightly browned. Add onion and water and cook until water evaporates and onion is soft and golden. Add tomatoes and cook over medium heat until soft. Add peppers, salt and pepper and cook until peppers are soft. Serve very hot. Serves 4.

Peppers Stuffed with Pipérade

A marvellous cold dish, filled with a delicious scrambled egg mixture. Serve it for lunch, or as a light supper dish.

**2 red peppers, halved, cored and seeded;
3 tbs olive oil; 125 g (4 oz) cooked ham or bacon,
chopped; 1 large onion, chopped;
¹/₂ cup chopped green pepper; 1 tomato, peeled,
seeded and chopped; salt and freshly ground black
pepper; ¹/₂ cup fresh breadcrumbs;
¹/₄ cup cream; 3 eggs, beaten; chopped parsley.**

Blanch red peppers for a few minutes in boiling water, then drain and cool. Heat 1 tbs oil in a heavy frying pan and lightly brown ham or bacon. Add onion and sauté until soft, adding chopped green pepper halfway through cooking. Stir in tomato and season with salt and pepper. Cover and cook over a low heat for 5 minutes. Allow to cool. Soak breadcrumbs in cream in a small bowl. Add eggs. Heat remaining oil in a heavy frying pan, add egg mixture and scramble until soft and creamy. Put eggs into a dish and cool. Fold together tomato mixture and scrambled egg and spoon carefully into prepared red pepper shells. Sprinkle tops liberally with chopped parsley before serving. Serves 4.

Stuffed Peppers

**4 large red or green peppers;
1¹/₂ cups Fresh Tomato Sauce (page 339).**

**STUFFING: 45 g (1¹/₂ oz) butter; 1 onion, finely
chopped; ¹/₂ cup short-grain rice;
60 g (2 oz) mushrooms, chopped;
1¹/₂ cups chicken stock; 125 g (4 oz) cooked ham,
veal or chicken, finely chopped;
salt and freshly ground black pepper.**

Cut tops off peppers and scoop out seeds. Blanch in boiling water for 2–3 minutes, see page 354. Pat dry with paper towels and set aside.

STUFFING: Melt 30 g (1 oz) of the butter in a saucepan and fry onion until softened. Add rice, stir over medium heat for 1–2 minutes, then add mushrooms. Pour stock over, bring to the boil, cover and simmer for 20 minutes or until rice is tender and stock absorbed. Stir in remaining butter and cooked ham, veal or chicken and season with salt and pepper. Put stuffing into peppers and pack them closely together in an oven-proof casserole. Heat tomato sauce and pour over and around peppers. Cover dish with greased foil and cook in a preheated moderate oven (180°C/350°F) for 25–30 minutes or until peppers are tender. Serves 4.

Tomato and Pepper Salad

2 green peppers, cored, seeded and cut into strips;
4 firm tomatoes, sliced; ¹/₂ Spanish onion
and 6 shallots, finely chopped;
1 bunch fresh coriander or flat-leaved Italian
parsley; salt and freshly ground black pepper;
4 tbs olive oil; 1–2 tbs wine vinegar.

Put peppers in a serving bowl with tomatoes, onion and coriander or parsley. Season with salt and pepper, pour on oil and vinegar and toss well. Increase amount of oil and vinegar if you wish. Serve as first course with bread (Lebanese pita or crusty French) to mop up the juices. Serves 4.

Stuffed Peppers, Piedmont–Style

3 cloves garlic, chopped; 2 large tomatoes, peeled,
seeded and diced; 1 cup fresh breadcrumbs;
3 green or red peppers, skinned , cored, seeded and
quartered lengthways; 12 anchovy fillets;
30 g (1 oz) butter; ¹/₄ cup olive oil;
salt and freshly ground black pepper.

Combine garlic, tomatoes and breadcrumbs and divide among the 12 pepper boat shapes. Place an anchovy fillet on top of each, then a small piece of butter. Put in a greased baking dish. Drizzle oil over and sprinkle with salt and pepper. Bake in a preheated moderate oven (180°C/350°F) for 15–20 minutes; the peppers should not become too soft. Serve cold. Serves 4–6 as part of an antipasto tray and serves as a lunch dish.

Peperonata
(Peppers with Tomatoes and Onions)

This dish may be served cold as antipasto or hot as an accompaniment to roast or grilled chicken, lamb or pork.

4 tbs olive oil; 3–4 medium onions, chopped;
2 cloves garlic, sliced; 2 bay leaves; 6 large peppers
(any colour or mixed), cored, seeded and cut into
thick strips; 500 g (1 lb) tomatoes, peeled and
quartered; salt and freshly ground black pepper.

Heat oil in a frying pan and fry onions, garlic and bay leaves for about 5 minutes, stirring occasionally. Stir in peppers, cover pan and cook gently for about 10 minutes. Add tomatoes, salt and pepper and cook, uncovered and stirring frequently, until most of the liquid has evaporated and mixture is fairly thick, This may take about 30 minutes. Remove bay leaves, season again if necessary and serve cold or hot. Serves 4–6.

Tabouleh–Stuffed Peppers

1 cup burghul (cracked wheat); 8 small green
peppers; ²/₃ cup olive oil; ¹/₂ cup lemon juice;
¹/₄ cup chopped fresh mint; ¹/₄ cup chopped
parsley; 2 tsp salt; freshly ground black pepper;
2 cups alfalfa sprouts; 1 cup peeled, seeded and
chopped cucumber; 2 tomatoes, chopped;
¹/₂ cup chopped shallots.

Soak burghul in water overnight in a glass or ceramic bowl. Drain and squeeze out as much water as possible, then spread out on a tea-towel to dry. Cook peppers in boiling salted water for 5 minutes. Drain and refresh under cold running water. Cut off tops, discard seeds and ribs and let peppers drain. Combine oil, lemon juice, herbs, salt and pepper in a large bowl. Add burghul, then rest of ingredients. Divide mixture among the peppers, mounding it high, and arrange peppers on a serving dish. Serves 8.

PEPPERMINT

One of the many varieties of mint, and one of the most useful herbs in industry. Its leaves yield, on distillation, peppermint oil, which flavours confectionery, ice cream, toothpaste, chewing gum, perfumes, liqueurs and pharmaceutical preparations. Peppermint oil and peppermint tea have traditionally been used in medicine for the relief of cramps, headaches, indigestion and the common cold, among other ailments.

Chocolate and peppermint seem to have a particular affinity – peppermint-flavoured chocolate, or chocolate with a peppermint cream filling, is a delicious accompaniment to after-dinner coffee.

Small bottles of peppermint essence are available for flavouring cakes, biscuits and confectionery. See recipes.

Peppermint Sticks

125 g (4 oz) butter, melted; ¹/₂ cup sugar;
1 cup desiccated coconut; 1 cup flour, sifted;
1 tbs cocoa powder; ¹/₂ tsp peppermint essence;
1 tsp baking powder; 1 cup cornflakes,
lightly crushed.

PEPPERMINT BUTTER ICING: 90 g (3oz) butter;
²/₃ cup icing sugar, sifted; peppermint essence.

DECORATION: 30 g (1 oz) dark chocolate, melted with 15 g (½ oz) butter.

Cream butter with sugar, then beat in coconut, flour, cocoa powder, peppermint essence and baking powder. Mix well. Stir in cornflakes. Press into a 30 x 25 cm (12 x 10 in) Swiss roll tin; mixture should be nearly 1 cm (½ in) thick. Bake in a preheated moderate oven (180°C/350°F) for about 20 minutes. Cool. **PEPPERMINT BUTTER ICING**: Cream butter until light, then gradually beat in icing sugar. Flavour to taste with peppermint essence. When cake is cold spread roughly with icing and drizzle over melted chocolate mixture. Cut into fingers to serve. Makes 50 6 x 2.5 cm (2½ x 1 in) biscuits.

Double Delight Cake

CHOCOLATE FROSTING: 185 g (6 oz) cream cheese; 125 g (4 oz) butter; ½ tsp vanilla; ½ tsp peppermint essence; 6 cups icing sugar, sifted; ¼ cup hot water; 125 g (4 oz) dark cooking chocolate, melted.

CAKE: 60 g (2 oz) butter; 3 eggs; 2¼ cups flour; 1½ tsp bicarbonate of soda; 1 tsp salt; ¾ cup milk.

CHOCOLATE FROSTING: Beat together cheese, butter and essences, blending well. Beat in half icing sugar, then add remaining icing sugar alternately with hot water. Blend in melted chocolate and mix until smooth.
CAKE: Blend butter with 2 cups of the chocolate frosting. Add eggs, one at a time, and beat for 1 minute. Sift flour, soda and salt, and stir into creamed mixture alternately with milk, beginning and ending with dry ingredients. Spoon into 2 greased and lightly floured 20 cm (8 in) round sandwich tins. Bake in a preheated moderate oven (180°C/350°F) for 30–40 minutes. Cool on wire rack. Sandwich cake together with a little of the remaining frosting or jam. Decorate cake by spreading rest of frosting over top and side.

PERSIMMON

This fruit is a rare treat, because when properly ripe, it is very fragile and soft and needs delicate handling. A ripe persimmon is not unlike a tomato, slightly more orange than red, and almost translucent. The season for persimmons is late autumn to early winter.

Another variety of persimmon, called Sharon Fruit, and grown in Israel, is sometimes available. This has an edible skin, no pips and a very sweet flesh; it can be eaten while still firm unlike the ordinary persimmon, which tastes very astringent if not fully ripe and soft.

The persimmon tree is of Japanese origin where it is called *kaki*, but it has been cultivated in Mediterranean areas for many centuries. The fruit is most often eaten raw but may be stewed or made into jam.

TO EAT PERSIMMONS: With a small sharp knife, cut around the centre stalk of the persimmon and remove. Scoop out flesh with a small teaspoon. The jelly-like flesh around the seeds is also edible, but the seeds are not.

PESTO

See *Pasta Sauces.*

PESTO ALLA GENOVESE (BASIL, CHEESE AND PINE NUT SAUCE)

This pungent sauce, with its main ingredient basil, is used to flavour pasta dishes by tossing the hot pasta with pesto to taste and enough butter to coat the strands. A little of the sauce is excellent, too, in soups, as well as spooned over poached fish or boiled or baked potatoes. It can be stored, covered with a layer of oil, in a jar in the refrigerator where it will keep for months. For recipe, see *Pasta Sauces.*

PETITS FOURS

The French name 'Petits fours' is used to describe a variety of small cakes and biscuits often highly decorated, which are served after dessert and with coffee. They must be very small and elegant, just the size of one mouthful.

The term, which translates as 'little oven', is thought to have originated because these cakes were baked in a slower oven than big cakes. Such a difference is no longer relevant; the essential for Petits fours is that they be very small and very attractive.

Petits fours may simply be small-scale versions of the standard range of pâtisserie, such as tiny cream puffs or éclairs, or miniscule fruit tarts. Or they may be based on Almond Paste (see page 3), or on the Genoise Cake (see page 176) cut into attractive shapes, iced and decorated. For serving, tiny paper patty cases are available.

PHEASANT

One of the most popular of game birds, often raised commercially these days. It is a smallish, white-fleshed bird; its flavour can be rather delicate and not very 'gamey', especially if the bird did not grow up in the wild and fatten among grape vines.

An average pheasant weights about 1 kg (2 lb) and will serve 3–4 persons. For ease of carving, and especially if the bird is stuffed, it is often semi-boned – that is, the drumsticks and wings are left intact, but the thigh bones and main carcase bones are removed. Start from the middle of the back and gradually separate flesh from bone around to breast. **See recipes.**

Roast Stuffed Pheasant

1 x 1 kg (2 lb) pheasant; salt and freshly ground black pepper; 4 chicken livers; 60 g (2 oz) butter, 1/2 cup cooked rice; 1 tbs juniper berries; 1 tbs slivered almonds; 2 tbs strong pheasant or chicken stock; 1 small onion, finely chopped and softened in butter; port or Madeira.

Season pheasant lightly with salt and pepper. Lightly sauté chicken livers in half of the butter. Chop roughly, then mix with rice, juniper berries, almonds, stock and onion. Season with salt and pepper. Spoon stuffing into bird and truss. Rub remaining butter over pheasant and place, breast down, in roasting tin. Pour a little port or Madeira into the tin. Roast in a preheated hot oven (200°C/400°F), basting bird occasionally with pan juices. After 45 minutes, test with skewer through thigh; pheasant is cooked when juices that run out are still faintly pink. If necessary, leave in turned-off oven for 5–10 minutes longer. Serve with Cumberland Sauce (see pages 106–7), if desired; alternatively, make sauce with pan juices and pheasant stock. Serves 3–4.

Roast Pheasant

1 x 1 kg (2 lb) pheasant; 2 rashers bacon, rind removed; 60 g (2 oz) butter, melted; 1/2 cup sherry; 1 tbs redcurrant jelly; juice 1/2 lemon; flour.

Truss pheasant, and tie bacon around bird. Rub all over with butter. Roast in a preheated moderate oven (180°C/350°F) for 40 minutes. Meanwhile, combine butter, sherry, jelly and lemon juice. Remove bacon from pheasant. Dredge breast lightly with flour and pour liquid over. Continue roasting a further 15 minutes, basting 2–3 times with pan liquid. Serve this liquid as sauce. Serves 3–4.

PICKLES

The word 'pickles' usually describes coarsely chopped fruits and vegetables which are preserved in brine or vinegar. Home-made pickles add flavour and variety to all sorts of foods, and with chutneys, belong to the tradition of the English kitchen; the art of making them should not be allowed to die out.

They are, in a way, a legacy from the days of the British Raj in India, when these condiments were a very welcome addition to English food, especially simple cold meats. The British took to these exotic spicy products with open arms, and there was hardly a cookery book of the nineteenth century which didn't include recipes for relishes, pickles, chutneys and sauces. At the same time, silver cruet sets, filled with glass sauce bottles, were introduced and became a stand utensil on every table.

There is no special equipment needed for pickles, but because of their acidity, be sure to use stoneware, pottery, glass or plastic bowls for brining. Saucepans used should be unchipped enamel or stainless steel. Use clean, wooden spoons for stirring.

Store pickles in clean glass jars, preferably with glass lids. Plastic-plated metal lids can be used but *never* use metal ones. Glass coffee jars with plastic seals are also good.

A special mixture of spices is prepared as pickling spice, containing many of the necessary spices. **See recipes.**

See also *Chutney.*

Crisp Bread–and–Butter Pickles

1/4 cup coarse salt; 1/2 cup water; 10 cups very finely sliced cucumbers; 4 medium onions, sliced into rings; 1 large red or green pepper cored, seeded and sliced; 1 1/4 cups sugar; 1 1/4 cups vinegar; 1/2 tbs mustard seeds; 1/4 tsp turmeric; 1/4 tsp whole cloves.

Dissolve salt in water and pour over sliced vegetables. Put some ice cubes on top of cucumbers. Use about 3 cups ice; it is the ice and salt that give an almost brittle, crisp pickle. Let stand for 3 hours, weighted with a plate. Drain. Combine sugar, vinegar and spices and bring to the boil. Add vegetables and return to boiling point. Do not boil. Pack into sterilised jars, fill to overflowing, and seal. Makes 10 cups.

Zucchini Pickles

1 kg (2 lb) small zucchini, finely sliced; 2 medium onions, finely sliced; 1/4 cup salt; 2 cups white vinegar; 1 cup sugar; 1 tsp celery seeds; 1 tsp mustard seeds; 1 tsp turmeric; 1/2 tsp dry mustard.

Place zucchini and onion slices in a crock or bowl. Cover with water and add salt. Let stand for 1 hour, then drain. Mix remaining ingredients in a saucepan and bring to the boil. Pour over zucchini and onion. Let stand for 1 hour. Put in pan, bring to the boil and cook for 3 minutes. Pack into hot sterilised jars and seal. Makes 6 cups.

Cauliflower Pickles

1 medium head cauliflower, broken into florets; 1 cup tiny white onions, peeled; 1/3 cup salt; 5 cups white vinegar; 3/4 cup sugar; 1 tsp turmeric; 1 tbs mustard seeds; 1/2 tbs celery seeds; 1 red chilli.

Mix vegetables with salt and ice cubes, and cover with more ice cubes. Let stand for 3 hours. Drain. Mix remaining ingredients in a large saucepan and bring to the boil, stirring to dissolve sugar. Add cauliflower and onions. Cooks for 10 minutes or until tender but not soft. Pack into hot sterilised jars. Reheat liquid to boiling. Pour over vegetables and seal. Makes 5–6 cups.

p

Chow–Chow

A lovely, golden relish with a mustardy tang – good with pickled meats.

500 g (1 lb) green tomatoes, chopped;
3 small cucumbers, chopped; 1 red or green pepper, cored, seeded and chopped; 1/2 small cauliflower, chopped; 1 bunch celery, chopped;
500 g (1 lb) small white onions, peeled;
250 g (8 oz) green beans, cut into short lengths;
4 cups boiling water; 1/4 cup salt; 2 cups cider vinegar; 1 cup sugar; 2 tbs celery seeds; 2 tbs dry mustard; 2 tbs turmeric; 1/2 tbs whole allspice;
1/2 tbs pepper; 1/2 tbs ground cloves.

Combine vegetables in a large bowl. Cover with boiling water, add salt and let stand for 1 hour. Drain. Rinse well in cold water and drain again. Mix remaining ingredients in a large saucepan and bring to the boil. Add vegetables and cook until tender, stirring frequently. Spoon vegetables into hot, sterilised jars. Fill with cooking liquid and seal. Makes 10 cups.

Dill Cucumber Pickles

25 cucumbers, 8–10 cm (3–4 in) long; 2 cups cider vinegar; 2/3 cup salt; 5 cups water; sprigs fresh dill; cloves garlic, peeled.

Put cucumbers in a large bowl, cover with cold water and let stand overnight. Drain and pack into hot, sterilised jars. Combine vinegar, salt and water in a saucepan and bring to the boil. Pour over the cucumbers. Add 1–2 sprigs of dill and a clove garlic to each jar and seal. Makes about 4 jars.

Mustard Pickles (Piccalilli)

750 g (1 1/2 lb) small cucumbers, sliced;
250 g (8 oz) green tomatoes, diced; 500 g (1 lb) small white onions, peeled; 3 green peppers, cored, seeded and diced; 1/2 cauliflower, cut into small pieces; 1/4 cup salt; 5 cups cold water; 1/2 cup flour;
3 tbs dry mustard; 1 tbs turmeric;
4 cups cider vinegar; 1 cup sugar.

Put cucumbers, tomatoes, onions, peppers and cauliflower in a large bowl. Mix salt with water, pour over vegetables, cover and let stand for 8 hours or overnight. Drain and rinse under cold running water. Put vegetables in a large saucepan, cover them with fresh cold water and bring to the boil. Drain in a colander once again. Put flour, mustard and turmeric in the pan. Stir in enough vinegar to make smooth paste, then gradually add remaining vinegar and sugar, stirring well. Bring to the boil, stirring constantly, and cook until thick and smooth. Add vegetables and cook, stirring, until heated through. Spoon into hot, sterilised jars filling completely and seal. Makes about 10 cups.

Curried Eggplant Pickle

8 dried red chillies; 5 tsp chopped garlic;
4 tsp chopped fresh ginger; 2 tbs black mustard seeds; 2 1/2 tsp turmeric; 1 3/4 cups oil;
1.5 kg (3 lb) eggplants, cubed; 3 tsp salt;
1/2 cup firmly packed brown sugar; 3/4 cup vinegar;
2 tsp Garam Masala (page 171).

Soak chillies in hot water for 5 minutes. Drain, reserving water. Place chillies, garlic, ginger, mustard seeds and some of the water in which the chillies soaked in a blender or food processor and blend on high speed until puréed. Combine with turmeric. Heat oil and fry blended mixture for a few minutes, then add eggplant cubes. Cover and cook on low heat until eggplant is soft, stirring now and then. Add salt, sugar and vinegar and simmer until thick, stirring frequently to prevent burning. Stir in garam masala. Bottle in sterilised jars. Store covered. Makes about 4 cups.

Red or Green Pepper Relish

You can chop the vegetables for this and other relishes coarse or fine, according to your preference. Use a food processor, if you have one, to save time and effort.

12 red or green peppers, or a combination, cored, seeded and chopped; 6 onions, chopped;
6 sticks celery, chopped; 2 cups cider vinegar;
1 cup sugar; 1 tbs salt; 1/2 tbs mustard or celery seeds.

Cover vegetables with boiling water, then drain. Put them in a large saucepan, cover with cold water, bring to the boil and drain again. Mix vinegar, sugar, salt and mustard or celery seeds in pan and bring to the boil. Add vegetables and simmer for about 10 minutes. Adjust seasoning if necessary. Spoon vegetables into hot, sterilised jars. Fill to overflowing with cooking liquid and seal. Makes 7 cups.

Fresh Dill Pickles (Kosher Style)

3 cups vinegar; 3 cups water; 6 tbs salt; fresh or dried dill; cloves garlic, sliced; mustard seeds;
30–36 cucumbers, 8–10 cm (3–4 in) long.

Make a brine of the vinegar, water and salt. Bring to the boil. Put a generous layer of dill, 1/2–1 clove garlic and 1 1/2 tsp mustard seeds in each sterilised jar. Pack cucumbers tightly in jars. When half filled with cucumbers, add another layer of dill and complete packing. Fill jars with boiling brine, leaving 1 cm (1/2 in) in headspace. Put caps on jars, screwing bands tight. Process for 5 minutes in boiling water bath. Pickles will shrivel somewhat after processing, but they will later plump in sealed jar. Makes 5–6 x 2 1/2-cup jars.

p

Mixed Pickles

A sweet and spicy pickle, good with cold meats and toasted cheese.

6 green tomatoes, chopped; 2 green peppers, cored, seeded and chopped; I red pepper, cored, seeded and chopped; 3 onions, chopped; ¹/₂ small cabbage, chopped; 2 tbs salt; ¹/₂ tbs whole cloves; I cinnamon stick; ¹/₂ tbs whole allspice; I¹/₂ cups firmly packed brown sugar; I tsp celery seeds; I tbs mustard seeds; I cup cider vinegar.

Sprinkle vegetables with salt, cover and let stand overnight. Cover with cold water, then drain. Tie cloves, cinnamon and allspice in a muslin bag and place with remaining ingredients in a large saucepan. Add vegetables and bring to the boil. Reduce heat and simmer for about 15 minutes. Spoon vegetables into hot, sterilised jars. Remove bag of spices from cooking liquid, fill jars to overflowing with cooking liquid and seal. Makes 8 cups.

Celery Relish

Sweet and crunchy.

¹/₂ cup sugar; 2 tsp salt; ¹/₂ tsp dry mustard; ¹/₄ tsp ground cloves; ¹/₄ tsp ground allspice; ¹/₄ cinnamon; ¹/₄ tsp celery seeds; I–I¹/₂ cups cider vinegar; 2 bunches celery, chopped; 6 large tomatoes, chopped; I red pepper, cored, seeded and chopped.

Mix all ingredients well in a large saucepan. Bring to the boil, then reduce heat and simmer until thick, about 1 hour. Spoon vegetables into hot, sterilised jars. Fill to overflowing with cooking liquid, and seal. Makes 8 cups.

Watermelon Pickles

rind from I large watermelon; salt; I lemon, finely sliced.

PICKLING SYRUP: I0 cups cider vinegar; 2 cups water; 9 cups sugar; 2 tbs whole cloves; 2 tbs whole all spice; I piece fresh ginger; 3 tbs cracked cinnamon stick.

Trim off green skin and pink flesh from watermelon rind. Cut rind into squares or small oblong pieces. Measure: there should be 20 cups or 5 litres. Cover with cold salted water (¹/₄ cup salt to 10 cups water) and let stand overnight. Drain. Place rind in a large saucepan, cover with fresh cold water and bring to the boil. Simmer until tender.

PICKLING SYRUP: Place vinegar, water and sugar in a large saucepan. Tie spices in a cheesecloth bag and add to pan. Bring to the boil and boil rapidly for 5 minutes. Drain watermelon rind and add to the pickling syrup with lemon. Bring back to the boil and simmer for 1 hour or until clear. Remove spice bag. Pack pickle in hot, sterilised jars and seal. Makes about 10 cups.

PIE

Although there are exceptions, a pie usually consists of a filling topped with a crust; it may or may not have a bottom crust as well. Fillings range from hearty meats to delicate fruits, and the crust can be made from various kinds of pastry, crumbs, scone dough, meringue or even mashed potato. What they all have in common is that a pie is invariably acclaimed as a treat and a sign of a caring cook. See recipes.

ONE-CRUST PIES

To make a pie with a top pastry crust only, prepare filling and, if it is cooked, cool it completely. Place in a pie dish or tart plate just large enough to hold it, mounding it up in the centre to support the crust. If filling is not firm enough to mound, provide support by placing a pie funnel or an upturned egg cup in the centre of the dish before putting in filling.

Roll out pastry 5 mm (¼ in) thick, and cut a shape about 4 cm (1½ in) larger than top of dish. Cut a strip from the outside edge of this piece, slightly wider than rim of dish. Dampen rim with water and press pastry strip on to it, cutting ends to fit and dampening them to join. Moisten top of pastry strip.

Lift remaining pastry on a lightly floured rolling pin and lay it loosely over dish. Press pastry lid firmly on to dampened strip. Trim off overhang with a sharp knife, holding up the dish on one hand and cutting with the other, slanting the knife slightly under the rim, as you turn the dish round.

IF USING FLAKY PASTRY: With the back of a finger, press round the pastry lid so that it is pushed out slightly beyond the rim of the dish. At the same time, with a knife held horizontally, lightly tap cut edges of pastry all round. This is called 'knocking up' the pastry and will give a flaky finish to the edge.

Flute the crust by drawing the back of a knife across the edge at 1 cm (½ in) intervals, bringing the knife up and in, while with your other thumb you press the pastry down just in front of the knife. Pull the pastry with the knife, do not cut it. Cut a few small slits in pastry and pierce through centre into pie funnel, if using. Glaze (avoiding cut edges) and bake as directed in recipe.

IF USING SHORT PASTRY: Press edge of pastry out so that it is pushed slightly beyond the rim of the dish. Flute edge with your fingers or mark by pressing all round with the tines of a fork. Cut a few small slits in the pastry and pierce through centre into pie funnel, if using. Glaze and bake as directed in recipe.

TWO-CRUST PIES

A two-crust pie can be made with both top and bottom crusts of short or flaky pastry, or it can be made with short pastry underneath and flaky pastry on top.

Divide pastry into two portions, one a little larger than the other. Roll out larger portion about 3 mm (¹/₈ in) thick, and cut a shape which will line the dish with about 2 cm (¾ in) overhang. Lift pastry on a lightly floured rolling pin and fit it into the dish, easing it in loosely without stretching it. Use fingertips or a small ball of pastry, dipped in flour, to press crust against the dish so that no air is trapped between.

If filling is very juicy, brush bottom and sides of crust with lightly beaten egg, egg white or, for a sweet pie, melted jam, and allow it to dry for a few minutes. Place filling in dish as described under 'One-crust Pies'.

Roll other portion of pastry about 5 mm (¼ in) thick to a shape about 2.5 cm (1 in) larger than top of dish. Moisten rim of bottom crust with water. Lift top crust on to a lightly floured rolling pin and lay it loosely over the dish. Press top and bottom crust firmly together. Trim off overhang with a sharp knife, as for One-crust Pies.

With the back of a finger, press round the pastry lid, so that it is pushed out slightly beyond the rim of the dish. Then 'knock up' the edges and flute or mark as described under 'One-crust Pies'. Cut a few small slits in pastry and pierce through centre. Glaze and bake as directed in recipe.

DECORATE A PIE

Pastry-covered pies may be decorated with flowers, leaves, tassels or tiny fruits made from the pastry trimmings. Secure to the crust with beaten egg or egg white, and glaze. Cover decorations with foil if they are browning too much before pie is ready.

Pastry Fruits: Shape several tiny pastry balls and join to make a cluster of berries; or shape small apples, pears, etc. Poke holes in the tops with a fine skewer and insert pastry stems or leaves.

Pastry Leaves: Cut pastry into strips, cut diagonally across into diamonds and trim to leaf shapes. Make veins with the blunt edge of a knife and arrange on pie.

Pastry Rose: Cut 3 pastry strips about 1 x 5 cm (½ x 2 in). Roll one strip into a cylinder, wrap a second strip loosely round it and pinch base in to open out top; then wrap the third strip round from the opposite side and pinch base in again.

Pastry Tassel: Cut a pastry strip about 8 x 2.5 cm (3 x 1 in). Cut this strip across like a fringe to about two thirds of its width, then roll up lengthways, pinching the base together. Place in centre of pie and open out the fringe.

LATTICE-TOP PIES

A lattice top is a decorative finish to a pie with an attractive filling such as fruit. Roll out dough and cut strips 1–2 cm (½–¾ in) wide. Arrange the strips on the filling in rows at right angles to each other.

Or weave strips as follows: lay half the strips across the dish, about 2 cm (¾ in) apart. Fold back every second strip halfway. Place a strip at right angles across the unfolded strips. Unfold the doubled strips and fold back the alternate ones. Lay another cross strip about 2 cm (¾ in) from the first. Continue, working towards the edge, then repeat the process, starting from the other side of the centre line. Strips should be loosely arranged, without stretching.

When the whole pie is latticed, dampen the ends of the strips and press them to the bottom crust or to the edge of the dish. Fold edge of bottom crust over ends of strips, or for a one-crust pie, cover ends with a strip of pastry round the dampened rim of the dish.

Australian Meat Pies

Meat pies are an Australian favourite and are sold in cake and sandwich shops from one end of the land to the other. The classic version is simple – an individual, double-crust pie full of chopped beef in a rich gravy.

500 g (1 lb) chuck or blade steak; 2 tbs flour; 1 tsp salt; freshly ground black pepper; ½ cup water; 1 x 375 g (12 oz) packet frozen puff pastry, thawed; beaten egg to glaze.

Trim gristle and fat from steak and cut into thin shreds, then chop finely. Dust with flour, salt and pepper and place in a pudding basin or other heat-proof bowl with water. Cover with foil and tie in place with string, or use a snap-on lid. Place in a saucepan with enough boiling water to come halfway up sides of bowl, and simmer for 2 hours or until meat is very tender. Replace water as necessary to maintain level. Allow to cool completely. Roll out pastry dough thin and cut three quarters of it into round, oblong or square shapes to fit individual pie tins. Line tins with dough, and fill about three quarters full with meat filling. Cut lids from remaining dough, dampen edges and press into place. Cut a vent in top of each pie for steam to escape. Chill for 15 minutes, then brush with beaten egg. Bake in preheated hot oven (200°C/400°F) for 25 minutes or until pastry is puffed and golden. Serve with Tomato Sauce (see page 340). Makes 4–6 small pies.

VARIATION

POTATO PIES: Follow recipe for Meat Pies using three quarters of a packet of pastry, but instead of pastry lids, cover pies with creamy mashed potato made from 4 medium potatoes, ¼ cup boiling milk and 30 g (1 oz) butter. Season well with salt and pepper, spread over filling and roughen surface with a fork. Bake as for meat pies, covering pies loosely with foil if potato is browning too much.

Beef and Burgundy Pie

A restaurant favourite, this rich beef filling can be made into one large pie or individual ones, and topped with flaky pastry or a tender scone crust.

2 tbs oil; 30 g (1 oz) butter; 60 g (2 oz) pickled (salt) pork, diced; 12 button onions, peeled; 250 g (8 oz) button mushrooms; 1 kg (2 lb) chuck steak or beef shin, cubed; 3 tbs seasoned flour; 1 large onion, chopped; 1 tsp chopped fresh marjoram, or 1/4 tsp dried; 2 tsp chopped fresh thyme, or 1/2 tsp dried; 1 cup burgundy or other red wine; 1 cup beef stock; salt and freshly ground black pepper; 1 quantity Flaky or Rough Puff Pastry (pages 343–4), or 1 quantity Scone Dough (page 472); beaten egg or milk to glaze.

Heat oil and butter in a large, heavy saucepan or flameproof casserole Dry pickled pork well and fry until crisp and golden. Remove pork with a slotted spoon and reserve. Brown first button onions, then mushrooms, in fat in pan removing each when done. Toss beef with seasoned flour and brown, a few pieces at a time. Add chopped onion and cook gently until soft, then return pork and beef to the saucepan and add herbs, wine and stock. Cover and simmer very gently on top of stove, or place in a preheated slow oven (150°C/300°F). Cook until beef is tender, 1½–2½ hours. Add button onions and cook a further 15 minutes, then add mushrooms and cook 10 minutes more. Taste and adjust seasoning. Cool completely.

For pie with pastry crust: Spoon beef into a pie dish just large enough to hold it, mounded slightly, or into 6 individual pie dishes. Roll out pastry dough and cover dish. Decorate with roses or tassels and leaves made from pastry trimmings (see page 361). Chill 20 minutes. Cut a few small slits in crust and glaze with beaten egg. Bake in a preheated very hot oven (230°C/450°F) about 10 minutes or until pastry is well risen and beginning to colour, then reduce heat to moderate (180°C/350°F) and continue baking until pastry is golden brown and filling heated through, 25–35 minutes more for a large pie, 15–20 minutes for individual pies. Cover loosely with foil if pastry is browning too much.

For pie with scone crust: Spoon filling into pie dish, casserole or 6 individual ramekins, to come 1 cm (½ in) below rim. For a large pie, pat out scone dough to 1 cm (½ in) thick and cut into 12 scones. Place scones close together on top of filling. For small pies, pat out dough, cut 6 rounds to fit ramekins and place on filling. Brush tops with milk. Bake in a preheated very hot oven (230°C/450°F) for 8–10 minutes or until scone crust is well risen and golden, then reduce heat to moderate (180°C/350°F), cover loosely with foil and continue baking until filling is heated through, 20–30 minutes more. Serves 6.

Fisherman's Pie

500 g (1 lb) fillets white fish; 60 g (2 oz) butter; 1 tbs lemon juice; 2 cups milk; 1 onion, finely chopped; 1 bouquet garni; pinch nutmeg; 3 tbs flour; 1/4 cup cream; 1/3 cup grated Cheddar cheese; large pinch dry mustard; salt and freshly ground black pepper; 2 tbs chopped parsley; 1/2 cup cooked peas; 3 hard-boiled eggs, quartered; 1 quantity Rough Puff or Flaky Pastry (pages 343–4), or 1 x 375 g (12 oz) packet frozen puff pastry, thawed; beaten egg.

Place fish in an ovenproof dish, dot with half the butter and drizzle lemon juice over. Cover with foil and cook in a preheated moderate oven (180°C/350°F) for 20 minutes. Remove any skin or bones and flake fish, reserving juices. Heat milk in a saucepan with onion, bouquet garni and nutmeg until bubbles form round edge. Remove from heat and stand 5 minutes, then remove bouquet garni. Melt remaining butter in a heavy saucepan, stir in flour and cook on low heat 1 minute. Remove from heat, cool a little and add milk, stirring until smoothly blended. Return to medium heat and stir until boiling. Remove from heat, stir in cream, cheese and mustard and season with salt and pepper. Fold fish and its juices, parsley, peas and eggs into sauce. Cool completely, then spoon into pie dish just large enough to hold it. Cover with pastry dough and chill 20 minutes. Cut a few small slits in top and brush with beaten egg. Bake in a preheated very hot oven (230°C/450°F) for 10–15 minutes or until pastry is well-risen and beginning to brown, then reduce heat to moderate (180°C/350°F) and continue baking until pastry is golden-brown and filling is heated through, a further 25–30 minutes. Cover top loosely with foil if pastry is overbrowning. Serves 6.

VARIATIONS

This pie is easy to vary for special occasions. Substitute shelled, cooked prawns or crab, lightly poached scallops or fresh oysters for up to 250 g (8 oz) of the fish, and uses scallop poaching liquid, oyster liquor or white wine in place of ½ cup of the milk.

Vegetable Pie

2 cups milk; 1 onion, finely chopped; 1 bouquet garni; pinch nutmeg; 60 g (2 oz) butter; 3 tbs flour; 1/4 cup grated mild cheese; large pinch dry mustard; small pinch cayenne; salt and freshly ground black pepper; 3 cups diced or sliced cooked vegetables (beans, peas, carrots, corn, fennel, broccoli, cauliflower, peppers, mushrooms, celery); 1 quantity Rough Puff or Flaky Pastry (pages 343–4), or 1 x 375 g (12 oz) packet frozen puff pastry, thawed; beaten egg to glaze.

Heat milk in a saucepan with onion, bouquet garni and nutmeg until bubbles form round edge. Remove from heat and stand 5 minutes, then remove bouquet garni. Melt butter in a heavy saucepan, stir in flour and cook on low heat 1 minute. Remove from heat, cool a little and add milk, stirring until smoothly blended. Return to medium heat and stir until boiling. Remove from heat, stir in cheese, mustard and cayenne and season with salt and pepper. Fold vegetables into sauce and cool completely. Spoon mixture into a pie dish just large enough to hold it. Cover with pastry dough and chill 20 minutes. Cut a few small slits in top and brush with beaten egg. Bake in preheated very hot oven (230°C/450°F) for 10–15 minutes or until pastry is well risen and beginning to brown, then reduce heat to moderate (180°C/350°F) and continue baking until pastry is golden-brown and filling is heated through, a further 25–30 minutes. Cover top loosely with foil if pastry is browning too much. Serve very hot. Serves 6.

Savoury Mince Pie

double quantity Savoury Mince (page 269);
1 quantity Shortcrust Pastry (page 342);
beaten egg to glaze.

Spoon cool mince into pie plate or dish which will just hold it, and mound up a little in the centre. Roll out pastry dough and cover dish. If you have surplus dough, roll out, cut into triangles and bake with pie for extra servings. Chill 20 minutes. Cut a few small slits in crust and glaze with beaten egg. Bake the pie in a preheated hot oven (220°C/425°F) about 10 minutes or until pastry is beginning to colour, then reduce heat to moderate (180°C/350°F) and continue baking until pastry is golden-brown and filling heated through, 20–30 minutes more. Cover loosely with foil if pastry is over-browning. Serves 8.

Little Scottish Mutton Pies

These Glasgow favourites were once called 'Tuppenny Struggles' – and wonderful value they were with their generous meat filling and good gravy. Today, we make them more often with lamb than mutton but otherwise they are the same – a perfect example of how delicious simple, old recipes can be.

500 g (1 lb) lean, boneless lamb, diced;
1 small onion, grated; $^1/_4$ tsp nutmeg;
4 tbs beef stock; 2 tsp Worcestershire sauce;
salt and freshly ground black pepper;
1 quantity Hot Water Pastry (page 344);
beaten egg to glaze.

Mix lamb with onion, nutmeg, stock, Worcestershire sauce, salt and pepper. Divide pastry dough into 4 even portions. For each pie, take a portion and set aside half for lid (keep all dough you are not using in a covered bowl over hot water). Have ready a glass jar

8 cm (3 in) in diameter which has been rinsed out with hot water, dried and floured on the outside. Mould dough round jar, fasten on paper collar, fill and cover with pastry lid as described in Individual Raised Pork Pies. Glaze tops with beaten egg and cut a slit in each for steam to escape. Bake in a preheated moderate oven (180°C/350°F) for 45 minutes, removing paper collars after 20 minutes and covering tops with foil if pastry is browning too much. Serve hot. Makes 4.

Spanish Fish Pie

Perfect for lunch or for picnics.

4 tbs olive oil; 1 large onion, finely chopped;
750 g (1$^1/_2$ lb) firm fillets white fish; 1 large tomato,
peeled, seeded and finely chopped; 1 clove garlic,
crushed; 2 tbs finely chopped parsley; 1$^1/_2$ tsp salt;
$^1/_2$ tsp freshly ground black pepper; 1 tsp grated
lemon rind; $^1/_4$ cup chopped stuffed olives;
3 hard-boiled eggs, coarsely chopped;
double quantity Rich Shortcrust Pastry (page 342).

Heat 3 tbs of the oil in a heavy frying pan and cook onion until soft and golden. Remove any skin and bones from fish, cut into fingers and add to pan with tomato, garlic, parsley, salt, pepper and lemon rind. Simmer for 10 minutes, stirring gently several times. Check seasoning, then allow to cool. Add olives and eggs. Roll out just over half the pastry dough thinly and use to line 25 cm (10 in) pie plate. Spoon in cold filling. Roll out remaining dough and cover pie. Chill 20 minutes. Cut a few slits in the top for steam to escape and brush with remaining oil. Bake in a preheated hot oven (200°C/400°F) for 25 minutes or until pastry is golden brown. Cut into wedges to serve. Serves 4–6.

Bacon and Egg Pie

Plain Shortcrust Pastry made with 2 cups flour
(page 342); 250 g (8 oz) lean rashers bacon, rind
removed and chopped; 4 eggs; $^1/_2$ cup cream;
2$^1/_2$ tbs chopped parsley; salt and freshly ground
black pepper; pinch nutmeg; beaten egg to glaze.

Roll out just over half the pastry dough and use to line a 20–23 cm (8–9 in) pie plate. Arrange bacon in pie shell. Break eggs and slip them in on top of bacon. Mix cream with parsley and season with salt, pepper and nutmeg. Pour over eggs. Roll out remaining pastry dough to make a lid and cover the pie. Make a slit in centre and decorate with pastry leaves made from trimmings, if liked. Rest in a cool place for 20 minutes, then glaze with beaten egg and bake in a preheated hot oven (200°C/400°F) for about 30 minute or until golden-brown. Serve warm or cold. Serves 4–5.

Easter Cheese and Spinach Pie
(Torta Pasqualina)

This savoury pie from Italy was originally made with 33 sheets of pastry, one for each year of our Lord's life. As the pastry had to be made by hand, it could take the cook all morning just to mix and roll it. Today, we use less pastry in line with a lighter approach to food, and packaged filo makes the job even easier.

¹/₂ pack (12 sheets) filo pastry; 90 g (3 oz) butter, melted.

FILLING: 1 large bunch silverbeet, or 2 bunches English spinach; 2 tbs olive oil; 1 medium onion, finely chopped; salt and freshly ground black pepper; 500 g (1 lb) ricotta cheese; ¹/₂ cup cream or evaporated milk; 30 g (1 oz) butter; 6 eggs; ¹/₂ tsp dried marjoram; ³/₄ cup grated Parmesan cheese.

FILLING: Cut tough white stalks from silverbeet or spinach, rinse leaves well and steam until tender. Drain and chop finely by hand or in a food processor fitted with a steel blade. Press in a sieve to remove any remaining moisture. Heat oil in a heavy saucepan and gently fry onion until soft but not brown. Add silverbeet or spinach and stir together for 1–2 minutes. Season with salt and pepper and set aside. Mash ricotta in a bowl and stir in cream or evaporated milk and a good pinch of salt.

Line a greased 23–25 cm (9–10 in) pie dish with 6 sheets of filo pastry, brushing each with melted butter. (The filo will stay pliable as you work if you place it between 2 dry tea-towels with a dampened tea-towel on top.) Spread sixth layer of pastry with spinach mixture and spoon ricotta over top. Make 6 hollows in ricotta and put a little knob of butter in each. Break an egg into each hollow and season with salt, pepper and marjoram. Sprinkle Parmesan cheese over all. Cover filling with remaining sheets of filo, brushing each sheet with melted butter. Press edges firmly together and trim excess pastry. Prick top layer of filo with a fork and brush generously with butter. Bake pie in a preheated hot oven (200°C/400°F) for 40 minutes or until the pastry is golden-brown. Serve hot or cold. Serves 6 generously.

Finnish Meat Pie

In Finland, mashed potatoes are often added to the pastry for savoury pies and the filling may contain a mixture of meats. If you can get coarse sea salt at your supermarket or delicatessen, do use it. The Finns consider it more nutritious than ordinary salt, and it does something special for the flavour.

PASTRY: 2 cups flour, sifted; ¹/₂ tsp sea salt; 1¹/₂ cups cold mashed potatoes; 125 g (4 oz) butter, cut into small pieces; 2–4 tbs iced water; beaten egg to glaze.

FILLING: 1 large onion, finely chopped; 30 g (1 oz) butter 500 g (1 lb) topside mince; 250 g (8 oz) minced pork; 1 cup beef stock; ³/₄ cup cream; 1¹/₂ tsp sea salt; freshly ground black pepper; 2 tbs chopped parsley; 1 cup cooked brown rice (¹/₃ cup raw).

PASTRY: Combine flour, salt and mashed potatoes in a large bowl. Add butter and rub into mixture with the fingertips. Add enough iced water to make a firm dough. Wrap in plastic wrap and chill for 30 minutes or longer.

FILLING: Fry onion in butter until soft and golden. Add meats and fry until brown, stirring and breaking up any lumps with a fork. Add stock, cream, salt and pepper and simmer for 15 minutes. Stir in parsley and rice. Check seasoning and allow to cool. Divide pastry dough in half and roll out one piece to a rectangle about 25 x 30 cm (10 x 12 in). Place on a greased shallow baking tin and cover with cold filling, leaving a margin of 2.5 cm (1 in) all around. Dampen edges. Roll out second piece of dough and cover filling, pressing edges firmly to seal. Prick top all over with a fork, glaze with beaten egg and decorate with dough trimmings. Bake in a preheated hot oven (200°C/400°F) for 30 minutes or until crust is crisp and golden-brown. Serve hot, warm or cold. Serves 6–8 as main course, or 12 as an appetiser.
NOTE: 750 g (1¹/₂ lb) lean pork and veal mince may be used instead of topside and pork.

Raised Pork Pie

A true raised pie is made without a supporting mound, using hot water pastry which sets, when cool, into a sturdy shell that will stand by itself even before baking. The same pastry is used for the large cold pies which are called 'raised' but are made in decorative moulds – a splendid British tradition for cold buffets, pub meals and picnics.

1 kg (2 lb) pork, a mixture of lean and fat (neck of pork is a good cut), cut into 1 cm (¹/₂ in) cubes; 1 tsp salt; 1 tbs chopped mixed fresh herbs, or 1 tbs chopped parsley mixed with 1 tsp dried herbs; pinch cayenne; freshly ground white pepper; 1 quantity Hot Water Pastry (page 344); beaten egg to glaze.

JELLIED STOCK: 375 g (12 oz) pork bones; 1 onion; 6 cups water; salt; 1 bouquet garni; 6 white peppercorns.

Make jellied stock the day before preparing pie. Place all ingredients in a heavy saucepan, cover and simmer very, very gently for about 4 hours, replenishing water as needed. Strain and allow to cool. Adjust seasoning if necessary. Chill and lift off fat.

Combine pork with salt, herbs, cayenne and plenty of pepper. Set aside. Set aside one third of pastry dough for the lid, keeping it covered in a basin over hot water to prevent it hardening. Flatten remaining dough with your fist, lift into a loose-sided 20 cm (8 in) pie mould or springform tin and press it quickly on to the bottom and sides of the mould, bringing pastry just above rim. Fill mould to brim with pork filling, doming it slightly to support top crust. Roll out remaining dough and cover pie, pressing top crust on to sides. Trim off overhang (return it to warm basin), press edge all round to push it out a little and flute with fingers. Cut a hole in centre of pie; decorate with a pastry rose, placed over hole, and some pastry leaves made from trimmings (see page 361). Glaze pie with beaten egg. Bake in a preheated moderate oven (180°C/350°F) for 2 hours covering top with a piece of foil if pastry is browning too much. Remove from oven and allow to cool in the mould. Warm jellied stock gently until just melted. Remove pastry rose from pie, place a funnel in the hole and gradually pour in stock to fill pie. Allow to cool and set. To serve, replace pastry rose, remove sides of mould and lift pie on to a serving platter. If the pie is for a picnic, carry it in its mould and remove when you get there. Serves 6–8.

VARIATIONS

VEAL AND HAM PIE: Follow recipe for Pork Pie, but substitute veal bones for pork bones to make the stock and use the following filling instead of pork filling: 750 g (1½ lb) boneless shoulder of veal, cut into 2.5 cm (1 in) cubes; 125 g (4 oz) lean cooked ham, cut into small strips; 1 small onion, finely chopped; 2 tsp finely chopped parsley; 1 tsp grated lemon rind; salt and freshly ground black pepper. Arrange veal, ham and onion in layers, scattering with parsley and lemon rind and seasoning with salt and pepper. Dome top slightly. For a variation, hard-boiled eggs may be placed end to end when the pie is half-filled and covered with remaining filling. This gives a slice of egg in the middle of each slice of pie when it is cut.

INDIVIDUAL RAISED PORK PIES: The ingredients given for Raised Pork Pie will make 2 small pies 10–13 cm (4–5 in) in diameter. Prepare jellied stock and filling as directed in recipe. Make Hot Water Pastry and divide in half. For each pie, take half of pastry dough and set aside one third for lid (keep all dough you are not using in a covered bowl over hot water). Have ready a large glass jar 10–13 cm (4–5 in) in diameter which has been rinsed out with hot water, dried and floured on the outside. Press dough out to a round, stand jar in the middle and mould dough quickly around it, working up the sides. Turn jar upside-down with dough on it and continue to mould, pulling dough gently until it is about 10 cm (4 in) in depth. Place a collar of double greaseproof paper around the dough and secure it with a paper clip. Allow dough to cool, then carefully ease jar out of the dough case. Stand case on a baking tray. Spoon in

filling, mounding it up. Roll out reserved dough for lid, dampen edges and cover pie, pinching lid on to sides. Make a hole in centre of lid and decorate with a pastry rose or leaves and berries placed over hole (see page 361). Glaze top with beaten egg and bake in a preheated moderate oven (180°C/350°F) for 1–1½ hours, removing paper collar after 30 minutes and covering top with a piece of foil if necessary to prevent over-browning. When cool, fill up carefully with stock as for large pie. Makes 2.

Lemon Chiffon Pie

Although it has no top crust, its American origin gives this lovely dessert the name of 'pie' – Americans, a nation of pie-lovers, use the name for open and covered varieties.

CRUMB CRUST: 1½ cups fine sweet biscuit crumbs; ⅓ cup caster sugar; 75 g (2½ oz) butter, melted.

FILLING: 3 tsp (1 envelope) gelatine; ¼ cup cold water; 1 cup sugar; pinch salt; 1 tsp grated lemon rind; ½ cup lemon juice; 4 eggs, separated; whipped cream to decorate.

CRUMB CRUST: Mix crumbs, sugar and butter in a bowl. Turn mixture into a 23 cm (9 in) tart plate and press and pat it out evenly on to the bottom and sides. Bake in a preheated moderate oven (180°C/350°F) for 8–10 minutes. Remove and cool.

FILLING: Soften gelatine in cold water, then stir over simmering water until dissolved. Place ½ cup of the sugar, the salt, lemon rind and lemon juice in the top of a double saucepan or a heatproof bowl which will fit over a saucepan. Add egg yolks and gelatine mixture, stirring until well blended. Place over simmering water and stir until mixture thickens a little. Pour into a bowl and chill until mixture mounds when dropped from a spoon. Beat egg whites until foamy, then gradually beat in remaining sugar, beating until smooth and shiny. Fold egg whites into lemon mixture. Spread into pie shell and chill until serving time. Decorate with whipped cream. Serves 6–8.

VARIATIONS

LIME CHIFFON PIE: Follow recipe for Lemon Chiffon Pie, using gingersnap biscuits crumbs in the crust, and substituting grated lime rind and juice for lemon rind and juice.

ORANGE CHIFFON PIE: Follow recipe for Lemon Chiffon Pie, substituting 1 tsp grated orange rind and ½ cup orange juice plus 2 tbs lemon juice for the lemon rind and juice.

Latticed Raisin Pie

1 cup orange juice; ½ cup water; 1 cup seeded raisins; 1½ cups sugar; 4 tbs flour;
3 tbs lemon juice; large pinch salt; unsweetened Rich Shortcrust Pastry make with
2 cups flour (page 342).

GLAZE: lightly beaten egg white; caster sugar.

Bring orange juice and water to the boil, remove from heat and stir in raisins. Stand 2 hours, then stir in sugar, flour, lemon juice and salt. Return to low heat and stir constantly until boiling and well thickened. Cool completely. Divide pastry dough into 2 portions, one a little larger than the other. Roll out larger portion and use to line a 23 cm (9 in) pie plate. Spoon in raisin mixture, mounding it slightly. Roll out remaining dough and cover pie with a lattice top (see Lattice-Top Pies on page 361). Brush with egg white and sprinkle with caster sugar. Bake in a preheated very hot oven (220°C/425°F) for 10 minutes, then reduce heat to moderate (180°C/350°F) and bake 25–30 minutes longer or until top is browned. Serves 6–8.

Brandy Alexander Pie

3 tsp (1 envelope) gelatine; ½ cup cold water;
⅔ cup sugar; ⅛ tsp salt; 3 eggs, separated;
¼ cup brandy; ¼ cup crème de cacao;
2 cups cream, whipped; chocolate curls to decorate (see page 83).

**CRUMB CRUST: 1¼ cups sweet biscuit crumbs (Nice are ideal); ¼ cup sugar;
75 g (2½ oz) butter, melted.**

Soften gelatine in cold water in a saucepan. Add half of the sugar, the salt and egg yolks. Stir to blend. Heat over low heat, stirring, until gelatine dissolves and mixture thickens. Do not boil. Remove from heat and stir in brandy and crème de cacao. Chill until mixture starts to thicken slightly.
CRUMB CRUST: Combine all ingredients and press evenly over bottom and sides of 23 cm (9 in) pie plate. Chill until ready to use. Beat egg whites until stiff. Gradually beat in remaining sugar and fold into the thickened mixture. Fold in half of the whipped cream. Turn into chilled crust and chill for several hours or overnight. Decorate with remaining cream and chocolate curls. Serves 6–8.

PIGEON

A small game bird with a distinctive, almost sweet flavour, which is highlighted by a tangy, sweet-sour sauce. If young and tender, pigeon may be roasted, with a slice of bacon or pork fat or a lump of butter to keep it moist. Alternatively, and especially if it is older, pigeon may be braised or stewed.

Young fledgling pigeons, bred especially for the table, are called squab. They have a more delicate, tender flesh and are better suited to roasting in a very hot oven.

In general, allow one squab or one pigeon per person. If pigeon breasts only are offered, allow 3–4 breasts per person.

PIKELET

The Australian version of an old Scottish scone or 'girdle' cake, which is a popular item on the afternoon tea tray. Pikelets can be served warm or cold with butter and honey or jam, or cold with jam and cream. Pikelets can be reheated briefly in a warm oven or under a slow grill.

Pikelets

1 cup self-raising flour; ½ tsp salt;
2 tbs sugar; 1 egg; 1 cup milk;
30 g (1 oz) butter, melted; fat for frying.

Sift flour and salt into a bowl. Stir in sugar and make a well in centre. Beat egg, add milk and butter and mix well. Pour into well in dry ingredients all at once and stir to make a smooth batter. Drop scant tablespoons of batter on to a hot, greased griddle or shallow frying pan. Cook until golden, then turn and cook other side until golden. Cool, wrapped in a clean tea-towel or napkin. Serve warm with butter or cold with jam and cream. Makes 25–30 x 8 cm (3 in) pikelets.

PILAF, PILAU OR PILAW

See *Rice*.

PIMENTO

See *Allspice*.

PIMIENTO

Skinned sweet red peppers of a small, elongated variety, available canned in oil or brine. They add bright colour and Mediterranean flavour to salads and are invaluable, drained and cut into strips or other shapes, for garnishing.

Potato, Prawn and Pimiento Salad

A salad to serve as part of hors d'oeuvre varies or on an antipasto tray.

3 canned pimientos, drained; 4 medium waxy potatoes, cooked and diced; 3 hard-boiled eggs, cut into wedges; 125 g (4 oz) small shelled deveined prawns; 1 tbs finely chopped onion; salt and freshly ground black pepper; 1/4 cup Vinaigrette Dressing (page 442); 1/3 cup Mayonnaise (page 256).

Cut 2 pimientos into squares and reserve the third. Lightly fold together all ingredients, except reserved pimiento and 8–10 of the prawns. Spoon into a shallow square or oblong dish. Cut reserved pimiento into strips and garnish salad with pimiento strips arranged lattice-fashion, with a prawn in each space. Serves 4–6.

PINEAPPLE

A year-round favourite, doubly welcome in the cold winter months, when its golden sweetness reminds us that sunnier days are not too far away.

Pineapples are grown in tropical and subtropical climates, and with modern agricultural techniques, fresh pineapples are available at any time of the year. There is also the convenience of canned pineapple – in rings or chunks, crushed or as juice.

Fresh pineapple contains an enzyme, bromeline, similar to papain found in pawpaw which acts on protein. For this reason, fresh pineapple can never be used in any preparation containing gelatine, or fresh cream. However, the enzyme is destroyed by heat and is not present in canned pineapple, which is an ideal base for many desserts.

Fresh pineapple is best served simply, at the end of a rich meal or at breakfast. If fully ripe, it will need very little, if any, sugar. A ripe pineapple should be golden, with a rich sweet perfume and firm yet tender flesh. The green plumes should pull out easily.

Fresh or canned pineapple may also be added to a salad. And rings of pineapple, lightly fried in butter, are a good flavour contrast to hot baked ham, ham steaks or grilled pork chops.

■ BASIC PREPARATION: To peel a fresh pineapple, using a sharp stainless steel knife, cut off top and base of pineapple. Hold pineapple firmly with one hand and cut downwards, between eyes, at an angle of 45 degrees. Remove strips of skin between eyes. This method eliminates waste and also gives the pineapple an attractive appearance. See recipes.

Pineapple Buttermilk Sherbet

2 cups buttermilk; 1/2 cup sugar; 1 cup canned crushed pineapple; 1 egg white; 1 1/2 tsp vanilla.

Combine buttermilk, sugar and pineapple. Chill in freezer until mushy. Place in a chilled bowl. Add egg white and vanilla and beat mixture until light and fluffy. Pour into ice cream tray and freeze until firm, stirring occasionally. Serves 4.

Pineapple in Kirsch

Kirsch and pineapple make a classic combination.

1 ripe pineapple, peeled; sugar; 2 tbs Kirsch.

Cut pineapple into quarters lengthways and remove core from each wedge. Cut each wedge into halves or quarters as desired. Arrange on dish, sprinkle with sugar to taste and Kirsch. Chill before serving. Serves 4–6.

VARIATIONS
Other fruits may be added to Pineapple in Kirsch – try strawberries, orange or mandarin segments, fresh grapes, passionfruit, kiwi fruit. Cointreau may be substituted for Kirsch. If warmed and poured over the pineapple just before serving, it may be flamed for presentation.

Pineapple Caribbean

1 small ripe pineapple, peeled; 2 tbs brown sugar; grated rind 1 orange; pinch cinnamon; pinch nutmeg; 1/2 cup orange juice; 30 g (1 oz) butter; 4 tbs rum; cream or ice cream to serve.

Cut pineapple into quarters lengthways and remove core from each wedge. Cut each wedge into slices. Arrange slices in buttered ovenproof dish. Mix brown sugar, orange rind and spices, sprinkle over pineapple then pour over juice, Dot with butter. Bake in preheated hot oven (200°C/400°F) for about 15 minutes. Warm rum, ignite and pour flaming over pineapple at table. Serve with cream or ice cream. Serves 4–6.

VARIATION
A medium can pineapple rings, drained, may be substituted for fresh.

Chafing Dish Pineapple

1 ripe pineapple, peeled, cored and diced; 125 g (4 oz) butter; 1 1/2 tbs brown sugar; 1/3 cup rum; 1 cup cream.

Cook pineapple pieces in butter until golden-brown. Sprinkle with sugar and rum and continue cooking until liquid is absorbed. Add cream, heat through and serve immediately. Serves 4–6.

Pineapple Whip

1 tbs gelatine; 1/4 cup cold water; 1 medium can pineapple chunks; 1 tbs grated orange rind; 1/2 cup plain yogurt; 1 tbs honey.

Soften gelatine in cold water in small saucepan for 5 minutes, then dissolve over gentle heat. Drain juice from pineapple, add enough water to make 1 1/2 cups, then stir in dissolved gelatine. Chill to consistency of unbeaten egg white. Add orange rind, yogurt and honey and beat until thick. Fold in pineapple. Turn into bowl and chill until set. Serves 6–8.

Pineapple Upside-down Cake

Serve this dessert cake hot with ice cream, egg custard or a sweet sauce.

CARAMEL: 75 g (2¹/₂ oz) butter; ¹/₃ cup firmly packed brown sugar.

DECORATION: 3 rings canned pineapple; 6 glacé cherries; 6 walnut halves.

CAKE: 1¹/₂ cups self-raising flour; ¹/₂ tsp salt; 60 g (2 oz) butter; ³/₄ cup caster sugar; 1 egg, well whisked; ¹/₂ cup milk.

CARAMEL: Cream butter with sugar. Spread over bottom and sides of a greased and lined 20 cm (8 in) round cake tin.

DECORATION: Cut through pineapple rings to make 6 thin rings; arrange these on caramel and decorate with cherries and walnuts.

CAKE: Sift flour and salt together 3 times. Cream butter with sugar, then beat in egg until light and fluffy. Stir in sifted flour alternately with milk. Spoon cake mixture carefully on top of the pineapple arrangement in the tin. Bake in preheated moderate oven (180°C/350°F) for 50–60 minutes. Invert on to serving plate immediately cake is removed from oven. Leave for a few minutes then remove tin. Serves 6–8.

PINE NUT

The kernel from the cone of certain types of pine tree, some of which are very common, in Mediterranean counties. Naturally, pine nuts often feature in traditional dishes of this region.

In Italy, pine nuts (called *pignoli*) go into the famous sauce, *Pesto alla Genovese* (see *Pasta Sauces*). In Nice, France, a sweet tart is made with silverbeet, apples, pine nuts and sultanas. Often a decorative pattern of pine nuts will stud Lebanese kibbi, or toasted pine nuts will be used to garnish a rice pilaf or rice salad. Roasted and salted, pine nuts can be substituted for salted almonds.

Although they are more commonly used in savoury dished, pine nuts are also made into macaroon-type biscuits and sweets. **See recipes.**

Pine Nut Sauce for Fish

60 g (2 oz) butter; ¹/₂ cup pine nuts, sliced; 2 tbs lemon juice.

Melt butter over low heat. Add pine nuts and cook gently for 5 minutes or until butter is slightly browned. Add lemon juice and heat. Pour over grilled or pan-fried fish fillets. Makes about ³/₄ cup, sufficient for 4 fillets.

Spinach with Sultanas and Pine Nuts

1 bunch fresh spinach; 2 tbs olive oil; salt and freshly ground black pepper; ¹/₂ cup sultanas; 60 g (2 oz) butter; ³/₄ cup pine nuts.

Remove stalks and rinse spinach leaves. Pat leaves as dry as possible, then slice into fine shreds. Heat oil in large frying pan. Add spinach, salt and pepper and toss over heat until spinach starts to give out juices. Add sultanas and continue cooking over moderate heat until spinach is tender and juices have evaporated, turning and tossing often. In separate pan, heat butter and cook pine nuts until golden. Add to spinach and serve at once. Serves 4.

PIPERADE

This open-faced omelette is a specialty of the Basque country. It is quick to make if the pipérade mixture (onions, peppers, tomatoes) is made ahead. It makes a lovely luncheon dish.

Pipérade

2 tbs oil; 2 onions, finely sliced; 1 red or green pepper, cored, seeded and cut into thin strips; 1 clove garlic, crushed; 2–3 tomatoes, peeled seeded and sliced; salt and freshly ground black pepper; 1 tbs butter; 8 eggs; 2–3 slices cooked ham, cut into strips; 2–3 tbs chopped parsley.

Heat oil in a frying pan and cook onions and pepper gently, covered, until they are tender but not browned. Add garlic and tomatoes, and cook gently about 5 minutes longer. Season with salt and pepper. Remove from pan and keep hot. In the frying pan heat butter. Beat eggs with ¹/₄ tsp salt and pepper and add to pan. Cook rapidly, stirring with a fork, to a creamy mass. Remove from pan and top with vegetable mixture, mixing a bit of it delicately into the eggs. Heat strips of ham in frying pan and strew over pipérade. Sprinkle with parsley. Serves 4.

PIROSHKI (PIROZHKI)

Some say that the Russians were the first to think of the delicious tidbits served with cocktails. We know for a fact that they did invent piroshki, the little pies that now appear in all shapes and sizes all over the world.

Piroshki, made into tiny cocktail sizes, served piping hot from the oven, make wonderful accompaniments to clear chicken or beef soups, with drinks, or may be served all on their own as a first course. Allow at least 3 or 4 for each person, although you may need more.

There are several versions and many varied fillings. piroshki may be made with yeast dough, or shortcrust, cream cheese or choux pastry, and filled with smoked pork and onion, vegetables, cream cheese or fish. Fried piroshki are a great favourite in Europe, and are mostly filled with a meat or cabbage filling. **See recipes.**

Piroshki (*with Cream Cheese Pastry*)

**PASTRY: 125 g (4 oz) cream cheese;
125 g (4 oz) butter; I¹/₂ cups flour;
beaten egg to glaze.**

**FILLING: 60 g (2 oz) butter; I onion, chopped;
2–3 rashers bacon, or 90 g (3 oz) speck,
rind removed and chopped;
salt and freshly ground black pepper.**

PASTRY: Beat cream cheese with butter in a mixing bowl. Add sifted flour and mix to a dough. Wrap in greaseproof paper and chill overnight or for several hours. (If left overnight, allow to stand at room temperature for 1 hour or so before rolling out.)

FILLING: Melt butter in a frying pan and fry onion and bacon or speck until onion is transparent and bacon is crisp. Season with salt and pepper. Roll out pastry dough thinly and cut into 5 cm (2 in) rounds with a pastry cutter. Put 1 teaspoonful of filling on to each round, moisten edges with a little beaten egg and fold dough over to form a crescent shape. Seal edges well. Place on baking trays. Brush with beaten egg and bake in a preheated hot oven (200°C/400°F) for 10 minutes or until golden-brown. Makes about 24.

Piroshki

Piroshki freeze well and once thawed, piroshki just need 20 minutes reheating, wrapped in foil, in a moderate oven before serving.

**30 g (I oz) compressed yeast; 2¹/₂ tbs sugar;
3 cups flour; I¹/₄ cups milk; 125 g (4 oz) butter;
2 tsp salt; I egg yolk, beaten; beaten egg to glaze.**

**FILLING: 3 large onions, finely chopped;
60 g (2 oz) butter; 250 g (8 oz) speck or thick rasher
bacon, rind removed and finely chopped;
freshly ground white pepper.**

Combine yeast with ¹/₂ tbs of sugar in s small bowl. Stir until yeast becomes liquid. Sprinkle with 1 tsp of flour and leave in a warm place. Meanwhile, heat milk, butter, salt and remaining sugar in a saucepan, stirring occasionally until milk is lukewarm. Sift remaining flour into a large mixing bowl. Make a well in centre and pour in milk mixture, yeast mixture and egg yolk. Stir with a wooden spoon, gradually incorporating flour. Beat dough with your hand for 3 minutes until it is smooth and elastic. Sprinkle with a little flour, cover with damp tea-towel and leave dough to rise in a warm place until dough has doubled in bulk – about 1 hour.

FILLING: Fry onions in butter until golden. Allow to cool. Mix the speck or bacon with onion and season with pepper. Turn dough on to a floured work surface and knead lightly. This is a soft dough. Tear off pieces of dough the size of a large tablespoon. Place 1 teaspoon of filling in middle of each piece of dough, fold over to enclose filling and mould dough into little balls.

Place piroshki on lightly greased baking trays and leave to rise in warm place for 15 minutes. Brush with beaten egg and bake in a preheated very hot oven (230°C/450°F) for 10–15 minutes or until golden. Slide on to a clean tea-towel to keep warm. Makes 60 tiny cocktail, or 30 larger, piroshki.

NOTE: If using dry yeast see *Yeast Cookery*.

Fried Piroshki

These dainty fried pastries are made to accompany soups in Russia. They have fillings appropriate to the soup they accompany – tiny bacon cubes, minced fish or meat, mushrooms, hard-boiled eggs, cheese or cabbage. They may be made larger and enjoyed as a large snack or for lunch.

**YEAST DOUGH: 15 g (¹/₂ oz) compressed yeast;
¹/₄ cup lukewarm water; ¹/₂ tsp sugar; ¹/₂ cup milk;
15 g (¹/₂ oz) butter; I tbs sour cream; 2 cups flour;
¹/₂ tsp salt; I egg, beaten; oil for deep-frying.**

**FILLING: I medium onion, finely chopped;
I tbs oil; 250 g (8 oz) minced steak; 250 g (8 oz)
mixed minced pork and veal; 2 hard-boiled eggs,
chopped; 15 g (¹/₂ oz) butter; 2 tbs stock or water;
I tsp salt; freshly ground black pepper.**

Combine compressed yeast, water and sugar in a small bowl. Stir and set aside. Place milk, butter and sour cream in saucepan and heat until just warm, stirring occasionally. Sift flour and salt into a large mixing bowl and make a well in centre. Pour in yeast and milk mixtures and beaten egg. Stir with a wooden spoon, gradually incorporating flour. Remove from bowl and knead lightly on a floured work surface. Place dough back in bowl, sprinkle with a little flour, cover and leave to rise in a warm place for about 1 hour or until doubled in bulk.

FILLING: Cook onion in oil until soft; remove to a bowl. Lightly fry meat until brown and crumbly. Combine with onions, hard-boiled eggs, butter, stock, salt and pepper. Leave to cool. Turn out dough on to a floured work surface and knead lightly. Roll out thinly and cut into rounds with an 8 cm (3 in) cutter. Place 2 teaspoons of filling in centre of each round and fold over to enclose filling and mould into oval shapes. Stand on a baking tray and keep covered with a clean tea-towel. As soon as all the piroshki have been filled and shaped, deep-fry in batches in hot oil until golden-brown. Drain on paper towels. Serve hot. Makes about 30.

NOTE: Piroshki are best served fresh but may be made ahead and reheated in a moderate oven for 10 minutes. If using dry yeast see *Yeast Cookery*.

PISSALADIERE

A wonderful warm, savoury open tart from the south of France. It is often sold in market places where it can be bought, sliced and still hot, with onions, herbs, anchovies and black olives, spread over pastry or bread dough – an irresistable combination that can easily be prepared at home.

Pissaladière Nicoise

1 x 20 cm (8 in) Shortcrust Pastry Flan Case, baked blind (page 342); 6–8 medium onions, sliced; 4 tbs oil; 1 bouquet garni; salt and freshly ground black pepper; 2 cloves garlic, crushed; 12–16 anchovy fillets; 8–10 black olives.

Put flan case on a baking tray. Cook onions gently in 3 tbs oil, with bouquet garni, salt and pepper, for about 45 minutes. The onions should almost melt and become a rich golden colour. Stir in garlic after 20 minutes. Transfer onion mixture to pastry case, discarding bouquet garni, and make a lattice pattern on top with anchovies and olives. Sprinkle remaining oil on top and bake pissaladière in a preheated hot oven (200°C/400°F) for about 15 minutes or until very hot. If pissaladière is to be a lunch or supper dish, serve with a bowl of tossed green salad. Serves 4–6.

NOTE: The pissaladière can be made using Pizza Dough (see pages 371–2) instead of shortcrust pastry if you wish. In this case use a pizza tray and form the dough as for a pizza.

PISTACHIO NUT

Throughout the Middle East you will find street vendors with snacks of salted pistachio nuts. Greek and Lebanese delicatessens in other countries stock them, and often the unsalted nuts as well.

The pistachio needs a hot climate for the small nuts to ripen properly. When ripe, the shell cracks open spontaneously, the nuts are usually salted in the shell. The small, pale green kernels have a unique flavour which is equally appropriate in sweet and savoury dishes. For example, pistachio nuts are often added to a terrine or to pork sausages; tossed in butter to garnish a pilaf. Pistachio ice cream is very popular in France and Italy, and chopped pistachios may be included in the filling for Baklava (see page 20). The favourite confections of the Middle East, halva and Turkish delight, often include pistachios, especially the luxury versions. Chopped or sliced, shelled pistachios add an attractive touch if used to decorate desserts, ices and cakes.

PISTOU

The Provençal name for basil and, by extension, it is also the name of the typical soup of Provence – *Soupe au pistou* – in southern France, in which basil is an essential ingredient. This soup is rather similar to the Italian minestrone, with its combination of vegetables and pasta. The basil enrichment added at the end is not too distant from the sauce *Pesto alla Genovese* (see page 339) – which is not really surprising, given the proximity of Provence and Italy and their respective histories.

Soupe au Pistou

2 large onions, chopped; $^1/_2$–1 cup plus 2 tbs olive oil; 1 cup dried white beans, soaked overnight and drained; 500 g (1 lb) green beans, cut into short lengths; 500 g (1 lb) zucchini, diced; 2 large tomatoes, peeled, seeded and chopped; 3 potatoes, diced; 8 cups water; salt and freshly ground black pepper; 200 g (7 oz) vermicelli; 5 cloves garlic; about 1 cup fresh basil leaves, loosely packed; 5 tbs grated Parmesan cheese; extra grated Parmesan cheese to serve (optional).

Cook onions in 2 tbs oil in a saucepan until soft. Add remaining vegetables and cover with water. Season with salt and pepper. Bring to the boil, then cover and simmer for about 1 hour or until white beans are almost tender. Add vermicelli and continue cooking until soft.

Meanwhile, pound the garlic and basil to a paste in a large mortar or bowl. Slowly add about $^1/_2$ cup remaining oil to obtain a thick but pouring consistency. Taste soup and adjust seasoning. Pour basil mixture into soup, or offer it separately. Pass around a bowl of additional Parmesan if desired. Serves 8–10.

PITA BREAD

The unleavened bread of the Middle East, sometimes called Lebanese bread or pocket bread, because it is flat and hollow inside, like a pocket. Both white and wholemeal varieties are available.

Pita bread is soft, and can be rolled or folded around a filling; cubes of grilled meat, or a couple of Falafel (chick pea croquettes – see page 397), or simply salad with Tahini Sauce (see page 525). In the Middle East, it is always served with dips such as *Hummus bi Tahini* (see page 200) or *Baba Ghannouj* (see page 18), and it can also be folded into a sort of spoon for eating stews or rice.

In today's kitchen, pita bread finds a place as a base for a quick pizza: cover it with thin slices of tomato or a thick tomato purée, add slices of cheese, anchovies, olives and a sprinkling of oregano and pop into a hot oven for 5–10 minutes.

Or for an individual *pissaladière à la minute*: top pita bread with finely sliced onions, cooked until very soft in oil or butter, then a lattice of anchovy fillets and black olives, and cook as for the quick pizza above.

Pita bread is available from delicatessens and supermarkets, and is a very useful standby to have in your freezer.

PITHIVIERS

Gâteau Pithiviers is a much-loved pastry of France, named after the French town of Pithiviers. It becomes the traditional epiphany cake served on Twelfth Night (6th January) in France when it is called Galette des Rois (cake of kings). It was the traditional gift of the baker to his favourite customers, the almond paste sometimes hiding a dried bean or silver trinket, and the cake accompanied by a cardboard cut-out crown. The lucky person who found the bean in his mouth would wear the crown for the day.

It is fairly easy to make with frozen puff pastry sheets being readily available.

Gâteau Pithiviers

2 sheets ready-rolled frozen puff pastry; 1 egg, beaten for glaze; 2 tbs caster sugar.

FILLING: 125 g (4 oz) unsalted butter; $^1/_2$ cup caster sugar; 1 egg and 1 egg yolk; 150 g (5 oz) ground almonds; 1 tbs plain flour; 2 tbs rum.

FILLING: Cream the butter and beat in the sugar until light and fluffy. Beat in the egg and yolk. Stir in the ground almonds, flour and rum.

With a sharp knife and using a cake tin as a guide, cut out a 25 cm (10 in) round from each sheet of pastry. Set one round on a baking tray and mound the filling in the centre, leaving a 25 mm (1 in) border. Brush the border with some of the egg glaze. Lay the remaining round on top and press the edges together firmly. Scallop the edge of the gâteau by pulling it in at regular intervals with the back of a knife. Chill until ready to bake, as this is delicious served warm. Brush with egg glaze and, working from the centre, score the top in curves like the petals of a flower without cutting through to the filling. Cut a hole in the centre to allow steam to escape.

Bake in a preheated (220°C/425°F) oven for 20 minutes, reduce the heat to (180°C/350°F) and bake a further 10 minutes. Sprinkle with the extra caster sugar and return to the oven for a further 5–10 minutes to give pastry a crisp, caramelised glaze. Serve warm with coffee or with whipped cream as a dessert. Serves 8.

PIZZA

Probably no other food has had such a quick rise to fame as the pizza. From Italy, it has spread to almost every country in the world. Its power to please lies in the aroma of the fresh baked yeast crust, the savoury topping, and its versatility as a snack, first course, or meal in itself.

The word 'pizza' in Italian actually means any kind of cake or pie, but the pizza most familiar is the *Pizza alla Napoletana*, a dish typical of Naples. It consists of a layer of dough, rolled or patted to a preferred thickness, and is beautiful to look at topped with a wonderful fresh tomato sauce or sliced tomatoes, black olives, anchovies, mozzarella cheese and sometimes a sprinkling of oregano leaves. Today, round pizza ovens, with their glowing coals, are to be found at work from the narrow alleyways among the washing of Naples to all over the south and into the north of Italy as well. Indeed, pizza shops are all over the world.

Pizza is traditionally cooked in a round pan, in a hot oven until the edges are brown and crisp and the cheese bubbly and golden. It is cut into wedges to serve, and eaten with the fingers. For parties bake pizza in a rectangular or square tin, which makes it easier to cut into serving-sized portions.

There are countless varieties of pizza, ranging from the simplest – just a crust, tomato sauce and mozzarella cheese – to the elaborate Four Seasons Pizza, each section representing a season of the year. Washed down with a goodly quantity of light wine, pizza makes a delicious and substantial meal prepared before your very eyes. **See recipes.**

Pizza Dough (1)

If you like a high, fluffy, bread-like crust, use this dough to make 1 x 30 cm (12 in) pizza. For a thinner, crisper crust, divide dough roll or pat out into 2 x 30 cm (12 in) rounds.

30 g (1 oz) compressed yeast, or 1 sachet (1$^1/_2$ tsp) active dried yeast; 1 cup lukewarm water; $^1/_2$ tsp sugar; 3 tbs olive oil; 3 cups flour; 1$^1/_2$ tsp salt; freshly ground white pepper.

Combine compressed yeast, water and sugar in a large bowl. (If using dried yeast see *Yeast Cookery*.) Set aside for about 15 minutes or until surface is foamy. Stir in olive oil. Sift flour and salt over yeast mixture, season with pepper and blend with a wooden spoon. Turn dough on to a lightly floured work surface and knead gently until smooth and elastic. Place dough in a large, greased bowl, turn dough to grease it all over. Cover with a tea-towel and leave in a warm place for 2 hours, or until doubled in bulk, light and spongy. Turn out on to a lightly floured work surface, knock down and knead 4–5 times. Roll out to a 30 cm (12 in) round about 1 cm ($^1/_2$ in) thick, or divide dough in half and roll out into 2 rounds 5 mm (¼ in) thick. Place on a greased baking tray, cover and leave to rise in a warm place for about 15 minutes before adding toppings. Makes 1–2 pizza crusts.

NOTE: After the first rising, pizza dough can be wrapped in plastic wrap and refrigerated overnight. The next day, simply knock down, knead lightly, roll out, and allow to rise for 15 minutes before filling and baking.

Pizza Dough (2)

This recipe makes a dough that can be successfully reheated. You can make the pizzas beforehand and reheat them in a slow oven for 7–10 minutes before serving, or freeze them until required. The quantity is enough for 12 individual pizzas, about 12 cm (5 in) diameter, or 1 large rectangular pizza about 35 x 30 cm (14 x 12 in).

4 cups flour; 2 tsp salt; ¹/₂ cup lukewarm milk; 30 g (10 oz) compressed yeast, or 1 sachet (1¹/₂ tsp) active dried yeast; 1 egg; 2–4 tbs olive oil.

Sift flour and salt into a large, warmed bowl. Combine a little of milk and compressed yeast and stir until smooth. (If using dried yeast, see *Yeast Cookery*.) Make a well in centre of flour and pour in yeast mixture, remaining milk, egg and 2 tbs olive oil. Stir with a wooden spoon to form a dough, adding more olive oil if required until dough can be shaped into a ball which comes away cleanly from sides of bowl. Cover with a tea-towel and leave to rise in a warm place for about 2 hours or until doubled in bulk and spongy. Knock dough down, knead 4–5 times and pat out in a greased rectangular baking tray, or shape into 12 individual round pizzas and arrange on greased baking trays. Allow dough to rise in a warm place for 15 minutes before adding toppings. Makes 1 large or 12 small pizza crusts.

Pizza Sauce

This rich, flavourful tomato sauce is used as a base for many pizzas. It is spread over the bread dough before other toppings are added. Instead of fresh tomatoes, drained canned whole tomatoes may be used.

750 g (1¹/₂ lb) ripe tomatoes, peeled and chopped; 2 cloves garlic, crushed; 1 tsp dried oregano; 1 tbs chopped fresh basil, or 1 tsp dried; 1 bay leaf; 1 tbs brown sugar; salt and freshly ground black pepper.

Place all ingredients in a saucepan and simmer gently for 30–40 minutes, stirring often. Taste for seasoning, remove bay leaf and cool before using. Makes sufficient for two 30 cm (12 in) rounds, or two 35 x 30 cm (14 x 12 in) rectangles.

Four Seasons Pizza

A choice of four toppings makes this pizza especially colourful and interesting.

¹/₂ quantity Pizza Dough (1), patted out to a 30 cm (12 in) round (page 371); 1 quantity Pizza Sauce (above).

TOPPING 1: 2 slices cooked ham, cut into strips; 4 medium mushrooms, thinly sliced; salt and freshly ground black pepper.

TOPPING 2: 4 anchovy fillets, halved; 2 tbs diced mozzarella cheese; 2 tsp drained capers.

TOPPING 3: 4–5 slices salami, cut into strips; 8 black olives, stoned.

TOPPING 4: 6 prawns, shelled and deveined, or ¹/₄ cup flaked tuna or 1 x 125 g can mussels, drained; 4 thin slices mozzarella cheese.

TO FINISH: 2 tbs olive oil; ¹/₄ cup grated Parmesan cheese.

Spread cooled sauce over dough and add toppings, a different one for each quarter. Sprinkle olive oil and cheese over whole pizza and bake in a preheated hot oven (200°C/400°F) for 18–20 minutes or until crust is golden and crisp around edges. Serves 6–8.

Salami Pizza

double quantity Pizza Dough (2), patted out to two 35 x 30 cm (14 x 12 in) rectangles or two 30 cm (12 in) rounds (opposite); 4 tbs olive oil; ¹/₂ cup grated Parmesan cheese; 1 quantity Pizza Sauce (opposite); 1 x 50 g can flat anchovy fillets; 125 g (4 oz) Italian salami, cut into strips; 12 black olives, stoned and quartered.

Brush pizza dough with half of the olive oil and sprinkle with half of the Parmesan cheese. Spoon sauce over each, then add anchovy fillets, salami and black olives. Sprinkle with remaining oil and cheese. Bake pizzas in a preheated hot oven (200°C/400°F) for 18–20 minutes or until crust is golden and cooked. Serves 12.

VARIATION

NEAPOLITAN PIZZA: Make as for Salami Pizza but replace salami with slices of mozzarella cheese, and omit Parmesan cheese. Olives are optional.

Ham and Mushroom Pizza

double quantity Pizza Dough (2), patted out to two 35 x 30 cm (14 x 12 in) rectangles or two 30 cm (12 in) rounds (opposite); 4 tbs olive oil; ¹/₂ cup grated Parmesan cheese; 1 quantity Pizza Sauce (opposite); 250 g (8 oz) cooked ham, cut into strips; 6–8 mushrooms, finely sliced; salt and freshly ground black pepper.

Brush pizza dough with half olive oil and sprinkle with half of the Parmesan cheese. Spoon sauce over each pizza and then add ham and mushrooms, seasoning with salt and pepper. Sprinkle remaining olive oil and Parmesan cheese over and bake in a preheated hot oven (200°C/400°F) for 18–20 minutes or until crust is golden and cooked. Serves 12.

VARIATION

PIZZA MARGHERITA: Make as for Ham and Mushroom Pizza, substituting 2 cups diced mozzarella cheese and 12 leaves fresh basil, finely chopped, for the ham and mushrooms.

PLUM

A round, stone fruit that comes in an abundance of colours, shapes and sizes throughout summer and the early part of autumn. There are large, red-skinned, yellow-fleshed varieties around; deep crimson blood plums; small, oval, purplish angelinas; large prune plums and sweet greengage plums.

Some varieties of plum are best eaten raw, or combined with other stone fruits, sprinkled with caster sugar and lemon juice and a little brandy and chilled. Others are equally good cooked, or made into a fruit tart; choose the least juicy varieties for a tart.

Spiced pickled plums make a good accompaniment to cold meats, or to a simple meat loaf. **See recipes.**

Plums in Port

12 plums; 3 cups water; 1 cup sugar; ²/₃ cup port.

TO SERVE: Crème Fraîche (page 102) or ice cream and crisp biscuits.

Wash plums. Place water and sugar in a saucepan and bring slowly to the boil, stirring until sugar dissolves. Boil, without stirring, for 5 minutes. Add port and plums and poach gently for about 5 minutes or until plums are tender. Remove plums and set aside. Boil the syrup until it is reduced by about one third, then pour over the plums. Chill. Serve in a glass bowl with Crème Fraîche or ice cream, and a crisp biscuit. Serves 4.

Oven–Baked Plums

1 kg (2 lb) plums; 3/4 cup sugar; 1/4 cup water.

Make shallow cut around each plum, then arrange in an ovenproof dish. Sprinkle with sugar and water, cook in a preheated slow oven (150°C/300°F) for 20–25 minutes or until soft. Serve warm. Serves 6.

VARIATIONS
Use brown or vanilla sugar in place of ordinary crystal sugar, or substitute 2 tbs each port and water for water.

Peach and Plum Compote

1 cup sugar; 1 cup water; thinly peeled rind 1 orange, cut into fine strips; 1 tbs lemon juice; about 2 tbs Cointreau; 4 large ripe peaches, peeled; 4 large ripe plums, peeled.

Dissolve sugar in water in a saucepan over low heat. Bring to the boil, then add orange rind strips and boil 5 minutes. Cool. Add lemon juice and Cointreau to cooled syrup. Place whole fruit in serving bowl and pour over syrup. Cover and chill before serving. Serves 4.

Pickled Plums

An unusual accompaniment to cold meats, especially ham or pork.

1¹/₂ cups sugar; 1¹/₂ cups wine vinegar; 1 small cinnamon stick; 1 tbs whole cloves; 1 kg (2 lb) plums.

Dissolve sugar in vinegar in a large saucepan over low heat. Bring to the boil and boil for 2–3 minutes, then add cinnamon and cloves. Prick plums in several places with a fine skewer and add to syrup. Bring to the boil again, skimming off any scum. Lift out plums and place in a bowl. Boil syrup 3–4 minutes, then pour over plums. Leave in a cold place 24 hours. Drain off syrup into a saucepan and bring to the boil. Add plums, return to the boil, then lift out plums. Boil syrup 2 minutes longer and pour over plums. Cool. Place in sterilised jars and seal. Leave in a cool dark place for 6 weeks before using.

PLUM PUDDING

See *Christmas Pudding.*

POLENTA

A yellow maize or cornmeal grown in northern Italy, where it is regarded as one of the staple foods. Polenta is used in many different ways after it has first been prepared as a rather thick porridge. Polenta is graded according to its texture and can be fine, medium or coarse ground. It is available from most supermarkets, delicatessens and health food stores.

Plain boiled polenta can be grilled, baked or fried and served with a meat or tomato sauce, or simply with butter and grated cheese. It can be made into gnocchi (see pages 179–80), served in a ring with a chicken liver filling, or with chicken and mushrooms in a casserole. **See recipes.**

Basic Polenta

6 cups water; 2 tsp salt; 250 g (8 oz) finely ground polenta; freshly ground black pepper.

Bring water and salt to the boil in a saucepan over medium heat. Slowly pour in polenta, stirring constantly with a wooden spoon until a smooth mixture forms. Lower heat and simmer, stirring frequently, for 20–25 minutes or until polenta comes away cleanly from sides of pan. Season to taste with pepper. Serves 4.

VARIATION
THICK POLENTA: If a thicket polenta is needed, continue cooking over a low heat for about 50 minutes or until it reaches the required thickness.

Polenta in Tomato Sauce

1 quantity Basic Polenta (above); 1 cup Tomato Sauce (page 340); grated Parmesan cheese.

Turn warm polenta into a greased baking dish. Spread out evenly. When cool, cut into 5 cm (2 in) squares. Place squares in a lightly greased, shallow ovenproof dish, spoon over tomato sauce and sprinkle generously with grated Parmesan cheese. Bake in a preheated moderately hot oven (190°C/375°F) for 30–40 minutes or until golden-brown. Serve hot, with extra grated Parmesan cheese. Serves 4.

Polenta with Chicken Livers

1 quantity Basic Polenta (page 373); 3 rashers bacon, rind removed and diced; 30 g (1 oz) butter; 500 g (1 lb) chicken livers; 250 g (8 oz) mushrooms, sliced; salt and freshly ground black pepper; 3 leaves fresh sage; 1/4 cup dry white wine; finely chopped parsley.

Turn warm polenta into a greased 18 cm (7 in) cake tin and keep warm in a larger pan of hot water while preparing filling. Fry bacon in a frying pan until crisp. Add butter, chicken livers and mushrooms and sauté over medium heat about 2 minutes or until chicken livers are just brown. Season with salt and pepper, add sage and wine. When wine starts to boil, turn down heat and cook for 2–3 minutes. Remove sage leaves. Ease polenta away from edges of tin and turn carefully on to a serving plate. Serve wedges with mixture and sprinkle with parsley. Serves 6–8.

Polenta Casserole

1 quantity thick Basic Polenta (page 373); 500 g (1 lb) mushrooms, sliced; 30 g (1 oz) butter; 3 cups diced cooked chicken; 1 cup Tomato Sauce (page 340); 1/2 cup grated Parmesan cheese.

Serve warm polenta in a buttered casserole dish. Sauté mushrooms in butter for 3 minutes and scatter over polenta with the chicken. Coat with sauce and sprinkle with Parmesan cheese. Bake in a preheated moderate oven (180°C/350°F) for 45 minutes. Serves 6.

POMEGRANATE

A late summer fruit, about the size of an apple. Its thick, reddish-golden skin contains a mass of tiny seeds, each enclosed in a capsule of deep pink jelly.

A pomegranate may be halved and squeezed like an orange; its juice is very refreshing and thirst-quenching, and forms the basis for Grenadine syrup. The fleshy seeds may be eaten with a teaspoon, after all the skin and membrane of the pomegranate has been removed. In mediaeval times, pomegranate seeds were used to decorate a dish of fish, poultry and salads and still are today.

POPCORN

A perennial children's favourite for snacks and for birthday parties. It is a special type of dried corn, and may be bought ready-popped, either plain, toffee-coated or candy-coated. Popping your own corn, though, is very

simple and much more fun. Automatic popcorn poppers are available, but an ordinary frying pan with a lid, or an electric frypan, will do the same job.

TO POP CORN: Heat 1–2 tbs oil in the pan, just enough to film the base, and add enough popcorn to cover half the base of the pan in one layer. Shake over high heat until popping starts, then cover with lid. Shake pan from time to time as long as popping continues (if you remove the lid you will have popcorn all over the room!). When all corn has popped, toss with melted butter and sprinkle lightly with salt.

POPOVER

First cousin to the Yorkshire pudding, popovers are made with the same basic ingredients, in slightly different proportions, and baked in the same way.

Popovers may be sweet or savoury. They may be eaten with butter and sugar, with honey, jam or golden syrup, or they may be split open and filled with a savoury meat, chicken or vegetable mixture. But no matter how they are eaten, they should be served as soon as they come out of the oven, nicely puffed and crisp.

Popovers

1 cup flour; pinch salt; 2 eggs, beaten with 1 cup milk; 1 tbs oil or melted butter.

Sift flour and salt into a bowl. Make well in centre and pour in egg mixture. Add oil or melted butter and mix until batter is smooth, then beat well until surface is covered with bubbles. Allow to stand in a cool place for 1 hour. Grease deep patty pan tins or custard cups well and half fill with batter. Bake in a preheated hot oven (220°C/425°F) for about 40 minutes or until puffed and golden. Serve at once. Makes 8–10.

POPPY SEED

The tiny seed of a poppy plant, used a lot in European and Asian cooking. Although the plant belongs to the same family as the opium poppy, it is non-narcotic but does have some medicinal value – an infusion is said to relieve the pain of toothache.

Poppy seeds are often sprinkled on bread, rolls and savoury biscuits before baking, and baking enhances their nutty flavour. In central European countries, such as Austria and Hungary, poppy seeds are combined with sugar and raisins, peel or spice to make a strudel filling. For cakes, they may either be cooked in milk until soft or ground into a sort of flour.

The best poppy seeds are said to come from Holland, and are slate-blue in colour. In some countries, poppy seeds are crushed for their oil (they contain about 50% oil), which may be used as salad oil. **See recipes.**

Poppy Seed Noodles

noodles, cooked; butter; 1–2 tbs poppy seeds.

Drain noodles and return to pan. Add butter and poppy seeds and toss well. Serve with goulash, casseroles of meat or poultry.

Poppy Seed Cake

An unusual but delicious cake. Serve as a dessert or as a tea-time treat.

**1¹/₂ cups poppy seeds; 6 eggs, separated;
1 cup sugar; ¹/₂ cup chopped mixed candied peel;
1 tsp ground allspice; whipped cream.**

Grind poppy seeds in blender. Beat egg yolks until thick, then gradually add sugar and continue beating until very thick and pale. Stir in peel, allspice and poppy seeds. Beat egg whites until stiff and fold into yolk mixture. Pour mixture into a greased and floured 23 cm (9 in) springform tin. Bake in a preheated moderate oven (180°C/350°F) for about 50 minutes. Allow cake to cool in tin, then remove sides. Spread top with whipped cream before serving.

PORK

Pork sold in butchers' shops is from young animals and is a tender meat. Good pork should have pale pink, fine-grained flesh, pearly white fat and thin, smooth skin.

It used to be considered essential to cook pork thoroughly but modern commercial methods of feeding and raising pigs have made this unnecessary. Small cuts, grilled and fried, are more succulent if not cooked too well-done; however, most people still enjoy a larger cut best if it is served traditionally well-cooked.

Please read *Meat* for amount to buy, factors determining tenderness, testing meat for doneness, carving etc. See recipes.

ROAST PORK

■ **CHOICE CUTS FOR ROASTING:**

Leg: A very large roast if left whole, but many butchers sell half legs. The shank end is easier to cook evenly and to carve if it is boned and tied.

Loin: Can be bone-in or boned and tied. A full loin serves 8–10, but can be cut in two to make smaller roasts.

Rib on the Bone: Consists of 6–8 rib chops in a piece.

Crown Roast: Made from two sets of ribs bent round and tied together to make a circle with the meat inside and the bones outside. The skin and excess fat are removed before tying.

Fillet: A small, skinless and very tender piece of meat which is usually baked *en croûte* (pastry-wrapped), rather than truly roasted.

Suckling Pig: A whole very young pig, still being milk-fed, hence its name. An impressive party dish.

■ **ECONOMICAL CUTS FOR ROASTING:**

Shoulder: Can be bone-in or boned, rolled and tied. It may be stuffed before being tied.

Hand: Easier to cook evenly and to carve if it is boned and tied.

Foreloin or Cushion.

Belly or Spring: Used as the outer wrapping for a pork and veal-stuffed rolled roast. Belly is a flat and rather fatty cut which gives lots of crackling but has only a thin layer or two of lean meat. It can be slit through the centre and filled with a meaty stuffing for an economical roast.

■ **TO ROAST:** Choice and economical cuts which still have the skin on may be roasted in the same way. Have skin scored by the butcher or score it yourself with a sharp knife, cutting about 3 mm (⅛ in) deep at 1 cm (½ in) intervals. Tie meat into a compact shape if necessary, so that it will cook evenly, and weigh it. Sprinkle skin with cooking salt and rub well in (this makes the crackling crisp). Place pork, skin side up, on a rack in a roasting tin. Roast in a preheated very hot oven (260°C/500°F) until the skin starts to bubble and crisp (about 20–30 minutes), then lower heat to moderate (180°C/350°F) for remainder of cooking time. Do not baste pork or cover dish, or the crackling will lose its crispness. Allow a total roasting time of approximately 30 minutes per 500 g (1 lb), plus an extra 30 minutes. To test for doneness, see *Meat*. Rest for 15–30 minutes in turned-off oven, with door ajar, or other warm place, before carving.

For pork roasts, which have had the skin removed, follow instructions above but omit initial searing to crisp skin. Instead, place pork fatty side up in a preheated hot oven (220°C/425°F) for 10 minutes, then turn down heat to moderate (180°C/350°F) and continue cooking, allowing about 35 minutes per 500 g (1 lb), plus an extra 35 minutes.

CROWN ROAST: Cook in the same manner as other skinless roasts, but allow about 25 minutes per 500 g (1 lb). Stand crown roast directly in the pan, and protect tops of bones with foil to prevent charring.

GRILLED PORK

It is best to have pork chops and steaks cut 2–2.5 cm (¾–1 in) thick for grilling.

■ **CHOICE CUTS FOR GRILLING:**

Pork Loin Chops or the 'New-style' Cuts: From the loin and chump (rump) area: Medallions, Butterfly steaks, Porkacue steaks.

■ **ECONOMICAL CUTS FOR GRILLING:**

Leg Chops and Chump Chops: These are inclined to be dry, so need to be marinated before grilling or basted very frequently during grilling.

Spareribs: Delicious barbecued; these are usually pre-baked or simmered to melt away excess fat, and are often marinated and always basted with spicy sauce.

■ **TO GRILL:** Have meat at room temperature. Use a sharp knife to cut through the skin and fat around the edge at 1 cm (½ in) intervals to prevent buckling. Season with freshly ground black pepper and brush with oil or melted butter. Place on a greased grill rack under a preheated moderate grill or over coals. Brush every 2–3 minutes with more oil or melted butter to keep meat moist, and turn 2–3 times. Allow 12–16 minutes, depending on cut and thickness. To test for doneness, see *Meat*.

PAN-FRIED PORK

This method is suitable for slices of fillet, chops or steaks (any cut) and for the small 'new–style' cuts such as medallions or pork schnitzel cut from the leg. Prepare meat as for grilling. Use a thick, heavy pan; heat on high heat for a few minutes, add just enough oil, or butter and oil, to coat the base and when it gives off a slight haze, put in the meat. Cook 30 seconds–1 minute on each side until browned, then lower heat to moderate and continue to cook, turning once, until done as desired. To test for doneness, see *Meat*.

If meat is coated with breadcrumbs, cook as described but use a little more fat, enough to come halfway up the pieces.

A pan sauce, such as those given below, can be made after the meat is removed.

PAN SAUCES FOR PORK

These quantities are enough for 4 large chops or 6–8 small medallions.

Juniper and Herb Sauce: Dust pork with flour and pan-fry in butter and oil. Remove meat and keep warm for a few minutes. Pour all but 1 tbs fat from the pan and add ⅓ cup dry white wine, ⅓ cup beef stock, 3 crushed juniper berries and 1 tsp chopped fresh thyme, or ¼ tsp dried thyme. Boil 3 minutes, stirring and scraping up brown bits from pan. Season and pour over pork.

Cider and Cream Sauce: Pan-fry pork in a little oil, remove it from pan and keep warm for a few minutes. Pour off fat from pan, add 1 tbs butter and melt it. Add 2 tbs finely chopped shallot and cook gently 2 minutes. Add ⅓ cup cider and boil, stirring and scraping up brown bits from pan, 2–3 minutes. Stir in ¼ cup cream, simmer a minute or two longer, season and pour over pork.

Piquant Caper Sauce: (for crumbed pork or schnitzel) Coat pork with flour, egg and fresh or dried breadcrumbs, and pan-fry in butter and oil. Remove it from pan and keep warm. Add a little extra butter to pan, if necessary, to make about 2 tbs. Add 1 onion, chopped, and cook gently a few minutes until softened. Add 3 canned anchovy fillets, finely chopped, ½ cup brown stock and 1 tbs wine vinegar. Boil, stirring and scraping up brown bits from pan, for about 3 minutes. Season, remove from heat and swirl in a knob of butter. Pour over pork and serve immediately.

Braised or Casseroled Pork: Cuts for braising or casseroling include chops and steaks (any cut) and also diced meat from belly or forequarter.

Pork and Sauerkraut Goulash

Sauerkraut is a good foil for the richness of pork – this is an old Hungarian recipe.

60 g (2 oz) butter; 1 tbs oil; 4 onions, finely sliced; 1 kg (2 lb) boneless pork shoulder, cut into 2.5 cm (1 in) cubes; 2 tbs paprika; 1 tbs tomato paste; 1 cup water; salt; 1 x 440 g can sauerkraut, drained; 1 tsp caraway seeds; 1 tbs flour; ½ cup sour light cream.

Melt butter and oil in a large flameproof casserole and cook onions until golden. Stir in pork and paprika and sauté for 5 minutes. Stir in tomato paste and water and bring to the boil, stirring constantly. Season with salt, cover and simmer for 30 minutes. Place sauerkraut in a colander and rinse well under cold running water. Drain. Add to casserole with caraway seeds and enough water just to cover. Simmer, covered, for 45 minutes or until pork is just tender. Combine flour with a little sour cream and stir into goulash. Simmer, stirring constantly, for 10 minutes, then add remaining sour cream and heat through. Adjust seasoning to taste. Serves 4–6.

Mediterranean–Style Pork Chops

30 g (1 oz) butter; 1 tbs oil; 4 pork chops; salt and freshly ground black pepper; 375 g (¾ lb) mushrooms, sliced; 2 large green or red peppers, cored, seeded and chopped; 375 g (¾ lb) tomatoes, skinned and sliced; 1 tbs chopped fresh basil; 1 tsp sugar; 1 cup chicken stock.

Melt butter and oil and fry chops quickly until browned on both sides; season and remove from pan. Fry mushrooms and peppers until soft. Add tomatoes, basil, sugar and stock. Boil for 3 minutes then return chops to pan and simmer, uncovered, for about 30 minutes. The sauce should be thick. Arrange chops on a heated dish with sauce and garnish with lemon wedges. Serves 4.

Pork Chops Lyonnais

Onions are a feature of Lyonnais cooking, typified by this hearty dish which should be served with lots of mashed potato to absorb the flavoursome juices.

8 pork chops; salt and freshly ground black pepper; 1 kg (2 lb) onions, finely chopped; 3 tbs cider vinegar; 3 tbs dry white wine; 1 sprig fresh thyme, or pinch dried.

Trim any excess fat from chops, season them with a little salt and pepper and set aside. Melt a little pork fat in heavy pan and cook onions gently until starting to turn brown. Remove from pan and keep warm. Melt a little more pork fat if necessary and cook chops about 20 minutes, turning once. Remove to heated serving platter and keep warm. Add vinegar and wine to pan and bring to the boil, scraping up any bits stuck to bottom. Reduce liquid by half, then stir in onions and season with salt, pepper and thyme. Cook, stirring, for 3–4 minutes, then pour around chops. Remove fresh thyme if using. Serve with creamy mashed potatoes. Serves 6.

Spiced Pork Chops with Apple Slices

4 pork loin chops, cut about 2 cm (³⁄4 in) thick; salt and freshly ground black pepper; I tbs oil; 2 cloves garlic, crushed; I tbs Worcestershire sauce; ¹⁄2 tsp dry mustard; 60 g (2 oz) butter; 4 apples, cored and thickly sliced.

Use a sharp knife to cut through fat around chops at 2 cm (¾ in) intervals (this is to prevent chops curling during grilling). Season with salt and pepper. Combine oil, garlic, Worcestershire sauce and mustard and spread over chops. Melt half the butter. Grill chops as described in introduction, brushing every 2 minutes with melted butter. Meanwhile, fry apple slices gently in remaining butter until golden-brown on both sides. Serve with chops. Serves 4.

Spareribs in Plum Sauce

8–10 meaty pork spareribs; fluffy boiled rice to serve.

MARINADE: 2 tbs sherry; I tbs light soy sauce; I tbs hoisin sauce; I clove garlic, crushed; 2 tsp finely grated fresh ginger.

SAUCE: I x 425 g can purple plums; I tsp chilli sauce; ¹⁄2 cup water; I tbs cornflour; ¹⁄4 cup malt vinegar.

Blanch spareribs in boiling water for 2 minutes, then drain and pat dry with paper towels. Place spareribs in a flat dish.

MARINADE: Combine ingredients, spoon over spareribs and stand 2 hours, turning often, or cover and refrigerate overnight.

SAUCE: Drain plums and measure ¾ cup syrup into a saucepan. Blend in remaining ingredients. Stone plums, then purée and add to sauce. Bring to the boil, stirring, until thickened. Simmer 5 minutes. Drain spareribs, reserving marinade. Cook spareribs under a preheated hot grill, on a barbecue or on a rack in a preheated moderate oven (180°C/350°F), for 25–40 minutes, turning during the cooking. Add any marinade to plum sauce, then pour over spareribs and serve with fluffy boiled rice with a tossed salad. Serves 4–6.

Finnish Karelian Pot

This old Finnish dish is so popular it is sold in cans in Finland. The recipe couldn't be simpler, but the combination of meats and the long, slow cooking gives a unique flavour. In Finland, it would be served with boiled potatoes and tart-sweet lingonberries or cranberries, both available in cans from delicatessens.

500 g (I lb) lean, boneless pork; 500 g (I lb) lean, boneless beef; 500 g (I lb) lean, boneless lamb; I tbs coarse salt (sea salt); I tsp black peppercorns; 3–4 juniper berries (optional); I cup water.

Cut meat into bite-sized cubes and combine. Arrange in layers in a deep, round casserole, sprinkling each layer with a little salt. Add peppercorns, juniper berries and water and cover very tightly. (This amount of water seems small, but juices will come from meat.) Bake in a preheated slow oven (150°C/300°F) for 4 hours, or in a slow cooker set on low for 6–8 hours. Adjust seasoning, and serve from the pot. Serves 6–8.

Pork Chops with Green Peppercorns

4 pork butterfly chops, loin chops or steaks; salt and freshly ground black pepper; I tbs oil; 2 tsp green peppercorns; I tbs French mustard; ¹⁄2–²⁄3 cup cream; watercress or parsley to garnish.

Season pork with salt and pepper. Heat oil in a large frying pan and fry pork 4–5 minutes on each side. Remove to a heated platter and keep warm. Pour off all but 1 tbs fat from pan. Add peppercorns and fry for a few seconds, then add mustard and cream. Shake pan or stir with rounded side of a spoon to pick up brown bits on bottom of pan. Continue to cook until sauce thickens. Spoon sauce over pork and garnish with watercress or parsley. Serve with creamy, mashed potatoes or ribbon noodles and a green salad. Serves 4.

NOTE: Many people may be allergic to pink peppercorns so use with caution.

Pork Schnitzels with Lemon

Pork schnitzels look like and can be treated in the same way as veal schnitzels. This is an Italian way of treating tender, thin steaks.

6–8 pork schnitzels; juice I lemon; salt and freshly ground black pepper; flour; 30 g (I oz) butter; 3 tbs oil.

TO FINISH: 2 tsp butter; 6–8 slices lemon.

Season each schnitzel with lemon juice, salt and pepper and let meat stand for 30 minutes. Dry and dust lightly with flour. Heat half the butter and oil in a large frying pan and sauté half the steaks about

3 minutes on each side. Remove to a plate and keep warm. Fry remaining schnitzels, using remaining butter and oil. It is important not to crowd the pan or the meat steams.

TO FINISH: Heat butter in pan and lightly sauté lemon slices. Top schnitzels with lemon, serve with mashed or sautéed potatoes and a salad. Serves 4–6.

Pickled (Salt) Pork

This is a useful cold meat to have on hand for summer eating. Slices of the pork are good mixed with shredded lettuce as a sandwich filling, or diced and added to omelettes. Thin slices top rye bread with a dill pickle and a spot of mustard for open sandwiches. Smear slices with mustard, toss in breadcrumbs and pan-fry or grill for a hot dish. Cubes of pickled (salt) pork can be added to rice or potato salad, and of course it is delicious simply served as part of a cold meat platter.

1 x 1.5 kg (3 lb) pickled belly pork or hand of pork; 2 carrots, sliced; 1 onion, sliced; 6 black peppercorns; 2 cloves; 2–3 stalks parsley; 3 tbs wine vinegar.

Soak pork in cold water for 3–4 hours. Drain, put in a saucepan with fresh cold water to cover and add remaining ingredients. Bring to simmering point, skimming off the scum, then cover pan and simmer gently for 1½–2 hours or until very tender. Drain pork, cool slightly and slip out bones. Place in a flat dish, cover with plastic wrap and press with a weight until cold. Chill, then remove to a fresh plate or cover with fresh wrap. Serve in thin slices with hot English mustard and vinegar, or use in any of the ways suggested above. Serves 6.
NOTE: If using a hand of pork, there is no need to press it.

Pork Cheese

For this excellent old-fashioned cold meat dish, fresh or pickled (salt) pork is cooked slowly until it falls from the bone and is pressed in its own savoury juices which form a jelly.

1 fresh or pickled (salt) hand of pork; salt and freshly ground black pepper; 4 leaves fresh sage, finely chopped.

If using pickled (salt) pork, soak in water to cover overnight. Drain. Place in a heavy pan with enough fresh water just to cover. Cover and cook over low heat for 4 hours. Drain, reserving liquid, and discard bones. Place meat, including skin, in a bowl and season with salt, if needed, and pepper. Sprinkle sage over pork. Strain a little cooking liquid on to meat in bowl and leave to cool, pressed down with a weight. Chill until set. Turn out and serve with a green salad. Serves 6.

Spareribs with Spiced Barbecue Sauce

Meaty spareribs are lightly simmered, marinated overnight in a sweet and spicy sauce, then grilled until brown and crisp.

2 kg (4 lb) meaty pork spareribs; fresh coriander or shredded spring onion tops to garnish; boiled rice to serve.

BARBECUE SAUCE: ¹/₂ cup tomato paste; ¹/₂ cup olive oil; ¹/₄ cup red wine vinegar; **1 x 2.5 cm (1 in) piece fresh ginger, chopped; 2 tbs turmeric; 2 tbs hoisin sauce; 4 cloves garlic, chopped; 1 tsp hot chilli sauce, or ¹/₄ tsp Tabasco sauce; salt and freshly ground black pepper.**

Place spareribs in a large saucepan, cover with water and bring to the boil. Reduce heat and simmer 20 minutes. Drain. Make barbecue sauce by whirling all ingredients in a food processor fitted with a steel blade or in a blender about 30 seconds or until well combined, then transfer to a large bowl. Add spareribs, covering them well with sauce, cover bowl and chill overnight. Drain spareribs and place on an oiled rack under a preheated grill or over hot coals. Grill, turning once, for 15 minutes or until browned and crisp. Arrange spareribs on a heated platter. If liked strew fresh coriander or shredded spring onion tops over spareribs. Serve with boiled rice. Serves 6–8.

Fragrant Pork Balls with Cabbage

Unlike many Chinese dishes, this one can be made beforehand if necessary and gently reheated. Pork mince is available from many butchers and supermarkets.

500 g (1 lb) pork mince; 8 spring onions, finely chopped; 1 tsp grated fresh ginger; ¹/₂ cup drained, chopped water chestnuts (optional); 1 egg, lightly beaten; 3 tbs dry sherry; 1 tsp salt; ¹/₄ tsp pepper; ¹/₂ tsp Chinese five-spice powder; 3 tbs soy sauce; 1 tbs cornflour mixed to a paste with 2 tbs water; ¹/₂ cup peanut oil; 1 small head cabbage or Chinese cabbage, chopped; 2 cups water; 2 tsp sugar.

Mix mince with spring onions, ginger, water chestnuts, egg, 1 tbs sherry, salt, pepper, five-spice powder and 1 tbs soy sauce. Wet hands with cornflour mixture and shape pork mixture into 4 large balls. Heat oil in a wok or deep frying pan and fry meatballs until golden-brown on all sides, about 5 minutes. Drain on paper towels and set aside. Reheat oil in wok and fry cabbage, tossing, for 2–3 minutes until coated with oil. Arrange meatballs on top, add water, remaining soy sauce and sherry and sugar and cover pan. Simmer for 1 hour. Serve with plain boiled rice and side dishes of soy sauce and hot mustard. Serves 4.

Barbecued Pork Spareribs

Ask your butcher to cut spareribs into individual ribs.

**1.5 kg (3 lb) meaty pork spareribs; 3 tbs oil;
5 tbs soy sauce; 5 tbs water; 2 tbs hoisin sauce;
1 tsp sugar; 4 slices fresh ginger, shredded;
2 onions, finely sliced; 5 tbs dry sherry;
salt and freshly ground white pepper;
5 tbs chicken stock.**

Blanch spareribs in boiling water for 2 minutes, then drain and pat dry with paper towels. Put ribs and oil into a flameproof casserole. Heat until oil just begins to bubble, then stir-fry for 5 minutes over medium heat, to brown ribs. Add soy sauce, water, hoisin sauce, sugar, ginger and onions. Stir until well blended, turning ribs to coat. Put casserole into a preheated slow oven (150°C/300°F). Cook for 20 minutes, then stir in sherry and season with salt and pepper. Cook for a further 40 minutes, stirring halfway through. Take dish from oven, remove spareribs and place them side by side on bottom of a baking dish. Return to oven and increase temperature to very hot (230°C/450°F). Roast for 12–15 minutes or until crisp and rich golden-brown. Arrange spareribs on a heated platter. Pour chicken stock into casserole dish with onion mixture and stir over moderate heat for 2–3 minutes. Pour into a separate dish and serve with spareribs. Serves 4–6.

Stir-fried Pork with Spring Onions

Other vegetables may be substituted for the spring onions.

315 g (about 10 oz) boneless pork loin or fillet.

**MARINADE: 1 clove garlic, crushed; 1 tbs soy sauce;
1/2 tbs sugar; 1 tbs cornflour.**

**TO COOK: 2–3 tbs oil; 2 tbs soy sauce; 1 tsp sugar;
8 spring onions, cut into finger lengths.**

Remove any fat and tough membranes from pork, and cut into slices about 5 mm (1/4 in) thick. Using blunt edge of a chopper, or a heavy saucer, pound meat lightly to tenderise and flatten it. Mix marinade ingredients together, pour over pork and allow to stand for 30 minutes. Heat oil in a wok or a large, heavy frying pan. Fry pork slices on both sides until golden-brown (add a little more oil if necessary to prevent sticking). This should take about 4 minutes altogether. Add soy sauce and sugar. Stir in the spring onions, quickly mix through pork, then transfer to a heated serving plate and serve at once. This will serve 4–6 as part of a Chinese meal, or 2 as a main course with rice.

Cha Shao Quick Roast Pork

1 kg (2 lb) pork fillet.

**MARINADE: 1 1/2 tbs soy sauce; 1 1/2 tsp red bean curd;
1 1/2 tbs dry sherry; 1 tbs hoisin sauce; 1/2 tsp salt;
1 1/2 tsp sugar or honey; 1 tbs oil.**

Place pork fillet in a shallow dish. Combine marinade ingredients, pour over pork and turn meat until well coated with marinade. Leave for 2 hours, turning every 20 minutes. Place pork on a wire rack in a baking dish and roast in a preheated hot oven (220°C/425°F) for 12 minutes, turning halfway through cooking. Remove from oven and cut into 5 mm (1/4 in) thick slices. Arrange on a serving platter. Serves 4–6.

NOTE: Red bean curd can be purchased in cans from Chinese grocery stores.

Island Roast Pork

A good party dish. Serve with rice salad and glazed sweet potatoes.

**2.5 kg (5 lb) loin of pork, on the bone or boned,
rolled and tied; 1 tbs light soy sauce; 1 1/2 tsp grated
fresh ginger; 1 clove garlic, crushed; 2 tsp salt;
2 tsp oil.**

Have skin of pork well scored. Mix soy sauce, ginger, garlic, salt and oil. Rub over pork. Cover and chill overnight. Next day, bring back to room temperature then place pork in a shallow roasting tin. Roast in a preheated very hot oven (260°C/500°F) for 15–20 minutes or until skin is starting to bubble and crisp. Lower heat to moderate (180°C/350°F) and roast for 2 hours. Do not cover pork while roasting. Serves 8–10.

Roast Suckling Pig

Measure your oven and, when ordering the pig, specify the size you require. If necessary ask the butcher to saw it in half across the middle and arrange to have one half cooked in a friend's or neighbour's oven. Also ask the butcher to score the sides of the pig diagonally at 2.5 cm (1 in) intervals from behind the head to the tail.

**1 suckling pig, weighing 6–7 kg (12–15 lb); olive oil;
2 onions, finely chopped; 6 spring onions, finely
chopped; 125 g (4 oz) butter; grated rind 1 lemon;
6 cups fresh white breadcrumbs; 4 tbs finely
chopped mixed fresh herbs (marjoram, parsley,
sage and thyme), or 3 tbs chopped parsley mixed with
1 tbs mixed dried herbs; salt and freshly ground
black pepper; 2 eggs, lightly beaten.**

GARNISH: watercress; baked apples (optional).

Make stuffing first. Fry onions and spring onions in half the butter until soft. Stir in remaining butter then lemon rind, breadcrumbs, herbs, salt, pepper and

p

eggs. Pack loosely into pig. Sew up opening, or secure with skewers and lace them with string. Cover ears and tail with foil to protect them from burning. Place pig in a large baking dish, brush with oil and rub with salt. Bake in a preheated very hot oven (230°C/450°F) for about 45 minutes or until skin starts to crisp, then lower heat to moderate (180°C/350°F) and roast a further 3 hours or until cooked. A small pig of 6 kg (12 lb) will take about 2½ hours. If the pig is cut in half, cooking time will be the same. Check for doneness with a meat thermometer inserted in thickest part of flesh, not touching bone; the pig will be cooked when internal temperature reaches 85°C/185°F. Failing a meat thermometer, pierce thickest part with a skewer and check juice that comes out; when pig is done, it will be quite clear with no tinge of pink. Leave pig in turned-off oven with door ajar for 20 minutes before serving. Place pig on a large platter or board. Serve hot or at room temperature, garnishing platter with watercress and baked apples or other garnish of your choice. If pig is in 2 halves, arrange a watercress garland, secured with toothpicks, over the join. To carve suckling pig, please see *Meat*. Serves 12–15.

Potted Hough

The rightly famous potted meat of Scotland.

**1.5 kg (3 lb) shin of beef, cut into thick slices;
2 pig's trotters, or 2 veal knuckles, each cut into
3 pieces; 6 black peppercorns; 1 blade mace;
1 bay leaf; 3–4 anchovy fillets, mashed;
salt and freshly ground black pepper.**

**TO SERVE: cucumber slices; vinegar;
hot English mustard; tomatoes; potato salad.**

Put beef, pig's trotters or veal knuckles, peppercorns, mace and bay leaf into a large, heavy saucepan and cover with cold water. Bring to the boil and skim top. Cover and simmer for 3 hours. Cool, then remove meat from broth. Strain broth. Trim away fat and gristle and remove bones from meat. With 2 forks, pull meat apart into fine shreds. Return shredded meat to strained broth and boil uncovered for 20 minutes to reduce. Add anchovies and season with salt and pepper. Boil a further 5 minutes to blend flavours. Pour into 1 large or 2 small bowls which have first been rinsed with cold water. Cover with plastic wrap or a plate and chill until firm. Turn out on to a serving plate and garnish with cucumber slices. Serve the potted hough with vinegar, hot English mustard, tomatoes and a potato salad. Serves 8.

PORRIDGE

This is a relic of the gruel which was a staple item in the daily diet of poor peasants, particularly in the winter months, during many centuries past.

Basically, porridge is a mixture of partially milled grain and water, boiled until thick. Today it is more often a breakfast food, eaten with milk or cream, and may be sweetened with sugar or honey. It is usually made with rolled oats (see *Oatmeal*), but rolled wheat (wheatmeal) can also be used for porridge. Buckwheat is used in Russia to make a similar kind of porridge, called *kasha* (see *Kasha*), and in those areas of Europe where maize is grown, coarsely ground maize is the preferred grain.

Scottish Oatmeal Porridge

**2 cups water; ¹/₂ cup medium ground oatmeal,
¹/₄ tsp salt.**

Bring water to the boil in a heavy saucepan or top of a double saucepan. Add oatmeal in a constant stream, stirring continuously. When boiling again, lower heat, cover and simmer very gently for 10 minutes. Add salt and stir. Cover and simmer a further 10 minutes or until oatmeal is well swollen and tender. Serve piping hot in cold soup plates and dip each spoonful into individual bowls of cold milk or cream before eating. Serves 2.

PORT

A rich, sweet, fortified wine, usually drunk at the end of a meal but sometimes offered as an aperitif. In cooking it is used in a similar fashion to Madeira; for example, as a final enrichment to sauces. A simple sauce for roast duck can be made with pan juices, orange juice and port; Cumberland Sauce (see pages 106–7), served with game and cold meats calls for port, and a basic brown sauce for roast meat may be varied by the addition of a little port. The once popular dessert of port wine jelly was made with port, redcurrant jelly, a little sugar, gelatine and water.

See also *Jelly: Port Wine Jelly*.

POTATO

There are numerous varieties of potato with the more readily available depending on consumer demand and growers. Growers are constantly seeking hardier varieties according to their resistance to disease, keeping qualities and percentage yield that are also acceptable to the consumer. The consumer needs to know what potato is best for each method of cooking. Some make wonderful chips and baked potatoes; the more waxy ones are best for salads, while some are best for mashing. Much depends on how much starch a potato has.

Generally, the best potatoes for flavour and all-purpose use are those with a creamy flesh such as Desiree, Kipfler, Bintje and Pink Eye, among others. However, some of the more yellow-fleshed potatoes such as Nicola, though delicious, are often too waxy to be good for mashing. Those with a white flesh such as Pontiac, Russet Burbank and Sebago, are mostly used for mashing and chips.

New or Early Potatoes: Proper new potatoes come on to the market in late spring and are available through most of the summer. They have a thin pearly skin and firm waxy flesh, are moister than older potatoes, and are best boiled or steamed. Chats are new season potatoes which are graded to be round or oval in shape.

Old and Floury or Mealy Potatoes: These are good for baking in their skins or 'jackets', or for boiling and mashing.

Slightly Yellow or White-flesh Waxy Potatoes: Best for roasting, frying as chips, French fries, shoestrings or game chips; noisette, or sautéed potatoes. Very waxy potatoes are best for salads.

Bintje: A long, oval-shaped potato with dense creamy flesh, best used for steaming, frying, boiling and salads.

Desiree: Oval potatoes with a pinkish red skin and pale yellow creamy flesh. An excellent all-rounder, they are good for roasting, steaming, mashing and in sliced potato dishes.

Kipfler: These have yellow skin and flesh and an elongated knobbly shape and nutty flavour. Excellent boiled, steamed and in salads; good to roast. Rub with oil, sprinkle with sea salt and roast in a dry pan.

Nicola: Oval-shaped with creamy-coloured skin and yellow flesh. Good for boiling, potato salad, roasting, frying or microwaving, but the waxy texture means it is not suitable for mashing.

Patrone: Small, smooth-skinned, oval potatoes that can be slightly pear-shaped. The skin and flesh are light yellow. These potatoes have a firm waxy texture, which makes them excellent for steaming and boiling. They are good for salads, roasting and gratin dishes, but are not well suited to mashing.

Toolangi Delight: This potato was developed by the Department of Agriculture and Rural Affairs, Potato Research Station, Toolangi, in Victoria. Mostly round with moderately deep eyes, it has purple skin and white flesh. Has very good culinary qualities and will mash, bake, make very good chips and is excellent for gnocchi.

Pink Eye: Small irregular roundish potatoes with pink-mauve skin, the pink being more prominent around the eyes, with a yellow flesh. They will cook in much the same way as Patrone.

Pink Fir Apple: Creamy pink skin, waxy yellow flesh. Boil or bake; very good for salads.

Russet Burbank: A long, oval potato, brown skin with chocolate and red tones, and white flesh. Excellent for baking and chips (used by that famous hamburger franchise), and are similar to the famous American Idaho potato.

Do not buy any variety of potato that has green skin or flesh. Potatoes should feel very firm, and have a faint earthy smell. Buy new potatoes in small quantities as you need them because they do not keep well. Store old potatoes in a cool, dark place; they keep particularly well if they are left unwashed, with earth still clinging to the skins.

INSTANT MASHED POTATOES: This convenience food cannot rival freshly cooked potatoes for flavour, but it can be useful when mashed potato is called for as an ingredient. It can also be used as a thickener for soups and stews – simply sprinkle over and stir in.

NOTE: Potato flour is a thickening agent used by Continental cooks in soups and gravies, and also in baking. **See recipes.**

Boiled New Potatoes

Choose small, new potatoes of uniform size with pearly skins.

**500 g (1 lb) new potatoes; 2 cups water; pinch salt; 2 small sprigs fresh mint (optional);
30 g (1 oz) butter; 1 tbs finely chopped fresh mint, parsley or dill.**

Scrape skins of potatoes lightly. Bring water to the boil in a saucepan, add potatoes, salt and mint sprigs, if using, and return to a gentle boil. Cover and cook gently for 10–15 minutes, depending on size of potatoes. Drain immediately. Return potatoes to saucepan and shake over low heat until quite dry. Add butter and toss potatoes until each is glistening. Place in heated serving dish and sprinkle with chopped mint, parsley or dill. Serves 4.

NOTE: Omit sprigs of mint in cooking water if garnishing with chopped parsley or dill.

Crispy Olive Potatoes

16 small new potatoes; 60 g (2 oz) butter, melted; 3 tbs flour; 1 tsp salt; pinch cayenne; 1 tsp paprika; 1/2 cup chopped stuffed olives.

Cook potatoes in boiling salted water until just tender. Drain and peel when cool enough to handle. Toss in melted butter to coat evenly, then coat in flour mixed with salt, cayenne and paprika. Place in a buttered, shallow casserole. Sprinkle with olives and bake in a preheated hot oven (200°C/400°F) for 20 minutes (turn potatoes after first 10 minutes to brown evenly) until piping hot and crispy. Serves 4.

Herbed New Potatoes with Fresh Peas

750 g (1 1/2 lb) new potatoes, scraped; 1 1/4 tsp salt; 1 cup shelled fresh peas; freshly ground black pepper; 2 tbs shredded fresh mint or basil; 30 g (1 oz) butter; 1/4 cup cream; parsley to garnish.

Cook potatoes in boiling water, with salt, until just tender. Ten minutes before potatoes are completely cooked, add peas. When peas are cooked, remove from heat and drain off water. Add pepper, mint or basil, butter and cream and heat a few seconds. Turn into a serving dish and garnish with parsley. Serve immediately. Serves 6.

Sugar–Glazed New Potatoes

New potatoes taste and look delectable with a caramel coating. Serve with ham, chicken or pork – meats that take well to a sweet sauce or fruit.

500 g (1 lb) new potatoes; 45 g (1¹/₂ oz) butter; 2 tbs sugar; salt.

Cook potatoes in boiling salted water until just tender. Drain and peel as soon as they are cool enough to handle. Melt butter in a heavy frying pan big enough to take potatoes in a single layer. Add sugar and stir over low heat until a light golden-brown. Add potatoes and cook, stirring, until heated through and evenly coated with glaze. Sprinkle with salt and serve at once. Serve 4.

Creamy Mashed Potatoes

When cooked sufficiently the potatoes should break under pressure of a fork but not be mushy. Over-cooking or cutting potatoes into small pieces makes them water-soaked and they lose flavour. Always add hot milk for fluffy potatoes as cold makes them sticky.

6 medium potatoes, peeled, halved if large; salt and freshly ground pepper; 60 g (2 oz) butter; ¹/₂–1 cup hot milk; nutmeg (optional).

Put potatoes into a saucepan with cold water to cover. Add a little salt and bring to the boil. Cook, covered, until potatoes are easily pierced with a skewer, about 20–30 minutes. Drain, return to saucepan and shake pan over a low heat for a few minutes until potatoes are thoroughly dry. Mash with a potato masher or fork. Using a wooden spoon beat until very smooth. Add butter to potatoes, then gradually beat in hot milk until potatoes are light and fluffy. Season with salt and pepper, and a pinch of nutmeg, if liked.
To keep hot: After mashing potatoes push them down well in saucepan, packing tightly. Level top, add butter and spoon about 4 tbs hot milk over. Cover and leave in a warm place. Before serving beat well, adding more hot milk if necessary. The potatoes will keep for up to 20 minutes. Serves 4–6.

VARIATIONS

CHEESE POTATOES: Spread Creamy Mashed Potatoes in a buttered flameproof dish. Sprinkle top generously with grated cheese such as Parmesan, Gruyère or Cheddar and brush with melted butter. Or spread with cream to which grated cheese has been added. Place under a preheated hot grill or in a hot oven until cheese has melted.

POTATOES WITH CHIVES OR SPRING ONIONS: Fold snipped chives or chopped spring onions through Creamy Mashed Potato just before serving.

EGG GRATIN: Divide hot Creamy Mashed Potatoes among 4 greased individual ramekins and make a depression in each one. Drop an egg into each depression, spoon over a little cream, or cream mixed with grated cheese. Bake in a preheated moderately hot oven (190°C/375°F) until eggs are set.

POTATOES WITH ONIONS: Prepare Creamy Mashed Potatoes and keep warm. Melt 60 g (2 oz) butter in a frying pan and cook 3 medium onions, finely sliced, until golden-brown and tender. Sprinkle with ¹/₂ tsp dried sage, salt and pepper. Gently fold through potatoes and serve.

Mousseline Potatoes
(Pureé of Potatoes)

750 g (1¹/₂ lb) old, floury potatoes, peeled; 30 g (1 oz) butter; 1¹/₄ cups hot milk; salt and freshly ground black pepper; ¹/₄ tsp nutmeg.

Place potatoes in a large saucepan, cover with cold water and bring to the boil. Cook gently for about 20 minutes or until tender. Drain and cool slightly, then return to the pan 2or 3 at a time and cook over very gentle heat to dry off any moisture. Rub potatoes through a sieve, or process in a food processor using the double-sided steel blade. Return potatoes to the hot pan, place over gentle heat and gradually beat in butter and hot milk. Continue beating until very smooth and soft. Add salt, pepper and nutmeg and serve immediately. Serves 4.

Baked Jacket Potatoes

In America the Idaho potato is most often chosen for baking. Choose old, floury potatoes for this popular and easy way to serve them.

4 large even-sized baking potatoes; 30 g (1 oz) butter, quartered.

Scrub potatoes, dry and pierce each 4–6 times with a skewer. Bake directly on the shelf in a preheated hot oven (200°C/400°F) for about 1 hour, depending on size of potatoes. Test by pressing between fingers. When done, cut a cross on top with a pointed knife and squeeze gently to open. Top with butter. Serves 4.
NOTE: The above method produces crisp skin. If softer skin is required rub all over the surface of potatoes with oil before baking.

TOPPINGS: Add a dollop of sour cream and sprinkle with snipped chives; crumble crisp fried bacon over sour cream topping. Sprinkle with crisp bacon and grated cheese; top with butter, grated orange rind and chopped mint.

Potatoes Czarina

Baked potatoes are scooped out, seasoned, reheated in the jackets and topped with caviar. An unexpected but superb combination which may be served for lunch with a crisp salad, or as a first course before a simple main dish.

6 large baking potatoes; 30 g (1 oz) butter;
3/4 cup sour cream; 2 tbs snipped chives or finely
chopped spring onions; 1 tbs finely chopped parsley
or fresh dill; 1/2 tsp nutmeg; salt and freshly ground
black pepper; 125 g (4 oz) caviar or lumpfish roe,
chilled.

Scrub potatoes, dry and pierce each 4–6 times with a
skewer. Bake in a preheated hot oven (200°C/400°F)
for about 1 hour or until tender when pressed
between the fingers. Cut a lid from top of each
potato and scoop out pulp with a sharp spoon, being
careful not to pierce skins. Place potato shells in
a turned-off oven to keep warm. Put flesh in a
saucepan over low heat and add butter, sour cream,
chives or spring onions, parsley or dill, nutmeg, salt
and pepper. Stir thoroughly with a wooden spoon,
mashing pulp and blending ingredients until mixture
is piping hot. Arrange potato shells on a heated
platter, stuff with seasoned potato, and top each
serving with a spoonful of cold caviar. Serves 6.

VARIATION
Potatoes can be topped with crisp cooked bacon.

Roast Potatoes

Choose potatoes of medium and uniform size. They
should be old and slightly waxy for best results. Too
small potatoes tend to dry out during roasting.

6 medium potatoes, peeled; salt; oil for roasting.

Place potatoes in a saucepan, cover with cold water
and bring to the boil. Boil for 5 minutes. Drain and
dry well on paper towels. Run the tines of a fork
over surface of potatoes and sprinkle very lightly
with salt. Put enough oil into a baking dish to come
1 cm (1/2 in) up the sides. Heat oil, then put in potatoes
and roast in a preheated hot oven (200°C/400°F) for
40–50 minutes or until golden and crusty, turning
and basting occasionally. Drain on crumpled paper
towels and serve hot. Serves 4–6.

NOTE: If you would like to roast potatoes at the same
time as a joint of meat, prepares as above then place in
the roasting pan alongside the joint during the last 45
minutes to 1 hour of cooking time, turning and
basting with pan juices 3 or 4 times.

Potato Chips

French fried potatoes, the popular 'pommes frites' of
France, have become equally well liked as potato
chips in many other countries. Choose old, dry, slightly
waxy potatoes for best results, and cut into uniform
lengths and thickness. Soak the potatoes in cold water
before frying to help get rid of some of the starch
released when the potatoes are cut. Dry the potatoes
well before immersing in hot oil; damp potatoes take
longer to cook and become greasy. Care should
always be taken when deep frying to lower the food

gently into the hot oil to avoid splashing or overflowing.
Do not have the frying container more than half full
of oil or the oil will overflow when the chips are
added.

**4 large even-sized potatoes, peeled;
oil for deep-frying; salt.**

Cut potatoes into 5 cm (2 in) lengths, 1 cm (1/2 in)
wide. Soak for 30 minutes in ice-cold water. Drain
and dry well with paper towels. Place enough oil in a
deep heavy pan to come not more than halfway up
the sides and heat gently to 145°C/300°F or until a
bread cube placed in the hot oil turns brown in less
than 1 minute. Put potatoes in a frying basket and
lower into hot oil. Cook until soft but not brown,
about 4–5 minutes. Lift out. Increase the temperature
of the oil to 190°C/375°F or until a bread cube turns
brown in 30 seconds. Gently lower chips into hot oil
and cook until brown and crisp, about 1–2 minutes.
Drain on crumpled paper towels, sprinkle with salt
and serve immediately. Serves 4.

VARIATIONS
MATCHSTICK POTATOES: Cut potatoes into strips the
size of matchsticks and proceed as for Potato Chips,
frying once only in oil (190°C/375°F) for about 1–2
minutes until crisp and golden.
SHOESTRING POTATOES: Cut potatoes into strips not
more than 5 mm (1/4 in) thick and proceed as for
Potato Chips, frying once only in oil (190°C/375°F) for
about 2–3 minutes.

Game Chips

Game chips are the classic accompaniment for game
and are sometimes served at Christmas with the
festive roast turkey. Game chips should be of uniform
shape, thickness and diameter, resembling fine wafers
of potato.

2 large potatoes, peeled; oil for deep-frying; salt.

Shape potatoes into thick cylinders so each slice will
be approximately the same diameter. Slice very fine.
Soak slices in ice-cold water for 20 minutes, then
drain and dry thoroughly. Heat oil to 200°C/400°F or
until a bread cube turns brown in 30 seconds. Place
one quarter of potatoes at a time in a frying basket

and lower gently into hot oil. Keep slices moving about so that they do not stick together. After 1–2 minutes, slices will float to the surface when they are nearly cooked. When golden and crisp, remove and drain on crumpled paper towels. Sprinkle with salt and serve immediately on a folded napkin. Serves 4.

VARIATIONS

SARATOGA CHIPS: These chips are sliced very fine using a vegetable peeler. They should be of uniform thickness but the diameter of each chip may vary. Soak, dry and fry as for Game Chips.

STRAW POTATOES: Cut potatoes into sticks 3 mm (⅛ in) thick, then into very thin matchsticks, 3 mm (⅛ in) wide. Soak, dry and fry as for Game Chips.

Pommes de Terre Noisette
(Noisette Potatoes)

Slightly waxy, yellow or white-fleshed old potatoes are best for this method.

1 kg (2 lb) potatoes, peeled; 4 tbs butter; salt.

Using a melon baller scoop out balls of potato. Keep in cold water until all potatoes have been prepared. Drain and place in a saucepan with fresh cold water to cover. Bring to the boil and simmer for 2 minutes. Drain and dry thoroughly on paper towels. Heat butter in a frying pan and sauté potatoes, shaking pan occasionally, until they are golden-brown all over. Season with salt. Serve with meat, poultry or fish. Serves 4–6.

Sauté Potatoes

Potatoes for this dish should be old and slightly waxy. They are boiled whole first then peeled. Serve with fish, chicken or steak.

1 kg (2 lb) potatoes; salt; 60 g (2 oz) butter; 1 tbs oil.

Place potatoes in a large saucepan. Cover with cold water and add salt. Cover, bring to the boil and simmer for 15–20 minutes or until just tender. Drain, then peel when cool enough to handle. Cut into thick slices. Heat butter and oil in a heavy frying pan and when foaming add potatoes. Cook briskly, shaking pan and turning potatoes continually. They should never be left to fry. The constant turning gives outside of potatoes a crumbly texture, characteristic of this dish. Sprinkle with salt and serve immediately without draining potatoes. Serves 4–6.

Scalloped Potatoes

1 kg (2 lb) old potatoes, peeled and finely sliced; 1 clove garlic, halved; 90 g (3 oz) butter; salt and freshly ground white pepper; 1 cup milk; nutmeg; 60 g (2 oz) Gruyère cheese, finely sliced.

Dry potato slices thoroughly. Rub a shallow oven-proof dish with cut sides of garlic and smear with 30 g (1 oz) butter. Carefully arrange potato slices in layers in the dish, seasoning each layer with salt and pepper. Scald mild and add a little nutmeg, salt and pepper. Arrange cheese on top of potatoes. Carefully pour over milk and add rest of butter, cut into small pieces. Bake in a preheated moderate oven (180°C/350°F) for 40–45 minutes or until tender and golden. Cut in wedges and serve from the dish. Serves 6–8.

Savoury Potato Cakes

These cakes go well with a fresh green salad. Serve them immediately while the outside is still brown and crispy and the inside fluffy.

750 g (1½ lb) potatoes, peeled; 60 g (2 oz) butter; salt and freshly ground black pepper; 4 rashers bacon, rind removed and finely chopped; 3 tbs flour; lard or extra butter, if needed, for frying.

Cook potatoes in boiling salted water until tender. Drain well, return to heat for a minute or so to dry off, and mash until smooth with butter, salt and pepper. Cook bacon in a heavy frying pan over a medium heat, without extra fat, for 5 minutes. Remove bacon with a slotted spoon. Beat flour into potatoes and mix in bacon. Pat out on a well-floured work surface until about 5 mm (¼ in) thick. Cut into rounds with a floured pastry cutter. Heat bacon fat in frying pan, adding a little lard or butter if needed. Add potato cakes and cook over a medium-high heat for about 2 minutes on each side, until golden-brown. Serve at once. Serves 4.

Potato Croquettes

1 quantity Duchess Potatoes (see page 130); oil for deep-frying.

COATING: flour; egg; breadcrumbs.

Roll potato mixture into small balls or barrel shapes. Coat with flour, then beaten egg and finally bread-crumbs. Deep-fry for 5–6 minutes and drain on paper towels. If preferred, mould potato mixture into flat cakes, coat with flour, egg and breadcrumbs and shallow-fry in a small amount of butter. Serves 6–8.

Gratin Dauphinois

The mountain province of Dauphine in France produces excellent potatoes which are used in 'gratins'. The addition of cheese does not play any part in the genuine Gratin Dauphinois but is particularly good when the Gratin is served with a baked ham or roast beef.

1 kg (2 lb) potatoes, peeled; 1 clove garlic, crushed; salt and freshly ground black pepper; nutmeg; 125 g (4 oz) Gruyère or Emmenthal Cheese, grated (optional); 1 cup cream; 30 g (1 oz) butter.

Slice potatoes as thin as a 20 cent piece. Rub garlic around inside of an ovenproof dish, then butter it well. Arrange potato slices in concentric circles in dish, seasoning each with salt, pepper and nutmeg and sprinkling with grated cheese if using. Pour cream over layers, scatter butter, which has been cut into small pieces, over top and sprinkle with remaining cheese. Bake in a preheated moderate oven (180°C/350°F) for 1 hour or until potatoes are tender and top golden and crisp. Serves 6–8.

Pan Haggerty

This traditional dish from northern England combines potatoes, onions and cheese. It is hearty enough for a main course if you add a green vegetable or salad.

4 tbs oil; 1 kg (2 lb) potatoes, peeled and finely sliced; 500 g (1 lb) onions, finely sliced; 125 g (4 oz) well-flavoured Cheddar cheese, grated; salt and freshly ground black pepper; butter; finely chopped parsley.

You will need a large frying pan with a heavy base and a well-fitting lid for this dish. Heat oil in the pan and put in layers of potatoes, onions and cheese, seasoning each layer with salt and pepper and beginning and ending with potatoes. Put lid on pan and cook over gentle heat until underside is crisp and brown and vegetables are tender, about 20–30 minutes. Dot top of potatoes with butter and place pan under a preheated grill for a few minutes until top is browned. Serve on a heated platter, cut in wedges like a pie and sprinkle with parsley. Serves 6–8.

Sour Cream Potato Cakes

A lighter alternative to savoury potato cakes.

3 large boiled potatoes, coarsely grated (enough to make 2 cups); 1 tsp salt; freshly ground black pepper; 2 tbs snipped chives or finely chopped spring onions; 1 cup flour, sifted; about 1 cup sour cream; 60 g (2 oz) butter; chopped parsley or chives.

Combine grated potatoes with salt, pepper, chives or spring onions and flour in a large bowl. Stir in enough sour cream to make a soft dough, about the same consistency as scone dough. Roll or pat out on a lightly floured work surface to a thickness of about 1 cm (½ in). Cut into rounds with a floured 5 cm (2 in) scone cutter. Heat butter in a large, heavy frying pan and brown potato cakes for about 3 minutes on each side. Serve at once, sprinkled with a little parsley or chives. Serves 6.

Potatoes Anna

This is a round 'cake' of thinly sliced potatoes, which is turned out and cut into wedges for serving. In kitchenware shops a special Anna tin is available, but you can get good results using a small, heavy frying pan. Choose potatoes the same size, to give even rounds.

1 kg (2 lb) old potatoes, peeled and finely sliced; 90 g (3 oz) butter; salt and freshly ground black pepper.

Dry potato slices well. Rub frying pan generously with butter and arrange a layer of potatoes in neat, overlapping circles. Season with salt and pepper and dot with small pieces of butter. Arrange another layer of potato slices on top, with more seasoning and butter, and continue until potatoes and butter are used up. Place pan on top of stove over low heat, cover with buttered greaseproof paper and a lid, and cook gently for 20 minutes. Remove lid and paper, transfer pan to a preheated moderate oven (180°C/350°F). Continue cooking for 30–40 minutes or until potatoes are brown and crusty on the bottom and cooked through when tested with a skewer. Rest for 1–2 minutes, then invert potatoes on to a heated platter. Cut in wedges to serve. Serves 6–8.

Potatoes in White Wine with Anchovies

Serve this simple appetiser at room temperature for the best flavour. Perfect for summer brunches.

6 large, old potatoes; ¼ cup dry white wine; 2 tbs wine vinegar; ⅓ cup olive oil; freshly ground black pepper; 2 x 50 g cans rolled anchovy fillets, drained; coriander leaves or flat-leaved parsley to garnish.

Place potatoes in a saucepan, cover with cold water and bring to the boil. Simmer until tender. Drain and peel when cool enough to handle. Cut into thick slices. Sprinkle with wine and cool to room temperature. Combine vinegar, olive oil and pepper and pour over potatoes. Scatter anchovies over potatoes and garnish with coriander leaves or parsley. Serves 6–8.

Rösti

Rösti is the national Swiss potato dish made in the shape of a thick, crispy, golden-brown cake. Sometimes the Rösti is flavoured with crisp bacon and sometimes with onion. It is cut in ample wedges and served with all meat dishes or with fried eggs for breakfast.

1.5 kg (3 lb) old potatoes; ½ tsp salt; 125 g (4 oz) speck or smoked bacon, diced; 30 g (1 oz) butter.

Place potatoes in a saucepan and cover with cold salted water. Bring to the boil and cook for about 10 minutes. Drain and peel when cool enough to handle. Grate potatoes. Fry speck or bacon in half the butter in a heavy frying pan. Cook gently until bacon fat is transparent. Spread potatoes in frying pan to form a thick cake. Cook over a low heat for about 10 minutes. Slip a knife or spatula under potato cake occasionally to ensure underside is not becoming too brown. Turn cake out on to a large plate. Add remaining butter to frying pan and when foam has subsided slide potato cake back into it. Cook over a gentle heat for 8 minutes, making sure it does not become too brown. Turn out on to a large heated dish and serve. Serves 6.

NOTES: The Rösti can be browned quickly on both sides over a high heat and then placed in a preheated moderate oven (180°C/350°F) for 20 minutes to finish cooking. Rösti will keep for about 30 minutes in a warm oven, if necessary.

VARIATION

If making a simple Rösti without speck or bacon, heat 3 tbs olive oil in the frying pan before adding the butter. To add onions to Rösti, cook 2 chopped onions in oil and butter until they become transparent, then add potatoes.

Hot Potato Salad

2 rashers streaky bacon, rind removed; 1 onion, chopped; 1 tbs flour; ¼ cup white vinegar; ½ cup water; ¼ tsp salt; 1 tsp sugar; freshly ground black pepper; 2 tbs prepared mild mustard; 4 medium potatoes, peeled, cooked and sliced; chopped parsley.

Fry bacon until crisp. Remove from pan with tongs, crumble and set aside. Cook onion in bacon fat until soft and lightly browned. Blend in flour, then stir in bacon, vinegar, water, salt, sugar, pepper and mustard. Bring to the boil, stirring well. Add potatoes, tossing to coat lightly, and heat through. Sprinkle with parsley and serve hot, or let cool, store in refrigerator and reheat before serving. Serves 4.

VARIATION

HOT POTATO SALAD WITH PIQUANT MUSTARD DRESSING: Make as above, using Dijon mustard instead of mild mustard and adding a pinch of cayenne to dressing. If liked, garnish with snipped chives instead of parsley.

Creamy Potato Salad with Ham

This may be served as a first course at dinner, or as the main course for lunch. Cold sliced tongue, corned beef, or any of the Continental-type sausages can replace the more expensive ham.

500 g (1 lb) new potatoes; 3 tbs oil; 1 tbs vinegar; 1 small onion, finely chopped; salt and freshly ground black pepper; ½ cup Mayonnaise (page 256); ½ cup sour cream; 3 thick slices cooked ham or tongue, cut into julienne (matchstick) strips; chopped parsley; 1–2 canned pimientos, drained and cut into strips (optional).

Cook potatoes in boiling salted water until just tender. Peel while hot and cut into thick slices. Put oil, vinegar and onion in a bowl, beat until thick and season with salt and pepper. Add warm potatoes, folding them into dressing. Allow to cool. Combine mayonnaise and sour cream in another bowl and lightly fold into potatoes. Turn into a salad bowl. Arrange ham or tongue on top of potatoes. Sprinkle with chopped parsley to serve, and, if liked, strips of red pimiento. This salad is best served at room temperature. Serves 4.

Potato Salad

1 kg (2 lb) potatoes; ½ cup Vinaigrette Dressing (page 256); 1 tbs snipped chives to garnish.

If using tiny new potatoes, scrape skins with a small sharp knife, plunge them into boiling salted water and cook until tender. If using large older potatoes, cover with cold salted water, bring to the boil and simmer until tender, then peel and cut into large dice. The potatoes should be moistened with vinaigrette while still warm. To serve, pile into a bowl and garnish with chives. Serves 4–6.

Potato and Cucumber Soup

4 large old, floury potatoes, peeled and sliced; 2¼ cups water; 1 onion, sliced; 60 g (2 oz) butter; ½ tbs salt; 2 cucumbers, peeled, seeded and diced; 1 cup milk; 1 cup cream; 1 tbs caraway seeds.

Put potatoes in a large heavy saucepan with water, onion, butter and salt. Bring to the boil, then cover and simmer for 20 minutes or until potatoes are soft. Purée mixture through a food mill, or in several batches in a blender or food processor. Return mixture to the pan and add cucumber. Scald milk and cream and stir into pan. Bring to the simmer, then stir in caraway seeds and cook for 5 minutes. Season with salt and pepper. Serves 6.

POULTRY

The name given to all domesticated fowl, i.e., chicken, duck, goose, turkey, guinea fowl.

See individual entries.

PRALINE

A confection of caramelised sugar and almonds, crushed or ground to a fine powder. Equal quantities of sugar and whole almonds are used. Sometimes about half the almonds are replaced by hazelnuts, but the method remains the same, as do the uses for the final product.

Praline may be sprinkled on ice cream, a cold or hot soufflé or custard; added to a butter cream or crème pâtissière, to fill cakes and cream puffs; or used to decorate the top and sides of large cakes.

Praline keeps well in an airtight container; it may also be stored frozen. **See recipes.**

Praline

250 g (8 oz) sugar; 250 g (8 oz) whole unblanched almonds.

Cook sugar and almonds in a heavy-based saucepan over low heat until sugar melts, turning nuts over to brown evenly. Continue cooking until sugar has become nut brown in colour. Pour into an oiled tin or plate. Allow to become quite cold and hard, then break into small pieces and crush with a rolling pin, or grind in a blender or nut mill. Store in airtight container. Makes about 1 cup.

Crème Anglaise au Praliner

A rich and creamy stirred custard, with a generous topping of praline is one of the most delectable creams. Serve with poached fruit – pears in burgundy, fresh strawberries or raspberries, fresh or poached peaches.

2 tbs sugar; 4 egg yolks; I tsp cornflour; I cup cream; ²/₃ cup milk; 5 tbs Praline (above).

Beat sugar with egg yolks until thick and light-coloured. Stir in cornflour. Bring cream and milk to the boil. Pour a little on to beaten yolks, stirring all the time, then return yolk mixture to saucepan. Cook over a gentle heat, stirring constantly with a wooden spoon, until custard thickens and coats back of spoon thinly. Be sure to stir into corners and all over bottom of pan to prevent custard catching and burning. Remove from heat and beat for 2 minutes to help custard cool, then pour into a serving dish. Cool and chill. Just before serving coat top evenly with praline. Serves 6.

PRAWN

Small clawless crustaceans, possibly the most popular of all seafood. Prawns, and their relatives scampi and shrimp, are a delicacy enjoyed by people all over the world. Prawns are delicious eaten freshly boiled, either warm or chilled and served with plenty of brown bread and butter, a squeeze of lemon juice and freshly ground black pepper.

Cooked prawns are used in some recipes but in most cases it is best to use fresh green or raw prawns. The delicate flesh of prawns does not stand up to being cooked twice – it will toughen and lose much flavour. The appearance of some deep-sea prawns, such as the Royal Reds, make them unsuitable for some cold prawn dishes, but they are splendid in many cooked dishes.

■ **TO BUY:** Whether green or freshly boiled, prawns should be whole and undamaged. The heads should be firm and unbroken and the tails unsquashed and intact. Green prawns should be washed and free of any mud, and the flesh firm and translucent. The colour of cooked prawns varies according to the variety. Some are rich red while others turn a pale pink. Green or cooked prawns should each be stored by the fishmonger with plenty of crushed ice mixed through them; they should be reminiscent of the sea, with a mild, prawny smell.

■ **TO BOIL:** Wash thoroughly, then put into a large container of briskly boiling seawater, or fresh water with 2 tsp salt added to it for each 1 kg (2 lb) prawns. Too much salt will toughen the prawns. Boil for 2–3 minutes or until the prawns rise to the surface. Remove immediately, cool quickly in fresh cold water, drain and mix with crushed ice. Or, if you prefer, eat them while still warm with plenty of freshly ground black pepper, brown bread and butter and lemon juice.

■ **TO CLEAN:** Remove the head, shell, legs and tail (unless recipe specifies otherwise). Remove the black vein, which may be gritty, particularly in large prawns, by slitting along the back and pulling it out.

FROZEN AND CANNED PRAWNS

Choose untorn, well-wrapped packs without clumps of ice on the package. Prawns coated with breadcrumbs and frozen ready for cooking do not have to be thawed before frying. Use frozen or canned prawns in sauces, fillings and stuffing.

See also Garlic Prawns (see *Garlic*) and Prawn Curry (see *Curry*). See recipes.

Prawn Cocktail

A 1960s dish enjoying a revamp.

¹/₂ cup tomato purée; 2 drops Tabasco sauce; ¹/₂ tsp lemon juice; 2–3 tbs cream; shredded lettuce; I kg (2 lb) medium prawns, cooked, shelled and deveined; thin buttered brown bread; 4 lemon wedges.

Combine tomato purée, Tabasco sauce, lemon juice and cream. Placed shredded lettuce in 4 individual dishes, arrange prawns on top and spoon sauce over. Serve with triangles of buttered bread and wedges of lemon. Serves 4.

Orange, Avocado and Prawn Salad

This luxury salad would make a good main course for a small dinner party, yet takes only 10 minutes or so to put together. Heat bread rolls or crusty bread in the oven to serve with the salad.

2 ripe avocados, peeled, stoned and sliced lengthways; 2 large oranges; 500 g (I lb) prawns, cooked, shelled and deveined; 4 sticks celery, chopped; I tbs snipped chives; 2 cos or I head lettuce; 8–10 walnut halves.

FRENCH DRESSING: 2 tbs lemon juice; 6 tbs olive oil; I tsp chopped fresh oregano, or pinch dried; salt and freshly ground black pepper.

Mix all ingredients for dressing together by shaking in a screw-top container. Pour half over sliced avocados. Peel oranges, removing outside membrane, and cut between membranes to remove skinless segments. Combine prawns, oranges, celery and chives. Line a large bowl with lettuce leaves. Place prawn mixture in centre and arrange avocado slices and walnut halves over it. At the table, pour remaining dressing over salad and toss lightly to combine. Serves 4.

Prawn and Grapefruit Salad

1 kg (2 lb) prawns, cooked, shelled and deveined; lettuce leaves; $^1/_2$ cup julienne (matchstick) strips celery; $^1/_2$ cup julienne (matchstick) strips red pepper; $^1/_4$ cup julienne (matchstick) strips shallots; 2 tbs lime or lemon juice; salt and freshly ground black pepper; $^3/_4$ cup Mayonnaise (page 256); 2 tbs chopped parsley; 2 grapefruit, segmented; 16 cherry tomatoes, or 4 small tomatoes, quartered.

Chill prawns until ready to serve. Arrange lettuce leaves on 4 small serving plates and top with prawns. Sprinkle over celery, red pepper and shallots, reserving some for garnish. Season with lime or lemon juice, salt and pepper. Thin mayonnaise carefully with a little boiling water to make a light coating consistency. Spoon over salad. Sprinkle with reserved vegetables and parsley, then arrange grapefruit segments and tomatoes around top. Serves 4.

Sugar-Roasted Prawns

A popular dish on Chinese restaurant menus.

12 large green king prawns; peanut oil; 4 thin slices fresh ginger, finely chopped; 4 spring onions (with some green tops), finely chopped; $^1/_2$ cup chicken stock; $^1/_2$ tsp salt; $^1/_2$ tsp chilli powder; $^1/_2$ cup sugar; 2 tsp sesame oil; coriander sprigs or shredded spring onions to garnish.

Remove legs and feelers from prawns, leaving on heads and shells. Heat enough peanut oil in a wok or large, heavy frying pan to come to a depth of 5 cm (2 in). Cook prawns in hot oil for 3–4 minutes or until they turn pink. Drain prawns. Pour off oil from pan to leave only a thin film. Stir-fry ginger and spring onions until the aroma is released, about 30 seconds, then pour in chicken stock and add salt, chilli powder and sugar. Cook over very high heat, so liquid reduces rapidly. When mixture starts to caramelise, turn heat to low and add prawns, stirring and turning them over in caramel so they are well coated. Sprinkle with sesame oil, and stir through. Serve at once, garnished with coriander sprigs or shredded spring onions. Serves 4.

Cold Prawns in Dill Sauce

A Scandinavian way with prawns.

1 kg (2 lb) green medium prawns; $^1/_2$ cup lemon juice; 1 tsp dried dill; 1 small onion, grated; 2 tsp sugar; 1 tsp salt; $^1/_4$ tsp ground allspice; thinly sliced buttered rye bread to serve.

GARNISH: sprigs fresh dill; lemon wedges.

Cook prawns in boiling salted water to cover. As soon as they turn pink, drain, reserving ¾ cup of the liquid. Mix liquid with lemon juice, dill, onion, sugar, salt and allspice. Shell prawns, leaving on tail segments, and devein. Place in a bowl and pour sauce over. Cover and chill overnight. To serve, arrange in an attractive bowl and garnish with dill sprigs and lemon wedges. Serve with buttered rye bread. Serves 4–6.

NOTE: Cooked prawns may be used instead of green prawns. Peel, reserving shells and heads. Simmer shells and heads for 2 minutes in 1 cup water with a pinch of salt. Strain and use this liquid for the sauce.

Prawn and Mushroom Vol-au-Vent

8 x 8 cm (3 in) vol-au-vent cases, bought or home-made (page 571); 60 g (2 oz) button mushrooms, sliced; 45 g ($1^1/_2$ oz) butter; 250 g (8 oz) shelled, cooked prawns, deveined; 2 cups hot Béchamel Sauce (page 456); 1 tbs chopped parsley; 2–3 drops Tabasco sauce; 2–3 tsp lemon juice; salt and freshly ground black pepper; sprigs parsley to garnish.

Heat pastry cases in a preheated moderate oven (180°C/350°F) for 5–10 minutes. Meanwhile, gently fry mushrooms in butter for 1 minute, then stir in prawns and heat through. Add to the hot sauce with chopped parsley, Tabasco, lemon juice, salt and pepper. Spoon sauce into warm pastry cases. Garnish each with a sprig of parsley. Serves 8.

Prawn Cutlets

12 green king prawns; 2 eggs; 1 tbs soy sauce; salt; cornflour; fine dry breadcrumbs; oil for deep-frying; lemon wedges to garnish.

Shell prawns, leaving tails intact, and devein. Using a sharp knife, slit prawns down back, being careful not to cut right through. Beat eggs with soy sauce and salt. Dip prawns in cornflour to coat lightly, then into egg mixture and lastly in breadcrumbs. Press cut sides of prawns gently with palm to flatten. Deep-fry 'cutlets' in hot oil until golden, about 5 minutes, taking care not to overcrowd the pan. Drain on paper towels and serve immediately, garnished with lemon wedges. Serves 2–4.

Potted Prawns

A traditional English favourite.

185 g (6 oz) butter; 500 g (1 lb) green prawns, shelled, deveined and chopped; ¼ tsp ground mace; ¼ tsp nutmeg; pinch of cayenne; 1 tsp ground mixed spice; freshly ground black pepper.

Melt butter in a large frying pan and add prawns, mace, nutmeg, cayenne, mixed spice and pepper. Toss in butter for a few minutes until cooked. Spoon prawns and butter into small soufflé dish or 6 individual pots. Press down lightly, then cover with foil and chill overnight. Serve with Melba Toast (see page 263). Serves 6.

King Prawns in Shell with Tomato Sauce

If you are serving this dish the authentic Chinese way, with the heads and shells intact, don't forget finger bowls and plenty of paper napkins, or set each diner's place with a rolled, moist towel in its own little bamboo basket.

1 kg (2 lb) green king prawns; 2 tbs oil; 2 tbs Chinese rice wine or dry sherry; 1 tsp sesame oil.

SAUCE: 1½ tbs tomato sauce; 1 tbs chilli sauce; pinch salt; ¼ tsp sugar; 2 tbs chicken stock; 1 tbs shredded fresh ginger; ½ tsp cornflour; 2 tsp water.

If prawns are very large, cut each in half. Rinse lightly and dry thoroughly. Heat a wok or frying pan, add oil and stir-fry prawns until a good red colour, about 2 minutes. Sprinkle with wine or sherry.
SAUCE: Combine ingredients in a bowl, add to prawns, cover and bring to the boil. Reduce heat and simmer gently for 3–4 minutes. Add sesame oil for a final touch and serve hot. Serves 4.
NOTE: You may shell the prawns, removing heads but leaving tail shells intact, and devein before cooking.

Prawns with Rémoulade Sauce

A delightfully piquant dressing makes prawns a special treat.

1 kg (2 lb) prawns, cooked, shelled and deveined; 2 tbs chopped dill pickle or gherkin; 1 tbs chopped capers; 1 cup Mayonnaise (page 256); 1½ tsp prepared mustard; 1 tbs chopped chives or parsley.

Arrange prawns on a chilled plate. Combine remaining ingredients and pile in a bowl. Chill until serving time. Serve prawns and sauce with crisp salad greens and thin buttered brown bread, if liked. Serves 4.

Braised Prawns with Snowpeas

750 g (1½ lb) green prawns, shelled and deveined; 1 tbs Chinese rice wine or dry sherry; 1 tsp cornflour; 1 tsp soy sauce; 125 g (4 oz) snowpeas; 5–6 tbs oil.

SEASONINGS: 1 tsp salt; ½ tsp sugar; 1 tsp soy sauce.

If prawns are large, cut in half. Put into bowl with wine or sherry, cornflour and soy sauce. Mix well, then cover and chill for at least 30 minutes. String snowpeas, if necessary. Mix all ingredients for seasoning together. Heat 4 tbs oil in a wok or frying pan and cook prawns, stirring over a high heat until colour changes. Remove. Add further 1–2 tbs oil to wok and stir-fry snowpeas for 2 minutes. Return prawns to wok and add seasonings. Toss until heated through, and serve immediately. Serves 4.

Scandinavian Prawns

1 cup dry white wine; 2 tbs fresh chopped dill or 2 tsp dried; 2 sticks celery, chopped; 1 tsp salt; 750 g (1½ lb) green prawns; sour cream or Mayonnaise (page 256) to serve.

Place wine, dill, celery and salt in a saucepan and bring to the boil. Drop in prawns. Stir until prawns take on a pink tinge, then cover and simmer gently for 2–3 minutes. Allow to cool in the liquid. Shell and devein. Serve chilled, with a bowl of sour cream or mayonnaise. Fresh dill may be snipped over prawns to garnish. Serves 4–6 as a main course with rice, or 8–10 as an appetiser without rice.

Prawn Bisque

250 g (8 oz) cooked prawns; 30 g (1 oz) butter; 1 tbs flour; 4 cups Fish Stock (page 509) or water; ¼ tsp paprika; ¼ tsp salt; ½ cup cream; 2 tbs dry sherry; salt and freshly ground black pepper.

GARNISH: 1 tbs chopped parsley; 1 tbs snipped chives.

Shell and devein prawns, reserving heads and shells. Melt butter in a saucepan and sauté prawn heads and shells for 5 minutes. Sprinkle with flour and pound well with a wooden spoon. Add fish stock or water, paprika and salt. Bring to the boil and simmer for 10 minutes, then strain. Reserve a few prawns for garnish and place remaining prawns and strained stock in blender or food processor. Blend or process until smooth. Heat gently, stirring continuously, then add cream, sherry, salt and pepper. Do not let soup boil. Serve immediately, garnished with reserved prawns, chopped, and parsley and chives. Serves 6.
NOTE: If you do not have a blender or food processor, chop prawns very finely before adding to strained stock.

Devilled Barbecued Prawns

**1 kg (2 lb) green prawns; 2 tbs butter;
1 small green pepper, cored, seeded and diced;
1 tbs Dijon mustard; 1 tsp Worcestershire sauce;
few drops Tabasco sauce; 1 tbs mango chutney;
1 tsp tomato paste; 2 tsp barbecue sauce;
2 spring onions, chopped; ¹⁄₄ tsp cayenne;
salt and freshly ground black pepper; ¹⁄₂ cup cream.**

Shell prawns, leaving heads on, and devein. Melt butter in a saucepan and sauté green pepper for 1 minute. Add remaining ingredients, except cream and prawns, and cook, stirring, over low heat for 1–2 minutes or until amalgamated. Remove from heat and stir in cream. Barbecue or grill prawns, brushing liberally with sauce during cooking. Serve with rice, or without as an appetiser. Serves 4–6.

PROFITEROLE

Profiteroles are small choux pastry puffs with a sweet or savoury filling. They make superb party savouries or glamorous desserts or can star at afternoon tea. Tiny profiteroles, filled or unfilled, are an elegant accompaniment to clear soup. **See recipes.**

Cocktail-size Profiteroles: (to serve with drinks or to accompany soup): Make mounds about 2 cm (³⁄₄ in) in diameter, and bake 10 minutes in a very hot oven (230°C/450°F), then for about 10 minutes more at moderate (180°C/350°F). Dry out in turned-off oven 20 minutes.

Tiny Unfilled Puffs (to accompany soup): Make dots of pastry by squeezing it from a piping bag fitted with a plain 5 mm (¹⁄₄ in) tube and cutting off in 5 mm (¹⁄₄ in) lengths. Bake in a preheated moderate oven (180°C/350°F) for about 10 minutes or until crisp and brown.

Cream Puffs: Make mounds about 4 cm (1¹⁄₂ in) in diameter and bake 10 minutes in a very hot oven (230°C/450°F), then 20–25 minutes at moderate (180°C/350°F). Cover loosely with a sheet of foil if puffs brown too much before they feel firm and light in the hand. Slit sides and return to turned-off oven with door ajar for 30 minutes to dry out.

NOTE: Crème Pâtissière fillings may be added to sweet Profiteroles 1–2 hours ahead of time, but whipped cream fillings should not be added more than 30 minutes ahead or profiteroles may go soggy.

Cold fillings which do not contain cream may be added 1–2 hours ahead of time; those with cream should not be added more than 30 minutes ahead, or profiteroles may go soggy. Hot fillings may be added at the last minute and the filled profiteroles placed in the oven for a few minutes if necessary to ensure they are very hot. Or, for cocktail-size profiteroles, the filling may be put in cold and heated in the shells, in one layer on a baking tray, in a preheated moderate oven (180°C/350°F) for about 20–25 minutes.

Fill with one of the following, to serve cold with drinks or soup.

- Softened pâté.
- Mashed salmon or finely chopped cooked ham, chicken or prawns, mixed with enough Mayonnaise (see page 256) to bind.
- Softened blue cheese mashed with a little cream.
- Caviar mixed with a little sour cream and onion juice.
- Chopped roast beef mixed with enough Béarnaise Sauce (see pages 459–60) to bind.
- Avocado mashed with a little cream cheese, lemon juice and seasonings.
- Finely chopped smoked salmon or other flaked, smoked fish mixed with cream cheese and seasoned with pepper and lemon juice.

Fill with one of the following, to serve hot with drinks or in cream-puff-sized shells as a first course.

- Chopped cooked spinach, flaked crab, chopped prawns or asparagus, mixed with Mornay Sauce (see page 457).
- Chopped cooked chicken, ham, brains, sweetbreads or seafood, fried mushrooms or Duxelles (see page 133) mixed with Béchamel or Velouté Sauce (see pages 456–7).
- Sautéed chicken livers and golden shallots in a sauce made in the pan with cream and a little sherry, thickened with cornflour.

Basic Profiteroles

1 quantity sweetened or unsweetened Choux Pastry (page 345); 1 egg; pinch salt.

Using a piping bag fitted with a 1 cm (¹⁄₂ in) plain tube, pipe choux pastry into small, high mounds, well apart, on a lightly greased baking tray. Pipe each mound with one steady pressure, and release pressure before lifting bag away, to avoid a long tail. Alternatively, take spoonfuls of the pasty and push off on to baking tray. Do not try to change shape of choux pastry when putting it out, or it will rise in bumpy shapes instead of round ones. For 5 cm (2 in) profiteroles, make mounds about 3 cm (1¹⁄₄ in) in diameter. Beat egg with salt and brush over pastry mounds, pushing down tails (egg glaze may be omitted if puffs are to be iced; just push down tails with a damp finger).

Bake in a preheated very hot oven (230°C/450°F) for 10 minutes, then reduce heat to moderate (180°C/350°F) and bake 15–20 minutes more or until profiteroles are golden-brown, firm and light in the hand. If pastry is becoming too brown before it is cooked through, cover loosely with a sheet of foil. Make a slit or hole with the point of a knife in the side of each profiterole. Return to turned-off oven and leave with door ajar for 20 minutes to ensure that puffs are thoroughly dried out (this is the secret of puffs that will hold their shape without collapsing). Cool on a wire rack. Fill by piping filling through the holes in the sides, or by carefully cutting off tops with a serrated knife, spooning in filling and replacing lids. Unfilled profiteroles will keep in an airtight container for 1–2 weeks. Makes about 16 x 5 cm (2 in) profiteroles.

Profiteroles au Chocolat
(Chocolate Profiteroles)

16 x 5 cm (2 in) Profiteroles (above); ¹/₂ cup cream, whipped with 2 tsp icing sugar and a few drops vanilla, or ³/₄ cup Crème Pâtissière (page 207); sifted icing sugar.

HOT CHOCOLATE SAUCE: 185 g (6 oz) dark chocolate; 6 tbs water; 1 tbs rum or brandy (optional).

Fill profiteroles with whipped cream or crème pâtissière. Pile them into a serving dish and sift a little icing sugar over the top.
HOT CHOCOLATE SAUCE: Break chocolate into pieces and place in a heatproof bowl with water and rum or brandy, if using. Set bowl over a saucepan of simmering water and stir until chocolate melts. Cook 1 minute longer, then pour into a heated jug and serve with profiteroles. Serves 6–8.
VARIATION
CHOCOLATE PROFITEROLES FOR AFTERNOON TEA: Fill profiteroles as described, then dip tops into Chocolate Glaze (see page 83). Place on a wire rack to set. Omit chocolate sauce.

Profiteroles à l'Orange
(Orange Profiteroles)

3 sugar cubes; 1 orange; ¹/₂ cup cream; 2 tsp brandy (optional); 16 x 5 cm (2 in) Profiteroles (page 390); 90 g (3 oz) caster sugar.

Rub sugar cubes over rind of orange until sugar is saturated with orange oils. Squeeze juice from half the orange, and pound sugar cubes with 2 tsp of the juice until dissolved. Whip cream with this orange syrup and brandy. Use to fill profiteroles. To make toffee topping, place caster sugar in a small, heavy saucepan and cook slowly, tilting pan frequently from side to side so that sugar heats evenly, until it melts and caramelises to a golden-brown. Dip base of saucepan in cold water to stop further cooking. Dip top of each profiterole in toffee and place on a wire rack to set. Serves 6–8.

Profiteroles Pralinées (Praline Profiteroles)

¹/₂ cup cream; ¹/₄ cup Crème Pâtissière (page 207); 2 tbs Praline (page 387); 16 x 5 cm (2 in) Profiteroles (page 390); icing sugar.

Whip cream and mix with crème pâtissière and praline. Fill profiteroles and sift a little icing sugar over tops. Serves 6–8.

Coffee Profiteroles

1 tsp instant coffee powder; 2 tsp hot water; ¹/₂ cup cream; 2 tsp icing sugar, sifted; 2 tsp brandy or whisky (optional); 16 x 5 cm (2 in) Profiteroles (page 390); 1 quantity Coffee Glacé Icing (page 205).

Dissolve coffee in hot water and allow to cool. Whip cream with icing sugar, coffee and brandy or whisky, if using. Fill profiteroles and ice tops with coffee glacé icing. Serves 6–8.

Cream Puffs

These are delicate little puffs of feather-light choux pastry, filled with sweetened whipped cream. Alternatively, use Crème Pâtissière (see page 207).

1 cup cream; icing sugar, sifted; few drops vanilla; 12 Profiteroles (page 390).

Whip cream with 1 tbs icing sugar and vanilla. Fill shells and sift more icing sugar over the tops. Makes 12.

PROSCIUTTO

The general Italian term for ham, although it has come to refer more particularly to raw, uncooked ham (*prosciutto crudo*).

Prosciutto is made throughout Italy (and the same method is followed in many other countries), but the prosciutto of Parma has the highest reputation. It is traditionally prepared in the cold months of the year; proscuitto is cut from the hind thigh of the pig, salted, then allowed to dry for about 12–18 months.

A good prosciutto should be a deep, rosy pink colour, with a thin edge of white fat; it should be quite firm and dry. It is usually cut in paper-thin slices, since it contains very little moisture and its flavour is quite intense. It is often served as antipasto or hors d'oeuvre, either by itself or accompanied by fresh ripe figs or melon. It may also be used with pasta, in which case thicker slices are required.

See also *Ham*.

Prosciutto con Melone
(Raw Ham with Melon)

There is no substitute for the delicate flavour of raw smoked ham. It combines exquisitely with the sweetness of ripe cantaloupe (rockmelon) or honeydew melon and, when in season, ripe figs.

1 ripe melon, chilled; 6–8 paper-thin slices prosciutto.

Seed and cut melon into 6–8 slices. Serve each portion of melon with a slice of prosciutto draped over it. Serves 6–8.

PRUNE

Any kind of dried plum. Certain varieties of plums are particularly suitable for drying. Prunes should be black and shiny, with a moist dark, sweet flesh. They may often be eaten or used for cooking without any preliminary soaking, but soaking will soften them and reduce cooking time. Red or white wine may be used to give a slightly different flavour, and soaking in weak tea is said to enhance the prunes' flavour.

A simple dish of stewed prunes may be offered for breakfast or as a dessert, and many more elaborate desserts are based on prunes. Halved prunes may be added to a plain cake, a steamed pudding or a custard in place of raisins or sultanas, and the inclusion of nicely-plumped prunes in a winter fruit salad makes a welcome change.

The rich flavour of prunes also combines well with meats such as pork and rabbit. In Germany, prunes are often associated with goose – for example, in a stuffing with apples; with goose giblets; with haricot beans or lentils, to accompany goose or duck.

Large stoned dessert prunes may be stuffed with a whole almond or walnut, with marzipan or fondant, or with ground walnuts, sweetened with sugar or honey. Overnight soaking in port or Madeira beforehand will add a delightfully subtle difference to their flavour. See recipes.

Pork with Prunes

500 g (1 lb) large dessert prunes; 1¹/₂ cups white wine; 6 thick pork chops, trimmed of rind and excess fat; flour; salt and freshly ground black pepper; 30 g (1 oz) butter; 1 tbs redcurrant jelly; 1 cup cream; squeeze lemon juice.

Soak prunes overnight in wine. Next day, drain off one quarter cup wine and reserve. Simmer prunes very gently in remaining wine until soft. Remove stones. Lightly flour chops and season with salt and pepper. Brown on both sides in butter, then add reserved wine, cover and simmer gently about 40 minutes. Drain prunes, and add liquid to pan. Cook for about 3 minutes, then remove chops to heated serving dish. Arrange prunes with chops. Reduce pan liquid, then add redcurrant jelly and gradually stir in cream. Adjust seasoning, add lemon juice and pour sauce over chops. Serves 6.

Prune Mousse

500 g (1 lb) prunes, stoned; grated rind and juice 1 orange; grated rind and juice 1 lemon; 1 tbs port; 3 tsp (1 envelope) gelatine; 2 egg whites; ¹/₂ cup caster sugar; whipped cream to decorate.

Cook prunes in water to cover until tender. Purée in a blender or through sieve. If necessary, add a little water to make 1¹/₂ cups purée. Set aside ¹/₄ cup orange juice. Add remaining juices, rinds and port to purée. Soften gelatine in reserved juice, then dissolve over gentle heat. Add to purée and chill until starting to thicken. Beat egg whites until stiff, and gradually beat in sugar. Fold meringue into prune mixture. Spoon into individual dishes or large serving bowl and chill at least 1 hour. Decorate with whipped cream before serving. Serves 6.

Prune Hors d'oeuvre

large dessert prunes; walnut or pecan halves; rashers lean bacon, rind removed.

Soak prunes in boiling water or hot tea for 15 minutes, if desired. Drain, remove stones and stuff with nuts. Wrap in bacon and secure with wooden toothpicks. Grill, turning frequently, or bake in a preheated hot oven (200°C/400°F) until bacon is crisp, about 7–10 minutes. Drain on paper towels and serve hot.

Prune Tart

3 cups boiling water; 1 tsp tea leaves; 500 g (1 lb) large dessert prunes; 1 quantity Rich Shortcrust Pastry (page 342); 1 egg; ¹/₂ cup cream; 1 tsp cornflour; ¹/₄ cup caster sugar; 2 tbs Grand Marnier or Cointreau; 30 g (1 oz) butter.

Pour boiling water over tea and leave to steep for 5 minutes then drain. Soak prunes in weak tea for 4 hours. Drain and remove stones. Roll out pastry dough to about 5 mm (¼ in) thick. Line 23 cm (9 in) tart tin, and arrange prunes in tin. Bake in a preheated hot oven (200°C/400°F) for about 15 minutes. Meanwhile, beat egg with cream, cornflour, caster sugar and liqueur. Pour mixture over prunes, dot with butter and bake for 10–15 minutes longer. Serve warm or cold with cream. Serves 6–8.

PUDDINGS

See *Desserts and Puddings*.

PUFF PASTRY

See *Pastry*.

PUFTALOON (FRIED SCONE)

It seems that puftaloons are particular to Australia where, traditionally, they are eaten hot with golden syrup or treacle. Puftaloons are a type of scone dough, fried in plenty of hot dripping or a light vegetable cooking oil.

Puftaloons

2 cups self-raising flour; ¹/₂ tsp salt; 30 g (1 oz) butter; ²/₃ cup milk; oil for deep-frying.

Sift flour and salt into a bowl. Rub in butter. Make a

well in centre and mix in milk, adding more milk if necessary to make a soft dough. Knead lightly, then roll out on a floured work surface to 1 cm (½ in) thickness. Cut into rounds with a 4 cm (1½ in) cutter. Heat oil in a saucepan or deep frying pan and fry scones, turning once, until puffed and golden and cooked through. Drain on paper towels and serve hot. Makes about 12.

PULSES: DRIED BEANS, PEAS AND LENTILS

Dried beans, peas and lentils are classified as 'pulses', a word taken from the Latin 'puls' or 'pottage'. There are hundreds of varieties of pulses with differing flavours and textures, but they are regarded as a good source of protein.

Pulses are readily available from supermarkets, health food stores and delicatessens. They can be stored for up to 1 year in airtight containers, but longer storage will harden them. Buy pulses that are clean and of uniform size and quality. Most are available ready-wrapped, but some can be purchased loose.

Pulses make delicious soups, salads, or main course dishes. They are economical, easy to prepare and help stretch the menu.

DRIED BEANS

Haricot or White Beans: Smooth, oval beans of which there is more than one variety. Each is virtually inter-changeable with another in most recipes. Haricot beans are used in soups, baked bean dishes, stews, with meats and in salads. Varieties of haricot or white beans include:

Navy Beans: Excellent in dishes such as Boston Baked Beans.

Flageolets: Used with lamb dishes in France.

Soissons: Often considered to be the finest haricot beans and used to great effect in the superb *cassoulet* dishes of France.

Cannellini: The Italian variety of haricot beans and slightly fatter than their French and English equivalents. Cannellini are delicious in soups as well as many dishes from Tuscany, including Beans with Tuna, served with a garlicky dressing.

Butter Beans: Also known as Lima Beans, and can be large or small. Use the large beans in soups and purées, and the small butter beans in dishes instead of haricot beans or in their own right. Either large or small butter beans are delicious in salads.

Borlotti Beans: Pinky-brown, black-speckled beans used in Italian soup-stews, and sometimes mixed with pasta.

Chick Peas: Also known as Spanish beans, *garbanzo* or *ceci* peas. They are not strictly speaking, peas. Their nutty flavour and crisp texture are perfect in salads, soups, stews and in many other dishes such as *Hummus bi Tahini* (see pages 199–200), a delicious Middle Eastern spread.

Dried chick peas may need soaking for up to 10 hours before cooking, and sometimes need 5–6 hours of gently simmering to become completely tender. Chick peas can also be purchased canned, which eliminates the soaking and long cooking processes. Simply drain, rinse and use as specified in your recipe.

Red Kidney Beans: Kidney-shaped as their name suggests, and are probably most often associated with Chile Con Carne (see page 82), or salads. They are also the major component in *frijoles refritos* (Refried Beans), one of the basic dishes of Mexico.

Broad Beans or Fava Beans: These are strongly flavoured beans that form the basis of the Middle Eastern dish Falafel, little bean patties flavoured with herbs, garlic and onion (see page 397).

Mung Beans: These can be cooked as for other dried beans, but are probably best used after sprouting, in salads and Chinese dishes (see *Bean Sprouts*).

Black-eyed Peas or Beans: Creamy white beans which derive their name from the little black eye or spot in the centre. Often served in southern USA with pork and cornbread. Black-eyed peas are the essential ingredient in 'Hopping John' – a mixture of beans, brown rice, bacon and oil.

Soy Beans: Highly nutritious, containing complete protein, and used extensively as food and oil, particularly in countries where other sources of complete protein are scarce. Soy bean curds or *tofu* are used in Asian dishes as a meat substitute. Tofu is a rather bland substance that readily takes on flavours from other ingredients in the dish. Soy sauce is made from fermented soy beans. The distinctive flavour of soy beans blends well when used with other beans in recipes.

■ **BASIC PREPARATION**: When buying in bulk discard any broken or defective beans. Rinse well, until the water runs clear. Packaged beans usually need rinsing only. Most beans need soaking to restore the water lost during drying. The soaking water may be used in most recipes. Soak beans by one of the two methods below:

QUICK SOAKING: Put beans in a large saucepan, add cold water to cover and bring to the boil. Cover pan and cook for 2 minutes; remove from heat. Let stand for 1 hour, then cook according to recipe.

OVERNIGHT SOAKING: Put beans in a large bowl, cover with water and soak for 6–8 hours but no longer or they may ferment.

■ **TO COOK**: Cook beans in the soaking water or fresh water to cover. Cover the saucepan, bring to the boil, reduce heat and simmer for the time stated in the recipe or for 1½–2 hours (except chick peas which take longer – up to 5–6 hours). Red kidney beans should boil rapidly for the first 10 minutes of cooking to ensure harmful toxins are destroyed. Stir occasionally, being careful not to break the beans. When ready, they should be tender and hold their shape. Sugar, salt or acids (this includes tomatoes) added to the beans during simmering will toughen them, so add after beans are tender.

If beans are to be used for soups or in baked dishes, they should be cooked until they are just barely tender. Add flavourings such as onion, carrot, celery, bouquet garni, bay leaf, garlic or bacon bones according to the dish.

Most dried beans are also available precooked in cans, which precludes the soaking and long slow cooking. Drain, rinse and use according to recipe.

DRIED PEAS

Split Peas: Usually sold packaged, skinned and split; they may be bright green or golden yellow, and are often used in soups. Rinse thoroughly and soak in cold water overnight unless otherwise specified on the package or in the recipe.

LENTILS

Red, Brown and Green Lentils: These need less cooking and preparation than dried peas and beans. The small red lentil needs no pre-soaking and becomes tender after 20 minutes cooking. The brown and green lentils take a little longer to cook. Lentils are excellent in purées and soups.

In Germany, brown lentils accompany roast duck and in France, when cooked with garlic and flavoured with lemon juice, the purée is eaten with pickled (salt) pork. Some lentils can be used in salads.

Dhal: This is the Hindi word for pulses, and most packages labelled '*dhal*' contain a mixture of lentils with some dried beans and peas. Dhal is a delicious spiced purée served with Indian curries, and most take about 45 minutes to cook. **See recipes.**

Boston Baked Beans

2 cups small white haricot beans, soaked in water overnight; 125 g (4 oz) pickled (salt) pork or speck, cut into 2.5 cm (1 in) strips; 2 tsp dry mustard; $^1/_2$ cup firmly packed brown sugar; $^1/_3$ cup dark molasses; 1 tsp salt.

Drain beans, reserving liquid. Place one third of salt or pork speck in bottom of an ovenproof casserole and add drained beans. Blend together mustard, brown sugar and molasses with reserved bean liquid

and pour over beans. Cut several gashes in remaining salt pork or speck and place on top of beans. Cover and bake in a preheated very slow oven (120°C/250°F) for about 6 hours, adding extra water as needed. Uncover for final hour of cooking so pork will brown and crisp. Season. Serves 6–8.

NOTE: If you have a slow cooker this dish is an excellent one to try.

Beans with Tuna

A perfect light lunch dish.

$^3/_4$ cup dried haricot or cannellini beans, soaked in water overnight and drained; $^1/_2$ cup olive oil; juice 1 lemon; 2 cloves garlic, crushed; salt and freshly ground black pepper; 1 onion, finely sliced; 1 x 200 g can solid pack tuna, drained and flaked; chopped parsley.

Place beans in a saucepan and cover with fresh cold water. Bring to the boil, then cover and simmer 2½ hours or until tender. Drain. Mix together olive oil, lemon juice, garlic, salt and pepper and add to hot beans. Stir in onion. Cover and chill for several hours. Fold in tuna, sprinkle with parsley and serve in individual bowls. Serves 4.

Cassoulet

The traditional French meat, sausage and bean casserole.

125 g (4 oz) bacon; 750 g (1½ lb) pork spareribs, 500 g (1 lb) dried white haricot beans, soaked in water overnight and drained; 1 onion, halved; bouquet garni; 2 cloves garlic, lightly crushed; 500 g (1 lb) breast or shoulder of lamb, boned; 500 g (1 lb) garlic-flavoured boiling sausage such as clobassi; $^3/_4$ cup fresh breadcrumbs.

Trim rind from bacon and also any rind from pork. Dice bacon. Place beans in a heavy saucepan with bacon, onion, bouquet garni and garlic. Cover with water, bring to the boil and simmer for 1¼ hours. Meanwhile, roast pork spareribs and lamb in a preheated moderately slow oven (160°C/325°F) for 30 minutes. Add whole sausage to beans and simmer for a further 15 minutes. When beans are almost cooked, drain off and reserve liquid, discarding onion, bouquet garni and garlic. Place half the beans in a deep casserole. On top place sausage, thickly sliced, then lamb and pork, cut into serving-size pieces. Cover with the remaining beans and moisten with 1 cup of reserved liquid. Sprinkle breadcrumbs on top. Bake in a very slow oven (120°C/250°F) for 1½ hours, adding more liquid if dish becomes too dry. The breadcrumbs should form a fine golden crust on top by the end of cooking. Serves 6.

Quick Barbecued Baked Beans

2 tbs dark molasses; 2 tbs prepared spicy mustard;
juice $^1/_2$ lemon; 2 tsp Worcestershire sauce;
4 cups (2 x 420 g) cans baked beans in tomato sauce;
500 g (1 lb) frankfurts, thickly sliced.

Combine molasses, mustard, lemon juice and
Worcestershire sauce in a saucepan and heat gently.
Add beans and frankfurts and simmer for about 10
minutes, or place in a casserole, top with frankfurts
and bake in a preheated moderate oven (180°C/350°F)
for about 30 minutes. Serves 4–6.

Pasta with Beans

1 cup dried haricot or borlotti beans;
$4^1/_2$ cups cold water; 3 cups macaroni;
3 tbs olive oil; 1 large onion, chopped;
2 large carrots, sliced; 1 cup chopped celery;
1 clove garlic, crushed; 2 cups peeled, chopped
tomatoes; 1 tsp chopped fresh sage; 1 tsp chopped
fresh oregano; salt and freshly ground black
pepper; chopped parsley; grated Parmesan cheese.

Soak beans in water overnight. Next day, put beans
and water into a large saucepan. Bring to the boil,
then cover and simmer for 2–3 hours or until beans
are tender. Stir several times during cooking. Drain,
reserving $2^1/_2$ cups liquid. Cook macaroni according
to directions on packet. Drain. Heat oil in a large
heavy saucepan and sauté onion, carrots, celery and
garlic until soft but not coloured. Add tomatoes,
sage, oregano, salt and pepper. Cover and cook over
a gentle heat for 20 minutes. Add beans, macaroni
and $1^1/_2$ cups reserved bean liquid. Bring to the boil,
then cover and simmer for 35–40 minutes, stirring
occasionally, and adding more bean liquid if necessary.
Adjust seasoning. Turn into a serving bowl or
casserole and sprinkle with chopped parsley and
Parmesan cheese. Serves 8.

Chick Peas in Garlic Oil

1 cup dried chick peas, or 2 x 375 g cans garbanzos;
$^1/_2$ cup olive oil; 4 cloves garlic, crushed;
salt and freshly ground black pepper; juice 1 lemon;
3 tbs chopped parsley.

If using dried peas, cover with cold water and bring
to the boil, then turn off heat. Cover and leave
for 1 hour. Drain, cover with fresh cold water and
cook, covered, over a low heat for 2–3 hours or until
tender. Add a little more water if necessary to
prevent sticking. Drain. If using canned peas, drain
and rinse in a sieve under cold water before cooking.
Heat oil in a frying pan and sauté garlic and chick
peas on medium heat until lightly browned, stirring
gently from time to time. Season with salt, pepper
and lemon juice. Stir in half parsley. Serve hot or at

room temperature, sprinkled with remaining
parsley. Serves 6–8 as a first course.

Chick Pea Salad

1 cup dried chick peas, or 2 x 375 g cans garbanzos;
2 small onions, 1 halved and 1 sliced into rings;
1 bay leaf; 1 clove garlic; 1 tsp salt; 1 orange;
2 sticks celery, sliced; $^1/_2$ green or red pepper,
cored, seeded and sliced.

DRESSING: 1 tbs vinegar; 3 tbs oil; pinch dry
mustard; salt and freshly ground black pepper.

Soak dried chick peas in water overnight. Next day,
drain, place in saucepan, cover with fresh cold water
and add halved onion, bay leaf and garlic. Bring
to the boil, skimming off any scum that rises to the
surface. Cook, covered, on low heat for 2–3 hours or
until tender. Drain, discarding flavourings, add salt
and leave to cool. If using canned garbanzos, drain
them and rinse in a sieve under cold water. Holding
orange over a bowl to catch all the juice, remove all
rind and white pith with a serrated knife. Loosen
segments by cutting down each side of membranes.
Lift out segments in one piece and remove any seeds.
Squeeze core with remaining membrane over
segments. This juice may be added to dressing. Mix
orange segments, celery, green or red pepper, beans
and onion rings. Beat dressing ingredients together
until slightly thickened. Pour over salad and toss
well. Serves 4.

Spanish Cocido

A traditional Spanish soup-stew. Serve in deep soup
plates.

500 g (1 lb) dried chick peas; $^1/_4$ cup olive oil;
1 x 1 kg (2 lb) piece chuck steak or breast of veal;
3–4 large onions, chopped; 2 cloves garlic,
crushed; 2 tomatoes, quartered; 4 carrots, sliced;
$^1/_2$ cup chopped parsley; 1 ham bone or ham hock
(optional); 2 tsp salt; 2 chorizos (Spanish sausages)
or salami, sliced.

Place chick peas in a saucepan, cover with water and
bring to the boil. Boil 2 minutes, then remove from
heat and soak 1 hour. Drain. Cover with fresh water
and simmer $1^1/_2$ hours. Heat oil in a large saucepan
and sear meat over high heat. When brown all over,
add onions, garlic, tomatoes, carrots, parsley, ham
bone or hock, salt, sausages and chick peas with their
cooking water. Bring slowly to the boil, then cover
and simmer $1^1/_2$ hours or until chick peas are tender.
Add more hot water during cooking if necessary; the
peas must be well covered throughout cooking time.
To serve, discard ham bone or hock (return meat to
soup, if liked), slice meat and spoon chick pea sauce
over. Serves 6.

Garbanzo Spread

This spread is good for sandwiches or as a dip. Try it in an open-face sandwich with cucumber and tomato slices, or serve with wholemeal cracker biscuits.

1 x 375 g can garbanzos; ¹/₂ small onion, finely chopped; 1 clove garlic, crushed; 1 tbs oil; ¹/₄ cup chopped parsley; 1 tsp chopped fresh basil, or ¹/₄ tsp dried; 1 tsp chopped fresh oregano, or ¹/₄ tsp dried; 1 tsp ground cumin; lemon juice; salt and freshly ground black pepper.

Drain garbanzos, reserving liquid from can, and mash or purée in a food processor. Cook onion and garlic gently in oil until soft. Stir in herbs and cumin and cook 1 minute longer. Remove from heat and mix in garbanzo purée and enough of their liquid to give a spreading or dipping consistency, with lemon juice to taste. Season with salt and pepper. Makes 1–1¹/₂ cups.

Chick Pea and Pasta Soup

This soup from Italy is both filling and nutritious. The pancetta (or bacon) and parsley give a rich and fresh flavour. Pancetta is available at specialty Italian delicatessens.

1 x 375 g can garbanzos, drained; 6 cups chicken or beef stock; 2–3 slices pancetta or rashers streaky bacon, rind removed and finely chopped; 4 tbs olive oil; 2 cloves garlic, finely chopped; 4 tbs chopped parsley; salt and freshly ground black pepper; 2 cups ditalini or small pasta shells; grated Parmesan or Pecorino cheese.

Place garbanzos and stock in a saucepan and simmer gently for 5 minutes. Spoon out about half the chick peas and reduce to a purée with a little of the stock – use a food processor, blender or food mill. Return purée to pan. Fry pancetta or bacon in oil with garlic and parsley until cooked. Add this mixture (known as the soffrito) to chick pea mixture and bring to the boil. Season with salt and pepper. Add pasta and cook until tender. The soup will thicken considerably during this last cooking. Serve with cheese sprinkled over. Serves 4–6.

Refried Beans (Frijoles Refritos)

With minor variations these appear at every meal in Mexico.

2 cups dried red kidney beans, soaked in water overnight; salt; 125 g (4 oz) bacon dripping or lard; 1 large onion, finely chopped; 1 clove garlic, crushed; 1 small dried red chilli, seeded and finely chopped, or 1¹/₂ tsp Mexican chilli powder.

Boil beans rapidly in soaking liquid for 10 minutes, then reduce heat and cook gently until tender, about 2 hours. Add salt during last 30 minutes cooking time. Drain beans, reserving cooking liquid. Heat half the dripping or lard in a large frying pan. Add some of the beans and mash into hot fat. Add a little liquid and stir, then mash more beans into pan. Keep on adding beans and liquid until all are used, then stir over medium heat until mixture thickens. Turn into a bowl and clean frying pan. Refrigerate bean mixture until required. Heat remaining fat in pan and gently fry onion, garlic and chilli or chilli powder for a few minutes, stirring. Add beans and continue cooking and stirring until beans are dry. Taste and add more salt if necessary. Serves 6–8 as a side dish or as a filling for tacos.

NOTE: This dish can be made using canned kidney beans. Omit the first frying. Mash the beans in their liquid, then fry with onion, garlic and chilli until dry.

Bean Salad

1 onion, chopped; 1 tbs olive oil; 2 cloves garlic, 1 whole and 1 crushed; 1 bay leaf; 1 tsp salt; 5³/₄ cups water; 1 cup dried kidney or lima beans, soaked in water overnight and drained; 1 green pepper, cored, seeded and diced; ¹/₂ cup Vinaigrette Dressing (page 442); 3 tbs chopped parsley; 1 tsp prepared mustard.

Gently fry half the chopped onion in oil in a heavy saucepan until beginning to colour. Add whole garlic clove, bay leaf, salt and water. Add beans, boil rapidly for 10 minutes then simmer until tender, 2–2¹/₂ hours. Drain and cool. Add green pepper to beans. Combine dressing, crushed garlic, parsley, mustard and remaining onion. Pour over beans and toss well to mix. Chill, and toss again just before serving. Serves 6–8.

NOTE: This salad may be served as a first course on a bed of shredded lettuce on individual plates.

Hopping John
(Black-Eyed Peas and Rice)

1 cup black-eyed peas, soaked in water overnight and drained; 1 smoked pork hock, or 1 small piece pickled (salt) pork, or 1 ham bone; 1 large onion, chopped; 1 cup long-grain rice; salt and freshly ground black pepper.

Rinse peas in cold water and place in a large saucepan with pork, onion and enough water to measure twice depth of peas. Bring to the boil, then cover and simmer for 1 hour or until peas are tender. Remove pork with slotted spoon; discard any bone and gristle and chop meat into small pieces. Drain peas into a sieve placed over a bowl. Add enough water to liquid, if necessary, to measure 2 cups. Return chopped meat, peas and liquid to saucepan, bring to the boil and add rice. Simmer, covered, until rice is tender and liquid is absorbed. Stir in salt and pepper and spoon into a heated serving bowl. Serves 6.

Falafel *(Bean Croquettes)*

This is a deliciously spicy appetiser from the Middle East. The fava or broad beans used in falafel need long soaking to help the skins slip off more easily.

I cup dried fava or broad beans; I cup dried chick peas; I medium onion, chopped; 2 cloves garlic, chopped; ¹/₂ cup finely chopped parsley; pinch chilli powder; I tsp ground coriander; ¹/₂ tsp ground cumin; I tsp bicarbonate of soda; salt and freshly ground black pepper; oil for deep-frying.

Soak fava or broad beans in water to cover for 48 hours, changing water twice each day. It is best to cover beans and refrigerate during soaking process to prevent fermentation. Soak chick peas in cold water for 12–15 hours. Drain beans and peas. Remove skins from beans by squeezing each firmly in the fingers until the seed pops out of the skin. You may have to slit the skin of some beans with the point of a sharp knife and then squeeze. Leave skin on chick peas. Combine beans and peas with onion and garlic and process in a food processor in 2 batches, or push through a food mill twice. Add parsley, chilli powder, coriander, cumin and soda and season with salt and pepper. Knead well and leave for 30 minutes. Shape a tablespoon of the mixture into a ball and flatten into a thick patty, 4 cm (1¹/₂ in) in diameter. Repeat until all mixture is used. Deep-fry in hot oil, 6–8 at a time, for 5–6 minutes, turning to brown evenly. Drain on paper towels. Serve hot as an appetiser or in split pita bread with Tahini Sauce (see page 525). Makes about 30.

DRIED PEAS
Pea with Ham Soup

500 g (I lb) split green peas, soaked in water overnight and drained; 8 cups water; I ham bone; salt and freshly ground black pepper; 4 bratwurst sausages, or 6 frankfurts (optional).

Place peas, water and ham bone in a large saucepan and bring to the boil. Season with salt and pepper, and simmer for 30 minutes. Remove ham bone and cut off meat. Chop meat and set aside. Strain soup through a sieve, return to pan and reheat. Heat sausages or frankfurts, if using, in hot water, then drain and slice. Add to soup with ham. Adjust seasoning. Serves 6.

Kichadi

This is very much like pilaf – a combination of rice and split peas.

2 cloves; very small piece cinnamon stick; cardamom seeds from 3 pods; I tsp turmeric; 2 tsp ground fenugreek seeds; 4 tbs oil; 2 onions, chopped; I green pepper, cored, seeded and diced; 2 cups brown rice; 6 cups water; I tsp salt; I cup yellow split peas.

Sauté all the spices in 2 tbs oil in a large, heavy saucepan. Add onions and green pepper and cook, stirring, until onions are soft. Stir in rice and continue to cook for about 5 minutes or until rice begins to turn white. Add water and salt and bring to the boil. Cover and cook on low heat for 20 minutes. Sauté yellow split peas in remaining oil. Add split peas to rice and continue cooking for 30 minutes. Makes 6 cups.

VARIATION

Add chopped cooked vegetables or a diced raw tomato at end of cooking time.

LENTILS
Sausages with Lentils

3 rashers bacon, rind removed and halved; 6 large pork sausages; 250 g (8 oz) lentils; 2 onions, each studded with 3 cloves; I bouquet garni; salt and freshly ground black pepper.

GARNISH (OPTIONAL): Chopped parsley.

Place bacon in a large saucepan over low heat and cook until fat melts. Add sausages to pan and fry, turning occasionally, until evenly browned. Add lentils, onions, bouquet garni, salt and pepper. Pour in sufficient water just to cover the ingredients. Bring to the boil, then cover and simmer gently for 30–40 minutes or until lentils are tender and liquid has been absorbed. Remove bouquet garni and onions and serve hot, garnished with parsley, if desired. Serves 6.

Lentils with Mint

I cup brown lentils; salt and freshly ground black pepper; I clove garlic, crushed; ²/₃ cup plain yogurt; ¹/₂ bunch watercress, stalks removed, or ¹/₂ cup chopped parsley; I¹/₂ tbs chopped fresh mint; 2 tomatoes, peeled, seeded and diced.

Place lentils in a saucepan with enough fresh cold water to cover. Bring to the boil slowly and simmer 15 minutes or until just tender but not mushy. Drain lentils, reserving liquid. Stir in salt, pepper and garlic. Measure ¹/₂ cup lentil stock and mix it with yogurt. Stir into lentil mixture. Just before serving, lightly mix watercress or parsley into lentils. Finally add mint and tomatoes. Serve as salad, or use to fill small pita breads. May be served with cold meats – for non-vegetarians – or other vegetable dishes. Serves 4.

Mediterranean Lentil Stew

Lentils do not need soaking before cooking. Mixed with vegetables they make a delicious stew in which most of the liquid is absorbed to give a moist sauce.

2 tbs oil; 2 onions, chopped; I clove garlic, crushed; 2 sticks celery, sliced; 4 small zucchini, sliced; 4 tomatoes, peeled and quartered; 3³/₄ cups water or stock; I tsp ground coriander; salt and freshly ground black pepper; I cup brown lentils; 2 tbs chopped coriander or parsley (optional).

Heat oil in a large saucepan. Add onions, garlic, celery and zucchini and fry gently for 5 minutes or until lightly browned, stirring frequently. Add tomatoes, water or stock, ground coriander, salt and pepper. Bring to the boil. Add lentils, then cover and simmer for 1 hour or until lentils are tender. Alternatively, transfer ingredients to a casserole, cover and bake in a preheated moderate oven (180°C/350°F) for 1½–2 hours. Sprinkle with chopped coriander or parsley before serving. Serve hot. Serves 4.

Lentil Salad

2 cups brown lentils; I large onion, studded with
2 cloves; I bay leaf; I tsp salt; 3 cloves garlic, bruised;
I strip orange rind; ½ cup chopped parsley;
I cup finely chopped spring onions;
½ cup olive oil; I tsp red wine vinegar;
I tbs lemon juice.

GARNISH: 2 rashers bacon, grilled until crisp and crumbled; 2 hard-boiled eggs, chopped;
¼ cup chopped parsley; 12–15 black olives.

Cover lentils with cold water in a saucepan and bring slowly to the boil, then remove from heat, cover and stand 1 hour. Drain and return to pan. Cover again with cold water to come 5 cm (2 in) above lentils. Add onion, bay leaf, salt, garlic and orange rind. Bring to the boil, then cover and simmer until just tender, about 20–30 minutes. Drain and discard flavouring ingredients. Cool. Put lentils into a bowl and toss gently with parsley, spring onions, oil, vinegar and lemon juice. Cover and stand for 1 hour. Fold bacon gently through lentils. Spoon salad into a serving dish and garnish with eggs, parsley and black olives. Serves 8.

Cauliflower and Lentil Curry

½ cup red or brown lentils; 2 onions, finely
chopped; 60 g (2 oz) butter or ghee;
½ tsp chilli powder, or to taste; ¼ tsp turmeric;
½ tsp curry powder; 2 tbs desiccated coconut;
I medium cauliflower, cut into florets; I tsp salt;
I cup water; juice I lemon.

Place lentils in a saucepan, cover with fresh cold water and simmer gently for about 20 minutes or until almost tender. Drain. Fry onions in butter or ghee until soft. Add spices and coconut and cook gently, stirring, for 3 minutes. Add cauliflower, salt, lentils and water. Cover tightly and cook on low heat for 15–20 minutes or until cauliflower and lentils are soft. Stir in lemon juice. Taste and add more salt if needed. Serve as a main course with rice, pappadams and 1–2 side dishes, or as an accompaniment to a meat curry. Serves 4 as a main course, 6 as an accompaniment.

Dhal (Red Lentils)

250 g (8 oz) red lentils; ½ tsp chilli powder;
I tsp salt; I tsp turmeric; 4½ cups boiling water;
3 tomatoes, quartered; 2 onions, finely chopped;
30 g (I oz); 2 tsp grated fresh ginger.

Put lentils, chill, salt and turmeric into a saucepan with boiling water, and cook until tender. Purée lentils in a blender or push through a sieve. Fry tomatoes and onions in butter until golden. Add to lentils with ginger and cook for 5 minutes. Dhal should have the consistency of a thick sauce and is best eaten with boiled rice. Serves 4–6.

PUMPKIN

To trick-or-treat children at Halloween, this vegetable is perhaps more of a joy than something to be eaten. Historically, pumpkin is from the most ancient of vegetable families, the gourds, which were eaten in soups in Europe well before America and its pumpkins were discovered. There are many varieties of pumpkin, of all shapes and sizes. Some are available almost throughout the entire year; others wait for the first frosts before being harvested, when they are said to keep better and to have a sweeter flesh. Look for golden nuggets, japs and Queensland blues.

Pumpkin has a sweetish, nutty flavour which may be enhanced with herbs, cheese or spices, as in the traditional Pumpkin Pie. A dash of grated nutmeg is good with mashed pumpkin, too.

Whole pumpkins may be stuffed with bread, cheese, cream and seasonings and baked in the oven for a couple of hours; if the mixture is more liquid, the result is thick pumpkin soup in its own tureen. Small butternut pumpkins, halved and the centre flesh and seeds removed, may be parboiled and used as a 'cup' for another vegetable, such as spinach or broccoli.

Pumpkin Soup – whether cooked in the pumpkin or not – is always a winter favourite; in some Asian countries it is made with coconut milk and flavoured with coriander and shallots.

■ TO COOK: It may be boiled, steamed or baked. Steaming is usually preferable to boiling, unless the pumpkin is to be mashed afterwards, since the pumpkin will keep its shape better and not become waterlogged. Pumpkin is generally peeled before cooking, although the skin of some varieties (such as butternut) is edible when young. See recipes.

BAKED PUMPKIN: Cook with the roast meat, if the tin is large enough. Roll pumpkin pieces in meat drippings, arrange around meat and cook for 30–45 minutes. Otherwise, cook in a separate tin with 1–2 tbs oil or dripping.

BOILED PUMPKIN: Cook pieces of pumpkin, not too small, in boiling salted water until tender. Drain, dry briefly over heat then toss with butter and chopped fresh parsley. Alternatively, mash with butter and seasonings to taste.

Pumpkin is often mashed with potato, which can absorb some of the excess moisture from the pumpkin. The pumpkin needs less cooking time, and should be added about 5 minutes after potato.

STEAMED PUMPKIN: Place even-sized pieces of pumpkin in steaming basket and steam until tender, about 10–15 minutes. Alternatively, cook in 5 mm (1/4 in) water over high heat, but make sure the pan does not boil dry.

Pumpkin Soup

4^1/$_2$ cups peeled, seeded and chopped pumpkin;
^{1}/$_2$ cup finely chopped onion; 90 g (3 oz) butter;
3 cups water; 1 cup milk; 2 tbs flour; salt and freshly ground white pepper; 1 egg yolk (optional).

Cook pumpkin and onion in 60 g (2 oz) butter in a saucepan for 10 minutes, stirring constantly. Add water and cook gently until pumpkin is very tender. Push through sieve or purée in blender or food processor with a little of the milk. Melt remaining butter in clean pan and stir in flour, then pumpkin purée and remaining milk, stirring constantly until well blended. Season with salt and pepper. Simmer 20 minutes. If desired, take out a little soup, blend with egg yolk and stir into remaining soup, just before serving. Serves 4–6.

VARIATION
Add a little grated fresh ginger with onion.

Pumpkin Gratin

500 g (1 lb) pumpkin, peeled, seeded and chopped;
2 tbs rice; ^{3}/$_4$ cup water; salt and freshly ground black pepper; ^{1}/$_4$ cup cream; nutmeg;
3 tbs grated cheese.

Place pumpkin in a saucepan with rice and water. Season lightly with salt and pepper. Bring to the boil, then cover, reduce heat and cook for 12–15 minutes, by which time pumpkin and rice should be tender and water absorbed. Mash pumpkin and rice, or purée in blender. Add cream, nutmeg and extra seasoning if required. Turn into buttered, shallow ovenproof dish. Sprinkle with cheese and place in a preheated hot oven (200°C/400°F) to warm through and brown surface. Serves 6.

Pumpkin Pie

Gramma, or bugle, pumpkin is the variety traditionally used for pumpkin pie, but if it is not available, use butternut instead.

1 kg (2 lb) pumpkin, peeled, seeded and chopped;
^{1}/$_2$ tsp salt; ^{3}/$_4$ cup firmly packed brown sugar;
^{1}/$_2$ cup sultanas; 1 tsp cinnamon; ^{1}/$_2$ tsp nutmeg;
1 tbs flour; grated rind and juice 1 lemon; Rich Shortcrust Pastry for a two crust pie made using 2 cups flour (page 342); 30 g (1 oz) butter;
beaten egg white or milk; caster sugar.

Place pumpkin in a saucepan, cover with boiling water, add salt and cook for 5 minutes. Drain. Combine pumpkin with brown sugar, sultanas, spices, flour, lemon juice and rind. Line greased 23 cm (9 in) pie plate with just over half pastry dough. Add pumpkin filling and dot with butter. With remaining dough, make lid for pie, or cut pastry into strips and arrange as lattice. Cut small steam vents in lid. Brush dough with egg white or milk and sprinkle with caster sugar. Bake in a preheated hot oven (200°C/400°F) for 30 minutes, then reduce heat to moderate (180°C/350°F) and bake for further 40 minutes or until pastry is crisp and golden. Serves 6–8.

Pumpkin Pie (American Style)

The traditional American recipe made without the top pastry crust.

2 cups cooked, mashed pumpkin; 2 eggs, lightly beaten; 1^1/$_2$ cups evaporated milk; ^{1}/$_2$ cup sugar;
1 tsp cinnamon; ^{1}/$_2$ tsp ground ginger;
^{1}/$_4$ tsp ground cloves; ^{1}/$_2$ tsp salt;
1 quantity Rich Shortcrust Pastry (page 342).

Combine pumpkin with eggs, milk, sugar, spices and salt, blending well. Roll out pastry dough and use to line 23 cm (9 in) pie plate. Fill with pumpkin mixture. Bake in a preheated hot oven (200°C/400°F) for 40 minutes. Serve warm or cool, with whipped cream, if liked. Serves 6–8.

PUNCH

Originally, punch was a drink based on rum and flavoured with lemon juice and cinnamon. Today, it is a beverage made in large quantities, usually containing fruit or fruit juice but not necessarily made with alcohol. A bowl of punch is useful at large parties when it is not possible to offer a range of different drinks. In the time of Brillat-Savarin, the famous eighteenth-century French gourmet and writer, a bowl of punch was served at the end of the evening, after coffee and liqueurs. See recipes.

Wassail Bowl

The Wassail bowl, symbolising good cheer, is a traditional drink whose origins go back to Anglo-Saxon times. It should be quaffed with the toast, 'Wassail!' ('Good health!').

12 small red apples; 2 cups water; 1 tsp freshly grated nutmeg; 2 tsp ground ginger; 1 cinnamon stick;
6 whole cloves; 6 whole allspice; 4 coriander seeds;
4 cups sugar; 2^1/$_2$ litres (10 cups) ale; 2 bottles sherry or Madeira; 12 eggs, separated; 1 cup brandy.

Prick apples all over and bake them in a preheated moderate oven (180°C/350°F) for 40–50 minutes or until soft. Mix water, spices and sugar in a large saucepan and bring to the boil, stirring until sugar is dissolved. Simmer for 10 minutes, then add ale and sherry or Madeira and heat, do not boil. Beat egg yolks until thick and pale. Whisk egg whites to a firm snow and fold into yolks. Slowly strain half the spiced mixture over the eggs, stirring constantly. Pour into a warmed punch bowl. Bring the remaining spiced mixture almost to boiling point and strain it into the bowl. Add brandy, stir to combine and add apples. Serve hot in punch cups. The apples may be served after the punch. Serves 25–30.

Champagne Cup

Champagne or sparkling wine may by used for this cup.

¹/₄ cup brandy; ¹/₄ cup Curaçao; I x 750 ml (I¹/₄ pint) bottle champagne; soda water; fresh grapes, strawberries or sliced fresh peaches to garnish.

Pour brandy, Curaçao and champagne over ice in large punch bowl and mix well. Add soda water as desired just before serving, and garnish with fresh fruit. Quantities may be doubled if desired. Serves 6–8.

Rum Punch

FOR EACH DRINK: crushed ice; 60 ml (2 oz) rum; juice ¹/₂ lime; I tsp sugar; mint sprigs to garnish.

Half-fill a tall glass with ice and add rum, lime juice and sugar. Stir, and serve garnished with mint sprigs.

Tea Punch (Alcoholic)

3 tbs tea leaves, 5 cups boiling water; 5 cups sweet white wine (Sauternes, Barsac); ¹/₂ cup lemon juice; ice cubes; fresh fruit to garnish (orange and lemon slices, strawberries or cherries, sliced peaches, pineapple chunks).

Steep tea leaves in boiling water for 5 minutes. Add wine and lemon juice and strain over ice in a punch bowl. Float fruit on top and stand for 10 minutes before serving. Serves 10.

Tea Punch (Non-Alcoholic)

3 tbs lemon juice; ³/₄ cup orange juice; I¹/₂ cups apricot nectar; I x 750 ml (I¹/₄ pint) bottle ginger ale; I¹/₂ cups strong tea; 3 tbs sugar; ice cubes; mint sprigs to garnish.

Have fruit juices, apricot nectar and ginger ale well chilled. Strain tea into a large jug and stir in sugar, lemon and orange juices and apricot nectar. Add ginger ale, stirring gently. Serve over ice cubes in tall glasses, garnishing each drink with a sprig of fresh mint. Serves 8.

PURI

An Indian deep-fried unleavened bread made from *atta* or *roti* flour.

The dough is well kneaded to give the necessary light texture, rolled into thin rounds, then deep-fried. Puris are very light, puffed golden and hollow inside. They are served warm to accompany curries, dhal or vegetable purées. *Atta* or *roti* flours are available from health food shops and good delicatessens.

Puri

3 cups atta or roti flour; I tsp salt; I tbs ghee or peanut oil; I cup lukewarm water; oil for deep-frying.

Place flour in a bowl, reserving ¹/₂ cup. Add salt to flour. Rub in ghee or add oil. Make a well in the centre and add water all at once, mixing with one hand to form a dough. Knead dough for at least 10 minutes. Wrap in plastic wrap and chill for 1 hour. Shape dough into 14–16 small balls about the size of a large walnut. Roll each one into thin rounds about 10 cm (4 in) diameter using reserved flour for dusting the work surface. In a deep frying pan heat about 2.5 cm (1 in) oil until a faint haze rises from the surface. Fry puris one at a time, pressing on the edges with an egg slice to encourage them to puff. When risen, turn to cook the other side. Drain on crumpled paper towels and serve hot. Makes about 14–16.

q

q

QUAIL

A small game bird, which has been adapted to commercial production. Almost all the quail eaten now has been bred for the table. The bird is white-fleshed, and has a faint gamey taste. Quail is usually very tender, and should be cooked quickly in a hot oven or grilled over hot coals; because the flesh is rather dry, a piece of pork fat or fatty bacon is placed on the breast or wrapped around the bird.

Quail can be eaten with a knife and fork, but it is easier to eat wings and drumsticks with the fingers; for this reason, finger bowls should always be offered when quail are served. Allow 1 to 2 quail per person for a main course; if serving as an entrée, before the main course, one quail per person is sufficient.

■ **TO COOK:** Season inside lightly with salt and pepper. Rub with butter, place a piece of pork fat or bacon on breast and truss securely. Roast, breast side up, in a preheated hot oven (200°C/400°F) for 10–12 minutes or until juices run clear when thigh is pricked with fine skewer. Remove trussing string and serve each quail on a round of fried bread.

Quail can be stuffed before roasting; choose a rice stuffing or a walnut and celery stuffing. **See recipes.**

Quail with Grapes

6 quail; salt and freshly ground black pepper; 60 g (2 oz) butter; $^1/_2$ cup dry white wine; juice $^1/_2$ lemon; $^1/_2$ cup sultana grapes, stalks removed.

Season quail lightly with salt and pepper. Heat butter in a shallow flameproof casserole and cook quail until lightly brown all over. Add wine and lemon juice, cover and cook over low heat for about 15 minutes. Add grapes and cook for about 5 minutes longer. Reduce sauce over high heat if necessary. Serves 6 as a first course, 3–4 as a main course.

Minute Quail

8 quail; salt and freshly ground black pepper; 60 g (2 oz) butter; 3 golden shallots, finely chopped; 3 thin slices prosciutto, cut into strips; 1 cup chicken stock.

Split quail down back, open out flat and remove any small bones from inside. Season with salt and pepper. Heat butter in a shallow flameproof casserole and cook quail for 4–5 minutes on one side. Turn, add shallots and prosciutto to casserole and cook a further 4–5 minutes. Remove quail to heated plate. Deglaze pan with stock and boil to reduce by about half. Pour over quail and serve immediately. Serves 4–6.

NOTE: Quail may be cooked in 2 or 3 lots.

Grilled Quail

In this recipe the quail are marinated with herbs in oil, which helps ensure that they do not dry out during grilling. Take care not to overcook the quail.

8 quail; $^1/_2$ cup olive oil; 2 tbs dried oregano or marjoram; 4 bay leaves, crumbled; salt and freshly ground black pepper; lemon wedges to serve.

Split quail down back and open out flat. Flatten with blade of cleaver. Place in a large shallow dish and sprinkle with olive oil, herbs, salt and pepper. Cover and marinate 2–3 hours, turning quail once or twice. Grill over hot coals, or under a preheated grill, for 10–15 minutes or until just cooked and brown. Serve with lemon wedges. Serves 4–6.

QUEEN OF PUDDINGS

This is an elaborate version of baked bread custard. A creamy base topped with jam then a layer of meringue perfectly combines flavours and textures, and makes a lovely ending to a dinner.

Queen of Puddings

2 cups fresh breadcrumbs, white or brown; 2 tbs vanilla sugar; grated rind 1 lemon; $2^1/_2$ cups milk; 60 g (2 oz) butter; 4 eggs, separated; 2 tbs berry jam, or jelly; $^1/_2$ cup caster sugar.

Mix breadcrumbs, vanilla sugar and lemon rind. Heat milk and butter almost to boiling, pour over breadcrumb mixture and allow to stand for 10 minutes. Beat in egg yolks. Pour into a greased shallow ovenproof dish. Bake in preheated moderate oven (180°C/350°F) for about 30 minutes or until just firm. Warm jam or jelly and spread evenly over custard without breaking surface. Beat egg whites until stiff. Add half caster sugar and whisk again until glossy. Fold in remaining caster sugar, reserving 1 teaspoon. Pile meringue on to custard and sprinkle with reserved caster sugar. Return to oven to bake for about 15 minutes or until meringue is slightly browned and crisp. Serve hot. Serves 6.

QUENELLE

An ethereal souffléed dumpling, poached in water or stock. Quenelles are made from a mousseline mixture or from a purée of fish, shellfish, veal or chicken beaten into a panada of choux pastry. Panada-type quenelles, though light, tender and a little easier to handle, are less delicate than the mousseline type.

Quenelles are a classic garnish for elegant soups and for certain dishes presented in the grand manner. For example, *Ris de Veau à la Financière* is a dish of richly sauced sweetbreads in a vol-au-vent case, garnished with veal quenelles, truffles, olives, 'turned' or 'fluted' mushrooms and sometimes cockscombs and cocks' kidneys! However, quenelles are usually served with a good sauce nowadays, as a superb entrée or lunch dish in their own right. **See recipes.**

Quenelles *(Mousseline Type)*

1 quantity Mousseline mixture (page 278); butter; hot water or stock; sauce (see recipe).

Prepare mousseline mixture of your choice, using fish, shellfish or chicken, or you may use 500 g (1 lb) very lean veal in the same way as chicken. Chill mixture well.

To shape each quenelle, dip 2 spoons into very hot water, scoop out some mixture on one spoon and round it off with inverted bowl of second spoon. Dip second spoon again into hot water, slip it under quenelle and, holding spoons just above surface of a buttered large, deep flameproof dish, slide quenelle off. It should be a neat egg shape. Use small or large spoons depending on size quenelles you want to make; they will swell to almost double their original size when cooked. Shape remaining mixture in same way, placing quenelles a little apart in dish.

Place dish on stove and gently pour round quenelles enough hot water or stock to cover them. Use fish stock for fish quenelles, chicken for others. Bring to just below simmering point (liquid should quiver, but no bubbles rise) and poach over low heat for 10–15 minutes or until quenelles are firm and roll over easily. Remove with a slotted spoon and drain on a tea-towel. They may be served at once, or can be covered and stored in refrigerator for up to 24 hours. To reheat quenelles, return them to buttered baking dish, cover with hot water or stock and poach very gently for 6–8 minutes or until heated through.

Serve 2–3 small quenelles in each bowl of soup, or 2–3 of the size shaped with a dessertspoon or small tablespoon for an entrée. Mask entrée quenelles with a good sauce such as Velouté, Beurre Blanc or Sauce Suprême (see *Sauces*). Quenelles can be placed on a bed of mushrooms or other vegetable purée before sauce is added, and top can be sprinkled with buttered breadcrumbs or grated cheese and browned under a preheated moderate grill. Makes about 15 entrée quenelles.

Quenelles *(Panada Type)*

**1 quantity Choux Pastry (page 345);
500 g (1 lb) finely minced shellfish or fresh fish,
or finely minced and sieved chicken or veal;
salt and freshly ground white pepper; nutmeg;
2–6 tbs chilled cream; butter;
hot water or stock; sauce.**

Mix together choux pastry, minced fish or meat, ½ tsp salt, ¼ tsp pepper and a large pinch of nutmeg. Chill mixture thoroughly, then beat in chilled cream little by little, using only sufficient to make a mixture firm enough to hold its shape on a spoon. Adjust seasoning. Shape, poach and serve the quenelles in the same manner as for mousseline-type quenelles. Makes about 15 entrée quenelles.

QUICHE

An open-faced tart with a savoury custard filling, thought to have originated in Lorraine, a province of eastern France. It was originally made with bread dough, but short pastry has been substituted in modern recipes.

There should be a lot of creamy filling in very little pastry. The pastry should be rolled out as thinly as possible. Today it is made in a metal flan ring, with straight sides (although many use one with fluted edges), which can stand on a baking tray. The tart can then be slid on to a plate for serving. Metal flan rings can be bought in chain stores and leading kitchenware shops, some having a metal base that lifts out for easy removal of the quiche.

Most widely known is *Quiche Lorraine*, which traditionally contains only eggs, cream or milk, and bacon or ham. However, there are many other popular fillings including cheese, tomatoes and onions, crab, smoked salmon, mushrooms or other vegetables, combined with a rich savoury custard, poured into the pastry shell and baked until puffed and brown.

A quiche is the perfect luncheon or supper dish served with a green salad, hot French bread and cold white wine. It also makes a good first course for dinner. Miniature quiches make delicious hot hors d'oeuvre.

Quiche lends itself to advance preparation. The flan ring, lined with pastry, may be prepared well ahead of time and chilled, the filling prepared and stored in the refrigerator. Half an hour before serving, the filling is placed in the flan, the custard poured in and the quiche baked in a preheated moderately hot oven (190°C/375°F) for about 30 minutes until a knife inserted in the centre comes out clean. Serve as soon as possible, but if guests are not ready, leave the quiche in the turned-off oven, door ajar, and it will stay puffed and brown for about 10 minutes.

A cold quiche is good picnic fare or makes a quick and satisfying snack. **See recipes.**

Herb Quiche

**30 g (1 oz) butter; 8 spring onions, finely chopped;
2 eggs; 1 cup cream; 1 tbs snipped chives;
1 tbs chopped watercress; 1 tbs chopped parsley;
salt and freshly ground black pepper; 1 x 20 cm
(8 in) Shortcrust Pastry Flan Case (page 342).**

Melt butter in a frying pan and sauté spring onions lightly. Beat together eggs and cream, and stir in spring onions, herbs, salt and pepper. Pour into a flan case. Bake in a preheated moderately hot oven (190°C/375°F) for 30–40 minutes or until filling is set. Serves 4–6.

q

Quiche Lorraine

While the classic Quiche Lorraine contains no cheese, this is a popular variation that is accepted by many.

3–4 rashers bacon, rind removed; 3 thin slices Swiss or Gruyère cheese; 1 x 20–23 cm (8–9 in) Shortcrust Pastry Flan Case (page 342); 2 eggs; 1 tsp flour; pinch nutmeg; 1/2 tsp salt; pinch cayenne; 1/2 cup cream; 1/2 cup milk; 1 tbs melted butter; watercress or parsley to garnish.

Grill bacon until crisp. Drain and crumble into bite-sized pieces. Cut cheese same size as bacon. Place bacon and cheese in flan case in layers. Beat together eggs, flour, nutmeg, salt, cayenne, cream and milk, only until combined. (Overbeating causes bubbles on top.) Stir in melted butter. Strain over bacon and cheese. Bake in a preheated hot oven (200°C/400°F) for 10 minutes, then reduce heat to moderate (180°C/350°F) and bake for a further 20 minutes or until a knife inserted in filling comes out clean. Garnish with watercress and serve warm with tossed salad. Serves 4–6.

Herbed Tomato Quiche

1 1/2 cups cream; 2 eggs; 2 egg yolks; 2 tbs tomato paste; salt and freshly ground black pepper; 4 tbs grated Swiss or Gruyère cheese; 1 x 25 cm (10 in) Shortcrust Pastry Flan Case (page 342); 2 tomatoes, cut into 1 cm (1/2 in) slices; 2 tbs chopped parsley; 1 tbs chopped fresh mixed herbs (lemon thyme, oregano, basil, chives); 3 tbs grated Parmesan cheese; 2 tsp butter.

Combine cream, whole eggs, egg yolks, tomato paste, salt and pepper and beat lightly. Add 2 tbs Swiss cheese. Spoon custard into flan case. Arrange tomato slices on top, sprinkle with salt, pepper and herbs and top with remaining Swiss and Parmesan cheeses. Dot with small pieces of butter. Bake on top shelf of a pre-heated moderately hot oven (190°C/375°F) for 20-25 minutes or until filling is set and top is golden. Remove quiche from pan and let it cool on a wire rack. Serves 6–8.

Roquefort Quiche

90 g (3 oz) Roquefort cheese; 185 g (6 oz) cream cheese; 2 eggs; 2/3 cup cream; salt and freshly ground black pepper; pinch nutmeg; 1 x 20–23 cm (8–9 in) Shortcrust Pastry Flan Case (page 342).

Beat cheeses with eggs and beat in cream gradually. Season with salt, pepper and nutmeg. Spoon into flan case. Bake in a preheated hot oven (200°C/400°F) for 10 minutes, then reduce heat to moderate (180°C/350°F) and bake for a further 20 minutes. Serves 4–6.

Seafood Quiche

3/4 cup fresh, frozen or canned crab, drained and flaked, or cooked shelled prawns; 1 tbs finely chopped spring onions; 1 tbs finely chopped parsley; 1 tbs dry sherry or vermouth; 1 x 20–23 cm (8–9 in) Shortcrust Pastry Flan Case (page 342); 2 eggs, lightly beaten; 1 cup cream, or 1/2 cup cream and 1/2 cup milk; pinch nutmeg; 1 tsp salt; pinch white pepper.

Remove any bony tissue from crab. Combine seafood with spring onions, parsley and sherry or vermouth. Chill, covered, for 1 hour. Sprinkle seafood mixture over bottom of flan case. Combine eggs, cream, nutmeg, salt and pepper. Strain over seafood mixture in flan. Bake quiche in a preheated hot oven (200°C/400°F) for 10 minutes, then reduce heat to moderate (180°C/350°F) and bake for a further 15 minutes or until filling is set and golden. Serve hot or warm. Serves 4–6.

Leek Quiche

30 g (1 oz) plus 2 tsp butter; 1/4 cup water; 1/2 tsp salt; 2 cups sliced leeks; 2 eggs; 1/4 –1/2 cup cream; 1/2 cup milk; pinch nutmeg; pinch pepper; 1/4 cup grated Swiss cheese; 1 x 20–23 cm (8–9 in) Shortcrust Pastry Flan Case (page 342); 1–2 slices Swiss cheese, cut into triangles.

Heat 30 g (1 oz) butter with water and salt in a heavy saucepan. Add leeks, cover and cook 6–8 minutes or until liquid in pan has almost evaporated. Lower heat and cook gently until leeks are soft. Drain. Beat eggs, cream, milk, nutmeg and pepper until just combined. Add leeks and grated Swiss cheese. Pour into flan case and arrange cheese triangles in pattern on top. Dot with small pieces of remaining butter. Bake in a preheated hot oven (200°C/400°F) for 10 minutes, then reduce heat to moderate (180°C/350°F) and bake for a further 20 minutes or until filling is set. Serves 4–6.

Spinach Quiche

500 g (1 lb) spinach; 30 g (1 oz) butter; 1 small onion, finely chopped; 2 eggs; 1 egg yolk; 1 cup cream; salt and freshly ground black pepper; 1 tsp chopped fresh oregano, or pinch nutmeg; 1 x 20–23 cm (8–9 in) Shortcrust Pastry Flan Case, baked blind (page 342).

Remove tough stalks from spinach, rinse well under cold running water and shake off excess. Place in a saucepan, cover tightly and simmer for 4–5 minutes. Drain spinach, pressing well to remove all liquid. Chop finely. Melt butter in a frying pan and cook onion until soft but not coloured. Add spinach. Cook over a high heat for 2–3 minutes to remove any

q

remaining moisture, then place in a bowl and allow to cool. Beat eggs and egg yolk together, add cream and mix well. Season with salt and pepper. Add spinach mixture and stir in oregano or nutmeg. Pour into flan case. Bake in a preheated moderately hot oven (190°C/375°F) for 30 minutes or until golden. Serves 4–6.

QUINCE

Looking rather like an ungainly, over-sized pear, the quince comes on to the market in late summer, about the same time as the early pears. Because of its tart flavour, it is not eaten raw, but makes a lovely dessert when cooked with sugar.

The quince is rich in pectin, and can be made into a beautiful, deep pink jelly. The cooked, sweetened pulp can be dried to yield a thick, jelly-like paste; this is especially popular in Spain, where it is called *membrillo*. Quinces are best if picked before they are fully ripe, then left to mature in a warm place. The fruit is ripe when it is yellow and strongly perfumed.

The addition of a quince, peeled and grated, to the apples for a pie gives a pleasant flavour variation; quinces may also be included in a dish of cooked, spiced pears. See recipes.

Quince Compote

**I cup sugar; 2 cups water; juice ¹/₂ lemon;
I kg (2 lb) quinces, peeled, cored and thickly sliced.**

Combine sugar, water and lemon juice in a saucepan. Add quince cores and peelings and simmer for 30 minutes. Strain syrup, return to pan and bring back to the boil. Poach quince slices until soft. Serve hot or cold, with cream or yogurt. Serves 8.

Quince Snow

**2 large quinces, peeled, cored and thinly sliced;
2 egg whites; about ¹/₄ cup caster sugar.**

Cook quinces in very little water until quite soft. Purée through sieve or in blender and cool. Beat egg whites until stiff. Gradually fold in quince purée and sugar to taste until smooth and well mixed. Chill. Serve with cream or custard, if desired. Serves 4.

Spiced Quinces

Pickled or spiced quinces make an excellent and unusual accompaniment to cold meats.

**4 large quinces, peeled, cored and cut into chunks;
salt; sugar; wine vinegar; coriander seeds.**

Place quinces in a saucepan, cover with cold water, add salt and bring to the boil. Boil for 10 minutes, then drain, reserving liquid. To each cup of liquid, add 2 cups sugar; ¹/₄ cup vinegar and ¹/₂ tsp coriander seeds. Bring to the boil, stirring to dissolve sugar. Add fruit and simmer until tender. Cool. Next day drain off syrup and bring to the boil. Pack quinces into sterilised jars, pour over boiling syrup and seal while still warm. Serve with ham, pork, mutton and turkey.

Quince Paste (*Quince Cheese*)

A delicious sweetmeat made from the reduced and sweetened purée of quince, so slowly cooked that it becomes a rich deep amethyst colour. Serve it with cheese, particularly the fresh soft cheeses, or cut it into squares, roll in sugar and serve with coffee.

6 quinces; ¹/₂ cup water; white sugar.

Rub quinces with a cloth to remove the down. Put them whole and unpeeled into a preheated moderate oven (180°C/350°F) and cook until tender, about 3 hours. Alternatively, quarter them (do not peel), remove seeds and steam them in the ¹/₂ cup water. When quinces are cool, slice them (without peeling) into a bowl, discarding cores and any bruised or hard pieces. Put sliced fruit through a food mill or sieve. Weigh purée and add an equal weight of white sugar. Heat in a heavy pan until sugar has dissolved, then boil, stirring nearly all the time, until cheese begins to candy and come away from bottom as well as sides of pan. (The boiling paste erupts and spits so take care.) Turn off heat and continue stirring until boiling has ceased. Fill shallow rectangular earthenware or tin dishes, or one dish, with cheese and leave overnight for mixture to get quite cold.

Next day put these moulds into lowest possible oven until cheese has dried out and is quite firm, about 3–4 hours, although it may take longer. Turn out slabs of paste and cut into portions you are likely to use at one time. Wrap them in greaseproof paper or plastic wrap or foil, and store in tins in a dry place.

NOTE: For the cheese board, the quince cheese may be cut into small pieces. For sweetmeats, coat square or oblong shapes, or walnut-sized balls, of quince cheese in caster sugar and set in tiny paper cups or wrap in cellophane paper.

RABBIT

A wonderfully versatile meat, blending equally well with red or white wine in sauces, with herbs and spices, and with mushrooms and prunes.

Once denigrated in Australia as 'underground mutton', rabbit has nonetheless remained popular. It represents good value, and, since it is very lean, rabbit is valuable in diets where cholesterol content should be minimised. A whole rabbit usually weighs around 1 kg (2 lb) and will serve 4–5 persons. Very small, young rabbits are sometimes available in spring; these have a milder flavour and are very tender. Some shops sell rabbit pieces, so that you can buy the choicest part of the rabbit, the loin section, and avoid the bony rib section.

Rabbit flesh does tend to be dry, so it is best cooked with liquid, such as wine or stock. Cooking time will depend on the age of the rabbit; older rabbits may need up to 1½ hours cooking, while young rabbits will be cooked in less than 30 minutes.

Many recipes call for a rabbit to be jointed. Cutting up a rabbit is similar to cutting up a chicken; separate the rabbit at leg joints, to give 2 thighs; cut the loin into 1 or 2 sections through the backbone and cut the rib cage section in 2, along the backbone. **See recipes.**

Sauté of Rabbit with Herbs

1 rabbit, jointed; 2 tbs oil; 1 tbs finely chopped onion or golden shallot; salt and freshly ground black pepper; 2 tsp Herbes de Provence (see below); ¹/₂ cup white wine.

Slowly brown rabbit pieces on all sides in oil in a flameproof casserole. Add onion or shallot and cook 1 minute longer. Season with salt and pepper, sprinkle over herbs and add wine. Bring to the boil, stirring, then cover and simmer until rabbit is tender, about 1–1½ hours. Add more wine or stock during cooking if necessary. Adjust seasoning before serving. Serves 4.
NOTE: Herbes de Provence is a mixture of dried thyme, rosemary, marjoram, fennel seeds and savory.

Sauté of Rabbit with Red Wine

2 rabbits, jointed; seasoned flour; 1 tbs oil; 30 g (1 oz) butter; 125 g (4 oz) bacon, rind removed and cut into small strips; ³/₄ cup red wine; 1 clove garlic, crushed; 3 tbs tomato purée; salt and freshly ground black pepper; chopped fresh parsley.

Lightly dust rabbit pieces with seasoned flour, then brown all over in oil and butter in a flameproof casserole. Remove rabbit from pan. Add bacon and fry 2 minutes. Add wine, bring to the boil and reduce a little. Stir in garlic and tomato purée, season with salt and pepper and return rabbit to pan. Simmer, covered, for about 1–1½ hours or until rabbit is

tender. Adjust seasoning, and sprinkle with chopped parsley before serving. Serves 6.

Rabbit with Mustard

1 rabbit, jointed; seasoned flour; 6 small onions, quartered; 1 tbs oil; 30 g (1 oz) butter; 125 g (4 oz) streaky bacon, rind removed and diced; 2 cups stock; salt and freshly ground black pepper; 2 tbs French mustard; 1 bouquet garni; ¹/₂ cup cream; chopped fresh parsley.

Lightly dust rabbit pieces with seasoned flour. Cook onions in oil and butter in a flameproof casserole for 3 minutes. Remove and add rabbit and bacon. Brown rabbit on all sides. Pour in stock, season with salt and pepper and add mustard and bouquet garni. Return onions to pan and simmer, covered, for about 1–1½ hours or until rabbit is tender. Remove rabbit to heated dish. Discard bouquet garni; reduce sauce by fast boiling if necessary. Add cream and parsley, and adjust seasoning. Pour sauce over rabbit and serve with boiled or mashed potatoes. Serves 4.

Rabbit and Pistachio Terrine

You will need 2 large or 3 small rabbits to obtain the amount of meat required – or you may be lucky enough to live near a butcher or delicatessen that stocks rabbit fillets.

750 g (1¹/₂ lb) boneless rabbit meat, minced; 500 g (1 lb) sausage mince; 4 rashers bacon, rind removed and finely chopped; 2¹/₂ cups fresh white breadcrumbs; 1 small onion, finely chopped; 1 clove garlic, crushed; ¹/₂ tsp dried thyme; 2 tbs Pernod; 1 tsp salt; freshly ground black pepper; 1 egg, beaten; ¹/₂ cup chopped, shelled pistachio nuts or walnuts; 250 g (8 oz) rashers streaky bacon, rind removed.

Place rabbit meat in a large bowl with sausage mince, chopped bacon and breadcrumbs. Add remaining ingredients, except bacon rashers, and blend together thoroughly with a wooden spoon. Line a 10-cup terrine or loaf tin with bacon rashers, cover bottom and sides. Spoon rabbit mixture into tin and level top. Cut remaining bacon rashers into thin strips and arrange on top of mixture in a lattice design. Cover tightly with foil or a lid. Bake in a preheated moderate oven (180°C/350°F) for 1½ hours. Take from oven, remove lid and place a weight on top. Leave until cool then refrigerate until required. Allow to mellow for 30 minutes at room temperature before serving. Serve in slices with tiny gherkins and crunchy French bread. Serves 10–12.
NOTE: Pernod gives a subtle aniseed flavour to the loaf, and is available in quarter bottles from your liquor store. Otherwise, you may substitute a pinch of ground aniseed and 1 tbs of sherry or gin.

r

Rabbit with Green Olives

1 tbs olive oil; 125 g (4 oz) pickled (salt) pork, diced; 3 onions, thickly sliced; 2 sticks celery, thickly sliced; 1 rabbit, jointed; 1 tbs flour; 2 cups hot chicken stock; 1 bay leaf; 1 sprig fresh rosemary, or 1/2 tsp dried; salt and freshly ground black pepper; 8 green olives, stoned; 1 tbs capers (optional).

Put oil, pork, onions and celery into a large flame-proof casserole and heat gently, stirring occasionally, until fat runs from pork. Add rabbit and fry gently, turning, until lightly browned on all sides, about 10 minutes. Sprinkle in flour and stir for 1 minute. Stir in hot stock, bay leaf, rosemary, salt and pepper. Bring to the boil, then cover tightly and simmer for 45 minutes to 1½ hours or until rabbit is tender. Add olives and capers, and simmer a further 10 minutes. Discard bay leaf. Serves 4.

RADICCHIO

Radicchio is a member of the chicory family, a beautiful deep red with creamy streaks. It has a bitterness and crispness that is particularly good in salads. It is also good braised, grilled or shredded or added to quickly made pasta sauces. Its cousin, treviso, can be used the same way.

Radicchio, Beetroot and Pear Salad

1 small French stick or baguette; oil for frying; 1 bunch baby beetroot; 2 radicchio; 1 endive (witlof), bases trimmed; 2 firm pears.

DRESSING: 2 tbs balsamic vinegar; 1 tbs Dijon-style mustard; 6 tbs extra virgin olive oil; salt and freshly ground black pepper.

Cut the baguette across into thin slices. Heat the oil in a shallow frying pan and fry the bread slices quickly until lightly golden on both sides. Drain on crumpled paper towels and set aside. If making ahead, store air-tight. Cut off the tops about 1 cm (1/3 in) above the beetroot, keeping only the tiny young leaves for the salad. Wash, leave whole and do not peel. Cover with cold water in a large saucepan. Cook, covered, for 15 minutes or until tender. Drain, cool slightly and slip off the skins. Halve if large.

Wash radicchio and endive and remove any discoloured outer leaves. Quarter, core and slice the pears. In a large bowl, whisk together the vinegar, mustard and oil. Season with salt and pepper and set aside. To serve, toss the beetroot and leaves, radicchio, endive, pears and croûtons with the dressing. Season with freshly cracked black pepper and serve. Serves 4.

RADISH

One of the delights of spring is a bowl of rosy-pink radishes, fresh and crisp, to be eaten simply with butter, salt and crusty bread, in the French manner. Offer them at the start of a meal, since they are said to stimulate the appetite. Sliced radishes are often added to mixed salads, and small whole radishes make an attractive garnish, cut decoratively or simply trimmed.

Radishes are best eaten when very young; older ones and those which have grown too slowly, are sometimes too hot-tasting to enjoy. Growing your own is the best way to ensure your radishes are fresh, and they are, perhaps, the easiest of all vegetables to grow. Although the small red radish, long or round, is the most common variety, there are many others, including the long white radish (*mooli*) often used in Oriental cookery.

TO MAKE RADISH ROSES: Wash small round radishes, remove all but the smallest leaf and trim off the roots. Using a sharp, thin-bladed vegetable knife, cut a small slice from root and then cut 4 slices around radish from root and almost to stem. Chill in iced water until 'petals' open.

TO MAKE RADISH FANS: Wash radishes and trim off leaves and root. Put each radish into a wooden spoon and, holding it firmly on the work surface, cut across into thin slices – the sides of the spoon will stop the knife from going all the way through. Chill in iced water until slices open into a fan.

Radish and Zucchini Salad

1 bunch radishes, cut into small matchsticks; 125 g (4 oz) small zucchini, cut into small matchsticks; salt and freshly ground black pepper; 1/2 cup Vinaigrette Dressing (page 442); 1 tbs very finely chopped fresh dill or parsley.

Season radishes and zucchini lightly with salt and pepper, then toss with vinaigrette and dill or parsley. Serve chilled. Serves 4–6.

RAGOUT

The French term *ragoût* usually describes a dish of meat, fish or poultry cooked with vegetables and liquid, although a dish of spring vegetables, such as peas, carrots, onions and potatoes, can also be called a *ragoût*.

The similar Italian term *ragù* usually describes the rich tomato and meat sauce, namely *Ragù alla Bolognese*, that is served with piping hot pasta.

Ragoût of Lamb with Turnips

2 tbs oil; 1 kg (2 lb) lamb shoulder, boned and cubed; 1 tbs flour; 4 onions, quartered; 1 bouquet garni; 1 clove garlic, crushed; 1 cup stock or water; 500 g (1 lb) small white turnips, peeled and quartered; 30 g (1 oz) butter; salt and freshly ground black pepper; 6–8 small potatoes, peeled.

Heat oil in a frying pan and brown lamb cubes all over. Transfer to a flameproof casserole. Sprinkle flour over lamb and cook, stirring, until lightly browned. Add onions, bouquet garni, garlic and stock or water and bring rapidly to the boil, stirring. Cover and leave to simmer gently. Meanwhile, slowly brown turnips in butter in same frying pan as used for lamb. Add to casserole, and season with salt and pepper. Continue to simmer, covered, over gentle heat, or cook in a preheated moderate oven (180°C/350°F), for about 1¼ hours. Add potatoes and cook further 20–30 minutes or until potatoes and lamb are tender. Remove bouquet garni before serving. Serves 6.

RAISINS

Dried grapes of different varieties; they are dried in the sun or artificially, which makes their skins wrinkle, the flavour change and the sugar content increase.

Raisins make nutritious snacks eaten on their own; they are indispensable in fruit cakes, Christmas puddings and mincemeat, delicious in breads, biscuits and cakes, and in a sauce to accompany some meats such as ham or in a stuffing for poultry, veal or pork. Raisins dried on the vine are superb eaten with cream cheese or fresh plain yogurt to finish a meal.

When using raisins in a cake batter, dust them lightly with some of the flour specified in the recipe, then fold them into the batter, scattering well. The flour helps prevent them clumping together.

Raisins may be plumped if necessary, by soaking in hot water for 10 minutes or overnight in fruit juice in the refrigerator. Drain well and use according to your recipe.

Do not buy raisins in large quantities; it is best to keep a small stock on hand, stored in an airtight container – in the refrigerator or freezer. The seedless white raisins of USA are those we recognise as sultanas (see page 517). See recipes.

Raisin Sauce

²⁄₃ cup raisins; 2 cups water; 1 cup firmly packed brown sugar; 1½ tbs cornflour; ¼ tsp ground ginger; 2 tbs cider vinegar.

Simmer raisins in water for 5 minutes. Combine brown sugar, cornflour, ginger and vinegar, add to pan and cook, stirring, until thickened. Serve hot or cold with ham steaks or tongue. Makes about 2½ cups.

Raisin Ham with Cheese Sauce

An excellent way to use up leftover cooked ham, serve with a tossed salad.

½ cup raisins; ½ cup water; 1 tbs horseradish relish; 8 thin slices cooked ham; 1½ cups cooked rice; 2 tbs butter; 2 tbs flour; 2 cups milk; ½ tsp salt; pinch cayenne; 1 cup grated Cheddar cheese; parsley to garnish.

Bring raisins and water to the boil in a covered saucepan. Simmer 10 minutes, then cool. Drain raisins and chop finely. Mix with half the horseradish and spread over each ham slice. Roll up. Spread rice in a greased shallow ovenproof dish and arrange ham rolls on top. Melt butter in a saucepan, stir in flour and cook for 2 minutes without browning. Gradually stir in milk and bring to the boil, stirring. Simmer until thickened. Add salt, cayenne, remaining horseradish and grated cheese. Stir until cheese melts, then pour sauce over ham rolls. Bake in a preheated moderate oven (180°C/350°F) for 20 minutes. Serve hot, garnished with parsley. Serves 4.

Raisin and Nut Stuffing

3 cups fresh breadcrumbs; ½ cup raisins; ²⁄₃ cup chopped nuts; 2 tbs chopped parsley; 60–75 g (2–2½ oz) butter, softened; salt and freshly ground black pepper; 1 egg.

Mix all ingredients together well and use as a stuffing for poultry, veal or pork. Makes about 4 cups.

Raisin and Walnut Loaf

A beautiful loaf that keeps fresh for days if stored in an airtight container. Leave for 12 hours before cutting and serve sliced, with butter if liked.

2 cups self-raising flour; pinch salt; 60 g (2 oz) butter; ¼ cup sugar; ²⁄₃ cup raisins, roughly chopped; 1 cup chopped walnuts; 1 egg, beaten; 1 tbs golden syrup; ½ cup buttermilk.

TOPPING: 1 tbs sugar; 2 tbs chopped walnuts; little buttermilk.

Sift flour and salt into a mixing bowl. Rub in butter, then add sugar, raisins, walnuts and egg and mix well until combined. Stir golden syrup into buttermilk. Add to dry ingredients and beat well. Spoon into a greased 21 x 11 cm (8 x 4½ in) loaf tin. Level top with a spatula.

TOPPING: Mix sugar and walnuts. Brush loaf with buttermilk, and sprinkle sugar and nuts over top. Press gently with a spatula to make sure topping sticks to loaf. Bake in a preheated moderate oven (180°C/350°F) for 45–50 minutes or until quite firm to touch. Cool in tin for 5 minutes, then turn out on to a wire rack.

Raisin Marmalade Cake

2 cups self-raising flour; 125 g (4 oz) butter; 3/4 cup firmly packed brown sugar; 1/2 cup raisins; 2 eggs, beaten; 6 tbs thick cut marmalade.

Sift flour into a bowl and rub in butter. Add sugar and raisins and mix well. Gradually add eggs and beat well. The mixture should be fairly stiff, but if necessary add 1 tbs milk. Put two thirds of mixture into a greased and lined 15 cm (6 in) square cake tin. Smooth top and spread 2 tbs marmalade over it. Spread over half the remaining cake mixture, add another 2 tbs marmalade and then rest of cake mixture. Top with remaining marmalade. Bake in a preheated moderate oven (180°C/350°F) for 1 hour 25 minutes or until golden-brown and well risen. Cool on a wire rack. When cold cut cake into squares to serve.

Veal with Raisins

90 g (3 oz) butter; 1.5 kg (3 lb) breast of veal, boned and cubed; 3 tbs hot dry sherry or vermouth; 1/2 cup raisins; 125 g (4 oz) mushrooms, sliced; 1 tbs tomato paste; 3 tbs flour; 1 1/2 cups beef stock; 1 bay leaf; 1 cup sour cream; 1 tbs redcurrant jelly; salt; pinch cayenne; 1 tsp ground coriander.

Melt butter over moderate heat in a flameproof casserole and brown meat quickly. Pour hot sherry or vermouth over meat. Add raisins and cook briskly for 2–3 minutes, stirring. Mix in mushrooms, tomato paste and flour. When well blended pour on stock, and add bay leaf. Stir until boiling. Cover, reduce heat and cook gently for about 1 hour or until veal is tender. Remove veal using a slotted spoon and keep warm. Whisk sour cream into cooking liquid with redcurrant jelly, salt, cayenne and coriander. Return veal and simmer very gently for 10–15 minutes. Discard bay leaf. Serve with buttered noodles and a tossed salad. Serves 6.

RASPBERRY

Raspberries can be the most elusive of summer fruits. They arrive with the first of the summer fruits, the apricots and cherries, then all too quickly disappear during the very hot months, only to return when we had all but forgotten them, at the start of autumn. Fortunately, frozen raspberries can be found throughout the year, and although their appearance and flavour might not equal those of the fresh fruits, they can be profitably used in a raspberry sauce (sieve them to remove the tiny seeds).

Fresh raspberries can be served simply with sugar, cream, or a soft, creamy, fresh cheese such as mascarpone, but they combine superbly with other fruits, either fresh or cooked. Fill small melon halves with raspberries, or a pineapple shell with pineapple chunks and raspberries; toss sliced peaches or pears, fresh or cooked, with raspberries.

If you have an excess of raspberries, they may be made into jam or jelly (unlike strawberry jam, raspberry jam sets well). Alternatively freeze whole or make into purée and freeze in small containers. Frozen purée can be kept for about 6 months. It should be thawed in the refrigerator and stirred well before use. **See recipes.**

Raspberry Sauce

A versatile sauce that can be poured over ice cream, yogurt or fresh cream cheese; pour over orange segments, sliced poached pears or peaches; serve as sauce with lemon ice cream; use to make a raspberry bavarois; serve with a cream-filled sponge cake or roll; drizzle over a trifle; spread on crêpes before rolling; combine with thick cream for a raspberry fool or use in Pêche Melba (see page 353). Makes about 1 1/2 cups.

250 g (8 oz) raspberries; 1/4 – 1/2 cup sugar; squeeze lemon juice.

Purée raspberries with sugar in blender, then strain through sieve to remove seeds. Or push fruit through sieve to purée and stir in caster sugar to taste. Add lemon juice to sharpen flavour.

Clear Raspberry Sauce

1 cup fresh or frozen raspberries; 3/4 cup water; 3 tbs sugar; 2 tsp cornflour dissolved in 1 tbs water.

Place raspberries in a saucepan with water and sugar and bring to the boil. Add cornflour paste and cook the sauce, stirring, until it thickens. Push through a sieve and allow to cool. Makes 1 1/2 cups.
NOTE: If fresh or frozen raspberries are not available, use canned raspberries with their juice instead of water and sugar.

Classic Raspberry Mousse

1/2 cup sugar; 3/4 cup water; 500 g (1 lb) raspberries; 1 tbs gelatine; 2 tbs orange juice; 1/2 cup cream, whipped; 3 egg whites.

Dissolve sugar in water in a saucepan. Add raspberries and cook gently for about 3 minutes or until juice is starting to run out. Press through sieve, and allow purée to cool. Soften gelatine in orange juice, then dissolve over low heat. Stir into purée, then fold in whipped cream. Beat egg whites until stiff and fold lightly into raspberry mixture. Pour into serving bowl and chill until set. Serve with additional whipped cream, if desired. Serves 6.

Raspberry Sorbet

Making sorbets is easier if you have a small, electrically powered machine known as a sorbetière. The paddles of the machine keep the mixture in motion as it freezes, thus preventing the formation of large ice crystals. However, sorbets can be made very successfully without such a machine, as long as the mixture is whisked every half hour or so while freezing.

500 g (1 lb) raspberries; juice 2 oranges; juice 1 lemon; 1¹/₂ cups caster sugar.

Place raspberries in blender with juices and blend to a purée. (Alternatively, push through sieve.) Sieve purée to remove seeds, then add sugar and whisk until sugar has dissolved. If desired, sharpen taste with a little more lemon juice. Pour into container of sorbetière and freeze (or freeze in a shallow dish or ice cream trays and whisk frequently). Allow sorbet to ripen (mellow) in refrigerator for 30 minutes or so before serving. Serves 6–8.

RATATOUILLE

Summer vegetables were never combined better than in this colourful French medley so popular in Provence. Even when you have a surfeit of tomatoes, peppers and zucchini in salads, these same vegetables cooked in a ratatouille will tempt the most jaded appetite.

Ratatouille is a most versatile dish. It may be eaten cold, with cold meats or hard-boiled eggs, or simply with bread, as a dip. Or it may be eaten hot, as an accompaniment to grilled or roast lamb, pork chops or steaks (although lamb seems best suited to the accompaniment of this robust, garlicky flavour). A plain omelette is enhanced by ratatouille; a quick and easy lunch or supper dish is made by breaking eggs into hollows in a pan of hot ratatouille, and covering the pan until the eggs are set.

■ **TO PREPARE:** The easy way to make ratatouille is simply to layer the prepared vegetables in a pan, starting with sliced onions, then eggplants, peppers, zucchini and tomatoes. Season each layer with salt and pepper and drizzle of olive oil, tuck a few whole garlic cloves between the layers and cook over low heat for about 1 hour. Remove lid towards the end of cooking to allow excess liquid to evaporate. Proportions of each vegetable are not too important in this method, nor does it matter if there are no zucchini, but there must be tomatoes.

Ratatouille

This recipe is a little more time-consuming than the simple method, but it gives an even better result as the vegetables retain their fresh taste and texture.

2 medium eggplants, cubed; salt; 2 large onions, finely chopped; ¹/₂ cup olive oil; 2 peppers, cored, seeded and cut into fine strips; 4 zucchini, cut into ¹/₂ cm (¹/₄ in) slices; 2 cloves garlic; freshly ground black pepper; 4 ripe tomatoes, peeled, seeded and quartered; finely chopped parsley.

Place eggplant cubes in a colander, sprinkle with coarse salt and leave for 30 minutes. Drain and pat dry with paper towels. Cook onions in oil in a large saucepan until soft and golden. Add eggplant cubes, and cook 2 minutes longer. Add peppers, zucchini and garlic, season with pepper, cover and cook gently for about 15 minutes. Add tomatoes and cook about 5 minutes longer. Serve warm or chilled, sprinkled with finely chopped parsley. Ratatouille keeps well in the refrigerator for 3–4 days. Store covered. Serves 4–6.

RED CABBAGE

See *Cabbage*.

REDCURRANT

A fruit that seems to be even more elusive than raspberries, but there is some consolation in the knowledge that frozen redcurrants are not too difficult to find, and that their delicious, tangy flavour can be preserved in redcurrant jelly. Redcurrants are often combined with other summer berry fruits, such as raspberries, in fruit salads, compotes and in Summer Pudding (see pages 518–19). Cooked in syrup, redcurrants can flavour a plain yogurt or accompany fresh cream cheese.

Redcurrant Jelly is one of the most useful ingredients of any pantry. It can be melted and used to glaze red fruits in tarts or on cakes. Many sauces, especially those for game, call for redcurrant jelly, which also gives a touch of piquancy to Cumberland Sauce (see pages 106–7). **See recipes.**

Redcurrants with Raspberry Juice

2 cups redcurrants; ¹/₂ cup raspberries; ¹/₂ cup vanilla sugar; juice ¹/₂ lemon.

Place redcurrants in serving dish. Sieve raspberries, or purée in a blender and then sieve to remove seeds. Pour over redcurrants. Sprinkle with sugar, then lemon juice. Allow to macerate at least 3 hours. Serve chilled. Serves 2–3.

Redcurrant Jelly

This jelly is not as firm as most commercial jellies, but is very good for making Cumberland and other sauces. Redcurrant jelly should be melted over gentle heat, or in a bowl over hot water, before mixing with other ingredients for a sauce. It is sometimes necessary to sieve the melted jelly to remove any remaining jelly globules.

1 kg (2 lb) redcurrants; 4 cups caster sugar.

r

Place fruit in large saucepan and mix with sugar. Bring to the boil and boil, stirring constantly, for 8 minutes, carefully removing all scum as it rises. Strain through a fine sieve. Spoon resulting jelly into small jars. Seal when cold. Makes about 4 cups.

Redcurrant Sauce

A good accompaniment to duck or goose.

2 tbs redcurrant jelly; 2 tbs prepared mustard; pinch cayenne; juice I lemon; ¹/₄ cup port.

Melt redcurrant jelly, and sieve if necessary to remove lumps. Add remaining ingredients and simmer gently 5 minutes. Serve immediately. Makes about ¹/₂ cup.

REMOULADE SAUCE

This classic, mayonnaise-based sauce is served with cold seafood, particularly lobster and crab, with poultry and cold meats.

See *Mayonnaise* for recipe.

RHUBARB

This is available all year round, although it is most plentiful in the autumn.

Rhubarb is always eaten cooked, and can also be used for jams and jellies, either on its own or mixed with other fruits. It blends beautifully with other fruits, particularly apples and strawberries. It is also delicious with citrus flavourings, and with spices, especially ginger. A simple compote of rhubarb with plain yogurt makes a light, refreshing dessert or breakfast dish.

■ **BASIC PREPARATION:** Simply remove and discard the leaves, trim the root end and cut the stalks into convenient-sized pieces.

■ **TO COOK:** Cook rhubarb on top of the stove or in the oven, but use very little water, since the rhubarb will give out moisture and shrink as it cooks. Take care not to overcook, or the rhubarb will lose its bright red colour.

Cooked rhubarb may be puréed and used in the same way as strawberry or raspberry purée, or combined with thick cream or custard to make a Rhubarb Fool. See recipes.

Rhubarb Crumble

I cup sugar; ¹/₂ cup water; 4 cups rhubarb, cut into short pieces; I tsp grated orange rind.

CRUMBLE TOPPING: I cup flour; 60 g (2 oz) butter; ¹/₄ cup sugar; pinch cinnamon.

Dissolve sugar in water over heat to make a syrup. Bring to the boil, then add rhubarb and orange rind. Cover and simmer for 5 minutes or until rhubarb is tender but not mushy. Turn into greased ovenproof dish.

CRUMBLE TOPPING: Sift flour into a bowl and rub in butter until mixture resembles crumbs. Mix in sugar and cinnamon. Sprinkle topping over fruit. Bake in a preheated moderate oven (180°C/350°F) for 30 minutes or until crumble is golden-brown. Serves 6.

VARIATIONS

Substitute 2 cups sliced apple for 2 cups rhubarb, or add a little sliced preserved ginger to rhubarb.

Baked Rhubarb and Orange Sponge

I bunch rhubarb, trimmed and chopped; ¹/₄ cup firmly packed brown sugar; 2 tsp grated orange rind; 3 tbs warmed honey; 60 g (2 oz) butter; ¹/₄ cup caster sugar; I egg, lightly beaten; ³/₄ cup self-raising flour; ¹/₄ cup milk.

Place rhubarb in buttered ovenproof dish, sprinkle with brown sugar and half the orange rind, and pour over honey. Cream butter with remaining sugar until light and fluffy. Beat in egg, then fold in sifted flour alternately with milk. Spread over rhubarb. Bake in a preheated moderately hot oven (190°C/375°F) for about 40 minutes or until golden. Serve hot, with custard or cream. Serves 6.

Rhubarb Fool

I bunch rhubarb, trimmed and cut into 5 cm (2 in) lengths; ¹/₃ cup firmly packed brown sugar; grated rind I orange; I cup cream; 2 tsp Pernod (optional).

Place rhubarb in saucepan with sugar, orange rind and a little water and simmer gently until just tender. Drain, then push through a sieve or purée in a blender. Cool. Lightly whip cream and fold cooled purée with Pernod, if using. Serve cold in individual dishes, with sponge fingers or thin, crisp biscuits. Serves 4.

RICE

Learn to cook this great staple perfectly and you have the base for hundreds of splendid hot or cold savoury dishes, sustaining puddings and interesting accompaniments to meat, seafood and poultry.

There are many varieties of rice and it is important to choose the right kind for your purpose.

TYPES OF GRAIN

Rice may be short-, medium- or long-grain.

Short-grain Rice: Best for puddings because it clings together when cooked to give a creamy texture. Short or medium-grain rice is also the traditional choice for Chinese fried rice or other dishes, since clinging grains are best for eating with chopsticks, though long-grain rice can be used.

The Italian rices such as Arborio, Cannaroli or Vialone Nano are short- to medium-grain varieties, with large, round grains; available at Italian groceries and delicatessens, they are often labelled risotto rice. These rices are able to absorb liquid and stand up to long, slow cooking without becoming soft and mushy. Look for Calasparra for paella. If not available use one of the Italian rice varieties.

Medium-grain Rice: Suitable for savoury dishes where the rice should be in distinct grains but holding together – e.g., rice rings, moulds and croquettes. If medium-grain is not available, use long-grain for rice rings and moulds, short-grain for croquettes.

Long-grain Rice: Cooks to give the separate, fluffy grains required for plain boiled rice and for most savoury dishes, stuffings and rice salads.

Basmati Rice from Pakistan is a superb, light-textured long-grain rice, with a wonderful aromatic flavour. It is expensive, but worth it for dishes like Indian Ghee Rice, pilaf, pilau and Biryani (see page 35). Other fragrant rices to look for are jasmine, used in many Southeast Asian recipes and Thai white rice, a slightly sticky rice with a distinctive aroma.

TYPES OF RICE

White (polished) Rice: This has been hulled and had the bran coating removed. It is tender and easily digested, and is remarkable in its ability to complement, contrast or provide a vehicle for the flavours and textures of many other foods.

Brown Rice: This has been hulled but has not lost its bran coating. It is more nutritious and rather more filling than white rice, and has a nutty taste and slightly chewy texture. Brown rice is particularly good in vegetable dishes or used as a stuffing, and is an excellent binder for meat loaves. It takes longer to cook than white rice (about 40 minutes).

Parboiled Rice: Long-grain polished rice which has been treated before milling with a steam pressure process; this forces some of the bran's nutrients into the grain so that it retains more food value than ordinary white rice. It is not washed before cooking as the steam process has removed surface starch. Since the steam has also hardened it, it takes longer to cook than ordinary white rice (20–25 minutes) and absorbs more liquid (2½ parts water to 1 part rice). Apart from its nutritive value, the advantage of parboiled rice is that it is almost foolproof in giving beautifully fluffy, separate grains and it has a good nutty flavour.

Quick-cooking or 'Instant' Rice: This has been cooked, then dehydrated. It usually needs only 4–6 minutes' heating in boiling water; follow directions on the pack.

Wild Rice: The seed of a grass related to the rice family. It is very expensive but a great treat – its rare, nutty flavour is the perfect complement to poultry and game. For economy, cooked wild rice can be combined with cooked brown or white rice.

BUYING, STORING AND REHEATING RICE

Buy only as much as you expect to use within a month. It may develop weevils if held for too long. Store all rice airtight in a cool, dry place.

SERVINGS: One cup of raw rice weighs about 200 g (7 oz), and will swell to about 3 cups when cooked, enough for 6–7 servings of plain boiled rice as an accompaniment.

Cooked rice will remain in good condition in a covered container in the refrigerator for 5–6 days. To reheat, place in a sieve or colander and run hot water through it, then stand colander over a saucepan about one third full of boiling water, cover with a cloth and steam 10–15 minutes. Or spread out in a baking dish, sprinkle with a little milk and dot with butter, cover with a cloth, or foil with a few holes poked in it, and place in a preheated very slow oven (120°C/250°F) until heated through.

Rice can be frozen, though this changes the texture a little and is seldom worthwhile since it is almost as quick to cook rice freshly as to thaw it. Thaw by placing in a sieve and running hot water through it, then steaming over boiling water as described above. Do not freeze rice in liquid, e.g. in a soup, as it goes mushy. **See recipes.**

Boiled Rice

**1 cup rice; 8 cups water; 2 tsp salt;
1 slice lemon (optional).**

Rinse rice in a sieve under cold running water until the water runs clear. Bring measured water to the boil in a large saucepan and add salt. Lemon slice may be added to help keep rice white. Slowly sprinkle in rice through your fingers so that water does not go off the boil. Stir once, then cook uncovered, keeping water at a brisk boil, until rice is tender but still firm. Test by lifting out a grain or two and biting it. The rice is cooked when it is soft but slightly resistant to the teeth; this is called *al dente*. Basmati rice will take 7–10 minutes, other long-grain rice about 12 minutes, short-grain rice a little longer. Start testing a few minutes ahead of time. Drain rice in a sieve or colander and run cold, then hot, water through it to separate grains and wash out any remaining starch.

For very dry, fluffy grains, boil a little water in the saucepan, place colander of boiled rice over it, cover with a cloth and leave to steam for 5–10 minutes; or spread rice out in a baking dish, dot with butter, cover dish with a cloth, or foil with a few holes in it, and place in a preheated very slow oven (120°C/250°F) for 10–15 minutes. Makes 3 cups.

NOTE: If not required immediately, rice can be kept hot by steaming. Alternatively, place on a baking sheet, dot with butter, cover and keep warm in the oven (see above).

VARIATION

BOILED BROWN RICE: If possible soak brown rice in cold water for 20 minutes before cooking as above. Brown rice will take 40 minutes or longer to cook.

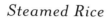

Steamed Rice

This method retains the flavour of the rice.

1 cup rice; 2 cups water; $^1/_2$ tsp salt.

Rinse rice in a sieve under cold running water until the water runs clear. Bring measured water and salt to the boil in a heavy saucepan. Slowly sprinkle in rice through your fingers so that water does not go off the boil. Stir once, then cover with a well-fitting lid and turn heat very low. Do not lift lid until last few minutes of cooking. Cook very gently for 10–15 minutes or until a test grain is tender but still firm when bitten. Remove from heat and fork up lightly. For very dry, fluffy grains, set the rice aside, still covered, for 5 minutes before forking up. Makes 3 cups.

VARIATION

STEAMED BROWN RICE: Follow recipe above but if possible soak brown rice in cold water for 20 minutes before cooking. It will take 40 minutes or more to cook.

Chinese-Style Rice

For Chinese fried rice cooked this way, spread it out in a shallow dish, cover and refrigerate overnight before using.

2 cups short-grain rice; $^1/_2$ tsp salt.

Rinse rice in a sieve under cold running water until the water runs clear. Place rice in a heavy saucepan and add salt and enough water to come about 2 cm (¾ in) above level of rice. Bring to the boil, then lower heat to medium and continue cooking until water has almost evaporated and steam holes appear in rice. Reduce heat to very low, cover with tight-fitting lid and steam 15–20 minutes or until rice is tender. Do not lift lid until last few minutes of cooking. Set aside, still covered, for 5 minutes, then fork up lightly. Makes about 6 cups.

Wild Rice

1 cup wild rice; salt.

Cover rice with cold salted water in a saucepan. Bring to the boil, skim any foreign particles from top and drain. Bring 3 cups fresh water to the boil, add 1 tsp salt and stir in rice slowly. Cook without stirring for about 30 minutes or until grains are tender, adding a little more boiling water if necessary. Fluff up with a fork before serving. Makes about 3 cups.

Rice Ring or Mould

butter; Boiled or Steamed Rice.

Generously butter a ring mould, or dariole or other individual moulds. Drain boiled rice well but do not run water through it. Pack hot rice firmly into moulds, rest in a warm place 3–4 minutes, then place a heated serving plate over each mould and invert it and plate together. Rap sharply on table to release rice and lift mould off carefully.

Indian Ghee Rice

Serve with a curry, grilled spiced chicken or pork, lamb or chicken satays. To get the best flavour, onions must be allowed to cook gently for a long time. Do not stir rice once it has come to the boil.

60 g (2 oz) ghee (clarified butter); 1 onion, finely sliced; 1 tsp turmeric; 2 cups long-grain rice, preferably Basmati; 3$^1/_2$ cup boiling chicken stock; 8 black peppercorns; 2 whole cloves; 4 cardamom pods; 1 tsp salt; 1 cinnamon stick; 1 cup hot cooked peas.

Heat ghee in a heavy saucepan, add half the onion and fry gently until golden-brown. Make sure onion is well cooked but do not allow to burn. Add turmeric and cook, stirring, for 1 minute. Add rice and fry 5–10 minutes, stirring constantly, until it is golden. Add boiling stock with peppercorns, cloves, cardamom, salt, cinnamon and remaining onion. Bring to the boil, stirring from time to time, then turn heat down very low, cover pan tightly and cook gently 10–20 minutes or until rice is tender and liquid is absorbed. Turn off heat and leave covered until serving time, then remove lid and fluff rice up with a fork. Serve garnished with peas. Serves 4–6.

VARIATION

CURRIED RICE: Follow recipe for Indian Ghee Rice, adding 2 tsp curry powder with the turmeric.

Basic Rice Pilaf

Pilaf can be an accompaniment, or can be a whole meal with fish, poultry, meat and vegetables added.

2 cups long-grain rice; 30 g (1 oz) butter; 1 small onion, finely chopped; salt and freshly ground black pepper; 4 cups boiling stock.

Rinse rice in a sieve under cold running water until water runs clear. Drain thoroughly. Melt butter in a heavy saucepan, add onion and cook gently until soft and golden. Stir in rice, season with salt and pepper and cook, stirring frequently, until rice become translucent. Pour in boiling stock and bring to the boil again, then lower heat, cover tightly and cook very gently for about 20 minutes or until all liquid is absorbed and rice is tender (small holes will appear on the surface). Remove lid and cooked uncovered for 1–2 minutes. Fluff up with fork before serving. Serves 8–10 as an accompaniment.

VARIATIONS

CASHEW AND SULTANA PILAF: Follow recipe for Basic Rice Pilaf. Fry 60 g (2 oz) cashew nuts and 60 g (2 oz) sultanas in a little ghee or butter until golden. Fork through finished pilaf.

MUSHROOM PILAF: Follow recipe for Basic Rice Pilaf, but add 1 cup mushrooms, sautéed in 30 g (1 oz) butter, to the pilaf with the stock.

MAIN-DISH PILAF: Follow recipe for Basic Rice Pilaf and fold through the finished pilaf 1 cup diced cooked chicken, flaked fish, shellfish, roast lamb or other meat, 1 cup cooked or raw vegetables and 2 tbs toasted almond halves. For vegetables, use sliced sautéed mushrooms, diced celery or pepper, diced cooked carrot, lightly cooked cauliflower or broccoli florets, cooked peas or beans. Serves 4–6.

TURKISH PILAF: Follow recipe for Basic Rice Pilaf but add 1 bay leaf, a 5 cm (2 in) piece cinnamon stick broken into 2 or 3 pieces, ½ cup raisins and ½ cup diced dried apricots with the stock. Serve with curries or lamb.

Fried Rice

Try to get Chinese rice wine – the best is Shaosing, a yellow rice wine. It is available from good Chinese supply shops. It really does give the authentic taste to fried rice.

8–10 dried Chinese mushrooms; salt; 6 tbs oil; 3 eggs; 6 spring onions, chopped; 125 g (4 oz) barbecued pork or ham, cut into small slices; 1 cup shelled small cooked prawns; 4 cups cooked Chinese-Style Rice, refrigerated overnight (page 414); ½ cup cooked peas.

SEASONING: 2 tbs Chinese rice wine or dry sherry; ¼ cup chicken stock; 2 tsp soy sauce.

Soak mushrooms in water to cover for 30 minutes, then drain. Simmer gently in salted water for 5 minutes. Drain. Remove stalks, slice mushrooms thinly and set aside. Heat 2 tbs of the oil in a wok or frying pan. Beat eggs with a pinch of salt and add to pan. Cook until firm, stirring so that cooked egg is broken into small pieces. Remove from pan and set aside.

Heat wok or pan and add remaining oil. When hot add spring onions, meat, prawns and mushrooms. Fry for a few seconds, then add rice, tossing constantly to mix and heat through. Season with salt, and add peas and cooked egg. Combine seasoning ingredients and sprinkle over rice. Mix well and serve. Serves 6.

NOTE: Chinese often used dried shrimp for this dish. Simply soak ½ cup dried shrimp in water until softened, about 30 minutes.

Saffron Rice

This superb rice is one of the most useful of all recipes. It makes a simple but stylish accompaniment to poultry, meat or seafood that is spicy – Indian, Southeast Asian, etc. Saffron is expensive but makes the subtle difference. Use a heavy saucepan or an iron casserole for absolutely carefree cooking.

½ tsp crumbled saffron; 1½ cups Basmati or other long-grain rice; 15 g (½ oz) butter; 1 tbs oil; 1 small onion, finely chopped; 3 cups boiling chicken stock or water; salt.

Soak saffron in enough warm water barely to cover. Rinse rice in a sieve under cold running water until water runs clear. Drain thoroughly. Heat butter and oil in a deep saucepan and cook onion until soft without colouring. Add rice and cook for a further few minutes, stirring all the time until rice is well coated with butter and oil. Pour on stock or water, and add saffron with water in which it was soaked and a large pinch of salt (or less if your stock is salty). Stir once, then cover tightly and cook gently for 15–20 minutes or until rice is tender and liquid has been absorbed. Remove lid and stand for a few minutes to let steam escape. Fluff up with a fork and serve. Serves 8.

Ham Rice Salad

Good for picnics and summer luncheons. The salad can be varied by using chicken, seafood, salami or other cold meat instead of ham, and other vegetables such as sliced celery, pepper or radish.

6 cups Steamed Rice (page 414), cooled to room temperature; 250 g (8 oz) cooked ham, sliced 1 cm (½ in) thick and diced; 1 cup cooked green peas; 1 cup chopped parsley; 1 cup finely chopped spring onions, including green stalks; salt and freshly ground black pepper; ½ cup Mayonnaise (page 256).

DRESSING: 2 tsp Dijon mustard; ½ cup olive oil; ¼ cup good vinegar; 1 clove garlic, crushed; salt and freshly ground black pepper.

Beat dressing ingredients together well, or shake in a jar. Mix rice with dressing, then add ham, peas, parsley and spring onions, and season with salt and pepper, if necessary. Lastly, add mayonnaise. Serves 8.

NOTE: Make ahead and store in refrigerator.

Shrimp (Prawn) Jambalaya

This colourful Creole dish derives from Spanish Paella (New Orleans was ruled by Spain in the eighteenth century). Like paella, it is a meal in itself.

r

1 cup long-grain rice; 2 thick rashers streaky bacon, rind removed and cut into strips; 1 tbs oil or butter; 1 large onion, finely chopped; 2 cloves garlic, crushed; 2 tender sticks celery, sliced; 1 large green pepper, cored, seeded and cut into strips; 1¹/₂–2 cups boiling chicken stock; 1 cup drained canned tomatoes, coarsely chopped; 2 tsp chopped fresh thyme, or ¹/₂ tsp dried; pinch cayenne; 125 g (4 oz) cooked ham, thickly sliced, and cut into small strips; salt and freshly ground black pepper; 500 g (1 lb) medium green prawns, shelled and deveined; 2 tbs finely chopped parsley.

Rinse rice in a sieve under cold running water until water runs clear. Drain well. Fry bacon in a large, flameproof casserole until crisp. Remove with a slotted spoon and set aside. Add oil or butter to bacon fat in pan and gently cook onion and garlic until soft but not brown. Add celery and green pepper and cook about 2 minutes or until slightly wilted. Add rice and cook, stirring frequently, about 5 minutes or until rice becomes translucent. Add 1½ cups boiling stock with tomatoes, thyme, cayenne, ham, salt and pepper. (Remember that ham may make mixture a little saltier as it cooks.)

Bring to the boil and stir once, then cover tightly and place in a preheated moderately slow oven (160°C/325°F). Cook 10 minutes. Add prawns, pushing them down beneath the surface. Cover again and cook a further 10–15 minutes or until rice is tender and liquid is absorbed. Check once or twice during this time and if race appears dry, add a few more spoonfuls of boiling stock. Add parsley and fork through. Serve Jambalaya from the casserole or pile it on to a large, heated serving dish. Serves 6.

VARIATION

CHICKEN JAMBALAYA: Follow recipe for Shrimp Jambalaya, but substitute 3 chicken fillets, (skinned, boned half-breasts), each cut crossways in half and sautéed 5 minutes in a little butter, for the prawns.

Brown Rice Pudding

A pudding so nourishing and satisfying that it would take only soup and a side salad to complete the meal.

3 cups Boiled Brown Rice (page 414); 3 cups milk; 3 eggs, beaten; ¹/₂ cup firmly packed brown sugar; ¹/₂ tsp mixed spice; ¹/₂ cup mixed dried fruit.

TO SERVE: brown sugar; sour cream.

Mix rice with remaining ingredients. Spoon pudding into a greased shallow ovenproof dish. Bake in a preheated moderate oven (180°C/350°F) for 30 minutes. Remove from oven and sprinkle a little more brown sugar evenly over top. Return to oven and bake 10 minutes more. Serve warm with sour cream slightly sweetened with brown sugar. Serves 6–8.

Saffron Pilau

A marvellous dish for a party, barbecue or large luncheon. It goes beautifully with cold roast beef or other meats, hot or cold chicken or grilled meat. It is good hot or cold and looks magnificent piled into a big dish. It is also excellent heaped into tomato cases, or moulded into a ring and filled with a savoury mixture. It is a failproof recipe – adding the liquid in 3 parts ensures that the rice will not go soggy.

3 tbs oil; 2 onions, finely sliced; ¹/₂ tsp crumbled saffron; 2 cups long-grain rice; 3¹/₂ cups boiling stock; 8 black peppercorns; 2 whole cloves; 4 cardamom pods, bruised; 1 cinnamon stick; 2 tsp salt; ¹/₂ cup sultanas or raisins; ¹/₂ cup halved, toasted almonds; 6 hard-boiled eggs, halved (optional).

Heat oil in a heavy saucepan and gently fry onions until a pale golden colour. Make sure onions are soft but do not allow to burn; this will take quite a while. Add saffron and cook for 1 minute, stirring. Add rice and fry gently, stirring constantly, for 5 minutes until all rice is coated with oil and golden. Add 1³/₄ cups boiling stock, with peppercorns, cloves, cardamom, cinnamon and salt (reduce if stock is salty). Bring to the boil, then cover and simmer gently for 20–25 minutes or until rice is tender, adding more stock as it is absorbed. Add sultanas or raisins, cover and allow to plump. Turn off heat and keep covered until ready to serve. A few minutes before serving, uncover pan to allow steam to escape, fluff up rice with a fork and add almonds. Turn on to a large heated serving dish. For a main dish, garnish with eggs. Serve 8–10.

NOTE: 1 tsp turmeric may be substituted for the saffron. It gives good colour but not the same flavour.

VARIATIONS

PILAU-STUFFED TOMATOES: Peel 12 firm tomatoes, scoop out centres with a teaspoon, salt inside and turn upside-down on paper towels for 10 minutes to drain. Brush tomatoes lightly with oil, then pile hot Saffron Pilau into the centres and place in a baking dish. Heat in a preheated moderate oven (180°C/350°F) for 10 minutes.

PILAU RING: Pack Saffron Pilau firmly into an oiled 7-cup ring mould. Rest in a warm place 3–4 minutes, then put a heated platter over the mould and invert. Tap mould to release rice, and remove mould. If liked, fill centre with cooked mushrooms and peas, sautéed chicken livers tossed in a little cream or any other savoury filling.

SAFFRON RICE SALAD: Prepare Saffron Pilau or Saffron Rice. Combine 2 tbs vinegar, 2 tsp prepared mustard (Dijon is best) and 6 tbs oil. Season with salt and pepper and beat with a fork until thick. Toss through rice. To this basic rice salad you can add 1 cup diced cooked chicken; ¹/₂ cup chopped green peppers and some chopped parsley. Shelled prawns and sliced canned water chestnuts for a crispy contrast make another good combination. For a creamy salad, fold in a little Mayonnaise (see page 256).

Green Rice

Rice combined with fresh green herbs and vegetables, cream and cheese makes a colourful and complete accompaniment to meats or fish, or it could be an interesting part of a meatless meal.

^{1}/$_2$ cup olive oil; ^{1}/$_2$ cup chopped green pepper; 3 cups Boiled or Steamed Rice (pages 413–4); 3 cups chopped cooked spinach; ^{3}/$_4$ cup chopped parsley; ^{1}/$_2$ cup snipped chives; I tsp salt; ^{1}/$_4$ tsp pepper; ^{1}/$_2$ cup cream; 2 cups grated Parmesan cheese.

Heat oil in a large saucepan and sauté green pepper for 5 minutes. Sir in rice, spinach, parsley, chives, salt and pepper and toss together until hot. Remove from heat and toss with cream and 1 cup of cheese. Turn into a heated serving dish and sprinkle remaining cheese on top. Serves 8.

Buttered Rice

This is a good way of using leftover cooked rice. It can be an accompaniment or a meal in itself, depending on what you add to the basic recipe.

60 g (2 oz) butter; 2 cups Steamed Rice (page 414); flavouring (see below).

Melt butter in a heavy saucepan, stir in rice and mix well, tossing lightly over gentle heat. Or heat through in a preheated moderately slow oven (160°C/325°F), shaking dish occasionally, until thoroughly heated through. After buttering rice and before heating, any of the following may be added: sliced mushrooms; strips of canned pimiento; diced celery or pepper; any cooked vegetables; cooked prawns, scallops or mussels; chopped parsley or mixed herbs; Pesto alla Genovese (see page 339); chopped shallot; desiccated coconut and grated fresh ginger. Serves 4.

Khichri

An Indian dish of split peas and rice, a combination which produces a good quality protein essential for a vegetarian meal.

2 cups long-grain rice; ^{1}/$_4$ cup oil; 4 small onions, sliced; ^{1}/$_2$ cup yellow split peas, soaked overnight and drained; I^1/$_2$ tsp salt; I tsp ground cumin; I tsp Garam Masala (page 171); I clove garlic, crushed; I cm (^{1}/$_2$ in) slice fresh ginger, peeled and finely chopped; 3^1/$_2$ cups water.

Soak rice in water to cover for 3 minutes, then drain well. Heat oil in a heavy saucepan and add half the onions. Cook over a moderate heat for 5–10 minutes or until crisp and golden. Lift out onions and drain on paper towels. Set aside. Add remaining onions to oil and cook gently until soft. Add rice, split peas, salt, cumin, garam masala, garlic and ginger. Reduce heat to moderately slow and cook mixture, stirring constantly, for 7–10 minutes or until rice and peas are coated with oil. Add water. Bring to the boil and cook over moderate heat, stirring, for 4 minutes. Cover pan with foil and tight-fitting lid and simmer gently for 25 minutes. Serve on a heated serving dish, garnished with reserved fried onions. Serves 4–6.

RICE PAPER SHEETS (BANH TRANG)

Packets of dried rice paper wrappers are sold in good Asian food stores and delicatessens. They are brittle and can take a few times to master rolling without breaking. The Vietnamese in particular use them for their fresh spring rolls (*cha gio*). Once they are softened with warm water they become pliable and can be used to wrap delicious salad fillings.

Prawn Rice Paper Rolls

There are many versions of these deliciously different fresh spring rolls.

8–10 small round rice paper sheets (banh trang); I red chilli, seeded and sliced; 2 tsp Thai fish sauce (nam pla); I tsp lime juice; I tsp sugar; 8–10 cooked prawns, shelled and deveined; I medium carrot; 4 spring onions; ^{1}/$_2$ cup bean sprouts; small handful each of Thai basil or Thai mint or coriander leaves.

CLEAR DIPPING SAUCE: 4 tbs sugar; ^{1}/$_2$ cup cold water; 2 tbs fish sauce; finely sliced red or green chilli; I tbs lime juice.

Brush a rice paper sheet with warm water or quickly dip into a bowl of warm water. Lay on a flat surface on kitchen paper towels until softened. Place another dampened sheet on top and repeat until all the sheets have been moistened.

Take care not to overwet the sheets; they should be soft enough to handle without tearing and becoming soggy, and not stick together.

In a small bowl add the chilli, fish sauce, lime juice and sugar and mix together. Cut the prawns in half lengthways. Peel and cut the carrot into fine shreds with the spring onions, including some of the green tops. Trim off the straggly brown tails from the bean sprouts.

Place a prawn half on one side of the rice paper. Cover with a basil, mint or coriander leaf. Add the shredded carrot and spring onions and a few bean sprouts. Sprinkle over with a little of the chilli mixture. Bring the ends of the rice paper up and roll up, enclosing the filling firmly, the basil leaf showing through on top and the seam underneath. If the rice paper tears, start again with a new sheet.

Cover the spring rolls with dampened paper towels or plastic wrap as you go. Serve piled on a plate with clear dipping sauce.

CLEAR DIPPING SAUCE: Stir the sugar and water until the sugar dissolves, then add the fish sauce, chilli and lime juice. This gives a very clear, glossy sauce.

RILLETTES

Better known in English as potted pork, this French dish is basically a pork spread, flavoured with herbs, spices, pepper and garlic. Rillettes are most commonly made with pork, but may also be made with goose, rabbit, turkey or duck, although each of these will include some pork.

Pork rillettes are made from belly pork, one of the most economical of pork cuts, but also one of the most fatty. The fat is essential to the rillettes, so don't be dismayed by the quantity.

Rillettes are eaten with plain (unbuttered) bread or toast, often accompanied by pickled gherkins. They may be served as a first course, or simply as something to nibble on with drinks.

Rillettes

I kg (2 lb) boneless belly pork, rind removed and cut into small cubes; I large clove garlic, bruised; I sprig fresh thyme; salt and freshly ground black pepper; ¼ cup water; ¼ tsp ground cloves; ¼ tsp nutmeg; ½ tsp cinnamon.

Place pork cubes in large, heavy saucepan with garlic, thyme and a little salt and pepper. Add water to prevent mixture sticking. Cook over very gentle heat for about 2 hours or until pork is extremely tender. Drain in a sieve. Discard garlic and thyme, and set fat aside. Using 2 forks, tear pork into shreds. Taste and season as desired with salt, pepper and spices; rillettes should be well seasoned. Return pork mixture to saucepan with a little of the reserved fat and heat, stirring well to mix seasonings through meat. Pack into small pots. Cover surface of each with layer of pork fat then cover with foil. Store in refrigerator. Remove 1–2 hours before serving. Covered with fat, rillettes will keep in the refrigerator for several weeks. Serves 4–6.

RISOTTO

A rice-based dish from the northern provinces of Italy, where rice is to the people of northern Italy what pasta is to those of the south.

Risotto should be made with either Arborio, Cannaroli, Vialone Nano, Roma or Baldo rice, most of which are grown along the Po River Valley in Italy's north. These rices can absorb liquid and stand up to long, slow cooking without becoming soft and mushy. The perfect risotto should be a creamy mass, with each grain having a slightly resistant core to the bite. It can be served plain, flavoured simply with butter and cheese, or more elaborately with such ingredients as mushrooms, tomatoes, meat, poultry, seafood or chicken livers, to name a few.

Risotto is usually served as a dish on its own with grated Parmesan cheese passed separately. One exception to this rule is Risotto Milanese which is served as an accompaniment to Osso Buco Milanese (see page 321). See recipes.

Risotto Milanese

The rice in this dish should be cooked to a melting creaminess with a little 'bite' still left in each grain.

125 g (4 oz) butter; I small onion, finely chopped; 30 g (I oz) beef marrow, sliced (optional); 2 cups Italian risotto rice or short-grain rice; ½ cup dry white wine; 4–5 cups hot chicken stock; ¼ tsp saffron powder or threads dissolved in I tbs hot water; ½ cup grated Parmesan cheese.

Melt 60 g (2 oz) of the butter in a heavy saucepan and fry onion gently until soft. Add beef marrow, if using. Stir in rice until it is well coated with butter. Pour in wine and cook over medium heat until wine has nearly evaporated. Stir in 1 cup of hot stock. Simmer, stirring occasionally, for 10 minutes and gradually add about 2 cups more stock. Continue simmer, stirring, for a further 5–10 minutes, gradually adding remaining stock, by which time the rice should have absorbed all the liquid. Do not let rice dry out. Stir in dissolved saffron and add remaining butter and Parmesan cheese. Serve immediately as an accompaniment to Osso Buco Milanese or on its own with extra butter and grated Parmesan cheese. Serves 4.

Risotto

125 g (4 oz) butter; I onion, chopped; I clove garlic; 2 tbs finely chopped parsley; 3 cups Italian Arborio rice; 8 cups boiling chicken stock; salt and freshly ground black pepper; 4–6 tbs grated Parmesan cheese; extra grated Parmesan cheese to serve.

Melt 60 g (2 oz) of the butter in a heavy saucepan and sauté onion and whole garlic clove. When onion is soft and golden add parsley. Cook over a low heat for a few minutes, then discard garlic and add rice. Fry for 5 minutes, stirring constantly, then add 1 cup boiling stock and cook gently until it is absorbed. Continue cooking gently, adding stock a cupful at a time and stirring occasionally, for 20–30 minutes or until rice is tender and all liquid is absorbed. Season with salt and pepper, stir in remaining butter and the cheese and leave risotto over low heat for a few minutes before serving. Serve with plenty of extra grated Parmesan cheese handed separately. Serves 6.

VARIATION

RISOTTO WITH MUSHROOMS: Make Risotto as per recipe, adding 2 rashers bacon, rind removed and finely chopped, with the onion, and 250 g (8 oz) mushrooms, sliced, with the parsley. Use only 60 g (2 oz) butter for frying the onion: do not add more with the cheese.

NOTE: Risotto may be prepared in this way using other vegetables such as tomatoes or zucchini. Shelled prawns, mussels, chicken meat or chopped sautéed chicken livers may also be added with the mushrooms.

RISOTTO WITH PRAWNS: Make Risotto as per recipe and keep hot. Melt 90 g (3 oz) butter in a frying pan and sauté 1 clove garlic and 1 kg (2 lb) green prawns, shelled and deveined, for 5–8 minutes or until prawns are cooked. Discard garlic, then season prawns with salt and pepper. Add to risotto and fold together.

RISSOLE

Strictly speaking, rissoles ought to be made with finely minced meat, fish or poultry, wrapped in thin shortcrust or puff pastry to form little turnovers, before being deep-fried. Or the pastry might be coated with egg and breadcrumbs or crushed vermicelli before frying. They were then served hot, often to accompany cocktails.

Today rissoles have become more informal; the pastry coating is usually omitted and egg and breadcrumbs used instead. They are larger and more likely to be served at lunch or family meals. Nevertheless, they remain a delicious way of stretching the budget. **See recipes.**

Chicken Rissoles

1 x 375 g (12 oz) packet frozen puff pastry, thawed; 1 quantity Chicken Croquette mixture (page 105); 1 egg, beaten; oil for frying; parsley sprigs to garnish.

Roll out pastry dough to about 3 mm (⅛ in) thick. Cut it into 6 cm (2½ in) rounds or squares. Place 1 teaspoon of croquette mixture in centre of each pastry round or square. Brush edges lightly with water and fold dough over, pressing edges together. Be careful not to fill pastries too much, and seal edges firmly so that none of the filling escapes. Brush tops with beaten eggs. Deep-fry in hot oil for 1–2 minutes or until golden-brown. Drain on paper towels. Serve immediately, garnished with parsley sprigs. Makes about 24.

Rissoles with Mushrooms

RISSOLES: 4 tbs oil; 1 onion, finely chopped; 4 slices bread, cubed; 4 tbs milk; 750 g (1½ lb) minced steak; 2 eggs, lightly beaten; 2 tbs tomato paste; ½ tsp salt; ½ tsp white pepper; ½ cup flour; dry breadcrumbs.

SAUCE: 45 g (1½ oz) butter; 6–8 mushrooms, finely sliced; 2 tbs flour; 2 tsp paprika; 1 cup beef stock; ½ cup sour cream.

RISSOLES: Heat 2 tbs oil and gently fry onion until soft. Soak bread cubes in milk for 10 minutes. Put steak, 1 egg, tomato paste, salt and pepper in a bowl and blend well together. Add onion and soaked bread cubes and blend again. Shape mixture into 8 rissoles. Dip in flour, then in remaining egg and coat with breadcrumbs. Heat remaining oil and fry rissoles until well browned on each side. Drain and keep warm.

SAUCE: Melt butter in a saucepan and gently fry mushrooms for 2 minutes. Blend in flour and paprika, then stir in stock. Cook gently until boiling, stirring constantly. Remove from heat, stir in sour cream and serve immediately with rissoles. Serves 4.

Cooked Meat Rissoles

250 g (8 oz) cooked meat, minced; ½ cup plus 2 tbs flour; 2 tbs fresh breadcrumbs; 2 tbs chopped parsley; ½ tsp dried thyme; salt and freshly ground black pepper; ⅔ cup stock; 1 egg, beaten; ½ cup dry breadcrumbs; oil for frying.

In a saucepan mix together minced meat, 2 tbs flour, fresh breadcrumbs, parsley, thyme, salt, pepper and stock. Stir over gentle heat until mixture becomes thick. Allow to cool. Shape into flat cakes. Dip in remaining flour, then beaten egg and coat with dry breadcrumbs. Shallow-fry in hot oil until golden-brown on both sides. Serves 2.

NOTE: Use leftover roast beef, lamb or chicken, corned beef, cooked ham, or well-drained and flaked canned tuna or salmon.

ROCK CAKE

A batch of Rock Cakes is quickly and easily made and a family favourite for picnics, lunch-boxes or as a quick snack with morning coffee or afternoon tea. Eat them warm or cold, buttered or plain.

Rock Cakes

2 cups self-raising flour; 90 g (3 oz) butter; ½ cup sugar; ½ tsp mixed spice; 2 tbs currants; 2 tbs sultanas; 2 tbs chopped mixed candied peel; 1 egg; 4–5 tbs milk.

Sift flour into a bowl and rub in butter until mixture resembles crumbs. Add sugar, spice and fruits and mix in well. Beat egg and add milk. Mix with dry ingredients to a stiff dough. Place tablespoons of mixture in little rough heaps on lightly greased baking trays. Bake in a preheated hot oven (200°C/400°F) for 10–15 minutes or until golden-brown. Makes about 25.

ROCKEFELLER OYSTERS

This recipe was created at Antoine's, one of the long-established and famous restaurants of New Orleans.

Rockefeller Oysters

125 g (4 oz) butter; 6 tbs finely chopped fresh spinach; 3 tbs finely chopped onion; 3 tbs finely chopped parsley; 3 tbs finely chopped celery; 5 tbs fresh breadcrumbs; dash Tabasco sauce; about ½ tsp salt; 36 freshly opened oysters, on the half-shell; rock salt.

Melt butter in a saucepan and add all ingredients except oysters and rock salt. Cook, stirring constantly, for 15 minutes or until soft. Press through sieve or purée in blender. Cool. Place a layer of rock salt in shallow ovenproof dishes and arrange oysters in half-shells on top. Place a spoonful of sauce on top of each oyster. Cook under a preheated medium grill until sauce begins to brown. Serve immediately. Serves 6.

ROCKMELON (CANTALOUPE)

See *Melon*.

ROE

Both the milt (soft roe) of male fish and the eggs (hard roe) of female fish are delicacies. Soft Roes on Toast, once a popular savoury course for the end of a formal dinner, make a splendid snack. Smoked roe is served like pâté with toast or brown bread and butter, and the salted, dried, pressed roe of the grey mullet, known in Greece as *tarama*, is used to make Taramasalata (see page 527).

The salted roe of the sturgeon is, of course, that great luxury, caviar; red salmon roe (keta), also costly, is used in the same way. Salted lumpfish roe, coloured orange or black, is a less expensive substitute and is commonly available.

Soft Roes on Toast

250 g (8 oz) fresh or canned soft roes; seasoned flour; 60 g (2 oz) butter; salt and freshly ground black pepper; pinch cayenne; lemon juice; 2 slices hot buttered toast; lemon wedges to serve.

If using fresh roes, poach gently in salted water to cover for 3–4 minutes. Drain fresh or canned roes and remove any dark vein. Dry roes well and dust with seasoned flour. Heat butter and, when foaming, add roes. Brown on both sides, then season with salt, pepper, cayenne and a little lemon juice. Arrange roes on toast, pour seasoned butter over and serve very hot, with lemon wedges. Serves 2.

ROLLMOP

See *Herring*.

ROSEMARY

The herb of remembrance, which grows wild in the countries of southern Europe but is cultivated in the north and in other parts of the world. It grows quite happily in pots in a warm dry place in many gardens.

A sprig of rosemary or its crushed leaves impart a unique aromatic fragrance reminiscent of dry summer hillsides around the Mediterranean shores. The special flavour of rosemary has a great affinity with lamb, veal and pork.

Place a sprig under the rack when roasting or grilling, or insert a few leaves with some slivers of garlic under the skin before roasting meat. Scent butter with rosemary and in it quickly sauté some tomatoes or mushrooms, or use to toss new potatoes, zucchini or patty pan squash.

Rosemary is best used fresh but dried rosemary is especially good to flavour sugar for an unusual touch in puddings and creams, or sprinkled over plain butter cakes. **See recipes.**

Rosemary Butter

Delicious with boiled new potatoes, patty pan squash, zucchini, on grilled lamb chops or pork steaks, and spread on hot breads.

125 g (4 oz) butter; 2 tsp lemon juice; 2 tsp finely chopped fresh rosemary, or 1 tsp dried; salt and freshly ground black pepper.

Cream butter until softened, then beat in lemon juice. Add rosemary, beat well and season with salt and pepper. Shape into a long roll, chill and slice as required. Makes 125 g (4 oz).

Veal Rosemary

2 tbs oil; 30 g (1 oz) butter; 750 g (1½ lb) boned veal shoulder, cubed; 1 onion, chopped; 2 tbs flour; 1 tbs chopped fresh rosemary, or 1 tsp dried; 2 cups peeled and chopped tomatoes; ½ cup dry white wine; 1 cup chicken stock; salt and freshly ground black pepper; 125 g (4 oz) mushrooms, sliced.

Heat oil and butter in a flameproof casserole, add veal and onion and cook until browned (do this in

2 batches if necessary to avoid overcrowding pan). Stir in flour and rosemary and cook until flour coats meat. Add tomatoes, wine and stock, and bring to the boil, stirring constantly. Season with salt and pepper. Add mushrooms. Cover and cook in a preheated moderately slow oven (160°C/325°F) for 1 hour or until veal is tender. Serve with buttered rice or creamy mashed potatoes and a green salad. Serves 4–6.

Rosemary Chicken in Cream

¹/₄ cup flour; ¹/₂ tsp salt; ¹/₂ tsp white pepper; 2 tsp chopped fresh rosemary, or I tsp dried; 4 large half-breasts of chicken; 2 cups cream; 2 tbs chopped parsley.

Season flour with salt, pepper and rosemary and use to coat chicken pieces. Put in a lightly buttered shallow baking dish and carefully pour over cream. Bake in a preheated moderately slow oven (160°C/325°F) for 30–40 minutes or until chicken is tender, turning after first 15–20 minutes of cooking. Remove pieces to a serving platter and keep warm. Reheat cream sauce, thinning if necessary with a little extra cream or hot milk. Pour over chicken and sprinkle with parsley. Serve with Poppy Seed Noodles (see page 375) and a crisp green salad. Serves 4.

Rosemary Soda Bread

2 cups wholemeal flour; 2 cups plain flour; 2 tsp salt; 2 tsp sugar; I tsp bicarbonate of soda; ³/₄ tsp baking powder; 90 g (3 oz) butter; ¹/₂ cup chopped parsley; I tbs snipped chives; I tbs chopped fresh rosemary, or I tsp dried; 2 cups buttermilk.

Sift flours, salt, sugar, soda and baking powder into a large bowl. Rub in butter until mixture resembles breadcrumbs. Stir in herbs, then buttermilk until dough forms a ball. Knead very lightly until smooth. Place on a greased baking tray and form into a 20 cm (8 in) round. Using a sharp, floured knife cut a cross 1 cm (½ in) deep in the top. Bake in a preheated moderately hot oven (190°C/375°F) for 40–50 minutes or until loaf sounds hollow when tapped on bottom. Serve warm or at room temperature sliced, with plenty of butter and a sharp Cheddar if liked.

Rosemary Sugar

2 cups sugar, crystal or caster; 2 sprigs fresh rosemary, or 2 tsp dried.

Combine sugar and rosemary in an airtight jar and shake well. Leave for 24 hours. Shake again and store for at least a week before using. Delicious in puddings, creams or sprinkled over hot cakes or biscuits. Makes 2 cups.

Spinach Rosemary

500 g (I lb) spinach; I tbs finely chopped parsley; 4 spring onions, finely chopped; 60 g (2 oz) butter; salt; ¹/₄ tsp white pepper; I sprig fresh rosemary; or ¹/₂ tsp dried.

Place spinach in a large heavy saucepan and add parsley, spring onions, butter, salt, pepper and rosemary. Cover pan and cook over a low heat for 5–10 minutes. Shake pan occasionally to prevent spinach sticking. Serves 4.

ROSE WATER

A fragrant essence distilled from rose petals, with a history as romantic as its name. Rose water has been used for thousands of years in countries of the Middle East, India and the Balkans, not only in the kitchen but also as a cosmetic ingredient and as purification water during religious ceremonies.

Rose water may be used as a flavouring instead of vanilla or almond essence, and lends its exotic perfume to many creams, sweet dishes and drinks. It can be purchased from health food shops, specialty delicatessens or at some chemists. Rose essence is also available from the same outlets and is highly concentrated. Use only a few drops if substituting for rose water. **See recipes.**

Rose Water Syrup

2 cups sugar; I cup water; strained juice ¹/₂ lemon; few drops pink food colouring; ¹/₃ cup rose water.

Put sugar and water in a heavy saucepan and stir over gentle heat until sugar has dissolved. Bring to the boil and add lemon juice. Boil, without stirring, for 10 minutes, skimming when necessary. Add enough food colouring to syrup to tint it a deep pink. Stir in rose water and boil for a further 3 minutes. Cool, then bottle and seal. Serve over cracked ice, using 2–3 tbs per glass. Top each serving with iced water and float a rose petal on top. Makes about 2½ cups syrup.

Persian Cream

I tbs gelatine; ¹/₄ cup cold water; I¹/₂ cups milk; ¹/₃ cup sugar; 2 eggs, separated; I tbs rose water.

TO SERVE: 2 cups partially frozen or well-chilled fresh berry fruits; whipped cream; 2 tsp rose water.

Sprinkle gelatine over cold water and allow to soften. Heat milk and sugar in a heavy saucepan or top of a double saucepan. Beat egg yolks and add to warm milk and sugar, off the heat. Stir over very low heat, or over hot water, until custard begins to thicken. Add softened gelatine and stir until dissolved. Allow to cool, then stir in rose water. Beat egg whites until stiff and fold into custard mixture. Chill for at least 4 hours. Serve with partially frozen or fresh berry fruits, and whipped cream flavoured with rose water. Serves 6.

Gulab Jamun

A delicately flavoured sweetmeat from India soaked in rose water syrup.

4 tbs full cream milk powder; 1¹/₂ tbs self-raising flour; pinch bicarbonate of soda; ¹/₂ tsp ground cardamom; 15 g (¹/₂ oz) ghee or softened butter; about 2 tbs water; ghee or oil for frying.

SYRUP: 1 cup sugar; 2 cups water; 3 cardamom pods, bruised; 3 tbs rose water.

Sift milk powder, flour, bicarbonate of soda and ground cardamom into a large bowl. Rub in butter or ghee, and add sufficient water to make a firm but pliable dough. Shape into balls the size of small walnuts. Fry slowly over gentle heat in hot ghee or oil, turning until well browned. Drain on paper towels.

SYRUP: In a large heavy saucepan combine sugar, water and cardamom pods and heat until sugar dissolves, stirring occasionally. Put fried gulab jamun into syrup and simmer for 30 minutes or until almost double in size and soft and spongy. Cool slightly, then add rose water and cool completely. Serve at room temperature or slightly chilled. Makes about 10.

Almond Cream

¹/₄ cup ground rice; 3 cups milk; pinch salt; ¹/₄ cup sugar; ³/₄ cup ground almonds; 2 tbs rose water.

DECORATION: toasted slivered almonds; pomegranate seeds (optional).

Make a thin paste from ground rice and ¹/₄ cup milk. Place remaining milk in a saucepan and bring to the boil. Stir in ground rice paste, salt and sugar. Cook, stirring constantly, over medium heat until mixture begins to bubble. Lower heat and simmer for 5 minutes, stirring often. Stir in ground almonds, blending well. Remove from heat and allow to cool a little, stirring occasionally. Stir in rose water and pour into serving dish. Chill at least 3 hours. Serve decorated with toasted slivered almonds and pomegranate seeds. Serves 6.

Iced Melon and Peaches

1 large ripe honeydew melon; ¹/₂ cup caster sugar; 4 ripe peaches, peeled, stoned and sliced; juice 1 lemon; 3 tbs rose water; shaved or crushed ice to serve.

Halve melon, remove seeds and dice flesh or scoop into balls. Sprinkle with sugar. Coat peach slices in lemon juice to prevent discoloration. Add peaches and lemon juice to melon balls, stirring gently. Mix in rose water. Cover bowl and chill for 3 hours. Serve piled into individual glasses and topped with ice. Serves 6–8.

ROUGH PUFF PASTRY

See *Pastry*.

ROUILLE

This peppery-hot sauce is a traditional accompaniment to Bouillabaisse (see page 488) and other fish soups of the Mediterranean region. It may be thickened with either bread or a potato, cooked in the soup.

Rouille

2 cloves garlic; 1 red pepper, skinned, cored, seeded and roughly chopped; 1 dried red chilli, soaked in warm water until soft; 1 x 5 cm (2 in) slice French bread, soaked in water or Fish Stock (page 509) and squeezed to remove excess liquid; 2 tbs olive oil; ¹/₂ cup hot Fish Stock; salt and freshly ground black pepper.

Pound garlic, pepper, chilli and bread to a smooth paste in a mortar with a pestle. Gradually add olive oil, blending until thick and smooth. Stir in hot fish stock, and season with salt and pepper. Serve separately with fish soups and stews. Rouille may also be made using a blender; add extra 2 tbs water or stock when blending garlic, peppers and bread. Makes about 1 cup.

ROULADE

The French word for 'roll' applies to different cuts of meat or minced meat mixtures rolled around a filling; to a galantine when shaped as a roll, or to thin slices of bread or pastry when rolled around a filling.

Deliciously light roulades can be made from a soufflé-type mixture that is cooked in a Swiss roll tin, spread with a filling either savoury or sweet, rolled and served hot or cold. They can be made in advance and reheated – perfect for entertaining.

Appropriate roulades such as Smoked Mackerel, Smoked Salmon or Prawn Roulades can be served as hors d'oeuvre or for any course of a meal, or try a Chocolate Roll (see page 85) with coffee.

METHOD FOR SOUFFLE-TYPE MIXTURE

PREPARING THE TIN: Choose a Swiss roll tin 25 x 38 x 2.5 cm (10 x 15 x 1 in). Oil the tin lightly and line with greaseproof paper, leaving an overhang of 5 cm (2 in) at each end. Grease the paper, dust lightly with sifted flour and shake out excess. Add mixture and spread evenly.

TO TEST WHEN COOKED: The top should be golden-brown and firm and a fine skewer inserted in the centre should come out clean.

TURNING OUT: Have ready a slightly dampened, clean tea-towel, covered with greaseproof paper. Quickly turn out the roulade from the tin on to the lined tea-towel. Immediately and carefully peel the paper lining from the roulade, trim the crusty ends, fill and roll up, or roll up and allow to cool before filling, according to your recipe.

FILLING AND ROLLING: Spread the prepared filling quickly and lightly over the surface. Immediately roll up as for a Swiss roll, using the tea-towel as a guide. Grasp the corners of the edge nearest you, lift the paper and cloth and the roulade will fall into a roll as you lift and remove them. Roll on to a serving platter, seam side down, and serve hot or cold as directed. **See recipes.**

Mushroom Roulade

Serve this superb roulade as a first course at a dinner party. It can be made ahead and reheated: make roulade, cool and store in refrigerator covered loosely with oiled foil. Remove from refrigerator 1½ hours before serving time and heat in a preheated slow oven (150°C/300°F) for 30 minutes, removing foil for last 5 minutes.

90 g (3 oz) butter; ½ cup flour; 2 cups warm milk; 1 tsp salt; ½ tsp white pepper; 1 tbs brandy; 1 tbs sour cream; 4 eggs, separated; parsley sprigs to garnish.

MUSHROOM FILLING: 125 g (4 oz) butter; 250 (8 oz) button mushrooms, sliced; 2 tsp lemon juice; 4 tbs flour; 1 cup warm milk; ½ tsp salt; freshly ground black pepper; ½ tsp nutmeg; ½ cup cream; 2 tbs finely chopped parsley.

Prepare and line a Swiss roll tin 25 x 38 x 2.5 cm (10 x 15 x 1 in) (see page 422). Melt butter in a heavy saucepan, blend in flour over low heat and cook, stirring, for 1 minute. Remove from heat, cool a little and add warm milk all at once, stirring until smooth. Return to moderate heat and stir constantly until boiling. Remove from heat, cool a little and add warm milk all at once, stirring until smooth. Return to moderate heat and stir constantly until boiling. Remove from heat and stir in salt, pepper, brandy and sour cream. Whisk in egg yolks one at a time. Beat egg whites until they stand in soft peaks and fold into egg yolk mixture. Spoon into prepared tin, spreading evenly with a spatula. Bake in a preheated moderately slow oven (160°C/325°F) for about 40 minutes or until golden on top.

MUSHROOM FILLING: Melt half the butter in a saucepan, add mushrooms and sauté quickly. Sprinkle with lemon juice. Remove mushrooms with a slotted spoon. Melt remaining butter in same saucepan, stir in flour and cook over low heat for 1 minute. Remove from heat, cool a little, then add milk all at once and stir, off heat, until smooth. Return to medium heat and stir constantly until boiling. Stir in salt, pepper, nutmeg, cream and parsley. Reserve 6–8 mushroom slices for garnish, and add remainder to saucepan. Cover pan and keep warm over gentle heat until roulade is ready. Turn out roulade. Gently peel off lining paper and trim crusty edges. Spread with hot filling. Roll up (see above) and

transfer to an ovenproof platter. Reheat in a moderate oven (180°C/350°F) for 5–10 minutes. Garnish with reserved mushroom slices and parsley sprigs. Serve sliced. Serves 6.

Red Caviar Roulade

This light, tender roll is not difficult to make for a party because, unlike the classic high soufflé, a roulade can be prepared in advance.

90 g (3 oz) butter; ½ cup flour; 2 cups warm milk; 1 tsp salt; ¾ tsp pepper; 1 tbs brandy; 1 tbs sour cream; 4 eggs, separated.

CAVIAR FILLING: 125 g (4 oz) Philadelphia cream cheese; 1 tbs lemon juice; 2 tbs sour cream; freshly ground black pepper; ½ cup cream, whipped; 1 x 100 g jar red caviar or salmon roe.

GARNISH: sour cream; caviar.

Prepare and line a Swiss roll tin 25 x 38 x 2.5 cm (10 x 15 x 1 in) (see page 422). Melt butter in a large heavy saucepan, blend in flour over low heat and cook for 1 minute, stirring. Remove from heat, cool a little, and add milk all at once. Stir until smooth, then return to a medium heat and cook, stirring constantly, until sauce boils. Remove from heat and stir in salt, pepper, brandy and sour cream. Whisk in egg yolks, one at a time. Beat egg whites until they stand in soft peaks and fold into yolk mixture. Spoon into prepared tin, spreading evenly with spatula. Bake in a preheated moderately slow oven (160°C/325°F) for 30–35 minutes or until golden on top. Turn out roulade (see page 422) and allow to cool.

CAVIAR FILLING: Soften cream cheese and beat in lemon juice and sour cream. Season with pepper and fold in whipped cream and caviar. At serving time, unroll roulade, spread with filing and roll up again (see page 423). Serve cut in thin slices, each garnished with a spoonful of sour cream and a teaspoon of caviar. Serves 8.

Stuffed Beef Roll

500–750 g (1–1½ lb) topside, or round steak, cut as 1 slice about 1 cm (½ in) thick; salt and freshly ground black pepper; 4 thin slices cooked ham; 3 small hard-boiled eggs; 30 g (1 oz) butter; 2 tbs oil; 2 leaves fresh sage, or ½ tsp dried; ½ cup dry white wine.

Flatten meat using a meat mallet or broad side of a cleaver. Season well with salt and pepper. Place ham slices, slightly overlapping, down centre, then top with whole hard-boiled eggs. Carefully roll up meat, tucking in ends. Tie securely with white string. Heat butter and oil in a flameproof casserole dish just large enough to hold roll without leaving too much space around it. Brown roll all over. Add sage and wine.

Cover and simmer very gently for 2–2½ hours or until meat is tender. Remove string. Serve sliced with pan juices poured over. Accompany beef roll with a selection of vegetables. Serves 6.

NOTE: This dish is also good cold, in which case the sauce should be poured off and left to cool separately so that the fat can be taken off the top when it solidifies.

Ham Stuffed Beef Rolls

6 thin slices topside or round steak, halved to give 12 pieces; 12 thin slices cooked ham; 2 sticks celery, finely chopped; 1 small carrot, finely chopped; salt and freshly ground black pepper; ½ cup flour; 60 g (2 oz) ham or bacon fat, finely chopped; 1 clove garlic, finely chopped; 1 medium onion, finely chopped; 2 tbs oil; ½ cup dry white wine; 2 x 425 g cans tomatoes; 1 bay leaf; 1 whole clove; 2 tbs finely chopped parsley.

Flatten steak pieces as thin as possible. Top each with a slice of ham and sprinkle with half the celery and the carrot. Season with salt and pepper. Roll up slices and tie each little roll with white string. Dust lightly with flour. Combine ham or bacon fat, remaining celery, garlic and onion. Heat oil in a flameproof casserole wide enough to take rolls in one layer. Add chopped mixture and cook, stirring, for 1 minute. Add beef rolls and brown quickly on all sides. Pour in wine and stir over medium heat until it has almost evaporated. Add tomatoes, bay leaf, clove, salt and pepper. Bring to the boil, then cover and simmer over very gentle heat for about 1 hour or until beef is tender. Stir occasionally. Transfer rolls to a heated serving platter, remove string and pour sauce over through a sieve. Sprinkle with chopped parsley. Serves 6.

Polpettone (Meat Roll)

An excellent Italian dish, equally good hot or cold.

1 kg (2 lb) very finely minced veal, beef or pork or a combination of these; 4 eggs; 2 cloves garlic, crushed; 1 onion, minced; ½ cup finely chopped parsley; salt and freshly ground black pepper; 2 hard-boiled eggs, chopped; 60 g (2 oz) cooked ham, chopped; 60 g (2 oz) Gruyère cheese, grated; about ½ cup water or stock.

Combine meat, eggs, garlic, onion, parsley, salt and pepper and mix well. Knead mixture until it adheres well together. Flour your hands and a board. Turn mixture on to board and knead again, then flatten mixture. Put hard-boiled eggs, ham and cheese down centre, then carefully roll meat into a large sausage shape. Place on a well-greased baking dish and cover roll with greased greaseproof paper. Cook

in a preheated slow oven (150°C/300°F) for about 1½ hours. Add a little stock or water during cooking if necessary to keep roll moist. Serves 8.

Smoked Mackerel Roulades

1 x 500 g (1 lb) smoked mackerel, skinned and boned; ½ cup sour cream; 2 tsp horseradish cream; juice ½ lemon; freshly ground black pepper; about 12 very thin slices buttered brown bread, crusts removed; watercress to garnish.

Flake mackerel and mix with sour cream, horseradish cream, lemon juice and pepper. Cover and chill for several hours. Spread mixture thinly over bread slices and roll up firmly, securing with toothpicks if necessary. Cover and chill for 1 hour before serving, garnished with watercress sprigs. Makes 12.

VARIATIONS

SMOKED SALMON ROULADES: Use 125 g (4 oz) chopped smoked salmon instead of the mackerel and mix with ½ cup sour cream, lemon juice and black pepper. Add some finely chopped white pickled onions if liked. Proceed as above.

PRAWN ROULADES: Combine 250 g (8 oz) cooked prawns, shelled, deveined and chopped, 4 tbs thick cream or Mayonnaise (see page 256), 2 drops Tabasco Sauce, 1 tsp lemon juice and freshly ground black pepper. Proceed as above.

Walnut Roll

3 tbs fine cake crumbs or fresh breadcrumbs; 3 eggs, separated; ½ cup caster sugar; ½ cup ground walnuts; ¼ cup self-raising flour; 1 cup cream, whipped and sweetened with 1 tbs icing sugar; extra sifted icing sugar.

Butter a Swiss roll tin 25 x 38 x 2.5 cm (10 x 15 x 1 in) and line with buttered greaseproof paper allowing 5 cm (2 in) overhang at each end. Sprinkle with the cake crumbs or breadcrumbs, coating surface evenly, then tip out any excess crumbs. Beat egg whites until holding stiff peaks. Beat yolks with caster sugar until mixture is light and creamy. Gently fold in walnuts and sifted flour alternately with stiffly beaten egg whites. Spread in prepared tin. Bake in a preheated moderate oven (180°C/350°F) for about 15 minutes or until cake springs back when centre is lightly touched. Turn out on to a clean tea-towel sprinkled with caster sugar, remove paper, trim cake and roll up (see page 422), and allow to cool. Unroll the cake, spread with sweetened whipped cream and re-roll (see page 423). Roll on to a serving platter seam side down and dust lightly with icing sugar. Serve sliced. Serves 8.

RUM

This distilled spirit is one of the products of the sugar industry. In the kitchen its use is mainly in desserts, although it may also be used in meat dishes, especially those of Caribbean origin or inspiration.

Light rum – whether clear or caramel-coloured – is preferred in cooking. Overproof (O.P.) rum has a much higher alcohol content, and is more expensive, but for Christmas cakes, for example, a little O.P. rum could be added to the prepared fruits.

In French cooking, rum is a very common ingredient of desserts. A rum syrup may be brushed over a sponge before filling; babas and savarins are steeped in rum syrup. Fruits, such as pineapples, bananas and apples, take nicely to a touch of rum, and rum can alternate with brandy in flambé desserts. A sweet soufflé omelette may be flavoured with rum, or a rum sabayon spooned over carefully poached fruits.

Chocolate is one of the best partners to rum, whether as a chocolate cake with a rum cream filling, or chocolate truffles with a hint of rum, or rich rum balls to serve with after-dinner coffee. **See recipes.**

Baked Stuffed Apples

6 large cooking apples, peeled and cored;
$^{1}/_{2}$ cup chopped glacé fruit (apricots, cherries, pineapple); $^{1}/_{4}$ cup sultanas; $^{1}/_{4}$ cup rum;
1 tbs sugar; 30 g (1 oz) butter.

Extract some of the inside of the apples and chop. Mix with glacé fruit, sultanas and rum. Fill apples with this mixture, sprinkle with sugar and dot with butter. Bake in a preheated hot oven (200°C/400°F) for about 35 minutes, sprinkling with water from time to time. Serve warm, with cream if desired. Serves 6.

Ricotta Cheese with Sugar and Rum

500 g (1 lb) ricotta cheese; 2 tbs sour cream;
$^{1}/_{2}$ cup caster sugar; 4 eggs, separated;
6 tbs rum; amaretti biscuits to serve (pages 2–3).

Beat ricotta with sour cream, then mix in sugar. Add egg yolks one at a time, beating until mixture is light and creamy, then stir in rum. Beat egg whites until stiff and fold into mixture. Spoon into 6 individual glasses. Chill for several hours before serving, accompanied by amaretti biscuits. Serves 6.

Bananas with Rum

6 bananas; $^{1}/_{2}$ cup rum; $^{1}/_{2}$ cup dry breadcrumbs;
60 g (2 oz) butter; 3 tbs redcurrant jelly.

Macerate bananas in rum for 1 hour. Drain, reserving rum. Roll bananas in breadcrumbs and fry in butter until golden. Meanwhile, heat rum with redcurrant jelly, stirring until thick and smooth. Spoon sauce over bananas to serve. Serves 4.

Rum Balls

1 cup stale cake crumbs; 4 tbs caster sugar;
1 cup ground almonds; 1 tbs cocoa powder;
2–3 tbs rum; grated chocolate or
chocolate sprinkles.

Combine cake crumbs, sugar, ground almonds, cocoa and enough rum to bind mixture together. Form into small balls, roll in grated chocolate or chocolate sprinkles and place in tiny paper cases. Serve with after-dinner coffee. Makes about 50 x 2.5 cm (1 in) balls.

Rum Mousse

3 egg yolks; $^{1}/_{2}$ cup caster sugar; 2 tsp gelatine;
$^{1}/_{4}$ cup water; 1 cup cream; $^{1}/_{2}$ cup rum;
grated chocolate.

Beat egg yolks with sugar until light. Sprinkle gelatine over water and leave to soften, then dissolve over hot water. Add dissolved gelatine to egg mixture and beat well. Whip cream until stiff and fold into egg mixture. Stir in rum. Pour into serving bowl and sprinkle with grated chocolate. Chill thoroughly before serving, with additional whipped cream if desired. Serves 6.

RUM BABA

See *Baba (au Rhum)*.

RUSKS

Pieces of bread which have been dried out in the oven, a process which produces a good nutty flavour as well as a crisp texture, transforming stale bread into something quite desirable. One of Italy's favourite nibbles, remembered with nostalgia by many travellers, consists of oven-dried slices of an especially made, slightly sweet, anise-flavoured bread. Another type of rusk, produced commercially for teething babies, is made by slowly baking fingers of bread dough until they are hard; *grissini*, the thin, crisp Italian-style bread sticks, are made in the same way.

■ **TO BAKE:** Cut sliced, crustless bread of any kind into fingers or other shapes such as small triangles, rounds or squares. Arrange in one layer on an ungreased baking tray and place in a preheated slow oven (150°C/300°F) until they are completely dried, crisp and several shades deeper in colour. The time needed will depend on the type and thickness of the bread. Check frequently, turning the pieces over when the upper side is crisp and rearranging them as necessary to colour evenly. Do not allow to become too dark or the flavour will be spoiled. Rusks may curl as they dry; if you want to keep them flat, put a wire rack upside-down on top of them. Cool on a rack and store in an airtight container.

Use, cold or slightly rewarmed, within a week or two; after that, the rusks with gradually get a 'tired' flavour.

You can use rusks in most of the ways you would use bread or toast. Serve them buttered or with peanut butter or honey or as snacks for hungry children. Or serve with soup, savoury mince or any other dish with a sauce or gravy; use to scoop up a dip, or as bases for hot or cold canapés. Sprinkle rusks generously with cheese, put 2 or 3 in the bottom of individual soup bowls and ladle hot onion soup over. See recipes.

Pane d'Anise *(Anise Bread)*

These nutty rusks, gently anise-flavoured, are traditionally dipped into a glass of red or rosé wine. They're lovely with coffee, too. Serve plain, buttered or with cheese.

125 g (4 oz) butter; 1 cup sugar; 2 tbs Pernod; 1 tsp crushed aniseed; 1½ tbs brandy or whisky; 3 eggs; 3 cups flour; 2 tsp baking powder; 1 cup coarsely chopped almonds, walnuts or pecans.

Cream butter with sugar until fluffy, then beat in Pernod, aniseed and brandy or whisky followed by eggs, one at a time. Sift flour and baking powder together and fold in with nuts. Scrape mixture on to a piece of plastic wrap, wrap and chill for 2 hours. Divide dough into 4 and keep each piece chilled until ready to shape (the dough will be sticky). Put one piece of dough on to one half of a well-greased baking tray and, with wet hands, shape it into a long loaf 5 cm (2 in) wide and 1 cm (½ in) thick. Form remaining pieces of dough into loaves in same manner, putting 2 loaves on each tray. Bake in a preheated moderately hot oven (190°C/375°F) for 20 minutes or until pale gold. Cool on trays. Cut loaves diagonally into 2 cm (¾ in) slices. Arrange slices, cut side down, close together, in one layer on baking trays. Toast in a preheated moderately hot oven (190°C/375°F) until they are dry, about 10 minutes. Cool on wire racks and store in airtight container. Makes about 48.

Crisp Wholemeal Sticks

Serve these with drinks or as a snack at any time. They're good for a packed lunch, too – add cheese, radishes and celery sticks.

6 x 2 cm (¾ in) thick slices day-old wholemeal bread, crusts removed; 1 clove garlic, crushed; 1½ tbs oil; salt; 1 tbs poppy seeds.

Cut each slice of bread into 4 fingers. Mix garlic into oil, brush over bread sticks and sprinkle lightly on all sides with salt, then poppy seeds. Arrange, well apart, on baking trays. Bake in a preheated moderate oven (180°C/350°F) for 20–25 minutes, turning once or twice to brown evenly. Cool on a wire rack and store in an airtight container. Serve cold or warm. Makes 24.

VARIATION

HERBED WHOLEMEAL STICKS: Omit garlic and use melted butter instead of oil. Mix butter with ½ spring onion, very finely chopped, and 1 tbs chopped, fresh, mixed herbs, or 1 tsp dried herbs chopped with 1 tbs parsley. Sprinkle with sesame seeds instead of poppy seeds.

Crisp Bread Shells

A variation on the rusk theme, these easy and economical little shells can be filled with any hot savoury mixture to serve as appetisers and are an alternative to *Croustades* (see page 105).

Use sliced fresh white or wholemeal bread, shaping it into tiny bite-sized cases.

sliced fresh bread, crusts removed; oil or melted butter.

TO SHAPE FLOWERS: Brush one side of each bread slice with oil or melted butter. Press, oiled side down, into patty pans. Press well down to fit pans, and corners of bread will sit up to form a pretty flower cup. Bake in a preheated moderate oven (180°C/350°F) until crisp and golden, 15–20 minutes. Remove from pans, cool on a wire rack and store in an airtight container.

TO SERVE: When appetisers are required, fill shells with any hot, savoury mixture (see suggestions in *Hors d'oeuvre*, Hot Filled Hors d'oeuvre). Place on baking trays and heat through for 10–15 minutes in a preheated moderate oven (180°C/350°F).

RUTABAGA

See *Turnip*.

S

SABAYON SAUCE

A lovely sweet sauce flavoured with wine or fruit juice. Serve cold with poached fresh fruits or fruit jellies, or hot with hot sponge or fruit puddings or warm poached fruits (see *Pear*).

Sabayon Sauce (Hot)

3 egg yolks, ⅓ cup caster sugar; pinch arrowroot; ½ cup white wine, sweet sherry or fruit juice.

Beat yolks with sugar and arrowroot in a heatproof bowl until very pale and thick. Add wine, sherry or juice and whisk vigorously. Place bowl over a saucepan of simmering water and continue whisking vigorously until sauce thickens. Do not allow water to get hotter than a simmer, or let water touch bowl. Remove from heat and beat for another few minutes. Serve immediately. Makes about 1½ cups.

VARIATION

COLD SABAYON SAUCE: Proceed as above, using an extra egg yolk. After removing from the heat and beating for a few minutes, place bowl over ice and continue whisking until sauce is thoroughly chilled.

SACHER TORTE

Lawsuits have been fought over the right to call a cake by this name. This recipe is close to the one served at the Hotel Sacher in Vienna.

Sacher Torte

185 g (6 oz) cooking chocolate; 155 g (5 oz) butter; 1½ cups caster sugar; 2 tbs rum; 1 tbs water; 5 eggs, separated; 1½ cups flour; apricot jam.

CHOCOLATE GLAZE: 90 g (3 oz) chocolate, chopped; ¾ cup cream; 1¼ cups caster sugar; 1 tsp golden syrup; 1 egg; 1 tsp vanilla.

Melt chocolate in a small heatproof bowl over simmering water, then cool. Cream butter with sugar until light and fluffy. Stir rum and water into cooled chocolate and add to creamed mixture, beating well. Add egg yolks one at a time, beating well after each addition. Fold in sifted flour. Beat egg whites until stiff, and fold through cake mixture lightly until just incorporated. Divide mixture between 2 greased, lined and floured 20 cm (8 in) sandwich tins. Bake in a preheated moderate oven (180°C/350°F) for 40–45 minutes or until a fine skewer inserted in centre comes out clean. Cool on wire racks. When cold sandwich together with warmed and sieved apricot jam.

CHOCOLATE GLAZE: Combine chocolate, cream, sugar and syrup in a small heavy saucepan. Stir constantly over low heat until chocolate and sugar melt. Increase heat to medium and cook, without stirring, for 5 minutes or to soft ball stage (mixture forms a soft ball when a little is dropped into cold water). Lightly beat egg and stir in 4 tablespoons of chocolate mixture. Return this to remaining chocolate mixture in pan and cook over low heat, stirring constantly, for 3–4 minutes or until glaze coats back of spoon thickly. Remove from heat and add vanilla. Cool to room temperature before using. Place cake on a wire rack over a baking tray. Pour glaze on to cake and smooth with a palette knife. When glaze stops dripping, transfer cake to a serving plate and refrigerate for 3 hours. Remove from refrigerator 30 minutes before serving.

SAFFRON

One of the most common spices of mediaeval cookery, saffron is now too expensive to be used with such abandon, although it is an essential ingredient of the Provençal bouillabaisse, the Milanese risotto and Spanish rice dishes, such as the traditional paella. It is also widely used in Indian cookery, especially in rice dishes and biryani. See separate entries.

Saffron comes from the orange stigmas of a type of crocus flower. The plant is native to Asia and parts of Europe, but was also grown extensively in England at one time, and has given its name to the town of Saffron Walden.

Saffron is available either as the dried stigmas or as a powder. The former may be ground, crumbled or used whole before being mixed with hot stock or liquid called for in a recipe, while the powder is simply infused in the liquid. See recipes.

Mussels in Saffron Sauce

½ tsp saffron threads, crumbled; ¼ cup warm water; 1 kg (2 lb) mussels, cleaned (see *Mussels*); 1 small onion, chopped; 1 bay leaf; 3 sprigs parsley; 1 sprig thyme; 3–4 fennel seeds; ⅔ cup water; 1 cup Béchamel Sauce (see page 456); 1 tbs cooked, finely chopped spinach; ½ cup fresh breadcrumbs; 30 g (1 oz) butter, cut into small pieces.

Soak saffron in ¼ cup warm water for 1–2 hours. Place prepared mussels in a wide flameproof casserole and add onion, bay leaf, parsley, thyme, fennel seeds and ⅔ cup water. Cover and cook over high heat for about 5 minutes, shaking pan occasionally. Remove mussels as soon as they are open, and discard shells. Strain cooking liquid and add 1 cup to Béchamel, stirring over very low heat. Discard any remaining cooking liquid. Stir in saffron threads and their soaking liquid, spinach and shelled mussels. Turn mixture into a flameproof gratin dish, sprinkle with breadcrumbs and dot with butter. Grill under a preheated high grill for about 5 minutes or until crumbs are crisp and golden. Serve immediately with crusty French bread. Serves 2.

Spanish Rice Soup

$^1/_2$ tsp saffron threads, crumbled;
$^1/_4$ cup warm water; 90 g (3 oz) butter;
2 large onions, chopped; 1–1$^1/_2$ cups long-grain
rice; $^1/_2$ tsp white pepper, 8 cups hot chicken stock.

Soak saffron threads in measured water for 1–2
hours. Melt butter in a large heavy saucepan and
sauté onions for 5 minutes. Lower heat, add rice
and stir until grains are coated with butter and
translucent. Season with pepper and add half the
stock. Cover and cook over low heat for 25 minutes.
Add remaining stock, saffron threads and liquid and
cook, uncovered, for a further 10 minutes. Serves 6–8.

Cornish Saffron Cake

$^1/_2$ tsp saffron threads, crumbled;
$^1/_4$ cup warm water; 4 cups flour; $^1/_2$ tsp salt;
125 g (4 oz) butter; 30 g (1 oz) compressed yeast;
$^3/_4$ cup warm milk; $^1/_4$ cup caster sugar;
2 eggs, beaten; $^3/_4$ cup sultanas;
2 tbs chopped mixed candied peel; 2 tbs milk.

Soak saffron in measured warm water for 1–2 hours.
Sift flour and salt together, add butter and rub in until
mixture resembles crumbs. Dissolve yeast in warm
milk, stir in saffron threads and their soaking liquid
and add to flour mixture with sugar and eggs. Beat
until smooth and elastic. Put into a clean, greased
bowl and turn dough over so it is greased lightly all
over. Cover bowl with a cloth and leave to rise in a
warm place for about 45–50 minutes or until doubled
in bulk.

Mix in sultanas and peel and turn dough into a
greased 20 cm (8 in) deep cake tin. Set aside in a warm
place to prove for about 15–20 minutes or until dough
reaches the top of the tin.

Brush cake with milk and bake in a preheated hot
oven (200°C/400°F) for 45–50 minutes. Cool on a
wire rack and serve warm or cold with cream.
Serves 8.

NOTE: $^1/_2$ tsp powered saffron may be used in place of
saffron threads. Dissolve in $^1/_4$ cup warm water and
use without soaking.

SAGE

An easily grown, perennial herb with a strong, pungent
and slightly bitter flavour. The leaves may be dried, but
for best flavour use young, fresh sage leaves. Always use
sage sparingly; too much can completely overpower
a dish.

Sage is common in both English and European cuisine.
In Britain it is used as a flavouring in stuffings, especially
the traditional Sage and Onion Stuffing for roast duck. It
is also one of the components of mixed herbs, and it is
used to flavour cheese (e.g. Sage Derby) and special
breads. Although in French cooking sage is not as widely
used as thyme or rosemary, it is often used to flavour a
roast of pork in Provence; Italian cooks combine sage
with veal, as in *Saltimbocca*, and Veal Chops with Sage
and White Wine. **See recipes.**

Veal Chops with Sage and White Wine

4 veal loin chops, 2 cm ($^3/_4$ in) thick; $^1/_4$ cup flour;
3 tbs oil; 12 leaves dried or fresh sage;
salt and freshly ground black pepper;
$^1/_2$ cup dry white wine; 30 g (1 oz) butter.

Lightly coat chops in flour. Heat oil in a frying pan
and add chops and sage. Brown chops on both sides
for about 8–10 minutes, turning 2 or 3 times. Remove
chops to warmed plate when cooked and season with
salt and pepper. Tilt pan and drain off excess oil. Add
wine to pan and deglaze, scraping up any residue.
Boil until almost completely evaporated, then reduce
heat and mix in butter. Return chops to pan to warm
through. Serves 4.

Sage and Onion Stuffing

4 leaves fresh sage; 2 mild onions, finely chopped;
2 cups fresh breadcrumbs;
grated rind $^1/_2$ lemon; 2–3 tbs melted butter;
salt and freshly ground black pepper.

Blanch sage leaves in boiling water for 5 minutes,
then drain and chop finely. Combine sage, onions,
breadcrumbs, lemon rind, melted butter, salt and
pepper. If necessary, add a little stock to bind mixture.
Sufficient to stuff 1 large duckling.

Roast Port with Sage

1 x 2 kg (4 lb) boned pork loin, in one piece, and
trimmed of rind and excess fat;
6 young leaves fresh sage; 1 bay leaf;
$^1/_2$ tsp dried thyme; 2 tsp salt; olive oil;
2–3 cloves garlic, halved.

Prepare meat the day before cooking. Make small
cuts in meat and insert sage leaves. Crumble bay leaf,
mix with dried thyme and salt and rub mixture over
pork. Drizzle 2–3 tbs olive oil over pork and place
halved garlic cloves on top. Cover and leave for at
least 12 hours. Next day, place meat in roasting tin,
with garlic underneath, and drizzle a little more oil
over meat. Roast in preheated moderately slow oven
(160°C/325°F) for about 2 hours, basting from time to
time with pan juices, until juices from meat run clear.
Remove to heated plate. If desired, deglaze tin with a
little white or rosé wine and serve pan juices with
meat. Serves 8.

S

SAGO

The tiny grains of sago are made from a type of paste, derived from the sago palm, which grows in tropical regions.

Sago is basically a carbohydrate with little distinct flavour of its own. Like other starchy products, however, it can absorb liquids and act as a thickener. It is sometimes used to thicken soups, but its principal use is in desserts. **See recipes.**

Lemon Sago

1 cup sago; 3 cups water; grated rind 2 lemons; juice 3 lemons; 3 tbs golden syrup; 3 tbs sugar.

Soak sago in water for 30 minutes, then add remaining ingredients and pour into a saucepan. Bring to the boil, stirring, and simmer until quite thick. Pour into a mould. Cool and chill. Serve with cream or custard. Serves 6.

Sago Pudding

2 tbs sago; 3 cups milk; $^1/_4$ cup sugar; 3 eggs; $^1/_2$ tsp vanilla.

Simmer sago in milk until grains have swelled, then pour into bowl and cool. Beat in sugar, eggs and vanilla. Pour into buttered ovenproof dish. Place dish in tin of hot water and bake in a preheated moderate oven (180°C/350°F) for about 1 hour. Serve warm or chilled. Serves 4–6.

SALAD

There are few edible foods that cannot be used in salads. The first salad that springs to mind is perhaps the simple green, tossed salad so beloved of the epicurean French.

The English used to favour mixed salads, the most popular being lettuce with tomatoes, cucumber and probably beetroot, dressed with vinaigrette or salad dressing. The Americans introduced fruit to green salads. Today, the whole world, from the super chefs of great kitchens, to imaginative home cooks in search of good, healthy, fresh-tasting meals, have taken to salad-making with the same delight as ducks to water.

Fresh vegetables are the richest and cheapest source of the numerous vitamins and minerals essential to our health. With the herbs, meats, fish, eggs, cheese and oil that are mixed with these, a salad can be a complete balanced meal.

To make the most of salads buy only young, tender, fresh greens, vegetables and fruits. Use imagination with the additional foods. The other golden rule is that the dressing should be added at the last moment (there are, of course, exceptions). Also, a salad looks fluffier and more bouncy when just prepared; it seems to settle on standing and lose its light, freshly made look.

Included in this section are salads that have become classics, salads that you will find on restaurant menus, and many that are made in homes for family meals and for entertaining. The foods that go to make many salads have been listed as well as the 'dressings' that add distinction to salads. For other salads see the Index, because many delicious salads are distributed throughout the book. **See also recipes.**

SALAD GREENS

SELECTION AND CARE: Greens must be very fresh and unwilted. Buy or pick only enough for a day or two. Discard any tough or dry outer leaves and wash them as you require them. Don't break up the heads before storing them in the refrigerator; separate the leaves and wash them as required. Salad greens need careful washing in cold water, as sand hides in their crevices.

It is very important to dry greens thoroughly. Fold the wet leaves in a tea-towel and shake them gently over the sink. When the leaves are dry, break them up, wrap in a dry tea-towel and return to the refrigerator until it is time to make the salad. A most useful gadget, looking like a hand-operated spin dryer, is a plastic salad dryer; it really makes a splendid job of drying salad greens, without bruising or crushing tender leaves.

TYPES OF SALAD GREENS

Cabbage: The main varieties used for salads are Savoy, drumhead and red cabbages. Discard the outside wilted leaves before slicing. Cabbage has a strong distinctive flavour. **See also *Cabbage.***

Chicory (Belgian Endive or Witlof): Tightly clustered white leaves, with yellow, tender tips. The leaves can be used whole or sliced. Chicory has a slightly tangy taste. **See also *Chicory.***

Endive, Curly: Tightly curled bunchy head. The leaves graduate from dark green to yellow-green at the heart. Use the crisp young leaves and centre stalk. Endive has a slightly bitter taste. **See also *Endive, Curly.***

Escarole: Slightly curly, rich green outer leaves, with a fresh yellow heart. Use only the tender centre leaves for salad. The flavour is slightly bitter. **See also *Escarole.***

Lettuce: The iceberg lettuce, with its firm heart and crisp outer leaves, is the basis of many salads. Mignonette lettuce, with its small soft leaves, is a favourite with home gardeners. Look for other varieties such as cos and romaine. Flavours are mild. **See also *Lettuce.***

Parsley, Italian: This has a flatter and larger leaf than the more common, tightly curled parsley, and a slightly stronger flavour.

Spring Onions: This is the term used in this book to describe immature onions with the slender green leaves (sometimes called green onions). There is also a green onion where the white base has developed into a round bulb. Remove outside leaves and root base. Cut off tough green leaves. Spring onions have a fresh onion flavour. Look also for the true French shallot, a small purple bulb with a red-brown or golden skin (sometimes called a golden shallot) and a mild flavour. See also *Onion*.

Spinach, English: Dark green leaves on slim stalks, with reddish, fibrous roots. Use when very fresh. Don't confuse spinach with silverbeet, which has larger, tougher leaves; only the very young tender leaves of silverbeet are suitable for salads. Spinach has a mild flavour. See also *Spinach*.

TYPES OF SALAD VEGETABLES

Avocado: Once a great favourite with the Aztecs, this pear-shaped fruit, with its rich buttery flesh, is greatly appreciated for its delicate but distinctive flavour. There are many varieties and they are found the year round. The perfect partner for cold seafood, avocado is equally good combined with a green salad or served alone with Vinaigrette Dressing (see page 442). See also *Avocado*.

Bean Sprouts: Sprouted mung beans are crisp and crunchy and enjoyed in many salads. The sprouted bean of the shoot (minus the bean) is used. Other shoots like alfalfa are also popular in salads. See also *Bean Sprouts*.

Beans, Green: Small whole beans or long slender snake beans make an interesting fresh salad. Just top and tail them. If very young, they do not need stringing. Blanch in boiling salted water for 5 minutes, then drain and rinse in cold water to preserve their bright green colour and crisp texture. Season with a little grated nutmeg and toss in a garlic-flavoured Vinaigrette Dressing (see page 442). Scatter snipped fresh chives and chopped parsley over the top. A few mashed anchovies added to the dressing give an excellent flavour to a bean salad. See also *Beans, Green*.

Cabbage, Chinese: Shaped much like a large romaine lettuce, with long, thin, mild-flavoured leaves. The leaves are green-edged and nearly white in the centre. See also *Cabbage*.

Carrots: Carrots for salads must be young and crisp; either grate them or cut into julienne (matchstick) strips. They combine well with all salad vegetables. See also *Carrot*.

Cauliflower: Just as good in salads as it is eaten as a hot vegetable. Break off sprigs, cutting away the tough stems, and cook in boiling salted water for a few minutes. Then drain and rinse under cold running water. Try it combined with celery, ham and a mustard-flavoured Vinaigrette Dressing (see page 442), served chilled, sprinkled with a few chopped fresh herbs. See also *Cauliflower*.

Chicory, Italian: Long, dark green, smooth stems with leaves resembling spinach. The leaves can be cooked like spinach and any tender stalks sliced and added to salads.

Cucumber: The perfect summer salad vegetable, with its cool distinctive taste. It combines perfectly with salad dressings, and is delicious with sour cream to which a little grated fresh ginger and fresh garlic may be added. It is not necessary to remove the skin when cucumber is sliced thinly. Lightly salt the slices, placed in a colander, and allow to stand for 30 minutes to extract indigestible juices. Drain and rinse well with cold water. Toss in a little Vinaigrette Dressing (see page 442) and scatter with a few freshly snipped chives or finely chopped dill. See also *Cucumber*.

Fennel: One of the nine herbs the early Anglo-Saxons believed guarded against evil. The other kind of fennel – the vegetable Florence fennel – with its white celery-like stem is the one used for salads. Sliced thinly, its distinctive aniseed flavour mixes well with salad greens and tomatoes. Its feathery leaves, when finely chopped, give an aromatic flavour to cream sauces for fish. See also *Fennel*.

Garlic: This pungent bulb is a necessity in today's kitchen. Before using, remove the thin, papery skin surrounding each clove. A cut clove rubbed around a salad bowl gives a lift to a simple green salad. Rubbed with some olive oil on slices of French bread (in France called *chapons*), and then tossed with the greens it imparts its full aromatic flavour to a green salad. A touch of garlic, for many, is an indispensable part of a salad. See also *Garlic*.

Mushrooms: Small button mushrooms are best for salads. They are good eaten raw, and may be left whole or thinly sliced. It's not necessary to peel them: just wipe them with a cloth, dipped in water and a little lemon juice. Toss in a light Vinaigrette Dressing (see page 442), with plenty of freshly chopped parsley. See also *Mushroom*.

Peppers, Green and Red: These glossy vegetables are, perhaps, the most beautiful of all salad ingredients. Their sweet peppery flavour is greatly appreciated in rice salads, potato salads and the delicious Provençal ratatouille and Salade Niçoise. See also *Peppers (Sweet)*.

Radish: These are sold in tightly clustered bunches. Ideal for salads or served whole with hard-boiled eggs, olives and cherry tomatoes. See also *Radish*.

Tomatoes: Choose firm, red tomatoes. These can be peeled, if liked, and sliced or quartered and tossed in a good dressing; excellent, too, with chopped basil, oregano or parsley. Tomatoes are often added to other salad vegetables to make a mixed salad. Alternatively, scoop out centre and fill with diced cucumber, or a rice or seafood salad. Cherry tomatoes, sometimes called 'Tom Thumbs', are now available and are good eaten whole or tossed in a mixed salad. See also *Tomato*.

Watercress, and Mustard and Cress: These herbs are now available from nurseries and specialty kitchen shops for the home gardener. Watercress is bought in tight bunches, and its small, attractive sprigs, with their slightly bitter, peppery taste, make a perfect salad ingredient. Cut off tough stems, tie the dark leafy heads into bunches and stand in ice-cold water to keep them crisp and fresh. Dress them with a mustard-flavoured Vinaigrette Dressing (see page 442).

Mustard and cress are bought already sprouted in punnets. Snip off tops only and sprinkle over salads. See also *Cress*.

Zucchini: These small, dark green marrows, which are particularly favoured by Southern Europeans, combine beautifully with quartered tomatoes and peppers. Blanch them in boiling salted water and refresh in ice-cold water before using. Add them to a green salad or toss with mushroom slices, some oregano and a garlic-flavoured Vinaigrette Dressing (see page 442). Excellent with terrines and cold meats. See also *Zucchini*.

OTHER SALAD INGREDIENTS

Anchovies: A little goes a long way. These distinctively flavoured fish are featured in Caesar Salad (see page 58), and Salad Niçoise (see page 296). See also *Anchovy*.

Cheese: Wedges, cubes, slivers, julienne (matchstick) strips, and finger-sized sticks of all kinds of cheese can add richness and flavour to a salad. Blue cheese is often crumbled into a dressing; Parmesan or Pecorino is grated and sprinkled over some salads. Soft cream and ricotta cheeses make great luncheon salads: sprinkle mounds of cheese with snipped chives, chopped green onions and dust with paprika; accompany with a few salad greens and tomatoes. See also *Cheese*.

Croûtons, pasta, Potatoes, or Rice: These provide a pleasant contrast to the crispness of vegetables, and add substance to a salad. See also *Croûtes and Croûtons, Pasta, Potato or Rice*.

Eggs, Hard-boiled: Chopped or quartered eggs are most suitable for a substantial salad; grated or sieved, they can give an attractive mimosa effect to a green salad. Particularly good with strong or bitter greens like endive, chicory, or escarole, eggs seem to round them off. See also *Egg*.

Fish, Meats and Poultry: These add substance to a salad, and are the base on which to build a 'meal-in-itself' salad. Leftover meats, if a little dry, may be marinated in a good dressing. Often meats, poultry and seafood are cooked especially for salad-making; canned varieties are often featured in salads.

Herbs, fresh: Tossed with a green salad or mixed in with the dressing, herbs give that distinctive taste to a salad. *Fines herbes*, beloved of the French, is the great classic mixture, and is made, traditionally, with chopped parsley, chives, tarragon and chervil; but any combination of these can be used. Use basil in tomato salads; chives with cheese; dill is good with fish and cucumber; Chinese parsley with chicken (particularly if the dressing is Oriental), and ordinary parsley goes with just about all salads. See also *Herbs*, and individual entries for different herbs.

Nuts: Soft yet crunchy walnuts or pecans, roughly chopped, can be particularly good as an accent in a winter salad of tart greens. See also individual entries.

Olives, Green, Black or Stuffed: Stone and slice or sliver. Use them sparingly in a green salad; they are more appropriate for a mixed concoction or a composed salad (in which case leave them whole). See also *Olive*.

Pimiento: Bright red, canned pimiento adds a bright touch to many salads. Drain before using. See also *Pimiento*.

TYPES OF SALADS

Green Salad, Tossed: Often called a French salad, this mixture of crisp greens, torn into bite-sized pieces only, is tossed in a light Vinaigrette Dressing (see page 442) at the last moment and liberally sprinkled with chopped parsley and other herbs. It is a classic accompaniment to French roast chicken. It is often served with, or after, a main course, particularly if there are no green vegetables with the dish.

Green salads can be made up of plain lettuce, cos or iceberg lettuce, depending on the season, or be a mixture of salad greens and vegetables, such as water-cress, sliced cucumber and shallots. Chicory can also be added in season. Tomato and beetroot, etc., are not included in a true French tossed green salad.

Mixed Salad, Tossed: A green salad with other additions, e.g. tomatoes, cheese, etc., that can make it a light meal in itself. The dressing (see *Salad Dressings*) may be a standard Vinaigrette or varied with herbs or canned anchovy fillets.

Composed Salad: The ingredients are arranged attractively in a bowl, and a little dressing is spooned over. The diners takes portions of salad and help themselves to additional dressing.

Substantial Salad: Often based on rice, macaroni or other pastas, potatoes with crispy, crunchy salad greens and vegetables added. The dressings used can be as varied as the ingredients.

Vegetable Salad, Cooked: Cooked vegetables may be marinated in a dressing and served as a salad or as part of an hors d'oeuvre tray. Choose young, tender ones and do not overcook them: they should still be a little crisp inside.

Starter Salad: A light salad, refreshing to the palate and not too filling. Particularly popular is a salad based on eggs or fish. Sometimes a selection of salads is presented as hors d'oeuvre, in little white oblong or oval dishes; they are a feature in French and Italian restaurants, particularly for lunch.

Light Meal Salad: When a salad has protein in the form of egg, fish, cheese or meat, plus vegetables, it makes a delicious complete meal. Simply add crusty bread and a glass of light wine.

Side Salad: This is where a salad comes truly into its own, as an accompaniment to a more grand dish. Instead of only serving hot vegetables with cooked meats, etc., serve a salad either alone or as well.

The salad should be vegetable-based but can vary from a simple tossed salad to a composed salad – take your pick. Dress it carefully with a delicate dressing just before serving, using your imagination for what goes with what.

Mixed Green Salad with Chapons

Chapons are slices of French bread (flavoured liberally with garlic, a good olive oil and pepper) which are tossed with a salad of mixed greens to add a distinct garlic flavour. Much better than merely smearing the serving bowl with garlic!

selection of salad greens (lettuce, curly endive, spinach, spring onions, sliced, parsley and watercress); 1 cucumber; 2 cloves garlic, crushed; 3–4 tbs olive oil; freshly ground black pepper; 6 slices French bread; Vinaigrette Dressing (page 442).

Rinse, dry and chill salad greens. Tear into bite-sized pieces. Peel cucumber leaving a little green colour on the flesh. Cut in half lengthways and scoop out seeds with a spoon. Cut into 5 cm (2 in) lengths. Put garlic in a small bowl with olive oil and a good grinding of black pepper. Mix well, then brush on slices of French bread. Add to bowl with salad greens and cucumber, and just before serving toss with a little vinaigrette dressing. Serves 4.

Green Salad

1 lettuce, or selection of salad greens; ⅓ cup Vinaigrette Dressing (page 442); garlic (optional); chopped mixed fresh herbs (thyme, chives, mint and parsley).

If lettuce leaves are large, pull rather than cut them apart. Wash well, spin-dry in a salad basket or clean cloth (see *Salad Greens*, page 430). Make sure this is thoroughly done. If lettuce is at all limp, put it into refrigerator (in salad drawer or hydrator) until crisp. Tear into bite-sized pieces and put into a salad bowl with other greens. Watercress should be well rinsed in the bunch under cold running water, then shaken to get rid of moisture. Carefully pick over and remove some of the stalk; use sprigs only. Watercress gives a slightly peppery taste to salads.

Garlic may be used to flavour a green salad, but use it cautiously. Either rub bowl with a peeled clove or, better still, rub a clove well over a crust of French or ordinary bread. Having put salad into bowl, bury this *chapon*, as it is called, among leaves (not forgetting to remove it before serving the salad at the table).

Add vinaigrette dressing by sprinkling it over leaves, tossing lightly to make them glisten. A green salad should be dressed at the last moment, otherwise leaves will wilt and be unappetising. For a large amount of salad, you will find it easier to mix it with its dressing in a really big bowl, and then to transfer it to your salad bowl.

To make salad the Italian way: sprinkle in enough oil on its own, tossing leaves all the time to make them glisten. Mix vinegar (one third of the quantity of oil used) and seasoning together, and sprinkle over greens. For stronger flavour, crush garlic with a little salt and add to this dressing. Stir once or twice before serving salad, so that dressing is evenly distributed. Before serving, sprinkle with chopped herbs and parsley. Serves 4–6.

NOTE: ⅓ cup of vinaigrette is usually enough for one lettuce plus 1–2 cups other greens.

Chicory and Orange Salad

2 oranges; 3 heads chicory, cut diagonally into 6 mm (¼ in) slices; 2 carrots, grated.

VINAIGRETTE DRESSING: 2 tbs olive oil; 1 tbs walnut oil; 1 tbs vinegar; 1 tsp Dijon mustard; pinch sugar; salt and freshly ground black pepper.

Remove peel and pith from oranges and cut between membrane to remove segments. Combine chicory slices, orange segments and carrot in a salad bowl. **VINAIGRETTE DRESSING:** Whisk together ingredients. Add to salad and toss well. Serves 4–6.

Salade Périgordine

1 lettuce; 4–6 tomatoes, cut into wedges; 4 hard-boiled eggs, chopped; 9–10 walnuts, roughly chopped; 3 rashers streaky bacon, rind removed and cut into strips.

DRESSING: 1½ tbs wine vinegar; 1 tsp lemon juice; 5 tbs walnut, sunflower or corn oil; ½ tsp sugar; ½ tsp French mustard; 1 clove garlic, crushed; salt and freshly ground black pepper.

Put lettuce leaves, tomato wedges, chopped eggs and walnuts in a large salad bowl and mix gently. Fry bacon, without extra fat, over moderate heat until crisp.
DRESSING: Combine ingredients in a screw-top jar and shake well. Add dressing to salad and toss thoroughly. Drain bacon, stir into salad and serve immediately. Serves 4.

Spinach and Walnut Salad

1/4 cup chopped walnuts; 3 shallots, finely chopped;
1/2 bunch young spinach leaves, torn into pieces;
2 tsp white wine vinegar; 2 tbs walnut or olive oil;
salt and freshly ground black pepper.

Put walnuts, shallots and spinach in a salad bowl.
Cover and chill for 1 hour. Combine vinegar, oil, salt
and pepper in a screw-top jar and shake well. When
ready to serve, pour dressing over salad, toss well to
coat the leaves and serve immediately. Serves 4.

Lettuce Wedges with Cream Dressing

1 firm iceberg lettuce; 1/2 tsp prepared English
mustard; 1 tsp sugar; 2 tsp wine vinegar;
1/2 tsp dried tarragon; 1 clove garlic, crushed;
1 hard-boiled egg, separated; 1/2 cup cream;
salt and freshly ground black pepper;
snipped chives or chopped parsley to garnish.

Remove outside leaves of lettuce, and cut away core at
bottom. Cut lettuce into wedges, and arrange on a
large platter or 6 individual plates. Mix together
mustard, sugar, vinegar, tarragon, garlic and egg
yolk. Stir in cream and season with salt and pepper.
Spoon this dressing over lettuce wedges. Chop egg
white and sprinkle over lettuce with chives and parsley.
Serves 6.
NOTE: Make dressing just before serving, or vinegar
will sour cream and make the dressing too thick.

Chicken Waldorf

As served in the New York restaurant of that name.

4 half-breasts of chicken, or skinless, boneless
fillets; 1 cup apple cider; salt and freshly ground
black pepper; 2 eating apples, cut into thin wedges;
juice 1 lemon; 6–8 spring onions, shredded;
3 sticks tender celery, cut into julienne
(matchstick) strips; 1/2 cup walnut pieces;
parsley to garnish.

WALNUT SAUCE: 1 egg, lightly beaten; 1/2 tbs sugar;
2 tsp flour; 1/2 tsp dry mustard; 1/2 cup cream;
1/4 cup finely chopped walnuts; little extra cream;
salt and freshly ground black pepper.

Carefully remove skin and bones from chicken
breasts. Poach breasts or fillets in cider, seasoned
with salt and pepper, about 8 minutes. Cool in liquid.
Lift out chicken and cut breasts diagonally into
3 even-shaped fillets. Lay on a large dish, cover with
plastic wrap and refrigerate until required. Strain
liquid and reserve for sauce. Coat apple wedges with
lemon juice.
WALNUT SAUCE: Place reserved chicken cooking
liquid in a stainless steel or enamel saucepan and boil

to reduce to 1/2 cup. Remove from heat and stir in egg,
sugar, flour and mustard. Whisk in cream. Return to
medium heat and bring to the boil, whisking
constantly. Strain through fine sieve and add walnuts.
Cool to room temperature, and thin to desired consistency with extra cream. Season with salt and pepper.

One hour before serving, arrange salad on a large
platter as follows: place apple wedges down centre
and strew over spring onions and celery, leaving
a few for garnish. Arrange chicken breasts over
vegetables. Spoon some walnut sauce over chicken,
top with walnut pieces and strew with remaining
celery and spring onions. Serve remaining sauce
separately. Garnish with parsley. Serves 6.

Cathay Salad

The Asian use of ginger gave this salad its name.

2 cups bean sprouts; 6 spring onions, finely
chopped; 1 avocado, peeled, stoned and finely
sliced; 250 g (8 oz) medium prawns, cooked,
shelled and deveined; 2 chicken breasts, poached,
skinned, boned and finely sliced; 125 g (4 oz) fresh
champignons (tiny button mushrooms),
finely sliced; watercress or mignonette lettuce.

MUSTARD AND GINGER DRESSING: 1 tbs lemon juice;
3 tbs safflower oil; 1 clove garlic, crushed;
1 tsp grated fresh ginger; 1 tsp tarragon-flavoured
mustard or plain French mustard; 1 tbs cream.

Combine bean sprouts, spring onions, avocado,
prawns, chicken and champignons. Place in a chilled
bowl on a bed of watercress or mignonette lettuce.
MUSTARD AND GINGER DRESSING: Combine all ingredients in a jar and shake well. Toss salad lightly
in dressing just before serving. Serves 2–3.

Curried Pecan Chicken Salad

3 half-breasts of chicken; 1 carrot, sliced;
1 onion, sliced; 7 sticks celery, sliced; salt;
3 medium Jonathan apples, cored and diced;
juice 1 lemon; 1/3 cup pecan halves or walnuts;
1 tbs oil; 2 tsp curry powder; 1 small onion,
chopped; 1/2 cup Mayonnaise (page 256);
lettuce leaves to serve.

Poach chicken breasts in enough water to cover,
with carrot, sliced onion, 1 celery stick and a little
salt for 8 minutes or until tender. Drain and cool.
Discard skin and bones and dice meat. Sprinkle
apples with lemon juice. Place in a bowl with chicken,
pecan halves and remaining celery. Heat oil in a frying
pan, add curry powder and chopped onion and cook
gently about 5 minutes. Add to mayonnaise. Toss
chicken salad with well-seasoned mayonnaise and
chill. Serve piled up on crisp lettuce leaves. Serves
6 as a first course or 4 as a main course.

Oriental Salad

I lettuce or a mixture of young spinach, watercress or various kinds of lettuce – whatever is leafy and interesting at the greengrocers; I cup mung bean sprouts; $^{1}/_{2}$ cup thinly sliced water chestnuts; $^{1}/_{4}$ cup slivered toasted almonds.

ORIENTAL DRESSING: $^{1}/_{4}$ cup chopped spring onions; I tsp chopped fresh coriander; $^{1}/_{4}$ cup chopped parsley; I tsp grated fresh ginger; I tbs soy sauce; I cup sour light cream; 2 tbs Mayonnaise (page 256).

Rinse and dry lettuce or other greens and refrigerate until crisp. Tear into serving pieces, place in salad bowl and scatter bean sprouts and water chestnuts over.

ORIENTAL DRESSING: Mix all dressing ingredients together and drizzle over salad. Scatter almonds on top and toss lightly. Serve immediately. Serves 6–8.

Duck and Pawpaw Salad

This salad may also be made very successfully with cold turkey and is a good salad for those days after Christmas when leftover turkey is on the menu.

500 g (I lb) cooked duck, turkey or chicken meat, sliced; jellied turkey or duck juices (if available); I good-sized ripe pawpaw, peeled, seeded and finely sliced; juice $^{1}/_{2}$ lemon; $^{1}/_{2}$ cup walnut pieces; curly endive or mignonette lettuce.

DRESSING: 2 tbs walnut oil; 2 tbs safflower oil; 2 tbs finely snipped chives; salt and freshly ground black pepper.

Moisten meat with any jellied meat juices. Sprinkle pawpaw slices with lemon juice. Stand 10 minutes, then drain, reserving juice. Toast walnuts, then drain, reserving juice. Toast walnuts lightly in a preheated moderate oven (180°C/350°F).
DRESSING: Combine 2 tbs of the reserved pawpaw juice with oil, chives, salt and pepper. Shake well to combine. Line a salad bowl or dish with endive or lettuce and arrange meat and pawpaw on it. Spoon over dressing and garnish with walnut pieces. Serves 4.
NOTE: If walnut oil is not available, use 4 tbs safflower oil.

Chicken Citrus Salad

A lovely salad of cool colours and fresh flavours which looks best in a clear glass bowl.

I cucumber, peeled and seeded; 4 half-breasts of chicken, poached, skinned, boned, and cut into small pieces; 2 sticks tender celery, finely sliced; I small green pepper, cored, seeded and finely sliced; I grapefruit, segmented; combination of mignonette or iceberg lettuce and watercress.

DRESSING: $^{1}/_{3}$ cup Mayonnaise (page 256); $^{1}/_{3}$ cup Vinaigrette Dressing (page 442); I tsp mild Dijon mustard; $^{1}/_{2}$ small onion, grated; I tsp finely chopped chives; salt and freshly ground black pepper.

GARNISH: I tbs finely chopped parsley; 2 tsp capers.

Cut cucumber into balls with a melon baller. Place in a bowl with chicken, celery, green pepper and grapefruit.
DRESSING: Whisk all ingredients together until well blended. Pour over salad and toss carefully. Serve in a chilled salad bowl on a bed of lettuce and watercress. Garnish with parsley and capers. Serves 2.

Roast Beef Salad

500 g (I lb) cold roast beef, cut into strips; 4 medium tomatoes, cut into wedges; I celery heart, finely sliced; 50 g ($^{1}/_{2}$ cup) stuffed olives; watercress; lettuce.

BLUE CHEESE DRESSING: 2 tbs cream; I tbs red wine vinegar; 2 tbs oil; freshly ground black pepper; 60 g (2 oz) blue cheese (preferably French Roquefort), crumbled.

Combine beef with tomatoes, celery and olives. Place on a bed of watercress and lettuce.
BLUE CHEESE DRESSING: Shake together cream, vinegar, oil and pepper in a jar until well combined. Carefully stir in crumbled cheese just before dressing is used. Spoon over salad. Serves 4.

Mexican Salad

Young nasturtium leaves give a delicious piquant flavour to salads.

$^{1}/_{2}$ Savoy cabbage, finely sliced; I bunch watercress; young nasturtium leaves, or mustard and cress; I avocado, peeled, stoned and sliced; 4 rashers lean bacon, rind removed, grilled until crisp and crumbled; I chilli, seeded and finely chopped; I half-breast of chicken, poached, skinned, boned and sliced; 6 small radishes, sliced; I red pepper, cored, seeded and sliced.

ANCHOVY DRESSING: 2 anchovy fillets; milk; I tbs wine vinegar; 3 tbs olive oil; I clove garlic, crushed; I tsp finely chopped fresh oregano, or pinch dried; freshly ground black pepper.

Combine cabbage in a large bowl with watercress and nasturtium leaves, avocado, bacon, chilli, chicken, radishes and red pepper.
ANCHOVY DRESSING: Soak anchovies in milk for 10 minutes. Drain and pat dry. Mash them to a paste and blend in vinegar and oil. Add garlic and oregano, and season with pepper. Spoon dressing over salad and toss very carefully so as not to break avocado. Serves 4–6.

Tuna Pasta Salad

350 g (12 oz) green tagliatelle noodles;
1 x 200 g can tuna fish, drained; 2 small onions,
finely sliced; 2 ripe tomatoes, peeled and
quartered; 2 hard-boiled eggs, quartered;
10 black olives, stoned, chopped parsley.

DRESSING: 1 tbs tarragon vinegar; 1 tbs sherry;
salt and freshly ground black pepper; 2 tbs chopped
spring onions or shallots; 2 tbs chopped parsley;
4 tbs olive oil.

Cook pasta in boiling salted water until 'al dente', or
tender but still firm. Drain well and cool. Flake tuna
lightly with a fork (be careful as tuna can easily
become mushy). Mix with cooked pasta, onions,
tomatoes, eggs and olives.
DRESSING: Combine vinegar, sherry, salt, pepper,
spring onions or shallots and parsley in a bowl. Add
oil in a stream, beating dressing until it is well
combined. Pour dressing over salad and toss gently.
Sprinkle with chopped parsley. Serves 4.

Fettucini and Pepper Salad

Sunday lunches in the garden call for relaxed meals.
Serve this salad with barbecued meats or a platter of
cold, sliced meats.

250 g (8 oz) fettucini noodles; 2 red or green
peppers, halved, cored and seeded;
125 g (4 oz) Gruyère cheese, diced;
6–8 walnuts, chopped.

DRESSING: 4 tbs olive oil; 1 tbs walnut oil;
1 tbs vinegar; 1 tsp Dijon mustard;
salt and freshly ground black pepper.

Cook noodles in boiling salted water for 8–10 minutes or until 'al dente', or tender but still firm. Drain.
Grill peppers, cut sides down, under a preheated high
grill until skins blacken and blister. When cool
enough to handle, pull off thin outer skin and cut
flesh into long, even strips. Mix pepper strips with
cheese and walnuts in a salad bowl.
DRESSING: Combine all ingredients for dressing. Add
to noodles, mix lightly and toss with salad. Chill for at
least 1 hour before serving. Serves 4.

Italian Ham Salad

1 cup pasta shells; 125 g (4 oz) cooked ham, sliced
and shredded; 6–8 black olives, halved and stoned;
2–3 tbs thick Mayonnaise (page 256); 1 tsp Dijon
mustard.

Cook pasta shells in boiling salted water for about 10
minutes or until 'al dente' or just tender. Drain and
refresh under cold running water. Mix ham with
olives and pasta. Add mayonnaise and stir enough
into salad to bind. Serves 4.

Penne, Tuna and Olive Salad

Penne is the name for pen-nib shaped lengths of
hollow pasta which are lovely in a salad because they
take in the flavour of the dressing and other ingredients. Serve this economical main-course salad with
crusty bread, red wine and fresh fruit for a complete
Italian-style summer meal.

250 g (8 oz) penne; 1 large red or green pepper,
cored, seeded and finely shredded;
1 medium onion, finely sliced; 4 tender sticks
celery, finely sliced; 1/4 cup finely chopped parsley;
10 black olives, halved and stoned; lettuce leaves;
1 x 200 g can tuna in oil, drained; 2 ripe tomatoes,
quartered; sprigs of parsley or watercress to garnish.

TARRAGON DRESSING: 1 clove garlic, crushed;
1/2 tsp salt; freshly ground black pepper; 2 tsp Dijon
mustard; 1 tbs wine vinegar; 3 tbs olive oil;
1 tsp chopped fresh tarragon, or 1/4 tsp dried.

Cook penne in boiling salted water until 'al dente' or
tender but still firm.
DRESSING: Place ingredients in a screw-top jar and
shake until creamy and well blended. Drain penne
and rinse under hot running water. Place in a bowl,
toss with dressing and leave to cool. Add pepper,
onion, celery, parsley and olives and toss again. Line
a serving bowl with lettuce leaves and pile salad in
middle. Separate tuna into chunks and arrange on
top of salad with tomato quarters. Garnish with
sprigs of parsley or watercress and serve at room
temperature. Serves 6–8.

Seafood Salad

Any combinations of seafood may be used in this
salad, and rice, boiled for 14 minutes, may be substituted for the pasta.

125 g (4 oz) penne or other short tubular pasta;
1 tbs curry powder; 500 g (1 lb) fresh mussels,
scrubbed and steamed open; 250 g (8 oz) cooked
prawns, shelled and deveined; 1 x 200 g can tuna in
oil, drained and flaked; 1 celery heart, or 1 head
fennel, finely sliced; 1 red and 1 yellow or green
pepper, cored, seeded and finely sliced;
50 g (1/2 cup) black olives, stoned;
salt and freshly ground black pepper.

CURRY AND HERB-FLAVOURED DRESSING:
1 tbs red or white wine vinegar; 3 tbs olive oil;
1 tbs finely chopped fresh herbs (thyme, parsley,
chives, oregano, basil); 1 tsp French mustard;
1 tbs sour cream; 1/2 tsp curry powder;
salt and freshly ground black pepper.

Cook pasta in boiling salted water, flavoured with
curry powder, until 'al dente' or tender but still firm
to the bite. Drain well and cool. Remove mussels
from their shells. In a salad bowl, combine pasta,
mussels, prawns, tuna, celery or fennel, peppers and
olives. Season with salt and plenty of pepper.
CURRY AND HERB-FLAVOURED DRESSING: Whisk all
ingredients together until well blended. Toss salad
with dressing just before serving. Serves 4–6.
NOTE: This salad may be served on a bed of crisp
curly endive.

Roquefort Salad

You can buy small portions of the lovely ewe's milk
cheese of France. While it is a little expensive, this is
an excellent way of enjoying its unique taste.

selection of salad greens (lettuce, chicory,
curly endive); 1 clove garlic, halved; salt;
1/4 cup olive oil; 1 tbs cider vinegar;
1 1/2 tbs fresh lemon juice; 1/4 tsp black pepper;
1/2 cup crumbled Roquefort cheese.

Rinse and dry greens, and crisp in refrigerator. Place
greens in a salad bowl that has been rubbed with
garlic. Add salt, oil, vinegar, lemon juice, pepper and
Roquefort. Toss lightly. Serve at once. Serves 6.

Nut and Cheese Salad

3 tbs Vinaigrette Dressing (page 442);
1 lettuce, crisped and torn into pieces;
1 head chicory or tender sprigs curly endive;
2 tbs chopped walnuts;
125 g (4 oz) Gruyère cheese, diced.

Make vinaigrette in the salad bowl. Add lettuce,
chicory, cut in chunky pieces or leaves left whole if
tiny, nuts and cheese. Just before serving toss lightly
with dressing. Serves 4.

Fennel, Pear and Watercress Salad

Serve this salad in a large flattish dish; it makes more
of a display and makes it easy to select each serving.

2 tbs wine vinegar; 1 tbs French mustard; 1 tsp finely
grated fresh ginger; salt and freshly ground black
pepper; crushed garlic to taste; 1/2 cup olive oil;
1 tbs walnut oil; 1 bunch watercress; 1 head fennel,
finely sliced; 4 ripe pears, peeled, cored and sliced.

Place vinaigrette in a bowl with mustard, ginger, salt
pepper, and garlic. Using a fork, gradually beat in

olive and walnut oils until a thick dressing is formed.
Place remaining ingredients in a salad bowl, pour
over dressing and toss together gently before serving.
Serves 6–8.
NOTE: For something a little out of the ordinary, add
snowpeas topped and tailed and lightly blanched in
boiling water for 30 seconds.

Watercress and Violet Salad

A lovely early spring-time salad

1 bunch violets; 2 tbs olive oil; 2 tsp wine vinegar;
1 tsp Grand Marnier; 1 bunch watercress;
2 tbs chopped pecans.

Snip stems off violets. Place olive oil, vinegar and
Grand Marnier in a screw-top jar and shake well to
blend. Place watercress in salad bowl, top with violets
and nuts, add dressing, toss and serve. Serves 6.

Beetroot Salad with Horseradish Sauce

2 cups diced cooked beetroot; 1 cup sour cream;
2 tbs cream; 2 tbs lemon juice; 2 tbs grated onion;
2 tbs drained, pickled, grated horseradish;
1 tsp salt; 2 cups peeled and diced apple;
1 cup diced tender celery; few shallots, cut into
fine julienne (matchstick) strips, or snipped
chives to garnish.

Combine diced beetroot with sour cream, cream,
lemon juice, onion, horseradish and salt. Add diced
apple and celery, then toss. Cover and chill for 1 hour
before serving. Garnish with julienne of shallots or
snipped chives. Serves 6–8.

Radish and Red Lettuce Salad

Use radicchio, red oak or mignonette in this recipe.

2–3 red leaf lettuce or other soft-leaved lettuce,
torn into bite-sized pieces; 8 radishes, finely sliced;
1/4 cup Vinaigrette Dressing made with lime juice
(page 442); coarsely ground black pepper.

Combine lettuce and radishes in a bowl, drizzle
dressing over and toss salad well. Divide salad
between two salad bowls and sprinkle each serving
with pepper. Serves 2.

Zucchini Salad

4 tbs olive oil; 4 golden shallots, finely chopped;
500 g (1 lb) zucchini, thinly sliced; 1 tsp paprika;
1/4 tsp sugar; 1 tsp dill seeds or chopped fresh dill;
2 tbs red or white wine vinegar;
salt and freshly ground black pepper;
chopped fresh dill to garnish.

Heat olive oil in a deep frying pan, add shallots and zucchini and sauté over gentle heat for 2–3 minutes or until zucchini are tender but still crisp. Add paprika, sugar, dill seeds or fresh dill, vinegar, salt and pepper. Toss through and cook 1 minute longer. Cool, then chill before serving, garnished with extra chopped fresh dill. Serves 4.

Spinach Salad with Yogurt

500 g (1 lb) fresh spinach, stems removed; 1/2 cup plain yogurt; 1 clove garlic, crushed; salt and freshly ground black pepper.

Chop spinach roughly, then cook in covered saucepan, without any water except that which clings to leaves after washing, for about 5 minutes. Drain and cool, then squeeze out excess liquid. Combine yogurt and garlic and mix with spinach. Season with salt and pepper. Serves 4.

New Potato Salad

1 kg (2 lb) new potatoes; salt.

DRESSING: 2 tbs vinegar; 1 tbs Dijon mustard; freshly ground black pepper; 6 tbs olive oil; 1/4 cup chopped fresh herbs (parsley, chives, oregano and mint).

Boil potatoes in their skins in boiling salted water until tender.
DRESSING: Place vinegar, mustard and pepper in a small bowl and gradually whisk in olive oil until thick. Stir in herbs and pour into salad bowl. Drain potatoes, then peel and chop. While potatoes are still warm, toss in dressing. Do not chill. Serves 6–8.

Avocado Salad

1 mignonette lettuce; 1 avocado, peeled, stoned and sliced.

DRESSING: 1 tbs white wine vinegar; salt and freshly ground black pepper; 2 tbs olive oil; few poppy seeds.

DRESSING: Whisk vinegar, salt, pepper and oil together until well blended, then add poppy seeds. Pour dressing over lettuce and toss well. Add avocado and toss again gently, but avoid breaking avocado. Serves 4.

Curried Potato Salad

500 g (1 lb) small new potatoes; 1/2 cup Vinaigrette Dressing (page 442); 1/2 cup thick Mayonnaise (page 256).

CURRY MIXTURE: 1 golden shallot, or 1/2 small onion, sliced; 2 tbs olive oil; 1 tbs curry powder; 1 tsp paprika; 2 tsp tomato paste; 1/2 cup water; 1 slice lemon; 2 tsp apricot jam or redcurrant jelly.

CURRY MIXTURE: Quickly soften shallot or onion in oil, then add curry powder and paprika and cook for 1 minute, stirring well. Add tomato paste mixed with water, lemon and jam or jelly. Cover and simmer for 7–10 minutes, then strain. Keep mixture in a small jar or covered container until wanted. Boil potatoes in their skins. Drain, peel and toss them in dressing while still hot. Add enough curry mixture to flavour mayonnaise to taste. Put potatoes in a serving dish, and coat with mayonnaise. Serves 4.

Polish Potato Salad

A lovely pinkish salad with horseradish.

750 g (1 1/2 lb) new potatoes; 2 tbs white wine; 1 raw beetroot, peeled and finely grated; 1 tbs grated horseradish; 3 tbs Mayonnaise (page 256); pinch dry mustard; salt and freshly ground black pepper; 1/2 cup plain yogurt.

Cook potatoes in their skins until tender, then peel while still hot and sprinkle with white wine. Allow to cool. Mix beetroot with horseradish and add to mayonnaise. Mix mustard, salt and pepper into yogurt and add this to beetroot mixture. Spoon this dressing over the potatoes and serve. Serves 4–6.

Russian Ham Salad

250 g (8 oz) cooked ham, thickly sliced and cubed; 3 large potatoes, cooked, peeled and cubed; 1 large crisp apple, cored and cubed; 4 sticks celery, finely chopped; 1 large dill pickle, or 4–5 gherkins, finely chopped; 1 cup Mayonnaise (page 256); 2 tbs chopped parsley; 1/2 tsp dried tarragon; salt; 1 small lettuce.

GARNISH: slices cooked beetroot; cubes unpeeled apple; onion rings.

Place ham, potatoes, apple, celery and pickle in a bowl. Mix mayonnaise with parsley and tarragon, add to bowl and toss lightly. Taste and season with salt as required. Line a serving bowl with lettuce leaves and spoon salad into the middle. Garnish with beetroot, apple and onion rings and chill until serving time. Serves 4–6.

German Salad

A meal in itself, great for lunches and weekend suppers.

4 medium potatoes; 2 Continental frankfurts; 250 g (8 oz) Polish clobassi or kransky sausage; 4 ripe tomatoes, peeled and cut into wedges; 1/4 small cabbage, finely shredded (about 2 cups).

DRESSING: 1 tbs red wine vinegar; 1/2 tsp sugar; pinch salt; pinch nutmeg; 1 large clove garlic, crushed; 1 tbs German or French mustard; 4 tbs salad oil; 1 tbs snipped chives; 1 tbs chopped parsley.

Boil potatoes in their skins.

DRESSING: Mix together vinegar, sugar, salt, nutmeg, garlic and mustard. Gradually beat in oil, then stir in chives and parsley. Drain potatoes and peel when cool enough to handle. Cut into cubes, place in a large bowl, and pour dressing over while they are still warm. Cover frankfurts and clobassi with cold water, bring to the boil and simmer for 3 minutes. Allow to cool in the water, then drain and skin. Cut frankfurts into diagonal slices and clobassi into bite-sized cubes. Add frankfurts, clobassi, tomatoes and cabbage to bowl of potatoes, and mix lightly together with your hands. Taste and adjust seasoning. Serves 4.

German Potato Salad

For this salad marinate potato slices in boiling stock, then fold in sour cream or mayonnaise before serving.

6 medium potatoes; I onion, finely chopped; $1^{1}/_{4}$ cups chicken stock; 4 tbs white vinegar; 5 tbs salad oil; 2 tsp prepared mustard; salt and freshly ground white pepper; $^{1}/_{2}$ cup sour cream; parsley or other fresh herbs to garnish.

Boil potatoes in their skins until just tender. Drain. Peel potatoes while still hot and cut into slices. Place in a bowl with onion. Bring stock to the boil with vinegar, and while boiling pour over potatoes. Leave to marinate until almost all liquid is absorbed, about 20–30 minutes. Pour off any excess liquid, then gently fold in oil mixed with mustard. Taste, and season with salt and pepper if necessary. Lastly, fold in sour cream. Serve at room temperature, garnished with parsley or other fresh herbs. Serves 6–8.

Potato and Ham Salad

500 g (I lb) new or waxy potatoes; 6 sticks celery, cut into julienne (matchstick) strips; $^{1}/_{2}$ cup cream; salt and freshly ground white pepper; I tbs lemon juice; I thick slice cooked ham, cut into thin strips; 2 tbs chopped mixed fresh herbs (parsley, chives, mint, chervil).

Boil potatoes in their skins in salted water until just tender. Drain and, when cool, peel and cut into thick slices. Add celery. Whip cream until thick, season well with salt and pepper and stir in lemon juice. Add to potato and celery and mix gently but thoroughly. Arrange in a salad bowl. Sprinkle ham strips and herbs over salad. Chill until ready to serve. Serves 4.

Rice Salad

Cooked rice, mixed with diced salad vegetables and pineapple, then tossed in a vinaigrette dressing. Serve with cold meats.

I cup long-grain rice; 90 g (3 oz) button mushrooms, sliced; I cucumber, peeled, seeded and diced; 6 crisp radishes, finely sliced; 3 slices fresh or canned pineapple, diced; salt and freshly ground black pepper; 2 ripe tomatoes, quartered, to garnish.

DRESSING: I clove garlic, crushed; I tsp dry mustard; $^{1}/_{2}$ tsp salt; 2 tbs wine vinegar; 6 tbs olive oil; $^{1}/_{2}$ cup finely chopped parsley.

Cook rice in plenty of boiling salted water for 15 minutes. Drain well. Toss hot rice in a bowl with remaining ingredients except tomatoes.

DRESSING: Combine ingredients, pour over rice salad and mix together. Cover and chill until needed. At serving time, bring to room temperature, adjust seasoning, and garnish with tomatoes. Serves 4.

Persian Rice Salad

A rather different rice salad – well spiced, and dotted with fruits and nuts. Serve with roast lamb, kebabs or curries.

$1^{3}/_{4}$ cups long-grain rice; 2 slices fresh ginger, finely chopped; I tsp ground coriander; I tsp ground cumin; $^{1}/_{2}$ tsp nutmeg; 6 spring onions, finely chopped (including some green tops); $^{1}/_{2}$ cup each raisins and sultanas, soaked in boiling water for 5 minutes and drained; I tbs grated orange rind; 6 ripe apricots, stoned and finely sliced; 60 g (2 oz) toasted pine nuts; about $^{1}/_{2}$ cup olive oil; salt and freshly ground black pepper.

GARNISH: fresh or canned apricot halves; pine nuts.

Cook rice in plenty of boiling salted water for 15 minutes. Drain well. Place warm rice in a large bowl and add remaining ingredients, seasoning with salt and pepper. You need just enough oil to moisten rice without making it mushy, so add it gradually. Serve salad warm or at room temperature, garnished with apricot halves and pine nuts. Serves 6–8.

Spanish Salad

The best saffron comes from Spain. The Spaniards use it lavishly in their rice and seafood dishes, giving them superb flavour and colour.

$1^{2}/_{3}$ cups long-grain rice; $^{1}/_{2}$ tsp saffron powder, or good pinch crumbled saffron; 2 red peppers; $^{1}/_{2}$ cup each black and green olives, stoned; I x 200 g can tuna, drained and flaked; 250 g (8 oz) medium cooked prawns, shelled and deveined; 3 rashers bacon, rind removed, grilled until crisp and crumbled; salt and freshly ground black pepper; mignonette lettuce.

DRESSING: I tbs lemon juice; 4 tbs olive oil;
salt and freshly ground black pepper;
grated rind ¹/₂ lemon; I clove garlic, crushed;
I tbs sliced fresh basil.

Cook rice in plenty of boiling salted water, with saffron, for 15 minutes. Drain. Char peppers all over under a preheated grill, place in a paper bag to steam for 10 minutes then rub off skins under cold running water. Remove skins, core and seeds and cut into strips. Add to rice with olives, tuna, prawns and bacon. Season salad with salt and pepper while rice is still warm.

DRESSING: Combine all ingredients in a screw-top jar and shake well. Pour over salad and toss. Serve cold on a bed of mignonette lettuce. Serves 4.

NOTE: Pots of basil may be bought at many green-grocers during the summer months.

Rice, Prawn and Almond Salad

¹/₂ cup long-grain rice; I large onion, finely chopped; 30 g (I oz) butter; 250 g (8 oz) prawns, cooked, shelled, deveined and chopped;
60 g (2 oz) almonds, blanched and shredded;
¹/₂ cup Vinaigrette Dressing (page 442).

Cook rice in plenty of boiling salted water for 15 minutes. Drain well. Cook onion in butter until soft. Add to rice with prawns and almonds. Stir in dressing. Serve salad in a bowl or hors d'oeuvre dish. Serves 4.

Italian Rice Salad

¹/₂ cup long-grain rice; 6–8 button mushrooms, quartered; 2 tbs water; squeeze lemon juice;
4 firm, ripe tomatoes, peeled, seeded and cut into thin wedges; 4–6 black olives, halved and stoned;
salt and freshly ground black pepper;
2–3 tbs Vinaigrette Dressing (made with dry white wine instead of vinegar, page 442).

Cook rice in plenty of boiling salted water for 15 minutes. Drain well and dry. Cook mushrooms in water with lemon juice for 2–3 minutes. Cook quickly, uncovered, so that liquid is well reduced by the time mushrooms are cooked; shake pan and stir well. Add mushrooms to rice with tomatoes and olives. Mix all ingredients with a fork, season well with salt and pepper and moisten with dressing. Serves 4.

Provençal Salad

A richly flavoured salad combining the flavours and colours of the Mediterranean. French mustard with Provençal herbs gives the dressing an authentic flavour.

I mignonette lettuce; 4 hard-boiled eggs, quartered; I x 200 g can tuna, drained and flaked;
8 small new potatoes, cooked, peeled and sliced;
I green, yellow or red pepper, cored, seeded and sliced; 2 tbs black olives, stoned;
6 ripe egg tomatoes, or 4 ripe tomatoes, quartered;
3 anchovy fillets, finely chopped;
I tbs grated Parmesan cheese.

DRESSING: I tbs wine vinegar (preferably red);
3 tbs good olive oil; I clove garlic, crushed;
I tsp mustard flavoured with Provençal herbs, or French mustard; I sprig fresh thyme, finely chopped (if available); salt and freshly ground black pepper.

Make a bed of lettuce leaves in a salad bowl. On this, arrange hard-boiled eggs, tuna, potatoes, pepper, olives, tomatoes and anchovy fillets. Chill. Sprinkle with cheese.

DRESSING: Shake ingredients in a screw-top jar until well combined. Spoon dressing over salad just before serving and toss at the table. Serves 4.

Green Bean Salad

Use tender, plump, stringless beans or snake beans for this salad. Serve as a first course or as an accompaniment to roasted or grilled meats.

750 g (I¹/₂ lb) young green beans; salt and freshly ground black pepper; 2–3 tbs wine vinegar;
¹/₂ tsp Dijon mustard; 6–8 tbs olive oil;
lettuce leaves; 6–8 spring onions, shredded;
2 tbs finely chopped parsley.

Cook green beans in boiling salted water until they are barely tender. Meanwhile, beat together vinegar, mustard and oil and season with salt and pepper. Drain beans and toss immediately while still warm in dressing. Chill. When ready to serve, line a salad bowl or rectangular hors d'oeurve dish with lettuce leaves. Add bean salad and sprinkle with spring onions and parsley. Serves 4–6.

Bacon and Egg Lentil Salad

A salad that's a satisfying, total meal.

2 cups red or brown lentils; I large onion, studded with 2 cloves; I bay leaf; I tbs salt;
3 cloves garlic, bruised; I strip orange rind;
¹/₂ cup chopped parsley; I cup finely chopped spring onions (including some green tops);
¹/₂ cup olive oil; I tsp red wine vinegar;
I tbs lemon juice; freshly ground black pepper;
2 rashers bacon, rind removed, grilled until crisp and crumbled.

GARNISH: 2 hard-boiled eggs, finely chopped;
¹/₄ cup chopped parsley; 12–15 black olives.

Place lentils in a saucepan and cover with cold water. Bring slowly to the boil, then remove from heat, cover and stand for 1 hour. Drain and cover with fresh cold water to come 5 cm (2 in) above lentils. Add onion stuck with cloves, bay leaf, salt, garlic and orange rind. Bring to the boil, then cover and simmer until just tender, about 20–30 minutes. Drain and cool. Remove flavouring ingredients and discard them. Put lentils into a bowl and toss gently with parsley, spring onions, oil, vinegar and lemon juice. Let stand, covered, for 1 hour. Taste and adjust seasoning if necessary. Cover and keep cool but not refrigerated until ready to serve. Toss bacon gently through lentils. Spoon salad into a serving dish and garnish with hard-boiled eggs, parsley and olives. Serves 8.

Three–Bean Salad

I cup dried red kidney beans; I cup dried haricot beans; I cup dried butter beans; 6 cups chicken stock; 3 bay leaves; 3 sprigs parsley; I onion, halved; 3 whole cloves; 18 black peppercorns; 3 tsp salt; I red pepper, cored, seeded and diced; 6 spring onions, sliced; 3/4 cup Vinaigrette Dressing (page 442); chopped parsley to garnish.

Soak kidney, haricot and butter beans separately overnight in water to cover. Next day drain and put in separate saucepans. Put 2 cups stock, 1 bay leaf, 1 parsley sprig, 1/3 onion, 1 clove, 6 peppercorns and 1 tsp salt in each pan and bring to the boil. Simmer until beans are tender, about 1 1/4 hours for kidney beans and 1 1/2 hours for haricot and butter beans. Drain, removing seasonings, and chill. Combine all beans, diced pepper and spring onions in a large serving bowl. Toss with vinaigrette dressing and sprinkle with chopped parsley. Serves 6–8.

Broccoli Salad

This chilled salad may be part of a plate of hors d'oeuvre or a separate course. It will keep in the refrigerator, covered with plastic wrap, for a few days.

2–3 heads broccoli; salt; 1/2 cup dry white wine; 4 tbs olive oil; 5 spring onions, chopped; 2 tbs chopped parsley; 2 cloves garlic, crushed; juice 2 lemons; 2 tsp thyme or 1/2 tsp dried; I tbs black peppercorns.

Pull off leaves from broccoli, cut off tough base of stems, and pare stems with a vegetable peeler. Cook in boiling salted water for 10 minutes. Rinse under cold water and drain. Cut into 5 cm (2 in) pieces. Put wine, oil, spring onions, parsley, garlic, lemon juice, thyme and peppercorns in a saucepan, cover and simmer for 20 minutes. Add broccoli and cook, uncovered, for 2 minutes more (broccoli should still be slightly crisp). Adjust seasoning and pour into a shallow dish. Serve at room temperature or slightly chilled. Serves 6.

Eggplant Salad

Eggplants (aubergines) make a super salad, good with crusty Italian bread.

I large or 2 medium eggplants.

DRESSING: 2 cloves garlic, chopped; 1/4 cup red wine vinegar; 1/3 cup olive oil; 1/3 cup vegetable oil; 1/3 cup chopped fresh parsley; chopped fresh dill; salt and freshly ground black pepper.

GARNISH: 1/2 red salad onion, chopped; I small red pepper, cored, seeded and diced.

Bake eggplant, wrapped in foil, in a preheated hot oven (200°C/400°F) for 40 minutes or until it is tender. Unwrap and let it cool on a wire rack. Peel and dice flesh, and arrange it in a serving dish.

DRESSING: In a food processor fitted with a steel blade or in a blender, purée garlic, vinegar, oils, parsley, dill, salt and pepper until smooth. Toss eggplant with dressing, and garnish salad with onion and red pepper. Chill salad, covered, for 2 hours, and serve with Italian bread. Serves 4–6.

Coleslaw with Sour Cream

1/2 medium cabbage, finely shredded; 1/4 cup Mayonnaise (page 256); I tbs Dijon mustard; 2 tbs chopped celery; dash Tabasco sauce; 3/4 cup sour cream; 1/2 red pepper, cored, seeded and finely sliced; 1/2 green pepper, cored, seeded and finely sliced; 3–4 tbs finely chopped spring onions.

Put cabbage in a large salad bowl. Combine remaining ingredients, pour over cabbage, toss thoroughly and chill well before serving. Serves 6.

Waldorf Coleslaw

I small cabbage, shredded; 4 spring onions, chopped (including some green tops); 2 sticks celery, chopped; I green pepper, cored, seeded and chopped; I Granny Smith apple, cored and chopped; 1/2 cup sultanas; 1/2 cup Mayonnaise (page 256) or sour cream; 1/2 cup walnut pieces.

DRESSING: I tbs wine vinegar; salt and freshly ground black pepper; 2 tsp Dijon mustard; 2 1/2 tbs oil.

Put cabbage, spring onions, celery, green pepper and apple into salad bowl and add sultanas. Whisk together dressing ingredients. Add to bowl and mix lightly. Cover and refrigerate for 2–3 hours. At serving time, add mayonnaise or sour cream, sprinkle with walnuts and toss. Serves 8.

Mixed Coleslaw

1/4 red cabbage, finely shredded; 1/4 white cabbage, finely shredded; 1/2 red pepper, cored, seeded and finely sliced; 1/2 bunch radishes, sliced; 1/2 cup Vinaigrette Dressing (page 442); chopped parsley to garnish.

Bring a large saucepan of water to the boil and add red cabbage. Stir vigorously for 1 minute, then drain immediately in a colander. Rinse cabbage under cold running water to set colour and cool. Leave to drain, then pat red cabbage with cloth to dry. Put in a large salad bowl with white cabbage, red pepper and radishes. Toss well with dressing and sprinkle salad with parsley before serving. Serves 8.

VARIATION

CREAMY MIXED SLAW: Prepare as above, but add ½ cup sour cream or Mayonnaise (see page 256) with the dressing.

SALAD DRESSINGS

The sauce for a salad may be a simple dressing of oil and vinegar, a creamy, thick mayonnaise, or it may be one of the imaginative variations of these two great basics. Whether simple or intricate, all good dressings have one thing in common: they must be made with the freshest and choicest ingredients available.

Vinaigrette Dressing (oil, lemon juice, vinegar, herbs) can be varied in a multitude of ways, by changing the herbs used, or using different oils and vinegars. And the best quality oil and vinegar you can afford, the freshest eggs you can find, and garden herbs freshly picked, will make a world of difference to the quality of the dressings you make.

Among the oils, there's olive oil, or a wide of choice of nut oils (walnut, almond, or peanut), or those made from seeds (sunflower, safflower or sesame) – all have their uses. Like wine, it's worth shopping around for the one that really suits your palate.

Vinegars, too, should be explored. A harsh vinegar will still taste harsh in a dressing. Look for different flavours – tarragon, wine, or cider.

Good dressings are one of the easiest ways to make food interesting. Remember, it is the actual flavour of the ingredients used which is important to the dressing – nothing else can give the same taste and appearance. So make sure everything you use is of the best quality and in the best condition.

VINAIGRETTE OR FRENCH DRESSSING

The most widely used dressing in the world is the basic oil-and-vinegar dressing of France – a mixture of good olive oil, wine vinegar, salt and freshly ground black pepper. Add a dollop of good prepared French mustard, if you like it, or a little hot powdered English mustard. Fresh herbs in season are added to suit the food the dressing is going to flavour and season. Garlic is used by those who like the flavour, and features in more robust salads. Be sure the salad greens are perfectly dry, so that the dressing will adhere to the leaves. It's best added to green salad at the moment of eating.

The usual proportion of oil to vinegar is three parts to one, but this can be varied to suit your own taste. Some salads call for a dressing where the oil is only lightly spiked with vinegar. If you find the one in three proportion too oily, add salt rather than increase the vinegar to cut the oiliness.

A squeeze of lemon juice is sometimes added at the last moment. Cider vinegar, red wine vinegar or any of the flavoured vinegars, such as tarragon, are excellent.

The choice of oil can vary. A good olive oil is the choice of many. Walnut oil has a distinctive taste and is good on tender green salads; it can also be used in combination with olive oil. The polyunsaturated oils are increasing in popularity, sunflower and safflower being the natural choices for those on low cholesterol diets. See recipes.

See also *Mayonnaise* and *Green Goddess Dressing*.

Vinaigrette Dressing

2 tbs good vinegar; ¼ tsp salt; 1 tsp French mustard; freshly ground black pepper; 6 tbs olive oil; pinch caster sugar (optional).

Put vinegar into a small bowl with salt, mustard and pepper. Mix well with a fork or birch whisk, then slowly add oil, beating until mixture thickens slightly. If dressing tastes sharp, add more oil or a pinch of caster sugar. If dressing is too oily for your taste, add more salt – this cuts oiliness. An alternative method is to combine all ingredients in a screw-top jar and shake well until mixture thickens. The main drawback to this method is the tendency to re-use the jar over and over, even adding little quantities of dressing left over. Makes about ¾ cup.

VARIATIONS

GARLIC VINAIGRETTE DRESSING: There are several ways to add garlic to your dressing. If you like a pungent dressing, crush 1–2 cloves garlic to a paste with salt, add vinegar, mustard and pepper and then oil. You can chop garlic and add it to the finished dressing for a more rustic salad. For a more delicate flavour, bruise peeled garlic clove and steep in the vinegar for 1–2 hours. The vinegar brings out a more delicate flavour of the garlic, while oil brings out the strong flavour.

MUSTARD VINAIGRETTE DRESSING: Increase the amount of French mustard to taste, or add 1 tsp English mustard instead.

FRESH HERB VINAIGRETTE DRESSING: When adding herbs it is best to sprinkle half of the freshly chopped herbs over the salad, and add the remaining herbs to the dressing. Tarragon, basil, chives and parsley add their own distinctive flavours. They may be used separately or in combination. 1–2 tbs chopped fresh herbs is sufficient for this quantity of Vinaigrette.

CHIFFONADE DRESSING: To ¾ cup Vinaigrette Dressing; add 2 hard-boiled eggs, finely chopped, and 1 tbs each finely chopped green olives, onion and parsley. Good on tart salads with chicory, curly endive, etc.

Fines Herbes Vinaigrette

**I tbs tarragon vinegar; ^{1}/$_4$ cup dry red wine;
I tsp Dijon mustard; I tsp salt; I tsp paprika;
^{1}/$_2$ tsp black pepper; I tsp finely chopped fresh basil,
marjoram or oregano; ^{1}/$_2$ cup chopped parsley;
2 cloves garlic, crushed; ^{1}/$_2$ cup olive oil.**

Combine all ingredients and beat well with fork or
whisk, or shake well in a screw-top jar. Use over
salad greens or sliced tomatoes, or as a dressing for
lightly cooked vegetables. Makes 1 cup.

Green Mayonnaise

**I cup fresh watercress; 2 leaves spinach;
^{1}/$_4$ cup fresh tarragon, chervil or parsley;
I tsp lemon juice; I cup Mayonnaise (page 256).**

Simmer greens in unsalted water 2 minutes. Drain
and rinse in cold water. Press out water, then pound
in mortar until greens are reduced to a pulp, or purée
in blender. Add lemon juice and combine mixture
with mayonnaise. Use with vegetable or fish salads.
Makes 1½ cups.

Yogurt Mayonnaise

This is sometimes referred to as eggless mayonnaise.
It is the one to use when on a low cholesterol diet or
dieting.

**3 tsp Dijon mustard; I^1/$_2$ tbs olive oil;
^{3}/$_4$ cup low fat plain yogurt; I tbs lemon juice;
salt and freshly ground white pepper.**

Place mustard in a mixing bowl. Add oil gradually,
beating vigorously with a fork or whisk. Blend in
yogurt. Add remaining ingredients until mixture is
smooth. Refrigerate until required. Makes 1 cup.

Sauce Verte

This very green, herby sauce is a favourite in France
and Italy. It is served with chilled seafood, hot boiled
beef and some salads, or can be folded through
2 cups cooked rice to make an interesting rice salad.

**I cup parsley; I tbs chopped onion; ^{1}/$_4$ cup capers;
^{1}/$_2$ x 50 g can anchovy fillets, drained; I–2 cloves
garlic; 2 small sour gherkins; I small boiled potato,
or I slice white bread, softened in water and
drained; ^{1}/$_2$ cup olive oil; salt and freshly ground
black pepper; I tbs wine vinegar.**

Chop together very finely (or chop in blender or
food processor fitted with steel blade), first parsley,
then onion, capers, anchovies, garlic and gherkins.
Add potato or bread and mix until a coarse, dry,
green paste is formed. Place mixture in a bowl and
work in just enough oil (about 1 tsp) to form a slightly
thinner but smooth paste. Add salt and pepper.
Continue to add remaining oil slowly, mixing

constantly until paste is of a smooth consistency.
Add vinegar and mix thoroughly. Makes 1½ cups.

Buttermilk Dressing

**I cup buttermilk; 3 tbs lemon or lime juice;
^{1}/$_2$ tsp Dijon mustard; ^{1}/$_2$ tsp paprika;
salt and freshly ground white pepper; pinch salt.**

Combine all ingredients in a screw-top jar and shake
well. Good with egg and cheese salads. Makes about
1¼ cups.

Sour Cream and Horseradish Sauce

Serve with cold smoked fish, such as trout or
salmon, or cold roast beef. Good also with fish
moulds or loaves.

**I cup sour light cream or plain yogurt;
6 spring onions, chopped; 2 tbs grated horseradish;
I tsp Dijon mustard; salt and freshly
ground black pepper.**

Combine all ingredients in a bowl, mixing thoroughly. Makes 1½ cups.

Old–fashioned Cooked Salad Dressing

Use this in the same way as Mayonnaise, and use the
same variations (see page 256).

**I tbs sugar; I^1/$_2$ tbs flour; I tsp salt;
2 tsp dry mustard; 2 egg yolks; 60 g (2 oz) butter,
melted; I^1/$_2$ cups milk; ^{1}/$_3$ cup vinegar;
dash paprika (optional).**

Combine dry ingredients in top of double saucepan or
a heatproof bowl which will fit over a saucepan. Add
egg yolks, butter and milk and blend well. Gradually
stir in vinegar. Cook over simmering water, stirring
constantly, until thick. Add paprika if desired. Makes
about 2 cups.

SALMON

Fresh wild salmon is considered one of the great fish
delicacies of the world; it is beautifully coloured,
the pink flesh is both firm and succulent, the flavour
unique, and it is rich in Omega-3 fatty acids, so good for
our hearts.

Worldwide, salmon farming has expanded enormously
over the past decade, with major producers in Norway,
Scotland, Chile and Australia. Many consider wild
salmon (not farmed) from the rivers of Scotland and
Ireland the very best. Introduced into NSW in 1963, and
transferred for aquaculture in Tasmania in the mid-
1980s, fresh Atlantic salmon and ocean trout have
become readily available at Australian fish markets.
However, because salmon farming has been subject to

S

broad and persistent attack by environmentalists, it is still best seen as a luxury, to keep farming less intensive and more environmental.

Atlantic salmon and ocean trout are reared in freshwater hatcheries for 9–12 months. They are pre-adapted to life in seawater and are transferred to net cages in the sea. The farm sites are generally in sheltered bays or estuaries around Tasmania.

Organic Salmon: As the call for organic foods grows it is encouraging to find organic salmon is becoming available. Yarra Valley in Victoria, Australia is one such supplier.

Fresh Salmon and Ocean Trout: There is no substitute for fresh salmon cooked to perfection. It can be purchased whole where they usually weigh 3–4 kg (6–8 lb), or ready cut into fillets or steaks (cutlets). A whole baked or poached salmon is a fitting dish to take the place of turkey or ham at the Christmas or celebration table. Salmon fillets, or steaks, too, are the epitome of luxury – delicious, yet easy to cook.

Canned Salmon: Probably the most familiar type, and enormous amounts are processed every year. One of the most sought-after varieties is sockeye salmon, considered outstanding for canning because of its rich red, very firm flesh. Canned sockeye salmon is always marked as such on the label, whereas other varieties may only be described as either red or pink salmon.

Smoked Salmon: A superb delicacy. Wafer-thin slices of smoked salmon may be served with lemon wedges and brown bread and butter, with cream cheese and bagels, or on rye bread with sour cream. Smoked salmon lends a touch of luxury to homely scrambled eggs, transforming them into a dish for princes – try it for a special brunch with fine champagne. Choose smoked salmon that has pale pink-gold flesh and is as fresh as possible.

A dark red or deep orange colour usually means a dye or over-cured fish. It may be bought freshly sliced from a whole side of salmon, or ready sliced, and vacuum-packed. Smoked salmon is also available canned or in pieces in jars.

Salmon Trout are closely related to trout but feed in the sea and spawn in fresh water. They are found in northern Europe and combine the beautiful flavour and pink-coloured flesh of salmon with the texture of trout. They may be prepared and served in the same way as salmon.

Salmon Roe Eggs: The eggs are larger than lumpfish eggs, they are salted and are a bright orange colour. Store in refrigerator once opened. Use in same ways as Caviar - as an hors d'oeuvre. See *Caviar*.

Poached Salmon

Probably the finest way to serve fresh salmon. May be served hot or cold.

1 x 1 kg (2 lb) salmon steak; 4¹/₂ cups water;
juice ¹/₂ lemon; 1 cup white wine; 1 tsp salt;

6 black peppercorns; 1 bouquet garni
(sprig thyme, bay leaf, sprig parsley and
stick celery).

Tie fish into shape carefully with white tape, but not tightly as the fish swells during cooking, or wrap in muslin. Place in a shallow flameproof dish. Combine remaining ingredients in a saucepan and bring to just below simmering point. Pour this court bouillon over fish and bring just to the boil. Reduce heat to low, cover dish and poach (the liquid should just shiver throughout cooking – do not let it boil or the delicate fish will spoil). Continue poaching for 20–30 minutes or until fish flakes easily when tested with a fine skewer. Drain fish, remove skin and serve with parsley, buttered new potatoes and Hollandaise Sauce (see page 459). Serves 6–8.

NOTE: If fish is to be served cold, allow to cool in liquid before skinning. Serve with potato and cucumber salads and Mayonnaise (see page 256) or sour cream.

Grilled Salmon Steaks

4 salmon steaks, cut 2 cm (³/4 in) thick;
2 tbs ground black pepper; juice ¹/2 lemon;
60 g (2 oz) Maître d'Hôtel Butter (page 52).

Put fish in a glass or earthenware dish. Combine remaining ingredients, except Maître d'Hôtel Butter, and pour over fish. Leave to marinate for about 1 hour, turning steaks several times. Drain fish and place on oiled grill. Cook using a preheated grill for 5 minutes on each side and then a further 2 minutes on each side. Spread ¹/3 of Maître d'Hôtel Butter on a warm dish – butter should soften, not melt. Remove skin and centre bone from steaks, arrange on prepared dish and place remaining butter on top of each steak. Serves 4.

Baked Atlantic Salmon

Atlantic salmon and ocean trout are two great dishes worthy of a festive meal, especially Christmas dinner. Serve the salmon warm or at room temperature, with a home-made Mayonnaise (page 256), or in the mango season, Mango and Mint Sauce (page 248). Complete the meal with boiled new potatoes and a green salad.

3 kg (6 lb) whole fresh Atlantic salmon or ocean trout, organic for preference; few lemon slices; 1 tsp sea salt.

Lay a piece of aluminium foil on a baking dish that will accommodate the fish, and sprinkle with half the sea salt. Arrange the whole fish on top and place a few lemon slices in the cavity. Sprinkle fish with remaining salt. Cover with another sheet of aluminium foil and wrap up loosely. Bake in a preheated moderate oven (180°C/350°F), for 35–40 minutes, until the eyes have turned white and a skewer inserted into the thickest part feels warm when tested on your lip. Leave to cool, still covered with foil, for 15 minutes.

Remove skin while fish is still warm. Make a shallow cut around the top of the tail section, along the back of the fish and across the start of the head section. Carefully pull away the skin, then rather than turn fish, pull skin on the other side from underneath. When fish has cooled transfer to a long platter, draining off any juice. Garnish with sprigs of mint and strips of lime rind and offer with the Mayonnaise (page 256) or Mango and Mint Sauce (page 248). To serve, lift serving-sized pieces carefully from the bone on each side of the length from the head down to the backbone. When all of the first side is served, turn the fish to repeat with other side. Serves 8.

Smoked Salmon Open Sandwiches

sprigs fresh dill, cress or lettuce leaves; 2 slices rye or black bread; butter; 4–6 slices smoked salmon; 2 slices lemon to garnish; 2 tbs sour cream.

Place chilled dill, cress or lettuce on buttered rye or black bread. Fold slices smoked salmon and place on top. Garnish with lemon slices and top with sour cream. Serves 1–2.

Roasted Salmon Salad with Basil Aïoli

Use organic salmon or ocean trout fillets for preference. Fillets tend to be more melt-in-the-mouth than the steaks or cutlets.

4 x 250 g (8 oz) salmon fillets or steaks, skin left on; 4 fresh bay leaves; 2–4 tbs extra virgin olive oil; sea salt and freshly ground pepper; 2 cups baby rocket leaves or watercress sprigs; 250 g (8 oz) baby spinach leaves; 4 firm tomatoes, peeled, seeded and cut into thin strips; 1–2 tbs lemon juice.

BASIL AIOLI: 2 cloves garlic; 1/2 tsp salt; 6 spring onions, chopped (including some green); 1/4 cup freshly chopped basil leaves; 1 egg; 2 tbs lemon juice; 1 cup olive oil.

Using a sharp knife, make a small cut just under the skin of each salmon fillet or steak and insert a bay leaf. Place the salmon, skin side up, on a lightly oiled baking tray. Brush the salmon with the olive oil and season to taste with salt and pepper. Roast in a preheated slow oven (120°C/300°F), for 15 minutes. Remove from the oven and lay a sheet of aluminium foil on top. Allow to rest for 5–10 minutes. Toss the salad leaves with the tomato julienne, adding the lemon juice and just enough extra virgin olive oil to coat, without being drenched. Remove skin from salmon if liked. Arrange the mixed leaves on serving plates, place salmon on top with spoonful of Basil Aïoli and serve at once. Serves 4.

BASIL AIOLI: Crush the garlic to a paste with the salt. In a food processor or blender, place the spring onions, basil, egg, lemon juice and garlic, process with an on/off action until the basil mixture is finely blended. With the motor running add the oil in a slow stream and blend well until thick. Season with salt and pepper to taste.

Scrambled Egg with Smoked Salmon

For a special brunch serve this elegant dish with hot toast and champagne.

6 eggs; salt and freshly ground black pepper; 60 g (2 oz) butter; 125 g (4 oz) smoked salmon, flaked; 3 tbs cream; 1/4 cup Mayonnaise (page 256) or thick cream; 2 tsp snipped fresh dill; 4 slices smoked salmon; sprigs fresh dill to garnish.

Beat eggs and season with salt and pepper. Cook gently in butter, stirring, until set. Fold in flaked smoked salmon and cream. Allow to cool a little. Serve piled on a dish, with mayonnaise or thick cream spooned over and sprinkled with snipped dill. Fold slices of smoked salmon and garnish dish with these and sprigs of fresh dill. Serves 4.

Salmon and Potato Bake

A lunch or supper dish, serve with green salad.

60 g (2 oz) butter; 3 tbs flour; 1/2 tsp salt; freshly ground black pepper; 2 cups milk; 1 x 440 g can (2 cups) salmon, drained; 4 cups sliced cooked potatoes; 1/2 cup Mayonnaise (page 256); 1 cup grated Cheddar cheese; 1 tsp Worcestershire sauce; 1/2 tsp French mustard; paprika.

Melt butter in a saucepan and blend in flour, salt and pepper. Gradually add milk off heat, then cook, stirring constantly, until thickened. Remove any bones and skin from salmon and flake. Stir into sauce. Arrange in alternate layers with potatoes in a shallow ovenproof dish. Combine mayonnaise, 1/2 cup cheese,

Worcestershire sauce and mustard. Spread over salmon mixture. Top with remaining grated cheese and sprinkle with paprika. Bake in a preheated moderate oven (180°C/350°F) for about 30 minutes. Serves 4.

Smoked Salmon with Cucumber

¹/₂ cup sour cream; 2 tbs cider vinegar;
I tbs snipped chives; ¹/₂ tsp snipped fresh dill;
¹/₂ tsp salt; ¹/₄ tsp pepper; 2 medium cucumbers,
peeled and finely sliced; 6 slices pumpernickel
bread; butter; 125 g (4 oz) smoked salmon, sliced.

Mix sour cream, vinegar, chives, dill, salt and pepper. Pour over cucumbers and mix. Cover and chill for 2–3 hours. Spread pumpernickel with butter and put a slice of smoked salmon on each piece. Top with cucumber mixture and serve as an appetiser. Serves 6.

Salmon Cakes

2 cups mashed potatoes; 60 g (2 oz) butter;
I tbs finely chopped onion or chives;
I x 220 g can (I cup) salmon or tuna, drained;
I tsp lemon juice; salt and freshly ground black
pepper; ¹/₄ cup flour; I egg, beaten;
¹/₂ cup dry breadcrumbs; oil or butter for frying.

Beat mashed potatoes with butter and onion. Remove any bones and skin from fish and flake. Combine with potatoes and lemon juice, and season with salt and pepper. Form into 6 small cakes. Dip in flour, then egg, then in breadcrumbs. Fry in a little oil or butter until nicely browned. Serve with Sauce Tartare (see page 256). Serves 4.

Salmon Puffs

I x 440 g can (2 cups) salmon, drained;
¹/₂ cup fresh breadcrumbs; 2 tbs grated onion;
I tbs lemon juice; 30 g (I oz) butter, melted;
salt and freshly ground black pepper; I egg;
¹/₂ cup milk; sour cream; snipped chives.

Remove any bones and skin from fish and flake. Combine salmon, breadcrumbs, onion, lemon juice, butter, salt and pepper. Beat egg and add milk. Stir into salmon mixture. Place in 4–6 well-greased individual ramekin dishes. Set dishes in a baking tin with water to come halfway up the sides and bake in a preheated moderate oven (180°C/350°F) for about 45 minutes or until set and golden. Top each with a spoonful of sour cream and sprinkle with snipped chives. Serves 4.

Salmon Soufflé

I x 220 g can (I cup) salmon; milk; 60 g (2 oz) butter;
¹/₄ cup flour; ¹/₄ tsp dry mustard; salt; cayenne;
6 eggs, separated; I tbs chopped parsley.

Drain salmon, reserving liquid. Remove any bones and skin from fish and flake. Add enough milk to reserved liquid to make 1 cup. Melt butter in a saucepan and blend in flour, mustard, salt and cayenne. Gradually add milk mixture and cook over medium heat, stirring constantly, until it boils and thickens. Beat egg yolks until pale and thick. Stir a little of the hot sauce into yolks, then add to remaining sauce in pan. Remove from heat. Fold in salmon and parsley. Beat egg whites until they hold soft peaks. Stir 1 tablespoonful of egg whites into salmon mixture, then gently and quickly fold in remaining whites. Pour into a well-greased 6-cup soufflé dish (see *Soufflé* for preparation of dish). Bake in a preheated moderate oven (180°C/350°F) for 45 minutes or until firm. Serve immediately. Serves 4.

Italian Salmon Salad

150 g pasta bows; I x 220 g can (I cup) salmon,
drained and flaked; I red pepper, cored, seeded and
diced; ¹/₂ cucumber, finely diced; 10 black olives,
stoned; ¹/₂ cup Vinaigrette Dressing (page 442);
watercress to garnish.

Cook pasta in boiling water until 'al dente'. Drain thoroughly and leave to cool. Mix flaked salmon with the pepper, cucumber, olives and pasta. Pour over the dressing and toss lightly. Arrange in a serving dish and garnish with sprigs of watercress. Serves 4.

Salmon Kedgeree

I cup raw rice; I x 440 g can (2 cups) salmon;
60 g (2 oz) butter; 2 hard-boiled eggs, finely
chopped; 2–3 tbs cream; salt and freshly ground
black pepper; pinch cayenne pepper;
I tbs chopped parsley.

Cook rice in boiling salted water until tender, drain well. Keep hot over boiling water or in a slow oven. Remove bones and skin from salmon and flake gently. Melt butter in a saucepan, add salmon, eggs, cream, salt and pepper and stir until hot. Combine fish mixture with hot rice and add parsley. Turn into a serving dish and serve. Serves 5–6.

Smoked Salmon and Dill Dip

250 g (8 oz) cream cheese, softened;
¹/₃ cup sour light cream; 2 tbs lemon juice;
I tbs grated horseradish; 90 g (3 oz) smoked
salmon, finely chopped; I tbs snipped fresh dill,
or I tbs chopped parsley mixed with ¹/₂ tsp dill seeds;
salt and freshly ground black pepper; cayenne;
sprigs fresh dill or parsley to garnish.

Stir cream cheese with a wooden spoon until smooth, then stir in sour cream, lemon juice and horseradish and combine thoroughly. Fold in smoked salmon, dill, salt, pepper and cayenne. Spoon into a serving bowl and garnish with sprigs of dill or parsley. Makes about 1¹/₂ cups.

SALSIFY

A white-skinned root vegetable, sometimes called oyster plant because its flavour is akin to that of oysters.

■ **BASIC PREPARATION:** Wash the roots, then thinly peel; drop them into a bowl of acidulated water to prevent discolouration.

Salsify may be served in white or cream sauce, or tossed in butter and parsley, or fried in a light batter, but the vegetable must be pre-cooked before proceeding with any of these preparations.

■ **TO PRE-COOK:** Simply drop the prepared vegetable, cut into lengths of about 5 cm (2 in) into boiling salted water and cook for 20–25 minutes. Drain, then finish as desired. *Scorzonera* (*Black Salsify*) has a brownish-black skin otherwise it closely resembles salsify in flavour and texture. Prepare and use the same way as white-skinned salsify.

Buttered Salsify

I kg (2 lb) salsify roots; 60 g (2 oz) butter; salt and freshly ground black pepper; finely chopped parsley.

Prepare salsify as described above, and pre-cook in boiling salted water. Drain. Heat butter in frying pan and cook salsify for about 10 minutes, turning often, until golden. Season with salt and pepper and toss with chopped parsley. Serves 6.

SALT

Salt for the table, an almost pure form of sodium chloride, has since ancient times been a valuable commodity to man. It imparts flavour to food and is indispensable in cooking. Our bodies need salt to survive. There are two types of salt: rock (or mined) salt and sea salt (called solar salt). Seasoned salts such as celery salt or vegetable salt are simply a blend of salt with herbs or spices.

Rock Salt: Rock salt is mined from where it occurs in layers from the evaporation of land-locked seas of past geological ages. Untreated rock salt is said to have the best flavour of all salts. Most cooking or kitchen salt is finely ground refined rock salt with magnesium carbonate added to make it free-running. Rock salt is also used for pickling salt which has no additives, and iodized salt, with iodine added as the name suggests, for its health benefits.

Sea Salt: Sea salt is obtained from seawater, either by direct evaporation or by the factory-finishing of saline concentrations from seawater pans. Sea salt is evaporated slowly by the sun, which makes large, irregular crystals and is best as a topping to a dish or offered at the table in a salt dish. It is a waste to use the delicate crystals in cooking, when their delightful crunch is lost. Look for kosher salt to use for sauces, in soups and stocks and in seasoning liquid mixtures.

Gourmet Salts: There is a growing number of 'boutique' salts available; all are best used where their contrasting textures contribute to overall flavour. The varying sizes and shapes depend on how their brines were evaporated.

'Fleur de sel' comes from the French Atlantic coast and is regarded by many as the world's finest salt, being texturally superior to most. When sun and wind conditions are ideal, fleur de sel, 'flower of salt', blossoms on the surface of the solar evaporation ponds. Its crystals have unique shapes because they can grow only downward from the surface of the ponds.

Maldon Sea Salt: The coastal town of Maldon, Essex, England, has been a salt-producing centre since the Middle Ages. In fact, legend has it that the secret of salt making from seawater was discovered there almost 2000 years ago, when the Romans ruled Britain. Maldon sea salt is considered to be one of the finest English sea salts. It has a powerful flavour and the pyramid-shaped crystals give a wonderful crunch and sparkle to food.

Australian Murray River Salt Flakes: These pale, apricot-coloured salt flakes are a favourite with gourmets. Salinity is a major and growing problem in Australia and an area of particular concern is the Murray Darling Basin. Support for this salt helps towards stimulating the removal of salt from this sensitive area and assists in solving the inland salinity problem. Various other natural sea salt crystals are available, including Southern Ocean Salt from the Great Australian Bight.

SAMBAL

See *Curry*.

SAMOOSAS (SAMOSAS)

These Indian savouries are semi-circular pastries filled with minced lamb, subtly flavoured with spices and herbs. They are deep-fried until golden and crisp and are wonderful with pre-dinner drinks.

Samoosas

PASTRY: I cup flour; $^1/_2$ tsp salt; I tbs ghee or butter; 3–4 tbs lukewarm water; milk; oil for deep frying.

FILLING: I tbs ghee; 2.5 cm (I in) piece fresh ginger, grated; 2 onions, chopped; 2 tbs chopped fresh mint; 2 tsp curry paste or powder; I tsp salt; 250 g (8 oz) minced lamb; $^1/_2$ tsp saffron, crumbled; I cup hot water; I tomato, peeled and chopped; juice $^1/_2$ lemon; $^1/_2$ tsp Garam Masala (page 171).

PASTRY: Sift flour and salt into a bowl. Rub in ghee or butter with fingertips. Add water and knead to form a stiff dough. Cover bowl with a cloth and allow to stand while preparing filling.

FILLING: Heat ghee and gently fry ginger, half the onions and the mint until onions are soft and golden. Stir in curry paste or powder and salt and fry for 2–3 minutes. Add lamb and cook for 5 minutes, stirring frequently. Meanwhile, soak saffron in hot water. Stir into meat mixture with tomato. Bring to the boil, then turn heat very low and cook, uncovered, for 30–40 minutes, stirring occasionally. The meat should be tender and moisture evaporated. Add lemon juice and garam masala. Allow to cool then mix in remaining onions.

Divide dough into 14–16 even-sized pieces. Shape each into a ball and roll out on a lightly floured board as thinly as possible, keeping the shape round. Cut each round in half and moisten edges with milk. Place a small spoonful of filling on one side of each half-round and fold other side over. Press edges together and trim with a fluted cutter if liked. Heat oil in a heavy pan and deep-fry samoosas, a few at a time, until golden-brown. Drain on crumpled paper towels. Serve hot. A bowl of mint or coriander chutney may be offered for dipping. Makes about 30.

SANDWICHES

Some sandwiches are famous – the Hero, the Shooter's Sandwich, the Club Sandwich, the thin, perfect, cucumber sandwiches of English tea tables – and there are many others that make a satisfying, nourishing light meal. Some are designed for rugged appetites; and at the other extreme, Mrs Beeton gave instructions for making small tea sandwiches to be eaten with gloved fingers! In between, there are hundreds of good ways to combine fillings and toppings with one or another of the bread family. **See recipes.**

TO KEEP FRESH: They will keep in excellent condition for up to 24 hours if wrapped in the following way: stack them 3–4 at a time, place a lettuce leaf on top and wrap closely in plastic wrap. Wrap packages in a damp tea-towel, then slip the whole parcel into a plastic bag and close tightly. Store in the refrigerator or in a cool place. Leave sandwiches whole and crusts on, and trim and cut up just before serving.

TO FREEZE: They may be frozen for a week or two but great care must be taken to prevent sogginess or drying out. Fillings that are rather high in fat, such as cheese, canned fish or meat, work best. Do not include mayonnaise, cooked egg whites, jellies, fresh fruits or vegetables with a high water content such as cucumber, lettuce, celery, tomato, apple, banana or pineapple.

Have butter soft at room temperature. Butter the bread liberally, being sure to go right to the edges, make sandwiches and wrap closely in plastic wrap, 3–4 sandwiches at a time or in quantities required for school lunches etc. An extra slice or crust of bread at each end of the package will help prevent drying out. Leave

crusts on and sandwiches whole, if possible, or in large pieces. Over-wrap in foil or plastic.

Thaw in wrappings – about 2–3 hours; an inner parcel may be taken frozen in a lunch-box.

See also *Danish Open Sandwiches*.

PARTY SANDWICHES

Ribbon Sandwiches: Make these with three layers of buttered bread (the middle slice buttered on both sides) with filling in between. Alternate white and brown bread, if you wish. Some good combinations are:

- Sardine mashed with a little chopped parsley and lemon juice on one layer, cream cheese with chopped chives or spring onions on the other.
- Thin cucumber slices on one layer, peanut butter or cream cheese on the other.
- Grated cheese or cottage cheese on one layer, cream cheese mixed with chopped celery and walnuts on the other.
- Finely chopped smoked salmon or drained, canned salmon seasoned well with black pepper on one layer, cream cheese and chopped capers on the other.

Pinwheel Sandwiches: Cut the crusts from an unsliced sandwich loaf and cut loaf lengthways into slices. Butter, then spread with any desired filling and roll up each slice from end to end. Wrap tightly in plastic wrap and leave at least 1 hour. Slice across to serve.

Rolled Sandwiches: Remove crusts from fresh sliced white or brown bread and roll lightly with a rolling pin. Butter right to edge and spread with cream cheese, mayonnaise or a home-made spread, or cover with a thin slice of ham, salami or cheese. Place a thin stick of celery, dill pickle, cucumber or an asparagus spear on one edge and roll up, pressing lightly to seal. Lay sandwiches, seam side down, close together on plastic wrap and wrap tightly. Leave at least 1 hour before using.

LUNCH-BOX SANDWICHES

These fillings make nourishing sandwiches that carry well.

- Finely chopped green pepper and radish, or grated carrot and bean sprouts on wholemeal bread spread with devilled ham and mayonnaise.
- Raisins, dates or mixed dried fruits, sprinkled with a little mixed spice and a few drops of lemon juice, on wholemeal bread spread with cream cheese.
- Hummus, bean sprouts and thinly sliced cucumber, on wholemeal bread or spread thickly inside pita bread. Finely chopped shallots or spring onions, celery or pepper, or grated raw beetroot or carrot can be added.
- Well-drained, flaked tuna mixed with finely chopped shallot, celery and green pepper, a little chopped mango chutney, a dash of soy sauce and enough mayonnaise to bind.
- Drained, mashed baked beans mixed with crumbled crisp-fried bacon. Spread on wholemeal or rye bread, spread with mayonnaise. Thinly sliced cheese may be added.

- Peanut butter and thinly sliced cucumber (leave the skin on for extra crunch).
- Peanut butter, grated carrot and raisins.
- Diced cooked ham or chicken (or both) mixed with mayonnaise, chopped tomato, radish and shallot or spring onion.
- Hard-boiled egg, chopped and bound with cream cheese thinned with cream or mayonnaise, and seasoned with salt, pepper and paprika.
- Devilled egg: mix 2 chopped hard-boiled eggs with 1 tsp Worcestershire sauce, $1/4$ tsp French mustard, 1 tsp chutney, $1/2$ tsp curry powder, salt, cayenne and 1 tbs melted butter. Layer with lettuce on brown bread.
- Cream cheese, chopped almonds and bean sprouts.
- Cream cheese, marmalade, raisins and chopped peanuts.
- Cottage cheese, chopped chives and bean sprouts or shredded spinach leaves.
- Cream cheese, grated orange rind and walnut pieces.
- Sliced corned beef (which may be canned) on sweet and sour or rye bread, which has been spread with a mixture of softened cream cheese, a little Dijon-style mustard and bottled horseradish to taste. Pack a few dill pickles with the sandwich.
- Shredded cabbage and grated carrot, chopped spring onions and bean sprouts, seasoned with salt and pepper and bound with mayonnaise. Nice on caraway-seed rye bread.
- Cold cooked or canned fish (or fish fingers), flaked and mixed with a little chopped spring onion, celery and cucumber, and bound with tartare sauce. Use brown bread for this.
- Liverwurst mixed with a little grated nutmeg, a spoonful of mayonnaise and chopped chives and parsley, layered with lettuce in white bread.

FILLED ROLLS FOR PICNICS OR LUNCH-BOXES

Use crusty or soft rolls, long or round. Split, pull out some of the crumb if you wish, butter and fill generously. Some especially successful ideas:

- A cold sausage or hamburger (better still if it's put in while hot so that the juices flavour the bread). Add crisp fried or raw onion, fresh herbs, mustard, tomato sauce or chutney.
- Finely chopped tomato, onion, zucchini, cucumber and mint or basil, seasoned with salt and pepper and drained in a sieve before filling the roll.
- Liverwurst, crisp-cooked crumbled bacon, chopped tomato, lettuce and thinly sliced cucumber.
- Feta cheese, sliced olives, chopped tomato and bean sprouts.
- Drained flaked tuna, hard-boiled egg, chopped spring onions, bean sprouts and mayonnaise.
- Corned beef and well-drained coleslaw.
- Potato salad and ham, bacon or salami.
- Don't butter the roll but sprinkle the inside with olive oil

and spread with tomato paste. Fill with grated cheese mixed with two or three of the following: chopped spring onions, chopped green pepper, mashed anchovies, strips of ham or salami, drained tuna, sliced olives, capers, sliced mushrooms, fresh chopped herbs or dried herbs re-chopped with parsley. If desired, wrap in foil and heat before taking on a picnic.

Pita Sandwiches: Pita or pocket bread with a generous filling makes an excellent portable meal. Use any combination of meat, cheese, fish or vegetables, such as the following:

- Tabouleh with sliced roast beef or lamb, tomatoes and shredded lettuce.
- Sliced cooked chicken with mayonnaise, chopped celery and spring onions, cooked peas and diced, cooked carrot.
- Garbanzo Spread (see page 396) with sliced cucumber and tomato.

NOTE: Pita bread is available from delicatessens and some supermarkets.

Home–made Sandwich Spreads and Fillings

These nutritious spreads are good on bread or crispbread.

Savoury Tomato Spread

Lovely alone or with chicken, cold meat or fish fillings.

1 onion, finely chopped; 1 tbs butter; 3 tomatoes, peeled and chopped; 2 tbs grated cheese; 2 tsp chopped mixed fresh thyme, sage and marjoram or $1/2$ tsp dried mixed herbs with 2 tsp chopped parsley; about $1/2$ cup fresh breadcrumbs; salt and freshly ground black pepper.

Gently fry onion in butter until soft. Add tomatoes and cook until thick. Stir in cheese and herbs and remove from heat. Add enough breadcrumbs to give a spreading consistency and season with salt and pepper. Store, covered, in refrigerator. Keeps 1 week to 10 days. Makes about $1\frac{1}{2}$ cups.

Piquant Sardine Spread

Good with thinly sliced cucumber.

1 x 105 g can sardines, drained and mashed; 2 spring onions, finely chopped; 5 tbs Mayonnaise (page 256); 2 tsp Dijon mustard; $1/2$ tsp curry powder; 2 hard-boiled eggs, finely chopped; 1 tbs lemon juice; salt and freshly ground black pepper.

Mix all ingredients together well. Store, covered, in refrigerator. Keeps 4–5 days. Makes about 1 cup.

Peanut Butter, Bacon and Carrot Spread

Layer with paper-thin, well-drained tomato slices and lettuce leaves.

¹/₂ cup peanut butter; ¹/₂ cup grated carrot; 2 rashers bacon, rind removed, grilled until crisp and crumbled; about 2 tbs Mayonnaise (page 256).

Mix peanut butter, carrot and bacon until well blended and add enough mayonnaise to give a spreading consistency. Store, covered, in refrigerator. Keeps 1 week. Makes about 1¹/₄ cups.

Apricot and Nut Spread

Use dark bread or raisin bread spread with butter or cream cheese.

³/₄ cup diced dried apricots; ¹/₄ cup firmly packed brown sugar; ¹/₂ cup orange juice; ¹/₂ cup finely chopped almonds, walnuts or peanuts; 2 tbs currants.

Simmer apricots with brown sugar and orange juice until mixture is soft and liquid has evaporated, about 35 minutes. Watch carefully and stir often to ensure that the mixture does not scorch. Remove from heat and mash with a fork, then stir in nuts and currants. Store, covered, in refrigerator. Keeps several weeks. Makes about 1 cup.

Hearty Sandwiches

Great sandwiches for substantial snacking or meals on the run.

The Reuben

The name tells us that we owe the Reuben to the traditions of Jewish cookery. Anyone who knows New York's wonderful delicatessens will remember hot sandwiches like this.

1 large, thick slice rye bread; 1 tbs Thousand Island Dressing (page 257); sauerkraut, rinsed in cold water and squeezed dry; 2 thin slices corned beef; 1 slice Swiss cheese.

Toast bread on one side, then spread other side with dressing. Cover with a generous layer of sauerkraut and top with corned beef then with cheese. Grill under a preheated grill until filling is heated through and cheese melted. Serves 1.

Omelette in a Roll

This makes wonderful cocktail food, too, cut across into slices. Flavour the omelette well, turn straight into the roll while hot and eat warm or cool.

1 oval-shaped soft bread roll, plain or wholemeal; butter.

OMELETTE: 2 eggs; 3 tsp water; ¹/₂ tsp salt; freshly ground black pepper; flavouring (see below); 2 tsp butter.

Slice top from roll, pull out most of the crumb, and butter inside of shell.

OMELETTE: Beat eggs, water, salt and pepper lightly together with a fork. Stir in chosen flavouring. Heat butter in an omelette pan or small frying pan and when foam has subsided, pour in egg mixture. Cook over fairly high heat, pulling mixture from edge toward centre with a fork or spatula, so that uncooked mixture runs underneath. When omelette is set underneath but top is still quite moist remove from heat. Flip over one third of omelette toward centre, then turn over again so that it is folded in 3. Roll out onto bread shell, put lid on and wrap tightly in plastic wrap or foil Leave at least 1 hour before eating. Rolls can be refrigerated if you want to leave them overnight, but bring back to room temperature or warm gently in oven before eating. Serves 1.

FLAVOURINGS: 1 tbs chopped mixed fresh herbs or 1 tsp mixed dried herbs chopped with 1 tbs parsley; 2 tbs grated well-flavoured cheese mixed with 2 tsp flaked crab, salmon or smoked fish; 1 spring onion, chopped, with a grating of cheese; 2 tbs finely chopped cooked ham with 1 shallot, chopped, and a little chutney.

Club Sandwich

An American creation, it became a favoured light meal or hearty snack.

3 slices white bread; butter; Mayonnaise (page 256); 4 thin slices cooked chicken breast; salt and freshly ground black pepper; 4 thin slices firm, ripe tomato; 3 rashers bacon, rind removed and fried crisp; stuffed olive to garnish; dill pickles to serve.

Toast bread on both sides. Spread one side of each slice with butter and mayonnaise. Cover one slice with chicken, season with salt and pepper and top with second slice of toast, buttered side up. Cover with tomato and bacon, season and place third slice of toast on top, buttered side down. Cut diagonally in half and garnish with an olive secured with a toothpick. Serve with a few dill pickles. Serves 1.

Shooter's Sandwich

As the name implies, nourishment for times spent in the woods.

1 long loaf crusty bread, such as Italian bread; 1 thick rump steak, about 300 g (10 oz); salt and freshly ground black pepper; English or French mustard; 2–3 dill pickles, thinly sliced.

Cut loaf in half lengthways and remove some of the crumb. Grill steak until medium-rare. Slice across thinly and pile, while hot, into bottom of loaf. Drizzle over any juices that have escaped while slicing. Season with salt, pepper, mustard and top with sliced dill pickle. Put top of loaf on and tie with string. Wrap tightly in foil or plastic wrap and put a heavy weight on top. Leave for about 6 hours. Cut across into thick slices to serve. Serves 4.

The Hero

A substantial snack for any hero bent on conquest.

2 crusty bread sticks (small baguettes); butter; 4–6 lettuce leaves; 185 g (6 oz) cooked ham, thinly sliced; 60 g (2 oz) Gruyère, Jarlsberg or other cheese, thinly sliced; 2 firm, ripe tomatoes; 2 thin slices onion, separated into rings; salt and freshly ground black pepper; sliced stuffed olives or dill pickles (optional).

Cut bread sticks in half lengthways, pull out some of the crumb and butter insides. Fill with layers of lettuce, ham, cheese, tomatoes and onion rings. Season with salt and pepper and add sliced stuffed olives or dill pickles, if desired. Place tops on and tie ends and middles with string. Wrap tightly in foil or plastic wrap and leave 1 hour or longer. Cut across into pieces to serve. Serves 4–6.

An Englishman's Bacon Sandwich

English aficionados of the bacon sandwich have it this way.

3–4 rashers bacon, rind removed; 2 slices white bread; butter; HP sauce.

Fry bacon until crisp and drain on a paper towel. Butter the bread. Pile bacon on one slice, sprinkle liberally with HP sauce and top with second slice of bread. Serve immediately. Serves 1.

The Submarine or Poor Boy

The Submarine or Poor Boy is a close relation of The Hero. It can be hot or cold.

1 long French loaf, or 2 small Italian loaves or bread sticks; 1/4 cup olive oil; 185 g (6 oz) Swiss or other cheese, thinly sliced; 4 firm, ripe tomatoes, thinly sliced; 185 g (6 oz) salami, thinly sliced; 1 x 50g can anchovy fillets, drained and halved lengthways; 2–3 canned pimientos, drained and halved or quartered; freshly ground black pepper; chopped parsley; green or black olives to garnish.

Cut loaf or loaves in half lengthways and remove some of the crumb. Brush insides of bread with oil. Place cheese slices, overlapping, on one half of the bread, and top with overlapping slices of tomato then salami. Arrange anchovies and pimientos alternately on top, grind a little black pepper over and sprinkle generously with parsley. Put other pieces of bread on top, tie at intervals with string and wrap tightly in foil. Place in refrigerator with a weight on top and leave for several hours, or overnight. To serve cold, unwrap and cut across in thick slices. To serve hot, place the wrapped bread in a preheated moderate oven (180°C/350°F) for 15 minutes. Unwrap and cut across in thick slices. Serve garnished with olives. Serves 4–6.

NOTE: The submarine may also be served open-faced. Divide the filling evenly between top and bottom halves of bread, making the final topping cheese. Place under a preheated grill until cheese is bubbling.

VARIATIONS

ROAST BEEF SUBMARINE: Follow recipe for The Submarine, but spread bread with butter instead of olive oil and fill with layers of thinly sliced roast beef and tomatoes or mushrooms. Season with salt, pepper and Dijon mustard. For a hot sandwich, you might smear the beef with leftover gravy.

CHICKEN SUBMARINE: Follow recipe for The Submarine, but spread bread with mayonnaise instead of olive oil and fill with layers of thinly sliced cooked chicken, tomatoes, green pepper, celery, coleslaw or other vegetables. Season with salt and pepper.

HAM AND PINEAPPLE SUBMARINE: Follow recipe for The Submarine, but spread bread with butter and a little mustard instead of olive oil and fill with layers of thinly sliced cooked ham and pineapple sprinkled with chopped green pepper, toasted almonds and spring onions.

The BLT
(Bacon, Lettuce and Tomato Sandwich)

A great American favourite.

3–4 rashers bacon, rind removed; 2 slices white bread; 2 tsp Mayonnaise (page 256); 4 large slices tomato; salt; 1 crisp lettuce leaf.

Fry bacon until crisp and drain on a paper towel. Toast bread and spread each slice with mayonnaise. Pile tomatoes on one slice, salt and top with bacon, lettuce and second slice of toast, mayonnaise side down. Serve immediately. Serves 1.

Steak Sandwich

A minute steak is a small steak cut thin for quick cooking. A cube steak is a small, thin steak which has been tenderised by breaking some of the meat fibres under pressure. It has a waffle-like surface.

1 onion, thinly sliced; 1 tbs oil; 1 minute or cube steak; 2 slices white or wholemeal bread; butter; salt and freshly ground black pepper; dash Worcestershire sauce.

Fry onion in oil until lightly browned. Remove onion with a slotted spoon and keep warm. Heat pan until oil begins to give off a slight haze, then add steak and brown for about 2 minutes on each side. Meantime, toast and butter bread. Place steak on one slice of toast, season with salt, pepper and Worcestershire sauce, pile onion on top and cover with second slice of toast. Serve immediately. Serves 1.

Bratwurst Rolls

These little warm rolls with their herby, mustard sausage stuffing are superb for an outdoor wedding or any casual party. You make them a day ahead and they couldn't be easier to heat and serve – guests can help themselves from a basket or serving dish decorated with flowers or leaves.

25 long, soft bread rolls; 250 g (8 oz) butter, melted; 12 spring onions, finely chopped; ¹/₂ cup chopped mixed fresh herbs, or ¹/₂ cup chopped parsley with 1 tbs mixed dried herbs; 25 hot grilled bratwurst or similar Continental sausages; Dijon mustard; salt and freshly ground black pepper.

Slit open rolls lengthways and pull out some of the crumb from each piece. Brush insides with melted butter and sprinkle with chopped spring onions and herbs. Split sausages lengthways, spread insides generously with mustard and put back together. Place a sausage in each hollowed roll (trim to fit if necessary), season with salt and pepper and press roll back together. Wrap rolls, in batches of 6–8, tightly in foil and leave overnight in refrigerator. When rolls are required, heat packages straight from refrigerator in a preheated moderate oven (180°C/350°F) for 20 minutes. Unwrap and pile up in a basket or serving dish. Makes 25.

NOTE: If you are going to have the wedding feast away from home, take the hot rolls in their foil wrapping. They will carry perfectly and remain pleasantly warm.

Tea and Cocktail Sandwiches

Small sandwiches that can be eaten in 2 or 3 bites are some of the nicest things to serve on a tea table or offer with drinks. They can be made an hour or two ahead of time, arranged on a plate or in a napkin-lined basket and covered with a damp cloth until required.

Cucumber Sandwiches

cucumber, finely sliced; salt; thin slices fresh white bread; butter; freshly ground white pepper.

Sprinkle cucumber slices with salt. Leave on a tilted plate 20 minutes to allow juice to escape, then drain on paper towels. Butter bread and make sandwiches with cucumber, seasoned with salt and white pepper. Remove crusts and cut into small triangles.

NOTE: If using ready-sliced bread, roll slices lightly with a rolling pin to make them thinner before buttering.

Watercress Sandwiches

thin slices brown bread; butter; chopped watercress; salt; lemon juice.

Butter bread generously and make sandwiches with watercress seasoned with salt and a few drops of lemon juice. Roll each sandwich lightly with a rolling pin. Remove crusts and cut into small triangles.

Ham and Watercress Fingers

¹/₂ cup thick Mayonnaise (page 256); 2 tbs finely chopped green olives; 1 tbs finely chopped cornichons or gherkins; 1 tbs chopped parsley; 1 tbs chopped spring onions; 2 tsp Dijon mustard; salt and freshly ground black pepper; 14 thin slices pumpernickel or rye bread; 150 g (5 oz) cooked ham, thinly sliced; watercress leaves.

Combine mayonnaise, olives, cornichons, parsley, spring onion, mustard, salt and pepper. Spread bread with mayonnaise mixture. Top half the slices with ham, then watercress. Cover with remaining slices, mayonnaise side down, and press lightly together. Remove crusts and cut each sandwich into 3 fingers. Makes 21.

Cream Cheese and Herb Sandwiches

125 g (4 oz) cream cheese; 3 tsp lemon juice; salt and freshly ground black pepper; ¹/₄ cup chopped parsley; ¹/₄ cup chopped mixed herbs (chives, thyme, oregano, a little sage); 1 tbs finely chopped spring onions (if chives are not available); butter; 12 slices white or brown bread.

Soften cream cheese, then mash well with lemon juice, salt and pepper. Mix in herbs. Butter bread and make sandwiches with cheese and herb mixture. Remove crusts and cut into fingers or small triangles. Makes 18 fingers, 24 small triangles.

Chicken and Avocado Triangles

These look and taste luxurious, but really make one avocado and a little chicken go a long way.

6 slices white bread, 6 slices brown bread; butter;
1 ripe avocado, peeled and stoned; 2 tsp lemon
juice; salt and freshly ground black pepper;
1¹/₂ cups chopped, cooked chicken meat;
2 tbs Mayonnaise (page 256);
finely chopped parsley to garnish.

Butter bread lightly. Mash avocado with lemon juice, and season with salt and pepper. Combine chicken and mayonnaise. Spread white bread with a layer of avocado, then chicken. Top with brown bread. Trim crusts and cut each sandwich into 4 triangles. Arrange on a platter and garnish with a little finely chopped parsley. Serves 4.

SARDINE

The true sardine is a Mediterranean fish, of the same family as herring, anchovy and pilchard. In the summer it migrates to cooler Atlantic waters, off the French and Portuguese coasts; the canning of sardines is an important industry in these regions.

Sardines, anchovies and similar small fish called sardines in other parts of the world, are usually around 12–15 cm (5–6 in) in length.

■ **BASIC PREPARATION:** Because the bones are soft enough to eat, the fish need little preparation before cooking – simply cut away the head from the body and gently pull out the insides and the backbone if you wish. Wash and pat dry with paper towels. The sardines can now be coated in flour and fried, or grilled, or barbecued in a hinged wire fish grill over hot coals.

Fresh sardines are very popular in Mediterranean countries. They are usually fried, but may also be stuffed with a garlic-flavoured spinach mixture, as in Provence, or with a mixture of capers, olives, sultanas and pine nuts, as in Sicily.

Sardines are available salted or canned in oil. Salted sardines are prepared in the same way as salted anchovies – they must be thoroughly cleaned and washed, then packed in a jar with fresh olive oil. They can then be used in the same ways as canned sardines – in salads, especially with tomatoes and hard-boiled eggs; in sandwiches, and in cocktail savouries. See recipes.

Hors d'oeuvre of Canned Sardines:
- Arrange whole canned sardines on a dish, dress with lemon juice and olive oil, and sprinkle with very finely chopped spring onion, a few onion rings or sieved hard-boiled egg yolk.
- Dress whole canned sardines with a Fresh Herb Vinaigrette Dressing (see page 442), made with lemon juice, and sprinkle over lots of chopped parsley.

Sardine Canapés:
- Spread toast rectangles with Garlic Butter (see page 172). Slip an onion ring over each canned sardine and place on toast. Decorate with finely chopped hard-boiled egg and chives, or with strips of canned pimiento, or sliced stuffed olives.
- Remove bones from 1 can sardines. Mash, then season with lemon juice and grated onion. Bind with a little mayonnaise and pile on buttered toast rounds. Serve as is, or top each with a small square of cheese and grill until melted. Serve hot.
- Spread toast rectangles with Garlic Butter (see page 172). Arrange slices of hard-boiled egg on toast. Top with a small sardine and a little Green Mayonnaise (see page 443).

Fried Fresh Sardines

500 g (1 lb) fresh sardines, cleaned;
3–4 tbs seasoned flour; oil for frying;
lemon wedges to serve.

Roll sardines in seasoned flour to coat. Heat 2.5 cm (1 in) oil in a frying pan and fry sardines until golden. (Sardines may need to be cooked in several batches.) Remove with a slotted spoon. Reheat oil, return sardines to pan and fry for 30 seconds to crisp coating. Drain on paper towels and serve immediately, with lemon wedges. Serves 4.

Lemon Grilled Sardines

24 fresh sardines or anchovies, cleaned; salt and
freshly ground black pepper; juice 1 lemon;
¹/₄ cup oil; 3 lemons, quartered, to garnish.

Place sardines or anchovies in a bowl, season lightly with salt and pepper and add lemon juice and oil. Mix lightly so that each sardine is well coated. Arrange on rack of grill and cook under a preheated high grill for 2–3 minutes on each side. Arrange fish on a heated serving platter and garnish with lemon quarters. Serves 2–3.

Gratin of Fresh Sardines

1 lemon; few sprigs fresh fennel or thyme;
500 g (1 lb) fresh sardines, cleaned; salt and freshly
ground black pepper; ¹/₂ cup dry white wine;
1 tbs olive oil; ¹/₂ cup fresh white breadcrumbs;
1 tbs finely chopped parsley.

Squeeze juice from ¹/₂ lemon; cut other half into thin slices. Lay herbs and lemon slices on bottom of oiled shallow ovenproof dish. Arrange sardines on top and season well with salt and pepper. Sprinkle over lemon juice, white wine and oil. Combine breadcrumbs and parsley and scatter over sardines. Cook in a preheated hot oven (200°C/400°F) for 10–15 minutes, basting with pan juices from time to time. Serves 4.

Baked Sardines

500 g (1 lb) fresh sardines or anchovies, cleaned;
salt and freshly ground black pepper;
3 tbs lemon juice; 2 tbs chopped parsley;
2 cloves garlic, crushed; 1 cup fresh breadcrumbs;
30 g (1 oz) butter.

Arrange fish in an oiled ovenproof dish large enough
to hold fish in one layer. Season lightly with salt and
pepper and sprinkle lemon juice over them. Sauté
parsley, garlic and breadcrumbs in butter in a frying
pan over high heat, then spread over fish. Heat dish
for 1 minute on top of stove over medium heat, then
place it in a preheated very hot oven (230°C/450°F).
Cook for 10–12 minutes or until fish is golden and
breadcrumbs crisp. Serves 4.

Sicilian Baked Sardines

1 kg (2 lb) fresh sardines or anchovies, cleaned;
1/2 cup olive oil; 2 cups fresh breadcrumbs;
1/2 cup chopped parsley; 1 small onion, finely
chopped; 3 tbs pine nuts; grated rind and
juice 1 lemon; salt and freshly ground black pepper;
2 bay leaves.

Cut heads off sardines or anchovies if preferred. Split
open down belly, turn skin up on a board and press
firmly down backbone. Turn again and lift out backbone. Rinse quickly in salted water and dry well on
paper towels. Heat oil in pan and toss 1 1/2 cups breadcrumbs until crisp. Place fried crumbs in a bowl. Add
parsley, onion, pine nuts, lemon rind, salt and pepper.
Mix ingredients lightly together. Put a little of this
stuffing into each fish and roll sides together round it.
Arrange sardines in one layer in an oiled ovenproof
dish. Tear bay leaves into pieces and sprinkle on top
with any remaining stuffing. Top with remaining
breadcrumbs. Bake in a preheated moderate oven
(180°C/350°F) 30 minutes. Squeeze lemon juice over
and serve immediately. Serves 6.

SASHIMI

A highly regarded Japanese dish, consisting of slices of
raw fish garnished with slivers of cabbage, white radish
or other vegetables, and always accompanied by
wasabi, a hot, green horseradish paste, and soy sauce
for dipping. The fish selected for sashimi must be very
fresh, ideally caught and eaten on the same day. The
most prized fish is the tuna from the Northern Pacific.

The fish can be prepared either cut in small, square
slabs with 5 or 6 pieces arranged resting on each other
for one serving, or it can be sliced transparently thin.

Sashimi is nearly always served at a formal meal and is
considered a course on its own.

Sashimi

750 g (1 1/2 lb) very fresh tuna, bream, kingfish,
mackerel or jewfish; 2 cups shredded daikon (giant
white radish available from Asian greengrocers);
1 carrot, shredded; 6 spring onions, shredded;
6 snowpeas; 6 cooked, unshelled king prawns;
1 tbs wasabi (available from Asian grocers);
6 lemon wedges; 1 tbs grated fresh ginger;
shoyu (Japanese light soy sauce).

Fillet fish, removing all skin and bones, and cut into
thin slices. Arrange daikon, carrot and spring onions
in mounds on a serving platter, together with snowpeas. Arrange fish and prawns in centre of platter.
Mix wasabi to a thick paste with a little water and
place on platter, with lemon wedges and ginger.
To serve, pour shoyu into individual bowls, then
allow each diner to add wasabi and ginger to their
own bowl of shoyu according to taste. The fish
and vegetables are then dipped into this sauce before
eating. Serves 6.

SATAY (SATE)

Visitors to Malaysia and Singapore never forget the satay
– grilled skewered meat, poultry or fish. Satay vendors,
with their charcoal braziers, are part of the charm of the
city streets, and the smell of grilled meats and spices is
irresistible.

Beef, pork, lamb, poultry and seafood are suitable for
satay. Small cubes of meat are marinated in a spicy
mixture, then threaded on bamboo or wooden skewers
and grilled over charcoal. They can also be grilled under
a domestic grill.

Indonesian satay is often served with a spicy peanut
sauce, or you may prefer to buy a commercial satay
sauce available at supermarkets and delicatessens.

Bamboo or wooden skewers should be well soaked in
water for at least 2 hours before using to prevent them
burning.

Serve small satays as a first course or more substantial
ones as a main course, accompanied by rice and salad.
See recipes.

See also *Peanut*.

Malaysian Satay Sauce

4–8 dried chillies, soaked and drained;
8 spring onions, chopped; 1 clove garlic, crushed;
4 macadamia nuts, chopped; 1 small strip lemon
rind, chopped; 1/2 cup raw peanuts; 2 tbs oil;
1 cup Coconut Milk (page 91); 2 tsp tamarind pulp
soaked in 1/4 cup water for 10 minutes;
1 tsp brown sugar; salt.

Pound chillies, spring onions, garlic, macadamia nuts
and lemon rind, or grind finely in a food processor.
Lightly roast peanuts in a dry, heavy frying pan, then

chop or pound coarsely. Heat oil in a saucepan and gently fry chilli mixture for 5 minutes, stirring frequently. Add coconut milk and bring slowly to the boil, stirring constantly. Strain tamarind over a bowl, squeezing out and reserving as much water as possible. Discard tamarind. Add tamarind water to sauce with brown sugar, roasted peanuts and salt. Simmer gently for 2–3 minutes. Serve sauce at room temperature. Makes about 2 cups.

NOTE: Tamarind pulp is available from health food or Asian grocery stores. If not available use 2 tsp lemon juice.

Quick Peanut Sauce

**3 tbs peanut butter; 1/2 tsp sugar;
1/2 tsp Tabasco sauce; 30 g (1 oz) butter;
1 clove garlic, crushed; juice 1/2 lemon;
1–2 tbs light soy sauce; 1/4 cup cream.**

Combine all ingredients, except cream, in a heavy saucepan. Cook over low heat, stirring constantly, until thick. Remove from heat and gradually stir in cream. Serve poured over pork, beef, lamb or chicken satays or use as a dipping sauce. Makes about 1/2 cup.

Mild Peanut Sauce

**6 tbs smooth or crunchy peanut butter;
1 cup water; 3/4 tsp garlic salt; 2 tsp brown sugar;
2 tbs light soy sauce; lemon juice;
1/2 tsp anchovy paste or essence (optional);
Coconut Milk (page 91) or water.**

Combine peanut butter and water in a saucepan and stir over a gentle heat until mixed. Remove from heat and add all other ingredients, adding enough coconut milk or water to make the paste a thick pouring consistency. Adjust seasoning and add more salt and lemon juice if necessary. Makes about 1 cup.

Prawn Satay

**3 tbs lemon juice; 1/2 cup thick Coconut Milk
(page 91); 1/2 tsp sambal ulek (see Note);
1/2 tsp dried shrimp paste (trasi); 1 tbs dark soy
sauce; 1 tsp dark brown sugar; finely grated rind
1 lemon; 2 cloves garlic, crushed with 1/2 tsp salt;
750 g (1 1/2 lb) green prawns, shelled and
deveined; oil.**

Combine lemon juice, coconut milk, sambal ulek, trasi, soy sauce, brown sugar, lemon rind and garlic in a glass or earthenware bowl. Stir until sugar dissolves. Add prawns and stir. Cover and marinate for 2–3 hours in the refrigerator. Drain prawns, reserving marinade. Thread prawns on bamboo skewers (previously soaked in water to prevent burning), allowing 3–4 prawns per skewer. Brush with oil and grill over hot coals for about 5 minutes or under a

preheated grill until prawns are lightly browned. Simmer reserved marinade for 1 minute, stirring constantly, and add more coconut milk or soy sauce to taste if necessary. Serve separately as a sauce. Serves 4.
NOTE: Sambal ulek and Trasi are available from health food shops and Asian delicatessens.

Spicy Chicken Satay

**1 kg (2 lb) chicken breast, skinned and boned or
chicken fillets; 1 tbs tamarind pulp soaked in
1/4 cup water for 10 minutes; 1 tbs ground
coriander; 1 tsp ground cumin; 1/2 tsp ground
fennel; 8 spring onions, chopped; 2 cloves garlic,
crushed; 1 strip lemon rind; 2.5 cm (1 in) fresh
ginger, chopped; 1/2 tsp salt; 1 tsp turmeric;
2 tsp brown sugar; 4 tbs oil; sprigs fresh coriander
to garnish.**

Cut chicken into pieces 2 cm (3/4 in) square. Strain tamarind over a bowl, squeezing out and reserving as much water as possible. Discard tamarind. Place tamarind water in an earthenware or glass bowl and add the remaining ingredients, except oil and fresh coriander. Add chicken, cover and refrigerate several hours. Drain chicken pieces and thread on to bamboo skewers (previously soaked in water for 2 hours). Cook over charcoal or until golden-brown. Garnish with fresh coriander sprigs. Serve with Malaysian Satay Sauce, steamed rice and chunks of cucumber and raw onion. Serves 6–8.
NOTE: If tamarind pulp is not available, use 2 tsp lemon juice.

Indonesian Satay

**1 tbs peanut oil; juice 1 lemon; 1 clove garlic,
crushed; 1 tbs dark soy sauce or Indonesian soy
sauce (ketjap manis); 500 g (1 lb) pork fillet,
cut into 2 cm (3/4 in) cubes.**

Combine peanut oil, lemon juice, garlic and soy sauce. Marinate pork cubes in this mixture, turning occasionally, for 2–4 hours. Drain, reserving marinade. Thread cubes on bamboo skewers (previously soaked in water for 2 hours), allowing 3–4 cubes per skewer. Grill under a preheated grill for 10–15 minutes or until well done, basting occasionally with reserved marinade. Serve hot with Quick Peanut Sauce or Malaysian Satay Sauce. Serves 12 as a first course, 6 as a main course.

Malayan Beef Satay

**1 kg (2 lb) steak, scotch fillet or rump,
cut into 2 cm (3/4 in) cubes; 1/3 cup light soy sauce;
1/3 cup peanut oil; 2 onions, finely chopped;
2 cloves garlic, crushed; 3 tbs toasted sesame seeds;
2 tsp ground cumin; 1 tsp lemon juice;
salt and freshly ground black pepper.**

S

Put steak cubes into an earthenware bowl. Combine soy sauce, peanut oil, onions, garlic and sesame seeds, pour over meat and leave to marinate at least 3 hours, turning from time to time. Drain meat, reserving marinade. Thread meat cubes on to small bamboo skewers (previously soaked in water for 2 hours), allowing 4–5 cubes per skewer. Mix cumin and lemon juice together and brush over meat. Grill over hot coals of a barbecue or under a preheated grill, basting with marinade and turning frequently. Grill 6–8 minutes for rare, 8–10 minutes for medium, 10–12 minutes for well-done. Season before serving. Serves 6–8.

NOTE: To toast sesame seeds, sprinkle into a large, heavy frying pan and cook over a medium heat for 2–3 minutes or until well browned. Do not use any oil. A less expensive cut of meat, such as topside, can be used – just add $^1/_2$ cup vinegar to the marinade and marinate overnight if possible.

Singapore Beef Satay

750 g ($1^1/_2$ lb) rump steak; 2 tsp turmeric; 2 tsp ground cumin; 2 tsp ground fennel finely grated rind $^1/_2$ lemon; $^1/_2$ tsp salt; 1 tbs sugar; 4 tbs thick Coconut Milk (page 91).

Trim fat from steak and cut fat into small pieces. Cut beef into 2 cm (¾ in) cubes. Combine turmeric, cumin, fennel, lemon rind, salt, sugar and coconut milk in an earthenware or glass bowl. Stir to dissolve sugar. Add beef cubes and mix well, then cover and leave to marinate for 1–2 hours. Thread meat on bamboo skewers (previously soaked in water for 2 hours) with 2–3 little pieces of fat on each skewer between some of the meat cubes. Put about 5–6 pieces of meat on each skewer. Grill over hot coals or under a preheated grill for 8–10 minutes or until beef is tender and brown on all sides. Serve immediately with Peanut Sauce or Malaysian Satay Sauce (see pages 454–5). Serves 6.

SAUCES

A good sauce can add distinction to everyday foods – as nice for family meals as for special occasions. It is reassuring to know that there are really only three main groups of sauce: *white*, *brown*, and *emulsion*.

When you become proficient at the basic recipes, you can make virtually any sauce recipe you come across. Also, there are a myriad of pan sauces which fit perfectly into today's lifestyle – light, quick and foolproof to make; and simple fruit sauces, made from puréed and sweetened fruit.

Remember that a sauce should have body, but must never be so thick that it sits heavily on the food. A pouring or flowing sauce should run freely off a spoon, a coating sauce should be just dense enough to cling to the food but not to blanket it thickly. Be ready to add a little more liquid if your sauce is too heavy.

■ **TO STORE:** Most sauces to be served separately with food can be prepared ahead and reheated when needed. Place hot sauce in a heatproof sauce container. Cover with plastic wrap, placed directly on the surface of the sauce, then with a lid. When cool, store in the refrigerator. To reheat, remove plastic wrap, place sauce container in a pan of hot water and stir over very gentle heat until sauce is hot.

Emulsion sauces, such as Hollandaise and Béarnaise, must not be heated beyond lukewarm (it is quite correct to serve them at this temperature) or else they will separate; place the sauce container in a pan of warm water off the heat and stir until smooth.

TYPES OF SAUCES

SAUCES BASED ON A ROUX: The basis of many sauces is a *roux*, a cooked mixture of fat and flour. The longer it is cooked, the darker the colour becomes and the nuttier the flavour. A white or golden (blond) roux is used for the lighter-coloured sauces, and a brown one for the dark sauces. It is important for a smooth result to cook the roux slowly, stirring, until it is the desired colour. When the liquid is added, the sauce must be stirred or whisked constantly until boiling so that it will thicken evenly without lumps.

White Sauce

These are light in colour, usually creamy white or a light straw colour, delicate in taste and smooth as satin. This smooth texture is achieved by a well-made roux and the liquid being carefully added.

The two main white sauces are Béchamel and Velouté. Béchamel is made with butter, flour and milk, flavoured with aromatic vegetables and herbs; Velouté is made with butter, flour and white stock – fish, chicken or veal according to what food it is to accompany. A knob of butter is sometimes swirled into the sauce at the last moment for extra richness. A Velouté sauce may also be enriched with egg yolks and cream.

Béchamel Sauce

1 cup milk; $^1/_2$ bay leaf; 1 slice onion; 5 black peppercorns; 1 small piece celery; 1 blade mace; 30 g (1 oz) butter; $1^1/_2$ tbs flour; salt and freshly ground white pepper; nutmeg.

Heat milk with bay leaf, onion, peppercorns, celery and mace in a small heavy saucepan until bubbles form around edge. Remove from heat, cover and let stand 20 minutes. Strain and reserve. Wipe out saucepan. Melt butter in it. Stir in flour. Stir over low heat 1 minute. Remove from heat and cool a little, then add strained milk and stir until smooth. Return to medium heat and stir constantly until boiling.

Lower heat and cook very gently 5 minutes, stirring frequently. Season with salt, pepper and nutmeg. Makes about 1½ cups.

NOTE: This recipe makes a coating sauce – the right consistency for covering food in the dish in which it is to be served. For a flowing sauce to be served separately, follow the recipe but use only 1 tbs flour. For panada thickness (used to bind croquettes and as a soufflé base), follow the recipe but use 3 tbs flour.

VARIATIONS

MORNAY (CHEESE) SAUCE: To 1 quantity Béchamel Sauce, add 30 g (1 oz) grated Parmesan, Gruyère or sharp Cheddar cheese and a pinch of dry mustard. Stir over low heat just until cheese has melted. Use to coat fish, vegetables, chicken or eggs. To make a dish into a gratin, pour sauce over and place under a preheated hot grill or in a hot oven until top is golden-brown (sprinkle first with a little more cheese and/or breadcrumbs tossed in butter if you wish).

CREAM SAUCE: To 1 quantity Béchamel Sauce add 2 tbs cream. Bring to the boil, then add a few drops lemon juice. Use for food that is served creamed – eggs, chicken, vegetables, veal.

CAPER SAUCE: To 1 quantity Cream Sauce add 1½ tbs capers and 1 tbs chopped parsley. Serve with hot ox tongue, lamb tongue, and grilled or poached fish.

CURRY CREAM SAUCE: Fry 1 finely chopped onion in 1 tbs butter. Add 1 tbs curry powder and fry, stirring 1 minute. Add to 1 quantity Cream Sauce and simmer gently 5–10 minutes. A little shredded or desiccated coconut may be fried with the curry powder if desired. Adjust seasoning, adding a few extra drops lemon juice if necessary. Serve on hard-boiled eggs or mix with 1½ cups chopped cooked chicken, turkey or lamb or 1 x 440 g can (2 cups) salmon or tuna, and reheat.

PARSLEY SAUCE: To 1 quantity Béchamel Sauce, add 2 tbs finely chopped parsley and a few drops lemon juice. Serve on boiled potatoes or with tripe, tongue, poached chicken or fish.

MUSTARD SAUCE: To 1 quantity Béchamel Sauce, add 2 tsp dry mustard blended with 1 tsp vinegar, or 1 tbs Dijon mustard. Serve with boiled meats such as corned beef or with hot poached Continental sausage such as rookwurst.

ONION SAUCE: Boil 4 finely chopped white onions in water to cover until tender. Drain and stir into 1 quantity Béchamel Sauce. Stir in 1 tsp cream and heat gently. Sliced hard-boiled eggs, coated with this sauce and sprinkled with parsley, become Oeufs à la Tripe, a breakfast or luncheon dish. Use also with corned beef and other boiled meats.

WHITE OR MELTED BUTTER SAUCE: Make Béchamel Sauce as above without flavouring the milk first. White sauce can be nice on foods with pronounced flavour such as cauliflower or smoked fish, and can be used as the base for Mornay, Onion and other well-flavoured sauces. For more delicately flavoured foods or as the base for sauces such as Cream Sauce or Parsley Sauce, Béchamel is better.

Velouté Sauce

Serve on vegetables, chicken, meats and fish, and as the basis for many variations.

30 g (1 oz) butter; 2 tbs flour;
1½ cups warm stock (chicken, veal or fish
according to dish for which sauce will be used);
salt and freshly ground white pepper;
few drops lemon juice; 1 egg yolk; 1 tbs cream.

Melt butter in a heavy saucepan and stir in flour. Stir over low heat until straw-coloured. Remove from heat and cool a little, then add hot stock and stir until smooth. Return to medium heat and stir constantly until boiling. Lower heat and cook very gently 15 minutes, stirring frequently. Season with salt, pepper and lemon juice. Stir egg yolk into cream in a small bowl (this is called the liaison). Stir in a little of the hot sauce. Cook, stirring, until sauce is glossy and a little thicker, but do not allow it to boil. Makes about 1½ cups.

VARIATIONS

POULETTE SAUCE: To 1 quantity chicken Velouté Sauce, add ½ tsp lemon juice and 2 tsp chopped parsley. Good on broad beans or other green vegetables, brains or grilled or poached chicken.

SOUR CREAM SAUCE: Follow recipe for Velouté Sauce using fish or veal stock. Omit egg yolk and cream liaison and add ⅓ cup sour cream. Excellent with seafood or veal.

BERCY SAUCE: Boil 1 finely chopped shallot in ½ cup white wine until liquid has almost evaporated. Stir in 1 quantity fish or chicken Velouté Sauce, 1 tsp lemon juice and 2 tsp chopped parsley and reheat. Serve with seafood or chicken.

SAUCE SUPREME: Follow recipe for Velouté Sauce, using strong chicken stock as the liquid and 3 egg yolks with ½ cup cream as the liaison. Use this rich sauce to coat Sautéed Suprêmes of Chicken (see page 519) and mousselines of chicken, veal or ham (see *Mousseline*).

Brown Sauce

The basic brown sauce is a simplified version of the elaborate *Sauce Espagnole* of classic cuisine, but is still a fine luxury sauce. It and its variations are served with grills and sautés of red meat, and also with browned poultry and game. It is an essential ingredient in French cooking for some of the great savoury meat dishes.

Brown Sauce

60 g (2 oz) clarified butter, or 3 tbs oil;
1 small onion, diced; 1 small carrot, diced;
1 small piece celery, diced; 1 tbs flour;
2½ cups warm brown stock; 1 tbs tomato paste;
1 bouquet garni; 5 black peppercorns;
¼ cup dry sherry; mushroom trimmings
(optional); salt and freshly ground black pepper.

Heat clarified butter or oil in a heavy saucepan, add diced vegetables (called a mirepoix) and cook on low heat, stirring occasionally, until vegetables shrivel slightly without colouring. Stir in flour and continue to cook very slowly, stirring, until roux is hazelnut brown. Remove from heat and cool a little, then add 1½ cups stock and stir until smoothly blended. Stir in tomato paste and add bouquet garni, peppercorns, sherry and mushroom trimmings if using. Return to medium heat and stir until boiling. Half-cover with a lid and simmer 25 minutes. Add half the remaining stock, return to boil and skim. Simmer 5 minutes. Add remaining stock, boil up and skim again. The addition of cool stock accelerates rising of fat and scum and helps to clear sauce. If pan is tilted slightly the scum and fat will rise on one side only and can be easily removed. Simmer 5 minutes more. Adjust seasoning. Strain, pressing vegetables through sieve to extract juice. Makes about 2 cups.

NOTE: This sauce can be stored in the refrigerator as described in introduction (page 456), for 1 week. If you want to keep it longer, bring to the boil and return to refrigerator in a clean container.

VARIATIONS

BURGUNDY SAUCE: Follow recipe for Brown Sauce but substitute ½ cup dry red wine for the sherry. Serve with steak, roast beef and game.

MADEIRA OR MARSALA SAUCE: Follow recipe for Brown Sauce but substitute ¼ cup Madeira or Marsala for the sherry. Serve with Beef Wellington, ham, or with grilled or sautéed kidneys or liver.

CHASSEUR SAUCE: Gently cook 2 finely chopped golden shallots in 15 g (½ oz) butter until soft but not coloured. Turn heat up, add 60 g (2 oz) sliced mushrooms and shake until just coloured. Add ¼ cup white wine and boil until reduced to a few tablespoons of liquid. Stir in 1 tsp tomato paste and 1 cup Brown Sauce and simmer 2–3 minutes. Serve with steaks, cutlets and roasts.

SAUCE ROBERT: Gently fry 1 tbs finely chopped onion in 1 tbs butter until softened. Add ¼ cup dry white wine and 1 tsp wine vinegar and boil until reduced by half. Stir in 1 cup Brown Sauce and add 1 tbs Dijon mustard and a pinch or two of sugar to taste. Piquant with lamb, pork or calf liver.

Pan Sauces

The preceding Brown Sauce, with its deep, rich flavour and velvety texture, though well worth making for special occasions, is too time-consuming for regular use by most of today's busy cooks. Fortunately, it is easy to make simple and excellent pan sauces in minutes, to enhance meats, chicken or fish.

See also *Supreme of Chicken*.

Marsala and Lemon Sauce

Thin veal stakes (escalopes) with this sauce make a quick and delicious dish. Just add buttered noodles and a salad.

3 tbs Marsala; 1 tbs lemon juice; 4 tbs cream;
salt and freshly ground black pepper.

Dust veal steaks with flour and sauté in butter until lightly browned on both sides. Pour over Marsala and let it bubble for a few minutes until it looks syrupy. Add lemon juice and cream. Stir well, scraping up veal juices from pan. Season with salt and pepper and simmer 1 minute longer. Serves 4.

Lemon and Parsley Sauce

For chicken or fish.

30 g (1 oz) butter; 2 tbs lemon juice;
1 tbs chopped parsley;
salt and freshly ground black pepper.

Cook chicken pieces or fish fillets or steaks in a little oil and butter, then remove to a heated dish. Slowly pour off fat from pan, then add butter and heat until foaming, stirring and scraping up brown bits from pan. Add lemon juice and parsley. Taste, and season with salt (if needed) and pepper. Spoon over chicken or fish. Serves 2–4.

Quick Mushroom Sauce

For hamburgers, steak or lamb cutlets.

butter; 1 cup thickly sliced or quartered
mushrooms; 1 tsp cornflour (optional);
⅔ cup cream or stock; 1–2 tbs lemon juice;
salt and freshly ground black pepper.

Cook meat in a little oil and butter, then remove to a heated dish. Add butter to pan if necessary to make about 2 tbs fat and heat on high heat until foaming. Add mushrooms and cook undisturbed about 45 seconds, then turn over and cook other side a further 45 seconds. Sprinkle with cornflour, if using, and stir a few moments. Add cream or stock and bring to the boil, stirring and scraping up brown bits from bottom of pan. Cook 1 minute. Add lemon juice, salt and pepper. Spoon sauce over meat or serve separately. Serves 4.

Wine or Vermouth Sauce

For steak or hamburgers.

$^{1}/_{2}$ **cup red or white wine or dry vermouth;**
salt and freshly ground black pepper;
30 g (1 oz) butter, cut into pieces.

Cook steaks or hamburgers in a little oil and butter, then remove to a hot dish. Slowly pour off fat from pan. Add wine or vermouth and bring to the boil over high heat, stirring and scraping up brown bits from bottom of pan. When liquid is reduced by about half, season with salt and pepper and remove from heat. Add butter pieces. Do not stir but swirl butter in by swinging pan in a circular motion. Pour over meat and serve immediately. Serves 4.

Emulsion Sauces

These luscious egg and butter sauces are thickened by the emulsifying action of egg yolk when it is whisked with other ingredients. A wire whisk is a worthwhile investment if you are making these sauces by hand – it really does make the difference in blending them smoothly together. Egg and butter sauces can also be made, effortlessly and speedily, in a blender or food processor. Note that these are warm, not hot, sauces; if overheated they will curdle. **See recipes.**

Hollandaise Sauce

Marvellous with asparagus and other vegetables, fish and chicken.

2 egg yolks; 1 tbs water; lemon juice;
125 g (4 oz) unsalted butter, cut into small pieces;
small pinch salt.

Heat about 2.5 cm (1 in) water in the bottom of a double saucepan or a saucepan over which a heatproof bowl will fit. Bring just to simmering point. Place egg yolks, water and 1 tsp lemon juice in top of double saucepan or bowl, place over gently simmering water (which must not touch bottom of upper container) and whisk until yolks thicken slightly. This stage is called a sabayon and is reached when you begin to see bottom of bowl between strokes and mixture clings to whisk when it is raised from bowl. Now add butter, a

piece at a time, slipping it through your fingers to soften it slightly. Whisk all the time, incorporating each piece of butter thoroughly before adding next piece. When all butter has been added and sauce is thick and creamy, add salt and a little more lemon juice. The sauce should have a delicate lemon flavour but should not be too sharp. Makes about $^{3}/_{4}$ cup.

NOTE: If the sauce refuses to thicken or curdles (probably because it has got too hot), do not worry, there is a remedy. Rinse out another mixing bowl with hot water, then put in 1 tsp lemon juice and 1 tbs of the sauce. Beat with a wire whisk until they thicken together, then beat in the rest of the sauce a little at a time, whisking each addition well until quite smooth before adding the next.

VARIATIONS

HOLLANDAISE WITH EGG WHITES: Fold 2 egg whites, beaten until they hold soft peaks, into 1 quantity Hollandaise Sauce just before serving. This makes a lighter sauce and gives more servings. Serve with fish, asparagus or eggs.

SAUCE MOUSSELINE: Fold $^{1}/_{2}$ cup cream, lightly whipped, into 1 quantity Hollandaise Sauce just before serving. Serve with mousselines of shellfish and chicken (see *Mousseline*), sautéed veal, chicken, asparagus or artichokes.

SAUCE VIN BLANC: Place $^{1}/_{2}$ cup Fish Stock (see page 509 or cooking liquor from poached fish) and $^{1}/_{4}$ cup dry white wine in a saucepan and boil rapidly until reduced to 2 tbs. Follow recipe for Hollandaise Sauce using this reduced liquid in place of the lemon juice and water. Serve on poached fish.

Béarnaise Sauce

Serve with grilled steak, tournedos or roast beef, also with shellfish and some vegetables (green peas with Béarnaise are delicious). Any leftover sauce should be kept for serving on cold roast beef or chicken sandwiches.

$^{1}/_{4}$ **cup white wine vinegar; 1 golden shallot or**
spring onion, chopped; 4 black peppercorns;
1 bay leaf; $^{1}/_{4}$ tsp dried tarragon;
1 sprig fresh thyme, or pinch dried; 2 egg yolks;
125 g (4 oz) butter, cut into small pieces;
salt and freshly ground white pepper;
1 tsp finely chopped fresh tarragon or parsley
(optional).

Put vinegar, shallot (or spring onion), peppercorns, bay leaf, dried tarragon and thyme into a small saucepan and boil until reduced to 1 tbs liquid. Strain, pressing to extract all flavour. Place reduced flavoured vinegar and egg yolks in the top of a double saucepan or in a heatproof bowl that will fit over a saucepan. Bring 2.5 cm (1 in) water just to simmering point in bottom of double saucepan or saucepan, place container with egg yolks over water (which must not touch container) and whisk until yolks thicken slightly. This stage is called sabayon and is reached when you begin to see bottom of bowl between strokes and mixture clings to whisk when it is raised from bowl. Now add butter, a piece at a time, slipping it through your fingers to soften it slightly. Whisk continuously, incorporating each piece of butter thoroughly before adding next piece. When all butter has been added and sauce is thickened and creamy, season lightly with salt and pepper and fold in tarragon or parsley, if using. Makes ¾ cup.

NOTE: If sauce refuses to thicken or curdles, it can be remedied as described for Hollandaise Sauce.

VARIATIONS

PALOISE SAUCE: Follow recipe for Béarnaise Sauce but substitute 2 tbs chopped fresh mint (including stalks) for dried tarragon and thyme for making reduced flavoured vinegar, and 1 tsp shredded fresh mint for chopped fresh tarragon or parsley to fold through finished sauce. Serve with roast or grilled lamb.

SAUCE CHORON: Stir 1–1½ tbs tomato paste into 1 quantity Béarnaise Sauce. Serve with grilled or sautéed veal or lamb.

Hot Butter Sauces

These superbly simple sauces depend on the wonderful fragrance and flavour of butter.

Beurre Blanc

Beurre Blanc, light and creamy, goes back to Escoffier and beyond but is newly popular as a sauce of the Nouvelle Cuisine. It is easy to make with a wire whisk – an essential tool to achieve the liaison between liquid and butter which gives the sauce body. Serve with mousselines (see page 278) or quenelles (see pages 402–3), shellfish, poached or grilled fish, chicken, eggs and vegetables such as broccoli, cauliflower or artichokes.

I cup poaching liquid (Court Bouillon, page 98) from fish or shellfish, or I cup dry white wine with good squeeze lemon juice added; I tbs finely chopped golden shallot; 250 g (8 oz) chilled butter, cut into large dice; salt and freshly ground white pepper.

Put poaching liquid, or wine and lemon juice, into a small, heavy saucepan, add shallot and boil until reduced to about 2 tbs liquid. Remove from heat and whisk in 2 pieces of chilled butter. Return to very low heat and continue whisking in butter one piece at a time. The sauce will thicken to consistency of pouring cream. As soon as all butter has been added, remove from heat and whisk in salt and pepper. Makes about ¾ cup.

NOTE: The reduction of liquid and shallot can be prepared ahead and reheated when needed, but do not try to hold or reheat the completed sauce – it is quite correct to serve it warm rather than hot.

Beurre Noisette (Brown Butter)

'Noisette' means hazelnut, the golden-brown colour of this sauce. Beurre Noisette is excellent on fish, sweetbreads, eggs and vegetables. Chopped parsley, other herbs or toasted nuts are nice additions.

90 g (3 oz) butter; I tbs lemon juice.

Heat butter slowly in a small frying pan, shaking pan occasionally to ensure even browning. When butter is golden-brown add any herbs etc., remove from heat and stir in lemon juice. Pour over food while still frothing. Serve very hot. Makes about ½ cup.

Beurre Noir (Black Butter)

Despite the name the butter is cooked until it is brown, not black. Beurre Noir is the classic sauce to serve on brains and is good with fresh or smoked fish, chicken, vegetables and eggs. Oeufs au Beurre Noir – poached eggs in rich shortcrust tartlet cases or on rounds of toasted French bread, sauced with Beurre Noir with capers and chopped herbs – makes a first-course or luncheon dish.

90 g (3 oz) butter; I tbs chopped parsley; I tbs drained capers (optional, but always used for brains); I tbs vinegar.

Heat butter slowly in a small frying pan, shaking pan occasionally to ensure even browning, until it is nut-brown. Stir in parsley and capers, if using, remove from heat and add vinegar. Pour over food while still frothing. Serve very hot. Makes about ½ cup.

Other Useful Sauces

A selection of easy-to-prepare savoury sauces that can add variety to everyday dishes.

Smooth Tomato Sauce

An excellent sauce for pasta, gnocchi, grilled meats and green vegetables.

3 tbs olive oil; I onion, finely chopped; I carrot, finely chopped; I stick celery finely chopped; 2 cloves garlic, crushed; I sprig fresh marjoram, finely chopped, or ½ tsp dried; few sprigs parsley, finely chopped; I kg (2 lb) ripe tomatoes, chopped; salt and freshly ground black pepper; ½ tsp sugar.

Heat olive oil in a saucepan and add onion, carrot, celery, garlic, marjoram and parsley. Cook over low heat until golden. Add tomatoes and season with salt, pepper and sugar. Simmer until tomatoes have turned almost to a purée. Push through a sieve, or blender or food processor and then sieve. Makes about 2 cups.

Mushroom Sauce

To serve with pasties, Finnan Haddie (see page 149), grilled hamburgers, vegetables or grilled meats.

60 g (2 oz) mushrooms, preferably flat ones, chopped or sliced; 2 golden shallots, finely chopped; 45 g (1¹/₂ oz) butter; 2 tsp flour; 1¹/₄ cups warm chicken stock; 2 tbs cream; 1 tbs chopped mixed fresh herbs or parsley; salt and freshly ground black pepper; few drops lemon juice.

Gently cook mushrooms and shallots in half the butter in a saucepan until soft. Add remaining butter and melt it, then stir in flour. Cook gently 1 minute. Remove from heat and add stock, stirring until smoothly blended. Return to medium heat and stir until boiling. Simmer 2 minutes, then add cream and herbs and simmer 1 minute longer. Season with salt, pepper and lemon juice. Makes about 1¹/₄ cups.

Balinese Curry Sauce

This fragrant curry sauce is one of the most adaptable of bases. Chicken, pork, beef or lamb, cut into bite-sized pieces, can be cooked gently in it. For a vegetable curry add cabbage, green beans, eggplant, cauliflower, potato. It is also a good base for leftover cooked poultry or meats – just heat gently in the sauce.

¹/₂ cup water; 1 tsp turmeric; 4 curry leaves, or pinch curry powder; 2.5 cm (1 in) piece fresh ginger; 1 tsp ground coriander, or 1 tbs chopped fresh coriander; ¹/₂ tsp grated lemon rind; 1–2 chillies, seeded (or to taste); 4 spring onions, chopped (including some green tops); 2 cloves garlic; 45 g (1¹/₂ oz) butter; 1 tsp salt; 1¹/₂ cups Coconut Milk (page 91); 2 macadamia nuts or 4 cashew nuts, crushed; 1 tsp sugar.

Put water, turmeric, curry leaves or powder, ginger, coriander, lemon rind, chillies, spring onions and garlic into a blender or food processor fitted with a steel blade and process until smooth. If making by hand, pound all these ingredients, except water, in a mortar, then mix in water. Heat butter in a wok or small frying pan, add onion mixture and cook briskly, stirring, 5 minutes. Stir in salt and coconut milk, then crushed nuts and sugar.

Vegetables, hard-boiled eggs or diced cooked meat are now added and simmered in the sauce for 15 minutes or until vegetables are done. Raw chicken pieces or diced meat should be cooked gently about 45 minutes or until tender. This recipe makes enough sauce for about 2 cups meat or vegetables. Serves 4.

NOTE: The sauce can be made ahead, ready for use. Simmer 5 minutes after adding crushed nuts and sugar, then cool and store in a covered container in the refrigerator. Keeps 1 week.

Beer or Cider Sauce with Sultanas

To serve with hot or cold ham or smoked tongue.

¹/₄ cup firmly packed brown sugar; 1 tbs cornflour; large pinch salt; 1 cup cider or beer; ¹/₄ cup sultanas; 8 cloves; 8 cm (3 in) cinnamon stick; 15 g (¹/₂ oz) butter.

Mix brown sugar, cornflour and salt in a small, heavy saucepan. Stir in cider or beer and add sultanas. Tie spices in a bag and add them. Boil gently 10 minutes, stirring often. Remove spice bag and swirl in butter. Serve immediately. Makes about 1 cup.

Devil Sauce

Devil Sauce is a hot, spicy mixture used to coat foods for grilling. Devilled chicken joints or small, split chickens, thick lamb or pork chops, fish fillets or fish steaks are all delicious. Devilling is also an excellent way to use cooked meat or poultry. Use the following for uncooked chicken, lamb or pork chops.

DRY DEVIL MIXTURE: 1 tsp salt; 2 tsp sugar; 1 tsp black pepper; 1 tsp ground ginger; 1 tsp dry mustard; ¹/₂ tsp curry powder; 30 g (1 oz) butter, melted, for grilling.

SAUCE: 2 tbs tomato relish; 1 tbs Worcestershire sauce; 1 tbs soy sauce; 1 tbs fruit chutney; dash Tabasco sauce; 30 g (1 oz) butter; shredded spring onions to garnish.

Mix ingredients for dry devil mixture and rub into surface of chicken or meat. Leave at least 1 hour. Brush food with melted butter for grilling and grill under a preheated grill until browned on both sides. SAUCE: Add sauce ingredients to remaining butter for grilling and heat gently. Spoon over browned chicken or meat and continue cooking, basting frequently with juices in grill pan, until done to your liking. Juices and sauce remaining in grill pan may be diluted with hot stock or vegetable water and spooned over for serving. Garnish with shredded spring onions. Makes sufficient for 4 large chicken joints.

VARIATIONS

DEVIL SAUCE FOR FISH: Mix together all the ingredients for dry devil mixture, plus butter for grilling and sauce ingredients. Spread over surface of fish and leave 1 hour. Place in well-heated, greased grill pan under a preheated hot grill and grill on one side only for fillets or small steaks, or turning once for thick steaks. Garnish with shredded spring onions. Sufficient for 4–8 fish fillets or 4 fish steaks.

DEVIL SAUCE FOR COOKED MEAT OR CHICKEN: Cut meat into thick slices; slash chicken flesh at intervals. Mix together all ingredients for dry devil mixture, plus butter for grilling and sauce ingredients. Spread over surface, working well in. Leave at least 2 hours. Brown quickly under a preheated grill, basting several times with remaining mixture. Garnish with shredded spring onions. Makes sufficient for 4 servings.

Plum Sauce

Superb with ham, pork or duck. Keeps 2–3 weeks in the refrigerator.

2 large onions, finely chopped; 90 g (3 oz) butter; 500 g (1 lb) plums, stoned; 1¹/₂ cups dry red wine; 1 tbs sugar; salt and freshly ground black pepper.

Cook onion slowly in butter until soft but not brown. Simmer plums with 1 cup wine for 10 minutes, then add onions with their butter and season with sugar, salt and pepper. Simmer 10 minutes longer. Add remaining red wine, cover and simmer 40 minutes. Serve hot or at room temperature. Makes about 3 cups.

Dessert Sauces

Sweet sauces can be served with a variety of desserts – fresh fruit, ice cream, steamed or milk puddings.

Quick Apricot Sauce

Nice on ice cream, cream-filled meringues, chocolate cake or apple tart.

1¹/₂ cups apricot jam; ¹/₂ cup water; 2 tbs sugar; squeeze lemon juice; 2 tbs Kirsch or Grand Marnier; ¹/₄ cup toasted, slivered almonds.

Boil jam, water and sugar together slowly for 10 minutes, stirring frequently. Rub through a sieve and add lemon juice and liqueur. Serve warm, adding almonds at last minute. Makes about 2 cups.

Dipping Sauce for Fruit

Arrange a selection of prepared fresh fruits on individual plates and place a small bowl of this sauce on each.

1 cup sour cream; ¹/₄ cup desiccated coconut; 2 tbs chopped walnuts; 2 tbs sieved apricot jam; 2 tsp finely chopped preserved ginger; 1 tbs rum or brandy (optional).

Mix all ingredients together. Serves 4.

Lemon Sauce

Serve with a lemon-flavoured sponge pudding.

2 tsp cornflour; 1¹/₄ cups water; 3 tbs lemon juice; 1 tbs sugar; 1 tbs golden syrup; 1 tsp butter.

Blend cornflour with a little of the water. Put all remaining ingredients into a small, heavy saucepan and bring to the boil, stirring. Stir in blended cornflour and bring to the boil again, stirring constantly. Makes about 1¹/₂ cups.

VARIATION

LEMON RUM OR BRANDY SAUCE: Follow recipe for Lemon Sauce. Add 3 tbs rum or brandy after removing sauce from heat.

Sweet White Sauce

A simple, old-fashioned sauce, very good with steamed pudding.

1 tbs cornflour; 1 cup milk; 1 tbs sugar; ¹/₂ tsp vanilla.

Blend cornflour with a little of the milk. Put remaining milk and sugar into a small, heavy saucepan and bring to the boil, stirring. Stir in blended cornflour and bring to the boil again, stirring constantly. Simmer gently 3 minutes, then add vanilla. Makes 1 cup.

Simple Fruit Sauces

Any canned or stewed fruit, soft fresh fruit or frozen berries, etc., can be made into a sauce for ice cream, sponge or milk puddings, cake or waffles.

fresh or canned fruit; 1 tbs arrowroot or cornflour; sugar; lemon juice; 1–2 tbs brandy, rum, sherry, or liqueur (optional).

Purée fruit in a blender or food processor or rub through a sieve. Add syrup if using canned or stewed fruit. Thicken, if necessary, by blending arrowroot or cornflour with a little juice or water, heating puréed fruit to boiling point and stirring in enough blended arrowroot to give desired thickness. Sweeten with sugar and sharpen the flavour with lemon juice. Add brandy, rum, sherry or liqueur to taste, if desired. Serve hot or cold.

SAUERKRAUT

Called *choucroute* in French, this is basically shredded cabbage fermented with salt, and flavoured with juniper berries. This fermentation has been used for centuries as a method of preserving cabbage, an important consideration during the long, snow-bound months of winter in northern Europe.

Sauerkraut is most often combined with salted or smoked meats or sausages to make a one-dish meal. These dishes almost always require long cooking, during which the meat imparts some of its flavour to the sauerkraut.

Bulk sauerkraut is sometimes available from big barrels, but more often sauerkraut is bought in jars, canned or in vacuum-packs. If the sauerkraut is packed in brine, it should be washed and thoroughly drained before use. See recipes.

Knackwurst with Sauerkraut

2 onions, finely chopped; 30 g (1 oz) butter; 1 tbs oil; 1 kg (2 lb) sauerkraut, rinsed if necessary; 2 cooking apples, peeled, cored and sliced; 1 tbs brown sugar; 1 tsp dry mustard; ¹/₂ cup dry white wine; salt and freshly ground black pepper; 500 g (1 lb) knackwurst sausage, or Polish clobassi.

Fry onions in butter and oil in a frying pan until transparent. Toss sauerkraut with fork to separate, then add to pan with apples, sugar, mustard and wine. Season with salt and pepper. Spread out in a large greased shallow ovenproof dish. Place sausage in pan of cold water, bring to the boil then drain. Cut into thick diagonal slices and arrange on top of sauerkraut mixture. Cover with foil and bake in a preheated moderate oven (180°C/350°F) for 20–30 minutes or until heated through. Serve accompanied by mustard and dill pickles. Serves 6.

Choucroute Soup

500 g (1 lb) sauerkraut; 2 medium potatoes, peeled and diced; 2 rashers bacon, rind removed; 6 juniper berries; 1 bay leaf; salt and freshly ground black pepper; 2 tsp sugar; 5 cups stock or water; 2–3 smoked frankfurts, cut into short lengths; ¹/₄ cup cream.

Place sauerkraut in a large saucepan with potatoes, bacon, juniper berries, bay leaf, salt, pepper and sugar. Add stock or water and simmer about 1 hour. Push through a sieve or purée using a food mill. Return to pan, add frankfurts and cook further 15 minutes. Adjust seasoning, and stir in cream just before serving. Serves 6–8.

Juniper Sauerkraut

1 onion, finely chopped; 1 apple, peeled, cored and chopped; 1 clove garlic, crushed; 60 g (2 oz) butter; 6 juniper berries, crushed; 500 g (1 lb) sauerkraut; 1 tsp celery seeds; 1 cup stock; 1 cup plain yogurt or sour cream.

Cook onion, apple and garlic in butter in a flame-proof casserole over low heat until soft. Add juniper berries, sauerkraut, celery seeds and stock and simmer

for 2–3 minutes. Cover, reduce heat to very low and cook for 45–60 minutes, or cook in a preheated slow oven (150°C/300°F). Stir in yogurt or sour cream just before serving. Serve hot as an accompaniment to grilled pork chops or sausages. Serves 6.

SAUERBRATEN

A dish of marinated, spiced beef or pork pot-roasted to melting tenderness is one of Germany's most celebrated dishes. The old way to tenderise tough meat was to cover it in a vinegar marinade. Today the marinade is often based on red wine and used more for flavour than as a tenderiser. Serve sauerbraten with dumplings and red cabbage.

Sauerbraten

1 x 3 kg (6 lb) boned and rolled top round of beef or fresh silverside; ¹/₂ cup red wine vinegar; 1¹/₂ cups red wine; 10 black peppercorns; 1 tsp salt; 1 bay leaf; 6 cloves; 2 cloves garlic; 2 strips lemon rind; 1 onion, sliced; ¹/₄ tsp nutmeg; 3 sticks celery, chopped; 2 carrots, chopped; 3 sprigs parsley; 2 cups beef stock; 3 tbs cornflour; ¹/₂ cup sour cream.

Place beef in a large china or glass bowl. Combine vinegar, red wine, peppercorns, salt, bay leaf, cloves, garlic, lemon rind, onion, nutmeg, celery, carrots and parsley. Add to beef, cover and refrigerate for 3 days, turning occasionally. Remove meat and reserve marinade. Dry meat well with paper towels. Bring marinade to the boil in a saucepan and leave to simmer over low heat while the meat is cooking; it will be used to baste the meat. Heat a heavy flameproof casserole, add meat, fat side down, and brown well on all sides over moderate heat. Pour off excess fat. Add 1 cup beef stock, then cover and simmer over very low heat for 3–3¹/₂ hours or until meat is tender. Baste occasionally with remaining stock and the hot marinade until all the marinade has been added. Remove meat to a hot platter. Strain cooking liquid, pressing vegetables through the sieve. Remove fat from surface and return to casserole. Thicken with cornflour mixed with a little water. Add sour cream. The sauce should be served separately from the meat. Serves 8–10.
NOTE: If liked, the gravy may be thickened with ¹/₂ cup broken gingersnap biscuits and ¹/₄ cup raisins or currants added for sweetness.

SAUSAGE

Salame, saucisson, wurst – the simple sausage speaks many languages. The art of sausage-making can be traced back many centuries, and sausages have probably been made for as long as the pig has been slaughtered, around Christmas time in the northern hemisphere.

The skill and ingenuity of these early sausage-makers is still in evidence today, with different towns and regions still producing their own particular and traditional types of sausage. It might be fresh or salted, cooked or smoked, herb or garlic-flavoured, large or small.

Butchers are now offering a wide range of sausages that are competing with prime cuts for an agreeable main meal.

TYPES OF SAUSAGE

Fresh Sausages: These may be made of pork or beef, and are seasoned or spiced. The meat may be very finely ground and combined with cereal or some other 'filler', or the sausage may contain meat only. Most fresh Continental sausages are of this latter type; the *Toulouse* sausage is a particular type of pure pork sausage, which comes as one long coiled length.

Raw Sausages: Also called air-dried sausages, these are typified by the Italian *salame*. These are generally made of pork, or a mixture of pork and beef. The meat is minced and salted, in the same way as ham is salted, flavourings and spices are added and the sausages are hung up to dry for several months. Salami-type sausages are marvellous in salads; as part of an hors d'oeuvre; combined with fresh melon or figs; on savouries and open sandwiches. They should be quite firm when bought, and should be sliced very thinly.

Cooked Sausages: There is an enormous range of cooked sausages, some of which are also smoked. Polish *clobassi* is one of these, as is the Italian *mortadella*, and many German sausages – *frankfurt*, *bierwurst*, *presswurst*. These may be eaten as they are, with a salad and perhaps mustards and pickles, or potato salad and dill cucumbers. Or they may be simmered in stock or water for about 10–20 minutes, depending on size, and eaten hot with starchy vegetables such as mashed potatoes, sauerkraut, cooked lentils, haricot beans or red cabbage.

Soft Sausages: These include all forms of liver sausage, which is eaten as it is, on bread or biscuits. German *mettwurst* is another soft, spreading sausage. German sausages may also be made with tongue, or a mixture similar to brawn, or liver mixture studded with cubes of pork fat.

Black Puddings: Also known as *boudins* in France, or blood sausages, are made with pig's blood, onions and seasonings. These may be cooked by simmering or frying, and are usually accompanied by mashed potato, onions and fried apple rings.

Andouilles and Andouillettes: French names for smoked and salted sausages made from pork tripe. They are found throughout France; *andouille* is eaten cold, usually as an hors d'oeuvre, while *andouillettes* are gently fried or simmered.

■ **TO COOK FRESH SAUSAGES:** Fresh sausages may be grilled or fried, and if desired cooking may be preceded by parboiling. Prick the sausages lightly with a sharp-pronged fork or the point of a knife, in order to prevent them bursting. Parboiling also helps to prevent bursting.

When frying sausages, it is rarely necessary to add any fat except just enough to prevent them from sticking. If sausages give out a lot of fat during cooking, drain this off.

When barbecuing sausages, thread them on long skewers to make them easy to turn.

Tomato, onion or mustard sauces go well with cooked fresh sausages, as do mustard or horseradish condiments. See recipes.

Risotto with Italian Sausage

2 tbs finely chopped onion; 45 g (1^1/2 oz) butter; 2 tbs oil; 2 cups long-grain rice; 4 cups boiling chicken stock; 375 g (12 oz) Italian sausage; ^{1}/4 cup dry white wine; salt and freshly ground black pepper; 3 tbs grated Parmesan cheese.

Gently fry onion in 30 g (1 oz) butter and the oil in a saucepan until translucent. Add rice and stir until well coated. Add ^{1}/2 cup stock, stirring. As stock is absorbed, add another ^{1}/2 cup stock and mix in. Continue adding stock in this way until it is all added and rice is tender. Meanwhile, cook sausage in frying pan with wine. Allow wine to evaporate, then cook sausages in their fat for 12–15 minutes. Remove and set aside. When rice is cooked, add salt and pepper. Stir in remaining butter and Parmesan and mix thoroughly. Turn on to heated serving dish. Pour all but 2 tbs fat from frying pan in which sausages cooked. Add about 2 tbs water and deglaze frying pan over high heat, scraping any residue from bottom. Return sausages to pan to heat through, then arrange on risotto and pour pan liquid over. Serve immediately, with additional Parmesan if desired. Serves 4.

Scotch Eggs

500 g (1 lb) sausage mince; few drops Tabasco sauce; few drops Worcestershire sauce; 6 hard-boiled eggs; ^{1}/2 cup flour; salt and freshly ground black pepper; 1 egg, beaten; dry breadcrumbs; oil for deep-frying.

Mix sausage mince with sauces. Divide into 6 equal portions. Dust eggs lightly with flour seasoned with salt and pepper, then cover each egg with sausage mixture, pressing and moulding on well. Brush with beaten egg and roll in breadcrumbs. Chill for at least 1 hour. Deep-fry eggs in hot oil until golden-brown. Drain on paper towels. Cool and chill. Serve cold with salads. Makes 6.

Sausages with Onion Gravy

8 sausages; 60 g (2 oz) butter; 6 onions, sliced; 2 tbs flour; 1 tsp dry mustard; 1 cup beef stock; ^{3}/4 cup flat beer; 1 tsp sugar; 1 tsp chopped fresh thyme, or ^{1}/4 tsp dried; salt and freshly ground black pepper.

Prick sausages, place in a saucepan and cover with cold water. Bring to the boil and simmer for 10 minutes. Drain. Peel off skin. Melt butter in a saucepan and sauté onion until softened. Stir in flour and dry mustard and cook for 1 minute. Stir in remaining ingredients, bring to the boil and simmer 15 minutes. Add sausages and continue to simmer for 5 minutes or until heated through. Serves 4.

German Bean Soup

I cup dried white beans, soaked overnight and drained; freshly ground black pepper;
I tbs finely chopped parsley; 2 bay leaves; salt;
I tbs oil; 2 medium carrots, sliced; 8 cups stock;
I large cabbage leaf, cut into chunks;
2 medium leeks, cut into 5 cm (2 in) pieces;
pinch nutmeg; 250 g (8 oz) German bratwurst
or frankfurts, thickly sliced.

Cover beans with fresh cold water and bring to the boil. Add pepper, parsley and bay leaves and simmer gently for 1 hour or until beans are tender, adding salt towards the end of cooking. Drain and discard bay leaves. Heat oil in a saucepan, add carrots and cook gently for 10 minutes. Add stock, cabbage, leeks and cooked beans. Adjust seasoning and add nutmeg. Cook over moderate heat for 15 minutes, then add sliced sausage and simmer gently 15 minutes longer. Serves 8–10.

Italian Salad with Cheese and Salami

I lettuce, torn into pieces; 2 firm, ripe tomatoes, seeded and cut into wedges; 4 anchovy fillets, chopped; salt and freshly ground black pepper;
2 tbs wine vinegar; 5 tbs olive oil; pinch dried oregano; 125 g (4 oz) Italian salami (milano or veneto), thinly sliced and cut into strips;
125 g (4 oz) mozzarella cheese, cut into strips.

Place lettuce leaves in a bowl with tomatoes. Add anchovy fillets, salt and pepper to vinegar, then gradually whisk in oil. Add oregano. Taste and add more oil or vinegar if desired. Pour dressing over lettuce and tomato and toss lightly. Arrange salami and cheese around top of salad, and serve immediately with crusty bread. Serves 4.

Frankfurt and Cabbage Salad

4 frankfurts; 4 slices cooked ham, cut into fine strips; 4 ripe tomatoes, peeled, seeded and diced;
I red or green pepper, cored, seeded and cut into strips; 1/2 cup Vinaigrette Dressing (page 442);
1/4 tsp paprika; I tsp tomato paste; I tsp prepared French mustard; 1/2 small white cabbage, finely shredded; 3–4 tbs oil; salt and freshly ground black pepper; I tbs white wine vinegar.

Poach frankfurts, drain, cool and slice thickly. Place frankfurts, ham, tomatoes and pepper in a large bowl. Combine dressing with paprika, tomato purée and mustard. Toss frankfurt mixture with this dressing. Arrange salad on half of large platter. Toss cabbage with oil, salt and pepper, then add vinegar and toss again. Arrange cabbage salad next to frankfurt salad. Serves 4.

Sausages with Peppers and Wine

500 g (1 lb) chorizo or similar spiced pork sausages;
I tbs olive oil; 1/4 cup water; 3 golden shallots, sliced;
I small red or green pepper, cored, seeded and
finely chopped; I rasher bacon, rind removed
and diced; 1/2 cup white wine; I tbs Madeira;
salt and freshly ground black pepper.

Gently fry sausages in oil until browned all over. Transfer to ovenproof dish. Add water and complete cooking in a preheated moderate oven (180°C/350°F). In pan in which sausages were browned, cook shallots, pepper and bacon for 2–3 minutes. Add wine and Madeira and bring to boil, then simmer for 10–15 minutes or until sausages are ready. Season sauce with salt and pepper, serve with sausages. Serves 3–4.

Bean and Sausage Platter

8 Italian pork sausages; 2 tbs olive oil; 1/2 cup
tomato purée or Fresh Tomato Sauce (page 339);
1/2 cup water; salt and freshly ground black pepper;
2 cups dried haricot beans, soaked and cooked in
water until tender, or 4 cups drained canned
haricot beans.

Prick sausages, place in frying pan and cover with cold water. Slowly bring to the boil, then drain. In same pan, cook sausages in oil until cooked through and well coloured on all sides. Remove and keep warm. Add tomato purée or sauce to pan and cook for 1–2 minutes. Add water and simmer gently 10 minutes. Season with salt and pepper. Add beans, stir well to mix and reheat for 5 minutes. Return sausages to pan to heat through. Arrange beans on heated serving platter and top with sausages. Serve immediately. Serves 6–8.

Sausages with Apples

500 g (1 lb) pork sausages; 4 apples, cored and
sliced; 30 g (1 oz) butter; 1/2 cup dry cider or white
wine; I tbs brandy; 1/2 cup cream; salt and freshly
ground black pepper.

Prick sausages and fry over moderate heat. In another pan, cook apples in butter until golden. Remove from pan and keep warm. Add cider or wine to pan, bring to the boil and reduce slightly, then add brandy and cream. Reduce heat and stir well. Reduce over high heat if thicker sauce required. Season well with salt and pepper and pour sauce over sausages and apples. Serve immediately. Serves 3–4.

Polish Sausage in Red Wine

I cup finely chopped onions; 3 cups red wine; I kg (2 lb) Polish clobassi or kransky sausage.

Combine onions with red wine in large heavy frying pan or electric frypan. Add sausage and bring to the boil, then reduce heat and simmer for 20–25 minutes, turning several times, or until sausages are glazed with wine. Slice thickly, and serve on bed of creamy mashed potatoes. The sausage is also delicious cold. Serves 8.

Sausage Rolls

I x 375 g (12 oz) packet frozen puff pastry, thawed; 500 g (I lb) sausage mince; salt and pepper; I egg, beaten.

Roll pastry out thinly and divide into 2 strips about 10 cm (4 in) wide. Trim edges. Form sausage mince into 2 neat rolls and place each roll on a strip of pastry. Brush edges lightly with egg, fold pastry over sausage mince and seal it to opposite edge. Cut each roll into 12 sections. Rinse baking tray with cold water, place sausage rolls on tray and make 2 diagonal slashes in top of each roll. Brush tops with remaining egg. Chill 20 minutes. Bake in a preheated very hot oven (230°C/450°F) for 10 minutes, then reduce heat to moderate (180°C/350°F) and cook 10 minutes longer. Serve hot. Makes 24

NOTE: If made in advance, cool rolls on a wire rack, then, when needed, reheat for 5–8 minutes in a moderate oven (180°C/350°F).

Glazed Pork Sausages

8 pork sausages; ¹/₃ cup firmly packed brown sugar; 2 cups water; I tbs vinegar.

Put all ingredients into a large frying pan and simmer gently until water has evaporated. Tilt pan back and forth to roll sausages and coat them with light glaze that has formed on bottom. Serve immediately with hot boiled rice mixed with chopped red pepper, pineapple and spring onions. Serves 4.

Toad-in-the-Hole

An old English favourite.

I cup flour; ¹/₄ tsp salt; I egg; I¹/₄ cups milk; 500 g (I lb) sausages; 30 g (I oz) dripping or lard.

Sift flour and salt in a bowl. Make well in centre, add egg and milk and gradually mix to a smooth batter. Set aside for 30 minutes. Fry sausages in fat in

flameproof baking dish for 5 minutes until brown on all sides. Pour batter over sausages and bake in a preheated hot oven (200°C/400°F) for about 30 minutes. Serves 4.

Chick Peas with Tomatoes and Sausages

I¹/₂ cups dried chick peas, soaked overnight and drained; 250 g (8 oz) pork sausages; 150 g (5 oz) bacon, diced; I large onion, finely chopped; 2 cloves garlic, chopped; I large green pepper, cored, seeded and diced; 4 large ripe tomatoes, peeled, seeded and chopped; nutmeg or cinnamon; ¹/₄ tsp dried thyme; salt and freshly ground black pepper.

Place chick peas in saucepan and add fresh cold water to cover. Simmer, covered, for about 1 hour. Prick sausages and brown in frying pan. Remove and cut into 2.5 cm (1 in) pieces. Set aside. Blanch bacon in boiling water for 1 minute, then drain. Brown bacon, onion, garlic and green pepper in fat from sausages in frying pan, stirring from time to time. Add tomatoes, spice, thyme, salt and pepper. Cover and cook over low heat for 10 minutes. Fold in sausage pieces. Drain chick peas, reserving 2 cups liquid. Turn into greased ovenproof baking dish and cover with tomato and sausage mixture. Moisten with reserved liquid. Cover and bake in a preheated moderately hot oven (190°C/375°F) for about 1½ hours, stirring from time to time. Serve in wide soup plates. Serves 4–6.

Baked Sausage, Cabbage and Apples

500 g (I lb) sausage mince; I small onion, finely chopped; 3 tbs vinegar; 2 tbs brown sugar; salt and freshly ground black pepper; ¹/₂ small cabbage, finely shredded; 3 medium cooking apples, peeled, cored and thinly sliced; nutmeg.

Shape sausage mince into 8 flat patties and brown quickly on both sides in a greased frying pan. Remove patties. Add onion to fat in pan and brown lightly. Add vinegar, sugar, ½ tsp salt and a grinding of pepper, and remove from heat. Arrange alternate layers of cabbage and apple in a greased casserole, seasoning each layer with salt, pepper and nutmeg. Place sausage patties in a single layer on top and pour vinegar mixture over. Cover and bake in a preheated moderate oven (180°C/350°F) 40 minutes. Uncover and bake 10 minutes longer. Serve with buttered noodles. Serves 4.

Curried Sausages

8 sausages; I large onion, chopped; ¹/₄ cup diced
celery; I cooking apple, peeled, cored and diced;
I clove garlic, crushed; I–2 tbs curry powder;
2 tbs flour; 2 tsp tomato paste; 2 cups chicken stock;
salt and freshly ground black pepper.

Prick sausages, place in a baking dish and bake in a
preheated moderately slow oven (160°C/325°F) for
15–20 minutes or until well cooked. Drain sausages,
reserving 3 tbs of fat. Place fat in a saucepan and fry
onion, celery, apple and garlic until soft. Add curry
powder and fry 2 minutes. Blend in flour and tomato
paste, then add stock gradually, stirring constantly
until boiling. Season with salt and pepper. Add
sausages to sauce and simmer until heated through.
Serve with fluffy boiled rice and simple store cupboard
accompaniments such as sultanas, chutneys and
cashews. Serves 4.

Sausage Roll in Flaky Pastry

2 large onions, thinly sliced; 30 g (I oz) butter;
2 tbs brandy, whisky or Calvados; 2 tsp chopped
fresh thyme, or ¹/₂ tsp dried; ¹/₂ tsp chopped fresh
sage, or pinch dried; large pinch nutmeg; small
pinch ground cloves; about ¹/₂ tsp salt (depending
on seasoning of sausage mince); freshly ground
black pepper; 750 g (I¹/₂ lb) sausage mince;
I quantity Flaky Pastry (page 343), or
I x 375 g (12 oz) frozen puff pastry, thawed;
I egg yolk, lightly beaten.

Cook onions gently in butter until soft but not brown.
Set aside. Knead liquor, herbs, spices, salt and pepper
into sausage mince. Roll meat between 2 sheets of
floured plastic wrap to a rectangle about 1 cm (1¹/₂ in)
thick. Peel off top sheet of wrap and spread meat
evenly with onions. Using bottom sheet of wrap to
help, roll up meat like a Swiss roll. Lift into a greased
shallow baking tin, seam side down, and bake in a
preheated moderately slow oven (160°C/325°F) for 30
minutes, turning occasionally. Remove from oven
and cool. Increase temperature to very hot
(230°C/450°F). Roll out pastry to a sheet large enough
to wrap around the meat. Place meat on pastry and
wrap it around, brushing a little egg yolk on to seam
and pressing it together. Place seam side down on
baking tray and chill 20 minutes. Cut a few slashes in
pastry and brush with egg yolk. Bake in very hot oven
(230°C/450°F) for 10–15 minutes or until pastry is
lightly coloured. Reduce heat to moderate
(180°C/350°F) and bake 15 minutes longer or until
pastry is golden-brown and meat is heated through.
Serve hot or warm. Serves 6.

SAUSAGE ROLLS

See *Sausage*.

SAVARIN

A wonderful liqueur-soaked yeast cake, said to have
been invented by the great French chef Brillat-Savarin.
He used a yeast dough similar to that used for the earlier
Rum Baba (see page 18), but omitted the raisins in the
mixture, changed the shape and the name, and introduced it to Paris where it became a triumph.

A savarin is baked in a special savarin ring mould. The
syrup is usually flavoured with Kirsch, and the centre can
be filled with whipped cream, custard or a fruit filling. A
savarin is usually glazed, and can be decorated with
almonds, glacé fruits or fresh berry fruits.

Savarin

2 cups flour; ¹/₄ tsp salt; 15 g (¹/₂ oz) compressed
yeast; 3 tsp sugar; ¹/₂ cup warm milk;
2 eggs (60 g size); 125 g (4 oz) butter, softened;
¹/₂ cup Apricot Glaze (page 9); I cup fruit
(strawberries, raspberries, cherries, blackberries,
etc.), sprinkled with 2 tbs Kirsch and I tbs sugar.

SYRUP: I cup water; I cup sugar; 2.5 cm (I in) piece
vanilla bean; 4 tbs Kirsch.

Sift flour and salt into a large warmed bowl. In a
small bowl cream yeast with sugar, then add warm
milk. Make a well in centre of flour and add yeast
mixture. Sprinkle a little flour from side over top,
cover with a cloth and leave in a warm place for 15
minutes for yeast to sponge. Beat eggs into butter
and add yeast to mixture. Beat vigorously using the
hand until all flour is incorporated and the dough is
smooth and elastic. Cover with a cloth and leave
dough to rise in a warm place until doubled in bulk.
This will take 30–40 minutes. Spoon dough into a
well-greased 23 cm (9 in) savarin mould or ring
tin. Allow to rise in a warm place until dough
reaches top of tin. Bake in a preheated hot oven
(200°C/400°F) for about 20 minutes or until golden-
brown and beginning to shrink a little from sides
of mould.

SYRUP: Combine water, sugar and vanilla bean in
a saucepan. Stir over medium heat until sugar
dissolves. Bring to the boil and boil for 10 minutes.
Discard vanilla bean. Stir in Kirsch. Remove savarin
from oven and cool in tin for 5 minutes. Turn out on
to a cake rack and place a dish under rack to catch
any syrup if it runs off cake. Prick savarin with a fine
skewer all over and while still hot spoon warm syrup
over, a little at a time, until all syrup has been
absorbed. Allow savarin to cool. Carefully slide on to
a serving dish, brush lightly with apricot glaze and
fill centre with fruit. Serves 6–8.

NOTE: The centre of the Savarin may be filled with
2 cups whipped cream flavoured with Kirsch, 2 cups
Crème Pâtissière (see page 207) flavoured with vanilla
and Kirsch, or a macédoine of fresh fruits such as

cherries, pears, apricots and pineapple sprinkled with sugar and Kirsch. A bowl of whipped cream may accompany the Savarin if you wish.

SCALLOPINE

The Italian name for the thinly beaten veal steak that the French call *escalope*; the tiny ones, *escapolines* in French, become *piccate* in Italy. Italian cooks use *scalop-pine* to make exquisite quick dishes, both simple and sumptuous. For description and basic preparation, see *Escalope*. **See recipes.**

Scaloppine Passetto

4 large scaloppini; 1 tbs flour; 8 slices prosciutto or ham deluxe; 8 thin slices mozzarella cheese; 1/2 tsp dried sage; salt and freshly ground black pepper; butter; 1/2 cup grated Parmesan cheese.

Cut each scaloppine in half. Sprinkle with flour and place between 2 sheets of plastic wrap. Flatten with a cutlet bat, rolling pin or flat side of a meat mallet. Place a slice of prosciutto, then mozzarella cheese on each steak and sprinkle with sage, salt and pepper. Roll up each steak and secure with a wooden toothpick, Heat enough butter in a frying pan to cover bottom generously. Quickly sauté veal rolls in 2 lots, until they are browned on all sides. Place rolls in an ovenproof dish and sprinkle with Parmesan cheese and a little melted butter. Bake in a preheated moderately hot oven (190°C/375°F) for 10 minutes and serve piping hot. Serves 4.

Saltimbocca

The name means 'jump in the mouth': it is so quick to cook, it jumps into the pan and then into the mouth.

6 large scaloppini, halved and beaten flat; 12 slices prosciutto; 12 leaves fresh sage; 75g (2 1/2 oz) butter; salt and freshly ground black pepper; 1/2 cup dry white wine.

Cover each slice of veal with a slice of prosciutto and place a sage leaf on each. Secure with wooden toothpicks, Heat 60 g (2 oz) butter in a frying pan, add veal slices when foam subsides and brown quickly, about 2 minutes on each side. Season very lightly with salt and generously with pepper. Arrange slices, ham side up, on a heated serving dish. Remove toothpicks and keep saltimbocca warm. Add wine to pan and boil 1–2 minutes, stirring and scraping up brown bits with a wooden spoon. Season with salt and pepper. Remove from heat and swirl in remaining butter. Pour sauce over meat and serve immediately. Serves 6.

Scaloppine with Marsala
(Scaloppine alla Marsala)

A famous Sicilian treatment of scaloppine, using the fortified wine which originated on the island.

4 large scaloppini, halved and beaten flat; salt and freshly ground black pepper; 2 eggs, beaten; 3 tbs flour; 45 g (1 1/2 oz) butter; 1/2 cup dry Marsala or sherry; 1/2 cup beef stock or consommé.

Season scaloppine with salt and pepper, dip in beaten egg and coat with flour. Heat about 30 g (1 oz) butter in a frying pan (use enough butter to cover completely) and brown meat, taking care not to burn, for about 5 minutes on each side. When well browned, add Marsala and swirl liquid round so that it will be thickened by flour and butter. Remove scaloppini to heated plates. Add stock and remaining butter to pan, scraping brown bits from bottom and sides. Swirl to make gravy and pour over meat. Serves 4.

Piccata in Tomato Cream Sauce
(Piccata con Pomodoro)

A much-loved Italian dish.

18 piccata, beaten flat; salt and freshly ground black pepper; flour; 125 g (4 oz) butter; 1/2 cup dry white wine; 1/2 cup brown stock; 1 tbs chopped golden shallot; 4 ripe tomatoes, peeled, seeded and chopped; pinch sugar; 1 cup cream; 2 tbs lemon juice.

Season piccata with salt and pepper and dust with flour. Reserve about 1 tbs butter and heat remainder in a large frying pan over fairly high heat. Brown veal, a few slices at a time, about 2 minutes on each side. Remove slices to a heated serving platter and keep hot. Add wine and stock to pan and boil rapidly until reduced by half. Add shallot and tomatoes, season with sugar, salt and pepper and cook about 5 minutes. Add cream, reduce heat slightly and simmer 5 minutes longer. Remove from heat, add lemon juice and swirl in reserved butter bit by bit. Pour sauce over piccata and serve immediately. Serves 6.

Piccata with Parsley and Lemon
(Piccata al Prezzemolo e Limone)

18 piccata, beaten flat; salt and freshly ground black pepper; flour; 125 g (4 oz) butter; 1/3 cup lemon juice; 2 tbs chopped parsley.

Season piccata with salt and pepper and dust with flour. Set aside about 1 tbs butter and heat remainder in a large, heavy frying pan, Brown veal, a few pieces at a time, about 2 minutes each side. Transfer them to a heated serving platter and keep warm. Add lemon juice and parsley to pan, remove from heat and swirl in reserved butter bit by bit. Pour over veal and serve immediately. Serves 6.

SCALLOP

A shellfish known by its French name, *coquille St Jacques*, belonging to a group of bivalve molluscs, the most familiar species having scalloped, fan-shaped shells that are both beautiful and symbolic. The exquisite scallop design has been used in paintings through the ages (notably Botticelli's *The Birth of Venus*). The shell has long been a symbol of Christianity and a badge of the Pilgrims.

Scallops are usually purchased shucked or split, the edible flesh (white adductor muscle and orange coral or roe) removed from the shells. They can be bought fresh or frozen and usually require little preparation, except the removal of any small brown parts that may be left after cleaning.

Scallops have a delicate, subtle flavour, admirably suited to simple dishes. They should be cooked for short periods only and can be baked, poached, grilled or fried in many ways. Whichever, way you choose, don't overcook or reheat them too long or they will shrink and toughen.

Try scallops fried or baked in the oven in butter with chopped parsley, garlic and lemon juice, or sautéed and served with a little port and cream stirred in to make a sauce. Grill them with bacon, speared on a skewer, or roll them in breadcrumbs and fry in butter; use them in soups and chowders, or poach them lightly and serve in a white wine or vermouth sauce, sprinkled with breadcrumbs and browned under the grill. **See recipes.**

Scallop Chowder

4 cups milk; 1¹/₂ cups cream; 60 g (2 oz) butter; 2 tsp sugar; I tsp Worcestershire sauce; ¹/₂ tsp salt; ¹/₄ tsp white pepper; 500 g (I lb) scallops, minced or finely chopped; lemon juice; paprika; 2 tbs finely chopped parsley.

Combine milk, cream, butter, sugar, Worcestershire sauce, salt and pepper in a heatproof bowl or top of a double saucepan. Heat over simmering water, stirring. Add scallops and simmer for 5 minutes. Season with lemon juice. Serve sprinkled with paprika and chopped parsley. Serves 4–6.

Scallops with Garlic Butter Sauce

500 g (I lb) scallops; seasoned flour; 75 g (2¹/₂ oz) butter; I tbs olive oil; I small clove garlic, finely chopped; 2 tbs finely chopped parsley; lemon wedges to garnish.

Remove any brown parts from scallops but keep coral. Dust with seasoned flour, shaking well to remove any excess. Melt 15 g (¹/₂ oz) butter with the oil in a sauté pan. When foam subsides, sauté scallops for 2–3 minutes or until light golden. Transfer to a heated dish and keep warm. Clarify remaining butter by melting it slowly and skimming off foam. Spoon clear butter into a container and discard milky solids left at bottom. Return clarified butter to pan and heat until it sizzles without colouring. Remove from heat and stir in garlic. Pour over scallops and serve at once, sprinkled with chopped parsley and garnished with lemon wedges. Serves 4.

Chinese Steamed Scallops

Most fish markets sell fresh scallops in their shells, a treat when cooked in this light, easy, and quick and fragrant way. If scallops in their shells are not available, arrange 4–5 scallops in each of 4 small buttered ramekins and cook in this way.

250 g (8 oz) baby spinach leaves; 12 scallops, in shells; 6–8 spring onions, cut into matchsticks; 6 slices fresh ginger, shredded; ¹/₄ cup coriander sprigs; 4 tsp soy sauce; 2 tbs peanut oil; 2 tsp sesame oil.

Wash the spinach leaves. Shake the excess water off the leaves, drop them in a saucepan and allow to cook over a low heat, covered, until wilted. Drain well. Spoon evenly small amounts of the cooked spinach on the shells, top with scallop. Arrange the shells on a rack in a steamer (a large bamboo steamer is ideal, or use a cake rack in a wok). Scatter half the spring onions and ginger over the scallops, reserving the rest for garnish.

Cover well with aluminium foil or a lid and cook gently over a moderate heat until cooked, about 5 minutes. Remove the shells to a heated serving dish and garnish the scallops with the reserved spring onions, ginger and coriander sprigs. Heat the soy sauce, peanut and sesame oil in a small saucepan, pour over the scallops and serve immediately. Serves 3–4.

Curried Scallops

A curry flavour seems to go particularly well with scallops, and adds a golden colour to the creamy sauce.

I kg (2 lb) scallops; 90 g (3 oz) plus 2 tsp butter; 3–4 spring onions, chopped; 2 tsp curry powder; 2 cups dry white wine; I bouquet garni (2 sprigs parsley, I bay leaf and 2 sprigs fresh thyme); 2 tsp flour; ¹/₂ cup cream; salt and freshly ground black pepper; finely chopped parsley.

Remove any brown parts from scallops, keeping coral. Melt 90 g (3 oz) butter in a heavy saucepan over a medium heat and add spring onions and curry powder. Stir for 1 minute. Add wine, scallops and bouquet garni and bring to the boil. Reduce heat and poach for 3–4 minutes. Using a slotted spoon, transfer scallops to a serving dish, or 6 individual scallop shells or dishes, and keep warm. Reduce cooking liquid to 1½ cups by rapid boiling, and discard bouquet garni. Make a beurre manié by blending butter and flour together. Gradually stir into stock in small pieces, and bring to boiling point. Add cream, season with salt and pepper and cook gently, stirring, for a few minutes, but do not allow to boil. Pour sauce over scallops and sprinkle with parsley. Serves 6.

Precious Jade Cocktail

Fascinating presentation makes this seafood cocktail the highlight of the meal. Offer a choice of 2 interesting sauces.

2 cucumbers; 375 g (12 oz) cooked prawns;
250 g (8 oz) scallops; ¼ cup dry white wine;
¼ cup water; salt and freshly ground black pepper;
1 tbs lemon juice; 3 tbs oil; fresh dill, parsley or
watercress to garnish.

FRESH TOMATO SAUCE: 2 ripe tomatoes, peeled,
seeded and finely chopped; ¾ cup cream, lightly
whipped; 2 tbs horseradish;
salt and freshly ground black pepper.

CURRIED MAYONNAISE: 1 cup Mayonnaise (page 256);
2 spring onions, finely chopped; 2 tsp chutney;
2 tsp curry powder; salt and freshly ground black
pepper; 1 egg white.

Lightly peel cucumbers, leaving a little pale green, then, with a swivel-bladed potato peeler, shave off thin ribbons of flesh. Drop them into iced water, which will make them curl into pretty shapes. Shell prawns, leaving tails intact, and devein. Remove any brown parts from scallops, keeping coral. Poach for 2 minutes in wine and water seasoned with little salt and pepper. Drain. Whisk together lemon juice, oil, salt and pepper and pour over scallops, turning to coat them with this dressing. Drain cucumber and arrange in middle of 6 individual serving plates. Arrange prawns on one side and scallops on the other. Garnish with dill, parsley or watercress.
FRESH TOMATO SAUCE: Fold tomatoes into cream, with horseradish, salt and pepper to taste.
CURRIED MAYONAISE: Mix mayonnaise with spring onions, chutney, curry powder, salt and pepper. Beat egg white until it forms soft peaks, and fold in. Pass sauces separately, so each guest may choose which they prefer. Serves 6.

Scallops Beurre Bianc

Creamy-white scallops with their pretty orange corals sit in a golden butter sauce and are topped with a scattering of chives to make a lovely picture.

500 g (1lb) scallops; salt and freshly ground white
pepper; 1 cup white wine; little lemon juice;
1 tbs chopped spring onions; 125 g (4 oz) butter,
cut into pieces; 8–10 chives to garnish.

Remove any brown parts from scallops, keeping coral. Season with salt and pepper. Poach scallops in wine and lemon juice for about 1 minute. Remove scallops and keep warm. Add spring onions to poaching liquid and boil to reduce to about ⅓ cup. Over a gentle head, add butter a little at a time, whisking it in to make a sauce (the consistency of pouring cream). Season sauce with salt and pepper and spoon on to 4 heated entrée plates. Arrange scallops on top and garnish with matchstick lengths of chives. Serves 4.

Scallops with Avocados

The combination of lightly poached scallops and avocado is perfect for a light luncheon followed by a green salad.

250 g (8 oz) scallops; white wine; 1 canned
pimiento, cut into strips; 2 ripe avocados chilled,
halved and stoned; chopped parsley; lemon wedges.

VINAIGRETTE DRESSING: 1 tbs lemon juice 1 small
clove garlic, crushed with a little salt;
4 tbs olive oil; salt and freshly ground black pepper;
dash Tabasco sauce.

Remove any brown parts from scallops, keeping coral. Poach gently in a little wine and water about 5 minutes. Drain. Mix all ingredients for dressing in a small bowl and pour over scallops. Add pimiento. Cover and chill for at least 1 hour. Scoop out some of the avocado flesh and add to seafood mixture. Blend lightly. Spoon some marinated seafood into each avocado half and sprinkle with chopped parsley. Serve with wedges of lemon. Serves 4.

Scallops in White Wine Sauce

500 g (1 lb) scallops; 1 cup dry white wine;
salt and freshly ground white pepper;
2 spring onions, halved; ¹/₂ cup water;
60 g (2 oz) butter; 2 tsp flour; ¹/₂ cup cream;
1 cup fresh breadcrumbs

Remove any brown parts from scallops, keeping coral. Put wine in saucepan with salt, pepper, spring onions and water. Add scallops, bring to the simmer and poach for 1 minute. Drain scallops and cut large ones in 2 or 3 slices. Strain cooking liquid and reduce by boiling over medium heat to ¹/₂ cup. Melt 45 g (1¹/₂ oz) butter in a saucepan, add flour and blend until smooth. Add reduced poaching liquid, then cream, stirring until sauce boils. Spoon a little sauce over bottom of 4 scallop shells or ovenproof ramekins, divide scallops among shells and cover with remaining sauce. Sprinkle with breadcrumbs. Put a piece of remaining butter on top of each and brown quickly under preheated grill. Serves 4.

Sautéed Scallops

This recipe can be used as a filling for vol-au-vent cases or crêpes, or served over rice or on its own with crusty bread to mop up the juices.

60 g (2 oz) butter; 6 spring onions, chopped; 1 stick celery, diced; 1 carrot, diced; 2 bay leaves; ¹/₄ cup dry sherry; 500 g (1 lb) scallops; 1 tbs chopped fresh dill or fennel; salt and freshly ground black pepper; sprigs of fresh dill or fennel to garnish.

Melt 30 g (1 oz) butter in a saucepan and fry spring onions, celery, carrot and bay leaves for 3–5 minutes. Add sherry, cover and simmer gently for 10 minutes or until vegetables are soft but not mushy. Remove bay leaves. Remove any brown parts from scallops, keeping coral. Sauté scallops and dill or fennel in remaining butter in a frying pan for 2 minutes. Season with salt and pepper. Add scallops and pan juices to vegetables and serve as above, garnished with sprigs of dill or fennel. Serves 6.

Scallops Newburg

500 g (1 lb) scallops; 60 g (2 oz) butter;
1 sprig fresh thyme; 1 sprig parsley; 2 tbs brandy;
2 tbs Madeira or sweet sherry; 1 cup cream;
2 egg yolks; ¹/₂ cup fresh breadcrumbs;
2 tbs grated Parmesan cheese.

Remove any brown parts from scallops, keeping coral. Melt butter in a saucepan, add scallops, herbs, brandy and Madeira or sherry, cover and simmer for 1 minute. Blend cream with egg yolks in a double saucepan and thicken over a low heat, stirring constantly. Arrange scallop mixture in a flameproof dish. Pour cream sauce over scallops and sprinkle with a mixture of breadcrumbs and cheese. Place under a preheated grill until top is golden-brown. Serves 4.

SCAMPI

See *Prawns*.

SCHNITZEL

A favourite in Germany and Austria, schnitzel is the same thin cut of veal as the French *escalope* and the Italian *scaloppine*. The Viennese version, *Wienerschnitzel*, is found on menus all over the world. **See recipes.**

Vienna Schnitzel (Wienerschnitzel)

Some cooks coat their schnitzels with fine fresh bread-crumbs, some with dry crumbs. In either case, the crumbs should be sieved first so that the coating will cook to an even golden-brown – if crumbs are of uneven size, some will darken too much. The crumbed schnitzels are left 20–30 minutes before frying to allow the egg to harden so that the coating will stay on when cooked. It should puff up in a few places, but never fall away from the veal. Schnitzels can be fried in butter, butter and oil, vegetable shortening or lard.

4 large or 8 small schnitzels, beaten flat to about
3 mm (¹/₈ in) thick; juice 1 lemon (optional);
2 eggs; 2 tbs cold water; 4 tbs vegetable oil; seasoned
flour; fine, sieved fresh or dry breadcrumbs;
60 g (2 oz) butter; 4 thin lemon wedges to garnish.

If desired, marinate schnitzels in lemon juice for 30 minutes before coating. Beat eggs with water, and beat in 2 tbs oil if liked – the oil is supposed to hold breading on securely and help make it crisp. Dry schnitzel well, then coat on both sides with seasoned flour and pat off excess. Dip into egg mixture, allow excess to drip off then dip into breadcrumbs, firming them on with your hand. Chill 30 minutes. Heat remaining oil in a large frying pan, add butter and when foam begins to sub-side, add schnitzels; do not overcrowd pan, cook them in 2 batches if necessary. Cook 2–4 minutes on each side until golden-brown. Put finished schnitzels, uncovered, into a low oven to keep hot while the rest are being fried. Arrange schnitzels on a heated serving platter and garnish with lemon wedges. Serve immediately. Serves 4.

VARIATIONS

HOLSTEIN SCHNITZEL: Follow recipe for Vienna Schnitzel. Garnish each schnitzel with a fried egg topped with 2 crossed anchovy fillets, and sprinkle with a few capers.

CHEESE SCHNITZEL: Follow recipe for Vienna Schnitzel, but use ³/₄ cup breadcrumbs mixed with ¹/₂ cup grated Parmesan cheese instead of plain bread-crumbs to coat them. Before serving, sprinkle with a little grated cheese and some paprika, and a slice of lemon.

ALMOND SCHNITZEL: Follow recipe for Vienna Schnitzel. Garnish each schnitzel with slivered almonds fried in butter.

Plain Schnitzel (Naturschnitzel)

Purists say that a true Naturschnitzel should be floured on one side only, the floured side being browned first, since if both sides are floured the second one will be soggy.

4 large or 8 small schnitzels, beaten flat to about 5 mm (¼ in) thick; seasoned flour; butter; ½ cup beef or veal stock; salt and freshly ground black pepper; lemon juice.

Flour schnitzels on one side and pat off excess. Brown both sides slowly (floured side first) in hot butter. Keep finished schnitzels hot in a low oven while you make the sauce. Add 30 g (1 oz) butter to pan and when it begins to bubble up, add stock and stir and scrape up brown bits from bottom of pan. Season with salt, pepper and lemon juice. Bring to the boil and pour over schnitzels. Serve immediately. Serves 4.

VARIATION

CREAM SCHNITZEL: Substitute ½ cup sour cream for cup stock when making sauce.

SCONES

The fragrance of freshly baked scones promises a treat that is never out of style. These most popular of quick breads can be mixed and baked in 15 minutes to enjoy with tea or coffee, or to provide hot savoury snacks or even the basis of a casual meal. Hot scones with cream and a good berry jam make that delight known the world over as Devonshire Tea. The original West England version uses clotted cream, but whipped cream does very well. See recipes.

Scones

3 cups self-raising flour; I tsp salt; 60 g (2 oz) butter; I¼ cups milk or buttermilk.

Sift flour and salt into a bowl. Rub in butter. Add nearly all the milk at once and mix in quickly with a knife. Add remaining milk only if necessary to mix to a soft dough. Turn on to a floured board and knead by turning and pressing with heel of hand 3 or 4 times. Pat out to a round 2 cm (¾ in) thick and cut into 4 cm (1½ in) rounds with a floured cutter. Place scones close together on a lightly greased baking tray. Brush tops with a little milk and bake in the top of a preheated very hot oven (230°C/450°F) for 10–15 minutes or until well risen and golden. For soft scones, wrap in a tea-towel as soon as they come from oven. For crusty scones, do not wrap, cool on a wire rack. Serve warm with butter or with jam and cream. Makes 12.

VARIATIONS

FRUIT SCONES: Follow recipe for Scones, but stir in 1 tbs sugar and ½ cup sultanas or other dried fruit after rubbing in butter. A little grated orange or lemon rind, or mixed spice, may also be added.

CHEESE SCONES: Follow recipe for Scones, but stir in ⅓ cup grated well-flavoured cheese, ¼ tsp dry mustard and a good grinding of black pepper or a pinch of cayenne after rubbing in butter. Bake scones in a preheated hot oven (220°C/425°F) for about 10 minutes.

CHEESE-TOPPED SCONE LOAF: Prepare dough as for Cheese Scones, place on a lightly greased baking sheet, and shape into a round or rectangular loaf 2.5 cm (1 in) thick. Mix together 45 g (1½ oz) softened butter, a pinch of salt, ½ cup grated cheese, and a pinch of cayenne, dry mustard and nutmeg. Spread mixture over loaf. Sprinkle with a little paprika and bake in a preheated hot oven (220°C/425°F) for 12–18 minutes. Cool on a wire rack. Serve cut in slices and buttered.

HERB SCONES: Follow recipe for Scones, but add 1 tbs chopped mixed fresh herbs, or 1 tsp dried herbs with 1 tbs chopped parsley, 2 tsp finely chopped shallot and 1 tsp sugar after rubbing in butter. Serve with morning coffee or as a savoury alternative at tea time.

CRUSTED ORANGE SCONES: Follow recipe for Scones, but add 1 tbs sugar after rubbing in butter, and use ¼ cup orange juice and ¾ cup milk for the liquid. Press a piece of loaf sugar dipped on orange juice on top of each scone before baking.

SPICED FRUIT PINWHEELS: Prepare dough as for Scones. Roll out to a rectangle 5 mm (¼ in) thick, brush with melted butter and sprinkle with sugar and cinnamon. Sprinkle with mixed dried fruit, roll up and cut into 2 cm (¾ in) thick slices. Place, cut sides up, in a greased, shallow baking tin and bake in a preheated hot oven (220°C/425°F) for 10–12 minutes or until browned.

Wholemeal Scones

2 cups self-raising flour; ½ tsp salt; I½ cups wholemeal self-raising flour; 90 g (3 oz) butter; I¼ cups milk.

Sift self-raising flour and salt into a mixing bowl. Stir in wholemeal flour. Rub in butter, then make well in centre and add sufficient milk to mix to a soft but not sticky dough. Turn on to a lightly floured board and knead gently. Pat out into a round shape, 2–2.5 cm (¾–1 in) thick. Place on a floured baking tray and mark into 8–12 triangles with a sharp, floured knife. Bake in a preheated hot oven (200°C/400°F) for 25–30 minutes or until firm to touch. Cool on wire rack. Break into triangles, split in half and spread with butter or serve with whipped cream and home-made jam. Makes 8–12.

NOTE: Variations given for Scones may be used for Wholemeal Scones.

Gem Scones

For these little 'gems' you need the special irons that have been part of Australia's cooking scene for generations. Country cooks treasure them, many are passed from mother to daughter. You can use small patty tins, heating them in the oven first.

30 g (1 oz) butter; 2 tbs sugar; 1 egg; pinch salt;
1/2 cup milk; 1 cup self-raising flour.

Heat gem scone irons in a preheated hot oven (200°C/400°F). Cream butter with sugar. Add egg, salt and milk and combine with creamed mixture. Sift flour and fold lightly into mixture until blended. Grease hot irons well. Spoon mixture in to three quarters fill each cup. Bake in hot oven for 10–15 minutes. Serve warm with butter. Makes 12.

Pumpkin Scones

60 g (2 oz) butter; 2 tbs caster sugar;
3/4 cup cold cooked, mashed pumpkin (well drained); 1 egg, beaten; 1/2 cup milk;
2 1/2 cups self-raising flour, sifted;
1/2 tsp cinnamon; 1/2 tsp nutmeg;
little milk to glaze.

Cream butter with sugar. Add pumpkin and mix well. Add egg, then stir in milk a little at a time. Add flour and spices and mix to a soft dough. Turn out on to a floured board and knead lightly, then roll out to about 2 cm (3/4 in) thickness. Cut into rounds with a floured scone cutter. Place rounds on a greased baking tray, brush tops with milk and bake in a preheated hot oven (200°C/400°F) for 15–20 minutes or until golden-brown on top and cooked through. Serve hot, split and buttered. Makes about 20.

Savoury Scone Ring

SCONE MIXTURE: 2 cups self-raising flour; 1 tsp salt; pinch cayenne; 60 g (2 oz) butter; 1/2 cup grated cheese; 1 egg, lightly beaten; 3/4 cup milk.

FILLING: 125 g (4 oz) salami, luncheon sausage or corned beef, finely diced; 2–3 gherkins, finely diced; 2 tsp melted butter; 2 tsp finely chopped parsley; 1 small onion, finely chopped;
1/4 cup grated cheese; 1 tbs tomato sauce;
1 tsp French mustard; salt and freshly ground black pepper.

Sift flour, salt and cayenne into a bowl. Rub in butter and stir in cheese. Mix egg and milk; reserve about 1 tbs and stir remainder into flour mixture with a knife. Pat dough out to a rectangle about 20 x 30 cm (8 x 12 in).

FILLING: Mix ingredients together and spread over dough. Roll up from a long side and form into a ring, pressing ends together to join. Cut two thirds of the way through ring at 3 cm (1 1/4 in) intervals and spread slices a little apart. Brush with reserved egg and milk. Place on a greased baking tray and bake into a preheated moderately hot oven (190°C/370°F) 30–35 minutes. Serve scone ring warm. Makes 10 slices.

Fruit and Nut Tea Ring

SCONE MIXTURE: 2 cups self-raising flour; pinch salt; 60 g (2 oz) butter; 1/4 cup sugar;
1/2 cup finely chopped dates or raisins; 1 egg yolk;
3/4 cup milk.

FILLING: 30 g (1 oz) butter, melted;
1/3 cup firmly packed brown sugar;
1/4 cup finely chopped walnuts; 1 tsp cinnamon.

GLAZE: egg white; white sugar

Sift flour and salt into a bowl. Rub in butter and stir in sugar and dates or raisins. Mix egg yolk and milk and stir in quickly with a knife. Pat out dough to a rectangle 2 cm (3/4 in) thick.
FILLING: Mix ingredients and spread over. Roll up from a long side and form into a ring, pressing ends together to join. Cut two thirds of the way through ring at 3 cm (1 1/4 in) intervals and spread slices a little apart. Brush with egg white and sprinkle with sugar. Place on a greased baking tray and bake in a preheated very hot oven (220°C/425°F) for 20–25 minutes. Serve warm. Makes 10 slices.

Crusted Steak Squares

750 g (1 1/2 lb) minced steak; 1/4 cup diced green or red pepper; 1 small onion, finely chopped;
1 cup finely chopped mushrooms; 1/2 cup grated cheese; 1 tbs tomato sauce; 2 tsp Worcestershire sauce; 1/2 cup fresh breadcrumbs; 1 egg; 1 tsp salt;
1/2 tsp black pepper; double quantity Scone Dough (page 472); milk to glaze.

Mix steak with vegetables, cheese, sauces, breadcrumbs, egg, salt and pepper. Press into bottom of a greased, shallow square or rectangular baking dish to make a layer about 2 cm (3/4 in) thick. Pat out scone dough to size of dish and place on meat mixture. Brush with milk and bake in a preheated very hot oven (220°C/450°F) for 10 minutes. Reduce heat to moderate (180°C/350°F) and continue baking 20–25 minutes. Cut into squares to serve. Serves 8.

SCOTCH EGG

See *Sausage.*

SEA URCHIN

A small creature, with a hard, spiny shell, found on rocky coastal shores. Despite their ferocious appearance, sea urchins are edible, and must be prised from the rocks. Wearing strong gloves, cut them horizontally across the middle with kitchen shears. Drain them, and scoop out the orange-pink coral, which is the only edible part. The coral is usually scooped out and eaten raw, with a dash of lemon juice if desired, and fresh crusty bread. Sea urchins are commonly used in Mediterranean countries, being added to a fish soup or an omelette, or used as a basis of sauce for cooked fish.

SEMOLINA

A cereal obtained from wheat grains in the middle stages of flour-milling when the bran, wheat germ and endosperm (the floury part of the grain) are separated. The first millings of the creamy-coloured endosperm is known as semolina.

Semolina can be purchased fine, medium or coarse ground, and is used to make some types of gnocchi (see pages 179–80), as well as breads, puddings and cakes, the latter two particularly in the Middle East and India. Semolina made from hard durum wheat is used commercially for pasta, and flour-coated coarse semolina grains make couscous, an integral part of substantial stews and some desserts in North Africa. Couscous is available from Middle Eastern and Greek grocery stores (see also page 98). Buy semolina ready packed or in bulk from supermarkets, delicatessens or health food shops. See recipes.

Indian Halva

$^1/_2$ cup sugar; $I^1/_4$ cups plus I tsp water; 8 cardamom pods, bruised; $^1/_4$ tsp saffron threads; 125 g (4 oz) ghee; $^3/_4$ cup semolina; $^1/_4$ cup blanched pistachio nuts, shredded; 30 g (I oz) slivered almonds.

Dissolve sugar in $1^1/_4$ cups water, with cardamom pods, and boil for 5 minutes. Remove from heat and cool, then strain, reserving cardamom pods. Heat saffron in a spoon over a direct heat, then pound in a small bowl with remaining water to a paste. Stir into strained syrup. Heat ghee in a saucepan and stir in semolina. Cook over a gentle heat until semolina thickens and mixture is creamy. Add syrup and stir over high heat until mixture is thoroughly incorporated. Remove seeds from cardamoms and crush seeds with a rolling pin. Stir into semolina mixture with pistachios and almonds. Serve warm, piled into individual sweet dishes, or spread out into a thick oblong and leave to cool completely before cutting into diamonds or squares. Serves 8–10.

NOTE: $^1/_4$ tsp powdered saffron may be used in place of saffron threads. Dissolve in 1 tsp water and stir into strained syrup.

Greek Walnut Cake

250 g (8 oz) butter; I cup caster sugar; I tsp grated orange rind; 4 eggs, separated; I cup flour; I cup fine semolina; 4 tsp baking powder; I tsp cinnamon; $^1/_2$ cup milk; 2 cups coarsely ground walnuts.

SYRUP: I cup sugar; I cup water; 2 whole cloves; 5 cm (2 in) cinnamon stick; I tbs lemon juice; thin strip lemon rind.

Cream butter with sugar and orange rind until light and fluffy. Add egg yolks, beating well after each addition. Sift flour, semolina, baking powder and cinnamon. Fold into creamed mixture alternately with milk, and add walnuts, mixing gently. Beat egg whites until stiff and fold into mixture. Pour into a well-greased 33 x 23 x 5 cm (13 x 9 x 2 in) baking dish. Bake in a preheated moderate oven (180°C/350°F) for 45 minutes or until a fine skewer inserted in centre comes out clean.

SYRUP: Combine ingredients in a heavy saucepan and stir over medium heat until sugar dissolves. Bring to the boil and boil over moderately high heat for 10 minutes. Strain. Remove cake from oven and pour hot syrup over cake while still in tin. Allow to cool in tin. When cold cut into square or diamond shapes.

Semolina Cake

125 g (4 oz) butter; $^1/_2$ cup caster sugar; I tbs grated orange rind; 2 eggs; 2 tbs brandy; I cup semolina; I tsp baking powder; 125 g (4 oz) ground almonds.

SYRUP: $^1/_2$ cup sugar; $I^1/_4$ cups orange juice; 3 tbs Grand Marnier, Cointreau or brandy.

Cream butter with sugar and orange rind until light and fluffy. Beat in eggs one at a time, beating thoroughly after each addition. Stir in brandy. Combine semolina, baking powder and almonds and fold lightly into egg mixture. Turn into greased and lined 20 cm (8 in) round cake tin. Place in a preheated hot oven (200°C/400°F), then lower heat to moderate (180°C/350°F) and bake for 30 minutes or until golden on top and a fine skewer inserted in centre comes out clean.

SYRUP: Place sugar and juice in a heavy saucepan, bring to the boil, stirring occasionally, and boil briskly for 5 minutes. Cool slightly, then stir in spirits. Leave cake in tin and pour syrup over, then return to oven and bake for a further 15 minutes. Remove from oven and allow cake to cool in tin. Turn out for serving, sliced, on its own or accompanied by whipped cream flavoured with 1 tsp grated orange rind.

Greek Halva

I cup sugar; $2^1/_2$ cups water; 125 g (4 oz) butter; I cup coarse semolina; 2 tbs pine nuts or raw peanuts; I tsp cinnamon; extra cinnamon to dredge.

Dissolve sugar in water and bring to the boil. Boil for 5 minutes, then set aside. Melt butter in a heavy saucepan and stir in semolina and nuts. Stir constantly over moderate heat for 10–15 minutes or until semolina is a golden-brown. Remove from heat. Reheat sugar syrup to boiling and pour into semolina, off the heat, stirring constantly. Add cinnamon and stir over low heat until smooth and bubbling. Cook very gently for 2 minutes. Turn off heat, cover pan with a clean folded tea-towel and put lid on. Leave for 15 minutes. Spread halva in a lamington tin. Decorate top using tines of a fork to make a crisscross pattern. Sprinkle with cinnamon and leave until cool. Cut into 5 cm (2 in) diamond shapes to serve. Makes about 20 pieces.

Semolina Shortbread

125 g (4 oz) ghee; $^1/_2$ cup sugar; I cup fine semolina, sifted; $^1/_4$ cup flour, sifted; I tsp ground cardamom.

Cream ghee with sugar until light. Add semolina, flour and cardamom and mix well. Leave for 30 minutes. Take a scant tablespoon of mixture, roll into a ball, then flatten slightly and put on an ungreased baking tray. Repeat with remaining mixture, leaving a little space around biscuits. Bake in a preheated slow oven (150°C/300°F) for about 30 minutes or until pale golden. Cool on a wire rack. Makes about 24.

Semolina Pudding

$2^1/_4$ cups milk; 3 tbs semolina (coarse or fine); 15 g ($^1/_2$ oz) butter; I egg, separated; pinch nutmeg, or $^1/_2$ tsp grated lemon rind; I tbs sugar; caster sugar to dredge.

Heat milk, stir in semolina and cook over gentle heat, stirring occasionally, for 5–6 minutes. Remove from heat and beat in butter, egg yolk, nutmeg or lemon rind and sugar. Whisk egg white until stiff and fold into mixture. Turn into a well-buttered 4-cup oven-proof dish and sprinkle top with caster sugar. Bake in a preheated moderate oven (180°C/350°F) for 15-20 minutes or until top is lightly browned and slightly puffy. Serves 4.

SESAME

The seeds of this plant have a multitude of uses. Their nutty flavour and crunchy texture are always appreciated, whether sprinkled on cooked vegetables or salads, scattered over breads and biscuits, or thickly mixed with toffee in sticky sweets.

Sesame seeds have a high oil content, and contain protein and minerals. They are crushed to yield either a pale-coloured, almost flavourless oil which may be used for cooking or salads (it contains a high proportion of unsaturated oils), or a quite different, darker, more viscous and strongly flavoured oil, frequently used in Chinese cooking. This latter oil is sold as 'Oriental' or 'Chinese' sesame oil.

Sesame seeds may also be crushed to produce a thick, oily paste known as *tahini*, which is very widely used in the Middle East (see page 525).

WAYS TO USE

Toasting, or frying in butter, brings out the flavour of sesame seeds.

- Lightly cooked carrot sticks are delicious when tossed with butter and sesame seeds.
- Fried sesame seeds may be added to mashed potato or sprinkled on a cauliflower au gratin.
- Yogurt may be topped with honey and toasted sesame seeds, or they may be mixed into a fruit salad.
- A simple sweet is made by cooking honey to a toffee and adding an equal amount of sesame seeds. **See recipes.**

Sesame Chicken with Rice Noodles

This soup/stew from China's Fukien province is said to rejuvenate the body. The pungent, nutty sesame oil beautifully offsets the chicken and delicate rice noodles.

750 g (1$^1/_2$ lb) chicken joints (thighs, breasts); 250 g (8 oz) Chinese rice noodles; I tbs dark Oriental sesame oil; 2 tbs vegetable oil; I tbs shredded fresh ginger; $^1/_2$ cup Chinese rice wine or dry sherry; 3 cups chicken stock; I tsp sugar; I tsp salt; I small bunch spinach or silverbeet, chopped.

With a cleaver or heavy knife chop chicken into bite-sized pieces. Soak noodles in warm water to cover for 5 minutes, then drain in a colander. Heat sesame oil with vegetable oil in a wok until it forms a haze. Add ginger and stir-fry for 30 seconds., then add chicken and stir-fry until pieces are golden, about 3 minutes. Add wine, bring to the boil and add stock, sugar and salt. Simmer for 30 minutes or until chicken is tender. Stir in noodles and cook 5 minutes. Stir in spinach, remove wok from heat and stand a few minutes. Ladle mixture into heated bowls. Serves 3–4.

Grilled Sesame Chicken Breasts

I tbs oil; $^1/_4$ cup soy sauce; $^1/_4$ cup dry white wine; I tsp dried tarragon; I tsp dry mustard; 4 boned half-breasts of chicken; sesame seeds to coat.

Combine oil, soy sauce, wine, tarragon and mustard. Marinate chicken in this mixture for 2–3 hours. Grill chicken breasts gently under a preheated grill for 4 minutes each side, basting with a little marinade from time to time. Remove from heat, brush all over with marinade and roll in sesame seeds. Return to grill to brown sesame seeds. Serves 4.

NOTE: Chicken fillets may also be cooked over hot charcoal, or in a preheated hot oven (200°C/400°F) for about 15 minutes, basting from time to time.

Sesame Seed Salad

1 lettuce, torn into pieces; 1/2 cup stoned black olives; 2 large ripe tomatoes, cut into wedges; 2 tbs sesame seeds; 15 g (1/2 oz) butter; 1/4 cup Vinaigrette Dressing (page 442)

Place lettuce in bowl with olives and tomatoes. Gently fry sesame seeds in butter until golden. Add to salad and toss with dressing. Serves 4–6.

Sesame Oat Fingers

3/4 cup rolled oats; 1/4 cup sesame seeds; 2/3 cup firmly packed brown sugar; 3/4 cup desiccated coconut; 1 tsp salt; 125 g (4 oz) butter, melted.

Combine rolled oats, sesame seeds, sugar, coconut and salt. Add melted butter and mix well. Press mixture into a greased shallow tin. Bake in a preheated moderately hot oven (190°C/375°F) for about 30 minutes. Cut into fingers when cold. Makes about 20.

Greek Sesame Rings

250 g (8 oz) unsalted butter; 1 cup caster sugar; 3 eggs; 1/4 cup milk; 1 tsp vanilla; 1/2 tsp grated orange rind; 1/2 tsp cinnamon; 1/2 tsp nutmeg; 5 cups flour, sifted; 3 tsp baking powder; 1/2–1 cup sesame seeds.

Cream butter with sugar until light. Add 2 eggs, one at a time, beating well after each addition. Lightly beat remaining egg. Take out 1 tbs egg, add to milk and set aside. Add remainder of egg to creamed mixture with vanilla and orange rind. Sift spices with flour and baking powder, and add to mixture gradually to form smooth dough. Knead for several minutes, then chill dough in refrigerator for 1 hour. To shape biscuits, take a piece of dough and roll into a thick rope about 1 cm (1/2 in) in diameter. Form into rings or figure-eight shapes, brush tops with reserved egg-milk mixture and dip into sesame seeds. Place on greased baking trays. Bake in a preheated moderate oven (180°C/350°F) for 25 minutes or until just lightly coloured. Cool slightly on trays before transferring to wire racks. Store in airtight containers. Makes about 60.

SHALLOT AND SPRING ONION

These members of the onion family are both known by each other's name in different parts of the world. Although a misnomer, what are bought in some parts of Australia as shallots are really non-bulbous fresh green onions.

Shallot: The true shallot or eschalot is often considered the queen of all the onions. Its flavour is intense without being too pungent. Shallots usually grow in clusters, though they can be single, and have long stems and a purplish flesh; the skins can vary from a greyish to a golden copper colour – these are called golden shallots. The shallot is much used in the cooking of northern France to flavour sauces, or in steak, fish or vegetable dishes.

Spring Onion: Two types of fresh spring onion are available. The first is slim and bulbless, except for a tiny bulge above the root, and is sold complete with its long, tubular green leaves. Spring onions may also be called green onions or scallions. Both the white and green parts are used. It is mild, delicious in salads and their dressings. Spring onion is also used to great effect in soups, sauces, savoury butters, casseroles, omelettes and other egg dishes, and in many Chinese dishes as both ingredient and garnish.

The second type of spring onion has a shiny, round white bulb about the size of a walnut, on a long, green stem. This onion is excellent sliced into salads, glazed whole in butter or used to give a delicious onion flavour to soups, stews, sauces, fish, meat or poultry dishes. It is superb with other vegetables such as fresh young green peas (see Petits Pois à Française, page 351).

SHASLIK

See *Kebab*.

SHELLFISH

See *Crab, Lobster* and *Prawn*.

SHEPHERD'S PIE

A great homely dish invented to use up leftover roast lamb but so good in its own right that it's worth cooking more lamb than you need for the first meal just to enjoy it.

Shepherd's Pie

**375 g (12 oz) cooked boneless lamb (weight after
trimming off skin, gristle and larger pieces of fat);
30 g (1 oz) bacon dripping or butter;
1 onion, chopped; 1 cup leftover gravy, or
1¹/2 tbs flour and 1 cup warm beef stock;
salt and freshly ground black pepper;
1 tsp Worcestershire sauce; 500 g (1 lb) potatoes,
peeled; 30 g (1 oz) butter; 2 tbs hot milk.**

Mince lamb or chop it very fine. Melt dripping or butter
in a saucepan and fry onion gently until golden, about
5 minutes. Stir in gravy and bring to simmering
point. Or stir flour into onion, cook 1 minute, remove
from heat and cool a little. Add stock, stirring
until smoothly blended, then return to heat and stir
until boiling. Add lamb, salt, pepper and
Worcestershire sauce. Cover and simmer gently 30
minutes. Meantime, cook potatoes until tender, Drain
well, dry off over low heat and mash with butter and
hot milk. Transfer meat mixture to a pie dish. Spread
potato over and rough up surface with a fork. Place
under a preheated moderate grill until top is golden-
brown. Serve at once. Serves 4–6.

NOTE: To extend meat, 1 can of baked beans and a
pinch of nutmeg can be added 5 minutes before the
end of cooking.

VARIATION

COTTAGE PIE: This is the name for a similar pie when
the dish has been varied by using beef instead of lamb
or by adding diced, cooked vegetables to the filling.

SHERBET

See *Ices, Sorbets, Granite and Sherbets.*

SHERRY

A fortified wine, usually offered as a pre-dinner drink. It is
available in varying degrees of sweetness, dry sherry
being the least sweet and sweet sherry the sweetest.

Sherry is often added to a dish at the last minute rather
than being used in its cooking. Many soups and sauces
benefit from a dash of sherry just before serving.

Rich fruit cakes can be enhanced with sherry, preferably the sweet type. Soak the prepared fruit overnight in
sherry, and when the cake comes out of the oven sprinkle
a little sherry over. Sweet sherry is also sprinkled over
plain cake when used to prepare a trifle, and impromptu
desserts can be quickly made with cake, sherry, fresh or
stewed fruit and cream. **See recipes.**

Sherried Mushroom Soup

**375 g (12oz) mushrooms; 90 g (3oz) butter;
2 tbs flour; 4 cups warm milk; 1 egg yolk;
¹/4 cup dry sherry; salt and freshly ground
black pepper.**

Slice mushroom caps; finely chop stems. Gently fry in
butter until soft. Sprinkle with flour and cook over
low heat, stirring, for 4 minutes. Stir in milk. Simmer
soup 10 minutes, stirring occasionally. Mix egg yolk
with sherry and add to soup. Season with salt and
pepper. Heat carefully, stirring constantly. Do not let
soup boil. Serves 4.

Sherried Veal with Cream

**1 kg (2lb) boneless veal shoulder or leg, cubed;
60 g (2oz) butter; 2 tbs dry sherry; 2 small onions,
finely chopped; 2 tbs flour; 1 clove garlic, crushed;
3 tomatoes, peeled, seeded and roughly chopped;
1 tbs tomato paste; ¹/2 cup veal or chicken stock;
¹/2 cup sour light cream; salt and freshly ground
black pepper; 1 bay leaf; chopped chives.**

Brown veal in butter in heavy saucepan. Pour in
sherry, allow to bubble a little, then remove veal and
set aside. Add onions to pan and cook 2 minutes.
Sprinkle with flour and stir well, then add garlic
and tomatoes and cook for 3 minutes. Remove from
heat and stir in tomato paste and stock. Return to
low heat and bring to the boil, stirring. Carefully
blend in sour cream, and season with salt and
pepper. Add bay leaf and return veal to pan. Cook
over very gentle heat for 45 minutes, or in a preheated
moderate oven (180°C/350°F) for 1–1½ hours.
Remove bay leaf before serving, sprinkled with
chopped chives. Accompany with buttered noodles.
Serves 6.

Spanish Chicken in Sherry

Sweet sherry is not frequently used in savoury dishes
but, in this interesting recipe, it adds fascinating
flavour to otherwise simple ingredients. The chicken
is partially cooked the night before and refrigerated in
its sauce – the marinating is part of the flavour secret
– a deliciously easy main course for a special dinner.

**1.5 kg (3 lb) chicken joints (thighs and drumsticks or
a mixture); about 2 ¹/2 cups medium-sweet sherry;
125 g (4 oz) butter; tiny white onions, or 4 onions,
quartered; 1 x 820 g can tomatoes; 2 bay leaves;
salt and freshly ground black pepper;
¹/2 cup stuffed olives, sliced.**

Place chicken in a deep glass or plastic bowl and pour
over enough sherry to cover. Refrigerate, covered for
2–3 hours or longer. Drain chicken, reserving sherry.
Heat butter in a large flameproof casserole and
brown chicken pieces on both sides over medium
heat. (This will be easier to do if you brown just a few
pieces at a time.) Return all chicken to casserole and
add onions, tomatoes with their juice, bay leaves and
enough reserved sherry to cover ingredients. Season
with salt and pepper. Cover casserole and simmer for
30 minutes. Allow to cool, then refrigerate overnight.

Next day, bring casserole to room temperature and bake, uncovered, in a preheated moderate oven (180°C/350°F) for 40 minutes or until chicken is tender and sauce reduced. Stir olives into casserole and cook for a further 2–3 minutes to heat through. Discard bay leaves. Serve with rice or noodles and mixed salad. Serves 6.

Sherry Sultana Cake

500 g (1 lb) sultanas; 3/4 cup water; 1/4 cup sweet sherry; 250 g (8 oz) butter; 1 cup sugar; 2 tsp cornflour mixed with 1/2 cup cold water; 3 eggs; 1 1/2 cups plain flour; 1 1/2 cups self-raising flour; pinch salt; 1/4 cup blanched almonds.

Simmer sultanas in water and sherry until all liquid is absorbed. Cool. Cream butter with sugar until light and fluffy. Add cornflour mixture and beat well. Add eggs one at a time, beating well after each addition. Sift flours with salt and fold into creamed mixture. Lastly, fold in sultanas. Turn into 20 cm (8 in) round or square cake tin lined with greaseproof paper. Arrange blanched almonds on top. Bake in preheated slow oven (150°C/300°F) for 1–1 1/2 hours or until a skewer inserted in centre comes out clean.

SHISH KEBAB

See *Kebab*.

SHORTBREAD

Eaten all year round but especially at New Year, Scottish Shortbread is famous all over the world, but how many people really know how to make it the Scottish way? The dough must be kneaded for about 15 minutes until it becomes smooth and very buttery before it is pressed into a tin or ring and decorated. If you do as the Scots do, you will have a superb shortbread, crisp yet tender. If making ahead, recrisp in a moderate oven for 15 minutes before serving.

Shortbread

250 g (8oz) butter; 1/2 cup caster sugar; 4 cups flour.

Cream butter until it resembles whipped cream, then add sugar gradually, beating until mixture is light and fluffy. Work in flour gradually, then knead dough for about 15 minutes or until very smooth. Divide dough into 2 pieces and press into 2 x 20 cm (8 in) flan rings standing on baking trays, or sandwich tins. With the heel of the hand push dough out until mixture is very smooth, then smooth over surface with a palette knife. Remove flan ring and crimp edges by pressing edge of dough with the finger and then pinching edge together. If using a sandwich tin, fork edge for decoration. Prick surface of shortbread with a fork. (This is done to release moisture as it cooks, making shortbread crisp.) Bake in centre of a preheated moderate oven (180°C/350°F) for 10 minutes, then reduce temperature to slow (150°C/300°F) and bake for a further 40 minutes.

SHORTCAKE

American shortcake is a luscious dessert consisting of a tender, scone-like cake which is split, filled and topped with fruit and cream, and served warm. Rounds of rich pastry can also be layered with cream and fruit, lemon cheese or passionfruit butter to make a Continental-style afternoon tea or dessert shortcake. **See recipes.**

American Strawberry Shortcake

2 cups flour; 1/4 cup caster sugar; 2 tsp baking powder; 1/2 tsp salt; 125 g (4 oz) butter; 1 egg; milk; 1 tbs butter, melted.

FILLING: 2 punnets (500 g/1 lb) strawberries; 1/2 cup sugar; 1 cup cream; 2 tbs icing sugar, sifted.

Make filling first. Reserve a few of the best strawberries, unhulled, to decorate. Hull remainder and divide in half. Slice one lot in halves, place in a bowl and toss with 1/4 cup sugar. Crush other half of strawberries with remaining sugar. Whip cream with icing sugar until soft peaks form. Refrigerate filling. Sift flour, sugar, baking powder and salt into a bowl. Cut butter into mixture with 2 knives until size of small peas. Break egg into a measuring cup and add enough milk to measure 3/4 cup; mix lightly. Make a well in centre of flour mixture, add milk and egg all at once and mix quickly with a fork until moistened. Turn mixture into a greased 20 cm (8 in) sandwich tin and smooth top. Bake in a preheated very hot oven (220°C/425°F) 25–30 minutes or until a skewer inserted in centre comes out clean.

To serve, immediately turn shortcake out on to a wire rack and split into 2 layers. Place bottom layer, cut side up, on a serving plate and brush with melted butter. Spoon on half of crushed and sliced strawberries, put other layer of cake on top with remaining strawberries. Pile cream in centre and decorate with reserved whole strawberries. Serve immediately while still warm. Serves 8.

Continental Strawberry Shortcake

SHORTCAKE PASTRY: 2 cups flour; pinch of salt; 185 g (6 oz) butter; 5 tbs icing sugar, sifted; 2 egg yolks; few drops vanilla.

FILLING: 2 punnets (500 g/1 lb) strawberries; 1 cup cream; 2 tbs icing sugar, sifted; few drops vanilla.

Sift flour and salt on to work surface and make a well in centre. Place remaining pastry ingredients in well and work together with fingertips of one hand. With other hand, use a metal spatula to draw flour quickly into centre to make a smooth dough. Shape into a ball, wrap in plastic wrap and chill 30 minutes. Divide dough in half and roll or pat out into 2 x 23 cm (9 in) rounds, about 5 mm (¼ in) thick. Place rounds on lightly greased baking trays. Prick all over with a fork and crimp edges with fingers and thumb. Bake in a preheated moderately hot oven (190°C/375°F) 15–20 minutes or until pastry is a pale biscuit colour. Do not allow to brown. Remove from oven and, while pastry is warm, cut one round into 8 segments. Cool pastry on a wire rack. Reserve 8 unhulled strawberries for decoration; hull and slice remainder with sliced strawberries. Place whole pastry round on a serving plate and cover with strawberry and cream mixture. Smooth over and arrange 8 pastry segments on top. Dust with extra sifted icing sugar and decorate with rosettes of cream topped with reserved whole strawberries. Leave 1 hour before serving. Serves 8.

NOTE: Other prepared fresh fruit (sliced peaches, plums, whole raspberries) can be substituted for strawberries, or use about 1½ cups cooked, puréed dried apricots or 1 quantity Lemon Cheese or Passionfruit Cheese (see pages 233 and 332).

Danish Raspberry Shortcake

¹/₂ **quantity Shortcake Pastry (opposite).**

TOPPING: 2 punnets (500 g/1 lb) raspberries; 4 tbs redcurrant jelly; 1 tbs water; ¹/₂ cup cream.

Wrap pastry in plastic wrap and chill 30 minutes. Roll or pat out to an 18–20 cm (7–8 in) round and crimp edges. Place on a lightly greased baking tray. Bake in a preheated moderately hot oven (190°C/375°F) 15–20 minutes or until pastry is a pale biscuit colour; do not allow to brown. Remove from oven and cool on a wire rack. Place pastry on a serving plate and cover with raspberries. Rub redcurrant jelly through a sieve into a small, heavy saucepan. Add water and heat slowly to boiling point, stirring, then boil until thick enough to coat a spoon lightly and last drops are sticky as they fall from spoon. Brush warm glaze over raspberries. When quite cold, whip cream, and, using a piping bag fitted with a 1 cm (½ in) star tube, pipe a border round top of shortcake. Serves 6.

VARIATION

APRICOT SHORTCAKE: Follow recipe for Danish Raspberry Shortcake but use well-drained poached or canned apricots instead of raspberries, and 5–6 tbs Apricot Glaze (see page 9) instead of redcurrant glaze. Brush pastry base with 2–3 tbs glaze before arranging fruit on top, to prevent juices from soaking into pastry, then use remaining glaze to brush over fruit.

SHORT CRUST (SHORTCRUST)

See *Pastry.*

SHORT SOUP

Also known as Wonton Soup, a specialty found on Chinese menus thoughout the world. Wonton are the little meat-filled dumplings wrapped in a square of pasta – short as opposed to the long strands of pasta that go into Long Soup, hence the name. The wonton wrappers are available from most Chinese grocery suppliers, or ask at the local Chinese restaurant.

Short Soup

SOUP: 6 cups chicken stock; 3 spring onions, finely chopped; ¹/₂ tsp sesame oil.

WONTONS: 375 g (12 oz) minced pork; 2 tbs chopped water chestnuts; 3–4 green prawns, shelled deveined and chopped (optional); 1 tbs soy sauce; ¹/₂ tsp Oriental sesame oil; 1 tsp grated fresh ginger; 24 wonton wrappers; 1 egg, beaten; salt.

Place all soup ingredients in a saucepan and bring to the boil. Reduce heat and simmer 3 minutes.

WONTONS: Combine pork with water chestnuts, prawns, soy sauce, sesame oil and grated ginger, mixing well. Place 1 teaspoon filling slightly below centre of each wonton wrapper. Brush around edges of wrapper with lightly beaten egg. Fold wrapper diagonally in half to form a triangle. Press edges to seal, and press out any air pockets around filling. Brush a dab of egg on front of right corner of each triangle and on back of left corner. With a twisting action, bring 2 moistened surfaces together. Pinch to seal. Drop wontons into vigorously boiling salted water and cook until they float to top, about 5–7 minutes. Drain. Place 4 wontons in bottom of each soup bowl and pour hot soup over. Serves 6.

SHRIMP

See *Prawn.*

SIENA CAKE

This 'flat' cake with a nougat-like texture, rich with candied peel, toasted nuts and spices is a particular specialty of the town of Siena, Italy.

Siena Cake

²/₃ **cup hazelnuts, toasted, skinned and chopped; ³/₄ cup coarsely chopped, blanched almonds; 1 cup finely chopped candied peel; ¹/₄ cup cocoa; ¹/₂ cup plain flour; ¹/₂ tsp ground cinnamon; ¹/₄ cup ground nutmeg; ¹/₂ cup sugar; ¹/₃ cup clear honey.**

TOPPING: 2 tbs icing sugar; 1 tsp ground cinnamon.

Mix together hazelnuts, almonds, candied peel, cocoa, flour and spices. Put sugar and honey into a small pan, heat gently until sugar dissolves, then boil steadily until a sugar thermometer registers 115°C (240°F) or until a little of the mixture dropped into a cup of cold water forms a soft ball. Take off the heat immediately and stir in nut mixture. Turn into a lined and greased 20 cm (8 in) flan ring, spread evenly and press down firmly. Bake in a cool oven (150°C/300°F), for 30–50 minutes. Allow to cool then turn out and sprinkle the top liberally with the icing sugar sifted with cinnamon. Cut into small wedges before serving. Serves 8–12.

SILVERBEET

See *Spinach*.

SILVERSIDE

See *Beef*.

SIRLOIN

See *Beef*.

SMØRREBRØD

See *Danish Open Sandwiches*.

SNAIL

A small land mollusc, very popular in France, where it is called *escargot* and found in all wine-growing areas. Snails are also a favourite dish in other Mediterranean countries, where they can be cooked in a spicy tomato stew.

Outside France, it is more common to buy snails, already prepared and cooked, in cans. The large shells are usually sold with the cans, so that the snails can be returned to their shells with a garlic butter, often called snail butter, or *beurre pour escargots*, before heating. This is the most common way of serving snails in France. Allow about 6–8 per person.

Escargots à la Bourguignonne
(Snails with Garlic Butter)

125 g (4 oz) butter; 2 tbs finely chopped golden shallots; 1–2 cloves garlic, crushed; 2 tbs finely chopped parsley; salt and freshly ground black pepper; 24 snail shells; 24 canned snails.

Cream butter well, then beat in shallots, garlic, parsley, salt and pepper. Put a little garlic butter in each snail shell, then add a snail, and fill shells with remaining butter mixture. Place snails in special plates (with indentations for shells, so that they stay upright and butter does not spill). Bake in a preheated very hot oven (230°C/450°F) for about 7 minutes or until butter sizzles. Serve hot, with plenty of crusty bread. Serves 4.

SNOWPEA

Know as *mange-tout* in French, because all of the pea is edible, this delicately flavoured vegetable is one of the easiest to prepare and cook.

The sugar snap pea is a similar tender pea but plumper and shorter than the snowpea. Use as for snowpea.
■ **BASIC PREPARATION:** Simply top and tail them, removing strings at the same time, as though they were young beans.
■ **TO COOK:** Snowpeas are best when lightly cooked to retain some of their crispness. They can be quickly cooked in boiling water, then tossed in butter, or steamed.

Snowpeas are a common ingredient in Chinese cooking, when they may be used whole or cut into short diagonal sections, and stir-fried quickly in a wok.

Braised Snowpeas

2 tbs oil; 500 g (1 lb) snowpeas, trimmed and stringed; ¹/₂ tsp salt; 2 tbs stock or water; ¹/₂ tsp sugar; 2 tsp light soy sauce.

Heat oil in a wok or frying pan, add peas and stir-fry for 30 seconds without browning. Add remaining ingredients, stir to coat peas and cook 1 minute longer. Peas should be tender but still crisp. Serve immediately. Serves 6.

SORBET

See *Ices, Sorbets, Granite and Sherbets*.

SORREL

This plant is sometimes considered a herb, sometimes a vegetable. In appearance it is rather like English spinach but its flavour is lemony and fairly sharp, even bitter, although not unpleasant. It is because of its strong flavour that it is often used sparingly, like a herb.

Sorrel is a spring and summer plant, very easy to grow – the leaves should be picked often and while they are young and fresh. They may be added to other greens in a salad, or cooked like spinach and finished with cream or butter. In France, a handful of sorrel is often added to spinach; in this way, the sharpness of its taste is offset by the mild flavour of the spinach.

Cooked, squeezed dry and puréed, sorrel can be combined with fresh cheese and hard-boiled egg yolks, to refill the egg whites. Delicious soups are also made with sorrel and other greens, or with potato, cooked in chicken stock and finished with cream. A hot purée of sorrel, with or without spinach, goes well with pork or veal, and sorrel makes a classic accompaniment to salmon – indeed, it goes well with any fish. **See recipes.**

Fish with Sorrel

Poached fish fillets coated in a creamy sorrel and spinach sauce.

12 small fish fillets, about 100 g (3¹/₂ oz) each,
skinned; salt and freshly ground black pepper;
90 g (3 oz) butter; 3 tbs finely chopped golden
shallot; 1 clove garlic; 1 bouquet garni (4 sprigs each
fresh parsley and tarragon, 1 sprig fresh thyme);
2 cups dry white wine; 155 g (5 oz) sorrel, chopped;
155 g (5 oz) spinach, chopped; 4 sticks tender celery,
finely chopped; 2 tsp chopped parsley;
2 tsp chopped chives; 1 tbs flour; 1 tsp prepared
mustard; ¹/₂ cup cream; lemon juice.

Season fish fillets lightly and fold in 2, skinned side
in. Heat 30 g (1 oz) butter in a saucepan and cook
shallot until soft. Add garlic, bouquet garni and wine.
Bring to the boil and simmer until reduced by about
half. Strain and set aside. Heat remaining butter in a
frying pan. Add sorrel, spinach, celery and herbs and
cook for 5 minutes. Sprinkle with flour and stir well,
then pour on reduced wine. Bring to the boil, stirring
constantly, and simmer gently 10 minutes. Add fish
fillets, cover and cook over very low heat for 5–7
minutes. Carefully remove fish to heated plates.
Blend mustard and cream, and add to sauce with
lemon juice to taste. Adjust seasoning. Pour sauce
over fish and serve immediately. Serves 6.

Sorrel Soup

1 small onion, finely chopped; 45 g (1¹/₂ oz) butter;
2 medium potatoes, peeled and diced;
4 cups chicken stock; salt and freshly ground
pepper; 2 cups sorrel leaves; pinch sugar;
pinch nutmeg; 3–4 tbs cream.

Cook onion in butter in saucepan until soft. Add
potatoes and chicken stock, season with salt and
pepper and simmer until potatoes are soft. Place
sorrel leaves in blender with potato soup and blend
until smooth. (Do this in several lots.) Reheat gently,
then add sugar and nutmeg, stir in cream and adjust
seasoning. If desired, serve sprinkled with chopped
chives or small croûtons. Serves 4.

SOUFFLE

Highly renowned as a creation of French cuisine, a
soufflé is one of the lightest, most delectable and useful
dishes in a cook's repertoire. Any chef, worth their salt,
can whip up a soufflé on command. And most people
who like to cook and care about what they eat will, with
a little leftover chicken or cheese, reach for the eggs to
make a superb Cheese Soufflé or *Soufflé de Volaille à la
Reine* – a right royal chicken soufflé.

To make a soufflé you need eggs, milk, butter and flour.
You make a sauce, add egg yolks then fold in beaten egg
whites, bake in the oven and, *voilà* – a light-as-air soufflé.
For flavour you can add grated cheese, chopped cooked
chicken, seafood, ham or vegetables – the range is limit-
less. If you want a sweet soufflé, sugar and vanilla are a

natural choice. Liqueurs like Grand Marnier or Cognac,
fruits, fresh or candied and, of course, that great
favourite chocolate, make a sweet soufflé one of the
most popular dishes on restaurant menus.

A word of reassurance, a soufflé is not as difficult
to make as many people think. The soufflé gained a
reputation for being difficult in the days of wood-burning
stoves. With today's excellent thermostatically
controlled ovens, baking a perfect soufflé is assured.

■ **BASIC PREPARATION:** Success with soufflés is simply
a matter of following basic rules:

A soufflé does have to be eaten as soon as it's ready.
During baking, the air trapped in the whites expands and
the soufflé puffs up, but because of its delicate structure
it will not hold up for more than a few minutes.

The flavourings are added in different ways. Cooked
chicken, seafood and vegetables are often chopped
finely, almost to a purée; cheese may be grated. These
are folded into the basic sauce before adding egg
whites. Sometimes the food is cut into thin slices and
folded into the finished mixture, and for some soufflés,
whole, lightly cooked food is added, like a poached
egg, or strawberries.

Eggs should be at room temperature. The main point
to watch when making a soufflé is that the egg whites
are beaten correctly. The whites must have no trace of
yolk, and the bowl and beaters must be dry and free of
grease. Beat the whites until foamy, add cream of tartar
or salt (as indicated in recipe) and beat to a velvety
snow. Test by gathering a little mixture on the beater
and holding it upright; at the right consistency, the
beaten whites will stand on the beater in a firm peak
with a slightly drooping top.

It is the air beaten into the egg whites that makes the
soufflé expand and rise, so it is important to fold them
into the sauce as lightly as possible. Have the sauce
warm (if you have made it ahead, stand the bowl in warm
water). Stir a big spoonful of the whites into the base
mixture to lighten it, then scoop the rest of the whites on
to the surface and fold in, by cutting down through the
mixture with a large metal spoon or rubber spatula.
Folding in the whites should only take a minute or so.
The mixture will blend a little more as you turn it into the
soufflé dish.

COOKING TIMES: A soufflé made with about 1¹/₂ cups
sauce and 3–4 eggs in a 5–6 cup soufflé dish, will take
about 30 minutes to cook in a preheated moderately hot
oven (190°C/375°F). It will rise well above the rim of the
dish. At this stage the centre will be creamy, as some
people prefer. For a well-cooked soufflé, leave for a
further 5 minutes in oven.

A soufflé made with 5–6 eggs requires a 7–8 cup dish,
and will take 40–45 minutes to cook.

TO PREPARE A SOUFFLE DISH: For a savoury soufflé,
grease the dish and dust with fine dry breadcrumbs or a
mixture of breadcrumbs and finely grated Parmesan

cheese. For a sweet soufflé, grease, then dust the dish with a little caster sugar. Remove excess crumbs or sugar by turning the dish upside-down and tapping it lightly on the table.

For a high cold soufflé, to stand above the rim of the dish, cut a strip of foil or greaseproof paper wide enough to be doubled and come 8 cm (3 in) above the dish and long enough to fit around the dish with an overlap of 8–10 cm (3–4 in). Fold over to make a double strip. If a smooth effect on the soufflé is desired, brush one side of the strip with oil. Tie the strip around the dish, oiled side in and fold at the bottom, so that it stands like a collar above the edge.

COLD DESSERT SOUFFLE: The charm of a cold soufflé, apart from its delectable flavour and airy texture, is its spectacular appearance. Its height above the top rim of the dish in which it is set is the clue to its fragile lightness.

The size of the soufflé dish determines the height of the finished soufflé. Sizes vary from individual serving dishes through 12, 15, 18 cm (5, 6, 7 in) diameter and larger. They are usually made with straight sides in ovenproof earthenware, and invariably have a fluted outside and indented rim.

A 3-egg soufflé is made in a 15 cm (6 in) dish, while a larger 6-egg Sweet Sherry Soufflé (see page 483) is made in a large 18 cm (7 in) dish.

Cheese Soufflé

45 g (1½ oz) butter; 3 tbs flour; I cup warm milk; ½ cup grated Gruyère, Emmenthal or similar Swiss cheese; I tbs grated Parmesan cheese; ½ tsp salt; freshly ground black pepper; pinch cayenne; pinch nutmeg; 4 egg yolks; 5 egg whites; ½ tsp cream of tartar.

Prepare a 5–6 cup soufflé dish or 4 individual 1-cup soufflé dishes. Place a baking tray on a shelf in the centre of a preheated hot oven (200°C/400°F). Melt butter in a saucepan, stir in flour and cook over low heat for 1 minute. Remove from heat, cool a little, and blend in milk, stirring until smooth. Return to heat and stir until boiling, then take from heat and stir in cheeses, salt, pepper, cayenne and nutmeg. Beat in egg yolks, one at a time. Whisk egg whites with cream of tartar until stiff but not brittle and fold into cheese mixture. Pour mixture into prepared soufflé dish, tap bottom of dish lightly on work surface to expel any large air pockets, and smooth top of soufflé. Quickly run a spoon around the top of the mixture about 2.5 cm (1 in) from the edge to make soufflé rise evenly in a 'crown'. Immediately place dish on baking tray in oven, close door gently, and turn oven down to moderately hot (190°C/275°F). Bake soufflé about 24 minutes (18 minutes for small soufflés) until it is well puffed up, golden-brown on top and just firm. Have a heated serving platter ready and a warmed serving spoon

and fork. Place soufflé dish on platter, and take immediately to table. To serve, pierce top lightly with spoon and fork held vertically, and spread soufflé apart. Include some crust and some creamy centre with each serving. Serves 4.

VARIATIONS

HERB SOUFFLE: Follow recipe for Cheese Soufflé, folding in 1 golden shallot or spring onion, finely chopped, and 1 tbs finely chopped fresh herbs, such as chives, parsley, marjoram, oregano, in any combination, with the cheese and seasonings. Bake as above.

CHEESE AND MUSHROOM SOUFFLE: Follow recipe for Cheese Soufflé. Sauté 6–8 mushrooms, sliced, in a little butter. Half fill prepared soufflé dish with soufflé mixture, scatter over mushrooms and fill with remaining mixture. Top with mixture of grated Parmesan cheese and buttered crumbs and bake as per recipe.

SPINACH SOUFFLE: Follow recipe for Cheese Soufflé but use 2 tbs grated Swiss cheese, 1 tbs grated Parmesan and ½ cup finely chopped cooked spinach as the flavouring. Measure the spinach after cooking, squeezing as dry as possible and chopping.

Chicken Soufflé

3–4 golden shallots or spring onions, chopped; 60 g (2 oz) butter; 3 tbs flour; 1½ cups warm milk; ½ tsp dried marjoram; I tsp chopped parsley; salt and freshly ground black pepper; 4 egg yolks; ¾ cup chopped cooked chicken meat; 5 egg whites.

Prepare a 6-cup soufflé dish (see pages 481–2). Place a baking tray on a shelf in the centre of a preheated hot oven (200°C/400°F). Cook shallots (or spring onions) in butter for 1–2 minutes. Add flour and cook, stirring, for a few minutes. Remove from heat and add warm milk, herbs, salt and pepper. Return to heat, bring slowly to the boil and boil for 2 minutes, stirring constantly. Remove sauce from heat and cool slightly. Beat in egg yolks one at a time. Add chicken. Beat egg whites with pinch of salt until stiff. Lightly fold into chicken mixture, then pour into prepared dish. Immediately place dish on baking tray, close oven door, and turn oven down to moderately hot (190°C/375°F). Bake soufflé for about 35 minutes. Serves 4.

VARIATIONS

Replace chicken with ¾ cup of any of the following: canned tuna, drained and flaked; diced cooked lobster, prawns or crab; finely chopped cooked brains or sweetbreads.

Vanilla Soufflé

45 g (1½ oz) butter; I tbs flour; I cup warm milk; ¼ tsp salt; ½ cup sugar; piece vanilla bean; 4 egg yolks; 5 egg whites.

Prepare a 6-cup soufflé dish (see pages 481–2) and sprinkle inside with sugar. Melt butter in saucepan, blend in flour and cook 1 minute. Remove from heat and gradually add milk. Add salt, sugar and vanilla bean. Return to heat and cook, stirring constantly, until thick and smooth. Allow to cool. Remove vanilla bean. Beat in egg yolks one at a time. Beat egg whites until stiff and fold into vanilla mixture.

Pour into prepared dish and run a spoon around top about 2.5 cm (1 in) from edge. Stand dish in roasting tin of hot water and bake in a preheated moderately hot oven (190°C/375°F) for 15 minutes. Reduce heat to moderate (180°C/350°F) and cook further 25 minutes. Serve immediately with fruit sauce. Serves 6.

VARIATIONS

CHOCOLATE SOUFFLE: Chop 60 g (2 oz) cooking chocolate finely and melt over hot water. Add to Vanilla Soufflé mixture before egg yolks, then proceed as above.

COFFEE SOUFFLE: Follow recipe for Vanilla Soufflé, but substitute ½ cup strong black coffee for ½ cup of the milk.

ALMOND SOUFFLE: Follow recipe for Vanilla Soufflé, but add ½ cup ground almonds before the egg yolks and substitute ¼ tsp almond essence for the vanilla. Sprinkle with shredded almonds before baking.

Iced Vanilla Soufflé

I vanilla bean, or ¹/₂ tsp vanilla; 2 cups milk;
3 eggs, separated; ¹/₃ cup sugar; I tbs gelatine;
2–3 tbs water; ¹/₂ cup cream, whipped;
I punnet (250 g/8 oz) strawberries, hulled;
caster sugar to taste; dash Kirsch;
shaved chocolate or whipped cream to decorate.

Prepare a 5-cup soufflé dish (see pages 481–2). Split vanilla bean and scald with milk. Cream egg yolks with sugar and pour on milk. Return to saucepan and stir over low heat, without boiling, until thickened. Strain, cool and add vanilla if using. Soften gelatine in water, then dissolve over hot water and add to custard. Stir over ice until beginning to set. Fold in cream. Stiffly beat egg whites and fold in. Put a small tall oiled jam jar or bottle in centre of prepared dish. Pour mixture into dish. Chill until set. Before serving remove jar and fill centre of soufflé with whole or sliced sugared strawberries flavoured with Kirsch. Carefully peel off collar and decorate sides with shaved chocolate or whipped cream. Serve 5–6.

Sweet Sherry Soufflé

I tbs gelatine; ¹/₂ cup cold water;
I¹/₂ cups sweet sherry; 6 eggs, separated;
³/₄ cup caster sugar; I¹/₄ cups cream, whipped;
I scant tbs lemon juice; 9–10 Savoy or sponge
finger biscuits; extra whipped cream to decorate.

Prepare a 7–8 cup soufflé dish (see pages 481–2). Soften gelatine in cold water for 5 minutes, then dissolve over hot water. Stir in sherry and cool, then chill for 30 minutes or until mixture begins to thicken. Meanwhile, beat egg yolks until frothy. Add ¼ cup sugar gradually and beat until mixture is thick and lemon-coloured. Add sherry mixture to egg yolks and combine well. Fold in whipped cream. Beat egg whites until foamy. Add remaining sugar gradually, beating constantly, then add lemon juice and beat until mixture is stiff but not dry. Fold into sherry mixture gently but thoroughly. Spoon about half mixture into dish and stand biscuits at equal intervals round edge, pushing them down to the bottom. Spoon in remaining mixture. Chill until firm. Remove collar from dish and serve decorated with whipped cream. Serves 12.

Strawberry Soufflé

I punnet (250 g) (18 oz) strawberries, hulled;
I tbs gelatine; ¹/₄ cup cold water;
4 eggs, separated; ³/₄ cup caster sugar;
I¹/₄ cups cream, whipped; pinch salt;
few drops red food colouring.

Prepare a 5–6 cup soufflé dish or 6 individual 1-cup dishes (see pages 481–2). Sieve strawberries or blend to a purée. Soften gelatine in cold water, then dissolve over hot water. Put egg yolks with ½ cup sugar in top of double saucepan and cook over simmering water, stirring constantly, until slightly thickened. Stir in gelatine and cool, stirring occasionally. When cold mix in strawberry purée. Fold in cream. Beat egg whites with salt until they hold soft peaks. Gradually add remaining sugar and continue beating until mixture is shiny and holds a definite peak. Fold into strawberry mixture very gently and add a few drops of red food colouring. Pour into prepared dish or dishes and chill until firm. Remove paper collar before serving. Serves 6.

Liqueur Soufflé

(Benedictine or Grand Marnier)

5 eggs, separated; ¹/₂ cup caster sugar;
³/₄ cup brandy; ¹/₂ cup sherry; I tbs lemon juice;
I tbs Benedictine or Grand Marnier;
I¹/₂ tbs gelatine; ¹/₂ cup water;
I¹/₄ cups cream, whipped.

Prepare a 6–7 cup soufflé dish (see pages 481–2). Beat egg yolks with sugar until thick and light. Stir in brandy, sherry, lemon juice and liqueur. Soften gelatine in water, then dissolve over hot water and add to mixture. Fold in cream. Stiffly beat egg whites and fold in. Pour into prepared dish and chill until firm. Remove collar before serving. Serves 8–10.

SOUPS

Originally, soup was basic sustenance – a pot of warming nourishment that brought the family together. Soup was a meal in itself: with a generous chunk of bread and a warm hearth to enjoy it by, it revived many a flagging body and spirit. These hearty soups are still with us today: Scotch Broth, Minestrone, Bouillabaisse, Pea and Ham Bone, chowder and many more, the recipes unchanged by time.

More sophisticated concepts of dining have altered the role of soup. Restaurant chefs have created lighter and more delicate soups for their customers, fond mothers have created soups to nourish a sick and ailing child or more robust ones for the family, home cooks have sought soups to star at a dinner party. Whether you want to make a soup that is a meal in itself, a first course for a family meal, a luxury one for a dinner party, or a chilled soup to tempt jaded appetites on a hot summer day, you will be able to find a recipe for there is a soup for almost any occasion.

Although soup does not necessarily need to be made from stock, and very few households these days have a stock pot simmering on the stove all day, it is good to have stock either in the refrigerator or the freezer ready to turn into soup with freshly cooked vegetables. See *Stock* for stocks used in soup-making.

Stock cubes can be used but they tend to be salty and give a 'sameness' to soups. Liquid packaged stocks now available are useful.

Canned consommé is quite expensive, whereas home-made stock is usually made from ingredients which are very cheap or would otherwise be discarded, and a home-made stock, when made correctly, is nutritious in itself. Canned consommé does have its place, though. When time is short, it is a comforting thought to go to the cupboard and make a lovely soup with this as a base. A touch of sherry, a few herbs, a handful of diced or julienne (matchstick) vegetables, and you have a delicious soup. See recipes.

Soups can be divided into several categories – Consommé and Clear Soups; Cream Soups, usually made with softened vegetables as the base; Fish Soups; nutritious Pulse Soups made from dried beans, peas or lentils; Quick Soups that take only minutes to prepare; Hearty Soups which are often served as a complete meal; and Chilled Soups, refreshing to serve on a hot summer's day.

Consommé and Clear Soups

The term 'consommé' is generally used these days to describe any clear soup. A good consommé starts with a good rich bouillon, clear of fat, then made crystal-clear, and any existing fat cleared by clarification. Beaten egg whites and lean minced beef, or, in the case of chicken bouillon, egg whites and chicken backs, are added to the simmering bouillon. As the egg whites and meat cook, they attract and hold the tiny particles of fat and other matter that cloud the soup. When this mass of solids is discarded you have a sparkling, clear consommé. Serve with a garnish and, if liked, a dash of sherry or Madeira, and you have the perfect start to a meal.

Consommé Double

A consommé made with strongly flavoured clear stock, having a rich brown colour. It may be served hot or cold and jellied, and is usually garnished. It becomes double when the basic soup is clarified with additional beef. Good consommé 'jels' naturally on cooling.

6 cups cold brown stock; 2 egg whites, lightly beaten; 2 egg shells; 250 g (8 oz) finely minced lean beef; 1/4 cup dry flor sherry.

TO CLARIFY CONSOMMÉ: Remove any fat from stock, then place stock in a saucepan with egg whites, egg shells and beef. Bring slowly to the boil, whisking occasionally with a wire whisk. Allow liquid to rise in pan as it reaches boiling point, then draw pan aside. Boil up carefully once more, taking care not to break crust which will form on top. Draw pan aside, lower heat and then simmer soup very gently for 30 minutes. This slow simmering will extract all flavour from meat. Strain through a colander lined with butter muslin, holding back egg white crust with a spoon and then at the end, sliding it out on to cloth. The consommé should now be clear. If not, filter it again through egg white on cloth into a clean bowl. Return to heat and add sherry and garnish. Serves 6.

NOTE: A little sherry can make a consommé but too much can break it. Use a good dry flor sherry – 1–2 tsp for each serving according to your taste. Sherry-flavoured consommé is excellent on its own, but it is often garnished and takes its name from the particular garnish.

VARIATIONS

CONSOMME ROYALE: Break up 2 eggs with a whisk or fork but do not make them frothy. Add 4 tbs cream and season with salt and white pepper. Pour into a small mould or cup and steam or poach this custard for 20 minutes or until set. Allow to cool completely, then turn out and slice into strips or cut into shapes. Add to the hot Consommé just before serving.

CONSOMME CHIFFONADE: Parboil finely shredded tender sorrel or lettuce leaves in boiling salted water for 1 minute and drain them. Add to the hot Consommé just before serving.

Spiced Tomato Consommé

This is similar to the classic Consommé Madrilène, which is a clear soup strongly flavoured with tomato.

This version is lightly thickened and has a well-spiced flavour.

I medium onion, finely chopped; 30 g (I oz) butter; 8 cups strong chicken stock; I x 425 g can tomatoes; I large bouquet garni containing strip lemon rind; salt and freshly ground black pepper; ¹/₂ cup dry sherry; I tbs arrowroot; 2 tbs water or stock; lemon juice.

GARNISH: cream; chopped chives.

Soften onion in butter in a saucepan, and add stock, tomatoes and bouquet garni. Season with salt and pepper. Cover and simmer for 40 minutes, then rub through a sieve. Rinse out pan, add sherry and boil to reduce by half. Stir in sieved soup. Dissolve arrowroot in water or stock and add to soup. Bring to the boil, stirring until thickened. Add a few drops of lemon juice. Adjust seasoning, and serve with a spoonful of cream swirled into each cup and a sprinkling of chopped chives. Serves 8.

NOTE: The soup may also be served iced with a slice of lemon in each cup. In this case, omit the cream.

Borsch Julienne

A light, ruby-red soup. Serve chilled as a first course or, should the weather change, you can serve it hot.

4 cups strong beef stock; 4 beetroot, peeled and grated; I cup red wine; 2 tbs tomato paste; I bay leaf; 3 egg whites, beaten; I beetroot, cooked, peeled and cut into fine julienne (matchstick) strips; ³/₄ cup sour cream; grated rind I lemon; salt; pinch cayenne.

Put stock into a heavy saucepan. Add grated beetroot, wine, tomato paste, bay leaf and egg whites. Cook over a moderate heat, whisking constantly, until mixture comes to the boil, then draw aside and leave for 10 minutes. Strain through a fine damp cloth and place in refrigerator until cold. Add fine julienne of beetroot. Season sour cream with lemon rind, salt and cayenne. Serve soup in bowls and offer cream separately. Serves 6.

Cream Soups

These delicious soups are made with the simplest of ingredients, and their tender, melting qualities appeal to many people who are quite indifferent about eating vegetables.

Cooking the chopped vegetables in a little butter until soft is an important step in making cream soups, but care has to be taken not to brown the vegetables or the colour and flavour of the finished soup will be spoilt. The easiest way to soften the vegetables is to melt the butter in the saucepan, add the vegetables and toss well; then place on top a double circle of greaseproof paper, pushing it well down over the vegetables, cover the saucepan and cook over very gentle heat for about 15 minutes, shaking the pan occasionally.

The addition of cream gives a very smooth texture to the finished purée, but do not overdo it. With cream especially, it's no use imagining that if a little is good, more will be better. Too much 'softens' the flavour of the vegetables and, of course, adds to the calories. Sour light cream, which has fewer calories than regular cream, can also be used.

Use about 2–3 tsp cream, yogurt or sour light cream to each plate of soup.

Green Velvet Soup

2 large, dark green cucumbers; 2¹/₂ cups chicken stock; 30 g (I oz) butter; I¹/₂ tbs flour; I cup warm milk; I tsp chopped fresh dill, or ¹/₄ tsp dried; salt and freshly ground white pepper; ¹/₄ cup cream; snipped fresh dill or chives to garnish.

Peel cucumbers thinly, so that green beneath skin is left on. Halve lengthways, scoop out seeds and cut into pieces. Pureé in a food processor or blender until smooth, adding a little stock to help if necessary. Pour into a jug, add remaining stock and set aside. Melt butter in a large saucepan, stir in flour and cook gently for 1 minute. Remove from heat, cool a little, and stir in milk. Blend smoothly together, then return to heat and stir until boiling. Add cucumber mixture, dill, salt and pepper. Stir in cream. Reheat gently until piping hot. Serve in heated bowls, garnished with dill or chives. Serves 6.

Walnut Soup

125 g (4 oz) peeled walnuts, chopped; I clove garlic, crushed; 4 cups beef or chicken stock; ³/₄ cup cream; salt and freshly ground black pepper.

Using a mortar and pestle, food processor or blender, process walnuts with garlic and a little of the stock until quite smooth. Add to remaining stock. Heat cream to boiling point in a large saucepan, then stir in walnut mixture. Heat gently and season with salt and pepper. Serve hot or chilled. Serves 6.

NOTE: Peeled walnuts are the secret to this recipe. Peeled walnuts can be bought in cans or at a good Chinese grocer. If you have to prepare them yourself, cover the walnuts with water, bring slowly to the boil, simmer for a few minutes, then drain and peel.

Danablu Soup

This soup can be made with your choice of blue cheese.

**155 g (5 oz) Danablu (Danish Blue Cheese);
30 g (1 oz) butter; 2 tbs flour; 4 cups chicken stock;
1 cup cream.**

**GARNISH: 3/4 cup cream, whipped;
3 tbs chopped parsley.**

Mash cheese with a fork. Melt butter in a saucepan, add flour and cook for 1 minute, stirring. Gradually stir in stock and cook, stirring constantly, until slightly thickened. Beat together mashed cheese and cream, and add to soup, beating with a wire whisk. Bring to the boil. Serve in soup plates or small bowls. Garnish each with a spoonful of whipped cream, sprinkled with chopped parsley. Serves 6–8.

Creamy Onion Soup

**125 (4 oz) butter; 4 large white onions, finely
sliced; 1 clove garlic, crushed; 2 cups chicken stock;
2 cups milk; 1 cup very thin, raw vermicelli or
noodles, broken into small pieces; 3 egg yolks,
beaten; 1/2 cup cream; pinch nutmeg; salt and
freshly ground white pepper; 1/2 cup grated
Cheddar cheese; chopped parsley to garnish.**

Heat butter in a large, heavy saucepan and gently cook onions and garlic until very soft but not brown. This will take at least 20 minutes, and they should be stirred often to prevent sticking. Push mixture through a sieve, or pureé in a blender or food processor. Return to saucepan, add stock and milk and bring to the boil. Add vermicelli and simmer gently until vermicelli is cooked, about 5 minutes. Pour a little hot soup into egg yolks and stir well, then add to remaining soup. Cook over a very low heat, stirring constantly with a whisk, until thickened. Add cream, nutmeg, salt and pepper, and stir in cheese. Do not allow to boil. Serve in hot soup bowls, sprinkled with a little chopped parsley. Serves 4–6.

Cream of Cauliflower Soup

An excellent winter soup, this is good chilled as well as hot.

**4 cups water; 1 small cauliflower, broken into small
florets; 60 g (2 oz) butter; 3 tbs flour;
2 cups chicken stock; 1/4 tsp nutmeg;**
**salt and freshly ground white pepper; 2 egg yolks;
1/3 cup cream; finely chopped parsley or
snipped fresh dill to garnish.**

Bring water to the boil in a saucepan. Drop in cauliflower florets and cook for about 10 minutes. Drain, reserving cooking liquid. Reserve about 2 cups cooked florets, and sieve or pureé remander with 1 cup reserved liquid in a blender or food processor. Melt butter in a saucepan, blend in flour and cook, stirring, until a pale straw colour. Remove from heat and add remaining reserved cooking liquid and stock, stirring until mixture is smooth. Add cauliflower pureé, return to heat and stir until boiling. Simmer for about 15 minutes, stirring occasionally. Add reserved cauliflower florets, nutmeg, salt and pepper and simmer for a further 5 minutes. Beat egg yolks with cream. Stir in a ladle of hot soup, then add this mixture to remaining soup, stirring. Heat gently without boiling, then pour into a heated tureen or bowls and sprinkle with parsley. Or chill and serve sprinkled with parsley or dill. Serves 6.

Potage Cressonière
(Watercress Soup)

**60 g (2 oz) butter; 1 clove garlic, chopped;
1 onion, chopped; 2 potatoes, peeled and thinly
sliced; 1 tbs salt; 1/4 tsp black pepper; 1 cup water;
1 bunch watercress; 2 cups milk; 2 egg yolks;
1/2 cup cream.**

Heat butter in a large saucepan. Add garlic and onions and cook, covered, until tender, about 5 minutes. Add potatoes, salt, pepper and water. Cover and bring to boil. Reduce heat and simmer 15 minutes or until potatoes are almost tender. Discard thick hairy stems from watercress. Cut remaining watercress stems into short lengths. Coarsely chop leaves. Add all the watercress stems, half the leaves and milk to potato mixture and continue cooking 15 minutes. Purée in blender or food processor. Return to saucepan and reheat. Beat together egg yolks and cream. Add a ladle of hot soup, mix well, and stir into remaining soup. Cook gently, stirring constantly, until slightly thickened. Garnish with remaining watercress leaves and serve immediately. Serves 4–6.

Cream of Broccoli Soup

**1 onion, sliced; 1 carrot, sliced; 1 small stick celery
with leaves, sliced; 1 clove garlic; 1/2 cup water;
2 cups coarsely chopped cooked broccoli;
1 tsp salt; generous pinch cayenne; 1/2 cup cooked
macaroni; 2 cups chicken stock; 1/2 cup cream;
sour cream to serve.**

Place onion, carrot, celery, garlic and water in a saucepan, bring to the boil and simmer, covered, for 10 minutes. Add broccoli, salt, cayenne and macaroni.

Purée in a blender or food processor. With motor running, add stock and cream. Alternatively, sieve broccoli mixture and stir in stock and cream. Chill and serve topped with sour cream. Serve 4–6.

Fresh Mushroom Cream Soup

Raw mushrooms are pureéd then merely reheated giving a true fresh mushroom taste.

5 cups chicken stock; I clove garlic, crushed; 250 g (8 oz) large mushrooms; 60 g (2 oz) butter; I egg yolk; ¹/₂ cup cream; 2 button mushrooms, thinly sliced; Croûtons (page 105) to serve.

Heat stock and garlic. Roughly chop large mushrooms. Place about one third in a blender or food processor with one third of the butter and stock. Purée until smooth then transfer to a saucepan. Purée remaining mushrooms, butter and stock in 2 batches. Heat mixture gently until very hot, season with salt and pepper. Beat egg yolk with cream until blended. Stir in a little hot soup then pour this mixture back into the saucepan. Heat gently, stirring, until soup becomes glossy and thickens slightly. Do not boil. Serve immediately garnished with mushroom slices. Pass croûtons around separately. Serves 6.

Cream of Pimiento Soup

I small onion, chopped; 2 canned pimientos (peppers), chopped; 45 g (I¹/₂ oz) butter; 3 tbs flour; I¹/₂ cups chicken stock; I¹/₂ cups milk; ³/₄ cup grated cheese; salt and freshly ground black pepper; ¹/₂ cup cream.

Sauté onion and pimientos in butter until onion is tender but not brown. Blend in flour, then gradually add stock and milk and cook, stirring, until thickened. Add cheese and stir until melted. Season with salt and pepper. Swirl in cream. Serve 4.

Cream of Tomato Soup

5–6 medium, ripe tomatoes, peeled and chopped; I tbs chopped onion; ¹/₂ tsp celery seeds; ¹/₂ bay leaf; 2 cloves; 60 g (2 oz) butter; ¹/₄ cup flour; 3 cups warm milk; I¹/₂ tsp salt; freshly ground black pepper; 2 tbs tomato paste.

Place tomatoes in saucepan with onion, celery seeds, bay leaf and cloves and simmer gently for 15 minutes or until tomatoes are very soft. Stir occasionally. Meanwhile, melt butter in another saucepan, add flour and cook for 1 minute, stirring. Add milk and cook, stirring vigorously with a whisk, until thickened and smooth. Season with salt and pepper and add tomato paste. Press tomato mixture through a sieve. There should be about 2 cups. Reheat tomato pureé, then gradually add to soup base, stirring. If mixture curdles, whisk until smooth. Serves 6.

Cream of Carrot Soup (*Potage Crécy*)

30 g (I oz) butter; 4 medium carrots, sliced; I onion, sliced; 3 cups hot chicken stock or water; salt; generous pinch cayenne; 6 tbs cream; chopped parsley to garnish.

Melt butter in saucepan, add carrots and onion and cook gently until softened, about 10 minutes. Add 2 cups chicken stock or water and bring to the boil. Reduce heat, cover and simmer for 10 minutes. Rub through a sieve or pureé in a blender. Return soup to pan and heat gently with remaining stock. Season with salt and cayenne, then swirl in cream. Sprinkle with chopped parsley before serving. Serves 4.

Fish Soups

Not eaten as much as they should be, fish soups can be very welcome additions to our menus – whether as a hearty chowder, a light delicate bisque, or a luxury soup like Oyster Chowder.

Home-made fish stock is no trouble to make – and what is more the ingredients are virtually free! Your fish merchant will often give you the bones and skins of the fish he has been filleting or will sell you a couple of bream or snapper heads for very little. They will make an excellent foundation for many different soups.

See also *Stocks*.

Oyster Chowder

An American favourite.

2 medium potatoes, peeled and diced; I carrot, finely chopped; 2 sticks celery, chopped; 6 cups milk; I tbs chopped onion; salt and freshly ground black pepper; 2 tbs flour; 60 g (2 oz) butter; 24 fresh oysters, removed from shells; 2 tbs chopped parsley.

Cook potatoes, carrot and celery in a small amount of boiling salted water in a large saucepan until tender. Drain. Add milk, onion, salt and pepper to vegetables and bring to the boil. Cream flour with half the butter to make a paste and add, in small pieces, to boiling mixture. Cook, stirring, until thickened. Cook oysters, with their liquid, in remaining butter until edges curl. Add to soup and serve immediately, sprinkled with parsley. Serves 4–6.

Fish Chowder

4 fish heads, or bones from 4 fish (any kind saved when fish were cooked for a meal); 2 cups water; I small onion, chopped; I clove garlic, crushed; 2 tbs chopped green pepper; 2 tbs butter or olive oil; 2 cups chopped peeled ripe tomatoes; 2 potatoes, peeled and finely diced; ¹/₂ cup chopped celery; I bay leaf; I tsp salt; ¹/₈ tsp black pepper; 250 g (8 oz) fish fillet, cut into strips; I tbs chopped parsley.

Rinse heads or bones and simmer in water 10 minutes. Strain broth and discard bones. Sauté onion, garlic and green pepper in butter or oil until onion is transparent. Add reserved broth, tomatoes, potatoes, celery, bay leaf, salt and pepper. Simmer until potatoes are tender. Add fish strips and parsley and cook gently 5–8 minutes. Discard bay leaf. Serves 4.

Maryland Crab Bisque

1 onion, finely chopped; 60 g (2oz) butter; 2 cups crabmeat, picked over to remove bits of shell and cartilage; 1/2 tsp salt; freshly ground black pepper; 3 cups milk; 1 cup cream; 2 tbs Scotch whisky; a few drops Tabasco sauce; chopped chives to garnish.

Sauté onion in butter until transparent. Stir in crabmeat, salt and pepper and cook over low heat 5 minutes, stirring occasionally. Scald milk, add to crab and cook 5–10 minutes. Add cream and, when mixture is piping hot, stir in whisky and Tabasco. Serve immediately, sprinkled with chopped chives. Serves 6.

Italian Clam Soup

1/4 cup olive oil; 1 onion, chopped; 1 clove garlic; 3 anchovy fillets, chopped; 1 tbs chopped parsley; 1/2 cup dry red wine; 1 tbs tomato paste; 1 1/2 cups warm water; 1/2 tsp salt; 1/2 tsp black pepper; 1 x 290 g can clams, drained; 1 tsp chopped fresh oregano; 8 thin slices Italian bread, fried in olive oil.

Heat oil in a large saucepan, add onion and garlic and fry until brown. Discard garlic. Add anchovies, parsley and wine to oil and cook 5 minutes. Stir in tomato paste, water, salt and pepper and cook 3–4 minutes. Add clams and oregano and cook 2 minutes longer. Place 2 slices fried bread in each soup dish and pour hot soup over them. Serves 4.

Bouillabaisse

An Australian version of this classic Mediterranean soup.

3 tbs olive oil; 1 onion, chopped; 2 tbs chopped celery leaves; 1–2 cloves garlic, crushed; good pinch saffron powder; 4 tomatoes, peeled and chopped; 2 cups water; 3/4 cup dry white wine; salt and freshly ground black pepper; pinch cayenne; 1.5 kg (3 lb) mixed seafood, such as fish steaks or fillets, cubed; shelled cooked prawns and lobster (optional); squeeze lemon juice; chopped parsley to garnish.

Heat oil in heavy saucepan, add onion and cook until translucent. Add celery leaves, garlic and saffron, then tomatoes. Cook, stirring occasionally, until reduced to a pulp. Add water and wine. Season with salt, pepper and cayenne. Simmer for 5 minutes. If too thick, add a little more water. Add raw seafood and cook gently; the fish will take about 5–8 minutes, but cooked prawns and lobster only need to be heated through. Squeeze lemon juice over and serve garnished with chopped parsley. Serves 4–6.

Dried Bean, Pea and Lentil Soups

Dried beans, peas and lentils make nourishing and inexpensive soups, and should be served frequently by budget-minded people. Although the proteins they contain lack some of the essential amino acids, this can be rectified by serving cheese, milk or eggs separately, or adding a little meat to the soup.

Beans vary in cooking time according to variety and age, and are usually soaked in water overnight before cooking. If you have forgotten to soak them, a quick method to tenderise them for cooking is to cover with cold water, bring to the boil and simmer for 2 minutes. Remove from heat and let stand, tightly covered, for 1 hour; this is the equivalent of 8 hours' soaking. Or you can use canned beans.

Remember that 1 cup bean, peas or lentils will expand to 2 1/2 cups after cooking – this equals two 300 g cans.

See also *Pulses: Dried Beans, Peas and Lentils.*

Haricot Bean Soup

Haricot beans are cooked to the stage where they are soft but not disintegrated to make a thick bean purée. The celery, leeks and tomato should also be very soft, so that they can easily be pushed through a sieve. An egg yolk liaison binds the soup.

1 cup dried haricot beans, soaked overnight and drained; 5 cups water; 1 bouquet garni; 1 medium onion; 1 clove garlic; 4–5 sticks celery, finely chopped; 2 leeks (white part only), or 2 onions, finely chopped; 60 g (2 oz) butter; 4 large tomatoes, chopped; salt; 2 egg yolks; Garlic Croûtons (page 105) to serve.

Cook beans in the 5 cups water with bouquet garni, onion and garlic until tender, about 1 hour. Cook celery and leeks or onions in half the butter until soft but not coloured. Add tomatoes and cook gently for about 10 minutes. Discard onion, garlic and bouquet garni from beans. Combine beans and liquid with vegetables and rub through a sieve or purée in a blender. Return to pan. Season with salt and bring to the boil, stirring. Beat egg yolks with 2 tbs hot soup. Add to remaining soup with rest of the butter. Reheat but do not allow to boil. Serve with croûtons fried in garlic-flavoured oil. Serve 6–8.

Italian Bean Soup

I cup dried haricot beans, soaked overnight and drained; I bouquet garni; salt; I tbs oil; 60 g (2 oz) pickled (salt) pork or bacon, finely chopped; I onion, finely chopped; I stick celery, finely chopped; I clove garlic, crushed; 2 tomatoes, peeled and chopped; I tsp salt; freshly ground black pepper; 8 cups hot water; I cup elbow macaroni; grated Parmesan cheese to serve.

Place beans in a large saucepan with fresh water to cover. Add bouquet garni, cover and simmer until tender, about 1 hour. Season with salt at end of cooking time. Drain. Heat oil in saucepan, add pork, onion, celery and garlic and sauté until golden. Add tomatoes with salt, pepper, hot water and cooked beans. Simmer for 5 minutes. Add elbow macaroni and cook a further 8–10 minutes or until macaroni is tender, adding more water if necessary. Serve hot with a bowl of Parmesan cheese handed separately. Serves 6–8.

Yellow Split Pea Soup

An English speciality.

500 g (I lb) yellow split peas; 10 cups water; I ham hock; 3 onions, chopped; 2 carrots, diced; handful celery leaves; few parsley stalks; 2 bay leaves; I tsp chopped fresh summer savory (if available); salt and freshly ground black pepper; Croûtons (page 105) to serve.

Soak split peas overnight in the water. Next day, put in a large pan and add remaining ingredients. Bring slowly to the boil, cover and simmer gently for 2–3 hours or until peas are very tender. It may be necessary to add more water during cooking to maintain right consistency. To serve, remove hock, celery leaves, parsley and bay leaves and adjust seasoning. Take any meat from hock, chop and return it to the soup. Serve with croûtons. Serves 8–10.

Dhal Soup

60 g (2 oz) ghee or butter; I medium onion, finely chopped; 2 cloves garlic, crushed; I tbs ground coriander; 5 cm (2 in) cinnamon stick; I tsp turmeric; I tsp ground cumin; ¹/₂ tsp ground fenugreek; ¹/₄ tsp chilli powder (or to taste); I cup red lentils; 6 cups water; 2 tbs tomato paste; salt; lemon juice; Croûtons (page 105) to serve.

Heat ghee or butter in saucepan and gently fry onion and garlic until golden. Add spices and cook for 2 minutes, stirring constantly. Add lentils and water with tomato paste and salt. Simmer, covered, for 30 minutes. Remove cinnamon stick. With a wooden spoon, mash some lentils against side of pan, so you have a thickened soup with some whole lentils in it or

purée in a blender until smooth. Add lemon juice, adjust seasoning and serve with croûtons. Serves 6.

Lentil and Lemon Soup

I cup red lentils; 6 cups water; salt and freshly ground black pepper; 3 rashers streaky bacon, rind removed and diced; 3 potatoes, peeled and diced; I tbs lemon juice.

Put lentils into a large saucepan with the water, and add a large pinch each of salt and pepper and the bacon. Bring to the boil, then reduce heat and simmer, covered, for 1¹/₂ hours or until lentils are soft. Add diced potatoes and simmer for 20 minutes longer or until potatoes are soft. Mix well so potatoes thicken soup, then add lemon juice. Serve very hot. Serves 6.

Pea Soup

A Canadian recipe, good with crisp, butter-fried croûtons or sour black bread.

I cup yellow split peas; 6 cups cold water; 250 g (8 oz) pickled (salt) pork, finely chopped; I large onion, chopped; 2 sticks celery, chopped; 2 medium carrots, chopped; ¹/₄ cup chopped parsley; salt and freshly ground black pepper; ¹/₂ tsp ground allspice.

Soak peas overnight in water to cover. Next day, boil in soaking water for 10 minutes and drain. Return peas to saucepan and add the cold water and remaining ingredients. Cover pan and simmer over very low heat for 2–3 hours or until peas have become a mush. Adjust seasoning. Serves 6.

Quickly Made Soups

There are times when you want to supplement a meal with another course, or decide at the last minute to make a soup. Perhaps the avocado you planned to use is overripe, or you have more tomatoes than you can use in salads. Here are some soups that can be made in minutes even without home-made stock. A few cans of beef or chicken consommé, stock cubes or packets, or those interesting packets of Japanese soups, are all useful to have on hand for such emergencies, and in some of the recipes no stock is needed – just a few vegetables.

Italian Egg Drop Soup

In many different parts of the world, egg is added to clear broth to make a light, nourishing soup. This Italian version has a fluffy, creamy texture – with cheese for extra flavour.

6 cups beef or chicken stock; salt and freshly ground black pepper; 3 eggs, separated; 4 tbs grated Parmesan cheese; nutmeg.

Heat stock in a large saucepan and season with salt and pepper. Beat egg whites until they form soft peaks; beat yolks lightly. Combine whites and yolks with cheese and a few gratings of nutmeg. When soup boils, stir in egg mixture, then remove from heat and serve immediately. Pass a basket of crusty bread. Serves 6.

Clear Soup with Ravioli

7 cups beef stock; $1/2$ cup dry white wine or vermouth; 3 tbs tomato paste; I bay leaf; salt and freshly ground black pepper; 24–30 frozen ravioli (about $1/2$ x 500 g/I lb packet); grated Parmesan cheese to serve.

Place stock, wine or vermouth, tomato paste and bay leaf in a large saucepan and blend together. Heat until soup boils, then season with salt and pepper. Add ravioli to pan and simmer until tender, about 20 minutes. Remove bay leaf and ladle soup into bowls. Sprinkle with a little grated Parmesan cheese and serve with extra Parmesan. Serves 6.

Meatball and Spinach Soup
(Chinese)

SOUP: 8 cups beef or chicken stock; I leek or 8 spring onions, finely sliced; I tsp finely chopped fresh ginger; 2 tbs Chinese rice wine or medium dry sherry; 6 tender spinach leaves, finely sliced; salt and freshly ground black pepper.

MEATBALLS: 250 g (8 oz) lean minced beef; 4 shallots, finely chopped; I tsp finely chopped fresh ginger; $1/2$ tsp salt; I tbs cornflour; I tbs light soy sauce; I egg.

Place soup ingredients in a large saucepan. Bring to the boil and simmer for 5 minutes.
MEATBALLS: Mix ingredients and form into small, marble-sized balls. Drop into simmering soup and cook a further 6–8 minutes or until meatballs are cooked through. Serves 6.

Zuppa alla Pavese

A simple chicken broth is enriched with egg, Parmesan cheese and toasted bread to become a soup fit for a king: this soup was served to King Francis I of France by an enterprising Italian farmer's wife. His Royal Highness enjoyed it so much he declared: 'What you have given me is a king's soup!'

90 g (3 oz) butter; 6 thick slices Vienna bread; 6 eggs; salt; $1/2$ cup grated Parmesan cheese; 6 cups boiling chicken stock.

Melt butter in a frying pan and sauté bread until golden. Place bread slices in heated soup bowls. Carefully break an egg into each bowl. Sprinkle each with a little salt and grated cheese. Very carefully ladle a cup of boiling stock into each bowl. Keep stock over heat while working so that it remains hot enough to poach eggs in the bowls. Serve immediately. Serves 6.

Quick Vegetable Soup

You can use any combination of vegetables for this soup, whatever is on hand. It is one of the simplest and quickest soups to make as it doesn't require stock. It is ready as soon as the vegetables are tender. This soup is a meal in itself.

2 tbs oil; 2 cloves garlic, crushed or finely chopped; 3 onions, chopped; I leek, sliced; 250 g (8 oz) streaky bacon, rind removed and diced; $1/2$ bunch broccoli, sliced; 2 carrots, diced; 2 white turnips, diced; 4 potatoes, peeled and diced; $1/2$ Savoy cabbage, shredded; 250 g (8 oz) green beans, cut diagonally into 2 cm ($3/4$ in) slices; 9 cups hot water; salt and freshly ground black pepper; chopped parsley.

Heat oil in large saucepan, add garlic, onions, leek and bacon and cook very gently until onion is soft but not brown. Add remaining vegetables and cook, stirring occasionally, for 10 minutes. Add hot water, bring to the boil, then lower heat and season with salt and pepper. (The bacon may be salty.) Simmer until vegetables are tender – about 20 minutes. Lastly add some chopped parsley. Serve with fresh crusty bread. Serves 8–10.

Soup of a Thousand Infants

This Portuguese soup gets its charming name from the egg, herbs and breadcrumb drops whisked through it.

4 cups chicken stock; I egg, lightly beaten; $3/4$ cup fine fresh breadcrumbs (process in a blender, then push through a sieve); $1/4$ cup finely chopped parsley; I tsp chopped fresh thyme, or $1/4$ tsp dried; juice $1/2$ lemon; salt and freshly ground black pepper.

Bring stock to the boil in a saucepan. Meanwhile, mix together egg, breadcrumbs, parsley and thyme. Drop mixture by spoonfuls into boiling stock, beating constantly with a wire whisk. Stir in lemon juice, season with salt and pepper to taste and serve at once. Serves 4.

Ten–Minute Tomato Soup

750 g ($1 1/2$ lb) tomatoes, peeled and chopped; I clove garlic, crushed; 2 tbs chopped parsley; 3 tbs olive oil; 3 cups chicken stock; salt and freshly ground black pepper; pinch sugar.

Place tomatoes in saucepan with garlic, parsley and olive oil. Cook gently for about 5 minutes. Add stock, salt, pepper and sugar and cook for a further 5 minutes. This soup can be eaten hot or chilled. Serves 4–6.

Beetroot Soup

3 beetroot, peeled and shredded; $^1/_2$ onion, finely
chopped; 4 cups chicken stock; 2 tomatoes, peeled,
seeded and chopped; pinch nutmeg;
salt and freshly ground black pepper;
1–2 sweet and sour gherkins, chopped;
sour cream to serve (optional).

Place beetroot in a heavy saucepan with onion and
$^3/_4$ cup chicken stock. Cover and cook gently for 5
minutes. Add tomatoes with remaining heated stock
and bring to the boil. Season with nutmeg and – only
if necessary – salt and pepper. Add gherkins. Serve
with a swirl of sour cream, if liked. Serves 6.

Hearty Soups

Some soups are almost a meal in themselves. It is a
mistake to serve such soups as part of a substantial
three-course meal. Their role is quite different. Serve
them for weekend lunches or suppers, followed by a
crisp green salad and a piece of fruit, and you have a
nourishing and satisfying meal.

Many of these soups are old traditional recipes,
brought up to date, and made more in keeping with
today's healthy approach to eating by using a good
stock that is prepared in advance, and then only quickly
and lightly cooking vegetables. This way you get the
maximum nutrition, the minerals drawn out from the
long, slow cooking of the bones, and the vitamins
retained in the quickly cooked vegetables. Soups taste
better for this treatment.

In almost all of these soups a generous handful of
parsley or a choice of fresh herbs added to the soup
plate on serving can only be an added bonus.

Mutton Broth

A Scottish soup. Serve with fresh crusty bread.

750 g (1$^1/_2$ lb) scrag neck of mutton or lamb;
8 cups water or white stock; 1 tbs salt;
$^1/_2$ cup chopped celery; 2 carrots, diced;
1 parsnip, diced; 1 turnip, diced; 2 onions, diced;
freshly ground black pepper; chopped parsley.

Remove as much fat as possible from mutton/lamb
and cut meat into small pieces. Cover the meat and
bones with the water or stock and bring slowly to the
boil. Remove scum, then add salt and simmer for 1
hour. Add diced vegetables and pepper. Continue
cooking gently, covered, for another hour. Remove
bones, cut any pieces of meat off bones and return
these to broth. Skim to remove any fat using
absorbent paper towels if necessary, adjust seasoning
to taste and serve sprinkled with parsley. Serves 8.

Portuguese Chicken Soup with Mint

1 x size 20 roasting chicken, or 2 kg (4 lb) chicken
pieces; 1 large onion, finely chopped; 1 tsp salt;
8 cups water, stock or vegetable cooking liquid;
3 tbs rice; $^1/_3$ cup lemon juice;
6 tbs chopped fresh mint.

TO SERVE: sprigs fresh mint; lemon slices.

Put chicken or pieces, onion and salt in a very large
saucepan. Add water, stock or vegetable cooking
liquid and bring slowly to the boil. Simmer for about
1 hour for a whole chicken, less for chicken pieces.
They should be tender without being overcooked.
Using a slotted spoon remove chicken to a plate and
allow to cool. Add rice to broth and simmer for about
20 minutes. Meanwhile, skin and bone chicken and
cut flesh into thin strips. Add chicken to broth with
lemon juice and mint. Reheat gently and serve in
heated bowls over sprigs of mint. Garnish each
serving with lemon slices. Serves 6–8.

Meat and Vegetable Soup

1 tbs oil; 30 g (1 oz) butter; 1 kg (2 lb) meaty soup
bones; 2 onions, chopped; 2 carrots, chopped;
$^1/_2$ turnip, chopped; 1 ripe tomato, peeled and
chopped; 2 sticks celery, chopped;
$^1/_2$ cup parsley sprigs; 2 tsp brown sugar;
3 beef stock cubes, crumbled (optional);
8 cups water; salt and freshly ground black pepper;
$^3/_4$ cup shelled peas (fresh or frozen);
2 tbs chopped parsley; toast points to serve.

Heat oil and butter in a large, heavy saucepan. Add
bones and brown over medium heat. Remove bones.
Add chopped vegetables and cook for 5 minutes,
stirring several times. Add parsley sprigs, sugar, stock
cubes and water. Season lightly with salt and pepper,
return bones to pan and simmer gently, covered, for
2$^1/_2$ hours. Take bones out, remove meat and dice.
Return the meat to saucepan with peas. Simmer
uncovered until peas are tender, about 10 minutes for
fresh peas or 3 minutes for frozen. Adjust seasoning
and stir in chopped parsley. Serve soup with toast
points. Serves 8–10.

Chicken Corn Soup

1 chicken, cut into pieces; 8 cups water; 1 tbs salt;
$^1/_4$ tsp saffron powder; 125 g (4 oz) noodles;
2 cups fresh corn kernels, cut from cob; freshly
ground black pepper; chopped parsley;
2 hard-boiled eggs, chopped.

Cover chicken with water in a saucepan, add salt and
saffron and bring to the boil. Lower heat, cover and
simmer until tender, about 2 hours. Remove chicken
from stock and take meat from skin and bones. Chop

meat and return to stock. Bring back to the boil. Add noodles and corn and cook until noodles are tender. Season with salt and pepper, and stir in a little chopped parsley and the eggs. Serves 6.

Herbed Pumpkin Soup

60 g (2 oz) butter; 1 large onion, finely chopped; 1.5 kg (3 lb) pumpkin, peeled, seeded and chopped; 1 tbs flour; 5 cups boiling water; 1 chicken stock cube; 1 cup hot milk; 1 tbs butter, or 3 tbs cream; salt and freshly ground black pepper; nutmeg; 2 tbs chopped mixed fresh herbs (parsley with a little oregano, thyme); Croûtons (page 105) to garnish.

Melt butter in a heavy saucepan and add onion and pumpkin. Cover and cook over a low heat about 10 minutes. Sprinkle flour over vegetables and cook over moderate heat for about 5 minutes, stirring frequently. Combine water and stock cube, add to pan and simmer, covered, until tender. Cool slightly, then sieve, or purèe in blender with a little milk. Gradually stir in hot milk and simmer gently for about 5 minutes. Just before serving, and for a richer soup, swirl in butter or cream. Season with salt, pepper and a little nutmeg, and stir in herbs. Serve hot, garnished with croûtons. Serves 6.

Pot Herb Soup

1 leek, sliced; 1 cup shelled fresh green peas; 3 cups chicken stock; 6 sprigs fresh chives; 6 sprigs fresh chervil; 6 sprigs parsley; 30 g (1 oz) butter; 1 tbs flour; 1/2 cup milk; salt and freshly ground black pepper; 2 spring onions, finely chopped; 2 egg yolks; 1/4 cup cream.

Cook leek and peas in 2½ cups stock until tender. Meanwhile, finely chop chives, chervil and parsley. Melt butter in a saucepan, add flour and cook for 1 minute, stirring. Bring milk and remaining stock to the boil, then add to butter-flour mixture, stirring vigorously with a whisk. Season with salt and pepper. Add leek and peas with liquid in which they were cooked, spring onions and herbs and mix well. Beat egg yolks with cream and add to soup.

Cook gently, stirring constantly until thickened, but do not let boil. Adjust seasoning to taste and serve hot. Serves 6.

Potato Soup with Gruyère and Parmesan Cheese

4 large potatoes, peeled and diced; 3 cups chicken stock; 1½ cups milk, scalded; pinch nutmeg; salt and freshly ground white pepper; 2/3 cup grated Gruyère or Emmenthal cheese; 1/3 cup grated Parmesan cheese.

Cook potatoes in boiling stock for about 20 minutes or until very tender. Purée potatoes and stock in a blender or rub through a sieve until very smooth. Stir in milk, nutmeg, salt and pepper and simmer until heated through. Divide soup among 4 flameproof bowls and sprinkle each with 2 tbs of Gruyère then 1 tbs of Parmesan. Place under a preheated grill for about 2 minutes or until cheese is melted and bubbling. Serves 4.

Lyons Velvet (Onion Soup Lyonnaise)

45 g (1½ oz) butter; 1 tbs oil; 750 g (1½ lb) onions, finely sliced; 1 tsp salt; 2 tbs flour; 6 cups boiling beef stock; 1/2 cup dry white wine or vermouth; freshly ground black pepper; 4 eggs; 155 g (5 oz) Swiss cheese, finely grated; 2 tbs brandy; 6 slices dry, crustless toast to serve.

Heat butter and oil in a large, heavy saucepan and cook onions gently for 25–30 minutes or until very soft, stirring occasionally. Be careful not to let them burn. Sprinkle salt and flour into pan and stir over medium heat for 2 minutes. Remove from heat and blend in boiling stock. Add wine, season with pepper and strain soup into a large earthenware bowl. (Save the onions to use in a meat loaf, scrambled eggs etc.) Tip soup back into pan and reheat. Beat eggs until light in bowl that has been heated with soup, and stir in cheese. When soup is boiling, pour slowly into bowl, beating all the time. The boiling liquid will partially cook eggs, and soup will turn thick and creamy. Still beating, add brandy and blend into soup. Have ready slices of dry toast in 6 deep, heated bowls, and ladle soup over. Serve immediately. Serves 6.

French Onion Soup

45 g (1½ oz) butter; 1 tbs oil; 4–5 onions, finely sliced; 1 tbs salt; 2 tbs flour; 8 cups boiling beef stock; 1/2 cup dry white wine or dry vermouth; freshly ground black pepper; 2 tbs brandy (optional).

GARNISH: slices French bread; 1 cup grated Swiss, or 1/2 cup Parmesan cheese.

Melt butter in a large heavy saucepan, add oil and cook onions gently for 20–30 minutes, stirring occasionally. Be careful not to burn onions. Sprinkle in salt and flour and stir over moderate heat 3 minutes. Remove from heat and blend in boiling stock. Add wine. Season with pepper. Return to heat, cover and simmer for 30–40 minutes, skimming occasionally.

GARNISH: Put bread in one layer in shallow baking tin. Bake in a preheated moderately slow oven (160°C/325°F) for about 30 minutes or until crisp and lightly coloured. If desired, bread can be brushed with a little olive oil halfway through cooking, and after baking, each slice rubbed lightly with cut clove of garlic.

Just before serving soup, adjust seasoning and stir in brandy. Pour into heated soup tureen or soup cups over bread slices. Serve cheese separately. Serves 6–8.

VARIATION

FRENCH ONION SOUP GRATINEE: Follow recipe for French Onion Soup. Put prepared bread into a heat-proof deep casserole dish or soup tureen or individual heatproof bowls and top with 125 g (4 oz) Swiss cheese, cut into fine slivers. Pour boiling soup over. Sprinkle 3 tbs grated Parmesan cheese over and put under a preheated hot grill until cheese melts and browns lightly. Serve immediately.

Leek and Potato Soup
(Potage Bonne Femme)

30 g (I oz) butter; 2 leeks, finely sliced; salt and freshly ground black pepper; 2 medium potatoes, peeled and diced; 3 cups chicken stock; I cup hot milk; little extra butter; Croûtons (page I05) or chopped parsley to garnish.

Melt butter in a heavy saucepan, add leeks and cook over a low heat until soft but not brown. Season with a little salt and pepper, then add potatoes. Stir in chicken stock. Cover and simmer gently for about 30 minutes or until potato is tender. Blend in hot milk and a little extra butter. Adjust seasoning. Serve hot garnished with croûtons or chopped parsley. Serves 6.

VARIATION

POTAGE PARMENTIER: Follow recipe for Leek and Potato Soup, or use any left over, then sieve or purée in blender or food processor fitted with a steel blade (this should be done a few cupfuls at a time). Reheat and serve hot, sprinkled with parsley or croûtons.

Goulash Soup

Make this hearty soup the day before eating. It is often served in the crowded beer halls in Munich, Germany.

60 g (2 oz) speck or bacon, cut into strips; I large onion, finely chopped; I¹/₂ tbs paprika; 500 g (I lb) shin of beef, cubed; I tsp salt; freshly ground black pepper; 2 tbs vinegar; I tbs tomato paste; I tbs caraway seeds (optional); I clove garlic, crushed; ¹/₂ tsp dried marjoram; 8 cups beef stock; 3 medium potatoes, peeled and diced.

Heat speck or bacon strips in a large pan until fat runs. If speck is very lean, add a little oil. Add onion and cook with speck until it is golden. Sprinkle with paprika and stir for 1 minute, then add meat and brown very lightly. Stir in salt, pepper, vinegar and tomato paste. Simmer for 3–4 minutes, then add caraway seeds, garlic, marjoram and stock. Bring to the boil, cover and simmer over a very low heat for 45 minutes or until meat is almost tender. Add potatoes and cook for a further 20 minutes or until potato is tender. Adjust seasoning before serving. Serves 6.

Chilled Soups

These seem to have a special charm on hot summer days – and, of course, they have the added bonus for the cook in that they can be prepared in the morning, left in the refrigerator ready to be served … and should the weather turn chilly, most of them can be heated gently.

Take care when seasoning cold soups – they may need a little extra salt before serving and, if a cream soup, don't have it too thick; it should be of a pleasantly flowing consistency.

Finely chopped fresh herbs give a pretty finish to a chilled soup, and a wonderful perfume as well. Add a swirl of cream or sour cream to chilled creamy soups before serving.

Cream of Curried Pea Soup

I cup shelled fresh or frozen peas; I onion, sliced; I carrot, sliced; I stick celery with leaves, sliced; I potato, peeled and sliced; I clove garlic; I tsp salt; I tsp curry powder; 3 cups chicken stock; I cup cream; whipped cream to serve.

Place vegetables, garlic, salt, curry powder and 1 cup stock in a saucepan and bring to the boil. Cover, reduce heat and simmer for 15 minutes. Sieve or purée in a blender, then stir in remaining stock and cream. Chill, and serve topped with whipped cream. Serves 6.

Vichyssoise

A classic cold soup that can be served hot.

60 g (2 oz) butter; 4 leeks, finely sliced; salt and freshly ground white pepper; 4 medium potatoes, peeled and diced; 6 cups chicken stock; 2 cups hot milk; I cup cream.

GARNISH: sour cream; snipped chives.

Melt butter in a saucepan, add leeks and cook over a low heat until soft but not brown. Season with a little salt and pepper, and add potatoes. Stir in stock. Cover and simmer for about 30 minutes or until potato is tender. Blend in hot milk. Allow soup to cool, then sieve or purée in a blender or food processor. Chill. Stir in cream. To serve, top with a spoonful of sour cream if liked, and sprinkle with finely snipped chives. Serves 6–8.

Cucumber Buttermilk Soup

2 small cucumbers, peeled, seeded and diced; 3 cups buttermilk; salt and freshly ground black pepper; dash Tabasco sauce.

Place cucumbers in a bowl, cover with ice cubes and soak for about 2 hours. Drain cucumbers thoroughly. Add buttermilk, seasoning and Tabasco. Chill well. Serves 4.

Iced Lebanese Soup

I large green cucumber, peeled, seeded and diced; salt and freshly ground black pepper; $^1/_2$ cup strong chicken stock; $^1/_2$ cup tomato juice; 3 cups plain yogurt; $^1/_2$ cup cream; 600 g (I$^1/_4$ lb) small cooked prawns, shelled and deveined; I clove garlic, halved.

GARNISH: I tbs chopped fresh mint; I hard-boiled egg, finely chopped.

Place cucumber on a plate set at a slight tilt (put a wooden spoon under one side) and sprinkle lightly with salt. Leave aside for salt to draw out some juice from cucumber. Mix stock, tomato juice and yogurt together until well combined and smooth, and stir in cream. Rinse cucumber, drain well and add to soup with prawns. Season with salt and pepper and chill thoroughly. Adjust seasoning again just before serving. Rub chilled soup bowls or tureen with cut clove of garlic, ladle soup in and sprinkle with chopped mint and hard-boiled egg. Serves 6.

Balkan Chlodnik

This chilled soup is something like a Russian borsch, but with intriguing additions which include chopped prawns, eggs and beer. With buttered rye bread or pumpernickel, it's almost a meal in itself.

2 large beetroot; 2 cups chicken stock; 250 g (8 oz) cooked prawns, shelled, deveined and chopped; 3 hard-boiled eggs, chopped; I cucumber, peeled, seeded and chopped; I lemon, thinly sliced; $^1/_2$ tbs snipped chives; I tbs chopped fresh dill or parsley; I cup sour light cream; I cup beer; salt and freshly ground black pepper; chopped fresh dill or parsley to garnish.

Cook beetroot in boiling salted water to cover until tender. Drain. Peel and chop beetroot, and combine with chicken stock in a large bowl. Add remaining ingredients, stir well and chill. At serving time, place an ice cube in 6 bowls and ladle chilled soup into bowls. Sprinkle with chopped dill or parsley. Serves 6.

Chilled Curried Zucchini Soup

90 g (3 oz) butter; 750 g (I$^1/_2$) zucchini, chopped; I cup chopped spring onions; 2 tsp curry powder; I tbs ground cumin; 2 cups chicken stock; 3 cups buttermilk; salt and freshly ground black pepper.

GARNISH: $^1/_2$ carrot; $^1/_2$ zucchini; 2 radishes.

Melt butter in a large saucepan and add zucchini and spring onions. Cover and cook over a low heat for 10 minutes, shaking pan occasionally and checking that vegetables do not colour. Add spices and cook for 2 minutes, stirring, then stir in stock. Pureé mixture in a blender or food processor. Pour into a large bowl, stir in buttermilk and season with salt and pepper. Chill for 4 hours. For garnish, slice vegetables thinly on a slant. Chill in iced water for at least 1 hour, then pat dry. Divide soup among chilled bowls, and garnish with vegetables. Serves 6.

Cold Vegetable Soup

A variation on the Spanish gazpacho, a lovely beginning to a meal, summer or winter.

4 tomatoes, peeled and chopped; I cucumber, peeled and diced; I onion, finely chopped; I red or green pepper, cored, seeded and chopped; 2 cloves garlic, finely chopped; $^1/_2$ cup fresh white breadcrumbs; I tbs red wine vinegar; 3 cups chicken stock; 2 tbs olive oil; leaves fresh basil or coriander (Chinese parsley); salt and freshly ground black pepper; $^1/_2$ cup cream.

Mix together tomatoes, cucumber, onion, pepper, garlic and breadcrumbs. Add vinegar, stock oil, and 3 basil leaves or a few sprigs coriander. Season with salt and pepper. Cover and marinate for 12 hours or overnight in refrigerator. Purée in a blender or food processor and strain through a sieve. Stir in cream and adjust seasoning. Serve very cold, topped with thin strips of basil or chopped coriander. Serves 4–6.

Beetroot and Orange Soup

4–5 beetroot, peeled and grated; I tsp salt; I tsp dried thyme; $^1/_4$ tsp pepper; I bay leaf; 6 cups water; 2 cups canned vegetable tomato juice; I cup orange juice; 2 tbs gelatine.

GARNISH: sour cream; 2 tbs snipped chives.

Combine grated beetroot, salt, thyme, pepper, bay leaf and water in a large saucepan. Bring to the boil and simmer 20 minutes. Strain mixture into a large bowl, pressing hard on solids. Reserve 1 cup cooked grated beetroot. Heat vegetable tomato juice in saucepan and stir in beetroot liquid, orange juice and reserved grated beetroot. Take out ¾ cup liquid and sprinkle gelatine over it. When spongy, stir into hot liquid until dissolved. Transfer mixture to a large bowl and cool, then chill, covered. Break up with a fork. Serve in chilled bowls garnished with a dollop of sour cream and a sprinkling of snipped chives. Serves 8.

Cold Tomato Soup

3 cups tomato juice; 2 tbs tomato paste;
1 x 425 g can tomatoes, chopped with their juice;
4 spring onions, chopped; 2 sticks celery, chopped;
1 tsp curry powder; freshly ground black pepper;
grated rind ½ lemon; 2 tbs lemon juice;
2 tsp sugar; 1 tsp chopped fresh thyme, or pinch
dried; ½ cup sour light cream; chopped parsley.

Mix together all ingredients except sour cream and parsley. Chill well, covered. To serve, spoon chilled soup into 6 bowls, swirl a little sour cream into each and sprinkle with chopped parsley. If liked, 1–2 ice cubes may be put into each bowl before adding soup. Serves 6.

Rød Grød Med Fløde
(Fruit Soup with Cream)

Fruit soup is often served as a dessert in Denmark, but it makes a perfect light first course for a rich meal. It's easy to make with canned rhubarb, canned plums or cherries.

2 x 450 g cans rhubarb; 4 cups water;
¼ cup lemon juice; 2 tbs arrowroot or cornflour;
sour cream to serve.

Sieve rhubarb, and its syrup, or purée in a blender or food processor. Mix purée with water and lemon juice in a saucepan and bring to the boil. Mix arrowroot or cornflour with a little water to make a thin paste. Stir in a little hot soup, then pour this back into saucepan, stirring constantly until soup boils and thickens. Cover and allow to cool, then cover and chill. Serve chilled, with a spoonful of sour cream swirled into each bowl. Serves 8.

Chilled Cucumber Soup

30 g (1 oz) butter; 1 small onion, chopped;
1 large green cucumber, seeded and diced;
1 cup watercress sprigs or shredded outside leaves
of lettuce; 1 medium potato, peeled and diced;
2 cups chicken stock; 2 sprigs parsley; ½ tsp salt;
¼ tsp pepper; ¼ tsp dry mustard; 1 cup cream.

GARNISH: chopped chives; diced cucumber; diced radish.

Melt butter in saucepan and cook onion gently until soft but not brown. Add all remaining ingredients except cream and bring to the boil. Simmer until potatoes are tender, about 15 minutes. Sieve or pureé soup in blender or food processor. Adjust seasoning and chill, covered, until required. Before serving, stir in cream and sprinkle with chopped chives, cucumber and radish. Serves 6.

Iced Pepper Soup

A nutritious, refreshing soup that can be made in a few seconds.

2 large peppers, cored, seeded and diced;
2 cups chicken stock; 2 tbs lemon juice;
salt and freshly ground black pepper;
2 cloves garlic, chopped; ¼ tsp Worcestershire
sauce; sour cream to serve.

Place peppers in a blender or food processor with 1 cup stock, lemon juice, salt, pepper, garlic and Worcestershire sauce. Pureé until fairly smooth, then add remaining stock. Adjust seasoning. Chill well. Serve topped with sour cream. Serves 2–3.

Chilled Butternut Soup

1 onion, sliced; 60 g (2 oz) butter;
750 g (1½ lb) butternut pumpkin, peeled,
seeded and chopped; 4 thin slices lemon, seeds
removed; ¼ cup flour; 6 cups warm chicken stock;
salt and freshly ground white pepper;
1 cup cream; lemon juice.

Cook onion gently in butter in large saucepan until soft. Stir in pumpkin and lemon slices, sprinkle with flour and stir over low heat for 3 minutes. Remove from heat and cool a little, then add chicken stock, stirring until smoothly blended. Return to heat and stir until boiling. Season lightly with salt and pepper and simmer, partially covered with a lid, for 1 hour. Discard lemon slices. Purée mixture in a blender and pour into a bowl. Allow to cool, then chill, covered, for at least 4 hours. Stir in chilled cream and lemon juice, and adjust seasoning. Serves 6–8.

Iced Spinach Soup

I onion, finely chopped; I clove garlic, crushed;
30 g (I oz) butter; I x 250 g can spinach, drained,
or I x 250 g (8 oz) packet frozen spinach, thawed;
4 cups chicken stock; salt and freshly ground black
pepper; I cup cream; snipped chives to garnish.

Sauté onion and garlic in butter until transparent.
Add spinach, chicken stock, salt and pepper. Bring to
the boil and simmer for about 8 minutes. Chill. Just
before serving, adjust seasoning and add cream. To
garnish, sprinkle with snipped chives. Serves 4–6.
NOTE: When fresh spinach is available, use it instead
of canned. Rinse 1 bunch spinach, remove white
stalks and roughly chop leaves. Place in large
saucepan, cover and steam, in water left on leaves
after rinsing, about 5 minutes, shaking pan to prevent
burning. Drain well, then chop spinach or purée in a
blender or food processor.

Chilled Melon Soup

I large rockmelon, peeled, seeded and diced;
20 g (²/₃ oz) butter; I tbs sugar; grated rind and
juice ¹/₂ lemon; ¹/₄ tsp ground ginger;
¹/₄ tsp nutmeg; ¹/₄ tsp salt; I¹/₂ cups water;
¹/₂ cup sweet white wine; few sprigs fresh mint
and melon balls to garnish.

Place diced melon in saucepan and add butter, sugar,
lemon rind and juice, ginger nutmeg and salt. Cook
over gentle heat, stirring occasionally, until melon
becomes soft and pulpy, about 10 minutes. Sieve or
puré mixture in a blender. Stir in water and wine
and chill for at least 3 hours. Adjust seasoning, and
serve garnished with mint and melon balls. Serves 4.

Chilled Pumpkin Soup

1.25 kg (2¹/₂ lb) pumpkin, peeled, seeded and
cubed; 4 cups chicken stock; I cup chopped onion;
³/₄ cup chopped spring onions (white parts only);
I cup cream; salt and freshly ground black pepper.

GARNISH: 6 thin slices red-ripe tomatoes;
¹/₂ cup cream, whipped; ³/₄ cup finely chopped
spring onions (green parts only).

Combine pumpkin, chicken stock, onion and spring
onions in a large saucepan. Bring to the boil and
simmer until pumpkin is tender. Sieve or puré
mixture in a blender or food processor. Cool. Stir
cream into soup and season with salt and pepper. Pour
soup into 6 chilled cups and float a thin slice of tomato
on each serving. Spoon whipped cream on to each slice
and sprinkle with green part of onions. Serves 6.

SOY SAUCE

The pungent, salty brown sauce that is essential to
Chinese, Japanese and Southeast Asian cooking. The
best is brewed from naturally fermented soya beans and
can be distinguished by the thick head of foam, like that
on stout, which forms and remains for some time if the
bottle is vigorously shaken.

Different types of soy sauce, some salt-reduced are
available.
Chinese Soy Sauce can be dark or light; both types are
used in cooking and the light sauce, which is the thinner
and saltier of the two, is also used as a table condiment.
Japanese Soy Sauce (*shoyu*), lighter again, should
always be used in Japanese dishes. It is used as an
ingredient and as a dip at the table.
Indonesian Soy Sauce (*ketjap manis*) is thick and sweet
with a salty tang.

All types of soy sauce are available from Asian food
stores. When a recipe calls for 'soy sauce' without further
qualification, it is usually best to use a light Chinese or
Japanese one.

SOYA (SOY) BEAN

See *Pulses: Dried Beans, Peas and Lentils.*

SPAGHETTI

See *Pasta.*

SPARERIBS

There are two types of pork spareribs. The first are cut
from the belly area, giving meaty slices with layers of fat
and lean and some small, cross-cut bones; the second
are the rib bones, together with what little meat joins
them after outer cuts have been removed.

Beef spareribs, often called short ribs, are cut from the
lower end of the set of ribs. They have a fairly high
proportion of bone but are quite meaty.

Spareribs may be sold in individual slices or joined in a
set. They are good barbecued or grilled, often served
with a spicy American-style or Chinese sauce; the
spareribs are usually pre-baked or boiled in order to melt
off excess fat.

Many people like to eat spareribs in the fingers, so be
sure to supply plenty of paper napkins. Ribs can also be
baked, and pork spareribs are braised for wonderful,
hearty Middle European dishes with sauerkraut, apples
and sometimes potatoes, dumplings, sausages or other
meats. See recipes.

Spareribs with Sauerkraut

2 kg (4 lb) meaty pork spareribs;
I x 820 g can sauerkraut, drained;
I large onion, finely chopped; 2 tsp caraway seeds
(optional); dry white wine; I large apple, peeled,
cored and sliced; 6–8 medium new potatoes;
I kg (2 lb) knackwurst, frankfurts, thickly sliced
cooked ham, smoked pork chops or a mixture; salt.

Cut spareribs into individual portions. Rinse sauerkraut under cold running water, drain and squeeze dry in a cloth. Heat a large, heavy flameproof casserole and brown spareribs slowly in their own fat. Remove ribs. Add onion and sauerkraut and brown in fat remaining in pot. Return ribs to casserole, burying them in sauerkraut. Add caraway seeds, if using, and enough white wine just to cover. Cover tightly, bring to simmering point (180°C/350°F). Cook for 1½ hours. Add apple, potatoes and meats, burying them in sauerkraut. Cover again and cook 1 hour longer or until meats are very tender.

Alternatively, the dish can be cooked 40 minutes longer, cooled and reheated next day for about 1 hour in a moderate oven (180°C/350°F). Add salt before serving. Serves 6–8.

Baked Spareribs with Raisins

**1 kg (2 lb) pork or beef spareribs; 2 tsp salt;
¼ tsp pepper; 1 onion, finely chopped;
½ cup finely chopped celery; 60 g (2 oz) butter;
1 egg; ¾ cup water; 6 cups fresh bread cubes;
1 cup raisins; ¼ tsp dried sage; ¼ tsp dried thyme
or marjoram.**

Cut spareribs into individual portions. Place in saucepan, cover with water and add 1 tsp salt and the pepper. Bring to the boil and simmer gently for 45 minutes – 1 hour. Drain and pat dry with paper towels. Sauté onion and celery in butter until soft. Beat egg and water in a large bowl, then stir in bread cubes, raisins, herbs, remaining salt and cooked onion mixture. Mix thoroughly and spread in large baking tin. Put spareribs on top and bake in a preheated moderate oven (180°C/350°F) about 1–1½ hours or until crisp and tender. Serves 4.

SPECULAAS

These are special crisp biscuits rich in butter and flavoured with brown sugar, spices and rum made especially for Saint Nicholas' Eve in Holland. Sometimes the biscuits are in the shape of small rectangles sprinkled with almonds and sometimes the biscuit mixture is pressed into elaborate moulds in the shape of men and women or Saint Nicholas himself.

Speculaas

**3 cups flour; 4 tsp baking powder; 1 tbs cinnamon;
1 tsp ground cloves; 1 tsp nutmeg; ½ tsp ground
aniseed; ½ tsp salt; ½ tsp ground ginger or
white pepper; 250 g (8 oz) butter; 1½ cups firmly
packed brown sugar; 3 tbs rum or brandy; 1 egg white
to glaze; 125 g (4 oz) slivered blanched almonds
to decorate.**

Sift together flour, baking powder, cinnamon, cloves, nutmeg, ground aniseed, salt and ginger or pepper.

Beat butter with brown sugar until mixture is light and fluffy. Stir in rum or brandy. Gradually add flour mixture, stirring until well combined, then form dough into a ball. Knead dough on a board sprinkled with about ¼ cup sifted flour. Roll out dough into a rectangle about 5 mm (¼ in) thick. With a sharp knife or cutter cut dough into 6 x 3 cm (2½ x 1½ in) rectangles. Place on a buttered baking tray, brush with lightly beaten egg white and decorate with slivered almonds. Bake in a preheated moderately hot oven (190°C/375°F) for 12 minutes or until browned and firm. Cool and store in an airtight tin. Makes about 40.

SPICE

The word covers a wide variety of aromatic and pungent seasonings used to flavour savoury and sweet dishes. There are hot spices, sweet spices and spicy-sweet spices. They are not gathered from any one part of a plant or tree but from whichever part is most aromatic and most pungent: for example, cinnamon bark is exactly that, and vanilla beans are the pods of a type of orchid. Seeds, buds, berries, roots and pods all provide spices with which we are familiar.

The addition of spices to vinegars for salad dressings, fresh or dried fruits, or to creams and custards, gives a remarkably subtle aroma and flavour to simple dishes. Delicious home-made preserves, such as pickled onions or eggs, use pickling spices to flavour the preserving vinegar.

Characteristic spices impart vastly different flavours and aromas to the foods of Asia, China and the Middle East, yet they are indispensable, too, when baking our homely cakes, breads and biscuits.

Spices lose their value as a flavouring agent if they are stale, so purchase in very small quantities and store away from the light in small airtight containers. Use them as soon as possible after purchase.

Pickling Spice: Usually made from mustard seeds, bay leaf, allspice, cinnamon stick, coriander seeds and black peppercorns. Sometimes fresh ginger chilli and mace are added. The proportions vary in different recipes but excellent mixtures of pickling spice can be bought, ready-packaged for use, by spice companies. **See recipes.**

Middle East Spice Mix (Baharat): This is the ground spice mix used in the Gulf States and generally throughout the Middle East. It may be made up and used to flavour meatballs or kebabs, and many Middle Eastern sauces, soups, curries and seafood dishes.

Za'atar: A dry spice mix with walnuts from Iraq, used as a dip for bread previously dipped in olive oil. Use it to sprinkle over meat, chicken or vegetable dishes. Sumac is a souring agent often used in the Middle East. Lemon juice or grated lemon rind may be used instead. **See recipes.**

See also individual names of spices; *Garam Masala* and *Onion:* Spiced Pickled Onions.

Spice Cake

1/4 cup sugar; 3/4–1 cup mixed dried fruit;
2 tsp mixed spice; 90 g (3 oz) butter; 3/4 cup water;
2 cups self-raising flour, sifted; 1 tbs treacle or
golden syrup; 1 1/2 tsp bicarbonate of soda;
2–3 tbs warm milk.

Place sugar, mixed fruit, spice, butter and water in a saucepan and heat gently, stirring, until sugar dissolves. Bring to the boil and simmer for 5 minutes. Remove from heat and cool slightly. Fold in flour with treacle or syrup and soda dissolved in warm milk. Pour into a greased and lined 18 cm (7 in) round cake tin. Bake in a preheated moderate oven (180°C/350°F) for 1 hour. Turn out and cool on a wire rack.

Pfeffernusse *(Spice Biscuits)*

These sweet spicy-flavoured biscuits keep well for up to 6 weeks in an airtight container.

4 cups flour; 1 tsp baking powder; 1 tsp ground
cloves; 1 tsp ground allspice; a grinding of black
pepper; 1 tsp cinnamon; 2/3 cup honey;
1 cup golden syrup; 3/4 cup sugar;
45 g (1 1/2 oz) butter.

Sift together flour, baking powder, cloves, allspice, pepper and cinnamon. Place honey, golden syrup and sugar in a large, heavy saucepan. Stir over low heat until sugar dissolves, then bring to the boil, without stirring. Reduce heat to low and simmer for 5 minutes. Remove from heat, and stir in butter. Add flour mixture, one quarter at a time, beating well until smooth. Place teaspoons of mixture on 2 greased baking trays, leaving about 2.5 cm (1 in) between each biscuit. Bake in a preheated hot oven (200°C/400°F) for 10–15 minutes or until light brown. Cool on a wire rack. Makes about 30.

Spiced Apples

8 cups sugar; 1 tsp salt; 5 cups white vinegar;
12 clovers; 10 cm (4 in) cinnamon stick;
1 tsp whole allspice; 1.5 kg (3 lb) small firm apples,
weighed after peeling, coring and slicing.

Combine sugar, salt, vinegar and spices tied in a muslin bag in a large heavy saucepan. Bring to the boil. Add sliced apples and simmer very gently until tender. Discard spice bag. Using a slotted spoon, lift out apple slices and pack in sterilised jars. Boil syrup steadily until thick and pour over the fruit. Seal jars and store in a cool dark place. Makes about 4 x 500 g (1 lb) jars.

Spiced Prunes

Serve as an accompaniment to roast pork or cold meats.

500 g (1 lb) dessert prunes; 1 1/2 cups cold tea;
1 cup sugar; 2 cups mild white vinegar; 4 cloves;
8 cm (3 in) cinnamon stick.

Put prunes in a bowl, cover with cold tea and soak overnight. Combine sugar, vinegar and spices in a heavy saucepan. Bring to the boil and boil steadily for 15 minutes. Remove from heat. Pour prunes and tea into another pan and simmer for about 15 minutes or until soft. Drain, reserving 1 cup tea, and pack prunes into sterilised jars. Add reserved tea to spiced vinegar and pour over prunes. Seal jars and store in a cool, dark place. Leave for 24 hours before using. Makes about 3 x 250 g (8 oz) jars.

Spicy Fruit Nuts

oil for frying; 2 cups raw cashews; 2 cups blanched
almonds; 4 cups raw peanuts; 1 tbs salt;
2 tsp Garam Masala (page 171); 2 tsp chilli powder.

Heat oil in a deep frying pan and fry nuts, in batches of about 1 cup at a time, over medium heat until golden-brown and crisp. Drain on crumpled paper towels. Place fried nuts in a bowl and add salt, garam masala and chilli powder. Mix well to coat nuts thoroughly. Cool completely before storing in an airtight container. Makes 6 x 250 g (8 oz) jars.

Spiced Canned Peaches

2 x 425 g cans peach halves; 1 cup sugar;
3/4 cup cider vinegar; 1 tbs cloves; 1 tbs whole
allspice; 10 cm (4 in) cinnamon stick.

Drain syrup from peach halves into a heavy saucepan. Add sugar, vinegar, and spices tied in a muslin bag. Boil for 10 minutes, then add peaches and cook for 5 minutes or until peaches are heated through. Remove spice bag. Pack peaches in hot sterilised jars and fill with hot syrup. Seal and store in a cool, dark place. Makes about 4 x 250 g (8 oz) jars. Good with cold ham.

Buttered Spiced Beetroot

8 small whole beetroot, cooked and peeled,
or 1 x 425 g can baby beetroot, drained;
60 g (2 oz) butter; pinch salt; freshly ground black
pepper; 1/2 tsp cinnamon; 1/4 tsp ground ginger;
1/4 cup firmly packed brown sugar; juice 1 lemon.

Dice beetroot. Combine remaining ingredients in a saucepan, and stir over gentle heat until butter melts. Add beetroot and stir until heated through. Serve hot with pork, ham steaks or hamburgers. Serves 4.

Hot Spiced Wine Punch

2 bottles burgundy or claret; thinly pared rind
1 small orange; thinly pared rind 1 lemon;
8 cm (3 in) cinnamon stick; $^{1}/_{2}$ whole nutmeg,
crushed; 6 cloves; 2 tbs sugar (or more to taste).

Combine all ingredients in a large saucepan. Bring
to just under boiling point, then turn off heat and
stand for 10 minutes. Strain into mugs and serve hot.
Serves 10–12.
NOTE: If you prefer a sweeter drink, stir in more
sugar before serving.

Spiced Beef Loaf

1 kg (2 lb) finely minced steak;
90 g (3 oz) rashers bacon, rind removed and
minced; $^{1}/_{2}$ tsp dried basil; $^{1}/_{2}$ tsp ground allspice;
$^{1}/_{2}$ tsp salt; 6 black peppercorns, crushed;
1 clove garlic, crushed; 2 tbs port, sherry or red
wine; 2 tsp red wine vinegar.

Combine all ingredients in a large bowl and mix very
thoroughly. Cover, refrigerate and leave at least
3 hours or overnight. Pack into a 21 x 15 cm (8½ x 6 in)
loaf tin. Stand tin in a baking dish filled with enough
water to come halfway up sides and cook in a preheated moderately slow oven (160°C/325°F) for about
1½ hours. If top of loaf begins to brown too much,
cover loosely with foil. Leave to cool in tin. To turn
out, run a knife around edges and invert tin on to a
serving platter. Cut in thin slices and serve with
spiced fruit, chutney or a mustardy sauce. Serves 6–8.

Baharat

3 tbs black peppercorns; 1$^{1}/_{2}$ tbs coriander seeds;
1$^{1}/_{2}$ tbs crumbled cinnamon stick or cassia;
1$^{1}/_{2}$ tbs whole cloves; 2 tbs cumin seeds;
1 tsp cardamom seeds; 1 whole nutmeg;
3 tbs paprika.

Place peppercorns, coriander seeds, cinnamon stick or
cassia, cloves and cumin and cardamom seeds in a
blender and grind to a powder. Grate nutmeg and
blend into spices with paprika. Store in airtight jar.

Za'atar

2 tbs sesame seeds; 1 tbs coriander seeds;
1 tbs cumin seeds; $^{1}/_{2}$ cup walnut halves;
2 tsp ground cinnamon; salt and freshly ground
black pepper; 2 tsp sumac powder or
1 tsp grated lemon rind.

In a heated dry frying pan dry-roast the sesame seeds
until they pop and turn golden-brown, shaking the
pan constantly. Remove to a mortar or blender. Toast
the coriander and cumin seeds in the same way and
add to the sesame seeds. Toast the walnuts until light
golden and add to the spices. Using a pestle or with

the motor of the blender grind the seeds, spices and
nuts to a fine powder, being careful not to overwork
and let the oils be released. Add cinnamon, salt and
pepper to taste and the sumac or lemon rind. Mix well
then pile the mixture in a shallow bowl. Serve
alongside a bowl of extra virgin olive oil and pieces of
pita or good crusty bread.

Honey Spiced Sponge Roll

3 eggs; $^{1}/_{2}$ cup caster sugar; $^{1}/_{2}$ cup arrowroot;
1 tbs flour; $^{1}/_{2}$ tsp cinnamon; 1 tsp mixed spice;
1 tsp cream of tartar; $^{1}/_{2}$ tsp bicarbonate of soda;
1 tbs honey (at room temperature).

HONEY CREAM FILLING: 90 g (3 oz) butter;
2 tbs honey; 1 tbs water.

Beat eggs until thick. Gradually add sugar and
continue beating until mixture is thick and will hold
its shape, about 10 minutes. Sift together 3 times the
arrowroot, flour, cinnamon, mixed spice, cream of
tartar and soda. Lightly fold into egg mixture, then
add honey, mixing gently until evenly distributed.
Turn into greased and lined 30 x 25 cm (12 x 10 in)
Swiss roll tin and gently shake to spread mixture
evenly. Bake in a preheated moderately hot oven
(190°C/375°F) for 15–20 minutes. Turn out on to a
tea-towel which has been lightly dusted with caster
sugar. Quickly peel off lining paper and trim edges.
Roll up immediately in tea-towel from a short side.
Allow to cool.
HONEY CREAM FILLING: Beat butter until light, then
add honey a tablespoon at a time. Add water and
continue beating until mixture is smooth and creamy.
Unroll cake and spread over filling. Roll up again.
(If serving as dessert, roll cake beginning with wider
side, and cut into diagonal slices.) Serves 8.

Cinnamon Layered Cake

1$^{1}/_{2}$ cups sugar; $^{1}/_{2}$ cup mixed chopped nuts;
1 tbs cinnamon; 125 g (4 oz) butter; 2 eggs;
1 tsp vanilla; 1 tbs lemon juice; 2 cups flour;
$^{1}/_{2}$ tsp baking powder; $^{1}/_{2}$ tsp bicarbonate of soda;
$^{1}/_{4}$ tsp salt; 1 cup sour cream.

Combine $^{1}/_{2}$ cup sugar with the nuts and cinnamon
and set aside. Cream butter with remaining sugar until
light and fluffy. Add eggs, vanilla and lemon juice,
beating well. Sift flour with baking powder, soda and
salt and add alternately to butter mixture with sour
cream. Pour half the batter into a greased and bottom-
lined 23 cm (9 in) square cake tin. Sprinkle with half
the cinnamon mixture and over it spread remaining
batter. Sprinkle rest of cinnamon mixture on top. Bake
in a preheated moderate oven (180°C/350°F) for 35–40
minutes or until a skewer inserted in centre comes out
clean. Serve warm on its own or with whipped cream
flavoured with cinnamon.

SPINACH

If you ask in an Australian greengrocer's simply for 'spinach', you are likely to get silverbeet, which has larger and tougher leaves than true spinach. True spinach, with thin, tender, arrowhead-shaped leaves, is usually sold as 'English spinach'. There is also Italian spinach, similar to the English type but a little stronger in flavour, which is often available at Italian greengrocers. The three vegetables are similar in flavour and can be used in the same way.

Here, the word 'spinach' will be used to cover all types, and instructions and recipes may be applied to any one. Any can serve as an excellent accompanying vegetable, as a bed for other foods such as eggs and fish, as the basis of a soufflé, tart filling, mould, salad or stuffing, or as partner to other vegetables, pasta, rice, cheese, meats, seafood and poultry in scores of savoury dishes. Baby spinach leaves are used in salads or folded into hot pasta or rice. Spinach in a dish is often given the name 'Florentine' (*alla Florentina* in Italian), a tribute to the skill with which the Italians raise this vegetable and the imagination with which they use it.

Choose spinach which is bright, intense green and unwilted. The ends of the stems should be unwithered. Since it shrinks greatly in cooking, allow 250 g (8 oz) raw spinach per person. Cut stems short and store unwashed in a plastic bag in the refrigerator crisper until required. Stems can be stored separately, then boiled and served with cheese sauce as a vegetable in their own right.

■ **BASIC PREPARATION:** If spinach is young and tender, cut off stems at base of leaves. If it is more mature, fold each leaf inward and pull off stem toward the tip. Wash, immediately before cooking, by plunging up and down in several changes of cold water until there is no grit to be seen in the bottom of the sink or bowl. Shake to remove most of the water.

■ **TO COOK:** Unless it is to be served *en branche* (whole), chop coarsely. Drop into a heavy saucepan, season with salt, pepper and grated nutmeg and cover tightly. Do not add water. Cook on low heat, lifting the lid and stirring frequently until steam has formed and spinach has begun to wilt, then cook covered 1–2 minutes more. Spinach is cooked when it is wilted and tender.

Drain in a colander, refresh under cold running water, then squeeze well to remove as much moisture as possible. This preparation may be carried out ahead of time and the spinach refrigerated, covered, until required. It can be reheated gently in butter to be served s a vegetable, or used as directed in recipes. **See recipes.**

Spinach en Branche

1 kg (2 lb) spinach; 30 g (1 oz) butter; salt and freshly ground black pepper; nutmeg; lemon juice.

Cook spinach as described above, leaving leaves whole, and press dry. Melt butter in a wide, heavy saucepan, add spinach and heat gently, separating leaves gently with a fork. Season with salt, pepper, nutmeg and a few drops of lemon juice and serve very hot. Serves 4.

VARIATION

CHOPPED BUTTERED SPINACH: Follow recipe for Spinach en Branche, but chop leaves coarsely before cooking, then chop finely after squeezing dry.

Italian Spinach

1 large bunch spinach, coarsely shredded; 2 tbs butter; 1 tbs olive oil; 1 clove garlic, finely chopped; salt; 1/4 tsp cayenne; coarsely grated Parmesan cheese.

Place spinach in large saucepan and cook, covered, for 2–4 minutes – toss or turn spinach over occasionally to speed cooking. Drain well. Heat 1 tbs butter and olive oil in a frying pan. Add garlic, salt, cayenne and spinach and toss lightly. Place in a flameproof serving dish and sprinkle with cheese and remaining butter, melted. Brown quickly under a preheated hot grill. Serves 4.

Purée of Spinach

1 kg (2 lb) spinach, cooked and squeezed dry; 45 g (1 1/2 oz) butter; salt and freshly ground black pepper; nutmeg; lemon juice; triangular Croûtes, page 105 (optional).

Sieve spinach or purée in a food mill or food processor. Melt butter in a saucepan, add spinach purée and stir on low heat until all surplus moisture has been driven off. Season with salt, pepper, nutmeg and a few drops of lemon juice, and serve domed up in a heated dish, surrounded by triangular croûtes, if desired. Serves 4.

VARIATION

PUREE OF SPINACH WITH CREAM: Follow recipe for Pureé of Spinach, but stir in 1/4 cup cream after moisture has been driven off, and cook 2–3 minutes longer before seasoning.

Spinach and Rice (Spanakaryzo)

A Greek way with spinach.

1 cup rice; 1 medium onion, finely chopped; 1/3 cup olive oil; 2 cups boiling water; 1 1/2 tsp salt; 500 g (1 lb) spinach, cut into strips or use baby spinach leaves.

Sauté rice and onion in olive oil, stirring occasionally, for 15 minutes. Add boiling water and salt. Cover and simmer for 10 minutes. Add spinach and mix thoroughly. Cover and continue to cook, stirring occasionally, for 15 minutes. Serves 4.

Spinach and Herb Terrine

625 g (1¹/₄ lb) minced pork; 1 kg (2 lb) English spinach; 3 rashers bacon, rind removed and diced; 125 g (4 oz) cooked ham, diced; 125 g (4 oz) cooked tongue, diced; 4 eggs, beaten; 1 onion, chopped; 2 cloves garlic, crushed; 3 tbs finely chopped parsley; 1 tbs chopped fresh basil; 1 tbs chopped fresh chervil; ¹/₂ tsp chopped fresh rosemary; 2 tsp salt; ¹/₄ tsp cayenne; freshly ground black pepper; 2 tbs butter; 125 g (4 oz) chicken livers, cut into 1 cm (¹/₂ in) pieces; ¹/₂ cup cream; 250 g (8 oz) fresh pork back fat, cut into thin strips.

Place minced pork in a bowl. Cook spinach 2 minutes and drain. Chop finely and add to pork with bacon, ham, tongue, eggs, onion, garlic, herbs, salt, cayenne and pepper. Mix well. Melt butter in a saucepan. Add chicken livers and cook until lightly browned. Stir into pork with cream. Place pork fat strips on a board and stretch with back of a knife until they are 3 mm (¹/₈ in) thick. Use most of the strips to line a 6-cup terrine. Spoon pork and spinach mixture into terrine. Use all the mixture, even if it comes above sides of terrine – it will shrink as it cooks. Cover top with remaining pork strips, tucking them into sides of mixture. Cover with foil, or seal a lid with a flour-and-water paste made from 1 cup flour mixed with 4 tbs water. Place terrine in a baking dish of hot water and bake in a preheated moderate oven (180°C/350°F) for 1½ hours. Take from oven, remove lid and place a weight on top. Leave until cool and set. Serve in thin slices. Serves 8–10.
NOTE: If no chervil is available, use extra parsley.

Spinach and Bacon Salad

6 rashers streaky bacon, rind removed and cut into strips; 1 tsp olive oil; 500 g (1 lb) young spinach, rinsed, dried and chilled.

DRESSING: 3 tbs olive oil; 1 tbs wine vinegar; pinch sugar; salt and freshly ground black pepper.

Fry bacon in olive oil until golden.
DRESSING: Whisk all ingredients together. Toss spinach with dressing in a salad bowl. Pour hot bacon and fat over salad and serve at once. Serves 6.

Cream of Spinach Soup

6 cups chicken stock; 2 medium potatoes, peeled and sliced; 2 medium onions, sliced; 1 medium bunch spinach; good pinch nutmeg; salt and freshly ground black pepper; ¹/₂ cup cream or evaporated milk.

Bring stock to the boil in a large saucepan. Add potatoes and onions, cover and cook for 20 minutes. Reserve 1 spinach leaf for garnish, and roughly chop remainder. Add to pan and cook for another

10 minutes, uncovered. Pureé soup in a blender or food processor, return to saucepan and season with nutmeg, salt and pepper. Thin with a little water if necessary, stir in cream or evaporated milk and reheat to boiling. Serve in heated bowls, garnished with reserved spinach, finely shredded. Serves 6.

SPONGE CAKE

See *Cakes.*

SPRING ONION

See *Shallot and Spring Onion.*

SPRING ROLL

Variations of spring roll exist throughout Southeast Asia, their popularity extending to many countries of the Pacific. Spring rolls may be large or small, eaten as snack food or as part of a meal, their fillings differing from region to region. However, all share some characteristics: wafer-thin wrappers encasing a delectable filling, each one, whether large or small, being rolled up and deep-fried until crisp and golden.

Spring rolls are usually served with a dipping sauce, which again varies from region to region. Preparation of spring rolls is simpler now we can buy freshly made or frozen wrappers from most good supermarkets, delicatessens or health food stores. There are usually about 20 wrappers per packet. **See recipes.**

See *Rice Paper Sheets.*

Spring Rolls (Chinese)

250 g (8 oz) pork fillet, shredded; 1 tbs dry sherry; ³/₄ tsp salt; 1 tsp cornflour; ¹/₂ cup oil; ¹/₂ cup shredded leek or spring onions; 1 cup shredded canned bamboo shoots; ¹/₄ cup shredded dried Chinese mushrooms, soaked in warm water for 30 minutes and drained before shredding; 2 cups bean sprouts; 2 tbs soy sauce; 8 x 20 cm (8 in) Spring Roll Wrappers , or use bought ready-made fresh or frozen; beaten egg to seal; oil for deep-frying.

Mix together pork, dry sherry, ½ tsp salt and cornflour. Heat half the oil and sauté pork mixture for about 2 minutes. Remove from pan and place in a bowl. Add remaining oil to pan and sauté leek or spring onions, bamboo shoots, mushrooms and bean sprouts for about 2 minutes. Remove from pan and place in bowl with pork mixture. Add remaining salt and soy sauce and mix all ingredients together. Allow filling to cool before using. When ready to assemble, remove wrappers from freezer and allow to thaw until pliable to prevent tearing when separating the delicate layers. Lay on a flat surface and keep wrappers covered with a clean tea-towel as

S

you work so they do not dry out. Place 2 tbs of filling on lower half of each spring roll wrapper. Brush left and right edges with beaten egg. Fold bottom edge up, left and right edges over, and roll up. Brush top edge with egg and press to seal. Heat oil to 185°C/360°F or until a bread cube turns golden-brown in 60 seconds. Deep-fry rolls until crisp and golden, about 5–8 minutes. Drain on crumpled paper towels and serve immediately. Makes 8.

Singapore Chinese Spring Rolls

6 dried Chinese mushrooms, soaked in warm water for 30 minutes and drained; 3 tbs peanut oil; I tbs sesame oil; I clove garlic, crushed; ¹/₂ tsp finely grated fresh ginger; 250 g (8 oz) boneless pork, finely chopped; 250 g (8 oz) green prawns, shelled, deveined and chopped; 2 cups finely shredded Chinese cabbage; I cup shredded giant white radish; 12 water chestnuts, chopped; I cup chopped canned bamboo shoots; 125 g (4 oz) bean sprouts; 6 spring onions, finely chopped; I tbs light soy sauce; I tbs oyster sauce; ¹/₂ tsp salt; 3 tsp cornflour; I packet frozen spring roll wrappers; beaten egg to seal; oil for deep-frying.

Remove stems from mushrooms, and finely chop caps. Heat peanut and sesame oils in a wok or large frying pan and fry garlic and ginger for a few seconds. Add pork, increase heat and stir-fry about 1 minutes. Mix in vegetables, sauces and salt. Mix cornflour to a thin paste with a little cold water. Tilt pan so liquid gathers at one edge and add cornflour paste to liquid, stirring until thickened. Stir through mixture. Remove from heat and cool completely. Put 2 tbs of filling on lower half of each wrapper. Brush left and right edges with beaten egg. Fold bottom edge up, left and right edges over, and roll up. Brush top edge with egg and press firmly to seal. Heat oil to 185°C/360°F or until a bread cube turns golden-brown in 60 seconds. Deep-fry rolls until crisp and golden, about 5–8 minutes. Drain on crumpled paper towels and serve immediately, with chilli sauce for dipping. Makes about 16.
NOTE: Dried mushrooms and fresh Chinese vegetables (Chinese cabbage, white radish) can be purchased at Chinese greengrocers. Water chestnuts and bamboo shoots are available canned at most good supermarkets, delicatessens and health food stores.

Chicken Spring Rolls (Vietnamese)

30 g (I oz) transparent noodles, cooked in water for 10 minutes, drained and cut into 2.5 cm (I in) pieces; 250 g (8 oz) chicken breast meat, skinned and cut into thin strips; I tbs dried wood ears (mushrooms, available from Chinese and Asian

grocery stores), soaked in warm water for 30 minutes, drained and finely chopped; 2 spring onions, finely chopped; 125 g (4 oz) crabmeat; ¹/₂ tsp black pepper; I packet frozen spring roll wrappers, each cut in half to form 2 rectangles; beaten egg to seal; oil for deep-frying; shredded spring onions to garnish.

NUOC CHAM SAUCE: 2 cloves garlic, crushed; I fresh red chilli; 5 tsp sugar; juice and pulp ¹/₄ lime or lemon; ¹/₃ cup nuoc man (fish sauce available from Asian grocery stores); ¹/₃ cup water.

Combine noodles, chicken, mushrooms, spring onions, crabmeat and pepper. Place 3–4 tsp of filling on lower half of each spring roll wrapper. Brush left and right edges with beaten egg. Fold bottom edge up, left and right edges over, and roll up. Brush top edge with egg and press to seal. Set aside while making sauce.
NUOC CHAM SAUCE: Pound garlic, chilli and sugar using a pestle and mortar, or mash with back of a spoon. Add lime or lemon juice and pulp, then fish sauce and water. Mix well to combine ingredients. Heat oil to 185°C/360°F or until bread cube turns golden-brown in 60 seconds. Deep-fry rolls for 3–4 minutes or until crisp and golden. Drain on paper towels and serve immediately, garnished with shredded spring onions. Serve with nuoc cham sauce. Makes 20.

SPROUTS, BRUSSELS

See *Brussels Sprouts*.

SPUMONE

An Italian moulded ice cream, usually consisting of an outer coating of ice cream, and a filling of whipped cream, contrasting flavoured ice cream or liqueur-soaked fruits, and served sliced. A delicious and less elaborate version is based on a Zabaglione mixture (see *Zabaglione*) that is moulded and served in wedges.

Spumone makes a festive centre piece, and can be made and frozen days ahead of serving time if you wish. It may be moulded in a metal loaf tin or cylinder.
TO ASSEMBLE: Soften the ice cream to be used for the outer layer and spoon about three quarters of it into the base and sides of the chilled metal mould. The layer should be about 2 cm (³⁄4 in) thick. Cover the mould and freeze until solid. Remove from freezer, spoon in the filling and top with the remaining one quarter of ice cream (softened). Cover securely and freeze.
TO UNMOULD: Remove from freezer, rub the mould with a cold damp cloth, uncover and invert on to a chilled serving platter. If the spumone sticks, a hot cloth rubbed over the mould should help to release the cream.

Decorate with whipped cream, fruit and nuts if desired. See recipes.

Spumone Coppelia

3 cups Chocolate Ice Cream, softened (page 202);
5 cups hazelnut ice cream, softened (see below);
$^1/_4$ cup whole hazelnuts; whipped cream to
decorate (optional).

Line bottom and sides of an 8-cup chilled loaf tin with
2 cups chocolate ice cream. Cover mould with foil and
freeze. When frozen, fill centre with hazelnut ice
cream, then cover with remaining softened chocolate
ice cream. Cover mould and freeze for at least
3 hours. Unmould on to a chilled serving platter,
decorate top with hazelnuts and rosettes of cream if
liked. Serve sliced. Serves 8 –10.
NOTE: Make hazelnut ice cream by combining 5 cups
slightly softened vanilla ice cream (see page 202) with
1 cup finely ground hazelnuts.

Spumone Zabaglione

3 egg yolks; 2 tsp water; 3 tbs caster sugar;
$^1/_2$ cup marsala or similar sweet wine;
$^3/_4$ cup cream.

Combine egg yolks, water, sugar and wine in top of a
double saucepan or heatproof bowl. Whisk until lukewarm over a pan of hot, not boiling, water, then remove
from heat and continue beating until mixture is foamy
and slightly thickened. Whip cream until it holds soft
peaks and fold into egg mixture. Pour into a 4-cup
mould, cover with foil and freeze for 3–4 hours.
Unmould on to a chilled serving platter, and cut into
wedges to serve. Accompany with fresh strawberries,
raspberries, peaches, apricots or crisp biscuits. Serves 4.

SQUAB

See *Pigeon*.

SQUASH

The American name for certain members of the gourd
family. In Australia it is usually applied to the creamy or
golden pie-shaped variety called custard squash, to their
tiny, bright green relations called patty pan or button
squash, and to the yellow crook-necked squash which is
rather like a large zucchini. All these squash are thin-
skinned, with juicy flesh, and should be eaten when they
are young and tender.

Butternut squash (also called butternut pumpkin) and
acorn squash have harder rinds and firm, dryish flesh; in
Australian terms, this brings them into the category of
pumpkins rather than squash. For preparation and cooking
see *Pumpkin*.

When buying squash, look for small, firm, unblemished
ones whose skins have a sheen. Store in the refrigerator
crisper and use within a day or two.
■ **BASIC PREPARATION:** Wash the squash and lightly
trim the stem end and, if necessary, any little brown mark

at the other end. Leave whole, halve or slice according to
the recipe. Peel large custard squash thinly; young ones
should not need this.

Squash beyond the baby stage may have developed
slightly bitter juices: to remove this, 'dégorge' (see
Eggplant) by sprinkling salt on cut surfaces and leaving
in a colander to drain for 20 minutes. Rinse under cold
running water and dry before using.
■ **TO COOK:** Squash may be boiled, steamed or sautéed.
See also recipes.
BOILED SQUASH: For firm-tender, brilliant green patty
pan squash, drop them into a generous amount of fast-
boiling salted water and boil for 4–8 minutes, depending
on size. Drain in a colander and run cold water over
squash to stop cooking and set the colour. Reheat gently
in butter when required, and season with pepper and
lemon juice.
STEAMED SQUASH: This is a good way to cook custard
or crook-necked squash. Leave whole or cut up. Cook,
tightly covered, in about 1 cm ($^1/_2$ in) of salted water, or in
a steamer over boiling water, until tender. Time will
depend on size of squash pieces. Serve with butter,
pepper and lemon juice, or a sauce such as Mornay or
Poulette (see *Sauce*) or Fresh Tomato (see *Pasta*).
SAUTEED SQUASH: Slice thickly and dégorge as
described above. Heat enough butter to cover bottom
of a frying pan generously, and when foaming add
squash. Cook, stirring and tossing frequently, for 3–4
minutes or until just tender.

A few serving suggestions:
- Add shredded spring onions to sautéed squash.
- Sprinkle with chopped fresh herbs, or dried herbs with
  chopped parsley, before serving.
- Add fresh breadcrumbs (about $^3/_4$ cup to 500 g/1 lb
  squash) as you sauté the squash.
- Sprinkle with grated cheese or crumbled crisply fried
  bacon before serving.

Baked Stuffed Custard Squash

4 custard squash, about 10 cm (4 in) across,
or 2 larger ones, steamed.

STUFFING: 2 rashers streaky bacon, rind removed
and chopped; 30 g (1 oz) butter; 1 small onion,
chopped; 90 g (3 oz) mushrooms, chopped;
2 tbs chopped green or red pepper; 1 tomato,
peeled, seeded and chopped; 1 cup cooked rice;
salt and freshly ground black pepper.

Cut a lid off each steamed squash and scoop out some
flesh with a sharp spoon, discarding any large seeds.
Chop this flesh and drain in a sieve. Turn squash
shells upside-down to drain.
STUFFING: Gently fry bacon in a dry frying pan until
fat runs. Add butter and fry onion, mushrooms and
pepper until soft. Stir in tomato and rice and season
with salt and pepper. Fill squash with stuffing,

S

replace lids and place in a buttered ovenproof dish. Brush squash with melted butter and bake in a preheated moderate oven (180°C/350°F) for 20–30 minutes. Serves 4.

Squash and Tomato Medley

For those who enjoy vegetables lightly cooked with a natural fresh flavour.

500 g (1 lb) zucchini; 2 tbs olive oil; 300 g (10 oz) patty pan or button squash; 1 clove garlic, crushed; salt and freshly ground black pepper; 1/4 cup chopped parsley; 1 tsp chopped fresh thyme or oregano; 1 punnet cherry tomatoes, halved; 1/4 cup water.

Cut the zucchini into chunks and the squash through the middle. Heat the oil in a heavy frying pan. Add the garlic, squash, zucchini, and cook over a moderate heat, tossing the pan frequently, for about 3 minutes. Take care not to let the garlic burn. Season with salt and pepper and add the herbs, tomatoes and water. Cover and simmer until just tender for about 5 minutes. Serves 4–6.

SQUASH, FRUIT

Fresh fruit squash is deliciously refreshing, topped with iced water and soda water. It is made with sweetened fruit pulp and/or juice, usually from citrus fruits.

Commercial squash is sold in concentrated form to which water is added for serving. The components of the drink are usually specified on the label by law and may consist solely of chemicals.

Orange Squash

6 (or more) oranges; 3 cups sugar; 3 cups water; 30 g (1 oz) citric acid.

Lightly grate rind from the oranges and squeeze out juice. There should be 2 cups juice, so if necessary squeeze more oranges. Add grated rind to sugar and water in a saucepan and heat until sugar dissolves. Add orange juice and citric acid, mix well and bottle. If you wish to keep squash longer than a week, use special ginger beer preserving bottles available from kitchenware shops and sterilise in simmering water for 30 minutes. Serve topped with crushed ice, iced water or soda water and float an orange slice on top. Makes 6 cups.

SQUID (CALAMARI)

The fine delicate flavour of squid has been known for many centuries to people living around the Mediterranean. Squid are related to the octopus and cuttlefish, but the flesh is more tender and sweet; they are all cephalopods.

Squid can be bought from fishmongers fresh and ready-cleaned, and frozen; squid freeze very well, with little loss of flavour or texture. When buying fresh squid choose those with firm flesh that is white and almost translucent. The edible parts are the tentacles and the sac-like body.

See also *Fritto Misto*.

■ **BASIC PREPARATION:** Pull out the head and tentacles from the body. Remove the eyes, ink sac and parrot-like beak at the base of the tentacles and discard. Cut the fins off the body. Remove the skin by rubbing it off the body and tentacles with your fingers (dip your fingers in salt to act as an abrasive). Remove any remaining yellowish deposit and the long internal quill-like bone, which resembles hard cellophane. Wash the squid thoroughly in cold running water and dry well before using according to your recipe.

■ **TO COOK:** Squid can be fried, baked, grilled or stewed but, as with all seafood, must not be overcooked or the flesh will become tough. See also recipes.

Pan-fried Squid: Cut prepared squid into thin slices. Place in a dish with oil, salt and pepper to season and let stand 1 hour, turning occasionally. Heat a heavy frying pan, drop in squid slices and cook gently for 3–4 minutes, adding a little more oil if necessary. Serve with lemon wedges.

Grilled Squid: Cut prepared squid into pieces. Place in a dish with oil, salt and pepper to taste and let stand 1 hour, turning occasionally. Place squid under a pre-heated medium grill and cook 4–5 minutes on each side, brushing occasionally with oil. Serve with lemon wedges.

Squid Fried in Piquant Sauce: Pan-fry squid as above with the addition of 3 cloves garlic, peeled and ½ fresh chilli or ¼ tsp chilli powder. When tender, remove garlic and chilli. Combine 1 tbs each of bread-crumbs, chopped parsley and butter and toss over squid, stirring over a high heat for 1 minute. Serve with lemon wedges.

Stuffed Baby Squid

12–18 baby squid, cleaned; 1 clove garlic; 4 anchovy fillets; 3–4 sprigs parsley; 2 eggs, lightly beaten; 1 cup fresh breadcrumbs; salt and freshly ground black pepper; 2–3 tsp olive oil; lemon wedges to serve.

Cut tentacles from squid and chop them as fine as possible with garlic, anchovies and parsley. This may be done in a blender, food processor or mincer. Combine eggs, breadcrumbs, salt, pepper and olive oil and work to a paste. Add anchovy mixture. Stuff squid bodies with this mixture and sew up openings with strong thread. Sprinkle with salt and pepper and brush with oil. Cook under a preheated moderate grill for 15 minutes, turning occasionally and basting with oil. Cook under a preheated moderate grill for 15 minutes, turning occasionally and basting with oil. Serve very hot, with lemon wedges to garnish. Serves 6.

VARIATION

SQUID IN TOMATO SAUCE: Make stuffing as described, using tentacles from 6 large squid, cleaned. Spoon stuffing into 6 squid. Heat 2 tbs olive oil in a heavy shallow pan and fry 1 medium onion, finely chopped, and 2 cloves garlic, crushed, until soft. Stir in 1 x 425 g can tomatoes, season well with salt and pepper and simmer for 15 minutes. Add stuffed squid, cover and simmer gently for 1–1¼ hours. Serves 6.

Baby Squid with Parsley

When you can get the tiny squid or cuttlefish, try them this way. Do not overcook or they will become tough.

I kg (2 lb) baby squid, cleaned; ¼ cup olive oil; 2 cloves garlic, bruised; salt and freshly ground black pepper; ½ cup chopped parsley; juice ½ lemon; triangular Croûtes (page 105) to serve.

Cut squid into rings, or lengthways into 4. If liked, the tentacles may also be cooked. Heat oil gently with garlic cloves until they begin to brown; discard garlic. Add squid, season with salt and pepper and cook over a brisk heat for 1–2 minutes. Sprinkle with parsley and lemon juice and serve very hot, with triangular croûtes. Serves 4.

Calamari (Fried Squid)

This is a dish often found in Italian restaurants, and is one of the simplest but most delicious ways of serving squid. Serve as a starter or as a main course with salads.

500 g (I lb) squid, cleaned; I egg; ½ cup milk, flour; salt and freshly ground black pepper; I cup fine, dry breadcrumbs; oil for deep-frying.

Cut squid tentacles into pieces about 8 cm (3 in) long, and cut body into rings. Beat egg with milk in a shallow dish. Dredge squid in flour, seasoned with salt and pepper, then dip in egg mixture, and roll in breadcrumbs. Heat 8–10 cm (3–4 in) of oil in a deep-fryer to 200°C/400°F. Fry squid in oil until golden, about 2 minutes. This should be done in several batches; do not overcrowd the pan. Drain on paper

towels, sprinkle with salt and serve with Sauce Tartare (see page 256). Serve 6.

Deep-fried Squid

4–6 squid, cleaned; ½ cup flour; salt and freshly ground black pepper; oil for deep-frying; lemon wedges to serve.

Cut squid tentacles into pieces about 8 cm (3 in) long, and cut body into rings. Season flour with salt and pepper and roll squid pieces in it. Heat oil in a deep-fryer to 185°C/360°F or until a bread cube turns golden-brown in 40 seconds. Deep-fry squid for 2–3 minutes or until golden-brown. If necessary fry in several batches to avoid overcrowding pan. Drain on paper towels and serve immediately, with lemon wedges. Serves 4–6.

STEAK DIANE

A superb dish of tender fillet steak, flamed in brandy and sherry, the delicious pan juices forming the sauce. Steak Diane is a popular restaurant dish, well worth trying at home when you are dining *à deux*. Have all the ingredients ready before you begin cooking as this will take only a minute or two. Make the dish for two people only as no more than two steaks can be successfully sautéed at the one time in the average sauté or frying pan.

Steak Diane

2 x I cm (½ in) thick pieces fillet steak; salt and freshly ground black pepper; 60 g (2 oz) butter; I clove garlic, crushed; I tbs Worcestershire sauce; I tbs brandy; 2 tbs dry sherry; I tbs finely chopped parsley.

Trim all fat from steak and beat to flatten until 5 mm (¼ in) thick. Season with salt and pepper. Heat butter in a large frying pan and when it is foaming add steaks. Sauté for about 40 seconds (rare) or for about 1 minute (medium) on each side. Add garlic and allow it to cook for 30 seconds. Stir in the Worcestershire sauce. Heat brandy and sherry until warm, seat alight and pour over steaks. Shake pan until flames die down. Remove steaks to a heated serving dish and sprinkle with parsley. Give sauce a good stir and pour it sizzling hot over steaks. Serve immediately. Serves 2.

STEAK TARTARE

The classic raw beef mixture that is popular in much of Europe. Traditionally, it is served topped with a raw egg yolk for the diner to mix through the beef, and with small bowls of chopped onion and capers. Steak Tartare also makes excellent appetisers and cocktail or larger open-face sandwiches. Beef for Steak Tartare should not be minced, but scraped with a metal spoon or chopped in a food processor to give very fine-textured juicy meat.

S

Steak Tartare

500 g (1 lb) lean round steak; ¼ tsp dry mustard;
dash Worcestershire sauce; few drops Tabasco sauce;
salt and freshly ground black pepper;
chopped parsley; 4 egg yolks.

TO SERVE: finely chopped onion; capers.

Scrape meat with edge of a metal spoon until it become a fine mince, discarding any fat or gristle as you go. To prepare in a food processor, remove all fat and gristle first, cut lean meat into pieces and process, using steel blade, until almost smooth. Lightly mix steak with mustard, Worcestershire sauce, Tabasco, salt and pepper. Shape into 4 patties and place on individual serving plates. Cover surface of meat with chopped parsley, pressing it on lightly, and mark a trellis pattern with a knife. Chill well before serving. At serving time, make an indentation in top of each patty with a soup spoon and place a raw egg yolk in it. Serve with separate bowls of chopped onion and capers. Serves 4.

VARIATIONS

STEAK TARTARE BALLS: Follow recipe for Steak Tartare, but mix 1 egg yolk, 1 tsp grated onion, 2 tbs finely chopped capers and 1 tbs finely chopped parsley through meat with seasonings. Roll mixture lightly into 2.5 cm (1 in) balls and roll in finely chopped parsley. Chill well before serving. Makes about 40.

STEAK TARTARE SANDWICHES: Make steak mixture as for Steak Tartare Balls. Mound on rounds of lightly buttered French bread to serve as appetisers, or larger Italian bread for a sandwich meal. Cover with parsley and mark a trellis pattern with a knife. Makes about 20 small or 8 large sandwiches.

STEAK AND KIDNEY PUDDING/PIE

The perennial favourite, Steak and Kidney Pudding or Pie, with rich, thick peppery gravy, has travelled far beyond its origins in Sussex, and can be found on the tables of English-speaking people across the world. It is good, hearty fare, ideal for serving on cold winter nights, and remains a nourishing, economical dish for family and friends.

The basic steak and kidney mixture can be steamed in a suet crust, when it is called Steak and Kidney Pudding, or it can be baked with a puff or flaky pastry crust. Many people also enjoy steak and kidney topped with a sponge mixture, or with some parsley dumplings steamed with the meat during the last half hour of cooking.

A few bottled oysters or sliced mushrooms make a superb addition to steak and kidney, enriching the dish sufficiently for serving at even the smartest of dinner parties. **See recipes.**

Basic Steak and Kidney

1 kg (2 lb) chuck or blade steak, cut into
2.5 cm (1 in) cubes; ½–1 calf's kidney,
or 2–3 sheep's kidneys, cored and chopped;
1 tbs flour; 1 tsp salt; 1 tsp freshly ground black
pepper; ½ tsp mixed dried herbs; ½ cup water;
2 tsp Worcestershire sauce (optional);
¼ tsp nutmeg (optional).

Sprinkle meats with flour, salt, pepper and herbs. Spoon into a heavy saucepan and pour water over. Cover tightly and simmer very gently over low heat for about 2 hours, or in a preheated moderately slow oven (160°C/325°F) for about 1½ hours or until meat is tender. If necessary add a little more water. When cooked, stir in Worcestershire sauce and nutmeg, if using. Serves 4–6.

NOTE: Steak and kidney may be steamed. Combine the ingredients in a pudding basin. Cover with 2 thicknesses of greased greaseproof paper or foil and tie with string. Put into a large saucepan with boiling water coming halfway up sides of basin. Steam for 3½–4 hours or until meat is tender, replenishing water in pan as it evaporates with more boiling water.

VARIATION

STEAK AND KIDNEY WITH DUMPLINGS: Follow recipe for Basic Steak and Kidney. About 30 minutes before cooking is finished, add 6–8 Fluffy Herb Dumplings (see page 133). Cover casserole or saucepan and cook further 20–30 minutes or until dumplings are swollen and tender. Do not lift lid of pan during first 20 minutes of cooking.

Steak and Kidney Pudding

1 quantity Suet Pastry (page 344); 1 quantity
uncooked Basic Steak and Kidney (above).

Roll out about one third of suet pastry dough on a lightly floured work surface to make a round 30 cm (12 in) in diameter and about 5 mm (¼ in) thick. Use to line a 4-cup pudding basin, draping dough loosely over a rolling pin to help lift it into basin. Gently press dough into basin, being careful not to stretch or tear it. Roll out remaining dough into a round about 18–20 cm (7–8 in) diameter. Spoon uncooked steak and kidney mixture into pastry-lined basin, filling it to within 1 cm (½ in) of top. Mound meat a little in centre. Trim excess dough from rim of basin and brush dough rim with cold water. Place round of dough on top, trim off excess and crimp edges all around rim to seal tightly.

Place a lightly greased round of double thickness greaseproof paper or single thickness foil over top of pudding, turning edges down all around to a depth of about 5 cm (2 in). Dip a clean tea-towel in cold water and wring it dry. Spread it flat, sprinkle with flour and shake to remove excess. Place towel over top of pudding, floured side down, and tie securely with string about 4–5 cm (1½–2 in) under rim. Knot 4 corners of cloth over top. Place basin in a large pan of fast boiling water to come three quarters up sides of basin. Cover and boil steadily over moderate heat for 3½–4 hours. As water evaporates pour in more boiling water to maintain level. To serve, remove towel and paper or foil and pin a folded napkin round basin. Serve straight from basin. Serves 4–6.

NOTE: If the pudding seems a little dry after cutting, pour in a small amount of boiling water to augment the gravy.

Steak and Kidney Pie

I quantity Basic Steak and Kidney, cooked and cooled (opposite); I x 375 g (12 oz) packet frozen puff pastry, thawed; egg yolk, beaten with a little water to glaze.

Spoon cooked steak and kidney mixture into a round or oval pie dish just large enough to hold it, mounding it up in the centre. Allow to cool. Roll out pastry dough on lightly floured board to 2.5 cm (1 in) larger all round than top of dish. Cut off a strip of dough all round, 2.5 cm (1 in) wide, and place strip on edge of dish. Brush with a little egg glaze and cover with dough round or oval. Press on to strip to seal and trim edge. Cut an air vent in centre of dough lid. Decorate with pastry rose and leaves (see page 361). Chill 30 minutes. Brush with egg glaze and bake in a preheated hot oven (200°C/400°F) for 20–30 minutes. Reduce heat to moderate (180°C/350°F) and bake further 30–40 minutes. It may be necessary to cover pastry with foil to prevent over-browning. Serves 4–6.

NOTE: ½ quantity home-made Puff Pastry or ¾ quantity Flaky Pastry may be used instead of commercial pastry (see *Pastry*).

VARIATIONS

STEAK AND KIDNEY PIE WITH OYSTERS: Follow recipe for Steak and Kidney Pie. After cooking, carefully insert a funnel into centre vent and push in 1 bottle of oysters, drained (you may have to halve them first).

STEAK AND KIDNEY PIE WITH MUSHROOMS: Add 125 g (4 oz) mushrooms, sliced, to Basic Steak and Kidney mixture before cooking.

Steak and Kidney Sponge

This light and tender sponge topping absorbs the delicious flavours of the steak and kidney mixture.

I quantity Basic Steak and Kidney, steamed (opposite); I cup self-raising flour; ½ tsp salt; 2 eggs, separated, I cup milk; 60 g (2 oz) butter, melted.

After steaming steak and kidney mixture, leave basin standing in saucepan of hot water while you prepare topping. Sift flour and salt into a bowl and make a

well in centre. Beat egg yolks and stir in milk. Pour into flour mixture, add butter and stir until smooth. Beat egg whites until stiff and fold into mixture. Spoon sponge mixture carefully over steak and kidney mixture in basin so meat is completely covered. Add more boiling water to saucepan to come half way up sides of basin if necessary. Put lid on saucepan and boil steadily for about 20 minutes. Serve immediately, with a napkin tied around basin. Serves 4–6.

NOTE: Steak and kidney may be cooked in a saucepan or casserole, as described in basic recipe if preferred. Turn into pudding basin and proceed as above.

STEAMBOAT

A spectacular Chinese meal of meats and seafood cooked at the table by the diners themselves. The name refers to the traditional cooking vessel, a Mongolian fire pot whose base holds hot coals (available from Chinese grocery stores). A fondue set may be substituted. The pot of simmering stock is set in the centre of the table with the foods and sauces arranged round it. Guests use small strainers to lift their choice of food into the stock, and when cooked, it is plucked out of the strainer with chopsticks, dipped into sauce and eaten. After the meat and seafood are eaten, noodles and vegetables are cooked in the remaining stock and served in soup bowls as a last course.

Steamboat

STOCK: I kg (2 lb) chicken soup bones; 10 cups water; 4 slices fresh ginger; 5 spring onions, coarsely chopped; 2 cloves garlic, bruised; I tsp salt; 4 black peppercorns.

MEATS AND SEAFOOD: 4 chicken fillets (skinless, boneless, half-breasts); 250 g (8 oz) pork fillet; 250 g (8 oz) beef fillet or Scotch fillet; 250 g (8 oz) chicken livers, lamb or calf liver; 250 g (8 oz) firm-fleshed white fish fillets, skinned and any bones removed.

NOODLES AND VEGETABLES: 500 g (I lb) Chinese cabbage, cut into 8 cm (3 in) strips; 250 g (8 oz) transparent noodles (rice vermicelli), soaked in boiling water for 30 minutes and drained; 500 g (I lb) fresh, crisp English spinach or silverbeet, shredded; handful snowpeas (if available); 125 g (4 oz) bean curd, thickly sliced.

SAUCES: See recipe.

To make stock, simmer all ingredients together in a saucepan for 2–3 hours. Strain, cool, then chill. Skim fat from surface.

MEATS AND SEAFOOD: Remove any fat from chicken breasts and pull out white tendon which runs down underside of each half-breast. Remove gristle and fat from pork and beef. Remove sinews and membrane from livers.

Wrap all meats and fish separately in plastic wrap and place in freezer to become firm before slicing. Slice meats and fish as thinly as possible into pieces about 8 x 2 cm (3 x ¾ in), keeping slices in order as they are cut. Arrange on plates and cover.

NOODLES AND VEGETABLES: Drop cabbage into boiling water for 1 minute, then drain and refresh under cold water. If you are using a fire pot, light about 20 heat beads in a fireplace or barbecue and burn about 15 minutes until a white ash forms on surface. Transfer with tongs to grate of fire pot, pushing them well in.

Meantime, bring prepared stock to the boil. If using a fondue set, light burner and set pot over it. Pour stock into pot and place on a thick board in centre of table. Arrange meats, fish and sauces round it, garnishing plates with a little green spinach or cabbage. Provide a plate, a strainer, chopsticks, a soup bowl and spoon for each guest. Guests now cook and eat meats and fish as described earlier. When they have done so, drop prepared noodles, vegetables and bean curd into pot, adding a little more stock or water if necessary. Cook for 1 minute, then ladle into soup bowls. Serves 6–8.

SAUCES: Choose from soy sauce, Chinese chilli sauce, hoisin sauce, Chinese barbecue sauce, Chinese lemon sauce (all available at Chinese stores) or one of the following: soy sauce mixed with a little chilli sauce; soy sauce with a little chilli sauce and Chinese sesame oil.

STEAMED PUDDING

See *Desserts and Puddings*.

STOCK

The importance of stock cannot be overestimated in flavouring sauces, casseroles and soups, gravies and many other savoury dishes. Stock is not hard to make; it is simply the flavourful liquid obtained from simmering together the bones, trimmings and flesh of meat, chicken or fish with vegetables, seasonings and water. The liquid is then strained through a fine strainer or cheesecloth and chilled, so that the fat which rises to the top can be easily removed. Slow cooking and skimming the surface of the stock when if first comes to the boil are important, because they help to give a clear stock.

The success of good stock depends on its distinctive flavour. Whether beef, chicken or fish, it should taste of that food, and only a few vegetables should be cooked with the meat or bones so that their flavour does not intrude. Make sure the butcher gives you beef bones for beef stock – lamb does not give the same richness. Lamb or mutton stock has its place, and excellent Scottish soups are made from them, but beef and lamb together do not combine well.

Veal is used for white stock, and the Chinese make a light stock with pork bones or a combination of pork and chicken. Each meat with its bones has a use.

Stock will keep in the refrigerator for 1 week, if protected by the layer of fat that would otherwise be removed, or 6 months in a freezer. Particles of meat or vegetables in the stock will reduce the storage time, so care should be taken when straining. It is a good idea, especially if you make a lot of soup, to make a large pot of stock and refrigerate or freeze it for later use.

Although not all soups are made from stock, carefully made stock is so essential to good cooking, that it's well worth making. The ingredients are cheap and easily obtainable. Consider the pressure cooker and crock-pot (electric slow cooker: as modern aids to stock-making. Basic stocks are referred to in the recipes throughout this book and here is how to make them.

Stock or bouillon cubes, canned beef or chicken consommé may be used to replace stock in recipes. These tend to have a 'sameness' about them, though, that reflects in the dishes in which they are used. They do have their place, however. Some butchers and delicatessans sell good stock, frozen.

TO CLARIFY STOCK: Remove fat from cold stock, then place stock in a saucepan with 2 egg whites, lightly beaten, and the 2 egg shells. Bring slowly to the boil, whisking occasionally with an egg whisk. Allow the liquid to rise in the pan as it reaches boiling point, then lower the heat, and simmer very gently for 20 minutes.

You will find that as the egg whites cook they attract and hold any remaining particles of fat and residue that might cloud the stock. Strain through a colander, lined with butter muslin, and you have a clear liquid ready to use as the basis of many delicious soups. **See recipes.**

Brown Stock: For this you use the same ingredients and method as for Beef Stock (see recipes) but the bones and vegetables are first browned to give a richer colour to the stock. Place the bones in a roasting tin with the carrot and onion, and roast in a hot oven (200°C/400°F) until a good, rich, brown colour; place them in a large saucepan.

Rinse out the roasting tin with a little water, scraping any brown sediment from the bottom, add to the bones and proceed with the recipe for Beef Stock.

White Stock: This is made as for Chicken Stock but veal bones (knuckle is ideal) are used in place of the chicken, or half veal and half chicken. If using veal bones, save the bone from a shoulder or ask the butcher for a veal knuckle, sawn in two to fit your saucepan.

See also *Yabbies*: Shellfish Stock for Yabbies.

Chicken Stock

This stock is used for white sauce as well as soups.

500 g (1 lb) chicken bones (carcase, backs or wings); about 6 cups cold water (enough to cover bones); 1 tsp salt; 1 carrot, halved; 1 tsp black peppercorns; 1 bouquet garni (1 stick celery, 3 sprigs parsley, 1 sprig fresh thyme, 1 bay leaf).

Place bones in a large, heavy saucepan and add remaining ingredients. Bring to the boil, carefully skimming surface. Cover pan and simmer very gently for 3–4 hours. Strain through a fine sieve and cool. Refrigerate until needed, then remove fat which has risen to top of stock, leaving flavoured jelly underneath. This stock keeps for a week in refrigerator. Makes about 4–5 cups.

NOTE: Use fresh bones for clear, well-flavoured stock. Your poultry supplier often has a bag of bone pieces (carcases, wing tips, etc.) at a very reasonable price, or you may use necks and backs. Giblets, if available, may also be added to the stock, except the chicken liver, which is inclined to give a bitter taste.

Beef Stock

This stock is used in brown sauces and soups. Clarified, it is also used in clear soups.

1 kg (2 lb) beef bones (shank, marrow bone or rib bones or a combination); 500 g (1 lb) shin of beef, chopped; 1 carrot, thickly sliced; 1 onion, thickly sliced; 2 tsp salt; about 12 cups cold water (enough to cover bones); 1 tsp black peppercorns; 1 bouquet garni (2 sticks celery, 4 sprigs parsley, 1 sprig fresh thyme, 1 bay leaf).

Put bones into a large saucepan, then add remaining ingredients. Bring slowly to the boil, skimming surface well, then simmer very gently, half-covered, for 4–5 hours (very slow simmering for a long time is the secret of well-flavoured stock). Strain through a fine sieve, cool, then chill. Remove surface fat before using. Makes about 9–10 cups.

Fish Stock

This stock is used in may fish sauces and soups, and can be frozen or will keep well in the refrigerator for a week.

1 fish head and bones (a snapper head is ideal); 5 cups cold water; 1 cup white wine, or juice 1 lemon with enough water to make 1 cup; 1 tsp white peppercorns; 1 bouquet garni (1 stick celery, 3 sprigs parsley, 1 sprig fresh thyme, 1 bay leaf).

Place all ingredients in a large saucepan and bring to the boil. Skim surface, then simmer gently for 20 minutes. Strain through a fine sieve or cheesecloth. Makes about 5½ cups.

NOTE: For the best flavour, fish stock must be simmered, never boiled. Instead of a snapper head, you can use 2–3 heads of smaller fish, or bones and trimmings left after filleting fish. You will need about 500 g (1 lb) altogether.

Chinese–Style Stock

A stock which combines chicken with pork bones gives a very delicate flavour which is characteristic of Chinese soups. Pork rib bones are good ones to use, and your butcher will save these for you if you give a little notice.

500 g (1 lb) chicken bones; 500 g (1 lb) pork bones; 1 carrot, halved; 1 onion, halved; 1 slice fresh ginger; 2 spring onions, chopped; 1 tsp salt; 1 tsp white peppercorns; 5 cups water (or enough to cover bones).

Put bones into a deep saucepan and add remaining ingredients. Bring to the boil, skimming surface, then simmer very gently for 2–3 hours. Strain and cool, then chill until needed. Makes about 4 cups.

STOLLEN

One of the most popular German fruit breads. Various Stollen are made for Christmas, a time of great rejoicing, and the most famous was developed in Dresden. Its rather dry dough holds together the lovely fruit and nut treats of Christmas – almonds, raisins, currants and brightly coloured glacé fruits. It is customary to bake two at a time – one for the household and one to give away. Stollen improves on keeping and once it becomes over-dry, it is almost as good to eat cut into slices and toasted back to freshness.

Stollen

2 strips candied angelica, cut into 1 cm (½ in) dice; ⅓ cup raisins; ½ cup currants; ½ cup glacé cherries, halved; ⅔ cup chopped mixed candied peel; ⅓ cup rum; 5 cups flour; large pinch salt; ⅓ cup warm milk; 4 g (1½ oz) compressed yeast; 185 g (6 oz) butter; ½ cup caster sugar; 2 eggs, lightly beaten; ½ cup blanched slivered almonds.

TO FINISH: melted butter; caster sugar; sifted icing sugar.

Place angelica, raisins, currants, cherries and peel in a bowl and pour rum over. Toss well and allow to stand for 2 hours or preferably overnight. Sift flour and salt into a bowl. Place warm milk in another bowl, add yeast and butter and stir until yeast is dissolved. Mix in sugar and eggs. Make a well in centre of flour, pour in yeast mixture and mix until smooth, commencing with a wooden spoon and then finishing off with the hand. When dough leaves sides of bowl, turn on to a lightly floured board and knead until smooth and elastic – this may take 10–15 minutes. Place dough into a clean greased bowl, cover with a damp cloth and leave to rise in a warm place until doubled in bulk, 50 minutes – 1 hour.

When risen, knock dough down and shape into a square. Drain rum-soaked fruits, dry well on paper towels and toss in a little flour. Spoon into middle of dough square with almonds. Fold dough over fruits, and knead fruits lightly into dough. Return to greased bowl, cover and leave in a warm place to rise for 30–45 minutes. Knock dough down and turn on to floured board. Halve dough. Roll out each portion into an oval about 2 cm (¾ in) thick. Brush with melted butter, and sprinkle with a little caster sugar. Fold into three lengthways, overlapping centre with each edge by about 2.5 cm (1 in).

Press edges gently to keep in place. Lightly flour hands, taper ends slightly and pat sides to mound stollen in centre. The finished loaf should be about 8 cm (3 in) wide. Place on a greased baking tray. Repeat with second portion of dough. Brush with a little butter and let rise in a warm place for about 1 hour or until doubled in bulk. Bake in a preheated moderately hot oven (190°C/375°F) for about 45 minutes or until golden-brown and crusty. Cool on a wire rack. Dust heavily with sifted icing sugar before slicing and buttering. Makes 2.

VARIATION

POPPY SEED STOLLEN (MOHNSTOLLEN): Omit all fruits, using almonds only. When each portion of dough is rolled into a flat oval, brush with melted butter and fill each with half of following mixture: 250 g (8 oz) poppy seeds, ground and simmered in 1 cup milk with ⅔ cup raisins for 5 minutes; ⅔ cup chopped mixed candied peel, ½ cup sugar; ½ tsp cinnamon; 1 tbs rum; few drops rosewater. Fold and bake as for basic Stollen.

STRAWBERRY

Once called 'strayberry' because it propagated itself by runners, the strawberry was known to epicures in Roman times. Today's varieties are no doubt much changed but let us be thankful for those experiments which have given us a berry not only beautiful in shape and colour but delicately perfumed and refreshing.

Nothing compares with the flavour and fragrance of ripe strawberries. They have enough natural sweetness not to need sugar but this is really a matter of choice. They are wonderful on their own but take to other ingredients extremely kindly – cream, sprinkled with red wine or orange juice, fresh cream and, oddly enough, freshly ground black pepper. And when the time is ripe for an old-fashioned Loving Cup, fill 2 wine glasses with chilled demi-sec champagne, place a dish of sugar-strewn strawberries close by – and the rest is up to you. See recipes.

Strawberries Sarah Bernhardt

2 punnets (500 g/1 lb) strawberries, hulled; 3 tbs caster sugar; ⅓ cup Cointreau; vanilla ice cream; 2 slices glacé pineapple, finely sliced.

CREAM: 1 cup cream; sugar; 1 tbs Cointreau.

Place strawberries in a bowl, reserving 6 of the best for decoration. Sprinkle with caster sugar and Cointreau and chill for a few hours, covered. Place a scoop of vanilla ice cream in 6 individual dishes, sprinkle with glacé pineapple and spoon over strawberries. Mask dessert with whipped cream, which has been sweetened and flavoured with Cointreau. Decorate each portion with a whole strawberry. Serves 6.

Strawberries Romanoff

8 pieces lump sugar; 2 oranges; 6 tbs Curaçao; 2 punnets (500 g/1 lb) strawberries, hulled; 1 cup Crème Chantilly (page 102).

Rub lumps of sugar over skins of oranges until they are well impregnated with flavour of rind. Crush sugar and mix with Curaçao. Add strawberries and macerate in a covered container in refrigerator until serving time. Arrange strawberries in a bowl in a pyramid shape. Put crème chantilly into a piping bag with a rose piping tube and decorate strawberries. Serves 6.

Venetian Strawberries

Believe it or not, the pepper enhances the strawberries' delicate flavour.

2 punnets (500 g/1 lb) strawberries, hulled; 4 tbs caster sugar; freshly ground black pepper; 1 cup demi-sec champagne.

Place strawberries in a bowl. Sprinkle with sugar and allow to stand for 10 minutes. Grind some black pepper over them, then pour over champagne. Stir carefully to combine the flavours. Serves 6.

Strawberries in the Snow

2 punnets (500 g/1 lb) strawberries, hulled and sliced; ½ cup caster sugar; 2 tbs Kirsch (optional); 4 egg whites; 1 cup cream.

Sprinkle strawberries with 1 tbs caster sugar and the Kirsch. Allow to macerate for 15 minutes. Beat egg whites stiffly and gradually beat in remaining sugar. Whip cream stiffly. Fold egg whites into cream, then gently and carefully mix with macerated strawberries. Spoon into a large bowl or individual dishes and serve chilled. Serves 6.

NOTE: A few whole ripe strawberries may be used for decoration.

Strawberries Wilhemine

strawberries; Kirsch; caster sugar; orange juice; Crème Chantilly (page 102) to serve.

Macerate some fine large strawberries in Kirsch, caster sugar and orange juice. Serve with crème chantilly.

Strawberry Fool

Next to strawberries, sugar and cream, this must be the easiest and one of the nicest strawberry desserts. It may be frozen for a delicious strawberry ice cream.

strawberries (enough to make 2 cups purée), hulled; ¹/₄ cup caster sugar; 1 cup cream.

Crush strawberries or purée in a blender. Sweeten with sugar. Whip cream until thick and fold into purée. Serve well chilled. Serves 4–6.

Baked Strawberry Soufflés

1 punnet (250 g/8 oz) strawberries, hulled and sliced; ¹/₂ cup plus 2 tbs sugar; 2 tbs Kirsch; 5 egg whites; whipped cream to serve.

Sprinkle sliced strawberries with 2 tbs sugar and the Kirsch, and macerate for 1 hour. Butter 6 small soufflé dishes and use 2 tbs sugar to coat sides and bottom. Beat egg whites until stiff, then gradually beat in remaining sugar to form a stiff meringue. Drain strawberries and fold through meringue, then spoon into dishes. Stand in a baking tin and add enough hot water to come halfway up sides of dishes. Bake in a preheated moderate oven (180°C/350°F) for 15–18 minutes or until puffed and lightly browned. Serve at once, with whipped cream. Serves 6.

Strawberries à la Ritz

2 punnets (500 g/1 lb) strawberries, hulled; sugar; 1 punnet (250 g/8 oz) raspberries; ³/₄ cup cream; candied violets or slivers candied angelica to decorate.

Place ²/₃ of the strawberries in a glass serving bowl and sprinkle with sugar to taste. Sieve remaining strawberries with raspberries or purée in a blender or food processor. Spoon purée over whole strawberries and chill until serving time. When ready to serve, whip cream and spread over fruit, masking it completely. Decorate with candied violets or slivers of angelica. Serves 4.

NOTE: If fresh raspberries are not available, use frozen raspberries.

STROGANOFF

This superb dish of strips of fillet of beef, lightly sautéed and finished off with sour cream, was said to have been created for a Russian Count (Stroganoff) as a light after-theatre supper dish. There are several schools of thought on how it is made and served. One is that it contained only beef, seasonings, a touch of tomato paste, sour cream and, just before serving, a hint of grated raw onion, then served with straw potatoes as texture contrast. The accompaniment had to be ready at the same time as the Stroganoff, which should only take 15 minutes from start to finish. Triangles of hot buttered toast are another acceptable accompaniment.

A second popular version includes sautéed onions and mushrooms and is often served at dinner parties, accompanied by rice.

The two versions are given below, the first just right for a little after-theatre supper for two. For those who have come to enjoy onions and mushrooms in their Stroganoff as a main course, the quantities have been increased to cater for four.

It is not recommended making Stroganoff for a crowd; the large quantity of meat tends to weep and alter the freshness of the dish. The exception is, of course, when being made in a professional kitchen with very large sauté pans. See recipes.

Beef Stroganoff (1)

375 g (12 oz) fillet steak, in one piece; salt and freshly ground black pepper; 2 tsp flour; 30 g (1 oz) butter; 2 tsp tomato paste; ¹/₃ cup sour cream; 1 tsp grated onion.

Carefully trim away any fat and sinews from steak. Cut into slices about 5 mm (¹/₄ in) thick, and then into strips about 5 cm (2 in) long and 5 mm (¹/₄ in) wide. Season well with salt and pepper and toss in flour. Heat butter in a heavy frying pan. When foam subsides, add beef strips. Fry briskly over high heat for 3–4 minutes, keeping pieces of meat on the move by shaking pan. When meat is brown, lower heat and add tomato paste and sour cream. Stir gently to get up brown crusty bits from bottom of pan and to coat meat with creamy sauce. Adjust seasoning. Transfer to a small saucepan and place in a larger saucepan of boiling water to keep warm and mellow for about 5 minutes. Just before serving, stir in grated onion. Serve on heated plates with buttered toast points or crisp straw potatoes. Serves 2.

NOTE: Packaged straw potatoes will do. Spread out on a baking tray and crisp in a preheated hot oven (200°C/400°F) for about 5 minutes, while making the Stroganoff.

Beef Stroganoff (2)

750 g (1¹/₂ lb) fillet steak, in one piece; salt and freshly ground black pepper; 1 tbs flour; 60 g (2 oz) butter; 2 medium onions, finely sliced into rings; 250 g (8 oz) button mushrooms, finely sliced; 1 tbs tomato paste; ²/₃ cup sour cream.

Prepare strips of steak as in Beef Stroganoff (1). Season well with salt and pepper and toss in flour. Heat 30 g (1 oz) of the butter in a heavy frying pan and fry onion rings until just coloured, about 10 minutes. Remove to a plate with a slotted spoon. Add mushrooms to pan and fry for a few minutes or until softened. Remove to plate with onions. Add remaining butter to pan and heat. Fry beef strips over high heat for 3–4 minutes, shaking pan to keep pieces of meat on the move. Return onions and mushrooms to pan and shake over medium heat for 1 minute to heat through. Season generously with salt and pepper. Add tomato paste and sour cream and cook a few minutes longer, stirring gently to combine ingredients. Serve at once, or keep warm by transferring mixture to a saucepan and standing in a pan of hot water for 10 minutes with lid on. Serve with straw potatoes, buttered noodles or boiled rice. Serves 4 as a main course or 6 as a first course.

STRUDEL

A delicate filled pastry which is usually associated with Austrian cooking, but is claimed as a specialty also by other parts of the former Austro-Hungarian Empire. It is one of the best and most famous of desserts or, with a savoury filling, a handsome luncheon dish or entrée – a wonderfully crisp, tender and flaky construction of paper-thin pastry layers rolled round a filling.

True strudel pastry is fascinating but time-consuming to make. Filo pastry sheets or puff pastry, rolled as thin as possible, can be substituted with good results. **See** recipes.

See also *Apple*: Quick Apple Strudel.

Strudel Pastry

Strudel pastry should be made with high-gluten bread flour so that it will be strong enough to be stretched without tearing. The process of gently pulling and stretching the dough to paper thinness is easier if 2 people work from opposite sides. Be sure to take off any rings, which may tear the dough, before you begin. Have the strudel filling ready before stretching dough – once stretched, it should be used within 5 minutes or it will become brittle.

1½ cups bread flour; ¼ tsp salt; I egg;
½ cup lukewarm water; 2 tbs white vinegar;
2 tbs vegetable oil; melted butter.

Sift flour and salt into a bowl. Beat egg until frothy, stir in water, vinegar and oil and add to flour. Mix with a wooden spoon until smooth, then turn dough out on to a lightly floured work surface. Knead thoroughly, scraping dough off surface as necessary with a knife. As you knead, keep lifting dough and slapping it down hard on the surface. It will be sticky at first but as you continue it will become elastic, smooth and shiny, leaving the hands clean. Kneading will take about 15 minutes and dough should be beaten 100–150 times. Shape it into a ball and cover with a warm bowl. Leave 20 minutes. Meantime, cover a table with a cloth that hangs over edges. Flour cloth well. Brush top of dough with melted butter and lift it on to the floured cloth. Roll

out to 3 mm (⅛ in) thickness. Now slip your closed fists, thumbs tucked in and palms downward, under dough. Working from centre, lift and pull it out gently by pulling your hands apart. Work toward edges and move round table so that dough is evenly stretched on all sides. If dry patches appear in dough, brush with melted butter to keep them supple. If dough tears, pinch it together. When dough is as thin as paper, brush generously all over with melted butter and trim off thick edges with scissors. This quantity of dough will make one large strudel to serve 10–12. Fill and bake as directed in recipe.

Apple Strudel

6 large cooking apples, peeled, cored and thinly sliced; ½ cup caster sugar; 1½ tsp cinnamon;
½ cup sultanas; 2 tsp grated lemon rind;
I quantity Strudel Pastry (opposite); melted butter;
I cup fresh breadcrumbs fried in butter.

Mix apples, sugar, cinnamon, sultanas and lemon rind together and set aside. Brush stretched-out strudel dough with melted butter and sprinkle with fried breadcrumbs. Spoon apple mixture in an 8–10 cm (3–4 in) wide line along one side, to within 5 cm (2 in) of the edges. Fold edges of pastry over filling, and roll up, starting from filling end, by lifting the cloth to make the dough roll over and over on itself. Lift strudel on to a greased baking tray, curving it into a horseshoe if too long for the tray. Brush with more melted butter. Bake in a preheated very hot oven (230°C/450°F) for 10 minutes, then reduce heat to hot (200°C/400°F) and bake a further 20 minutes or until strudel is crisp and brown. Brush several more times with melted butter while cooking, and again after removing from oven. Serve warm, cut into wide diagonal slices. Serves 10–12.

NOTE: Strudel should be served freshly baked, as the pastry toughens when cold. However, it can be frozen unbaked and then baked straight from the freezer. Remove from freezer wrapping and place on a greased baking tray. Bake as directed in recipe, but allow an extra 15–20 minutes' baking time after reducing heat to hot (200°C/400°F). Test by inserting a fine skewer into the centre; tip should be hot when withdrawn. Cover strudel loosely with foil if pastry is over-browning before filling is cooked through.

Cheese Strudel

I quantity Strudel Pastry (opposite); I cup fresh breadcrumbs fried in butter; melted butter.

FILLING: 60 g (2 oz) butter; grated rind I lemon;
⅓ cup caster sugar; 375 g (12 oz) creamed cottage cheese; 2 tsp flour; I egg; ½ cup sultanas,
soaked in 2 tbs rum or brandy.

To make filling, cream butter with lemon rind and sugar, beating until mixture resembles whipped cream. Rub cottage cheese through a sieve, or purée in a food processor until smooth. Using a wooden spoon, work cheese and flour into butter mixture. Beat in egg, and stir in fruit. Sprinkle stretched-out strudel dough with breadcrumbs, then spoon filling in a line along one side to within 5 cm (2 in) of the edges. Fold edges of dough over filling and brush with melted butter. Roll up, starting from filling end, by lifting cloth to make dough roll over and over on itself. With the last roll, roll strudel on to a greased baking tray; curve it into a horseshoe if too long for tray. Brush with more melted butter. Bake in a preheated hot oven (200°C/400°F) for 20 minutes, then reduce heat to moderate (180°C/350°F) and bake a further 10 minutes. Brush several more times with melted butter while cooking. Strudel is done when pastry is as crisp as parchment and golden-brown. Serve warm. Strudel can be made ahead and re-warmed in a low oven. Serves 8.

Savoury Fish or Chicken Strudels

These strudels are made with filo pastry. The recipe makes 2 strudels which will cut into 5 servings each – nice for a luncheon or small buffet party. Can be frozen.

90 g (3 oz) butter; 6 spring onions, finely chopped; 4 tbs flour; 2 cups warm milk; salt and freshly ground white pepper; $^1/_4$ tsp nutmeg; 6 hard-boiled eggs, coarsely chopped; 750 g (1$^1/_2$ lb) fish fillets, poached, drained and flaked, or 2 cups cooked chicken meat, chopped; $^1/_4$ cup finely chopped parsley; $^1/_2$ cup grated cheese; $^1/_2$ tsp Dijon mustard; 16 sheets filo pasty; melted butter.

Melt butter in a heavy saucepan, add spring onions and cook gently for 3 minutes. Stir in flour and cook for 1 minute. Remove from heat, cool a little and add warm milk, stirring until smoothly blended. Return to heat and stir until boiling. Season to taste with salt, pepper and nutmeg. Allow to cool, then mix with chopped eggs, fish or chicken, parsley, cheese and mustard.

Make one strudel at a time. Remove 8 sheets filo from packet, unfold on to a dry tea-towel and cover with another dry tea-towel and brush lightly with melted butter. Top with another sheet, butter it, and so on with the remaining sheets. Spoon half the filling in a line along one long side of stacked pastry, to within 5 cm (2 in) of edges. Fold edges of pastry over filling and brush with melted butter. Using the tea-towel to help, gently roll up strudel from filling end. With the last roll, roll strudel on to a greased baking tray. Brush with melted butter. Make another strudel in the same way. Bake the strudels in a preheated hot oven (200°C/400°F) for 20 minutes, then reduce heat to moderate (180°C/350°F) and bake a further 10 minutes. Brush several more times with melted butter while cooking. Strudel is done when pastry is as crisp as parchment and golden-brown. Serve hot, cut into wide slices.

Strudels can be made ahead and reheated in a preheated moderate oven (180°C/350°F), covering them loosely with foil if tops are browning too much. Serves 10.

NOTE: Flaked canned salmon may be used instead of poached fish fillets to make the filling.

STUFFING

Stuffings are made with a wide variety of ingredients – breadcrumbs, sausage and other minced meats, fruit and rice. As well as adding an interesting flavour, a stuffing can help the cook by holding the food in shape, keeping it moist and making it go further.

It is important to mix and handle stuffings lightly so as not to compact them, and to leave room for the stuffings to expand during cooking and stay light. If some stuffing is left over after filling food, cook it separately in a greased baking dish.

It is best to cook onion and garlic lightly before adding them to a stuffing, as this improves the flavour and aides digestion. You should also pre-cook pork or sausage mince until it changes colour, to make sure that it will cook through. Always stuff poultry just before cooking; this is a safety measure.

Make fresh breadcrumbs for stuffings, using bread 2–4 days old, by pulling it apart very lightly with your fingers or with two forks. Do not put bread through a mincer, as the stuffing will be too compact. Of course if you have a blender or food processor, beautiful crumbs can be made in a trice. See recipes.

Basic Breadcrumb Stuffing

1 small onion, chopped; 1 stick celery with leaves, chopped; 90 g (3 oz) butter; 1–2 tsp poultry seasoning or dried sage; $^1/_2$ tsp salt; freshly ground black pepper; 2 tbs chopped parsley (optional); 5 cups bread cubes or crumbs; water, milk or chicken stock (optional).

Sauté onion and celery in butter until soft but not brown. Combine with poultry seasoning or sage, salt, pepper, parsley and bread cubes or crumbs. If a moist dressing is desired, add enough liquid barely to moisten crumbs. Makes sufficient for 2 chickens or 1 small turkey.

VARIATIONS

BREADCRUMB CHESTNUT STUFFING: Follow recipe for Basic Breadcrumb Stuffing, reducing quantity of breadcrumbs to 3$^1/_2$ cups, and adding 1 cup boiled, coarsely chopped chestnuts. To prepare chestnuts, cut a cross in flat side of each shell. Boil in water to cover 20 minutes or until tender. Shell, peel and chop. (Alternatively, use canned.)

MUSHROOM STUFFING: Cook 250 g (8 oz) sliced mushrooms with onion, then proceed as for Basic Breadcrumb Stuffing.

GIBLET STUFFING: Simmer giblets in water until tender. Chop and measure. Substitute for an equal amount of the breadcrumbs, then proceed as for Basic Breadcrumb Stuffing.

SAUSAGE STUFFING: Crumble 125–185 g (4–6 oz) sausage mince and brown in a frying pan. Remove sausage and sauté onion and celery in part sausage fat and part butter. Add all to crumbs and proceed as for Basic Breadcrumb Stuffing.

Apple, Prune and Nut Stuffing

90 g (3 oz) butter; 1 onion, finely chopped; 2 cooking apples, peeled, cored and finely diced; 4 cups cubed day-old bread; 1 cup chopped stoned prunes; 1/4 cup chopped walnuts; 1/2 cup pine nuts; 1/2 cup chopped parsley; 1 tsp chopped fresh sage, or pinch dried; salt and freshly ground black pepper.

Melt butter in a heavy frying pan and sauté onion until soft and golden. Add apples to pan and cook for 3–4 minutes or until apple is soft. Meanwhile, lightly toast bread cubes in a preheated moderately slow oven (160°C/325°F) for 10 minutes or until crisp. Remove apples and onion with a slotted spoon and place in a bowl with prunes. In same pan, lightly fry walnuts and pine nuts until golden. Combine nuts with apple mixture and bread cubes, and fold through parsley and sage. Season with salt and pepper, and use at once. Makes sufficient for a goose or large duckling.

Mushroom Rice Stuffing

Use for fish, tomatoes, peppers and marrow.

2 rashers streaky bacon, rind removed and chopped; 30 g (1 oz) butter; 1 tbs finely chopped onion; 90 g (3 oz) mushrooms, finely chopped; 1 cup cooked rice; 1 tbs chopped parsley; 2 tbs chopped mixed fresh herbs, or 1 tsp dried; salt and freshly ground black pepper; lemon juice.

Gently fry bacon over medium heat until fat runs. Add butter, onion and mushrooms and fry until soft. Stir in rice, parsley and herbs, and season with salt, pepper and lemon juice. Makes sufficient to stuff 4 tomatoes or peppers, or 1 large fish or marrow.

Ham and Spinach Stuffing

This stuffing is superb with veal.

1/2 bunch spinach; salt and freshly ground black pepper; nutmeg; 1 cup finely chopped cooked ham;

1 small onion, finely chopped; 30 g (1 oz) butter; 1 cup fresh breadcrumbs.

Place spinach in a heavy saucepan with a little salt, pepper and nutmeg. Cover pan and cook for 3–4 minutes until softened, shaking occasionally to prevent sticking. Drain well and, when cool enough to handle, squeeze out as much water as possible with your hands. Chop spinach finely and place in a bowl with ham. Season with salt and pepper. Cook onion gently in butter until soft and golden. Add to spinach and ham with a pinch of nutmeg and breadcrumbs and mix ingredients lightly together with a fork. Adjust seasoning. Makes sufficient to stuff a shoulder of veal for roasting or a breast of veal for braising.

Sausage or Meat Stuffing

Use for turkey, chicken and veal.

1 medium onion, finely chopped; 1 tbs butter; 500 g (1 lb) minced pork or sausage mince; 1 tbs chopped parsley; 1 tsp dried sage; good pinch ground mace; 1 cup fresh white breadcrumbs; salt and freshly ground black pepper.

Cook onion in butter until soft, then add meat and cook, stirring and breaking down lumps with a fork, until meat changes colour. Remove from heat and lightly mix in remaining ingredients. Cool before using. Makes sufficient to stuff breast of 1 x 6 kg (12 lb) turkey, or 2 chickens or boned shoulders of veal.

Herb Stuffing

Use for fish, poultry or meat.

1 small onion, finely chopped; 30 g (1 oz) butter; 2 cups fresh breadcrumbs; 1 tbs chopped fresh herbs, or 1 tsp dried (see below); 2 tbs chopped parsley; 1 tsp grated lemon rind; 1/2 tsp salt; freshly ground black pepper; 1 egg, beaten; stock or water.

Cook onion gently in butter until golden. In a bowl, mix together breadcrumbs, herbs, parsley, lemon rind, salt and a generous amount of pepper. Add onion and butter, egg, and enough stock or water to moisten stuffing very lightly. Do not overmix, just stir through with a fork. Makes sufficient to stuff a chicken, a large whole fish, or a shoulder of lamb.

NOTE: Use sage or savory for duck or goose; lemon thyme for fish, chicken or veal; mint for lamb.

Baltimore Oyster Stuffing

2 tbs bacon fat; 1 tbs chopped parsley; 2 tsp snipped chives; 5 cups stale bread cubes or crumbs; 1 tsp chopped fresh marjoram or thyme; 1 tsp salt; freshly ground black pepper; 25 bottled or fresh oysters, drained.

Melt bacon fat, add parsley and chives and cook until wilted. Add herb mixture to bread with marjoram, salt and pepper. Lightly mix in oysters. If stuffing seems too dry, moisten with a little oyster liquor. Makes sufficient for 2 chickens or 1 x 3 kg (6 lb) turkey.

Mandarin Stuffing for Goose

250 g (8 oz) chestnuts; 60 g (2 oz) butter; ¹/₂ cup diced celery with leaves; 3 mandarins; I x 250 g (8 oz) packet prepared bread stuffing; ¹/₂ tsp poultry seasoning; 3 cups cooked rice; ¹/₂ cup stock or water.

Cut a cross in flat side of each chestnut. Boil in water to cover for 20 minutes or until tender. Shell, peel and chop. There should be about 1 cup. Melt butter in a frying pan, add celery and cook over medium heat about 10 minutes. Meanwhile, peel mandarins, removing white membranes. Cut segments in half and remove seeds. Combine mandarins, bread stuffing, chestnuts, poultry seasoning, rice and stock. Add cooked celery and butter and mix together lightly with a fork. Makes sufficient for 1 x 4.5 kg (9 lb) goose. **NOTE:** Canned chestnuts may be used instead of fresh. Just drain and chop.

Peach and Rosemary Stuffing

This is an unusual stuffing that goes well with lamb or chicken.

I cup fresh white breadcrumbs; I tsp chopped fresh rosemary or ¹/₂ tsp dried; 4 canned peach halves, chopped; ¹/₂ egg, beaten; salt and freshly ground black pepper.

Combine all ingredients. Makes sufficient to stuff a 2 kg (4 lb) boned shoulder of lamb. **NOTE:** 2 fresh peaches can be used.

Potato and Parsley Stuffing

Uses as a stuffing for duck or chicken. For a goose or small turkey, double the quantities.

I tbs beef dripping; I onion, chopped; 250 g (8 oz) pork sausage mince; I cup freshly mashed potatoes; salt and freshly ground black pepper; ¹/₂ cup chopped parsley.

Melt dripping in a frying pan and fry onion until pale golden. Stir in sausage mince, breaking it up as it cooks and browns. Remove pan from heat and mix in potatoes, salt, pepper and parsley. Cool before using. Makes sufficient for a chicken or duckling.

Rice Stuffing with Herbs

Use as a stuffing for vegetables such as red or green peppers, tomatoes, cucumbers, squash, marrow or wrapped in cabbage or vine leaves. It is also excellent as a stuffing for a roasting chicken.

I¹/₃ cups long-grain rice; 45 g (I¹/₂ oz) butter; I onion, chopped; 4 rashers streaky bacon, rind removed and chopped; salt and freshly ground black pepper; 6 tbs chopped mixed fresh herbs (chervil, tarragon, dill, mint, parsley and chives).

Cook rice in boiling salted water until almost tender; drain. Melt butter in a frying pan and cook onion until translucent. Add bacon and fry, stirring, until lightly coloured. Remove from heat and stir in rice, salt and pepper. Stir in herbs. Makes about 3 cups.

SUCCOTASH

Americans learned to make succotash from the Indians, who cooked corn and beans in a pot together. In winter succotash was made with dried corn and beans, while in summer the fresh vegetables were used. Today canned or frozen corn and beans make suitable substitutes. Serve succotash hot, well seasoned with plenty of pepper, as a side dish for roast pork, poultry or beef, or with ham steaks.

Succotash

I cup canned baby lima beans, drained; I cup canned sweetcorn kernels, drained; salt; ¹/₂ tsp black pepper; pinch cayenne; ¹/₂ tsp sugar; 30 g (I oz) butter; chopped parsley.

Rinse lima beans and corn under cold running water. Place in a saucepan with salt, pepper, cayenne, sugar and butter. Heat very gently, stirring now and again, until piping hot. Sprinkle with chopped parsley to serve. Serves 4.

SUCKING PIG

See *Pork*.

SUET

The firm, white fat around lamb and beef kidneys. Beef suet is the kind you will usually find, and is the one to use when a recipe calls for suet. It can be bought in solid form from the butcher, or grated and packaged, usually with a little added flour, ready to use. To prepare butcher's suet, chill it first to make it firmer, then remove membrane and grate or chop fine. A little flour from the recipe sprinkled on the suet, will help to keep it from sticking to the knife.

Boiled Plum Pudding

This is not as heavy as the usual pudding and has no spices, but develops a marvellous flavour after two weeks' maturation. This is the pudding of Dickens' England.

155 g (5 oz) raisins, coarsely chopped; 125 g (4 oz) stoned dates, coarsely copped; 155 g (5 oz) sultanas; 125 g (4 oz) currants; 90 g (3 oz) chopped mixed candied peel; ¼ cup brandy; 4 cups self-raising flour; 1 tsp salt; 250 g (8 oz) beef suet, grated; 1 cup caster sugar; ½ cup treacle; 1½ cups water; extra brandy to serve.

Soak fruit and peel in brandy overnight. Sift flour and salt into a large mixing bowl. Rub suet into flour until mixture resembles breadcrumbs. Stir in sugar, brandy-soaked fruit and treacle mixed with water. Mix thoroughly to a firm batter. Rinse a large pudding cloth in boiling water, remove (using rubber gloves) and wring out well. Sift flour over and shake off any excess. Turn pudding mixture into centre of cloth and gather cloth firmly around pudding. Secure cloth tightly with string. Tie ends of pudding cloth around a wooden spoon and reset wooden spoon on edges of saucepan to prevent pudding touching bottom of pan. Pour boiling water into pan to cover pudding and place a lid on top. Steam for 1 hour. By this time, pudding will have taken shape and wooden spoon may be removed. Steam for a further 1½ hours. Hang pudding in a dark, dry place for at least 2 weeks to mature. On day it is to be eaten, steam pudding for a further 1-1½ hours. Unwrap and turn on to a heated platter. Heat some brandy, set alight and pour flaming over pudding, taking it immediately to the table. Serve with vanilla ice cream, whipped cream or Hard Sauce (see page 191). Serves 8–10.

NOTE: Do not worry if a little mould forms on the cloth while the pudding is maturing. Just wipe it off if possible and boil pudding as instructed in the recipe. Never, never place the pudding in a clean cloth. This will let the water in as soon as you boil it, ruining your pudding.

SUGAR

A sweet substance extracted from many plants, chiefly sugar cane, sugar beet, sugar maple and various species of palm.

Cane Sugar: Different varieties of cane sugar have somewhat different applications. Despite the preference for raw sugar by health food enthusiasts there is no significant difference between raw and refined sugars; the only difference is taste. Raw sugar, brown sugar and syrups are higher in mineral content than white sugar but shouldn't be regarded as an important food source of any nutrient other than carbohydrate.

Ordinary White Granulated Sugar: The most common sugar, used as an everyday sweetener. It is the best to use in the making of syrups and toffees as it gives the clearest results.

Caster Sugar: A fine white sugar; best for creaming and beating cake and icing mixtures and where a less grainy result is wanted.

Brown Sugar: Sugar that is refined further and then coated with a film of molasses. Brown sugar can replace white in any recipe where the flavour will not be harmed by a note of molasses.

Icing Sugar: A powdered sugar with grains so fine as to be almost intangible. Pure icing sugar is used to make icing for fine 'piped' decoration of cakes as well as a firm covering. Soft icing mixture is pure icing sugar with cornflour, which helps keep the grains soft. It is used in icings and frostings where a soft finish is required.

Demerara Sugar: The least refined sugar we can buy. Centrifuges spin the raw sugar and, much like a clothes dryer, force the liquid off the crystals. This is how white sugar is made. Demerara sugar still has much of the molasses left in the crystals, giving it a distinctive rich flavour which is excellent for baking, making chutneys and desserts. New to the Australian market but well known in the United Kingdom, it is produced in Mauritius, although presently Australian production is being considered.

Cubed or Loaf Sugar: Dates from the time before we had the technology to crystallise sugar, when sugar was sold in large hard chunks (it still is in some parts of the world). When sugar was needed a small tool was used to chip away at the rock of sugar. After a time sugar refineries began to cut these loafs into smaller and smaller chunks, eventually producing the sugar cube we know today. It is a convenient product for adding to hot drinks and for rubbing over citrus rind to add flavour to a dish.

Palm Sugar: Made from the sap of many types of palm it is used in different Asian foods. Available in Asian stores, it is dominant in the cuisines of Southeast Asia. Palm sugar is now widely used in preserving, snacks, cakes, drinks and sweetmeats.

Beet Sugar: In Europe and the US, sugar made from sugar beet is common. The sugar beet plant is a root crop, that grows underground. When fully grown, a sugar beet weighs 1–2 kg (2–4 lb) and produces about 3 teaspoons of sugar. Sugar beets are white in colour, and quite sweet when eaten raw. Sugar made from sugar beets is identical to that made from sugar cane; however, sugar and molasses (the kind for human consumption) come only from the processing of sugar cane.

SUKIYAKI

Perhaps Japan's most famous dish: beef and vegetables cooked with soy sauce and sake at the table. An electric frypan is ideal for the purpose. The cooking time is brief and the food is cooked and eaten in several batches. To cut the beef into paper-thin slices, wrap first in plastic wrap and place in freezer until firm enough to slice easily.

Sukiyaki

2 onions, finely sliced; 6 spring onions, cut into 5 cm (2 in) lengths; I eggplant, finely sliced; 125 g (4 oz) Chinese cabbage, cut into 6 cm (2¹/₂ in) strips; 6 dried mushrooms, soaked in warm water for 30 minutes, drained, stalks removed and sliced; 125 g (4 oz) bean sprouts; I x 225 g can bamboo shoots, drained and cut into wedges; I kg (2 lb) beef fillet or Scotch fillet, cut into paper-thin slices; 60 g (2 oz) beef suet, chopped; light soy sauce; sugar; I–2 tbs sake or dry sherry; I cup beef stock; 125 g (4 oz) bean curd; 60 g (2 oz) rice vermicelli, cut into 10 cm (4 in) lengths.

TO SERVE: eggs; soy sauce; boiled rice.

Arrange vegetables and beef in separate rows on a platter. Heat a large iron pan or electric frypan. Rub with some suet, then fry fat for about 5 minutes or until pan is well greased. Remove any remaining pieces of suet. Sauté batch of onions and spring onions for 5 minutes, stirring frequently. Add batch of remaining vegetables, soy sauce and sugar to taste and wine, then moisten with stock. Add some bean curd and cook over high heat for 5 minutes, stirring frequently. Push all ingredients to side of pan, add batch of beef and cook, stirring, for 3 minutes, adding some vermicelli for the last minute. The guests help themselves from pan, to which more meat and vegetables are added for second helpings. Before cooking second helping add more suet. Traditionally, each diner breaks a raw egg into their bowl, beats it lightly with chopsticks, adds a little soy sauce if liked, and then dips hot food in it before eating, but some prefer to omit this step. Serve with boiled rice. Serve 6–8.

SULTANA

A variety of seedless, white grape once grown only in Smyrna, Turkey. Today sultanas are grown in many parts of the world where they are dried either naturally in the sun or artificially. In North America seedless white raisins or sultanas are classified as part of the raisin variety of grape.

Sultanas have become among the most well-loved of all dried fruits, and most are available washed, packaged and ready for use. Some can be bought in bulk and these, too, are usually ready-prepared; if not, remove any stalks or grit, rinse and dry well on paper towels before using.

Sultanas are nutritious and delicious eaten as a snack on their own. Children love to find a little packet of sultanas in their school lunch-boxes or mixed with a little salad of grated carrot and cheese. Sultanas also appear in many cakes, biscuits, puddings and in some savoury dishes, particularly those containing rice.

Store sultanas in an airtight container after opening the pack, and buy only about as many as you need at the time to keep them at their peak. To hold in top condition for longer than a week or two, store in refrigerator or freezer. See recipes.

See also *Fruit*, *Dried* and *Candied*.

Sultana Rice

2 cups water; I tsp salt; I slice lemon; ¹/₄ cup sultanas; I cup long-grain rice; 2 tbs chopped parsley.

Place water in saucepan and bring to the boil. Add salt, lemon slice and sultanas and sprinkle in rice. Return to the boil and stir once or twice, then turn heat as low as possible, cover pan and steam gently for 20–25 minutes. Do not lift lid or stir during steaming time. Remove from heat, fork through rice to allow steam to escape and fold in parsley. Serve with pork, poultry, ham and veal dishes. Serves 4.

Turkish Sultana Compote

2 cups sultanas; ¹/₂ cup warm water; ¹/₂ cup honey; grated rind I lemon; ¹/₂ cup pine nuts; I cup plain yogurt to serve.

Soak sultanas in cold water to cover for 1 hour. Drain. Boil together warm water and honey for 2–3 minutes. Stir in sultanas and lemon rind. Simmer over gentle heat for 10 minutes, skimming with slotted spoon if necessary. Stir in pine nuts. Chill thoroughly before serving with yogurt. Serves 4–6.

Sultana and Cashew Pilau

Serve as an accompaniment to spiced chicken or lamb dishes.

60 g (2 oz) ghee; I onion, finely chopped; 2 cups long-grain rice; salt and freshly ground black pepper; 4 cups boiling chicken stock; ¹/₂ cup cashew nuts; ¹/₂ cup sultanas.

Melt 30 g (1 oz) ghee in a heavy saucepan, add onion and cook gently until golden. Stir in rice, season with salt and pepper and cook gently until rice becomes coated with ghee and turns translucent. Pour boiling stock over rice, stir once and return to the boil. Lower heat, cover and simmer very gently for about 20 minutes or until liquid is absorbed and rice is tender. Remove lid and cook for 2 minutes more. Heat remaining ghee and fry cashews and sultanas for 2–3 minutes, stirring constantly. Turn contents of pan into rice and fork through. Serves 8–10.

Sultana Bread

3 cups flour; 2 tsp baking powder; 185 g (6 oz) butter; ³/₄ cup caster sugar; I¹/₄ cups sultanas; 3 eggs; I tsp vanilla; about ¹/₂ cup milk.

Sift flour and baking powder into a large mixing bowl. Rub in butter with fingertips, then add sugar and sultanas. Make a well in centre. Lightly mix eggs and vanilla and pour into well. Mix with a fork to a soft dough, adding milk as necessary. Spoon into a greased and lined 23 x 12 cm (9 x 5 in) loaf tin, spreading evenly. Bake in a preheated moderate oven (180°C/350°F) for 1½ hours. Reduce temperature to moderately slow (160°C/325°F) after baking for 1 hour if loaf is getting too brown. When baked a skewer inserted in centre will come out clean. Serve sliced and buttered.

Sultana Cake

This cake is beautifully moist and will keep for up to 10 days when stored in an airtight container. Excellent for lunch-boxes, picnics, with tea or coffee, or simply to have on hand to offer guests when they drop in.

250 g (8 oz) butter; I cup sugar; 3 eggs; ²/₃ cup milk; I¹/₂ cups sultanas; 3 tbs almonds, blanched and chopped; 3 tbs chopped mixed candied peel; 3 cups flour; I¹/₂ tsp baking powder.

Beat butter and sugar until light and fluffy. Add eggs and mix well. Stir in milk gradually, then add sultanas, almonds and peel. Fold in flour and baking powder sifted together. Spoon into a greased and bottom-lined 20 cm (8 in) round or square cake tin. Bake in a preheated moderately slow oven (160°C/325°F) for about 1½ hours or until a skewer inserted in centre comes out clean. Cool on a wire rack.

Sultana Spice Cake

I cup firmly packed brown sugar; I cup sultanas; I¹/₄ cups water; 125 g (4 oz) butter; I tsp cinnamon; ¹/₂ tsp nutmeg; ¹/₂ tsp ground allspice; 2 cups flour; I tsp bicarbonate of soda; I tsp baking powder; ¹/₂ tsp salt.

Combine sugar, sultanas, water, butter and spices in a heavy saucepan. Bring to the boil and boil for 5 minutes. Allow to become completely cold. Sift flour, soda, baking powder and salt, and stir into boiled mixture. Pour into a greased and lined 21 x 15 cm (8½ x 6 in) loaf tin or a 20 cm (8 in) ring tin. Bake in a preheated moderate oven (180°C/350°F) for 50–60 minutes or until a skewer inserted comes out clean. Turn out on to a wire rack, carefully remove lining paper and cool.

Sultana Fingers

Easy-to-make biscuit bars that require no cooking.

125 g (4 oz) butter; I cup sultanas; ¹/₂ cup sugar; I egg, lightly beaten; I tsp vanilla; 250 g (8 oz) milk arrowroot biscuits, finely crushed; ¹/₄ cup crushed mixed nuts.

CHOCOLATE ICING: I cup icing sugar; 2 tbs cocoa powder; 30 g (I oz) butter, melted; I tbs hot water; ¹/₂ tsp vanilla.

Place butter, sultanas and sugar in a large saucepan and bring slowly to the boil, stirring to dissolve sugar. Remove from heat and cool slightly, then add egg and vanilla, beating well. Add biscuit crumbs and blend together thoroughly. Press mixture into a well-greased 28 x 19 cm (11 x 7½ in) lamington tin. **CHOCOLATE ICING:** Sift icing sugar and cocoa together, add remaining ingredients and mix well until smooth and glossy. When biscuit mixture is cold, spread with chocolate icing and sprinkle with chopped nuts. Leave until icing is set then cut into 2.5 cm (1 in) fingers before serving. Makes about 20.

Sultana Sesame Biscuits

125 g (4 oz) butter; ¹/₂ cup sugar; I egg; I tsp cinnamon; ¹/₂ cup toasted sesame seeds; ¹/₂ cup sultanas; I cup wholemeal flour, sifted.

Cream butter with sugar until light and fluffy. Add egg and beat well. Stir in remaining ingredients and blend well. Spread mixture in a greased 28 x 19 cm (11 x 7½ in) lamington tin. Bake in a preheated moderate oven (180°C/350°F) for 20 minutes. Remove from oven, cut into fingers and allow to cool in tin. Makes 24.

NOTE: To toast sesame seeds, heat a dry frying pan until moderately hot, add sesame seeds and stir for 1–2 minutes until toasted and golden-brown.

SUMMER PUDDING

One of the loveliest fruit puddings of the world is English Summer Pudding. Humble white bread is used as a container for the delicious berry fruits of summer. The pudding is weighted, chilled, unmoulded and served with thick cream. Individual Summer Puddings make a lovely finale to any summer dinner party. Make Summer Pudding with fresh or frozen raspberries, loganberries, red or blackcurrants, boysenberries, blackberries or strawberries.

Summer Pudding

¹/₂ loaf thick sliced white bread, slightly stale, crusts removed; 500 g (I lb) strawberries, hulled; 500 g (I lb) raspberries or other berry fruit of your choice (fresh or frozen); ³/₄ cup sugar; thick cream to serve.

Use most of bread slices to line bottom and sides of a greased 6–8 cup pudding basin. Cut slices to fit basin and overlap bread to ensure there are no spaces through which fruit juice can escape. Place fruit in a saucepan with just water clinging to it from rinsing. (Frozen fruit is not rinsed.) Sprinkle sugar over.

Cover and cook very gently for 3 minutes or until sugar has dissolved. Leave to cool. Fill bread-lined basin with cold fruit, adding enough fruit juice to soak surrounding bread. Reserve remaining juice. Cover top of pudding with more bread slices cut to fit, place a plate on top and weight with a couple of cans. Chill overnight. Unmould pudding on to a deep serving platter, pour reserved juice over and serve with thick cream. Serves 6–8.

NOTE: You may omit the strawberries and substitute other berry fruits if you wish.

VARIATION

INDIVIDUAL SUMMER PUDDINGS: Line 6 x 1-cup individual soufflé dishes with bread (you may need to use more bread than in above recipe) and proceed as above. Weight each dish with small plates, saucers or several thicknesses of foil with a can on top. Chill overnight. Serve as above. Serves 6.

SUNDAE

A concoction of ice cream and sauce, syrup, fruit, whipped cream, chopped nuts, grated chocolate – the combinations limited only by your imagination and degree of nonchalance about digestion or waistline. The name and the dish are attributed to the ingenuity of an American, who complied with a law forbidding the sale of ice cream sodas on a Sunday, by simply omitting the soda water and calling the new dish after the day. Serve a sundae in a long, shallow dish, in a tall glass or, for a grand effect, in a brandy balloon. See recipes.

Banana Split

2–3 scoops vanilla ice cream; 1 banana, halved lengthways; Hot Chocolate Sauce (page 84); whipped cream; chopped nuts; 1 glacé cherry; 1 cream wafer biscuit.

Arrange ice cream along a shallow dish. Place half banana on each side of ice cream. Spoon over chocolate sauce, decorate with whipped cream and nuts and top with a cherry. Serve at once, with a wafer cream biscuit pushed into one end. Serves 1.

Triple Strawberry Sundae

4–6 strawberries; 1/2 cup whipped cream; 1 scoop strawberry ice cream; 2 scoops vanilla or chocolate ice cream; 1 langue de chat or other crisp finger biscuit.

STRAWBERRY SAUCE: 6–8 strawberries, hulled; 1 tbs caster sugar.

To make sauce, mash strawberries with caster sugar. Chill well.

Reserve one large, perfect, unhulled strawberry for decoration. Take out about 2 tbs whipped cream and set aside for decoration. Hull and slice remaining

strawberries and fold into remaining cream. Arrange 1 scoop each strawberry and vanilla ice cream in a dish or glass. Pile strawberry and cream mixture on top, then remaining scoop of vanilla ice cream. Spoon sauce over and decorate with reserved cream and strawberry. Serve with langue de chat or other biscuit. Serves 1.

Hot Marshmallow Sundae

3 scoops coffee or chocolate ice cream; 2 halves canned or fresh pears or peaches, or 4 halves apricots; 3/4 cup hot Marshmallow Sauce (page 255); slivered, toasted almonds.

Arrange ice cream and fruit in a dish or glass. Pour over hot sauce and scatter with almonds. Serve immediately. Serves 1.

SUPREME OF CHICKEN (SUPREME DE VOLAILLE)

A boneless, skinless half-breast of chicken, often sold in poultry shops as a 'chicken fillet'.

Supremes are wonderfully versatile morsels, easy to turn into a speedy dinner for one or a stylish dinner party dish. They can be cooked in the oven so that they remain white, for serving with a good sauce, or can be sautéed to a delicate golden-brown. They can also be beaten flat and cooked in the same way as Chicken Schnitzel (see pages 76–7), or rolled round a stuffing.

■ **BASIC PREPARATION:** Cut and pull out the white tendon that runs down the underside of the meat. Trim edges neatly, then flatten and shape the supremes with your hands. To beat a supreme flat, place it between 2 sheets of greased greaseproof paper and beat gently with a cutlet bat, rolling pin or the flat side of a meat mallet, to a thickness of 5 mm (1/4 in). See recipes.

Sautéed Supremes of Chicken

4 supremes chicken; seasoned flour; 2 tbs oil; 60 g (2 oz) butter; lemon wedges or pan sauce of your choice (page 520) to serve.

Turn the supremes in seasoned flour and pat off excess. Heat oil in a frying pan, add butter and, just as it begins to turn brown, add supremes, flat side down. Sauté on moderately high heat for 3 minutes, turn and sauté other side for 2 minutes. Press chicken with your finger. If it feels springy, it is ready. If still soft and yielding, cook 1 minute longer and check again. Be careful not to overcook; if cooked until there is no springiness, supremes are overdone and will be tough and dry. Remove to a heated serving dish and serve with lemon wedges, or keep hot a minute or two while making one of the following pan sauces, or one of the Pan Sauces on pages 458–9. Serves 2–4.

White–Cooked Supremes of Chicken

4 supremes chicken; $^1/_2$ tsp lemon juice; salt and freshly ground white pepper; 60 g (2 oz) butter; I quantity hot Sauce Suprême, Poulette, Bercy, Mushroom or other sauce of your choice to serve (see *Sauces*); bouquet of fresh watercress or parsley sprigs to garnish.

Rub supremes with lemon juice and season lightly with salt and pepper. Heat butter in a flameproof casserole or baking dish large enough to take supremes in one layer. When butter is foaming, add supremes and turn over quickly so that they are coated with butter. Lay a piece of buttered grease-proof paper over chicken, cover dish and place in a preheated hot oven (200°C/400°F). Cook for 6 minutes, then press chicken with your finger. If it feels springy, it is ready. If still soft and yielding, cover, cook 1 minute longer and check again. Be careful not to overcook; if cooked until there is no springiness, supremes will be overdone and will be tough and dry. Remove supremes to a heated serving platter and mask with sauce. Garnish with a bouquet of watercress or parsley and serve immediately. Serves 2–4.

NOTE: If preferred, supremes can be served with any of the pan sauces below, using butter and juices remaining in the dish.

PAN SAUCES TO SERVE WITH SUPREMES OF CHICKEN

Fines Herbes Sauce

30 g (I oz) butter; 2 tsp lemon juice; 2 tbs finely chopped mixed herbs (parsley, chives, tarragon, chervil).

After removing supremes, add butter to pan in which they were sautéed and heat. When foaming, add lemon juice and herbs. Remove from heat, swirl sauce in pan to combine ingredients and pour over supremes.

Shallot and Wine Sauce

I tbs finely chopped golden shallots; $^1/_4$ cup port or Madeira; $^1/_2$ cup brown beef stock; salt and freshly ground white pepper; I tbs chopped parsley.

After removing supremes, add shallots to fat remaining in pan and sauté on moderate heat for 1 minute. Stir in port or Madeira and stock and boil on high heat until reduced by half. Season with salt and pepper, stir in chopped parsley and pour over supremes; serve immediately.

Mushroom Cream Sauce

30 g (I oz) butter; I small leek or onion, finely chopped; 8 button mushrooms, thinly sliced; $^1/_3$ cup cream; salt and freshly ground white pepper.

After removing supremes, add butter to pan in which they were sautéed and heat. When foaming, add leek or onion and mushrooms. Sauté on fairly high heat, stirring once or twice, for 3 minutes. Stir in cream and boil until sauce thickens a little. Season to taste with salt and pepper and spoon over supremes.

Cognac Cream Sauce

2 tbs cognac; $^1/_3$ cup cream or Crème Fraîche (page 102); I tbs dry sherry; salt and freshly ground white pepper.

Cook supremes for only 2 minutes on each side. Leave them in the pan, pour over cognac and set alight. When flames subside, add cream or crème fraîche and dry sherry. Allow to boil up, season to taste with salt and pepper. Pour over supremes and serve immediately.

SWEDE TURNIP

See *Turnip and Swede*.

SWEET AND SOUR SAUCE

This famous Chinese sauce varies a little from region to region. It is often cooked as part of a dish such as Sweet and Sour Pork, but the sauce below can be prepared separately to use as a dip for meatballs, fried wonton and other hot hors d'oeuvre. See recipes.

Sweet and Sour Sauce for Dipping

3 tbs soy sauce; 3 tbs sugar; 3 tbs vinegar; 2 tbs tomato sauce; 2 tbs dry sherry; I$^1/_2$ tbs cornflour mixed with 8 tbs cold water.

Mix all ingredients, except cornflour and water, in a small saucepan and bring to the boil. Stir cornflour mixture again and pour into boiling liquid. Cook, stirring constantly until sauce clears and thickens. Makes about 1½ cups.

Sweet and Sour Pork

750 g (I$^1/_2$ lb) fairly lean boneless pork, cut into 2 cm (3/4 in) cubes; $^1/_2$ tsp salt; I tbs soy sauce; I tbs cornflour; 4 tbs water; I egg, beaten; I medium onion; oil; I green or red pepper, cored, seeded and cut into strips.

SAUCE: 2$^1/_2$ tbs sugar; 2 tbs vinegar; 2 tsp cornflour; I$^1/_2$ tbs soy sauce; I tbs sherry; I$^1/_2$ tbs tomato purée; 5 tbs water.

Sprinkle pork cubes with salt and rub meat between your hands to work salt in, then sprinkle with soy sauce and leave for 1 hour, turning meat over several times. Mix cornflour with water and beat in egg to make a batter. Add pork and mix well to coat pieces. Cut onion downward into quarters, then eighths and separate into petals. Mix sauce ingredients together and set aside. Deep-fry pork in hot oil for about 3 minutes. Drain and keep pork hot in a low oven. Heat 2 tbs oil in a wok or frying pan and stir-fry onion for 1 minute, then add pepper and stir-fry 1 minute longer. Lower heat, stir sauce mixture and pour in. Stir until sauce is clear and thickened. Add pork to pan and turn pieces gently in sauce for 30 seconds. Serve immediately with boiled or steamed rice. Serves 4–6.

SWEETBREADS

These are considered a delicacy by a great many people, and classic French cuisine includes a number of famous dishes based on sweetbreads.

They are an animal's pancreas and thymus glands, usually taken from a calf. In appearance and texture, sweetbreads are very similar to brains and, like the latter, they must be given special soaking and blanching treatments before cooking.

Once prepared, sweetbreads may be cooked whole or sliced, pan-fried or coated in breadcrumbs and fried. They may also be braised, whole, with aromatic vegetables, herbs and wine and served with a rich mushroom sauce or a delicate creamy sauce. Creamed sweetbreads can be used to fill small savoury tartlets, vol-au-vent cases, croûstades or crisp bread shells (see page 426).

■ **BASIC PREPARATION:** Soak sweetbreads in cold water for several hours, changing water frequently. This will allow the blood and impurities to seep out. Then blanch by placing them in a large pan of fresh cold water, bringing it slowly to the boil and boiling for 2 minutes. Drain and rinse them well under cold running water. The sweetbreads can then be trimmed of pieces of cartilage, ducts and skin. If they are to be sliced, they should be pressed between two plates or boards.

Once prepared, sweetbreads can be stored in the refrigerator for a day before they are cooked as desired. See recipes.

Sweetbreads with Poulette Sauce

500 g (1 lb) prepared sweetbreads; 1 onion, sliced; 1 carrot, sliced; 1 bouquet garni; veal or chicken stock; 45 g (1¹/₂ oz) butter; 2 tbs flour; 1 egg yolk; ¹/₃ cup cream; squeeze lemon juice; 1 tbs finely chopped parsley; salt and freshly ground black pepper.

Place sweetbreads in a saucepan with onion, carrot, bouquet garni and stock just to cover. Bring to the boil and simmer for about 45 minutes. Strain off 1¹/₂–2 cups stock and reserve. Slice sweetbreads thickly and keep warm. Melt butter in a clean saucepan, stir in flour and cook for a few seconds, then pour on reserved stock and bring to boil, stirring constantly. Cook until sauce is of coating consistency. Beat egg yolk with cream, add to sauce and reheat without boiling. Add lemon juice, parsley, salt and pepper. Serve sweetbreads with sauce. Serves 6.

Sautéed Sweetbreads

500 g (1 lb) prepared sweetbreads, thickly sliced; salt and freshly ground white pepper; flour; 30 g (1 oz) butter; ¹/₂ cup strong veal or chicken stock; finely chopped parsley.

Season sweetbreads lightly with salt and pepper and lightly coat with flour. Sauté in foaming butter for 3–4 minutes each side, them remove to warmed plate. Deglaze pan with stock, reduce as desired and pour over sweetbreads. Sprinkle with finely chopped parsley. Serves 6.

VARIATION
Serve Sautéed Sweetbreads with a sauce such as Onion Sauce, Brown Butter Sauce, Fresh Tomato Sauce (see *Sauces*).

SWEETCORN

See *Corn*.

SWEET POTATO

Not a true potato but the tuber of a large, leafy plant which can be grown in any warm climate. Sweet potatoes can be either white, or orange-fleshed, and take the shape of a large, fat sausage. Despite the name, sweet potatoes are quite different from potatoes in taste and texture. However, they can be cooked in the same ways as potatoes, such as oven-baked in their skin, or boiled and peeled, then tossed in butter, or mashed. See recipes.

Candied Sweet Potatoes

1 kg (2 lb) sweet potatoes; salt; 90 g (3 oz) butter; ¹/₂ cup lightly packed brown sugar; ¹/₂ cup water.

Cook sweet potatoes in boiling salted water until tender but still firm. Peel, then cut into halves or quarters. Heat butter, sugar and water in a heavy saucepan to simmering point. Add potatoes and cook on top of stove over very low heat, turning occasionally, for about 15 minutes or until potatoes are delicately golden-brown on all sides. Serves 6.

Glazed Sweet Potatoes

1 kg (2 lb) sweet potatoes, peeled and cut into even-sized pieces; salt; 60 g (2 oz) butter; 1 tbs oil; 1 tbs honey; pinch ground ginger.

Drop sweet potatoes into pan of boiling salted water and simmer 5 minutes. Drain. Melt half butter with oil in baking dish and stir in honey and ginger. Add sweet potatoes and toss in honey mixture. Dot with remaining butter. Bake in a preheated moderate oven (180°C/350°F) for 40 minutes or until tender. Brush potatoes with glaze in pan and turn occasionally during cooking. Serves 6.

SWISS ROLL

This impressive rolled sponge cake is baked in a shallow baking tin, spread with jam and rolled while still hot, or rolled, cooled and then spread with warm jam.

Some Swiss rolls are also flavoured with spices and honey, and, of course, there is the famous Chocolate Roll.

See also *Chocolate*: Chocolate Roll and *Spice*: Honey Spiced Sponge Roll.

Swiss Roll

3/4 cup self-raising flour; pinch salt; 3 eggs;
1/2 cup caster sugar; I tbs hot water;
3—4 tbs jam or lemon curd; caster sugar.

Grease a 30 x 25 cm (12 x 10 in) Swiss roll tin and line with greased greaseproof paper, or make a paper case this size using thick greaseproof paper (see Chocolate Roll). Sift flour with salt. Place eggs and sugar in a heatproof bowl and stand over a pan of gently simmering water, not boiling. Whisk together until mixture is very thick and creamy, about 10 minutes. If using an electric mixer whisking over hot water is not necessary. Remove bowl from water and continue whisking mixture until cool. Fold in flour as lightly as possible with a metal spoon. Lastly, fold in hot water. Pour into prepared tin, shake into corners and spread evenly using a metal spatula. Bake in a preheated very hot oven (220°C/425°F) for 7–12 minutes or until pale golden and springy. Do not overcook as it makes rolling up difficult.

Quickly turn out the sponge on to a tea-towel well sprinkled with caster sugar. Carefully strip off lining paper. Trim off crisp edges with a sharp knife. Roll in towel and cool. Unroll sponge. Place jar of jam or curd in saucepan of hot water and when warm spread jam or curd over sponge, taking it almost to the edges. Lifting edges of sugared tea-towel nearest you, roll sponge into a neat firm roll. Stand roll on a wire rack with join underneath. Leave until cold, away from any draughts. Sprinkle with a little more caster sugar before serving. Serves 8.

t

TABASCO SAUCE

An orange-red fiery liquid made from hot red peppers and known by its trade name 'Tabasco'. Tabasco sauce should always be used with discretion – 1 or 2 drops is often enough. Use in soups, cocktails and barbecue sauces, salad dressings, savoury butters, tomato juice, chilli dishes, and some egg or fish dishes. A drop added to scrambled eggs, fish cakes or salmon mornay enhances the flavour.

Green Tabasco is also available but is not as popular as the fiery red.

Spicy Avocado Sauce

1 large avocado, halved and stoned; 1 tbs lemon juice; 3 drops Tabasco sauce; salt and freshly ground black pepper; 1 tomato, peeled, seeded and chopped; 1/4 cup finely chopped parsley; 1/2 tsp ground coriander; 1 tbs oil; 1 tbs white vinegar.

Scoop flesh from avocado into a bowl. Add lemon juice and mash roughly. Mix in Tabasco, salt, pepper and tomato. Blend to a smooth purée or push through a sieve, then beat in parsley, coriander, oil and vinegar. Cover and refrigerate for 1 hour. Serve with poultry or fish, or as a dipping sauce for meatballs. Makes about 1 1/2 cups.

TABLET

A Scottish version of fudge. Take care to stir gently or the mixture will become grainy before it has caramelised thoroughly.

Tablet

1 1/4 cups milk; 4 cups sugar; 60 g (2 oz) butter; 1 x 400 g can sweetened condensed milk; 1/4 tsp vanilla; walnut halves to decorate.

Combine milk, sugar and butter in a heavy saucepan. Stir over low heat until sugar dissolves, about 20 minutes, then stir in condensed milk and bring to the boil. Boil steadily over medium heat for about 25 minutes or until dark golden-brown. Add vanilla and stir well. Remove from heat and allow to cool for a few minutes. Beat with a wooden spoon or hand-held electric beater for about 10 minutes or until mixture is thick. Pour into a well-greased 28 x 19 cm (11 x 7 1/2 in) lamington tin. Place walnut halves on top, mark into pieces with a knife and leave to cool. When set, break into squares. Makes about 60 pieces.

TABOULEH (TABBOULI, TABBOULEH)

One of the most popular dishes from the Middle East, and Lebanon in particular. Burghul (or cracked wheat), on which the salad is based, gives a delicious nutty flavour that appeals to most people. Plenty of fresh mint and parsley is mixed through and lemon juice imparts a refreshing tang. Serve Tabouleh with flat pita bread as part of an hors d'oeuvre tray or traditional *mezze* of the Middle East, or use as an accompaniment to grilled or barbecued lamb or chicken.

Burghul is available from most delicatessens, health food shops and good supermarkets. It is always soaked in cold water for about 2 hours before use, to soften and swell the grains.

Tabouleh

1 cup burghul; 2 large tomatoes, peeled and chopped; 3 tbs finely chopped spring onions; salt and freshly ground black pepper; 1–1 1/2 cups finely chopped fresh parsley; 1/2 cup finely chopped fresh mint; 3–4 tbs olive oil; 3–4 tbs lemon juice; lettuce leaves to serve (optional).

Soak burghul in cold water to cover for about 2 hours. Drain, squeeze out as much water as possible (use your hands to do this) and spread on a clean tea-towel or paper towel to dry. Put burghul in a bowl. Add tomatoes and spring onions to burghul and season with salt and pepper. Add parsley, mint, oil and lemon juice and mix well. Adjust seasoning – salad should taste fresh and lemony. Serve on lettuce leaves on a flat platter or piled in a bowl. Serves 6.

VARIATION

TABOULEH STUFFED TOMATOES: Make Tabouleh, omitting tomatoes. Remove tops from 6 tomatoes and scoop out flesh, leaving shell. Sprinkle tomatoes with salt, turn upside-down and leave to drain for about 30 minutes. Dry with paper towels. Mix chopped tomato flesh with tabouleh and use to fill centres of tomatoes. Arrange on a platter with any leftover tabouleh spooned down centre.

TACO

A tortilla (Mexican corn pancake), folded or rolled around a filling and often fried crisp. It can be filled with a savoury filling before rolling and then fried, or fried first with fillings added afterwards. Crisp taco shells are available in packages and a complete 'taco kit' containing taco shells, sauce and seasonings, is also available at most health food shops and supermarkets. Tacos are eaten at all hours of the day in Mexico, and they have become a popular 'fast food' in other countries. They are good for a party because you can put out the fillings and sauce and let each guest assemble their own. **See recipes.**

See also *Tortilla*.

Tacos

10–12 packaged taco shells or soft tortillas.

FILLING: 1 tbs oil; 1 clove garlic, crushed; 1 medium onion, finely chopped; 500 g (1 lb) lean minced beef; 1 tsp Mexican chilli powder; 1 tsp ground cumin; 2 tbs tomato paste; 1/2 cup water; salt and freshly ground black pepper; 2 tbs chopped fresh coriander or parsley.

SAUCE: $^1/_2$ cup tomato purée; I small onion, grated; I tsp chopped fresh oregano, or $^1/_4$ tsp dried; I tsp salt; 2 tsp vinegar; pinch sugar; I small fresh or dried chilli, seeded and finely chopped.

TOPPINGS: I cup grated, well-flavoured cheese; I cup shredded lettuce; I cup finely chopped onions; 2 medium tomatoes, chopped; I ripe avocado, peeled, stoned and diced (optional, but delicious).

Heat taco shells according to packet instructions, or fold soft tortillas in half and fry in a little hot oil until crisp.

FILLING: Heat oil in a large saucepan and fry garlic and onion until softened, about 4 minutes. Add minced beef, and stir over medium heat until it turns brown and crumbly. Add chilli powder, cumin, tomato paste, water, salt and pepper. Cook gently, covered, for 10 minutes. Stir in coriander or parsley and adjust seasoning.

SAUCE: Combine all ingredients in a saucepan and simmer for 3 minutes. Set taco shells on a platter, with filling, toppings and sauce in separate bowls. About 2 tbs of meat filling is placed in every taco, then toppings and sauce added according to taste. Tacos are eaten in the hand, so be sure to provide plenty of paper napkins! Serves 5–10.

NOTE: For vegetarian tacos, use refried beans (see page 396) as the filling instead of meat or create meatless fillings of your choice.

Salad Tacos

I cup cooked or canned red kidney beans, drained; I leafy lettuce, torn into bite-sized pieces; I avocado, peeled, stoned and cubed; $^1/_2$ green pepper, cored, seeded and diced; 2 tomatoes, chopped; I tsp chopped fresh oregano; 8 taco shells; $^1/_2$ cup grated Cheddar cheese.

MARINADE: $^1/_2$ tsp dry mustard; $^1/_2$ tsp ground cumin; 2 tbs wine vinegar; $^1/_4$ cup oil; $^1/_4$ tsp salt.

FRENCH DRESSING: I tbs vinegar; 3 tbs oil; I clove garlic, crushed; pinch sugar.

Beat marinade ingredients together with a fork. Chill kidney beans in marinade for 2–3 hours. Combine dressing ingredients. Add lettuce, avocado, green pepper, tomatoes and oregano. Drain beans, add to salad and toss lightly. Crisp taco shells as directed on packet. Spoon salad into tacos. Sprinkle cheese over top and serve immediately. Serves 4.

TAHINI (TAHINA)

A paste made from toasted sesame seeds, widely used in the Middle East where it is made into delicious creamy sauces and salad dressings, is used to flavour cakes and biscuits and is an essential ingredient in the wonderful garlicky chick pea dip, Hummus bi Tahini (see pages 199–200). See recipes.

Yogurt and Tahini Salad

I small lettuce, torn into pieces; 2 small carrots, very finely sliced; I cucumber, thinly peeled and diced; 2 sticks celery, sliced; 3–4 spring onions, diagonally sliced into 2.5 cm (I in) lengths; $^1/_4$ cup roasted cashew nuts; 2 tbs grated Cheddar or crumbled blue cheese; $^1/_2$ cup alfalfa sprouts.

DRESSING: I cup plain yogurt; $^1/_2$ cup tahini; I clove garlic, crushed; I tbs lemon juice; salt; I tbs chopped parsley.

Put vegetables into a salad bowl and mix lightly. DRESSING: Whisk together all ingredients except parsley; fold parsley in lightly. Spoon dressing over salad, sprinkle on cashews and cheese and top with alfalfa. Serves 4–6.

Tahini Sauce

2 cloves garlic; $^1/_2$ cup tahini (sesame paste); $^1/_4$–$^1/_2$ cup cold water; $^1/_2$ cup lemon juice; salt.

Place garlic and tahini in blender or food processor and process to crush garlic. Add water and lemon juice alternately, a little at a time, until desired consistency is reached. Add salt to taste. If mixing by hand, crush garlic with salt in a mixing bowl, and gradually beat in tahini. Mix in water and lemon juice alternately until mixture is desired consistency. Makes about 1$^1/_4$ cups.

TAMALE

A Mexican speciality; a hearty snack made by spreading cornmeal dough on a corn husk, covering it with a sweet or savoury filling, then rolling it up inside the husk and steaming it. The Mexican cornmeal, *masa*, is not readily available commercially in Australia, but canned tamales can be found in some good food stores.

Tamale Pie

A savoury Mexican-style pie with a cornbread crust. Yellow cornmeal (polenta) is used in place of the Mexican cornmeal (*masa*).

750g (1½ lb) minced steak; I large onion, chopped; I green pepper, cored, seeded and chopped; I x 425 g can tomatoes; I x 310 g can sweetcorn kernels, drained; ½ cup stoned black olives; I tbs sugar, I tsp salt and 2–3 tsp Mexican chilli powder, or I packet commercial chilli seasoning mix.

CRUST: I cup yellow cornmeal; I tsp salt; 2½ cups cold water; ½ cup grated Cheddar cheese.

Brown minced beef in a dry frying pan, stirring and breaking down lumps with 2 forks, until crumbly. Add onion, green pepper, tomatoes with their juice (snipping into pieces with scissors as you add them), sweetcorn, olives and seasonings. Turn mixture into a pie or other ovenproof dish and spread evenly. CRUST: Mix cornmeal, salt and cold water in a heavy saucepan and cook, stirring, for 15 minutes or until thick. Spread mixture over meat mixture. It may sink, but will rise during baking. Bake in a preheated moderate oven (180°C/350°F) for about 40 minutes or until topping is firm. Sprinkle with grated cheese and bake 5 minutes longer. Serves 6–8.

TAMARILLO (TREE TOMATO)

A glossy, plum-red fruit the size and shape of a large egg. There are also yellow and purplish varieties. Tamarillos, natives of South America, have juicy, slightly acid flesh.

Raw tamarillos may be used for fruit salads or on fruit platter, or arranged in slices or wedges on a cheese board to accompany soft, creamy cheeses. The puréed flesh is used as an ingredient in sweet and savoury dishes, and the sliced fruit as a garnish.

Tamarillos may be poached in sugar syrup and served warm or cold with cream, ice cream or custard.

■ BASIC PREPARATION: Raw tamarillos need no preparation beyond washing. The skin and seeds can be eaten, but as the skin can be bitter, you may prefer to peel the fruit with a knife, or by covering with boiling water for 1 minute, then slipping the skins off with your fingers. TO PREPARE TAMARILLO PUREE: Skin the fruit, then rub flesh through a sieve.

Creamy Tamarillo Sauce

Serve on ice cream, or on poached fruit.

½ cup sugar; ½ cup water; ½ cup dry white wine; 6 tamarillos, skinned and puréed (see above); I tsp lemon juice; 2 tsp brandy; ½ cup cream.

Heat sugar, water and wine together, stirring until sugar has dissolved. Bring to the boil and boil for 5 minutes. Add tamarillo purée and simmer until reduced and a little thickened. Stir in lemon juice and brandy. Cool and chill. At serving time, whip cream until it just holds its shape and fold into tamarillo mixture. Makes about 1½ cups.

TANDOORI CHICKEN

A great and famous dish of northern India, named after the tandoor (clay oven) in which the spiced chicken is baked. Tandoori chicken came into India from across the North West Frontier and beyond, from the Turks and the descendants of Genghis Khan – a fascinating example of the way in which food interlocks with history.

When cooked in the traditional way, the chicken is threaded on a spit and baked in the tandoor over hot coals, but it can be cooked on an electric rotisserie or on a rack set in a roasting tin, and finished on the barbecue if you wish.

Tandoori Chicken

I x 1.5 kg (3 lb) chicken.

YOGURT MASALA: 3–4 cloves garlic, chopped; 2.5 cm (I in) piece fresh ginger, chopped; I tsp cumin seeds; pinch nutmeg; I½ tsp salt; ¾ cup plain yogurt; I tbs peanut oil; I tbs tomato sauce; 2 tsp lemon juice; 2–3 drops red food colouring.

LEMON SPICE SAUCE: ½ tsp pepper; ¼ tsp ground cardamom; I tbs peanut oil; 2 tsp lemon juice.

TO SERVE: onion rings, radishes; red or green pepper; chillies; flat bread.

Remove chicken skin but leave chicken whole. Cut 2 slits about 1 cm (½ in) deep in thighs and breast. YOGURT MASALA: Put all ingredients in a blender and purée, or grind garlic, ginger, cumin seeds, nutmeg and salt to a paste with a mortar and pestle or end of a rolling pin in a bowl, then mix in remaining ingredients. Spread masala over chicken, rubbing well in, and refrigerate overnight. Next day, bring chicken to room temperature, then place on a rotisserie over a pan, or on a rack in a shallow roasting tin. Pour over remaining masala. Bake in a preheated hot oven (200°C/400°F) for 15 minutes, then reduce heat to moderate (180°C/350°F) and bake 1 hour more, basting frequently with pan juices.

LEMON SPICE SAUCE: Mix together ingredients. Remove chicken from oven and cut into 6 pieces. Coat chicken pieces with any remaining masala and sprinkle with lemon spice sauce. Return to a hot oven (200°C/400°F) for 10–15 minutes, or grill under a preheated grill or over hot coals until dark reddish-brown and crisp. Serve chicken on a large heated platter, with onion rings, radishes, sliced green or red pepper and, for those who appreciate something hot, a few chillies. Pass a flat bread such as Chapatis (see page 69). Serves 3–4.

TANGERINE

See *Mandarin and Tangerine*.

TAPENADE

Whether for a picnic, quick snack or a light lunch there is nothing nicer than a bowl of this delicious paste of olives, anchovies, capers and canned tuna. Tapenade is all the better for being made a few days ahead and stored airtight in the refrigerator.

Tapenade

125 g (4 oz) black olives; 6 anchovy fillets, drained and rinsed; 3 tbs capers, drained; 100 g (3¹/₂ oz) can tuna in oil, drained; juice 1 lemon; ¹/₃ cup olive oil.

Stone the olives and crush in a mortar or chop in a food processor. Add the anchovy fillets, capers, tuna and the juice of half a lemon. Pound or process until mixture has formed a fairly smooth paste. Still pounding or with the motor still running, add the oil in a slow, steady stream. Taste and add more lemon juice, if liked, to taste. Turn into a small serving bowl, and serve with halved hard-boiled eggs, some crusty bread and a few crisp vegetables.

TAPIOCA

A product extracted from the roots of the cassava plant; it forms into small balls during processing.

It is a starchy product, and thus sometimes used for thickening, but more commonly it is used in desserts, like sago. Tapioca pudding is made by substituting tapioca for sago in the recipe for Sago Pudding (see page 430).

Tapioca Almond Cream

250 g (8 oz) ground almonds; 6 cups water; pinch salt; ¹/₂ cup tapioca; 2 eggs, separated; sugar; ¹/₄ cup cream, whipped.

Pound ground almonds in a mortar, gradually adding enough water to produce a smooth, thick liquid. Turn into colander lined with a clean tea-towel. Wring and squeeze to extract almond milk. Repeat with remaining water. Alternatively, blend briefly in a blender, then squeeze out almond milk. Pour almond milk into saucepan, bring to the boil, add salt and sprinkle over tapioca. Cook over low heat, stirring or whisking constantly, until tapioca is clear and mixture has thickened. Beat in egg yolks off heat, and add sugar to taste. Beat egg whites until stiff, and fold into mixture with cream. Serve warm or cold. Serves 8.

TARAMASALATA

A splendid Greek dip made from tarama, the smoked, dried roe of the grey mullet. Tarama is available in cans. Serve taramasalata as an hors d'oeuvre with olives and crusty bread, pita bread or fresh vegetables such as pepper strips, celery sticks and radishes for dipping.

Taramasalata

4 thick slices day-old white bread, crusts removed; ¹/₂ cup milk; 125 g (4 oz) tarama; 1 small onion, grated; 1 clove garlic, crushed; ¹/₄ cup lemon juice; ³/₄ cup olive oil; freshly ground white pepper.

Soak bread in milk for 5 minutes, then squeeze dry, discarding milk. Mash bread until smooth with a mortar and pestle or with back of a wooden spoon in a bowl. Beat in tarama little by little, then onion, garlic and lemon juice. Mixture should be a smooth paste. Now add olive oil little by little, beating it in with a whisk or rotary beater and making sure that each addition is absorbed before adding more. Taramasalata should be thick and creamy; it will firm more on chilling. Taste and beat in a little more lemon juice if required. Chill well before serving. Makes about 1¹/₂ cups.

VARIATION

BLENDER TARAMASALATA: Taramasalata is beautifully simple to make in a blender or food processor. For this method, the onion and garlic need only be chopped. Place soaked and squeezed bread and all other ingredients except oil in container of blender or processor and process until smooth. Then, with motor running, add oil gradually through feed tube, making sure each addition is absorbed before adding more. Taste, add a little more lemon juice if required. Chill well before serving.

TARRAGON

A profuse-growing summer herb. Its long, slender leaves are often used to decorate a cold dish, such as jellied chicken, but its role in the kitchen goes far beyond that of a mere garnish.

Tarragon is one of the four fresh herbs found in *fines herbes* (the others being chives, chervil and parsley). Tarragon lends its tang to Béarnaise Sauce (see pages 459–60), and does wonders for chicken in any form. It can be used in salads and salad dressings, either as the fresh herb or in the form of tarragon vinegar. Tarragon may be added to pâtés, especially chicken pâté, to soups and to seafood dishes, hot or cold.

Dried tarragon is more pungent than the fresh, and for many dishes it is advisable to add dried tarragon as well as fresh.

There are two variants of tarragon, French tarragon and Russian tarragon. The former has a more distinct aroma and flavour, the latter is more bland. It is advisable to buy only French dried tarragon, and this, together with fresh Russian tarragon, makes a quite satisfactory combination. **See recipes.**

Tarragon Vinegar: Fill a glass or bottle with fresh tarragon leaves, add good quality wine vinegar to cover and leave to infuse for 2 weeks. Strain and bottle, adding a sprig fresh tarragon to each bottle if desired. If fresh tarragon is unavailable, use 1–2 tbs dried tarragon to 2 cups wine vinegar.

Tarragon Butter

Serve on grilled meals, fish and chicken.

**125 g (4 oz) butter; 1 tbs lemon juice;
2–3 tbs finely chopped fresh tarragon,
or mixture of fresh and dried tarragon;
salt and freshly ground black pepper.**

Cream butter until soft, then gradually beat in lemon juice. Blend in tarragon, and season with salt and pepper. Form into a log. Chill and slice into rounds when firm. Makes enough for 8 pieces of meat, fish or chicken.

Chicken Breasts with Tarragon

**6 chicken half-breasts or fillets, boned;
60 g (2 oz) butter; salt and freshly ground black
pepper; 1 tsp dried tarragon; 1/2 cup chicken stock;
1/2 cup cream; 1 tbs chopped fresh tarragon.**

Trim chicken if necessary. Cook in frying pan in foaming butter for 3–4 minutes each side. Season with salt and pepper and sprinkle with tarragon after turning. When both sides are browned, turn once more and cook for a further 2–3 minutes. Remove and keep warm. Deglaze pan with stock, and boil to reduce by half. Stir in cream and chopped fresh tarragon. Reduce over heat if desired. Pour sauce over chicken and serve immediately. Serves 6.

Tournedos with Tarragon

**6 fillet steaks, about 2.5 cm (1 in) thick;
45 g (1 1/2 oz) butter; salt and freshly ground
black pepper; 2 tbs Madeira or port;
1 tbs chopped fresh tarragon.**

Cook steaks in heavy frying pan in about 15 g (1/2 oz) butter for 2–3 minutes each side. Season cooked side with salt and pepper after turning. When little drops of red juice appear on surface of meat, pour over Madeira or port. Allow it to bubble for about 30 seconds, then stir in tarragon and remaining butter. Serve immediately. Serves 6.
NOTE: Cooked in this way, steaks will be rare. If medium steaks are desired, turn steaks a second time and cook for 2–3 minutes before adding Madeira.

TARTARE SAUCE

See *Mayonnaise*.

TARTS AND TARTLETS

The combinations of food, both sweet and savoury, that can be presented in an open pastry shell are almost endless. There is hardly an occasion from afternoon tea or cocktails to a lunch or dinner party, a picnic or a relaxed family meal, when one or another of the great tart family would not be welcome.

The terms 'tart' and 'flan' are virtually interchangeable. The French lean towards the former, the English toward the latter, while Americans often call a filled pastry shell an open pie.

■ **TO SHAPE TART SHELLS:** For directions on lining large or individual-size flan rings, see *Pastry*, page 341.

TO LINE INDIVIDUAL PLAIN TARTLET TINS: For the tiny, saucer-shaped tartlet tins that are joined in a set of 12, roll pastry thin and, using a round cutter, stamp out rounds a little larger than the top of the tins. If using pastry containing sugar or eggs, grease tins lightly. Fit pastry rounds into tins, pressing lightly to ensure that no air remains between pastry and tin. Prick shells before baking.

TO LINE INDIVIDUAL FANCY TARTLET TINS: Place the tins close together, about six in a group. If using pastry containing sugar or eggs, grease tins lightly. Roll pastry thin, lift on the rolling pin and lay it loosely over all the tins together. Shape a small piece of pastry into a ball, dip it in flour and use it to press pastry into the tins. Flour rolling pin and roll over tins, first one way, then the other, to remove surplus pastry. Fold trimmings together and roll out again to line more tins. Take each tin, press edges up lightly with the thumb and prick pastry bottom before baking until dried out and pale golden.

TO BAKE UNFILLED TART SHELLS: See directions for baking blind under Pastry, page 341. **See recipes.**

    See also *Flan* and *Quiche*.

Savoury Tarts

Savoury tarts can be created from store cupboard ingredients – eggs, milk, cheese, vegetables, even leftover meat and fish.

Basque Tart

**1 large onion, finely chopped; 2 cloves garlic,
crushed; 30 g (1 oz) butter; 3 large tomatoes,
peeled, seeded and chopped; 1 small red pepper and
1 small green pepper, cored, seeded and cut into
short strips; 60 g (2 oz) cooked ham or prosciutto,
cut into strips, 1 tsp tomato paste; 2 eggs, beaten;
1/2 cup cream; 1 cup fresh breadcrumbs;
1 tbs grated Parmesan cheese; salt and freshly
ground black pepper; 1 x 23 cm (9 in) Plain
Shortcrust Pastry Tart Shell (page 342).**

Cook onion and garlic in butter until soft but not browned. Remove from heat and add tomatoes. Blanch peppers in boiling water for 5 minutes and drain. Add peppers, ham, tomato paste, eggs, cream, breadcrumbs, cheese, salt and pepper to tomato mixture and mix lightly. Turn into tart shell and bake in a preheated moderately hot oven (190°C/375°F) for about 40 minutes or until filling is set and pastry golden. Serves 4–6.

Cheese Soufflé Tart

This tart should be served while the filling is still puffed up. You can prepare the tart shell and the filling, up to the point of folding in the egg whites, ahead of time.

3 rashers streaky bacon, rind removed and finely chopped; I onion, finely chopped; I x 20–23 cm (8–9 in) Rich Shortcrust Pastry Tart Shell, partially baked blind (page 342); 30 g (I oz) butter; 2 tbs flour; ²/₃ cup warm milk; salt and freshly ground black pepper; pinch dry mustard; 60 g (2 oz) Gruyère cheese, grated; 2 eggs, separated.

Fry bacon gently in a dry frying pan until fat runs. Add onion and cook until golden-brown. Spread onion and bacon on bottom of tart shell. Melt butter in saucepan, add flour and stir on low heat for 1 minute. Remove from heat, cool a little and add milk, stirring until smoothly blended. Season with salt, pepper and mustard. Return to heat and stir until boiling, then remove from heat, stir in cheese and beat in egg yolks one at a time. Beat egg whites until they hold soft peaks and fold into cheese mixture. Turn mixture into tart shell and bake in a preheated hot oven (200°C/400°F) for 20 minutes or until filling is puffed and golden. Serves 4–6.

VARIATION

CHEESE SOUFFLE TARTLETS: Follow recipe for Cheese Soufflé Tart, but use pastry to line 12 x 5 cm (2 in) shallow tartlet tins, and bake blind. Divide filling among tartlets and bake for 8–10 minutes.

Tomato and Cheese Tart

A good tart to take on a picnic or, baked in a 20 cm (8 in) shallow square tin and cut into squares, to serve with drinks.

3–4 firm, ripe tomatoes, cut into I cm (¹/₂ in) thick slices; 375 g (12 oz) Gruyère cheese, finely sliced; I x 23 cm (9 in) Plain Shortcrust Pastry Tart Shell, partially baked blind (page 342); 2 spring onions, finely chopped; 4–5 leaves fresh basil, cut into fine ribbons, or ¹/₂ tsp dried; salt and freshly ground black pepper; 2 tbs grated Parmesan cheese; 30 g (I oz) butter, melted.

Sprinkle tomato slices with salt and place on a rack for about 30 minutes to drain. Arrange cheese slices, overlapping, in a layer in tart shell. Scatter chopped spring onions and basil over and place drained tomato slices on top to cover cheese completely. Season with salt and pepper, sprinkle with Parmesan cheese and drizzle melted butter over. Bake in a preheated moderately hot oven (190°C/375°F) for about 25 minutes or until lightly coloured. Serve warm. Serves 4–6 or makes 16 x 5 cm (2 in) squares.

Spanish Tarts

Make in 10 cm (4 in) rings for a first course, or in tart-let tins for party savouries.

Rich Shortcrust Pastry made with I ¹/₂ cups flour (page 342); I kg (2 lb) spinach, chopped; salt and freshly ground black pepper; nutmeg; 30 g (I oz) butter; 2 onions, finely chopped; 2 tbs flour; I cup warm milk; ¹/₂ cup grated Swiss cheese; I tsp lemon juice; ¹/₂ tsp paprika; ¹/₂ cup fresh breadcrumbs.

Roll out pastry dough and use to line 4 x 10 cm (4 in) flan rings or 16–18 x 5 cm (2 in) tartlet tins. Prick well, chill 30 minutes, then bake blind (see page 341) in a preheated hot oven (200°C/400°F) until golden. Cool in tins. Pack spinach into a saucepan and season with salt, pepper and nutmeg. Cover tightly and cook, in water that clings to leaves after rinsing, 5–6 minutes or until soft. Drain well and, when cool enough to handle, squeeze out as much moisture as possible. Chop spinach finely.

Melt butter in saucepan and cook onions gently until soft but not brown. Add flour and stir over low heat 1 minute. Remove from heat and cool slightly, then add milk, stirring until smoothly blended. Return to heat and stir until boiling. Season with salt, pepper and a little nutmeg. Fold in spinach. Remove from heat and stir in ¹/₄ cup cheese and the lemon juice. Adjust seasoning. Fill tart shells with mixture. Mix remaining cheese, paprika and breadcrumbs and sprinkle over the tops. Place under a preheated grill or in a preheated hot oven (200°C/400°F), until tops are browned. Serve hot or warm. Makes 4 entrée tarts, 16–18 party savouries.

Fruit Tarts

The French are masters at the art of producing a fine fruit tart. Attractively arranged fruit in a crisp pastry case, the most delectable tarts are made with fresh fruit, served warm from the oven.

Glazed Apple Tart

A light French dessert tart, beautiful to look at and good to serve with coffee.

3 large dessert apples, such as Golden Delicious, peeled, halved and cored; I x 23 cm (9 in) Sweet Rich Shortcrust Pastry Tart Shell, partially baked blind (page 342); 30 g (I oz) butter, melted; ¹/₄ cup sugar.

GLAZE: ¹/₄ cup sieved apricot jam; I tbs water.

Put each apple half, cut side down, on a board and cut across into very thin slices, keeping shape of half intact. Arrange halves in tart shell, fanning slices out somewhat. Brush with melted butter, sprinkle with sugar and bake in a preheated moderately hot oven (190°C/375°F) for 5 minutes. Brush again with butter and bake 5 minutes more or until pastry is browned and apples tender. Cool 10 minutes in flan ring, then remove sides and place tart on a wire rack. Stir apricot jam and water over low heat until boiling and glaze hangs in heavy drops from spoon. Brush over apples. Serve tart lukewarm. Serves 6–8.

VARIATION
Halved, stoned fresh apricots or well-drained canned apricot halves may be substituted for apples.

French Fruit Tart *(Tarte aux Fruites)*

This tart has the tempting, glamorous look of the tarts seen in those superb French pâtisseries. The trick is to work in a tidy area, with nothing else on the go at the same time. The French Fruit Tart needs your undivided attention!

1 x 20 cm (8 in) Pâte Sucrée Tart Shell, baked blind (page 342); ¹/₂ quantity Crème Pâtissière (page 207); few mixed fruits (strawberries, grapes, cherries, mandarin or orange segments, apricots or pears); ¹/₄ cup sieved apricot jam; 1 tbs water; squeeze lemon juice.

Fill cooled tart shell with crème pâtissière. Have prepared fruit ready and arrange over cream in a decorative fashion, in concentric circles, in any order. The cream should be completed covered with fruit. Make glaze by heating apricot jam, water and lemon juice together, stirring, until mixture hangs in heavy drops from spoon. Brush over fruit while still warm. Put in refrigerator to set glaze until ready to serve. Serves 6.

NOTE: For best results this tart should be put together 1–2 hours before serving. Have the tart shell baked, the crème pâtissière and the glaze at the ready (it will have to be reheated) and then settle down to create a beautiful work of art.

Plum Tart

PASTRY: 1 cup flour; 60 g (2 oz) butter; 1 tbs caster sugar; ¹/₄ cup ground almonds; ¹/₂ egg, beaten; little grated lemon rind; 2 tsp rum.

FILLING: ¹/₂ cup ground almonds; ¹/₂ cup sugar; 1.5 kg (3 lb) ripe plums (President or Angelina plums are best), slit open and stoned; 3 tbs icing sugar; ¹/₂ tsp cinnamon.

To make pastry, work all pastry ingredients together. Roll into a ball, wrap in plastic wrap and refrigerate for 1 hour before using. When chilled, roll out on a floured work surface and use to line a 25 cm (10 in) flan tin with a removable base. Chill tart shell for 30 minutes. **FILLING:** Sprinkle tart shell with ground almonds and 1 tbs sugar. Arrange plums, cut side up, in circles,

packing them tightly and reversing direction of fruit with each circle. Sprinkle with remaining sugar. Place on a baking tray and bake on lowest rack in a preheated moderate oven (180°C/350°F) for 1 hour or until plums are soft. Cool a few minutes, then remove flan ring and allow to stand until just warm. Combine icing sugar and cinnamon and sift over plums before serving. Pass around a bowl of whipped cream if liked. Serves 8.

Tart Tatin

This luscious dessert of caramelised apples on a pastry crust appears on the menu of nearly every French restaurant. Golden Delicious apples must be used. To make this tart you need a heavy, round flameproof dish – a cast iron frying pan with a screw-on handle is one idea, a small paella pan another – it is worth looking for a special pan for this famous dish. These are now available at specialty kitchen shops.

PASTRY: 1 cup flour; 2 tsp caster sugar; 90 g (3 oz) butter, cut into small dice; 1 egg yolk; 1 tbs cold water.

FILLING: 125 g (4 oz) butter; 1¹/₃ cups sugar; 10 large, ripe Golden Delicious apples, peeled, cored and cut into thin slices.

To make pastry, sift flour and sugar into a bowl, make a well in centre and place butter, egg yolk and water in well. Mix quickly with a fork to form a dough. Roll in plastic wrap and chill 1 hour. To make this pastry with an electric beater, cream sugar with butter and incorporate egg and water. Mix for a few seconds, then add flour all at once. Do not beat any more when dough is formed. Chill before using.

FILLING: Place butter and sugar in a 23 cm (9 in) round flameproof dish. Allow butter to melt on a gentle heat. Remove from heat and arrange apples, cut side up, in circles in dish, packing them very tightly together. Return to heat and cook gently until butter and sugar form a pale caramel. This will take about 15 minutes. Do not allow caramel to become

t

dark. While the apples are cooking carefully roll out dough to a 28 cm (11 in) round. Remove dish from heat and cover apples with dough round, pushing edges inside dish. Place on a baking tray and bake in a preheated moderately hot oven (190°C/375°F) for 45 minutes, covering loosely with foil if browning too much. Stand for 10 minutes before inverting tart on to a heated dish. Serve tart warm, with lightly whipped cream if desired. Serves 8.

Fruit Tartlets

These fruit-filled glazed tartlets may be made with any fruits in season.

**1 quantity Pâte Sucrée (pages 344–5);
500 g (1 lb) fresh fruit in season (see recipe).**

**GLAZE: 1 cup sieved jam (use apricot for pale fruits and redcurrant for red fruits); 3 tbs water;
1 tbs lemon juice.**

Roll out pastry dough thinly and use to line 6 individual 8 cm (3 in) tartlet tins. Chill. Prick bottom of each tartlet with a fork, chill 20 minutes and then bake blind (see page 341) in a preheated moderately hot oven (190°C/375°F) for 8–10 minutes or until pastry is a pale biscuit colour. Do not allow to brown. Allow to cool.

TO PREPARE FRUITS FOR TARTS:

STRAWBERRIES: Wash, dry carefully and hull. They can be left whole if small, or sliced or halved.

APRICOTS: Poach in a light syrup (½ cup sugar dissolved in 1 cup water) until just tender. Drain. Slit and remove stones. Small fruits may be used whole, larger fruits sliced or halved. Good quality canned fruit may also be used.

PEACHES AND PLUMS: Prepare in the same way as apricots.

GRAPES: Wash, halve if desired and seed if necessary (see *Grapes*).

PEARS: If using ripe pears, peel, slice finely and arrange in the tartlet shells. Brush with a little lemon juice to prevent discolouring. If the pears are not quite ripe, peel and poach in a light syrup until tender. Drain before slicing.

RHUBARB: Use young rhubarb; wash well and cut into 4 cm (1½ in) lengths. Poach in a light syrup and drain well.

MANDARINS: Peel, remove outside skins with a sharp knife and cut between membranes to separate skinless segments. Dry segments on paper towels before using.

CHERRIES: Wash, then remove stones with a cherry stoner, or halve cherries and lift stones out with a small sharp knife. Dry before placing in tartlet shells.

GLAZE: Heat all ingredients over gentle heat, stirring until glaze hangs in heavy drops from spoon. Brush tartlet shells with hot glaze. Pile fruit into tartlet shells and brush fruit carefully with glaze until it glistens. Allow to set. Makes 6.

Individual Pear Tarts

An example of the French way with fruit tarts. The fruit is arranged in a design that shows its lovely shape, over a layer of crème pâtissière.

**1 quantity Biscuit Pastry (page 343); 2 firm ripe pears, peeled, halved and cored; lemon juice;
¼ cup sugar; ½ cup water; 1 strip lemon rind;
½ quantity Crème Pâtissière (page 207).**

Roll out pastry dough and use to line 4 x 10 cm (4 in) loose-bottomed flan rings. Chill 30 minutes, then bake blind (see page 341) in a preheated moderate oven (180°C/350°F) for 8 minutes. Remove lining paper and rice or beans, return to oven and bake 5–10 minutes more or until shells are golden. Remove from oven and cool. Brush each pear half with lemon juice as it is prepared, to prevent discolouration. Put sugar, water and lemon rind into a heavy saucepan and bring to the boil. Add pears, cover tightly and poach gently (just below a simmer) for 8–10 minutes or until pears are just tender. Remove saucepan from heat and cool pears in syrup for 20 minutes. Remove them and drain on a cloth. Spread a layer of crème pâtissière in each tart shell. Place each pear half over crème pâtissière in a tart shell, fanning slices out. Boil down remaining poaching syrup until it is sticky, and brush over pears. Warm the tarts slightly in a cool oven (120°C/250°F) before serving. Serves 4.

Hot Apple Tarts
(Tartes Fines Chaudes aux Pommes)

The French way of making fruit tarts that look as beautiful as they taste is quite traditional. This is an up-to-date version from a top Paris restaurant.

**1 x 375 g (12 oz) packet frozen puff pastry, thawed;
4–6 eating apples, peeled and cored;
½ cup caster sugar; 125 g (4 oz) butter;
little warmed honey; Crème Fraîche
(page 102) to serve.**

Roll out pastry dough thinly on a floured work surface. With a 15 cm (6 in) round cutter or saucer, cut out 6 rounds. Turn rounds over on to a dampened baking tray and chill for 30 minutes. Slice apples downward very thinly. Arrange on pastry rounds in overlapping rows. Sprinkle with sugar and dot with butter. Bake in a preheated hot oven (220°C/425°F) for 20–25 minutes or until apples and pastry are golden. Brush tops with honey, and serve warm with chilled crème fraîche. Serves 6.

Other Sweet Tarts

To serve as dessert or at afternoon tea.

Cream Cheese Tart

I quantity Pâte Sucrée (pages 344–5); 125 g (4 oz) unsalted butter, softened; ½ cup caster sugar; 250 g (8 oz) cream cheese, softened; 2 eggs, beaten; pinch nutmeg; icing sugar.

Roll out pastry dough and use to line a 20 cm (8 in) flan ring. Chill 20 minutes. Cream butter with sugar until light and fluffy. Add cheese, beating until light and fluffy. Beat in eggs little by little. Spread mixture in tart shell and sprinkle with nutmeg. Bake in a preheated moderately hot oven (190°C/375°F) for 30 minutes or until filling is puffed and golden and pastry a pale gold. Protect sides with crumpled foil if pastry is browning too much. Sift icing sugar over surface and serve warm or cold. Serves 6.

Brown Sugar Tart

double quantity Pâte Sucrée (pages 344–5); 2 cups firmly packed brown sugar; I cup cream; 30 g (I oz) butter; ¼ tsp vanilla; pinch salt; 2 egg, beaten.

Use two thirds of dough to line a 23 cm (9 in) flan ring. Place brown sugar and cream in a saucepan and bring to the boil, stirring. Simmer gently for about 15 minutes. Remove pan from heat and stir in butter, vanilla and salt. Let mixture cool to lukewarm. Add eggs and beat until well blended. Pour into tart shell. Roll out remaining one third of dough, then cut into strips. Arrange strips lattice-fashion over tart, pressing lightly at ends to join them to sides. Bake in a preheated hot oven (200°C/400°F) for about 20–25 minutes or until pastry is cooked and filling is barely set. Cool on a wire rack. Serves 6–8.

Neenish Tarts

PASTRY: 125 g (4 oz) butter; ½ cup sugar; ½ tsp almond essence; I egg; 2 cups flour, sifted; I tsp baking powder; pinch salt.

FILLING: 90 g (3 oz) butter; ½ cup sifted icing sugar; 3 tbs sweetened condensed milk; I tbs lemon juice.

ICING: I cup icing sugar; drop vanilla; I tbs cocoa powder; I tsp butter.

To make pastry, cream butter with sugar and almond essence until light and fluffy. Add egg and beat well. Stir in flour, baking powder and salt. Knead lightly, then form into a ball, wrap in plastic wrap and chill for 30 minutes. Roll out and cut into 24 x 6 cm (2½ in) rounds. Fit into greased patty tins, prick lightly and chill 20 minutes. Bake in a preheated moderate oven (180°C/350°F) for 10–15 minutes or until a pale biscuit colour. Cool on wire racks.

FILLING: Beat butter until fluffy, then beat in icing sugar, condensed milk and lemon juice. Spoon into cooled tarts, smooth flat with palette knife and leave to set.

ICING: Sift icing sugar into a small heatproof bowl, add 1 tbs hot water and heat over gently simmering water. Stir in vanilla and when icing will coat back of a spoon use immediately to ice one half of each tart. Add cocoa and butter to remaining white icing in bowl. Stand over simmering water and stir until butter melts and icing is smooth and glossy (you may have to beat in a little more hot water). Use at once to ice other halves. Makes 24.

Jam Tarts

½ quantity Biscuit Pastry (page 343); 12 tsp jam (apricot, raspberry, strawberry, blackberry).

Roll out pastry dough thinly and use to line 12 shallow tartlet tins. Prick bases and put 1 tsp of jam into each. Roll pastry trimmings and cut narrow strips to make pastry crosses on top of jam, if liked; press ends on to edges. Chill 20 minutes, then bake in a preheated moderate oven (180°C/350°F) for about 15 minutes. Makes 12.

Lemon Cheese Tarts

½ quantity Biscuit Pastry (page 343); lemon cheese (page 233); whipped cream (optional).

Roll out pastry dough thinly and use to line 12 shallow tartlet tins. Prick bases and chill 20 minutes, then bake blind in a preheated moderate oven (180°C/350°F) for about 15 minutes or until pastry is golden. Remove from tins and cool on a wire rack. Fill each tart shell with lemon cheese and top with a dab whipped cream, if liked. Serve within 20 minutes. Makes 12.

TEACAKE

In England, traditional teacakes are large round baked buns of yeast dough, irresistible when served hot, split, toasted and buttered.

Other varieties of teacake are made from simple quick-mix batters, sometimes sprinkled with sugar and spices or other toppings, and often served sliced and buttered while still warm. Whichever variety you prefer, teacakes are a comforting treat at the close of a cold afternoon. See recipes.

See also *Yeast Cookery* and *Cinnamon*.

Apple Teacake

I egg, separated; ½ cup caster sugar; ½ cup milk; ½ tsp vanilla; 30 g (I oz) butter, melted; I cup self-raising flour, sifted; I apple, peeled, cored and thinly sliced.

TOPPING: melted butter; $^1/_2$ tsp cinnamon mixed with I tbs sugar.

Whisk egg white until stiff and gradually beat in sugar, then egg yolk. Stir in milk, vanilla and melted butter. Fold flour carefully into mixture. Pour into a greased 18 cm (7 in) sandwich tin and arrange apple slices on top of batter. Bake in a preheated moderately hot oven (190°C/375°F) for 20–25 minutes. While still hot, brush with melted butter and sprinkle with cinnamon and sugar. Serve warm or cold.

Yorkshire Teacakes

15 g ($^1/_2$ oz) compressed yeast; I$^1/_4$ cups warm milk; 4 cups flour; I tsp salt; 45 g (I$^1/_2$ oz) lard or butter; I$^1/_2$ tbs caster sugar; $^3/_4$ cup currants; 2 tbs chopped mixed candied peel; milk to glaze.

Dissolve yeast in warm milk and leave in a warm place for about 10 minutes or until mixture becomes frothy. Sift flour and salt into a large bowl and rub in lard or butter. Stir in sugar, currants and peel. Add milk and yeast mixture and mix to a firm dough (you may need to add a little more flour). Turn dough on to a lightly floured work surface and knead until smooth and elastic – about 10 minutes. Form into a ball, return to clean, very lightly oiled bowl and turn dough round to coat lightly with oil. Cover with a tea-towel and leave to rise in a warm place for about 1 hour or until dough has doubled in bulk.

Turn on to a lightly floured surface, knock dough down and knead until smooth. Divide into 6 pieces. Shape each into a ball, then roll out to a round 15–18 cm (6–7 in) in diameter. Place teacakes on 2–3 greased baking trays, brush tops with milk and cover with oiled plastic wrap. Allow to rise in a warm place for about 40 minutes or until almost doubled in size. Bake in a preheated hot oven (200°C/400°F) for about 20 minutes or until well risen and golden-brown. Cool on a wire rack. Serve warm or toasted, split open and spread with plenty of butter. Makes 6.

NOTE: If you would like the buns to have a sticky top, brush with clear honey or syrup as soon as you remove them from the oven.

Honey Teacake

I$^1/_4$ cups sour cream; $^3/_4$ cup firmly packed brown sugar; I egg; 2$^1/_4$ cups wholemeal flour, sifted; I tsp bicarbonate of soda; 3 tbs warmed honey; $^1/_2$ cup chopped mixed nuts.

TOPPING: I tbs caster sugar; $^1/_4$ tsp nutmeg; 2 tsp butter, softened.

Beat together sour cream, sugar and egg, then stir in flour and bicarbonate of soda. Mix well. Beat in warmed honey and chopped nuts. Spoon mixture into a well-greased 20 cm (8 in) round cake tin and bake in a preheated slow oven (150°C/300°F) for about

1$^1/_2$ hours. Turn on to a wire rack. Mix topping ingredients and brush over top of loaf. Serve warm or cold, sliced, either buttered or plain.

TERIYAKI

The splendid Japanese dish of marinated, grilled and glazed beef or chicken. It can be cooked at the table on an Hibachi barbecue, or on a griddle or in an electric frypan. Prepared teriyaki sauce, available bottled from Asian stores and many supermarkets, may be substituted for that given in the recipe.

Beef Teriyaki

6–8 slices fillet steak, each about 5 mm ($^1/_4$ in) thick; oil.

SAUCE: I clove garlic; $^1/_2$ tsp sugar; $^1/_2$ tsp grated fresh ginger; $^1/_2$ cup Japanese soy sauce; $^1/_2$ cup mirin (sweet sake) or dry sherry.

GLAZE: 2 tsp sugar; 3 tbs water; I tsp cornflour mixed with I tbs cold water.

GARNISH: I tbs dry mustard, sprigs fresh coriander or parsley.

Trim any fat and gristle from steaks.

SAUCE: Crush garlic with sugar, then mix with remaining ingredients. Dip both sides of each steak into sauce, then remove from sauce and set aside for 30 minutes.

GLAZE: Put 3 tbs sauce into a small saucepan and add sugar and water. Bring to the boil. Stir cornflour mixture again, and stir into saucepan. Stir until mixture boils and becomes clear; set aside. Mix mustard with just enough hot water to make a thick paste; set aside.

Heat grill or griddle, brush with oil and cook steak at high heat for about 1 minute each side or until lightly browned. This will give medium-rare steak. For well-done meat, cook 1 minute more. To serve, slice each steak into strips and assemble again into original shape. Heat glaze to boiling point and spoon over steaks. Garnish each plate with a dab of mustard and a sprig of coriander or parsley. Serves 6 as part of Japanese meal, 4 as a main course.

VARIATION

CHICKEN TERIYAKI: Follow recipe for Beef Teriyaki, but substitute 4–6 half-breasts of chicken, boned but with skin left on, for the steaks. After marinating, grill skin side up for 2–3 minutes or until a light golden-brown. Dip again into sauce and grill other side 2–3 minutes, then dip a third time into sauce and grill skin side up until a rich brown. Cut into strips and reassemble to serve. Glaze and garnish as for Beef Teriyaki.

TERRINE

See Pâté and Terrine.

THYME

Whether fresh or dried, the herb thyme is indispensable in the kitchen. It is one of the elements of the classic *bouquet garni* and a 'must' in stocks and stews. It goes into wine marinades for meat and poultry, into hearty, one-dish soups, and is particularly good with rabbit.

There are many varieties of thyme, all of them perennial herbs. The wild thyme which grows in Mediterranean regions is one of these; in addition, there are lemon thyme and variegated thyme, plus other varieties used mainly as ornamental plants. The easiest way to have your own thyme is to get a rooted branch from a friend's bush, which will quickly spread.

Branches of thyme may be dried, but since the herb is perennial it is often easier to use sprigs of fresh thyme. Dried thyme, however, is more convenient if the recipe calls for crumbled thyme – for example for a stuffing or to add to a meatball mixture. **See recipes.**

Sauce Marchand de Vin

This sauce should be made in the same pan as the one used to cook steaks. Pour off excess fat before starting sauce.

2 tbs finely chopped onion; 60 g (2 oz) butter; 5 tbs red wine; 1 clove garlic, crushed; 1 sprig fresh thyme; ½ tsp French mustard; salt and freshly ground black pepper.

Cook onion in about 15 g (½ oz) butter in frying pan for about 2 minutes over high heat. Add wine, garlic and thyme, and boil to reduce to 3–4 tbs. Remove from heat. Whisk in remaining butter, cut into small pieces, then add mustard, salt and pepper. Stir in any juices which have run out of steaks. Remove thyme from sauce. Arrange steaks on heated plates, and strain sauce over them and serve immediately. Makes enough for 2 steaks.

Papeton d'Aubergines (Eggplant)

This was a dish created in the fifteenth century in Avignon by the French papal chef – thus the corruption of French and Italian words.

1.5 kg (3 lb) eggplants, peeled and finely sliced; salt; about ½ cup olive oil; freshly ground black pepper; 2–3 sprigs fresh thyme; 5 eggs; ½ cup grated cheese.

Place eggplant slices in large colander, sprinkle with salt and leave to dégorge for about 1 hour. Drain and pat dry with paper towels. Heat a little olive oil in a frying pan, and quickly brown eggplant slices, 3–4 at a time, on both sides. Add more oil to pan as needed. Purée eggplant through food mill or in blender. Season with salt and pepper and add thyme leaves. Add eggs one at a time, beating well. Pour mixture into greased 6-cup soufflé dish, and bake in a preheated hot oven (200°C/400°F) for 10–15 minutes

or until a crust forms on top. Sprinkle with grated cheese, reduce oven temperature to moderate (180°C/350°F) and cook for 25–30 minutes longer. Serve warm as an accompaniment to grilled or roast lamb or beef, or cold as hors d'oeuvre. Serves 6–8.

TIMBALE

The name given to a deep round mould, usually small, made from metal, earthenware or ovenproof china, with either straight or sloping sides. It also applies to the dish prepared in the mould.

A timbale is made with a delicious creamy custard mixture of fish, poultry, meat or vegetables which is steamed, resulting in a texture resembling that of a soufflé. It is usually served with a sauce.

Sometimes the mould can be filled with potato, macaroni or rice and turned out as a garnish for fish, meat or poultry.

A timbale provides an elegant method for using leftover ingredients, and also makes a superb first course for a dinner party. **See recipes.**

Zucchini Timbale

A rather moist mixture reminiscent of the soft centre in a soufflé and an excellent first course or luncheon dish.

1 kg (2 lb) zucchini, grated; salt; 4 medium onions, minced; 45 g (1½ oz) butter; 1 tbs oil; 1 cup grated mixed Parmesan and Gruyère cheeses; 1 cup cream; 8 large eggs, well beaten; freshly ground white pepper.

GARNISH: 60 g (2 oz) butter; 1 cup fresh white breadcrumbs; 4 tbs chopped parsley.

Sprinkle grated zucchini with salt and leave for 30 minutes to drain. Dry well with paper towels. Cook onions gently in butter and oil until translucent. Increase heat to medium, stir in zucchini and cook for about 5 minutes, stirring frequently. Cover pan and cook over low heat 2–3 minutes longer or until zucchini is tender. Remove from heat and cool. Add cheese to zucchini mixture and stir in cream. Mix in beaten eggs, salt and pepper. Carefully pour into a greased and bottom-lined 6-cup mould (or 6 individual 1-cup moulds). Set mould in a baking dish filled with enough hot water to come about two thirds way up sides of mould. Bake on middle shelf of a preheated moderate oven (180°C/350°F) for 35–40 minutes or until set. Test with a thin-bladed knife inserted in centre – it should come out clean and look slightly buttery when custard is ready. Remove from heat and from water bath. Rest timbale for 15 minutes before unmoulding.

GARNISH: Melt butter in a small frying pan, stir in breadcrumbs and sauté until golden-brown. Remove from heat and stir in parsley. Run a knife around edge of mould and invert timbale on to serving plate.

Sprinkle with parsley and breadcrumb garnish and serve immediately. Serves 6.

NOTE: If using individual moulds, bake for 20–25 minutes, depending on their depth.

VARIATIONS

BROCCOLI TIMBALE: Follow recipe for Zucchini Timbale, using 2½–3 cups cooked, well drained and puréed broccoli instead of zucchini. Serve with Hollandaise Sauce, if desired (see page 459).

SPINACH TIMBALE: Follow recipe for Zucchini Timbale, using 2½–3 cups cooked, well drained and puréed spinach instead of zucchini. Serve with Hollandaise or Tomato Sauce (see *Sauces*).

Timbales of Smoked Salmon

A stunning way to present smoked salmon for a very special dinner. Crème fraîche makes a delicate filling.

125 g (4 oz) smoked salmon, thinly sliced;
¹/₂ cup Crème Fraîche, chilled (page 102);
2 tbs salmon roe; pinch cayenne,
or dash Tabasco sauce.

FRESH TOMATO PUREE: 4 ripe tomatoes, peeled,
seeded and chopped; salt and freshly ground
black pepper.

GARNISH: snipped chives or fresh dill;
whole chives or sprigs fresh dill.

Rinse 4 individual soufflé dishes or other small moulds (about ⅓-cup size) and line bottoms with dampened greaseproof paper. Line with smoked salmon slices, trimming them level with rims. Chop trimmings finely. Beat crème fraîche until soft peaks form, and fold in chopped salmon, caviar and cayenne or Tabasco. Fill moulds with mixture. Cover and chill overnight.

FRESH TOMATO PUREE: Mash tomato flesh with a fork or purée in a food processor fitted with the steel blade, then rub purée through a fine sieve. Season with salt and pepper and chill. Run a thin knife around inside of each mould. Invert a serving plate over each, hold plate and mould firmly together and turn them over. Rap plate sharply on table to release timbale, and lift mould off carefully. Spoon tomato purée in a cordon around each timbale and sprinkle with snipped chives or dill. Garnish each plate with chives or dill. Serves 4.

Fish Timbales

2 cups boned and very finely chopped cooked fish;
¹/₄ tsp salt; pinch paprika; ¹/₂ tsp grated lemon
rind; 2 tsp lemon juice; ¹/₂ cup cream; 3 egg whites;
Sauce Tartare (page 256) to serve.

Combine fish, salt, paprika, lemon rind and lemon juice. Whip cream until it holds stiff peaks and fold into fish mixture. Whisk egg whites until stiff and fold in gently. Spoon into a greased and bottom-lined

4-cup mould (or 4 x 1-cup individual moulds). Set in a baking dish with hot water to come three quarters of the way up sides of mould. Bake in a preheated moderate oven (180°C/350°F) for 30–40 minutes, depending on depth of moulds. Test with a thin-bladed knife inserted in centre – it should come out clean when timbales are ready. Remove from heat and from water bath. Unmould on to serving plates and serve with tartare sauce. Serves 4.

Chicken Timbales

2 cups minced cooked chicken; 3/4 cup cream;
¹/₄ tsp salt; ¹/₄ tsp paprika; 4 egg whites;
I small canned pimiento, drained and cut into
strips; Velouté Sauce (page 457) to serve.

Combine minced chicken, cream, salt and paprika and blend well. Whisk egg whites until stiff peaks form and fold into chicken mixture. Line 6 greased 1-cup moulds with strips of pimiento and spoon in chicken mixture. Set in a baking dish with hot water to come three quarters of the way up sides of moulds. Bake in a preheated moderate oven (180°C/350°F) or 20–25 minutes or until set. Test with a thin-bladed knife inserted in centre – it should come out clean when timbales are ready. Remove from heat and from water bath. Unmould and serve with velouté sauce. Serves 6.

VARIATION

HAM TIMBALES: Follow recipe for Chicken Timbales using 1 cup minced cooked chicken and 1 cup minced cooked ham instead of 2 cups chicken. Serve with Sauce Suprême (see page 457).

TIPSY CAKE

A dessert resembling trifle, made from firm sponge cake either whole or in two layers. The cake is soaked in sweet white wine, sherry or brandy, then decorated with split, blanched almonds and whipped cream. It was once served surrounded with custard and when cut, the soaked cake slid and toppled sideways as though it was a bit 'tipsy' – a nice explanation for the name.

Tipsy Cake

2 x 18 cm (7 in) Whisked Sponge or Sponge sandwich
layers (page 59); 3/4 cup sweet white wine, sherry or
brandy; ¹/₂ cup warm apricot jam; ¹/₂ cup split,
blanched almonds.

DECORATION: I cup cream, whipped and sweetened
with I tbs sifted icing sugar;
¹/₄ cup toasted flaked almonds.

Prepare each sponge layer separately. Slowly spoon wine, sherry or brandy on cake to moisten evenly. Brush with warm jam and put layers together. Chill for 2–3 hours or overnight. Stud cake with almonds and decorate with whipped cream and toasted flaked almonds. Serves 8–10.

NOTE: Use a combination of wine, sherry or brandy if you wish.

TISANE

A herbal tea or infusion, sometimes sweetened with honey but rarely drunk with milk. Almost any herb can be used to make an infusion, together with the flowers of some plants.

Some tisanes have health-giving reputations. Camomile tea is an old remedy for upset stomachs (Mrs Rabbit gave it to Peter Rabbit after he had gorged himself in the vegetable garden).

Peppermint tea is recommended as a prevention against colds. Angelica tea is said to help digestion. When caffeine is not allowed in the diet, herbal teas are often advised instead. Many have a soothing effect, such as linden flower (*tilleul*) tea.

A tisane may be made from either fresh or dried herbs or flowers. Little sachets of herbs or flowers for infusions may also be bought; these look like tea bags but must be left to infuse for much longer. Camomile, rose hip and linden flower are among the most common.

Rosemary Tea: Pour boiling water over a fresh sprig of rosemary in a cup. Cover, and leave to infuse for 5 minutes. For more than one person, use several sprigs rosemary in a teapot.

Peppermint Tea: Put a handful of fresh peppermint leaves in a china or earthenware teapot, pour over boiling water and leave to infuse for 5 minutes. Sweeten to taste with a little honey and add a squeeze of fresh lemon juice. Dried peppermint leaves may be used in the same way. Cut branches of mint and spread out or hang in a dry, airy place until leaves are dried. Strip off leaves and store in an airtight container.

TOFFEE (TAFFY, TOFFY)

A very popular sweetmeat of ancient origin, that was probably once made with black treacle flavoured with rum. Today the basic recipe contains sugar, water and sometimes butter. It is boiled at a high temperature (this varies according to type of toffee) to give the texture required after cooling.

TIPS WHEN MAKING TOFFEE:

- Always use a large heavy-based pan and oil the sides.
- Use a sugar thermometer for best results.
- Do not stir unless the recipe specifies this.
- Reduce the heat to a low simmer after the toffee has reached a temperature of 127°C/260°F.
- When the toffee reaches the required temperature, pour the mixture immediately into an oiled tin.
- Cool at an even room temperature, and when it is lukewarm, mark into squares with an oiled knife. See recipes.

Simple Toffee

2 cups sugar; 3/4 cup cold water; 1 tbs vinegar.

Place all ingredients in a heavy 8-cup saucepan. Stir over medium heat until sugar has dissolved. Bring to the boil, without stirring, and cook until syrup is golden-brown. Remove from heat and allow bubbles to settle. Pour into small paper cases (standing in metal pans), or pour into an oiled 18 cm (7 in) square shallow tin and mark into squares with an oiled knife. Makes about 50 x 2.5 cm (1 in) pieces.

Treacle Toffee

2 cups raw sugar; 1/2 cup water; 90 g (3 oz) butter; pinch cream of tartar; 1/3 cup treacle; 1/3 cup golden syrup.

Dissolve sugar in water in a heavy 8-cup saucepan over low heat. Add remaining ingredients and bring back to the boil, without stirring. Boil to soft-crack stage, or 132°C/270°F if using a sugar thermometer. To test when soft-crack stage is reached, drop 1/2 tsp toffee syrup into 1 cup cold water. Work it with your fingers: hard separate threads that bend when removed from water should form.

Pour toffee into an oiled 18 cm (7 in) square shallow tin. Cool for 5 minutes, then mark into squares with an oiled knife and leave to set. When cold, break into squares and wrap in waxed paper. Makes about 50 x 2.5 cm (1 in) pieces.

Toffee Apples

8 medium apples; 2 cups sugar; 2/3 cup water; 2 tsp vinegar; pinch cream of tartar; red food colouring (optional).

Push a wooden butcher's skewer into each apple. Place sugar, water, vinegar and cream of tartar in a deep, heavy saucepan. Stir over gentle heat until sugar has dissolved, then cover and bring to the boil. Remove lid and boil syrup rapidly, without stirring, for about 15 minutes or until temperature reaches 150°C/300°F, or hard-crack stage. To test when hard-crack stage is reached, drop 1/2 tsp toffee syrup in 1 cup cold water. Work it with your fingers for 1–2 seconds: if toffee makes brittle threads that stay brittle out of the water, it is ready. Remove from heat and colour syrup with red food colouring, if liked. Twirl apples quickly in toffee mixture until well coated. Place on a greased baking tray to become hard. Makes 8.

VARIATION

TOFFEE SPRINKLES: Cook toffee as for Toffee Apples. Set paper cases in patty cake pans and 3/4 fill with toffee. Sprinkle with hundreds and thousands or desiccated coconut. Makes about 10.

TOFU (BEAN CURD)

Known as 'tofu' in Japan and 'doufu' in China and some-times 'the boneless meat of China', bean curd is made from dried soy beans. High in protein, low in carb-ohydrates and cholesterol, bean curd generally has a bland nutty flavour, which is its strength. It is invaluable throughout Asia for absorbing the flavour of any dish to which it is added. It can be used in salads, stir-fries, soups and other healthy Asian dishes and is a great addition to a vegetarian diet.

To make bean curd, soy beans are soaked, skins removed then blended with water to make soy milk. Magnesium chloride is added to heated soy milk to separate the curds and whey. The curds are turned into many different forms: firm, soft silken puffs, sheets, fermented cakes and liquid. Pressed firm tofu is creamy in colour and comes in firm blocks; the softer silken firm tofu is fragile and also comes in blocks. It needs to be handled carefully. Puffed tofu has been cut into pieces and deep-fried; tempeh is fermented tofu with a nutty, smoky flavour made from cooked beans fermented with a mould until they form a chunky tasty bean cake. Bean curd also comes preserved in brine, sometimes flavoured with chilli or sesame oil.

Agedashi Tofu

600 g (20 oz) silken firm tofu; cornflour, potato or rice flour for dusting; oil for frying; 1 sheet of nori (dried seaweed).

SAUCE: 1 cup dashi broth (instant can be used); 2 tbs soy sauce; 3 tbs mirin; 1 tsp sugar; 1 spring onion, finely sliced.

Drain and rinse the tofu in water. Place on a rack over a plate, cover with paper towel and place a small weight on top. Allow to drain for about 30 minutes to remove excess liquid. Cut the tofu into 5 x 1.5 cm (2 x ¾ in) cubes. To make sauce, gently heat together dashi broth, soy sauce, mirin and sugar, and simmer for a few minutes. Add spring onion and set aside.

Dust the cubes of tofu carefully with cornflour to coat evenly. In a wok or heavy frying pan, add enough oil to coat the tofu and heat until hot but not smoking. Add the tofu a few at a time and deep-fry, turning, until golden and crisp. Remove carefully with a slotted spoon and drain on crumpled paper towels. Arrange fried tofu on serving plates and pour a little dashi sauce over each. Alternatively, simply accompany the fried tofu with soy sauce for dipping. Serve immediately garnished with nori cut into thin strips using scissors. Serves 4 as a starter.

Salt and Pepper Doufu

Szechwan seasoning can be purchased at any good delicatessen or supermarket.

600 g (20 oz) silken firm tofu; 1 cup peanut or vegetable oil; 1 tbs Szechwan seasoning; 1 tsp salt; 1 tsp sugar; 2 cloves garlic, finely chopped; 2.5 cm (1 in) piece fresh ginger, finely grated; ½–1 red bird's-eye chilli, chopped; 2 spring onions, sliced.

Drain and rinse the tofu in water. Place the tofu on a rack on a plate, cover with clean paper towels and place a small weight on top. Drain for about 30 min-utes to remove excess liquid. Cut the tofu into thick slices and cut again into triangles or squares. Heat a wok or heavy frying pan, add the oil and heat until hot but not smoking. Add the tofu, a few at a time, and deep-fry until lightly golden on both sides. Tofu is very fragile, so remove carefully with a slotted spoon and drain on paper towels.

In a small bowl mix the Szechwan seasoning, salt and sugar together. Pour off most of the oil, leaving 1–2 tablespoons in the wok or frying pan. Reheat the oil and add the garlic, ginger and chilli and stir-fry very gently for 30 seconds. Return the tofu to the pan and continue to stir-fry very gently until heated through. Serve immediately. Garnish with the spring onions. Serves 4 as a starter or as a main meal with rice and a stir-fried vegetable.

TOMATO

Indispensable as the fresh tomato is for eating either raw or cooked, it is only the beginning of this great fruit's use-fulness to the cook. The tomato takes so well to being canned, puréed and concentrated that these forms are considered equal in status to the fresh product – indeed, they are sometimes the first choice for their rich colour and deep flavour, especially when fresh tomatoes are a little out of season and may lack flavour. Tomato juice, tomato sauce or ketchup, tomato relish or chutney find a place in most kitchens, and are used both to accompany food and as ingredients.

The tomato comes in a number of varieties from the large, ridged ones (which usually have especially good flavour), through smooth red globes to egg tomatoes, just right for lunch-boxes. There are also yellow varieties. Tiny cherry tomatoes (sometimes called 'Tom Thumb'), now widely available, are brilliant for garnishing. They can be used in salads and, dipped first into gin then into coarse salt, make a sensational nibble to have with drinks. Tomatoes are often sold on the vine; these make an attractive display.

■ TO BUY: The very best fresh tomato is one that has been sun-ripened on the bush, but those available commercially have usually been picked at the stage where they are mature but still green or just beginning to redden. They are often fully ripe by the time they reach the shop; buy bright red ones for immediate use, paler ones if you want to use them in a day or two.

Tomatoes to be eaten raw or cooked whole or with a stuffing would be bright coloured but firm, with smooth, tight skins and no soft spots. Tomatoes which are a little beyond this stage and are very soft but still sound are usually cheaper and are excellent for cooking.

■ **TO STORE:** Remove from any plastic wrapping and store ripe tomatoes in a cool, dark place; refrigerate (in a plastic bag in the crisper) only if you have more than you can use immediately, and remove half an hour before serving for fullest flavour. Store underripe tomatoes in good light but not in sunlight, and they will redden well in a day or two. You can speed the process by keeping them in a closed paper bag with a ripe apple. Tomatoes which have been picked before reaching maturity will not ripen and are best used for making pickles and chutney or, if they are not too hard, for frying; slice thickly, dust with seasoned flour and fry slowly in bacon fat or butter.

■ **BASIC PREPARATION:**

TO PEEL: Cover tomatoes with boiling water, in a saucepan or bowl, count to 10, then remove and place them under cold running water. Make a tiny slit in the skin at the base and strip the skin off toward the stem end.

If the skin does not come away easily, drop tomatoes back into boiling water for a few seconds more, then place under cold running water again. After peeling, use the point of a knife to cut out the blossom at the stem end. Use peeled tomatoes in casseroles, sauces, salads and for garnish.

TO SEED: Cut tomatoes in half crossways; squeeze them in the palm of your hand, giving a little shake as you do so, over a sieve set over a bowl. Scrape out any remaining seeds with a teaspoon or grapefruit knife, and discard the seeds. Use the liquid in the bowl for the dish you are making, or add it to a stock or sauce.

TO SEASON: The correct basic seasoning for tomatoes is salt, pepper and just a touch of sugar to bring out the flavour. A little sugar added to dressings for tomato salads or to dishes using cooked tomatoes will give the fullest flavour. See recipes.

Basic Tomato Sauce

This is a good sauce to make in quantity and freeze – the recipe can easily be doubled. Use it as a base for a superb home-made soup; with spaghetti or other pasta; with meatballs; for cooking mussels or other seafood.

700 g (23 oz) can peeled tomatoes; 3 tbs tomato paste; 6 sprigs parsley; 2 cloves garlic; 1 medium onion, quartered; 1 tsp sugar; 1 tbs chopped basil leaves; $^{1}/_{4}$ cup olive oil; 1 bay leaf; 1 tsp salt; $^{1}/_{4}$ tsp freshly ground black pepper.

With the metal blade of a food processor or blender in place, add tomatoes, tomato paste, parsley, garlic, onion, sugar and basil. Process, turning on and off rapidly, until ingredients are finely chopped. Pour

into a large saucepan. Add olive oil, bay leaf, salt and pepper. Simmer for 30 minutes and remove the bay leaf. Taste for seasoning, adding more salt if needed. If a smoother sauce is desired, process the mixture until puréed, again using the food processor with the metal blade. Makes about 2 cups.

Tomato Meatball Soup

1 tbs soy sauce; 1 tbs sherry; 1 spring onion, chopped; $^{1}/_{2}$ tsp grated fresh ginger; 1 egg, beaten; 2 tbs cornflour; 250 g (8 oz) minced lean pork or beef; 4 cups stock; 1 leek, thinly sliced; 4 medium, ripe tomatoes, peeled and diced; 1 tsp peanut oil; chopped fresh coriander or spring onions to garnish.

Mix soy sauce, sherry, spring onion, ginger, egg and cornflour with minced meat and set aside. Place stock in large saucepan and add leek and tomatoes. Bring to the boil and simmer for a few minutes. Add oil, then drop teaspoons of meat mixture into simmering soup. Cover and cook gently for 5–8 minutes. Serve sprinkled with fresh coriander or spring onions. Serves 4.

NOTE: When tomatoes are expensive, use 1 x 425 g can tomatoes. Chop the tomatoes and measure juice to replace some of the stock.

Tomato Soup with Fresh Basil Paste

Make the basil paste in the summer when the fresh herb is available, and keep it, covered with oil, in the refrigerator for the winter months.

1 tsp olive oil; 1 medium carrot, sliced; 1 small leek (white part only), sliced, or 8 spring onions, chopped; 1 clove garlic, crushed; 1 sprig fresh thyme, or small pinch dried; $^{1}/_{2}$ bay leaf; 3 ripe tomatoes, chopped; 1 tbs tomato paste; 5 cups chicken stock; 1 tsp salt; freshly ground black pepper.

BASIL PASTE: 2 handfuls fresh basil leaves; 2 tsp olive oil.

Heat olive oil in a large heavy saucepan, add carrot, leek or spring onions and garlic and cook gently for 5 minutes. Stir in thyme, bay leaf, tomatoes and tomato paste, then the chicken stock. Heat until simmering. Season with salt and pepper, and simmer, half covered, for 20 minutes.

BASIL PASTE: Put basil leaves and olive oil in a blender or food processor fitted with steel blade and blend to a paste. Rub soup through a sieve and return to saucepan (or purée in a blender or food processor and strain back into pan). Reheat and serve, swirling a small dollop of basil paste into each serving. Serves 6.

Creamy Tomato Soup (Hot or Cold)

I cup Basic Tomato Sauce (page 538);
3 cups chicken stock; I cup cream;
salt and freshly ground black pepper;
snipped chives, fresh basil or nutmeg, to serve.

Purée sauce in a blender until it is very smooth, or rub it through a sieve. Combine with stock and, if soup is to be served hot, bring cream to the boil and stir in tomato mixture gradually. Adjust seasoning. Serve scattered with chives or basil, or grate a little nutmeg over each serving. Serves 4.

Salad of Roasted Tomatoes with Shallots

This dish relies on flavoursome red tomatoes and delicious little golden shallots, both roasted, and good olive oil.

8 golden shallots, peeled and halved;
about 8 tbs olive oil; 2 tsp caster sugar;
8 ripe red tomatoes, peeled; 250 g (8 oz) green
beans, tipped; I cup shelled cooked broad beans;
I tbs balsamic or wine vinegar;
sea salt and freshly ground pepper.

Arrange the shallots on a sheet of foil, sprinkle with 2 tbs olive oil and caster sugar. Fold up the sides of the foil and seal the edges to make an airtight parcel. Bake in a preheated hot oven (200°C/400°F) for 30 minutes. Meanwhile, halve the peeled tomatoes, drizzle with olive oil and roast in the oven for 30 minutes. Remove and set tomatoes and shallots aside.

Drop the beans into boiling salted water and cook for about 4 minutes until crisp-tender. Drain and refresh under cold water. If time allows, remove the white skin from each broad bean to reveal the bright green bean underneath and set aside.

Add the vinegar to a small bowl with salt and pepper and gradually whisk in 4 tbs olive oil until a thickened dressing is formed. Whisk in the juice from the tomatoes. Arrange the beans on a salad platter and top with the roasted tomatoes and shallots. Scatter with the broad beans and spoon around the dressing. Serves 4–6.

Pan-fried Cherry Tomatoes

Now that many back gardens are growing a few plants of these prolific tomatoes and the greengrocer has them in punnets, use them as a vegetable with all kinds of foods.

24–30 cherry tomatoes, depending on size;
2 tbs light olive oil; I clove garlic, chopped;
I tbs chopped parsley; 6 fresh basil leaves, torn;
sea salt and a fresh grinding of pepper.

Wash and stem the tomatoes. Heat the oil in a frying pan, add the tomatoes, garlic and parsley and, over a moderate heat, cook the mixture for 2–3 minutes or until tomatoes are heated through. Take care not to allow the skins to split. Just before serving, toss in the basil and season with salt and pepper. Serves 4–6.

Buttered Tomatoes with Basil

6 small tomatoes, peeled and cored;
30 g (I oz) butter, melted; salt and freshly ground
black pepper; fresh basil, cut into fine ribbons,
or chopped parsley.

Arrange tomatoes in a buttered baking dish, blossom ends down. Brush with melted butter, and sprinkle with salt and pepper. Bake in a preheated moderately hot oven (190°C/375°F) for 10–15 minutes or until slightly softened and heated through. Brush with melted butter and sprinkle lightly with salt every 5 minutes. Serve at once, sprinkled with basil or parsley. Serves 6.

Tomates à la Provençale (Tomatoes, Provençal Style)

Tomatoes and garlic are the basis for most dishes from Provence – in fact, tomatoes are referred to as 'pommes d'amour' there. If you're a garlic lover, once you eat tomatoes cooked in this way, you won't eat them simply grilled again. Tomates à la Provençale is often served in France as a first course, with plenty of the light, crusty French bread to mop up the garlicky oil.

6 large ripe tomatoes, halved; salt and freshly
ground black pepper; olive oil;
3 cloves garlic (more if desired),
finely chopped; finely chopped parsley.

Squeeze tomato halves gently to remove seeds and juice. Season lightly with salt and pepper. Heat oil in a heavy frying pan to a depth of about 1 cm (½ in). Add tomatoes, cut sides up, with garlic. Cover and cook gently until tender, about 20 minutes. Remove to a heated serving dish, pour over cooking oil and sprinkle with chopped parsley. Serve hot with crusty bread, as an accompaniment to grills or as a separate vegetable dish. Serves 6.

Anchovy-Stuffed Tomatoes

6–8 even-sized tomatoes; 30 g (I oz) butter; 2 spring
onions, chopped; 3 tbs fresh white breadcrumbs;
6 anchovy fillets; grated cheese; butter.

Slice stem ends off tomatoes. Carefully scoop out seeds and discard. Remove and chop some of the pulp. Melt butter in a frying pan and gently fry spring onions until soft. Remove with a slotted spoon, and fry breadcrumbs until golden. Mash anchovy fillets and mix with spring onions, tomato pulp and fried breadcrumbs. Fill tomatoes with mixture and sprinkle with grated cheese. Bake in a preheated moderate oven (180°C/350°F) for 10–15 minutes. Dot with butter before serving. Serves 6–8.

Tomates Garni

This special way with tomatoes is often used as a garnish for dishes such as roast chicken, rack of lamb or roast fillet of beef.

6 medium, firm, ripe tomatoes; salt; sugar; 60 g (2 oz) butter; 1¹/₂ cups hot freshly cooked peas.

Cut tops off tomatoes and carefully scoop out seeds. Sprinkle insides with salt and a touch of sugar, then turn upside-down to drain for 30 minutes. Pat insides dry with paper towels. Put ½ tsp butter into each tomato and arrange in a buttered baking dish. Melt remaining butter, reserve 1 tbs and mix rest with peas. Fill tomatoes with peas and brush skins with reserved butter. Bake in a preheated moderately hot oven (190°C/375°F) for 10 minutes, brushing skins again with butter after 5 minutes. Serves 6.

Tomatoes au Gratin

4 ripe tomatoes, thickly sliced; salt and freshly ground black pepper; 1 cup fresh breadcrumbs; ¹/₄ cup grated Parmesan cheese, 4 tbs oil.

Arrange tomato slices, overlapping, in a lightly oiled flameproof dish. Season generously with salt and pepper, sprinkle with breadcrumbs, then cheese, and finally oil. Cook under a preheated medium grill for 5–6 minutes or until tomatoes are tender and surface is lightly browned. Serve from dish. Serves 4.

VARIATION

TOMATOES AND EGGPLANT AU GRATIN: Follow recipe for Tomatoes au Gratin, but before grilling, interleave overlapping slices of tomatoes in the dish with 8 slices of eggplant, which have been dusted with flour and very quickly browned in oil over a fairly high heat.

Tomatoes Baked with Herbs

A most versatile yet simple dish, adding a touch of colour and robust flavour to roast chicken or a mixed grill. The amount of garlic used depends on personal liking for this pungent little bulb.

6 ripe tomatoes; salt and freshly ground black pepper; 1–2 cloves garlic, chopped; 2 tbs chopped fresh herbs (basil, parsley, thyme); ³/₄ cup fresh breadcrumbs (optional); 30 g (1 oz) butter.

Cut tops off tomatoes and season generously with salt and pepper. Sprinkle each with garlic and herbs

and top with breadcrumbs (if using). Put a generous dot of butter on top of each tomato. Arrange in a buttered gratin dish and bake in a preheated moderate oven (180°C/350°F) for 10 minutes. Serve from dish. Serves 4–6.

Tomato and Onion Savoury

An excellent old-fashioned accompaniment to bake in the oven with a roast. It is good with barbecued chops or sausages, too. Tomatoes which are a little too soft for salad are right for this dish.

4 ripe tomatoes, peeled and sliced; 2 onions, finely sliced, 1¹/₂ cups fresh breadcrumbs; 30 g (1 oz) butter, melted; sugar; salt and freshly ground black pepper.

Arrange tomatoes, onions and breadcrumbs mixed with butter in layers in a shallow ovenproof dish, seasoning tomato layers with a little sugar, salt and pepper, and finishing with a layer of crumbs. Bake in a preheated moderate oven (180°C/350°F) for 45 minutes or until vegetables are soft and top browned. Serves 6.

VARIATION

HERBED TOMATO SAVOURY: Follow recipe for Tomato and Onion Savoury, but sprinkle tomato layers with 2 tsp chopped fresh mixed herbs, or ½ tsp dried herbs mixed with 2 tsp chopped parsley.

Sliced Tomatoes with Basil

One of the simplest and best ways to feast on tomatoes in summer when they, and basil, are in season.

4 ripe tomatoes, thickly sliced; 2 tsp wine vinegar; ¹/₂ tsp Dijon mustard; sea salt and freshly ground black pepper; pinch sugar; 1¹/₂ tbs olive oil; 2 tbs fresh basil leaves, cut into fine ribbons.

Place tomato slices in a shallow dish. Mix vinegar with mustard, salt, pepper and sugar in a small bowl, and beat in oil little by little to make a thick dressing. Spoon over tomatoes and scatter with basil. Serves 4.

Luncheon Tomatoes

Tomatoes filled with a delicious salad can be a main dish or an accompaniment to cold meats.

6 ripe tomatoes; $^1/_2$ cup plain yogurt;
$^1/_4$ cup Mayonnaise (page 256); I small cucumber,
diced; 2 spring onions, finely chopped (including
some green tops); I stick celery, diced;
$^1/_2$ green or red pepper, cored, seeded and diced;
3 hard-boiled eggs, chopped; salt and freshly
ground black pepper.

Have ingredients chilled. Cut a slice from the top of
each tomato and carefully scoop out most of the pulp
and seeds, leaving a shell about 1 cm ($^1/_2$ in) thick. Salt
shells lightly inside and turn upside-down to drain.
(Reserve scooped-out pulp and seeds for a stew, soup,
casserole, etc.) Mix yogurt and mayonnaise, and fold
in cucumber, spring onions, celery, pepper and eggs.
Season with salt and pepper. Spoon mixture into
tomato shells, mounding it up. Serves 6.

VARIATIONS
Instead of hard-boiled eggs, use 1 cup chopped
cooked ham or corned beef, or 1 small can tuna fish
or salmon, drained and flaked.

Tomato Relish

Home-made tomato relish is lovely with cold meats,
grilled chops or cheese, or on sandwiches.

1.5 kg (3 lb) very ripe tomatoes, peeled and
chopped; 500 g (I lb) onions, chopped;
2 cups sugar; 2$^1/_2$ cups malt vinegar; I tbs flour;
I tbs curry powder; pinch cayenne;
I tbs dry mustard; I tbs salt.

Drain off $^3/_4$ cup juice from tomatoes. Put tomatoes,
onions, sugar and vinegar into a saucepan and
simmer, uncovered, until mixture is thick. Blend
remaining ingredients with reserved tomato juice
and stir in. Stir until boiling, then simmer 5 minutes.
Bottle in clean, warm jars and seal when cool. Makes
about 8 x 250 g (8 oz) jars.

Tomato Ketchup

4 kg (8 lb) ripe tomatoes, chopped; 2 cloves garlic,
chopped; 500 g (I lb) onions, chopped;
2$^1/_2$ cups firmly packed brown sugar; 8 whole cloves;
2 tbs rock salt; pinch cayenne; I tsp cinnamon;
$^1/_2$ tsp ground ginger; 3$^1/_2$ cups vinegar.

Put all ingredients in a heavy saucepan. Bring to the
boil slowly, then simmer until tomatoes and onions
are very soft. Stir from time to time with a wooden
spoon to prevent burning. Strain mixture through a
nylon sieve, bottle in clean, warm bottles and cork.
This sauce keeps well for a long time. Makes about
6 x 300 ml ($^1/_2$ pint) bottles.

Fresh Tomato Juice

Nothing matches the flavour of home-made juice.
When tomatoes are cheap, make this in double or
triple quantities and keep tightly covered in the
refrigerator.

12 medium, ripe tomatoes, chopped; $^1/_2$ cup water;
I medium onion, sliced; 2 sticks celery (with
leaves), sliced; I bay leaf; 3 sprigs parsley.

SEASONING: I–2 tsp salt; freshly ground black
pepper; I tsp Worcestershire sauce; I tsp sugar.

Place tomatoes in a saucepan with water, onion,
celery, bay leaf and parsley. Simmer for 15 minutes.
Strain and add seasoning ingredients to taste. Chill
well before serving. Serves 4–6.

Tomato Salsa

A tangy, hot salsa for dipping corn chips into, or for
dressing up hamburgers or grilled meats, even fish.

2 medium onions, chopped; 2 cloves garlic, finely
chopped; 8 large tomatoes, peeled and roughly
chopped; 2 canned serrano chillies or
2 fresh green chillies, finely chopped;
2 tsp sugar; salt to taste; 6 tbs light olive oil;
$^1/_2$ cup tomato paste; $^1/_4$ cup chopped
fresh coriander.

Using a food processor and doing in several lots,
lightly purée together the onions, garlic, tomatoes
and chillies. The purée should still have a chunky
texture. Season with sugar and salt. Heat the oil in
a heavy medium pan and add the tomato mixture
and tomato paste. Bring slowly to the boil and cook,
stirring frequently over a moderate heat, until thick
and well blended. This should take about 10 minutes. Stir in the coriander and cook a further
minute. Cool slightly; pour into small jars and seal.
Best kept in the refrigerator. Makes about 4 x 250 g
(8 oz) jars.

Fresh Tomato Bruschetta

4–6 ripe red tomatoes; I red salad onion, chopped;
4 tbs virgin olive oil; sea salt; I tsp balsamic vinegar;
I tbs chopped parsley or basil; 4–6 slices of a small
baguette, cut lengthwise.

Dice the tomatoes finely. Combine with the onion,
adding 2 tbs olive oil, sea salt and balsamic vinegar.
Stir in the parsley or basil. Drizzle the remaining
olive oil lightly on both sides of each bread slice. Heat
the grill and toast the bread on both sides. Arrange
the bread slices on a platter and spoon the tomato and
onion mixture over each. Serves 4.

VARIATIONS
PISSALADIERE: Prepare as above, spooning the tomato
mixture on toasted bread. Arrange 2 anchovy fillets,
crisscrossed on each bruschetta, and scatter with a few
halved black olives. Drizzle with extra olive oil and
heat through under a preheated grill, about 2 minutes.

PARMIGIANA: Prepare bruschetta, spooning the tomato mixture on toasted bread. Top each with 2 thin slices of mozzarella cheese and a shaving of Parmesan cheese. Drizzle with olive oil and heat through to melt the cheese under a preheated grill.

Stuffed Tomatoes, Italian Style

6 large tomatoes; 1¹/₂ cups cooked long-grain rice (²/₃ cup uncooked); 2 tbs each chopped fresh basil and parsley; ¹/₄ cup olive oil; 4 canned anchovy fillets, drained and chopped; 2 cloves garlic, crushed; salt and freshly ground pepper.

Slice caps off tomatoes and set aside. Use a teaspoon to scoop out some of the flesh, leaving a thick shell. Roughly chop the scooped-out tomato and mix with the remaining ingredients, seasoning with salt and pepper. Stand tomatoes in an oiled shallow ovenproof dish just large enough to hold them in one layer and fill with the rice mixture. Top with caps. Bake in a moderately hot oven (190°C/360°F) for 15 minutes, basting with cooking juices every now and then. Serve hot or at room temperature with crusty bread and a salad. Serves 4–6.

Tomato Bocconcini Salad

8 perfect vine-ripened tomatoes; 8 baby fresh mozzarella cheeses (bocconcini); sea salt crystals; small fresh basil leaves; 3 tbs extra virgin olive oil; balsamic vinegar; freshly ground pepper.

Wash tomatoes and cut into even slices. Cut each bocconcini through into 4–6 slices. Arrange tomato slices overlapping on a serving plate, alternating with the bocconcini slices. Season with sea salt and scatter with basil leaves, tearing them if they are large. Drizzle over the olive oil, and sprinkle with a little balsamic vinegar. Lastly, season with pepper. Serve with crusty bread. Serves 6.

TONGUE

Smooth, richly flavoured tongue, sold fresh, salted or smoked, is one of the best of cold meats and is excellent served hot with a piquant sauce. Cooked, sliced tongue can be crumbed and fried or used in hearty savoury dishes. Canned tongues (usually lambs') are a useful store-cupboard item, especially popular with the elderly because they are easy to eat and can be bought in small cans.

Ox, calf and lamb tongues are available; pig's tongue is usually available with the head. Whatever the variety, smaller tongues are usually better than larger; for prime texture, an ox tongue should be under 1.5 kg (3 lb). Fresh or salted tongues should be soft to the touch, smoked tongue should be firm but not hard.

■ **BASIC PREPARATION:** If salted or smoked tongue has been heavily salted (ask the butcher), it must be blanched before cooking. Cover with cold water, bring very slowly to the boil and drain.

■ **TO COOK:** Place tongue (fresh, salted or smoked) in a saucepan and cover with cold water. For 1 ox tongue or 6–8 lamb tongues, add 6 whole allspice, 6 whole cloves, 6 black peppercorns, a bouquet garni, 1 sliced onion, 1 sliced carrot and 1 sliced stalk celery. Add 1¹/₂ tsp salt if cooking fresh tongue. Bring slowly to the boil, skim the surface and simmer, covered, for about 3 hours for ox tongue and 1–1¹/₂ hours for lamb tongues.

The boiled tongue is cooked when one of the small bones near the root end can be easily pulled out. Cool in liquid until cool enough to handle, then take tongue out, remove remaining bones and trim off root. Slit underside of skin and remove. Skin should come off easily if you push thumbs underneath it to ease edges, then peel off. Tongue is then finished as the recipe directs.

TO CARVE: Cut ox or calf tongue into slices straight across starting from the thickest part. Toward the thin end, change direction to carve diagonal slices. Carve lamb tongues in long diagonal slices. Carve pressed tongue in thin slices across the top.

Braised Tongue with Sour Cream

1 onion, chopped; 1 carrot, chopped; 1 stalk celery, chopped; 1 fresh ox tongue, cooked; 125g (4 oz) butter, melted; ¹/₂–1 cup cooking liquid from tongue; 1 cup sour cream; salt and freshly ground pepper.

To braise tongue, place vegetables in a large roasting pan. Place tongue on top and pour over melted butter. Cook uncovered in a preheated moderate oven (180°C/350°F) for 45 minutes–1 hour or until tongue is nicely browned. Baste every 10 minutes with pan juices, adding a little of the liquid in which tongue was cooked if juices are drying out.

Remove tongue to a heated platter. Rub contents of roasting pan through a sieve and return to pan. Boil down, stirring if necessary, until thick. Stir in sour cream and heat to just under boiling point. Season with salt and pepper and serve over tongue. Serves 6.

Pressed Tongue

1 fresh, salted or smoked ox tongue, freshly cooked; sauce of your choice (page 543) to serve.

After trimming and skinning tongue, curl it while still warm into an 18 cm (7 in) soufflé dish or cake tin. Place on top a plate which will just fit inside the dish or tin, then put a heavy weight, at least 3 kg (7 lb), on the plate. Chill overnight.

Run a knife round the edge and unmould tongue on to a serving plate. Serve in thin slices with Cumberland Sauce (pages 106–7), Rémoulade Sauce (page 256) or one of the following sauces. Serves 6–8.

NOTE: 6–8 lamb tongues can be substituted for the ox tongue.

Apple and Horseradish Sauce

3 cooking apples, peeled, cored and sliced;
2 tbs water; 2 tbs sugar; 1 strip lemon rind;
2 tbs grated horseradish.

Put apples into a heavy saucepan with water, sugar
and lemon rind. Cover and cook gently to a pulp.
Cool, remove lemon rind and mash. Stir in horseradish. Makes about 1½ cups.

Spiced Mustard Sauce

2 tbs brown sugar; 3 tbs cider or white wine vinegar;
4 tbs olive oil; 1 tsp prepared English mustard;
½ tsp salt; freshly ground black pepper;
pinch ground cloves.

Mix ingredients. Makes about ⅔ cup.

Crumbed Tongue

8–10 x 1 cm (½ in) thick slices cooked tongue;
seasoned flour; 2 eggs, beaten; 2 tbs cold water;
1 cup fresh breadcrumbs; 2 tbs oil;
60 g (2 oz) butter; Rémoulade Sauce
(page 256) to serve.

Turn slices of tongue in seasoned flour and pat off
excess. Mix egg and water and coat slices with
mixture, then with breadcrumbs. Chill for 20 minutes.
Fry in oil and butter, turning once, until golden-
brown. Drain on crumpled paper towels and serve
with Rémoulade Sauce. Serves 4.

Ox Tongue au Gratin

1 fresh or salted, cooked ox tongue; 3 onions, sliced;
90 g (3 oz) butter; 1 tbs flour; ½ cup dry white wine;
½ cup beef stock; 8–10 mushrooms, sliced;
1 cup fresh breadcrumbs.

Cut tongue into 1 cm (½ in) thick slices and arrange
the slices in a shallow ovenproof dish. Cook onions
gently in half butter until soft. Sprinkle in flour, blend
thoroughly and stir in wine and stock. Simmer until
thickened and spread over tongue. Heat remaining
butter, add mushrooms and breadcrumbs and toss
until coated with butter. Top dish with mixture and
place in a preheated hot oven (200°C/400°F) for 15–25
minutes, or under a preheated grill, until top is crisp
and golden. Serves 6.

TORTE

The German word for an open tart of rich cake, containing
such ingredients as ground nuts, spices, fruit, chocolate
and cream. Some tortes are a cake-like mixture, baked in a
pastry case; some have many layers interspersed with
butter cream, while others are split and filled with sweet
cream and fresh fruits.

Many tortes are made with little or no flour, ground nuts
taking its place and whisked eggs providing aeration and
structure. See recipes.

See also *Sacher Torte*, *Linzer Torte* and *Black Forest
Cherry Torte*.

Hazelnut Torte

6 eggs, separated; 1 whole egg; ¾ cup caster sugar;
1 cup ground hazelnuts; ¾ cup fresh white
breadcrumbs; 1 tsp flour.

FILLING: 1½ cups cream; 1 tsp caster sugar;
1 tsp vanilla; ½ cup ground hazelnuts.

Beat egg yolks and whole egg together until thick
and pale yellow. Gradually beat in ½ cup sugar, then
nuts and breadcrumbs. Continue to beat until
mixture forms a dense, moist mass. Whisk egg
whites in another bowl until they begin to foam,
then gradually add remaining sugar. Continue to
whisk until whites form stiff glossy peaks. Mix
about half the egg whites into hazelnut mixture,
sprinkle flour over and fold in remaining egg
whites. Pour into a buttered and floured 25 cm
(10 in) springform tin. Bake in a preheated slow
oven (150°C/300°F) for 35–45 minutes or until cake
shrinks away slightly from sides of tin. Remove
from oven, release spring on tin and remove sides.
Allow cake to cool.

FILLING: Whip cream and add sugar and vanilla. Slice
cake into 2 layers and sandwich back together with a
third of cream. Using a spatula, cover top and sides of
cake with remaining cream, and scatter ground
hazelnuts over top and sides. Serves 10.

Griestorte

3 eggs, separated; ½ cup caster sugar;
grated rind and juice ½ lemon;
⅓ cup fine ground semolina;
2 tbs ground almonds; ⅔ cup cream, whipped;
1 punnet (250 g/8 oz) raspberries or strawberries,
sprinkled with 1 tbs caster sugar.

Beat egg yolks with sugar over a pan of hot water
until thick and mousse-like. Remove from heat, add
lemon rind and juice and continue beating until very
thick and pale. Stir in semolina and ground
almonds. Whisk egg whites until stiff peaks form,
then fold into mixture. Turn at once into a greased
and bottom-lined 20 cm (8 in) cake tin that has been
dusted with caster sugar and flour. Bake in a
preheated moderate oven (180°C/350°F) for 30–40
minutes or until cake shrinks a little from sides of
tin. Cool on a wire rack. When cold, split cake into
2 layers and fill with whipped cream. Cover top
of cake with raspberries or strawberries. Serves 8.

VARIATION

GRIESTORTE WITH FRESH PEACHES OR PEARS: Peel, stone or core and slice 2 fresh peaches or pears, dip in water acidulated with lemon juice to prevent browning, remove, dry well and put in between cake layers with whipped cream. Dust top of cake with sifted icing sugar.

Mocha Torte

2–3 packets Savoy or sponge fingers (about 18); 4 cups cream; 3 tbs drinking chocolate powder; 1 tsp instant coffee powder; 1 cup sweet sherry.

DECORATION: 1 cup cream (optional); 100 g (3 1/2 oz) bar milk chocolate or chocolate buttons.

Cup sponge fingers in half diagonally to give 2 pointed wedges from each biscuit. Whip cream with drinking chocolate and instant coffee until it just begins to hold its shape. Pour sherry into a shallow dish. Dip sponge finger halves, one at a time, in sherry, quickly to prevent them becoming soggy, and arrange one layer, cartwheel fashion, on bottom of greased and bottom-lined 28 cm (11 in) spring-form tin. Top with a third whipped cream. Repeat with another layer of sherried sponge fingers, then cream, and repeat again. You will have 3 layers each of biscuits and cream. Cover with foil and refrigerate overnight. Remove sides of tin and place on a large serving plate.

DECORATION: Lightly whip well-chilled cream until it holds its shape and pipe rosettes around edge of cake. Using a swivel-bladed vegetable peeler, shave curls of chocolate from narrow edge of chocolate bar and strew over cream, or place chocolate buttons around edge, between cream rosettes. Serve cut into wedges. Serves 12.

Caramel Almond Torte

3 eggs, separated; 1/2 cup caster sugar; 1/2 tsp vanilla; 1/4 cup Caramel Syrup (page 64); 6 tbs flour; 1/2 tsp baking powder; 1/2 tsp salt; 1/4 tsp cream of tartar; 1/2 cup chopped toasted almonds.

TOPPING: 1 cup cream, whipped with 1 tbs brown sugar; few whole toasted almonds.

Beat egg yolks until thick, pale and creamy, then beat in 1/4 cup sugar and the vanilla. Gradually add caramel syrup and beat until well blended. Sift flour, baking powder and salt over mixture and gently fold in. Whisk egg whites until foamy, add cream of tartar and whisk until whites hold their shape. Gradually whisk in remaining sugar and continue whisking until whites are a stiff snow. Fold whites into yolk mixture with chopped almonds. Pour into a lightly greased 23 cm (9 in) springform tin. Bake in

a preheated moderate oven (180°C/350°F) for 25 minutes or until golden-brown on top and beginning to shrink away slightly from sides of tin. Remove sides of tin and cool on a wire rack. Top with whipped cream and almonds to serve. Serves 8.

Coffee and Nut Dobostorte

4 eggs, 3/4 cup caster sugar; 1 1/4 cups flour.

BUTTER CREAM: 1/3 cup sugar; 1/2 cup water; 3 egg yolks; 250 g (8 oz) unsalted butter, creamed; 1/2 cup ground hazelnuts; 1 tbs coffee essence.

CARAMEL: 2/3 cup sugar; 1/3 cup water.

DECORATION: 1/2 cup ground hazelnuts; 8 whole hazelnuts.

Grease 3 baking trays and dust lightly with flour, shaking off excess. Using a cake tin or plate as a guide, mark 5 x 20 cm (8 in) circles on trays, 2 circles on 2 of the trays and 1 on the third tray. Whisk eggs with sugar in a heatproof bowl over a saucepan of very hot water off the heat until mixture is thick and mousse-like. Remove from saucepan and continue whisking until bowl is cold. Using a metal spoon, fold in sifted flour, lightly and thoroughly. Divide mixture into 5 portions and spread inside each circle on prepared baking trays. Bake in a preheated moderately hot oven (190°C/375°F) for 5–8 minutes or until pale golden-brown. Remove from oven. Using a sharp knife, trim rounds if necessary. Cool on wire racks.

BUTTER CREAM: Dissolve sugar in water, stirring, over medium heat. Bring to the boil and boil for 5–6 minutes, without stirring, until syrup reaches thread stage. (To test, drop 1/2 tsp syrup into a cup of ice cold water; it should form threads.) Pour on to egg yolks and whisk until thick and mousse-like. Gradually beat in creamed butter, ground hazelnuts and coffee essence. Place one round of cake on an oiled baking tray ready to coat with caramel.

CARAMEL: Combine sugar and water in a heavy saucepan over very low heat and stir until sugar dissolves. Increase heat, bring to the boil and boil steadily, without stirring, until mixture is a rich dark brown. Pour at once over round of cake. Cool a few minutes until on point of setting, then mark into 8 portions with an oiled knife and trim around edges. To assemble torte, sandwich cake rounds together with 1/2 butter cream, placing caramel-covered round on top. Spread sides of cake with half remaining butter cream, and press ground hazelnuts on to sides. Using rest of butter cream, pipe a rosette on each portion and decorate with whole hazelnuts. Serves 8.

NOTE: Baking the rounds of cake can be done in rotation using one baking tray, but each time it must be wiped, re-greased and floured.

TORTILLA

The national bread of Mexico, a tortilla is a thin, flat cake made with cornmeal, from white corn, called *masa*. Tortillas are cooked on a griddle without browning, so they are quite soft and maybe eaten like this or fried briefly in oil to crisp them. *Masa* is not available commercially in Australia, but soft tortillas are available in cans and also in refrigerated packages in some delicatessens.

Tortillas may be used as a plate or scoop for other food, or stuffed with a filling and rolled up. They are also the basis for other dishes: a Mexican family might start the day with freshly made soft tortillas, then eat more tortillas at every meal throughout the day to accompany meat dishes or as *tacos* or *enchiladas*.

Tortilla is also the Spanish name for omelette.

See also *Tacos*, *Enchiladas* and *Omelette*: Spanish Omelette.

TOURNEDOS

The French name for a small thick steak cut from the centre of a beef fillet; trim fillet of all fat and gristle and remove outer sinew. A tournedos should be about 5 cm (2 in) thick when it is ready for cooking, but if it comes from the area toward the narrower end of the fillet, it may be cut thicker and flattened with the hand to make it a little wider. Shape it with your hands into a neat circular shape, and tie string around it to keep the shape, before cooking it.

A tournedos can be grilled but is usually pan-fried, and is often served on a fried bread croûte (see page 105), to catch the juices. It can be garnished in many ways to make luxury dishes which take their names from the garnish.

Tournedos

I tbs oil; 30 g (I oz) butter; 4 tournedos;
4 round Croûtes (white bread sautéed in clarified butter, see page 52); salt and freshly ground black pepper; sauce or garnish of your choice (see below).

Heat a large, heavy frying pan until a drop of water flicked on to the surface will bounce and sizzle. Add oil and heat, then add butter and, when just turning brown, put in tournedos. Sear for 2 minutes on each side. Reduce heat to moderately low and continue to cook, turning once, about 5 minutes more for rare, 7 minutes for medium-done. Remove strings from tournedos and place each on a hot croûte set on a heated plate. Season with salt and pepper. Garnish as desired and serve immediately. Serves 4.

VARIATIONS

TOURNEDOS ROSSINI: Place a slice of foie gras on each tournedos and spoon ¾ cup hot Madeira Sauce (see page 458) over them. Top each with a slice of truffle.
TOURNEDOS PARISIENNE: Garnish each plate with asparagus tips and Noisette Potatoes (see page 384), and spoon ¾ cup warm Béarnaise Sauce (see pages 459–60) over them.

TOURNEDOS CHASSEUR: Spoon ¾ cup hot Sauce Chasseur (see page 458) over tournedos and sprinkle with finely chopped parsley.
TOURNEDOS OPERA: Accompany tournedos with individual Rich Shortcrust Pastry Tart Shells (see page 342) filled with diced chicken livers, sautéed in butter, mixed with Madeira Sauce (see page 458).

TREACLE

A by-product of sugar refining; it is the fluid left after sugar cane has been processed.

There are two types of treacle: black treacle, which closely resembles molasses but is sweeter, and light treacle, better known as golden syrup (see page 181). Light treacle is used in the filling for the nursery favourite Treacle Tart. Black treacle enhances the flavour of rich fruit cakes, puddings and gingerbreads. It can also be used in barbecue sauces, or indeed in almost any recipe calling for molasses.

Treacle is obtainable from most good supermarkets, health food shops and delicatessens. See recipes.

See also *Ginger*: Rich Ginger Cake.

Rich Treacle Tart

I quantity Plain Shortcrust Pastry (page 342);
I¹/₂ cups fresh bread or plain cake crumbs;
I cup golden syrup; I egg, beaten; grated rind and juice ¹/₂ lemon.

Roll out pastry dough and use to line a 20 cm (8 in) pie plate. Combine remaining ingredients and pour into pastry case. Use any remaining pastry to decorate the tart with a lattice design. Bake in a preheated hot oven (200°C/400°F) for 10 minutes, then reduce heat to moderate (180°C/350°F) and bake for a further 20 minutes. Allow to cool, during which time filling will set. Serves 6.

Old-fashioned Ginger Cake

2 cups flour; I tsp mixed spice; 2 tsp ground ginger;
I tsp bicarbonate of soda; 125 g (4 oz) butter;
¹/₃ cup firmly packed brown sugar;
2 tbs black treacle; ¹/₂ cup golden syrup;
2 eggs, beaten; ¹/₂ cup milk.

Sift flour, spice, ginger and soda into a bowl. Combine butter, sugar, treacle and syrup in a small heavy saucepan. Heat gently until melted and dissolved, then allow to cool. Stir into dry ingredients with eggs and milk and beat thoroughly until smooth. Pour into a greased and lined 18 cm (7 in) square cake tin. Bake in a preheated slow oven (150°C/300°F) for 1¼–1½ hours or until a skewer inserted in centre comes out clean. Cool in tin for 15 minutes, then turn out. Serve plain or iced with Lemon Glacé Icing (see page 205).

t

Treacle Scones

2 cups self-raising flour; I tsp baking powder;
I tsp mixed spice; pinch salt; 60 g (2 oz) butter;
I¹⁄₂ tbs caster sugar; 2 tbs sultanas (optional);
I tbs treacle; about ²⁄₃ cup milk.

Sift flour, baking powder, spice and salt into a
bowl. Rub in butter until mixture resembles fine
breadcrumbs. Stir in sugar and sultanas, if using.
Gently heat treacle in a small saucepan and mix
thoroughly with half the milk. Add to dry ingredients
with enough of the remaining milk to make a soft
dough. Turn dough on to a floured work surface
and flatten out to about 2 cm (³⁄₄ in) thick. Cut into
rounds or squares using a floured scone cutter or
sharp knife. Place on a lightly greased baking tray.
Bake in a preheated very hot oven (230°C/450°F) for
10–12 minutes or until well risen and golden-brown.
Cool on a wire rack. Makes about 12.

Bara Brith

A Welsh fruit bread packed with flavour.

2 cups self-raising flour; pinch salt; I tsp mixed
spice; 60 g (2 oz) butter; ¹⁄₃ cup sugar; grated rind
I lemon; ³⁄₄ cup sultanas; ¹⁄₄ cup treacle; I egg,
beaten; ¹⁄₂ tsp bicarbonate of soda; ¹⁄₂ cup milk.

Sift flour, salt and spice into a bowl. Rub in butter
until mixture resembles fine breadcrumbs. Stir in
sugar, lemon rind and sultanas. Add treacle and egg.
Dissolve bicarbonate of soda in milk, add to flour
mixture and mix until well blended. Turn into a
greased and lined 21 x 15 cm (8¹⁄₂ x 6 in) loaf tin.
Bake in a preheated moderate oven (180°C/350°F)
for about 1¹⁄₄ hours or until a skewer inserted in
centre comes out clean. Turn on to a wire rack
to cool. Wrap in foil and store for 24 hours before
serving, sliced and buttered.

TRIFLE

English trifle is similar to tipsy cake. It contains sponge
cake, soaked in a combination of good sweet sherry and
brandy, rich egg custard, cream, nuts and jam. Although
not traditional, some people like to add fresh or canned
fruit to the sponge cake base.

A well-made trifle is a splendid dish to serve at a party,
piled up in your prettiest serving dish and decorated with
fresh or glacé fruits, crushed macaroons or nuts.

Trifle

2 x 18 cm (7 in) Sponge Sandwich layers, made the
day before (page 60); strawberry or raspberry jam;
¹⁄₂ cup sweet sherry; 2 tbs brandy; about I cup
Crème Anglaise (page III); I–I¹⁄₂ cups Crème
Chantilly (page 102); ¹⁄₂ cup almonds, blanched
and split.

DECORATION: 6 glacé cherries, halved; candied
angelica, rinsed in warm water to remove sugar
coating and cut into strips; ¹⁄₂ cup roughly
crushed macaroons (optional).

Cut sponge into 3.5 cm (1¹⁄₂ in) pieces and spread
each piece lightly with jam. Pile into a serving dish
and sprinkle with sherry and brandy. Allow to soak
while making the crème anglaise. Pour hot custard
over soaked cake, cover and chill overnight. Cover
trifle thickly with Crème Chantilly, piling it up
in decorative swirls. Sprinkle almonds over, and
decorate with glacé cherries, strips of angelica and
crushed macaroons. Serves 8–10.

TRIPE

The lining of the stomach of cattle or sheep, but particularly
the former. These animals actually have four different
stomachs, so tripe is available either quite smooth or
honeycombed. Tripe is nearly always sold blanched and
partly cooked, but it still needs further long, slow cooking.
This is usually preceded by a second blanching, in order
to freshen the flavour.

One of the classic accompaniments to tripe is onions,
whether in the English Tripe and Onions or the French
Tripes à la Lyonnaise. In Italy, tripe is often cooked with
tomatoes or served in a tomato sauce; in Nice, in the
south of France, tripe might be cooked with onions,
tomatoes, garlic and white wine. **See recipes.**

Tripe and Onions in Parsley Sauce

I kg (2 lb) tripe, cut into squares; I¹⁄₂ cups water;
5 onions, sliced; I tsp salt.

PARSLEY SAUCE: 60 g (2 oz) butter; 2 tbs flour;
I cup milk; salt and freshly ground black pepper;
2 tbs chopped parsley.

Place tripe in a large saucepan, cover with cold water
and bring to the boil. Boil for 5 minutes, then drain
and discard water. Add measured water, bring to the
boil, cover and simmer for 1 hour. Add onions and
salt and continue to cook until tripe is tender – about
a further hour. Take care not to overcook. When tender, drain off liquid and reserve 1 cup for the sauce.
PARSLEY SAUCE: Melt butter in a clean saucepan and
add flour. Cook without browning for 2 minutes.
Remove from heat and stir in reserved liquid from
tripe and milk. Return to heat and cook, stirring, until
sauce thickens. Season with salt and pepper. Add
parsley, tripe and onions, and serve very hot. Serves 6.

Tripes à la Lyonnaise

I kg (2 lb) tripe; I tsp salt; 4 large onions, finely
sliced; I clove garlic, chopped; 60 g (2 oz) butter;
salt and freshly ground white pepper; I¹⁄₂ cups dry
white wine; 2 tbs lemon juice; I tbs chopped parsley
to garnish.

Place piece of tripe in large saucepan, cover with water and bring to the boil. Drain off water, and add fresh water just to cover. Add salt, bring to the boil and simmer gently until tender, about 1 hour. Drain tripe and cut into thin strips about 5 cm (2 in) long. Fry onions and garlic in 30 g (1 oz) butter until golden. Add remaining butter with tripe and cook for a further 5 minutes. Season with salt and pepper, and stir in wine. Cook over high heat for 1 minute, then reduce heat, cover and simmer gently for 1 hour. Add lemon juice, and sprinkle with parsley before serving. Serves 6.

Casserole of Tripe

500 g (1 lb) tripe; 1 knuckle veal, split; 2 rashers lean bacon, rind removed and cut into squares; 1 large onion, sliced; 3–4 carrots, quartered; 30 g (1 oz) butter; 1 clove garlic, chopped; 1 tbs chopped parsley; 1 cup dry white wine; salt and freshly ground black pepper.

Place tripe and veal knuckle in a saucepan, cover with cold water and bring to the boil. Drain off water. Fry bacon, onion and carrots in butter for about 5 minutes. Cut tripe into small squares, and place on top of vegetables with knuckle. Sprinkle with garlic and parsley, add wine, and bring just to the boil. Cover tightly and cook very gently for 2–2½ hours. Remove veal knuckle and season with salt and pepper to taste before serving. Serves 4.

TROUT

The flavour of this freshwater fish is so delicate and the texture so fine it is regarded as one of the great fish of the world.

Trout are caught in mountain streams and lakes, and many fishermen consider the best method of cooking them is to dip them in flour and sauté each side in butter or bacon fat, with as little time as possible between catching and eating.

Indeed, they are absolutely delicious treated this way, but not everyone has the opportunity to fish for trout. Most people rely on the fishmonger to supply fresh trout. These are produced especially for the market at trout farms, and their quality is excellent. They are also available frozen, and can be purchased from good supermarkets and delicatessens.

Smoked trout is also considered a superb delicacy. Served skinned and filleted with thin brown bread and butter, a twist of lemon and a grinding of black pepper. Smoked trout is available at good delicatessens. For Ocean trout, see *Salmon*.

■ **TO BUY:** A trout about 300 g (10 oz) is sufficient for 1 serving. A larger trout about 600 g (1lb 40 oz) will serve 2. Allow an extra 2–3 minutes cooking time for larger trout.

■ **BASIC PREPARATION:**

TO CLEAN FRESH TROUT: Split the fish along the belly from the vent to the head. Remove the gills, entrails and stomach lining, leaving the head and tail intact. Rinse well in cold running water to remove all trace of blood. Dry well with paper towels.

TO PREPARE CLEANED FRESH TROUT: Simply rinse lightly in cold water and pat dry with paper towels.

TO PREPARE FROZEN TROUT: Allow fish to thaw according to instructions on the packet. Rinse lightly in cold water and pat dry with paper towels.

TO FILLET SMOKED OR COOKED TROUT: Cut the fish down the lateral line along the side. Hold the knife against the backbone and, with a fork, ease the flesh from the rib cage and backbone. Slide the 2 fillets off the fish to each side of it. Lift up the tail and slide the knife under the backbone, lifting it up and easing off the flesh. Discard the tail, backbone and head, leaving 4 fillets ready to eat.

■ **TO COOK:** Trout can be grilled, baked, poached, barbecued or pan-fried. Be careful not to overcook or the flesh will be dry and powdery, losing much flavour. The flesh should be moist and flake easily when sufficiently cooked. Leave the head on and when done the eye will be quite white and opaque.

BAKED TROUT: Season trout inside the cavity with black pepper and salt. Put in a buttered shallow ovenproof dish, dot with butter, pour over ¼ cup white wine, cover dish with foil and bake in a preheated moderate oven (180°C/350°F) for 15–20 minutes.

POACHED TROUT: Lower trout into boiling court bouillon (see page 98) and cook for 5 minutes. If serving hot, transfer drained trout to a heated platter and pour over a little melted butter. If trout is to be served cold, allow to cool in court bouillon and remove skin just before serving.

BARBECUED TROUT: Season trout with salt and black pepper, place a knob of butter or bacon fat in the cavity, spread fish with softened butter. Wrap in foil and cook over or in coals for 10–15 minutes.

GRILLED TROUT: Wrap each trout with a very thin bacon rasher. Place under a preheated moderate grill and grill for about 5 minutes on each side or until the bacon is crisp and trout is cooked.

PAN-FRIED TROUT: For 2 trout, (about 300 g/10 oz each) melt 30 g (1 oz) butter and 2 tsp oil in a large, heavy-based frying pan. Dip the fish lightly in seasoned flour and place in the pan when the butter stops foaming. Fry over moderate heat for 3–4 minutes on each side or until the eye is white and opaque and the flesh easily penetrated with a fine skewer. See recipes.

Trout Meunière

2 trout (about 300 g/10 oz each), cleaned; milk; seasoned flour; 90 g (3 oz) butter; 2 tbs oil; 1 lemon, sliced; squeeze lemon juice; salt and freshly ground black pepper; chopped parsley to garnish.

t

Dip trout in milk, then dust lightly with seasoned flour and shake off any excess. Melt 60 g (2 oz) butter and the oil in a large frying pan. When butter foams, add trout and cook for about 3–4 minutes on each side or until golden-brown and flesh flakes easily when tested with a fine skewer. Transfer to a heated serving dish and place a few slices of lemon on each fish. Heat remaining butter in frying pan and when it foams add lemon juice. Season with salt and pepper and pour sizzling butter over fish. Garnish with chopped parsley. Serves 2.

VARIATION

TROUT AMANDINE: Cook trout as for Trout Meunière. Remove to a serving platter and keep warm. Heat 60 g (2 oz) butter in pan and gently fry ¼ cup blanched, sliced almonds until golden-brown. Add 1 tbs lemon juice, salt and pepper. Pour over hot fish and serve at once.

Trout Nantua

2 cups water; ½ cup dry white wine;
I bay leaf; 2 sprigs parsley;
6 black peppercorns; salt; juice ½ lemon;
4 trout (about 300 g/10 oz each), cleaned.

SAUCE: ⅔ cup Mayonnaise (page 256);
⅓ cup tomato juice; dash Tabasco sauce;
salt and freshly ground black pepper;
60 g (2 oz) cooked shelled prawns, deveined.

GARNISH: I cucumber, finely sliced; watercress sprigs.

Combine water, wine, bay leaf, parsley, peppercorns, salt and lemon juice in a large frying pan. Bring to the boil, then reduce heat and place trout side by side in simmering liquid. Poach trout very gently for 5–8 minutes or until flesh will flake easily when tested with a fine skewer. Allow to cool in the liquid. Drain trout, and skin and fillet fish.

SAUCE: Combine mayonnaise, tomato juice, Tabasco, salt, pepper and prawns and spoon over fish. Garnish with cucumber slices and watercress sprigs. Serve with thin triangles of brown bread and butter. Serves 4.

VARIATION

COLD POACHED TROUT WITH CUCUMBER SAUCE: Poach trout as for Trout Nantua and allow to cool in liquid. Drain carefully, skin and arrange on a platter with lemon wedges and sprigs of parsley. To make sauce, peel 1 small cucumber, cut in half lengthways and scoop out seeds. Chop flesh very finely and mix with ½ cup Fromage Blanc (page 161) or sour light cream, 1 tbs lemon juice, pinch paprika, 1 tbs snipped chives and ½ tsp chopped fresh dill.

Smoked Trout with Horseradish Cream

2 smoked trout; slices or wedges lemon or lime;
citrus leaves or fresh dill; 2 tbs grated horseradish;

I cup sour cream; salt and freshly ground black pepper; thin brown bread-and-butter sandwiches.

With a sharp knife, slit trout skin along back and belly, and cut through skin just behind head and in front of tail on both sides. Carefully peel off skin and place whole trout on a serving platter or board. Garnish with lemon or lime and a spray of citrus leaves or dill. Mix horseradish and sour cream, and season with salt and pepper. Place in a bowl. To serve, cut through flesh along back and down centre, and loosen and lift off blocks of trout. When first side is served, turn over and repeat with other side. Serve with horseradish cream, freshly ground black pepper, and small brown bread and butter sandwiches. Serves 6–8.

Grilled Trout with Herbs

4 trout (about 300 g/10 oz each), cleaned;
salt and freshly ground black pepper;
lemon juice; 4 tbs chopped mixed fresh herbs
(parsley, chives, marjoram and basil);
flour; 60 g (2 oz) butter, melted.

SAUCE: 30 g (1 oz) butter; I tbs hot water; squeeze lemon juice.

Season trout inside and out with salt, pepper and lemon juice. Place 1 tbs chopped herbs inside each cavity. Sprinkle fish with a little flour, patting it in with the fingers. (This improves colour and also helps to keep fish moist.) Place melted butter in grill tray, add fish and turn fish over in butter to coat on all sides. Cook under a preheated high grill for 5–8 minutes, without turning, until skin is crispy and flesh flakes easily when tested with a fine skewer. The underside will also be cooked at this stage. Place fish on a heated serving platter. Add butter for sauce to grill tray with hot water and lemon juice. Swirl this around to heat through, then pour over fish and serve at once. Serves 4.

Trout del Nera

4 trout (about 300 g/10 oz), cleaned;
2–3 tbs olive oil; salt and freshly ground black
pepper; ¹/2 cup chopped parsley; few sprigs fresh
rosemary, chopped; sprigs fresh herbs to garnish;
4 lemon wedges to serve.

Arrange trout on greased preheated grill tray or pan,
brush with oil and season with salt and pepper.
Combine chopped herbs and sprinkle half over fish.
Cook under a preheated high grill for about 5–8
minutes, brushing occasionally with oil. Season with
salt and pepper and sprinkle over remaining
chopped herbs. Grill a further 1 minute or until fish
flakes easily when tested with a fine skewer. Just
before serving, trickle over a little more olive oil.
Garnish with herb sprigs and serve with lemon
wedges. Serves 4.

Smoked Trout Pâté

2 smoked trout, skinned and filleted;
I cup sour cream; I cup ricotta cheese;
juice ¹/2 lemon; salt and freshly ground black
pepper; Melba Toast to serve (page 263).

Flake trout and place in a blender with sour cream
and ricotta cheese. Blend until smooth. Or mash with
a fork or process in a food processor and push
through a sieve. The mixture should be very smooth.
Stir in lemon juice, salt and pepper. Pack into a 3-cup
soufflé dish or 6 x ¹/2-cup individual little pots. Cover
and chill overnight. Serve with Melba toast. Serves 6.

Trout in Cream Sauce

¹/4 cup flour; salt and freshly ground black pepper;
4 trout (about 300 g/10 oz), cleaned;
60 g (2 oz) butter, melted; ³/4 cup cream;
I tbs snipped chives.

Season flour with salt and pepper and dust trout
lightly, shaking off any excess flour. Brush a small
baking dish with melted butter and place trout in
dish. Brush fish with remaining butter to coat well.
Bake in a preheated hot oven (200°C/400°F) for 7–10
minutes or until skin is brown and crisp, basting occasionally with butter in dish. Meanwhile, season cream
with salt and pepper and bring to the boil. Continue
boiling for about 3 minutes or until thickened slightly.
Remove from heat and stir in chives. Place trout on a
heated serving platter and pour over hot cream sauce.
Serve immediately. Serves 4.

TRUFFLE

One of nature's best-kept secrets, the truffle has resisted
exploitation by modern agriculture until recent years. It is
an edible fungus which grows underground, usually near
oak trees, in many parts of the world. Not all truffles,
however, have the same quality. The most esteemed are
the black truffles from the Périgord in France, closely
followed by the white truffles found in the Piedmont area
of northern Italy. Excellent truffles are now grown in
Australia but are still very expensive to buy.

The harvest takes place around late autumn, with the
aid of specially trained pigs or dogs who sniff out the
elusive truffles. Some truffles are used fresh, particularly
for Christmas specialties such as roast truffled turkey,
truffled *boudin blanc* (white pudding), or truffled goose
liver pâté; others go into manufactured foods or are
canned for year-round use.

Outside France and Italy, truffles usually come in cans –
either as a whole small truffle, truffle pieces or peelings,
or truffle juice. Canned truffles or truffle pieces may
be used in any recipe calling for truffles and truffle juice
may be used in a sauce. Even the peelings can be used
to add flavour to a sauce, but should be removed
before serving.

Truffles are, arguably, the most expensive ingredient a
kitchen could have, but fortunately only a very small
amount is required to perfume and flavour a dish.

In almost all dishes, it is best to add the truffle to whatever it is intended to perfume and then leave for several
hours, at least, to allow the perfume of the truffle to
permeate the food. Canned truffles are not nearly as
flavoursome as fresh ones, but can be improved if
soaked in Madeira or port when removed from the can.

WAYS TO USE TRUFFLES

Fresh truffles finely shaved are good with steamed
potatoes, pasta, poached or scrambled eggs and
steamed chicken. When, as is almost always the case,
the supply of truffles is limited, use the truffle in a dish
which will make the most of its flavour, rather than
attempting to duplicate, with one small can of truffles, a
dish which requires several large truffles. Use a small
truffle to advantage in a terrine or pâté; with a loin of
pork for roasting; when slipped under the skin of a
plump chicken before gently poaching; or when added
to a flavoursome brown Madeira sauce and served with
perfectly cooked beef fillet or a warm, poached chicken
liver mousse. Italians shave thin slices over freshly
cooked pasta. **See recipes.**

Chicken Breasts with Truffle Sauce

I x 30 g can truffle pieces or small fresh truffles,
chopped; ¹/4 cup port or Madeira;
6 chicken fillets (skinless, boneless half-breasts);
salt and freshly ground black pepper;
about ¹/2 cup flour; 90 g (3 oz) clarified butter
(see page 52); I tbs chopped shallot;
¹/2 cup chicken stock.

Mix truffle pieces and juice with port or Madeira, and leave to stand for 30 minutes. Season chicken with salt and pepper and lightly coat with flour. Cook chicken in hot clarified butter in a frying pan for about 3 minutes each side or until springy to touch. Remove to a heated dish. Add shallot to pan and cook for about 1 minute. Stir in stock and truffle mixture, bring to the boil and reduce over high heat until slightly thickened and syrupy. Pour sauce over chicken and serve immediately. Serves 6.

Truffled Loin of Pork

1 x 1 kg (2 lb) boned pork loin, rind removed (bone and rind reserved); salt and freshly ground black pepper; 1 x 60 g can truffle pieces, or 1 whole small truffle, chopped; 1 small clove garlic, sliced; 2 cups chicken stock; 1/2 cup dry white wine.

Spread meat flat and season with salt and pepper. Drain can of truffle pieces, if using, and reserve liquid. Place pieces of truffle at intervals along meat, together with slivers of garlic. Roll up meat neatly and tie securely with fine string. Leave for 1 hour, then place in baking dish with bones, trimmings and rind cut into strips. Roast in a preheated moderately slow oven (160°C/325°F) for 30 minutes, then add stock, wine and liquid from truffle can, if available. Cover and leave to cook for 2–2½ hours longer. Remove pork and set aside to cool. Drain off liquid. Chill pork and liquid. Next day, remove layer of fat from jellied liquid. Slice pork and surround with chopped jelly. Serves 6.

TRUFFLE, CHOCOLATE

This is a rich, luscious, cocoa-covered ball, which earns its name from its similarity to the real truffle, fresh from the earth. Chocolate Truffles are perfect to serve with after-dinner coffee.

Chocolate Truffles

150 g (5 oz) dark chocolate; 1/3 cup thick cream; 30 g (1 oz) unsalted butter; rum or brandy (optional); sifted cocoa powder.

Melt chocolate in a basin placed over a pan of hot water. Bring cream to the boil in a pan, add to chocolate and mix well. Refrigerate overnight. Next day, heat mixture gently over hot water again; when melted, gradually blend in butter and flavour with a little rum or brandy if desired. Remove from heat and cool. Chill until firm. Form into small balls, and roll in cocoa. Store in refrigerator, but remove about 1 hour before serving. Makes about 24.

NOTE: Chocolate truffles are best made in the cold winter months.

TUILES

Crisp curled wafer biscuits, very thin and delicious as petits fours with coffee or as an accompaniment to ice creams. After baking, the pliable mixture is draped over a rolling pin to cool, which gives the characteristic tuile shape. Handle the mixture quickly and lightly at this point as it cools and crisps quickly. Bake in batches of no more than 4 at a time for ease of handling. Tuiles can be flavoured with almonds, orange or lemon rind or vanilla. Store in airtight containers.

Tuiles d'Amandes

2 egg whites; 1/2 cup caster sugar; 1/2 cup flour, sifted; 1/2 tsp vanilla; 1/4 cup blanched, slivered almonds; 60 g (2 oz) butter, melted and cooled.

Beat egg whites until stiff and gradually beat in sugar. Gently fold in flour, vanilla, almonds and butter. Spread 3–4 tsp of mixture to form flat rounds or ovals, well separated from each other, on greased baking trays. Bake in a preheated moderately hot oven (190°C/375°F) for 4–5 minutes or until golden. Remove from heat and, using a spatula, lift off carefully. Quickly drape over a rolling pin to cool. When cold, store in an airtight container. Makes 10–16 according to size required.

VARIATIONS

TUILES A LA VANILLE: Follow recipe for Tuiles d'Amandes, omitting slivered almonds and increasing vanilla to ¾ tsp.

TUILES A L'ORANGE: Follow recipe for Tuiles d'Amandes, omitting slivered almonds and vanilla and using 2 tsp finely grated orange rind instead (or lemon rind for lemon-flavoured Tuiles).

NOTE: For large tuiles, spread 2–3 tbs of the mixture on baking trays to form round or oval shapes up to 15 cm (6 in) across. Bake and finish as for Tuiles d'Amandes.

TUNA

Fresh tuna steaks are such a good food and comparatively economical with little waste to such dense meat. For those of us lucky enough to be able to shop at large fish markets, tuna has become a familiar sight. Ask for Yellowfin tuna as the sustainable choice. Southern Bluefin tuna has been declared by the Bureau of Rural Sciences as overfished and endangered. Steaks cut from the middle sections of the fish are really delicious grilled. Fresh tuna can also be baked or pan-fried, or sliced paper-thin for tuna carpaccio (see *Carpaccio*, page 65) or eaten raw in the Japanese dish Sashimi (see page 454).

Canned tuna is sold packed in oil or brine, in solid-pack style (large pieces), chunk style (smaller pieces) and sandwich or salad style (flaked). Various manufacturers also can it with flavourings such as onion, tomato, or curry etc. It is one of the best items to have on the emergency shelf. A can or two of tuna can be turned quickly into appetisers to serve with drinks, a hearty soup, a first course or main dish or, of course, into substantial salads and sandwiches.

■ **TO COOK:** Fresh tuna is often marinated before cooking and must be well basted while grilling or baking. For grilling, baking or poaching use steaks about 4 cm (1½ in) thick; for pan-frying use thinner ones, about 2 cm (¾ in) thick, or slice the tuna thinly into escalopes, flour lightly and fry 2–3 minutes on each side. In general, it is best to leave the skin on the steaks for cooking, to hold them in shape, but peel it off before serving as it is unattractively dark and can have a strong flavour. Do not overcook tuna; the centre of each steak should be pale pink. **See recipes.**

TUNA SPREADS
The spread on page 553 can be used for sandwiches, or can be piled on toasted French bread and grilled to make hot canapés. **See recipes.**

Fresh Tuna Burgers

500 g (1 lb) tuna, cut into chunks; ½ red onion, finely chopped; 2 tbs freshly chopped coriander and parsley; ½ tsp cumin; salt and freshly ground pepper; 1 tbs olive oil; salad greens to serve.

Put the tuna in the bowl of a food processor and process using an on/off action until finely chopped. Add the onion, herbs, cumin and salt and pepper to taste and mix well. Using an egg poacher or with wetted hands shape the mixture into 4 even-sized thick patties. Cover and refrigerate until ready to use.

Heat the oil in heavy frying pan, add the tuna burgers and cook over a high heat for 1 minute on each side. They should be golden on the outside and moist and very pink in the middle. Serve with creamy mashed potatoes or on toasted crusty bread with salad greens. Serves 4.

Grilled Tuna with Rocket Salad

6–8 patty pan squash, halved; 125 g (4 oz) sugar snap or snowpeas, topped and tailed; 1 bunch rocket leaves; 1 red salad onion; 4 tuna steaks; 1 tbs light olive oil; salt and freshly ground black pepper.

DRESSING: juice 1 lime; 1 tsp freshly grated ginger; 3 tbs olive oil.

Bring a saucepan of salted water to the boil, add the squash and boil for 2–3 minutes or until tender. Remove with a slotted spoon and refresh in iced water. Drop the peas in boiling water and cook for 1 minute or until bright green. Drain, refresh in cold water and drain thoroughly. Remove the stems from the rocket, thoroughly wash the leaves, and dry well. Halve the onion and cut into thin slices. In a large

bowl, whisk together the lime juice, ginger and oil. Toss the rocket and vegetables lightly in the dressing and set aside.

Brush the steaks with the olive oil and cook for a few minutes on each side under a preheated griller, a ribbed grill pan or heavy frying pan. The tuna should be seared on the outside and still pinkish on the inside. To serve, pile the salad on serving plates and top with the grilled tuna. Season to taste with salt and a good grinding of pepper. Serves 4.

Tuna Brochettes

1 kg (2 lb) tuna steaks, cut 2 cm (3/4 in) thick; ½ cup olive oil; ¼ cup lemon juice; 1 tsp salt; freshly ground black pepper; 2 sticks French bread, cut into 1 cm (½ in) slices; bay leaves.

Remove skin from tuna and cut meat into bite-sized pieces. Mix oil, lemon juice, salt and pepper, add tuna and marinate it for 1 hour, turning pieces gently once or twice. Thread a slice of bread on to a small bamboo or flat metal skewer, add a piece of fish and a bay leaf, and repeat until skewer contains 3 pieces of fish, 3 bay leaves and 4 pieces of bread. Do not push ingredients too close together. Repeat with more skewers and remaining bread, tuna and bay leaves. Brush filled skewers with marinade and cook under a preheated high grill for about 10 minutes or until browned, turning and basting with marinade several times. Serves 6.
NOTE: Soak bamboo skewers in hot water for 2 hours before using, to prevent charring.

Fresh Tuna with Coriander

4 tuna steaks, cut about 2 cm (3/4 in) thick; 1 cup dry white wine; seasoned flour; 2 tbs oil; 30 g (1 oz) butter; salt and freshly ground black pepper; 2 tsp lemon juice; 2 tbs chopped fresh coriander leaves.

Marinate tuna in white wine for 2 hours. Drain, reserving wine. Dry steaks and dust lightly with seasoned flour. Heat oil in a frying pan, add butter and, when just turning brown, put steaks in. Sauté 3–5 minutes on each side. Remove tuna to heated plates, peel off skin and keep warm. Add reserved wine to pan and boil over high heat for 30 seconds, stirring in brown bits from pan. Remove from heat, season with salt and pepper and stir in lemon juice and coriander. Pour over fish and serve immediately. Serves 4.

Vitello Tonnato *(Veal with Tuna Sauce)*

The famous and superb Italian summer dish of veal masked with a creamy tuna sauce. Serve with a green salad.

1 x 2 kg (4 lb) boned veal leg roast, rolled and tied;
6 anchovy fillets, chopped; 1 onion, sliced;
2 sticks celery, sliced; 2 carrots, sliced;
2 sprigs parsley; 2 cloves; salt and freshly ground
black pepper; 2–3 bay leaves; 1 cup dry white wine
(optional); lemon slices to garnish.

TUNA SAUCE: 1 x 200 g can tuna in oil, drained;
6 anchovy fillets; 1 tsp capers; 2 tbs lemon juice;
freshly ground black pepper; 1/2 cup Mayonnaise
(page 256).

With a sharp-pointed knife make holes in surface of
meat and insert pieces of anchovy. Place meat in a
flameproof casserole with onion, celery, carrots,
parsley, cloves, salt and pepper. Put bay leaves on top
of meat. Pour in wine if using and sufficient water to
cover meat. Bring slowly to the boil, then reduce heat,
cover and simmer for 1½–2 hours. When veal is
tender, remove string and allow to cool in stock.

TUNA SAUCE: Pound tuna with anchovy fillets, capers
and lemon juice, or purée in a food processor until
smooth. Season with pepper. Combine with mayonnaise. Add a little of the veal stock if sauce is too thick.

Drain veal well when cold, put into an earthenware
or glass bowl and cover with tuna sauce. Cover and
marinate overnight. A few hours before serving,
remove veal from sauce and slice thinly. Arrange slices
on serving platter and spoon over sauce thinned with a
little more veal stock or olive oil. Chill again until
ready to serve. Garnish with sliced lemon. Serves 8.

Fresh Tuna with Peas, Tuscan Style

Tuscan cooks sauté thin slices of tuna and serve
them in a superbly simple wine sauce with green
peas. Serve in deep plates, with lots of crusty bread
to mop up the delicious sauce.

1/4 cup olive oil; 1 clove garlic, crushed;
1 small onion, finely chopped; 500 g (1 lb) tuna
fillets, skinned and thinly sliced;
1/4 cup dry white wine; 2 tsp tomato paste;
salt and freshly ground black pepper;
1½ cups cooked green peas; 2 tsp finely
chopped parsley.

Heat oil in a large frying pan and brown garlic and
onion gently. Push vegetables to side of pan. Add tuna
and brown lightly. Add wine and tomato paste, and
season with salt and pepper. Cover and cook on very
low heat for 10–15 minutes. Add peas, heat through
for a few minutes and serve very hot, sprinkled with
finely chopped parsley. Serves 4–6.

Italian Tuna with Haricot Beans and Tomatoes

3/4 cup dried haricot beans, soaked overnight and
drained; 1/4 cup olive oil; 1 clove garlic, sliced;

3 large ripe tomatoes, peeled and chopped;
1 x 200 g can tuna in oil, drained and broken into
chunks; 1 tsp chopped fresh basil, or 1/2 tsp dried;
salt and freshly ground black pepper.

Cook beans in fresh water to cover until tender.
Drain. Heat oil in a large saucepan and brown garlic.
Discard garlic and add tomatoes. Salt lightly and
cook for 10 minutes. Stir in cooked beans and tuna
chunks, sprinkle with basil and plenty of pepper and
simmer for 10 minutes. Serve very hot. Serves 6.

Hot Tuna and Potato Salad

4 medium potatoes, peeled, cooked and cut into
chunks; 1/3 cup sliced celery; 1 medium onion,
chopped; 1/2 cup cooked peas; 1 x 200 g can tuna in
oil; 4 rashers streaky bacon, rind removed;
3 tbs sugar; 6 tbs vinegar; 2 tbs water;
1/2 tsp celery seeds; 1 egg, beaten;
salt and freshly ground black pepper.

Put potatoes, celery, onion, peas and tuna with its oil
into a shallow casserole. Put bacon into a cold frying
pan and simmer 5 minutes. Stir a little of the hot
mixture into egg, then stir this back into pan. Pour
over potato and tuna mixture. Season with salt and
pepper, mix lightly and level surface. Crumble bacon
over top. Bake, uncovered, in a preheated moderate
oven (180°C/350°F) for about 15 minutes or until
heated through. Serves 6.

Tuna and Apple Salad

1 large red apple, cored and finely sliced;
1 tbs lemon juice; 1/2 cup thinly sliced celery;
1 x 200 g can tuna in oil, drained and broken into
chunks; salt and freshly ground black pepper;
1/4 cup Mayonnaise (page 256);
1/4 cup sour cream; lettuce leaves.

Toss apple slices in lemon juice and place in a bowl
with celery and tuna. Season with salt and pepper,
add mayonnaise and sour cream and mix lightly.
Serve on a bed of lettuce. Serves 2 as a light luncheon,
4 as a first course.

Tuna Mornay

**60 g (2 oz) plus 2 tsp butter; 2 tbs flour;
2 tsp dry mustard; 1¹/₂ cups milk; salt and freshly
ground black pepper; ¹/₂ cup grated cheese;
2 x 200 g cans tuna in oil, drained and broken
into chunks; ¹/₃ cup fresh breadcrumbs.**

Melt 60 g (2 oz) butter in a saucepan, blend in flour
and cook over a gentle heat for 1 minute. Add mustard,
then milk, stirring until sauce thickens. Season with
salt and pepper and add 2 tbs grated cheese. Fold in
tuna and turn into a greased flameproof dish. Top
with remaining cheese mixed with breadcrumbs and
dot with remaining butter. Place under a preheated
grill until bubbly and golden. Serves 4.

Brandade of Tuna and Beans

A sturdy French provincial dish, needing only a
green salad, crusty bread and fresh fruit or the lightest
of desserts to complete the meal.

**I cup dried haricot beans, soaked overnight and
drained; I x 200 g can tuna in oil, drained;
3/4 cup grated mature Cheddar cheese;
60 g (2 oz) butter; I clove garlic, crushed;
salt and freshly ground black pepper;
3 tbs fine dry breadcrumbs.**

Cook beans in fresh water to cover until very tender.
Drain and mash beans thoroughly with a fork. Mash
tuna into beans. Beat in cheese, half the butter, the
garlic, salt and pepper. This can all be done in a food
processor – brandade should have a firm texture. Pile
mixture in a shallow, buttered baking dish. Sprinkle
with breadcrumbs and dot with remaining butter.
Bake in a preheated hot oven (200°C/400°F) for 25
minutes or until browned. Serve warm. Serves 4.

Tuna with Peas

A dish that can be created using the tuna, frozen peas,
pasta and can of tomato paste you always have on
hand in the kitchen pantry.

**2 x 200 g cans tuna in oil; I onion, finely chopped;
2 tbs tomato paste; I tbs chopped parsley;
500 g (I lb) green peas; salt and freshly
ground black pepper; pinch sugar;
freshly cooked pasta or rice to serve.**

Drain oil from cans of tuna into a large saucepan.
Heat oil and sauté onion over a medium heat until
soft. Stir in tomato paste, parsley, peas and enough
water barely to cover peas. Season with salt, pepper
and sugar. Cover and cook for 10 minutes. Add tuna,
broken into chunks, and simmer for 3 minutes more.
Serve over freshly cooked pasta tossed with butter
and Parmesan cheese, or with rice, noodles or crusty
bread and butter. Serves 6.

Taiba

(Algerian Chilled Tuna with Red Pepper)

The original recipe has enough chilli to make it
quite fiery – suit yourself about the amount you use.
Add slowly after the other vegetables and taste as
you go.

**2 red chillies, or to taste, seeded and chopped;
I small red pepper halved, cored and seeded;
6 ripe tomatoes, peeled, seeded and chopped;
4 tbs olive oil; 4 cloves garlic, crushed; 2 tbs tomato
paste; 3 x 200 g cans tuna in oil, drained and
coarsely flaked; ¹/₂ tsp ground coriander;
salt and freshly ground black pepper.**

When preparing chillies, work under cold running
water, and wash your hands immediately afterward.
Grill pepper halves, skin side up, under a preheated
high grill until skin blisters and blackens, then rub skin
off under running water. Chop finely. Heat oil in
saucepan and add vegetables, garlic and tomato paste.
Stir over moderate heat for 5 minutes. Add tuna,
coriander, salt and pepper. Simmer on low heat, stirring
gently once or twice, for 5 minutes or until liquid has
evaporated. Let taiba cool, then chill, covered, for
2 hours or overnight. Serve with crusty bread. Serves 6.

Savoury Tuna Spread

**I x 185 g can sandwich tuna, drained;
2 tbs finely chopped celery; I tbs finely chopped
shallot; 2 tbs finely chopped cucumber;
3 tbs Mayonnaise (page 256); dash Worcestershire
sauce; dash Tabasco sauce.**

Mix all ingredients together. Makes about 1¹/₂ cups.

TURKEY

Turkey breeding has changed over the years and the
present-day bird has more tender breast meat in proportion
to dark meat than the same-sized bird of years ago.

Turkeys are available now from a small 2.5 kg (5 lb) up to
a giant 12.5 kg (26 lb). It is also possible to buy half-
turkeys, turkey breasts and turkey hindquarters – so
there is a turkey to suit almost every family's size
and budget.

A good turkey is compact, with pearly-white skin and a
broad plum breast. Organic turkey is a wise choice.

- A 3–4 kg (6–8 lb) turkey, unstuffed weight, will serve
  8–10 people.
- A 4–6 kg (8–12 lb) bird will serve 10–14 people.
- A 6–8 kg (12–16 lb) bird will serve 14–16 people.

Most turkeys are purchased frozen, and they will take
up to 3 days to thaw in the refrigerator. It is most important that the bird is properly thawed before it is stuffed and
cooked, also that the stuffing is added just before
roasting. Make the stuffing the day before, as well as the
stock, so it is ready for making the gravy.

TO STUFF A TURKEY: A turkey is usually stuffed with 2 different stuffings – one in the crop and one in the main body cavity. When the turkey is cooked, the stuffing in the crop is carved into slices, so everyone gets a piece of stuffing surrounded by white breast meat and crispy skin. The stuffing from the main body cavity is spooned around the carved meat. Be careful to stuff the crop lightly as the stuffing will expand during cooking, and too much may cause the skin to split, spoiling the appearance of the turkey.

TO TRUSS A TURKEY: See Roast Stuffed Turkey recipe opposite.

■ **TO ROAST:** One important point to remember – if you are cooking a very large turkey, do make sure beforehand that your oven is large enough to hold it.

ROASTING TIMES: An unstuffed turkey takes 20–30 minutes less overall to cook than a stuffed one. The times given here are for stuffed turkeys. Since ovens vary considerably and the shape of your bird can make a difference, check frequently after suggested cooking time is two-thirds over. Roast in a moderately slow oven (160°C/325°F).

Ready-to-cook Weight	Cooking Time
3–4 kg (6–8 lb)	3–3½ hours
4–6 kg (8–12 lb)	3½ –4 hours
6–8 kg (12–16 lb)	4–6 hours

TO TELL WHEN COOKED: If a meat thermometer pushed into the thickest part of the thigh registers 90°C/190°F, the turkey is cooked.

If you don't own a thermometer, pierce the thickest part of the thigh with a fork or fine skewer. If the fork goes in easily and the juice which runs out is clear, the turkey is cooked. If the juice has a pink tinge, further cooking is required.

Rest turkey for 15 minutes in the turned-off oven, with door ajar, while making the gravy. This resting period allows the meat to firm up and makes carving easier.

■ **TO CARVE:** First make sure your carving knife is razor-sharp. Remove the trussing strings and skewers and set the bird on a large board or serving plate (a board is easier to carve on). Holding the bird steady with a carving fork, place a long-bladed sharp knife between the thigh and body of the bird and cut through the joint. Remove the leg by pressing it outward with the knife blade, while bending it back with the fork. Separate the thigh and drumstick, and slice off the dark meat. Repeat with the other leg. Remove the wings and cut into two if desired. Carve down the breast on each side with straight, even strokes.

Carve the stuffing in the crop, including some of the white breast meat, into thin slices; remove stuffing from the body cavity with a spoon.

■ **TO SERVE:** The white meat is usually arranged in over-lapping slices at one end of a heated platter, with slices of dark meat at the other. Stuffing may be served on two separate heated plates or, if your platter is large enough, arranged with the turkey meat.

ROAST TURKEY PORTIONS

To roast a half-turkey, turkey breast or turkey hindquarter, place it, skin side up, on a greased rack in a roasting tin. Spread with softened butter and roast, uncovered, in a preheated moderately slow oven (160°C/325°F), basting with pan juices every 15 minutes, until juices run clear when the thickest part of the meat is pierced with a fine skewer, or a meat thermometer inserted into the thickest part, away from the bone, reads 90°C/190°F. The time will depend on the size and shape of the portion but, as a guide, allow about 30 minutes per 500 g (1 lb). Rest for 15 minutes in the turned-off oven with door ajar, while making the gravy as described in the recipe for Roast Stuffed Turkey (below).

If you want to serve stuffing with turkey portions, prepare it and spread it in a buttered ovenproof dish. Moisten with a spoonful or two of the pan juices from the turkey and bake it in the oven with the turkey for the last 45 minutes of cooking. **See recipes.**

Turkey à la King: Follow recipe for Chicken à la King (see page 79), substituting cooked turkey for chicken.

Devilled Turkey: Devilled cooked turkey drumsticks or other joints, cut into pieces of suitable size, are a traditional and splendid Boxing Day dish. Follow directions for cooked meat or chicken under recipe for Devil Sauce (see page 461).

Roast Stuffed Turkey

1 x 6 kg (12 lb) turkey with giblets; 1 quantity Sausage or Meat Stuffing (page 514); 1 quantity Chestnut Stuffing (page 74); 60 g (2 oz) butter, softened; salt and freshly ground black pepper; 2 tbs flour.

GIBLET STOCK: 3½ cups chicken stock; 1 slice onion; 1 slice carrot; small piece celery.

Thaw turkey completely if frozen, and remove bag of giblets from cavity. Wipe cavity of turkey with damp paper towels. Spoon sausage or meat stuffing into the crop, being careful not to pack it too tightly, and press outside of breast to mould stuffing to a good shape. Bring neck flap over stuffing to the back and secure it with a poultry pin or small skewer. Spoon chestnut stuffing into body cavity. Shape bird nicely with both hands. Place turkey on its back, legs towards you. Place centre of a piece of string below breast at neck end, bring ends down over wings then down underneath bird. Cross string underneath, then bring it forward and up to tie ends of drumsticks and parson's nose together. Wipe bird with a paper towel and spread butter over, being sure to cover breast and legs well. Grind a little pepper over. Place turkey on a rack in a large roasting tin, propping up legs with crumpled foil if necessary. Cover pan with a tent of greased foil. Roast in a preheated moderately slow oven (160°C/325°F) for 4–4½ hours or until done (see Roasting Times). Baste every 25 minutes with juices in tin (unless you have a self-basting turkey). Remove foil for last 30 minutes to allow turkey to brown.

GIBLET STOCK: While turkey is roasting, put giblets into a saucepan with stock, onion, carrot and celery. Cover and simmer for 45 minutes or until giblets are tender. Strain and reserve 3 cups for the gravy. The diced heart and gizzard may be added to the gravy if desired.

Remove turkey to a heated serving platter or carving board and allow to rest in a warm place for 20 minutes while making gravy and finishing vegetables. Pour off all but about 3 tbs of turkey drippings from roasting tin. Put tin on medium heat, sprinkle in flour and stir briskly to prevent lumps from forming. Cook, stirring all the time, until browned. Stir in reserved giblet stock, scraping up all good brown bits on bottom of tin. Bring to the boil and simmer 2 minutes. Season with salt and pepper and strain. Stir in diced heart and gizzard, if using. Cranberry sauce, available in cans from many delicatessens and supermarkets, is a classic additional accompaniment. Serves 14.

Turkey Hash

**60 g (2 oz) butter; I onion, chopped;
2 cups cubed cooked turkey; 2 cups cubed cooked potatoes; I/2 cup leftover gravy or cream, or a mixture of both; salt and freshly ground black pepper; I tbs finely chopped parsley.**

Heat butter in a large frying pan and fry onion until golden-brown. Stir in turkey and potatoes and cook pressing down with a spatula to form a flat cake, for 3–4 minutes. Lower heat, pour in gravy or cream, and season with salt and pepper. Cook for a further 10 minutes. Serve cut into wedges, sprinkled with chopped parsley. Serves 4–6.

NOTE: Any leftover stuffing can be added with the turkey and potato.

Turkey Pie

**60 g (2 oz) butter; I¹/₂ tbs flour; I cup warm turkey stock (made from carcase) or chicken stock;
¹/₄ cup cream; salt and freshly ground black pepper;
2 tsp lemon juice; 12 button onions;
2 cups cubed cooked turkey; I cup cooked peas;
I quantity Plain Shortcrust Pastry (page 342),
or I x 375 g (12 oz) packet frozen puff pastry, thawed.**

Melt 30 g (1 oz) butter in a saucepan, add flour and stir over low heat 2 minutes. Remove from heat, cool a little and add stock, stirring until smoothly blended. Return to heat and stir until boiling. Stir in cream, salt, pepper and lemon juice. Remove from heat and cool. Cook onions in remaining butter until lightly browned. Arrange turkey in a layer in a pie dish, cover with onions with their butter, then peas, and

pour sauce over. Roll out pastry dough and use to cover dish. Cut slits in dough lid to allow steam to escape. Chill 20 minutes, then bake in a preheated very hot oven (230°C/450°F) for 10 minutes. Reduce heat to moderate (180°C/350°F) and bake for a further 20 minutes, covering loosely with foil if pastry is browning too much. Serves 4–6.

TURKISH DELIGHT

A jelly-type sweet most popular in the Middle East, delicious served with coffee when guests call. Flavour with citrus juices, rose water or peppermint; add chopped nuts; colour delicately with a few drops of food colouring and roll each morsel in sifted icing sugar. Turkish delight makes a lovely gift from your kitchen.

Turkish Delight

**2 tbs gelatine; I cup water; I lemon; I orange;
3 cups sugar; ²/₃ cup cornflour;
red or green food colouring; sifted icing sugar.**

Sprinkle gelatine over ¹/₄ cup of the water and set aside to soften. Peel lemon and orange thinly, without any white pith. Squeeze and strain juice. Place lemon and orange rinds and juice in a deep, heavy saucepan with sugar and ²/₃ cup water. Bring slowly to the boil, stirring to dissolve sugar before boiling point is reached. Boil steadily without stirring for 4–5 minutes until a sugar thermometer registers 105°C/221°F, or when ¹/₂ tsp of syrup dropped into a cup of cold water forms long threads. Mix cornflour with remaining cold water and add to syrup with softened gelatine. Simmer until clear and gelatine has dissolved, stirring occasionally. Add a few drops of food colouring, and strain into a lightly oiled 18 cm (7 in) shallow tin. Leave to set overnight. Next day, cut into squares and roll in sifted icing sugar. Package in layers separated with wax paper lightly dusted with sifted icing sugar. Makes about 50 x 2.5 cm (1 in) squares.

VARIATIONS

Chopped nuts – almonds, pistachios, walnuts – may be added to the mixture before pouring into tins.

CREME DE MENTHE TURKISH DELIGHT: Follow the recipe for Turkish Delight, but omit the orange and lemon rinds and juice, and instead flavour with ¹/₂ tsp oil of peppermint and colour with green food colouring.

ROSE WATER TURKISH DELIGHT: Follow the recipe for Turkish Delight, but omit the orange and lemon rinds and juice, and instead flavour with 2 tbs rose water and tint pink with red food colouring. Add ¹/₂ cup chopped pistachio nuts before pouring into prepared tins.

TURMERIC

One of the principal spices of India, and an ingredient in most commercial curry powders. The powder is obtained from the dried root of a plant of the ginger family. Fresh turmeric rhizomes resemble ginger and need to be peeled and grated or finely chopped before use.

The most obvious characteristic of turmeric is its colour – ranging from brilliant yellow to deep gold. It may be used as a fabric dye as well as for colouring and flavouring foods, such as curries and Indian rice dishes, as well as chutneys and pickles.

Turmeric can be used instead of saffron to give a yellow colour although the flavour is quite different. It goes into almost all vegetable curries in India, and many other vegetarian dishes. Indonesian curries, too, often call for turmeric.

Like all aromatic spices, turmeric loses its pungency if stored too long; it should be bought in small quantities, and replaced when its aroma fades. See recipes.

Mixed Vegetable Curry

Brussels sprouts, chokos or cabbage could replace any of the vegetables suggested in this recipe.

^{1}/$_2$ cup oil; ^{1}/$_2$ tsp mustard seeds; 2 tsp turmeric or I tbs grated fresh turmeric; 6–8 curry leaves (optional); 2 cloves garlic, crushed; 2 cm (^{3}/$_4$ in) piece fresh ginger, grated; pinch chilli powder; ^{1}/$_2$ small cauliflower, broken into florets; 250 g (8 oz) green beans, cut into short lengths; I carrot, finely sliced; 6 leaves spinach, torn into pieces; salt.

Heat oil in large saucepan and fry mustard seeds, turmeric, curry leaves (if using), garlic, ginger and chilli for a moment or two. Add cauliflower, beans and carrot and fry over medium heat, stirring, until vegetables are half cooked and still crisp. Add spinach and fry for a further 5 minutes. Add salt, cover and simmer over a low heat for 2–3 minutes. Serves 4.

Indian Lamb Kebabs

I kg (2 lb) boneless leg of lamb, cut into cubes; I small clove garlic; I tsp salt; I tsp finely grated fresh ginger; ^{1}/$_2$ tsp black pepper; ^{1}/$_2$ tsp turmeric; ^{1}/$_2$ tsp ground coriander; ^{1}/$_2$ tsp ground cumin; ^{1}/$_2$ tsp crushed dried curry leaves; ^{1}/$_2$ tsp crushed dried oregano; 2 tsp soy sauce; 2 tsp sesame oil; 2 tsp lemon juice; I tbs peanut oil.

Place lamb cubes in large bowl. Crush garlic with salt, and combine with remaining ingredients. Pour over lamb and stir well to ensure that each piece is covered with mixture. Cover well and refrigerate for at least 3 hours. Drain meat and thread on to small skewers. Cook under a preheated grill or over hot coals until nicely browned on all sides. Serve hot with boiled rice and Indian side dishes if desired. Serves 6.

TURNIP AND SWEDE (RUTABAGA, NEEP AND SWEDISH TURNIP)

These root vegetables grow wild in parts of eastern Europe and Siberia but are widely cultivated in many other countries.

TURNIP: It can be either round or long, has white flesh and is at its best when young and small. The round ones should be no bigger than tennis balls and the long ones about the size of a medium carrot. The green tops when very young and fresh can be prepared the same way as spinach. Buy turnips when young, and choose firm, heavy roots with no soft spots. Most turnips are peeled and cubed or sliced before cooking, with some exceptions such as the classic accompaniment to roast duckling – glazed whole baby turnips. Turnips are also delicious with ham, turkey and boiled lamb.

SWEDE: Also known as Swedish turnip, rutabaga in the USA and neep in Scotland. Swede has a pale yellow flesh, with a firm dense texture. The flavour is slightly milder than a turnip and it can grow to a much larger size without much impairment to taste and texture. Choose swedes that are heavy with no soft spots, holes or bruising. Peel thickly and cut into dice or slices according to your recipe. They are delicious boiled then mashed with butter; roasted around a joint of lamb, beef or pork; used in soups or stews, or combined with other ingredients such as cheese or bacon. See recipes.

Roast Turnips or Swedes

500 g (I lb) turnips or swedes, peeled and cut into 2.5 cm (I in) pieces; dripping, lard or oil.

Drop turnips or swedes into boiling water and cook for about 4 minutes. Drain and dry the pieces on paper towels. Have ready an ovenproof dish with enough hot dripping, lard or oil to come 1 cm (^{1}/$_2$ in) up sides. Put in dried vegetables and roast in top part of a preheated moderate oven (180°C/350°F) for about 40 minutes or until crisp and tender. Turn pieces several times during roasting. Serves 4.

NOTE: If you prefer to have the turnips or swedes soft and juicy, put the blanched pieces around the roasting joint of meat instead.

Glazed Baby Turnips

500 g (I lb) small whole baby turnips, peeled; 2 tsp caster sugar; 60 g (2 oz) butter.

Cook turnips in boiling salted water until just tender. Drain off all but 2 tbs of liquid. Add sugar and cool over low heat until dissolved. Stir in butter, increase heat and cook until sugar and butter mixture begins to brown. Keep shaking pan so turnips are thoroughly coated in mixture, making sure it does not burn. Serve with roast duckling. Serves 4–6.

Turnip Casserole

3 cups diced cooked turnips or swedes (or a combination of both); 90 g (3 oz) butter; 1 tbs sugar; ¹/₂ tsp salt; freshly ground black pepper; 1 cup fresh breadcrumbs; 125g (4 oz) Gruyère cheese, diced.

Mash turnips or swedes and combine with 60 g (2 oz) butter, the sugar, salt, pepper, ³/₄ cup of the breadcrumbs and the cheese. Turn into a buttered 4-cup ovenproof dish, top with remaining bread-crumbs and pour over remaining butter, melted. Bake in a preheated moderate oven (180°C/350°F) until top is browned, about 20 minutes. Serves 4–6.

Turnips in Butter

500 g (1 lb) turnips, peeled; about 60 g (2 oz) butter; freshly ground black pepper.

Cut turnips into wedges, quarters or thick slices. Cook in boiling lightly salted water for 10–15 mintues or until tender. Drain and cool. Heat butter in a frying pan and brown turnips on all sides, a few at a time. Do not crowd pan. Season with salt and pepper, remove to a heated serving dish and keep warm while browning remaining turnips, adding more butter when necessary. Serves 4.

Turnips in Sour Cream

4 turnips, peeled and diced; 2 tsp caraway seeds; ¹/₄ cup sour light cream; paprika; lemon juice.

Cook turnips in boiling salted water, with caraway seeds, for 5 minutes. Drain off water, then add sour cream. Heat through gently for a few minutes. Sprinkle with paprika and a little lemon juice and serve hot. Serves 4.

Mashed Swedes

500 g (1 lb) swedes, peeled and cubed; 2 medium potatoes, peeled and cubed; 30 g (1 oz) butter; ¹/₄ cup cream; salt and freshly ground black pepper.

Put swedes and potatoes in a saucepan of cold salted water, bring to the boil and boil until tender. Drain, and mash well, purée in a food processor or push through a sieve. Return purée to the cleaned saucepan and place over low heat. Beat in butter and cream, season with salt and plenty of black pepper to taste and serve very hot. Serves 4–6.

TURNOVER

A square or circle of pastry folded over a filling. It is quicker and easier to make than a pie, is portable and is a treat for many occasions. Serve turnovers, large or small, sweet or savoury, as a main course or dessert, for picnics, packed lunches or as nibbles with drinks.

Use plain or sweet shortcrust pastry, cream cheese or sour cream pastry, commercial or home-made flaky pastry or, speediest of all, frozen ready-rolled sheets of puff pastry. Turnovers can be baked or deep-fried. See recipes.

Basic Turnovers

Fillings must be completely cold when the pastry is folded around them.

1 quantity Plain or Sweet Shortcrust Pastry, Cream Cheese Pastry, Sour Cream Pastry or Rough Puff Pastry (see *Pastry*), or 1 x 375 g (12 oz) packet frozen puff pastry, thawed; filling of your choice (see below); lightly beaten egg or egg white; caster sugar (for sweet turnovers only).

Roll out dough 5mm (just under ¹/₄ in) thick and cut into squares or circles of desired size. Mound chosen cold filling in centre of one half of each piece of pastry (a triangular half for squares). Do not overfill; use about 1¹/₂ tbs filling for 10 cm (4 in) turnovers, 1 tbs filling for 8 cm (3 in) turnovers. Brush edges with beaten egg or egg white, fold other half over and press edges to seal. If using rough puff pastry, lightly tap cut edges to seal. If using shortcrust, cream cheese or sour cream pastry, press round sealed edges with tines of a fork or point of a teaspoon for a decorative effect. Place turnovers on greased baking trays and chill 20 minutes. Brush savoury turnovers with beaten egg; sweet ones with beaten egg white, then sprinkle over caster sugar.

Cut 2 or 3 slits in tops to allow steam to escape and bake in a preheated oven until pastry is golden-brown. Bake shortcrust, rough puff or puff pastry turnovers at 230°C/450°F and cream cheese or sour cream pastry turnovers at 200°C/400°F.

Turnovers may also be deep-fried. Shape as described above, but do not cut slits in pastry. Chill 20 minutes. Heat oil in a deep-fryer until a small piece of pastry will brown in 1 minute. Place turnovers in a frying basket, fry until golden (about 5 minutes), then drain on crumpled paper towels and serve hot. Makes about 12.

SAVOURY FILLINGS FOR BASIC TURNOVERS
CHEESE AND TOMATO: Peel, seed and chop 2 large tomatoes and mix with 1 tbs fresh breadcrumbs, 4 tbs grated cheese, 1 tbs grated onion, 1 egg, salt and pepper.
SAVOURY MINCE: Chop 1 small onion and fry, without extra fat, with 250 g (8 oz) hamburger mince, breaking the meat down with a fork. When meat has changed

t

colour, sprinkle with 2 tsp flour and stir until brown. Add ¼ cup water or beef stock, ¼ tsp Worcestershire sauce, 1 tsp tomato sauce, salt and pepper. Stir until thickened. 2 tsp chopped parsley or other fresh herbs, a pinch dried herbs, or ½ small carrot, grated, may be added. Cover and simmer for 10 minutes, then cool.

COOKED OR CANNED FISH, MEAT OR CHICKEN: Flake or chop finely and mix with your choice of chopped tomato, celery, herbs, green pepper, grated onion, mustard or grated lemon rind. Add just enough chutney, cream, plain yogurt, mayonnaise, gravy or any suitable sauce you may have to moisten slightly. Season well with salt and pepper. Half a thick slice of the softer type of Continental sausage, spread with Dijon mustard, is excellent too, or for tiny party turnovers rolled, stuffed anchovy seasoned with pepper and a few drops of lemon juice.

VEGETABLE: Sliced mushrooms or chopped cooked vegetables are good mixed with chopped herbs or grated cheese and seasoned well with salt and pepper. Moisten slightly, as for meat fillings, if needed.

SWEET FILLINGS FOR BASIC TURNOVERS

FRUIT: Use apples or pears, stewed or thinly sliced and sprinkled with sugar and lemon juice; or use berries or other fresh or canned fruits. Drain canned fruits well.

DRIED FRUIT: Use fruit mincemeat or raisins, sultanas or mixed dried fruit, sprinkled with brown sugar and lemon juice.

CREAM CHEESE OR RICOTTA: Use cream cheese, or ricotta cheese mixed with a little cream. Sweeten to taste with brown or white sugar, then add your choice of flavourings: ground cinnamon, cardamom or mixed spice, brandy or rum, chopped dried or glacé fruits, grated orange or lemon rind.

JAM OR LEMON CHEESE: Use a good berry jam, apricot jam (which may be mixed with slivered almonds), marmalade sprinkled with cinnamon or a few drops of orange liqueur, or lemon cheese.

Pork Turnovers

These are good hot or cold.

60 g (2 oz) butter; I large onion, finely chopped; 2 tbs flour; ¾ cup warm milk; ¼ cup cream; I cup finely chopped cooked pork; I cooking apple, peeled, cored and chopped; grated rind I lemon; I tbs lemon juice; ½ tsp crumbled dried rosemary; salt and freshly ground black pepper; Plain Shortcrust Pastry made with 2 cups flour (page 342); beaten egg to glaze.

Melt butter in a saucepan and cook onion gently until soft. Add flour, stir over low heat 1 minute and remove from heat. Cool a little, then add milk, stirring until smoothly blended. Return to heat and stir until boiling. Add cream, pork, apple, lemon

rind, lemon juice, rosemary, salt and pepper and mix well. Cool completely. Roll out dough 5 mm (¼ in) thick and cut into 8 x 10 cm (4 in) rounds. Divide filling among rounds, mounding it on one half of each and leaving a margin for sealing. Brush edges with beaten egg and fold other halves over, pressing edges to seal and crimping with fingers and thumb. Chill 20 minutes. Cut 2 slits in top of each turnover and glaze with beaten egg. Place on a greased baking tray and bake in a preheated very hot oven (230°C/450°F) for 15 minutes or until golden-brown. Makes 8.

Sausage and Apple Turnovers

3 thick beef or pork sausages; I tbs bacon fat or butter; I large cooking apple, peeled, cored and finely chopped; nutmeg; 3 tsp currants; 2 tsp lemon juice; Rich Shortcrust Pastry made with 2 cups flour (page 342); salt and freshly ground black pepper; beaten egg to glaze.

Prick sausages all over, cover with cold water and bring to the boil. Simmer 3 minutes, then drain, cool and skin. Heat bacon fat or butter in a frying pan and fry sausages until brown on all sides. Set aside to cool. Mix apple with nutmeg, currants and lemon juice. Roll out dough and cut 6 x 15 cm (6 in) rounds. Divide apple mixture among rounds, placing it on one side only and leaving a margin for sealing. Cut sausages in half and place on apple mixture. Season with salt and pepper. Brush edges of dough rounds with beaten egg and fold over, pressing edges to seal and crimping with fingers and thumb. Chill for 20 minutes. Brush tops with egg and cut 2 or 3 small slits in each turnover for steam to escape. Place on a greased baking tray and bake in a preheated hot oven (220°C/425°F) for 10 minutes, then lower heat to moderate (180°C/350°F) and bake 20 minutes longer, covering turnovers with foil if pastry is browning too much. Makes 6.

Apricot Turnovers

PASTRY: 1½ cups flour; 90 g (3 oz) butter; I tsp grated lemon rind; ⅓ cup ground almonds; I egg, beaten; I egg white; caster sugar to glaze.

FILLING: 125 g (4 oz) dried apricots; I cinnamon stick; ¼ cup sugar; 2 tsp brandy or Grand Marnier.

To make pastry, sift flour into a bowl and rub in butter until mixture resembles crumbs. Stir in lemon rind and almonds. Add egg and 1–2 tsp cold water, if necessary, to make a soft dough. Wrap in plastic wrap and chill 1 hour.

FILLING: Simmer apricots with cinnamon stick in water to cover until very soft. Add sugar, stir to dissolve and simmer for 10–15 minutes longer or until liquid is almost evaporated. Remove from heat, stir in brandy and cool completely. Roll out dough and cut 6 x 10 cm (4 in) rounds. Put a spoonful of filling on one side of each round, leaving a margin for sealing, and brush edges with egg white. Fold other sides over, pressing to seal, and mark edges with point of a teaspoon. Brush with egg white, sprinkle with caster sugar and cut 2 small slits in top of each turnover. Chill for 20 minutes, then place on a greased baking tray and bake in a preheated hot oven (200°C/400°F) for 15 minutes or until pastry is golden-brown. Serve warm, to accompany coffee, or with whipped cream as a dessert. Serves 6.

TZATZIKI

A refreshing Greek yogurt and cucumber dip to serve with triangles of toasted Lebanese bread, Melba toast, slices of French bread or crisp raw vegetables. Tzatziki is also used as a sauce to complement fried or grilled fish, lamb kebabs or any barbecued meats; or fold diced green pepper, celery, tomato and shallots through, garnish with fresh coriander or black olives and serve as a refreshing summer salad.

Tzatziki

1½ cups plain yogurt; 1 medium green cucumber; 1 tbs lemon juice; 1 large clove garlic, crushed; salt and freshly ground black pepper; 1 tbs chopped fresh mint.

Line a sieve with a double thickness of cheesecloth (or use a disposable cloth). Place over a bowl, spoon yogurt in and let it drain for 2 hours. Meantime, peel cucumber thinly with a vegetable peeler so that some of the green under the skin is left. Cut lengthways in half, scoop out seeds and grate flesh, or chop very fine. Place in a sieve and leave 20 minutes to drain off excess juice. Combine drained yogurt, cucumber, lemon juice and garlic in a bowl and season with salt and pepper. Fold in half the mint and sprinkle the rest over the top. Makes about 2 cups.

u v

UPSIDE-DOWN CAKE

The Americans are credited with inventing cakes whose decorative, caramelised fruit topping is baked underneath the cake layer. The important point about all upside-down cakes is that the bottom of the cake tin should be completely covered with butter and sugar mixture which forms a caramel, and this base is then completely covered with fruit. **See recipes.**

See also *Pineapple:* Pineapple Upside-down Cake.

Fruit Upside–down Cake

Use well-drained canned, poached or soft fresh fruit such as stoned plums or apricots, or berries. The cake layer in this recipe is light and short.

FRUIT LAYER: I cup well-drained canned or poached fruit (apples, pears, peaches, cherries) or prepared, soft fresh fruit; 30 g (I oz) butter; 3 tbs caster sugar.

CAKE: 60 g (2 oz) butter; ¼ cup caster sugar; I egg; ½ cup self-raising flour, sifted.

FRUIT LAYER: Leave berries whole; halve or slice other fruit. Melt butter in an 18 cm (7 in) round sandwich tin. Sprinkle evenly with sugar, and arrange fruit on caramel in a decorative pattern.

CAKE: Cream butter with sugar, then add egg and beat well. Fold in flour. Spoon cake mixture over fruit, being careful not to disturb arrangement. Bake in a preheated oven (180°C/350°F) for 30 minutes or until cake is cooked. Turn out, leaving fruit side up. Serve warm with cream, ice cream or custard, or cold with coffee.

Quick Upside–down Cupcakes

30 g (I oz) butter; 4 tbs brown sugar; 12 canned apricot halves, well-drained; I x 310 g packet buttercake mix.

Melt butter and spoon evenly into 12 deep patty-pans. Sprinkle bottom of each patty-pan with brown sugar. Place an apricot half, cut side up, in each. Make up cake mixture according to directions on packet and spoon on top of fruit, filling patty-pans two-thirds full. Bake in a preheated moderately hot oven (190°C/375°F) for 12–15 minutes or until cake is cooked. Turn out, leaving apricots on top. Makes 12.

Prune and Apricot Upside–down Cake

FRUIT LAYER: 30 g (I oz) butter; 4 tbs brown sugar; 12 dessert prunes, stoned; 12 dried apricots; 4 glacé cherries; 8 blanched almonds.

CAKE: 60 g (2 oz) butter; ¼ cup sugar; few drops vanilla; I egg, beaten; I cup self-raising flour; pinch salt; 2½ tbs milk.

FRUIT LAYER: Melt butter in an 18 cm (7 in) square cake tin. Sprinkle evenly with sugar, and arrange prunes, apricots, cherries and almonds on glaze in an attractive pattern.

CAKE: Cream butter with sugar until light and fluffy. Add vanilla and egg and mix well. Sift flour with salt and fold in alternately with milk. Spoon cake mixture carefully over fruit, taking care not to disturb arrangement. Bake in a preheated moderate oven (180°C/350°F) for 25 minutes or until cake is cooked. Turn out, leaving fruit side up. For a dessert, serve warm with cream; cool if serving as a cake.

VACHERIN

A luscious meringue dessert usually made into a case or basket to hold a filling of fruits, creams or ice creams. Sometimes the base is a disc of sweet pastry or almond paste with the meringue piped on in rings one on top of the other around the edge. The filling is then piled into the centre. Vacherins can also be assembled with discs of meringue layered with filling. **See recipes.**

Vacherin Melba

VACHERIN MERINGUE CASE: 4 eggs whites; I cup caster sugar; ½ tsp vanilla.

FILLING: 3 cups vanilla ice cream; I cup sliced canned or fresh peaches; ½ cup fresh, frozen or canned raspberries, puréed.

To make the meringue case, cut a round of greaseproof paper 20 cm (8 in) in diameter, place on a greased baking tray and spray with non-stick cooking spray. Whisk egg whites and sugar together until very thick and glossy. Fold in vanilla. Put mixture in a piping bag fitted with a plain 1 cm (½ in) tube. Pipe (or spread) layer of meringue over paper round, then pipe several rings around outer edge, one on top of the other, to form a case. Bake in a preheated slow oven (150°C/300°F) for 35–40 minutes or until crisp and pale golden. Turn off oven and allow to cool completely in oven with door open. Just before serving, fill case with softened ice cream. Arrange peach slices on top and pour raspberry purée over peaches. Serve immediately. Serves 8.

VACHERIN CHANTILLY WITH FRUITS: Make meringue case as above. Just before serving, whip 2 cups cream and fold in 2 tbs Grand Marnier and 1 tbs sifted icing sugar. Put a layer of fresh fruit, such as strawberries, or sliced peaches, bananas, apricots or grapes (or a mixture of fruits), in meringue case. Pile whipped cream on top and decorate with a little more fruit. If using peaches or bananas, sprinkle slices with lemon juice to prevent discolouration. Serve immediately.

Mocha Vacherin

VACHERIN MERINGUE CASE: 4 egg whites; I cup caster sugar; ½ tsp cinnamon; ¾ cup ground hazelnuts.

MOCHA SAUCE: $^1/_2$ **cup sugar;** $^3/_4$ **cup water;
1 tbs instant coffee powder; 2 tbs boiling water;
1 tbs rum.**

FILLING: $^1/_2$ **tsp instant coffee powder; 2 tbs brown
sugar; 1 tbs hot water;** $^3/_4$ **cup cream.**

DECORATION: sifted icing sugar; $^1/_2$ **cup whipped
cream; whole hazelnuts.**

Cut 2 rounds of greaseproof paper 20 cm (8 in) in
diameter. Place on a greased baking tray and spray
with non-stick cooking spray. Whisk egg whites until
stiff. Add 1 tbs caster sugar and beat for 30 seconds
longer. Sift remaining sugar with cinnamon and fold
into egg whites with ground hazelnuts. Spread or
pipe meringue over the 2 paper rounds. Bake in a
preheated cool oven (140°C/275°F) for 1–1¼ hours.
Turn off oven and allow to cool completely in oven
with door open.

MOCHA SAUCE: Dissolve sugar in $^1/_2$ cup of the water
over low heat. Increase heat and boil without stirring
until syrup is a rich golden-brown. Remove from heat
and carefully stir in remaining cold water. Return to
low heat and stir until caramel dissolves. Pour into a
heatproof bowl and allow to cool. As syrup cools and
begins to thicken, stir in instant coffee, dissolved in
boiling water, and rum. When cold, sauce should be
thick and syrupy.

FILLING: Mix coffee and brown sugar with hot water
and allow to cool. Whip cream and, as it begins to
thicken, add coffee and brown sugar mixture.
Continue beating until cream holds soft peaks.
Sandwich 2 meringue rounds with filling. Dust top of
gateau with sifted icing sugar and pipe rosettes of
cream around edge. Decorate rosettes with whole
hazelnuts. Serve with mocha sauce. Serves 8.

VANILLA

Vanilla beans can truly be called fragrant; their aroma is
one of the most pleasant of all flavourings. The vanilla
bean is actually the pod of a climbing orchid native to
Central America, and was first brought to Europe from
Mexico. The flavour of vanilla is available in the form of
beans, in vanilla essence and in the tiny sachets of vanilla
sugar. The essential flavouring of vanilla can be syn-
thesised, and both imitation vanilla essence and sugar
flavoured with imitation vanilla are to be found; neither of
these, however, is a proper substitute for real vanilla.
Vanilla finds its niche in the realm of desserts, and is also
used as a flavouring for chocolate. In cakes, creams,
custards, ice cream and sauces, vanilla is a vital ingredient. Poaching in a vanilla-flavoured syrup highlights the
flavour of many fruits, especially apricots and pears. For
custards and custard-based desserts, a piece of vanilla
bean is left to infuse in the hot milk. This piece of vanilla
bean may be washed, dried and re-used. Store it in a jar
of sugar or caster sugar, where it will gradually impart its

flavour to the sugar; this vanilla-flavoured sugar can be
used whenever a vanilla flavour is called for. When a
piece of vanilla bean is infused in milk or added to a
syrup, it is inevitable that tiny black specks of vanilla will
remain after the piece of vanilla bean is removed. It is not
necessary to remove these; anyway, they show that real
vanilla has been used.

Vanilla Sugar: The easiest way to make vanilla sugar is
simply to buy pieces of vanilla bean in a jar of sugar. A
more strongly flavoured vanilla sugar can be made by
blending a whole vanilla bean, cut into short sections,
with 1 cup sugar. Sieve before use. The flavour is even
better if the blended mixture is left for a week or so before
sieving. Store airtight. **See recipes.**

Syrup for Poaching Fruits

**1 cup sugar; 1½ cups water;
2.5 cm (1 in) piece vanilla bean, split lengthways.**

Dissolve sugar in water, then add vanilla bean and
bring to the boil. Simmer gently for 5–10 minutes.
Remove vanilla bean. Add fruit as desired (apricots,
pears, peaches, cherries, etc.) and poach gently until
tender. Cool in syrup. Makes about 2¼ cups.

Baked Apricots

**1 kg (2 lb) ripe apricots, halved and stoned;
2 tbs vanilla sugar (see above); ¼–½ cup water.**

Arrange apricots in an ovenproof baking dish.
Sprinkle with vanilla sugar and water (if apricots are
very ripe, very little water will be required). Bake in a
preheated slow oven (150°C/300°F) for about 1 hour
or until apricots are soft. Serve hot. Serves 6.

Vanilla Biscuits

**125 g (4 oz) butter or margarine; 4 tbs caster sugar;
1 tsp vanilla; 1 cup flour; ½ tsp baking powder;
blanched almond halves or glacé cherries to decorate.**

Melt butter or margarine; cook until it browns slightly.
Cool over cold water, then add sugar and cream until
light. Beat in vanilla. Gradually work in flour sifted
with baking powder. Using floured hands, shape into
small balls and flatten them slightly. Top each with
almond or cherry. Place on lightly greased baking tray.

Bake in a preheated moderately hot oven (190°C/375°F) for 12–15 minutes or until crisp and golden. Makes about 50.

Rich Vanilla Custard

5 cm (2 in) piece vanilla bean; 2 cups hot milk; 1 egg; 2 egg yolks; 2 tbs sugar; 15 g (¹/₂ oz) butter.

Infuse vanilla bean in hot milk in heavy saucepan for 5–10 minutes, then remove. Beat egg, egg yolks and sugar together, pour on milk and mix well. Return to saucepan with butter and cook over low heat, stirring constantly, until thick. Remove from heat and beat with rotary beater until slightly cooled. Pour into a bowl or jug and cool completely. Makes about 2¼ cups.

Strawberries in Vanilla Syrup

2 punnets (500 g/1 lb) strawberries, hulled; juice 1 lemon; 1¹/₂ cups sugar; ¹/₂ vanilla bean, split lengthways; 1 cup water.

Sprinkle strawberries with lemon juice and about ¹/₂ cup sugar. Leave to macerate for 30 minutes. Meanwhile, make a syrup with remaining sugar, vanilla bean and water. Poach strawberries in this syrup over very low heat for about 5 minutes. Cool, then chill for 5–6 hours before serving. Serves 6.

Vanilla Crescents

These crescent-shaped almond shortbreads are an Austrian specialty.

1¹/₄ cups flour; pinch salt; 155 g (5 oz) unsalted butter, softened; ¹/₄ cup icing sugar, sifted; 2 egg yolks; 1 tsp vanilla; 155 g (5 oz) ground almonds, preferably unblanched; extra icing sugar.

Sift flour with salt on to a work surface. Make a well in centre and put in butter, sugar, egg yolks and vanilla. Sprinkle ground almonds on to flour. Work ingredients in centre with fingertips of one hand until they are well blended. With other hand, use a metal spatula to draw dry ingredients quickly into centre, and mix to a ball of dough. Knead dough lightly, wrap in plastic wrap and chill 1 hour. Pinch off walnut-sized pieces of dough, roll into balls, then roll under your hand to form little cylinders and bend into crescents. Place on a greased baking tray. Bake in a preheated moderate oven (180°C/350°F) for 10–12 minutes or until lightly coloured. Remove to a wire rack, placing a sheet of greaseproof paper underneath. Dredge biscuits heavily with sifted icing sugar while they are still warm. Makes about 75.

VEAL

Since it comes from young animals, veal (calf meat) is tender and its flavour is delicate. Milk-fed veal, prized in Europe but not usually available in Australia, is very pale.

Grass-fed veal is a little more pink but should not be red. Good veal is fine-grained and smooth, with only a thin edge of white satiny fat. The bones are large in proportion to the size and should be bluish white.

Veal has only a small amount of external fat and little internal fat, so care must be taken to guard against dryness when cooking. It should be cooked with low to moderate heat, either by a moist-heat method (stewing, braising, pot-roasting) or, for roasting or grilling, with plenty of additional fat provided by very frequent basting and perhaps a covering of streaky bacon for a roast. The two exceptions to the moderate heat rule are pan-fried cutlets or chops which are browned quickly to seal them but then cooked gently until done, and the very thin slices called escalopes, which are sautéed briefly on medium to high heat.

Please read *Meat* for amount to buy, factors determining tenderness, testing meat for doneness, carving, etc.

■ THE CHOICE CUTS FOR ROASTING:

Leg: May be cut into 2 or more roasting pieces, on or off the bone.

Cushion (Topside): A boneless leg roast.

Rump: Boneless.

Loin: The most succulent cut, which may be on the bone or boned, rolled and tied.

Fillet: Small, boneless and fatless, the most tender cut of all.

■ OTHER CUTS FOR ROASTING:

Shoulder: On the bone or boned and rolled.

Forequarter Roasts: Boned and rolled breast, and foreloin rib, sold on or off the bone.

Pork and Veal Roast: A rolled roast with an outer layer of fatty pork made up by the butcher from various cuts of veal.

■ TO ROAST: Choice and other cuts are roasted in the same way (except for a pork and veal roast, which should be treated as a pork roast – see *Pork*). Weigh the veal roast and place it on a rack in a roasting tin. Smear the surface of the meat with butter and lay rindless rashers of streaky bacon or strips of fresh pork fat over the top. Place in a preheated moderately slow oven (160°C/325°F) and roast for about 45 minutes per 500 g (1 lb), basting with pan juices and extra butter, if necessary, every 15 minutes. Since underdone veal is indigestible and unpleasant, it should always be well-done. To test for doneness, use a meat thermometer or pierce with a fine skewer; juices should run clear. Rest for 15–20 minutes in a warm place, before carving.

GRILLED VEAL

Veal is rarely grilled since it lends itself better to other methods of cooking. However, some cuts can be grilled, as long as they receive constant brushing with oil or melted butter to prevent the close-grained texture of veal becoming dry and tough. Veal should always be served well-done.

v

■ **THE CHOICE CUTS FOR GRILLING**

Loin Chops: These may include a piece of kidney.

Cutlets: Rib chops.

NOTE: Both chops from the loin and those from the rib are sometimes called 'cutlets'. The name is sometimes given, too, to 1 cm (½ in) steaks cut from the leg, but these are better pan-fried.

■ **TO GRILL:** Have chops cut 2 cm (¾ in) thick and at room temperature. Cut through edge in several places to prevent buckling. Roll up tails of chops and secure with poultry pins or small skewers. Season on both sides with oil or melted butter. To give a golden finish, dust with a little flour. Place on a greased grill rack under a preheated grill and grill under moderate heat, brushing every 2 minutes with oil or melted butter. Turn the chops 2 or 3 times during grilling. Chops will take 12–14 minutes; they are cooked when the thickest part of the meat releases clear juice when pierced with a fine skewer.

SAUTEED VEAL

This method is suitable for loin chops, cutlets and leg or fillet steaks, cut about 2 cm (¾ in) thick, and for the thin delicate slices called escalopes or scaloppine.

To cook escalopes, see *Escalope and Scaloppine.*

TO SAUTE: Have meat at room temperature and prepare it as for grilling. Heat enough oil to cover the bottom of a heavy frying pan generously. Add an equal quantity of butter, and add meat when foaming subsides. Cook 30 seconds–1 minute on each side or until browned, then lower heat and continue to cook gently, turning once, until cooked through – when the meat feels firm if pressed, or when beads of juice are clear if meat is pierced with a fine skewer.

PAN SAUCES FOR SAUTEED VEAL

Serve sautéed veal chops, steaks or escalopes with lemon wedges, or with one of the following quickly made pan sauces. Quantities are sufficient for 4 large chops or escalopes.

Sour Cream and Caper Sauce: After sautéing veal, remove it to a heated platter and keep warm. Add ¾ cup sour cream to the pan, stir in 2 tsp Dijon mustard and bring to the boil, stirring in all the brown bits from the pan. Season with salt and pepper and stir in 2 tsp drained capers. Spoon over the veal and top each chop or steak with 2 crossed halves of anchovy fillets.

Cream and Lemon Sauce: After sautéing veal, remove it to a heated platter and keep warm. Add ½ cup cream and 2 tbs lemon juice to the pan and boil 1 minute, stirring in all the brown bits from the pan. Season with salt and pepper and spoon over the veal.

Port and Mushroom Sauce: While veal is cooking, gently cook 125 g (4 oz) sliced mushrooms in a separate, covered saucepan with 1 tbs each butter and lemon juice. When veal is done, remove to a heated platter and keep warm. Add 1 tbs finely chopped shallots to the pan and fry, stirring, 1 minute, then stir in ¼ cup port and

½ cup dry white wine and boil on high heat 2 minutes. Add mushrooms with their juices, season to taste and spoon over veal.

Ham Sauce: After sautéing veal, remove it to a heated platter and keep warm. Add 2 tbs finely chopped shallot and 60 g (2 oz) cooked ham, cut into thin strips, to the pan. Fry 2 minutes, then stir in ½ cup veal or chicken stock and 2 tsp wine vinegar. Boil, stirring in all the brown bits from the pan, for a minute or so, then season with salt and pepper. Remove from heat and swirl in a knob of butter and 1 tbs chopped parsley. Spoon over veal.

Apple and Onion Sauce: Dust veal with seasoned flour before sautéing as usual in oil and butter. Remove veal to a heated platter and keep warm. Add 30 g (1 oz) butter to the pan and when it is foaming, add 1 sliced apple. Fry until golden. Add ½ cup dry white wine, or ½ cup chicken stock and 2 tsp wine vinegar, and boil 1 minute, stirring gently. Season with salt and pepper and spoon over veal.

PAN-FRIED CRUMBED VEAL

The most famous example of veal cooked this way is Wienerschnitzel (see page 471), but thicker veal steaks and cutlets are juicy and delicious when fried with a crisp crumb coating. Coat meat with egg and breadcrumbs. In a heavy frying pan heat enough butter and oil to come halfway up the pieces of veal. When foam subsides arrange the pieces in one layer without crowding the pan. Cook over moderate heat until golden-brown then turn and cook other side, 12–15 minutes in all. Drain on crumpled paper towels and serve immediately.

BRAISED OR CASSEROLED VEAL

Braising (pot-roasting) in a covered casserole with aromatic vegetables is an excellent way to cook a large piece of veal for maximum juices and flavour. Serving size or smaller pieces from the breast, neck or other areas are tender and melting when cooked slowly with cream, wine or other liquid. **See recipes.**

See also *Blanquette, Escalope, Osso Buco Milanese, Scaloppine, Schnitzel.*

Veal Birds

Thin slices of veal escalopes, pounded with a meat mallet, are wrapped around a filling, browned and then simmered in liquid which is made into a pan sauce or gravy for serving.

8 veal escalopes, about 10 x 15 cm (4 x 6 in); flour; 60 g (2 oz) butter; ½ cup chicken stock; ½ dry white wine; 1 bouquet garni; salt and freshly ground black pepper; ¼ cup cream; chopped parsley to garnish.

STUFFING: 30 g (1 oz) butter; 1 small onion, finely chopped; 125 g (4 oz) mushrooms, finely chopped; 1½ cups fresh white breadcrumbs; 2 tbs chopped parsley; finely grated rind and juice 1 lemon.

To make the stuffing, melt butter in a frying pan, add onion and fry until golden. Stir in mushrooms and cook 1 minute. Remove pan from heat, stir in remaining stuffing ingredients and allow to cool. If escalopes are not already beaten out, pound them between 2 sheets of plastic wrap until very thin. Place stuffing along one end of each escalope, roll up securely and tie with thread. Roll in flour until evenly coated. Melt butter in a flameproof casserole, put in rolls and brown quickly on all sides. Pour in stock and wine and bring to the boil, stirring constantly. Lower heat, and add bouquet garni, salt and pepper. Cover and simmer gently for 30–40 minutes or until meat is tender. Remove bouquet garni, stir in cream just before serving, sprinkled with chopped parsley. Serve with creamy mashed potatoes. Serves 4.

VARIATION

VEAL OLIVES: These are also made by rolling veal escalopes around a stuffing, but they are smaller than Veal Birds. Trim the escalopes to a smaller size, 5 x 8 cm (2 x 3 in) and follow recipe for Veal Birds.

Veal and Ham Birds with Hazelnut Sauce

8 veal escalopes; 8 thin slices cooked ham; 2 tbs finely chopped parsley; 2 cloves garlic, crushed; 90 g (3 oz) butter; $^1/_2$ cup chopped hazelnuts or walnuts; 1 large onion, finely chopped; $^1/_2$ cup white wine; $^1/_2$ tsp cinnamon; salt and freshly ground black pepper; 2–3 tbs sour cream.

If escalopes are not already beaten out, pound between 2 sheets of plastic wrap until very thin. Place a slice of ham on each slice of veal, and sprinkle with parsley and garlic. Tuck sides in, and make into neat rolls, securing with white thread or fine string. Heat butter in a large, heavy frying pan and gently brown rolls on all sides. Remove, and arrange side by side in a casserole just large enough to take them comfortably. Add hazelnuts and onion to butter remaining in frying pan, and fry until onion is soft and golden. Add wine, cinnamon, salt and pepper. Stir well to get up any brown bits from bottom of pan, and pour over veal rolls. Cover casserole and bake in a preheated moderate oven (180°C/350°F) for 20–25 minutes or until veal is tender. Take rolls out, remove strings and arrange on a heated serving platter. Stir sour cream into juices in casserole, and return to oven for a minute to heat though. Adjust seasoning and pour over rolls. Serves 4.

Veal Breast with Spinach Stuffing

In Italy, veal is served in a number of interesting ways. This economical cut of veal is most delicious with its spinach and rice stuffing and is a meal in itself. Ask the butcher to cut you 4 slices of pickled (salt) pork belly or back fat; use these to cover the meat and give it richness.

1 x 1.5–2 kg (3–4 lb) boned veal breast, cut with a pocket; salt and freshly ground black pepper; 3 tbs butter; 1 medium onion, chopped; 250 g (8 oz) mushrooms, chopped; 1 bunch (500 g/1 lb) spinach; $^1/_2$ tsp chopped fresh rosemary or basil; 1 cup cooked rice; 1 egg, lightly beaten; 4 slices pickled (salt) pork back fat; 1 tbs flour; 1 cup stock.

Season veal with salt and pepper. Heat butter, add onion and fry until transparent. Add mushrooms and cook, stirring often, for about 3 minutes. Meanwhile, cook spinach, tightly covered, for 3–4 minutes. There is no need to add water; spinach will cook in water which clings to leaves. Drain and, when cool enough to handle, squeeze as dry as possible, then chop. Mix spinach, onion and mushrooms with herbs, salt and pepper, rice and egg. Use mixture to fill pocket in veal and close with metal skewers. Place meat on a rack in a roasting tin. Arrange slices of pickled pork or fat over veal and add enough water to tin to cover bottom by about 1 cm ($^1/_2$ in). Cover with foil and bake in a preheated moderate oven (180°C/350°F) for 2 hours. Uncover and bake 30 minutes longer. Remove meat to a heated plate and keep warm while you prepare gravy. Add flour to tin and allow to brown a little over a gentle heat, then add stock and stir into a smooth gravy. Serves 6–8.

Veal Cutlets Modena–Style

Plump veal loin cutlets cooked in a style commonly used in Modena, Italy. Just a little Marsala is added, but its distinctive qualities flavour the sauce and the meat.

6 veal cutlets, 2.5 cm (1 in) thick; 1 egg; salt; $^1/_4$ cup flour; dry breadcrumbs; 125 g (4 oz) butter; 1 tbs olive oil; 1 medium onion, finely chopped; 2 tbs Marsala; 2 tsp tomato paste; $^1/_2$ cup white stock (chicken or veal); freshly ground black pepper.

Fold tail end inside each cutlet and secure with a small skewer. Beat egg with a pinch of salt on a plate. Dip cutlets in flour, then egg, and coat with breadcrumbs. Heat butter with oil in a heavy sauté pan or frying pan. Add cutlets and brown well on both sides. Add onion and fry until it begins to brown. Pour on Marsala and cook until it evaporates to 1 tbs. Stir in tomato paste, stock, salt and pepper, and continue cooking for 15–20 minutes or until cutlets are tender when tested with a skewer. Remove skewers from cutlets. Arrange cutlets on a heated serving dish and spoon pan juices over. Serves 6.

v

Veal Pot Roast

2 tbs oil; 30 g (1 oz) butter; 1 x 2.5 kg (5 lb) shoulder of veal, boned, rolled and tied; 1 cup diced onions; 1 large carrot, sliced; 1 cup diced celery; 1 bay leaf; 10 black peppercorns; 1 clove garlic, crushed; 1 tsp salt; $1/4$ tsp paprika; $1/2$ cup dry white wine; 1 tbs Beurre Manié (page 35).

Heat oil in a heavy, flameproof casserole, add butter and, when turning brown, add meat and brown it on all sides. Lift meat out. Add all remaining ingredients, except wine and beurre manié, to casserole and cook for 1–2 minutes over moderate heat, stirring, until onion begins to soften. Set a rack over vegetables and put meat on it. Pour over wine and add enough water to cover vegetables. Cover casserole tightly and place in a preheated moderately slow oven (160°C/325°F). Cook for $2^{1/2}$ hours or until tender. Uncover and cook for a further 20 minutes. Remove meat to a heated platter. Remove rack and, on moderate heat on top of stove, whisk beurre manié little by little into gravy. Stir until smooth and cook gently 5 minutes. Discard bay leaf. Serve gravy with sliced meat. Serves 8.

Veal Braised with Vermouth

1 kg (2 lb) boneless lean veal, cut into 4 cm ($1^{1/2}$ in) cubes; 60 g (2 oz) butter; 4 medium onions, thinly sliced; 2 tbs flour; $1/2$ cup dry white wine; $1/4$ cup dry vermouth; $2^{1/2}$ cups chicken or veal stock; salt and freshly ground black pepper; 1 bouquet garni; 250 g (8 oz) button mushrooms; 1 egg yolk; 1 tsp lemon juice; $1/2$ cup cream; 1 tbs chopped parsley.

TO SERVE: hot buttered rice; 2 tbs grated Parmesan cheese.

Brown veal cubes in butter in a wide, heavy saucepan, deep sauté pan or flameproof casserole. Add onions and cook until they colour lightly, then stir in flour and cook stirring gently, 2 minutes. Add wine, vermouth and enough of the stock barely to cover meat, and stir until simmering. Season with salt and pepper and add bouquet garni. Cover and simmer 40 minutes. Add mushrooms and cook 10 minutes longer or until veal is tender. Beat egg yolk and lemon juice with cream, stir in a little hot liquid from veal, then stir this back into pan. Cook gently, stirring, until liquid thickens a little more and becomes glossy; do not allow to boil. Adjust seasoning and discard bouquet garni. Serve veal scattered with parsley, on a bed of hot buttered rice with 2 tbs grated Parmesan cheese folded through it. Serves 6–8.

Braised Veal Shoulder with Spinach and Mushroom Stuffing

1 x 2 kg (4 lb) boned shoulder of veal; 1 tbs Dijon mustard; 3 tbs oil; 60 g (2 oz) butter; 2 carrots, sliced; 2 medium onions, sliced; 1 bouquet garni; 1 cup dry white wine; 1 cup chicken or veal stock; salt and freshly ground black pepper.

STUFFING: 500 g (1 lb) spinach; 2 tbs finely chopped shallots; 30 g (1 oz) butter; 250 g (8 oz) mushrooms, thinly sliced; $1/3$ cup cream; $1/2$ cup fresh breadcrumbs; 90 g (3 oz) cooked ham, diced; $1/4$ cup grated Parmesan cheese; 1 egg, beaten; 1 tbs chopped parsley; salt and freshly ground black pepper; nutmeg.

Lay veal flat, slice part way through thickest part of meat and open it out. Spread cut surface of meat with mustard, and set aside.

STUFFING: Cook spinach, with only water that clings to leaves, in a tightly covered saucepan for 3–4 minutes. Drain, squeeze out as much moisture as possible and chop fine. Cook shallots gently in butter for 3 minutes, then add mushrooms and cook 5 minutes more, stirring several times. Remove from heat and mix in spinach and remaining ingredients for stuffing.

Spread stuffing over meat. Roll up and tie firmly with string at intervals along its length to make up plump sausage shape. Heat oil and butter in a heavy, flame-proof casserole and brown meat roll on all sides.

Remove meat. Add carrots and onions to casserole and brown them lightly. Add bouquet garni, wine and stock and bring to the boil, stirring and scraping bottom of casserole to mix in brown bits. Place meat on bed of vegetables. Cover tightly and cook in a preheated moderate oven (180°C/350°F) for 2 hours or until veal is tender, turning it after first hour.

Remove meat to a warm place and rest for 15 minutes, then remove strings and carve across into thick slices. Arrange veal down a heated serving platter. Bring pan juices to the boil, adjust seasoning, discard bouquet garni, and spoon a little over veal. Serve remainder in a sauceboat. Serves 8.

NOTE: The veal can be served cold: allow to cool before removing string, and slice a little thinner than for hot veal. Meantime, strain cooking liquid and boil it down until it is syrupy. Arrange veal slices on a serving platter and brush several times with the reduced liquid to glaze it.

Sautéed Veal with Lemon and Rosemary

4 veal cutlets or 8 small escalopes; 2 tbs olive oil; 60 g (2 oz) butter; 8 paper-thin slices lemon; $1/2$ tsp chopped fresh rosemary, or pinch dried; 4 tbs dry white wine; salt and freshly ground black pepper.

Sauté veal in oil and half the butter, adding lemon slices to pan for the last 5 minutes of cooking. Remove veal to a heated platter, arrange lemon slices on top and keep warm. Add remaining butter to pan and, when it is frothing, add rosemary and wine. Bring to the boil, stirring in all the brown bits from pan. Season with salt and pepper and spoon over veal. Serves 4.

Veal Chops Stuffed with Cheese

A speciality of the Piedmont region of Italy.

6 veal chops; 125 g (4 oz) Fontina, Gouda or Jarlsberg cheese, thinly sliced; salt and freshly ground white pepper; flour; beaten egg; dry breadcrumbs; 90 g (3 oz) butter.

Slit each chop horizontally almost to bone to make a pocket. Stuff pockets with slices of cheese. Lay chops flat and press edges together, then seal by beating with heel of heavy kitchen knife. Season chops on both sides with salt and pepper, dust with flour and coat with egg and breadcrumbs. Heat butter and fry chops on moderate heat for 10–15 minutes or until golden-brown on both sides and cooked through. Serves 6.

Veal Patties with Sour Cream Sauce

500 g (1 lb) minced veal; 1/2 cup fresh breadcrumbs; 1 tsp grated lemon rind; 1 tsp chopped fresh marjoram, or 1/4 tsp dried; 1/2 tsp chopped fresh rosemary, or 1/4 tsp dried; 1 tsp salt; 1/2 tsp pepper; 2 tbs sour cream; 1 egg; flour; 45 g (1 1/2 oz) butter.

SAUCE: 1 tbs butter; 1 onion, finely chopped; 1 cup sour cream; salt and freshly ground black pepper; pinch nutmeg.

Mix veal, breadcrumbs, lemon rind, herbs, salt, pepper, sour cream and egg. Shape into 8 patties about 2 cm (3/4 in) thick and flour lightly. Heat butter in a heavy frying pan and brown patties on both sides, then turn heat low and cook gently for about 5 minutes more on each side. Remove to a heated platter and keep warm. SAUCE: Add butter and onion to pan and cook until onion is lightly browned. Add sour cream and heat slowly, stirring in all brown bits from pan. Do not allow to boil. Season with salt, pepper and nutmeg, and spoon over patties. Serves 4.

Veal in White Wine

Shoulder veal is good for this, or your butcher may sell lean stewing veal already chopped into cubes.

3 tbs oil; 1.5 kg (3 lb) boneless lean veal, cut into bite-sized cubes; 1 large onion, finely chopped; 1/2 cup tomato pureé; 1 tbs flour; 2 cups chicken stock; 1 cup dry white wine; 1 clove garlic, crushed; 1 bay leaf; 1/2 tsp dried thyme; 1/2 tsp dried rosemary; salt and freshly ground black pepper; chopped parsley to garnish.

VEGETABLE ADDITION: 125 g (4 oz) butter; 12 small white onions; 1 tbs sugar; 12 small mushroom caps; 3 large tomatoes, peeled, quartered and seeded.

Heat oil in a deep, heavy saucepan and brown veal cubes on all sides over medium heat. Add onion and tomato pureé, and stir together for 2 minutes. Mix flour with a little stock, and add to pan with remaining stock and white wine. Add garlic, bay leaf, thyme and rosemary, and season generously with salt and pepper. Stir until boiling, then cover tightly and simmer for 1 hour. Meanwhile, heat half the butter in a heavy frying pan and slowly brown onions over medium heat. Sprinkle with sugar and stir until onions are glazed. Remove onions to a plate. Heat remaining butter in same pan. Add mushroom caps and toss until coated with butter. Remove. Add onions, mushrooms and tomatoes to veal and simmer for a further 30 minutes or until meat is tender. Adjust seasoning, discard bay leaf and spoon into a serving dish. Sprinkle with parsley and serve. Serves 8.

VEGETABLES

See individual entries.

VELOUTE SAUCE

See *Sauces*.

VENISON

Venison is the meat from several species of deer, which may be raised commercially or hunted as game, as in parts of northern Europe. Vension meat is very lean, and joints for roasting may need to be larded or covered with a fine sheet of pork fat. The farm-raised venison is milder in flavour, moister and often younger than game venison, and if cooked quickly and carefully does not need to be larded. Also, it does not need to be hung or marinated, as is sometimes recommended for game.

As with beef, the forequarter cuts of venison are best used in casseroles. The saddle, or both sides of the loin, is roasted while the leg may either be roasted or cut into steaks. Venison steaks should be pan-fried and served fairly rare; overcooked, they are too dry. Marinating

v

steaks in a basic wine-oil marinade helps counteract this dryness.

Traditional vegetable accompaniments to venison include chestnuts, potatoes, Brussels sprouts and lentils. Sauces for venison are usually based on red wine, and red-currant jelly may also accompany venison. See recipes.

Venison Casserole

1 kg (2 lb) boned shoulder venison, sinews removed and cubed; about 2 tbs flour; 2 onions, chopped; 2 tomatoes, peeled, seeded and chopped; 1 bouquet garni; small piece cinnamon stick; 5 pickled walnuts, sliced; salt and freshly ground black pepper; 1 tsp Angostura bitters; 3/4 cup dry red wine.

Coat meat cubes lightly in flour and place in greased casserole. Arrange onions and tomatoes on top, add bouquet garni; cinnamon and walnuts, and season with salt and pepper. Stir bitters into wine and add to the casserole. Cover lightly and cook in a preheated moderate oven (180°C/350°F) for about 2 hours. Discard bouquet garni. Serves 4–6.

Roast Saddle of Venison

1 x 3.5–4 kg (7–8 lb) saddle of venison; 1/2 tsp dried thyme; salt and freshly ground black pepper; 8–10 thin slices pickled (salt) pork; 1/2 cup fresh orange juice; 3 tbs redcurrant jelly; 2 tbs brandy.

Wipe meat with a damp cloth, and rub well with thyme, salt and pepper. Place on rack in roasting tin and cover with pork slices. Roast in a preheated very hot oven (230°C/450°F) for 45–60 minutes (venison is more tender if quite rare). Remove pickled pork, transfer venison to heated plate and keep warm. Skim off excess fat from roasting tin, place tin on heat and add orange juice, scraping up any residue from bottom of pan. Add redcurrant jelly, stirring constantly. Bring to the boil, pour in warmed brandy and flame. Serve immediately with venison. Serves 8.

VERJUICE

The word 'verjuice' comes from the French for green juice, *vert jus*. This gentle acidulant is made from green, unripe grapes or other sour fruits such as crab apples. Verjuice, or, to the Italians, 'agresto', was a common flavouring in the Middle Ages and Renaissance when it was used as we would use lemon juice or vinegar today, to add sharpness to the flavour of food.

Verjuice is excellent used for deglazing a pan to make a sauce. Remove any excess fat from the pan in which meat or vegetables have been roasted or fried, leaving just a little. Add 1 cup verjuice and place over a moderate heat. Scrape up the crusty bits, incorporating them into the verjuice. Reduce until *jus* is just beginning to coat the

spoon. Add a knob of butter for richness and shine and strain into a jug or spoon over the food. Use verjuice in place of vinegar in salad dressings, marinades, and splash a little over cooked vegetables to give them a special tang.

VERMOUTH

Vermouth is an aperitif wine, made by infusing selected herbs and spices in a base wine then fortifying the resultant wine with distilled spirits. There are many brands of vermouth, each with slightly different infusion mixtures, but most brands include a dry white, sweet white and sweet red vermouth.

Because their flavour is more concentrated than that of a table wine, vermouths are particularly useful when finishing a sauce, mixing a forcemeat stuffing or assembling the meats for a pâté or terrine – they flavour without making the mixture too liquid.

Simple and delicious sauces can be quickly made by deglazing a pan in which meat, chicken, scallops or prawns have been pan-fried; try deglazing with dry white vermouth for seafood or veal escalopes, with red vermouth for chicken breasts. Sweet vermouths can enhance the flavour of fresh summer fruit, lightly chilled, and red vermouth can substitute for red wine and some of the sugar when poaching fruits such as prunes or pears. Fresh or poached fruit may also be treated to a sabayon sauce, based on vermouth. See recipes.

Pears in Vermouth

2 cups sweet red vermouth; 1 cup sugar; 1/2 cup orange juice; 1 tsp grated orange rind; 6–8 pears, peeled, halved and cored; 1 lemon, halved.

Combine vermouth, sugar, and orange juice and rind in a saucepan. Bring to the boil, stirring to dissolve sugar, and simmer gently for 5 minutes. Rub pears with lemon to prevent browning. Place pears into simmering syrup, and simmer 8–10 minutes longer or until tender. Cool in syrup, then remove. Reduce syrup to 1 cup by rapid boiling and pour over pears. Cool then chill. Serve chilled, with sweetened whipped cream flavoured with orange liqueur if desired. Serves 6–8.

NOTE: It is preferable to peel and poach only 2 pears at a time in order to prevent any discolouration.

Veal Escalopes with Mushrooms

12 small, thin veal escalopes, trimmed; 60 g (2 oz) butter; 1 tbs oil; 3 tbs chopped shallots; 1/4 cup dry vermouth; 1/2 cup stock; 1 tbs cornflour mixed with 2 tsp water; 1 cup cream; salt and freshly ground black pepper; 250 g (8 oz) mushrooms, sliced.

Fry veal escalopes in 30 g (1 oz) of the butter and oil over moderately high heat for about 4 minutes each side. (It is preferable to cook veal in 3–4 batches, using a proportion of butter and oil for each batch.) Remove escalopes to heated dish when cooked. Pour off some of the oil/butter mixture, leaving 2 tbs. Add shallots and cook gently for 1 minute. Add vermouth and stock and scrape up residue from bottom of pan. Reduce over high heat to about 3 tbs. Blend cornflour mixture with cream, add and boil, stirring, until thickened. Season with salt and pepper, and remove from heat. In a separate pan, fry mushrooms in remaining butter for 4–5 minutes. Season, then add to cream sauce. Simmer for 1 minute. Season escalopes lightly with salt and pepper, and add to sauce in pan. Cover and warm through for 4–5 minutes, basting veal with sauce occasionally. To serve, arrange veal on heated dish and spoon sauce over. Serves 4–6.

VERTE SAUCE

See *Salad Dressing*.

VICTORIA SPONGE

A classic sponge sandwich layered with jam, the top lightly dusted with caster sugar. It keeps well, and was a great favourite at tea parties in Victorian times. The success of the cake depends on the air beaten into the mixture. Use an electric mixer if you wish, or beat by hand using a whisking movement from the wrist, lifting the mixture as you whisk.

Victoria Sponge

2 cups self-raising flour; pinch salt;
250 g (8 oz) butter; ¹/₂ tsp vanilla; 1 cup caster sugar;
4 eggs, beaten; jam; caster sugar to dust.

Sift flour with salt. Cream butter and vanilla thoroughly, then beat in sugar by degree until light and fluffy. Gradually beat in eggs until thoroughly combined. Be careful not to add eggs too quickly or mixture will curdle and texture of cake will be affected. Fold in flour. Spoon mixture into 2 x 20 cm (8 in) sandwich tins that have been greased, bottom-lined with greased greaseproof paper and dusted with flour. Bake in a preheated moderately hot oven (190°C/375°F) for 40–45 minutes or until cakes have shrunk slightly from sides of tins. Turn on to a wire rack to cool. When cold, sandwich together with a good jam of your choice and dust top with caster sugar.

VICHYSSOISE

One of the specialties created by the great French chef Louis Diat for the old Ritz-Carlton in New York. Vichyssoise now appears on restaurant menus throughout the world and is made in many homes. It had its origins in the simple leek and potato soup, *Potage Bonne Femme* of France, which when put through a mouli became *Potage Parmentier*. Both of these soups are served hot.

Casting around for a new cold soup to entice his clientele, Diat remembered how his mother used to cool her potage by adding cold rich milk to it. A cup of cream, an extra straining, a sprinkle of chives *et voilà!* He had his new soup. Diat named it after Vichy, the famous spa located near his boyhood home, as a tribute to the fine cooking of the region.

For recipe see *Soup*.

VINAIGRETTE

The classic vinaigrette or French dressing is a subtle mixture of good quality olive oil, wine vinegar, salt and pepper. To this basic mixture is sometimes added mustard, fresh herbs or, as in southern France, garlic. Flavourings depend on taste and the types of salad the vinaigrette is to dress. Vinaigrette can also be used as a dressing for cooked, cooled vegetables. Serve vegetable vinaigrette as an hors d'oeuvre, or accompaniment to hot or cold meats.

For vinaigrette dressing recipe see *Salad Dressings*.

Vegetable Vinaigrette

500 g (1 lb) vegetables (cauliflower, baby onions, carrots, button mushrooms, patty-pan squash, zucchini, asparagus, green beans, snow peas or mixture).

DRESSING: 3 tbs oil; 1 tbs wine vinegar; 1 clove garlic, crushed; ¹/₂ tsp finely chopped mixed fresh herbs, or 1 tbs parsley chopped with 1 tsp dried mixed herbs; salt and freshly ground black pepper.

Trim vegetables; break cauliflower into florets, cut carrots into sticks. Cook vegetables separately in boiling salted water just until crisp-tender – minutes only for most, 45–50 second for snow peas. Drain and refresh under cold running water. Make a dressing by combining remaining ingredients. Arrange vegetables on a serving dish, spoon dressing over, cover and marinate 2 hours. Serve slightly chilled. Serves 6.

VINEGAR

Vinegar is the acid liquid obtained from various fruits and grains after alcoholic and acetous fermentation takes place. Thus wine vinegar is fermented from fresh wine, malt vinegar is made from malt liquor, cider vinegar from cider, and sweet and sour vinegars from rice wine. They vary greatly in strength and flavour according to the grain or fruit from which they are made.

Vinegar is an essential ingredient in salad dressings, mint and horseradish sauces and can be used sparingly instead of lemon juice in hollandaise, béarnaise and mayonnaise sauces. Many marinades for meat and game contain vinegar (the acid has a tenderising effect), and it is used in pickling of all kinds – fruits, vegetables, meat, fish and eggs.

All vinegars are corrosive so when mixing pickles, or using marinades or any recipes containing vinegar, use utensils made of glass, earthenware, china, or stainless or enamelled steel.

TYPES OF VINEGAR

Wine Vinegar: Wine vinegars can be red or white and are sometimes quite strong, but always have a delicious flavour. They can be diluted according to taste with the additions of a little red or white wine as appropriate. The best and purest wine vinegar probably comes from Orléans in France. Use white wine vinegar in mayonnaise and red or white in vinaigrette.

Balsamic Vinegar: An aged reduction of sweet white grapes boiled to a syrup, produced in the regions of Modena and Reggio in Italy. The grapes are cooked very slowly in copper cauldrons until reduced by over 50 per cent. The resulting 'must' is placed into wooden barrels and an older balsamic vinegar is added to assist in the acetification. Each year the vinegar is transferred to different wood barrels so that the vinegar can obtain some of the flavours of the different woods. The only approved woods are oak, cherry, chestnut, mulberry, acacia, juniper and ash. True aceto balsamic vinegar must be aged a minimum of 10 years. The better balsamic vinegars are aged 25 to 50 years (these balsamics are not to be poured, but used by the drop). Find a good-quality medium-priced one to use in your cooking. In the Middle Ages, it was used as a disinfectant and enjoyed a reputation as a miracle cure, good for everything from sore throats to labour pains.

Cider Vinegar: This has a strong, distinctive flavour and is much sharper than wine vinegar. Makes an excellent vinaigrette to use with a fresh tomato salad.

Malt Vinegar: A strong, dark vinegar made from malted barley. The colour does not necessarily denote the strength as it is sometimes coloured with caramel to varying degrees of brown. Use for pickling.

Distilled or White Vinegar: Not as strong as malt vinegar; use for pickling when the vinegar needs to be clear to enhance the colour of the pickle.

Rice Vinegar: Often used in Asian cooking especially in the Japanese dish Sushi or Vinegared Rice. It has a sweet, delicate flavour.

Flavoured Vinegars: Red or white vinegar and distilled white vinegar can be flavoured with spices, herbs, chillies or garlic. These are steeped in the vinegar for some days, and the liquid is then strained and decanted into sterilised bottles for use. Use flavoured vinegars for salad dressings, sauces and vinaigrettes. See recipes.

Herb Vinegar

1 cup fresh herbs (thyme, mint, tarragon, or basil, etc.); 4 cups red or white wine vinegar.

Pack herbs into jars (use 4 x 1-cup jars or 2 x 2-cup jars), fill with vinegar, cover; store at room temperature. Leave for 2–3 weeks, shaking jars once each day. Strain vinegar into sterilised bottles, insert a few sprigs of chosen herbs, cover and store. Makes 4 cups.

Chilli Vinegar

Add a few drops of this hot vinegar to fresh chutneys that are to accompany curries or use when you want a hot spicy salad dressing.

4–6 fresh chillies, or 1 tbs dried; 2 cups white vinegar or malt vinegar.

Put chillies into a jar. Bring vinegar to the boil and pour over chillies. Cool, cover and store for 5–6 weeks before use, shaking jar occasionally. Makes 2 cups.

Spiced Vinegar

A good, all purpose spiced vinegar for use when pickling. Malt vinegar gives a good flavour, but for a clear pickle use distilled white vinegar.

4 cups vinegar (malt or white); 6 black peppercorns; 6 cloves; 1 cinnamon stick; 5 blades mace; 2 tsp whole allspice.

Place vinegar in saucepan with spices. Bring slowly to boiling point, then remove pan from heat, cover and leave for 2 hours. Strain if desired. Use spiced vinegar cold. Makes 4 cups.

VARIATION

Add one of the following: 1 tbs celery seeds or mustard seeds; 5 cm (2 in) piece fresh ginger; 1 clove garlic; 3 bay leaves.

Pickled Eggs in Spiced Vinegar

12 hard boiled eggs.

SPICED VINEGAR: 2.5 cm (2 in) piece fresh ginger, lightly crushed; 1 tbs white peppercorns; 4 cups white wine vinegar; 4 chillies.

Tie ginger and peppercorns in a muslin bag. Bring vinegar to boiling point and add ginger and peppercorns. Lower heat and simmer for 5 minutes. Allow to cool. Shell eggs and pack into sterilised jars. Put 1 or 2 chillies in each jar and fill with spiced vinegar, making certain eggs are covered completely. Cover and store for 3–4 weeks before using. Makes 4 x 1-cup jars or 2 x 2-cup jars.

Spiced Oranges

4 medium oranges, each cut into 8 wedges;
$^1/_4$ tsp bicarbonate of soda; 1 tsp whole allspice;
12 cloves; 2 cups malt vinegar; 8 cm (3 in) cinnamon
stick; 2.5 cm (1 in) piece fresh ginger; 2 cups sugar.

Put oranges into a saucepan and add water to cover and the bicarbonate of soda. Bring to the boil and simmer gently for 15 minutes. Place remaining ingredients in another saucepan and bring to the boil, stirring until sugar has dissolved. Drain orange wedges and place in vinegar syrup. Cover and simmer for 20 minutes. Remove orange wedges with a slotted spoon and pack into sterilised hot dry jars. Boil syrup and top up jars. Cover and seal. This pickle with be ready in a week. Makes about 6 cups.

VINE LEAVES

Probably the most familiar use of vine leaves in cookery is to stuff them with an aromatic mixture of meats or rice. The result is delicious. These little parcels are enjoyed in the Middle East and Mediterranean countries (see *Dolma, Dolmades*). They are served hot or cold, with or without a sauce.

Quail and other small birds acquire a faint lemony flavour when wrapped first in bacon and then in vine leaves before cooking in a casserole. Vine leaves can also be used to line baskets for bread or fruit for a fresh and pretty effect when entertaining.

Fresh vine leaves for cooking should be medium light green and not too young. Any leaves from any vine bearing edible grapes are suitable. If you do not have fresh vine leaves, buy those preserved in brine available from good delicatessens.

■ **BASIC PREPARATION (FRESH AND PRESERVED VINE LEAVES):** Rinse leaves in cold water. Boil a large saucepan of water, drop in leaves and blanch for 3 minutes to soften leaves. Remove with a slotted spoon to a bowl of cold water, drain and dry with paper towels before using. You may have to blanch leaves in several batches.

TO STUFF VINE LEAVES: Place the leaves shiny side down on a work surface. Trim off stalks. Place filling in centre of each leaf and roll up, turning in sides of leaf so filling is completely encased.

Vine Leaves and Mushrooms

500 g (1 lb) mushrooms; 1 clove garlic;
250 g (8 oz) fresh or preserved vine leaves, blanched;
olive oil; salt and freshly ground black pepper.

Remove and chop mushroom stems finely with garlic. Place vine leaves in layers in bottom of an oiled flameproof dish. Cover them with a film of olive oil and place over moderate heat until oil is hot. Add mushroom caps, stalk side up, cover dish with a lid or foil and cook in a preheated moderate oven (180°C/350°F) for 20 minutes. Remove from oven. Add chopped stems and garlic, and season with salt and pepper. Return to oven and cook for a further 10 minutes. Serve hot as a first course. Serves 4.

VOL-AU-VENT

Ever-popular vol-au-vent are tender light cases of puff pastry containing a filling of seafood, poultry, eggs, ham or vegetables, usually bound with a deliciously creamy sauce. They are versatile enough to be served as hors d'oeuvre in tiny little bite-sized cases or as large individual ones that are perfect as an entrée. Vol-au-vent can also have sweet fillings.

Vol-au-vent cases can be brought prepared and ready to be filled at cake shops, supermarkets and delicatessens or frozen, ready to be baked. You may prefer to shape your own cases using either commercial frozen or home-made puff pastry. **See recipes.**

Basic Vol-au-Vent Cases

1 x 375 g (12 oz) packet frozen puff pastry, thawed,
or 1 quantity Puff Pastry (page 343);
beaten egg yolk to glaze.

Roll out chilled pastry to a thickness of about 5 mm ($^1/_4$ in). Cut in to rounds with a floured pastry cutter to size of your choice. Arrange half the rounds on a dampened baking tray. Cut centre out of remaining rounds with a slightly smaller cutter to leave a ring of pastry about 3 cm (1$^1/_4$ in) wide. Gather trimmings together (do not knead) and roll out to make more vol-au-vent cases. Prick rounds previously placed on tray with a fork and brush edges with water. Carefully place a pastry ring on top of each round and press gently to seal. Mark a crisscross pattern with tip of a sharp knife around tops of rings and brush with a little beaten egg yolk.

Bake on top shelf of a preheated very hot oven (230°C/450°F) for 10 minutes or until well puffed, crisp and golden. Remove any soft dough from inside and cool cases on a wire rack.

One 375 g (12 oz) packet frozen pastry makes 3 x 10 cm (4 in) cases or 9 x 5 cm (2 in) cases. One quantity home-made puff pastry makes 4 x 10 cm (4 in) cases or 12 x 5 cm (2 in) cases.

NOTE: Vol-au-vent cases can be made ahead and stored in an airtight tin. Reheat for 5–6 minutes in a preheated moderate oven (180°C/350°F) when required and spoon hot filling into centre.

FILLINGS FOR VOL-AU-VENT:

The following quantities are sufficient for 2 x 10 cm (4 in) vol-au-vent cases or 12 x 5 cm (2 in) cases.

ASPARAGUS: To 1 cup hot Béchamel Sauce (see page 456), add ½ cup cooked, chopped asparagus. Season with 1 tsp lemon juice, salt and freshly ground black pepper.

CREAMED SPINACH: To 1 cup cooked, well dried, puréed spinach, add ¼ cup sour cream, ¼ tsp nutmeg, and 2 tbs finely chopped shallots fried in 1 tbs butter. Reheat, stirring, before filling cases.

SEAFOOD: To 1 cup cooked shelled prawns, crab or fresh bottled oysters, drained, add ½ cup hot thick Béchamel Sauce (see page 456), 1 tbs cream, 2 drops Tabasco sauce and a squeeze of lemon juice. Season with salt and pepper to taste.

Ham and Egg Vol–au–Vent

4 large vol-au-vent cases, about 10 cm (4 in) diameter; 1 cup diced cooked ham; 2 hard boiled eggs, chopped; 2 shallots, finely chopped; 1 tbs chopped green pepper; 45 g (1½ oz) butter; 1 cup hot Béchamel Sauce (page 456); 1 tsp Dijon mustard; salt and freshly ground black pepper.

Place vol-au-vent cases on a lightly greased baking tray and heat in a preheated moderate oven (180°C/350°F) for 5–6 minutes. Meanwhile, gently fry ham, eggs, shallots and green pepper in butter until hot. Stir into hot sauce with mustard, salt and pepper. Spoon into hot cases. Serves 4.

Chicken Vol–au–Vent

4 large vol-au-vent cases, about 10 cm (4 in) diameter; 1 cup cooked, chopped chicken; 6–8 button mushrooms, sliced; 45 g (1½ oz) butter; ½ tsp Worcestershire sauce; 2 tbs finely chopped pickled cucumbers; 1 cup hot Béchamel Sauce (page 456); salt and freshly ground black pepper; 2 tbs toasted slivered almonds to garnish.

Place vol-au-vent cases on a lightly greased baking tray and heat in a preheated moderate oven (180°C/350°F) for 5–6 minutes. Meanwhile, gently fry chicken and mushrooms in butter until heated through. Stir chicken, mushrooms, Worcestershire sauce and pickles into hot Béchamel Sauce, and season to taste. Spoon into hot cases and sprinkle with almonds. Serves 4.

w

WAFFLE

Waffles have been known and loved in Europe for hundreds of years, their popularity having extended more recently to America and other parts of the western world. French waffles, or *gaufre*, are made from a light spongy batter and emerge from the specially patterned irons puffed, crisp and golden. They are usually sweet and served piping hot with a flavoured butter cream. Scandinavian waffles are often heart-shaped, honeycomb-patterned and served with lingonberries and sour cream or fresh butter. Belgian waffles are sometimes made with a yeast batter and served with fresh strawberries and a very light fluffy cream. But perhaps more familiar are waffles American-style. These are eaten as either a sweet or savoury and at any meal from breakfast to supper.

TO PREPARE A WAFFLE IRON: Follow the manufacturer's directions for seasoning an electric waffle iron before using it for the first time. Once seasoned, the plates usually need not be greased or washed. Simply brush them to remove any crumbs after use and wipe the outside of the iron with a damp cloth.

■ **TO COOK:** Heat the waffle iron until the indicator shows it is ready to use. If using a non-electric iron, heat until a splash of water on its surface sizzles dry. Do not grease because most waffle batters contain enough butter not to need it. Put the batter into a jug. Pour enough batter on to the bottom plate to cover about two thirds of the surface. Close the lid and cook for 3–4 minutes. When the waffle is ready, the steam will have stopped coming from the side and the top will lift off easily. If it does not, leave for another minute to finish cooking. **See recipes.**

WAYS TO SERVE WAFFLES

Have savoury waffles at breakfast or brunch with eggs, ham, bacon or sausage; top them with grilled tomatoes, kidneys, mushrooms or cheese; or for luncheon topped with any creamed vegetable, poultry or ham mixture. Serve sweet waffles at any time with butter and honey or golden syrup; jam and whipped cream; ice cream and caramel or chocolate sauce; butter, lemon or orange juice and sugar; whipped cream and fresh or stewed fruits; or as do the Canadians with unique, delicious maple syrup.

Basic Waffle Batter

If serving with savoury foods, omit the sugar from this recipe. For tender waffles, mix the batter gently and quickly and do not beat.

1³/4 cups flour; 2 tsp baking powder; ¹/2 tsp salt; 1 tbs sugar; 3 eggs, separated; 1¹/2 cups milk; 90 g (3 oz) butter, melted.

Sift flour, baking powder, salt and sugar into a large bowl. Beat egg yolks with milk and melted butter.

Make a well in centre of flour mixture, pour in liquid and with just a few swift strokes combine liquid with flour. The batter will still have small lumps. Beat egg whites until stiff peaks form and fold quickly into batter until barely blended. Cook waffles as described earlier and serve hot. Makes 6–8.

Buttermilk Waffles

2 cups flour; ¹/4 tsp bicarbonate of soda; 1¹/2 tsp baking powder; 1 tbs sugar; ¹/2 tsp salt; 2 eggs, separated; 1³/4 cups buttermilk; 90 g (3 oz) butter, melted.

Sift dry ingredients into a bowl. Beat egg yolks with buttermilk and melted butter and combine with dry ingredients. Whisk egg whites until stiff, but not dry, and fold into batter. Cook waffles as described earlier. Makes 6–8.

Sour Cream Waffles

5 eggs; ¹/2 cup caster sugar; 1 cup flour; 1 tsp baking powder; 1 tsp bicarbonate of soda; 1 tsp ground cardamom or ginger; 1 cup sour cream; 60 g (2 oz) unsalted butter, melted.

Beat eggs and sugar until mixture falls back into bowl in a ribbon when beater is lifted out. Sift together dry ingredients. Using a large metal spoon, fold half dry ingredients into egg mixture, then sour cream and remaining dry ingredients. Stir in butter lightly. Set aside for 10 minutes before using. Cook waffles as described earlier. Serve with berry fruits and sour cream. Makes 12.

WALDORF SALAD

Invented for the opening of New York's Waldorf-Astoria Hotel, Waldorf salad has become a classic, especially good with ham and chicken.

See also *Chicken Waldorf* (page 434) and *Waldorf Coleslaw* (page 441).

Waldorf Salad

3 unpeeled green and red apples, cored and diced; 1 cup diced celery; ³/4 cup Mayonnaise (page 256); salt and freshly ground black pepper; ¹/2 cup walnut pieces.

Mix apples and celery in a bowl, add mayonnaise and fold through. Season, add walnuts and fold through. Turn into a salad bowl and serve at once. Serves 6–8.

VARIATION

WALDORF SALAD WITH SOUR CREAM: Follow recipe for Waldorf Salad, but use ¹/2 cup sour cream and ¹/4 cup mayonnaise for the dressing.

WALNUT

The walnut has a long history; the Romans considered it the nut of Jupiter, and food fit for the gods. Native to Persia, walnut trees were introduced to Rome by the Greeks, and Roman legionaries carried the nut with them to England, where they soon become established. Later, however, many trees in both Europe and England were cut down to satisfy the demand for walnut furniture. Walnuts contain a very high proportion of oil, and walnut oil is much sought after especially for salads, where it imparts a mild but distinctive taste. Because of the high oil content, however, it is difficult to make cakes with ground walnuts, in the same way as with ground almonds.

There are countless uses for walnuts, both sweet and savoury. Try walnuts with a blue vein cheese, especially Roquefort; add walnuts to a salad of cos lettuce; make a Waldorf Salad with walnuts, celery, apple and mayonnaise (opposite). Walnuts are combined with meat and chicken in Chinese cooking, and can be added into the stuffing for quail or other birds. Ground walnuts form the basis of several Middle Eastern sauces for cold fish or poultry.

Honey and walnuts make a superb combination in biscuits and desserts; in Greece, yogurt is often served drizzled with honey and topped with walnuts. Dates, raisins and other dried fruit go well with walnuts, and delectable caramel and chocolate fudges (see page 168) can be made with walnuts. Young green walnuts are sometimes pickled in a spiced vinegar, after first soaking in brine and may be served with cheese.

TO BLANCH (PEEL) WALNUTS: Walnuts are usually used unblanched, but for a few delicate dishes such as Walnut Soup (pages 485–6), the skin should be removed. Cover the shelled nuts with cold water, bring to the boil and simmer a few minutes. Remove from heat. Take nuts one at a time from water and use a sharp knife to peel off as much skin as possible. It is a time-consuming job. Peeled walnuts are available in cans or from Chinese food stores.

Compote of Pears and Prunes with Walnuts

750 g (1¹/₂ lb) small pears, peeled; 250 g (8 oz) prunes;
³/₄ cup walnut halves; 1¹/₂ cups dry red wine;
1¹/₄ cups sugar; small cinnamon stick; 2 bay leaves.

Place pears, prunes and walnuts in a saucepan, and add wine, sugar, cinnamon and bay leaves. Cook very gently for about 20 minutes or until pears are tender. Cool, then cover and allow to macerate for a day. Remove cinnamon and bay leaves, if liked, before serving. Serves 6.

Walnut Sauce for Pasta

¹/₂ cup cream; ³/₄ cup walnut pieces, finely chopped;
salt and freshly ground black pepper;
grated Parmesan cheese to serve.

Heat cream gently and stir in walnuts. Season well with salt and pepper. Pour sauce over hot cooked pasta, and offer grated Parmesan cheese separately. Makes about 1 cup sauce or enough for 2 servings of pasta.

Walnut Butter Biscuits

250 g (8 oz) butter; 1¹/₂ cups icing sugar, sifted; 1 egg;
1 tsp vanilla; 2¹/₂ cups flour; ¹/₂ tsp bicarbonate of
soda; 1 tsp baking powder; ¹/₄ tsp salt;
1¹/₂ cups finely chopped walnuts;
walnut halves to decorate.

Cream butter with icing sugar. Add egg and vanilla, and beat well. Sift flour with bicarbonate of soda, baking powder and salt. Stir into creamed mixture with chopped nuts. Form mixture into small balls, place on greased baking trays and top each with a walnut half. Bake in a preheated moderately hot oven (190°C/375°F) for 10–12 minutes or until lightly browned. Cool on wire racks. Makes about 36.

Walnut Bread

3 cups flour; 1 tsp salt; 3 tsp baking powder;
1 cup caster sugar; 1 cup walnut pieces;
1 egg, beaten; 1 cup milk.

Sift flour, salt and baking powder into a bowl. Add sugar and walnuts, then stir in egg and milk. Mix until smooth. Turn into two 21 x 11 cm (8¹/₂ x 4¹/₂ in) greased loaf tins. Bake in a preheated oven (180°C/350°F) for 45 minutes or until a skewer inserted in centre comes out clean. Cool on wire rack. Serve sliced with butter, and cheese if desired. Makes 2.

Maple Walnut Pie

1 cup maple syrup; ¹/₂ cup plus 3 tbs water;
3 tbs cornflour; 60 g (2 oz); Sweet Rich Shortcrust
Pastry, made with 2 cups flour (page 342);
1 cup coarsely chopped walnuts.

Bring maple syrup and ¹/₂ cup water to the boil and boil for 2 minutes. Mix cornflour and remaining water together in a small bowl, then add to boiling syrup, stirring constantly. Cook about 2 minutes or until mixture thickens. Remove from heat, stir in butter, and cool quickly by placing pan in refrigerator. Line a 20 cm (8 in) pie plate with a little more than half the pastry. Pour in cooled syrup mixture and sprinkle walnuts on top. Roll out remaining pastry and cover pie, crimping edges to seal. Cut a few slashes in centre of pastry lid to allow steam to escape. Bake in centre of a preheated hot oven (200°C/400°F) for 30 minutes. Serve warm or at room temperature with a bowl of whipped cream if liked. Serves 6–8.

Walnut Chocolate Cake

This cake, a specialty from northern Italy, is baked in a shallow tart or pie tin and is about 2.5 cm (1 in) thick when baked. It is a superb mixture with the tang of citrus.

30 g (1 oz) butter, melted; 2 tbs fine dry breadcrumbs; 5 eggs, separated; ²/₃ cup caster sugar; 1¹/₂ cups freshly ground walnuts; 155 g (5 oz) dark chocolate, grated; grated rind ¹/₂ lemon; ¹/₃ cup chopped mixed candied peel; icing sugar, sifted.

Brush melted butter over bottom and sides of a 25 cm (10 in) straight-sided tart or pie plate. Sprinkle breadcrumbs over bottom and side and shake out excess. Beat egg yolks with sugar until light and fluffy. Add ground walnuts, grated chocolate, lemon rind and peel, and mix thoroughly. Whisk egg whites until stiff peaks form and fold gently into walnut mixture. Pour into prepared tin. Bake cake in a preheated moderate oven (180°C/350°F) for about 1 hour or until a skewer inserted in centre comes out clean. Turn cake on to a wire rack to cool. Sprinkle sifted icing sugar over top and serve in thin wedges.

Cheese and Walnuts Rounds

Beautifully flavoured savoury biscuits with a crisp, tender shortbread texture.

220 g (7 oz) butter, softened; 1¹/₂ cups grated mature Cheddar cheese; 4 tbs finely chopped walnuts; 2 tsp finely snipped chives; 2¹/₄ cups flour; ¹/₄ cup ground rice; pinch cayenne; ¹/₂ tsp salt.

Cream butter and beat in cheese a little at a time. Stir in 2 tbs walnuts and chives. Sift flour, ground rice, cayenne and salt together and stir into butter mixture. Pinch off pieces of dough and roll into balls about 2.5 cm (1 in) diameter. Flatten between your hands. Place a little apart on greased baking trays, brush lightly with cold water and sprinkle with remaining walnuts. Bake in a preheated moderate oven (180°C/350°F) for about 15 minutes or until lightly browned. Cool on baking tray for 3 minutes, then remove and cool completely on a wire rack. Store in an airtight container and serve cold or slightly warmed. Makes about 60.

Walnut Sauce for Ice Cream

1¹/₂ cups caster sugar; ¹/₂ cup water; 1 cup walnut pieces; pinch salt; 1 tsp vanilla.

Bring sugar and water to the boil, stirring until sugar has dissolved. Boil, without stirring, until thick and syrupy. Add walnuts, salt and vanilla, and cook 2 minutes longer. Serve spooned over vanilla ice cream. Makes about 2 cups.

WASABI

Japanese wasabi is seldom found in its fresh form though it is now being grown in Tasmania. The fresh root is peeled and grated on tiny graters and is searingly hot, like common horseradish or hot English mustard, so you need only a little. It is found commercially in several forms: a light green powder which is reconstituted with a little water; and in squeezable tubes. Serve in a little mound in a small dish with Japanese dishes or add to salads and dressings. It is the traditional accompaniment to sashimi and sushi along with soy sauce.

Cured Tuna with Wasabi Dressing

At city fish markets you can buy top quality fresh tuna. Alternatively use salmon or ocean trout fillets.

1 tbs chopped dill; 1 tsp fine sea salt; 1 tsp coarsely ground white pepper; 1 tsp sugar; 500 g (1 lb) sashimi tuna or salmon; 2 tbs olive oil; 2 Lebanese cucumbers; 3 tbs lime juice; 1 tbs sesame oil; 1 tsp wasabi paste.

Mix together the dill, salt, pepper and sugar. Sprinkle half of this over a plate large enough to hold all the fish. Lay the fish on top and scatter over the remaining curing mixture. Sprinkle with 1 tbs of the olive oil. Cover with plastic wrap or foil and marinate for 24 to 36 hours, turning the fish a few times.

Lift the fish out on a board and scrape away the curing mixture. Cut into thin slices. Lightly peel the green from the cucumber and shred coarsely into long strips. Place a pile of cucumber on each serving plate. Arrange the cured fish slices on the cucumber decoratively. Mix the lime juice and olive oil together with the sesame oil and wasabi and drizzle this mixture over each serving. Serves 6.

WATER CHESTNUTS

These crunchy morsels are the bulb of an aquatic plant. Peeled, canned water chestnuts, whole or sliced, are available in most supermarkets as well as in Chinese food stores, and fresh water chestnuts are sometimes to be found in Chinese greengrocers. Use a sharp knife to peel the dark skin from fresh water chestnuts before using them. Store peeled, fresh or canned water chestnuts, covered with water, in the refrigerator, changing water daily. They will keep for about a week.

Water chestnuts are frequently used in Chinese cookery, and their delicate flavour and crisp texture are pleasant in salads and hors d'oeuvre, and with other vegetables. **See recipes.**

Chicken Liver and Water Chestnut Appetisers

1 x 230 g can whole water chestnuts, drained; 500g (1 lb) chicken livers; 250 g (8 oz) bacon rashers, cut thin, rind removed.

**FRENCH DRESSING: **1 tbs wine vinegar; $^1/_2$ tsp salt; freshly ground black pepper; 3 tbs vegetable oil.

Slice water chestnuts thickly if large. Place in a small bowl.

FRENCH DRESSING: Mix vinegar with salt and pepper, and beat in oil with a fork or whisk. Pour over water chestnuts and set aside. Trim membrane and any dark parts from livers and cut in halves or quarters if large. Stretch bacon with back of knife and cut into pieces about 9 cm (3$^1/_2$ in) long. Wrap a piece of chicken liver and water chestnut in each piece of bacon and secure with a wooden toothpick. Cook under a preheated medium grill for 3–4 minutes on each side. Makes about 20.

Stir-fried Beans and Water Chestnuts

1 tbs cornflour; $^1/_2$ cup chicken stock; 1 tbs oil (preferably peanut); 500 g (1 lb) green beans, cut into 5 cm (2 in) lengths; 1 tsp sugar; 1 x 230 g can water chestnuts, drained and sliced if whole; 1 tbs dry sherry; light soy sauce; hot steamed rice to serve.

Mix cornflour with 1 tbs chicken stop. Heat oil in a wok or heavy frying pan, add beans and stir-fry on moderate heat for 3 minutes. Stir in sugar, water chestnuts, remaining stock and sherry. Cover and simmer 2 minutes. Add soy sauce to taste. Stir cornflour mixture again, add to pan and stir until beans are lightly glazed. Serve immediately on hot steamed rice. Serves 4.

Stir-fried Pork with Water Chestnuts

2 tbs peanut oil; 1 large clove garlic, sliced; 1 tsp grated fresh ginger; 250 g (8 oz) pork fillet, cut across grain into strips about 8 x 1 cm (3 x $^1/_2$ in); 1 x 230 g can water chestnuts, drained and sliced if whole or $^1/_2$ cup fresh sliced; 2 tsp light soy sauce; 1 tsp sugar; 1 tsp Chinese rice wine, or 1 tsp gin; 1$^1/_2$ cups chicken stock; 1 tbs cornflour; 3 drops dark Oriental sesame oil; 2 spring onions, sliced on long diagonal into shreds; hot steamed rice to serve.

Heat a wok or heavy frying pan, add oil and when it begins to give off a slight haze, add garlic and ginger and stir-fry for 15 seconds. Add pork and stir-fry until browned, about 5 minutes. Add water chestnuts and stir-fry for 1 minute, then add soy sauce, sugar and wine or gin. Stir for 30 seconds, then add 1 cup stock, cover and cook on a moderate heat for 5 minutes. Mix cornflour with remaining stock, add and stir until liquid is thickened. Add sesame oil and half the spring onions, mix well and serve, garnished with remaining spring onions, on hot steamed rice. Serves 4.

WATERCRESS

See *Cress*.

WATERMELON

See *Melon*.

WATERZOOI (WATERZOOTJE)

A hearty Flemish dish resembling a soup stew and made with either chicken and vegetables or fish. Sometimes the liquid is served separately as soup, sometimes the solids are served over rice, and at other times the liquid and solids are served together. Whichever way it is served, Waterzooi is satisfying, warming and delicious. Have plenty of crusty bread to go with it and a good crisp tossed salad to follow. **See recipes.**

Waterzooi de Poisson
(Flemish Fish Soup)

60 g (2 oz) butter; 3 sticks celery, chopped; 1 kg (2 lb) mixed fish steaks, skinned and boned; salt and freshly ground black pepper; $^3/_4$ cup dry white wine; $^1/_4$ tsp dried thyme; 1 bay leaf; 1 sprig fresh basil; 2 cups hot boiled rice.

Melt half the butter in a deep, heavy saucepan. Add celery and arrange fish on top. Season well with salt and pepper. Add wine and enough water to cover fish. Sprinkle with herbs and add remaining butter, cut into small pieces. Bring to the boil, then cover and simmer very gently until fish is cooked, about 15–20 minutes depending on thickness of steaks. Put hot rice in 4 bowls, lift fish steaks from soup with an egg slice and place on top of rice. Pour hot cooking liquid over fish or serve it separately in other bowls. Serves 4–6.

Chicken Waterzooi

125 g (4 oz) butter; 1 kg (2 lb) boneless chicken meat, cut into large chunks; 6 sticks celery, chopped; 4 sprigs parsley; 4 leeks, sliced; 1 onion, chopped; 1 bay leaf; $^1/_4$ tsp nutmeg; 4 black peppercorns; salt; 6–8 cups chicken stock; 2 tsp lemon slices to garnish.

Heat butter in a deep, heavy saucepan and brown chicken pieces. Add celery, parsley, leeks, onion, bay leaf, nutmeg, peppercorns and salt. Pour in stock, adding a little extra if necessary to cover chicken, and bring to the boil. Skim surface, then lower heat, cover, and simmer very gently for about 30 minutes or until chicken is tender. Using a slotted spoon, remove chicken and keep warm. Strain liquid into a clean saucepan and add lemon juice. Beat together egg yolks and cream and add to liquid. Cook over a gentle heat, stirring constantly, until soup thickens slightly. Do not let it boil. Return chicken to soup, pour into a heated tureen and float lemon slices on top. Serves 6–8.

WELSH RAREBIT (RABBIT)

Versions of this dish have existed for a long time in England and Scotland as well as Wales. 'Rabbit' seems to be an older version of the name.

Welsh Rarebit

I cup grated mature cheese; ¹/₄ cup beer;
¹/₄ cup milk or cream; ¹/₂ tsp dry mustard; salt;
cayenne; 15 g (¹/₂ oz) butter; I egg, well beaten;
4 slices buttered toast.

Put cheese, beer and milk or cream into a small saucepan and heat gently, stirring, until cheese melts. Remove from heat and stir in mustard, salt, cayenne, butter and egg. Return to low heat and stir until mixture thickens a little, do not allow to boil. Pour over toast and serve at once. Serves 4.

VARIATION

BUCK RAREBIT: Top each serving of Welsh Rarebit with a poached egg.

WHISKY (WHISKEY)

Whisky or Scotch is, of course, the national drink of Scotland, and it is hardly surprising that it should find its way into many of the traditional dishes of that country. Scottish grouse might be cooked with whisky; Atholl Brose is a drink made of honey, oatmeal and whisky; the same basic ingredients, with cream, make a dessert know as Cranachan (see page 303); whisky is sprinkled over strawberries before serving; and whisky can flavour little after-dinner biscuits.

Apart from Scottish fare, whisky can be used for almost any chafing dish recipe. It can replace brandy in fruit cakes, giving a delightfully different flavour; a Christmas pudding can even be served with a whisky butter sauce. There is also the differently spelt 'whiskey' of Ireland and the bourbon whiskey of America. These can be used in the same way as Scotch or other whiskies for many culinary purposes. See recipes.

See also *Irish Coffee* and *Coffee: Ice Cream, Coffee and Scotch.*

Whisky Prawns

I tbs olive oil; 60 g (2 oz) butter; 2 tbs finely chopped shallots; I clove garlic, crushed;
500 g (I lb) green prawns, shelled and deveined;
2 ripe tomatoes, peeled, seeded and diced; salt and freshly ground black pepper; tiny pinch cayenne;
¹/₂ cup whisky; ¹/₂ cup dry white wine; hot steamed rice to serve; ¹/₃ cup cream; I tbs cornflour mixed with I tbs milk; I egg yolk.

Heat oil in a frying pan, add butter and, when melted, add shallot and garlic. Cook gently for 3 minutes. Add prawns, tomatoes, salt, pepper and cayenne and cook gently, turning over with an egg slice, for

3 minutes or until prawns change colour. Pour over half the whisky, set alight and shake pan until flames die down. Add wine and simmer 3 minutes. Remove prawns to a bed of hot steamed rice and keep warm. Add remaining whisky and cream to pan and heat until boiling, then add cornflour mixture, stirring until mixture boils again. Stir a little sauce into egg yolk, return to pan and stir for 1 minute without boiling. Adjust seasoning, pour over prawns and serve immediately. Serves 4–6.

Veal Kidneys with Whisky

2 veal kidneys, skinned, cored and cut into I cm
(¹/₂ in) slices; seasoned flour; 90 g (3 oz) butter;
¹/₄ cup whisky; ¹/₂ cup cream;
salt and freshly ground black pepper.

Soak kidney slices for 30 minutes in cold water. Drain and dry well on paper towels. Coat in seasoned flour. Heat butter until just beginning to brown, add kidneys and fry on moderate heat just until slices are stiffened and lightly browned on both sides. Remove slices as they are done, and keep them warm. Return all slices to pan. Pour whisky over and set alight. Shake pan until flames die down, then add cream and simmer gently for 5 minutes. Season with salt and pepper and serve immediately with boiled rice or toast points. Serves 3–4.

Atholl Brose

A strong drink; Scots keep it on hand to buck the spirits!

²/₃ cup oatmeal; about ²/₃ cup water; 2 tbs honey;
about 4 cups Scotch whisky.

Put oatmeal into a bowl and mix with water until it is a thick paste. Allow to stand for 30 minutes, then drain off liquid, pressing down well with a spoon so that oatmeal is quite dry. Discard oatmeal. Combine liquid and honey, stirring until well blended. Pour into two 750 ml (3-cup) bottles and fill up with whisky. Cork well. Shake before using. Serves about 25.

VARIATION

A pleasant dessert can be made by pouring 2 tbs liquid Atholl Brose into tall glasses, and topping up with whipped cream. Chill and serve sprinkled with oatmeal that has been toasted in a dry hot frying pan for a few minutes or until crisp, stirring frequently, to give a nutty flavour.

Whisky Boiled Fruit Cake

125 g (4 oz) butter or margarine; I cup milk;
I cup sugar; 500 g (I lb) mixed dried fruit;
I tsp mixed spice; ¹/₂ tsp cinnamon; ¹/₄ cup whisky;
I scant tsp bicarbonate of soda; 2 eggs, beaten;
I cup self-raising flour; I cup plain flour.

Place butter, milk, sugar, fruit and spices in a saucepan, bring to the boil, cover and simmer for 5 minutes. Cool a little, then stir in whisky and bicarbonate of soda and allow to cool completely. Add beaten eggs and mix well. Sift flours together and fold into mixture, then spoon into a greased and bottom-lined 20 cm (8 in) cake in. Bake in a preheated moderate oven (180°C/350°F) for 1 hour or until a skewer inserted in centre comes out clean. Cool in tin.

WHITEBAIT

Whitebait are tiny fish, the 'fry' or young of sprats and herrings and other similar fish. They are eaten whole, usually either fried or in fritters.

Purchase whitebait as fresh as possible from good reliable suppliers and cook on the same day. Allow 125 g (4 oz) whitebait per person.

Canned whitebait can be used in exactly the same ways as fresh whitebait. They should be well drained before use, and patted dry with paper towels if they are to be fried. **See recipes.**

Fried Whitebait

¹/₂ cup flour; salt and freshly ground black pepper; 500 g (1 lb) whitebait; oil for deep frying; lemon wedges to serve.

Sift flour with salt and pepper and lightly coat whitebait, shaking gently to remove excess flour. Heat oil until just starting to smoke. Fry whitebait for 2–3 minutes. Cook only as many whitebait as will cover bottom of frying basket. Drain on crumpled paper towels. When all are cooked, return all whitebait to frying basket and fry quickly for a few seconds a second time until crisp and golden. Drain on paper towels, and serve with lemon wedges and fingers of brown bread and butter. Serves 4.

Whitebait Fritters

2 eggs; 250 g (8 oz) fresh whitebait; salt and freshly ground black pepper; peanut oil for frying; sprigs parsley to garnish; lemon wedges to serve.

Beat eggs, add whitebait and stir until well mixed. Season with salt and pepper. Heat enough oil to cover bottom of frying pan with a thin film. Spoon in about 1 tbs whitebait mixture to make a large fritter. Fry 2 minutes each side or until golden. Garnish with parsley and serve with lemon wedges. Makes 4–6 large fritters.

WHITE SAUCE

See *Sauces; Béchamel Sauce.*

WITLOF

See *Chicory.*

WINE

The reason for cooking with wines is that they give depth and richness to the flavours of food. Now that well-made, inexpensive wines are available in the ingenious casks, which enable you to tap off just a glassful, as well as in flagons and bottles, it seems as natural to have wine at hand in the kitchen as to have onions or butter or eggs.

Quick dishes and family meals can benefit as much from wine as food for special occasions. Add a touch of white wine to a salad dressing or sprinkle a little on the potatoes for potato salad while they are still warm. Add a dash of white wine to the pan juices for basting a chicken. Swirl a glassful round the pan in which you have cooked ham steaks, pork chops, fish or veal; boil for a minute, stirring to pick up all the good brown bits, season and pour over the meat. Make a quick snack of toast with a wine and cheese topping, or a tasty wine-flavoured Savoury Charlotte with ingredients you probably have on the shelf. Poach or bake fruit in wine; add a little white wine to carrots as they glaze. Use ½ cup wine as the liquid for a pot roast; stir a spoonful of red or white wine into gravy or soup; make a quick red wine pan sauce for sausages, kidneys or hamburgers. All these ideas are easy, and all lift everyday eating.

WINES FOR COOKING

The only firm rule is that the wine you cook with should be one that you would drink. There is no need to sacrifice a fine bottle to the cooking pot, but wine for cooking should always be sound and pleasant to your palate. When it is added toward the end of cooking time or when the dish is cooked for only a short time, the full character of the wine comes through so it is worth using the best you can. This need not be extravagant since you usually add only a spoonful or so if the cooking time is short.

In general, cook with the wine that you would drink with the food – white wine for white meats, seafood and chicken, red wine for darker meats such as beef, lamb and duck. There are exceptions – Coq au Vin is an example of chicken cooked in red wine, Alsatian Lamb is cooked in white wine. Fruits, vegetables and cheese may go with either red or white wine in different dishes.

If you have leftover table wine to use for cooking, cork the bottle tightly and store it in the refrigerator. It will last 4–5 days before turning vinegary. Use wooden spoons and pans with a non-metal lining when you are cooking with wine, as it readily picks up a metallic taste.

HOW MUCH TO USE: Do not think that if a little wine improves a dish, a lot will make it better. Moderation is the key word. Think in terms of a wine glassful (about ½ cup) if it will be cooked with other ingredients for some time, a spoonful or two if it will be cooked briefly.

The purpose of the wine is to enhance the flavour of the food, not to dominate it. Follow a recipe or, if you are adding wine to a basic recipe, follow these guidelines and proceed with discretion, tasting often. **See recipes.**

White Wine Cheese Toast

**60 g (2 oz) butter; 1¹/₂ tbs flour; 1 cup warm milk;
1¹/₂ cups grated Gruyère cheese; ¹/₂ cup dry white wine;
1 clove garlic, crushed; 1 egg, beaten;
salt and freshly ground black pepper; nutmeg;
1 loaf French bread.**

Melt butter in a small heavy saucepan, add flour and stir over gentle heat for 1 minute. Remove from heat and cool a little, then add milk, stirring until smoothly blended. Return to heat and stir until boiling. Add cheese, wine, garlic, egg, salt, pepper and nutmeg. Stir just until cheese melts, then remove from heat. Slice bread on diagonal into 10–12 thick slices. Toast lightly on one side under a preheated grill, then spread other side generously with cheese mixture and grill under medium heat until lightly browned. Serves 6.

Savoury Charlotte

A substantial luncheon or supper dish made from ingredients you probably have on hand.

**1 clove garlic, crushed; salt; 60 g (2 oz) butter,
softened; 8 slices stale white bread; 6 eggs;
¹/₂ cup cream; ¹/₂ cup chicken stock; 1¹/₂ cups dry white
wine; 1 tbs chopped shallot; 250 g (8 oz) Cheddar
cheese, grated; 125 g (4 oz) button mushrooms, sliced
or 1 x 440 g can salmon, drained, skin and bones
removed and flesh coarsely flaked;
white pepper; lemon juice.**

Crush garlic with a little salt and beat into butter. Remove crusts from bread and spread slices with garlic butter. Cut into fingers and use to line bottom and sides of a 20 cm (8 in) soufflé dish, placing buttered side against dish. Reserve any leftover fingers for top of charlotte. Beat eggs with cream, and add chicken stock, wine, shallot, cheese and mushrooms or salmon. Season with salt, pepper and lemon juice. Pour gently into bread-lined dish and top with any remaining bread fingers, buttered side out. Bake in a preheated moderate oven (180°C/350°F) for 35–40 minutes or until a knife inserted in centre comes out clean. Serves 6.

Veal Chops Braised with Herbs

**1 tbs oil; 30 g (1 oz) butter; 4 thick veal chops;
salt and freshly ground black pepper;
2 tbs chopped shallot; ¹/₂ cup dry white wine or
vermouth; 2 tsp chopped fresh basil or tarragon,
or ¹/₂ tsp dried; ¹/₂ cup cream.**

Heat oil and butter and brown chops for 3–4 minutes on each side. Season with salt and pepper. Arrange in a single layer in a flameproof casserole. Add shallot to frying pan and cook gently 5 minutes. Add wine and basil or tarragon and simmer 3 minutes. Pour over chops. Cover and bake in a preheated moderate oven (180°C/350°F) for 20 minutes or until chops are tender. Lift out chops and place on a heated serving dish. Add cream to casserole and stir over gentle heat until heated through. Pour over veal and serve. Serves 4.

Dixie Steak

A vigneron's recipe for a savoury casserole that is almost magically easy.

**750 g (1¹/₂ lb) blade steak, cut into 2.5 cm (1 in) cubes;
¹/₂ tsp curry powder; 1¹/₂ tsp sugar; 1 tbs flour;
salt and freshly ground black pepper; 1 onion, sliced;
1 green or red pepper, cored, seeded and sliced;
1 cup red wine; 1 cup water.**

Place steak cubes in a casserole. Combine curry powder, sugar, flour, salt and pepper and sprinkle over meat. Cover with sliced onion and pepper; mix wine and water and pour over. Cook in a preheated moderately hot oven (190°C/375°F) for 1¹/₂ hours or until meat is tender. Serves 4–6.

Daube à l'Avignonnaise

A daube is a dish of meat cooked very slowly in a flavoursome wine stock. The meat is often larded with pickled (salt) pork or bacon and marinated first for deep, rich flavour. You can make the daube a day ahead, chill and remove fat from the surface, then reheat it gently when wanted.

**2 kg (4 lb) boned leg of lamb; 4 cloves of garlic;
2 tbs finely chopped parsley; 125 g (4 oz) bacon or
speck; 4 large onions, sliced; 2–3 carrots, chopped;
salt and freshly ground black pepper; 1 tsp crumbled
dried herbs (thyme, bay leaf, marjoram);
1¹/₂ cups red wine; ¹/₄ cup brandy;
4 tbs Beurre Manié (page 35, optional).**

Cut lamb into large pieces, each weighing about 90 g (3 oz), and cut a small, deep slit in each. Crush 1 clove garlic and mix with parsley. Cut bacon into pieces about thickness of your little finger and half the length, one for each piece of lamb. Roll these bacon pieces in parsley and garlic mixture and insert a piece of bacon into each piece of lamb. Put meat in a glass or earthware dish with half the onions, the carrots, salt, pepper and herbs. Pour over red wine and brandy and leave to marinate for 4–5 hours. Cut remaining bacon into squares and put bacon and oil into a heavy flameproof casserole. Cook gently until bacon fat runs, then add remaining onions and brown. Add meat, orange rind and remaining whole garlic cloves. Pour over marinade and simmer until liquid is reduced by one third. Cover very tightly and place in a preheated slow oven (150°C/300°F). Cook for 4–5 hours. If desired, thicken sauce by placing casserole over low heat on top of stove and whisking in beurre manié, a little at a time. Serves 8.

VARIATION

DAUBE MEDITERRANEE: Follow recipe for Daube à l'Avignonnaise, but add 12 stoned black olives and 125 g (4 oz) sliced mushrooms after 2 hours cooking in the oven.

Rhineland Pork Stew

60 g (2 oz) butter; 1 large onion, chopped; 2 tbs flour; 2 cups stock or water; salt and freshly ground black pepper; 6 cloves; 1 bay leaf; 1 x 425 g can tomatoes, drained; 1 kg (2 lb) boneless pork shoulder, cut into 2.5 cm (1 in) cubes; ¼ cup white wine.

Melt butter in a large heavy saucepan. Add onion and cook until softened but not browned. Sprinkle flour over onion and cook, stirring for 5 minutes or until flour has turned a golden colour. Add stock or water gradually and stir until smooth and thickened. Add salt, pepper, cloves, bay leaf and tomatoes. Cover and simmer 10 minutes. Add pork and wine and simmer, covered, for 1½ hours or until meat is tender. Discard bay leaf and cloves. Serves 4–6.

Alsatian Lamb

A recipe from the province of Alsace in France where they produce a lovely riesling of delicate flavour and bouquet.

1 small leg of lamb; 1½ cups dry white wine; 1 clove garlic, crushed; 1 onion, studded with 4 cloves; 1 bay leaf; 3 carrots, sliced; 1 tsp chopped fresh thyme, or ¼ tsp dried; salt and freshly ground black pepper; 250 g (8 oz) long bacon rashers; 1 cup stock or vegetable water; 1 tsp arrowroot (optional).

Remove excess fat from lamb. Combine wine, garlic, onion, bay leaf, carrots, thyme, salt and pepper in a large bowl. Marinate lamb in wine mixture for 12 hours. Drain, reserving marinade. Wrap lamb in bacon rasher, securing with wooden toothpicks. Place on a rack in a roasting tin and add about 1 cup marinade. Place in a preheated very hot oven (230°C/450°F) and reduce to moderate (180°C/350°F). Roast lamb for 1–1½ hours or until cooked, basting every 15 minutes with marinade. Remove lamb to a heated platter and leave in turned-off oven with door ajar while you make gravy.

Remove rack from roasting tin and place tin on top of stove. Add stock or vegetable water and boil rapidly, stirring often, until liquid is reduced to about 1 cup. If you like, thicken gravy slightly by stirring in arrowroot blended with a little cold water. Strain gravy into a heated sauceboat. Serve lamb with gravy, small boiled potatoes and whole green beans. Serves 4–6.

NOTE: Although white wine is used in the cooking of Alsatian Lamb, you might like to drink a good red wine with the meal.

Poulet au Citron

Chicken with lemon cream sauce is an example of using a good white table wine to add flavour to a sauce. Use the wine you intend to serve with the dish – serve it chilled, of course. Creamy mashed potatoes are lovely with this dish, followed by a crisp green salad tossed in a little Mustard Vinaigrette Dressing (see page 442).

1 lemon; 100 g (3½ oz) butter; 2 kg (4 lb) chicken pieces (half-breasts, thighs, drumsticks); 1 tbs sherry; ½ cup white wine; grated rind 1 orange; salt and freshly ground white pepper; ¾ cup cream; little grated cheese.

Grate rind from lemon and set aside. Peel lemon and slice thinly. Heat 90 g (3 oz) butter in a large frying pan and, when foaming, brown chicken on all sides. Reduce heat, cover pan and cook – shaking the pan and turning chicken every now and then – for 10–15 minutes or until chicken is nearly cooked.

Remove chicken, add sherry and wine to pan. Stir over moderate heat, picking up brown bits from bottom of pan, for a few minutes. Add orange and lemon rinds and season with salt and pepper. Turn heat to high and stir in cream slowly. The sauce should thicken a little. Put back chicken and turn to coat with sauce. Heat through for a few minutes. Arrange on a heated flameproof serving dish, spoon over sauce and sprinkle with cheese. Put a few slices of lemon and remaining butter, in small pieces, on top. Brown under a preheated grill. Serves 6.

Poulet Basque

8 chicken pieces (drumsticks, thighs, half-breasts); salt and freshly ground black pepper; 3 tbs oil; 4 large tomatoes, peeled, seeded and coarsely chopped; 1 large green and 1 large red pepper, seeded and cut in julienne (matchstick) strips; 90 g (3 oz) mushrooms, sliced; 185 g (6 oz) cooked ham, diced; ½ cup dry white wine; 1 tbs chopped parsley.

Season chicken with salt and pepper and brown in oil, using a large, heavy saucepan. Add tomato, peppers, mushrooms and ham and pour wine over. Cover and simmer 25–30 minutes or until chicken is tender. Arrange chicken pieces on a heated platter and keep warm. Boil sauce until slightly reduced, taste and adjust seasoning and pour over chicken. Sprinkle with parsley and serve. Serves 4.

Chicken and Rice Casserole

An easy one-pot meal.

1.5 kg (3 lb) chicken pieces (thighs, drumsticks, half-breasts); ¹/₂ cup seasoned flour; 2 tbs oil; 60 g (2 oz) butter; 1 cup long-grain rice; 12 small white onions; 250 g (8 oz) mushrooms, halved or quartered if large; 1 x 140 g can pimientos, drained and chopped (optional); 1 clove garlic, chopped; salt and freshly ground black pepper; 1 tsp dried tarragon; 1 cup hot chicken stock; ¹/₂ cup dry white wine.

Coat chicken pieces in seasoned flour. Heat oil and butter in a large flameproof casserole, and slowly brown chicken on all sides, doing this in several batches if necessary. When all chicken is browned, return it to casserole and add rice and onions. Stir gently for a few minutes, then add mushrooms, pimientos (if using) and garlic. Season with salt and pepper, sprinkle tarragon over and gently pour over stock and wine. Bring to the boil, then cover and bake in a preheated moderately hot oven (190°C/375°F) for about 40 minutes or until chicken and rice are tender. Add a little hot water or more stock during cooking, if necessary. Serves 6.

Kidneys in Mustard and Wine Sauce

6 lamb kidneys, skinned, cored and thinly sliced; seasoned flour; 60 g (2 oz) butter; 3 shallots, chopped; 2 tbs French mustard; ¹/₂ cup dry red or white wine; 2 tsp lemon juice; ¹/₄ cup chopped parsley.

Roll kidney slices in seasoned flour and brown quickly in half the butter in a frying pan. Remove kidney to a heated dish. Add shallots to pan and cook until soft. Blend mustard with remaining butter, and add with wine and lemon juice to pan. Return kidneys and cook gently until liquid is reduced by half. Add parsley and cook for 1 minute. Serve with boiled rice or noodles or hot toast. Serves 4.

Ham Steaks in White Wine Sauce

60 g (2 oz) butter; 6 ham steaks; 1 tbs flour; 1¹/₂ cups dry white wine; 3 tbs redcurrant jelly; 1 tsp Dijon mustard; salt and freshly ground black pepper.

Heat butter in a frying pan; when sizzling, brown ham steaks, in 2 or 3 batches, for about 2 minutes each side. Remove ham and keep warm. Stir flour into pan and cook for 1 minute. Add wine gradually, stirring until sauce boils and thickens. Stir in redcurrant jelly and mustard, season with a very little salt and pepper and simmer for 1 minute. Spoon sauce over ham. Serves 6.

Beef Casserole for a Crowd

An easily assembled, hearty casserole that is all the better for being made ahead and reheated.

45 g (1¹/₂ oz) butter; 3 onions, thinly sliced; 3 shallots, cut into short lengths; 2 carrots, sliced; 1 stick celery, sliced; 2 cloves garlic, crushed; 1 sprig fresh thyme, or pinch dried; 1 sprig fresh rosemary, or pinch dried; 2 bay leaves; few stalks parsley, chopped; 2.5 kg (5 lb) blade or chuck steak, cut into 5 cm (2 in) cubes; 2 tsp salt; freshly ground black pepper; 2 tsp paprika; ¹/₂ cup red wine.

Smear butter over bottom and sides of a large casserole, or 2 smaller ones. Put in half the vegetables and herbs, then meat, then remaining vegetables and herbs. Sprinkle with salt, pepper and paprika and pour wine over. Cut a piece of greaseproof paper the size of the casserole, butter it and place on top, then cover with a well-fitting lid. Bake in a preheated moderately slow oven (160°C/325°F) for 3–4 hours or until meat is tender. Serves 12–15.

Pokolbin Veal Paprika

Pokolbin in the Hunter Valley is one of Australia's famous wine-growing areas.

1 small onion, chopped; 30 g (1 oz) butter; 1 kg (2 lb) lean veal steak, cut into bite-sized cubes; 125 g (4 oz) whole button mushrooms; salt and freshly ground black pepper; 1 tbs paprika; 1 cup white wine; 1 tbs cornflour; 1¹/₂ cups sour cream.

Cook onion gently in butter in a saucepan until transparent. Lift out with a slotted spoon and set aside. Turn heat to high, add veal to pan and brown on all sides. Return onion to pan with mushrooms and sprinkle with salt, pepper and paprika. Add water to cover, cover pan and simmer for 1 hour or until meat is tender. Add a little more water if meat is drying out during this time. Tip contents of pan through a sieve into a bowl, and return liquid to pan. Add wine and boil over high heat until reduced by half. Blend cornflour with a little cold water and add to pan, stirring until sauce boils and thickens. Return veal and mushrooms, heat through gently and adjust seasoning. Just before serving, stir in sour cream and heat but do not boil. Serve with hot buttered rice or noodles. Serves 6–8.

Veal Casserole

1 kg (2 lb) boneless veal; 60 g (2 oz) bacon, rind removed and diced; 30 g (1 oz) butter; 4 tbs flour; 1 cup hot water or white stock; 1 cup red wine; salt and freshly ground black pepper; Bouquet Garni (page 43); 24 button onions, peeled; 2 cloves garlic, chopped.

Trim gristle from veal and cut into cubes. Brown with bacon in butter. Sprinkle flour over and stir 2 minutes then stir in hot water or stock and wine. Season with salt and pepper, add bouquet garni, onions and garlic, cover and simmer 2 hours. Adjust seasoning to taste, remove bouquet garni and serve with rice or noodles. Serves 4–6.

Baked Fish with Tomatoes and Mushrooms

1 x 1.5 kg (3 lb) whole fish, cleaned and scaled; 90 g (3 oz) butter; $^1/_4$ cup chopped onions; 1 cup chopped mushrooms; 1 tomato, peeled, seeded and chopped; 1 tsp chopped chives; 1 tbs chopped parsley; $^3/_4$ cup fresh breadcrumbs; salt and freshly ground black pepper; 1 tbs lemon juice; $^1/_2$ cup dry white wine.

Heat half the butter in a frying pan, add onion and cook until transparent. Add mushrooms and cook until wilted. Add tomato and simmer 5 minutes. Stir in chives, parsley, breadcrumbs, salt and pepper. Stuff fish loosely with herb mixture and close with skewers and string. Place fish in a baking pan lined with greased foil, and sprinkle with lemon juice, wine, salt and pepper. Dot with remaining butter. Bake, uncovered and basting occasionally, in a preheated hot oven (200°C/400°F) for 30–40 minutes or until the fish flakes easily when tested with a fine skewer. Sprinkle with additional butter and lemon juice. Serves 6.

Fish Fillets with Wine and Onion Sauce

6 fillets white fish, skinned; 3 small onions, thinly sliced; $^3/_4$ cup dry white wine; 2 tbs lemon juice; 1 bay leaf; 1 tsp salt; 6 black peppercorns; 30 g (1 oz) butter; 2 tbs flour; $^1/_4$ tsp dried mustard.

Arrange fish on a bed of sliced onion in a buttered shallow ovenproof dish. Add wine, lemon juice, bay leaf, salt and peppercorns. Cover with buttered paper and then bake in a preheated moderate oven (180°C/350°F) for 10–15 minutes. Remove fillets to a heatproof serving dish and keep warm. Strain contents of dish into a bowl, rubbing onion through sieve. If necessary, add water to make 1 cup. Melt

butter in a small saucepan, add flour and cook for 1 minute. Remove from heat and cool a little, then add mustard and strained liquid, stirring until smoothly blended. Return to heat and stir until boiling. Pour over fillets. Place in a preheated hot oven (200°C/400°F) for 2 minutes if fish has been allowed to cool. Serve immediately. Serves 4.

Oysters in White Wine

1 onion, finely chopped; 4 shallots, finely chopped; 45 g (1$^1/_2$ oz) butter; 1 cup dry white wine; salt and freshly ground white pepper; 1 tbs chopped parsley; 2$^1/_2$ tbs cream; squeeze lemon juice; 24 canned oysters, drained; $^1/_2$ cup fresh breadcrumbs tossed in butter.

Cook onion and shallots gently in butter until golden. Add wine, salt and pepper and simmer until reduced by half. Remove from heat and stir in parsley, cream and lemon juice. Add oysters. Turn into a flameproof dish and sprinkle with buttered breadcrumbs. Brown under a preheated hot grill. Serve immediately, with crusty bread to mop up juices. Serves 4 as a first course, 2 as a light meal.

Oeufs Bourguignonne

Eggs in red wine sauce, as cooked in France, introduces an unexpected combination.

90 g (3 oz) butter; 3 small onions, finely chopped; 3 tbs flour; 1$^3/_4$ cups red wine; salt and freshly ground pepper; pinch sugar; 6 large eggs, 6 slices bread, crusts removed.

Melt 30 g (1 oz) butter in a saucepan and cook onion gently until golden. Add flour and stir 5 minutes. Add wine, a little at a time, stirring constantly until smooth, then continue to stir until boiling. Season with salt, pepper and sugar and simmer very gently for 15 minutes. Meanwhile, heat remaining butter in a frying pan and fry bread until golden brown on both sides. Drain on crumpled paper towels, place on heated individual plates and keep warm.

Poach eggs in the red wine sauce, keeping them rather soft. Do this in 2 batches if necessary, keeping cooked eggs hot in a dish in a very low oven. To serve, place eggs on bread croûtes, spoon sauce over and serve immediately. Serves 6 as a first course, 3 as a luncheon or supper dish.

Red Cabbage with Wine

Excellent with sausages or with roast duck, pork or game.

$^1/_2$ large or 1 small red cabbage, cored and finely shredded; $^1/_2$ tsp salt; freshly ground black pepper; pinch nutmeg; 1 small onion, finely chopped; 30 g (1 oz) butter; 2 tsp white wine vinegar; 1 cup red or white wine; 1 cup water; 1 large green apple, peeled, cored and diced.

w

Drop cabbage into boiling water and boil for 10 minutes, then drain well again. Season with salt, pepper and nutmeg and set aside. Cook onion in butter until soft but not brown. Add vinegar, wine, water and cabbage. Cover and simmer 30 minutes. Add apple and cook 25–30 minutes longer, adding a little more water if drying out. Serves 6.

Wine Cream

I tbs cornflour; I cup dry white wine;
I cup caster sugar; grated rind and juice 1/2 lemon;
grated rind and juice I orange; 6 egg yolks;
2 egg whites; crisp biscuits, or sponge fingers to serve.

Mix cornflour with 1/4 cup of wine. Put the sugar, remaining wine, lemon and orange rinds and juice, and cornflour mixture into a saucepan and stir until boiling. Cook for 1 minute, stirring constantly. Beat egg yolks. Add a little of the hot mixture, then stir this back into pan and stir over low heat until thickens. Do not allow to boil. Strain mixture into a bowl, cool and chill. Just before serving, whisk egg whites until they hold soft peaks and fold lightly into custard. Serve with crisp biscuits or sponge fingers. Serves 6.

WONTON

Wonton, an important part of Chinese cookery, are little packages of savoury food wrapped in squares of fresh noodle dough and deep-fried, steamed or boiled. They are served as appetisers, as part of a meal with a sauce, or floating in a clear broth (see *Short Soup*, page 479).

Wonton skins (wrappers) can be made at home but are available ready-made in Chinese food stores. There are about 90 wrappers to 500 g (1 lb). Store tightly wrapped in plastic, in the refrigerator or freezer. They will keep for about a week under refrigeration.

Fried Wonton

250 g (8 oz) minced pork; 2 tbs soy sauce;
I tsp brown sugar; I tsp salt; 250 g (8 oz) frozen
spinach, thawed; 1/2 packet of 40 wonton wrappers;
oil for deep frying.

Combine pork, soy sauce, brown sugar and salt in a bowl and mix well. Squeeze spinach to remove excess water and dry in paper towels to remove as much moisture as possible. Chop very fine. Add pork mixture and mix thoroughly. Place about 1/2 tsp of mixture in centre of each wonton wrapper. Dampen edges with water, gather edges and sides together to enclose filling in a little parcel, and press firmly together to seal. Heat oil to moderately hot and deep-fry wonton (a few at a time) for about 5 minutes or until golden-brown. Drain on crumpled

paper towels and serve with Chinese Chilli Sauce, or Sweet and Sour Sauce (see page 520). Makes about 40.

WORCESTERSHIRE SAUCE

A spicy, piquant, commercially bottled sauce first made early last century from an old recipe belonging to Mr Lea and Mr Perrins. It is a thin, very dark brown sauce and contains among other ingredients soy sauce, vinegar, chilli, anchovies, garlic, fruits and numerous spices.

Use a little Worcestershire sauce to flavour stews, casseroles, meat pies, soups and sauces or sprinkle sparingly over steaks, hamburgers or chops according to individual taste. Try a few drops in iced tomato juice for a refreshing starter to the day, and enliven chicken, fish or cooked meats with *Devil Sauce* (see page 461) of which Worcestershire is an essential ingredient. Steak Diane and Bloody Mary are two much-loved treats that wouldn't be the same without a dash of Lea and Perrins' famous sauce. **See recipes.**

Devilled Skirt Steak

4 pieces skirt steak, about 125 g (4 oz) each;
I medium onion, grated; 1/2 tsp dry mustard;
I tbs vinegar; I tbs Worcestershire sauce; I tbs salt;
I clove garlic, crushed; freshly ground black pepper.

Place steak in a shallow earthenware or glass dish. Spread grated onion on steaks. Combine remaining ingredients, pour over and turn to coat steaks on both sides. Marinate for 2–3 hours, turning frequently. Grill over hot coals or under a preheated hot grill for about 2–3 minutes on each side. Serve immediately. Serves 4.

Creamy Tomato Juice

I1/2 cups well chilled tomato juice;
3/4 cup chilled cream; I tsp grated onion; pinch salt;
pinch celery salt; I tsp Worcestershire sauce;
1/2 cup crushed ice; cayenne to garnish.

Combine all ingredients, except cayenne, in a blender jar or hand shaker. Blend or shake until well mixed. Serve immediately, garnished with a shake of cayenne. Serves 4.

Bloody Mary

1/3 cup vodka; I cup chilled tomato juice;
I tsp lemon juice; I tsp Worcestershire sauce;
2 drops Tabasco sauce; 1/2 tsp celery salt;
pinch garlic salt; 3/4 cup crushed ice.

Combine all ingredients in a shaker or the goblet of a blender. Shake or blend until well mixed. Pour without straining into whisky sour glasses and serve immediately. Serves 2.

y

YABBIES

Yabbies are freshwater crayfish, rather similar to the French écrevisses. Although a few people have attempted – and succeeded – to raise yabbies commercially, most come from natural creeks and waterholes and consequently their supply in the cities is rather erratic. There seems to be no clearly defined yabbie season, but they are perhaps more plentiful in spring than in summer or winter. Yabbies have a taste vaguely similar to that of prawns, but without the salty sweetness of the latter. Some say they are best eaten straight from the pot, without the benefit of any sauce; others like them warm, in a salad, or cold with a lemony mayonnaise. Cooked yabbies may also garnish other fish or seafood dishes. Buy live yabbies when available at the fish markets. They should be clean, free of weed and react when touched. Grasp them firmly at the junction of the head and tail when handling. When purchased ready-cooked, they should be bright orange-red, stored on ice or refrigerated. Yabbies sometimes have a slight muddy taste and to overcome this live yabbies may be placed in a large bucket of cold water and left in a very cool place for about 5 hours or overnight. Alternatively, dill seeds may be added to the cooking liquid and the cooked yabbies left overnight in the cooking liquid with sprigs of fresh dill.
■ **TO COOK:** Kill yabbies by freezing, then drop into boiling salted water, *Court Bouillon* (see page 98) or *Shellfish Stock* (see below). Lower the heat and simmer for about 5–10 minutes or until the shell colour changes to orange-red. Remove with a slotted spoon. When cool enough to handle, separate tail from heads. Cut through tail shells with strong kitchen scissors and extract tail meat. **See Recipes.**

Shellfish Stock for Yabbies

small crabs, prawn heads and other shellfish oddments; I carrot; I leek or onion; I stick celery; few black peppercorns; I bay leaf; stalks parsley; little white wine.

In a large saucepan combine crabs, prawn heads and other shellfish oddments, carrot, leek or onion, celery, peppercorns, bay leaf and parsley stalks. Add water and a little white wine. Bring to the boil and simmer for about 30 minutes. Strain before use.

Yabbie Salad

I kg (2 lb) yabbies, cooked and shelled (above); Vinaigrette Dressing (page 442); salad greens.

Toss yabbies with vinaigrette dressing. Garnish with salad greens. Serves 2.

VARIATION

YABBIES DILL SALAD: Add 2 tbs finely chopped fresh dill to dressing. Alternatively, dress yabbies with a light tarragon-flavoured Mayonnaise (see page 256)

and garnish with slivers of just-cooked snow peas and artichoke hearts, or fresh watercress.

Yabbies in Fresh Tomato Sauce

I onion, finely chopped; 30g (I oz) butter; I clove garlic, chopped; I kg (2lb) ripe tomatoes, peeled, seeded and chopped; I bouquet garni; salt and freshly ground black pepper; 2 kg (4lb) yabbies, cooked and shelled (opposite); 2 tbs brandy; pinch cayenne; I tbs chopped chives.

Cook half onion in half butter for 2 minutes, then add garlic and cook briefly. Add tomatoes and bouquet garni. Season with salt and pepper. Cook over low heat for 10 minutes. Meantime, fry remaining onion in remaining butter, in a separate pan, for 2 minutes. Add yabbies and cook gently 2 minutes longer. Deglaze pan with brandy. Remove bouquet garni and add tomato mixture to yabbies. Stir in cayenne and chives and serve yabbies and sauce immediately. Serves 4.

YAM

In appearance, yams are rather like sweet potatoes but they taste more like ordinary potatoes when cooked. They are the tubers of a tropical vine which originated in China but is now found throughout the Pacific, the West Indies and Africa. Yams can be baked, boiled or fried.
■ **TO COOK:** Yams may be baked whole, in their skins, but should be peeled before boiling or frying. Yams quickly discolour when peeled, so drop into cold acidulated water (water with a little lemon juice or vinegar added) as soon as peeled. Add a little lemon juice to the water when boiling, too. **See Recipes.**

Sweet Yam Soufflé

750 g (1½ lb) yams; 155 g (5 oz) butter; ½ tsp salt; ¼ tsp pepper; 2 tbs brown sugar; 2 eggs, beaten; 2 tbs white wine; ½ tsp cinnamon.

Bake yams whole, without peeling, in a preheated very hot oven (230°C/450°F) for about 1 hour or until tender. Halve, scoop out flesh, and mash with 125g (4 oz) butter. Add salt, pepper, sugar, eggs and wine, and beat until fluffy. Pour into a greased ovenproof dish, sprinkle with cinnamon and dot with remaining butter. Bake in a preheated moderate oven (180°C/350°F) for about 45 minutes. Serve warm. Serves 6.

Boiled Yams with Cheese Sauce

500 g (1 lb) yams, peeled and thickly sliced; squeeze lemon juice; 60 g (2 oz) butter; 2 tbs flour; I cup hot milk; I cup grated Parmesan cheese; salt and freshly ground black pepper; pinch cayenne.

Cook yams in boiling salted water, with lemon juice, until soft. Drain and set aside. Melt butter in a saucepan, stir in flour and cook for about 1 minute. Add milk and mix well. Bring to the boil, stirring constantly. Add half the cheese, and season with salt, pepper and cayenne. Place yam slices in a greased ovenproof dish, cover with sauce, then sprinkle over remaining cheese. Warm through in a preheated hot oven (200°C/400°F) for 5–10 minutes. Serves 6.

YEAST COOKERY

Cooking with yeast – baking breads, rolls, sweet fruit loaves, spice buns, festive breads – is one of the joys of the kitchen. It is satisfying and relaxing to knead the dough, shape it and enjoy the warm spicy aroma while it bakes. Yeast is a living organism and needs food, warmth and moisture to grow. These essentials are provided when bread type doughs are mixed. The yeast starts to work and the carbon dioxide created makes the dough rise and gives breads and buns their characteristic light texture. Be careful the liquid added is only lukewarm because too much heat will kill the yeast. Tackle yeast cookery with confidence and enjoyment; the dough is not delicate like pastry and thorough kneading results in a light even textured product. You will not need a lot of time for preparation; most of the time is taken by the dough itself when it is set aside to rise.

■ **TO BUY AND STORE YEAST**

COMPRESSED OR FRESH YEAST: These may be purchased from good delicatessens and health food stores. Buy in small amounts or as much as you need for the recipe, keep wrapped in the refrigerator and use within 2–3 days. Larger amounts of yeast can be divided into packets of 15 g (1/2 oz), wrapped in foil, labelled and frozen. These are best used within 3 months of freezing. Compressed yeast should crumble easily, be a pale cream putty colour and have a fresh, pleasant, very faintly alcoholic smell. Do not use yeast if it smells strongly alcoholic or is a dark colour – this means it is stale. Quantities: 3 tsp compressed yeast equals 15 g (1/2 oz); 6 tsp compressed equals 30 g (1 oz).

TO SPONGE COMPRESSED YEAST: Some recipes recommend allowing the yeast to sponge first before mixing into the dry ingredients. Follow the recipe instructions and leave the yeast and liquid in a warm place for about 15 minutes. It is ready when a creamy foam covers the surface. Not all recipes use this method so read the instructions first before proceeding.

Dried (Active) or Dehydrated Yeast: Various types of dried yeast are available commercially, their dif-ferences being in the way they are used and in the quantities necessary for leavening. Be careful to check the instructions for use on the packet and use only those amounts specified as equivalent to compressed yeast when substituting. Too much yeast will spoil the product, making it course and sour. Some dried yeasts need to be reactivated before using.

Dry Yeast: Probably the most widely available of all, dry yeast may be purchased from supermarkets, groceries, delicatessens and health food shops. It is packaged in sachets which usually contain 7 g (1/4 oz) yeast or 1 1/2 tsp and will keep for about 1 year in a cool, dry place in the unopened sachets. Dry yeast may be substituted in recipes calling for fresh or compressed yeast. Follow the instructions on the packet or, as a guide, use 1 1/2 tsp or 1 x 7 g (1/4 oz) sachet in place of 15 g (1/2 oz) of com-pressed yeast, or 2 sachets in place of 30 g (1 oz) of compressed yeast. Dry yeast may be added directly to the flour in most recipes as it does not need to be reactivated before use, but if you prefer, combine 1 sachet dry yeast, 1/4 tsp sugar and 2 tbs hand-warm water and leave for 10 minutes until frothy on top. Use as your recipe instructs.

Dry Active Yeast: Similar to dry yeast. Available from health food shops and some delicatessens. It is packaged in sachets containing 7 g (1/4 oz) or 2 tsp and will keep for about 1 year in a cool, dry place in the unopened sachets. When substituting for compressed yeast, first check the instructions for use on the packet or, as a guide, use 2 tsp or 1 x 7 g (1/4 oz) sachet in place of 30 g (1 oz) compressed yeast. Some dry active yeasts need to be reactivated before use. Check packet instructions or, as a guide, combine 1 sachet of dry active yeast with 2 tbs hand-warm water and 1/4 tsp sugar and leave for 15 minutes or until a frothy cream has formed on top. Whisk for a few seconds, then use as your recipe indicates.

Dried Yeast Compound: This is not as well known as dried yeast. It may be purchased from health food stores in cans, usually 500 g (1 lb) weight, and is useful if you make bread regularly. Store in a cool, dry place and after opening the can, transfer the contents to an airtight container and store again in a cool, dry place. Always shake the container before using to distribute the yeast granules evenly through the compound mixture. Dried yeast compound may be substituted for compressed yeast. Use 3 tsp yeast in place of 15 g (1/2 oz) compressed yeast and reactivate first; combine 3 tsp dried yeast compound with 2 tsp sugar and 1/3 cup hand-warm water. Allow to stand for 40 minutes before using as your recipe indicates.

■ **TO PREPARE THE DOUGH:** Place dry ingredients into a warm bowl, make a well in the centre and pour in liquids and yeast (unless recipe specifies otherwise). Mix to a soft dough and beat well to develop the gluten in the flour.

KNEADING THE DOUGH: Not all yeast doughs require kneading but if recipe specifies, turn on to a lightly floured board and knead to a smooth, elastic ball. This will take about 10 minutes. Knead in as little extra flour as possible. The dough will be quite sticky when you first start kneading but will become smooth and satiny quite quickly. Dough is sufficiently kneaded when the impression of a finger, pressed into it, smooths out quickly.

RISING: Put ball of dough into a clean, very lightly oiled bowl and turn dough over so the surface is lightly greased. Cover bowl with lightly oiled plastic wrap or a damp tea-towel. Set the bowl in a warm place free from draughts for about 1–2 hours or until the dough doubles in bulk. A temperature of about 27°C/80°F is ideal. To test when ready, lightly and quickly press 2 fingers into the top of the dough to a depth of about 1 cm (½ in). If dents remain the dough is ready. If they fill up, leave for 15 minutes before testing again.

KNOCKING BACK DOUGH: After the first rising the dough is usually knocked back to expel excess carbon dioxide. Turn the dough on to a lightly floured board, punch your fist into the middle, then knead several times. Shape as required and leave to prove for 30 minutes – 1 hour, depending on size or as recipe states. Before baking test again with fingers.

■ **TO BAKE:** The shaped dough is usually put in a preheated hot oven (200°C/400°F) for the first 15 minutes to kill the yeast and prevent over-proving. When baked the bread or buns will sound hollow when tapped underneath. See recipes.

See also *Bread*, *Baps* and *Stollen*.

Basic Sweet Rich Dough

This basic dough makes many different loaves, rolls and twists of any size or shape you wish. Add spices, fruits, cherries or nuts; brush with melted butter and sprinkle with cinnamon and sugar before baking, or bake, cool and drizzle over some Glacé Icing (see page 205).

4½ cups flour; large pinch salt; ¾–1 cup milk;
125 g (4 oz) butter; 30 g (1 oz) compressed yeast;
½ cup caster sugar; 2 eggs, beaten.

Sift flour with salt into a large bowl. Heat ¾ cup of the milk to lukewarm, add butter and allow to melt, then add to yeast and stir until dissolved. Mix in sugar and beaten eggs. Make a well in flour, pour in milk mixture and stir until smooth, first with a wooden spoon and then with the hand. Add more warm milk if necessary to make a soft dough. When dough comes away cleanly from sides of bowl, turn on to a floured work surface and knead until smooth and elastic. Only add a little more flour if dough is too soft to knead. Place dough in a greased bowl and turn dough over in bowl so it is lightly greased. Cover with plastic or a damp cloth and leave to rise in a warm place for 45–50 minutes or until doubled in bulk. Knock back dough, pull sides to centre, turn over, then cover and allow to rise again for 30 minutes before shaping and baking.

WAYS TO USE BASIC SWEET RICH DOUGH

SUGARPLUM RING: Use half the quantity of Basic Sweet Rich Dough. Leave to rise in a warm place until doubled in bulk. Pinch off bits of dough and form into balls about 2.5cm (1 in) in diameter. Knead balls lightly on a floured work surface. Roll balls of dough in melted butter, then in a mixture of brown sugar and cinnamon and place in a greased 20 cm (8in) ring tin. Leave a little space between each to allow for rising. Cover with a floured, damp cloth and allow to rise in a warm place until almost doubled in bulk. Sprinkle over chopped walnuts or almonds. Bake in a preheated moderate oven (180°C/350°F) for 30–35 minutes.

CLOVERLEAF ROLLS: Use half the quantity of Basic Sweet Rich Dough. Leave to rise in a warm place until doubled in bulk. Shape risen dough into small walnut-sized balls. Grease muffin or patty tins and put 3 balls of dough in each. Cover and let rise in a warm place until doubled in bulk, 30–45 minutes. Brush rolls with milk or beaten egg and bake in a preheated hot oven (200°C/400°F) for about 15 minutes. Makes 12–18.

CRESCENTS: Use half the quantity of Basic Sweet Rich Dough. Leave to rise in a warm place until doubled in bulk. Roll out dough to the size of a dinner plate. Spread with softened butter, and sprinkle with poppy seeds or sesame seeds. Cut into 8 wedges, and roll up each wedge from the widest edge towards the point. Stretch the dough gently and shape into a crescent. Place crescents well apart on a greased baking tray. Cover with a cloth and allow to rise in a warm place until the rolls double in size. Brush with a little beaten egg or milk and sprinkle over a few poppy seeds or sesame seeds. Bake in a preheated very hot oven (230°C/450°F) for 10–15 minutes or until the rolls are golden. Makes 8.

Greek Easter Bread

It's an old Greek custom to bake eggs in a nest of sweet dough. Use raw eggs, either natural white or brown, or colour them with Easter egg dye obtainable from many Greek delicatessens.

1 quantity Basic Sweet Rich Dough (opposite);
½ cup finely chopped mixed candied peel;
¼ cup chopped almonds; ½ tsp aniseed (optional);
5 eggs; Glacé Icing (page 205); red food colouring;
chopped nuts or fruit jellies to decorate.

After second rising, turn dough on to a floured work surface. Combine peel, almonds and aniseed, if using, and knead into dough. Divide dough in half and roll each half into a long rope about 60 cm (24 in) long. Twist ropes loosely together and shape into a ring on a large greased baking tray. Arrange unshelled eggs in hollows evenly around ring. Cover and leave to rise in a warm place for 30–40 minutes. Bake the ring in a preheated moderately hot oven (190°C/ 375°F) for 30–35 minutes. Remove to a wire rack to cool. When cool, spread with glacé icing, tinted pale pink, leaving the eggs uncovered. Decorate with chopped nuts or brightly coloured fruit jellies.

Greek Feast Bread

This subtly lemon-flavoured loaf, with it's three-in-one design, represents the Holy Trinity. It is decorated with cherries and almonds. This quantity makes one very large bread. If your baking tray is small, use only two-thirds of dough to make the 3 balls, and use the remaining dough for small rolls. If desired, the rolls can be made in the shape of nests and a raw egg in the shell placed on top of each before rising, to be baked with the rolls as in the Greek Easter Bread.

**I quantity Basic Sweet Rich Dough (opposite);
I tbs grated lemon rind; I cup sultanas.**

**DECORATION: Glacé Icing (page 205);
glacé cherries; whole almonds.**

Prepare dough, adding lemon rind and sultanas with yeast mixture. Cover dough and leave to rise in a warm place until doubled in bulk, then knock back and leave to rise again. After the second rising, turn on to a floured work surface and knead lightly. Divide into 3 and roll each portion into a ball. Place on a large greased baking tray in a clover leaf pattern, 1–2.5 cm (½–1 in) apart. Cover and leave in a warm place to rise again until doubled, about 30 minutes. Bake in a preheated moderately hot oven (190°C375°F) for about 30 minutes or until lightly browned and a skewer inserted in centre comes out clean. Remove to a wire rack and cover loosely with a tea-towel. Ice when cool, and decorate with cherries and almonds.

Tea Ring

**½ quantity Basic Sweet Rich Dough (opposite);
30 g (I oz) softened butter; ¼ cup caster sugar;
⅓ cup raisins; 2 tsp cinnamon.**

**DECORATION: Glacé Icing (page 205); walnut halves;
glacé cherries; candied angelica.**

After second rising, turn dough onto a floured work surface and roll out to an oblong about 1 cm (½ in) thick. Dot surface with softened butter and sprinkle with sugar, raisins and cinnamon. Roll up dough tightly, beginning at longer side, and seal by pinching edges well together. Curl dough into a ring, joining ends together well, and place on a greased baking tray. Using scissors or a sharp knife, snip ring at 2.5 cm (1 in) intervals around outside edge, making each cut or snip two thirds through dough. Cover with a cloth and leave to rise for 15–20 minutes. Bake tea ring in a preheated moderately hot oven (190°C/375°F) for about 25 minutes or until golden-brown and a skewer inserted in centre comes out clean. Make a thin glacé icing and brush over ring while still warm, then decorate with nuts, cherries and angelica.

Cardamom Braid

**½ quantity Basic Sweet Rich Dough (opposite);
I–2 tsp ground cardamom; I egg; 2 tsp milk;
caster sugar.**

Make up Basic Sweet Dough as directed, adding ground cardamom to the flour before sifting, Leave in warm place until doubled in bulk. Turn on to floured surface and knead lightly. Divide into 3 equal portions and shape each piece into a roe about 1 cm (1 in) across. Line ropes up on a greased baking tray and, starting from middle, plait loosely towards ends, taking care not to stretch dough. Seal ends by pinching well together. Cover and leave in a warm place to rise until doubled in bulk. Beat egg and milk then brush over braid. Sprinkle generously with caster sugar and bake in preheated moderate oven (180°C/350°F) for 30–35 minutes or until brown. Remove to a wire rack and loosely cover with a tea-towel. Cool before slicing.

NOTE: This quantity makes one large braid, you can use it to make two smaller braids if liked.

Hot Cross Buns

A favourite Hot Cross Bun recipe that always works.

**4 cups flour; I tsp mixed spice; ½ tsp cinnamon;
I tsp salt; 60 g (2 oz) butter; ¼ cup currants or
sultanas; ¼ cup chopped mixed candied peel;
30 g (I oz) compressed yeast; ½ cup caster sugar;
½ cup lukewarm water; ½ cup lukewarm milk;
I egg, lightly beaten.**

**PASTE FOR CROSS: 4 tbs self-raising flour;
2 tbs cold water.**

GLAZE: ¼ tsp gelatine; 2 tbs water; I tbs sugar.

Sift flour, mixed spice, cinnamon and salt into a bowl. Rub in butter, then mix in currants or sultanas and peel. Make a well in centre. Cream yeast with sugar and add a little warm water to dissolve yeast completely. Blend remaining water and milk with yeast and add with beaten egg to flour. Mix to form a soft dough. Turn on to a lightly floured work surface and knead until smooth and elastic. Shape into a ball, place in a clean, greased bowl and turn over so that top of dough is greased. Cover and leave to rise in a warm place until doubled in bulk, 1¼–1½ hours. Turn risen dough on to a lightly floured work surface and gently press out to 1 cm (½ in) thick. Divide dough into 16 pieces and shape each into a small ball. Place balls on greased baking tray, at least 2.5 cm (1 in) apart, or arrange in greased round cake tins. Cover and leave to rise in a warm place for a further 20–30 minutes. To make paste for cross, combine flour and water and beat to a smooth paste. Put into a greaseproof paper funnel or small piping bag fitted with a plain nozzle. Using a sharp knife, make a slight indentation in shape of a cross on top of each bun just before baking and pipe prepared paste into cross. Bake in a preheated hot oven (200°C/400°F) for about 15 minutes. Meanwhile, to make glaze, sprinkle gelatine over water in a small saucepan. When softened, dissolve over a low heat. Add sugar and stir until dissolve over a low heat. Add sugar and stir until dissolved. Remove from heat. Remove buns from oven and brush with glaze while still hot. Stand buns in a warm place, such as on opened door of turned-off oven. This helps to set glaze. Makes 16.

VARIATION

If liked, omit the paste cross and decorate with a sweet icing cross. Mix 1 cup sifted icing sugar with enough hot milk to make a firm consistency, about 2 tsp. Put into a piping bag fitted with a plain tube and pipe crosses on bake warm buns.

Chelsea Buns

I quantity Basic Sweet Rich Dough (page 588); 60 g (2 oz) butter, softened; ¼ cup caster sugar; I cup currants; I tsp mixed spice; extra caster sugar.

GLAZE: ¼ cup sugar; ⅓ cup water.

After first rising, turn dough on to a floured work surface, knead lightly and roll out to a rectangle about 30 x 23 cm (12 x 9 in). Spread with softened butter, and sprinkle with 1 tbs sugar. Fold each end over to meet in centre, then fold dough in half and roll out again. Sprinkle with rest of sugar, the currants and spice. Roll up like a Swiss roll. Cut into slices about 4 cm (1½ in) thick. Arrange slices, cut side up and almost touching, and in a well-greased 20 cm (8 in) sandwich tin. Cover loosely with a clean tea-towel and leave to rise in a warm place for about 20 minutes. The buns should now be touching. Sprinkle with extra caster sugar. Bake the buns in a preheated hot oven (200°C/400°F) for about 20 minutes. Meanwhile, make glaze. Combine sugar and water in a saucepan and stir over gentle heat until sugar has dissolved. Increase heat and boil, without stirring, for 3 minutes. Remove buns from oven, brush with glaze

and return to oven for 30 seconds to dry glaze. Leave to cool before separating buns. Serve warm or cool with plenty of butter. Makes 12.

Cottage Loaf (Basic Milk Dough)

4 cups flour; I tsp salt; 15 g (½ oz) compressed yeast; 3 tsp sugar; 1¼ cups milk; 60 g (2 oz) butter.

Sift flour and salt into a large mixing bowl. Make a well in centre of flour. Cream yeast with sugar in a small bowl. Heat ½ cup milk to lukewarm and add to yeast and sugar mixture. Mix until dissolved, then pour into well in flour. Stir in a little of surrounding flour, then cover with a cloth and leave in a warm place for 30 minutes. Melt butter, add remaining milk and warm slightly. Pour into yeast batter in bowl and gradually mix in flour to make a medium soft dough. The dough for a cottage loaf should be quite stiff, so add more flour if necessary. Knead dough, then allow to rise until it is doubled in bulk. Knock dough back and knead lightly for 10 minutes. Shape two thirds of dough into a ball and place on greased baking tray. Shape remaining dough into a ball, place on top of the other dough, then press a floury finger right down the centre of both. Leave to rise until doubled in bulk, about 35 minutes. Brush with milk, sprinkle with a little flour and bake in centre of a preheated very hot oven (230°C/450°F) for 20 minutes. Reduce heat to moderate (180°C/350°F) and bake for a further 20–25 minutes. To test if bread is cooked, knock firmly on base: the bread should sound hollow. If it does not, bake for a little longer.

VARIATION

FRUIT LOAF: Prepare dough as for Cottage Loaf, using a little more liquid. When dough has doubled in bulk, knock dough back and knead in 125 g (4 oz) mixed dried fruit. Cut dough in half, shape and place in 2 well greased 21 x 11 cm (8½ x 4½ in) loaf tins. Cover and leave to rise for 35–40 minutes. Bake loaves in a preheated very hot oven (230°C/450°F) for 20 minutes, then reduce heat to moderate (180°C/350°F) and bake a further 20–25 minutes. Paint loaves with honey or thick milk and sugar syrup as soon as they come out of the oven. Cool on a wire rack. Makes 2.

Sourdough Rye Bread

Delicious rye bread made with a sourdough starter. Make the starter first and let it stand at room temperature for 2 days before using. The starter can then be refrigerated, where it will keep for 5–6 days. Return to room temperature before using to make more bread.

SOURDOUGH STARTER: 7 g (¼ oz) or 1½ tsp compressed yeast; ½ tsp sugar; ⅔ cup lukewarm water; ¾ cup plain flour.

BREAD: 15 g ($^1/_2$ oz) compressed yeast;
2 tsp brown sugar; $2^1/_2$ cups plain flour;
$1^1/_2$ cups lukewarm water; 2 cups rye flour; 1 tsp salt;
2 tsp caraway seeds; 1 tbs salad oil.

SOURDOUGH STARTER: Cream yeast with sugar, then stir in lukewarm water until dissolved. Sift in flour and mix until smooth. Cover bowl with plastic wrap and leave for 2 days, unrefrigerated, before using.

BREAD: Cream yeast with $^1/_2$ tsp brown sugar and $^1/_2$ tsp plain flour. Mix in $^1/_2$ cup lukewarm water until dissolved, and leave in a warm place for about 10 minutes or until the surface of mixture is frothy. Sift together remaining plain flour, rye flour, salt and remaining sugar, returning husks in sifter to bowl. Stir in caraway seeds. Make a well in centre. Combine creamed yeast mixture with remaining lukewarm water, 2 tbs sourdough starter and oil. Add to well in flour mixture and mix well. If dough is too dry, add extra water. Turn dough on to a lightly floured work surface and knead until smooth and elastic. Halve dough and shape into 2 rounds. Place both rounds side by side in a greased 21 x 15 cm ($8^1/_2$ x 6 in) loaf tin. Cover tin with a clean cloth and leave to rise in a warm place until dough reaches top edge of tin, about 45 minutes. Brush top of dough with water and bake in a preheated hot oven (200°C/400°F) for 35–40 minutes. Turn out and cool on a wire rack.

NOTE: This mixture can be doubled in quantity to make 2 loaves.

Norwegian Sweet Bread

In many parts of the world, beer is added to bread to give extra flavour and richness. This good-tasting Norwegian bread has a full flavour and delicious chewy texture.

30g (1 oz) compressed yeast; $1^1/_4$ cups lukewarm milk;
6 cups plain flour; $^1/_2$ cup sugar; 3 tsp salt;
$^1/_2$ tsp ground cloves; $^1/_2$ tsp black pepper;
$1^1/_2$ cups light beer; $^1/_2$ cup golden syrup;
2 cups rye flour; 1 cup raisins.

Soften yeast in warm milk in a large bowl and let stand for 5 minutes. Beat in 1 cup plain flour, the sugar, salt, cloves and pepper. Cover bowl with a tea-towel and stand in a warm place for 40 minutes or until dough is light and bubbly. Add beer and golden syrup. Beat in rye flour and raisins, and enough of the remaining plain flour to make a moderately stiff dough. Turn dough out on to a lightly floured work surface and knead until smooth and elastic, 8–10 minutes. Place in a greased bowl, turning dough to grease surface. Cover and allow to rise in a warm place until doubled in bulk, about 1 hour. Knock dough back and rest for 10 minutes. Divide dough into thirds and shape into 3 round loaves. Place on greased baking trays, cover and let rise until doubled in bulk, 35–40 minutes. Bake in a preheated moderately hot oven (190°C/375°F) for about 40 minutes. Makes 3.

Sally Lunn

4 cups flour; 1 tsp salt; 30g (1oz) compressed yeast;
1 tsp sugar; 2 eggs; 1 egg yolk; 1 cup cream;
$^1/_4$ cup lukewarm water.

GLAZE: $^1/_4$ cup milk; 3 tsp caster sugar.

Place flour and salt in a large bowl. In a separate bowl, cream yeast with sugar. Beat whole eggs with egg yolks and strain into creamed yeast mixture. Stir in cream and whisk until frothy. Add lukewarm water. Pour yeast mixture into flour and mix to a soft dough, adding a little more water if necessary. Beat well, then cover with lightly oiled plastic wrap and clean tea-towel. Put in a warm place to rise for about $1^1/_2$ hours or until doubled in bulk. Turn dough onto a lightly floured work surface and knead lightly. Halve dough and shape into 2 rounds about 20 cm (8 in) diameter. Put rounds into 2 greased 20cm (8 in) cake tins. Bake in a preheated hot oven (200°C/400°F) for 20–25 minutes. Combine milk and sugar and heat gently to dissolve sugar. Remove cakes from oven, brush with milk and sugar glaze and return to oven for 30 seconds to dry glaze. Serve warm with butter, or sliced, toasted and buttered. Makes 2.

Old-fashioned Penny Buns

5 cups flour; $^1/_2$ tsp salt; 15g ($^1/_2$ oz) compressed yeast;
$^1/_4$ cup plus $^1/_2$ tsp sugar; $2^1/_4$ cups lukewarm milk;
90g (3 oz) butter; 1 egg, beaten; $^1/_2$ cup currants.

GLAZE: $^1/_4$ cup sugar; $^1/_2$ cup water.

Place $2^1/_2$ cups flour and the salt in a large bowl. Cream yeast with $^1/_2$ tsp sugar in a small bowl. Stir in about $^1/_2$ cup milk until dissolved. Make a well in flour and pour in yeast mixture. Mix to a soft dough, using a little more milk if necessary, and beat well. Cover with lightly oiled plastic wrap and set aside to rise for 30–40 minutes. Warm remaining milk and melt butter in it. Allow to cool to lukewarm, and add egg. Stir into risen flour mixture together with currants, and remaining flour and sugar. Beat well, then cover bowl with lightly oiled plastic wrap and a clean tea-towel. Set aside to rise in a warm place for about 1½ hours or until doubled in bulk. Turn on to a floured work surface, punch your fist into dough and knead lightly. Shape pieces of dough into small buns and place on a greased baking tray so buns are just touching each other. Cover loosely with a cloth and allow to rise for 15 minutes. Bake the buns in a preheated hot oven (200°C/400°F) for 15–20 minutes. Meanwhile, make glaze. Put sugar and water in a small saucepan and heat gently, stirring until sugar dissolves. Increase heat and boil for 3 minutes, without stirring. Remove buns from oven, brush with glaze and replace in hot oven for about 30 seconds to dry glaze. Serve warm from oven, with or without butter; or cold, sliced and spread with butter, or toasted with butter. Makes about 15.

Berlin Doughnuts
(Russian Jam Doughnuts)

30 g (1 oz) compressed yeast; ¼ cup lukewarm water;
60 g (2 oz) butter; 1 cup milk; ¼ cup sugar;
2 eggs, beaten; 1 tsp salt; 3¾ cups flour;
1 tsp grated lemon rind; 1 egg white; raspberry jam;
oil for deep-frying; icing sugar.

Dissolve yeast in lukewarm water. Heat butter and milk in a saucepan, stirring until butter has melted. Cool to lukewarm. Combine yeast mixture, butter and milk mixture, sugar, eggs and salt in a large bowl and beat well. Add flour and lemon rind, beating well. Cover bowl with lightly oiled plastic wrap and a tea-towel and let rise in a warm place for about 45 minutes or until doubled in bulk. Turn on to a floured work surface and knead lightly. Wrap in plastic wrap and chill for 20 minutes. Roll out dough to a thickness of about 1 cm (½ in) and cut into rounds using a 5 cm (2 in) floured cutter. Brush half the rounds using lightly beaten egg white. Push 1 tsp raspberry jam into centres of other rounds. Top jam rounds with rounds topped with egg white, pinching edges firmly together. Cover very loosely with a clean tea-towel and let rise in a warm place until almost doubled in size, about 20 minutes. Heat oil in a deep saucepan until a cube of bread dropped into the oil turns brown in 60 seconds, or temperature reaches 180°C/350°F. Fry doughnuts a few at a time for 3–5 minutes or until golden brown, turning once. Drain on crumpled paper towels. Dust with sifted icing sugar and serve warm. Makes about 12.

VARIATION

RING DOUGHNUTS: Roll out dough and cut into 5 cm (2 in) rounds as above. Omit jam but cut a small circle in the centre of each round. Leave to rise and fry as for Berlin doughnuts, drain well then coat in caster sugar.

Swedish Coffee Breads

60 g (2 oz) butter or margarine; 4 cups flour;
⅓ cup sugar; pinch salt; 30 g (1 oz) compressed yeast;
1 cup lukewarm milk.

TO FINISH: beaten egg; sugar; chopped nuts;
melted butter; cinnamon; currants; sultanas.

Melt butter and allow to cool. Place flour in a bowl. Add sugar and salt, mix and make a well in centre. In a small bowl, cream yeast in a little of the milk and add to flour with butter and remaining milk. Mix with a spoon until all milk and butter have been absorbed, then cover with a damp cloth and leave to rise in a warm place for 2 hours or until dough has doubled in size. Knock back and knead dough until soft and smooth. Divide into 3 portions and shape as follows.

COFFEE TWIST: Take 1 portion of dough and divide it into 3 equal pieces. Roll each piece of dough between floured hands to a long strand. Plait strands together lightly, then cover and allow twist to rise on a baking tray for 45 minutes. Brush with beaten egg, and sprinkle with sugar and chopped nuts. Bake in a preheated moderate oven (180°C/350°F) for 15–20 minutes. Alternatively, bake without egg glaze, brush with honey and sprinkle with nuts when twist comes hot from the oven. Makes 1.

CINNAMON RING: Roll out second portion of dough as thinly as possible on a floured work surface. Brush with melted butter and sprinkle heavily with sugar and cinnamon. Roll up like a Swiss roll and join the ends together to make a ring. Make sure ends are well sealed. Place ring on baking tray to rise. Cut almost through dough at 2.5 cm (1 in) intervals with scissors. Turn leaves of dough thus formed to alternate sides to expose filling. Allow to rise again for 45 minutes. Brush with beaten egg and bake in a preheated moderate oven (180°C/350°F) for 15–20 minutes. Makes 1.

FRUIT AND NUT BUNS: Roll out remaining portion of dough as thinly as possible on a floured work surface. Brush with melted butter and sprinkle heavily with sugar, currants, sultanas and chopped nuts. Roll up like a Swiss roll and cut into 2.5 cm (1 in) slices to form small buns. Decorate each bun by cutting with scissors in different patterns according to your imagination. Allow to rise on a baking tray for 45 minutes. Brush with beaten egg and bake in a preheated hot oven (200°C/400°F) 5–10 minutes. Makes about 12.

Honey Potato Buns

Honey and freshly mashed potato make these buns beautifully tender and moist. Serve them with marmalade for tea or brunch, or split and toast them like English muffins.

15 g (¹/₂ oz) compressed yeast; ¹/₄ cup lukewarm water or potato cooking water; 3 tbs milk; ¹/₃ cup vegetable oil; ¹/₂ cup honey; ¹/₂ cup lukewarm, freshly cooked, sieved potatoes (no milk or seasoning added); 1¹/₂ tsp salt; 1 egg, beaten; about 3 cups flour; melted butter to glaze.

Stir yeast into water in a small bowl until dissolved. In a large bowl, mix milk, oil, honey, potatoes and salt. Add egg, then yeast mixture. Stir in flour, 1 cup at a time, to make a soft but not sticky dough. Turn out onto a floured work surface and knead until dough is smooth and elastic and small blisters appear just under the surface. Wash bowl in warm water, dry and oil lightly. Place dough in it and turn dough about so it is lightly oiled all over. Cover with oiled plastic wrap and let it rise in a warm place for about 1¹/₂ hours or until doubled in bulk. Pat dough out into a rectangle on a floured work surface and cut into 24 even pieces. Roll into balls and place in a greased, shallow baking tin, about 35 x 25 cm (14 x 10 in). Cover loosely with a damp cloth and let rise in a warm place until doubled in bulk, about 45 minutes. Brush with melted butter and bake in a preheated hot oven (220°C/425°F) for 12–15 minutes or until golden. Makes 24.

Mix and Drop Rolls

These rolls don't need any kneading or shaping, but they offer all the fun of working with yeast, plus scope for creative additions.

1 cup lukewarm water; 15 g (¹/₂ oz) compressed yeast; ¹/₄ cup sugar; 1 tsp salt; 1 egg, beaten; ¹/₄ cup vegetable oil; 3 cups flour.

Put water into a large bowl and sir in yeast until dissolved. Add sugar, salt and egg. Stir mixture well, then let stand for about 10 minutes until bubbly. Add oil and half the flour and beat with your hand until very smooth, then add remaining flour and beat in. Cover bowl with oiled plastic wrap and leave in a warm place for about 30 minutes or until dough has almost doubled in bulk. Drop dough into greased deep muffin tins so that each cup is half full. Let rise in a warm place until almost doubled in bulk. Bake in a preheated hot oven (200°C/400°F) for 15 minutes or until golden-brown. Makes 24.

VARIATIONS

FLAVOURINGS 1: After dough has risen in bowl, divide into 4 parts and place each in a bowl with one of the following: ¹/₄ cup drained, crushed pineapple; 4 tbs chopped raisins; 4 tbs chopped pecans, walnuts or almonds; ¹/₄ cup grated cheese; ¹/₄ cup crumbled crisp-fried bacon; 2 tbs mixed, chopped fresh herbs, or 2 tsp dried herbs mixed with 2 tbs chopped parsley; 1 tbs cocoa powder mixed with 1 tbs sugar; 2 tsp cinnamon or mixed spice. Mix each portion of dough

with the added ingredient until well blended. Then spoon into tins, let rise and bake as in the basic recipe.
FLAVOURINGS 2: Before putting dough into muffin tins, place one of the following ingredients into each greased tin: 1 tsp butter, 1 tsp brown sugar and 3 pecan or walnut halves; 1 tsp butter and 1 tsp shredded coconut; 1 tsp butter and 1 tsp jelly-style jam. Half fill prepared tins with dough, let rise and bake as in the basic recipe.

Bran Rolls

1 cup lukewarm water; 30 g (1 oz) compressed yeast; 1 cup boiling water; 250 g (8 oz) butter or margarine; ²/₃ cup sugar; 1 cup unprocessed bran; 1¹/₂ tsp salt; 2 eggs, beaten; 6 cups flour.

Put lukewarm water into a large bowl and stir in yeast until dissolved. In another bowl, pour boiling water over butter or margarine, stir in sugar, bran and salt and let stand until lukewarm. Stir eggs into bran mixture. Add yeast mixture and mix well. Stir in flour 1 cup at a time. Cover bowl with oiled plastic wrap and a cloth and let rise in a warm place until almost doubled in bulk, about 2¹/₂ hours. Knock dough down and drop by spoonfuls into greased muffin tins, filling cups half full. Let rise in a warm place until almost doubled in bulk, about 1 hour. Bake in a preheated moderately hot oven (190°C/375°F) for about 15 minutes or until golden. Makes 48.

YOGURT

Yogurt has a long history and reputation for promoting health and longevity. In the Middle East and India, yogurt is part of the basic daily diet and is frequently used in cooking.

Yogurt is a fermented milk product, with a pleasantly tangy taste and a smooth, refreshing texture. It can be made from cow's, sheep's or goat's milk, full cream or slim. Flavoured and sweetened yogurts are available commercially, as well as plain yogurts, but the latter is easily prepared at home.

WAYS TO USE YOGURT

Plain or flavoured yogurt is a delicious, soothing dessert. Plain yogurt may take the place of cream with an apple pie, steamed pudding or fruit salad; topped with honey and walnuts, in Greek fashion, it appeals to young and old; and it complements perfectly fresh berry fruits, such as strawberries and raspberries.

Yogurt accompanies curries and Indian vegetable dishes, Middle Eastern dishes such as lentils and rice, or fried eggplant. Meats and vegetables are often cooked in yogurt, and yogurt can serve as the base of a spicy marinade for chicken. Salads can be dressed with yogurt dressing, or the same basic ingredients may be combined as a dip or spread, or even a chilled summer soup. Hot vegetable soups can be enriched with yogurt, and in summer yogurt blended with water and garnished with mint makes a most refreshing and cooling drink (see *Lassi*).

COOKING WITH YOGURT: Yogurt curdles if cooked for a long time, for example in recipes such as meatballs in yogurt, or yogurt soup. To prevent this, the yogurt should be mixed with cornflour – 1 tsp of cornflour mixed in a little cold water to every 1½ cups yogurt – slowly brought to the boil and then allowed to simmer over very low heat, uncovered, for about 10 minutes. Stir constantly with a wooden spoon, in one direction only, while bringing to the boil. See recipes.

HOME-MADE YOGURT

Either fresh or powdered milk may be used, full cream or skim. If you want yogurt of a thick, junket-like consistency, evaporate some of the water from the milk by allowing it to simmer gently for about 20 minutes over low heat. Yogurt needs a 'starter' for fermentation; use 2 tbs commercial or home-made plain yogurt per 2 cups milk. Temperature is important for satisfactory fermentation to take place. If you have a thermometer, the milk should reach 45°C/115°F when it is cooled after heating and before the yogurt 'starter' is added. Or test by inserting a finger into the milk for a count of 10 by which time the heat from the milk will 'sting' your finger.

NOTE: Automatic yogurt makers, which keep the mixture at a constant temperature, can be used.

YOGURT CHEESE

If yogurt is turned into muslin-lined sieve and left to drain overnight, the result is a soft, creamy sort of cheese, called labna in the Middle East. It may be eaten as is, or flavoured with herbs, spices or garlic, or added to salads or vegetable dishes.

For a creamier cheese combine cream with plain yogurt before draining. The resulting soft cream cheese is delicious with fruit and has many other uses.

WAYS TO USE YOGURT CREAM CHEESE

- Halve a small ripe melon, remove seeds, fill with a few spoonfuls of Yogurt Cream Cheese and sprinkle with a little brown sugar.
- Serve melon and Yogurt Cream Cheese without the sugar.
- Curl a few slices of prosciutto and serve with Yogurt Cream Cheese as a first course.
- Mound about ½ cup Yogurt Cream Cheese on a dessert plate, mask with sweetened cream and surround with any fresh summer fruit, or sliced or halved stewed apricots, plums or peaches.
- Serve a bowl of Yogurt Cream Cheese with a square of Guava or Quince Cheese (see *Quince*).
- Offer a little black pumpernickel bread or Scottish oatcakes with Yogurt Cream Cheese to be served in place of a cheese board.

Home–made Yogurt (1)

2 cups milk; 2 tbs plain yogurt.

Heat milk to boiling and when froth starts to rise remove from heat. Leave until milk is warm, then beat 2 tbs milk into yogurt and set aside. Allow remaining milk to cool to a little more than blood heat (45°C/115°F), or test as described. Remove skin on top of milk and gently mix in yogurt starter, stirring only a few times to blend. Cover casserole dish with lid, wrap in a blanket or thick cloth and leave undisturbed in a warm place for 8–10 hours or until thickened. Chill for at least 4 hours before using. Makes about 1½ cups.

Home–made Yogurt (2)

This recipe makes a thick, creamy yogurt. Dieters should make the skim milk variation.

2 cups milk; ¼ cup full-cream milk powder; 2 tbs plain yogurt.

Set aside 2 tbs fresh milk and stir milk powder into remainder. Heat gently to boiling point, stirring occasionally to dissolve milk powder. Simmer very gently for 20 minutes. Remove skin from top of milk and pour milk into a small casserole dish. Leave to cool until a little warmer than blood heat (45°C/115°F), or test as described. Beat yogurt into reserved 2 tbs milk and mix very gently into warm milk, stirring only a few times to blend. Cover dish with a lid, wrap in a thick cloth or blanket and leave undisturbed in a warm place for 8–10 hours or until thickened. Chill at least 4 hours before using. Makes about 1¼ cups.

VARIATION

SKIM MILK YOGURT: Replace milk powder and fresh milk with 1 cup skim milk powder and 1½ cups water. Use low-fat yogurt as a starter.

Yogurt Cream Cheese

This soft creamy cheese is a excellent with fruit or fruit pastes (quince, guava). It can also be spooned over tomatoes, or combined with herbs and used to stuff tomatoes.

2 cups plain yogurt; 1 cup cream.

In a bowl combine yogurt and cream. Pour mixture into a sieve lined with a double thickness of dampened cheesecloth and set over a bowl. Let mixture drain for 8 hours or until whey has drained off and curds are firm. Makes about 1½ cups.

Yogurt Cheese with Fresh Herbs

This lovely fresh cheese is good with rye, black or any whole-grain bread; it makes a light meal served with a salad.

2$^{1}/_{2}$ cups plain yogurt; salt and freshly ground black pepper; 1 tbs sour cream; $^{1}/_{2}$ clove garlic, crushed; 2 tbs chopped parsley; 2 tsp chopped mixed fresh herbs (oregano, thyme, dill, chives).

Pour yogurt into a colander or sieve lined with muslin or cheesecloth and set over a bowl. Tie up with a string so that it forms a bag. Lift it out of colander and leave it to drain overnight, tying string to a wooden spoon across a bowl. Next day, tip drained curds from bag into a bowl and beat until smooth, adding a little salt and pepper and the sour cream. Mix garlic with half the herbs and fold in. Form into a round flat shape, or pile into a small dish, and sprinkle over remaining herbs. Chill for 1–2 hours before serving. Serves 4.

NOTE: To get a good shape to the cheese, line an empty, washed small margarine tub with cheesecloth, fill with cheese, then refrigerate several hours. Turn on to plate and sprinkle with remaining herbs.

Turkish Yogurt Soup

4 tbs rice; 5 cups good chicken or beef stock; 1 tbs cornflour; 2 cups plain yogurt; 2 egg yolks, beaten; 2 tbs chopped fresh mint.

Cook rice in stock for 20 minutes. In separate pan, blend cornflour with a little yogurt, then add remaining yogurt, beating until smooth. Add egg yolks and a few spoons hot stock and whisk well. Stir over low heat until thickened, but do not allow to boil. Add yogurt mixture to simmering stock. Cook for a further 2 minutes, stirring constantly. Thin with a little water if necessary. Serve sprinkled with chopped mint. Serves 6.

Quick Yogurt Soup

2 cups plain yogurt, chilled; 1 cup tomato juice, chilled; 2 tbs parsley sprigs; 2 tbs chopped shallot; 1 tbs fresh mint sprigs; 1 tsp fresh oregano sprigs or $^{1}/_{4}$ tsp dried; salt and freshly ground black pepper; 1 cup finely chopped cucumber; black olives and crusty bread, to serve.

Put yogurt, tomato juice and herbs into a blender or food processor and process until herbs are finely chopped. Pour into 4 soup bowls and top with cucumber. Serve with black olives and crusty bread. Serves 4.

Chicken in Yogurt

1.5 kg (3 lb) chicken joints, skinned; 1$^{1}/_{2}$ cups plain yogurt; 1 large red or green pepper, cored, seeded and finely chopped; 1 tsp paprika; 5 cm (2 in) piece fresh ginger, peeled and grated; 2 green chillies, seeded and crushed; 4 cloves garlic, crushed; 1 tsp salt; 5 tbs finely chopped parsley or fresh coriander.

Prick chicken all over with very sharp fork and place in a bowl. Combine yogurt with pepper, paprika, ginger, chillies, garlic and salt. Pour over chicken, cover and marinate overnight in refrigerator, turning from time to time. Next day, heat a large pan, add chicken and marinade and stir in parsley. Cover and cook on high heat for 5 minutes, then reduce heat to medium and cook for about 20 minutes or until chicken is tender. Turn chicken over to coat evenly in yogurt mixture, and serve immediately. Serves 6.

Mogul Chicken

Convenient chicken pieces, marinated in yogurt and spices and baked golden-brown, are delicious hot or cold.

6 half-breasts of chicken; 2 tsp grated lemon rind; $^{1}/_{2}$ cup plain yogurt; $^{1}/_{4}$ cup oil; 1 onion, grated; 2 cloves garlic, crushed; 2 tsp grated fresh ginger; 1 tbs curry powder; 1 tsp ground cumin; 1 tsp ground coriander; 1 tsp paprika; 8 cm (3 in) cinnamon stick, broken into pieces; 1 tsp salt.

Remove skin from chicken and make 3 or 4 deep diagonal slashes in each piece. Place chicken in one layer in a large shallow baking dish. Combine remaining ingredients and spoon over chicken, rubbing it in and coating thoroughly. Cover and refrigerate for 12 hours, turning pieces over and rubbing in marinade several times. Remove dish from refrigerator 1½ hours before serving time. Stand at room temperature for 1 hour, then remove chicken pieces, place a rack in dish and arrange chicken on it, bony side up, in one layer. Place in a preheated hot oven (200°C/400°F) and bake for 15 minutes or until lightly coloured, then turn pieces over and baste with marinade. Bake 10–15 minutes more, basting again after 7 minutes. Chicken is done when it is golden-brown and juices run clear when thickest part of flesh is pierced with a fine skewer. Serve hot or at room temperature. Serve 6.

NOTE: For cold chicken to eat in the fingers, you might like to lift the meat from the bone when it is cool enough, and cut each breast diagonally in half.

Yogurt Salad Dressing

1 cup plain yogurt; 1 tbs vinegar or lemon juice; 2 tsp grated onion or finely chopped shallot; salt and freshly ground black pepper; chopped fresh herbs as desired.

Whisk together yogurt, vinegar or lemon juice and onion or shallot. Season with salt and pepper and add herbs if desired. Use with green salads, chicken salads, cooked vegetable salads, beetroot. Makes 1 cup.

Yogurt Mousse

2 cups plain yogurt; 4 tbs brown sugar; grated rind and juice 2 lemons; grated rind and juice ¹/₂ orange; 2 tbs gelatine; ¹/₄ cup water: 3 egg whites.

TO SERVE: bananas, lemon juice and brown sugar.

Put yogurt into a large bowl and beat in sugar, lemon and orange juice and rind. Soak gelatine in water and dissolve over hot water. Fold gently into yogurt mixture. Whip egg whites until they hold soft peaks and fold into yogurt mixture. Chill for 2 hours and serve on the same day, the texture changes if kept too long. Serve with sliced bananas sprinkled with lemon juice and brown sugar. Serves 6.

Yogurt Honey Cakes

Light griddle type cakes, soaked in hot syrup then served warm with honey and cream.

3 cups water; 2¹/₂ cups sugar; 1¹/₂ tbs lemon juice; ¹/₂ tsp vanilla; 1 cup plain yogurt; ¹/₄ cup cream; 2 eggs; 2 cups plain flour; 1 tsp bicarbonate of soda; 250 g (8 oz) butter.

TO SERVE: honey and sweetened whipped cream.

Mix water, sugar and lemon juice in a saucepan, bring to the boil and simmer 5 minutes. Stir in vanilla and keep this syrup hot.

Beat yogurt with cream and eggs until smooth. Sift flour with bicarbonate of soda and gradually stir into yogurt mixture. Heat half the butter in a frying pan and drop in tablespoonfuls of the batter, space well apart. Cook until golden-brown underneath, turn and cook other side. As cakes are cooked, drop into hot sugar syrup, leave 5 minutes then remove to a platter.

When you have used up half the batter, pour off any remaining butter from the pan, wipe it out quickly and repeat the cooking process with remaining butter and remaining batter. Soak in hot syrup as before, remove to platter and allow to cool a little.

Split each cake into halves, spread with honey and top with whipped cream. Serve immediately. Makes about 20.

YORKSHIRE PUDDING

The Yorkshire Pudding of England should be crisp, light, well puffed and golden. It is made from a simple batter mixture that is baked in the oven and is traditionally served with roast beef. In Yorkshire it is sometimes served separately, before the meat. Yorkshire pudding can be baked in one tin or in individual muffin tins. Some people like to place the joint on a trivet and pour the batter directly into the baking dish beneath so the pudding bakes under the meat and catches the drippings as the meat roasts. Have the batter ingredients at room temperature before mixing for maximum rising. For recipes see page 25.

YULE LOG (BÛCHE DE NOËL)

The traditional French Christmas cake is log-shaped, covered with chocolate butter cream (Crème au Beurre) and patterned to represent the bark of a log. The origin of the yule log may have come from the custom of sending a log on Christmas Eve to the house to which you were invited for Christmas day, so guests could enjoy a roaring log fire.

Yule Log

¹/₂ cup flour; ¹/₂ tsp baking powder; ¹/₄ tsp salt; 60 g (2 oz) dark chocolate, chopped; 4 eggs; ³/₄ cup caster sugar; 1 tsp vanilla; ¹/₄ tsp bicarbonate of soda; 2 tbs cold water; extra caster sugar; 1 quantity Chocolate Crème au Beurre (see page 207).

Sift together flour, baking powder and salt. Melt chocolate in a heatproof bowl over hot water. Put eggs into a bowl, add sugar and beat over hot water, or on highest speed of electric mixer, until mixture is very light and thick and greatly increased in volume. Fold sifted flour mixture and vanilla into egg mixture all at once. Stir bicarbonate of soda and cold water into melted chocolate and fold quickly and evenly into cake mixture. Turn mixture into a greased and lined 38 x 25 x 2.5 cm (15 x 10 x 1 in) Swiss roll tin. Bake cake in a preheated hot oven (200°C/400°F) for 15 minutes or until cakes springs back when centre is lightly touched. Loosen edges and turn onto a tea-towel thickly dusted with caster sugar. Peel off lining paper and trim edges of cake with a sharp knife. Roll immediately in towel and leave to cool on a wire rack for at least 1 hour. When cold, carefully unroll cake and spread with a third of chocolate butter cream. Roll cake once more and cut off one end of cake at an angle. Place roll on plate or board, arrange cut piece of cake alongside to resemble a stump and cover whole 'log' with remaining butter cream. Make a bark-like finish with a fork and chill until serving time.

ZABAGLIONE (ZABAIONE AL MARSALA)

The famous Italian dessert, Zabaglione, is a superb mixture of egg yolks, Marsala and sugar whisked to perfection over hot water. Serve in warmed individual glasses accompanied with crisp biscuit or savoy fingers, or spoon over fresh strawberries. Chilled Zabaglione is a delicious variation for those who prefer a cold dessert, or the chilled mixture can be used to fill puffs or eclairs. **See recipes.**

Zabaglione

8 egg yolks; 2 tbs sugar; $1^1/4$ cups Marsala.

Combine egg yolks and sugar in a heatproof bowl or top of a double saucepan and beat together until white and fluffy. Stir in Marsala and place over hot, but not boiling, water. Whisk constantly over a low heat until mixture is frothy and thick. Be careful it does not boil or it will curdle. As soon as mixture is thick, pour into warmed glasses and serve immediately. Serves 4–6.

Chilled Zabaglione

1 tbs gelatine; 1–2 tbs water; 8 egg yolks; $^1/2$ cup sugar; 1 cup Marsala; $^1/2$ tsp vanilla; grated rind $^1/2$ lemon; $^1/4$ tsp cinnamon; $2^1/4$ cups cream.

Soften gelatine in water, then dissolve over simmering water. Set aside. Beat egg yolks and sugar in a heatproof bowl or top of a double saucepan until white and fluffy. Stir in Marsala and place over hot, but not boiling water. Whisk constantly over a low heat until mixture is frothy and thick. Remove from heat, stir in dissolved gelatine and continue beating until mixture is cool. Add vanilla, lemon rind and cinnamon. Place bowl or pan in a larger one containing crushed ice and continue beating until mixture is thoroughly chilled and thick. Whip cream until it holds stiff peaks and fold through ice-cold mixture. Place in individual glasses and chill for 2–3 hours. Serve with crisp biscuit. Serves 6–8.

ZEST

The name given to the outside coloured rind of any citrus fruit, such as lemon, orange, grapefruit and lime. Zest contains essential oils that lend a distinctive flavour to any dish in which it is used.

TO REMOVE ZEST: Scrape surface of fruit with a very fine grater using short sharp strokes; or rub surface with sugar lumps until they become impregnated with citrus oils; or pare very thinly with a vegetable peeler. Make certain you do not include any white pith with the rind as this can make the dish bitter.

See also *Lemon.*

ZUCCHINI (COURGETTE)

Zucchini are small young members of the marrow family, very popular in many of the superb dishes of Italy and France. They have a light delicate flavour and the texture, when cooked, should have a slight bite. Choose very young zucchini that are no more than 10 cm (4 in) long so they will be sweet and tender. They should be firm to the touch without any bruising of soft spots. Avoid any that are spongy as they may be bitter. Different varieties of zucchini are available, the most familiar being dark green and quite slender. Other plumper ones are a delicate pale green with a slightly deeper green stripe.

■ **BASIC PREPARATION:** Wash the zucchini gently, but do not peel. Trim off stem and any little brown mark at the other end, then cut diagonally into thick or thin slices or long strips, or if small and young enough, leave whole. If slices are to be deep-fried, sprinkle them with salt and leave to drain for 1 hour; use 2 tsp salt for 500 g (1 lb) zucchini. Rinse, drain and pat dry with paper towels. Or they can be soaked in milk, drained and dried before dusting with flour.

■ **TO COOK:** Boil quickly, uncovered, in a little lightly salted water for 3–4 minutes or until tender, depending on the thickness of the slices. Drain and toss in butter. Be careful not to overcook as zucchini softens a little after draining and the texture should be tender but still crisp. Toss in oil or a mixture of oil and butter and gently pan-fry until tender. Alternatively, grate raw zucchini and toss in butter over gentle heat for 1–2 minutes; stir in a little cream and a pinch of nutmeg. Grate raw into salads. **See recipes.**

Sautéed Zucchini

750 g ($1^1/2$ lb) zucchini, thinly sliced; salt and freshly ground black pepper; 3 tbs oil; 2 tsp chopped parsley; 1 tbs chopped fresh oregano.

Put zucchini slices in a colander, sprinkle with salt and leave for 1 hour. Rinse, drain and dry on paper towels. Heat oil in a large frying pan. Cook zucchini slices until translucent and edges are lightly browned, turning with a spatula to cook uniformly. This should take only 3–4 minutes. Add more oil if needed. Sprinkle with salt, pepper and herbs. Serve with grilled meats or poultry. Serves 6.

Buttered Zucchini

salt; 500 g (1 lb) small zucchini; 60 g (2 oz) butter; freshly grounded black pepper.

Bring about 5 cm (2 in) of water to the boil in a saucepan and add $^1/4$ tsp salt and zucchini. Keep heat fairly high so that water boils briskly, and cook zucchini for about 4 minutes if very small, 5–6 minutes if larger, turning over halfway through with a wooden spoon if water does not cover them. Drain zucchini and cut diagonally into 2 or 3 pieces or leave whole. Melt butter in saucepan, add zucchini and heat gently, rolling about by tilting pan, until very hot and coated in butter. Season lightly with salt and pepper and serve immediately. Serves 4.

NOTE: You can boil the zucchini ahead of time, cool quickly under cold running water and set aside. Cut into pieces and reheat in butter just before serving.

Grated Buttered Zucchini

Zucchini tastes and looks quite different when it is grated and heated through in foaming butter. If you wish, the watercress or lettuce may be left out and the quantity of zucchini increased to 750 g (1½ Ib). Leave the green skins on for colour.

500 g (1 Ib) zucchini; salt; 2 cups shredded watercress or lettuce; 60 g (2 oz) butter; freshly ground black pepper; pinch nutmeg.

Grate zucchini on coarse side of a hand grater, or with coarse grating attachment of a food processor. Toss with a little salt and stand for 30 minutes in a colander or sieve to drain. Rinse under cold water and dry using paper towels. Fold watercress or lettuce through zucchini. Heat butter and, when foaming, put in vegetables. Toss with 2 forks over medium heat. When very hot, season with salt, pepper and nutmeg. Serve immediately. Serves 4–6.

Deep-fried Zucchini

500 g (1 Ib) zucchini, thinly sliced length-ways; 2 tsp salt; ½ cup flour; freshly ground black pepper; oil for deep-frying.

Place zucchini in a colander, sprinkle with salt and leave to drain for 1 hour. Rinse in cold water, drain and dry well using paper towels. Combine flour and black pepper, and shake zucchini slices lightly in flour mixture. Heat oil in a deep saucepan and deep-fry zucchini for about 1 minute or until golden, crisp and tender. Fry slices in 4 or 5 batches to prevent their sticking together. Drain on crumpled paper towels and serve immediately, with a grinding of black pepper. Serves 4.

Zucchini Soup

15 g (½ oz) butter; 2 tsp oil; 1 small onion, chopped; 6 medium zucchini; thickly sliced; 1 medium potato, peeled and sliced; salt and freshly ground pepper; ½ tsp dried tarragon (optional); 4 cups chicken stock; 4 tbs cream (optional).

Heat butter and oil in a saucepan, add prepared vegetables and sprinkle with salt, pepper and tarragon. Cover and cook over a low heat for 10 minutes,

shaking pan occasionally and checking that vegetables do not colour. Add stock and simmer, covered, for 10 minutes or until vegetables are soft. Cool, then push through a sieve or purée in a blender or food processor. Reheat soup, adding more seasoning if necessary. For extra richness, 1 tbs cream may be added to each serving. Serves 4.

Zucchini Gratin

2 tbs olive oil; 1 clove garlic, crushed; 500 g (1 Ib) zucchini, cut into 5 mm (¼ in) slices; 2 tomatoes, peeled and sliced; salt and freshly ground black pepper; 2 tsp chopped fresh oregano, or ½ tsp dried; ¼ cup grated Parmesan cheese; ¾ cup grated Cheddar cheese.

Heat olive oil in a frying pan, add garlic and zucchini slices and fry gently for 4–5 minutes or until zucchini is tender but still crisp. Place zucchini in an ovenproof dish in alternating layers with sliced tomato. Season with salt, pepper and oregano. Sprinkle combined Parmesan and Cheddar cheeses over top. Bake in a preheated moderately hot oven (190°C/375°F) for 10 minutes or until cheese is golden-brown. Serves 4.

Zucchini Boortha

A deliciously spicy recipe for zucchini. Serve as part of a curry meal.

60 g (2 oz) ghee or butter; 1 onion, finely chopped; 1 small clove garlic, finely chopped; 1 tsp grated fresh ginger; ½ tsp ground cumin; 3 red or green chillies, seeded and chopped; 500 g (1 Ib) zucchini, thickly sliced; 30 g (1 oz) creamed coconut; salt; 1 tsp lemon juice.

Melt ghee or butter in a heavy pan and fry onion, garlic, ginger, cumin and chillies until soft, about 5 minutes. Add zucchini and cook until tender, about 15 minutes, then mash. Add creamed coconut, allow it to melt, then season with salt and lemon juice. Serves 4.

Zucchini à la Grecque

Serve chilled as a first course or with crusty French bread as a light luncheon dish.

**8–10 small zucchini, cut into 5 mm (¹/₄ in) slices;
1 tbs chopped fresh tarragon, or 1 tsp dried;
1 tbs lemon juice; 1 clove garlic, crushed;
1 tbs finely chopped parsley; 1 tomato, peeled and
seeded; pinch pepper; 1 bay leaf; ¹/₄ cup olive oil;
1 cup water.**

Place all ingredients in a heavy saucepan or flame-proof casserole. Cover and bring to the boil. Reduce heat and simmer gently until zucchini is tender but still firm, 5–6 minutes. Let mixture cool, then chill. Serves 3–4.

VARIATION

VEGETABLES A LA GRECQUE: Many vegetables can be served this way. Use 6 young leeks or artichokes, 8–10 tender sticks celery, 500 g (1 lb) button mushrooms or baby onions instead of zucchini.

Ricotta–Stuffed Zucchini

A delicately flavoured ricotta cheese filling blends beautifully with zucchini. Serve as a first course, for a light luncheon or at supper.

**8 plump zucchini, about 10–13 cm (4–5 in) long;
¹/₂ tsp salt; 1 thick slice white bread, crusts removed;
¹/₄ cup milk; 125 g (4 oz) ricotta cheese;
¹/₂ tsp chopped fresh oregano, or ¹/₄ tsp dried;
1 clove garlic, crushed; ¹/₄ cup grated Parmesan
cheese; 1 egg yolk; freshly ground black pepper.**

Drop zucchini into a saucepan of boiling salted water and boil for 3 minutes, then drain. Meanwhile, soak bread in milk and when soft, squeeze it dry. Slice zucchini in half lengthways and, using a teaspoon, scoop out the centres to make boat-shapes with shells about 5 mm (¹/₄ in) thick. These provide cases for filling. Finely chop scooped-out zucchini flesh and put into a bowl. Add bread, ricotta, oregano, garlic, Parmesan, egg yolk and pepper and beat thoroughly. The mixture should be fairly soft; if too stiff add a little milk. Fill zucchini cases with suffing. Oil a shallow baking dish and arrange zucchini close together in a single layer. Bake in a preheated moderately hot oven (190°C/375°F) for 20–25 minutes or until filling is golden-brown. Serves 4.

Tomatoes and Zucchini

From Italy comes a superb way with zucchini to serve hot or cold.

**2 tbs oil; 1 clove garlic, crushed;
500 g (1 lb) zucchini, cut into 5mm (¹/₄ in) slices;
2 tomatoes, peeled, seeded and diced;
salt and freshly ground black pepper.**

**GARNISH: 12 black olives, halved and stoned;
finely chopped parsley.**

Heat oil in a heavy frying pan, add garlic and zucchini and cook, stirring frequently, until softened. Add tomatoes and cook until they are soft. Season with salt and pepper. Garnish with olives and parsley. Serve hot or at room temperature. Serves 4.

Herbed Zucchini Salad

**500 g (1 lb) zucchini; 3 tbs olive oil;
1 tbs lemon juice; 1 tbs chopped parsley;
1 tbs snipped chives; 2 tbs chopped fresh basil,
oregano or marjoram; salt and freshly ground
black pepper.**

Cook zucchini in sufficient lightly salted boiling water to cover for 5–6 minutes or until just tender. Drain, then quarter zucchini. Combine olive oil and lemon juice, pour over hot zucchini and toss gently to coat thoroughly. Cool and chill. Just before serving, drain off any remaining liquid and add herbs, salt and pepper. Toss gently and serve immediately. Serves 4.

Ricotta–Stuffed Zucchini Flowers

During summer and autumn, zucchini flowers are sometimes sold in greengrocers, especially by green-grocers with Italian backgrounds. Occasionally, you may see tiny zucchini with the fresh flowers still attached. Either is delicious stuffed with this simple ricotta and herb mixture, dipped in a light batter and fried until golden and just tender.

**12 zucchini flowers, or 500 g (1 lb) baby zucchini with
flowers still attached; 250 g (8 oz) fresh ricotta cheese;
a grating of nutmeg; 1 bunch chives, snipped;
1 egg, beaten; 4 tbs grated Parmesan cheese;
salt and freshly ground black pepper;
light olive oil for frying.**

**BATTER: 2 eggs; ¹/₂ cup plain flour;
¹/₂ cup soda water or water with ¹/₂ teaspoon
bicarbonate of soda (more water may be necessary).**

Begin by making the batter. Beat the eggs in a shallow bowl, whisk in the flour with a fork and add the water to make a smooth consistency. The batter should not be too thick; the excess should drain off quickly. Set aside. Wash the flowers or zucchini gently and dry well with a kitchen cloth. In a small bowl mix the ricotta with the nutmeg, chives, egg, Parmesan and salt and pepper to taste. Carefully open the flowers and spoon the ricotta filling in each. Squeeze gently in the palm of the hand to enclose filling thoroughly.

Zwieback 601

To cook, heat 5–6 cm (1 in) of light olive oil in a pan or wok, dip the flowers into the batter, draining off excess, and fry a few at a time until golden-brown. Drain on paper towels then serve immediately. Serves 4–6.

Zucchini Bread

3 eggs; 2¼ cups caster sugar; 3 tsp vanilla; 1 cup oil; 2 cups grated zucchini; 3 cups flour; ¼ tsp baking powder; 1 tsp salt; 1 tsp bicarbonate of soda; 3 tsp cinnamon; 1 cup chopped walnuts.

Beat eggs until light and foamy, then add sugar, vanilla and oil and beat until thick and mousse-like, and mixture will leave a trail when poured from a spoon. Stir in grated zucchini. Sift together flour, baking powder, salt, soda and cinnamon. Fold this into zucchini mixture with walnuts. Pour into 2 greased and bottom-lined 21 x 11 cm (8½ x 4½ in) loaf tins. Bake in a preheated moderate oven (180°C/350°F) for 1–1½ hours or until a skewer inserted in centre comes out clean. Turn out and cool on a wire rack. Makes 2.

NOTE: Use only tender fresh zucchini. If they are tiny young ones, grate on a fine grater, or chop and purée in a blender. If zucchini are large, peel and seed before grating.

Zucchini Marinated with Garlic

This zesty salad can be part of the antipasto tray before an Italian meal or grill.

750 g (1½ lb) zucchini, sliced into thin strips about 8 x 2 cm (3 x ¾ in); ½ cup olive oil; ¼ cup lemon juice; 1 tbs chopped fresh oregano, or 1 tsp dried; 3 cloves garlic, crushed; ½ tsp salt; ¼ cup black olives; freshly ground black pepper.

Place zucchini in a shallow dish. Combine olive oil, lemon juice, oregano, garlic and salt, mix well and pour over zucchini. Cover, place in a refrigerator and marinate for at least 2 hours. One hour before serving, transfer zucchini to salad plates with a slotted spoon, reserving marinade. Garnish with olives, sprinkle with pepper and drizzle with reserved marinade. Serves 6–8.

ZWIEBACK

A twice-baked rusk of German origin made with a sweetened yeast dough usually flavoured with lemon and cinnamon. Zwieback is baked as a loaf, cooled and sliced. The slices are then dried out in the oven to become crisp and golden-brown. They keep well stored in an airtight container. Serve Zwieback to nibble with sherry or sweet white wine; top them with butter or a good plum or berry conserve. Zwieback may also be crushed and used as a crumb crust for unbaked desserts such as some cheesecakes or gelatine mixtures.

Zwieback

30 g (1 oz) compressed yeast; ⅔ cup luke-warm milk; 4 cups strong flour; 100 g (3½ oz) butter, melted and cooled; ⅓ cup sugar; grated rind ½ lemon; 1 tsp salt; ½ tsp cinnamon.

Dissolve yeast in milk and leave until frothy, about 15 minutes. Sift flour into a bowl and make a well in centre. Pour yeast mixture into well and mix in about ¼ of flour. Cover bowl and leave in a warm place for yeast sponge to rise, about 20 minutes. Beat in butter, sugar, lemon rind, salt and cinnamon. Mix to a fairly stiff dough and knead thoroughly for about 10 minutes or until smooth and elastic. Cover bowl with a clean cloth and leave to rise in a warm place until doubled in bulk, about 1½ hours. Turn onto a lightly floured work surface, knock dough down and knead briefly. Divide into 6 pieces and shape into ovals about 5 cm (2 in) thick. Place on 2 floured baking trays and leave in a warm place about 30 minutes or until doubled in bulk again. Brush with melted butter and bake in a preheated moderate oven (180°C/350°F) for about 25 minutes or until pale golden. Cool on wire racks. When quite cold, cut into 1 cm (½ in) slices, place on baking trays and bake in a preheated moderately slow oven (160°C/325°F) for about 20 minutes or until golden-brown on both sides. Makes about 50.

NOTE: Dry yeast may be used. See *Yeast Cookery*.

Recipe Index

Main entries (in bold) also include recipes.

Acknowledgements

This book by its very nature has to be authoritative, informative and useful both as an encyclopedia of food and cookery, and also as a practical source of recipes on every subject. In writing it, I have worked with people who have special qualifications, talents and experience of living, working and cooking in many different countries.

Amongst those who worked on the first edition of the encyclopedia, I would like to thank Meg Thomason, Julie Moses and Dr Barbara Santich.

Bringing out this new edition with Hardie Grant Books has been a wonderful experience. I would like to thank Sandy Grant and Julie Pinkham for their belief in the encyclopedia and for their enthusiasm; Jasmin Chua, my editor, who undertook the gigantic responsibility of managing the book and was involved in all the details that make this encyclopedia what it is; Foong Ling Kong, who skilfully copyedited the updated text; Hamish Freeman, who created a wonderful design and added a unique touch with his accomplished illustrations; Megan Ellis and Simone Wall, who undertook the mammoth task of typesetting the book; Jean Kingett, for her proofing skills; Geoff Lung for his evocative photographs that grace the cover; and Fay Donlevy, who prepared the comprehensive index – an essential part of what makes an encyclopedia work.

A special word of thanks to my daughter Suzanne Gibbs who contributed invaluable information on today's food and cookery for this edition.

Finally, a warm thank you to the readers who have sent me comments and feedback over the years. I have been delighted by the amount of attention the encyclopedia has received since its first publication.